Handbook of Research on Web Log Analysis

Bernard J. Jansen
Pennsylvania State University, USA

Amanda Spink
Queensland University of Technology, Australia

Isak Taksa
Baruch College, City University of New York, USA

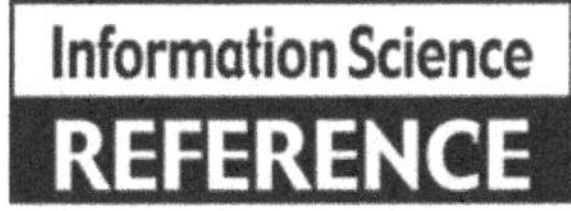

INFORMATION SCIENCE REFERENCE
Hershey · New York

Director of Editorial Content: Kristin Klinger
Director of Production: Jennifer Neidig
Managing Editor: Jamie Snavely
Assistant Managing Editor: Carole Coulson
Typesetter: Sean Woznicki
Cover Design: Lisa Tosheff
Printed at: Yurchak Printing Inc.

Published in the United States of America by
Information Science Reference (an imprint of IGI Global)
701 E. Chocolate Avenue, Suite 200
Hershey PA 17033
Tel: 717-533-8845
Fax: 717-533-8661
E-mail: cust@igi-global.com
Web site: http://www.igi-global.com

and in the United Kingdom by
Information Science Reference (an imprint of IGI Global)
3 Henrietta Street
Covent Garden
London WC2E 8LU
Tel: 44 20 7240 0856
Fax: 44 20 7379 0609
Web site: http://www.eurospanbookstore.com

Library of Congress Cataloging-in-Publication Data

Handbook of web log analysis / Bernard J. Jansen, Amanda Spink and Isak Taksa, editors.

p. cm.

Includes bibliographical references and index.

Summary: "This book reflects on the multifaceted themes of Web use and presents various approaches to log analysis"--Provided by publisher.

ISBN 978-1-60566-974-8 (hardcover) -- ISBN 978-1-60566-975-5 (ebook)
1. World Wide Web--Handbooks, manuals, etc. 2. Web usage mining--Handbooks, manuals, etc. I. Jansen, Bernard J. II. Spink, Amanda. III. Taksai, Isak, 1948-
TK5105.888.H3636 2008
006.3'12--dc22

2008016296

British Cataloguing in Publication Data
A Cataloguing in Publication record for this book is available from the British Library.

List of Contributors

Table of Contents

Preface xix

Chapter I
Research and Methodological Foundations of Transaction Log Analysis 1
Bernard J. Jansen, Pennsylvania State University, USA
Isak Taksa, Baruch College, City University of New York. USA
Amanda Spink, Queensland University of Technology, Australia

Section I
Web Log Analysis: Perspectives, Issues, and Directions

Chapter II
Historic Perspective of Log Analysis 18
W. David Penniman, Nylink, USA

Chapter III
Surveys as a Complementary Method for Web Log Analysis 39
Lee Rainie, Pew Internet & American Life Project, USA
Bernard J. Jansen, Pennsylvania State University, USA

Chapter IV
Watching the Web: An Ontological and Epistemological Critique of Web-Traffic Measurement 65
Sam Ladner, McMaster University, Canada

Chapter V
Privacy Concerns for Web Logging Data 80
Kirstie Hawkey, University of British Columbia, Canada

Section II
Methodology and Metrics

Chapter VI
The Methodology of Search Log Analysis 100
Bernard J. Jansen, Pennsylvania State University, USA

Chapter VII
Uses, Limitations, and Trends in Web Analytics 124
Anthony Ferrini, Acquiremarketing.com, USA
Jakki J. Mohr, University of Montana, USA

Chapter VIII
A Review of Methodologies for Analyzing Websites 143
Danielle Booth, Pennsylvania State University, USA
Bernard J. Jansen, Pennsylvania State University, USA

Chapter IX
The Unit of Analysis and the Validity of Web Log Data 165
Gi Woong Yun, Bowling Green State University, USA

Chapter X
Recommendations for Reporting Web Usage Studies 181
Kirstie Hawkey, University of British Columbia, Canada
Melanie Kellar, Google, USA

Section III
Behavior Analysis

Chapter XI
From Analysis to Estimation of User Behavior 206
Seda Ozmutlu, Uludag University, Turkey
Huseyin C. Ozmutlu, Uludag University, Turkey
Amanda Spink, Queensland University of Technology, Australia

Chapter XII
An Integrated Approach to Interaction Design and Log Analysis 227
Gheorghe Muresan, Microsoft Corporation, USA

Chapter XIII
Tips for Tracking Web Information Seeking Behavior 256
Brian Detlor, McMaster University, Canada
Maureen Hupfer, McMaster University, Canada
Umar Ruhi, University of Ottawa, Canada

Chapter XIV
Identifying Users Stereotypes for Dynamic Web Pages Customization 284
Sandro José Rigo, Universidade Federal do Rio Grande do Sul (UFRGS), Brazil
José Palazzo M. de Oliveira, Universidade Federal do Rio Grande do Sul (UFRGS), Brazil
Leandro Krug Wives, Universidade Federal do Rio Grande do Sul (UFRGS), Brazil

Chapter XV
Finding Meaning in Online, Very-Large Scale Conversations 307
Brian K. Smith, Pennsylvania State University, USA
Priya Sharma, Pennsylvania State University, USA
Kyu Yon Lim, Pennsylvania State University, USA
Goknur Kaplan Akilli, Pennsylvania State University, USA
KyoungNa Kim, Pennsylvania State University, USA
Toru Fujimoto, Pennsylvania State University, USA
Paula Hooper, TERC, USA

Section IV
Query Log Analysis

Chapter XVI
Machine Learning Approach to Search Query Classification 329
Isak Taksa, Baruch College, City University of New York, USA
Sarah Zelikovitz, The College of Staten Island, City University of New York, USA
Amanda Spink, Queensland University of Technology, Australia

Chapter XVII
Topic Analysis and Identification of Queries 345
Seda Ozmutlu, Uludag University, Turkey
Huseyin C. Ozmutlu, Uludag University, Turkey
Amanda Spink, Queensland University of Technology, Australia

Chapter XVIII
Query Log Analysis in Biomedicine 359
Elmer V. Bernstam, University of Texas Health Science Center at Houston, USA
Jorge R. Herskovic, University of Texas Health Science Center at Houston, USA
William R. Hersh, Oregon Health & Science University, USA

Chapter XIX
Processing and Analysis of Search Query Logs in Chinese 378
Michael Chau, The University of Hong Kong, Hong Kong
Yan Lu, The University of Hong Kong, Hong Kong
Xiao Fang, The University of Toledo, USA
Christopher C. Yang, Drexel University, USA

Chapter XX
Query Log Analysis for Adaptive Dialogue-Driven Search 389
Udo Kruschwitz, University of Essex, UK
Nick Webb, SUNY Albany, USA
Richard Sutcliffe, University of Limerick, Ireland

Section V
Contextual and Specialized Analysis

Chapter XXI
Using Action-Object Pairs as a Conceptual Framework for Transaction Log Analysis 416
Mimi Zhang, Pennsylvania State University, USA
Bernard J. Jansen, Pennsylvania State University, USA

Chapter XXII
Analysis and Evaluation of the Connector Website 436
Paul DiPerna, The Blau Exchange Project, USA

Chapter XXIII
Information Extraction from Blogs 469
Marie-Francine Moens, Katholieke Universiteit Leuven, Belgium

Chapter XXIV
Nethnography: A Naturalistic Approach Towards Online Interaction 488
Adriana Andrade Braga, Pontifícia Universidade Católica do Rio de Janeiro, Brazil

Chapter XXV
Web Log Analysis: Diversity of Research Methodologies 506
Isak Taksa, Baruch College, City University of New York, USA
Amanda Spink, Queensland University of Technology, Australia
Bernard J. Jansen, Pennsylvania State University, USA

Glossary 523

Compilation of References 538

About the Contributors 593

Index 601

Detailed Table of Contents

Preface xix

Chapter I
Research and Methodological Foundations of Transaction Log Analysis 1
Bernard J. Jansen, Pennsylvania State University, USA
Isak Taksa, Baruch College, City University of New York. USA
Amanda Spink, Queensland University of Technology, Australia

This chapter outlines and discusses theoretical and methodological foundations for transaction log analysis. It first addresses the fundamentals of transaction log analysis from a research viewpoint and the concept of transaction logs as a data collection technique from the perspective of behaviorism. From this research foundation, it then moves to the methodological aspects of transaction log analysis and examine the strengths and limitation of transaction logs as trace data. The chapter then reviews the conceptualization of transaction log analysis as an unobtrusive approach to research, and presents the power and deficiency of the unobtrusive methodological concept, including benefits and risks of transaction log analysis specifically from the perspective of an unobtrusive method. Some of the ethical questions concerning the collection of data via transaction log application are discussed.

Section I
Web Log Analysis: Perspectives, Issues, and Directions

Chapter II
Historic Perspective of Log Analysis 18
W. David Penniman, Nylink, USA

This historical review of the birth and evolution of transaction log analysis applied to information retrieval systems provides two perspectives. First, a detailed discussion of the early work in this area, and second, how this work has migrated into the evaluation of World Wide Web usage. The chapter describes the techniques and studies in the early years and makes suggestions for how that knowledge can be applied to current and future studies. A discussion of privacy issues with a framework for addressing the same is presented as well as an overview of the historical "eras" of transaction log analysis. The chapter concludes with the suggestion that a combination of transaction log analysis of the type used early in its

application along with additional more qualitative approaches will be essential for a deep understanding of user behavior (and needs) with respect to current and future retrieval systems and their design.

Every research methodology for data collection has both strengths and limitations, and this is certainly true for transaction log analysis. Therefore, researchers often need to use other data collection methods with transaction logs. This chapter discusses surveys as a viable alternate method for transaction log analysis. The chapter presents a brief review of survey research literature, with a focus on the use of surveys for Web-related research. We identify the steps in implementing survey research and designing a survey instrument. The chapter concludes with a case study of a large electronic survey to illustrate what surveys in conjunction with transaction logs can bring to a research study.

This chapter aims to improve the rigor and legitimacy of Web-traffic measurement as a social research method. The chapter compares two dominant forms of Web-traffic measurement and discusses the implicit and largely unexamined ontological and epistemological claims of both methods. Like all research methods, Web-traffic measurement has implicit ontological and epistemological assumptions embedded within it. An ontology determines what a researcher is able to discover, irrespective of method, because it provides a frame within which phenomena can be rendered intelligible. The chapter argues that Web-traffic measurement employs an ostensibly quantitative, positivistic ontology and epistemology in hopes of cementing the "scientific" legitimacy they engender. These claims to "scientific" method are unsubstantiated, thereby limiting the efficacy and adoption rates of log-file analysis in general. The chapter offers recommendations for improving these measurement tools, including more reflexivity and an explicit rejection of truth claims based on positivistic science.

This chapter examines two aspects of privacy concerns that must be considered when conducting studies that include the collection of Web logging data. After providing background about privacy concerns, the chapter first addresses the standard privacy issues when dealing with participant data. These include privacy implications of releasing data, methods of safeguarding data, and issues encountered with re-use of data. Second, the impact of data collection techniques on a researcher's ability to capture natural user behaviors is discussed. Key recommendations are offered about how to enhance participant privacy when collecting Web logging data to encourage these natural behaviors. The chapter aim is that understanding the privacy issues associated with the logging of user actions on the Web will assist researchers as they evaluate the tradeoffs inherent between the type of logging conducted, the richness of the data gathered, and the naturalness of captured user behavior.

Section II
Methodology and Metrics

Exploiting the data stored in search logs of Web search engines, Intranets, and Websites can provide important insights into understanding the information searching tactics of online searchers. This understanding can inform information system design, interface development, and information architecture construction for content collections. This chapter presents a review of and foundation for conducting Web search transaction log analysis. A search log analysis methodology is outlined consisting of three stages (i.e., collection, preparation, and analysis). The three stages of the methodology are presented in detail with discussions of the goals, metrics, and processes at each stage. The critical terms in transaction log analysis for Web searching are defined. Suggestions are provided on ways to leverage the strengths and addressing the limitations of transaction log analysis for Web searching research.

As the Web's popularity continues to grow and as new uses of the Web are developed, the importance of measuring the performance of a given Website as accurately as possible also increases. This chapter discusses the various uses of Web analytics (how Web log files are used to measure a Website's performance), as well as the limitations of these analytics. We discuss options for overcoming these limitations, new trends in Web analytics—including the integration of technology and marketing techniques—and challenges posed by new Web 2.0 technologies. After reading this chapter, readers should have a nuanced understanding of the "how-to's" of Web analytics.

This chapter is an overview of the process of Web analytics for Websites. It outlines how basic visitor information such as number of visitors and visit duration can be collected through the use of log files and page tagging. This basic information is then combined to create meaningful key performance indicators that are tailored not only to the business goals of the company running the Website, but also to the goals and content of the Website. Finally, this chapter presents several analytic tools and explains

This chapter summarizes the progress of search engine user behavior analysis from search engine transaction log analysis to estimation of user behavior. Correct estimation of user information searching behavior paves the way to more successful and even personalized search engines. However, estimation of user behavior is not a simple task. It closely relates to natural language processing and human computer interaction, and requires preliminary analysis of user behavior and careful user profiling. This chapter details the studies performed on analysis and estimation of search engine user behavior, and surveys analytical methods that have been and can be used, and the challenges and research opportunities related to search engine user behavior or transaction log query analysis and estimation.

Chapter XII
An Integrated Approach to Interaction Design and Log Analysis 227
Gheorghe Muresan, Microsoft Corporation, USA

This chapter describes and discusses a methodological framework that integrates analysis of interaction logs with the conceptual design of the user interaction. It is based on (i) formalizing the functionality that is supported by an interactive system and the valid interactions that can take place; (ii) deriving schemas for capturing the interactions in activity logs; (iii) deriving log parsers that reveal the system states and the state transitions that took place during the interaction; and (iv) analyzing the user activities and the system's state transitions in order to describe the user interaction or to test some research hypotheses. This approach is particularly useful for studying user behavior when using highly interactive systems. We present the details of the methodology, and exemplify its use in a mediated retrieval experiment, in which the focus of the study is on studying the information-seeking process and on finding interaction patterns.

Chapter XIII
Tips for Tracking Web Information Seeking Behavior 256
Brian Detlor, McMaster University, Canada
Maureen Hupfer, McMaster University, Canada
Umar Ruhi, University of Ottawa, Canada

This chapter provides various tips for practitioners and researchers who wish to track end-user Web information seeking behavior. These tips are derived in large part from the authors' own experience of collecting and analyzing individual differences, task, and Web tracking data to investigate people's online information seeking behaviors at a specific municipal community portal site (myhamilton.ca). The tips discussed in this chapter include: i) the need to account for both task and individual differences in any Web information seeking behavior analysis; ii) how to collect Web metrics through deployment of a unique ID that links individual differences, task, and Web tracking data together; iii) the types of Web log metrics to collect; iv) how to go about collecting and making sense of such metrics; and v) the importance of addressing privacy concerns at the start of any collection of Web tracking information.

Chapter XIV
Identifying Users Stereotypes for Dynamic Web Pages Customization 284
Sandro José Rigo, Universidade Federal do Rio Grande do Sul (UFRGS), Brazil
José Palazzo M. de Oliveira, Universidade Federal do Rio Grande do Sul (UFRGS), Brazil
Leandro Krug Wives, Universidade Federal do Rio Grande do Sul (UFRGS), Brazil

Adaptive Hypermedia is an effective approach to automatic personalization that overcomes the difficulties and deficiencies of traditional Web systems in delivering the appropriate content to users. One important issue regarding Adaptive Hypermedia systems is the construction and maintenance of the user profile. Another important concern is the use of Semantic Web resources to describe Web applications and to implement adaptation mechanisms. Web Usage Mining, in this context, allows the generation of Websites access patterns. This chapter describes the possibilities of integration of these usage patterns with semantic knowledge obtained from domain ontologies. Thus, it is possible to identify users' stereotypes for dynamic Web pages customization. This integration of semantic knowledge can provide personalization systems with better adaptation strategies.

Chapter XV
Finding Meaning in Online, Very-Large Scale Conversations 307
Brian K. Smith, Pennsylvania State University, USA
Priya Sharma, Pennsylvania State University, USA
Kyu Yon Lim, Pennsylvania State University, USA
Goknur Kaplan Akilli, Pennsylvania State University, USA
KyoungNa Kim, Pennsylvania State University, USA
Toru Fujimoto, Pennsylvania State University, USA
Paula Hooper, TERC, USA

Computers and networking technologies have led to increases in the development and sustenance of online communities, and much research has focused on examining the formation of and interactions within these virtual communities. The methods for collecting data and analyzing virtual online communities, especially very large-scale online discussion forums can be varied and complex. This chapter describes two analytical methods—qualitative data analysis and Social Network Analysis (SNA)–that we used to examine conversations within ESPN's Fast Break community, which focuses on fantasy basketball sports games. Two different levels of analyses—the individual and community level—allowed us to examine individual reflection on game strategy and decision-making as well as characteristics of the community and patterns of interactions between participants within community. The description of our use of these two analytical methods can help researchers and designers who may be attempting to analyze and characterize other large-scale virtual communities.

Section IV
Query Log Analysis

Chapter XVI
Machine Learning Approach to Search Query Classification 329
Isak Taksa, Baruch College, City University of New York, USA
Sarah Zelikovitz, The College of Staten Island, City University of New York, USA
Amanda Spink, Queensland University of Technology, Australia

Search query classification is a necessary step for a number of information retrieval tasks. This chapter presents an approach to non-hierarchical classification of search queries that focuses on two specific

areas of machine learning: short text classification and limited manual labeling. Typically, search queries are short, display little class specific information per single query and are therefore a weak source for traditional machine learning. To improve the effectiveness of the classification process the chapter introduces background knowledge discovery by using information retrieval techniques. The proposed approach is applied to a task of age classification of a corpus of queries from a commercial search engine. In the process, various classification scenarios are generated and executed, providing insight into choice, significance and range of tuning parameters.

Chapter XVII
Topic Analysis and Identification of Queries 345
Seda Ozmutlu, Uludag University, Turkey
Huseyin C. Ozmutlu, Uludag University, Turkey
Amanda Spink, Queensland University of Technology, Australia

This chapter emphasizes topic analysis and identification of search engine user queries. Topic analysis and identification of queries is an important task related to the discipline of information retrieval which is a key element for the development of successful personalized search engines. Topic identification of text is also no simple task, and a problem yet unsolved. The problem is even harder for search engine user queries due to real-time requirements and the limited number of terms in the user queries. The chapter includes a detailed literature review on topic analysis and identification, with an emphasis on search engine user queries, a survey of the analytical methods that have been and can be used, and the challenges and research opportunities related to topic analysis and identification.

Chapter XVIII
Query Log Analysis in Biomedicine 359
Elmer V. Bernstam, University of Texas Health Science Center at Houston, USA
Jorge R. Herskovic, University of Texas Health Science Center at Houston, USA
William R. Hersh, Oregon Health & Science University, USA

Clinicians, researchers and members of the general public are increasingly using information technology to cope with the explosion in biomedical knowledge. This chapter describes the purpose of query log analysis in the biomedical domain as well as features of the biomedical domain such as controlled vocabularies (ontologies) and existing infrastructure useful for query log analysis. This chapter focuses specifically on MEDLINE, which is the most comprehensive bibliographic database of the world's biomedical literature, the PubMed interface to MEDLINE, the Medical Subject Headings vocabulary and the Unified Medical Language System. However, the approaches discussed here can also be applied to other query logs. The chapter concludes with a look toward the future of biomedical query log analysis.

Chapter XIX
Processing and Analysis of Search Query Logs in Chinese 378
Michael Chau, The University of Hong Kong, Hong Kong
Yan Lu, The University of Hong Kong, Hong Kong
Xiao Fang, The University of Toledo, USA
Christopher C. Yang, Drexel University, USA

More non-English contents are now available on the World Wide Web and the number of non-English users on the Web is increasing. While it is important to understand the Web searching behavior of these non-English users, many previous studies on Web query logs have focused on analyzing English search logs and their results may not be directly applied to other languages. This chapter we discusses some methods and techniques that can be used to analyze search queries in Chinese. We also show an example of applying our methods on a Chinese Web search engine. Some interesting findings are reported.

Chapter XX
Query Log Analysis for Adaptive Dialogue-Driven Search 389
Udo Kruschwitz, University of Essex, UK
Nick Webb, SUNY Albany, USA
Richard Sutcliffe, University of Limerick, Ireland

The theme of this chapter is the improvement of Information Retrieval and Question Answering systems by the analysis of query logs. Two case studies are discussed. The first describes an intranet search engine working on a university campus which can present sophisticated query modifications to the user. It does this via a hierarchical domain model built using multi-word term co-occurrence data. The usage log was analysed using mutual information scores between a query and its refinement, between a query and its replacement, and between two queries occurring in the same session. The results can be used to validate refinements in the domain model, and to suggest replacements such as domain-dependent spelling corrections. The second case study describes a dialogue-based question answering system working over a closed document collection largely derived from the Web. Logs here are based around explicit sessions in which an analyst interacts with the system. Analysis of the logs has shown that certain types of interaction lead to increased precision of the results. Future versions of the system will encourage these forms of interaction. The conclusions of this chapter are firstly that there is a growing literature on query log analysis, much of it reviewed here, secondly that logs provide many forms of useful information for improving a system, and thirdly that mutual information measures taken with automatic term recognition algorithms and hierarchy construction techniques comprise one approach for enhancing system performance.

Section V
Contextual and Specialized Analysis

Chapter XXI
Using Action-Object Pairs as a Conceptual Framework for Transaction Log Analysis 416
Mimi Zhang, Pennsylvania State University, USA
Bernard J. Jansen, Pennsylvania State University, USA

This chapter presents the action-object pair approach as a conceptual framework for conducting transaction log analysis. We argue that there are two basic components in the interaction between the user and the system recorded in a transaction log, which are action and object. An action is a specific expression of the user. An object is a self-contained information object, the recipient of the action. These two components form one interaction set or an action-object pair. A series of action-object pairs represents the

interaction session. The action-object pair approach provides a conceptual framework for the collection, analysis, and understanding of data from transaction logs. The chapter proposes that this approach can benefit system design by providing the organizing principle for implicit feedback and other interactions concerning the user and delivering, for example, personalized service to the user based on this feedback. Action-object pairs also provide a worthwhile approach to advance our theoretical and conceptual understanding of transaction log analysis as a research method.

Chapter XXII
Analysis and Evaluation of the Connector Website 436
Paul DiPerna, The Blau Exchange Project, USA

This chapter proposes a new theoretical construct for evaluating websites that facilitate online social networks. The suggested model considers previous academic work related to social networks and online communities. This chapter's main purpose is to define a new kind of social institution, called a "connector website", and provide a means for objectively analyzing web-based organizations that empower users to form online social networks. Several statistical approaches are used to gauge website-level growth, trend lines, and volatility. This project sets out to determine whether or not particular connector websites can be mechanisms for social change, and to quantify the nature of the observed social change. The chapter's aim is to introduce new applications for Web log analysis by evaluating connector websites and their organizations.

Chapter XXIII
Information Extraction from Blogs 469
Marie-Francine Moens, Katholieke Universiteit Leuven, Belgium

This chapter introduces information extraction from blog texts. It argues that the classical techniques for information extraction that are commonly used for mining well-formed texts lose some of their validity in the context of blogs. This finding is demonstrated by considering each step in the information extraction process and by illustrating this problem in different applications. In order to tackle the problem of mining content from blogs, algorithms are developed that combine different sources of evidence in the most flexible way. The chapter concludes with ideas for future research.

Chapter XXIV
Nethnography: A Naturalistic Approach Towards Online Interaction 488
Adriana Andrade Braga, Pontifícia Universidade Católica do Rio de Janeiro, Brazil

This chapter explores the possibilities and limitations of nethnography, an ethnographic approach applied to the study of online interactions, particularly computer-mediated communication. In this chapter, a brief history of ethnography, including its relation to anthropological theories and its key methodological assumptions is addressed. Next, one of the most frequent methodologies applied to Internet settings, that is to treat logfiles as the only or main source of data, is explored, and its consequences are analyzed. In addition, some strategies related to a naturalistic perspective for data analysis are examined. Finally, an example of an ethnographic study that involves participants of a Weblog is presented to illustrate the potential for nethnography to enhance the study of computer-mediated communication.

Chapter XXV
Web Log Analysis: Diversity of Research Methodologies 506
Isak Taksa, Baruch College, City University of New York, USA
Amanda Spink, Queensland University of Technology, Australia
Bernard J. Jansen, Pennsylvania State University, USA

Web log analysis is an innovative and unique field constantly formed and changed by the convergence of various emerging Web technologies. Due to its interdisciplinary character, the diversity of issues it addresses, and the variety and number of Web applications, it is the subject of many distinctive and diverse research methodologies. This chapter examines research methodologies used by contributing authors in preparing the individual chapters for this handbook, summarizes research results, and proposes new directions for future research in this area.

Glossary 523

Compilation of References 538

About the Contributors 593

Index 601

Preface

Web use has become a ubiquitous online activity for people of all ages, cultures and pursuits. Whether searching, shopping, or socializing users leave behind a great deal of data revealing their information needs, mindset, and approaches used. Web designers collect these artifacts in a variety of Web logs for subsequent analysis. *The Handbook of Research on Web Log Analysis* reflects on the multifaceted themes of Web use and presents various approaches to log analysis. The handbook looks at the history of Web log analysis and examines new trends including the issues of privacy, social interaction and community building. It focuses on analysis of the user's behavior during the Web activities, and investigates current methodologies and metrics for Web log analysis. The handbook proposes new research directions and novel applications of existing knowledge. The handbook includes 25 chapters in five sections, contributed by a great variety of researchers and practitioners in the field of Web log analysis.

Chapter I "Research and Methodological Foundations of Transaction Log Analysis" by Bernard J. Jansen (Pennsylvania State University, USA), Isak Taksa (Baruch College, City University of New York, USA), Amanda Spink (Queensland University of Technology, Australia), introduces, outlines and discusses theoretical and methodological foundations for transaction log analysis. The chapter addresses the fundamentals of transaction log analysis from a research viewpoint and the concept of transaction logs as a data collection technique from the perspective of behaviorism. It continues with the methodological aspects of transaction log analysis and examines the strengths and limitations of transaction logs as trace data. It reviews the conceptualization of transaction log analysis as an unobtrusive approach to research, and presents the power and deficiency of the unobtrusive methodological concept, including benefits and risks of transaction log analysis specifically from the perspective of an unobtrusive method. Some of the ethical questions concerning the collection of data via transaction log application are discussed.

Section I, *Web Log Analysis: Perspectives, Issues, and Directions* consists of four chapters presenting a historic perspective of web log analysis, examining surveys as a complementary method for transaction log analysis, and investigating issues of privacy and traffic measurement.

Chapter II "Historic Perspective of Log Analysis" by W. David Penniman (Nylink, USA), provides a historical review of the birth and evolution of transaction log analysis applied to information retrieval systems. It offers a detailed discussion of the early work in this area and explains how this work has migrated into the evaluation of Web usage. The author describes the techniques and studies in the early years and makes suggestions for how that knowledge can be applied to current and future studies. A discussion of privacy issues with a framework for addressing the same is presented, as well as an overview of the historical "eras" of transaction log analysis.

Chapter III "Surveys as a Complementary Method for Web Log Analysis" by Lee Rainie (Pew Internet & American Life Project, USA), Bernard J. Jansen (Pennsylvania State University, USA) examines surveys as a viable complementary method for transaction log analysis. It presents a brief overview of survey research literature, with a focus on the use of surveys for Web-related research. The authors identify the steps in implementing survey research and designing a survey instrument. They conclude with a case study of a large electronic survey to illustrate what surveys in conjunction with transaction logs can bring to a research study.

Chapter IV "Watching the Web: An Ontological and Epistemological Critique of Web-Traffic Measurement" by Sam Ladner (York University, Canada), compares two dominant forms of Web-traffic measurement and discusses the implicit and largely unexamined ontological and epistemological claims of both methods. It suggests that like all research methods, Web-traffic measurement has implicit ontological and epistemological assumptions embedded within it. An ontology determines what a researcher is able to discover, irrespective of method, because it provides a framework within which phenomena can be rendered intelligible.

Chapter V "Privacy Concerns for Web Logging Data" by Kirstie Hawkey (University of British Columbia, Canada) examines two aspects of privacy that must be considered when conducting studies of user behavior that includes the collection of web logging data. First considered are the standard privacy concerns when dealing with participant data. These include privacy implications of releasing the data, methods of safeguarding the data, and issues encountered with re-use of data. Second, the impact of data collection techniques on the researchers' ability to capture natural user behaviors is discussed. Key recommendations are offered about how to enhance participant privacy when collecting Web logging data to encourage these natural behaviors.

Section II, *Methodology and Metrics*, consists of five chapters reviewing the foundations, trends and limitations of available and prospective methodologies, examining granularity and validity of log data, and recommending context for future log studies.

Chapter VI "The Methodology of Search Log Analysis" by Bernard J. Jansen (Pennsylvania State University, USA) presents a review of and foundation for conducting Web search transaction log analysis. A search log analysis methodology is outlined consisting of three stages (i.e., collection, preparation, and analysis). The three stages of the methodology are presented in detail with discussions of the goals, metrics, and processes at each stage. The critical terms in transaction log analysis for Web searching are defined. Suggestions are provided on ways to leverage the strengths and addressing the limitations of transaction log analysis for Web searching research.

Chapter VII "Uses, Limitations, and Trends in Web Analytics" by Tony Ferrini (Acquiremarketing.com, USA), Jakki J. Mohr (University of Montana, USA), emphasizes the importance of measuring the performance of a Website. The measuring includes tracking the traffic (number of visitors), visitors' activity and behavior while visiting the site. The authors examine various uses of Web Metrics (how to collect Web log files) and Web analytics (how Web log files are used to measure a Website's performance), as well as the limitations of these analytics. The authors also propose options for overcoming these limitations, new trends in Web analytics, including the integration of technology and marketing techniques, and challenges posed by new Web 2.0 technologies.

Chapter VIII "A Review of Methodologies for Analyzing Websites" by Danielle Booth (Pennsylvania State University, USA), Bernard J. Jansen, (Pennsylvania State University, USA) provides an overview of the process of Web analytics for Websites. It outlines how basic visitor information such as number of visitors and visit duration can be collected using log files and page tagging. This basic information is then combined to create meaningful key performance indicators that are tailored not only to the business goals of the company running the Website, but also to the goals and content of the Website. Finally, this chapter presents several analytic tools and explains how to choose the right tool for the needs of the Website. The ultimate goal of this chapter is to provide methods for increasing revenue and customer satisfaction through careful analysis of visitor interaction with a Website.

Chapter IX "The Unit of Analysis and the Validity of Web Log Data" by Gi Woong Yun (Bowling Green State University, USA), discusses challenges and limitations in defining units of analysis of Web site use. The author maintains that unit of analysis depends on the research topic and level of analysis, and therefore is complicated to predict ahead of data collection. Additionally, technical specifications of the Web log data sometimes limit what researchers can select as a unit of analysis for their research. The author also examines the validity of data collection and interpretation processes as well as sources of such data. The chapter concludes with proposed criteria for defining units of analysis of a Web site and measures for improving and authenticating validity of web log data.

Chapter X "Recommendations for Reporting Web Usage Studies" by Kirstie Hawkey (University of British Columbia, Canada), Melanie Kellar (Google Inc., USA), presents recommendations for reporting context in studies of Web usage including Web browsing behavior. These recommendations consist of eight categories of contextual information crucial to the reporting of results: user characteristics, temporal information, Web browsing environment, nature of the Web browsing task, data collection methods, descriptive data reporting, statistical analysis, and results in the context of prior work. This chapter argues that the Web and its user population are constantly growing and evolving. This changing temporal context can make it difficult for researchers to evaluate previous work in the proper context, particularly when detailed information about the user population, experimental methodology, and results is not presented. The adoption of these recommendations will allow researchers in the area of Web browsing behavior to more easily replicate previous work, make comparisons between their current work and previous work, and build upon previous work to advance the field.

Section III, *Behavior Analysis*, consists of five chapters summarizing research in user behavior analysis during various web activities and suggesting directions for identifying, finding meaning and tracking user behavior.

Chapter XI "From Analysis to Estimation of User Behavior" by Seda Ozmutlu (Uludag University, Turkey), Huseyin C. Ozmutlu (Uludag University, Turkey), Amanda Spink (Queensland University of Technology, Australia), summarizes the progress of search engine user behavior analysis from search engine transaction log analysis to estimation of user behavior. Correct estimation of user information searching behavior paves the way to more successful and even personalized search engines. However, estimation of user behavior is not a simple task. It closely relates to natural language processing and human computer interaction, and requires preliminary analysis of user behavior and careful user profiling. This chapter details the studies performed on analysis and estimation of search engine user behavior, and surveys analytical methods that have been and can be used, and the challenges and research opportunities related to search engine user behavior or transaction log query analysis and estimation.

Chapter XII "An Integrated Approach to Interaction Design and Log Analysis" by Gheorghe Muresan (Microsoft Corporation, USA), describes and discusses a methodological framework that integrates analysis of interaction logs with the conceptual design of the user interaction. It is based on (1) formalizing the functionality that is supported by an interactive system and the valid interactions that can take place; (2) deriving schemas for capturing the interactions in activity logs; (3) deriving log parsers that reveal the system states and the state transitions that took place during the interaction; and (4) analyzing the user activities and the system's state transitions in order to describe the user interaction or to test some research hypotheses. This approach is particularly useful for studying user behavior when using highly interactive systems. Details of the methodology and examples of use in a mediated retrieval experiment are presented.

Chapter XIII "Tips for Tracking Web Information Seeking Behavior" by Brian Detlor (McMaster University, Canada), Maureen Hupfer (McMaster University, Canada), Umar Ruhi (University of Ottawa, Canada), provides various tips for practitioners and researchers who wish to track end-user Web information seeking behavior. These tips are derived in large part from the authors' own experience in collecting and analyzing individual differences, task, and Web tracking data to investigate people's online information seeking behaviors at a specific municipal community portal site (myhamilton.ca). The tips discussed in this chapter include: (2) the need to account for both task and individual differences in any Web information seeking behavior analysis; (2) how to collect Web metrics through deployment of a unique ID that links individual differences, task, and Web tracking data together; (3) the types of Web log metrics to collect; (4) how to go about collecting and making sense of such metrics; and (5) the importance of addressing privacy concerns at the start of any collection of Web tracking information.

Chapter XIV "Identifying Users Stereotypes for Dynamic Web Pages Customization" by Sandro José Rigo, José Palazzo M. de Oliveira, Leandro Krug Wives, (Instituto de Informática, Universidade Federal do Rio Grande do Sul, Brazil), explores Adaptive Hypermedia as an effective approach to automatic personalization that overcomes the complexities and deficiencies of traditional Web systems in delivering user-relevant content. The chapter focuses on three important issues regarding Adaptive Hypermedia systems: the construction and maintenance of the user profile, the use of Semantic Web resources to describe Web applications, and implementation of adaptation mechanisms. Web Usage Mining, in this context, allows the discovery of Website access patterns. The chapter describes the possibilities of integration of these usage patterns with semantic knowledge obtained from domain ontology. Thus, it is possible to identify users' stereotypes for dynamic Web pages customization. This integration of semantic knowledge can provide personalization systems with better adaptation strategies.

Chapter XV "Finding Meaning in Online, Very-Large Scale Conversations" by Brian K. Smith, Priya Sharma, Kyu Yon Lim, Goknur Kaplan Akilli, KyoungNa Kim, Toru Fujimoto (Pennsylvania State University, USA), Paula Hooper (TERC, USA), provides understanding of how people come together to form virtual communities and how knowledge flows between participants over time. It examines ways to collect data and describes two methods–qualitative data analysis and Social Network Analysis (SNA)–which were used to analyze conversations within ESPN's *Fast Break* virtual community, which focuses on fantasy basketball sports games. Furthermore, the authors utilize the individual and community level analysis to examine individual reflection on game strategy and decision-making, as well as patterns of interactions between participants within the community.

Section IV, *Query Log Analysis*, consists of five chapters examining query classification and topic identification in search engines, analyzing queries in the biomedical domain and Chinese Information Retrieval, and presenting a comprehensive review of the research publications on query log analysis.

Chapter XVI "Machine Learning Approach to Search Query Classification" by Isak Taksa (Baruch College, City University of New York, USA), Sarah Zelikovitz (The College of Staten Island, City University of New York, USA), Amanda Spink (Queensland University of Technology, Australia), presents an approach to non-hierarchical classification of search queries that focuses on two specific areas of machine learning: short text classification and limited manual labeling. Typically, search queries are short, display little class specific information per single query and are therefore a weak source for traditional machine learning. To improve the effectiveness of the classification process the chapter introduces background knowledge discovery by using information retrieval techniques. The proposed approach is applied to a task of age classification of a corpus of queries from a commercial search engine. In the process, various classification scenarios are generated and executed, providing insight into choice, significance and range of tuning parameters.

Chapter XVII "Topic Analysis and Identification of Queries" by Seda Ozmutlu (Uludag University, Turkey), Huseyin C. Ozmutlu (Uludag University, Turkey), Amanda Spink (Queensland University of Technology, Australia), emphasizes topic analysis and identification of search engine user queries. Topic analysis and identification of queries is an important task related to the discipline of information retrieval, which is a key element for the development of successful personalized search engines. Topic identification of text is also no simple task, and a problem yet unsolved. The problem is even harder for search engine user queries due to real-time requirements and the limited number of terms in the user queries. The chapter includes a detailed literature review on topic analysis and identification, with an emphasis on search engine user queries, a survey of the analytical methods that have been and can be used, and the challenges and research opportunities related to topic analysis and identification.

Chapter XVIII "Query Log Analysis in Biomedicine" by Elmer V. Bernstam (UT-Houston, USA), Jorge R. Herskovic (UT-Houston, USA), William R. Hersh (Oregon Health & Science University, USA), describes the purpose of query log analysis in the biomedical domain as well as features of the biomedical domain such as controlled vocabularies (ontologies) and existing infrastructure useful for query log analysis. The chapter focuses specifically on MEDLINE, which is the most comprehensive bibliographic database of the world's biomedical literature, the PubMed interface to MEDLINE, the Medical Subject Headings vocabulary and the Unified Medical Language System. However, the approaches discussed here can also be applied to other query logs. The chapter concludes with a look toward the future of biomedical query log analysis.

Chapter XIX "Processing and Analysis of Search Query Logs in Chinese", by Michael Chau (The University of Hong Kong, Hong Kong), Yan Lu (The University of Hong Kong, Hong Kong), Xiao Fang (The University of Toledo, USA), Christopher C. Yang (Drexel University, USA), argues that more non-English content is now available on the World Wide Web and the number of non-English users on the Web is increasing. While it is important to understand the Web searching behavior of these non-English users, many previous studies on Web query logs have focused on analyzing English search logs and their results may not be directly applied to other languages. This chapter discusses some methods and techniques that can be used to analyze search queries in Chinese language. The authors show an example of applying these methods to a Chinese Web search engine.

Chapter XX "Query Log Analysis for Adaptive Dialogue-Driven Search" by Udo Kruschwitz (University of Essex, UK), Nick Webb (SUNY Albany, USA), Richard Sutcliffe (University of Limerick, Ireland), presents an extensive review of the research publications on query log analysis and analyses two case studies, both aimed at improving Information Retrieval and Question Answering systems. The first describes an intranet search engine that offers sophisticated query modifications to the user. It does this via a hierarchical domain model that was built using multi-word term co-occurrence data. The usage log is analyzed using mutual information scores between a query and its refinement, between a query and its replacement, and between two queries occurring in the same session. The second case study describes a dialogue-based Question Answering system working over a closed document collection largely derived from the Web. Logs are based around explicit sessions in which an analyst interacts with the system. Analysis of the logs has shown that certain types of interaction lead to increased precision of the results.

Section V, *Contextual and Specialized Analysis*, consists of four chapters presenting a conceptual framework for transaction log analysis, proposing a new theoretical model for evaluating connector websites that facilitate online social networks, introducing information extraction from blog texts, and exploring the use of nethnography in the study of computer-mediated communication (CMC).

Chapter XXI "Using Action-Object Pairs as a Conceptual Framework for Transaction Log Analysis" by Mimi Zhang (Pennsylvania State University, USA), Bernard J. Jansen (Pennsylvania State University, USA), presents the action-object pair approach as a conceptual framework for transaction log analysis. The authors argue that there are two basic components in the interaction between the user and the system recorded in a transaction log, which are action and object. An action is a specific utterance of the user. An object is a self-contained information object, the receipt of the action. These two components form one interaction set or an action-object pair. A series of action-object pairs represents the interaction session. The action-object pair approach provides a conceptual framework for the collection, analysis, and understanding of data from transaction logs. The authors suggest that this approach can benefit system design by providing the implicit feedback concerning the user and delivering, for example, personalized service to the user based on this feedback. Action–object pairs also provide a worthwhile approach to advance the theoretical and conceptual understanding of transaction log analysis as a research method.

Chapter XXII "Analysis and Evaluation of the Connector Website" by Paul DiPerna (The Blau Exchange Project, USA), proposes a new theoretical model for evaluating websites that facilitate online social networks. The suggested model considers previous academic work related to social networks and online communities. This study's main purpose is to define a new kind of social institution, called a "connector website", and provide a means for objectively analyzing web-based organizations that empower users to form online social networks. Several statistical approaches are used to gauge website-level growth, trend lines, and volatility. This project sets out to determine whether particular connector websites can be mechanisms for social change, and to quantify the nature of the observed social change. The author hopes this chapter introduces new applications for Web log analysis by evaluating connector websites and their organizations.

Chapter XXIII "Information Extraction from Blogs" by Marie-Francine Moens (Katholieke Universiteit Leuven, Belgium), introduces information extraction from blog texts. It argues that the classical techniques for information extraction that are commonly used for mining well-formed texts lose some of their validity in the context of blogs. This finding is demonstrated by considering each step in the information extraction process and by illustrating this problem in different applications. In order to tackle the problem of mining content from blogs, algorithms are developed that combine different sources of evidence in the most flexible way. The chapter concludes with ideas for future research.

Chapter XXIV "Nethnography: A Naturalistic Approach Towards Online Interaction" by Adriana Andrade Braga (Pontifícia Universidade Católica do Rio de Janeiro), explores the possibilities and limitations of nethnography, an ethnographic approach applied to the study of online interactions, particularly computer-mediated communication (CMC). The chapter presents a brief history of ethnography, including its relation to anthropological theories and its key methodological assumptions. The presentation focuses on common methodologies that treat log files as the only or main source of data and discusses results of such an approach. In addition, it examines some strategies related to a naturalistic perspective of data analysis. Finally, to illustrate the potential for nethnography to enhance the study of CMC, the authors present an example of an ethnographic study.

Finally, Chapter XXV "Web Log Analysis: Diversity of Research Methodologies" by Isak Taksa (Baruch College, City University of New York, USA), Amanda Spink (Queensland University of Technology, Australia), and Bernard J. Jansen (Pennsylvania State University) focuses on the innovative character of Web log analysis and the emergence of its new applications. Web log analysis is the subject of many distinctive and diverse research methodologies due to its interdisciplinary nature and the diversity of issues it addresses. This chapter examines research methodologies used by contributing authors in preparing the individual chapters for this handbook, summarizes research results, and proposes new directions for future research in this area.

The Handbook of Research on Web Log Analysis with its full spectrum of topics, styles of presentation and depth of coverage will be of value to faculty seeking an advanced textbook in the field of log analysis, and researchers and practitioners looking for answers to consistently evolving theoretical and practical challenges.

Bernard J. Jansen, Amanda Spink, and Isak Taksa
Editors

Chapter I
Research and Methodological Foundations of Transaction Log Analysis

Bernard J. Jansen
Pennsylvania State University, USA

Isak Taksa
Baruch College, City University of New York, USA

Amanda Spink
Queensland University of Technology, Australia

ABSTRACT

This chapter outlines and discusses theoretical and methodological foundations for transaction log analysis. We first address the fundamentals of transaction log analysis from a research viewpoint and the concept of transaction logs as a data collection technique from the perspective of behaviorism. From this research foundation, we move to the methodological aspects of transaction log analysis and examine the strengths and limitations of transaction logs as trace data. We then review the conceptualization of transaction log analysis as an unobtrusive approach to research, and present the power and deficiency of the unobtrusive methodological concept, including benefits and risks of transaction log analysis specifically from the perspective of an unobtrusive method. Some of the ethical questions concerning the collection of data via transaction log applications are discussed.

INTRODUCTION

Conducting research involves the use of both a set of theoretical constructs and methods for investigation. For empirical research, the results are linked conceptually to the data collection process. Quality research papers must contain a thorough methodology section. In order to understand empirical research and the implications of the results, one must thoroughly understand the techniques by which the researcher collected and analyzed the data. When conducting research concerning users and information systems, there are a variety of methods at ones disposal. These research methods are qualitative, quantitative, or mixed. The selection of an appropriate method is critically important if the research is to have effective outcomes and be efficient in execution. The data collection also involves a choice of methods. Transaction logs and transaction log analysis is one approach to data collection and a research method for both system performance and user behavior analysis that has been used since 1967 (Meister & Sullivan, 1967) and in peer reviewed research since 1975 (Penniman, 1975).

A transaction log is *an electronic record of interactions that have occurred between a system and users of that system*. These log files can come from a variety of computers and systems (Websites, OPAC, user computers, blogs, listserv, online newspapers, etc.), basically any application that can record the user – system – information interactions. Transaction log analysis is the methodological approach to studying online systems and users of these systems. Peters (1993) defines transaction log analysis as *the study of electronically recorded interactions between on-line information retrieval systems and the persons who search for information found in those systems*. Since the advent of the Internet, we have to modify Peter's (1993) definition, expanding it to include systems other than information retrieval systems.

Transaction log analysis is a broad categorization of methods that covers several sub-categorizations, including Web log analysis (i.e., analysis of Web system logs), blog analysis, and search log analysis (analysis of search engine logs). Transaction log analysis enables macro-analysis of aggregate user data and patterns and micro-analysis of individual search patterns. The results from the analyzed data help develop improved systems and services based on user behavior or system performance.

From the user behavior side, transaction log analysis is one of a class of unobtrusive methods (a.k.a., non-reactive or low-constraint). Unobtrusive methods allow data collection without directly interfacing with participants. The research literature specifically describes unobtrusive approaches as those that do not require a response from participants (c.f., McGrath, 1994; Page, 2000; Webb, Campbell, Schwarz, & Sechrest, 2000). This data can be observational or existing data. Unobtrusive methods are in contrast to obtrusive or reactive approaches such as questionnaires, tests, laboratory studies, and surveys (Webb, Campbell, Schwartz, Sechrest, & Grove, 1981). A laboratory experiment is an example of an extreme obtrusive method. Certainly, the line between unobtrusive and obtrusive methods is sometimes blurred. For example, conducting a survey to gauge the reaction of users to information systems is an obtrusive method. However, using the posted results from the survey is an unobtrusive method.

In this chapter, we address the research and methodological foundations of transaction log analysis. We first address the concept of transaction logs as a data collection technique from the perspective of behaviorism. We then review the conceptualization of transaction log analysis as trace data and an unobtrusive method. We present the strengths and shortcomings of the unobtrusive approach, including benefits and shortcomings of transaction log analysis specifically from the perspective of an unobtrusive method. We end with a short summary and open questions of transaction logging as a data collection method.

The use of transaction logs for academic purposes certainly falls conceptually within the confines of the behaviorism paradigm of research. The behaviorism approach is the conceptual basis for the transaction log methodology.

BEHAVIORISM

Behaviorism is a research approach that emphasizes the outward behavioral aspects of thought. Strictly speaking, behaviorism also dismisses the inward experiential and procedural aspects (Skinner, 1953; Watson, 1913); behaviorism has come under critical fire for this narrow viewpoint.

However, for transaction log analysis, we take a more open view of behaviorism. In this more encompassing view, behaviorism emphasizes the observed behaviors without discounting the inner aspects that may accompany these outward behaviors. This more open outlook ofbehaviorism supports the viewpoint that researchers can gain much from studying expressions (i.e., behaviors) of users when interacting with information systems. These expressed behaviors may reflect both aspects of the person's inner self but also contextual aspects of the environment within which the behavior occurs. These environmental aspects may influence behaviors that are also reflective of inner cognitive factors.

The underlying proposition of behaviorism is that all things that people do are behaviors. These behaviors include actions, thoughts, and feelings. With this underlying proposition, the behaviorism position is that all theories and models concerning people have observational correlates. The behaviors and any proposed theoretical constructs must be mutually complementary. Strict behaviorism would further state that there are no differences between the publicly observable behavioral processes (i.e., actions) and privately observable behavioral processes (i.e., thinking and feeling). We take the position that, due to contextual, situational, or environmental factors, there many times may be such disconnection between the cognitive and affective processes. Therefore, there are sources of behavior both internal (i.e., cognitive, affective, expertise) and external (i.e., environmental and situational). Behaviorism focuses primarily on only what an observer can see or manipulate.

We see the effects of behaviorism in many types of research and especially in transaction log analysis. Behaviorism is evident in any research where the observable evidence is critical to the research questions or methods. This is especially true in any experimental research where the operationalization of variables is required. A behaviorism approach at its core seeks to understand events in terms of behavioral criteria (Sellars, 1963, p. 22). Behaviorist research demands behavioral evidence. Within such a perspective, there is no knowable difference between two states unless there is a demonstrable difference in the behavior associated with each state.

Research grounded in behaviorism always involves *somebody* doing *something* in a *situation*. Therefore, all derived research questions focus on *who* (actors), *what* (behaviors), *when* (temporal), *where* (contexts), and *why* (cognitive). The actors in a behaviorism paradigm are people at whatever level of aggregation (e.g., individuals, groups, organizations, communities, nationalities, societies, etc.) whose behavior is studied. Such research must focus on behaviors, all aspects of what the actors do. These behaviors have a temporal element, when and how long these behaviors occur. The behaviors occur within some context, which are all the environmental and situational features in which these behaviors are embedded. The cognitive aspect to these behaviors is the rational and affective processes internal to the actors executing the behaviors.

From this research perspective, each of these (i.e., actor, behaviors, temporal, context, and cognitive) are behaviorist constructs. However, for transaction log analysis, one is primarily concerned with "what is a behavior?"

Behaviors

A variable in research is an entity representing a set of events where each event may have a different value. In log analysis, session duration or number of clicks may be variables that a researcher is interested in. The particular variables that a researcher is interested in are derived from the research questions driving the study.

One can define variables by their use in a research study (e.g., independent, dependent, extraneous, controlled, constant, and confounding) and by their nature. Defined by their nature, there are three types of variables, which are environments (i.e., events of the situation, environment, or context), subject (i.e., events or aspects of the subject being studied), and behavioral (i.e., observable events of the subject of interest).

For transaction log analysis, behavior is the essential construct. At its most basic, a behavior is an observable activity of a person, animal, team, organization, or system. Like many basic constructs, behavior is an overloaded term, as it also refers to the aggregate set of responses to both internal and external stimuli. Therefore, behaviors address a spectrum of actions. Because of the many associations with the term, it is difficult to characterize a term like behavior without specifying a context in which it takes place to provide meaning.

However, one can generally classify behaviors into four general categories, which are:

1. Behavior is something that one can detect and, therefore, record.
2. Behavior is an action or a specific goal-driven event with some purpose other than the specific action that is observable.
3. Behavior is some skill or skill set.
4. Behavior is a reactive response to environmental stimuli.

In some manner, the researcher must observe these behaviors. By observation, we mean studying and gathering information on a behavior concerning what the actor does. Classically, observation is visual, where the researcher uses his/her own eyes. However, observation is assisted with some recording device, such as a camera. We extend the concept of observation to include other recording devices, notably logging software. Transaction log analysis focuses on descriptive observation and logging the behaviors, as they would occur.

When studying behavioral patterns during transaction log analysis and other similar approaches, researchers use ethograms. An ethogram is an index of the behavioral patterns of a unit. An ethogram details the different forms of behavior that an actor displays. In most cases, it is desirable to create an ethogram in which the categories of behavior are objective, discrete, not overlapping with each other. The definitions of each behavior should be clear, detailed and distinguishable from each other. Ethograms can be as specific or general as the study or field warrants.

Spink and Jansen (2004), and Jansen and Pooch (2001) outline some of the key behaviors for search log analysis, a specific form of transaction log analysis. Hargittai (2004) and Jansen and McNeese (2005) present examples of detailed classifications of behaviors during Web searching. As an example, Table 1 presents an ethogram of user behaviors interacting with a Web browser during a searching session, with Table 2 (as an appendix) presenting the complete ethogram.

There are many way to observe behaviors. In transaction log analysis, we are primarily concerned with observing and recording these behaviors in a file. As such, one can view the recorded fields as trace data.

Trace Data

The researcher has several options to collect data for research, but there is no one single best method for collection. The decision about which approach or approaches to use depends upon the research questions (i.e., what needs to be investigated, how one needs to record the data, what resources are available, what is the timeframe available for data collection, how complex is the data, what is the

Table 1. Taxonomy of user-system interactions (Jansen & McNeese, 2005)

State	Description
View results	Interaction in which the user viewed or scrolled one or more pages from the results listing. If a results page was present and the user did not scroll, we counted this as a View Results Page.
With Scrolling	*User scrolled the results page.*
Without Scrolling	*User did not scroll the results page.*
but No Results in Window	*User was looking for results, but there were no results in the listing.*
Selection	Interaction in which the user makes a selection in the results listing.
Click URL (in results listing)	*Interaction in which the user clicked on a URL of one of the results in the results page.*
Next in Set of Results List	*User moved to the Next results page.*
Previous in Set of Results List	*User moved to the Previous results page.*
GoTo in Set of Results List	*User selected a specific results page.*
View document	Interaction in which the user viewed or scrolled a particular document in the results listings.
With Scrolling	*User scrolled the document.*
Without Scrolling	*User did not scroll the document.*
Execute	Interaction in which the user initiated an action in the interface.
Execute Query	*Interaction in which the user entered, modified, or submitted a query without visibly incorporating assistance from the system. This category includes submitting the original query, which was always the first interaction with system.*
Find Feature in Document	*Interaction in which the user used the FIND feature of the browser.*
Create Favorites Folder	*Interaction in which the user created a folder to store relevant URLs.*
Navigation	Interaction in which the user activated a navigation button on the browser, such as Back or Home.
Back	*User clicked the Back button.*
Home	*User clicked the Home button.*
Browser	Interaction in which the user opened, closed, or switched browsers.
Open new browser	*User opened a new browser.*
Switch /Close browser window	*User switched between two open browsers or closed a browser window.*
Relevance action	Interaction such as print, save, bookmark, or copy.
Bookmark	*User bookmarked a relevant document.*

frequency of data collection, and how the data is to be analyzed.).

For transaction log data collection, we are generally concerned with observations of behavior. The general objective of observation is to record the behavior, either in a natural state or in a laboratory study. In both settings, ideally, the researcher should not interfere with the behavior. However, when observing people, the knowledge that they are being observed is likely to alter participants' behavior. In laboratory studies, a researcher's instructions may change a participant's behavior. With logging software, the introduction of the application may change a user's behavior.

With these limitations of observational techniques in mind, when investigating user behaviors, the researcher must make a record of these behaviors to have access to this data for future analysis. The actor, a third party, or the researcher, can make the record of behaviors. Transaction logging is an indirect method of recording data about behaviors, and the actors themselves, with the help of logging software. Thus, transaction log records are a source of trace data.

The processes by which people conduct the activities of their daily lives many times create things, create marks, or reduce some existing material. Within the confines of research, these things, marks, and wear become data. Classically, trace data are the physical remains of interaction (Webb et al., 2000, p. 35 - 52). This creation can be intentional (i.e., notes in a diary) or accidental (i.e., footprints in the mud). However, trace data can also be through third party logging applications. In transaction log analysis, we are primarily interested in this data from third party logging. We refer to this data as trace data.

Researchers use physical or, as in the case of transaction log analysis, virtual traces as indicators of behavior. These traces are the facts or data that researchers use to describe or make inferences about events concerning the actors. Researchers (Webb et al., 2000) have classified trace data, into two general types. These two general types of trace measures are erosion and accretion. Erosion is the wearing away of material, leaving a trace. Accretion is the build-up of material, making a trace. Both erosion and accretion have several subcategories. In transaction log analysis, we are primarily concerned with accretion trace data.

Trace data or measures offer a sharp contrast to directly collected data. The greatest strength of trace data is that it is unobtrusive. The collection of the data does not interfere with the natural flow of behavior and events in the given context. Since the data is not directly collected, there is no observer present in the situation where the behaviors occur to affect the participants' actions. Trace data is unique; as unobtrusive and nonreactive data it can make a very valuable research source. In the past, trace data was often time consuming to gather and process, making such data costly. With the advent of transaction logging software, trace data for the studying of behaviors of users and systems has really taken off.

Interestingly, in the physical world, erosion data is what typically reveals usage patterns (i.e., trails worn in the woods, footprints in the snow, wear on a book cover). However, with transaction log analysis, logged accretion data provides us the usage patterns (i.e., access to a Website, submission of queries, Webpages viewed). Specifically, transaction logs are a form of controlled accretion data, where the researcher or some other entity alters the environment in order to create the accretion data (Webb et al., 2000, p. 35 - 52). With a variety of tracking applications, the Web is a natural environment for controlled accretion data collection.

Like all data collection methods, trace data for studying users and systems has strengths and limitations. Trace data are valuable for understanding behavior (i.e., trace actions) in naturalistic environments, offering insights into human activity obtainable in no other way. For example, data from transaction logs is on a scale available in few other places. However, one must interpret trace data carefully and with a fair amount of caution, as trace data can be misleading. For example, with the data in transaction logs, the research can report that a given number of search engine users only looked at the first result page. However, using trace data alone, the researcher could not conclude whether the users left because they found their information or because they were frustrated because they could not find it.

Trace data from transaction logs should be examined during analysis based on the same criteria as all research data. These criteria are credibility, validity, and reliability.

Credibility refers to how trustworthy or believable is the data collection method. The researcher must make the case that the data collection methodology records the data needed to address the underlying research questions.

Validity describes if the measurement actually measures what it is supposed to measure. There are generally three kinds of validity:

a. Face or internal validity addresses the extent to which the test or procedure the researcher is measuring looks like what they are supposed to measure.
b. Content or construct validity addresses the extent to which the test or procedure adequately represents all that is required.
c. External validity is the extent to which one can generalize the research results across populations, situations, environments, and contexts.

In inferential or predictive research, one must also be concerned with statistical validity (i.e., the degree of strength of the independent and dependent variable relationships).

Reliability is a term used to describe the stability of the measurement. Does the measurement measure the same thing, in the same way, in repeated tests.

How to address the issues of credibility, validity, reliability? Building on the work of (Holst, 1969), six questions must be addressed in every research project using trace data from transaction logs:

1. **Which data are analyzed?** The researcher must clearly articulate in a precise manner and format what trace data was recorded. With transaction log software, this is much easier than in other forms of trace data, as logging applications can be reverse engineered to clearly articulate exactly what behavioral data is recorded.
2. **How is this data defined?** The researcher must clearly define each trace measure in a manner that permits replication of the research on other systems and with other users. As transaction log analysis has proliferated in a variety of venues, more precise definitions of measures are developing (Park, Bae & Lee, 2005; Wang, Berry, & Yang, 2003; Wolfram, 1999).
3. **What is the population from which the researcher has drawn the data?** The researcher must be cognizant of the actors, both people and systems that created the trace data. With transaction logs on the Web, this is sometimes a difficult issue to address directly, unless the system requires some type of logon and these profiles are then available. In the absence of these profiles, the researcher must rely on demographic surveys, studies of the system's user population, or general Web demographics.
4. **What is the context in which the researcher analyzed the data?** It is important for the researcher to clearly articulate the environmental, situational, and contextual factors under which the trace data was recorded. With transaction log data, this refers to providing complete information about the temporal factors of the data collection (i.e., the time the data was recorded) and the make up of the system at the time of the data recording, as system features undergo continual change. Transaction logs have the significant advantage of time sampling of trace data. In time sampling, the researcher can make the observations at predefined points of time (e.g., every five minutes), and then record the action that is taking place, using the classification of action defined in the ethogram.
5. **What are the boundaries of the analysis?** Research using trace data from transaction logs is tricky, and the researcher must be careful not to over reach with the research questions and findings. The implications of the research are confined by the data and the method of the data collected. For example, with transaction log data, one can rather clearly state whether or not a user clicked on

a link. However, transaction log trace data itself will not inform the researcher why the user clicked on a link.

6. **What is the target of the inferences?** The researcher must clearly articulate the relationship among the separate measures in the trace data to either inform descriptively or in order to make inferences. Trace data can be used for both descriptive research for understanding and predictive research in terms of making inferences. These descriptions and inferences can be at any level of granularity (i.e., individual, collection of individuals, organization, etc.). However, Hilber and Redmiles (1998) point out that transaction log data is best used for aggregate level analysis, based on their experiences.

Transaction logs are an excellent way to collect trace data on users of Web and other information systems. The researcher then examines this data using transaction log analysis. The use of trace data to understand behaviors makes the use of transaction logs and transaction logs analysis an unobtrusive research method.

UNOBTRUSIVE METHOD

Unobtrusive methods are research practices that do not require the researcher to intrude in the context of the actors. Unobtrusive methods do not involve direct elicitation of data from the research participants or actors. This approach is in contrast to obtrusive methods such as laboratory experiments and surveys requiring that the researchers physically interject themselves into the environment being studied. This intrusion can lead the actors to alter their behavior in order to look good in the eyes of the researcher or for other reasons. For example, a questionnaire is an interruption in the natural stream of behavior. Respondents can get tired of filling out a survey or resentful of the questions asked. Unobtrusive measurement presumably reduces the biases that result from the intrusion of the researcher or measurement instrument. However, unobtrusive measures reduce the degree of control that the researcher has over the type of data collected. For some constructs, there may simply not be any available unobtrusive measures.

Why is it important for the researcher not to intrude upon the environment? There are at least three justifications. First, is the uncertainty principle (a.k.a., the Heisenberg uncertainty principle). The Heisenberg uncertainty principle is from the field of quantum physics. In quantum physics, the outcome of a measurement of some system is not deterministic or perfect. Instead, a measurement is characterized by a probability distribution. The larger the associated standard deviation is for this distribution, the more "uncertain" are the characteristics measured for the system. The Heisenberg uncertainty principle is commonly stated as "One cannot accurately and simultaneously measure both the position and momentum of a mass." (http://en.wikipedia.org/wiki/Uncertainty_principle). In this analogy, when researchers are interjected into an environment, they become part of the system. Therefore, their just being there will affect measurements. A common example in the information technology area is the interjection of a recording device into an existing information technology system just for the purposes of measuring may slow the response time of the system.

The second justification is the observer effect. The observer effect refers to the difference that is made to an activity or a person's behaviors by it being observed. People may not behave in their usual manner if they know that they are being watched or when being interviewed while carrying out an activity. In research, this observer effect specifically refers to changes that the act of observing will make on the phenomenon being observed. In information technology, the observer effect is the potential impact of the act of observing a process output while the process is running. A good example of the observer effect in transaction log analysis is pornographic searching behavior. Participants rarely search for porn in a laboratory study while studies employing trace data shows it is a common searching topic (Jansen & Spink, 2005).

The third justification is observer bias. Observer bias is error that the researcher introduces into measurement when observers overemphasize behavior they expect to find and fail to notice behavior they do not expect. Many fields have common procedures to address this, although seldom used in information and computer science. For example, the observer bias is why medical trials are normally double-blind rather than single-blind. Observer bias is introduced because researchers see a behavior and interpret it according to what it means to them, whereas it may mean something else to the person showing the behavior. Trace data helps in overcoming the observer bias in the data collection. However, as with other methods, it has no effect on the observer bias in interpretation of the results from data analysis.

We discuss three types of unobtrusive measurement that are applicable to transaction log analysis research, which are indirect analysis, context analysis, and second analysis. Transaction logs analysis is an indirect analysis method. The researcher is able to collect the data without introducing any formal measurement procedure. In this regard, transaction log analysis typically focuses in the interaction behaviors occurring among the users, system, and information. There are several examples of utilizing transaction analysis as an indirect approach (Abdulla, Liu & Fox, 1998; Beitzel, Jensen, Chowdhury, Grossman & Frieder, 2004; Cothey, 2002; Hölscher & Strube, 2000).

Content analysis is the analysis of text documents. The analysis can be quantitative, qualitative or a mixed methods approach. Typically, the major purpose of content analysis is to identify patterns in text. Content analysis has the advantage of being unobtrusive and depending on whether automated methods exist can be a relatively rapid method for analyzing large amounts of text. In transaction log analysis, content analysis typically focuses on search queries or analysis of retrieved results. There are a variety of examples in this area of transaction log research (Baeza-Yates, Calderón-Benavides & Gonźalez, 2006; Beitzel, Jensen, Lewis, Chowdhury & Frieder, 2007; Hargittai, 2002; Wang et al., 2003; Wolfram, 1999).

Secondary data analysis, like content analysis, makes use of already existing sources of data. However, secondary analysis typically refers to the re-analysis of quantitative data rather than text. Secondary data analysis is the analysis of preexisting data in a different way or to address different research questions than originally intended during data collection. Secondary data analysis utilizes the data that was collected by someone else. Transaction log data is commonly collected by Websites for system performance analysis. However, researchers can also use this data to address other questions. Several transaction log studies have focused on this aspect of research (Brooks, 2004a; Brooks, 2004b; Choo, Betlor, & Turnbull, 1998; Chowdhury & Soboroff 2002; Croft, Cook, & Wilder, 1995; Joachims, Granka, Pan, Hembrooke, & Gay, 2005; Montgomery & Faloutsos, 2001; Rose & Levinson, 2004).

As a secondary analysis method, transaction log analysis has several advantages. First, it is efficient in that it makes use of data collected by a Website application. Second, it often allows the researcher to extend the scope of the study considerably by providing access to a potentially large sample of users over a significant duration (Kay & Thomas, 1995). Third, since the data is already collected, the cost of existing transaction log data is cheaper than collecting primary data.

However, the use of secondary analysis is not without difficulties. First, secondary data is frequently not trivial to prepare, clean, and analyze, especially large transaction logs. Second, researchers must often make assumptions about how the data was collected as the logging applications were developed by third parties. Third, there is the ethics of using transaction logs as secondary data. By definition, the researcher is using the data in a manner that may violate the privacy of the system users. In fact, some point out a growing distaste for unobtrusive methods due to increased sensitivity toward the ethics involved in such research (Page, 2000).

Transaction Log Analysis as Unobtrusive Method

Transaction logs analysis has significant advantages as a methodology approach for the study and investigation of behaviors. These factors include:

- **Scale:** Transaction log applications can collect data to a degree that overcomes the critical limiting factor in laboratory user studies. User studies in laboratories are typically restricted in terms of sample size, location, scope, and duration.
- **Power:** The sample size of transaction log data can be quite large, so inference testing can highlight statistically significant relationships. Interestingly, sometimes the amount of data in transaction logs from the Web is so large, that nearly every relation is significantly correlated due to the large power.
- **Scope:** Since transaction log data is collected in natural context, the researchers can investigate the entire range of user – system interactions or system functionality in a multi-variable context.
- **Location:** Transaction log data can be collected in a naturalistic, distributed environment. Therefore, the users do not have to be in an artificial laboratory setting.
- **Duration:** Since there is no need for specific participants recruited for a user study, transaction log data can be collected over an extended period.

All methods of data collection have both strengths not available with other methods, but they also have inherent limitations. Transactions logs have several shortcomings. First, transaction log data is not nearly as versatile relative to primary data as the data may not have been collected with the particular research questions in mind. Second, transaction log data is not as rich as some other data collection methods and therefore not available for investigating the range of concepts some researchers may want to study. Third, the fields that the transaction log application records are many times only loosely linked to the concepts they are alleged to measure. Fourth, with transaction logs, the users may be aware that they are being recorded and may alter their actions. Therefore, the user behaviors may not be altogether natural.

Given the inherent limitations in the method of data collection, transaction log analysis also suffers from shortcomings deriving from the characteristics of the data collection. Hilbert and Redmiles (2000) maintain that all research methods suffer from some combination of abstraction, selection, reduction, context, and evolution problems that limit scalability and quality of results. Transaction log analysis suffers from these same five shortcomings:

- **Abstraction problem:** How does one relate low-level data to higher-level concepts?
- **Selection problem:** How does one separate the necessary from unnecessary data prior to reporting and analysis?
- **Reduction problem:** How does one reduce the complexity and size of the data set prior to reporting and analysis?
- **Context problem:** How does one interpret the significance of events or states within state chains?
- **Evolution problem:** How can one alter data collection applications without impacting application deployment or use?

Because each method has its own combination of abstraction, selection, reduction, context, and evolution problems, this points to the need for complementary methods of data collection and analysis. This is similar to the conflict inherent in any overall research approach. Each research method for data collection tries to maximize three desirable criteria: *generalizability* (i.e., the degree to which the data applies to overall populations), *precision* (i.e., the degree of granularity of the measurement), and *realism* (i.e., the relation between the context in which evidence is gathered relative to the contexts to which the evidence is to be applied). Although the researcher always wants to maximize all three of these criteria simultaneously - it cannot be done. This is one fundamental dilemma of the research process. The very things that increase one of these three features will reduce one or both of the others.

CONCLUSION

Recordings of behaviors via transaction log applications on the Web opens a new era for researchers by making large amounts of trace data available for use. The online behaviors and interactions among users, systems and information create digital traces that permit analysis of this data. Logging applications provide data obtained through unobtrusive methods, massively larger than any data set obtained via surveys or laboratory studies, and collected in naturalistic settings with little to no impact by the observer. Researchers can use these digital traces to analyze a nearly endless array of behavior topics.

The use of transaction log analysis is a behaviorist research method, with a natural reliance on the expressions of interactions as behaviors. The transaction log application records these interactions, creating a type of trace data. Trace data in transaction logs are records of interactions as people use these systems to locate information, navigate Websites, and execute services. The data in transaction logs is a record of user – system, user – information, or system – information interactions. As such, transaction logs provide an unobtrusive manner of collecting these behaviors. Transaction logs provide a method of collecting data on a scale well beyond what one could collect in confined laboratory studies.

The massive increased availability of Web trace data has sparked concern over the ethical aspects of using unobtrusively obtained data from transaction logs. For example, who does the trace data belong to - the user, the Website that logged the data, or the public domain? How does (or should one) seek consent to use such data? If researchers do seek consent, from whom does the researcher seek it? Is it realistic to require informed consent for unobtrusively collected data? These are open questions.

REFERENCES

Abdulla, G., Liu, B., & Fox, E. (1998). Searching the World-Wide Web: implications from studying different user behavior. *Paper presented at the World Conference of the World Wide Web, Internet, and Intranet, Orlando, FL.*

Baeza-Yates, R., Calderón-Benavides, L., & González, C. (2006, 11-13 October). The intention behind web queries. *Paper presented at the String Processing and Information Retrieval (SPIRE 2006), Glasgow, Scotland.*

Beitzel, S. M., Jensen, E. C., Chowdhury, A., Grossman, D., & Frieder, O. (2004, 25-29 July). Hourly analysis of a very large topically categorized web query log. *Paper presented at the 27th Annual International Conference on Research and Development in Information Retrieval, Sheffield, U.K.*

Beitzel, S. M., Jensen, E. C., Lewis, D. D., Chowdhury, A., & Frieder, O. (2007). Automatic classification of Web queries using very large unlabeled query logs. *ACM Transactions on Information Systems, 25*(2), Article No. 9.

Brooks, N. (2004a, July). *The Atlas Rank Report I: How Search Engine Rank Impacts Traffic.* Retrieved 1 August, 2004, from http://www.atlasdmt.com/media/pdfs/insights/RankReport.pdf

Brooks, N. (2004b, October). *The Atlas Rank Report II: How Search Engine Rank Impacts Conversions.* Retrieved 15 January, 2005, from http://www.atlasonepoint.com/pdf/AtlasRankReportPart2.pdf

Choo, C., Detlor, B., & Turnbull, D. (1998). A behavioral model of information seeking on the web: Preliminary results of a study of how managers and IT specialists use the web. *Paper presented at the 61st Annual Meeting of the American Society for Information Science, Pittsburgh, PA.*

Chowdhury, A., & Soboroff, I. (2002). Automatic evaluation of world wide web search services. *Paper presented at the 25th Annual International ACM SIGIR Conference on Research and Development in Information Retrieval, Tampere, Finland.*

Cothey, V. (2002). A longitudinal study of World Wide Web users' information searching behavior. *Journal of the American Society for Information Science and Technology, 53*(2), 67-78.

Croft, W. B., Cook, R., & Wilder, D. (1995, 11-13 June). Providing government information on the internet: Experiences with THOMAS. *Paper presented at the Digital Libraries Conference, Austin, TX.*

Hargittai, E. (2002). Beyond logs and surveys: In-depth measures of people's web use skills. *Journal of the American Society for Information Science and Technology, 53*(14), 1239-1244.

Hargittai, E. (2004). Classifying and coding online actions. *Social Science Computer Review, 22*(2), 210-227.

Hilbert, D., & Redmiles, D. (1998, 10-13 May). Agents for collecting application usage data over the internet. *Paper presented at the Second International Conference on Autonomous Agents (Agents '98), Minneapolis/St. Paul, MN.*

Hilbert, D. M., & Redmiles, D. F. (2000). Extracting usability information from user interface events. *ACM Computing Surveys 32*(4), 384-421.

Hölscher, C., & Strube, G. (2000). Web search behavior of internet experts and newbies. *International Journal of Computer and Telecommunications Networking, 33*(1-6), 337-346.

Holst, O. R. (1969). *Content Analysis for the Social Sciences and Humanities.* Reading, Massachusetts: Perseus Publishing.

Jansen, B. J., & McNeese, M. D. (2005). Evaluating the effectiveness of and patterns of interactions with automated searching assistance. *Journal of the American Society for Information Science and Technology, 56*(14), 1480-1503.

Jansen, B. J., & Pooch, U. (2001). Web user studies: A review and framework for future work. *Journal of the American Society of Information Science and Technology, 52*(3), 235-246.

Jansen, B. J., & Spink, A. (2005). How are we searching the world wide web? A comparison of nine search engine transaction logs. *Information Processing & Management, 42*(1), 248-263.

Joachims, T., Granka, L., Pan, B., Hembrooke, H., & Gay, G. (2005, 15-19 August). Accurately interpreting clickthrough data as implicit feedback. *Paper presented at the 28th Annual International ACM SIGIR conference on Research and Development in Information Retrieval, Salvador, Brazil.*

Kay, J., & Thomas, R. C. (1995). Studying long-term system use. *Communications of the ACM, 38*(7), 61-69.

McGrath, J. E. (1994). Methodology matters: Doing research in the behavioral and social sciences. In R. Baecker & W. A. S. Buxton (Eds.), *Readings in Human-Computer Interaction: An Interdisciplinary Approach* (2nd ed., pp. 152-169). San Mateo, CA: Morgan Kaufman Publishers.

Meister, D., & Sullivan, D. J. (1967). *Evaluation of User Reactions to a Prototype On-line Information Retrieval System: Report* prepared under Contract No. NASw-1369 *by Bunker-Ramo Corporation. Report Number NASA CR-918.* Oak Brook, IL: Bunker-Ramo Corporationo. Document Number N67-40083).

Montgomery, A., & Faloutsos, C. (2001). Identifying web browsing trends and patterns. *IEEE Computer, 34*(7), 94-95.

Page, S. (2000). Community research: The lost art of unobtrusive methods. *Journal of Applied Social Psychology, 30*(10), 2126- 2136.

Park, S., Bae, H., & Lee, J. (2005). End user searching: A web log analysis of NAVER, a Korean web search engine. *Library & Information Science Research, 27*(2), 203-221.

Penniman, W. D. (1975, 26-30 October). A stochastic process analysis of online user behavior. *Paper presented at the Annual Meeting of the American Society for Information Science, Washington, DC.*

Peters, T. (1993). The history and development of transaction log analysis. *Library Hi Tech, 42*(11), 41-66.

Rose, D. E., & Levinson, D. (2004, 17–22 May). Understanding user goals in web search. *Paper presented at the World Wide Web Conference (WWW 2004), New York, NY, USA.*

Sellars, W. (1963). Philosophy and the scientific image of man. In *Science, Perception, and Reality* (pp. 1 - 40). New York: Ridgeview Publishing Company.

Skinner, B. F. (1953). *Science and Human Behavior.* New York: Free Press.

Spink, A., & Jansen, B. J. (2004). *Web Search: Public Searching of the Web.* Dordrecht: Springer.

Wang, P., Berry, M., & Yang, Y. (2003). Mining longitudinal web queries: Trends and patterns. *Journal of the American Society for Information Science and Technology, 54*(8), 743-758.

Watson, J. B. (1913). Psychology as the behaviorist views it. *Psychological Review, 20*, 158-177.

Webb, E. J., Campbell, D. T., Schwartz, R. D. D., Sechrest, L., & Grove, J. B. (1981). *Nonreactive Measures in the Social Sciences* (2nd ed.). Boston, MA: Houghton Mifflin.

Webb, E. J., Campbell, D. T., Schwarz, R. D., & Sechrest, L. (2000). *Unobtrusive Measures (Revised Edition).* Thousand Oaks, California: Sage.

Wolfram, D. (1999). Term co-occurrence in internet search engine queries: An analysis of the Excite data set. *Canadian Journal of Information and Library Science, 24*(2/3), 12-33.

KEY TERMS

Behaviorism: A research approach that emphasizes the outward behavioral aspects of thought. For transaction log analysis, we take a more open view of behaviorism. In this more encompassing view, behaviorism emphasizes the observed behaviors without discounting the inner aspects that may accompany these outward behaviors.

Ethogram: An index of the behavioral patterns of a unit. An ethogram details the different forms of behavior that an actor displays. In most cases, it is desirable to create an ethogram in which the categories of behavior are objective, discrete, not overlapping with each other. The definitions of each behavior should be clear, detailed and distinguishable from each other. Ethograms can be as specific or general as the study or field warrants.

Trace Data (or measures): Offer a sharp contrast to directly collected data. The greatest strength of trace data is that it is unobtrusive. The collection of the data does not interfere with the natural flow of behavior and events in the given context. Since the data is not directly collected, there is no observer present in the situation where the behaviors occur to affect the participants' actions. Trace data is unique; as unobtrusive and nonreactive data, it can make a very valuable research course of action. In the past, trace data was often time consuming to gather and process, making such data costly. With the advent of transaction logging software, trace data for the studying of behaviors of users and systems has really taken off.

Transaction Log: *An electronic record of interactions that have occurred between a system and users of that system.* These log files can come from a variety of computers and systems (Websites, OPAC, user computers, blogs, listserv, online newspapers, etc.), basically any application that can record the user – system – information interactions. For transaction log analysis, behavior is the essential construct of the behaviorism paradigm. At its most basic, a behavior is an observable activity of a person, animal, team, organization, or system. Like many basic constructs, behavior is an overloaded term, as it also refers to the aggregate set of responses to both internal and external stimuli. Therefore, behaviors address a spectrum of actions. Because of the many associations with the term, it is difficult to characterize a term like behavior without specifying a context in which it takes place to provide meaning.

Transaction Log Analysis: A broad categorization of methods that covers several sub-categorizations, including Web log analysis (i.e., analysis of Web system logs), blog analysis and search log analysis (analysis of search engine logs).

Unobtrusive Methods: Research practices that do not require the researcher to intrude in the context of the actors. Unobtrusive methods do not involve direct elicitation of data from the research participants or actors. This approach is in contrast to obtrusive methods such as laboratory experiments and surveys requiring that the researchers physically interject themselves into the environment being studied.

APPENDIX

Table 2. Taxonomy of user-system interactions (Jansen & McNeese, 2005)

State	Description
View results	Interaction in which the user viewed or scrolled one or more pages from the results listing. If a results page was present and the user did not scroll, we counted this as a View Results Page.
View results: With Scrolling	*User scrolled the results page.*
View results: Without Scrolling	*User did not scroll the results page.*
View results: but No Results in Window	*User was looking for results, but there were no results in the listing.*
Selection	Interaction in which the user made some selection in the results listing.
Click URL(in results listing)	*Interaction in which the user clicked on a URL of one of the results in the results page.*
Next in Set of Results List	*User moved to the Next results page.*
GoTo in Set of Results List	*User selected a specific results page.*
Previous in Set of Results List	*User moved to the Previous results page.*
View document	Interaction in which the user viewed or scrolled a particular document in the results listings.
View document: With Scrolling	*User scrolled the document.*
View document: Without Scrolling	*User did not scroll the document.*
Execute	Interaction in which the user initiated an action in the interface.
Execute Query	*Interaction in which the user entered, modified, or submitted a query without visibly incorporating assistance from the system. This category includes submitting the original query, which was always the first interaction with system.*
Find Feature in Document	*Interaction in which the user used the FIND feature of the browser.*
Create Favorites Folder	*Interaction in which the user created a folder to store relevant URLs.*
Navigation	Interaction in which the user activated a navigation button on the browser, such as Back or Home.
Navigation: Back	*User clicked the Back button.*
Navigation: Home	*User clicked the Home button.*
Browser	Interaction in which the user opened, closed, or switched browsers.
Open new browser	*User opened a new browser.*
Switch /Close browser window	*User switched between two open browsers or closed a browser window.*
Relevance action	Interaction such as print, save, bookmark, or copy.
Relevance Action: Bookmark	*User bookmarked a relevant document.*
Relevance Action: Copy Paste	*User copy-pasted all of, a portion of, or the URL to a relevant document.*
Relevance Action: Print	*User printed a relevant document.*
Relevance Action: Save	*User saved a relevant document.*
View assistance	Interaction in which the user viewed the assistance offered by the application.
Implement Assistance	*Interaction in which the user entered, modified, or submitted a query, utilizing assistance offered by the application.*
Implement Assistance: PHRASE	*User implemented the PHRASE assistance.*

continued on following page

Table 2. (continued)

State	Description
Implement Assistance: Spelling	*User implemented the SPELLING assistance.*
Implement Assistance: Previous Queries	*User implemented the PREVIOUS QUERIES assistance.*
Implement Assistance: Synonyms	*User implemented the SYNONYMS assistance.*
Implement Assistance: Relevance Feedback	*User implemented the RELEVANCE FEEDBACK assistance.*
Implement Assistance: AND	*User implemented the AND assistance.*
Implement Assistance: OR	*User implemented the OR assistance.*

Section I
Web Log Analysis: Perspectives, Issues, and Directions

Chapter II
Historic Perspective of Log Analysis

W. David Penniman
Nylink, USA

ABSTRACT

This historical review of the birth and evolution of transaction log analysis applied to information retrieval systems provides two perspectives. First, a detailed discussion of the early work in this area, and second, how this work has migrated into the evaluation of World Wide Web usage. The author describes the techniques and studies in the early years and makes suggestions for how that knowledge can be applied to current and future studies. A discussion of privacy issues with a framework for addressing the same is presented as well as an overview of the historical "eras" of transaction log analysis. The author concludes with the suggestion that a combination of transaction log analysis of the type used early in its application along with additional more qualitative approaches will be essential for a deep understanding of user behavior (and needs) with respect to current and future retrieval systems and their design.

INTRODUCTION: GENERAL PERSPECIVE AND OBJECTIVES OF CHAPTER

This chapter is not an evaluation of current practice, but rather a look at the history of transaction logs and their evolution as a tool for studying user interaction. Much has been written about this tool, but there were just a few researchers who introduced this as a tool to study user interaction. This chapter is dedicated to those individuals (with apologies to any who are not cited, but were using this tool before it became well known and evident in the literature). At the same time, praise must be given to those who followed and assured that transaction log analysis evolved to the state it is at today, with a rich new "laboratory" represented by the Internet and the World-Wide Web.

Within this chapter, a variety of authors and studies are sampled to give a sense of the way in which transaction logs were first applied, how the study of on-line public access catalogs (OPACs) contributed to the evolution of transaction log analysis (and vice versa), and how particular projects (such as OPAC studies by the Council on Library Resources (CLR) and "IIDA" funded by the National Science Foundation (NSF) contributed to our understanding of user interaction. Previous surveys cited in the following paragraphs and sections of this chapter are drawn from as well as the author's own experience with transaction log analysis in the early days of its application.

As stated by Peters, Kurth, Flaherty, Sandore, and Kaske (1993, p.38):

Researchers most often use transaction logs data with the intention of improving the IR system, human utilization of the system, and human (and perhaps also system) understanding of how the system is used by information seekers. Transaction log analysis can provide system designers and managers with valuable information about how the system is being used by actual users. It also can be used to study prototype system improvements.

Penniman (1975a, p. 159) in one of the early studies using transaction logs stated, "The promise (of transaction logs) is unlimited for evaluating communicative behavior where human and computer interact to exchange information."

The promise of analyzing transaction logs has always been at least twofold: first to *describe* what users actually do while interacting with a system and second, to use this understanding to *predict* what should be the next actions they might take to use the system effectively (or to correct a difficulty they have encountered). Transaction logs continue to offer promise in both of these areas. The arena, in which this tool can be applied, however, is much larger. We now have the world (or at least the World-Wide Web) as a laboratory.

BACKGROUND: INFORMATION RETRIEVAL GOES ONLINE

In the late 1960's, before there was the Internet, there were a handful of online information retrieval system providers clamoring for attention (and a user base). Most systems had sprung from government-funded projects or were intended to serve such projects. Users were often restricted to a single proprietary system, and the competition was fierce to market the "best" system where most, in fact, appeared quite similar in features and functions (Walker, 1971; Gove, 1973). The ultimate system was yet to be, and still has not been, designed. If it were, it would certainly have the features so well articulated by Goodwin (1959) when retrieval was primarily a manual process or at best used batch-processing search software on large mainframes with extensive human intervention between end-user and information source. It was within this environment that Goodwin articulated the features of an "ideal" retrieval system as one in which the user would receive desired information:

- At the time it is needed (not before or after)
- In the briefest possible form
- In order of importance
- With necessary auxiliary information
- With reliability of information clearly indicated (which implies some critical analysis)
- With the source identified
- With little or no effort (i.e. automatically)
- Without clutter (undesired or untimely information eliminated)
- With assurance that no response means the information does not exist

This interesting and historical set of design specifications demonstrated a user-centric approach to system design that stands up well to the test of time. It could be argued that the disintermediation brought about by the evolution of online retrieval systems moved us further away from some of the desired features listed above. Today, much of the burden for searching rests now with the end user and not a skilled intermediary thereby increasing the effort of the end user – much like the trend toward end-user data entry for letters, memos, and other text oriented activities. At the same time, such systems have democratized information access and given those with the necessary skills immediate access to the fount of knowledge – or the fire hose of data that is now available on the World-Wide Web. This shift, which began in the late 1960's and early 1970's placed an even greater burden on system designers to understand how users were attempting to fill their information needs and what demands users were placing on the system to meet those needs.

As online interactive systems emerged in the late 1960's and early 1970's, so did the opportunity to unobtrusively study just how users were interacting with these new tools for retrieval. This ability was made possible simply because the computer systems upon which the retrieval software ran maintained files of all transactions, primarily for system recovery and audit purposes (Drummond, 1973). Such necessary insights into how systems were actually being used would have been difficult to achieve were it not for the ability to scan the transaction log files to see which commands were being used and in what pattern. The existence of such files, however, was often denied for fear that it would sound too much like "Big Brother" watching user actions. But exist they did, and they soon became a source for research as well as system recovery.

The practice of system-wide monitoring continues to this day, and thanks to legislated requirements such as Sarbanes-Oxley and HIPAA as well as system security needs, is likely to continue. According to Gorge (2007, p. 10):

It is best practice to collect, store and analyze logs with a view to being able to get complete, accurate and verifiable information. This will improve the organization's ability to comply with key standards and legislation as regards e-evidence. It could save an organization from potential liability and repair costs and will give visibility over mission critical and security systems, performance and usage.

There was early on, and should continue to be, concern regarding the privacy of individual activities on monitored systems, but the current environment encourages such monitoring more than ever before. Protection of individual privacy regarding such monitoring remains. A brief discussion of the historical and continuing examination of privacy issues in this domain appears later in this section.

TRANSACTION LOG ANALYSIS: THE EARLY YEARS

The transaction logs generated for system recovery and audit purposes contained date/time-stamped detail data on actual keystrokes and system responses. In the early days, with few users and few if any "public access" terminals, it was not difficult to determine who and where the input was coming from. Unique user identification was also available. With the introduction of systems within the public areas of libraries and elsewhere, it became increasingly difficult to determine the actual user or to isolate the human/computer dyad of a particular session of interaction. It is a little like trying to study a "conversation" when you have a record of everyone in a crowd talking at once. The question then becomes: "Who is talking to whom, and for how long?"

For some of the early systems, it was possible to incorporate an "information system monitor" much like the transaction log from the computer system, but with usage of the particular information retrieval system isolated from other system usage and data separated for that specific application usage. Such data could then be further massaged for analysis.

This monitoring capability provided a previously unavailable data source for studying the information seeking behavior of end users without the disruption (or corruption) of intermediary intervention. Techniques originally intended for the study of human-human communication (dyadic interaction) could now be applied to human-computer communication in a "natural" environment. It is not surprising, then, that research-oriented communication scholars such as Parker and Paisley (1966) identified the promise of transaction log analysis as a means of studying information-seeking behavior in an accurate and unobtrusive manner.

It also became clear early on in the introduction of online interactive information retrieval systems, that users were finding new and interesting ways to apply these systems in a manner not anticipated by the designers. In some cases there was interest by users who were managers in reshaping the systems to support management functions including early attempts at knowledge management (before it was even called by that name) (Penniman, 1971). Learning more about how systems were actually being used was not just an interesting area for study, it was essential to inform system designers about the requirements for the next versions of the systems they were building.

Some of the earliest reports of the development and/or application of transaction log analysis came from individuals such as Meister and Sullivan (1967), Treu (1971), and Mittman and Dominick (1973). This final citation is interesting in that Wayne Dominick was a graduate student at the time, and completed a master's thesis (Dominick, 1974) that focused on methodologies for system monitoring. He was one of a cadre of graduate students beginning to work in the area of user-system interaction. Others included Harry Back (1976), Jim Carlisle (1974), Dave Penniman (1975a), and Charles Stabell (1974). All of these individuals were early in the game of user-centric analysis of user-system interaction including some use of monitoring data. Such work formed the basis for the variety of research projects that followed and pointed out the need for a more user-centric design approach while calling attention to the availability of monitor data as a source of information for improved system design.

Stabell (1974) deserves particular attention among these early students of online interaction. Like Carlisle (1974), Stabell was studying complexity and its influence on information processing behavior. What makes his dissertation of particular interest, however, is the use of a state transition model to characterize the user interaction (in this case an investment decision-making support system). To build such a model, and the associated state transition graphs, the user interaction activity needed to be viewed as a continuous state string with frequency of particular state transitions recorded and transition probabilities calculated. Penniman (1975a) applied a similar approach to the domain of document retrieval systems in his study of user interaction with the BASIS-70 system. An example of a resulting transition graph is shown in Figure 1.

This illustration is important in that it shows the use of transaction log data for determining process and not merely frequency of particular actions. Modeling of user behavior over the duration of a particular session as opposed to simply counting frequencies is the difference between "zero order" analysis (involving sampling of frequency of occurrence of events) and higher order analysis where a sequence of events is viewed as a stochastic or probabilistic process. While Penniman presented some of the first data on user interaction in this manner, it was carried on significantly in later work involving adaptive prompting as well as use of OPACs as discussed later in this chapter. What this early work did, however, was provide a framework for treating transaction log data as a tool for studying the processes of communica-

Figure 1. Sample state transition graph (Source: Penniman, 1975a)

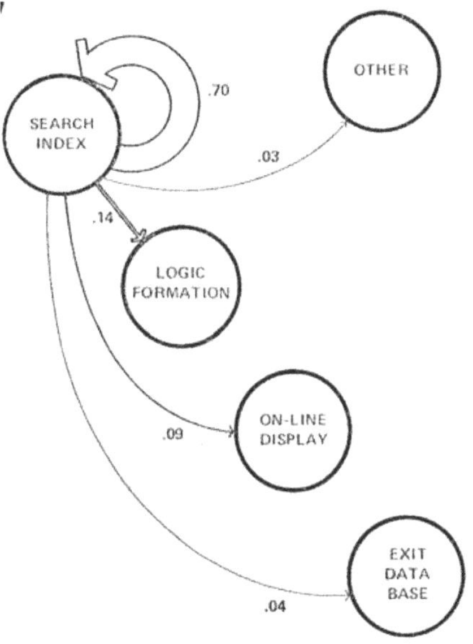

tion between human and computer in the realm of information retrieval rather than merely counting occurrence of single events.

More recently, Lin, Liebscher, and Marchionini (1991) described tools and methods for creating graphical representations of search patterns that built upon this concept. As discussed later, there is still a need for depicting user behavior in more sophisticated and informative ways. The state transition graph represents just one such method.

Penniman and Dominick (1980) worked together in developing additional aspects of online system monitoring. Penniman (who by that time was Vice-President for Planning and Research at the Online Computer Library Center (OCLC)) conducted his last transaction log research with a study of the National Library of Medicine's (NLM) Medline system (Penniman, 1982; Penniman, 1984). Dominick continued to explore and publish in the area of system monitoring into the 1990's providing a detailed framework for system monitoring and applying it in a variety of domains (Dominick, 1987; Dominick, 1990).

Penniman and Dominick (1980, p. 23) identified three general levels of data collection via transaction logs:

- **Complete protocol:** This level includes verbatim records of user/system interaction for an entire session or selected portions of the session. Also included would be an indication of system resources in use (status reports) and clock time.
- **Function or state traces:** This level maps the protocol onto a predetermined set of categories or states at the time of data capture. Such a technique can be used to mask specific user actions which might be considered confidential (subjects or topics searched, specific documents retrieved, etc.).
- **General session variables:** This level records such variables as sign-on and sign-off times, data bases accessed, resources used, and number of documents retrieved/displayed or printed. This represents a minimal level of data collection.

The implications of each level with respect to privacy issues are presented in the subsequent section on that topic. In general, however, it is clear that transaction logs can be used to generate anything from a full picture of what is happening within a user session to only the barest details useful for accounting or administrative purposes.

Rice and Borgman (1983, p. 248) identified the promise of transaction logs for evaluating computer-based communication systems (messaging and conferencing systems) as well as information retrieval systems and articulated a variety of data points that could be collected at a minimum. These included:

- Terminal and user identification numbers
- User start and end times

- Protocol commands
- Full text content
- Topic
- Code or system response
- Messages received or waiting including number, length and type
- Message audience category
- Number of matches retrieved
- Errors encountered
- User entries in response to computer-administered queries

Clearly, many of these data points or elements divulge a great deal about the users and their interests. It is this very aspect that is both the promise of online monitoring (to improve user interaction as described in the next section) and the threat (to invade the user's privacy as discussed in a subsequent section of this chapter).

USER TRACKING FOR ADAPTIVE PROMPTING

In addition to the early application of transaction log data to descriptive studies, "how the system is being used", there was the potential for the application of such data to create predictive models that could instruct and prompt users. Such studies could lead to automated adaptive prompting systems as suggested by Penniman (1976) and developed and tested by Meadow (1977).

The work by Meadow (Interactive Instruction for Data Access (IIDA) and Online Access to Knowledge (OAK)) is of particular interest because it explored in depth the use of transaction log data as an input to a user prompting system. This early work, funded by the National Science Foundation (Meadow, 1977; Meadow, Hewett and Aversa, 1982a and 1982b) and later by the Department of Energy (Borgman, Case and Meadow, 1989) also engaged several students, most notably Fenichel (1979) and Chapman (1981). Chapman employed state codes to conduct zero- through fourth-order stochastic process analysis of user behavior in order to structure an automated prompting system. Fenichel (1981) continued to analyze measures that could discriminate among users with different levels of experience as a means of selecting appropriate prompting or instruction methods.

The body of work produced by Meadow and his colleagues (Meadow, Hewett & Aversa 1982a; Borgman, Case and Meadow 1989) is landmark in the area of adaptive prompting. Meadow (1990, pp 793-794), in retrospect, concluded: a) "the front end or computer intermediary has not yet had a great success in wide commercial use" and b) that the "interface, in our opinion, has to be designed for a limited target group. It would be difficult, indeed, to have one that served both experienced searchers and novices equally well. Similarly, it would be difficult to serve users well who know the database content and structure and those who do not even understand the concept of database structure."

During the same period, Marcus (1982, p. 63), conducting similar studies concluded:

We must recognize the vital need for continued testing and analysis of intermediary systems in the context of the retrieval application and the basic information transfer process for which they serve" and "much more experimentation and analysis is required before the conclusions we have drawn from them can be verified with the desired quantifiable statistical precision.

In review of expert systems within the library domain, De Silva (1997) noted another search advisor, the Intelligent Database Enquiry Assistant (IDEA), comprised of a tutor, an advisor, and a user question handler being developed at about the same time. In addition, the NLS-Scholar system was under development to assist in teaching the use of a powerful editor system (Grignetti, Hausman, and Gould, 1975). Such front-end systems have continued to be an area of study (Belkin et al., 2001) and are still being called for (Markey 2007b, p. 1125):

Let us put research findings about system-feature use and multiple search sessions to work by building systems that are sensitive to the progress users are making on their ongoing searches, intervene with complex search features that are likely to solve user problems, and monitor users to determine whether these complex features help them achieve their goals.

OPACS ARE IMPLEMENTED AND STUDIED

As indicated, the initial application of transaction log analysis was focused on emerging database search systems such as Battelle's BASIS-70 (Penniman 1975b) where the contents were often "gray" literature such as technical or intelligence reports or even collections of numerical data. Such systems as Medline, Toxline and ERIC online were early and continuing targets for user-focused studies (Sewell, 1976; Brown and Agrawla, 1974; Bourne, Robinson, and Todd, 1974).

It was not until the late 1970's and early 1980's as online public access catalogs (OPACs) began to be implemented that a commensurate focus on the user interaction with library catalog systems emerged. Much of this focus can be attributed to the work of scientists at OCLC within the Department of Research. This included individuals such as John Tolle, Karen Markey, Charles Hildreth, and Neil Kaske. In addition, among these early "pioneers" of OPAC evaluation was Christine Borgman, who worked with OCLC in a visiting capacity to expand the work on OPACs. She wrestled with the early problems of identifying individual user sessions within large collections of monitor data available from public access terminals within libraries. (Borgman, 1983). Her dissertation (Borgman, 1984) incorporated her work at OCLC and drew on transaction logs as well as other collection techniques.

Borgman continued to explore this research tool with respect to online catalogs (Borgman, 1986; Borgman, 1996) as well as studies of children's searching behavior (Borgman, Hirsh and Hiller, 1996). She also spent some effort on front-end systems to aid in the search process (Borgman, Case, and Meadow, 1989) discussed more fully in the section on user tracking and intervention.

At that same time, another scientist in OCLC's Department of Research, John Tolle, extended the stochastic process analysis methods introduced by Penniman and employed them in the Council on Library Resources (CLR)-sponsored study of online catalogs (Tolle 1983a, Tolle 1983b). His focus on this modeling method (i.e. using stochastic process analysis and Markov chains) continued as a means of determining and describing user patterns (Tolle 1984 and Tolle 1985a) and culminated with the analysis of the National Library of Medicine's CATLINE system (Tolle, 1985b).

As suggested by Peters, Kaske, and Kurth (1993, p.152) the focus of transaction log studies on OPACs probably reached its zenith with the completion of the CLR study in the mid 1980's. This period is probably best documented by Markey (1984) where she analyzes logs she has collected of library catalog usage as well as other similar studies.

It is interesting to note that despite the extensive study of user interaction with OPACs at least one of the pioneers in OPAC studies concluded that there had been relatively little progress in the basic functionality of the online catalog, with searching functions not much better in the 1990's than those in the1980's (Hildreth, 1991).

Work continued on OPACs with dissertation projects continuing to apply transaction logs (Slack 1991). OPAC studies continued to build on the data analysis methods of previous studies (Peters, 1989; Hunter, 1991; Wallace, 1993;

Wyly, 1996; Slack, 1996). Studies continue today of OPACs and transaction log analysis of OPAC usage is being employed around the world (Lau and Goh, 2006).

The final "manifesto" of the *Library Hi Tech* survey of transaction log work during the 1980's was prophetic. Among the recommendations were: apply transaction log analysis to searching of databases beyond online catalogs, find a way to track users of graphical interface software, and find a way to track the users as they search many different databases (Sandore, Flaherty, Kaske, Kurth, and Peters, 1993, p. 105). These recommendations were certainly prescient regarding the requirements of later studies of user interaction with the Internet and World-Wide Web.

THE INTERNET AND THE WEB ENTER THE SCENE

A major transformation was occurring in the late 1980's and into the early to mid 1990's. As described by Markey (2007a, p. 1071):

...end users could go to libraries to search the most popular online IR databases on CD-ROMs or through the online catalog's familiar interface. WAIS and GOPHER were among the earliest tools that end users enlisted to search the Internet in the early 1990s. End user searching truly came into its own with the deployment of Web search engines in the mid 1990's.

It is true that the advent of search engines has revolutionized the way users seek information. Hidden behind the relatively simple interface of the typical search engine such concepts as term weighting and vector space models are at play. Despite such sophisticated underpinnings, as indicated by Berry and Browne (2005, p. 93) the standard response that users receive is "hundreds to thousands of results displayed in order of relevance with the search terms highlighted in brief or piecemeal descriptions ... there is room for improvement."

Markey (2007a, p. 1079) further characterizes the current situation succinctly:

For the vast majority of people's information needs, doing one's own searching is convenient, immediate, and instantaneous – connect to the Internet, launch a Web browser, type a query into a search engine's dialog box, browse ranked retrievals, and link to one or more full-length retrieved documents.

Just as Markey's book (1984) captured the essence of OPAC studies, so has the book by Spink and Jansen (2004) captured the essence (at least at the time of publication) of public searching of the Web. They drew from their own work as well as that of others to characterize changes across time, growth of, and stability of users' interaction with Web search engines. The patterns continue to evolve, however. For example, while "sex sites" were dominant in the early days of the Web and amounted to 13% of website visits within the United States in 2006, search sites overtook sex sites in Great Britain in October of 2006 – a first since tracking began (Sex and the Internet 2007, p. 74).

While other chapters will cover Web searching in more detail, it is useful to fit the emerging studies of Web searching within the historical context of transaction log analysis and to draw some conclusions regarding the future of this research and development tool.

Jansen's work is of particular interest in that he provides a framework for moving forward with future studies. This framework will allow comparison of results across a variety of studies including the earlier information retrieval system and OPAC work (Jansen and Spink, 2000; Jansen and Pooch, 2001). This framework includes: descriptive information, analysis presentation, and statistical analysis. Within the analysis presentation there are further segments at the session, query, and term level. He is continuing to refine this foundation for conducting Web search transaction log analysis (Jansen, 2006a). Finally, just as Penniman and Perry (1976) evaluated the "tempo" of user interaction with early information retrieval systems, Jansen (2006b) is looking at the temporal patterns of interactions with an eye towards providing user assistance at the right time in the interactive session on the Web.

Peters, along with Kaske and Kurth (1993), studied and summarized the extensive previous work regarding transaction logs and library systems. He then turned his attention to the remote use of library-created and library-supported Web sites (Peters,1998) and reached a number of interesting conclusions including:

Remote access has everything to do with access and little to do with distance and is changing the role of (scholarly) information in the (intellectual) lives of the (user) community (parentheses added by me to help generalize this statement).

While monitoring can provide demographic information more readily for remote users than easily obtained from onsite library users, such information is ultimately not very useful.

Instead, we should be interested in the more complex aspects of the user's "information landscape".

What is really needed is an understanding of the thought processes underway as people seek and use information (and computerized monitoring cannot provide insight as yet in that area).

Although surface-level analysis may be useful in determining the frequency with which library-owned Web resources are accessed or the time of day or day of week such sites are used (Abramson, 1998), a deeper analysis is certainly called for and harks back to the early days of transaction log analysis when patterns of interaction were being investigated. Qiu (1993) represents an example where the earlier stochastic process model and associated analysis was applied to a hypertext system with a small document set. In that case, he determined that a second-order process was exhibited and argues that his study was the first to actually attempt to determine the order of the process. Clearly more studies such as this are needed in which the environment is more representative of the current Web world and not the limited collection of Qiu's study.

Studies of the Web that combine monitoring with cognitive style instruments (Wang et al., 1998, Wang et al., 2000) and/or protocol analysis (Griffiths, Hartley and Willson, 2002) offer promise in understanding user information seeking behavior on the Web in that they go beyond the measure of "what" is being done and attempt to look at "why" there are differences in search behavior.

Even more sophisticated analysis of Web log transaction data is possible as demonstrated by Chen and Cooper (2001) where cluster-analytic techniques were used to identify six different user groups or types based on approximately 127,000 user sessions involving the University of California's MELVYL on-line library catalog system. Examples of groupings included sophisticated versus unsophisticated, known item searching, and help intensive searching. A continuous-time stochastic process was used to model user state transition behavior in a Web-based information system. Results of this analysis indicated that a higher order process than predicted by a Markov model was occurring. Third and fourth order sequential dependencies were observed depending upon the user group analyzed. This type of analysis is called for as opposed to the zero-order reporting of simple frequencies if we are to learn from all the Web data we now have at hand. An additional "rough approximation clustering" technique is reported by De and Krishna (2004) which resulted in eight user clusters based on pattern analysis using "rough set theory". While the system they studied was different than that of Chen and Cooper, and unlike Chen and Cooper they made no attempt to "name" each of their clusters, the point is evident that there are several different user types as exhibited by actual usage.

How far we have come, yet how little we still know about what the user considers a successful search experience. The final section of this chapter addresses that issue specifically and suggests how we still may be able to gain the insight so desperately needed to create the information systems for the next generation of users.

SUMMARIZING THE STAGES OF EVOLUTION OF TRANSACTION LOG ANALYSIS

With respect to the evolution of use of transaction logs, Peters (1993, pp. 42-43) described three stages in the development of transaction log analysis:

From the mid 1960's to the late 1970's the focus was on evaluating system performance.

From the late 1970's through the mid-1980's was an initial application to online catalog systems (with emphasis on both system use and user behavior).

From the mid 1980's was a period of "diversification" with a variety of aspects under investigation including specific search states, specific user groups, types of information systems, or types of data bases. Also during this period replication of studies appeared. For the most part, the studies focused on the use of actual systems.

It could be argued that this "diversification" continues to this day. It could also be argued that these phases greatly oversimplify the early days of transaction log research. While it is true that the OPAC studies appeared to dominate in the middle phase, the early phase was much more complex and was not just about system performance. Early on there was a period when system monitoring was explored as a tool for user assistance software (see the previous discussion of the IIDA project as an example). So, like most of history, while it is useful to think of eras, they often miss the nuances and richness of activity at any given time. For those researchers there at the time, the eras were not clearly that demarcated.

It is possible, however, to report, as shown in Figure 2, on the history of transaction log research in terms of the number of systems being studied (Peters 1993, pp. 44-45) as well as the rate of publication during the various periods as shown in Figure 3 (Peters, Kaske, and Kurth 1993, pp. 152-183).

More recently, Markey (2007a) has surveyed the past twenty-five years (roughly 1983 to 2006) of end-user searching with a selective focus on only those studies reporting the employment of transaction logs. Therefore, her work provides

Figure 2. Systems studied via transaction log analysis (Source: Peters 1993)

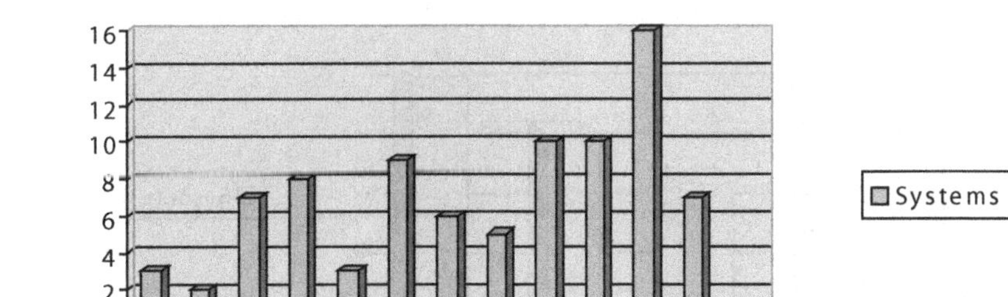

a surrogate update to the earlier survey, but the reader is cautioned not to compare actual counts with the previous chart, as Markey was much more selective in her publications cited. The data in Figure 4 do show, however, the continued publication of articles regarding transaction log analysis.

Markey (2007a, pp. 1071-1072) restricted her review to "intervention-free" studies (those using transaction log data) because she "wanted to learn how end users search IR systems left to their own devices and unaffected by potential biases such as the presence of an observer, their knowledge that a reviewer would scrutinize the search at a later time, their aptitude for or the potential biases of a researcher-assigned task." She acknowledges that despite these advantages, the transaction log method does, indeed, place restrictions on the type of research questions that can be addressed, referring to Kurth (1993, p. 99) who discussed both limits and limitations around a framework of four elements:

- The system being studied
- The user and the search process
- The analysis of transaction log data
- The ethical and legal issues

For purposes of his analysis, limits are "natural or logical boundaries of the phenomenon" while limitations are "practical boundaries" such as time and money. Despite a detailed discussion of each of the four elements, Kurth (1993, p. 102) concludes that the "trend of supplementing transaction log analysis with other methodologies is encouraging because it seeks to counteract the limits and limitations …". There is wisdom in the idea that one tool will not be adequate for bring-

Figure 3. Transaction log analysis publications (1966-1993). Source: Library Hi Tech Bibliography (1993)

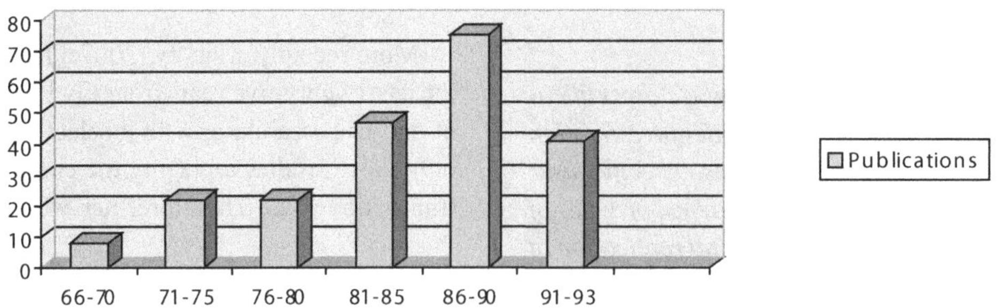

Figure 4. Selected citations in a 25-year study (Source: Markey, 2007)

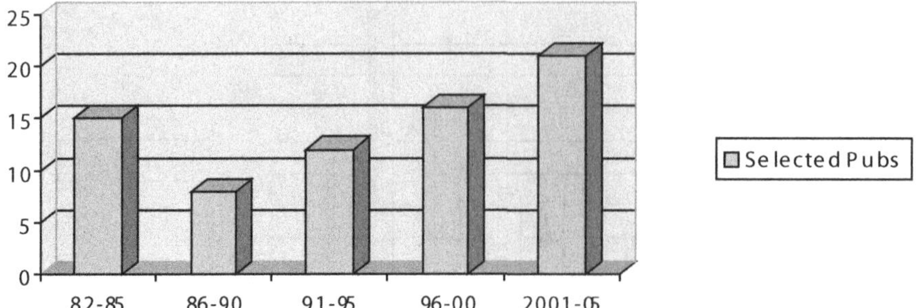

ing understanding to the world of user behavior, and that wisdom will be explored more fully in the final section of this chapter.

The question is, however, to what extent such past (or current) transaction log studies have actually improved our understanding of and enhancement of end user searching? Subsequent discussion of that issue within this book will cast some light on the answer, but Markey (2007b, p.1128) captures the essence of transaction logs as a research tool when she says:

logs are an unobtrusive approach to data collection, researchers can write custom programs to count, tally, and compare observations making it possible to analyze millions of cases in one fell swoop, and, for local systems such as online catalogs and locally mounted online databases they are usually available for the asking.

While unobtrusive, they can also be quite invasive. That is the subject of the following section on privacy and how it was viewed in the early days of transaction log analysis as well as some current thinking on the topic.

PRIVACY ISSUES

The issue of privacy was raised early on in the discussion of monitor data and its use in the study of user behavior. Tom Martin, one of the early information scientists with legal background to look at online retrieval systems and monitoring, suggested that system monitoring of all types (with the exception of such monitoring for system security and management) should require the prior consent of those using the system at the time of study (Martin, 1977). This, of course, failed to recognize that the transaction log files used in the earliest user studies were, in fact, already being collected for security and management purposes and used only secondarily for research into user behavior studies. Privacy was already being violated, the data just were not being exploited for beneficial purposes.

Penniman and Dominick (1980), who had individually and collectively conducted some of the earliest monitor studies, cautioned that privacy issues were a major barrier to widespread monitoring of information retrieval systems. A more realistic approach to protection of user privacy than that suggested by Martin was explicated by Penniman and Dominick (1980, p. 23) with definitions of the different levels of data disclosing increasing levels of user identification. These ranged from general session variables to complete recording of the entire protocol of interaction. (see Table 1)

Kurth (1993) suggested several methods for protecting user privacy where searcher identity must be revealed: (1) stripping patron information from the transaction log, (2) replacing patron id numbers with anonymous session identifier numbers, or (3) securing user permission for studying transaction logs of their sessions. Kurth (1993, p. 102) concluded in an extensive survey of early transaction log studies that: "At a time in which automated systems record and maintain more personal information about private citizens than ever before, we are justifiably suspicious of any automated system that has the potential to publicize information about our activities."

Such concern continues, as it should, with new researchers again proposing levels of disclosure as a means of protecting individuals while gaining insight into system usage.

As described earlier, adaptive prompting systems that could track user interaction and then suggest next actions for the user had been proposed and investigated (Penniman, 1976, Meadow, 1977). This concept clearly required a close tracking of user interactions with direct intervention during the user session. The fact that user actions were being "watched" would be obvious. Today, such systems are still suggested in terms of "personalized search" systems (Shen, Tan, & Zhai 2007, pp. 7-9) with the continuing concern for privacy protection. In this latest discussion, a four-level view of privacy is suggested:

- **Level 1: Pseudo Identity** – in which the actual user identity is replaced with less personally identifiable information, but the user information needs can still be aggregated at the individual level by the search engine.
- **Level 2: Group Identity** – in which a group of users share a single identity and the information needs are aggregated at the group level by the search engine.
- **Level 3: No Identity** – in which the user identity is not available to the search engine and the information needs can not be aggregated - even at a group level. (It could be possible, however to keep the user profile on the user's personal computer and provide personalized search help from that platform).
- **Level 4: No Personal Information** – neither the user identity nor the description of the user information need is available to the search engine.

This proposed multi-level privacy hierarchy is comparable to the earlier scheme of Penniman and Dominick (1980), but provides a more detailed approach to evaluating monitoring where complete or partial protocols are recorded. Clearly, privacy was of concern at the birth of transaction log research and continues to this day. It is interesting, however, that systems such as Amazon.com make no secret of the fact that they know what the user is doing and that the vendor is watching sales transactions closely to make suggestions of additional products in which they may be interested. Concern for privacy continues as indicated by the increase in legislation regarding protection and use of data but actual privacy seems to be diminishing in the world of online transactions.

At the same time, depending on the location (country/institution) of the intended research, collection and use of data may be restricted and serious researchers may find themselves highly constrained regarding access to data. This is a curious situation, indeed, where users are willingly relinquishing their rights to privacy as in the Amazon case, while law makers are working to protect (or merely restrict access to) personal data in other cases such as health records where improved sharing would be of benefit (Kohane et al., 2007)

Table 1. Privacy impacts of transaction log applications to system user studies (Source: Penniman and Dominick, 1980)

	Real-Time User Diagnostics	**Individual User Evaluation**	**Grouped User Evaluation**	**Computer System Protection**	**Computer System Evaluation**
General Session Variables	Low	Low	Low	Low	Low
Function or State Traces	Low	Medium	Low	Low	Low
Complete Protocol	Low (Note 1)	High	Medium (Note 2)	High (Note 3)	High

Note 1: Trace can be highly volatile and exist only long enough to provide assistance
Note 2: Could be high for proprietary groups and databases (corporate or intelligence agencies)
Note 3: Yet, this was (and is) a common practice.

CONCLUSION: WHAT WE CAN LEARN FROM HISTORY

Early users of transaction logs as a research or development tool had a strong focus on user-oriented design. This is still true of today's researchers who are beginning to raise questions about the context in which user interaction occurs. As this interest grows, additional tools augmenting transaction logs will take on even greater significance.

Penniman (1991) suggested a larger complexity to the study of user behavior and argued for system boundaries, when studying user system interaction, which included such elements as the educational, bureaucratic, and economic variables at play.

Jacobson (1993, p. 788) pointed out that "It is not always clear what cognitive conditions may be inferred from keyboard logs."

Markey (2007a, p. 1079) points out the current information retrieval models "acknowledge that information retrieval is a much more complex event, involving changes in cognition, feelings, and/or events during the information-seeking process." Markey (2007b, p. 1128) concludes that while transaction logs have been beneficial in giving researchers and system designers a view of end user activity, they will not be sufficient for answering the pressing research questions now being faced.

Merging transaction log data with other data, including demographic data (Nicholas et al., 2007) is promising. The author would caution researchers, however, to use demographic data carefully. To what extent such data can actually help in improved system design is open to question. Cluster analysis such as discussed earlier (Chen and Cooper 2001) is more likely to provide deeper insight into user characteristics than age, sex or annual income.

This author believes researchers and system designers need to return to the roots of the incentive for using transaction logs as a tool. The suggestions made by communication scholars such as Parker, and Paisley who saw the opportunity posed by this new data source never implied that it should be used in isolation. Combined with other tools, such as those suggested by Jacobson (1993) including structured or time-line interviews and Q-analysis of such interviews, and the earlier "talk aloud" method, transaction logs still represent a rich source of insight. Brophy (2004) suggests that storytelling is a means of enriching the understanding of the interactions within a library and that meaning and purpose can only be discerned within the context of the whole system. This supports the blended approaches reported by Wang et al. (2000) and Griffiths et al. (2002) as well.

It is encouraging that dissertations involving transaction logs as a research tool are continuing to be written by a new generation of researchers and that new vistas such as image retrieval are being explored (Tsai-Youn, 2006). What is even more encouraging, is that this tool is now being used in other domains than information or document retrieval involving the Web. A body of research literature is emerging in marketing and consumer behavior journals. This literature illustrates a sophistication in analytical methods for understanding user behavior while performing product searches on the Web (Jaillet, 2006) and determining how consumer behavior changes over time while using the Web (Moe and Fader 2004). In each of these cases, the methodology involved stochastic modeling techniques similar to those applied earlier in the evolution of transaction log analysis. Further, their conclusion supports the contention that simple summaries (frequency counts of events) provide little insight about individual usage patterns and that even detailed usage patterns change across time (are not stationary). One should expect such investigations within the marketing arena (using clickstream data) to increase as more companies rely on Web-based consumer action for purchases (Shankar and Malthouse, 2007).

Clearly, a return to some of the earliest work where transaction log data were analyzed as process data and not merely frequency counts or occurrences of single states (access to a particular url) is warranted (Chen and Cooper, 2001). As shown for both the user interaction domain as well as the marketing domain, frequency counts may be useful but will never provide the insight about user behavior that time-line data (via a variety of combined methods) can provide. Finally, we must be willing to create hybrid research designs that combine the highly quantitative approach of stochastic modeling with the more qualitative approaches available in order to arrive at a deep understanding of what is actually going on with the information seekers of this and the next generation.

REFERENCES

Abramson, A. D. (1998). Monitoring and evaluating use of the World Wide Web in an academic library: an exploratory study. In *Proceedings of the Annual Meeting of the American Society for Information Science* (pp. 315-326). Medford, N.J.: Information Today, Inc.

Back, H. B. (1976). *The design and evaluation of an interactive reference retrieval system for the management sciences.* Unpublished doctoral dissertation, Carnegie Mellon University.

Belkin, N. J., Cool, C., Kelly, D., Lin, S.-J., Park, S. Y., Perez-Carballo, J., & Sikora, C. (2001). Iterative exploration, design, and evaluation of support for query reformulaton in interactive information retrieval. *Information Processing and Management, 37(3),* 403-434.

Berry, M. W. and Browne, M. (2005). *Understanding search engines mathematical modeling and text retrieval, Second edition.* Philadelphia: Society For Industrial and Applied Mathematics.

Borgman, C. L. (1982). Online monitoring of users of the Ohio State University online catalog: methodological issues and results. In A. E. Petrarca, C.E. Taylor, and R. S. Kohn (Eds.), Information Interaction: Proceedings of the 45th ASIS annual meeting: Vol. 19 (pp. 35-36). White Plains, NY: Knowledge Industry Publications.

Borgman, C. L. (1983). *End user behavior on The Ohio State University libraries' online catalog* (Research report prepared for OCLC). Dublin, OH: Office of Research, OCLC.

Borgman, C. L. (1984). *The user's mental model of an information retrieval system: effects on performance.* Unpublished doctoral dissertation, Stanford University.

Borgman, C. L. (1986). Why are online catalogs hard to use? Lessons learned from information retrieval studies. *Journal of the American Society for Information Science, 37(6),* 387-400.

Borgman, C. L., Case, D. O., & Meadow, C. T. (1989). The design and evaluation of a front-end interface for energy researchers. *Journal of the American Society for Information Science, 40(2),* 99-109.

Borgman, C. L. (1996). Why are online catalogs *still* hard to use? *Journal of the American Society for Information Science, 47(7),* 493-503.

Borgman, C. L., Hirsh, S. G., & Hiller, J. (1996). Rethinking online monitoring methods for information retrieval systems: From search product to search process. *Journal of the American Society for Information Science, 47(7),* 568-583.

Brophy, P. (2004) Narrative-based librarianship. In *The area of information and social communication: Festschrift for Professor Wanda Pindlova (Studies in Library and Information Sciences Vol.10)* (pp. 188-195). Krakow: Jagiellonian University Press.

Carlisle, J. H. (1974). *Man computer interactive problem solving – relationships between user characteristics and interface complexity.* Unpublished doctoral dissertation, Yale University.

Chapman, J. L. (1981). A state transition analysis of online information-seeking behavior. *Journal of the American Society for Information Science, 32(5),* 325-333.

Chen, H. M. & Cooper, M. D. (2001). Using clustering techniques to detect usage patterns in a Web-based information system. *Journal of the American Society for Information Science, 52(11),* 888-904.

De, S. K., & Krishna, P. R. (2004). Clustering web transactions using rough approximation. *Fuzzy Sets and Systems, 148,* 131-138.

De Silva, S. M. (1997). A review of expert systems in library and information science. *Malaysian Journal of Library & Information Science, 2(2),* 57-92.

Dominick, W. D. (1974). *The man/machine interface, system monitoring and performance evaluation methodology for on-line interactive systems.* Unpublished masters thesis, Northwestern University.

Dominick, W. D. (1987). A performance measurement and evaluation environment for information systems. *Information Processing and Management, 23(10,* 7-15.

Dominick, W. D. (1990). The NASA RECON educational-program in interactive information-retrieval systems. *Computers & Education, 14(2),* 103-112.

Drummond, M. E. (1973). *Evaluation and Measurement Techniques for Digital Library Systems.* Englewood Cliffs, NJ: Prentice-Hall, Inc.

Fenichel, C. H. (1979). *Online information retrieval: Identification of measures that discriminate among users with different levels and types of experience.* Unpublished doctoral dissertation, Drexel University.

Fenichel, C. H. (1981). On-line searching measures that discriminate among users with different types of experiences. *Journal of the American Society for Information Science, 32(1),* 23-32.

Goodwin, H. B. (1959). Some thoughts on improved technical information service. *Special Libraries, 50(9),* 443-446.

Gorge, M. (2007). Making sense of log management for security purposes – an approach to best practice log collection, analysis and management. *Computer Fraud & Security, 2007(5),* 5-10.

Gove, N. B. (1973). Some good and bad features of present and future systems. In M. B. Henderson (Ed.) *Interactive Bibliographic Systems* (pp. 26-31). U.S. Atomic Energy Commission: Office of Information Services.

Griffiths, J. R., Hartley, R. J., & Willson, J. P. (2002). An improved method of studying user-system interaction by combining transaction log analysis and protocol analysis. *Information Research, 7(4).* Available at: http://InformationR/ir/7-4/paper139.html

Grignetti, M. C., Hausmann, C., & Gould, L. (1975). An intelligent online assistant and tutor – NLS Scholar. In *AFIPS Conference Proceedings NCC* (pp. 775-781)

Hildreth, C. R. (1991). Advances toward the E3OPAC: The imperative and the path. In *Proceedings of the Think Tank on the Present and Future of the Online Catalog* (pp. 17-38) Chicago: Reference and Adult Services Division, American Library Association.

Hunter, R. N. (1991). Successes and failures of patrons searching the online catalog at a large academic library: a transaction log analysis. *RQ 30(Spring),* 395-402.

Jaillet, H. F. (2006). Web metrics: measuring patterns in online shopping. *Journal of Consumer Behavior, 2(4),* 369-381.

Jansen, B. J. & Spink, A. (2000). Methodological approach in discovering user search patterns through Web log analysis. *Bulletin of the American Society for Information Science, 27(1),* 15-17.

Jansen, B. J. & Pooch, U. (2001). A review of Web searching studies and a framework for future research. *Journal of the American Society for Information Science, 52(3),* 235-246.

Jansen, B. J. (2006a). Using temporal patterns of interactions to design effective automated searching assistance. *Communications of the ACM, 49(4),* 72-74.

Jansen, B. J. (2006b). Search log analysis: What it is, what's been done. *Library and Information Science Research, 28(3),* 407-432.

Kohane, I. S., Mandl, K. D., Taylor, P. S., Holm, I. A., Nigrin, D. J., Kunkel, L. M. (2007). Reestablishing the Researcher-Patient Compact. *Science, 316(5826),* 836-837.

Kurth, M. (1993). The limits and limitations of transaction log analysis. *Library Hi Tech Issue 42, 11(2),* 98-104.

Lau, E. P. & Goh, D. H-L, (2006). In search of query patterns: A case study of a university OPAC. *Information Processing and Management, 42(5),* 1316-1329.

Lin, X., Liebscher, P., & Marchionini, G., (1991). Graphical representations of electronic search patterns. *Journal of the American Society for Information Science, 42(7),* 469-478.

Marcus, R. S. (1982). *Investigation of computer-aided document search strategies* (Report LIDS-R-1233). Boston:Laboratory for Information and Decision Systems, Massachusetts Institute of Technology.

Markey, K. (1984). *Subject searching in library catalogs: before and after the introduction of online catalogs.* Dublin, OH: OCLC.

Markey, K. (2007a). Twenty-five years of end-user searching, Part 1: Research findings. *JASIS, 58(8),* 1071-1081.

Markey, K. (2007b). Twenty-five years of end-user searching, Part 2: Future research directions. *JASIS, 58(8),* 1123-1130.

Martin, T. H. (1977). Monitoring and Individual Rights. In *Information management in the 1980's: Proceedings of the American Society for Information Science annual meeting* (p. 64) White Plains, NY: Knowledge Industry Publications.

Meadow, C. T. et al. (1977) *Individualized Instruction for Data Access (IIDA)* Final Design Report. Philadelphia, PA: Drexel University, Graduate School of Library Science, Franklin Institute Research Laboratories.

Meadow, C. T., Hewett, T. T. & Aversa, E. S. (1982a). A computer intermediary for interactive database searching. Part I: Design. *Journal of the American Society for Information Science, 33(5),* 325-332.

Meadow, C. T., Hewett, T. T. & Aversa, E. S. (1982b). A computer intermediary for interactive database searching. Part II: Evaluation. *Journal of the American Society for Information Science, 33(6),* 357-364.

Meadow, C. T. (1990). The making of an information retrieval interface. In *Information Technology 1990. Next decade in information technology, Proceedings of the 5th Jerusalem conference on information technology* (pp. 787-795). Los Alamitos, CA.: IEEE Computer Society.

Meister, D., & Sullivan, D. J. (1967) *Evaluation of user reactions to a prototype on-line information retrieval system* (Report No. NASA CR-918) Report to NASA by Bunker-Ramo Corporation under Contract No. NASA-1369, ERIC ED 019 094.

Mittman, B., & Dominick, W. D. (1973) Developing monitoring techniques for an on-line information retrieval system. *Information Processing and Management, 9(6),* 297-307.

Moe, W. W., & Fader, P. S. (2004). Capturing evolving visit behavior in clickstream data. *Journal of Interactive Marketing, 18(1),* 5-19.

Nicholas, D., Huntington, P., Jamali, H. R., & Dobrowolski, T. (2007). Characterizing and evaluating information seeking behavior in a digital environment: Spotlight on the 'bouncer'. *Information Processing and Management, 43,* 1085-1102

Parker, E. B., & Paisley, W. J. (1966). Research for Psychologists at the Interface of the Scientist and His Information System. *American Psychologist, 21(11),* 1061-1071.

Penniman, W. D. (1971, January). *BASIS-70 Design, Implementation, and Operation.* Paper presented at the joint meeting of the Central Ohio Chapters of the American Society for Information Science and the Association for Computing Machinery, Columbus, OH.

Penniman, W. D. (1974, October). *Rhythms of dialogue in BASIS – a preliminary report on doctoral research in human-computer conversational interaction.* Paper presented at the 37th annual meeting of the American Society for Information Science.

Penniman, W. D. (1975a). *Rhythms of dialog in human-computer conversation.* Unpublished doctoral dissertation, The Ohio State University.

Penniman, W. D. (1975b). A stochastic process analysis of on-line user behavior. In *Proceedings of the American Society for Information Science Vol. 12* (pp. 147-148). Washington, D.C.: ASIS.

Penniman, W. D. (1976). *A conceptual framework for adaptive prompting in interactive computer systems.* Unpublished paper included in correspondence to Dr. Sarah Rhodes, National Science Foundation, May 19, 1976.

Penniman, W. D. & Perry J. C. (1976). *Tempo of on-line user interaction.* Paper presented at the 5th Mid-year meeting of the American Society for Information Science, Nashville, TN.

Penniman, W. D. and Dominick, W. D. (1980). Monitoring and evaluation of on-line information system usage. *Information Processing and Management, 16(1),* 17-35.

Penniman, W. D. (1982). Modeling and evaluation of on-line user behavior. In *Proceedings American Society for Information Science, Vol. 19* (pp. 231-235).

Penniman, W. D. (1984). A methodology for evaluating interactive system usage. *SIGCHI Bulletin, 15(4),* 6-11.

Penniman, W. D. (1991). System interfaces revisited. In M. A. Siegel (Ed.), *Design and evaluation of computer/human interfaces: Issues for librarians and information scientists* (pp. 69-78). Urbana, IL: Graduate School of Library and Information Science, University of Illinois.

Peters, T. A. (1989). When smart people fail: an analysis of the transaction log of an online public access catalog. *The Journal of Academic Librarianship, 15(November),* 267-273.

Peters, T. A. (1993). The history and development of transaction log analysis. *Library Hi Tech Issue 42, 11(2),* 41-66.

Peters, T. A. (1998). Remotely familiar: Using computerized monitoring to study remote use. *Library Trends, 47(1),* 7-20.

Peters, T. A., Kaske, N. K., & Kurth, M. (1993) Transaction log analysis. *Library Hi Tech Bibliography, 8(9),* 151-183.

Peters, T. A., Kurth, M., Flaherty, P., Sandore, B., & Kaske, N. K. (1993) An introduction to the special section on transaction log analysis. *Library Hi Tech Issue 42, 11(2),* 38-40.

Qiu, L. (1993). Markov models of search state patterns in a hypertext information retrieval system. *Journal of the American Society for Information Science, 44(7),* 413-427.

Rice, R. E., & Borgman, C. L. (1983). The use of computer-monitored data in information science and communication research. *Journal of the American Society for Information Science, 34(4),* 247-256.

Sandore, B., Flaherty, P., Kaske, N. K., Kurth, M., & Peters, T. (1993). A manifesto regarding the future of transaction log analysis. *Library Hi Tech, Issue 42 11(2),* 105-106.

Sex and the Internet – devices and desires. (2007). *Economist, 383(8525),* 74.

Shankar, V., & Malthouse, E. C. (2007). The growth of interactions and dialogs in interactive marketing. *Journal of Interactive Marketing, 21(2),* 2-4.

Shen, X., Tan, B., & Zhai, C. X. (2007). Privacy protection in personalized search. *SIGIR forum, 41(1),* 4-17.

Slack, F. E. (1991) *OPACs: Using enhanced transaction logs to achieve more effective online help for subject searching.* Unpublished doctoral dissertation, Council for National Academy Awards, United Kingdom.

Slack, F. (1996). End-user searches and search path maps: a discussion. *Library Review 45(2).* 41-51.

Spink, A., & Jansen, B. J. (2004). *Web search: public searching on the Web.* Information science and knowledge management, v. 6. Dorndrecht, Netherlands: Kluwer Academic Publishers.

Stabell, C. B. (1974). *Individual differences in managerial decision making processes: A study of conversational computer system usage.* Unpublished doctoral dissertation, Massachusetts Institute of Technology.

Tolle, J. E. (1983a). *Current utilization of online catalogs: transaction analysis* (Final report to the Council on Library Resources, Vol. 1). Dublin, OH.: OCLC

Tolle, J. E. (1983b). Transaction log analysis online catalogs. In *Proceedings of the 6th annual international ACM SIGIR conference on research and development in information retrieval* (pp. 147-160). New York: ACM Press.

Tolle, J. E. (1984). Monitoring and evaluation of information systems via transaction log analysis. In *Proceedings of the 7th annual international ACM SIGIR conference on research and development in information retrieval* (pp. 247-258). Swinton, U.K.: British Computer Society.

Tolle, J. E. (1985a). Performance measurement and evaluation of online information systems. In *proceedings of the 1985 ACM thirteenth annual conference on computer science* (pp. 196-203). New York: ACM Press.

Tolle, J. E. (1985b). Online search patterns: NLM CATLINE database. *Journal of the American Society for Information Science, 36(2),* 82-93.

Treu, S. (1971). A conceptual framework for the searcher-system interface. In Walker, D. E. (Ed.), *Interactive bibliographic search: the user/computer interface* (pp. 53-66). Montvale, N.J.:AFIPS Press.

Treu, S. (1973) Techniques and tools for improving the interactive system interface. In *Interactive bibliographic systems: Proceedings of a forum held at Gaithersburg, Md. October 4-5, 1971* (pp.32-38). Oak ridge, TN: United States Atomic Energy Commission, Office of Information Services.

Tsai-Youn, H. (2006). *Search strategies for image retrieval in the field of journalism.* Unpublished doctoral dissertation, Rutgers The State University of New Jersey.

Walker, D. E. (Ed.). (1971). *Interactive bibliographic search: the user/computer interface.* Montvale, N.J.:AFIPS Press.

Wallace, P. M. (1993). How do patrons search the online catalog when no one's looking? Transaction log analysis and implications for BI and system design. *RQ 30(Winter),* 239-252.

Wang, P. L., Hawk, W. B. & Tenopir, C. (2000). Users' interaction with the World Wide Web resources: an exploratory study using a holistic approach. *Information Processing and Management, 36(2),* 229-251.

Wang, P. L., Tenopir, C., Layman, E., Penniman, W. D., & Collins, S. (1998). An exploratory study of user searching of the World Wide Web: A holistic approach. In *Proceedings of the Annual Meeting of the American Society for Information Science* (pp. 389-399). Medford, N.J.: Information Today, Inc.

Wyly, B. J. (1996). From access point to materials: a transaction log analysis of access point value for online catalog users. *Library Resources & Technical Services, 40(July),* 211-236.

KEY TERMS

Note: The author has borrowed freely from later work in this area for definitions, as some of the earlier studies had to "make it up as they went along". By the early 1990's, the techniques and thus the terminology had been fairly well developed.

Adaptive Prompting: A context sensitive method of issuing diagnostics based on patterns of actions as well as individual actions by the user (Penniman 1976, p. 3)

Analysis – First Order: An analysis of transaction patterns in which state pairs are evaluated and the immediately previous state is used to predict the current state

Analysis – Higher Order: An analysis of transaction patterns in which a sequence of states greater than two are evaluated and the current state is predicted on the basis of previous states (for example, a second-order process analysis would look at two previous states to predict the current state, a third order would look at three previous states, and so forth)

Analysis–Zero Order: An analysis of transactions in which only the current state is evaluated. This is usually characterized by studies in which frequency counts of particular states are reported irrespective of their context.

Markov Process: A stochastic process in which the transition probabilities can be estimated on the basis of first order data. Such a process is also stationary in that probability estimates do not change across the sample (generally across time)

Protocol: In this domain, a protocol is the "verbatim" record of user/system interaction for the entire user session (or selected portions) generally with time stamps on each action and perhaps some indication of system resources in use at the time. (Penniman and Dominick 1980, p. 23)

Protocol Analysis: The systematic evaluation of protocols using automated or manual content analysis tools. (Penniman and Dominick 1980, p. 31)

Search Engine: A software program that searches one or more databases and gathers the results related to the search query

Stochastic Process: A process that is probabilistic rather than deterministic in behavior. In the current context, a user state can be estimated but not determined with certainty when a sequence of previous states is available (e.g. a partial transaction log)

Transaction: A two-item set consisting of a query and a response, in which the IR system contributes either the query or the response and in which the response may be null. This definition allows human-to-machine, machine-to-human, and machin-to-machine transactions. It also allows for unanswered queries. (Peters, et al 1993, p. 39)

Transaction Log: An autonomous file (or log) containing records of the individual transactions processed by a computerized IR system. (Source: Peters, et al. 1993, p. 39)

Transaction Log Analysis: The study of electronically recorded interactions between online information retrieval systems and the persons who search for information found in those systems (Peters, et al 1993, p. 38 – narrow definition as applied to library and information science research)

Chapter III
Surveys as a Complementary Method for Web Log Analysis

Lee Rainie
Pew Internet & American Life Project, USA

Bernard J. Jansen
Pennsylvania State University, USA

ABSTRACT

Every research methodology for data collection has both strengths and limitations, and this is certainly true for transaction log analysis. Therefore, researchers often need to use other data collection methods with transaction logs. In this chapter, we discuss surveys as a viable alternate method for transaction log analysis and then present a brief review of survey research literature, with a focus on the use of surveys for Web-related research. The chapter then identifies the steps in implementing survey research and designing a survey instrument. We conclude with a case study of a large electronic survey to illustrate what surveys in conjunction with transaction logs can bring to a research study.

INTRODUCTION

Even the most ardent proponent of transaction log analysis must admit that the method has shortcomings (Jansen, 2006; Kurth, 1993), as do all methodological approaches. These shortcomings include a lack of understanding for the affective, situational, and cognitive aspects of system users. Therefore, the researcher employing transaction logs must look to other methods in order to address some of these shortcomings. Fortunately, the Web and other information technologies provide a convenient means for employing survey and survey research for such a purpose

Survey research is a method for gathering information by directly asking respondents about some aspect of themselves, others, objects, or their environment. Survey instruments are a data collection procedure that one can use in a variety of research designs. Researchers can use surveys to describe current characteristics of a sample population. One can also use surveys to try to discover the relationship among variables. Surveys gather data on respondents' recollections or opinions; therefore, surveys provide an excellent companion method for transaction logs that typically focus exclusively on actual behaviors of participants.

This chapter briefly reviews some previous studies that used surveys for Web research. We then discuss the types of surveys, the steps in survey research, and how to construct an appropriate survey instrument. We then present a case study and survey instrument to illustrate how surveys can supplement and enhance an overall research study that may also employ transaction logs.

REVIEW OF LITERATURE

Although surveys have been used for hundreds of years, the Web provides a remarkable channel for the use of surveys to conduct data collection (Jansen, Corley, & Jansen, 2006). Many of these Internet surveys have focused on demographical aspects of Web use over time (Kehoe & Pitkow, 1996) or one particular Website feature (Waite & Harrison, 2002). Treiblmaier (2007) presents an extensive review of the use of surveys for Website analysis.

Survey respondents may include general Web users or samples from specific population. For example, Jeong, Oh, and Gregoire (2003) surveyed travel and hotel shoppers. Huang (2003) surveyed users of continuing education programs, and Kim and Stoel (2004) surveyed female shoppers who had purchased apparel online.

For academic researchers, a convenience sample of students is often used to facilitate survey studies, including the users of Web search engines (Spink, Bateman, & Jansen, 1999). McKinney Yoon and Zahedi (2002) used both undergraduate and graduate students as their sample examining use of a Website. The major advantages of using students that are often cited include a homogeneous sample, access (Huizingh, 2002), their familiarity with the Internet (Jansen & McNeese, 2005), and creation of experimental settings (Rose, Meuter, & Curran, 2005). There are concerns in generalizing these results (Abdinnour-Helm, Chaparro, & Farmer, 2005), most notably for Websites and services where students have limited domain or system knowledge (Kim & Stoel, 2004; Koufaris, 2002). However, as a sample of demographic slice of the Web population, students appear to be a workable convenience sample with results from studies with students (c.f., Jansen & McNeese, 2005; Kellar, Watters, & Shepherd, 2007) similar to those using other sampling methods (c.f., Hargittai, 2002; Kehoe & Pitkow, 1996).

An increasing important type of survey instruments are electronic or Web surveys. Jansen, Corley, and Jansen (2006) define an electronic survey as "one in which a computer plays a major role in both the delivery of a survey to potential respondents and the collection of survey data from actual respondents" (p.1). Several researchers have examined electronic survey approaches, techniques, and instruments with respect to methodological issues associated with their use (Couper, 2000; Dillman, 1978; Fink, 1995; Fowler, 1995; Krosnick, 1999; Sudman, Bradburn, & Schwarz, 1996). There have been mixed research results concerning the benefits of electronic surveys (Kiesler & Sproull, 1986; Mehta & Sivadas, 1995; Sproull, 1986; Tse et al., 1995). However, researchers generally agree that electronic surveys offer faster response times and decreased costs. The electronic and Web-based surveys allow for a nearly instantaneous data collection into a backend database, which reduces potential errors caused by manual transcription.

Regardless of which delivery method used, survey research requires a detailed project planning approach.

PLANNING AND CONDUCTING A SURVEY

Although it may seem that conducting a survey is an easy task, one must employ a detailed planning process if survey research is to be successful. The goal of any survey is to shed insight into how the respondents perceive themselves, their environment, their context, their situation, their behaviors, or their perceptions of others.

To execute a survey, the researcher must identify the content area, construct the survey instrument, define the population, select a representative sample, administer the survey instrument, analyze and interpret the results, and communicate the results. These steps are somewhat linear but are also overlapping and may require several iterations. A 10-step survey research process is illustrated in Table 1, based on a process outlined in (Graziano & Raulin, 2004).

Step 1 and Step 2: *Determine the specific desired information* and *define the population that is being studied.* The information being sought and the population to be studied are the first tasks of the survey researcher. The answers to these questions are based on the goals of the survey research and drive both the construction and administration of the survey. If one uses a survey as a supplement to on-going Web log analysis, then these questions may already be partially answered.

Step 3: *Decide how to administer the survey.* There are many possibilities for administering a survey, ranging from face-to-face (i.e., an interview), to pen and paper, to the telephone (i.e., phone survey), to the Web (i.e., electronic survey). A survey can also be a mixed mode survey, combining more than one of these approaches. The exact method really depends on the answers to steps one and two (i.e., what information is needed and what population is studied). Used in conjunction with Web log analysis, surveys can be conducted prior to or after a lab study, or one can administer a survey to get insight into the demographics of the wider Web population.

Step 4: *Design a survey instrument.* Developing a survey instrument takes several steps. The researcher must determine what questions to ask, in what form, and in what order. The researcher must construct the survey so that it adequately gathers the information being sought. A basic rule of survey research is that the instrument should have a clear focus and should be guided by the research questions or hypotheses of the overall study. This implies that survey research is not well suited to early exploratory research because

Table 1. Ten step process for conducting a survey

STEP	ACTIONS
1	Determine the specific desire information
2	Define the population that is being studied
3	Decide how to administer the survey
4	Design a survey instrument
5	Pretest the survey instrument with a sub-sample
6	Select a sampling approach and representative sample
7	Administer the survey instrument to the sample
8	Analyze the data
9	Interpret the findings
10	Communicate the results to the appropriate audience

it requires some orderly expectations and focus of the researcher.

Step 5: *Pretest the survey instrument with a sub-sample.* Once the researcher has the survey instrument ready and refined, the researcher must pilot test the survey instrument. In this respect, a survey instrument is like developing a system artifact, where a system is beta tested prior to wider deployment. Generally, one conducts the pilot test on a sample that represents the population being studied, after which the researcher may (generally, will) refine the survey instrument further. Depending on the extent of the changes, the survey instrument may require another pilot test.

Step 6: *Select a sampling approach and representative sample.* Selecting an adequate and representative sample is a critical and challenging factor when conducting survey research. The population for a survey study is the larger group about or from whom the researcher desires to obtain information. From this population, one generally surveys a representative sample. If the researcher is administering a survey to the respondents of a laboratory study, the representativeness is not a problem, as the respondents are already the sample from the chosen population. However, if one is looking at the Web population, this population is large and diverse. It is impossible to question every member. One should carefully select a representative sample.

Whenever one uses a sample as a basis for generalizing to a population, the researcher is engaging in an inductive inference from the specific sample to the general population. In order to have confidence in inductive inferences from sample to population, the researcher must carefully choose the sample to represent the overall population. This is especially true for descriptive research, where the researcher wishes to describe some aspect of a population that may depend on demographic characteristics. In other cases, such as verifying the application of universal theoretical constructs, for example, Zipf's Law (Zipf, 1949), sampling is not as important since these universal construct should apply to everyone within the population.

Sampling procedures typically fall into three classifications, convenience sampling (i.e., selecting a sample with little concern for its representativeness to some overall population), probability sampling (i.e., selecting a sample where each respondent has some known probability of being included in the sample), and stratified sampling (i.e., selecting a sample that includes representative samples of each subgroup within a population).

Step 7. *Administer the survey instrument to the sample.* For actually gathering the survey data, the researcher must determine the most appropriate manner to administer the survey instrument. Many surveys are administered via the Web or electronically, as the Web offers substantial benefits in its easy access to a wide population sample. Additionally, administering a survey electronically, even in a laboratory study, has significant advantages in terms of data preparation for analysis. The survey can be administered once to a cross sectional portion of the population or one can administer the survey repeatedly over time to the same sample population.

Step 8. *Analyze the data.* Once the data is gathered, the researcher must determine the appropriate method for analysis. The appropriate form of analysis is dependent on the research questions, hypotheses, or types of question used in the survey instruments. The available approaches are qualitative, quantitative, or mixed methods.

Step 9: *Interpret the finding.* Like many research results, the interpretation of survey data can be in the eye of the beholder as to what the results mean. When results are in question, it may point to the need for further research. One of the best aids in interpreting results is the literature review. What have results from prior work pointed out? Are these results in line with those prior researches? Or, do the results highlight something new?

Step 10: *Communicate the results to the appropriate audience.* Finally, the results of any survey research must be packaged for the intended audience. For academic purposes, this may mean a scholarly paper or presentation. For commercial organizations, this may mean a white paper for system developers or marketing professionals.

Each of these steps can be challenging. However, designing a survey instrument (e.g., steps 4 and 5) can be the most difficult aspect of the survey research. We address this development in more detail in the following section.

DESIGNING A SURVEY INSTRUMENT

Before designing a survey instrument, the researcher must have a clear understanding of the type of data desired and must keep the instrument focused on that area. The key to obtaining good data via a survey is to develop a good survey instrument that is based on the research questions. The researcher should develop a set of objectives with a clear list of all needed data. These research goals and list of needed data will serve as the basis for the questions on the survey instrument.

A survey instrument is a data collection method that presents a set of questions to a respondent. The respondent's responses to the questions provide the data sought by the researcher. Although seemingly simple, it can be very difficult to develop a set of questions for a survey instrument. Some general guidelines for developing survey instruments are:

- **Provide instructions for completing the survey instrument:** To assist in ensuring that one collects valid survey results, include instructions on how to respond to questions on the survey instrument. Generally, there is a short introductory set of instructions usually at the top of the survey instrument. Provide additional instructions for specific questions if needed.
- **Place questions concerning personal information at the end of the survey:** Demographic information is often necessary for survey research. Place these questions at the end of the survey. Providing personal data may annoy some respondents, resulting in incomplete or inaccurate responses to the survey instrument.
- **Group questions on the instrument by subject:** If the survey instrument has more than ten or so questions, the questions need to be grouped by some classification method. Generally, grouping the questions by subject is a good organization method. If the instrument has multiple groups of questions, each group should have a heading identifying the grouping. Grouping questions allows the respondents to focus their responses around the central theme of the group of questions.
- **Present each questions and type of question in a consistent structure:** A consistent structure makes it much simpler for respondents and increases the likelihood of valid data. Explain the proper method for responding to each question and ensure that the response methods for similar questions are consistent throughout the instrument.

There are three general categories of survey questions, (1) multiple-choice, (2) Likert-scale, and (3) open-ended questions.

Multiple-Choice Question

Multiple-choice questions have a closed set of response items for the respondents to select. Multiple-choice questions are used when the researcher has a thorough understanding of the range of possible responses.

The items for multiple-choice questions must cover all reasonable alternatives that the respondents might select and each of the items must be

Examples of multiple-choice questions

What is your gender? a. Male b. Female	Which features of Instant Messaging programs do you find most useful when it comes to sharing information with teammates? a. Real-Time Chat b. File Sharing c. Chat logs d. None

Example of a Likert-scale rating question

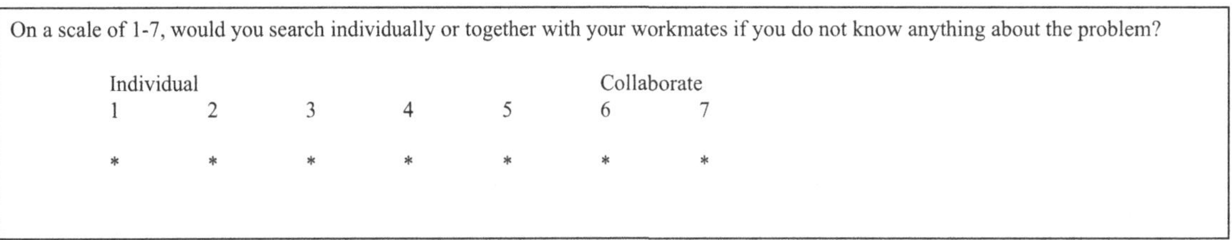

On a scale of 1-7, would you search individually or together with your workmates if you do not know anything about the problem?

Individual					Collaborate	
1	2	3	4	5	6	7
*	*	*	*	*	*	*

Example of a Likert-scale ranking question

On a scale of 1-5 (1-never used, 5-use every day), how experienced are you with using the following communication / collaboration applications for group projects?

a. _____ Email
b. _____ Instant messaging
c. _____ Face-to-face meetings
d. _____ Telephone
e. _____ Others (please elaborate)

unique (i.e. they do not overlap). Since presenting all reasonable alternatives is a difficult task, the researcher should include a general catch-all item (e.g., *None of the above* or *Don't know*) at the end of a list of item choices. This approach helps improve the accuracy of the data collected.

Likert-Scale Question

With Likert-scale questions, the items are arranged as a continuum with the extremes generally at the endpoints. Likert-scale questions may have the respondent indicate the degree to which they agree with a statement or rank a list of items.

Open-Ended Question

Open-ended questions have no list of items for the respondent to choose from.

Open-ended questions are best for exploring new ideas, for getting respondent's elaboration on previous answers, or for questions for which there are many possible answers. As such, the open-ended questions are great for qualitative research. The disadvantages to using open-ended questions are that it can be much more time consuming and difficult to analyze the data if one is doing quantitative research, as each question must be coded into order to derive variables.

If the researcher knows a partial list of possible responses, one can create a partially open-ended question.

Example of an open-ended question

> As part of your project, I believe that you must have confronted a situation when you did not really know how to proceed in order to solve a problem or perform a task on the Web.
>
> (a) Can you speak about a specific instance of your project work of this nature?
>
> ____
>
> ____

Example of a partially structured question

> Which features of Instant Messaging programs do you find most useful when it comes to sharing information with teammates?
>
> a. Real-Time Chat
> b. File Sharing
> c. Chat logs
> d. Others ______________
> e. None

A CASE STUDY USING SURVEY METHODOLOGY

Referring to the ten-step method outlined above for designing and conducting survey research and the procedures for developing a survey instrument, we present a case study of the survey research from the Pew Internet & American Life Project.

Pew Internet & American Life Project

Since December 1999, the Pew Internet & American Life Project based in Washington, D.C., USA regularly reports findings on subjects such as teenagers' and senior citizens' use of the Internet, broadband adoption, trends in email use, employment of search engines, use of the Internet to gather news (especially about politics), blog creation and readership, and trends in music and movie file sharing. The Pew Internet & American Life Project (the Project) has examined how people's Internet use affects their families, communities, health care, education, civic involvement, political life, and work places. Additionally, the Project uses regular surveys to track online life.

As of 2007, the Project has issued more than 100 reports based on social issues and online activities. It also has focused research on important public policy questions such as public attitudes about trust and privacy online, development of e-government, intellectual property issues, the impact of spam, and the status of digital divides. The Project is non-partisan and takes no positions on policy matters. All of its reports and datasets are available online for free at: http://www.pewinternet.org.

Exploratorium Survey Overview

Sponsored by the Pew Internet & American Life Project, the Exploratorium Survey obtained telephone interviews with a nationally representative sample of 2,000 adults age 18 and older living in the continental United States (US) telephone households. The survey was constructed by The Project and Princeton Survey Research Associates International (PSRAI). Interviews were conducted from 9 January to 6 February, 2006. Statistical results are weighted to correct known demographic discrepancies. The margin of sampling error for the complete set of weighted data is ±2.5%. The number of adult Internet users is 1,447 with a margin of sampling error of ±2.9%. Details on the design, execution and analysis of the survey are discussed below.

Design and Data Collection Procedures

Sample Design

The sample was designed to represent all continental US telephone households. The telephone sample was provided by Survey Sampling International, LLC according to PSRAI specifications. The sample was drawn using the standard *list-assisted random digit dialing* (RDD) methodology. Active blocks of telephone numbers (area code + exchange + two-digit block number) that contained three or more residential directory listings were selected with probabilities in proportion to their share of listed telephone households. After selection, two more digits were added randomly to complete the number. This method guarantees coverage of every assigned phone number regardless of whether that number is directory listed, purposely unlisted, or too new to be listed. After selection, the numbers were compared against business directories to match numbers purged.

Contact Procedures

Interviews were conducted from 9 January to 6 February 2006. As many as 10 attempts were made to contact every sampled telephone number. The sample was released for interviewing in replicates, which are representative sub-samples of the larger sample. Using replicates to control the release of sample ensures that complete call procedures are followed for the entire sample.

Calls were staggered over times of day and days of the week to maximize the chance of making contact with potential respondents. Each household received at least one daytime call in an attempt to find someone at home. In each contacted household, interviewers asked to speak with the youngest adult male currently at home. If no male was available, interviewers asked to speak with the oldest female at home. This systematic respondent selection technique has been shown to produce samples that closely mirror the population in terms of age and gender.

Weighting and Analysis

Weighting is generally used in survey analysis to compensate for patterns of non-responsiveness that might bias results. The weight variable balances the interviewed sample of all adults to match national parameters for sex, age, education, region based on US Census definitions, race, Hispanic origin, and population density. The White, non-Hispanic subgroup was also balanced on age, education and region. These parameters came from a special analysis of the U.S. Census Bureau's 2005 Annual Social and Economic Supplement (ASEC) that included all households in the continental US having a telephone.

Weighting was accomplished by using sample balancing, a special iterative sample weighting program that simultaneously balances the distributions of all variables using a statistical technique called the *Deming Algorithm*. Weights were trimmed to prevent individual interviews from having too much influence on the final results. The use of these weights in statistical analysis ensures that the demographic characteristics of the sample closely approximate the demographic characteristics of the national population. Table 2 compares weighted and un-weighted sample distributions to population parameters.

Effects of Sample Design on Statistical Inference

Post-data collection statistical adjustments require analysis procedures that reflect departures from simple random sampling. PSRAI calculates the effects of these design features so that an appro-

Table 2. Sample demographics

2005 PARAMETER		UN-WEIGHTED	DEMING WEIGHT (WEIGHT)
Gender			
Male	48.1%	44.9%	48.2%
Female	51.9%	55.2%	51.8%
Age			
18-24	12.6%	6.5%	12.4%
25-34	17.7%	12.6%	18.0%
35-44	19.9%	18.2%	19.9%
45-54	19.5%	20.8%	19.3%
55-64	13.8%	17.8%	13.5%
65+	16.5%	24.1%	16.8%
Education			
Less than HS Grad.	15.0%	8.9%	12.8%
HS Grad.	36.1%	31.9%	35.6%
Some College	23.1%	24.0%	24.0%
College Grad.	25.8%	35.2%	27.6%
Region			
Northeast	19.0%	17.5%	19.0%
Midwest	23.1%	25.7%	24.1%
South	35.9%	36.9%	35.2%
West	22.0%	20.0%	21.6%
Race/Ethnicity			
White/not Hispanic	71.2%	82.7%	73.5%
Black/not Hispanic	10.9%	8.8%	11.1%
Hispanic	12.1%	6.0%	10.7%
Other/not Hispanic	5.8%	2.4%	4.8%
Population Density			
1 - Lowest	20.1%	26.5%	20.9%
2	20.0%	22.8%	20.6%
3	20.1%	21.4%	20.5%
4	20.2%	15.6%	19.5%
5 - Highest	19.6%	13.8%	18.4%

priate adjustment can be incorporated into tests of statistical significance when using these data. The so-called "design effect" or *deff* represents the loss in statistical efficiency that results from systematic non-response. The total sample design effect for this survey is 1.28.

PSRAI calculates the composite design effect for a sample of size n, with each case having a weight, w_i as:

$$deff = \frac{n\sum_{i=1}^{n} w_i^2}{\left(\sum_{i=1}^{n} w_i\right)^2} \qquad (1)$$

In a wide range of situations, the adjusted *standard error* of a statistic should be calculated by multiplying the usual formula by the square root of the design effect ($\sqrt{deff}$). Thus, the formula for computing the 95% confidence interval around a percentage is:

$$\hat{p} \pm \left(\sqrt{deff} \times 1.96 \sqrt{\frac{\hat{p}(1-\hat{p})}{n}} \right) \quad (2)$$

where $\hat{p}$ is the sample estimate and n is the unweighted number of sample cases in the group being considered.

The survey's margin of error is the largest 95% confidence interval for any estimated proportion based on the total sample— the one around 50%. For example, the margin of error for the entire sample is ±2.5%. This means that in 95 out every 100 samples drawn using the same methodology, estimated proportions based on that the entire sample will be no more than 2.5 percentage points away from their true values in the population. The margin of error for estimates based on adult Internet users is ±2.9%. It is important to remember that sampling fluctuations are only one possible source of error in a survey estimate. Other sources, such as respondent selection bias, questionnaire wording and reporting inaccuracy, may contribute additional error of greater or less magnitude.

Response Rate

Table 3 reports the disposition of all sampled telephone numbers ever dialed from the original telephone number sample. The response rate estimates the fraction of all eligible respondents in the sample that were ultimately interviewed. At PSRAI, it is calculated by taking the product of three component rates:

- **Contact rate:** The proportion of working numbers where a request for interview was made – of 78 percent
- **Cooperation rate:** The proportion of contacted numbers where a consent for interview was at least initially obtained, versus those refused – of 43 percent
- **Completion rate:** The proportion of initially cooperating and eligible interviews that were completed – of 88 percent

Thus, the response rate for this survey was about 30 percent.

A complete exploratorium survey is presented in Appendix 1.

CONCLUSION

Transaction logs are an excellent means for recording the behaviors of system users and the responses of those systems. However, transaction logs are ineffective as a method of gaining an understanding of the underlying motivations, affective characteristics, cognitive factors, and contextual aspect that influence these behaviors. Used in conjunction with transaction logs, surveys can be an effective method for investigating these aspects. The combined methodological approach can provide a richer picture of the phenomenon under investigation.

In this chapter, we have reviewed a ten-step procedure for conducting survey research, with explanatory notes on each step. We then discussed the design of a survey instrument, with examples of various types of questions. Finally, we ended the chapter with a case study highlighting the telephone survey.

REFERENCES

Abdinnour-Helm, S. F., Chaparro, B. S., & Farmer, S. M. (2005). Using the end-user computing satisfaction (eucs) instrument to measure satisfaction with a Web site. *Decision Sciences, 36*(2), 341-364.

Table 3. Sample disposition

CATEGORY	OCCURRENCE/PERCENTAGE
Total Numbers Dialed	**13,087**
Business	1,156
Computer/Fax	891
Cell Phone	22
Other Not-Working	2,385
Additional Projected	757
Working Numbers	7,876
Working Rate	**60.2%**
No Answer	185
Busy	47
Answering Machine	1,276
Callbacks	74
Other Non-Contacts	132
Contacted Numbers	6,163
Contact Rate	**78.2%**
Initial Refusals	2,762
Second Refusals	749
Cooperating Numbers	2,652
Cooperation Rate	**43.0%**
No Adult in Household	25
Language Barrier	355
Eligible Numbers	2,272
Eligibility Rate	**85.7%**
Interrupted	272
Completes	2,000
Completion Rate	**88.0%**
Response Rate	**29.6%**

Couper, M. (2000). Web surveys: A review of issues and approaches. *Public Opinion Quarterly, 64*(4), 464-494.

Dillman, D. A. (1978). *Mail and telephone surveys.* New York: John Wiley & Sons.

Fink, A. (1995). *The survey handbook (vol. 1).* Thousands Oaks, CA: Sage Publications.

Fowler, F. J. (1995). *Improving survey questions: Design and evaluation (vol. 38).* Thousand Oaks, CA.: Sage Publications.

Graziano, A. M., & Raulin, M. L. (2004). *Research methods: A process of inquiry* (5th ed.). Boston: Pearsono.

Hargittai, E. (2002). Beyond logs and surveys: In-depth measures of people's web use skills. *Journal of the American Society for Information Science and Technology, 53*(14), 1239-1244.

Huang, M.-H. (2003). Designing website attributes to induce experiential encounters. *Computers in Human Behavior, 19*(4), 425-442.

Huizingh, E. K. R. E. (2002). The antecedents of Web site performance. *European Journal of Marketing, 36*(11/12), 1225-1247.

Jansen, B. J. (2006). Search log analysis: What is it; what's been done; how to do it. *Library and Information Science Research, 28*(3), 407-432.

Jansen, B. J., & McNeese, M. D. (2005). Evaluating the effectiveness of and patterns of interactions with automated searching assistance. *Journal of the American Society for Information Science and Technology, 56*(14), 1480-1503.

Jansen, K. J., Corley , K. G., & Jansen, B. J. (2006). E-survey methodology: A review, issues, and implications. In J. D. Baker & R. Woods (Eds.), *Encyclopedia of electronic surveys and measurements (eesm)* (pp. 1-8). Hershey, PA.: Idea Group Publishing.

Jeong, M., Oh, H., & Gregoire, M. (2003). Conceptualizing Web site quality and its consequences in the lodging industry. *Hospitality Management 22*(2), 161-175.

Kehoe, C. M., & Pitkow, J. (1996). Surveying the territory: Gvu's five WWW user surveys. *The World Wide Web Journal, 1*(3), 77-84.

Kellar, M., Watters, C., & Shepherd, M. (2007). A field study characterizing Web-based information seeking tasks. *Journal of the American Society for Information Science and Technology, 58*(7), 999-1018.

Kiesler, S., & Sproull, L. S. (1986). Response effects in the electronic survey. *Public Opinion Quarterly, 50*, 402-413.

Kim, S., & Stoel, L. (2004). Apparel retailers: Website quality dimensions and satisfaction. *Journal of Retailing and Consumer Services 11*(2), 109-117.

Koufaris, M. (2002). Applying the technology acceptance model and flow theory to online consumer behavior. *Information Systems Research 13*(2), 205-223.

Krosnick, J. A. (1999). Survey research. In *Annual review of psychology* (Vol. 50, pp. 537-367): Annual Review.

Kurth, M. (1993). The limits and limitations of transaction log analysis. *Library Hi Tech, 11*(2), 98-104.

McKinney, V., Yoon, K., & Zahedi, F. (2002). The measurement of Web-customer satisfaction: An expectation and disconfirmation approach. *Information Systems Research, 13*(3), 296-315.

Mehta, R., & Sivadas, E. (1995). Comparing response rates and response content in mail vs. Electronic mail surveys. *Journal of the Market Research Society, 37*(4), 429-439.

Rose, G. M., Meuter, M. L., & Curran, J. L. (2005). On-line waiting: The role of download time and other important predictors on attitude toward e-retailers. *Psychology & Marketing Research, 22*(2), 127-151.

Spink, A., Bateman, J., & Jansen, B. J. (1999). Searching the Web: A survey of excite users. *Journal of Internet Research: Electronic Networking Applications and Policy, 9*(2), 117-128.

Sproull, L. S. (1986). Using electronic mail for data collection in organizational research. *Academy of Management Journal, 29*(1), 159-169.

Sudman, S., Bradburn, N. M., & Schwarz, N. (1996). *Thinking about answers: The application of cognitive processes to survey methodology.* San Francisco: Jossey-Bass Publishers.

Treiblmaier, H. (2007). Web site analysis: A review and assessment of previous research. *Communications of the Association for Information Systems, 19*, 806-843.

Tse, A. C. B., Tse, K. C., Yin, C. H., Ting, C. B., Yi, K. W., Yee, K. P., et al. (1995). Comparing two methods of sending out questionnaires: E-mail vs. Mail. . *Journal of the Market Research Society, 37*(4), 441-446.

Waite, K., & Harrison, T. (2002). Consumer expectations of online information provided by bank websites. *Journal of Financial Services Marketing 6*(4), 309-322.

Zipf, G. K. (1949). *Human behavior and the principle of least effort.* Cambridge, MA: Addison-Wesley Press.

KEY TERMS

Electronic Survey: Is one in which a computer plays a major role in both the delivery of a survey to potential respondents and the collection of survey data from actual respondents.

Survey Instruments: A data collection procedure that one can use in a variety of research designs.

Survey Research: A method for gathering information by directly asking respondents about some aspect of themselves, others, objects, or their environment.

APPENDIX

Presented below are the questions from the survey that address aspects of the Web or Web usage. See the Pew Internet & American Life Website for a complete and updated version of the survey.

This the Exploratorium Survey as of 14 February 2006 designed by the Princeton Survey Research Associates International for the Pew Internet & American Life Project. The sample (n) was 2,000 adults 18 and older. Margin of error is plus or minus 3 percentage points for results based on the full sample [n=2,000]. Margin of error is plus or minus 3 percentage points for results based on Internet users [n=1,447].

Q1 Overall, are you satisfied or dissatisfied with the way things are going in this country today? (note: see the Pew Internet Life Project Website for details on each of the samples used for each survey implementation).

	Satisfied	Dissatisfied	Don't know/ refused
Current	36	55	8
Nov/Dec 2005	35	56	9
September 2005	32	61	8
May/June 2005	36	54	10
February 2005	41	49	10
January 2005	41	48	11
November 23-20, 2004	45	47	9
November 2004	46	46	8
May/June 2004	33	56	11
February 2004	40	50	10
November 2003	43	49	9
July 2003	46	45	9
June 2003	49	42	9
April/May 2003	54	37	8
March 12-19, 2003	42	49	10
March 3-11, 2003	41	51	8
February 2003	38	54	9
December 2002	41	47	11
November 2002	43	48	10
October 2002	40	49	11
September 2002	44	45	10
July 2002	45	43	11
March/May 2002	52	37	11
January 2002	58	33	9
December 2001	61	29	10
November 2001	62	28	9

continued on following page

October 2001	57	33	10
September 2001	46	44	11
August 2001	44	46	10
February 2001	53	38	10
December 2000	50	42	8
November 2000	50	41	9
October 2000	53	39	8
September 2000	51	40	9
July/August 2000	52	39	9
May/June 2000	51	41	8
March/April 2000	50	41	9

Q2 I'm going to read you a few statements. For each one, please tell me if this describes you very well, somewhat well, not too well, or not at all.

		Very well	Somewhat well	Not too well	Not at all	Don't know/ Refused
a	After I gather all the facts about something, I make up my mind pretty quickly					
	Current	55	31	8	4	1
	June/July 2004	52	32	9	5	1
b	I like to read about a lot of different things					
	Current	54	28	9	7	1
	June/July 2004	61	26	7	6	1
c	I find it difficult to make up my mind when I have too much information about something					
	Current	12	23	21	43	1
	June/July 2004	14	22	19	45	1
d	I enjoy learning about science and new scientific discoveries					
	Current	43	31	12	13	1

Q5 Do you use a computer at your workplace, at school, at home, or anywhere else on at least an occasional basis?

	Yes	No	Don't know/ Refused
Current	74	25	
Nov/Dec 2005	68	31	
September 2005	74	26	0
May/June 2005	72	28	

continued on following page

February 2005	70	30	
January 2005	69	31	
November 23-20, 2004	70	30	0
November 2004	68	32	0
May/June 2004	71	29	
February 2004	73	27	
November 2003	72	27	
July 2003	71	29	
June 2003	71	29	
April/May 2003	69	31	
March 20-25, 2003	70	30	
March 12-19, 2003	65	35	0
March 3-11, 2003	71	29	
February 2003	70	30	0
December 2002	68	32	0
November 2002	70	30	
October 2002	69	31	
September 2002	68	32	
July 2002	69	31	
March/May 2002	69	31	
January 2002	67	33	0
December 2001	64	36	
November 2001	65	35	
October 2001	62	38	
September 2001	63	37	
August 2001	66	34	0
February 2001	65	35	0
December 2000	69	31	
November 2000	65	35	
October 2000	64	36	
September 2000	62	38	
July/August 2000	63	37	
May/June 2000	60	40	
March/April 2000	63	37	

Q6a Do you use the internet, at least occasionally?

Q6b Do you send or receive email, at least occasionally?

	Uses Internet	Does not use Internet
Current	73	27
Nov/Dec 2005	66	34
September 2005	72	28
May/June 2005	68	32
February 2005	67	33
January 2005	66	34
November 23-20, 2004	59	41
November 2004	61	39
May/June 2004	63	37
February 2004	63	37
November 2003	64	36
July 2003	63	37
June 2003	62	38
April/May 2003	63	37
March 20-25, 2003	58	42
March 12-19, 2003	56	44
March 3-11, 2003	62	38
February 2003	64	36
December 2002	57	43
November 2002	61	39
October 2002	59	41
September 2002	61	39
July 2002	59	41
March/May 2002	58	42
January 2002	61	39
December 2001	58	42
November 2001	58	42
October 2001	56	44
September 2001	55	45
August 2001	59	41
February 2001	53	47
December 2000	59	41
November 2000	53	47
October 2000	52	48
September 2000	50	50
July/August 2000	49	51
May/June 2000	47	53
March/April 2000	48	52

Q12 About how many years have you been an Internet user?

Q12.1 About how many months is that?

Based on Internet users [N=1,447]

	Six months or less	A year ago	Two or three years ago	More than				Don't know/ Refused
				Three years ago	Four years ago	Five years ago	Six or more ago	
Current	2	3	9	85	7	14	64	1
November/ December 2005	1	4	12	80	5	14	61	3
September 2005	1	3	11	83	5	16	62	1
May/June 2005	2	4	14	79	7	14	58	1
February 2005	2	4	11	82	7	14	61	1
January 2005	2	4	12	81	8	17	56	1
November 23-30, 2004	1	4	11	83	6	17	60	2
May/June 2004	2	4	15	78	9	16	54	1
February 2004	2	3	14	79	10	16	53	2
November 2003	2	4	16	77	9	19	49	1
July 2003	2	5	19	74	9	20	44	1
June 2003	2	5	19	73	12	19	42	2
April/May 2003	2	5	18	74	11	19	45	1
March 20-25, 2003	3	6	16	74	10	18	46	1
March 12-19, 2003	2	7	16	74	12	18	44	1
March 3-11, 2003	2	5	14	77	12	20	45	1
February 2003	1	4	19	73	9	18	46	1
December 2002	1	6	23	68	13	19	36	2
November 2002	2	5	23	70	12	19	39	1
October 2002	3	6	22	68	12	18	38	1
September 2002	2	5	23	68	13	18	38	1
July 2002	2	6	24	65	13	19	33	2
March/ May 2002	7	10	31	52	10	15	25	
January 2002	8	13	36	43	8	13	21	
December 2001	6	13	34	47	10	14	20	
November 2001	7	12	34	47	12	12	20	
October 2001	5	15	32	47	12	14	19	1
September 2001	7	15	34	44	11	14	17	
August 2001	10	15	32	43	10	13	18	

continued on following page

February 2001	11	16	37	35	10	11	13	1
December 2000	12	19	35	34	n/a	n/a	n/a	
November 2000	11	19	33	37	n/a	n/a	n/a	
October 2000	12	20	33	35	n/a	n/a	n/a	
September 2000	11	21	37	31	n/a	n/a	n/a	
July/August 2000	14	21	33	32	n/a	n/a	n/a	
May/June 2000	15	19	33	33	n/a	n/a	n/a	
March/April 2000	18	20	32	30	n/a	n/a	n/a	
October 1999	15	22	32	31	n/a	n/a	n/a	0
November 1998	20	26	34	19	n/a	n/a	n/a	1
October 1996	26	38	24	12	n/a	n/a	n/a	

Q16 About how often do you go online from (INSERT) — several times a day, about once a day, 3-5 days a week, 1-2 days a week, every few weeks, every few months, or less often?

Based on Internet users [N=1,447]

	Several times a day	About once a day	3-5 days a week	1-2 days a week	Every few weeks	Less often	(VOL) Never	Don't know/ refused
a Home								
Current	29	25	17	12	5	6	6	
May/June 2005	27	22	15	13	6	7	10	
June/July 2004	27	27	17	13	5	5	7	
March 2004	29	24	15	13	6	5	8	
b Work								
Current	35	8	5	3	2	7	40	1
May/June 2005	35	9	5	4	2	6	39	
June/July 2004	28	12	5	4	1	5	44	
March 2004	28	10	5	6	2	4	44	
c Someplace other than home or work								
Current	3	3	4	5	9	21	56	
March 2004	3	3	3	6	6	15	64	1

BLG1 Have you, personally, ever created an online journal, a web log or "blog" that others can read on the web?

Based on internet users [N=1,447]

	CURRENT		NOV/DEC 2005	SEPT 2005	FEB 2005	JAN 2005	NOV 2004	FEB 2004	SEPT 2002	JULY 2002
%	13	Yes	8	9	9	10	6	5	7	3
	87	No	92	90	91	89	93	94	93	96
		Don't know/ Refused		1		1		1	1	

BLG2 Have you ever read someone else's online journal, web log or blog?

Based on internet users [N=1,447]

	CURRENT		SEPT 2005	FEB 2005	JAN 2005	NOV 2004	FEB 2004
%	39	Yes	27	23	27	27	17
	61	No	71	75	71	71	82
		Don't know/ Refused	2	2	2	1	1

Q18 Next, please tell me if you ever get news or information from each of the following sources. (First/Next)...

Q19 Did you happen to gets news or information from this source YESTERDAY, or not?

		Total EVER USE SOURCE	Total USED SOURCE Yesterday	Total NEVER USE SOURCE	Don't know/ refused
a	Newspapers				
	Current	85	49	15	
	June/July 2004	85	51	15	0
b	Television				
	Current	90	76	10	0
	June/July 2004	92	74	8	
c	Magazines				
	Current	56	21	44	0
	June/July 2004	56	21	44	
d	The radio				
	Current	72	54	28	
	June/July 2004	73	54	27	
e	The internet				
	Current	53	38	47	0
	June/July 2004	51	30	49	

EXPL1 On a slightly different topic...If you had to rate your own basic understanding of SCIENCE, would you say it is very good, good, just fair, or poor?

	CURRENT	
%	20	Very good
	38	Good
	32	Just fair
	9	Poor
	1	Don't know/Refused

EXPL2 Overall, how WELL INFORMED would you say you are about new scientific discoveries: very well informed, somewhat informed, not too informed, or not at all informed?

	CURRENT	
%	11	Very informed
	58	Somewhat informed
	23	Not too informed
	8	Not at all informed
		Don't know/Refused

EXPL3 In general, would you say you have a good idea of what it means to study something SCIENTIFICALLY, or are you not really sure what that means?

	CURRENT	
%	66	Have a good idea what it means
	33	Not really sure
	1	Don't know/Refused

EXPL4 In your own words, could you tell me what it means to study something scientifically?

Based on those who know what it means to study something scientifically [N=1,357]

	CURRENT	
%	93	Gave response
	6	Don't really know/Not sure what it means
	1	Refused

EXPL5 Please tell me if you strongly agree, agree, disagree or strongly disagree with each of the following statements.

		Strongly agree	Agree	Disagree	Strongly disagree	Don't know/ refused
a	Developments in science help make society better	31	58	8	1	3
b	In order to live their daily lives, people need a good understanding of basic scientific concepts and principles	19	58	18	2	2
c	Most scientific theories are eventually proven wrong and replaced by new theories	5	39	42	5	9
d	Scientific research is essential to improving the quality of human lives	35	56	7	1	2

continued on following page

e	Science creates more problems than solutions for us and our planet	3	19	52	19	6
f	Scientific research today doesn't pay enough attention to the moral values of society	11	38	36	7	8
g	To be a strong society, the United States needs to be competitive in science	39	50	8	1	2

EXPL6 We're interested in where you get your SCIENCE news and information. Do you ever get science news or information from the following sources?

		Yes	No	Don't know/ refused
a	Television	88	12	
b	Newspapers	69	31	
c	The radio	46	54	
d	Magazines	63	37	
e	The internet	54	46	

EXPL7 Where do you get MOST of your science news and information?

	CURRENT	
%	41	Television
	20	The internet
	14	Magazines
	14	Newspapers
	4	Radio
	7	Other/None of these
	1	Don't know/Refused

EXPL8 Next, please tell me if you have ever used the internet to do the following things. Have you ever used the internet to...?

Based on internet users [N=1,447]

		Yes	No	Don't know/ refused
a	Look up the meaning of a particular scientific term or concept	70	30	
b	Look for an answer to a question you have about a scientific concept or theory	68	31	1
c	Check the accuracy of a scientific fact or statistic	52	47	1
d	Compare different or opposing scientific theories	37	62	1
e	Download scientific data, graphs or charts	43	57	
f	Learn more about a science story or scientific discovery you first heard or read about offline	65	34	1
g	Complete a science assignment for school, either for yourself or for a child	55	45	
	Total yes to any item	87		

EXPL9 Which of the following comes closest to describing WHY you use the internet to get science news and information?

Based on those who get science news or information online [N=1,282]

	CURRENT	
%	71	Because getting science information online is easy and convenient
	13	Because you can get more accurate science information online
	12	Because you can get science information online that is not available anyplace else
	1	Some other reason (VOL)
	3	Don't know/Refused

EXPL10 Do you ever do any of the following to check the reliability of the science information you find online? Do you ever…?

Based on those who get science news or information online [N=1,282]

		Yes	No	Don't know/ refused
a	Compare it to other information you find online to make sure it's correct	62	38	1
b	Compare it to an OFFLINE source like a science journal or encyclopedia	54	46	
c	Look up the original source of the information or the original study it's based on	54	45	1
	Total yes to any item	80		

EXPL11 Is the internet usually the FIRST place you go when you want science news and information, or do you usually look someplace else first? IF OTHER SOURCE: Where do you usually look FIRST for science information?

Based on those who get science news or information online [N=1,282]

	CURRENT	
%	61	Internet first place respondent goes
	34	Go to other source first
	5	Magazines
	5	Books/Textbooks
	4	Library
	4	Television
	3	Encyclopedia/Periodicals
	3	Newspaper
	1	Journals
	9	Other
	3	Depends (VOL)
	2	Don't know/Refused

EXPL12 When using the internet, do you ever come across science news and information when you may have been going online for some other purpose?

Based on internet users [N=1,447]

	CURRENT	
%	65	Yes
	34	No
	1	Don't know/Refused

EXPL13 As I read a short list of science topics, please tell me if you are very interested, somewhat interested, or not at all interested in each topic.

		Very interested	Somewhat interested	Not at all interested	Don't know/ refused
a	The origins of the universe	29	37	33	1
b	The origins of life on this planet	35	40	24	1
c	Stem cell research	31	40	26	3
d	Global warming and changes in the Earth's climate	42	39	18	1
e	The human genome and DNA	36	41	22	1
f	Space and space exploration	31	41	28	1
	Total at least somewhat interested in one of the above items	96			

MODULE Distribution of respondents across follow-up modules

	CURRENT	
%	26	Stem cell module
	38	Global warming module
	29	Origins of life module
	7	No follow-up module

Stem Cell Module

SC1 How closely do you follow stories about stem cell research – very closely, fairly closely, not too closely, or not at all closely?

Based on those in stem cell module [N=539]

	CURRENT	
%	18	Very closely
	48	Fairly closely
	28	Not too closely
	6	Not at all closely
		Don't know/Refused

SC2 Do you ever get news or information about stem cell research from the INTERNET or through EMAIL?

Based on internet users in stem cell module [N=420]

	CURRENT	
%	38	Yes
	62	No
		Don't know/Refused

SC3 Can you recall any specific websites where you have gotten news or information online about stem cell research?

Based on internet users who get news/information about stem cell research online [N=159]

	CURRENT	
%	49	Gave response
	50	Can't recall
		Refused

SC4 How often do you get news or information about stem cell research from the Internet or through email – everyday day or almost everyday, several times a week, several times a month, or less often?

Based on internet users who get news/information about stem cell research online [N=159]

	CURRENT	
%	3	Everyday or almost everyday
	8	Several times a week
	32	Several times a month
	56	Less often
	1	Don't know/Refused

SC5 Where have you gotten MOST of your news and information about stem cell research? From school, from television, from newspapers, from radio, from magazines, or from the Internet and email?

Based on those in stem cell module [N=539] NOTE: Table exceeds 100% due to multiple responses

	CURRENT	
%	42	Television
	25	Newspapers
	20	The internet and email

continued on following page

	17	Magazines
	7	Radio
	5	School
	4	None of these/Someplace else (VOL)
	1	Don't know/Refused

SC6 Based on what you've heard or read, please tell me if you think the following statements about stem cell research are true or false. If you aren't sure, just say so and I'll move to the next item.

Based on those in stem cell module [N=539]

		True	False	Don't know	Refused
a	There are two major types of stem cells, adult stem cells and embryonic stem cells	54	18	27	1
b	Adult stem cells have been used for many years to treat cancers such as lymphoma and leukemia	37	27	36	1
c	There are over 100 stem cell lines available to federally-supported researchers in the United States	27	21	52	1

SC7 Overall, would you say it is EASY or DIFFICULT to find the scientific information you need to understand stem cell research?

Based on those in stem cell module [N=539]

	CURRENT	
%	56	Easy to find
	30	Difficult to find
	14	Don't know/Refused

SC8 If you wanted to learn more about stem cell research, where would you go FIRST for more information?

Based on those in stem cell module [N=539]

	CURRENT	
%	67	The internet
	11	Library
	4	Science magazines
	3	Scientific journals
	2	Television
	2	Newspapers
	2	Doctor
	5	Other
	4	Don't know
	0	Refused

Chapter IV
Watching the Web:
An Ontological and Epistemological Critique of Web-Traffic Measurement

Sam Ladner
McMaster University, Canada

ABSTRACT

This chapter aims to improve the rigor and legitimacy of Web-traffic measurement as a social research method. I compare two dominant forms of Web-traffic measurement and discuss the implicit and largely unexamined ontological and epistemological claims of both methods. Like all research methods, Web-traffic measurement has implicit ontological and epistemological assumptions embedded within it. An ontology determines what a researcher is able to discover, irrespective of method, because it provides a frame within which phenomena can be rendered intelligible. I argue that Web-traffic measurement employs an ostensibly quantitative, positivistic ontology and epistemology in hopes of cementing the "scientific" legitimacy they engender. But these claims to "scientific" method are unsubstantiated, thereby limiting the efficacy and adoption rates of log-file analysis in general. I offer recommendations for improving these measurement tools, including more reflexivity and an explicit rejection of truth claims based on positivistic science.

INTRODUCTION

The Internet's expansion afforded the opportunity for entirely new methods of research. Social researchers expressed initial enthusiasm primarily from the data provided by online surveys, which can be obtained more quickly and cheaply than in-person or telephone research (Couper, Traugott, & Lamias, 2001). Web-traffic measurement holds significantly slower adoption rates among social scientists than other online research methods such as online surveys and online focus groups. Web-traffic measurement is the analysis of data between so-called "client" computers and "server" computers. When client computers (such as the one I am using to write this chapter) request Web pages from server computers, a trail of data is created. Web-traffic measurement refers to the practice of capturing this data.

Web-traffic measurement can provide insight into how people use computers, and for this reason it is a method common among applied, private-sector user researchers (Kuniavsky, 2003; Rosenfeld & Wiggins, 2007). Web traffic measurement refers to the analysis of Web-generated quantitative data (and as this chapter will show, these data are generated both by server log files and the more contemporary javascript tags embedded in Web pages). But Web-traffic measurement also offers potential applications for non-profit, government and university-based social researchers. Non-profit researchers could use Web-traffic measurement to investigate public awareness of public health issues, for example. Government social researchers could investigate the efficacy of policy initiatives using indicators from Web-traffic measurement. University-based social-science researchers could apply Web-traffic measurement particularly fruitfully in investigating the patterns and efficacy of online pedagogy. Despite the potential benefits of this research method, Web-traffic measurement has not been embraced by non-profit, government or university-based researchers. In his description of various emerging Web-based methods, Bryman (2004), for example, describes new and even exotic sounding methods such as online surveys and focus groups, "virtual" ethnography and Web site content analysis. Notably missing from this list of Web-based methods is Web-traffic measurement.

It is my position that this gap is justified, in part, because Web-traffic measurement presents some troubling ontological and epistemological limitations for which practitioners of Web-traffic measurement have not fully provided remedies. Web-traffic measurement does offer a potentially fruitful method of research, however. This chapter is intended to show how Web-traffic measurement is currently limited by a lack of methodological reflexivity, how this may be remedied, and potential research applications of its use. Currently, Web-traffic measurement is used extensively in the private sector to track the effectiveness of online advertising campaigns, the popularity of online content, the source of visitors, and the efficacy of search-engine optimization. This chapter stems both from my role as a private-sector practitioner and as a university-based methodologist.

I argue that Web-traffic measurement has an incomplete and positivistic ontology that, when interrogated, reveals the gaps in understanding the entire user experience. This demonstrates how and in what ways Web-traffic measurement is insufficient as a user experience research method. Further, I argue that Web-traffic measurement has a clearly interactive relationship between researcher and research participant, and for this reason, this method overstates its ostensibly objective epistemology. Rather, Web-traffic measurement is better suited to an interpretivist ontology and epistemology, more characteristic of qualitative methods.

Because of this, I suggest that Web-traffic measurement can be improved by adopting a fully interpretivist position, which requires researchers to avoid generalizing results to large populations, and refusing to claim "statistical significance." Instead, Web-traffic researchers should move closer to theoretical tests and claim their results to be interpretations of events, rather than predictions of future events.

THE ORIGINATION OF WEB-TRAFFIC MEASUREMENT

Web-traffic measurement was not designed or intended to be a tool for social researchers. It emerged out of the technical need to monitor Web server performance. The World Wide Web, which was born in 1990 and popularized by the mid-1990s, was created when client computers, connected to the Internet, requested to see files from server computers (World Wide Web Consortium, 2007). These server computers were increasingly asked to "serve up" more and more files, making their response time and performance an issue.

The solution to this server-load problem was the creation of Web-traffic measurement, which could provide Web site managers with estimates of the computing power required of their servers. Similar to highway traffic measurement, Web-traffic measurement was intended to monitor and correct for "bottlenecks" in Web-traffic. At this time, the source of data was primarily through server log files. Server log files, which automatically recorded interactions between computers and Web servers, provided a rich data set to help Web site managers manage peak periods of traffic and plan upgrades to their server hardware. Typical findings from such log files included how long computers stayed connected to servers (or "session length"), Internet Protocol (IP) address of computer locations, Web pages visited, and overall number of computers or "visitors" that visited the site (Cohen, 2003b; Petersen, 2005b). These data were collected to monitor "server load," or as indicators of the total computing power required when computers downloaded files from the publicly available Web server. As a result, they were typically presented in raw form, which required significant interpretation and were cumbersome to analyze.

Web user experience practitioners embraced Web-traffic measurement as a *user experience research method* instead of as an *infrastructure monitoring tool.* "Log file analysis" came to refer to the practice of interpreting these Web server data (Kuniavsky, 2003; Petersen, 2004). As visitors come to and interact with a Web site, they create a digital trail of information that is automatically collected by many Web servers. Eventually, customized software (such as WebTrends) was created to provide a more useable format for these data. Customized software signaled an important shift in the use of Web-traffic measurement away from an IT diagnostic tool and toward an actual social research method.

Because of its non-research genesis, Web-traffic measurement was never subjected to a determination of its rigor as a method, which is typical of other emerging social research methods such as online surveys (e.g., see Couper, Traugott, & Lamias, 2001; Michaelidou & Dibb, 2006; Roster, Rogers, Hozler, Baker, & Albaum, 2007). While this approach provided potential insights for both Web site managers or practitioners and for university-based researchers, little scholarly attention has been paid to the potential of server logs (Cohen, 2003a). The new Web-traffic measurement provided the opportunity for Web site designers and usability specialists to enhance user interfaces and navigation systems, which were useful pieces of data for Web managers. New software tools collected and synthesized some of the more popular indicators of visitor behavior, such as entry and exit pages, most popular pages, and time spent on the Web site. One of the first such tools was WebTrends Log Analyzer first released in 1995 (WebTrends, 2001). Log Analyzer was originally positioned primarily as an IT monitoring tool not as a social research method. It was "designed and developed for Webmasters, Intranet Administrators, Internet Service Providers, Marketing Managers, Executive Management and Individuals" (Archive.org, 1997). The data that was collected using Log Analyzer was designed to help technical staff diagnose and correct server problems, as well as for Web usability specialists to diagnose and correct user interface problems. This kind of user research was a praxis-based method of fixing common problems such as broken links or missing images, but did not have a history of self-reflexivity common to similar research methods, such as usability testing and in-depth interviewing. Questions of reliability and validity were not asked in systematic ways.

RECENT FORMS OF WEB-TRAFFIC MEASUREMENT: ASP TOOLS

More recently, "application service provider" (ASP) tools have largely usurped server log files as the most prevalent form of Web-traffic measurement among private-sector practitioners. ASP tools differ from log file analysis in several key ways. First, where once Web-traffic measurement was largely completed by examining a server's logs, now Web site managers are likely to purchase a service agreement with a third party company, which will capture Web traffic data "mid-stream" (Petersen, 2004). In the ASP version, visitors are typically issued "cookies" (small text files) which sit on their computers and facilitate the recording of interactions between the visitor and a Web server. Interactions are simply "watched" by a third-party application, which in turn provides Web-based "dashboards" or summaries of major trends in Web traffic. Web site managers now log onto a Web-based interface to view the latest events, or download the raw data that the service provider collects from their traffic stream with visitors. Analysis typically happens through a combination of viewing the pre-configured dashboards and downloading data to Excel spreadsheets (Petersen, 2004).

The shift to the ASP model has also solidified Web-traffic measurement as a primary tool for researching Web user experience. In contrast to the first marketing materials for WebTrends Log Analyzer, contemporary marketing of ASP tools specifically targets aspects of user experience, such as navigation paths. WebSideStory, for example, makers of the HBX Analytics ASP tool, tells potential buyers that the tool will allow them to measure effectiveness of various online advertising, as well as gain knowledge of user behavior, "HBX Analytics highlights what visitors are clicking on, how long they are on each page, how they navigate around the site, and *provides detailed insight into how they interact* with your Web site forms. By understanding what visitors do while on your site, you can begin to refine your online strategy" (WebSideStory, 2007 emphasis mine). Omniture, makers of SiteCatalyst, also promise potential customers insight into revenue-generating links and locations, as well as, "Omniture SiteCatalyst helps organizations quickly identify and understand the most profitable paths through their Web sites, where visitors are dropping off, what's driving critical success events, and *how different segments of visitors interact* with the Web site" (Omniture, 2007 emphasis mine). Both SiteCatalyst and HBX Analytics are primarily Web-traffic measurement tools but their makers purport that these tools are a user experience research method as well. This expansion is due in part to the enormous economic potential of for-profit companies purchasing Web-traffic measurement tools. Log file analysis and ASP tools are collectively referred to as "Web analytics." Web analytics show all signs of continuing to grow as an industry (Petersen, 2005a). The market will continue to grow as more and more for-profit companies expand their Web presences.

WEB-TRAFFIC MEASUREMENT'S TURN TO POSITIVISM

Applied Web-traffic measurement has recently taken on a distinctly "scientific" tone in its approach to analysis. The practice is currently being constructed as a rigorous method that relies heavily on the positivistic rhetoric to justify its claims to predicting the "best" user experience. Persistent limitations of validity and reliability challenge these claims. But such limitations are secondary to the more fundamental problem with Web-traffic measurement: it purports to be an objectivist social research method yet employs an incomplete ontology and an implicitly interpretivist epistemology. The "scientific" claims of Web-traffic researchers are not consistent with these ontological and epistemological stances.

Web-traffic researchers have recently embarked on a project of adopting an explicitly "scientific" rhetoric in a misguided attempt to legitimate the practice as an authentic scientific method. This project makes the dubious assumption that quantitative validity is the only legitimate way to test truth claims, something very much in dispute among methodologists (Alasuutari, 1995; Schwandt, 2000). Kuniavsky argues that unlike other forms of user research, log file analysis is "objective and descriptive" (Kuniavsky, 2003, p. 474). Web-traffic researchers are now conducting "experiments" using so-called "A/B testing," which purports to be a "true scientific application" (Eisenberg, 2005). Web managers are exhorted to use "experimental design" and avoid "polluting results" by creating too many versions of a single page. Elements of the user experience are reduced to "variables" similar to the variables such as time, temperature and pressure that are manipulated in industrial processes (Chatham, 2004). Web-traffic researchers are told to "Apply the scientific method in these instances and make sure you can isolate the source of any measured differences" (Petersen, 2004, p. 78). This turn to "scientific experiments" signals that Web-traffic measurement is currently being constructed as a positivist, scientific method that can manipulate the user experience in the same way that industrial products are manipulated scientifically. The implication is that the user experience (like steel production, for example) can be predicted and controlled.

The adoption of positivistic rhetoric coincides with persistent and deep problems with validity and reliability. As Chatham finds, Web traffic researchers continue to struggle with accurate visitor counts and missing data points, compromising both the validity and reliability of the method (Chatham, 2005). Practitioners are dogged by day-to-day limitations in both the techniques and the underlying technology, which limit their ability to reliably produce analyses that are universally accepted as legitimate (Wiggins, 2007). Log files are notoriously unreliable, insofar as they will return differing results depending on the myriad of computer configurations of visitors to the site (Wiggins, 2007). They are also prone to the problem of "caching," in which computers store temporary copies of Web sites to provide faster load times (Kuniavsky, 2003). It is also common for practitioners to employ radically different techniques to get the same metrics from their log files (Petersen, 2005b). Common practice is to "customize" key performance indicators (or KPIs) to suit an individual analyst's needs. But there is no standardization of such procedures and as such, KPIs often differ significantly from analyst to analyst (Petersen, 2004). Moreover, even single analysts will find significant differences in consistently applied methods due to the constantly changing nature of Web technologies. Common discussions on the Web Analytics' Association listserv center on resolving day-to-day reliability problems regarding number of visitors and length of visits. Despite these continuing problems, analytics tools are increasingly positioned as tools for user research, specifically for improving Web site usability (Petersen, Bayriamova, Evans, Levy, & Matiesanu, 2004). This chapter will offer some suggestions for improving the efficacy of Web-traffic measurement for user experience problems.

More complete investigations of reliability and validity of Web-traffic measurement can be found elsewhere in this volume (e.g., Yun: The Unit of Analysis and the Validity of Web Log; Rigo, de Oliveira and Wives: Identifying users stereotypes for dynamic Web pages customization). This chapter, by contrast, focuses on the ontological and epistemological character of Web-traffic measurement as a research method. It is these questions that will enable social researchers to understand the limitations – and the potential – of this method.

Both log-file and ASP-based Web-traffic measurement methods are ostensibly quantitative in their approach to research, but they present some intriguing contradictions. Qualitative and quantitative research methods both rely on often implicit ontological and epistemological claims (Bryman, 2004; Creswell, 1994). Quantitative research ontologically assumes the nature of reality as objective and singular, and epistemologically assumes that the researcher is independent of the subject of research. Qualitative research, on the other hand, assumes that reality is fundamentally subjective, and that the researcher interacts with the subject of research. While there is more nuance to this debate than this binary, dichotomous view of research (e.g., Denzin & Lincoln, 2000; Schwandt, 2000), these ideal-types serve as a framework for comparison.

ONTOLOGICAL CLAIMS OF WEB TRAFFIC RESEARCH

To interrogate a method of scientific inquiry, one must understand first the ontological assumptions embedded within that method, and thereafter investigate the epistemological implications of that belief (Potter & Lopez, 2001). An ontology determines what a researcher is able to discover, irrespective of method, because it provides a frame within which phenomena can be rendered intelligible. An ontology describes one's understanding of reality itself. A researcher's ontology answers the question "What is there to know?" before the researcher determines a method for finding out *what is known* (Creswell, 1994). In other words, what one believes the nature of the world to be fundamentally influences how one would investigate any feature of that world. Ontological assumptions are often unspoken and implicit, but nonetheless are determinant of potential research findings (Schwandt, 2000).

In their critique of positivism, for example, Potter and Lopez (2001) argue that positivist researchers have transferred an ontology of natural science onto social science. The scientific method, with its reliance on systematic experimentation, has an implicit ontology of "actualism," which is the belief in the invariance of events. This is what allows scientific experimentation to be used as an inferential device; if researchers can engineer an event, they believe they can predict the likelihood of this same event occurring once more. Potter and Lopez (2001) argue that such positivist ontology is entirely inappropriate for social science (leaving aside how the inherent unpredictability of quantum physics troubles this ontology). They argue that social phenomena are "things" not "events" and as such cannot be known within a positivist ontological frame.

In turning our attention to Web-traffic measurement, it becomes rapidly apparent that Web-traffic measurement's unspoken assumptions are indeed both positivist and limited. Both log file analysis and ASP-based analysis base their data collection on the recorded interactions between a computer and a Web server. The data that are used are collected either from the host server or captured mid-stream between the host server and the client computer. No other data are collected, and no other data are used in analysis. *The unspoken belief within Web-traffic measurement is that these keystrokes and mouse clicks represent the sum total of what there is to know about a Web site visitor's experience.*

Further, Web-traffic researchers assume that measurement of single instances of interactions will predict future interactions. Within this ontology, there is an assumption that an individual person intentionally initiates these keystrokes and mouse clicks for meaningful reasons. The reality of Web-traffic measurement is limited to this small portion of the user experience but purports to encompass and infer the nature of the entire user experience. Based on this limited set of observations, Web-traffic researchers will typically infer the likelihood of any future "event" (i.e., series of mouse clicks or keystrokes). Not only is this ontology incomplete, but it also derives its logic from the positivist frame asserted by Potter and Lopez.

The Web visitor's mood, cognitive intent, physical ability, the physical location of her computer and individual status are all outside the realm of "what there is to know" for Web-traffic measurement. We may call this ontology "computer/server interaction" instead of "user experience." This ontology will never reveal, for example, that the person initiating the user-computer action is physically located in an Internet café in Johannesburg, using a dial-up connection, and is writing an email on behalf of her neighbor – an entirely reasonable scenario in South Africa (Hobbs, 2007). Computer/server interaction will not reveal that many of her mouse clicks are unintentional because she is disabled or has little experience using a mouse. Such an ontology could never discover, for example, that keystrokes on the user-computer were periodically interrupted by the Internet connection being dropped. Yet, Web-traffic researchers will attempt to infer the likelihood of how this person will again interact with the Web site, without any understanding of these *in situ* constraints.

This incomplete ontology is even more limited with the more recent and popular ASP-based Web-traffic measurement than in log file-based measurement. With ASP data collection, the user's data stream is not recorded directly on the Web server that serves up the pages the user requests, but through a third party server, which interprets the "clickstream" of the user. The "reality" of ASP-based Web-traffic measurement is not mouse clicks and keystrokes between the client computer and the server, but the mouse clicks and keystrokes that are captured by a third party server. The reality of Web-traffic measurement, especially ASP-based measurement, is decidedly narrow in its scope. Calling this reality "user experience" is entirely inappropriate first because it decidedly missed important aspects of the user experience, and also because it asserts the ability to predict future events based on an interpretivist approach. Yet this research method is frequently used to investigate user experience.

Consider, for example, the claim that usability problems can be diagnosed through Web-traffic measurement. "Usability," is defined as different by the International Organization for Standardization as "the efficiency, effectiveness and satisfaction with which specified users can achieve specified goals in particular environments" (as cited in Weir, Anderson, & Jack, 2006). Weir, Anderson and Jack note that "direct experience of the technology" is a fundamental aspect of usability. Yet, Web-traffic measurement is used as a means of investigating usability. This problem is recognized by Web analytics practitioners, such as Eric Peterson: "...there is no substitution to seeing how people really interact with the content and navigation systems you have built...One cannot describe the feeling one gets to see real users interacting with a system you have designed" (Petersen, 2004, p. 9).

What is observable is only the user's trail of mouse clicks and keystrokes, which may – or may not – be meaningful or even intentional. Yet researchers who use Web-traffic measurement underplay the significance of this oversight. Web-traffic measurement, which was originally intended to provide Web server performance monitoring, has now become a *bona fide* method for deriving insights into how humans use computers. Indeed, as some writers imply, it rivals in-depth human observation. Using the analogy that a Web site is like a closely monitored, high-service retail outlet such as a jewelry story, Kuniavsky suggests that the eyeless watch of the log file is as valuable as the deep observation of a jewelry store clerk:

> *A Web site visitor has to ask to see every piece they're interested in, like in a jewelry store. This is different from a supermarket, where he or she can spend all day squeezing every tomato, and no one would ever know. This is why a clerk at a jewelry store is likely to have a much better understanding of customers' behavior than a supermarket cashier.* (Kuniavsky, 2003, p. 402)

The computer/server interaction ontology is not equivalent to a jewelry store clerk gathering subtle, nuanced information about a person visiting their store. Rather, it is the equivalent of a blindfolded, deaf jewelry store clerk who uses a complex system of tapping to communicate with store visitors, who may or may not know the unique tapping language of that particular clerk.

This ontology is further limited by the assumption that future events can be predicted using Web-traffic measurement. Web-traffic researchers employ an implicit futural orientation to their analysis. Web-traffic data are considered not "things," but "events," which have a predictable likelihood of being repeated. Chatham argues that companies that incorporate "experimental design" in their uses of Web-traffic measurement can predict and quantify increases in sales (Chatham, 2004).

This ontological limitation of Web-traffic measurement does not suggest that it cannot be used to derive insight about user experience. But awareness of this limitation must be brought to the fore for Web-traffic measurement to be best implemented as a legitimate social research method. Potter and Lopez concede that their ontology of social phenomena as "things" limits their ability to be "objective" researchers. But, they argue, acknowledging this limitation and taking steps to overcome it (such as adopting an interpretivist rather than predictive stance in analysis) can only improve the nature of their research.

EPISTEMOLOGICAL CLAIMS OF WEB TRAFFIC RESEARCH

A researcher's understanding of what reality *is* determines their choice of method, and thereby, the relationship between the researcher and the research participant. In other words, epistemology follows ontology. Web-traffic measurement's epistemological claims emerge from this ontology of computer/server interaction. Log file analysis and ASP-based analysis both implicitly assume that the subject of research, typically referred to as "the user" or "the visitor" is an observable, stable unit of analysis, unaffected by the researcher's actions or assumptions. The advent of A/B testing further implies that the Web-measurement researcher assumes that she can actually manipulate the user's actions by changing pieces or "variables" in the user experience. In Creswell's (1994) framework, this would place Web-traffic measurement into the quantitative camp. According to Creswell, the quantitative researcher assumes that she is "objective," and removed from that which is being researched. The subject of research is assumed to be observable empirically. The quantitative researcher also assumes that her variables or categories of investigation are fixed before her study commences, and that analysis will continue with these fixed and stable indicators of what she considers reality. User mouse clicks and keystrokes are indeed observable but they are not "stable" representation of user experience – mostly because of the unreflective interference of the Web traffic research.

The Web traffic researcher is not an objective observer of user behavior but an *active participant* in the creation of data indicating such user behavior, insofar as the researcher selects, filters, and analyzes data without the benefit of rigorous self-reflexivity that is characteristic of qualitative researchers (McCorkel & Myers, 2003). The Web traffic researcher collects, counts and synthesizes various combinations of mouse clicks and keystrokes, but always assumes that these keystrokes represent an intelligible portrait of the user. In this sense, Web-traffic measurement epistemologically assumes that her actions are independent and do not affect the user's actions. She also assumes the stream of mouse clicks and keystrokes are indicators of behavior that may have even been elicited directly – or predicted and controlled – by the intentional manipulation of Web-site elements. But the very practice of Web-traffic measurement requires the active intervention of the researcher to render the data intelligible.

Practitioners typically configure their data collection methods in such a way as to further trouble the notion of intentionality behind the user's mouse clicks and keystrokes. While the ontology of Web-traffic measurement is computer/server interaction, we may call its epistemology "researcher-defined synthesis" of this interaction. Log file analysis tools typically will organize the raw data of mouse clicks and keystrokes into intelligible synthetic data points, such as "number of visitors" and "session length." Yet these intelligible indicators are not actually indicative of shifts in the patterns of mouse clicks and keystrokes; rather, they are either defined by the Web traffic researcher or pre-configured by the "default" settings of the log file analysis tool.

This synthesis may indicate a single, 40-minute long session, simply because the researcher pre-defined 40 minutes as a reasonable time to assume the user has simply walked away from the computer. In reality of course, the user could be continuously reading a single Web page for 40 minutes, only to have their 41st minute not counted. Or perhaps the user opened that window and left it idle, only to visit another Web site in an additional browser.

The epistemology of the Web traffic researcher in fact manipulates the representation of both of these events. In this sense, the researcher is defining the research findings, and not the manipulation of Web-site elements themselves. In effect, the "independent variable" is the setting on the Web-traffic measurement tool, and not the placement of a button or banner.

Again, the newer ASP-based measurement techniques present more troubling claims than the traditional log file systems. Unlike log files, ASP-based measurement does not include a standard set of measurements that exist regardless of the researcher's preferences. Log-file measurement is created through the installation of software on host servers, which in turn monitors how often that server is "called" by the client computers of end users. ASP-based measurement, by contrast, requires Web traffic researchers to choose how and where to place the JavaScript tags that produce measurement. This creates a researcher-generated conception of visitor behavior, not *actual* visitor behavior (Gassman, 2005). Log files can be interpreted in a myriad of ways, but their measurements are reliant on a standard set of traffic between servers and client computers. The interpretation of log files introduces an element of researcher bias. Javascript tags, on the other hand, have no "standard" placement, so in addition to interpretation after original measurement, ASP-based measurement introduces researcher bias before measurement even begins. Tags can be placed in so many different ways that both *measurement and interpretation* differ from researcher to researcher. The individual researcher chooses particular KPIs, for example, but could also choose to capture none of the flash-based traffic on a given page. Her analysis would portray users as not having interacted with any flash-based elements at all, even if they have. The placement of JavaScript tags thereby exaggerates the effect of the Web-traffic researcher directly affecting the measurement of traffic.

The common practice of abstracting the "visitor" further compounds the epistemological problem of researcher bias (more pronounced in ASP-based measurement, but present in all Web-traffic measurement). Epistemologically, this provides the analysis process with a veneer of "objectivity." Using Web-traffic measurement, the typical Web site visitor is never visible to the researcher, and becomes an abstract unit of analysis, not an immediate, observable one. Web traffic researchers have a fundamentally distal relationship with the user, making the visceral, in-person "experience" impossible to know. The user cannot be empirically observed through either log files or JavaScript-generated traffic data – simply her keystrokes and mouse clicks. The shift of Web-traffic measurement from Web traffic and server load information to user-experience research method has amplified the effects of this abstraction process. Web-traffic measurement, which is ostensibly a positivistic and objective research method, is mixed directly with qualitative and interpretivist research methods and design techniques. The discursive creation of "the visitor" allows for the researcher to project needs, ideas, and orientations toward technology onto a subject that she has never observed directly. This is particularly true in the creation of "design personas" which are visitor archetypes typically used to design and optimize Web sites. Personas are a frequent tool in Web design and are recommended as a "best practice" by practitioners (Manning, 2004). But recent authors have recommended merging Web-traffic data with qualitative persona data, making "the visitor" a subject of study without the researcher ever having interacted with an *actual* visitor (Petersen, 2004).

The relationship between researcher and end-user is, at best, distal. It is the equivalent of leafing through pages of economic data, without ever observing actual economic behavior. The symbolic practices of using a computer, surfing the Internet, and interacting with a Web site are abstracted unsystematically. This abstraction process yields very little insight into the general characteristics of users or the dynamics at play in the construction of the abstraction – something scholars have cautioned against (Ollman, 2001).

Using archetypes is not an inherently dubious research practice. In his examination of bureaucracy, for example, Weber argued that "ideal types" of bureaucratic organizations may not exist in such pure form in practice, but such types can be used to understand the inner workings of many organizations. But Weber, and other social theorists that employ archetypical forms, acknowledge that this is an interpretivist process, one that seeks *verstehen* or understanding of social processes and symbolic acts (Schwandt, 2000). But Web-traffic measurement relies on implicit positivistic claims. This type of method may be better suited to an interpretivist tradition, which accepts that the researcher's inferential interpretation of the data is an "unriddling" rather than an analysis of "true facts" (Alasuutari, 1995). Qualitative researchers typically concede that they stand "over and above" the subject of research, which sullies the true understanding of social experience (Smith, 2005). Web-traffic measurement can remedy these criticisms if it adopts an interpretivist stance, and ceases to claim to provide "objective" views of "reality."

RECOMMENDATIONS FOR IMPROVEMENT

In her defense of survey research, Marsh (1984) argues survey research is not wholly positivist in its approach, in that, unlike in experimentation, survey researchers do not attempt to establish causal explanations. Instead, they attempt to provide inferential explanation, based on robust social theory. For this reason, she argues, survey research has many redeemable qualities, first and foremost of which is that it is the most efficient way to ask large numbers of people about their beliefs and attitudes.

While Marsh may underestimate the many epistemological sins committed by survey researchers (e.g., see Bryman, 2004, pp. 78-79), her point is germane to the recovery and effective use of Web-traffic measurement. Web-traffic measurement can remedy these shortcomings, in part because, like survey research, Web-traffic measurement does not inherently entail *experimentation*, which seeks to create causal explanations. The shift toward A/B testing is troubling because it implies specific experimentation that is not appropriate. This begs the question of "statistical significance" as an important term that Web-traffic researchers are beginning to ask. I personally advised a member of the Web Analytics Association listserv about the correct process of determining statistical significance of two sets of

A/B data from a Web site. It was troubling to me epistemologically that this researcher believed he could predict and thereby control future visitor behavior simply by using "scientific" methods of statistical significance without ever interrogating the assumptions implicit in the method he chose. The pervasive and unquestioning valorization of "scientific" methods will continue to push Web-traffic measurement further into the positivist camp, without the requisite ontological and epistemological questions being asked.

The tempting desire to extend Web-traffic measurement as a method for understanding experience or social trends in general creates insoluble ontological and epistemological difficulties. It is my argument neither to ignore these problems, nor to abandon Web-traffic measurement altogether. Rather, I recommend that researchers remedy these problems by using Web traffic data reflexively and examining their methodological claims. First, Web-traffic measurement must include a systematic method of reflexivity. Second, Web traffic researchers ought explicitly to adopt a more interpretivist stance, based on qualitative approaches (See Table 1: Summary of Recommendations for Improvement). The method is best suited to understanding general trends and patterns in Web site navigation and can serve as *a complement* to other, more richly detailed methods of user research, which are qualitative in nature.

Systematizing self-reflexivity in Web-traffic measurement will prove difficult, but not impossible. The key to this approach is adopting a mixed-method conception of what Web-traffic measurement entails, one that includes reliability and validity "tests." Validity can be investigated through periodic "validity audits" of log files. These should be scheduled to investigate any potential trends that would trouble the *researcher's assumption of intentionality* behind mouse clicks and keystrokes. Web traffic researchers can, for example, periodically audit their geographic location files for indicators of potentially troubling locations. Researchers need not observe users *in situ,* but can rely on secondary sources that describe the entire user experience in such locations. Web traffic researchers can and should investigate if their logs indicate a high proportion of traffic for locations of which they know little of user ability level or reliability of computer equipment. Returning to our example above of the Internet café in Johannesburg, if a high proportion of users were arriving from such a location, it would behoove the Web traffic researcher to investigate these users' context. This approach can be extended beyond geographic location to specific social contexts. For example, if log files indicate that an inordinate number of people are visiting from a particular company domain, Web-traffic researchers should consider investigating how people at this company use their technology. Special attention should be paid to the *intentionality* of mouse clicks and keystrokes. Meaningful inferences cannot be drawn if mouse clicks and

Table 1. Summary of recommendations for improvement

Recommendation	Addresses this Limitation	Example
"Validity audits"	Ensures that Web-traffic measurement measures *Intentional* mouse clicks and key strokes	Periodic *in situ* observation of users
"Reliability tests"	Ensures quantitative data is not measuring a phenomenon not in existence	Regular interrogation of exceptional data patterns
Abandon any claim to quantitative validity	Accurately limits analysis to interpretation rather than prediction and control	Ceasing the practice of A/B testing

keystrokes lack intentionality, but this can only be determined through in-person observation.

Periodic "reliability tests" can also be scheduled, whereby Web-traffic researchers review shifts in seasonal traffic. Are patterns continuing as expected? Are there any unexpected or surprising spikes in activity? How might these spikes be related to any changes in the Web-traffic tool's configuration? Web-traffic researchers do typically search for changes in patterns, but may not have a systematic approach for completing "reliability tests" regularly.

My second recommendation is somewhat more radical. I suggest that Web-traffic researchers explicitly reject any quantitative, positivist claims to validity. This entails abandoning all claims of "scientific experimentation" which are so inappropriately typical of quantitative social researchers. Web-traffic researchers must adopt and accept that the process of tagging pages and the development of KPIs are fundamentally a practice of *interpreting* user behavior, and not predicting and controlling actual user behavior. This can be achieved by providing more nuanced explanations of how certain pages come to be tagged, and tying this process explicitly to theories of expected user behavior. For example, if a researcher chooses not to tag flash-based elements on a page, that researcher should also cite research that demonstrates flash-user interaction is limited or not important to the topic of study. Further, when developing KPIs, Web-traffic researchers should treat KPIs not as definitive *measurements* of user behavior but as *indicators* of behavior. In other words, Web-traffic measurement should be used as a guide to further, in-person observation of actual users. Web-traffic researchers should also completely abandon any attempts at experimentation or statistical significance. The underlying limitations of both log-file analysis tools and ASP-based tools, at the very least, make such claims dubious. But the social nature of the activities of users suggests that positivist claim of prediction and control is entirely inappropriate. And finally, and perhaps most radical, I assert that Web-traffic researchers cease to conduct A/B testing. This type of "experimentation" is quasi-scientific at best, and is frequently done in a haphazard manner (Chatham, 2004). The thin veil of rigor this method provides is simply window-dressing; provides no ontological or epistemological certainty to the method whatsoever.

Given the current limitations in reliability and validity, I predict the abandonment of scientific legitimacy will be the most difficult to implement. The pervasive acceptance of quantitative validity – characterized by large "sample sizes" and predictions of probability error – makes it exceedingly difficult for researchers to embrace fully qualitative notions of validity. Qualitative validity is characterized by notions of "trustworthiness" of results (Denzin & Lincoln, 2000), which appears to be flimsy in comparison to "hard numbers." Web-traffic researchers can appear to mitigate the influence of quantitative validity by fully integrating other qualitative research, such as ethnography, into their analyses. Ethnographic research does use numbers to summarize the events that researchers have witnessed but makes no attempts to predict future events (Lecompte & Shenshul, 1999).

Web-traffic measurement was not designed to be a social research method, but recent applications of this method have made it a frequent tool for understanding user behavior on Web sites. But as a social research tool, it presents some serious problems with validity and reliability. Moreover, it includes a set of ontological and epistemological contradictions that cannot be reconciled with positivist approaches to research. If Web-traffic researchers acknowledge these limitations, and respond accordingly, this method promises to offer rich data to a wide array of researchers from non-profit, public, and university-based settings.

REFERENCES

Alasuutari, P. (1995). *Researching Culture: Qualitative Methods and Cultural Studies.* Thousand Oaks: Sage.

Archive.org. (1997). Features, Technology and Strategy Overview: Why WebTrends v3.0 is the best solution for your business. http://web.archive.org/web/19970415212525/http://webtrends.com/: [April 7, 2007].

Bryman, A. (2004). *Social Research Methods* (2nd ed.). Oxford: Oxford University Press.

Chatham, B. (2004). *A Primer on A/B Testing.* Cambridge: Forrester Research.

Chatham, B. (2005). *What's On Web Analytics Users' Minds?* : Forrester Research.

Cohen, L. B. (2003a). A Two-tiered model for analyzing library Web site usage statistics, part 1: Web server logs. *Libraries and The Academy, 3*(2), 315.

Cohen, L. B. (2003b). A Two-tiered model for analyzing library Web site usage statistics, part 2: log file analysis. *Libraries and The Academy, 3*(3), 517.

Couper, M., Traugott, M., & Lamias, M. (2001). Web Survey Design and Administration. *Public Opinion Quarterly, 65*(2), 230-253.

Creswell, J. W. (1994). *Research Design: Qualitative and Quantitative Approaches.* Thousand Oaks: Sage.

Denzin, N., & Lincoln, Y. (2000). Introduction: The Discipline and Practice of Qualitative Research. In N. Denzin & Y. Lincoln (Eds.), *Handbook of Qualitative Research* (2nd ed., pp. 1-30). Thousand Oaks: Sage.

Eisenberg, B. (2005). How To Improve A/B Testing. www.clickz.com/experts/crm/traffic/article.php/3500811: [November 10, 2006].

Gassman, B. (2005). *How to Choose An Advanced Solution for Web Analytics.* Stamford: Gartner Research.

Hobbs, J. (2007). *Communal computing and shared spaces of usage: a study of Internet Cafes in developing contexts.* Paper presented at the American Society for Information Science and Technology. Las Vegas Nevada. Retrieved.

Kuniavsky, M. (2003). *Observing the User Experience: A Practioner's Guide to User Research.* San Francisco: Morgan Kaufman.

Lecompte, M., & Shenshul, J. (1999). *Designing and Conducting Ethnographic Research.* Walnut Creek: Altamira Press.

Manning, H. (2004). *Persona Best Practices.* Cambridge: Forrester Research.

Marsh, C. (1984). Problems with surveys: method or epistemology? In M. Blumer (Ed.), *Sociological Research Methods: An Introduction* (2nd ed., pp. 82-102). London: MacMillan.

McCorkel, J., & Myers, K. (2003). What difference does difference make? Position and privilege in the field. *Qualitative Sociology, 26*(2), 199-231.

Michaelidou, N., & Dibb, S. (2006). Using email queeztionnaires for research: good practice in tackling non-response. *Journal of Targeting, Measurement, and Analysis for Marketing, 14*(4), 289.

Ollman, B. (2001). Critical Realism in the Light of Marx's Process of Abstraction. In J. Lopez & G. Potter (Eds.), *After Postmodernism: An Introduction to Critical Realism* (pp. 285-298). London: Athlone Press.

Omniture. (2007). Omniture Site Catalyst. http://www.omniturc.com/products/web_analytics/sitecatalyst: [April 18, 2007].

Petersen, E. (2004). *Web Analytics Demystified*: Celilo Group Media/Cafe Press.

Petersen, E. (2005a). *US Web Analytics forecast 2004-2009*: Jupiter Research.

Petersen, E. (2005b). *Web Site Measurement Hacks*. San Franscisco: O'Reilly Media.

Petersen, E., Bayriamova, Z., Evans, P. F., Levy, M., & Matiesanu, C. (2004). *Key Performance Indicators: Using Analytics to Drive Action*. New York: Jupiter Research.

Potter, G., & Lopez, J. (2001). General Introduction: After Postmodernism: the Millennium. In J. Lopez & G. Potter (Eds.), *After Postmodernism: An Introduction to Critical Realism*. London: Athlone Press.

Rosenfeld, L., & Wiggins, R. (2007). *Using Search Analytics To Diagnose What's Ailing Your IA*. Paper presented at the American Society for Information Science and Technology. Las Vegas Nevada. Retrieved.

Roster, C., Rogers, R., Hozler, G. C., Baker, K., & Albaum, G. (2007). Management of marketing research projects: does delivery method matter anymore in survey research? *Journal of Marketing Theory and Practice, 15*(2), 127.

Schwandt, T. A. (2000). Three Epistemological Stances for Qualitative Inquiry: Interpretivism, Hermeneutics, and Social Constructionism. In N. Denzin & Y. Lincoln (Eds.), *Handbook of Qualitative Research* (pp. 189-215). Thousand Oaks: Sage.

Smith, D. E. (2005). *Institutional ethnography: a sociology for people*. Walnut Creek, CA: AltaMira Press.

WebSideStory. (2007). Web Site Analytics: On Demand Web Analytics for Optimizing Online Business Performance. http://www.websidestory.com/products/web-analytics/hbx-analytics/overview.html: [April 18, 2007].

WebTrends. (2001). WebTrends eBusiness Intelligence Solution Named "Best of 2000" By PC Magazine. [April 4, 2007].

Weir, C., Anderson, J., & Jack, M. (2006). On The Role Of Metaphor And Language In Design of Third Party Payments in eBanking: Usability and Quality. *International Journal of Human-Computer Studies, 64*, 770-787.

Wiggins, A. (2007). *Data Driven Design: Using Web Analytics To Improve Information Architecture*. Paper presented at the American Society for Information Science and Technology. Las Vegas Nevada. Retrieved.

World Wide Web Consortium. (2007). A Little History of the World Wide Web. http://www.w3.org/History.html: [February 19, 2007].

KEY TERMS

Clickstream Tracking: The passive collection of data that computer users generated when they click the mouse on a Web site. A computer user's "clickstream" is the list of events they have initiated by clicking their mouse.

Electronic Commerce Research: All forms of investigation of online selling of goods or services.

Interpretivism: A tradition in social and humanities research that assumes findings are to be interpreted by the researcher. This contrasts with positivism, which assumes the researcher "finds" or simply "observes" findings.

IS Research Methodologies: Refers to the common research methods used by information scientists.

Positivist Epistemology: Also referred to as "positivism," refers to the school of research thought that sees observable evidence as the only form of defensible scientific findings. Positivist epistemology, therefore, assumes that only "facts" derived from the scientific method can make legitimate knowledge claims. It also assumes the researcher is separate from and not affecting the outcomes of research.

Research Methodology: General knowledge approaches to conducting and designing research.

Sociology of Computing: A stream in sociology that researches the interactions between humans and computers as well as the social effects of using computers.

User Experience: Refers to the immersive character of technology use and is typically evoked by designers of technology. The "user experience" is assumed to be architected by interaction designers.

Web Analyst: A job title used by private-sector practitioners, which typically involves analyzing Web-traffic data.

Chapter V
Privacy Concerns for Web Logging Data

Kirstie Hawkey
University of British Columbia, Canada

ABSTRACT

This chapter examines two aspects of privacy concerns that must be considered when conducting studies that include the collection of Web logging data. After providing background about privacy concerns, we first address the standard privacy issues when dealing with participant data. These include privacy implications of releasing data, methods of safeguarding data, and issues encountered with re-use of data. Second, the impact of data collection techniques on a researcher's ability to capture natural user behaviors is discussed. Key recommendations are offered about how to enhance participant privacy when collecting Web logging data so as to encourage these natural behaviors. The author hopes that understanding the privacy issues associated with the logging of user actions on the Web will assist researchers as they evaluate the tradeoffs inherent between the type of logging conducted, the richness of the data gathered, and the naturalness of captured user behavior.

INTRODUCTION

Privacy is an important consideration when conducting research that utilizes Web logs for the capture and analysis of user behaviors. Two aspects of privacy will be discussed in this chapter. First, it is important that governmental regulations, such as the Personal Information Protection and Electronic Documents Act (PIPEDA) in Canada, or organizational regulations, such as a university's local research ethics board (REB) policies, are met. These regulations will dictate requirements for the storage and safeguarding of participant data as well as the use, re-use, and transfer of that data. Secondly, researchers may also find that providing privacy enhancing mechanisms for participants can impact the success of a study. Privacy assurances can ease study recruitment and encourage natural Web browsing behaviors. This is particularly important when capturing rich behavioral data beyond that which is ordinarily recorded in server transaction logs, as is generally the case for client-side logging. It is this second aspect of privacy that will be the primary focus of this chapter.

There are privacy concerns associated with viewing and releasing Web browsing data. Web browsers are typically used for a wide variety of tasks, both personal and work related (Hawkey & Inkpen, 2006a). The potentially sensitive information that may be visible within Web browsers and in data logs is tightly integrated with a person's actions within the Web browser (Lederer, Hong, Dey, & Landay, 2004). Increasingly the Internet has become a mechanism by which people can engage in activities to support their emotional needs such as surfing the Web, visiting personal support forums, blogging, and investigating health concerns (Westin, 2003). Content captured within Web browsers or on server logs may therefore include such sensitive items as socially inappropriate activities, confidential business items, and personal activities conducted on company time, as well as more neutral items such as situation-appropriate content (e.g., weather information). Visual privacy issues have been investigated with respect to traces of prior Web browsing activity visible within Web browsers during co-located collaboration (Hawkey, 2007; Hawkey & Inkpen, 2006b). Dispositional variables, such as age, computer experience, and inherent privacy concerns, combine with situational variables, such as device and location, to create contextual privacy concerns. Within each location, the social norms and Web usage policies, role of the person, and potential viewers of the display and users of the device impact both the Web browsing behaviors and privacy comfort levels in a given situation. The impacted Web browsing behaviors include both the Web sites visited, as well as convenience feature usage such as history settings and auto completes. Furthermore, most participants reported taking actions to further limit which traces are potentially visible if given advanced warning of collaboration.

Recently the sensitivity of search terms has been a topic in the mainstream news. In August 2006, AOL released the search terms used by 658,000 anonymous users over a three month period (McCullagh, 2006). These search terms revealed a great deal about the interests of AOL's users, and their release was considered to be a privacy violation. Even though only a few of the users were able to be identified by combining information found within the search terms they used, AOL soon removed the data from public access. This data highlighted the breadth of search terms with respect to content sensitivity as well as how much the terms could reveal about the users in terms of their concerns and personal activities.

In addition to taking actions to guard visual privacy within Web browsers, users may also take steps to guard the transmission of their personal information online. When concerned about privacy as they interact on the Web, users may opt to mask their identities by using a proxy server or other anonymizing (Cranor, 1999). The Platform for Privacy Preferences Project (www.w3.org/P3P/) has developed standards that facilitate user awareness of the privacy policies that govern the use of their personal information at participating websites. Research into online privacy generally examines issues concerning the transfer of personal data to business or governmental entities; the relationships are between consumers and corporations. This may be quite different from the privacy concerns associated with others viewing traces of previous Web browsing activity, as in the case of logged Web browsing data in a research context. Although in both cases personal information may be viewed, there are differences in the nature of the relationship to the viewer of the information. When the viewers of the captured information are not anonymous but are known to the user, privacy concerns may be heightened (Lederer, Mankoff, & Dey, 2003).

Field research theoretically allows the study of actual behaviors in a realistic environment.

However, the act of observing or recording participants' personal interactions may cause them to alter those behaviors (McGrath, 1995). This is often referred to as the Hawthorne Effect. For example, behaviors deemed to be socially inappropriate (Fisher, 1993) may be avoided during the period of the study. As well, participants may be unwilling to have logging software installed that may record personal interactions, particularly if that software logs data across applications. Software (e.g., a keystroke logger, or custom web browser) that has the potential of capturing user names and passwords may cause additional concerns (Weinreich, Obendorf, Herder, & Mayer, 2006). Privacy preserving mechanisms can help encourage participants to engage in their natural Web browsing behaviors and activities while allowing researchers to study the behaviors of interest. Appropriate methods of mitigating participants' privacy concerns depend on the research questions and the experimental logging environment in use.

The objectives of this chapter are to provide researchers with an understanding of the privacy issues associated with the logging of Web activity. Background will be provided in the areas of privacy theory in general and privacy concerns for Web browsing data in particular. It is important that privacy concerns are understood so that observational effects on behavior can be reduced during studies. Furthermore, the tradeoffs between participants' privacy and the collection of rich, yet natural data for various logging techniques will be discussed. Finally, guidelines for mitigating participants' privacy concerns during studies investigating Web behaviors will be presented.

BACKGROUND

General Privacy Theory

Westin (2003) defines individual privacy as "the claim of an individual to determine what information about himself or herself should be known to others." Over the past forty years, Westin has primarily dealt with consumer privacy rights, such as when personal information can be collected and how others can make use of the information. Westin also discusses how individuals seek a balance between maintaining privacy and fulfilling a need for communication and disclosure. How an individual manages this tradeoff depends on their personal situation including their family life, education, social class, and psychological composition. Furthermore, Westin states that an individual's privacy needs are highly contextual and continually shift depending on situational events.

This contextual nature of privacy is well established in the literature. Goffman (1959) first introduced the need to project different personas or faces during social interactions. The face presented in any given situation depends not only on the current audience but also on the current conditions. The combination of audience and situation determines how much and what information will be disclosed. Furthermore, as discussed by Palen and Dourish (2003), people can have many roles between which they fluidly move and can act in multiple capacities, often simultaneously. For example, one may act as an individual, a family member, and a representative of an organization. A person's role can influence their sense as to whether their behaviors would be considered socially acceptable. If information is conveyed that is out of character for the person's current role, the boundaries that have been maintained can collapse creating opportunities for social, bodily, emotional, and financial harm (Phillips, 2002). Lederer et al. (2003) discuss how activities convey the essence of a persona. Knowledge of an individual's prior activities is more sensitive when their identity is known as the activities can reveal hidden personae.

Privacy Concerns for Web Browsing Data

Web users conduct a wide range of activities within their Web browsers, resulting in visited web pages with a variety of content sensitivity (Hawkey & Inkpen, 2006a). Teltzrow and Kobsa (2004) summarized thirty published consumer surveys and studies investigating Internet privacy. Results consistently revealed that the majority of Internet users are concerned about the security of personal information as well as concerned about being tracked on the Internet, with a lesser amount being concerned that someone might know what websites they visited. Two field studies have specifically examined visual privacy concerns for visited Web pages. For the first study, conducted in 2004 (Hawkey & Inkpen, 2005), 42% of visited pages were classified as public (suitable for anybody to view), 25% as semi-public (suitable for a subset of viewers), 15% as private (suitable perhaps only for a close confident), and 18% as don't save (either irrelevant or extremely private). Similar results were found in the second study, conducted in 2005 (Hawkey & Inkpen, 2006a): 40% public, 20% semi-public, 25% private, 15% don't save. It must be noted that participants in both studies exhibited a great deal of individual variability in their privacy classifications with some participants having greater privacy concerns than others. This variability is both as a result of participants having differing privacy concerns for similar content and as a result of them having conducted browsing activities of differing sensitivity.

Studies have found that privacy concerns are highly nuanced and individual (Ackerman, Cranor, & Reagle, 1999; Hawkey & Inkpen, 2006a). Recent information sharing research has investigated privacy concerns for various types of information and recipients of that information. For example, one study investigated privacy comfort for participants when sharing information with a recipient (Olson, Grudin, & Horvitz, 2005). Privacy concerns differed depending on the person's relationship to the receiver of the information as well as on the type of information being shared. Their results suggest that some of the types of information that may be revealed in Web logs, such as personal activities like viewing non-work related websites and transgressions like viewing erotic material, are considered more sensitive than information such as contact and availability information. The amount of control that the individual retains over the disclosure of information may also impact their level of comfort (Palen & Dourish, 2003).

A person's demographics such as age and gender may affect their privacy disposition (Hawkey, 2007). However, a person's disposition to privacy, that is, their inherent privacy concern, is also grounded in their life experience. For example, their technical level or computer experience may impact their inherent privacy concerns. Additionally, dispositional variables may moderate the effect of situational variables. Someone with strong inherent privacy concerns may always be very private, someone with weak concerns may be less private, others may be more pragmatic and may more often modify their privacy comfort and browsing activities in response to the state of the environment (Hawkey, 2007; P&AB, 2003).

While inherent privacy concerns indicate someone's overall privacy preferences, the situational context will determine which information a person feels is appropriate to reveal (Joinson, Paine, Reips, & Buchanan, 2006; Westin, 2003). For example, in a study examining online disclosure of information, independent pathways were found for the dispositional variable of participant's general privacy concerns as well as the situational variables of perceived privacy (in terms of anonymity and confidentiality) and participants' trust in the receiver of the information (Joinson, Paine, Reips, & Buchanan, 2006). Similarly Malhotra et al. (2004) developed a causal model of online consumers' information privacy concerns. Their model considered the effect that Internet users' information privacy concerns have on trusting beliefs, risk beliefs, and their behavioral intention to reveal personal information. Furthermore, they incorporated the sensitivity of the information requested by marketers as a contextual variable and considered covariates such as sex, age, education, Internet experience, identity misrepresentation, past experiences with privacy invasion, and media exposure. They developed measures for new factors of privacy concerns including control (i.e., whether the user has control over the data) and awareness (i.e., whether the user is adequately informed as to use of the data) to augment existing scales for this domain which consider collection of information such as whether the exchange of personal information is equitable.

Privacy comfort for the viewing of Web browsing activity has also been found to depend not only on a person's disposition to privacy, but also on the situational context when the activity is revealed (Hawkey, 2007). Situational variables for privacy concerns associated with traces of activity in Web browsers include the computing device used and the location of use. Furthermore, within each location there may be other variables such as the current role of the user, social norms for the location, rules for personal Web browsing activities, and different types of viewers of the display and users of the device. These variables may constrain or shape both the browsing activities and the subsequent privacy concerns. For example, someone with Web access on both a home and a work computer may refrain from conducting many personal activities while at work, while someone with only access at work may conduct a broader range of activities in the workplace. A laptop user may perform the majority of their browsing activities on their laptop, but their viewing concerns may change as they move between different locations with different social norms. One's browser settings and preventative actions taken may also change depending on the usage environment. Beyond which traces are potentially visible as a result of these changes, the perceived sensitivity of the traces may also change as a result of the viewing situation. The cost and benefit of disclosure depends on the specifics of each situation (Joinson, Paine, Reips, & Buchanan, 2006).

Marx (2003) identified several privacy enhancing methods that people use when under surveillance, with *self-regulating*, *blocking*, *masking*, *switching*, and *refusal* activities being particularly applicable to mitigating privacy concerns associated with Web browsing data. For example, Web browsing activities may be *self-regulated* in the workplace to avoid surveillance by an employer, with more personal activities being conducted solely at home (Hawkey & Inkpen, 2006b). A person's attitudes and perceptions about privacy, trust, and social relationships or norms (e.g., workplace rules) will influence his behavior in a situation (Liu, Marchewka, Lu, & Yu, 2004). A common privacy preserving strategy employed within Web browsers is to *block* the recording of visited sites by turning off the convenience features such as history files and auto complete data (Hawkey, 2007). One downside to this approach is that a complete lack of visited sites within the browser's history files may be viewed as an indicator that there is an activity worth hiding. A more subtle approach would be to *mask* the activity rather than to block it completely (Marx, 2003). For example, to mask browsing activities in their personal bookmarks, users can rename stored sites to conceal the nature of the page (Hawkey, 2007). In order to guard privacy at the server level, users may opt to anonymize their browsing, thereby masking their identity (Cranor, 1999). Internet users in the studies surveyed by Teltzrow and Kobsa (2004) have taken steps such as *refusing* to give personal information to a Website and supplying false information to a Website when asked to register. *Switching* computers or browser applications to avoid logging software is a privacy enhancing mechanism that can impact the breadth of data recorded during studies (Kellar, Hawkey, Inkpen, & Watters, 2008). Finally, *refusing* to take part in studies altogether may also occur if the privacy concerns are too high (Tang, Liu, Muller, Lin, & Drews, 2006).

PRIVACY CHALLENGES ASSOCIATED WITH THE LOGGING OF WEB DATA

Much of the privacy background just presented was focused on the privacy concerns associated with the types of data that may be captured in Web logs. In this section, two facets of privacy challenges associated with Web logging data are discussed. The first are standard privacy concerns with respect to the capture, storage, transfer, and re-use of data. These are largely dictated by governmental and organizational regulations. The second are privacy concerns that participants may have about their activities being recorded. These concerns may affect their natural Web browsing behaviors during the study period and can be challenging to address.

Governmental and Organizational Regulations

The first concern when designing a study with Web log analysis is ensuring that governmental regulations (e.g., PIPEDA in Canada) or organizational regulations, such as a university's Research Ethics Board (REB) policies, with respect to privacy are met. These regulations will specify requirements for data collection including the storage and safeguarding of participant data as well as the use, re-use, and transfer of that data. As these regulations are specific to the country and institution where the research is located, they will not be extensively described here. However, some general areas for consideration will be presented. It is up to individual researchers to ensure that they are in compliance with the policies that govern their research.

Many REB and governmental policies address the period of time that data may be kept and the storage requirements for that data. In addition, data re-use may be limited to the purposes identified in the study materials and agreed to by participants. While it may be tempting to provide very broad potential use cases, more narrow usage possibilities may assuage participant concerns about the capture of what can be potentially sensitive data (Teltzrow & Kobsa, 2004).

Governmental regulations may even dictate which data logging software is used. For example, in Nova Scotia, Canada, the Personal Information International Disclosure Protection Act has recently been approved by the Nova Scotia provincial government (Dalhousie Research Services, 2006). This legislation deals with protection, storage, and management of personal information of Nova Scotians, and the issue of data transfer outside Canada is prominent. Special approval is required to use software, hardware, or services that store personal information of Nova Scotians outside of Canada, and permission must be granted to transfer data containing personal information to researchers outside of Canada.

Governmental regulations will likely apply to the storage and use of the data, although requirements may be lessened if the data is anonymized. Data collection itself may be anonymous (i.e., collected with no associated identifying information) or the data set may be anonymized through removal of any links between the data and identifying information. To be considered anonymized, there must be no way for an investigator to connect the data with a specific participant. This can be difficult with small data sets due to the potential triangulation of the data to a specific individual in the study population. Care must be taken that the data does not include potentially identifying information such as highly detailed demographic information or IP addresses (Dalhousie Research Services, 2006).

Depending on where the log data is captured (i.e., server-side, client-side) and the frequency with which the data needs to be transferred between the participant and the researchers, different security mechanisms are required to safeguard the data and ensure that participants' privacy is not inadvertently compromised. While discussion of security mechanisms is outside the scope of this chapter, there are several resources that may be useful (Garfinkel & Spafford, 2001; Huseby, 2004; Meier et al., 2003). The discussion in this section is limited to the tradeoffs inherent with different approaches.

When possible, researchers should take advantage of opportunities of anonymizing or otherwise transforming the data before receiving it. For example, with client-side storage of data, a data collection script can remove any identifying information such as IP addresses that may be stored in the data logs and assign a random user ID number that is not tied to recruitment or screening data. Furthermore, potentially identifying or sensitive information can be transformed into higher level data. For example, if a study would like to record where laptop users accessed the internet, a data collection script could take as input IP addresses and location labels and replace the personally identifying IP addresses in the data records with a general location field (whether home, work, or school) (Hawkey, 2007).

One question that arises during research that makes use of Web logs is where to store the data, and when and how to transfer the data between participant and researcher (Kellar, Hawkey, Inkpen, & Watters, 2008). When data is logged during a laboratory experiment, or with proxy or server-side logging applications, it is typically stored directly on a research computer. With proxy logging, researchers should provide a secure connection to the proxy server. Additional complexities arise for client-side data logging as data transfer and storage issues must be determined. Storing the data locally on the participant's machine for the duration of the study (and removing it physically during an uninstall session) may simplify the participants' duties and minimize privacy risks associated with the transfer of data; however, researchers run the risk of data loss if the participant's machine crashes. If data is transferred more frequently, the participant may be inconvenienced and there is a need to provide secure methods of transmission.

Impact of Privacy Concerns for Data Collection on Natural Web Browsing Behaviors

The remainder of this chapter will deal with the impact of privacy concerns on the ability of studies to capture natural Web browsing behaviors. It is important to consider that the act of recording visited sites may impact participants' normal Web browsing activity (McGrath, 1995). As previously discussed, there are privacy concerns associated with others viewing visited websites (Hawkey & Inkpen, 2006b; Olson, Grudin, & Horvitz, 2005; Teltzrow & Kobsa, 2004). Self-regulation of activity is one mechanism used to preserve privacy when under surveillance (Marx, 2003). However, for most studies involving the logging of Web data, it is important that participants conduct their Web-related activities as they normally would, regardless of the social desirability of the content (Fisher, 1993) or the personal information that may be captured.

Which traces of prior activity may be disclosed depend on the type of data logging being done. There are several challenges and tradeoffs when trying to capture rich contextual data (Kellar, Hawkey, Inkpen, & Watters, 2008). One key factor in determining an appropriate data logging strategy is the tradeoff between the amount of control the researcher retains and the amount of intrusiveness for the participant (McGrath, 1995). This chapter considers this tradeoff, extending the discussion of the impact on privacy concerns and the ability to capture natural Web browsing behavior for various Web logging strategies.

One approach is to use trace measures or archival records (McGrath, 1995). Archival records are records of user behavior that are collected for other purposes and may either be private or public knowledge. Examples of archival records include blogs or stored bookmarks in the Web browser. Trace measures are records of behavior inadvertently left by participants, such as Web server data logs created through server-side logging. If data is gathered after the fact, there will be no behavioral changes due to observation. However, there are several drawbacks to this approach, and the available data may not be appropriate depending on the research questions of interest.

Cockburn and McKenzie (2001) used archival data to conduct an empirical analysis of Web page revisitation. They analyzed the history records from academic user accounts captured on server backups. History records are stored within a Web browser to enable revisitation of previously visited sites. An advantage to their approach was that there were no behavioral changes due to observation as the participants were unaware at the time of web browsing that their browsing activities would be examined as part of a study. However, the data available was not complete. The history files only included the most recent timestamp for accessing a URL, so some visits were not captured temporally. Data collected in this fashion is generally limited in contextual information about the activities underway. Additionally, it may be difficult to get permission to use archival data if the participant is unclear about which sensitive activities may have been conducted during the study period.

The use of trace measures such as server logs will similarly remove behavioral changes due to observation. However, server-side logging generally limits the breadth of the data collected, either capturing only the access to a single website or access through a specific Web portal (Yun, Ford, Hawkins, Pingree, & McTavish, 2006). The data is also usually limited to the IP address of users, a time stamp, and the URL requested. Web server logs may be incomplete records of an activity, since page requests may not be received and recorded at the server if the page has been cached by the browser or a proxy server (Fenstermacher & Ginsburg, 2003). There is ongoing tension between Web users' privacy needs and a website's requirement for information about its users (Cooley, Mobasher, & Srivastava, 1999). While the use of cookies can alleviate problems of identifying returning individuals that are associated with dynamic IP addresses (Anick, 2003), users may turn off cookies in order to protect their privacy (Teltzrow & Kobsa, 2004). Users may also attempt to enforce privacy through obscurity, controlling release of personal information by using an anonymization service such as a proxy server (Sackmann, Struker, & Accorsi, 2006). A proxy server may assign many users to the same IP address and can make user identification difficult.

Observations consist of records of behavior intentionally collected by a researcher or their software; observations may or may not be visible to the participant (McGrath, 1995). For example, a researcher watching a person interacting with an application would be visible to the participant, while the application logs capturing user interactions would not. One of the main concerns with observational data is that natural behaviors will often be adjusted if the participant is aware of the observations. Software that captures observational data can be proxy-based or client-side.

If Web activity is captured through proxy logging, the user must login at the beginning of each session. Advantages to this approach are that it is easier to capture data across websites, and there are fewer participant identification issues than with server-side logging due to the use of a participant account. However, users may bypass the proxy server if concerned about the sensitivity of their browsing or if they are forgetful. This may limit the breadth of data collected. Another advantage to proxy logging is that participants can work within their normal Web browser environment. However, with traditional proxy logging, browser interactions cannot be captured; and there are still caching issues if pages are cached at the browser level (Barford, Bestavros, Bradley, & Crovella, 1999). One emerging method of data logging is to embed Javascript into delivered web pages through the proxy server (Atterer, Wnuk, & Schmidt, 2006). This method can be used to capture additional data including mouse movement, scroll bar use, and key presses. Proxy servers have also been found to be less reliable and accurate than client-side logging tools for temporal measurements of Web activity (Kelly & Belkin, 2004).

One advantage of field research over laboratory experiments is that participants have access to their usual Web tools, browsers, and physical environments (Kellar, Hawkey, Inkpen, & Watters, 2008). However, with client-side logging, there is a danger of altering the participants' Web browsing environment when attempting to capture natural Web browsing behavior that is also rich in detail. The Web browsing environment includes many factors such as the user's physical location and their usual browser application, including all its normal settings. One of the main reasons for selecting field studies as a methodology is to capture natural user behavior which can be important for studies which are investigating patterns of activity. It is therefore important that the experimental software not interrupt the flow of participants' Web browsing (Chatterjee, Hoffman, & Novak, 2003).

The choice of a client-side logging tool can help mitigate concerns about changing the Web browsing environment of the user. For example, a browser helper object (BHO) can be ideal for this purpose as participants can continue using Internet Explorer with their normal settings intact, including their Favorites, History, and Google toolbar (Kellar, Hawkey, Inkpen, & Watters, 2008). The automatic loading of the BHO means that participants do not have to remember to use the study instrument. However, a BHO can only record limited types of data (i.e., interactions at the Web document level). In order to record richer interactions with the Web browser itself, a custom Web browser must be used. Developing a custom Web browser that fully mimics the appearance and functionality of participants' commercial browser applications, including all installed features (e.g., user-installed toolbars) is challenging. In some instances, researchers may have access to the source code of a commercial browser. Adapting open source software (e.g., Mozilla Firefox) is a popular choice for researchers wanting to augment browser functionality to include logging (Weinreich, Obendorf, Herder, & Mayer, 2006); however, this can limit the user population or result in participants using a different Web browsing environment as the most common browser in use is still Internet Explorer.

There are additional privacy challenges if trying to capture participants' Web activities across all contexts of use with client-side logging. It can be difficult to install the software on all computers and devices in use, particularly if custom logging software is not robust and well-tested (Kellar, Hawkey, Inkpen, & Watters, 2008). If a computer in use is not owned by the participant (i.e., one located in the workplace), it may be difficult to receive corporate permission to record data (Tang, Liu, Muller, Lin, & Drews, 2006). Self-regulation of browsing activities that are not work-related may occur if the participant believes there is a chance that the employer may have access to the logs or be able to discern their identity in subsequent analysis. In such a case, it is very important to provide privacy preserving mechanisms to help alleviate concerns of both the participant and the employer.

As summarized in Table 1, while server-side logging has relatively few privacy concerns due to the difficulty of linking the data to specific users and their personal information, it suffers from a reduced amount of information that can be gathered. Data is primarily limited to navigation with a website and data entered at that site; it will not include navigation to cached pages or websites located on other servers. Client-side logging can

Table 1. Summary of tradeoffs by type of logging for richness of data, completeness of data, ability to discern individual participants, and naturalness of their Web browsing environment.

	Server-side Logging	**Proxy Logging**	**Client-side Logging**
Richness of data	Limited to navigation, data entry on site	Limited to navigation, some form data, - improved with scripting	Rich data including navigation, key strokes, browser interaction, but BHO more limited
Completeness of data	Caching issues, site specific	Caching issues, can be bypassed	Can be bypassed by using other browser or other computer
Ability to discern individual users participants	Can be difficult (anonymization services)	Good (must log in)	Good
Naturalness of participants' browsing environment	Completely natural	Participants aware of the logging /but browser environment unchanged	Participants aware at install. Environment depends on software (BHO generally transparent, but custom browsers may not have usual functionality and settings)

provide richer data, but the data collection is more invasive from a privacy perspective. As the software must be installed on client computers, the participants (and their personal information) are usually known to the researchers. Depending on the logging software, a great deal more information may be logged, including interactions with the Web browser and key strokes. Proxy logging, particularly if making use of Javascript to capture some of the user interactions, may be a viable compromise depending on the research objectives.

ENHANCING PRIVACY DURING OBSERVATIONAL DATA COLLECTION

Collection of observational data, particularly through client-side logging applications can provide researchers with rich data about Web browsing activities and behaviors, including interactions with the Web browser. However, the intrusiveness of this type of data collection may cause participants to alter their natural Web browsing behaviors, avoid using study software, or refuse to take part in the study altogether. It is important for researchers to provide mechanisms for participants to preserve their privacy. Recommendations for such privacy enhancing mechanisms are presented next.

Lederer et al. (2004) discuss how users should be able to maintain personal privacy through understanding and action. Understanding is required so that users are aware of potential privacy violations. Opportunities for action are required so that users can appropriately manage their privacy when necessary. Following this lead, the recommendations for providing privacy preserving mechanism in this chapter will be presented with two thrusts. The first is to increase participants' understanding of the data logging and its privacy implications and to also increase their trust in the researchers' ability to maintain their privacy. In addition to educating participants, trust can be increased by limiting the recorded data to that necessary to answer the research questions and providing opportunities for participants to inspect the recorded data. Second, recommendations will be given for privacy-enhancing actions that may be afforded to participants building on the methods identified by Marx (2003) for maintaining privacy in case of surveillance. These actions include the ability to pause recording as well as the ability to mask or delete sensitive records.

Recommendations for Increasing Understanding and Trust

Lederer et al. (2004) make the point that unless users can readily determine the nature and extent of potential information disclosure, they will not be able to fully understand the privacy implications as a result of system use. For participants to be comfortable enough with the logging software to engage in their usual Web browsing activities, it is important that they understand the data being captured. The issue of trust is also an important facet of privacy concerns. Internet users' willingness to share information with a website may depend on their level of trust towards the owner of the website (Teltzrow & Kobsa, 2004).

Recommendation 1: Educate Participants

The Platform for Privacy Preferences (P3P) Initiative provides mechanisms for Web users to understand the privacy policies of websites with which they interact. Privacy in this sense is based on transparency through policies; users can inspect an organization's privacy policies and must rely on their trust in an organization to follow the stated polices (Sackmann, Struker, & Accorsi, 2006). Similarly, transparency in the process can be used to educate participants in studies involving data logging.

Consent forms should explicitly describe data collection and use so that participants have a clear understanding of what data will be collected, who will be able to see it, how the data will be used, and how it will be reported. By explicitly providing this information to participants, as well as detailing any privacy preserving mechanisms in place, researchers should be able to assuage any general privacy concerns that may prevent potential participants from taking part in the study as well as address potential privacy violations specifically. Interestingly, participants may not always take advantage of the privacy preserving mechanisms provided (Kellar, Hawkey, Inkpen, & Watters, 2008); however, the very existence of these mechanisms can give potential participants a sense of control over the privacy of their Web browsing activities which may encourage them to take part in an intrusive field study (Obendorf, personal communication, January 2008).

Recommendation 2: Only Record / Receive as Much Information as Needed

In the E-Commerce domain, it is suggested that websites gathering personal information for the purposes of personalization only gather that information that is required for the immediate service (Teltzrow & Kobsa, 2004). Limiting data collection can also increase users' willingness to disclose the information. A similar policy should help with data logging for research purposes. While it is tempting to gather as much information as possible, privacy concerns may be minimized by only recording that data which is necessary to answer the research questions. By limiting the data collected (and providing details to participants about how it will be used), participants should feel more secure that their data is being respected and being used to further research in the area of interest.

Furthermore, there may be times when very detailed raw data will be collected, but the measures of interest are aggregate scores or temporal patterns. In such cases, it may be possible to collect and process the data on the client's machine, only receiving the processed data (Hawkey, 2007). For example, if the data of interest is revisitation patterns, the URL may be necessary to identify unique pages, but otherwise irrelevant to the research questions. A script could process the data, assigning a unique ID to each URL. This would preserve the data necessary for calculations while obscuring the actual sites visited which should alleviate privacy concerns. One disadvantage to this approach is that the researcher must be well-prepared and be sure of all data analysis that will be required.

Hawkey and Inkpen (2005) were interested in investigating overall privacy concerns and temporal privacy patterns associated with the later viewing of visited Web pages. The page title and URL of visited pages were collected in order to allow participants to annotate their browsing with a privacy level in an electronic diary. In order to provide participants with as much privacy as possible, the page title and URL were stripped from the records after annotation, so that only a browser window ID, date/time stamp, and privacy level were sent to the researchers. These data were sufficient to investigate the preliminary research questions, and it was hoped that this reduction in information would encourage participants to engage in their regular Web browsing activities regardless of the sensitivity of visited pages. After an informal survey of privacy concerns associated with their longitudinal field study of Web browsing behavior, Weinreich, Obendorf, Herder & Mayer (2006) opted to use a capturing system that did not record user names and passwords entered in the browser and that ignored activity on secure connections.

Recommendation 3: Provide Opportunities for Inspection of Data

Recent research discussions have suggested providing evidence creation as a way to increase transparency and allow auditing of the data collected (Sackmann, Struker, & Accorsi, 2006). Privacy evidence is created by interpreting the collected logged data about an individual through the lens of the policies applicable to that data to illustrate compliance. Providing opportunities for participants to inspect the data being sent to researchers is a method of increasing this transparency and reassuring them that only the agreed upon data is being transferred.

This was a technique used by Hawkey and Inkpen (2005; 2006a). After using an electronic diary to annotate their visited Web pages with a privacy level, participants generated a report to email to the researchers. This report allowed participants to inspect (but not change) the data, which served as confirmation of precisely which aspects of their Web browsing activity were being transferred to the researchers. Weinreich et al. (2006) also took this approach, allowing participants to view their logged data prior to transmitting it to researchers; as discussed later, they did allow participants to take actions on that data.

Affording Privacy Preservation Through Action

Three of Lederer et al.'s (2004) pitfalls relate to privacy preserving actions. The authors state that users should not have to extensively configure a system a priori in order to maintain privacy, but rather should be able to manage privacy within their normal interaction with the system. Additionally, their normal interaction with the system should not be hampered by the actions they must take to preserve privacy, nor should their normal mechanisms of preserving privacy, such as taking advantage of plausible deniability, be hampered by the technology. Furthermore, users should be able to quickly stop the release of information (i.e., have mechanisms of coarse-grained control) so that they can respond to unanticipated or quickly changing situations of use. One difficulty with providing real-time privacy enhancing mechanisms for participants is that this feedback may impact the natural flow of their Web browsing activities and make them more conscious of being observed.

The amount of control a person has over what information is recorded in Web data logs must be balanced with the need for that data for the research purposes. While not all of these recommendations may be appropriate for a given study, providing participants with some level of control over their data should help alleviate privacy concerns (Teltzrow & Kobsa, 2004). The intent of these recommendations is to provide participants with similar privacy-preserving mechanisms to those that they might use in their normal Web interactions when trying to limit the data collected by Web-servers (Cranor, 1999) or when under surveillance (Marx, 2003).

Recommendation 4: Provide the Ability to Pause Recording

Client-side logging software can be developed to automatically log all Web browsing actions or to be manually started by participants on a periodic basis. As previously stated, browser helper objects automatically load when Internet Explorer is loaded; a similar method is the Cross Platform Component Object Model (XPCOM) for Mozilla's Firefox browser. Participants may still bypass the collection of data, however, by using a different Web browser. Custom Web browsers generally must be manually started by the participant. This provides participants with an opportunity to only log those browsing activities that they wish to share. This may be suitable for research investigating episodes of targeted activity such as information seeking tasks as in Kellar et al. (2007). In that case, participants were asked to use a custom web browser periodically to perform information seeking tasks. Their participants could opt not to use the custom browser when conducting sensitive browsing activities.

If periodic recording of data is suitable for the research question, custom logging software such as Web browsers or toolbars associated with browser helper objects or other browser plug-ins should include a recording button that can be toggled on and off. This will allow participants to pause recording of their browsing when engaging in sensitive activities such as visiting socially inappropriate websites or engaging in confidential transactions. This can be very important when recording keystroke data that may include passwords. Alternatively, data logging software could be developed to avoid collecting password data or form field data if this data is not pertinent to the research question (Weinreich, Obendorf, Herder, & Mayer, 2006).

Recommendation 5: Provide the Ability for Participants to Mask Data

Another way to provide privacy for participants is to allow them to mask sensitive data. This may be more appropriate for studies which would like to capture all of a participant's browsing activities. Depending on the research questions, one or more fields in a data log may be candidates for masking.

Kellar et al. (2007) used masking in their field study investigating information seeking tasks and their impact on the use of Web browser navigation mechanisms. Participants could remove details about specific visited pages deemed to be sensitive. Masking was also an approach taken by Hawkey and Inkpen (2006a) in a field study investigating participants' visual privacy concerns for traces of their Web browsing activity. In this study, the researchers wanted to investigate the impact of context (location, visited page) on privacy concerns. They therefore needed to not only collect the URL and page title for annotation by participants within the electronic diary (as in their 2005 study), but to also receive that information as part of the generated report. As they did not want receipt of this additional information to impact participants' willingness to visit sensitive sites, they provided participants with the ability to selectively blind any sensitive data contained in the URL and page title. The electronic diary in Hawkey and Inkpen's (2005) study was modified to allow participants to mask entries in the diary by removing the page title and URL after applying a privacy level to a visited web page. When masking an entry, participants were asked to give a general reason for the sanitized browsing such as "looking for medical information"; the default label was "no reason given." An inspection of the visited pages revealed that the proportion of participants in the field study with instances of adult content was comparable to frequency reports of erotica viewing as reported by participants in a related anonymous survey (Hawkey & Inkpen, 2006b). This may indicate that participants' normal Web usage, including those activities not considered to be socially desirable (Fisher, 1993), was recorded during the study.

Recommendation 6: Provide Participants with the Ability to Delete Data

Deletion of records may be feasible for some research questions. Deletion is similar to pausing of the recording but is done after the fact. Research questions that may be answered by investigating specific episodes of Web browsing would be candidates for this approach. In order to preserve the integrity of the data, researchers may want to limit how the data can be handled, perhaps providing a data viewer that allows deletion at the record level, but no modifications of individual fields. Alternatively, deletion could be offered at the session level by providing participants with the opportunity to consent to the session being included in the study data upon exiting the data collection software. Weinreich, Obendorf, Herder & Mayer (2006) allowed their participants to view the data logs (as text files) before transmitting them to researchers. The text files were editable, so participants could potentially modify the data at will, either through masking or deletion of specific records or entire files; however, no participants are believed to have actually modified their data (Obendorf, personal communication, January 2008).

FUTURE TRENDS

The previous sections presented current challenges for researchers attempting to capture observational data and provided several recommendations for enhancing participant privacy in an effort to encourage users to engage in their normal Web browsing behaviors (summarized in Table 2). Privacy concerns of participants can be expected to increase as researchers gather more contextual information during studies, including their users' activities, goals, attitudes, and processes, to augment logged data (Kellar, Hawkey, Inkpen, & Watters, 2008). Contextual information plays an important role in how we understand and interpret people's everyday behavior. Information that provides additional details about

Table 2. Summary of recommendations for enhancing participants' privacy and thereby encouraging natural Web browsing behaviors.

Recommendations for Enhancing Privacy when Logging Web Browsing Activity
Increase Privacy and Trust
1. Educate participants about what information is being collected
2. Only record/receive as much information as is needed for the research questions
3. Provide opportunities for participants to inspect the data collected
Afford Privacy Preservation Through Action
4. Provide the ability for participants to pause recording of the data
5. Provide the ability for participants to mask particularly sensitive data
6. Provide participants with the ability to delete data

people, such as their location or task, can help us better understand and interpret their actions. In a Web environment, contextual information can be used to determine the activities in which a user is engaging, their motivations for engaging in those activities, as well as perceptions about the current tool or the information being viewed. Participant annotation of log data is one emerging method of gaining additional context (Kellar, Hawkey, Inkpen, & Watters, 2008). Another method is to retrospectively discuss portions of the data logs with participants using critical incident techniques (Choo, Detlor, & Turnbull, 2000).

There is also an increasing need to capture Web activity across usage contexts. It is important during studies of natural browsing behaviors that we record specific aspects of context that may be influencing behaviors at the time and capture those behaviors across all normal usage contexts. Web usage can vary across different locations (e.g., home, work) and devices (laptop, desktop) (Hawkey, 2007). Additionally, different Web browsers or Web browser settings may be used in these environments, and browsing may be conducted for different purposes (e.g., personal, work-related). There will be many research challenges to ensure that participant privacy is considered across contexts of use, as well as the privacy of any companies or organizations involved. As the boundaries between personal time and work time decrease, more and more participants may be multi-tasking across contexts (Olson-Buchanan & Boswell, 2006).

Loggers that capture data across applications are becoming more common as researchers investigate behaviors at the level of the activity or are gathering more contextual information about multi-tasking. Such logging applications increase privacy concerns of participants, whether they are keystroke loggers or screen capture applications. Screen capture software gives context by revealing what the user sees while interacting with their Web browser including applications outside of the Web browser. If such applications are used, participants are essentially agreeing to have all of their computer activity logged. It can be very difficult to recruit users to take part in such studies, and there may be privacy concerns not only for the participants, but for those with whom they communicate (i.e., email correspondence) (Tang, Liu, Muller, Lin, & Drews, 2006). Research ethics boards may require informed consent from all collaborators before their data is recorded.

As more contextual data is captured and more logging is conducted across applications, it will be increasingly important for researchers to consider participants' privacy concerns (Kellar, Hawkey, Inkpen, & Watters, 2008). Providing privacy enhancing methods such as those suggested in the recommendations should help alleviate privacy concerns which may impact recruitment efforts and encourage participants to engage in their usual activities. Researchers will need to be innovative in their methodological techniques as they balance the participants' desires for privacy with researchers' need for rich data to answer questions of interest.

Researchers must also keep abreast of changing privacy regulations at the governmental and organizational level. Given current political climates, it is expected that more rigid protections of data and their re-use will be legislated. Keeping informed of current practices is particularly important if conducting research across borders, as regulations vary widely.

CONCLUSION

This chapter first presented relevant privacy literature including general privacy theories and privacy concerns specific to Web browsing activities. This background provided the necessary grounding for the subsequent discussions of privacy issues with respect to the collection of log data for analysis. The main privacy issues presented were 1) ensuring that governmental and organizational regulations with respect to the safeguarding of participant data are met and 2) providing privacy preserving mechanisms for participants in order to encourage natural Web browsing behaviors. Privacy concerns will depend on the type of data logging. Several tradeoffs were discussed according to the location of the data logging (see Table 1 for a summary). While server-side data is less intrusive for participants and allows them to engage in their normal privacy preserving mechanisms, the data collected is limited and often unreliable. Client-side logging can provide richer data including Web browser interactions; however, data collection is more intrusive.

Several key recommendations for mechanisms to enhance participants' privacy were suggested (see Table 2 for a summary). These include ways to increase participants' understanding and trust of the data logging for the study as well as methods to allow them to control the capture of particularly sensitive data through masking, blocking, or deleting it. The author hopes that these recommendations will prove to be useful for researchers designing research methodologies that include the capture of observational data.

REFERENCES

Ackerman, M., Cranor, L., & Reagle, J. (1999). Privacy in E-Commerce: Examining User Scenarios and Privacy Preferences. In *1st ACM conference on Electronic commerce* (pp. 1-8). Denver, CO: ACM.

Anick, P. (2003). Using Terminological Feedback for Web Search Refinement - A Log-based Study. In *26th annual international ACM SIGIR conference on research and development in information retrieval* (pp. 88 95). Toronto, Canada: ACM.

Atterer, R., Wnuk, M., & Schmidt, A. (2006). Knowing the user's every move: user activity tracking for website usability evaluation and implicit interaction. In *15th International Conference on World Wide Web* (pp. 203-212). Edinburgh, Scotland: ACM.

Barford, P., Bestavros, A., Bradley, A., & Crovella, M. (1999). Changes in Web client access patterns: Characteristics and Caching Implications. *World Wide Web, 2*(1-2), 15-28.

Chatterjee, P., Hoffman, D. L., & Novak, T. P. (2003). Modeling the Clickstream: Implications for Web-Based Advertising Efforts. *Marketing Science, 22*(4), 520-541.

Choo, C. W., Detlor, B., & Turnbull, D. (2000). Information Seeking on the Web: An Integrated Model of Browsing and Searching. *First Monday, 5*(2), Retrieved August 3, 2004, from http://firstmonday.org/issues/issue2005_2002/choo/index.html.

Cockburn, A., & McKenzie, B. (2001). What do web users do? An empirical analysis of web use. *International Journal of Human-Computer Studies, 54*(6), 903-922.

Cooley, R., Mobasher, B., & Srivastava, J. (1999). Data Preparation for Mining World Wide Web Browsing Patterns. *Knowledge and Information Systems, 1*(1), 5-32.

Cranor, L. F. (1999). Internet Privacy. *Communications of the ACM, 42*(2), 28-31.

Dalhousie Research Services. (2006). *Directives to Researchers regarding Compliance with the University Policy for the Protection of Personal Information from Access Outside Canada.* Retrieved July 29, 2007 from http://researchservices.dal.ca/files/Personal_Information_Protection_Guide.pdf.

Fenstermacher, K., & Ginsburg, M. (2003). Client-Side Monitoring for Web Mining. *Journal of the American Society for Information Science and Technology, 54*(7), 625-637.

Fisher, R. J. (1993). Social Desirability Bias and the Validity of Indirect Questioning. *Journal of Consumer Research, 20*(2), 303-315.

Garfinkel, S., & Spafford, G. (2001). *Web Security, Privacy & Commerce, 2nd Edition*: O'Reilly.

Goffman, E. (1959). *The Presentation of Self in Everyday Life*. Garden City, New York: Doubleday Anchor Books.

Hawkey, K. (2007). *Managing the visual privacy of incidental information in web browsers*. Unpublished PhD Dissertation, Dalhousie University, Halifax, Nova Scotia.

Hawkey, K., & Inkpen, K. (2005). Privacy Gradients: Exploring ways to manage incidental information during co-located collaboration. In *CHI '05 Extended Abstracts of Human Factors in Computing Systems* (pp. 1431-1434). Portland, Oregon: ACM.

Hawkey, K., & Inkpen, K. M. (2006a). Examining the Content and Privacy of Web Browsing Incidental Information. In *15th International Conference on World Wide Web* (pp. 123-132). Edinburgh, Scotland: ACM.

Hawkey, K., & Inkpen, K. M. (2006b). Keeping Up Appearances: Understanding the Dimensions of Incidental Information Privacy. In *SIGCHI Conference on Human Factors in Computer Systems* (pp. 821-830). Montreal, Quebec: ACM.

Huseby, S. H. (2004). *Innocent Code: A Security Wake-Up Call for Web Programmers*. UK: John Wiley & Sons Ltd.

Joinson, A. N., Paine, C., Reips, U.-D., & Buchanan, T. (2006). Privacy and Trust: The role of situational and dispositional variables in online disclosure. In *Privacy, Trust, and Identity Issues for Ambient Intelligence Workshop, Pervasive 2006* (pp. 1-6). Dublin, Ireland.

Kellar, M., Hawkey, K., Inkpen, K. M., & Watters, C. (2008). Challenges of Capturing Natural Web-based User Behaviours. *International Journal of Human Computer Interaction, 24*(4), 385-409.

Kellar, M., Watters, C., & Shepherd, M. (2007). A Field Study Characterizing Web-based Information Seeking Tasks. *Journal of the American Society for Information Science and Technology, 58*(7), 999-1018.

Kelly, D., & Belkin, N. (2004). Display Time as Implicit Feedback: Understanding Task Effects. In *27th Annual International ACM SIGIR Conference on Research and Development in Information Retrieval* (pp. 377-384). Sheffield, UK: ACM.

Lederer, S., Hong, J. I., Dey, A. K., & Landay, J. A. (2004). Personal privacy through understanding and action: five pitfalls for designers. *Personal and Ubiquitous Computing, 8*(6), 440-454.

Lederer, S., Mankoff, J., & Dey, A. K. (2003). Towards a Deconstruction of the Privacy Space. *Workshop on Ubicomp Communities: Privacy as Boundary Negotiation, UBICOMP 2003*: Retrieved August 12, 2005 from http://guir.berkeley.edu/pubs/ubicomp2003/privacyworkshop/papers/lederer-privacyspace.pdf

Liu, C., Marchewka, J. T., Lu, J., & Yu, C.-S. (2004). Beyond concern: a privacy-trust-behavioral intention model of electronic commerce. *Information & Management, 42*(1), 127-142.

Malhotra, N. K., Kim, S. S., & Agarwal, J. (2004). Internet Users' Information Privacy Concerns (IUIPC): The Construct, the Scale, and a Causal Model. *Information Systems Research, 15*(4), 336-355.

Marx, G. T. (2003). A Tack in the Shoe: Neutralizing and Resisting the New Surveillance. *Journal Of Social Issues, 59*(2), 369-390.

McCullagh, D. (2006). *AOL's disturbing glimpse into user's lives*. CNET News.com, Online at: http://news.com.com/2100-1030_3-6103098.html. Retrieved October 5, 2006.

McGrath, J. E. (1995). Methodology matters: doing research in the behavioral and social sciences. In J. G. R. Baeker, W. Buxton, and S. Greenberg (Ed.), *Human-Computer Interaction: Toward the Year 2000* (pp. 152-169).

Meier, J. D., Mackman, A., Dunner, M., Vasireddy, S., Escamilla, R., & Murakan, A. (2003). *Improving Web Application Security: Threats and Countermeasures*: Microsoft Press.

Olson-Buchanan, J. B., & Boswell, W. R. (2006). Blurring boundaries: Correlates of integration and segmentation between work and nonwork. *Journal of Vocational Behavior, 68*(3), 432-445.

Olson, J. S., Grudin, J., & Horvitz, E. (2005). A Study of Preferences for Sharing and Privacy, *in CHI '05 Extended Abstracts of Human Factors in Computing Systems* (pp. 1985-1988). Portland, Oregon: ACM.

P&AB. (2003). Consumer Privacy Attitudes: A Major Shift Since 2000 and Why. *Privacy & American Business Newsletter, 10*(6), 1,3-5.

Palen, L., & Dourish, P. (2003). Unpacking "Privacy" for a Networked World. In *SIGCHI Conference on Human Factors in Computing Systems* (pp. 129-136). Ft. Lauderdale, FL: ACM.

Phillips, D. J. (2002). Context, identity, and privacy in ubiquitous computing environments. In *Workshop on socially-informed design of privacy-enhancing solutions, Ubicomp 2002.* Goteborg, Sweden.

Sackmann, S., Struker, J., & Accorsi, R. (2006). Personalization in Privacy-Aware Highly Dynamic Systems. *Communications of the ACM, 49*(9), 32-38.

Tang, J. C., Liu, S. B., Muller, M., Lin, J., & Drews, C. (2006). Unobtrusive but invasive: using screen recording to collect field data on computer-mediated interaction. In *20th anniversary conference on Computer supported cooperative work* (pp. 479-482). Banff, Alberta: ACM.

Teltzrow, M., & Kobsa, A. (2004). Impacts of user preferences on personalized systems: a comparative study. In *Designing personalized user experiences in eCommerce* (pp. 315-332). Norwell, MA, USA: Kluwer Academic Publishers.

Weinreich, H., Obendorf, H., Herder, E., & Mayer, M. (2006). Off the Beaten tracks: Exploring Three Aspects of Web Navigation. In *15th International Conference on World Wide Web* (pp. 133-142). Edinburgh, Scotland: ACM.

Westin, A. F. (2003). Social and Political Dimensions of Privacy. *Journal of Social Issues, 59*(2), 431-453.

Yun, G. W., Ford, J., Hawkins, R. P., Pingree, S., & McTavish, F. (2006). On the validity of client-side vs server-side web log data analysis. *Internet Research, 16*(5), 537-552.

KEY TERMS

Anonymized Data: Data that has been collected with identifying information, but has had subsequent removal of any links between the data and identifying information so that the researcher can no longer discern the specific owner of the data.

Anonymous Data: Data that is collected without any associated identifying information.

Client-Side Logging: Software that records Web browsing behavior at the user's computer. This is generally achieved either through a custom web browser or through browser plug-ins such as tool bars or browser helper objects.

Contextual Privacy Concerns: Privacy concerns vary in any given instance according to the inherent privacy concerns of the user and the situational factors at play. These include the viewer of the information, level of control retained over the information, and the type of information.

Furthermore, these factors can vary according to the device in use and the location.

Inherent Privacy Concerns: An individual's general privacy concerns; their disposition to privacy. Factors which may impact a person's disposition to privacy include their age and computer experience.

Privacy: "The claim of an individual to determine what information about himself or herself should be known to others." (Westin, 2003).

Proxy Logging: Software that serves as an intermediary between the user's web browser and the web site servers. Users generally have to log-in to the proxy and the proxy server can be used to augment retrieved web pages.

Server-Side Logging: Software that records Web browsing behavior at the server. Data collection is generally limited to navigation information.

Web Browsing Behaviors: User behaviors on the Web including their browsing activities and Web browser interactions. Privacy concerns have been found to impact Web browsing behaviours.

Web Browsing Environment: The context within which Web browsing occurs. For studies of Web usage this includes the Web browser and its associated tools (e.g., history, specialized toolbars), the task, and the motivation for conducting the browsing.

Section II
Methodology and Metrics

Chapter VI
The Methodology of Search Log Analysis

Bernard J. Jansen
Pennsylvania State University, USA

ABSTRACT

Exploiting the data stored in search logs of Web search engines, Intranets, and Websites can provide important insights into understanding the information searching tactics of online searchers. This understanding can inform information system design, interface development, and information architecture construction for content collections. This chapter presents a review of and foundation for conducting Web search transaction log analysis. A search log analysis methodology is outlined consisting of three stages (i.e., collection, preparation, and analysis). The three stages of the methodology are presented in detail with discussions of the goals, metrics, and processes at each stage. The critical terms in transaction log analysis for Web searching are defined. Suggestions are provided on ways to leverage the strengths and addressing the limitations of transaction log analysis for Web searching research.

INTRODUCTION

Information searching researchers have employed search logs for analyzing a variety of Web information systems (Croft, Cook, & Wilder, 1995; Jansen, Spink, & Saracevic, 2000; Jones, Cunningham, & McNab, 1998; Wang, Berry, & Yang, 2003). Web search engine companies use search logs (also referred to as transaction logs) to investigate searching trends and effects of system improvements (c.f., Google at http://www.google.com/press/zeitgeist.html or Yahoo! at http://buzz.yahoo.com/buzz_log/?fr=fp-buzz-morebuzz). Search logs are an unobtrusive method of collecting significant amounts of searching data on a sizable number of system users. There are several researchers who have employed the search log analysis methodology to study Web searching; however, not as many as one might expect given the advantages of the method.

One possible reason is that there are limited published works concerning how to employ search logs to support the study of Web searching, the use of Web search engines, Intranet searching, or other Web searching applications. Few of the published works provide a comprehensive explanation of the methodology. This chapter addresses the use of search log analysis (also referred to as transaction log analysis) for the study of Web searching and Web search engines in order to facilitate its use as a research methodology. A three-stage process composed of data *collection, preparation, and analysis* is presented for transaction log analysis. Each stage is addressed in detail and a stepwise methodology to conduct transaction log analysis for the study of Web searching is described. The strengths and shortcomings of search log analysis are discussed.

REVIEW OF LITERATURE

What is a Search Log?

Not surprisingly, a search log is a file (i.e., log) of the communications (i.e., transactions) between a system and the users of that system. Rice and Borgman (1983) present transaction logs as a data collection method that automatically captures the type, content, or time of transactions made by a person from a terminal with that system. Peters (1993) views transaction logs as electronically recorded interactions between on-line information retrieval systems and the persons who search for the information found in those systems.

For Web searching, a search log is *an electronic record of interactions that have occurred during a searching episode between a Web search engine and users searching for information on that Web search engine.* A Web search engine may be a general-purpose search engine, a niche search engine, a searching application on a single Web site, or variations on these broad classifications. The users may be humans or computer programs acting on behalf of humans. Interactions are the communication exchanges that occur between users and the system. Either the user or the system may initiate elements of these exchanges.

How are These Interactions Collected?

The process of recording the data in the search log is relatively straightforward. Web servers record and store the interactions between searchers (i.e., actually Web browsers on a particular computer) and search engines in a log file (i.e., the transaction log) on the server using a software application. Thus, most search logs are server-side recordings of interactions. Major Web search engines execute millions of these interactions per day. The server software application can record various types of data and interactions depending on the file format that the server software supports.

Typical transaction log formats are access log, referrer log, or extended log. The W3C (http://www.w3.org/TR/WD-logfile.html) is one organizational body that defines transaction log formats. However, search logs are a special type of transaction log file. This search log format has most in common with the extended file format, which contains data such as the client computer's Internet Protocol (IP) address, user query, search engine access time, and referrer site, among other fields.

Why Collect This Data?

Once the server collects and records the data in a file, one must analyze this data in order to obtain beneficial information. The process of conducting this examination is referred to as *transaction log analysis* (TLA). TLA can focus on many interaction issues and research questions (Drott, 1998), but it typically addresses either issues of system performance, information structure, or user interactions.

In other views, Peters (1993) describes TLA as *the study of electronically recorded interactions between on-line information retrieval systems and the persons who search for information found in those systems.* Blecic and colleagues (1998) define TLA as the detailed and systematic examination of each search command or query by a user and the following database result or output. Phippen, Shepherd, and Furnell (2004) and Spink and Jansen (2004) also provide comparable definitions of TLA.

For Web searching research, we focus on a sub-set of TLA, namely search log analysis (SLA). One can use TLA to analyze the browsing or navigation patterns within a Website, while SLA is concerned exclusively with searching behaviors. SLA is defined as *the use of data collected in a search log to investigate particular research questions concerning interactions among Web users, the Web search engine, or the Web content during searching episodes.* Within this interaction context, SLA could use the data in search logs to discern attributes of the search process, such as the searcher's actions on the system, the system responses, or the evaluation of results by the searcher.

The goal of SLA is to gain a clearer understanding of the interactions among searcher, content and system or the interactions between two of these structural elements, based on whatever research questions are the drivers for the study. From this understanding, one achieves some stated objective, such as improved system design, advanced searching assistance, or better understanding of some user information searching behavior.

What is the Theoretical Basis of TLA (and SLA)?

TLA and its sub-component, SLA, lend themselves to a grounded theory approach (Glaser & Strauss, 1967). This approach emphasizes a systematic discovery of theory from data using methods of comparison and sampling. The resulting theories or models are grounded in observations of the "real world," rather than being abstractly generated. Therefore, grounded theory is an inductive approach to theory or model development, rather than the deductive alternative (Chamberlain, 1995).

Using SLA as a methodology in information searching, one examines the characteristics of searching episodes in order to isolate trends and identify typical interactions between searchers and the system. Interaction has several meanings in information searching, addressing a variety of transactions including query submission, query modification, results list viewing, and use of information objects (e.g., Web page, pdf file, video). Efthimiadis and Robertson (1989) categorize interaction at various stages in the information retrieval process by drawing from information-seeking research. SLA deals with the tangible interaction between user and system in each of these stages. SLA addresses levels one and two (*move* and *tactic*) of Bates' (1990) four levels of interaction, which are *move*, *tactic*, *stratagem*, and *strategy*. Belkin and fellow researchers (1995) have extensively explored user interaction based on user needs, from which they developed a multi-level view of searcher interactions. SLA focuses on the specific expressions of these user needs. Saracevic (1997) views interaction as the exchange of information between users and system. Increases in interaction result from increases in communication content. SLA is concerned with the exchanges and manner of these exchanges. Hancock-Beaulieu (2000) identifies three aspects of interaction, which are interaction within and across tasks, interaction as task sharing, and interaction as a discourse. One can use SLA to analyze the interactions within, across, and sharing.

For the purposes of SLA, interactions can be considered *the physical expressions of communication exchanges between the searcher and the system.* For example, a searcher may submit a query (i.e., an interaction). The system may respond with a results page (i.e., an interaction). The searcher may click on a uniform resource locator (URL) in the results listing (i.e., an interaction). Therefore, for SLA, interaction is a more mechanical expression of underlying information needs or motivations.

How is SLA Used?

Researchers and practitioners have used SLA (usually referred to as TLA in these studies) to evaluate library systems, traditional information retrieval (IR) systems, and more recently Web systems. Transaction logs have been used for many types of analysis; in this review, we focus on those studies that centered on or about searching. Peters (1993) provides a review of TLA in library and experimental IR systems. Some progress has been made in TLA methods since Peters' summary (1993) in terms of collection and ability to analyze data. Jansen and Pooch (2001) report on a variety of studies employing TLA for the study of Web search engines and searching on Web sites. Jansen and Spink (2005) provide a comprehensive review of Web searching TLA studies. Other review articles include Kinsella and Bryant (1987) and Fourie (2002).

Employing TLA in research projects, Meister and Sullivan (1967) may be the first to have conducted and documented TLA results, and Penniman (1975) appears to have published one of the first research articles using TLA. There have been a variety of TLA studies since (c.f., Baeza-Yates & Castillo, 2001; Chau, Fang, & Sheng, 2006; Fourie & van den Berg, 2003; Millsap & Ferl, 1993; Moukdad & Large, 2001; Park, Bae, & Lee, 2005).

Several papers have discussed the use of TLA as a methodological approach. Sandore and Kaske (1993) review methods of applying the results of TLA. Borgman, Hirsch, and Hiller (1996) comprehensively review past literature to identify the methodologies that these studies employed, including the goals of the studies. Several researchers have viewed TLA as a high-level designed process, including Copper (1998). Other researchers, such as Hancock-Beaulieu, Robertson, and Nielsen (1990), Griffiths, Hartley, and Willson (2002), Bains (1997), Hargittai (2002), and Yuan and Meadows (1999), have advocated using TLA in conjunction with other research methodologies or data collection. Alternatives for other data collection include questionnaires, interviews, video analysis, and verbal protocol analysis.

How is SLA Critiqued?

Almost from its first use, researchers have critiqued TLA as a research methodology (Blecic et al., 1998; Hancock-Beaulieu et al., 1990; Phippen et al., 2004). These critiques report that transaction logs do not record the users' perceptions of the search, cannot measure the underlying information need of the searchers, and cannot gauge the searchers' satisfaction with search results. In this vein, Kurth (1993) reports that transaction logs can only deal with the actions that the user takes, not their perceptions, emotions, or background skills.

Kurth (1993) further identifies three methodological issues with TLA, which are: *execution*, *conception*, and *communication*. Kurth (1993) states that TLA can be difficult to execute due to collection, storage, and analysis issues associated with the hefty volume and complexity of the dataset (i.e., significant number of variables). With complex datasets, it is sometimes difficult to develop a conceptual methodology for analyzing the dependent variables. Communication problems occur when researchers do not define terms and metrics in sufficient detail to allow other researchers to interpret and verify their results.

Certainly, any researcher who has used TLA would agree with these critiques. However, upon reflection, these are issues with many, if not all, empirical methodologies (McGrath, 1994). Further, although Kurth's critique (1993) is still somewhat valid, advances in transaction logging software, standardized transaction log formats, and improved data analysis software and methods have addressed many of these shortcomings. Certainly, the issue with terms and metrics still apply (Jansen & Pooch, 2001).

As an additional limitation, transaction logs are primarily a server-side data collection method; therefore, some interaction events (Hilbert & Redmiles, 2001) are masked from these logging mechanisms, such as when the user clicks on the *back* or *print* button on the browser software, or *cuts* or *pastes* information from one window to another on a client computer. Transaction logs also, as stated previously, do not record the underlying situational, cognitive, or affective elements of the searching process, although the collection of such data can inform system design (Hilbert & Redmiles, 1998).

What are the Tools to Support SLA?

In an effort to address these issues, Hancock-Beaulieu, Robertson, and Nielsen (1990) developed a transaction logging software package that included online questionnaires to enhance TLA of browsing behaviors. This application was able to gather searcher responses via the questionnaires, but it also took away the unobtrusiveness (one of the strengths of the method) of the transaction log approach. Some software has been developed for unobtrusively logging client-side types of events, for example, the *Tracker* research package (Choo, Betlor, & Turnbull, 1998; Choo & Turnbull, 2000), the Wrapper (Jansen, Ramadoss, Zhang, & Zang, 2006), and commercial spyware software systems.

In other tools for examining transaction log data, Wu, Yu, and Ballman (1998) present SpeedTracer, which is a tool for data mining Web server logs. However, given that transaction log data is usually stored in ASCII text files, relational databases or text-processing scripts work extremely well for TLA. Wang, Berry, and Yang (2003) used a relational database, as did Jansen, Spink, and Saracevic (2000) and Jansen, Spink, and Pederson (2005). Silverstein, Henzinger, Marais, and Moricz (1999) used text processing scripts. All approaches have advantages and disadvantages. With text processing scripts, the analysis can be done in one pass. However, if additional analysis needs to be done, the whole dataset must be reanalyzed. With the relational database approach, the analysis is done in incremental portions; and one can easily add additional analysis steps, building from what has already been done.

In another naturalistic study, Kelly (2004) used WinWhatWhere Investigator, which is a spy software package that covertly "monitors" a person's computer activities. Spy software has some inherent disadvantages for use in user studies and evaluation including granularity of data capture and privacy concerns. Toms, Freund, and Li (2004) developed the WiIRE system for conducting large scale evaluations. This system facilities the evaluation of dispersed study participants; however, it is a server-side application focusing on the participant's interactions with the Web server. As such, the entire "study" must occur within the WiIRE framework.

There are commercial applications for general purpose (i.e., not specifically IR) user studies. An example is Morae 1.1 (http://www.techsmith.com/products/morae/default.asp) offered by TechSmith. Morae provides extremely detailed tracking of user actions, including video capture over a network. However, Morae is not specifically tailored for information searching studies and captures so much information at such a fine granularity that it significantly complicates the data analysis process.

How to Conduct TLA for Web Searching Research?

Despite the abundant literature on TLA, there are few published manuscripts on how actually to conduct it, especially with respect to SLA for Web searching. Some works do provide fairly comprehensive descriptions of the methods employed including Cooper (1998), Nicholas,

Hunteytenn, and Lievestey (1999), Wang, Berry, and Yang (2003), and Spink and Jansen (2004). However, none of these articles presents a process or procedure for actually conducting TLA in sufficient detail to replicate the method. This chapter attempts to address this shortcoming building on work presented in (Jansen, 2006).

SLA PROCESS

Naturally, research questions need to be articulated to determine what data needs to be collected. However, search logs are typically of standard formats due to previously developed software applications. Given the interactions between users and Web browsers, which are the interfaces to Web search engines, the type of data that one can collect is standard. Therefore, the SLA methodology provided in this chapter is applicable to a wide range of studies.

SLA involves the following three major stages, which are:

- **Data Collection:** The process of collecting the interaction data for a given period in a transaction log;
- **Data Preparation:** The process of cleaning and preparing the transaction log data for analysis; and
- **Data Analysis:** The process of analyzing the prepared data.

Data Collection

The research questions define what information one must collect in a search log. Transaction logs provide a good balance between collecting a robust set of data and unobtrusively collecting that data (McGrath, 1994). Collecting data from real users pursuing needed information while interacting with real systems on the Web affects the type of data that one can realistically assemble. If one is conducting a naturalistic study (i.e., outside of the laboratory) on a real system (i.e., a system used by actual searchers), the method of data monitoring and collecting should not interfere with the information searching process. In addition to the loss of potential customers, a data collection method that interferes with the information searching process may unintentionally alter that process.

Fields in a Standard Search Log

Table 1 provides a sample of a standard search log format collected by a Web search engine.

The fields are common in standard Web search engine logs, although some systems may log additional fields. A common additional field is a cookie identification code that facilitates identifying individual searchers using a common computer. A cookie is a text message given by a Web server to a Web browser. The cookie is stored on the client machine.

In order to facilitate valid comparisons and contrasts with other analysis, a standard terminology and set of metrics (Jansen & Pooch, 2001) is advocated. This standardization will help address one of Kurth's critiques (1993) concerning the communication of SLA results across studies. Others have also noted terminology as an issue in Web research (Pitkow, 1997). The standard field labels and descriptors are presented below.

A *searching episode* is a series of searching interactions within a given temporal span by a single searcher. Each record, shown as a row in Table 1, is a *searching interaction*. The format of each *searching interaction* is:

- **User Identification:** The IP address of the client's computer. This is sometimes also an anonymous user code address assigned by the search engine server, which is our example in Table 1.
- **Date:** The date of the interaction as recorded by the search engine server.
- **The Time:** The time of the interaction as recorded by the search engine server.

Table 1. Snippet from a Web search engine search log

user identification	date	thetime	search_url
ce00160c04c4158087704275d69fbecd	25/Apr/2004	04:08:50	Sphagnum Moss Harvesting + New Jersey + Raking
38f04d74e651137587e9ba3f4f1af315	25/Apr/2004	04:08:50	emailanywhere
fabc953fe31996a0877732a1a970250a	25/Apr/2004	04:08:54	Tailpiece
5010dbbd750256bf4a2c3c77fb7f95c4	25/Apr/2004	04:08:54	1'personalities AND gender AND education'1
25/Apr/2004	**04:08:54**	**dmr panasonic**	
89bf2acc4b64e4570b89190f7694b301	25/Apr/2004	04:08:55	bawdy poems"
	"Mark Twain""	**25/Apr/2004**	
397e056655f01380cf181835dfc39426		**04:08:56**	**gay porn**
a9560248d1d8d7975ffc455fc921cdf6	25/Apr/2004	04:08:58	skin diagnostic
81347ea595323a15b18c08ba5167fbe3	25/Apr/2004	04:08:59	Pink Floyd cd label cover scans
3c5c399d3d7097d3d01aeea064305484	25/Apr/2004	04:09:00	freie stellen dangaard
9dafd20894b6d5f156846b56cd574f8d	25/Apr/2004	04:09:00	Moto.it
415154843dfe18f978ab6c63551f7c86	25/Apr/2004	04:09:00	Capablity Maturity Model VS.
c03488704a64d981e263e3e8cf1211ef	25/Apr/2004	04:09:01	ana cleonides paulo fontoura

Note: Bolded items are intentional errors

- **Search URL:** The query terms as entered by the user.

Web search engine server software normally always records these fields. Other common fields include *Results Page* (a code representing a set of result abstracts and URLs returned by the search engine in response to a query), *Language* (the user preferred language of the retrieved Web pages), *Source* (the federated content collection searched, also known as *Vertical*), and *Page Viewed* (the URL that the searcher visited after entering the query and viewing the results page, which is also known as *click-thru or click-through*).

Data Preparation

Once the data is collected, one moves to the data preparation stage of the SLA process. For data preparation, the focus is on importing the search log data into a relational database (or other analysis software), assigning each record a primary key, cleaning the data (i.e., checking each field for bad data), and calculating standard interaction metrics that will serve as the basis for further analysis.

Figure 1 shows an Entity – Relation (ER) diagram for the relational database that will be used to store and analyze the data from a search log.

An ER diagram models the concepts and perceptions of the data and displays the conceptual schema for the database using standard ER notation. Table 2 presents the legend for the schema constructs names.

Since search logs are in ASCII format, one can easily import the data into most relational databases. A key thing is to import the data in the same coding schema in which it was recorded (e.g., UTF-8, US-ASCII). Once imported, each record is assigned a unique identifier or primary key. Most modern databases can assign this au-

Figure 1. ER scheme diagram Web search log

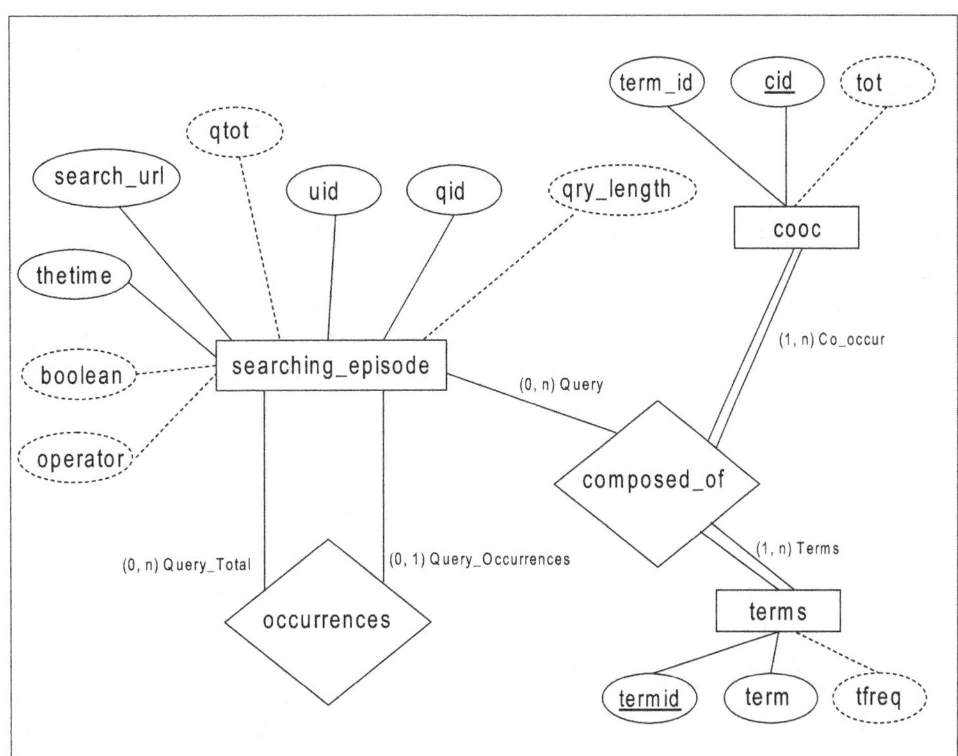

Table 2. Legend for ER schema constructs for search log

Entity Name	Construct
Searching_Episodes	a table containing the searching interactions
boolean	denotes if the query contains Boolean operators
operators	denotes if the query contains advanced query operators
q_length	query length in terms
qid	primary key for each record
qtot	number of results pages viewed
searcher_url	query terms as entered by the searcher
thetime	time of day as measured by the server
uid	user identification based on IP
Terms	table with terms and frequency
term_ID	term identification
term	term from the query set
tfreq	number of occurrences of term in the query set
Cooc	table term pairs and the number of occurrences of those pairs
term_ID	term identification
cid	the combined term identification for a pair of terms
tot	number of occurrences of the pair in the query set

tomatically on importation, or one can assign it later using scripts.

Cleaning the Data

Once the search log data is in a suitable analysis software package, the focus shifts to cleaning the data. Records in search logs can contain corrupted data. These corrupted records can be as a result of multiple reasons; but they are mostly related to errors when logging the data. In the example shown in Table 1, one can easily spot these records (additionally these records are bolded), but many times a search log will number millions if not billions of records. Therefore, a visual inspection is not practical for error identification. From experience, one method of rapidly identifying most errors is to sort each field in sequence. Since the erroneous data will not fit the pattern of the other data in the field, these errors will usually appear at the top of, bottom of, or grouped together in each sorted field. Standard database functions to sum and group key fields such as time and IP address will usually identify any further errors. One must remove all records with corrupted data from the transaction log database. Typically, the percentage of corrupted data is small relative to the overall database.

Parsing the Data

Using the three fields of *The Time*, *User Identification*, and *Search URL*, common to all Web search logs, the chronological series of actions in a searching episode is recreated. The Web query search logs usually contain queries from both human users and agents. Depending on the research objective, one may be interested in only individual human interactions, those from common user terminals, or those from agents. For the running example used in this chapter, we will consider the case of only having an interest in human searching episodes. To do this, all sessions with less than 101 queries are separated into an individual search log for this example.

Given that there is no way to accurately identify human from non-human searchers (Silverstein et al., 1999; Sullivan, 2001), most researchers using Web search log either ignore it (Cacheda & Viña, 2001) or assume some temporal or interaction cut-off (Montgomery & Faloutsos, 2001; Silverstein et al., 1999). Using a cut-off of 101 queries, the subset of the search log is weighted to queries submitted primarily by human searchers in a non-common user terminal, but 101 queries is high enough not to introduce bias by too low of a cut-off threshold. The selection of 101 is arbitrary, and other researchers have used a wide variety of cut-offs.

There are several methods to remove these large sessions. One can code a program to count the session lengths and then delete all sessions that have lengths over 100. For smaller log files (a few million or so records), it is just as easy to do with SQL queries. To do this, one must first remove records that do not contain queries. From experience, search logs may contain many such records (usually on the order of 35 to 40 percent of all records) as users go to Web sites for purposes other than searching, or they find what they are looking for on the search engine result page.

Normalizing Searching Episodes

When a searcher submits a query, then views a document, and returns to the search engine, the Web server typically logs this second visit with the identical user identification and query, but with a new time (i.e., the time of the second visit). This is beneficial information in determining how many of the retrieved *results pages* the searcher visited from the search engine, but unfortunately, it also skews the results in analyzing how the query level of analysis. In order to normalize the searching episodes, one must first separate these result page requests from query submissions for each searching episode. An example of how to do this can be found in the SQL query #00 (Appendix A).

From a *tbl_main*, this will create a new table *tbl_searching_episodes* which contains a count of multiple submissions (i.e., *qtot*) from each searcher within each record as shown in Figure 2. This collapses the search log by combining all identical queries submitted by the same user to give the unique queries in order to analyze sessions, queries and terms, and pages of results (i.e., *tbl_searching_episodes*). Use the complete un-collapsed sessions (i.e., *tbl_main*) in order to obtain an accurate measure of the temporal length of sessions. The *tbl_searching_episodes* will now be used for the remainder of our TLA. Use SQL query #01, Appendix A to identify the sessions with more than 100 records. Then, one can delete these records from *tbl_searching_episodes* using the SQL delete query #02, Appendix A.

In SLA, many times one is interested in terms and term usage, which can be an entire study in itself. In these cases, it is often cleaner to generate separate tables that contain each term and their frequency of occurrence. A term co-occurrence table that contains each term and its co-occurrence with other terms is also valuable for understanding the data. If using a relational database, one can generate these tables using scripts. If using text-parsing languages, one can parse these terms and associated data out during initial processing.

Figure 2. Records of searching episodes with number of duplicate queries (qtot) recorded

Microsoft Access - [tbl_searching_episodes : Table]

File Edit View Insert Format Records Tools Window Help

qid	uid	date	thetime	search_url	qtot	qry_length	boolean	operator
1	ce00160c04c4158087704275d69fbecd	25/Apr/2004	04:08:50	Sphagnum Moss Harvesting + New Jersey + Raking	4	6	☐	☑
2	38f04d74e651137587e9ba3f4f1af315	25/Apr/2004	04:08:50	emailanywhere	2	1	☐	☐
3	fabc953fe31996a0877732a1a970250a	25/Apr/2004	04:08:54	Tailpiece	1	1	☐	☐
4	5010dbbd750256bf4a2c3c77fb7f95c4	25/Apr/2004	04:08:54	1'personalities AND gender AND education'1	1	5	☑	☐
5	daade90d883432ddf6cf3fb509e3bf41	25/Apr/2004	04:08:54	dmr panasonic	1	2	☐	☐
6	89bf2acc4b64e4570b89190f7694b301	25/Apr/2004	04:08:55	bawdy poems"	1	2	☐	☑
7	9f6fa2a8d5b12a1f8380ed4ea1483b2b	25/Apr/2004	04:08:56	"Mark Twain""	1	2	☐	☑
8	397e056655f01380cf181835dfc39426	25/Apr/2004	04:08:56	gay porn	1	2	☐	☐
9	a9560248d1d8d7975ffc455fc921cdf6	25/Apr/2004	04:08:58	skin diagnostic	1	2	☐	☐
10	81347ea595323a15b18c08ba5167fbe3	25/Apr/2004	04:08:59	Pink Floyd cd label cover scans	1	6	☐	☐
11	3c5c399d3d7097d3d01aeea064305484	25/Apr/2004	04:09:00	freie stellen dangaard	1	3	☐	☐
12	9dafd20894b6d5f156846b56cd574f8d	25/Apr/2004	04:09:00	Moto.it	1	1	☐	☐
13	415154843dfe18f978ab6c63551f7c86	25/Apr/2004	04:09:00	Capablity Maturity Model VS.	1	4	☐	☐
14	c03488704a64d981e263e3e8cf1211ef	25/Apr/2004	04:09:01	ana cleonides paulo fontoura	1	4	☐	☐
15	7ab6a96ee504b5f54773f8cff3999354	25/Apr/2004	04:09:01	quetschrippen konstruktion kunststoff	2	3	☐	☐
16	01305f695166f2fc135bf26ee52d2a3b	25/Apr/2004	04:09:02	lovette password	3	2	☐	☐
17	eedec6d2ecc3519ea7747db9982abf57	25/Apr/2004	04:09:04	free porn	1	2	☐	☐
18	3438f445fa250f7377befde4f188a09b	25/Apr/2004	04:09:04	centro	2	1	☐	☐
19	ef8871c24d88b96ee8813cb361445040	25/Apr/2004	04:09:07	sex toys	1	2	☐	☐
20	cbf06662b4977b1b3161f1f3ea7e4ae4	25/Apr/2004	04:03:18	news "blue oak" "Quercus douglas"	1	5	☐	☑
21	9a44e9c5502a6b9ba9af1f0e443245b9	25/Apr/2004	04:09:09	international investment on nanotechnology	1	4	☐	☐
22	e40dab084acb6776a3aa57e8cea5b82f	25/Apr/2004	04:09:10	mosquito keychain	2	2	☐	☐
23	fabc953fe31996a0877732a1a970250a	25/Apr/2004	04:09:12	Valve Tailpiece	1	2	☐	☐
24	74574c974f7301ea4ba056fa00fab71b	25/Apr/2004	04:09:13	" wayne frocklage" Canadian pacific railway	1	5	☐	☑
25	143e559163fbf75e16a52a6d550fb01c	25/Apr/2004	04:02:46	matcho central	1	2	☐	☐
26	fc66620a68627983d416a8dd1afa0d73	25/Apr/2004	04:02:46	Pascal convert decimal to hex	2	5	☐	☐
27	7bff0819a1cdaf645f27f39842bde4b5	25/Apr/2004	04:02:46	bang bros"king chile"	1	4	☐	☑
28	59515ed43dfaa2dde796f3bab8045514	25/Apr/2004	04:02:46	CFISCO	1	1	☐	☐
29	3fb5e9a52e76f0fc344977c27e914ea8	25/Apr/2004	04:02:47	"Stargate" desktop themes	1	3	☐	☑
30	dacca5152e8e0975629cb994fbc0b447	25/Apr/2004	04:02:51	carrieland gallery	1	2	☐	☐
31	4167eb02168d2bc169ffa196d7b10fd5	25/Apr/2004	04:02:53	"femdom picture"	1	2	☐	☑
32	cd7b9dc409c60de204b94105830176ba	25/Apr/2004	04:02:55	"Carla Tonetti"	1	2	☐	☑
33	6b19f010e49a39d7103eabba4530fb74	25/Apr/2004	04:02:56	efficacy	1	1	☐	☐
34	5a20077ed4f1d8a7b41de52aca6ad756	25/Apr/2004	04:02:58	http://kickme.to/xaliasx	1	1	☐	☐
35	93cde4db94cc12cc852e7c4ad352620d	25/Apr/2004	04:03:14	P.M."	1	1	☐	☑
36	1c1c9d058d8dd3cfadb3ee54851f3624	25/Apr/2004	04:03:01	quattro elementi	1	2	☐	☐
37	bae5567110a17a941254661fda3205f0	25/Apr/2004	04:03:02	measurement high temp	1	3	☐	☐
38	606eb104503f078f5fdf20385e58544a	25/Apr/2004	04:03:02	levicom watercube	2	2	☐	☐
39	0fcec5c427a7a1b9393f538ff5373904	25/Apr/2004	04:03:03	notebook mediamarkt	1	2	☐	☐
40	082206ccd56dddc56894304522400d4d	25/Apr/2004	04:03:03	www.dancentury.com/cicada/wedding.html	1	1	☐	☐
41	5b43061638aef9d59dd351542c98f1fa	25/Apr/2004	04:03:04	mensajes subliminales un la publicidad"	1	5	☐	☑
42	07ff54fb225084bfe3c746c320222b5b	25/Apr/2004	04:03:13	online texting	1	2	☐	☐
43	07ff54fb225084bfe3c746c320222b5b	25/Apr/2004	04:03:04	onlinetexting	1	1	☐	☐
44	177219518313a13d3469e8ad9d1d5a7c	25/Apr/2004	04:03:12	Art	1	1	☐	☐
45	177219518313a13d3469e8ad9d1d5a7c	25/Apr/2004	04:03:14	Art history	1	1	☐	☐
46	cd7b9dc409c60de204b94105830176ba	25/Apr/2004	04:02:57	"Jim Jansen"	1	2	☐	☑
*						0	☐	☐

Record: 1 of 46

Datasheet View NUM

We see these as *tbl_terms* and *tbl_cooc* in our database (see Figure 1 and Table 2).

There are already several fields in our database, many of which can provide valuable information (see Figure 1 and Table 2). From these items, one can calculate several metrics, some of which take a long time to compute for large datasets.

DATA ANALYSIS

This stage focuses on three levels of analysis. These levels are discussed and the data analysis stage is stepped through.

Analysis Levels

The three common levels of analysis for examining transaction logs are *term, query, and session.*

Term Level Analysis

The term level of analysis naturally uses the *term* as the basis for analysis. A *term* is a string of characters separated by some delimiter such as a space or some other separator. At this level of analysis, one focuses on measures such as *term occurrence*, which is the frequency that a particular term occurs in the transaction log. *Total terms* is the number of terms in the dataset. *Unique terms* are the terms that appear in the data regardless of the number of times they occur. *High Usage Terms* are those terms that occur most frequently in the dataset. *Term co-occurrence* measures the occurrence of term pairs within queries in the entire search log. One can also calculate degrees of association of term pairs using various statistical measures (c.f., Ross & Wolfram, 2000; Silverstein et al., 1999; Wang et al., 2003).

The mutual information formula measures term association and does not assume mutual independence of the terms within the pair. One can calculate the mutual information statistic for all term pairs within the data set. Many times, a relatively low frequency term pair may be strongly associated (i.e., if the two terms always occur together). The mutual information statistic identifies the strength of this association. The mutual information formula used in this research is:

$$I(w_1, w_2) = \ln \frac{P(w_1, w_2)}{P(w_1)P(w_2)}$$

where $P(w_1)$, $P(w_2)$ are probabilities estimated by relative frequencies of the two words and $P(w_1, w_2)$ is the relative frequency of the word pair and order is not considered. Relative frequencies are observed frequencies (*F*) normalized by the number of the queries:

Table 3. Search log of user interactions

Time Stamp	Interaction
12:12:44	http://localhost/
12:12:44	Search RON (Back Space) BOTS
12:12:56	http://localhost/?TheQuery=robots View URL
12:12:57	View Results
12:13:02	SCROLLED RESULTS
12:13:29	http://localhost/wt01/webtrec/wt01-b01-18.html
12:13:30	View Doc
12:13:34	SCROLLED PAGE

$$P(w_1) = \frac{F_1}{Q'}; P(w_1) = \frac{F_2}{Q'}; P(w_1, w_2) = \frac{F_{12}}{Q'}$$

Both the frequency of term occurrence and the frequency of term pairs are the occurrence of the term or term pair within the set of queries. However, since a one term query cannot have a term pair, the set of queries for the frequency base differs. The number of queries for the terms is the number of non-duplicate queries in the data set. The number of queries for term pairs is defined as:

$$Q' = \sum_{n}^{m} (2n-3)Q_n$$

where Q_n is the number of queries with n words ($n > 1$), and m is the maximum query length. So, queries of length one have no pairs. Queries of length two have one pair. Queries of length three have three possible pairs. Queries of length four have five possible pairs. This continues up to the queries of maximum length in the data set. The formula for queries of term pairs (Q') account for this term pairing.

Query Level Analysis

The query level of analysis uses the query as the base metric. A *query* is defined as a string list of one or more terms submitted to a search engine. This is a mechanical definition as opposed to an information searching definition (Korfhage, 1997). The first query by a particular searcher is the *initial query*. A subsequent query by the same searcher that is different than any of the

Table 4. Queries ordered by use with descriptions for analysis of search log

Query Title	Query Description
qry_00_no_dups	this query removes all duplicates from the main table
qry_01_unique_ip_number_of_queries	this query identifies all the large sessions (i.e., sessions with more than 100 queries)
qry_02_remove_large_sessions	this query removes the large session
qry_03_list_of_unique_ips	this query provides the number of queries submitted by each uid
qry_04_average_queries_per_user	this query provides the average, max, min, and stdev of queries by uid
qry_05_session_length	this query provides the session length as measured by number of queries within a given time period
qry_06_number_of_result_pages	this query provides the count of the number of uid that viewed a certain number of result pages
qry_07_average_results_pages	this query provides the average, max, min, and stdev of the number of results pages
qry_08_repeat_queries	this query provides the repeat queries and a count of those repeat queries
qry_09_boolean_queries	this query updates a field indicating whether or not the query contains Boolean operators
qry_10_query_operators	this query updates a field indicating whether or not the query contains a query operator other than Boolean
qry_11_sum_total_terms	this query sums up the total number of terms in the transaction log
qry_12_avearge_query_length	this query provides the average, max, min, and stdev of query length as measured by the number of terms
qry_13_cooc	this query provides a list of the term co-occurrence pairs in descending order of frequency
qry_14_list_of_query_lengths	this query provides a list an count of frequency of each query length
qry_15_term_frequencies	this query provides a list of terms and frequency of those terms in descending order
qry_16_cooc_total	this query provides the number of term co-occurrence pairs in the data set

searcher's other queries is a *modified query*. There can be several occurrences of different modified queries by a particular searcher. A subsequent query by the same searcher that is identical to one or more of the searcher's previous queries is an *identical query*.

In many Web search engine logs, when the searcher traverses to a new results page, this interaction is also logged as an *identical query*. In other logging systems, the application records the page rank. A results page is the list of results, either sponsored or organic (i.e., non-sponsored), returned by a Web search engine in response to a query. Using either *identical queries* or some results page field, one can analyze the result page viewing patterns of Web searchers.

One can examine other measures at the query level of analysis. A *unique query* refers to a query that is different from all other queries in the transaction log, regardless of the searcher. A *repeat query* is a query that appears more than once within the dataset by two or more searchers.

Query complexity examines the query syntax, including the use of advanced searching techniques such as Boolean and other query operators. *Failure rate* is a measure of the deviation of queries from the published rules of the search engine. The use of query syntax that the particular IR system does not support, but may be common on other IR systems, is *carry over*.

Session Level Analysis

At the session level of analysis, one primarily examines the within-session interactions (Hancock-Beaulieu, 2000). However, if the search log spanned more than one day or assigns some temporal limit to interactions from a particular user, one could examine between-sessions interactions. A *session interaction* is any specific exchange between the searcher and the system (i.e., submitting a query, clicking a hyperlink, etc.). A *searching episode* is defined as a series of interactions within a limited duration to address one or more information needs. This session duration is typically short, with Web researchers using between five and 120 minutes as a cutoff (c.f., He, Göker, & Harper, 2002; Jansen & Spink, 2003; Montgomery & Faloutsos, 2001; Silverstein et al., 1999). Each choice of time has an impact on the results, of course. The searcher may be multitasking (Miwa, 2001; Spink, 2004) within a searching episode, or the episode may be an instance of the searcher engaged in successive searching (Lin, 2002; Özmutlu, Özmutlu, & Spink, 2003; Spink, Wilson, Ellis, & Ford, 1998). This *session* definition is similar to the definition of a *unique visitor* used by commercial search engines and organizations to measure Web site traffic. The number of queries per searcher is the *session length*.

Session duration is the total time the user spent interacting with the search engine, including the time spent viewing the first and subsequent Web documents, except the final document. Session duration can therefore be measured from the time the user submits the first query until the user departs the search engine for the last time (i.e., does not return). This viewing time of the final Web document is not available since the Web search engine server does not record the time stamp. Naturally, the time between visits from the Web document to the search engine may not have been entirely spent viewing the Web document, which is a limitation of the measure.

A *Web document* is the Web page referenced by the URL on the search engine's results page. A Web document may be text or multimedia and, if viewed hierarchically, may contain a nearly unlimited number of sub-Web documents. A Web document may also contain URLs linking to other Web documents. From the results page, a searcher may click on a URL, (i.e., visit) one or more results from the listings on the result page. This is *click through analysis* and measures the page viewing behavior of Web searchers. One measures *document viewing duration* as the time from when a searcher clicks on a URL on a results page to the time that searcher returns to the search engine. Some researchers and practitioners refer to this type of analysis as *page view analysis. Click through analysis* is possible if the transaction log contains the appropriate data.

Conducting the Data Analysis

The key to successful SLA is conducting the analysis with an organized approach. One method is to sequentially number and label the queries (or coded modules) to correspond to the order of execution and to their function, since many of these queries must be executed in a certain order to obtain valid results. Many relational database management systems provide mechanisms to add descriptive properties to the queries. These can provide further explanations of the query function or relate these queries directly to research questions. Figure 3 illustrates the application of such an approach.

Figure 3 shows each query in sequence and provides a descriptive tag describing that query's function. To aid in reading, a list of queries is also provided in Appendix A.

One approaches SLA by conducting a series of standard analyses that are common to a wide variety of Web searching studies. Some of these analyses may directly address certain research

Figure 3. Sequentially numbered and descriptively labeled queries for SLA

Microsoft Access - [transaction_log_example : Database (Access 2000 file format)]

Name	Description	Modified	Created	Type
Create query in Design view				
Create query by using wizard				
qry_00_no_dups	this query remove all duplicates from the main table	9/20/2005 9:10:39 PM	8/12/2004 6:36:42 PM	Query: Make Table Query
qry_01_unique_ip_number_of_queries	this query identifies all the large sessions (i.e., sessions with more than 100 queries)	9/20/2005 9:13:58 PM	8/12/2004 6:36:42 PM	Query: Select Query
qry_02_remove_large_sessions	this query removes the large session	9/20/2005 9:16:54 PM	8/12/2004 6:36:42 PM	Query: Delete Query
qry_03_list_of_unique_ips	this query provides the number of queries submitted by each uid	9/20/2005 9:18:08 PM	8/12/2004 6:36:42 PM	Query: Select Query
qry_04_average_queries_per_user	this query provides the average, max, min, and stdev of queries by uid	9/20/2005 10:28:4...	8/12/2004 6:36:42 PM	Query: Select Query
qry_05_session_length	this query provides the session length as measured by number of queries within a given time period	9/20/2005 10:16:0...	8/12/2004 6:36:42 PM	Query: Select Query
qry_06_number_of_result_pages	this query provides the count of the number of uid that viewed a certain number of result pages	9/20/2005 10:16:1...	8/12/2004 6:36:42 PM	Query: Select Query
qry_07_average_results_pages	this query provides the average, max, min, and stdev of the number of results pages	9/20/2005 10:16:2...	8/12/2004 6:36:42 PM	Query: Select Query
qry_08_repeat_queries	this query provides the repeat queries and a count of those repeat queries	9/20/2005 10:16:4...	8/12/2004 6:36:43 PM	Query: Select Query
qry_09_boolean_queries	this query updates a fiedl indicating whether or not the query contains Boolean operators	9/20/2005 10:30:2...	8/12/2004 6:36:43 PM	Query: Update Query
qry_10_query_operators	this query updates a field indicating whether or not the query contains a query operator other than Bool...	9/20/2005 10:30:0...	8/12/2004 6:36:43 PM	Query: Update Query
qry_11_sum_total_terms	this query sums up the total number of terms in the transaction log	9/20/2005 10:17:1...	8/12/2004 6:36:43 PM	Query: Select Query
qry_12_avearge_query_length	this query provides the average, max, min, and stdev of query length as measured by the number of terms	9/20/2005 10:25:2...	8/12/2004 6:36:43 PM	Query: Select Query
qry_13_cooc	this query provides a lsit of the term co-occurrence pairs in descending order of frequency	9/20/2005 10:17:3...	8/12/2004 6:36:43 PM	Query: Select Query
qry_14_list_of_query_lengths	this query provides a list an count of frequency of each query length	9/20/2005 10:17:4...	8/12/2004 6:36:43 PM	Query: Select Query
qry_15_term_frequencies	this query provides a list of terms and frequency of of those terms in descending order	9/20/2005 10:17:4...	8/30/2004 3:22:42 PM	Query: Select Query
qry_16_cooc_total	this query provides the number of term co-occurence pairs in the data set	9/20/2005 10:17:5...	8/30/2004 3:25:25 PM	Query: Select Query

questions. Others may be the basis for more in-depth research analysis.

One typical question is "How many searchers have visited the search engine during this period?" One can determine this by using SQL query 4, (Appendix A). This query will provide a list of unique searchers and the number of queries they have submitted during the period. One can modify this and determine "How many searchers have visited the search engine on each day during this period?" with the SQL query 5, Appendix A. Naturally, a variety of statistical results can be determined using the previous queries. For example, one can determine the standard deviation of number of queries per day using the SQL query #6, Appendix A.

One may want to know each of the session lengths (i.e., the number of queries within a session) for each searcher, which SQL query #7 will provide. Similarly, one may desire the number of searchers who viewed a certain number of results pages, addressed by query #8, Appendix A.

One can calculate various statistical results on results page viewing, such as the maximum number of result pages viewed using SQL query #10, Appendix A. SQL query #11, Appendix A will present the number of queries per day. An important aspect for system designers is results caching, because one needs to know the number of repeat queries submitted by the entire set of searchers during the period. The SQL query #12, Appendix A will tell us this information.

In order to understand how searchers are interacting with a search engine, the use of Boolean operators is an important feature. The SQL query #13, Appendix A makes a table of interactions with Boolean operators within the queries. Since most search engines offer other query syntax than just Boolean operators, the SQL query #14, Appendix A makes a table of queries containing other query syntax.

The SQL query #15, Appendix A provides a count of the number of terms within the transaction log. One certainly wants to know about query length; SQL query #16, Appendix A provides various statistics on query length: SQL query #17 provides the frequency of terms pairs within the transaction log, SQL query #18 provides a count of the various query lengths, SQL query #19 provides a count of the various term frequencies, and SQL query #20 provides a count of the term pairs within the transaction log.

The results from this series of queries both provides us a wealth of information about our data (e.g., occurrences of session lengths, occurrences of query length, occurrences of repeat queries, most used terms, most used term pairs) and serves as the basis for further investigations (e.g., session complexity, query structure, query modifications, term relationships).

DISCUSSION

It is certainly important to understand both the strengths and limitations of SLA for Web searching. First concerning the strengths, SLA provides a method of collecting data from a great number of users. Given the current nature of the Web, search logs appears to be a reasonable and non-intrusive means of collecting user–system interaction data during the Web information searching process from a large number of searchers. One can easily collect data on hundreds of thousands to millions of interactions, depending on the traffic of the Web site.

Second, one can collect this data inexpensively. The costs are the software and storage. Third, the data collection is unobtrusive, so the interactions represent the unaltered behavior of searchers, assuming the data is from an operational searching site. Finally, search logs are, at present, the only method for obtaining significant amounts of search data within the complex environment that is the Web (Dumais, 2002). Of course, researchers can also be doing SLA from research sites or capture client-side data across multiple sites using a custom Web browser (for the purpose of data collection) that does not completely mimic the searcher's natural environment.

There are limitations of SLA, as with any methodology. First, there may be certain types of data not in the transaction log, individuals' identities being the most common example. An IP address typically represents the "user" in a search log. Since more than one person may use a computer, an IP address is an imprecise representation of the user. Search engines are overcoming this limitation somewhat by the use of cookies and page tagging.

Second, there is no way to collect demographic data when using search logs in a naturalistic setting. This constraint is true of many non-intrusive naturalistic studies. However, there are several sources for demographic data on the Web population based on observational and survey data. From these data sources, one may get reasonable estimations of needed demographic data. However, this still not attributable specific search data to specific sub-populations.

Third, a search log does not record the reasons for the search, the searcher motivations, or other qualitative aspects of use. This is certainly a limitation. In the instances where one needs this data, one should use transaction log analysis in conjunction with other data collection methods. However, this invasiveness then lessens the unobtrusiveness, which is an inherent advantage of search logs as a data collection method.

Fourth, the logged data may not be complete due to caching of server data on the client machine or proxy servers. This is an often mentioned limitation. In reality, this is a relatively minor concern for Web search engine research due to the method with which most search engines dynamically produce their results pages. For example, a user accesses the page of results from a search engine using the *Back* button of a browser. This navigation accesses the results page via the cache on the client machine. The Web server will not record this action. However, if the user clicks on any URL on that results page, functions coded on the results page redirects the click first to the Web server, from which the Web server records the visit to the Web site.

CONCLUSION

In this chapter, following the literature review, we presented a three-step methodology for conducting SLA, namely collecting, preparing, and analyzing. We then reviewed each step in detail, providing observations, guides, and lessons learned. We discussed the organization of the database at the ER-level, and we discussed the table design for standard search engine transaction logs. Furthermore, we provided 16 queries (Appendix B) one can use to conduct analysis. This presentation of the methodology at a detailed level of granularity will serve as an excellent basis for novice or experienced search log researchers.

Search logs are powerful tools for collecting data on the interactions between users and systems. Using this data, SLA can provide significant insights into user–system interactions, and it complements other methods of analysis by overcoming the limitations inherent in these methods. With respect to shortcomings, one can combine SLA with other data collection methods or other research results to improve the robustness of the analysis, when possible. Overall, SLA is a powerful tool for Web searching research, and the SLA process outlined here can be helpful in future Web searching research endeavors.

REFERENCES

Baeza-Yates, R., & Castillo, C. (2001, 1-5 May). *In Relating Web structure and user search behavior* (pp. 1-2). Paper presented at the 10th World Wide Web Conference, Hong Kong, China. ACM.

Bains, S. (1997). End-user searching behavior: Considering methodologies. *The Katharine Sharp*

Review, 1(4), http://www.lis.uiuc.edu/review/winter1997/bains.html.

Bates, M.J. (1990). Where should the person stop and the information search interface start? *Information Processing & Management,* 26(5), 575-591.

Belkin, N., Cool, C., Stein, A., & Theil, S. (1995). Cases, scripts, and information-seeking strategies: On the design of interactive information retrieval systems. *Expert Systems With Applications,* 9(3), 379-395.

Blecic, D., Bangalore, N.S., Dorsch, J.L., Henderson, C.L., Koenig, M.H., & Weller, A.C. (1998). Using transaction log analysis to improve opac retrieval results. *College & Research Libraries,* 59(1), 39 - 50.

Borgman, C.L., Hirsh, S.G., & Hiller, J. (1996). Rethinking online monitoring methods for information retrieval systems: From search product to search process. *Journal of the American Society for Information Science,* 47(7), 568-583.

Cacheda, F., & Viña, Á. (2001, July). *In Experiences retrieving information in the World Wide Web* (pp. 72-79). Paper presented at the 6th IEEE Symposium on Computers and Communications, Hammamet, Tunisia. IEEE.

Chamberlain, K. (1995, 6 November). *What is grounded theory?* Retrieved 17 September, 2005, from http://kerlins.net/bobbi/research/qualresearch/bibliography/gt.html

Chau, M., Fang, X., & Sheng, O.R.L. (2006). Analyzing the query logs of a Website search engine. *Journal of the American Society for Information Science and Technology,* 56(13), 1363-1376.

Choo, C., Betlor, B., & Turnbull, D. (1998). In A *behavioral model of information seeking on the Web: Preliminary results of a study of how managers and it specialists use the Web* (pp. 290-302). Paper presented at the 61st Annual Meeting of the American Society for Information Science, Pittsburgh, PA. ASIS.

Choo, C., & Turnbull, D. (2000). Information seeking on the Web: An integrated model of browsing and searching. *First Monday,* 5(2), http://firstmonday.org/issues/issue5_2/choo/index.html.

Cooper, M.D. (1998). Design considerations in instrumenting and monitoring Web-based information retrieval systems. *Journal of the American Society for Information Science,* 49(10), 903–919.

Croft, W., Cook, R., & Wilder, D. (1995, 11 - 13 June). In *Providing government information on the internet: Experiences with thomas* (pp. 19-24). Paper presented at the the Digital Libraries Conference, Austin, TX.

Drott, M.C. (1998). *In Using Web server logs to improve site design* (pp. 43 - 50). Paper presented at the the 16th Annual International Conference on Computer Documentation, Quebec, Canada. ACM.

Dumais, S.T. (2002, 7-11 May). *Web experiments and test collections.* Retrieved 20 April, 2003, from http://www2002.org/presentations/dumais.pdf

Efthimiadis, E.N., & Robertson, S.E. (1989). Feedback and interaction in information retrieval. In C. Oppenheim (Ed.), *Perspectives in information management* (pp. 257-272). London: Butterworths.

Fourie, I. (2002, 24 -25 October). *A review of Web information-seeking/searching studies (2000 - 2002): Implications for research in the south african context* (pp. 49-75). Paper presented at the Progress in Library and Information Science in Southern Africa: 2d Biannial DISSAnet Conference, Pretoria, South Africa. SAOUG.

Fourie, I., & van den Berg, H. (2003, June). *A story told by nexus transaction logs: What to make of it* (pp. 1 - 19). Paper presented at the 7th

Southern African Online Meeting, Muldersdrift, South Africa. SAOUG.

Glaser, B., & Strauss, A. (1967). *The discovery of grounded theory: Strategies for qualitative research.* Chicago, IL: Aldine Publishing Co.

Griffiths, J.R., Hartley, R.J., & Willson, J.P. (2002). An improved method of studying user-system interaction by combining transaction log analysis and protocol analysis. *Information Research,* 7(4), http://InformationR.net/ir/7-4/paper139.html.

Hancock-Beaulieu, M. (2000). Interaction in information searching and retrieval. *Journal of Documentation,* 56(4), 431-439.

Hancock-Beaulieu, M., Robertson, S., & Nielsen, C. (1990). *Evaluation of online catalogues: An assessment of methods* (bl research paper 78). London: The British Library Research and Development Department.

Hargittai, E. (2002). Beyond logs and surveys: In-depth measures of people's web use skills. *Journal of the American Society for Information Science and Technology,* 53(14), 1239-1244.

He, D., Göker, A., & Harper, D.J. (2002). Combining evidence for automatic Web session identification. *Information Processing & Management,* 38(5), 727-742.

Hilbert, D., & Redmiles, D. (1998, 10-13 May). *Agents for collecting application usage data over the Internet* (pp. 149-156). Paper presented at the Second International Conference on Autonomous Agents (Agents '98), Minneapolis/St. Paul, MN.

Hilbert, D., & Redmiles, D. (2001, 9-13 July). *Large-scale collection of usage data to inform design* (pp. 569-576). Paper presented at the Eight IFIP TC 13 Conference on Human-Computer Interaction (INTERACT 2001), Tokyo, Japan.

Jansen, B.J. (2006). Search log analysis: What is it; what's been done; how to do it. *Library and Information Science Research,* 28(3), 407-432.

Jansen, B.J., & Pooch, U. (2001). Web user studies: A review and framework for future work. *Journal of the American Society of Information Science and Technology,* 52(3), 235-246.

Jansen, B.J., Ramadoss, R., Zhang, M., & Zang, N. (2006). Wrapper: An application for evaluating exploratory searching outside of the lab, SIGIR 2006 Workshop on Evaluating Exploratory Search Systems. *The 29th Annual International ACM SIGIR Conference on Research & Development on Information Retrieval (SIGIR2006).* Seattle, Washington, USA.

Jansen, B.J., & Spink, A. (2003, 23 - 26 June). *In An analysis of Web information seeking and use: Documents retrieved versus documents viewed* (pp. 65-69). Paper presented at the 4th International Conference on Internet Computing, Las Vegas, Nevada.

Jansen, B.J., & Spink, A. (2005). How are we searching the World Wide Web? A comparison of nine search engine transaction logs. *Information Processing & Management,* 42(1), 248-263.

Jansen, B.J., Spink, A., & Pedersen, J. (2005). Trend analysis of AltaVista Web searching. *Journal of the American Society for Information Science and Technology,* 56(6), 559-570.

Jansen, B.J., Spink, A., & Saracevic, T. (2000). Real life, real users, and real needs: A study and analysis of user queries on the Web. *Information Processing & Management,* 36(2), 207-227.

Jones, S., Cunningham, S., & McNab, R. (1998, June 1998). *In Usage analysis of a digital library* (pp. 293-294). Paper presented at the the Third ACM Conference on Digital Libraries, Pittsburgh, PA. ACM.

Kelly, D. (2004). *Understanding implicit feedback and document preference: A naturalistic user study.* New Brunswick: Rutgers, The State University of New Jersey.

Kinsella, J., & Bryant, P. (1987). Online public access catalogue research in the united kingdom: An overview. *Library Trends,* 35(4), 619 - 629.

Korfhage, R. (1997). *Information storage and retrieval.* New York: Wiley.

Kurth, M. (1993). The limits and limitations of transaction log analysis. *Library Hi Tech,* 11(2), 98-104.

Lin, S.-J. (2002, 9-11 August). *In Design space of personalized indexing: Enhancing successive Web searching for transmuting information problems* (pp. 1092 - 1100). Paper presented at the Eighth Americas Conference on Information Systems, Dallas, Texas. AIS.

McGrath, J.E. (1994). Methodology matters: Doing research in the behavioral and social sciences. In R. Baecker & W.A.S. Buxton (Eds.), *Readings in human-computer interaction: An interdisciplinary approach* (2nd ed., pp. 152-169). San Mateo, CA: Morgan Kaufman Publishers.

Meister, D., & Sullivan, D. (1967). *Evaluation of user reactions to a prototype on-line information retrieval system: Report to nasa by the bunker-ramo corporation.* Report number nasa cr-918. Oak Brook, IL: Bunker-Ramo Corporation.

Millsap, L., & Ferl, T. (1993). Search patterns of remote users: An analysis of opac transaction logs. *Information Technology and Libraries,* 11(3), 321-343.

Miwa, M. (2001, 2-4 February). *In User situations and multiple levels of users goals in information problem solving processes of askeric users* (Vol. 38, pp. 355-371). Paper presented at the the 2001 Annual Meeting of the American Society for Information Sciences and Technology, San Francisco, CA, USA. ASIS.

Montgomery, A., & Faloutsos, C. (2001). Identifying web browsing trends and patterns. *IEEE Computer,* 34(7), 94-95.

Moukdad, H., & Large, A. (2001). Users' perceptions of the web as revealed by transaction log analysis. *Online Information Review,* 25(6), 349-358.

Nicholas, D., Huntington, P., Lievesley, N., & Withey, R. (1999). Cracking the code: Web log analysis. *Online and CD ROM Review,* 23(5), 263-269.

Özmutlu, S., Özmutlu, H.C., & Spink, A. (2003, 23 - 26 June). *In A study of multitasking Web searching* (pp. 145-150). Paper presented at the the IEEE ITCC'03: international Conference on information Technology: Coding and Computing, Las Vegas, Nevada. IEEE.

Park, S., Bae, H., & Lee, J. (2005). End user searching: A Web log analysis of NAVER, a Korean Web search engine. *Library & Information Science Research,* 27(2), 203-221.

Penniman, W.D. (1975, 26-30 October). In C.W.H.L. Tighe (Ed.), *A stochastic process analysis of online user behavior* (pp. 147-148). Paper presented at the The Annual Meeting of the American Society for Information Science, Washington, DC. ASIS.

Peters, T. (1993). The history and development of transaction log analysis. *Library Hi Tech,* 42(11), 41-66.

Phippen, A., Sheppard, L., & Furnell, S. (2004). A practical evaluation of Web analytics. *Internet Research: Electronic Networking Applications and Policy,* 14(4), 284-293.

Pitkow, J.E. (1997, 7-11 April). *In search of reliable usage data on the www* (pp. 1343-1355). Paper presented at the Santa Clara, CA, the Sixth International World Wide Web Conference. Elsevier.

Rice, R.E., & Borgman, C.L. (1983). The use of computer-monitored data in information science. *Journal of the Amercian Society for Information Science,* 44(1), 247-256.

Ross, N., & Wolfram, D. (2000). End user searching on the internet: An analysis of term pair topics submitted to the excite search engine. *Journal of the American Society for Information Science, 51*(10), 949-958.

Sandore, B., Flaherty, P., & Kaske, N.K. (1993). A manifesto regarding the future of transaction log analysis. *Library Hi Tech, 11*(2), 105-111.

Saracevic, T. (1997, 1-6 November). *In Extension and application of the stratified model of information retrieval interaction* (Vol. 34, pp. 313-327). Paper presented at the The Annual Meeting of the American Society for Information Science, Washington, DC.

Silverstein, C., Henzinger, M., Marais, H., & Moricz, M. (1999). Analysis of a very large Web search engine query log. *SIGIR Forum, 33*(1), 6-12.

Spink, A. (2004). Multitasking information behavior and information task switching: An exploratory study. *Journal of Documentation, 60*(3), 336-345.

Spink, A., & Jansen, B.J. (2004). *Web search: Public searching of the Web.* New York: Kluwer.

Spink, A., Wilson, T., Ellis, D., & Ford, F. (1998, April 1998). Modeling users' successive searches in digital environments. *D-Lib Magazine.*

Sullivan, D. (2001, November 6). *Spiderspotting: When a search engine, robot or crawler visits.* Retrieved 5 August, 2003, from http://www.searchenginewatch.com/webmasters/article.php/2168001

Toms, E.G., Freund, L., & Li, C. (2004). Wiire: The Web interactive information retrieval experimentation system prototype. *Information Processing & Management, 40*(4), 655-675.

Wang, P., Berry, M., & Yang, Y. (2003). Mining longitudinal Web queries: Trends and patterns. *Journal of the American Society for Information Science and Technology, 54*(8), 743-758.

Wu, K.-L., Yu, P.S., & Ballman, A. (1998). Speedtracer: A Web usage mining and analysis tool. *IBM Systems Journal, 37*(1), 89-107.

Yuan, W., & Meadow, C.T. (1999). A study of the use of variables in information retrieval user studies. *Journal of the American Society for Information Science, 50*(2), 140-150.

KEY TERMS

Search Log: An electronic record of interactions that have occurred during a searching episode between a Web search engine and users searching for information on that Web search engine.

Search Log Analysis (SLA): The use of data collected in a search log to investigate particular research questions concerning interactions among Web users, the Web search engine, or the Web content during searching episodes.

Interactions: The physical expressions of communication exchanges between the searcher and the system.

Search Log Analysis (SLA) Process: A three stage process of collection, preparation and analysis.

APPENDIX A

SQL Query 00:

```
qry_00_no_dups
SELECT tbl_main.uid, tbl_main.date, tbl_main.search_url, Count(tbl_main.search_url)
    AS CountOfsearch_url, First(tbl_main.thetime) AS FirstOfthetime,
    First(tbl_main.qid) AS FirstOfqid INTO tbl_searching_episodes
FROM tbl_main
GROUP BY tbl_main.uid, tbl_main.date, tbl_main.search_url;
```

SQL Query 01:

```
qry_01_unique_ip_number_of_queries
SELECT tbl_searching_episodes.uid
FROM tbl_searching_episodes
GROUP BY tbl_searching_episodes.uid
HAVING (((Count(tbl_searching_episodes.uid))>=100));
```

SQL Query 02:

```
qry_02_remove_large_sessions
DELETE tbl_searching_episodes.qid, tbl_searching_episodes.uid,
tbl_searching_episodes.thetime, tbl_searching_episodes.search_url,
tbl_searching_episodes.qtot, tbl_searching_episodes.uid
FROM tbl_searching_episodes
WHERE (((tbl_searching_episodes.uid)="[inset values here]"));
```

SQL Query 03:

```
qry_03_list_of_unique_ips
SELECT tbl_searching_episodes.uid, Count(tbl_searching_episodes.search_url) AS
CountOfsearch_url
FROM tbl_searching_episodes
GROUP BY tbl_searching_episodes.uid
ORDER BY Count(tbl_searching_episodes.search_url) DESC;
```

SQL Query 04:

```
qry_04_average_queries_per_user
SELECT Avg(qry_03_list_of_unique_ips.CountOfsearch_url) AS
AvgOfCountOfsearch_url
FROM qry_03_list_of_unique_ips;
```

SQL Query 05:

qry_05_session_length
SELECT qry_03_list_of_unique_ips.CountOfsearch_url,
Count(qry_03_list_of_unique_ips.CountOfsearch_url) AS CountOfCountOfsearch_url
FROM qry_03_list_of_unique_ips
GROUP BY qry_03_list_of_unique_ips.CountOfsearch_url
ORDER BY Count(qry_03_list_of_unique_ips.CountOfsearch_url) DESC;

SQL Query 06:

qry_06_number_of_result_pages
SELECT tbl_searching_episodes.qtot, Count(tbl_searching_episodes.qtot) AS CountOfqtot
FROM tbl_searching_episodes
GROUP BY tbl_searching_episodes.qtot
ORDER BY tbl_searching_episodes.qtot;

SQL Query 07:

qry_07_average_results_pages
SELECT Avg(tbl_searching_episodes.qtot) AS AvgOfqtot
FROM tbl_searching_episodes;

SQL Query 08:

qry_08_repeat_queries
SELECT tbl_searching_episodes.search_url, Count(tbl_searching_episodes.search_url) AS CountOfsearch_url
FROM tbl_searching_episodes
GROUP BY tbl_searching_episodes.search_url
ORDER BY Count(tbl_searching_episodes.search_url) DESC;

SQL Query 09:

qry_09_boolean_queries
UPDATE tbl_searching_episodes SET tbl_searching_episodes.boolean = True
WHERE (((tbl_searching_episodes.search_url) Like " and *" Or*
(tbl_searching_episodes.search_url) Like " or *" Or*
(tbl_searching_episodes.search_url) Like " and not *"));*

SQL Query 10:

qry_10_query_operators
UPDATE tbl_searching_episodes SET tbl_searching_episodes.operator = True
WHERE (((tbl_searching_episodes.search_url) Like '"*' Or*
(tbl_searching_episodes.search_url) Like "+*" Or (tbl_searching_episodes.search_url)*
Like "[*]*" Or (tbl_searching_episodes.search_url) Like "*[?]*"));*

SQL Query 11:

qry_11_sum_total_terms
SELECT Sum(tblterms.tfreq) AS SumOftfreq
FROM tblterms;

SQL Query 12:

qry_12_average_query_length
SELECT Avg(tbl_searching_episodes.qry_length) AS AvgOfqry_length
FROM tbl_searching_episodes;

SQL Query 13:

qry_13_cooc
SELECT tblterms.term, tblterms.term, tblcooc.tot
FROM tblterms INNER JOIN tblcooc ON (tblterms.termid = tblcooc.cid2) AND
(tblterms.termid = tblcooc.cid1)
ORDER BY tblcooc.tot DESC;

SQL Query 14:

qry_14_list_of_query_lengths
SELECT tbl_searching_episodes.qry_length, Count(tbl_searching_episodes.qry_length)
AS CountOfqry_length
FROM tbl_searching_episodes
GROUP BY tbl_searching_episodes.qry_length
ORDER BY Count(tbl_searching_episodes.qry_length) DESC;

SQL Query 15:

qry_15_term_frequencies
SELECT tblterms.tfreq
FROM tblterms
GROUP BY tblterms.tfreq
ORDER BY tblterms.tfreq;

SQL Query 16:

qry_16_cooc_total
SELECT Sum(tblcooc.tot) AS SumOftot
FROM tblcooc;

Chapter VII
Uses, Limitations, and Trends in Web Analytics

Anthony Ferrini*
Acquiremarketing.com, USA

Jakki J. Mohr*
University of Montana, USA

ABSTRACT

As the Web's popularity continues to grow and as new uses of the Web are developed, the importance of measuring the performance of a given Website as accurately as possible also increases. In this chapter, we discuss the various uses of Web analytics (how Web log files are used to measure a Website's performance), as well as the limitations of these analytics. We discuss options for overcoming these limitations, new trends in Web analytics—including the integration of technology and marketing techniques—and challenges posed by new Web 2.0 technologies. After reading this chapter, readers should have a nuanced understanding of the "how-to's" of Web analytics.

INTRODUCTION

Effective Website management requires a way to track not only the traffic (number of visitors) at a particular Website, but also what those visitors are doing at the particular Website. Importantly, effective Website management requires a way to map the behavior of the visitors to the site against the particular objectives and purpose of the site.

Many tools have been devised to help assess Website performance; these tools are known generally as *Web metrics*, or the indicators used to measure Website performance (Napier, et al, 2003; Napier, et al, 2001; Schneider, 2007). Many Web metrics are available from the server (the computer) on which the Website is hosted, or "served up," on the Internet. In particular, the server records data for every time a browser hits a particular Web page, and includes information for every action a visitor at that particular Website takes; these data, known as *log files*, include, for example, who is visiting the Website (the visitor's URL, or Web address), the IP address (numeric identification) of the computer the visitor is browsing from, the date and time of each visit, which pages the visitor viewed, how long the visitor viewed the site, and other types of information (discussed subsequently). *Log file analysis*, also known as Web log analytics or more simply *Web analytics*, is the study of the log files from a particular Website. The purpose of log file analysis is to assess the performance of the Website; software (called log analysis software, such as that available from WebTrends, Web Side Story, or Urchin Web Analytics, cf. Schneider, 2007, p. 380) pulls data from the server log files and presents the information in a variety of useful templates.

Although Web analytics can provide very useful information, it also has several drawbacks. New techniques in Web analytics have been developed to overcome some of these drawbacks. Moreover, as the Internet has evolved with the use of new *Web 2.0* technologies (such as social networking, tagging, blogging, and so forth), the ability to effectively measure the performance of a given Website becomes more complicated.

The purpose of our chapter is three-fold. First, we will discuss the current ways in which log file data are used to evaluate Website performance; in addition, we discuss some of the limitations of, and remedies for, log file analysis. Second, we discuss new techniques in Web analytics that augment traditional log file analysis, providing a more robust picture of Website performance. Third, we discuss trends in Web analytics, highlighting issues related to the complications arising from Web 2.0 technologies. After reading this chapter, readers should have a nuanced understanding of the "how-to's" of Web analytics. Importantly, we note that our chapter does not address search engine positioning and how to evaluate it; nor does our chapter address privacy and trust issues, which are important topics in and of themselves.[1] Moreover, to be maximally useful, Web analytics should be used in conjunction with a robust strategic marketing process (e.g., Mohr, Sengupta, and Slater 2005).

CURRENT USES OF, AND PROBLEMS WITH, WEB ANALYTICS

This section addresses the state-of-the-art with respect to Web analytics, and is organized around the following issues:

- What data is collected in Web analytics?
- How is it obtained?
- Who uses the data?
- For what purposes are the data used?
- What are the deficiencies and limitations with Web analytics?
- How can these deficiencies be addressed?

Data Included In, and Uses Of, Web Analytics

Table 1 provides an overview of the data that are collected in Web analytics. As mentioned previously, these data are obtained by the computer server on which the Web page resides; the server records every action each visitor takes on a particular Website.

Web logs contain potentially useful information for anyone working with a Website—from server administrators to designers to marketers—who needs to assess Website usability and effectiveness. Website administrators use the data in log files to monitor the availability of a Website to make sure the site is online, available, and without technical errors that might prevent access. Administrators can also predict and plan for growth in server resources and monitor for unusual and possibly malicious activity. For instance, by monitoring past Web usage logs for

*Table 1. Types of data in log file analysis**

Hit	Refers to each element of a Web page downloaded to a viewer's Web browser (such as Internet Explorer, Mozilla, or Netscape); hits do *not* correspond in any direct fashion to the number of pages viewed or number of visitors to a site. For example, if a viewer downloads a Web page with three graphics, the Web log file will show four hits: one for the Web page and one for each of the three graphics.
Unique visitors	The actual number of viewers to the Website that came from a unique IP address (see IP address below).
New/Return visitors	The number of first-time visitors to the site compared to returning visitors.
Page views	The number of times a specified Web page has been viewed; shows exactly what content people are (or are not) viewing at a Website. Every time a visitor hits the page refresh button, another page view is logged.
Page views per visitor	The number of page views divided by the number of visitors; measures how many pages viewers look at each time they visit a Website.
IP address	A numeric identifier for a computer. (The format of an IP address is a 32-bit numeric address written as four numbers separated by periods; each number can be zero to 255. For example, 1.160.10.240 could be an IP address.) The IP address can be used to determine a viewer's origin (i.e., by country); it also can be used to determine the particular computer network a Website's visitors are coming from.
Visitor location	The geographic location of the visitor.
Visitor language	The language setting on the visitor's computer.
Referring pages/sites (URLs)	Indicates how visitors get to a Website (i.e., whether they type the URL, or Web address, directly into a Web browser or whether they click through from a link at another site).
Keywords	If the referring URL is a search engine, the keywords (search string) that the visitor used can be determined.
Browser type	The type of browser software a visitor is using (i.e., Netscape, Mozilla, Internet Explorer, etc.)
Operating system version	The specific operating system the site visitor uses.
Screen resolution	The display settings for the visitor's computer.
Java or Flash-enabled	Whether or not the visitor's computer allows Java (a programming language for applications on the Web) and/or Flash (a software tool that allows Web pages to be displayed with animation, or motion).
Connection speed	Whether visitors are accessing the Website from a slower dial-up connection, high-speed broadband, or T1.
Errors	The number of errors recorded by the server, such as a "404-file not found" error; can be used to identify broken links and other problems at the Website.
Visit duration	Average time spent on the site (length the visitor stays on the site before leaving). Sites that retain visitors longer are referred to as "sticky" sites.
Visitor paths/navigation	How visitors navigate the Website, by specific pages, most common entry pages (the first page accessed by a visitor at a Website) and exit points (the page from which a visitor exits a Website), etc. For example, if a large number of visitors leave the site after looking at a particular page, the analyst might infer that they either found the information they needed, or alternatively, there might be a problem with that page (is it the page where shipping and handling fees are posted, which maybe are large enough to turn visitors away?).
Bounce rate	The percentage of visitors who leave the site after the first page; calculated by the number of visitors who visit only a single page divided by the number of total visits. The bounce rate is sometimes used as another indicator of "stickiness."

** Napier, Judd, Rivers, and Adams (2003); see also www.webopedia.com*

visitor activity, a site administrator can predict future activity during holidays and other spikes in usage and plan to add more servers and bandwidth to accommodate the expected traffic. In order to watch for potential attacks on a Website, administrators can also monitor Web usage logs for abnormal activity on the Website such as repetitive login attempts, unusually large numbers of requests from a single IP address, and so forth.

Website designers use log files to assess the user experience and site usability. Understanding the user environment provides Web designers with the information they need to create a successful design. While ensuring a positive user experience on a Website requires more than merely good design, log files do provide readily-available information to assist with the initial design as well as continuous improvement of the Website. Web designers can find useful information about the type of operating system (e.g., Windows XP or Linux), screen settings (e.g., screen resolution), and the type of browser (e.g., Internet Explorer or Mozilla) used to access the site. This information allows designers to create Web pages which display well for the majority of users. For instance, many major Website destinations which have a wide variety of users, like Web portals such as Yahoo or MSN, can identify the computer environment for these many visitors, and design Web pages which cater to the most common environment.

Moreover, log files can show how a viewer navigates through the various pages of a given Website, or the *click trail*, also known as *clickstream data*. Clickstream data can show, say, what goods a customer looked at on an e-commerce site, whether the customer purchased those goods, what goods a customer looked at but did not purchase, what ads generated many click-throughs but resulted in few purchases, and so forth (Inmon, 2001). Because the details in log files give clues as to which Website features are successful, and which are not, they assist Website designers in the process of continuous improvement by adding new features, improving upon current features, or deleting unused features. Then, by monitoring the Web logs for user reaction (increased or decreased usage of the Website's features), and making adjustments based on those reactions, the Website designer can improve the overall experience for Website visitors on a continuous basis.

Another useful piece of information to provide input on Website design comes from analyzing the actual searches that visitors perform on the site itself. If the Website has a search form on its site (e.g., possibly it has downloaded a Google search bar for its own site visitors to use), the analyst can examine the keywords that visitors searched. This provides clues about the visitor's interests at the site, and, if enough visitors are looking for a particular piece of information, the site designer may want to add it or feature it more prominently.

Finally, Web logs are also used for marketing purposes to understand the effectiveness of various on- and off-line marketing efforts. By analyzing the Web logs, marketers can determine which marketing efforts are the most effective. Marketers can track the effectiveness of online advertising, such as banner ads and other links, through the use of the referrer logs ("referring URLs"). Examination of the referring URLs indicates how visitors got to the Website, showing, say, whether they typed the URL (Web address) directly into their Web browser or whether they clicked through from a link at another site.

In addition, marketers can assess the effectiveness of search engine listings by analyzing which search engines visitors came from and which search queries (keywords typed into the search engine) they used. Oftentimes, the best keywords to use (both for search engine positioning and paid search) are not always obvious. For example, a popcorn chain in New Jersey had been using keywords like "gourmet popcorn" and "popcorn tins." But, when it started using Web analytics, the company learned that more people were searching by "chocolate popcorn" and "caramel popcorn", so it boosted the use of those phrases, both in the site content as well as in its marketing efforts (Spors, 2007). Moreover, it found that most visitors were typing "kettle corn" as two words rather than the one word that the site was using, so it added a two-word version in its strategies as well.

Web logs can also be used to track the amount of activity from offline advertising, such as magazine and other print ads, by utilizing a unique URL in each offline ad that is run. Unlike online advertising which shows results in log information about the referring Website, offline advertising requires a way to track whether or not the ad generated a response from the viewer. One way to do this is to use the ad to drive traffic to a particular Website. So, many advertisers place a unique URL in each offline ad that they run; each unique URL directs viewers who saw the ad to a different Web address than the Website's regular URL. Web marketers can create a unique URL by buying a completely new domain name (Web address) or by using a subdomain, such as subdomain.domain.com, or by creating unique pages within the current site structure, such as www.domain.com/unique. Any visitor traffic that enters the Website via the unique URL is assumed to have been driven there by the offline ad – the only means by which a visitor could have discovered the specific URL. So, by tracking the number of visitors to each unique URL, the advertiser can evaluate the effectiveness of different offline ads.

Limitations of, and Remedies for, Log File Data

Despite the wealth of useful information available in log files, the data also suffer from limitations, creating challenges for the people using them. The limitations of Web log files generally arise because certain types of visitor data are not logged, such as information about the person visiting the site rather than just the computer visiting the site. Further, some of the data that are logged may be incomplete, such as visit duration as discussed below. As a result, conclusions based on this data may lead to unsound business decisions.

For example, visit duration is a commonly-reported statistic in Web log reports. However, Web logs do not provide an accurate way to determine visit duration. Visit duration is calculated based on the time spent between the first page request and the last page request. If the next page request never occurs, duration can't be calculated and will be under-reported. Web logs also can't account for the user who views a page, leaves the computer for twenty minutes, and comes back and clicks to the next page. In this situation, the visit duration would be highly inflated.

Another source of inaccuracy is in visitor count data. As discussed in the previous section (Table 1), most Web log reports give two possible ways to count visitors – hits and unique visits. The very definition of hits is a source of unreliability. By definition, each time a Web page is loaded, each element of the Web page (i.e., different graphics on the same page) is counted as a separate "hit." Therefore, even with one page view, multiple hits are recorded as a function of the number of different elements on a given Web page. The net result is that hits are highly inflated numbers.

Visit counts are also inaccurate because most Web analytics programs define a visit as a sequence of page requests from a unique visitor within a certain amount of time, usually 30 minutes. Counting visits in this manner is inaccurate because it relies on an arbitrary 30-minute timeframe to define a visit. Any visit longer than 30 minutes is counted as another visit. So, if a Website provides extensive information, or if a visitor is researching information on a Website for more than 30 minutes, visit counts will be inflated.

Another source of inaccuracy arises from the way in which unique visitors are measured. Web log reports measure unique visitors based on the IP address, or network address, recorded in the log file. However, as discussed in Table 2, due to the nature of different Internet technologies, IP addresses do not always correspond to an individual visitor in a one-to-one relationship. In other words, there is no accurate way to identify each individual visitor. Depending upon the particular situation, this causes the count of unique visitors to be either over- or under-reported. The main reason for this problem is that several Internet technologies make it difficult to identify individual users (or unique visitors). Table 2 describes these various Internet technologies and their impact on Web analytics.

When it comes to Web logs, decision makers must understand these potential inaccuracies caused by different technologies. Without the ability to accurately identify individual users, there isn't an accurate way to determine the exact number of unique visitors to a Website. As a result, many other items within a normal Web log report also provide inaccurate information, leading to erroneous conclusions about Website activity. For example, Web log reporting software often generates secondary reports based on the original log data. If the original log data, such as hits and unique visitors, are inflated or deflated, the secondary reports will also be inaccurate – leading to unsound business decisions. Say the secondary reports calculate the return on investment for marketing expenditure (the ratio of money gained or lost relative to the total amount of money invested). If the return on a specific marketing expenditure is computed as a function of the number of visitors the campaign attracted, and if this calculation incorporates an inaccurate visitor count, the conclusion regarding the effectiveness of the campaign will also be inaccurate. As a result, decision makers will base their decisions on misleading information.

In particular, the under-reporting of visitors is a serious issue for online advertising. If the ad is cached (see Table 2), nobody knows that the ad was delivered. As a result, the organization

Table 2. Internet technologies and complications for Web analytics

Proxy Servers	A proxy server is a network server which acts as an intermediary between the user's computer and the actual server on which the Website resides; they are used to improve service for groups of users. First, it saves the results of all requests for a particular Web page for a certain amount of time. Then, it intercepts all requests to the real server to see if it can fulfill the request itself. Say user X requests a certain Web page (called Page 1); sometime later, user Y requests the same page. Instead of forwarding the request to the Web server where Page 1 resides, which can be a time-consuming operation, the proxy server simply returns the Page 1 that it already fetched for user X. Since the proxy server is often on the same network as the user, this is a much faster operation. If the proxy server cannot serve a stored page, then it forwards the request to the real server. *Importantly, pages served by the proxy server are not logged in the log files, resulting in inaccuracies in counting site traffic.* Major online services (such as America Online, MSN and Yahoo) and other large organizations employ an array of proxy servers in which all user requests are made through a single IP address. This situation causes Web log files to significantly under-report unique visitor traffic. On the other hand, sometimes home users with an Internet Service Provider get assigned a new IP address each time they connect to the Internet. This causes the opposite effect of inflating the number of unique visits in the Web logs.
Firewalls	A proxy server can also function as a firewall in an organization, acting as an intermediary device, but for the purpose of security rather than efficiency. Firewalls are used by organizations to protect internal users from outside threats on the Internet, or to prevent employees from accessing a specific set of Websites. Firewalls hide the actual IP address for specific user computers and instead present a single generic IP address to the Internet for all its users. *Hence, this contributes to under-reporting unique visitor traffic in Web analytics.*
Caching	Although there are many nuances to it (such as "browser caching" and "server caching"), in general caching refers to the technique in which most Web browser software keeps a copy of each Web page, called a cache, in its memory. So, rather than requesting the same page again from the server (for example, if the user clicks the "back" button), the browser on her computer will display a copy of the page rather than make another new request to the server. Many Internet Service Providers and large organizations cache Web pages in an effort to serve content more quickly and reduce bandwidth usage. As with the use of proxy servers, caching poses a problem because *Web log files don't report these cached page views. As a result, once again, Web log files can significantly under-report the actual visitor count.*

delivering the ad doesn't get paid. *Cache busting* is a popular term that refers to technologies that solve this problem. These technologies, such as "page tagging," are discussed next.

Correcting Deficiencies in Log File Data

Some remedies exist for the visitor count inaccuracies commonly found in Web analytics: cookies and page tagging.

Cookies are small bits of data that a Website leaves on a visitor's hard drive after that visitor has hit a Website. Then, each time the user's Web browser requests a new Web page from the server, the cookie on the user's hard drive can be read by the server. These cookie data can be used in several ways. First—even if multiple viewers access the same Website through the same proxy server, for example—each viewer has a unique cookie; therefore, a unique session is recorded and a more accurate visitor count can be obtained. Cookies also make it possible to track users across multiple sessions (i.e., when they return to the site subsequently); this allows a computation of new versus returning visitors. Finally, third-party cookies – often set by advertising companies such as DoubleClick -- allow the Website to assess what other sites the visitor has visited; this enables personalization of the Website in terms of the content that is displayed.

Note, however, that cookies are *not* included in normal log files. Therefore, only a Web analytics solution which supports cookie tracking can utilize the benefits. (Alternatively, Web log files generally utilize a combination of the specific computer's numeric IP address and user agent—browser, search engine spider, or mobile phone—to identify a unique user, with the assumption that the two combined are a close estimation of a unique user.)

Due to concerns about privacy (cookies show which Websites a person has previously visited), many users dislike the idea of cookies being saved to their computer. As a result, many computer users have become savvy in removing cookies, deleting them from their hard drives on a regular basis. Many users even disable the cookie feature in their browser's security options.

As users become more sophisticated, the technologies to make it harder for users both to delete cookies and to surf anonymously become more sophisticated as well, and the cookie arena is no exception. One software program commonly used on the Internet, Macromedia Flash (which allows animation, or motion on the Webpage) offers an alternative that is harder for users to delete than the traditional browser cookie. Any computer user who has Flash software installed with their normal Web browser will have *Flash cookies* on their hard drive. These cookies are different (and separate) from the normal browser cookies. As a result, when users clear their browser cache to delete any stored cookies, the Flash cookies are not cleared out. Therefore, Flash cookies present a new opportunity for tracking unique visitors—although in the future users might also learn how to properly remove Flash cookies.

Another method for collecting information that overcomes some of the limitations in measuring Website activity is called *page tagging* (www.BruceClay.com). This technique has its origins in hit counters, a small image at the bottom of the Web page which looks and functions much like a car odometer; the hit counter increases by one count with each additional page view. Hit counters originated with many personal and small business Websites as a simple way to track how many people were visiting the site. As hit counters evolved, Website developers and marketers learned that they could identify additional information beyond the basic number of page views on the counter. Page tagging, which uses the same basic principle as hit counters, is a more robust system that relies on embedding a small piece of Javascript software code on the Web page itself. Then, when the computer user visits the Web page, the Java code is activated by the computer user's browser software. Referred to as "client-side technology" (because the tagging occurs on the user's computer when he loads the Web page) — as opposed to a server-side technology in which the log file records activity generated at the server — page tagging offers a significant advantage with respect to the "caching" problem found with server log files. Log files cannot track visitor activity from cached pages because the Web server never acknowledges the request. However, since page tagging is located on the Web page itself rather than on the server, each time the page is viewed, it is "tagged." Therefore, under-reporting of unique visitors is less of a problem with tagging than with Web log files. While server logs cannot keep track of requests for a cached page, a "tagged" page will still acknowledge and record a visit. Moreover, rather than recording a visit in a Web log file which is harder to access, page tagging records visitor information in a database, offering increased flexibility to access the information more quickly and with more options to further manipulate the data. Because of its increased flexibility (compared to traditional Web analytics based on server log files), most of the innovation in Web analytics is coming from page tagging. This method easily adapts to the rapidly changing Web environment and allows new ways to capture, manipulate, and display visitor information, as discussed in the next section.

Cookies and page tagging assist in an important marketing objective: identifying the most valuable customers (typically defined as those that account for a significant volume of purchases or Web-based activities). This objective can be difficult to accomplish when challenges in Web analytics software make it difficult to identify individual visitors. Flash cookies and page tagging are technologies available to deal with this problem.

NEW TECHNIQUES IN WEB ANALYTICS

Two new features of Web analytics software are site overlays and geo-mapping. In addition, other new features of Web analytics software make it easier to link the log analysis to specific online marketing activities and expenditures.

Many of the newer versions of Web analytics software provide a feature called a *site overlay*. As shown in Figure 1, the site overlay is a visual representation of the click activity on a specific page of the Website. The complete Web page is displayed as seen by the user in a browser, with the addition of the percentages of click activity for each link on the Web page. This overlay feature is a useful addition to the Web analytics software of the past. Rather than reviewing a numerical Web log report for the most popular links and paths through a site, the site overlay provides a detailed visual representation of each individual Web page, with all click activity represented. One benefit of a site overlay is that it provides an easy way to quickly identify which features visitors are clicking. Moreover, it gives a more complete picture of the activity on a specific Web page, as compared to traditional Web analytics which is usually limited to a simple list of the most popular click paths. Web developers and marketers alike can utilize a site overlay to analyze a specific Web page, and even each individual link within a Web page. For example, in Figure 1, the site overlay helps to quickly assess which fruits are the most popular and which are receiving little activity. As the Figure shows, site visitors clicked on mango much more frequently than kiwi fruit.

In addition to site overlays, another new technique in Web analytics arises from visual representations of the data. *Geo-mapping*, relying on new mapping technologies being made available by services such as Google Earth and Microsoft Virtual Earth, displays Web analytics with a richer geographic perspective. In the past, most Web analytics reports provided a

Figure 1. Example of site overlay

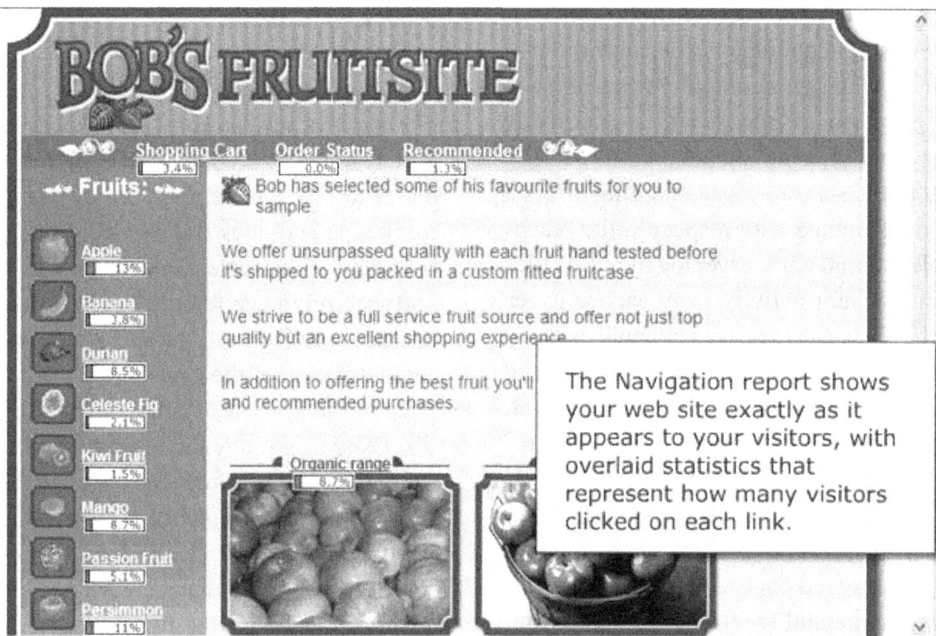

Figure 2. Example of geo-mapping

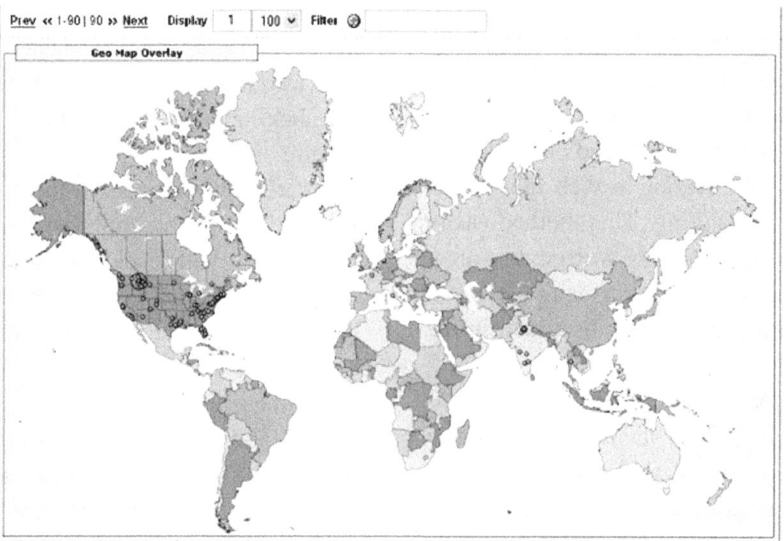

list of visitor countries (and number of visitors from each country) with little additional detail. Improvements in Web analytics and mapping software provide more detail on visitor locations. As shown in Figure 2, in addition to providing country of origin, geo-mapping provides detail on the specific cities visitors originate from, and creates a visual representation of all the visitors on a world map. This technique can be useful for tracking the penetration of a Website in a particular geographic region, or for tracking the effects of marketing activities in a specific city.

Other new tools in Web analytics provide a stronger link between online technologies and online marketing, giving marketers more essential information lacking in earlier versions of Web analytics software. For many years, Web analytics programs that delivered only simple measurements such as hits, visits, referrals, and search engine queries were not well linked to an organization's marketing efforts to drive online traffic. As a result, they provided very little insights to help the organization track and understand its online marketing efforts. Trends in Web analytics specifically improve both the method of data collection as well as the analysis of the data, providing significantly more value from a marketing perspective. These newer tools attempt to analyze the entire marketing process, from a user clicking an advertisement through to the actual sale of a product or service. This information helps to identify not merely which online advertising is driving traffic (number of clicks) to the Website and which search terms lead visitors to the site, but which advertising is most effective in actually generating sales (conversion rates) and profitability. This integration of the Web log files with other measures of advertising effectiveness is critical to provide guidance into further advertising spending.

For example, as shown in Figure 3, Web analytics software (e.g., Google Analytics) has the capability to perform more insightful, detailed reporting on the effectiveness of common online marketing activities such as search engine listings, pay-per-click advertising, and banner advertising. Marketing metrics to assess effectiveness can include:

Figure 3. Example of Google Analytics: Cost-Per-Click

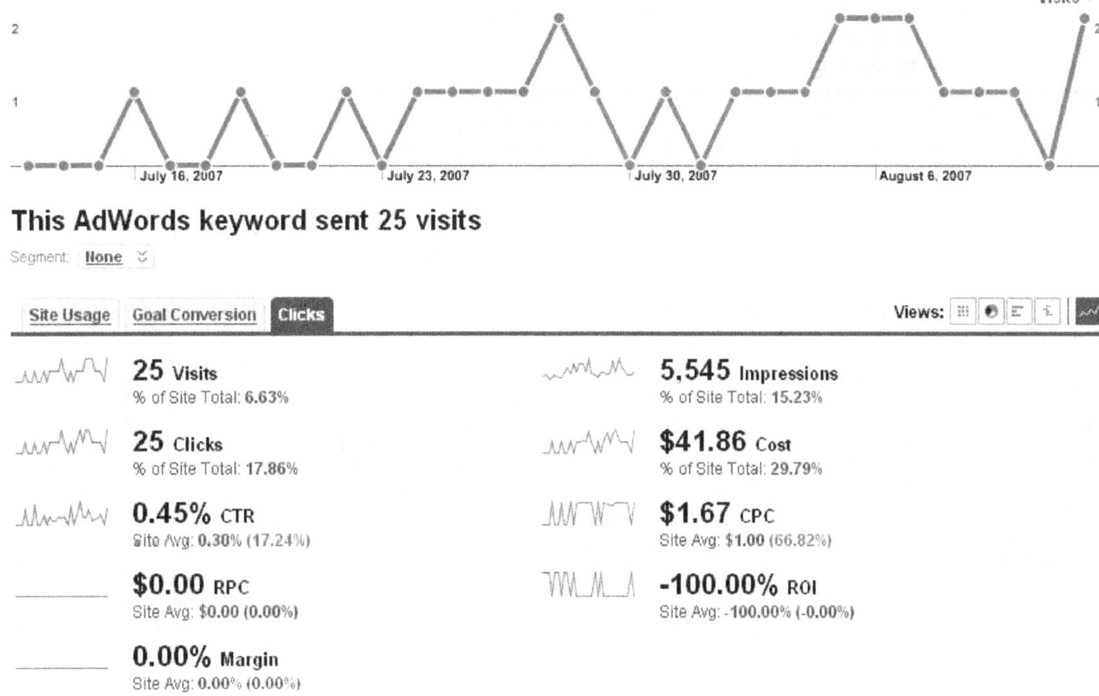

- **Cost-per-click:** The total online expenditure divided by the number of click-throughs to the site.
- **Conversion rate:** The percentage of the total number of visitors who make a purchase, signup for a service, or complete another specific action.
- **Return on marketing investment:** The advertising expense divided by the total revenue generated from the advertising expense.
- **Bounce rate:** The number of users that visit only a single page divided by the total number of visits; one indicator of the "stickiness" of a Web page.

An example of a report that links advertising to these metrics is shown in Figure 3. This figure was generated in Google Analytics from a campaign using the Google Adwords program. The Google Adwords program allows marketers to participate in a paid search advertising campaign. The advertiser buys specific keywords at a set price-per-click, and establishes a budget maximum and duration for the campaign. The figure illustrates a report generated for a single keyword, showing the click-through rate, cost-per-click, return-on-investment, and other information which might be helpful in determining a successful marketing campaign.

Figure 4 illustrates another report generated in Google Analytics for traffic to a Website from the top search engines. This report provides the average bounce rate for all traffic in addition to the specific bounce rate from each search engine. A consistently lower bounce rate from a specific search engine might indicate more valuable visitor referrals, in terms of visitor interest. This type of reporting enables a comparison of paid search traffic to, say, organic search engine traffic (which comes from the search engine's own listings using its algorithms), helping an organization to

Figure 4. Example of Google Analytics: Bounce Rate

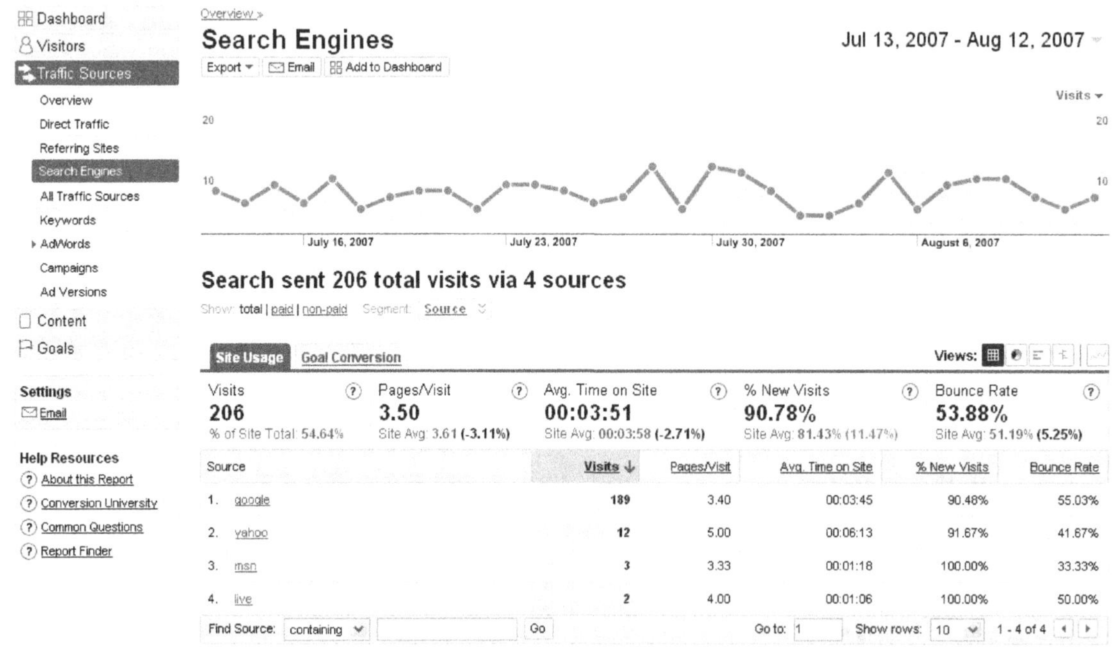

more effectively allocate its resources (Enright, 2006).

Another recent development in linking Web analytics to marketing is *behavioral targeting*, a technique that allows "supersmart, supertargeted display ads" based on a person's online behavior that not only do a better job of getting a Web surfer's attention, but also can be tracked with "laserlike precision" (Sloan, 2007). For example, in 2007 Yahoo had about 131 million monthly unique visitors to its sites. By dropping cookies onto every Web browser that looks up one of its sites, Yahoo analyzes this information and combines it with data about what people are doing on its search engine. Its sophisticated model can then be used to predict consumer behavior. In one campaign, Yahoo found that visitors who saw a specific brokerage ad were 160% more likely to search in that category over the next three weeks, typing in keywords like "online brokerages." Most importantly, the visitors who previously saw the ad overwhelmingly clicked on a display for this brokerage when it appeared in Yahoo's paid search results. The benefit is a user profile that goes well beyond a particular search episode (which search string, for example), and integrates the data with a host of other surfer behaviors. Say a person's cookie profile shows that he spent time at Yahoo Auto evaluating cars on fuel efficiency, and then clicked over to Yahoo's Green Center to read about alternative fuels, and then looked at cars on eBay (a Yahoo partner) (Sloan, 2007). Yahoo's behavioral targeting program can predict with 75% certainty which of the 300,000 monthly visitors to Yahoo Auto will actually purchase a car within the next three months. And, the next time this person visits Yahoo Sports, he will see an ad for hybrid cars. Indeed, based on this analysis, Yahoo is finding that ads on sites that seemingly have nothing to do with them (where the content seems irrelevant) can perform very well, because they are based on an elaborate analysis of a user's complete Internet behavior (and not merely a group of search terms.)

Despite these advances in integrating technology and marketing activities, Web logs alone do not answer a host of important business and marketing questions. User surveys and site registration both provide a start for Website owners to reliably identify each unique visitor as well as to collect more in-depth information about the people visiting the site that goes beyond simply how many are visiting. However, important questions still remain. Meaningful data about customer satisfaction is critical, as are insights into the reasons users visit and interact with a Website. Although Web log files provide the number of clicks from a site homepage to another page on the site, they don't provide information on why the users clicked that link. Are the users genuinely interested in the content of that link? Did the user find the information she was looking for at that link? Is the user satisfied with her overall experience with the Website? Moreover, Web logs do not include information about competitors and other market forces that are an important aspect of positioning the Website and its value to prospective site visitors. So, other techniques (beyond Web analytics) must be used to supply insights into other questions and concerns. Standard marketing research methods can be very useful in this regard. Quantitative research techniques such as customer satisfaction surveys can be used as a supplement, as can qualitative research techniques such as usability testing, interviews, and so forth.

WEB 2.0 CONSIDERATIONS

The tools mentioned previously that are used to evaluate Website performance work well when Internet users are viewing Web pages and seeking out information. However, new uses of the Internet are based on user-generated content and a more user-driven experience; they include, for example, blogging (or posting entries to a Website in the form of a diary or journal, also known as a 'web log'—not to be confused with Web log files), tagging, RSS feeds, wikis, interacting on social networking sites (such as MySpace, FaceBook, or LinkedIn) and sharing rich-media content such as videos (e.g., YouTube). Known collectively as *Web 2.0* (see Table 3), this cluster of collaborative technologies is designed to enhance the user experience on the Internet through enhanced connectivity and communications.

These new technologies pose new complications for Web analytics. First, some Web 2.0 technologies make it difficult to count Website traffic. If a person wants to determine how many readers are reading her blog, it becomes complicated when the blog is shared, say, via an RSS feed. In addition to monitoring traffic at the blog itself, one has to measure how many people access the blog via the RSS feed. The page views of the blog that occurs in GoogleReader, or Bloglines, or LiveJournal, or any place that the blog is syndicated are nearly impossible to track and count.

*Table 3. Web 2.0 technologies **

AJAX (*A*synchronous *J*avaScript *a*nd *X*ML)	A programming technique for Websites whose data are regularly refreshed by the user; it allows the Website to exchange small amounts of data with the server behind the scenes (rather than reloading the entire Web page each time the user requests an update), resulting in enhanced interactivity, speed, functionality, and usability.
Blogging (Blogs)	Short for We**b log**, a blog is a Web page that serves as a publicly accessible personal journal for an individual. Typically updated daily, blogs often reflect the personality of the author.
Podcasting (podcasts)	Allows subscribers to subscribe to a set of audio feeds to listen to the content on an iPod (or like device).
RSS (an acronym for *R*eal *S*imple *S*yndication)	Allows people to sign up to have news articles, blog posts, or audio interviews/podcasts from their favorite Websites sent directly to their computers—essentially, the syndication of Web content. A Website that wants to allow other sites to publish some of its content creates an RSS document and registers the document with an RSS publisher. A user that can read RSS-distributed content can then read content from a different site. Syndicated content can include data such as news feeds, events listings, news stories, headlines, project updates, excerpts from discussion forums or even corporate information.
Social networking sites	Websites whose "members" invite contacts and friends from their own personal networks to join the site. New members repeat the process, growing the total number of members and links in the network. Sites then offer features such as automatic address book updates, viewable profiles, the ability to form new links through "introduction services," and other forms of online social connections. MySpace, for example, builds on independent music and party scenes, and Facebook was originally designed to mirror a college community (though it has since expanded its scope to include high school, job-related, and regional networks). The newest social networks on the Internet are becoming more focused on niches such as travel, art, tennis, football (soccer), golf, cars, dog owners, and even cosmetic surgery. Other social networking sites focus on local communities, sharing local business and entertainment reviews, news, event calendars and happenings. Social networks can also be organized around business connections, as in the case of LinkedIn.
Twitter	A Web service that allows users to send "updates" about what they are doing at a particular moment in time via text messages (SMS), instant messaging or email to the Twitter Website; these updates can also be displayed on the user's profile page and can be delivered instantly to other users who have signed up to receive the updates. Also called "micro-blogging" because of the short nature of the frequently-updated posts. Twitter "look-alikes" include country-specific services (e.g. frazr) or sites that combine micro-blogging with other functions such as filesharing (e.g. Pownce).
Widgets	A portable chunk of code that can be installed and executed within any separate HTML-based Web page by an end user without requiring additional compilation; akin to plugins or extensions in desktop applications, these downloadable, interactive icons allow users to perform a task from their desktop without opening a Webpage.
Wiki	A collaborative Website comprised of the collective work of many authors. Similar to a blog in structure and logic, a wiki allows anyone using a browser interface to edit, delete or modify content that has been placed on the Website, including the work of previous authors. In contrast, a blog, typically authored by an individual, does not allow visitors to change the original posted material, only add comments to the original content. The term *wiki* refers to either the Website or the software used to create the site. *Wiki* means "quick" in Hawaiian.

** Web 2.0 is a second generation of Web-based communities and hosted services which facilitate collaboration and sharing user-generated content between and among Website visitors.*

Second, new technologies such as AJAX and widgets make it difficult to count site traffic. *AJAX* (for **A**synchronous **J**avaScript **a**nd **X**ML) is a programming technique that allows quick, incremental updates for the user without clicking a page refresh or reloading the entire Web page. Google Maps is one Website using AJAX technology. Essentially, in an interactive Web application, the Website exchanges small amounts of data with the server behind the scenes, so that the entire Web page does not have to be reloaded each time the user requests a change. As a result, the Web page's responsiveness (interactivity, speed, and functionality) are increased, and the user has a better browsing experience. However, AJAX technology that allows a page to update itself without reloading creates a problem for counting page views. When a visitor hits a page using AJAX, only the first page view is recorded, no matter how long that person stays and interacts with the page. (Recall that a page view is typically counted every time the same visitor visits/refreshes the page, cf. Web Analytics Association 2006). Hence, the use of a page view metric for Websites using AJAX can cause problems. For example, after deploying new versions of AJAX-intensive pages, many Websites lost all their traffic in comScore and Nielsen//NetRatings page-view counts (Picard, 2006). In fact, Yahoo's homepage was once listed as the most popular page based on the page-view metric. However, when Yahoo launched its new AJAX-enabled homepage, it lost the number-one ranking to MySpace. As a result, more emphasis is being placed on newer metrics such as visit duration and user interaction. In addition, AJAX does provide some capability for tracking refreshed page views through a tagging and "call back" to the server; however, most experts today find AJAX problematic for the mainstream, commercial analytics software that most companies use.

Widgets are little bits of programming (such as Javascript or Flash) that can be downloaded from one Website and then used or displayed by another. One popular Web widget is from YouTube, whose widget allows users to place videos on their social networking profiles and blogs. Google AdSense also has a popular widget that allows Website owners to display relevant advertisements and share in the ad revenue. The developers of a widget can track how many times their widgets are loaded elsewhere, but again, simple counting may be misleading. For example, if a widget is loaded into a sidebar of a Webpage without anyone paying attention to it, does the simple count convey meaningful data?

More important than the problems in counting site traffic per se are the metrics themselves. In the Web 2.0 environment, traditional metrics used to evaluate Website performance are called into question. Prior to Web 2.0, most visitor activity could be tied to simple page views. However, some argue that, at the extreme, "page views are obsolete" (Williams, 2006) and that "there will come a time when no one who wants to be taken seriously will talk about their Web traffic in terms of 'page views' any more than one would brag about their 'hits' today" (Zedowsky, 2006). In many cases, the sheer number of visitors to a particular site matters less than how engaged the visitors are. "Most bloggers would rather be read by a handful of key influencers who provide thoughtful commentary rather than by legions of regular Joes" (Zedowsky, 2006). Or, the bloggers are interested in the thoughtfulness of a handful of responses to their blogs rather than merely the number who read the blog. As one person stated on Zedowsky's (2006) blog:

I would much rather have 100 focused people reading my site than 100,000 people mindlessly wandering through. With a strong, well-defined niche, I can advertise to it, pull advice and knowledge from it, and learn a lot. This might be [only] a handful of page views. The analogy would be an airline company that brags about how many millions of people it is moving every day. If the quality of the interaction is low and people don't have a reason to come back, bragging about some number you counted up doesn't capture the reality of the situation.

Therefore, Web 2.0 presents a challenge for measuring Web activity because much of the key user activity is more complicated than simply viewing a page. Because user activity on Web 2.0 sites can involve watching a video, listening to a podcast, subscribing to RSS feeds, or creating rather than just viewing content, new metrics must be considered. For example, Web analytics of rich-media content might include, say, metrics such as the number of times a video has been played, the average duration of viewing, and completion rates. Or, in an interactive user environment, the quality of the user base may be more important than the quantity per se. Quality might be captured by visitors who stimulate word-of-mouth, for example.

Unfortunately, the dominant Web analytics companies provide little functionality to track these more nuanced issues posed by Web 2.0 technologies. However, new companies are springing up to address these issues. While there really isn't a comprehensive application to track all of the various Web 2.0 content, an assortment of new companies can provide information on the effectiveness of Web 2.0 sites. For example, TubeMogul.com provides information on various video Websites. FeedBurner.com can provide insight on the popularity of various blogs and analysis of RSS feeds and podcasts as well.

TubeMogul.com is a tool for those that publish, monitor, or advertise within online video. The service allows for viewership-related analytics that aren't provided by conventional Web analytics products. TubeMogul.com overcomes one obstacle with Web 2.0 content, related to the trend in publishing videos to popular video sites such as Metacafe and YouTube. Since this video content is published to an external site, conventional Web analytics does not track this content. TubeMogul can track the viewership of videos scattered across the popular video sites. The service will even aggregate the video comments and ratings from the various sites. Viewership is plotted over time which allows users to monitor spikes and trends. Figure 5 shows a TubeMogul report for viewership in YouTube for CBS versus NBC videos. The data indicate a close relationship between CBS and NBC in peak viewership.

FeedBurner.com, purchased in June 2007 by Google, provides a service for tracking several types of Web 2.0 media including blogs, podcasts, and RSS feeds. This service allows users to determine the number of subscribers, where subscribers are coming from, what they like best, and what they are downloading. FeedBurner, in much the same way as TubeMogul tracks video, overcomes the analytics challenge presented by blogs and other types of feeds by offering a solution to track content that is no longer contained in a single Website, but rather is distributed to other sites and feed readers across the Web. Figure 6 illustrates a FeedBurner report; it shows the most popular feed items, and the number of views and clicks for each item. This report also lists the number of feed subscribers. Feed activity is displayed visually in a graph to trend the activity over time.

As these two examples show, new companies are springing up to handle measurement and monitoring of new Websites based on Web 2.0 technologies. Although complications still exist, the evolving nature of the Internet implies that Web analytics will continue to evolve as well, providing better tools to manage such complications.

A final consideration in the metrics used for evaluating Web 2.0 sites that we address here is the concept of "the long tail" (Anderson, 2006), a reference to the tail of a demand curve. Although a relative handful of, say, blogs have many hits, the long tail consists of the millions of blogs that have only a handful of hits. Because the long tail is a potentially large market, this phenomenon has many implications for current and future business models (Anderson, 2006). For example, products

Figure 5. Example of TubeMogul.com statistics

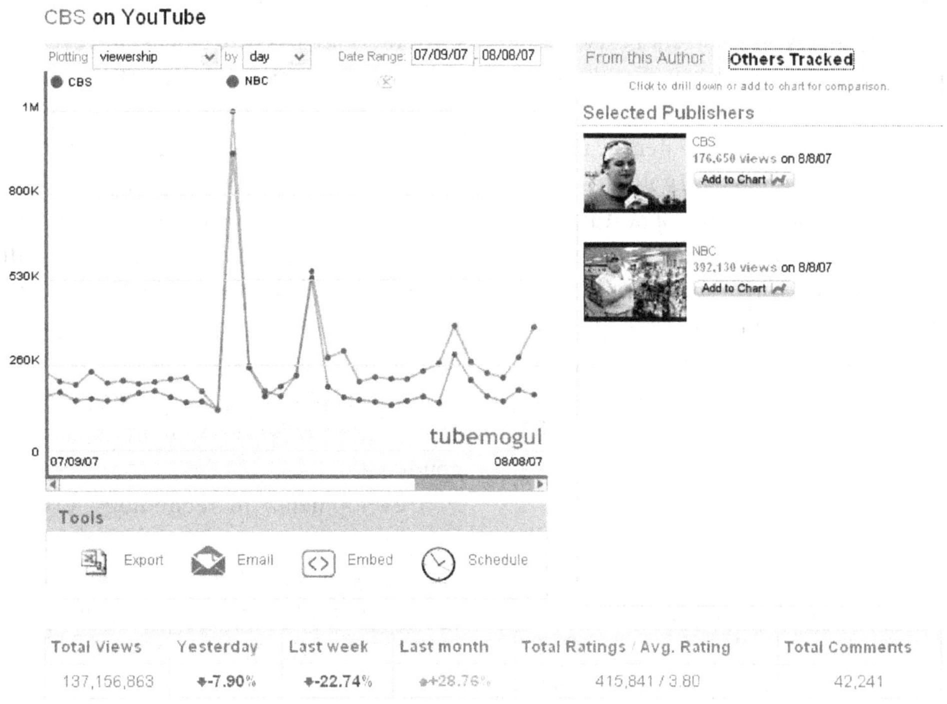

CBS on YouTube

Plotting viewership by day Date Range 07/09/07 08/08/07

CBS NBC

1M
800K
530K
260K
0

07/09/07 08/08/07

tubemogul

Tools

Export Email Embed Schedule

From this Author Others Tracked

Click to drill down or add to chart for comparison.

Selected Publishers

CBS
176,650 views on 8/8/07
Add to Chart

NBC
392,130 views on 8/8/07
Add to Chart

Total Views	Yesterday	Last week	Last month	Total Ratings / Avg. Rating	Total Comments
137,156,863	-7.90%	-22.74%	+28.76%	415,841 / 3.80	42,241

Figure 6. Example of FeedBurner.com statistics

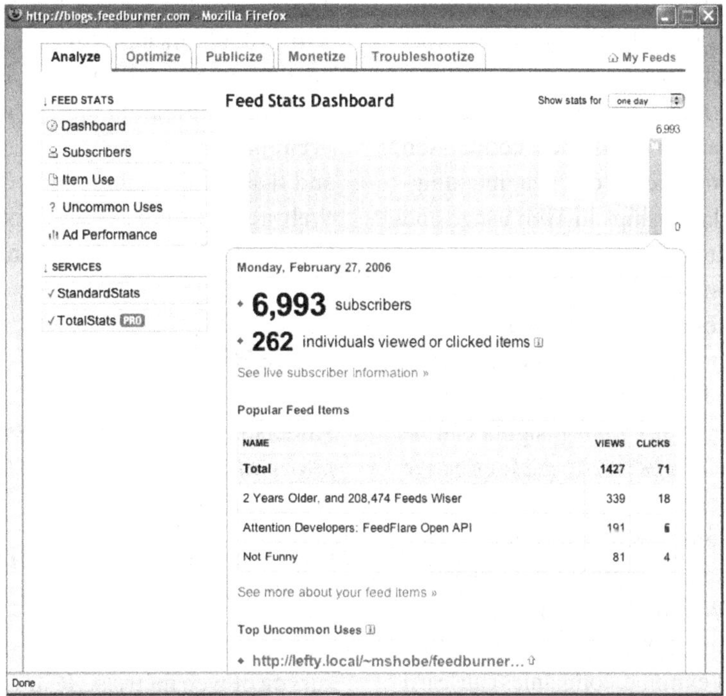

that are in low demand or have low sales volume can collectively make up a market share that rivals or exceeds the relatively few current bestsellers and blockbusters, if the store or distribution channel is large enough (think Netflix). Indeed, the total volume of low popularity items can exceed the volume of high popularity items—and the distribution and sales channel opportunities created by the Internet often enable businesses to tap into that long tail market successfully. The implication of the long tail phenomenon for Web analytics is that current metrics (counts of page views, visitors, etc.)—especially those based on averages—simply don't capture it.

CONCLUSION

This chapter has presented an overview of the traditional metrics used in Web analytics. Web analytics are a collection of tools and techniques that create meaning from the data derived from Web server log files. They can show a plethora of information, including, for example, how Internet users visitors navigated to a particular Website, which pages they visited, where they clicked, what they responded to, what information they supplied, what purchases they made, and which Website they visited next (www.Connectusdirect.com). Web analytics allow companies to discover meaningful patterns and relationships in Web usage and online behavior. Site overlays and geo-mapping are recent developments in Web analytics that provide visual representations of the data.

Integrating the technical perspective of Web log analytics with a business/marketing perspective can highlight not just *what* insights can be gained, but *how they can be used* to guide effective decision making about the specific Website. When combined with other types of information, Web analytics can be used by companies to optimize the conversion of Web traffic to sales and to increase their return on investment from marketing expenditures. At the extreme, companies can learn what motivates customer purchases, what drives customer satisfaction, what builds loyalty, which customers are likely to defect, and even, through behavioral targeting, what a particular customer's future behavior is likely to be.

Although the state-of-the-art in Web analytics is moving in this direction, there are still problems and complications with the existing tools and techniques. Some technologies make it difficult to count and identify unique visitors. When traffic data are inaccurate, subsequent reports based on that data can be very misleading. The use of cookies and page tagging are two techniques that can be used to generate more accurate visitor count data.

Developments in technology tax existing measurement systems. At the extreme, Web 2.0 technologies challenge the very idea of Web performance and measurement. New metrics and new companies are being developed to address these challenges.

To successfully use Web analytics, decision makers must have a clear understanding of the underlying goal and purpose of the Website itself. Then, they can choose the Web analytics that will provide meaningful answers. Importantly, no single approach or solution provides all the possible information that decision makers need. Web analytics that incorporate new technologies, and that use a combination of solutions to track Website performance, will ensure a rich analysis to ensure effective decision making.

REFERENCES

Anderson, C. (2006). *The long tail: Why the future of business is selling less of more.* New York, NY: Hyperion.

ConnectUsDirect.com. (2006). Online newsletter on Web analytics. (April).

Dhyani, D., Ng, W. G. & Bhowmick, S. (2002). A survey of web metrics. *ACM Computing Survey, 34*(December), 469-503.

Enright, A. (2006). Real-time analytics boost ROI, accountability. *Marketing News,* (October 1), 20-24.

Immon, B. (2001). Why clickstream data counts. *e-Business Advisor,* (April)

Mohr, J, Sengupta, S. and Slater, S. (2005). *Marketing of high-technology products and innovations*, Upper Saddle River, NJ: Prentice Hall.

Napier, H. A., Judd, P., Rivers, O., & Adams, A. (2001). *Creating a winning E-business* (pp. 364-369). Boston, MA: Thomas Course Technology.

Napier, H. A., Judd, P., Rivers, O., & Adams, A. (2003). *E-business technologies.* (pp. 372-380). Boston, MA: Thomas Course Technology.

Picard, E. (2006). *Ajax Counting Nightmares.* Retrieved 9/14/2007, http://www.clickz.com/showPage.html?page=3610786

Rosenkrans, L. G. (2006). Online banner ads and metrics challenges. *International Journal of Internet Marketing and Advertising, 3*(3), 193-218.

Schneider, G. (2007). *Electronic commerce.* (7th ed., pp. 380). Boston, MA: Thomson Course Technology.

Sloan, P. (2007). The quest for perfect online ad. *Business 2.0,* (February)

Sponder, M. (2006). *ComScore working on web 2.0 metrics.* Retrieved 4/20/2007, from http://www.webmetricsguru.com/2006/12/comscore_working_on_web_20_met.html

Spors, K. (2007, May 13). For the web, choose your words carefully. [Electronic version]. *Wall Street Journal,*

Sweiger, M. (2002). *Clickstream data warehousing.* New York: Wiley.

Web Analytics Association. (2006). Retrieved 09/14/2007, http://www.webanalyticsassociation.org/attachments/committees/5/WAA-Standards-Analytics-Definitions-Big-3-20061206.pdf.

Weischedel., B., Matear, S., & Deans, K. (2005). The use of e-metrics in strategic marketing decisions: A preliminary investigation. *International Journal of Internet Marketing and Advertising, 2*(1/2), 109-125.

Williams, E. (2006). Retrieved 06/12/2007, from www.evhead.com/2006/08/pageviews-are-obsolete.asp

Zawodny, J. (2006). *Hit counter 2.0, or web 2.0 metrics.* Retrieved 02/16/2007, from http://jeremy.zawodny.com/blog/archives/007665.html.

KEY TERMS

Behavioral Targeting: A technique used by online publishers and advertisers to increase the effectiveness of their campaigns. The idea is to observe a user's online behavior anonymously and then serve the most relevant advertisement based on their behavior. Theoretically, this helps advertisers deliver their online advertisement to the users who are most likely to be influenced by them.

Cache Busting: Techniques used to prevent browsers or proxy servers from serving content from their cache, in order to force the browser or proxy server to fetch a fresh copy for each user request. Cache busting is used to provide a more accurate count of the number of requests from users.

Clickstream Data/Clicktrail: The recording of Web pages that a computer user clicks on while Web browsing or using a personal computer.

Cookies (HTTP cookies or Web cookies): Parcels of text left by a Website on the computer user's hard disk drive; these data are then accessed by the Website's computer server each time the user re-visits the Website. Cookies are used to authenticate, track, and maintain specific information about users, such as site preferences and the contents of their electronic shopping carts.

Flash Cookies: Similar to "cookies" (above), but coded with Macromedia Flash software; Flash cookies are more difficult to remove than traditional cookies, and as a result, they tend to be more reliable.

Geo-Mapping: A visual representation of the geographical location of Website visitors layered on top of map or satellite imagery.

Log Files or Web Server Logs: A file (or several files) automatically created and maintained by a computer server on which a Website is hosted of the activity on that Website (traffic, hits, etc.). A typical example is a Web server log which maintains a history of page requests.

Log File Analysis: Analyzing log files (Web server logs) to review the aggregate results.

Page Tagging (Web Bug/Beacon): An object that is embedded in a Web page or e-mail and is usually invisible to the user but allows checking that a user has viewed the page or e-mail.

Server Logs: See log files.

Site Overlay: Any type of content that is superimposed over a Web page; for the purpose of Web analytics, the site overlay typically shows click and conversion data superimposed over the links on a Web page.

Web 2.0: A second generation of Web-based communities and hosted services, such as social-networking sites, wikis and blogs, which facilitate collaboration and sharing between users.

Web Analytics: The study of the behavior of Website visitors; the use of data collected from a Website to determine which aspects of the Website work towards the business objectives (for example, which landing pages encourage people to make a purchase).

Web Metrics: A generic term for the many types of measurements that can be made about a Website and its visitors.

ENDNOTES

* Both authors contributed equally to this project.

1 Quantifying site traffic is important for more than just an individual Website. Many companies rank Websites based on site traffic (e.g., Alexa.com; comScore.com; HitWise.com; Nielsen NetRatings.com) (cf. Lacy, 2006). They assess audience size, which allows various Websites to "monetize" their traffic by setting ad rates for banners and other forms of online marketing. Moreover, these metrics are sometimes used by investors to determine the valuation of a dot-com start-up. The issues related to measurement and auditing these measures for verified Website traffic statistics are beyond the scope of this chapter.

Chapter VIII
A Review of Methodologies for Analyzing Websites

Danielle Booth
Pennsylvania State University, USA

Bernard J. Jansen
Pennsylvania State University, USA

ABSTRACT

This chapter is an overview of the process of Web analytics for Websites. It outlines how visitor information such as number of visitors and visit duration can be collected using log files and page tagging. This information is then combined to create meaningful key performance indicators that are tailored not only to the business goals of the company running the Website but also to the goals and content of the Website. Finally, this chapter presents several analytic tools and explains how to choose the right tool for the needs of the Website. The ultimate goal of this chapter is to provide methods for increasing revenue and customer satisfaction through careful analysis of visitor interaction with a Website.

INTRODUCTION

Web analytics is the measure of visitor behavior on a Website. However, what kind of information is available from Website visitors, and what can be learned from studying such information? By collecting various Web analytics metrics, such as number of visits,visitors, and visit duration, one can develop key performance indicators (KPIs) – a versatile analytic model that measures several metrics against each other to define visitor trends. KPIs use these dynamic numbers to get an in-depth picture of visitor behavior on a site. This information allows businesses to align their Websites' goals with their business goals for the purpose of identifying areas of improvement, promoting popular parts of the site, testing new site functionality, and ultimately increasing revenue. This chapter covers the most common metrics, different methods for gathering metrics, how to utilize key performance indicators, best key practices, and choosing the right Web analytics tool.

The first section addresses metrics, information that can be collected from visitors on a Website. It covers types of metrics based on what kind of data is collected as well as specific metrics and how they can be utilized. The following section discusses the two main methods for gathering visitor information -- log files and page tagging. For each method, this section covers the advantages and disadvantages, types of supported information, and examples for data format. Following this is a section on how to choose the key performance indicators (KPIs). This includes outlining several business strategies for integrating Web analytics with the rest of an organization as well as identifying the type of Website and listing several specific KPIs for each site type. The following section provides the overall process and advice for Web analytics integration, and the final section deals with what to look for when choosing analytics tools as well as a comparison of several specific tools. Finally, the conclusion discusses the future of Web analytics.

METRICS

In order to understand the benefits of Website analysis, one must first understand metrics – the different kinds of available user information. Although the metrics may seem basic, once collected, they can be used to analyze Web traffic and improve a Website to better meet its overall goals. According to Panalysis (http://www.panalysis.com/), an Australian Web analytics company, these metrics generally fall into one of four categories: site usage, referrers (or how visitors arrived at your site), site content analysis, and quality assurance. Table 1 shows examples of types of metrics that might be found in these categories.

Although the type and overall number of metrics varies with different analytics vendors, there is still a common set of basic metrics common to most. Table 2 outlines eight widespread types of information that measure who is visiting a Website and what they do during their visits, relating each of these metrics to specific categories.

Each metric is discussed below.

Visitor Type

Since analyzing Website traffic first became popular in the 1990s with the Website counter, the measure of Website traffic has been one of the most closely watched metrics. This metric, however, has evolved from merely counting the number of hits a page receives into counting the number of individuals who visit the Website.

There are two types of visitors: those who have been to the site before, and those who have not. This difference is defined in terms of repeat and new visitors. In order to track visitors in such a way, a system must be able to determine individual users who access a Website; each individual visitor is called a unique visitor. Ideally, a unique visitor is just one visitor, but this is not always the case.

Table 1. Metrics categories (Jacka, n.d.)

Site Usage	Referrers	Site Content Analysis	Quality Assurance
• Numbers of visitors and sessions • How many people repeatedly visit the site • Geographic information • Search Engine Activity	• Which websites are sending visitors to your site • The search terms people used to find your site • How many people place bookmarks to the site	• Top entry pages • Most popular pages • Top pages for single page view sessions • Top exit pages • Top paths through the site • Effectiveness of key content	• Broken pages or server errors • Visitor response to errors

It is possible that multiple users access the site from the same computer (perhaps on a shared household computer or a public library). In addition, most analytic software relies on cookies to track unique users. If a user disables cookies in their browser or if they clear their cache, the visitor will be counted as new each time he or she enters the site.

Because of this, some companies have instead begun to track unique visits, or sessions. A session begins once a user enters the site and ends when a user exits the site or after a set amount of time of inactivity (usually 30 minutes). The session data does not rely on cookies and can be measured easily. Since there is less uncertainty with visits, it is considered to be a more concrete and reliable metric than unique visitors. This approach is also more sales-oriented because it considers each visit an opportunity to convert a visitor into a customer instead of looking at overall customer behavior (Belkin, 2006).

Visit Length

Also referred to as Visit Duration or Average Time on Site (ATOS), visit length is the total amount of time a visitor spends on a site during one session. One possible area of confusion when using this metric is handling missing data. This can be caused either by an error in data collection or by a session containing only one page visit or interaction. Since the visit length is calculated by subtracting the time of the visitor's first activity on the site from the time of the visitor's final activity, what happens to the measurement when one of those pieces of data is missing? According to the Web Analytics Association, the visit length in such cases is zero (Burby & Brown, 2007).

When analyzing the visit length, the measurements are often broken down into chunks of time. StatCounter, for example, uses the following time categories:

- Less than 5 seconds
- 5 seconds to 30 seconds
- 30 seconds to 5 minutes
- 5 minutes to 20 minutes
- 20 minutes to 1 hour
- Greater than 1 hour (Jackson, 2007)

The goal of measuring the data in this way is to keep the percentage of visitors who stay on the Website for less than five seconds as low as possible. If visitors stay on a Website for such a short amount of time it usually means they either arrived at the site by accident or the site did not

Table 2. Eight common metrics of Website analysis

Metric	Description	Category
Visitor Type	Who is accessing the Website (returning, unique, etc.)	Site Usage
Visit Length	The total amount of time a visitor spends on the Website	Site Usage
Demographics and System Statistics	The physical location and information of the system used to access the Website	Site Usage
Internal Search Information	Information on keywords and results pages viewed using a search engine embedded in the Website	Site Usage
Visitor Path	The route a visitor uses to navigate through the Website	Site Content Analysis
Top Pages	The pages that receive the most traffic	Site Content Analysis
Referrering URL and Keyword Analysis	Which sites have directed traffic to the Website and which keywords visitors are using to find the Website	Referrers
Errors	Any errors that occurred while attempting to retrieve the page	Quality Assurance

have relevant information. By combining this information with information from referrers and keyword analysis, one can tell which sites are referring well-targeted traffic and which sites are referring poor quality traffic.

Demographics and System Statistics

The demographic metric refers to the physical location of the system used to make a page request. This information can be useful for a Website that provides region-specific services. For example, if an e-commerce site can only ship its goods to people in Spain, any traffic to the site from outside of Spain is irrelevant. In addition, region-specific Websites also want to make sure they tailor their content to the group they are targeting. Demographic information can also be combined with information on referrers to determine if a referral site is directing traffic to a site from outside a company's regions of service.

System statistics are information about the hardware and software with which visitors access a Website. This can include information such as browser type, screen resolution, and operating system. It is important that a Website be accessible to all of its customers, and by using this information, the Website can be tailored to meet visitors' technical needs.

Internal Search

If a Website includes a site-specific search utility, then it is also possible to measure internal search information. This can include not only keywords but also information about which results pages visitors found useful. The Patricia Seybold Group (http://www.psgroup.com/) identifies the following seven uses for internal search data:

- Identify products and services for which customers are looking, but that are not yet provided by the company.
- Identify products that are offered, but which customers have a hard time finding.
- Identify customer trends.
- Improve personalized messages by using the customers' own words.
- Identify emerging customer service issues
- Determine if customers are provided with enough information to reach their goals.
- Make personalized offers. (Aldrich, 2006)

By analyzing internal search data, one can use the information to improve and personalize the visitors' experience.

Visitor Path

A visitor path is the route a visitor uses to navigate through a Website. Excluding visitors who leave the site as soon as they enter, each visitor creates a path of page views and actions while perusing the site. By studying these paths, one can identify any difficulties a user has viewing a specific area of the site or completing a certain action (such as making a transaction or completing a form).

According to the Web Analytics Association, there are two schools of thought regarding visitor path analysis. The first is that visitor actions are goal-driven and performed in a logical, linear fashion. For example, if a visitor wants to purchase an item, the visitor will first find the item, add it to the cart, and proceed to the checkout to complete the process. Any break in that path (i.e. not completing the order) signifies user confusion and is viewed as a problem.

The second school of thought is that visitor actions are random and illogical and that the only path that can provide accurate data on a visitor's behavior is the path from one page to the page immediately following it. In other words, the only page that influences visitor behavior on a Website is the one they are currently viewing. For example, visitors on a news site may merely peruse the articles with no particular goal in mind. This method of analysis is becoming increasingly popular because companies find it easier to examine path data in context without having to reference the entire site in order to study the visitors' behavior (Web Analytics Association, n. d.).

Top Pages

Panalysis mentions three types of top pages: top entry pages, top exit pages, and most popular pages. Top entry pages are important because the first page a visitor views makes the greatest impression about a Website. By knowing the top entry page, one can make sure that page has relevant information and provides adequate navigation to important parts of the site. Similarly, identifying popular exit pages makes it easier to pinpoint areas of confusion or missing content.

The most popular pages are the areas of a website that receive the most traffic. This metric gives insight into how visitors are utilizing the Website, and which pages are providing the most useful information. This is important because it shows whether the Website's functionality matches up with its business goals; if most of the Website's traffic is being directed away from the main pages of the site, the Website cannot function to its full potential (Jacka, n. d.).

Referrers and Keyword Analysis

A referral page is the page a user visits immediately before entering to a Website, or rather, a site that has directed traffic to the Website. A search engine result page link, a blog entry mentioning the Website, and a personal bookmark are examples of referrers. This metric is important because it can be used to determine advertising effectiveness and search engine popularity. As always, it is important to look at this information in context. If a certain referrer is doing worse than expected, it could be caused by the referring link text or placement. Conversely, an unexpected spike in referrals from a certain page could be either good or bad depending on the content of the referring page.

In the same way, keyword analysis deals specifically with referring search engines and shows which keywords have brought in the most traffic. By analyzing the keywords visitors use to find a page, one is able to determine what visitors expect to gain from the Website and use that information to better tailor the Website to their needs. It is also important to consider the quality of keywords. Keyword quality is directly proportional to revenue and can be determined by comparing keywords with visitor path and visit length (Marshall, n. d.). Good keywords will bring quality traffic and more income to your site.

Errors

Errors are the final metric. Tracking errors has the obvious benefit of being able to identify and fix any errors in the Website, but it is also useful to observe how visitors react to these errors. The fewer visitors who are confused by errors on a Website, the less likely visitors are to exit the site because of an error.

GATHERING INFORMATION

How does one gather these metrics? There are two major methods for collecting data for Web analysis: log files and page tagging. Most current Web analytic companies use a combination of the two methods for collecting data. Therefore, it is important to understand the strengths and weaknesses of each.

Log Files

The first method of metric gathering uses log files. Every Web server keeps a log of page requests that can include (but is not limited to) visitor IP address, date and time of the request, request page, referrer, and information on the visitor's

Web browser and operating system. The same basic collected information can be displayed in a variety of ways. Although the format of the log file is ultimately the decision of the company who runs the Web server, the following four formats are a few of the most popular:

- NCSA Common Log
- NCSA Combined Log
- NCSA Separate Log
- W3C Extended Log

The NCSA Common Log format (also known as Access Log format) contains only basic information on the page request. This includes the client IP address, client identifier, visitor username, date and time, HTTP request, status code for the request, and the number of bytes transferred during the request. The Combined Log format contains the same information as the common log with the following three additional fields: the referring URL, the visitor's Web browser and operating system information, and the cookie. The Separate Log format (or 3-Log format) contains the same information as the combined log, but it breaks it into three separate files – the access log, the referral log, and the agent log. The date and time fields in each of the three logs are the same. Table 3 shows examples of the common, combined, and separate log file formats (notice that default values are represented by a dash "-"):

Similarly, W3C provides an outline for standard formatting procedures. This format differs from the first three in that it aims to provide for better control and manipulation of data while still producing a log file readable by most Web analytics tools. The extended format contains user defined fields and identifiers followed by the actual entries, and default values are represented by a dash "-" (Hallam-Baker & Behlendorf, 1999). Table 4 shows an example of an extended log file.

There are several benefits of using system log files to gather data for analysis. The first is that it does not require any changes to the Website or any extra software installation to create the log files. Web servers automatically create these logs and store them on a company's own servers giving the company freedom to change their Web analytics tools and strategies at will. This method also does not require any extra bandwidth when loading a page, and since everything is recorded server-side, it is possible to log both page request successes and failures.

Using log files also has some disadvantages. One major disadvantage is that the collected data is limited to only transactions with the Web server. This means that they cannot log information independent from the servers such as the physical location of the visitor. Similarly, while it is possible to log cookies, the server must be specifically configured to assign cookies to visitors in order to do so. The final disadvantage is that while it is useful to have all the information stored on a company's own servers, the log file method is only available to those who own their Web servers.

Table 3. NCSA Log comparison (IBM, 2004)

NCSA Common Log	125.125.125.125 - dsmith [10/Oct/1999:21:15:05 +0500] "GET /index.html HTTP/1.0" 200 1043
NCSA Combined Log	125.125.125.125 - dsmith [10/Oct/1999:21:15:05 +0500] "GET /index.html HTTP/1.0" 200 1043 "http://www.ibm.com/" "Mozilla/4.05 [en] (WinNT; I)" "USERID=CustomerA;IMPID=01234"
NCSA Separate Log	Common Log: 125.125.125.125 - dsmith [10/Oct/1999:21:15:05 +0500] "GET /index.html HTTP/1.0" 200 1043 Referral Log: [10/Oct/1999:21:15:05 +0500] "http://www.ibm.com/index.html" Agent Log: [10/Oct/1999:21:15:05 +0500] "Microsoft Internet Explorer - 5.0"

Page Tagging

The second method for recording visitor activity is page tagging. Page tagging uses an invisible image to detect when a page has been successfully loaded and then uses JavaScript to send information about the page and the visitor back to a remote server. According to *Web Analytics Demystified* the variables used and amount of data collected in page tagging are dependent on the Web analytics vendor. Some vendors stress short, easy to use page tags while others emphasize specific tags that require little post-processing. The best thing to look for with this method, however, is flexibility – being able to use all, part, or none of the tag depending on the needs of the page (Peterson, 2004).

There are several benefits to using this method of gathering visitor data. The first is speed of reporting. Unlike a log file, the data received via page tagging is parsed as it comes in. This allows for near real-time reporting. Another benefit is flexibility of data collection. More specifically, it is easier to record additional information about the visitor that does not involve a request to the Web server. Examples of such information include information about a visitor's screen size, the price of purchased goods, and interactions within Flash animations. This is also a useful method of gathering data for companies that do not run their own Web servers or do not have access to the raw log files for their site (such as blogs).

There are also some disadvantages of page tagging, most of which are centered on the extra code that must be added to the Website. This causes it to use more bandwidth each time a page loads, and it also makes it harder to change analytics tools because the code embedded in the Website would have to be changed or deleted entirely. The final disadvantage is that page tagging is only capable of recording page loads, not page failures. If a page fails to load, it means that the tagging code also did not load, and there is therefore no way to retrieve information in that instance.

Although log files and page tagging are two distinct ways to collect information about the visitors to a Website, it is possible to use both together, and many analytics companies provide ways to use both methods to gather data. Even so, it is important to understand the strengths and weaknesses of both. Table 5 shows the advantages and disadvantages of log file analysis and page tagging.

The Problems with Data

One of the most prevalent problems in Web analytics is the difficulty identifying unique users. In order to determine repeat visitors, most Web analytic tools employ cookies that store unique identification information on the visitor's personal computer. Because of problems with users deleting or disabling cookies, however, some companies have moved towards using Macromedia Flash Local Shared Objects (LSOs). LSOs act like a cookie, but standard browsers lack the tools required to delete them, anti-spyware software does not delete them because it does not see them as a threat, and most users do not know how to delete them manually. Awareness is growing, however,

Table 4. W3C extended log file (Microsoft, 2005)

W3C Extended Log	#Software: Microsoft Internet Information Services 6.0 #Version: 1.0 #Date: 2002-05-24 20:18:01 #Fields: date time c-ip cs-username s-ip s-port cs-method cs-uri-stem cs-uri-query sc-status sc-bytes cs-bytes time-taken cs(User-Agent) cs(Referrer) 2002-05-24 20:18:01 172.224.24.114 - 206.73.118.24 80 GET /Default.htm - 200 7930 248 31 Mozilla/ 4.0+(compatible;+MSIE+5.01;+Windows+2000+Server) http://64.224.24.114/

Table 5. Log files vs. page tagging

Log Files		Page Tagging	
Advantages	*Disadvantages*	*Advantages*	*Disadvantages*
Does not require changes to the Website or extra hardware installation	Can only record interactions with the Web server	Near real-time reporting	Requires extra code added to the Website
Does not require extra bandwidth	Server must be configured to assign cookies to visitors	Easier to record additional information	Uses extra bandwidth each time the page loads
Freedom to change tools with a relatively small amount of hassle	Only available to companies who run their own Web servers	Able to capture visitor interactions within Flash animations	Can only record successful page loads, not failures
Logs both page request successes and failures	Cannot log physical location		Hard to switch analytic tools

and Firefox and Macromedia are working against LSOs and providing users with tools to delete them (Permadi, 2005).

Sen, Dacin, and Pattichis (2006) cite various other problems with log data from Websites including large data size and messy data. Problems with large data size are caused by massive amounts of traffic to a Website and also the amount of information stored in each record. Records with missing IP addresses and changes to Website content cause messy data. Even though the data may be hard to work with at first, once it is cleaned up, it provides an excellent tool for Web analytics.

CHOOSING KEY PERFORMANCE INDICATORS

In order to get the most out of Web analytics, one must know how to choose effectively which metrics to analyze and combine them in meaningful ways. This means knowing the Website's business goals and then determining which KPIs will provide the most insight.

Knowing Your Business Goals

Every company has specific business goals. Every part of the company works together to achieve them, and the company Website is no exception. In order for a Website to be beneficial, information gathered from its visitors must not merely show what has happened in the past, but it must also be able to improve the site for future visitors. The company must have clearly defined goals for the future and use this information to support strategies that will help it achieve those goals.

For a Website, the first step in achieving this is making sure the data collected from the site is actionable. According to the Web Analytics Association (McFadden, 2005), in order for a company to collect actionable data, it must meet these three criteria: "(1) the business goals must be clear, (2) technology, analytics, and the business must be aligned, and (3) the feedback loop must be complete" (Web Channel Performance Management section, para. 3).

There are many possible methods for meeting these criteria. One is Alignment-Centric Performance Management (Becher, 2005). This approach goes beyond merely reviewing past customer trends to carefully selecting a few key KPIs based on their future business objectives. Even though a wealth of metrics is available from a Website, this does not mean that all metrics are relevant to a company's needs. Reporting large quantities of data is overwhelming, so it is important to look at metrics in context and use them to create KPIs that focus on outcome and not activity. For example, a customer service Website might view the number of emails responded to on the same day they were sent as a measurement of customer satisfaction. A better way to measure customer satisfaction, however, might be to survey the customers on their experience. Although this measurement is subjective, it is a better representation of customer satisfaction because even if a customer receives a response the same day they send out an email, it does not mean that the experience was a good one (Becher, 2005).

Choosing the most beneficial KPIs using this method is achieved by following "The Four M's of Operational Management" as outlined by Becher (2005) which facilitate effective selection of KPIs:

- **Motivate:** Ensure that goals are relevant to everyone involved.
- **Manage:** Encourage collaboration and involvement for achieving these goals.
- **Monitor:** Once selected, track the KPIs and quickly deal with any problems that may arise.
- **Measure:** Identify the root causes of problems and test any assumptions associated with the strategy.

By carefully choosing a few, quality KPIs to monitor and making sure everyone is involved with the strategy, it becomes easier to align a Website's goals with the company's goals because the information is targeted and stakeholders are actively participating.

Another method for ensuring actionable data is Online Business Performance Management (OBPM) (Sapir, 2004). This approach integrates business tools with Web analytics to help companies make better decisions quickly in an ever-changing online environment where customer data is stored in a variety of different departments. The first step in this strategy is gathering all customer data in a central location and condensing it so that the result is all actionable data stored in the same place. Once this information is in place, the next step is choosing relevant KPIs that are aligned with the company's business strategy and then analyzing expected versus actual results (Sapir 2004).

In order to choose the best KPIs and measure the Website's performance against the goals of a business, there must be effective communication between senior executives and online managers. The two groups should work together to define the relevant performance metrics, the overall goals for the Website, and the performance measurements. This method is similar to Alignment-Centric Performance Management in that it aims to aid integration of the Website with the company's business objectives by involving major stakeholders. The ultimate goals of OBPM are increased confidence, organizational accountability, and efficiency (Sapir 2004).

Identifying KPIs Based on Website Type

Unlike metrics, which are numerical representations of data collected from a Website, KPIs are tied to a business strategy and are usually measured by a ratio of two metrics. By choosing KPIs based on the Website type, a business can save both time and money. Although Websites can have more than one function, each site belongs to at least one of the four main categories – commerce, lead generation, content/media, and support/self service (McFadden, 2005). Table 6 shows common KPIs for each Website type:

We discuss each Website type and related KPIs below.

Commerce

The goal of a commerce Website is to get visitors to purchase goods or services directly from the site, with success gauged by the amount of revenue the site brings in. According to Peterson, "commerce analysis tools should provide the 'who, what, when, where, and how' for your

Table 6. The four types of Websites and examples of associated KPIs (McFadden, 2005)

Website Type	KPIs
Commerce	• Conversion rates • Average order value • Average visit value • Customer loyalty • Bounce rate
Lead Generation	• Conversion rates • Cost per lead • Bounce rate • Traffic concentration
Content/Media	• Visit depth • Returning visitor ratio • New visitor ratio • Page depth
Support/Self service	• Page depth • Bounce rate • Customer satisfaction • Top internal search phrases

online purchasers (2004, p. 92)." In essence, the important information for a commerce Website is who made (or failed to make) a purchase, what was purchased, when purchases were made, where customers are coming from, and how customers are making their purchases. The most valuable KPIs used to answer these questions are conversion rates, average order value, average visit value, customer loyalty, and bounce rate (McFadden, 2005). Other metrics to consider with a commerce site are which products, categories, and brands are sold on the site and internal site product search that could signal navigation confusion or a new product niche (Peterson, 2004).

A conversion rate is the number of users who perform a specified action divided by the total of a certain type of visitor (i.e. repeat visitors, unique visitors, etc.) over a given period. Types of conversion rates will vary by the needs of the businesses using them, but two common conversion rates for commerce Websites are the order conversion rate (the percent of total visitors who place an order on a Website) and the checkout conversion rate (the percent of total visitors who begin the checkout process). There are also many methods for choosing the group of visitors on which to base your conversion rate. For example, a business may want to filter visitors by excluding visits from robots and Web crawlers (Ansari, Kohavi, Mason, & Zheng, 2001), or they may want to exclude the traffic that "bounces" from the Website or (a slightly trickier measurement) the traffic that is determined not to have intent to purchase anything from the Website (Kaushik, 2006).

It is common for commerce Websites to have conversion rates around 0.5%, but generally good conversion rates will fall in the 2% range depending on how a business structures its conversion rate (FoundPages, 2007). Again, the ultimate goal is to increase total revenue. According to eVision, for each dollar a company spends on improving this KPI, there is \$10 to \$100 return (2007). The methods a business uses to improve their conversion rate (or rates), however, are different depending on which target action that business chooses to measure.

Average order value (AOV) is a ratio of total order revenue to number of orders over a given period. This number is important because it allows the analyzer to derive a cost for each transaction. There are several ways for a business to use this KPI to its advantage. One way is to break down the AOV by advertising campaigns (i.e. email, keyword, banner ad etc.). This way, a business can see which campaigns are bringing in the best customers and spend more effort refining their strategies in those areas (Peterson, 2005). Overall, however, if the cost of making a transaction is greater than the amount of money customers spend for each transaction, the site is not fulfilling its goal. There are two main ways to correct this. The first is to increase the number of products customers order per transaction, and the second is to increase the overall cost of purchased products. A good technique for achieving this is through product promotions (McFadden, 2005), but many factors influence how and why customers purchase what they do on a Website. These factors are diverse and can range from displaying a certain security image on the site (MarketingSherpa, 2007) to updating the site's internal search (Young, 2007). Like many KPIs, improvement ultimately comes from ongoing research and a small amount of trial and error.

Another KPI, average visit value, measures the total number of visits to the total revenue. This is a measurement of quality traffic important to businesses. It is problematic for a commerce site when, even though it may have many visitors, each visit generates only a small amount of revenue. In that case, even if the total number of visits increased, it would not have a profound impact on overall profits. This KPI is also useful for evaluating the effectiveness of promotional campaigns. If the average visit value decreases after a specific campaign, it is likely that the advertisement is not attracting quality traffic to the site. Another less common factor in this situation could be broken links or a confusing layout in a site's "shopping cart" area. A business can improve the average visit value by using targeted advertising and employing a layout that reduces customer confusion.

Customer loyalty is the ratio of new to existing customers. Many Web analytics tools measure this using visit frequency and transactions, but there are several important factors in this measurement including the time between visits (Mason, 2007). Customer loyalty can even be measured simply with customer satisfaction surveys (SearchCRM, 2007). Loyal customers will not only increase revenue through purchases but also through referrals, potentially limiting advertising costs (QuestionPro).

Bounce rate is a measurement of how many people arrive at a homepage and leave immediately. There are two scenarios that generally qualify as a bounce. In the first scenario, a visitor views only one page on the Website. In the second scenario, a visitor navigates to a Website but only stays on the site for five seconds or less (Avinash, 2007). This could be due to several factors, but in general, visitors who bounce from a Website are not interested in the content. Like average order value, this KPI helps show how much quality traffic a Website receives. A high bounce rate may be a reflection of unintuitive site design or misdirected advertising.

Lead Generation

The goal for a lead generation Website is to obtain user contact information in order to inform them of a company's new products and developments and to gather data for market research; these sites primarily focus on products or services that cannot be purchased directly online. Examples of lead generation include requesting more information by mail or email, applying online, signing up for a newsletter, registering to download product information, and gathering referrals for a partner site (Burby, 2004). The most important KPIs for lead generation sites are conversion rates, cost per lead, bounce rate, and traffic concentration (McFadden, 2005).

Similar to commerce Website KPIs, a conversion rate is the ratio of total visitors to the amount of visitors who perform a specific action. In the case of lead generation Websites, the most common conversion rate is the ratio of total visitors to leads generated. The same visitor filtering techniques mentioned in the previous section can be applied to this measurement (i.e. filtering out robots and Web crawlers and excluding traffic that bounces from the site). This KPI is an essential tool in analyzing marketing strategies. Average lead generation sites have conversion rates ranging from 5-6% and 17-19% conversion rates for exceptionally good sites (Greenfield, 2006). If the conversion rate of a site increases after the implementation of a new marketing strategy, it indicates that the campaign was successful. If it decreases, it indicates that the campaign was not effective and might need to be reworked.

Cost per lead (CPL) refers to the ratio of total expenses to total number of leads, or how much it costs a company to generate a lead; a more targeted measurement of this KPI would be the ratio of total marketing expenses to total number of leads. Like the conversion rate, CPL helps a business gain insight into the effectiveness of its marketing campaigns. A good way to measure the success of this KPI is to make sure that the CPL for a specific marketing campaign is less than the overall CPL (WebSideStory, 2004). Ideally, the CPL should be low, and well-targeted advertising is usually the best way to achieve this.

Lead generation bounce rate is the same measurement as the bounce rate for commerce sites. This KPI is a measurement of visitor retention based off total number of bounces to total number of visitors; a bounce is a visit characterized by a visitor entering the site and immediately leaving. Lead generation sites differ from commerce sites in that they may not require the same level of user interaction. For example, a lead generation site could have a single page where users enter their contact information. Even though they only view one page, the visit is still successful if the Website is able to collect the user's information. In these situations, it is best to base the bounce rate solely off of time spent on the site. As with commerce sites, the best way to decrease a site's bounce rate is to increase advertising effectiveness and decrease visitor confusion.

The final KPI is traffic concentration, or the ratio of the number of visitors to a certain area in a Website to total visitors. This KPI shows which areas of a site have the most visitor interest. For this type of Website, it is ideal to have a high traffic concentration on the page or pages where users enter their contact information.

Content/Media

Content/media Websites focus mainly on advertising, and the main goal of these sites is to increase revenue by keeping visitors on the Website longer and also to keep visitors coming back to the site. In order for these types of sites to succeed, site content must be engaging and frequently updated. If content is only part of a company's Website, the content used in conjunction with other types of pages can be used to draw in visitors and provide a way to immerse them with the site. The main KPIs are visit depth, returning visitors, new visitor percentage, and page depth (McFadden, 2005).

Visit depth (also referred to as depth of visit or path length) is the measurement of the ratio between page views and unique visitors, or how many pages a visitor accesses each visit. As a general rule, visitors with a higher visit depth are interacting more with the Website. If visitors are only viewing a few pages per visit, it means that they are not engaged, and the effectiveness of the site is low. A way to increase a low average visit depth is by creating more targeted content that would be more interesting to the Website's target audience. Another strategy could be increasing the site's interactivity to encourage the users to become more involved with the site and keep them coming back.

Unlike the metric of simply counting the number of returning visitors on a site, the returning visitor KPI is the ratio of unique visitors to total visits. A factor in customer loyalty, this KPI measures the effectiveness of a Website to bring visitors back. A lower ratio for this KPI is best because a lower number means more repeat visitors and more visitors who are interested in and trust the content of the Website. If this KPI is too low, however, it might signal problems in other areas such as a high bounce rate or even click fraud. Click fraud occurs when a person or script is used to generate visits to a Website without having genuine interest in the site. According to a study by Blizzard Internet Marketing, the average for returning visitors to a Website is 23.7% (White, 2006). As with many of the other KPIs for content/media Websites, the best way to improve the returning visitor rate is by having quality content and encouraging interaction with the Website.

New visitor ratio is the measurement of new visitors to unique visitors and is used to determine if a site is attracting new people. When measuring this KPI, the age of the Website plays a role – newer sites will want to attract new people. Similarly, another factor to consider is if the Website is concerned more about customer retention or gaining new customers. As a rule, however, the new visitor ratio should decrease over time as the returning visitor ratio increases. New visitors can be brought to the Website in a variety of different ways, so a good way to increase this KPI is to try different marketing strategies and figure out which campaigns bring the most (and the best) traffic to the site.

The final KPI for content/media sites is page depth. This is the ratio of page views for a specific page and the number of unique visitors to that page. This KPI is similar to visit depth, but its measurements focus more on page popularity. Average page depth can be used to measure interest in specific areas of a Website over time and to make sure that the interests of the visitors match the goals of the Website. If one particular page on a Website has a high page depth, it is an indication that that page is of particular interest to visitors. An example of a page in a Website expected to have a higher page depth would be a news page. Information on a news page is constantly updated so that, while the page is still always in the same location, the content of that page is constantly changing. If a Website has high page depth in a relatively unimportant part of the site, it may signal visitor confusion with navigation in the site or an incorrectly targeted advertising campaign.

Support/Self Service

Websites offering support or self-service are interested in helping users find specialized answers for specific problems. The goals for this type of Website are increasing customer satisfaction and decreasing call center costs; it is more cost-effective for a company to have visitors find information through its Website than it is to operate a call center. The KPIs of interest are visit length, content depth, and bounce rate. In addition, other areas to examine are customer satisfaction metrics and top internal search phrases (McFadden, 2005).

Page depth for support/self service sites is the same measurement as page depth content/media sites – the ratio of page views to unique visitors. With support/self service sites, however, high page depth is not always a good sign. For example, a visitor viewing the same page multiple times may show that the visitor is having trouble finding helpful information on the Website or even that the information the visitor is looking for does not exist on the site. The goal of these types of sites is to help customers find what they need as quickly as possible and with the least amount of navigation through the site (CCMedia, 2007). The best way to keep page depth low is to keep visitor confusion low.

As with the bounce rate of other Website types, the bounce rate for support/self service sites reflects ease of use, advertising effectiveness, and visitor interest. A low bounce rate means that quality traffic is coming to the Website and deciding that the site's information is potentially useful.

Poor advertisement campaigns and poor Website layout will increase a site's bounce rate.

Customer satisfaction deals with how the users rate their experience on a site and is usually collected directly from the visitors (not from log files), either through online surveys or through satisfaction ratings. Although it is not a KPI in the traditional sense, gathering data directly from visitors to a Website is a valuable tool for figuring out exactly what visitors want. Customer satisfaction measurements can deal with customer ratings, concern reports, corrective actions, response time, and product delivery. Using these numbers, one can compare the online experience of the Website's customers to the industry average and make improvements according to visitors' expressed needs.

Similarly, top internal search phrases applies only to sites with internal search, but it can be used to measure what information customers are most interested in which can lead to improvement in site navigation. This information can be used to direct support resources to the areas generating the most user interest, as well as identify which parts of the Website users may have trouble accessing. In addition, if many visitors are searching for a product not supported on the Website, it could be a sign of ineffective marketing.

Regardless of Website type, the KPIs listed above are not the only KPIs that can prove useful in analyzing a site's traffic, but they provide a good starting point. The main thing to remember is that no matter what KPIs a company chooses, they must be aligned with its business goals, and more KPIs do not necessarily mean better analysis – quality is more important than quantity.

KEY BEST PRACTICES

In this chapter, we have addressed which metrics can be gathered from a Website, how to gather them, and how to determine which information is important. But how can this help improve a business? To answer this, the Web Analytics Association provides nine key best practices to follow when analyzing a Website (McFadden, 2005). Figure 1 outlines this process.

Identify Key Stakeholders

A stakeholder is anyone who holds an interest in a Website. This includes management, site developers, visitors, and anyone else who creates, maintains, uses, or is affected by the site. In order for the Website to be truly beneficial, it

Figure 1. The best key practices of Web analytics

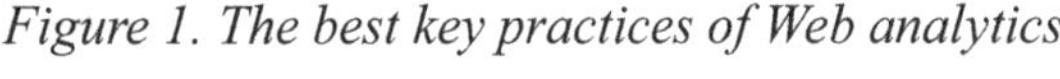

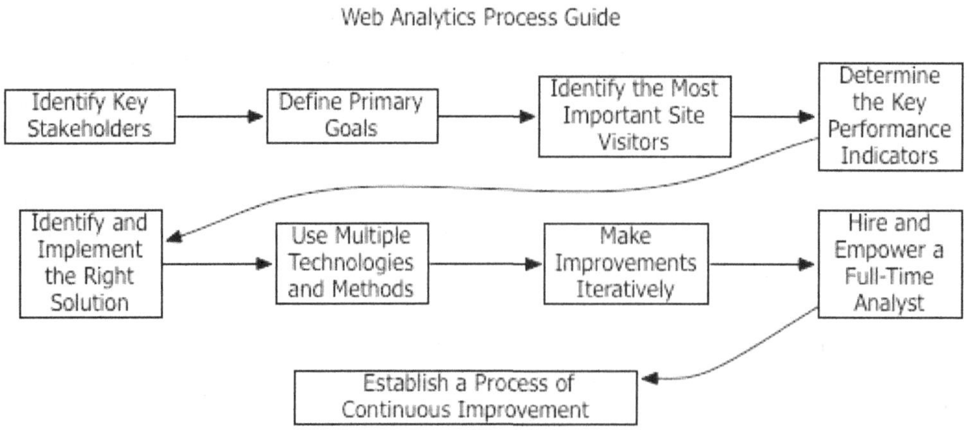

must integrate input from all major stakeholders. Involving people from different parts of the company also makes it more likely that they will embrace the Website as a valuable tool.

Define Primary Goals for Your Website

To know the primary goals of a Website, one must first understand the primary goals of its key stakeholders. This could include such goals as increasing revenue, cutting expenses, and increasing customer loyalty (McFadden, 2005). Once those goals have been defined, discuss each goal and prioritize them in terms of how the Website can most benefit the company. As always, beware of political conflict between stakeholders and their individual goals as well as assumptions they may have made while determining their goals that may not necessarily be true. By going through this process, a company can make sure that goals do not conflict and that stakeholders are kept happy.

Identify the Most Important Site Visitors

According to Sterne, corporate executives categorize their visitors differently in terms of importance. Most companies classify their most important visitors as ones who either visit the site regularly, stay the longest on the site, view the most pages, purchase the most goods or services, purchase goods most frequently, or spend the most money (Sterne, n. d.). There are three types of customers – (1) customers a company wants to keep who have a high current value and high future potential, (2) customers a company wants to grow who can either have a high current value and low future potential or low current value and high future potential, and (3) customers a company wants to eliminate who have a low current value and low future potential. The most important visitor to a Website, however, is the one who ultimately brings in the most revenue. Defining the different levels of customers will allow one to consider the goals of these visitors. What improvements can be made to the Website in order to improve their browsing experiences?

Determine the Key Performance Indicators

The next step is picking the metrics that will be most beneficial in improving the site and eliminating the ones that will provide little or no insight into its goals. One can then use these metrics to determine which KPI you wish to monitor. As mentioned in the previous section, the Website type – commerce, lead generation, media/content, or support/self service – plays a key role in which KPIs are most effective for analyzing site traffic.

Identify and Implement the Right Solution

This step deals with finding the right Web analytics technology to meet the business's specific needs. After the KPIs have been defined, this step should be easy. The most important things to consider are the budget, software flexibility and ease of use, and how well the technology will work with the needed metrics. McFadden suggests that it is also a good idea to run a pilot test of the top two vendor choices (McFadden, 2005). We will expand on this topic further in the next section.

Use Multiple Technologies and Methods

Web analytics is not the only method available for improving a Website. To achieve a more holistic view of a site's visitors, one can also use tools such as focus groups, online surveys, usability studies, and customer services contact analysis (McFadden, 2005).

Make Improvements Iteratively

When analyzing a Website's data, it is helpful to add gradual improvements to the Website instead of updating too many facets of the Website at once. By doing this one can monitor if a singular change is an improvement or if it is actually hurting the site.

Hire and Empower a Full-Time Analyst

It is important to put a person in charge of the data once it is collected. According to the Web Analytics Association, a good analyst understands business needs (which means communicating well with the stakeholders), has knowledge of technology and marketing, has respect, credibility, and authority, and is already a company employee. Although it may seem like hiring a full-time analyst is expensive, many experts agree that the return on revenue should be more than enough compensation to recoup the cost (McFadden, 2005).

Establish a Process of Continuous Improvement

Once the Web analysis process is decided upon, continuous evaluation is paramount. This means reviewing the goals and metrics and monitoring new changes and features which are added to the Website. It is important that the improvements are adding value to the site and meeting expectations.

SPECIFIC TOOLS

Choosing a Tool

Once the company decides what it wants out of the Web analysis, it is time to find the right tool. Kaushik outlines ten important questions to ask Web analytics vendors (2007):

1. *What is the difference between your tool and free Web analytics tools?* Since the company who owns the Website will be paying money for a service, it is important to know why that service is better than free services (for example, Google Analytics). Look for an answer that outlines the features and functionality of the vendor. Do not look for answers about increased costs because of privacy threats or poor support offered by free analytics tools.
2. *Do you offer a software version of your tool?* Generally, a business will want to look for a tool that is software based and can run on their own servers. If a tool does not have a software version but plans to make one in the future, it shows insight into how prepared they are to offer future products if there is interest.
3. *What methods do you use to capture data?* If you remember from the first section, there are two main ways to capture visitor data from a Website – log files and page tagging. Ideally, one should look for a vendor that offers both, but what they have used in the past is also important. Because technology is constantly changing, look for a company that has kept up with these changes in the past by providing creative solutions.
4. *Can you help me calculate the total cost of ownership for your tool?* The total cost of ownership for a Web analytics tool depends on the specific company, the systems they have in place, and the pricing of the prospective Web analytics tool. In order to make this calculation, one must consider the following:
   a. Cost per page view.
   b. Incremental costs (i.e. charges for overuse or advanced features).
   c. Annual support costs after the first year.

d. Cost of professional services (i.e. installation, troubleshooting, or customization).
e. Cost of additional hardware you may need.
f. Administration costs (which includes the cost of an analyst and any additional employees you may need to hire).

5. *What kind of support do you offer?* Many vendors advertise free support, but it is important to be aware of any limits that could incur additional costs. It is also important to note how extensive their support is and how willing they are to help.
6. *What features do you provide that will allow me to segment my data?* Segmentation allows companies to manipulate their data. Look for the vendor's ability to segment your data after it is recorded. Many vendors use JavaScript tags on each page to segment the data as it is captured, meaning that the company has to know exactly what it wants from the data before having the data itself; this approach is less flexible.
7. *What options do I have to export data into our system?* It is important to know who ultimately owns and stores the data and whether it is possible to obtain both raw and processed data. Most vendors will not provide companies with the data exactly as they need it, but it is a good idea to realize what kind of data is available before a final decision is made.
8. *Which features do you provide for integrating data from other sources into your tool?* This question deals with the previous section's Key Best Practice #6: Use Multiple Technologies and Methods. If a company has other data it wants to bring to the tool (such as survey data or data from your ad agency), bring them up to the potential analytics vendor and see if it is possible to integrate this information into their tool.
9. *What new features are you developing that would keep you ahead of your competition?* Not only will the answer to this question tell how much the vendor has thought about future functionality, it will also show how much they know about their competitors.
10. *Why did you lose your last two clients? Who are they using now?* The benefits of this question are obvious -- by knowing how they lost prior business, the business can be confident that it has made the right choice.

Some examples of free and commercially available analytics tools are discussed below.

Free Tools

One of the most popular free analytics tools on the Web now is Google Analytics (previously Urchin). Google Analytics (http://www.google.com/analytics/) uses page tagging to collect information from visitors to a site. In addition to expanding on the already highly regarded Urchin analytics tool, it also provides support for integrating other analytic information (for example, WordPress and AdWords). Google Analytics reports many of the KPIs discussed in the previous sections including depth of visit, returning visitors, and page depth.

There is, however, concern about privacy issues regarding Google Analytics because Google uses their default privacy policy for their analytics tools, but the company assures its Google Analytics users that only account owners and people to whom the owners give permission will have access to the data (Dodoo, 2006). Microsoft also provides a free Web analytic software called Gatineau (Thomas, 2007).

Paid Tools

InfoWorld provides an in-depth analysis comparing the top four Web analytic companies – Coremetrics, WebTrends, Omniture, and WebSide-

Story HBX (Heck, 2005). They created a scoring chart and measured each vendor on reporting, administration, performance, ease-of-use, support, and value. Coremetrics received a score of 8.3 with its highest ratings in administration and support. It is a hosted service that offers special configurations for financial, retail, and travel services. WebTrends also earned a score of 8.3 with its highest rating in reporting. This tool is expensive, but it offers a wide range of performance statistics and both client and server hosting. Omniture is next in line with a score of 8.4 with its highest ratings in reporting and support. It is an ASP reporting application that excels in providing relevant reports. WebSideStory had the highest score of 8.7 with its highest ratings in reporting, administration, ease-of-use, and support. This tool is easy to use and is appropriate for many different types of businesses.

CONCLUSION

The first step in analyzing your Website and Website visitors is understanding and analyzing your business goals and then using that information to carefully choose your metrics. In order to take full advantage of the information gathered from your site's visitors, you must consider alternative methods such as focus groups and online surveys, make site improvements gradually, hire a full-time analyst, and realize that your site's improvement is a process and not a one-time activity. Using these key best practices and choosing the right analytics vendor to fit your business will save your company money and ultimately increase revenue.

As Web analytics continues to mature, the methods vendors use to collect information are becoming more refined. One article speculates that companies will find concrete answers to the problems with cookies and unique visitors (Eisenberg, 2005). The Web analytics industry as a whole is also expanding. According to Eisenberg (2005), a recent Jupiter report predicts an increase in the Web analytics industry – 20 percent annually. More and more businesses are realizing the benefits of critically analyzing their Website traffic and are taking measures to improve their profits based off these numbers. Regardless of business size and objective, an effective Web analytics strategy is becoming increasingly essential for online success.

REFERENCES

Aldrich, S. E. (2006, May 2). *The Other Search: Making the Most of Site Search to Optimize the Total Customer Experience*. Patricia Seybold Group. Retrieved March 7, 2007, from WebSideStory database.

Ansari, S., Kohavi, R., Mason, L., & Zheng, Z. (2001). Integrating E-Commerce and Data Mining: Architecture and Challenges. *IEEE International Conference on Data Mining*.

Avinash, A. (2007, June 26). *Bounce Rate: Sexiest Web Metric Ever?* Retrieved December 2, 2007, from http://www.mpdailyfix.com/2007/06/bounce_rate_sexiest_web_metric.html.

Becher, J. D. (2005, March). Why Metrics-Centric Performance Management Solutions Fall Short. *DM Review Magazine*. Retrieved March 7, 2007, from http://www.dmreview.com/article_sub.cfm?articleId=1021509.

Belkin, M. (2006, April 8). *15 Reasons why all Unique Visitors are not created equal*. Retrieved March 7, 2007, from http://www.omniture.com/blog/node/16.

Burby, J. (2004, July 20). *Build a Solid Foundation With Key Performance Indicators, Part 1: Lead-Generation Sites*. Retrieved March 7, 2007, from http://www.clickz.com/showPage.html?page=3382981.

Burby, J. & Brown, A. (2007). *Web Analytics Definitions*. Retrieved October 30, 2007, from http://www.webanalyticsassociation.org/attachments/committees/5/WAA-Standards-Analytics-Definitions-Volume-I-20070816.pdf.

CCMedia. (2007, August 30). *How to Obtain a Cost-effective Operational Model for Support/ Self-service Websites?* Retrieved December 5, 2007, from www.webnibbler.com/en/WhitePaper/Online%20Support%20Website.pdf.

Dodoo, M. (2006, March 3). *Privacy & Google Analytics.* Retrieved March 7, 2007, from http://www.marteydodoo.com/2006/05/03/privacy-google-analytics/.

Eisenberg, B. (2005, April 1). *Web Analytics: Exciting Times Ahead.* Retrieved March 7, 2007, from http://www.clickz.com/showPage.html?page=3493976

eVision. (2007, September 27). *Websites that convert visitors into customers: Improving the ability of your Website to convert visitors into inquiries, leads, and new business.* Retrieved March 7, 2007, from http://www.evisionsem.com/marketing/webanalytics.htm

FoundPages. (2007, October 25). *Increasing Conversion Rates.* Retrieved October 31, 2007, from http://www.foundpages.com/calgary-internet-marketing/search-conversion.html

Greenfield, M. (2006, January 1). *Use Web Analytics to Improve Profits for New Year: Focus on four key statistics.* Retrieved March 7, 2007, from http://www.practicalecommerce.com/articles/132/Use-Web-Analytics-to-Improve-Profits-for-New-Year/

Hallam-Baker, P. M. & Behlendorf, B. (1999,February 4). *Extended Log File Format.* Retrieved March 7, 2007, from http://www.w3.org/TR/WD-logfile.html

Heck, M. (2005, February 18). *Chart Your Website's Success.* Retrieved March 7, 2007, from http://www.infoworld.com/Omniture_SiteCatalyst_11/product_56297.html?view=1&curNodeId=0&index=0

IBM. (2004, May 19). *Log File Formats.* Retrieved October 29, 2007, from http://publib.boulder.ibm.com/tividd/td/ITWSA/ITWSA_info45/en_US/HTML/guide/c-logs.html

Jacka, R. *Getting Results From Your Website.* Retrieved October 30, 2007, from http://www.panalysis.com/downloads/gettingresults.pdf

Jackson, M. (2007, January 22). *Analytics: Deciphering the Data.* Retrieved March 7, 2007, from http://www.ecommerce-guide.com/resources/article.php/3655251

Kaushik, A (2006, November 13). *Excellent Analytics Tip #8: Measure the Real Conversion Rate & 'Opportunity Pie.'* Retrieved November 3, 2007, from http://www.kaushik.net/avinash/2006/11/excellent-analytics-tip-8-measure-the-real-conversion-rate-opportunity-pie.html

Kaushik, A. (2007, January 23). *Web Analytics Tool Selection: 10 Questions to ask Vendors.* Retrieved March 7, 2007, from http://www.kaushik.net/avinash/2007/01/web-analytics-tool-selection-10-questions-to-ask-vendors.html

MarketingSherpa. (2007, October 20). *Security Logo in Email Lifts Average Order Value 28.3%.* Retrieved December 4, 2007, from https://www.marketingsherpa.com/barrier.html?ident=30183

Marshall, J. *Seven Deadly Web Analytics Sins.* Retrieved March 7, 2007, from http://www.clicktracks.com/insidetrack/articles/7_deadly_webanalytics_sins01.php

Mason, N. (2007, February 6). *Customer Loyalty Improves Retention.* Retrieved March 7, 2007, from http://www.clickz.com/showPage.html?page=3624868

McFadden, C. (2005, July 6). *Optimizing the Online Business Channel with Web Analytics.*

Retrieved March 7, 2007, from http://www.Webanalyticsassociation.org/en/art/?9

Microsoft. (2005, August 22). *W3C Extended Log File Examples*. Retrieved March 7, 2007, from http://technet2.microsoft.com/WindowsServer/en/library/b5b8a519-8f9b-456b-9040-018358f2c0c01033.mspx?mfr=true

Permadi, F. (2005, June 19). *Introduction to Flash Local Shared-Object*. Retrieved March 7, 2007, from http://www.permadi.com/tutorial/flashSharedObject/index.html

Peterson, E. T. (2004). *Web Analytics Demystified*. Celilo Group Media.

Peterson, E. T. (2005, July 31). *Average Order Value*. Retrieved November 3, 2007, from Web Analytics Demystified Blog Website: http://blog.webanalyticsdemystified.com/weblog/2005/07/average-order-value.html

QuestionPro. *Measuring Customer Loyalty and Customer Satisfaction*. Retrieved November 21, 2007, from http://www.questionpro.com/akira/showArticle.do?articleID=customerloyalty.

Sapir, D. (2004, August). Online Analytics and Business Performance Management. *BI Report*. Retrieved March 7, 2007, from http://www.dmreview.com/editorial/dmreview/print_action.cfm?articleId=1008820

SearchCRM. (2007, May 9). *Measuring Customer Loyalty*. Retrieved November 4, 2007, from http://searchcrm.techtarget.com/general/0,295582,sid11_gci1253794,00.html

Sen, A., Dacin, P. A., & Pattichis, C. (2006, November). Current trends in Web data analysis. *Communications of the ACM, 49(11),* 85 - 91.

Sterne, J. *10 Steps to Measuring Website Success*. Retrieved March 7, 2007, from http://www.marketingprofs.com/login/join.asp?adref=rdblk&source=/4/sterne13.asp

Thomas, I. (2007, January 9). *The rumors are true: Microsoft 'Gatineau' exists*. Retrieved March 7, 2007, from http://www.liesdamnedlies.com/2007/01/the_rumors_are_.html

Web Analytics Association. *Onsite Behavior-Path Analysis*. Retrieved March 7, 2007, from http://www.Webanalyticsassociation.org/attachments/contentmanagers/336/1%20Path%20AnAnalys.doc

WebSideStory. (2004). *Use of Key Performance Indicators in Web Analytics*. Retrieved December 2, 2007, from www.4everywhere.com/documents/KPI.pdf

White, K. (2006, May 10). *Unique vs. Returning Visitors Analyzed*. Retrieved March 7, 2007, from http://newsletter.blizzardinternet.com/unique-vs-returning-visitors-analyzed/2006/05/10/#more-532

Young, D. (2007, August 15). Site Search: Increases Conversion Rates, Average Order Value And Loyalty. *Practical Ecommerce*, Retrieved November 15, 2007, from http://www.practicalecommerce.com/articles/541/Site-Search-Increases-Conversion-Rates-Average-Order-Value-And-Loyalty/

KEY TERMS

Abandonment Rate: KPI that measures the percentage of visitors who got to that point on the site but decided not to perform the target action.

Alignment-Centric Performance Management: Method of defining a site's business goals by choosing only a few key performance indicators.

Average Order Value: KPI that measures the total revenue to the total number of orders.

Average Time on Site (ATOS): See *visit length*.

Checkout Conversion Rate: KPI that measures the percent of total visitors who begin the checkout process.

Commerce Website: A type of Website where the goal is to get visitors to purchase goods or services directly from the site.

Committed Visitor Index: KPI that measures the percentage of visitors that view more than one page or spend more than 1 minute on a site (these measurements should be adjusted according to site type).

Content/Media Website: A type of Website focused on advertising.

Conversion Rate: KPI that measures the percentage of total visitors to a Website that perform a specific action.

Cost Per Lead (CPL): KPI that measures the ratio of marketing expenses to total leads and shows how much it costs a company to generate a lead.

Customer Satisfaction Metrics: KPI that measures how the users rate their experience on a site.

Customer Loyalty: KPI that measures the ratio of new to existing customers.

Demographics and System Statistics: A metric that measures the physical location and information of the system used to access the Website.

Depth of Visit: KPI that measures the ratio between page views and visitors.

Internal Search: A metric that measures information on keywords and results pages viewed using a search engine embedded in the Website.

Key Performance Indicator (KPI): A combination of metrics tied to a business strategy.

Lead Generation Website: A type of Website that is used to obtain user contact information in order to inform them of a company's new products and developments, and to gather data for market research.

Log File: Log kept by a Web server of information about requests made to the Website including (but not limited to) visitor IP address, date and time of the request, request page, referrer, and information on the visitor's Web browser and operating system.

Log File Analysis: Method of gathering metrics that uses information gathered from a log file to gather Website statistics.

Metrics: Statistical data collected from a Website such as number of unique visitors, most popular pages, etc.

New Visitor: A user who is accessing a Website for the first time.

New Visitor Percentage: KPI that measures the ratio of new visitors to unique visitors.

Online Business Performance Management (OBPM): Method of defining a site's business goals that emphasizes the integration of business tools and Web analytics to make better decisions quickly in an ever-changing online environment.

Order Conversion Rate: KPI that measures the percent of total visitors who place an order on a Website.

Page Depth: KPI that measures the ratio of page views for a specific page and the number of unique visitors to that page.

Page Tagging: Method of gathering metrics that uses an invisible image to detect when a page has been successfully loaded and then uses JavaScript to send information about the page and the visitor back to a remote server.

Prospect Rate: KPI that measures the percentage of visitors who get to the point in a site where they can perform the target action (even if they do not actually complete it).

Referrers and Keyword Analysis: A metric that measures which sites have directed traffic to the Website and which keywords visitors are using to find the Website.

Repeat Visitor: A user who has been to a Website before and is now returning.

Returning Visitor: KPI that measures the ratio of unique visitors to total visits.

Search Engine Referrals: KPI that measures the ratio of referrals to a site from specific search engines compared to the industry average.

Single Access Ratio: KPI that measures the ratio of total single access pages (or pages where the visitor enters the site and exits immediately from the same page) to total entry pages.

Stickiness: KPI that measures how many people arrive at a homepage and proceed to traverse the rest of the site.

Support/Self Service Website: A type of Website that focuses on helping users find specialized answers for their particular problems.

Top Pages: A metric that measures the pages in a Website that receive the most traffic.

Total Bounce Rate: KPI that measures the percentage of visitors who scan the site and then leave.

Traffic Concentration: KPI that measures the ratio of number of visitors to a certain area in a Website to total visitors.

Unique Visit: One visit to a Website (regardless of if the user has previously visited the site); an alternative to unique visitors.

Unique Visitor: A specific user who accesses a Website.

Visit Length: A metric that measures total amount of time a visitor spends on the Website.

Visit Value: KPI that measures the total number of visits to total revenue.

Visitor Path: A metric that measures the route a visitor uses to navigate through the Website.

Visitor Type: A metric that measures users who access a Website. Each user who visits the Website is a unique user. If it is a user's first time to the Website, that visitor is a new visitor, and if it is not the user's first time, that visitor is a repeat visitor.

Web Analytics: The measurement of visitor behavior on a Website.

Chapter IX
The Unit of Analysis and the Validity of Web Log Data

Gi Woong Yun
Bowling Green State University, USA

ABSTRACT

This chapter discusses validity of units of analysis of Web log data. First, Web log units are compared to the unit of analysis of television to understand the conceptual issues of media use unit of analysis. Second, the validity of both Client-side and Server-side Web log data are examined along with benefits and shortcomings of each Web log data. Each method has implications on cost, privacy, cache memory, session, attention, and many other areas of concerns. The challenges were not only theoretical but, also, methodological. In the end, Server-side Web log data turns out to have more potentials than it is originally speculated. Nonetheless, researchers should decide the best research method for their research and they should carefully design research to claim the validity of their data. This chapter provides some valuable recommendations for both Client-side and Server-side Web log researchers.

INTRODUCTION

One of the main motivations of Internet content providers in expanding the availability of multimedia is the perception that the Internet provides unparalleled access to accurate usage data. It is generally felt that the Web log traces left by individual Internet users provide unprecedented quantity and quality of information to researchers and to those who would study consumer and market behavior. However, there were some warning signs about the validity of Web log data (Goldberg, 2001). This chapter will discuss most of the validity problems, but it should be noticed that many studies (e.g., Davis, 2004; Eveland & Dunwoody, 1998a; Eveland & Dunwoody, 1998b; Jansen & Resnick, 2005; Phippen, 2004) paid only minor attention to the validity of Web log data during the analysis. This might be because it is expected that the Internet use data collected from computers will provide precise and detailed information about users' Internet use behavior

(Eveland & Dunwoody, 1998a). Indeed, it is a reasonable assumption that Internet use behavior tracked by computer software will be more valid than previous media use tracking methods. This high expectation of validity is due to the pinpoint accuracy of the client computers' or server computers' data collection software.

Some researchers suspected the usefulness of the transaction log data (Peters, Kurth, Flaherty, Sandore, & Kaske, 1993; Kurth, 1993; Larson, 1991). Others argued that data structures and a complex collection algorithm should be explored for the meaningful analysis of the data, as this contributes greatly to the data quality and quantity (Phippen, 2004). For instance, a unit of analysis of the data needs more attention before scientific analysis of the Internet use data. Deciding a proper unit of analysis is difficult and it will influence predicting and including analysis units ahead of data collection.

The unit of analysis of Web site use can differ depending on researchers and the research topics. Hence, the unit of analysis of Web site use can be examined with various levels of analysis. Any research will need to choose a level or levels of analysis when they want to use Web log data to analyze user's navigation patterns or content access habits. The researcher's research concept will be a major factor determining the level of analysis. However, technical specifications of the Web log data sometimes limit what researchers can select as a unit of analysis for their research. Although many people have expectations of accuracy in Web log data, typical Web log data, both Server-side and Client-side data, have limitations and strengths.

The validity of Web logs cannot be taken for granted and there is much to learn about how to collect and accurately interpret online activity. This chapter will propose criteria in defining units of analysis of the Web site use with a media research paradigm after examining some theoretical frameworks of media use measurement.

A UNIT OF ANALYSIS

Many researchers already utilized Internet log data to understand individual patterns of knowledge seeking via the Internet. They created variables to track which Web pages users have visited (e.g., Eveland & Dunwoody, 1998a; Eveland & Dunwoody, 1998b; Phippen, Sheppard & Furnell, 2004), what users have queried (e.g., Jansen & Spink, 2005; Jansen, Spink & Pederson, 2005; Jones, Cunningham, McNab & Boddie, 2000; Sandore, 1993; Taha, 2004), what they wrote while they were using a computer, who they communicated with, what they communicated, or how they communicated (e.g., McTavish, Pingree, Hawkins, & Gustafson, 2003; Phippen, 2004). These units of analysis of Web site use have been operationalized based on the availability of Web log data.

Measurement Units

Internet use is different from watching a network TV program where millions of television viewers share a limited number of variations of channel surfing patterns. Each Internet user uniquely engages in non-linearly structured cyber space. Therefore, it is not an easy task to record and analyze all users' navigation behavior. However, some measurement units within a computerized recording system can be traced. The analysis units can be the amount of *time* spent during the navigation or the number of computer files *accessed.*

Time

One of the most frequently measured units in media research is time. The sheer volume of time exposure has been investigated since the beginning of the media research field. Survey respondents are asked to answer questions like 'how many hours did you spend reading a newspaper per week?', 'how many hours did you watch television last week?', or 'how many hours did you watch television news?' Such questions will also be applicable to computer users. In fact, computerized recording systems can trace smaller and more precise increments of time. The duration of stay on Web sites can represent 'time' spent for this medium and it can be measured in millisecond units.

Hawkins and Pingree (1997) have extensively discussed time as a unit of analysis for computer use. They have suggested five time levels for computer use where time represents the foundation of each measure. Their five levels are a lifestyle time frame, multi-episode segment of time, an episode of use, individual message, and within-message.

Each measure helps researchers explore the amount of time allocated to computer interaction as well as the nature of the interaction. 'A lifestyle time frame' measures the general use during the lifetime. 'Multi-episode segment of time' measures media use during the particular segments of the lifetime such as hours, weeks, or months. An 'episode of use' is a time frame used to measure a specific occasion of use. 'Individual message' measures the time spent for the specific message and 'within message' frame can measure the accesses to the certain section of the message (Hawkins & Pingree, 1997). Figure 1 represents Hawkins and Pingree's units of analysis and media use.

Figure 1. Units of analysis of media use

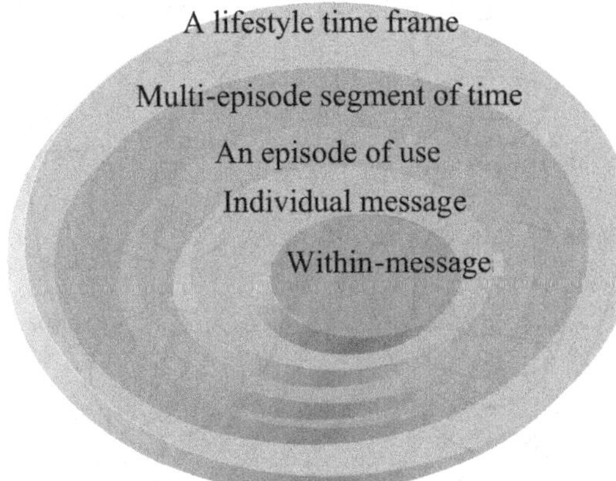

By targeting computer interaction in increasingly smaller segments or time intervals, researchers explored how computer use becomes beneficial to individual users (e.g., Booske & Saintfort, 1998; Smaglick et al., 1998). The five time levels proposed by Hawkins and Pingree can be applied to the Internet use with some modifications. Among five levels, 'Multi-episode segment of time' can be applied to two different time levels. Both computer and Internet use can be 'multi-episode segment of time'. For instance, turning the computer on and off multiple times creates multi-episode segments. At the same time, connection and disconnection to the Internet can create multi-episode segments through multiple log-ins and log-offs. Although both episodes can be treated as multi-episode segment of time, multi-episode of Internet happens only within the multi-episode of computer use because a computer must be turned on before an Internet use episode can start (Figure 2).

If we accept both computer use and Internet use as 'multi-episode segments of time', the rest of use time levels are relatively easy to apply. For Internet use measurements, 'an episode of use' will start with the Internet connection and it will end at the point of the Internet disconnection. Also, the 'individual message' can be a certain domain access (e.g., www.cnn.com) and the 'within message' can be Web page access within a domain (e.g., www.cnn.com/news/space.htm).

One of the many unique features of the Internet is the interactivity (Yun, 2007). As a private medium, the Internet provides highly interactive media use experience. Again, comparison between television and the Internet can draw a clearer picture. For instance, each person develops one's own pattern when they use media. People have their favorite channel and they go to that channel when they turn on the TV. However, combinations of TV surfing behavior are quite limited compared to the Internet. This is because TV does not provide unlimited information channels and the TV audience does not need to click a mouse to move on to the next scene or story. In sum, TV does not provide interactive media experience compared to the Internet which requires constant mouse clicks to move from one Web site to another.

We can discuss this issue more specifically comparing TV watching and Internet use (figure 3). TV viewers first decide which channel they are going to watch and, later, push the remote control buttons, but they do not have to actively navigate the story of the program. They can just sit and watch wherever the program plot leads them. They use the remote control only when they need to change the channel. However, Internet users have to actively choose where they want to go instead of sitting and watching where the program leads them. As we can see from Figure 4, Internet domain selection might be equivalent to TV channel selection. A comparison between Figure 4 and Figure 5 reveals that TV researchers can study the active involvement of the TV audience by simply analyzing each channel change in an episode. On the other hand, Internet researchers need to look at users' more micro level active involvement.

The solid arrow in Figure 5 stands for the passive involvement of the TV audience. Once the TV audience decides on the channel, the content watched by the audience is controlled by the flow of the TV program narrative. On the other hand, Internet users have active involvement even on this level. As shown in Figure 4, dotted arrows inside of the domain represent the Internet users' active involvement. They select each move inside the domain and go to wherever they want to go.

There are several consequences of this level of analysis in TV watching and Internet use. When the researcher analyzes TV content, the analysis unit is limited to the TV channel and program. However, Internet researchers can investigate more micro level activities, including each movement inside of the domain, because all these movements need users' active involvement. The only limitation is that the researchers

Figure 2. Units of analysis of computer use

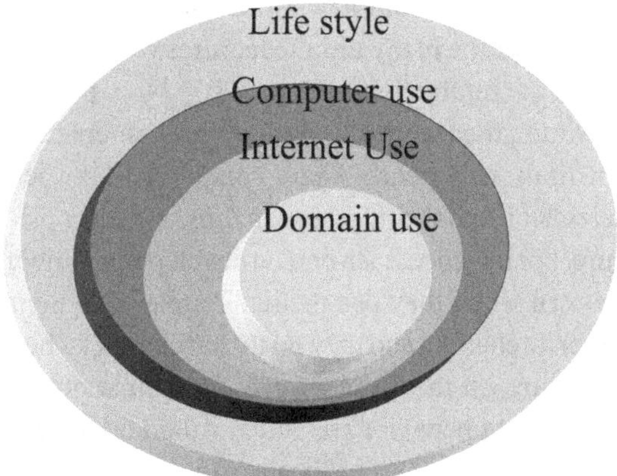

Figure 3. An example of TV use and Internet use episodes

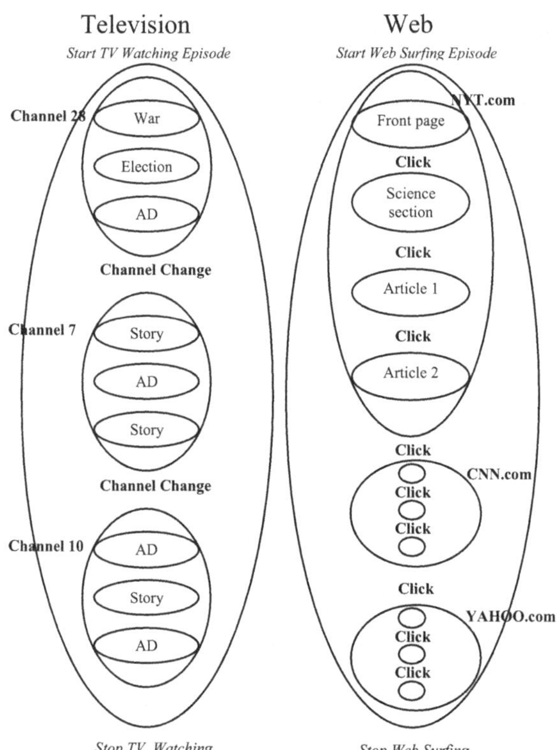

cannot analyze on this level unless s/he has all users' Internet use data.

Facing the limitations of collecting perfect Internet use data, one of the compromises adopted by Web log researchers is the concept of *session*. Session is defined as a set of sequentially or semantically related clicks and session units are very convenient to calculate time from the server-side Web log data (e.g., Jones, Cunningham, McNab, & Boddie, 2000; Jansen & Spink, 2005; Jansen, Spink & Pedersen, 2005, Peters, 1993). In fact, session is very similar to 'an episode of use'. A session starts when a user connects to the server and stops when a user leaves the Web site. One of the rationales for the Web log data miners to utilize the session is that it is a useful unit of analysis, which can be instrumental in calculating media use time. A more detailed discussion about session unit will appear in the latter part of this chapter.

Figure 4. Internet use episodes

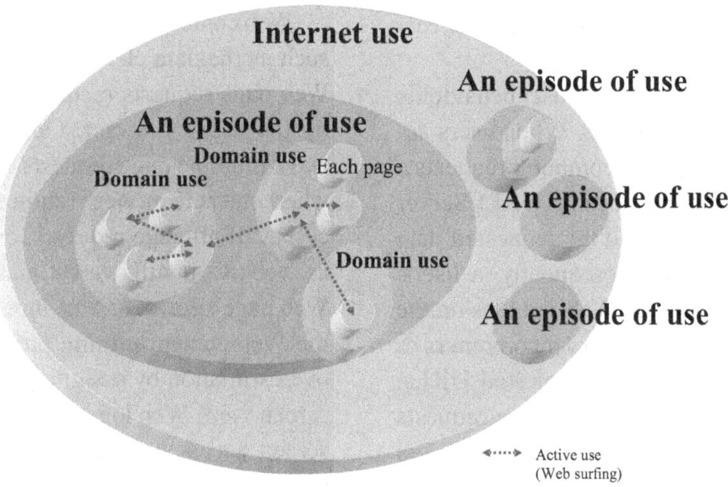

Figure 5. TV watching episodes

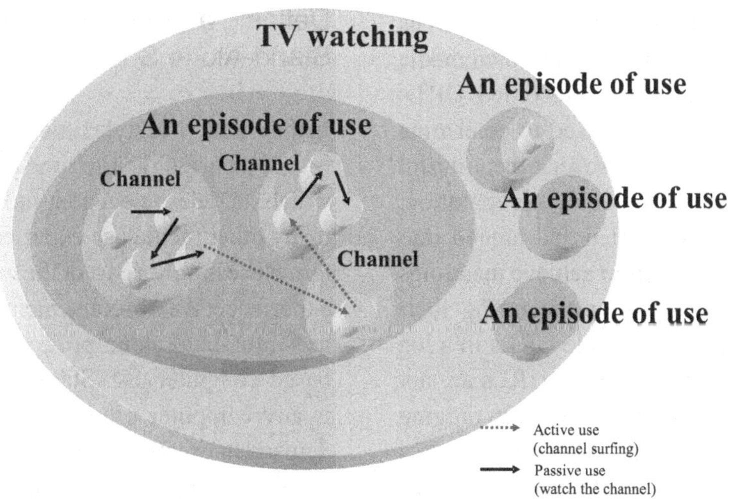

Frequency of Login vs. Page Request

Web log information such as the volume of data sent or received, the locations of users, or query strings can be measured in many ways. However, those measurements are less relevant to the individual's media use quantities and qualities. One of the more popular ways to measure the Internet use is the frequency of login, which is based on the record of users' points of entry to the Web site. Thus, the cumulated entries to the specific Web site or specific Internet program can be calculated. The frequency of login will be equivalent to the number of episodes of Internet use, or the number of sessions, in the Internet multi-episode time frame.

Another method of recording user behavior is the frequency of page requests. When users access any Web page, a user's computer requests a certain Uniform Resource Locator (URL). Server computers respond and send the requested data to the users' computer. Subsequently, a user's computer displays received Web site files on the screen. During this process, server computers or a user's computer can record requested URLs. And, the accumulated number of page requests can represent the amount of content accesses from the Web site.

The frequency of login and the page requests measurement are similar to the time measure for the media use. In fact, 'page requests' can tell us more about media use than the traditional media use measurement because the recorded URLs reveal filenames that can be used to determine the contents they contain. However, a meaningful analysis of the page requests requires preparation. That is, files should be sorted and tagged into specific categories in order to achieve meanings of the content accessed by users during their navigation. The revelation of the URLs in a log file may not mean anything when URLs are not clarified in some meaningful ways. Yet, tagging each file with some meaningful category requires a great deal of resources even for a moderate size Web site. In fact, creating this meta data for each Web page is one of the most time consuming processes in Web log data mining (e.g., Handschuh & Staab, 2002).

Conventional data mining scholars also worked on the Web log data mining. They used data mining theory as a frame of reference to analyze Web log mining. For instance, Web log mining scholars used the term 'Web content mining'. It is the process that categorizes content of the Web site and it is considered to be one of the most critical elements for the meaningful analysis of the data (Kanerva, Keeker, Risden, Schuh, & Czerwinski, 2004).

Web content mining includes important steps such as the data clean-up process. For instance, Web page requests record entire files requested by the user's browser. One screen access can leave multiple page requests in the Web log data when one screen view requires multiple file accesses. If all page requests, or hits, are counted as Web use, it will overestimate the access of the Web page (Bertot & McClure, 1997). Therefore, the Web content mining process should cut the overestimation by assigning a single count for a screen view. Web log mining scholars name one screen access as 'page access' or 'page view' and distinguish it from 'page requests' (Burton & Walther, 2001).

Defining an Episode of Use: Stand-Alone Software vs. Internet

In the whole "life style time frame", computer use is only a part of the life time media consumption which includes television, radio, newspaper and many other media use experience. Likewise, Internet use is only a part of the whole computer use experience. We can conveniently divide computer use into stand-alone program use and Internet based computer use. Stand-alone computer use is any computer program use, which does not demand Internet connection (Figure 6). Therefore, stand-alone programs include software such as stand-alone games, word processors, spreadsheets, DVD player, or graphic design software. Although stand-alone computer programs occasionally make connections to the Internet, it typically does not require a constant connection to the Internet. On the contrary, Internet based computer use requires a constant connection to the Internet. The gate to the Internet should be kept open continuously for the Internet experience and the data should be exchanged between user's computer and the computers on the Internet without any interruption.

Because stand-alone computer use occurs without an Internet connection, it is logical to consider that the stand-alone computer use is not Internet use. Only after the connection to the Internet and exchanges of data between user's computer and computers on the Internet, does an episode of Internet use starts. However, when a researcher includes stand-alone computer use in the study, turning on the computer will be the beginning of an episode.

Such a theoretical division between stand-alone program use and Internet use can be relatively clear, but it may not be practical to separate Internet use and stand-alone computer use in the contemporary computer use environment. In the real world, computer use includes a variety of use patterns among computer users. For instance, some users have constant network connections and they constantly switch applications between stand-alone software and Internet based software. In fact, they may even use stand-alone, Internet, and many other programs simultaneously by opening multiple windows and working on them at the same time. This type of user will constantly go in and out of the Internet. Thus, if a researcher defines an episode of Internet use by excluding stand-alone computer use, every switch between stand-alone computer use and Internet use will create an episode of Internet use. There is no doubt that this pattern of use will over-represent a number of episodes of Internet use from the traditional media use measurement perspective.

Figure 6. Units of analysis of stand alone software use and Internet use

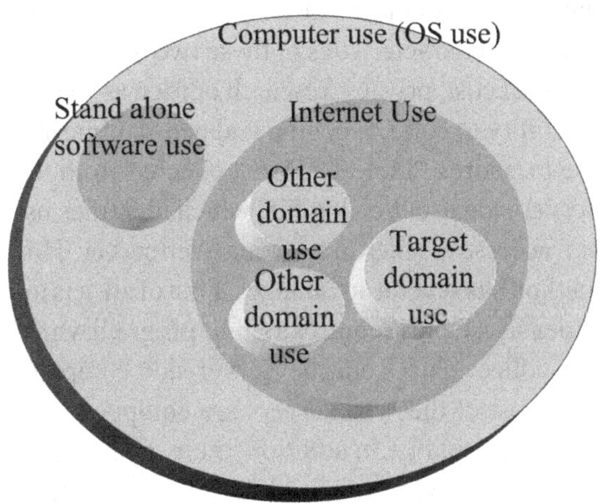

The distinction between stand-alone computer use and Internet use blurs even more when we adopt more micro level analysis. For instance, conventional electronic media use usually requires constant connections, such as watching television requires TV's constant connections to the broadcasting frequency or cable. Therefore, watching TV almost always means connecting to the broadcasting frequency or cable. On the other hand, Internet use does not always require constant connection. Once the content is downloaded or cached in the user's computer, Internet users can browse the content without a live connection.

This micro level analysis becomes more complicated when we consider the stand-alone software designed for the Internet communication such as e-mail. When users write e-mails with e-mail software, they typically open the program and start writing an e-mail. During an e-mail writing session, the e-mail program does not need to connect to the Internet, but it only momentarily connects to the Internet when users finish writing and push a send button. This example indicates that a boundary between stand-alone computer use and Internet use is quite complicated in contemporary computer use environment and it creates difficulties of measuring Internet use as media use. Internet use researchers should not only be aware of this problem, but also should clarify how they included or excluded stand-alone use in the analysis algorithm.

Attention to the Media

Another dimension that needs to be considered to obtain a valid measure of media use is an individual's attention to the media. The measurement of media use often requires the assumption that the audience paid some level of attention during the measured media use time. When we ask audiences 'how many hours do you spend watching TV?', we assume that they paid at least some attention to TV during the whole period rather than no attention at all during the answered amount of TV watching time (Danaher, 1995). It is a reasonable assumption since the answer is based on users' perceptual judgment of their media use time, although the answer is vulnerable to many measurement issues such as instrumental decays, history, or demand characteristics (Babbie, 2004).

However, when we are willing to adopt a detailed computer recording system, the minimal attention assumption should be carefully re-examined. In fact, there is a serious problem measuring a user's detailed behavior when the computer program cannot record users' movements. There are many scenarios where minimum attention level could not be satisfied. First of all, a Web log file cannot tell whether users are sitting in front of the monitor and reading information displayed on the screen. Users may work on something else while they are sitting in front of the computer such as organizing their desks or answering phone calls (Catledge & Pitkow, 1995; Jansen & Spink, 2005). Additionally, typical Web log data cannot accurately measure Web use when users activate multiple browsers or browser tabs and access many Web sites simultaneously. Furthermore, it is also possible that the users may not read an entire page but navigate only after reading the first line of the page (Burton & Walther, 2001). Therefore, the duration of time spent for specific Web site can misrepresent the real media use duration. The internal validity of the measured time from Web log file will be seriously threatened, if above instances are prevalent amongst Web users.

Two Types of Log Files (Client vs. Server)

Previous research on Transaction Log Analysis (TLA) reported that the validity of the log file can be triangulated and examined. Some researchers (e.g., Barber & Riccalton, 1988) confirmed the validity of the TLA and some (e.g., Nielsen, 1986) questioned the validity of TLA. I will discuss strengths and weaknesses of the two different types of Web log data: Client-side and Server-side.

Cost vs. Privacy

Ideally, Internet use data should be able to seamlessly collect each individual's entire Internet use in both time and page request units. However, the likelihood of getting ideal data is very low due to the limitations of research methods. Therefore, researchers frequently collect only partial information about how individuals use the Internet depending on the method available to them.

In general, there are two ways of collecting Internet use data: the Server-side collection and the Client-side collection. It is important to distinguish the characteristics of these two methods in terms of cost, privacy, research burden as well as its ability to collect specific and general Internet use measures (Table 1). Data collected from the Server-side use Web log file, which identifies users' accesses to files in a certain Web server. This method has several advantages. First of all, it is inexpensive. It only requires a single program which can collect data from the Server-side computer and most of the Web servers are equipped with this functionality. In addition, there are minimal human resources required for the Server-side

Table 1. Comparisons between client-side and server-side data

	Client Side	Server Side
Cost	High for user recruitment	Economical
Privacy	Invasive Higher concerns	Less Invasive Less ethical concerns
Demographic data	High validity	Low validity
Staff Involvement	High	Low
Data coverage	Whole Web use	Only from a specific Web server
Burden	Secure data storage Human subject approval	
Caching	No caching problem	Suffer caching problem

data collection which makes this method very economical. Second, Server-side data collection is less invasive and reduces the ethical concerns of privacy unless the data is collected in a closed system such as America Online (AOL). This is because typical Web server log cannot identify individuals. However, it should be noted that Web site users can be identified by their computer IP addresses, which can pin-point the locations of users' computers. Nonetheless, unless users willingly give away their private information to on-line surveys or registrations, the Server-side method is relatively free from privacy problems and it is not feasible for a researcher to link users' private information and their Web log data.

On the other hand, relative safety from privacy invasion is one of the critical shortcomings of this method. Because this method cannot provide individual information such as user demographics, studies based solely on Web log data can only produce limited research results. Although researchers can ask for voluntary responses from participants of the study, research that relies on online users' voluntary submission of their personal information can face severe sampling problems. Furthermore, the validity of the information is highly suspected considering the anonymous nature of the Internet.

Contrary to the Server-side method, Client-side data collection can be more accurate in measuring personal information. This is because the Client-side method requires some contacts with study participants. The Client-side method works by installing a monitoring program in users' computers and the researchers are then able to collect personal information during those contacts. Researchers can retrieve collected data from the user computer's hard drive after a certain period of time. In fact, some Client-side data collection software can constantly send accessed URLs from users' computers to a remote computer which is readily accessible to researchers. This simultaneous collection process can not only eliminate time delays of data collection, but it can also reduce required physical presence of researchers for periodical data collection.

Regardless of the specifics of each method, Client-side data collection provides detailed Internet use information. Indeed, the collected data is the whole Internet use data from the specific computer. However, contrary to the Server-side data collection method, the cost of user recruitment for the Client-side collection method can be high. This method does not only need software designed to collect data from research participants' computers, but it also requires a software installation on each participant's computer. Costs for software and human resources required for the installation process can be high enough to discourage many researchers from employing the Client-side data collection method. Furthermore, there are serious concerns about users' privacy. Participants' personal information is easily exposed to a researcher at the Internet user recruitment stage. Once a researcher gathered personal information, s/he can link it with the users' Internet use data. Every key stroke will be exposed to researchers including sensitive private information such as bank account numbers, credit card numbers, personal health information, social security numbers, and so on. The burden for a researcher to securely lock this type of data in the database might be overwhelming and it can hamper the human subject review board approval process.

Multiple Computer Access

Computers can save visited Web content on their cache memory and redistribute it when users want to visit the same Web content. This means that users' computers do not have to repeatedly request Web content to Web servers. Furthermore, proxy servers on the Web can sometimes save content files on their hard drives and transmit files to individual computers to conserve redundant Web traffics. This process is called *caching* and it can be a major problem for the Server-side data collection method because Web servers will never know users' Web content view when the content was redistributed from the users' or proxy servers' cache memory. Burton and Walther (2001) posit that the Client-side data collection method can overcome file caching problems because it records users' activities from client computers. However, more importantly and beyond this advantage, the Client-side collection method can produce more inclusive data collection by recording all activities from the client computers compared with the Server-side data collection method which can only record accesses to the content located in the specific Web server.

For these reasons, Client-side data covers a wider range of the user behavior. However, an important disadvantage of the Client-side data collection method is that the data collection program must be installed on *every* computer accessed by users to accomplish exhaustive Web use recording. If a study participant has a home computer and a work computer, the data collection program must be installed on both computers to truly capture use patterns. Indeed, a complete and perfect data collection requires all computers accessed by participants to have the Client-side log collection program. Obviously, the problem is that it is not only difficult to gain access to all users' computers, but, also, the installation process can consume a significant amount of research resources. As we discussed, Server-side data collection does not have this problem because the data only contains accesses to the specific Web server. It can record all access to the Web server no matter which computer a user accesses from. All access from users to the specific Web server leave traces in the Web server log file.

Client-side data collection will face more problems because the accelerated diffusion of the Internet will allow users to access Web sites not only from the designated computer but from many places such as the public library, Internet café, public university computer, refrigerator, IP TV, portable device, and so on. Yun et al. (2006) confirmed this concern. They found that 42% of users had accessed the Web site from multiple computers and 10% of users spent more than half of their access time in front of computers which did not have the tracking program.

Time vs. Page Request (Page Access)

Client-side recording systems can record virtually all mouse and keyboard moves (MacKenzie, Kauppinen & Silfverberg, 2001). Some of them have capabilities of recording point to point mouse moves and some computer programs can record events which represent activities of running software such as open file, close file, save, delete, copy, paste, and font size change. The event handler's report on some significant browsing behaviors such as focus, mouse down, resize, submit, hyperlink will be a valuable instrument for the media use time measurement (Etgen & Cantor, 1998).

Event recording is especially advantageous when a researcher wants to measure session time which is equivalent to 'episode of use' time. The Client-side recording system can record the moment when the user's Web browser is out-of-focus which means that the browser is not on the top of opened windows and a user stopped accessing the Web site. Also, it can record the moment of in-focus event or program-open event. Therefore, the Client-side data can tell the duration of time during an episode of use by subtracting the in-focus event time from the out-of-focus event time. In the same manner, it can even measure the duration of 'within episode of use'.

Such a function does not exist in the Server-side data collection method. The method's non-intrusive measurement characteristic cannot tell when a user minimizes or leaves the Web site. The only indicator is the Web server's session connection time function which is set to expire after a certain minutes of inactivity (typically 20 to 30 minutes). After the connection time expires, the server considers the user disconnected. This means that Server-side data almost always will indicate that the last page access will have maximum connection time because a Web server does not know when a user has actually left the Web site.

Time measurement for the Client-side data collection can be reasonably accurate because the out-of-focus function can detect the moment when users' attention leaves the Web site. Since Server-side data does not have this luxury, it is difficult to argue that the Server-side collection can present the duration of use. Although there are some software which attempt to measure time from the Server-side Web log data (e.g., Webtrends), the internal validity of the Server-side data's time measurement needs to be carefully examined (Burton & Walther, 2001).

On the other hand, there are no such validity problems when a researcher employs page requests, or page access, as a unit of analysis. Both collection methods can measure pages requested by users, although the Server-side collection method is recommended over the Client-side collection method due to the barriers of installing data collection software on subjects' computers.

In sum, it seems logical to assume that the Client-side Web log is better at measuring time and the Server-side Web log is better at reporting page requests. Additionally, knowledge on the degree of compatibility between two different measurement units will be beneficial to the researchers. If two measurement methods comparison resulted in having a great deal of resemblance, it will provide high confidence in these variables. Furthermore, if two data sets are compatible, we can interchangeably implement page request and duration of use in Internet use research. Indeed, Yun et al. (2006) reported that the time measurements as obtained from Server-side and Client-side log files did not perfectly match, but they are highly correlated. This means that Web log researchers can reasonably trust Server-side time measurement.

Methodological Challenges

There are methodological challenges that Web log researchers encounter such as caching, individual user recognition, sessions, and time calculation. These challenges can cause major threats to the validity of Web log data. Only careful preparations will prevent validity threats from them.

Caching

One of the most frequently criticized problems of the Server-side Web log analysis is the caching problem. It occurs when a local computer uses its own memory, intercepts user's page request to the Web server, and delivers the requested page from one's own memory. Caching can prevent Web page requests from leaving log records in the Web server log file.

The local gateway servers such as proxy servers can store the requested files in their own memory, intercept the next request of the same files, and provide them to the individual computers (Batista & Silva, 2001; Goldberg, 2001; Reips, 2000; Yu, Chen, & Tseng, 2004). This can be a fatal flaw in Server-side Web log file (Goldberg, 2001). However, dynamic content, which requires server-side script execution, are not generally cached in browsers or proxy servers. File names with the extensions such as 'asp', 'cgi', 'jsp', 'php', and many others are not designed to be cached in local memory due to their required script executions in Web servers. Therefore, those file types are supposed to be recognized by browsers and proxy servers and shouldn't be distributed from local memory unless browsers or proxy servers are misconfigured. However, misconfiguration rarely happens because of frequent browser updates and constant attention required for the network server maintenance.

A recent study on Cache memory problem confirmed the above concerns. Yun et al. (2006) reported 49% less number of page access files recorded on Server-side log compared to the same navigation recorded on Client-side log when only one fifth of the Web site was made of "html" files. Cached "html" files caused the problem. Thus, researchers should treat this problem as a major threat to validity and should devise countermeasures to compensate when they decide to use Server-side page access measures.

On the other hand, the same research indicated that the Server-side session time was not influenced by the caching problem because session time was calculated by subtracting the first page access time in the session from the last page access time in the session. Some missing cached pages between the first and the last access pages were included in the entire session time and, therefore, they did not influence the whole session time calculation.

Individual User Recognition and Sessions

Collected IP addresses are one of the most valuable pieces of information which enables individual user recognition. However, it becomes more difficult to identify individual users due to the diffusion of Dynamic Host Configuration Protocol (DHCP) and Network Address Translator (NAT). When DHCP or NAT is enabled, IP addresses are randomly assigned to computers and a computer is not designated with a fixed IP. Thus, IP address alone cannot identify a unique user (Burton & Walther, 2001; Goldberg, 2001; Jansen & Spink, 2005; Jones, Cunningham, & McNab, 1998; Wobus, 1998).

However, some Web sites with login systems can identify a user. Login systems force users to enter the assigned codename and password when they enter the Web site. Therefore, login systems can resolve many problems of identifying sessions and calculating time from the data. In addition, they can identify a user when a user accesses from multiple computers. Login systems can be very valuable for Web log researchers.

Time Calculation Algorithm

The problem of calculating time from Client-side data is relatively minor because it typically has an event recording function. However, it is still challenging to calculate time from the Server-side Web log. If Web log data can identify a unique user from codenames or IP addresses, several data mining and data cleaning processes can produce a reasonable time measurement.

First, the content of the Web page should be examined. Some users will show unreasonable amount of time spent for Web pages. The only way to validate those times is to examine the content of the Web page and decide maximum amount of time users could have spent viewing Web pages. For instance, a normal Web page may not require more than 20 minutes to read depending on the length of the Web page. However, discussion forum writing may take more than 30 minutes to write and edit the text message. Web log researchers should be aware of the content of the Web site they are analyzing and decide the maximum amount of time allowed for Web pages. Also, the last Web page access time in the session is recommended to be ignored. This is because Web servers cannot capture the user's exit points (Jansen, Spink, & Pederson, 2005).

The Server-side Web log is more available to researchers due to the convenient collection process. If the time calculation from the Server-side can be as valid as Client-side log, researchers can surrogate the Web use time variable with the Server-side Web log without sacrificing validity of the measurement. Fortunately, the Server-side measured session time and Client-side measured session time are reported to be very similar (Yun et al., 2006). Nonetheless, it should be noted that careful preparations (e.g., less html files on the server) should proceed before implementing Server-side session time measurement.

CONCLUSION

Previous research on Web log data analysis showed that several technical specifications should be carefully considered before any scientific analysis of Web log data. Most importantly, cache-able files can seriously damage the validity of Server-side Web log data. If the files on the Web server are cache-able, the validity of the data must be thoroughly examined. Thus, the researchers should check the Web site content structure and report the specifications of the Web site files and file structures in the report. In fact, understanding content structure of the Web site will inform and help researchers to better devise research questions and units of analysis.

One of the counter-intuitive research results of Web log analysis is that the Server-side session time calculation can be reliable and valid against all potential problems. However, it should be noted that the accurate time measure is limited to the *session* time units. Server-side time measure in other levels of analysis (e.g., individual page access time) cannot be accurate especially when cache-able files exist on the Web server.

One of the challenges of Client-side Web log research is the ubiquitous presence of the Internet in contemporary society. Client-side Web log data already misses lots of user navigation data due to users' multiple computer accesses from various locations. This problem will only grow as the number of devices available for the audience to access Web sites will increase as the technology evolves. Eventually, people will be able to access Web sites from everywhere. Thus, the Client-side Web log analysis will be criticized for missing some Web use by certain target audiences. Researchers should invest resources to collect data from the Client-side only after contemplating and resolving methodological challenges of the Client-side data collection method in their research.

Research on Web log data reminds us that the Internet is not developed for Web log researchers, although it is a great place to research user activities. In a sense, current Web log research is similar to the early Television rating research. Indeed, Web log researchers should be aware of the history of television audience rating system development, i.e. that it took decades to devise defective but, still, acceptable TV rating instruments. Web log analysis may follow the fate of TV rating systems and researchers may compromise by developing acceptable instruments rather than methodologically valid instruments. Nevertheless, more research on this topic will certainly contribute to the development of valid measures and analysis of the Web log data.

REFERENCES

Babbie, E. (2004). *The Practice of Social Research*. Belmont, CA: Wadsworth Publishing.

Barber, A. S., & Riccalton, C. (1988). The use of the LS/2000 online public access catalogue at Newcastle University Library (Grant No. SI/G/816): *British Library Research and Development Department Report.*

Batista, P., & Silva, M. J. (2001). Web access mining from an on-line newspaper logs. *Paper presented at the 12th International Meeting of the Euro Working Group on Decision Support Systems (EWG-DSS 2001),* Cascais, Portugal.

Bertot, J. C., & McClure, C. R. (1997). Web usage statistics: measurement issues and analytical techniques. *Government Information Quarterly*, 14(4), 373-396.

Booske, B. C., & Sainfort, F. (1998). Relation between quantitative and qualitative measures of information use. *International Journal of Human-Computer Interaction*, 10(1), 1-21.

Burton, M. C., & Walther, J. B. (2001). The value of Web log data in use-based design and testing. *Journal of Computer-Mediated Communication*, 6(3).

Catledge, L. D., & Pitkow, J. E. (1995). Characterizing browsing strategies in the World-Wide Web. *Paper presented at the Third International World Wide Web Conference*, Darmstadt, Germany.

Danaher, P. J. (1995). What happens to television ratings during commercial breaks?, *Journal of Advertising Research*, 35(1), 37-47.

Davis, M. P. (2004). Information-seeking behavior of chemists: A Transaction Log Analysis of referral URLs, *Journal of the American Society for Information Science and Technology*, 55(3), 326-332.

Etgen, M., & Cantor, J. (1998). *What does getting WET (Web Event-logging Tool) mean for Web usability?,* [Online]. Available: http://www.itl.nist.gov/iaui/vvrg/hfweb/proceedings/etgen-cantor/index.html [22 October, 2002].

Eveland, W. P., Jr., & Dunwoody, S. (1998a). Surfing the Web for science: Early data on the users and uses of The Why Files. *NISE Brief*, 2(2), 1-10.

Eveland, W. P., Jr., & Dunwoody, S. (1998b). Users and navigation patterns of a science World Wide Web site for the public. *Public Understanding of Science*, 7, 285-311.

Goldberg, J. (2001, 5/18). *Why Web usage statistics are (worse than) meaningless*, [Online]. Available: http://www.goldmark.org/netrants/webstats/ [15 October 2002].

Handschuh, S. & Staab, S. (2002). Authoring and annotation of Web pages in CREAM. *Proceedings of the 11th International Conference on World Wide Web*, Honolulu, Hawaii.

Hawkins, R. P., & Pingree, S. (1997). Measuring time frames of communication behaviors in computer use. *Paper presented at the International Communication Association*, Montreal, Canada.

Jansen, B., Jansen, K., & Spink, A. (2005). Using the Web to look for work: Implications for online job seeking and recruiting. *Internet Research*, 15(1), 49-66.

Jansen, B., & Resnick, M. (2005). Examining searcher perception of and interactions with sponsored results. *Paper presented at the ACM Conference on Electronic Commerce*, Vancouver, Canada.

Jansen, B., & Spink, A. (2005). An analysis of Web searching by European AlltheWeb.com users. *Information Processing and Management*, 41, 361-381.

Jansen, B. J., Spink, A., & Pedersen, J. (2005). A temporal comparison of AltaVista Web searching. *Journal of the American Society for Information Science and Technology*, 56(6), 559-570.

Jones, S., Cunningham, S. J., & McNab, R. (1998). Usage analysis of a digital library. *Paper presented at the Digital Libraries 98, Third ACM Conference on Digital Libraries*, Pittsburgh, PA.

Jones, S., Cunningham, S. J., McNab, R., & Boddie, S. (2000). A transation log analysis of a digital library. *International Journal of Digital Libraries*, 3, 152-169.

Kanerva, A., Keeker, K., Risden, K., Schuh, E., & Czerwinski, M. (2004). *Web usability research at Microsoft Corporation*. Microsoft Corporation [Online]. Available: http://research.microsoft.com/users/marycz/webchapter.html [12 January 2004].

Kurth, M. (1993). The limits and limitations of Transaction Log Analysis. *Library Hi Tech,* 42, 98-104.

Larson, R. R. (1991). Between Scylla and Charybdis: Subject searching in the online catalog. *Advances in Librarianship*, 15, 175-236.

Mackenzie, I. S., Kauppinen, T., & Silfverberg, M. (2001). Accuracy measures for evaluating computer printing devices. *CHI2001*, 9-16.

McTavish, F., Pingree, S., Hawkins, R., & Gustafson, D. (2003). Cultural differences in use of an electronic discussion group. *Journal of Health Psychology*, 8(1), 105-117.

Nielsen, B. (1986). What they say they do and what they do: Assessing online catalog use instruction through transaction monitoring. *Information Technology and Libraries*, 5, 28-34.

Peters, T. (1993). The history and development of Transaction Log Analysis. *Library Hi Tech*, 42, 41-66.

Peters, T. A., Kurth, M., Flaherty, P., Sandore, B., & Kaske, N. K. (1993). An introduction to the special section on Transaction Log Analysis. *Library Hi Tech*, 42, 38-39.

Phippen, A. (2004). An evaluation methodology for virtual communities using Web analytics. *Paper presented at the Proceedings of the International Networks Conference*, Plymouth, UK.

Phippen, A., Sheppard, L., & Furnell, S. (2004). A practical evaluation of Web analysis. *Internet Research*, 14(4), 284-293.

Reips, U.-D. (2000). The Web experiment method: advantages, disadvantages, and solutions. (*In* M. H. Birnbaum (eds.), *Psychological Experiments on the Internet,* San Diego, CA: Academic Press. p. 89-117.)

Sandore, B. (1993). Applying the results of Transaction Log Analysis. *Library Hi Tech*, 42, 87-97.

Smaglik, P., Hawkins, R. P., Pingree, S., Gustafson, D. H., Boberg, E., & Bricker, E. (1998). The quality of interactive computer use among HIV-infected individuals. *Journal of Health Communication*, 3, 53-68.

Taha, A. (2004). Wired Research: Transaction Log Analysis of E-journal databases to assess the research activities and trends in UAE university. *Paper presented at the Nordic Conference on Information and Documentation*, Aalborg, Denmark.

Wobus, J. (1998). *DHCP FAQ*. [Online] Available: http://www.dhcp-handbook.com/dhcp_faq.html [15 February 2004].

Yu, H.-F., Chen, Y.-M., & Tseng, L.-M. (2004). Archive knowledge discovery by proxy cache. *Internet Research*, 14(1), 34-47.

Yun, G. W. (2007). Interactivity concepts examined: Response time, hypertext, role taking, and multimodality. *Media Psychology*, *9*(5), 527-548

Yun, G. W., Ford, J., Hawkins, R. P., Pingree, S., McTavish, F., Gustafson, D., & Berhe, H. (2006). On the validity of client-side vs. server-side Web log data analysis. *Internet Research*, 16(5), 537-552.

KEY TERMS

Client-Side Log: All users' computer activities saved in a client's computer as a computer file.

Server-Side Log: All users' Web access activities on a Web server saved in a Web server as a computer file.

Lifestyle Time Frame: General media use during the lifetime.

Multi-Episode Segment of Time: Media use during the particular segments of the lifetime such as hours, weeks, or months.

An Episode of Use: A time frame used to measure a specific occasion of use.

Session: A set of sequentially or semantically related clicks.

Page Requests: Users' requests to the Web server to send files to the users' browser.

Page Access: Users' one screen access to the Web server content.

Cached Files: Some files that are saved and retrieved by browsers or proxy servers to save network resources

Chapter X
Recommendations for Reporting Web Usage Studies

Kirstie Hawkey
University of British Columbia, Canada

Melanie Kellar
Google, USA

ABSTRACT

This chapter presents recommendations for reporting context in studies of Web usage including Web browsing behavior. These recommendations consist of eight categories of contextual information crucial to the reporting of results: user characteristics, temporal information, Web browsing environment, nature of the Web browsing task, data collection methods, descriptive data reporting, statistical analysis, and results in the context of prior work. This chapter argues that the Web and its user population are constantly growing and evolving. This changing temporal context can make it difficult for researchers to evaluate previous work in the proper context, particularly when detailed information about the user population, experimental methodology, and results is not presented. The adoption of these recommendations will allow researchers in the area of Web browsing behavior to more easily replicate previous work, make comparisons between their current work and previous work, and build upon previous work to advance the field.

INTRODUCTION

Over the past dozen years there has been a wide variety of research conducted investigating user behavior on the Web, beginning most notably with Catledge and Pitkow's (1995) study of navigation strategies. This field of research has expanded to evaluate a variety of user behaviors on the Web such as information seeking behavior, navigational behavior, and general characteristics of Web usage. Aspects of Web browsing behavior motivate the design of tools and interfaces for Web applications. In this chapter, we use the term "Web browsing behavior" to include any interactions between a user and a Web browser, ranging from a user's use of the back button, to website revisitation patterns, information seeking behavior, and general Web usage. We want to make the distinction between our use of the term "Web browsing behavior" and the serendipitous task of "browsing the Web" as is defined in Web task categorizations (e.g., Kellar, Watters, & Shepherd, 2007). There are many applications of traces of Web browsing behavior (as captured in Web logs), particularly for the validation and comparison of models, algorithms or techniques.

Although much research has been conducted since the early studies of Catledge and Pitkow (1995) and Tauscher and Greenberg (1997), researchers are still using the results of this early research as statements of fact and as a basis for conducting research that builds upon it without challenging its current validity. However, the Web environment has changed along multiple dimensions since these early studies: it has become much larger, access speeds are much higher, and users have a wider variety of Web browsers and search tools at their disposal. The user population has also changed considerably as Web usage has become commonplace at work and at home; there is now a much greater variability in user characteristics and reasons for Web use.

It is important that researchers and practitioners currently developing algorithms, techniques, and applications based upon the behaviors of Web users have an understanding of the current state of the browsing behavior, including the amount of variability in behavior and trends over time. However, comparing previous research studies is complex because the studies need interpretation within the context of the Web browsing environment at the time of the study. This environment includes the population studied, the nature of the tasks performed, the browser or tools used, and the metrics recorded. Insufficient reporting of the study methodology and results in the literature can make this a challenging task. This inability to easily determine the design and procedure of studies and judge the external validity of results makes it difficult for researchers to replicate and build upon previous work.

Our objective in this chapter is to introduce a set of recommendations for reporting the contextual details of Web browsing behavioral studies. Adherence to these recommendations should enable more effective sharing of research results and allow other researchers to appropriately evaluate the applicability of the results to their own research problems. The study of Web browsing behavior is a research domain that is still growing and evolving (as the Web grows and evolves). It is important and worthwhile for the research community to engage in discussions about 'good practice' to ensure that research contributions can be placed correctly within the overall body of work.

BACKGROUND

A variety of Web browsing behaviors have been studied since the mid 1990's via a variety of methodological approaches. However, although standard recommendations for the reporting of results are used in other research domains, none exist for reporting of the methodological details and results for studies of Web browsing behavior. In this section, we first discuss standardized reporting of results. We then present the seminal papers in the field of Web browsing behavior and provide temporal context with respect to the Web browsing environment and user population at the time of the seminal studies. We also discuss methods of observing users' Web browsing behavior, as these will impact the data collected.

Standardized Reporting

Standardization of reporting is an approach that has worked in other disciplines to ease meta-analyses. The Controlled Standards of Reporting Trials (CONSORT) (www.consort-statement.org)

helps readers of randomized controlled trials understand the design and running of the study and the analysis and interpretation of the results. The Common Industry Format (CIF) (Laskowski, Morse, & Gray, 2001) is an ANSI approved standard for reporting the results of usability studies. This standard was developed to aid organizations in making decisions based on usability when choosing new software.

There has been some effort at creating standards for the reporting of on-line search behaviors. Jansen and Pooch (2000) proposed a framework for reporting Web searching studies to facilitate comparison of results. Their framework includes detailed descriptive information about the searchers, the information retrieval system (including the searching rules at the time of the study), the methods of data collection, and the transaction logs. When presenting analysis, they recommend that analysis is attempted at the level of session, query, and term (these terms are defined). They also recommend that statistical analysis is reported and that data is reported at low levels of detail as well as when aggregated to improve the ability of other researchers to compare their results. Wildemuth et al. (2004) have conducted multiple rounds of a Delphi study to investigate standard variables to collect for the study of online search behaviors. This research is still underway but after the second iteration, three main categories of variables have emerged: the search process, the search system, and the user. The goal of this work is to introduce an initial set of guidelines for reporting the contextual details of Web browsing behavioral studies.

Seminal Works

One of the first studies examining user behavior on the Web was conducted by Catledge and Pitkow (1995) in 1994. Participants' behavior was logged for three weeks while they browsed the Web using a modified version of XMosaic that collected browsing activity. The study highlighted two dominant methods of navigation: hyperlinks and the back button. As well, the browsing strategies of participants were classified into three categories: serendipitous, general purpose, and searcher.

One of the earlier applications of Web usage logs was conducted by Pirolli, Pitkow and Rao (1996). They used trace logs of Web usage from March through May of 1995, along with topology and textual similarity between nodes, to extract structures of websites.

Similar to Catledge & Pitkow, Tauscher and Greenberg (1997) observed user behavior with a modified version of XMosaic, in order to study revisitation patterns of users. Over a six week period in 1995, they observed that 58% of page visits were revisits and the back button was used in 30% of navigations.

Byrne et al. (1999) conducted a task analysis of user Web behavior through a 1998 study. Participants were videotaped in their offices, for a day, as they used the Web. The study revealed reading to be the most common Web activity and the most common method of navigation was hyperlinks, followed by the back button.

Choo, Detlor, and Turnbull (2000) investigated information seeking behavior on the Web in a two week study conducted circa 1998. Participants' Web behavior in the workplace was logged client-side during the course of the study. Through the analysis of users' clickstream data, interviews, and questionnaires, four modes of information seeking behavior were defined: undirected viewing, conditioned viewing, informal search, and formal search.

Cockburn and McKenzie (2001) conducted a four month retrospective observational study, from October 1999 to January 2000, of history and bookmark files retrieved from server backups. They found an average revisitation rate of 81% and in general, a small number of dominant web pages accounted for most of a participant's revisitation behavior. Analysis of participants' bookmark files found that they were either heavy or light users of bookmarks.

Sellen, Murphy & Shaw (2002) studied the activities and characteristics of knowledge workers on the Web. Participants were interviewed circa 2001 in front of their history lists and described the Web activities they had recently completed. Knowledge workers engaged in six types of activity on the Web: finding, information gathering, browsing, transacting, communicating, and housekeeping.

More recently, Herder (2005) logged the Web usage of 25 participants for varying periods between August 2004 and March 2005 (ranging from 51-104 days). A page revisitation rate of 51% was reported, which is much lower than the previous reported studies. Herder attributed this discrepancy to the way in which different researchers have calculated revisitation rate. Herder also noted that participants' revisitation rates stabilized after approximately 1000 page views, or on average after 10 days.

Weinreich et al. (2006) conducted a long term study (circa 2004-2005, average of 105 days captured, ranging from 52-195 days). Data was captured through a proxy server and augmented with client-side data for a subset of the participants. Weinreich et al. observed a significant decrease in back button usage from earlier studies. While the use of hyperlinks remained fairly constant, accounting for 43% of all navigation, the back button only accounted for 14%. They also reported an overall revisitation rate of 46%.

The Evolution of the Web Environment and Its Users

This section presents snapshots of the state of the World Wide Web and its users, at the time of the seminal research that was previously presented. It must be noted that the data reported has been selected from a variety of sources with varying methodologies, populations, and metrics. Therefore, direct comparisons are not always appropriate. These snapshots have been provided to illustrate the changing nature of user behavior on the Web and their Web browsing environment that gives the temporal context for the seminal papers in the area. A timeline of this activity is shown in Figure 1 which positions the seminal papers in the context of newly-emerging web activities.

Figure 1. Timeline of seminal papers (author names) within the context of newly-emerging web activities and products

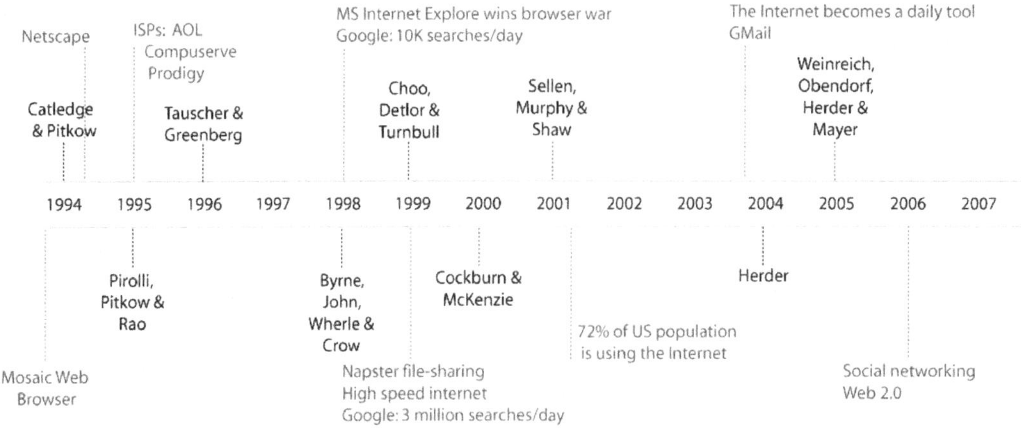

In the Beginning

Fall/94: The typical user is a 31 year-old educated male who works with computers and has authored about 30 Web documents (Pitkow & Recker, 1994). He uses a Mosaic browser 1-4 times a day for about 5 hours per week; however, Netscape has just been released (Pitkow & Recker, 1994). He uses the Web to browse, for entertainment, for work or business, and for research (Pitkow & Recker, 1994). He has a choice of about 10,000 websites (Marsh, 2003).

Fall/95: Worldwide Web traffic has surpassed FTP data and search engines are now available (Marsh, 2003). Users are shifting towards "early adopters/seekers of technology" instead of the "technology developers/pioneers" of a year before (Pitkow & Kehoe, 1996) with the start of commercial internet providers such as Compuserve, AOL and Prodigy (Infoplease, 2004b). Women now account for about 30% of Web users and there has been some increase in the number of younger and older users (Pitkow & Kehoe, 1996). Most users have 14.4 or 28.8 kbs modems (Pitkow & Kehoe, 1996).

Home Users and Browser Wars

Fall/98: Women now account for almost 40% of Web users (GVUOnlineSurvey, 1997). About one third of users have a 56K modem (Kehoe, Pitkow, Sutton, Aggarwal, & Rogers, 1999) and 84% are interested in high speed internet access (Pastore, 1998b). Microsoft Internet Explorer wins the browser wars, just surpassing 1997's dominant browser, Netscape Navigator, to capture 50% of the market (Pastore, 1998a). More than 40% of people between the ages of 9 and 49 now have on-line access (Infoplease, 2001); the average online user is 38 (Kehoe, Pitkow, Sutton, Aggarwal, & Rogers, 1999). Almost one third of users shop on-line (Pastore, 2000a). Google arrives and10,000 searches are performed per day (Google, 2007).

Work and Home: The Need for Speed

Fall/99: The year 2000 is looming and the 150 million Web users (Infoplease, 2004b) worldwide are looking for information about Y2K as the Lycos 50 listing of the top Web searches debuts (Lycos, 1999). Google performs 3 million searches per day (Google, 2007). Napster allows swapping of music and 'E-Commerce' is the new buzz word (Infoplease, 2004b). The 6% of users with high speed internet access view 130% more pages and surf the Web 83% more often than the 45% of users that still have a 28.8/33.6 K modem (Pastore, 2000c). According to Nielsen//NetRatings, the average Web user had 17 29-minute sessions each month, viewing an average of 32 pages per session (Pastore, 2000b).

In the Mainstream: Just Google it

Fall/01: Google has become a verb: with over 3 billion Web documents (Google, 2007) available to be searched and the Google toolbar to help them do it, users all over the world are telling each other to Google it. Napster has lost its court case (Infoplease, 2004b) but other file sharing applications are quick to fill the void. The structure of the population on-line is much closer to that from census data than in previous years (Pastore, 2001). There is an equal split of male/female users, but household incomes for Web users are still higher than for the general population ($49,800 vs. $40,800) and the Web user population is still younger (75% of adults 18-49 are on-line vs. 63% of the population, 24% of adults 50+ are on-line vs. 37% of population) (Pastore, 2001). Our average Web user now has 33 33-minute sessions per month, viewing an average of 36 pages per session (ClickZStatsStaff, 2002). Seventy-two percent of the population are now using the Internet (58% at home, 73% at school, 51% at work) (Kerner, 2004).

As a Daily Tool

Fall/04: The Internet has become a daily tool: 56% of those with access to the Internet go on-line daily; 48% send email, 27% get news, and 19% do research for a job (Infoplease, 2004a). Google has added Gmail and Desktop Search (Google, 2007) and the division between on-line and off-line blurs. Our average Web user now has 31 Web sessions per month at home during the almost 26 hours of home PC use (Nielsen//NetRatings, 2004a) and 65 sessions at work during the 76 hours of work PC use (Nielsen//NetRatings, 2004b).

Web 2.0 and Wide Spread Social Networking

Fall/06 and Onwards: Web 2.0 is the new buzzword and users are contributing content and participating in Web activities in new ways (Madden & Fox, 2006). Blogs are replacing personal Web pages and are used for creative expression and to share stories of personal experiences (Lenhart & Fox, 2006). Online services such as Flickr for photos and del.icio.us for bookmarks allow users to organize their information and share their interests through tagging; 28% of online Americans have tagged content and 7% report doing so on a typical day (Rainie, 2007). Social networking sites such as Facebook and MySpace continue to grow in popularity with hundreds of millions of users (Madden & Fox, 2006).

Temporal Context

As can be seen from the above timeline, the state of the Web has changed quickly and drastically since its inception. It is important that seminal works are acknowledged; but, given the ever-changing state of the Web, there is a concern that data that is no longer relevant is being used to support current research. Care must be taken to ensure that the context in which the data was recorded does not differ significantly from the current context with respect to the aspects of Web browsing behavior under study. These seminal works do however provide us with a baseline from which we can measure the changes in user behavior through the evolution of the Web.

The reliance on older data sets was noted in a recent survey (Hawkey & Kellar, 2004). Of the papers surveyed, 17 papers published in 2003-2004 reported an applied use of Web browsing data (i.e., validating a model, evaluating algorithms, evaluating an application or architecture). Existing traces were used in 64.7% of these 17 studies. For those using existing traces, older trace data sets were generally used (i.e., before 2000). In some cases, this appeared to be due to a lack of newer trace data available to the public. There may be some benefit in evaluating new algorithms with the same data sets used in previous evaluations, but there also needs to be some validation that algorithms scale to the much busier and larger Web environment of today. Those researchers needing to use existing Web traces to investigate research questions should examine the temporal contexts of the existing traces and the current environment in order to evaluate whether or not it is reasonable to assume that the older traces are still representative of the behavior of current Web users.

One example of changing user patterns is research about back button usage. Catledge & Pitkow (1995) reported the back button was used in 41% of all navigation, while one year later Tauscher (1997) reported the back button was used in only 30% of all navigation. In the two studies reported in the Smartback paper (Milic-Frayling et al., 2004) (dates unknown, approximately 12 months apart, and published in 2004), back button usage was down to 22% (exploratory study) and approximately 8% (back button and Smartback button equivalent, evaluation study) of all navigation. In a recent study (completed in March 2005), Kellar et al. (2006) found that the back button was responsible for 18% of all navigation. Weinreich et al. (2006) found the back button only accounted for 14.3% of all navigation mechanisms. However, each of these studies had a relatively small number of participants and there may be individual differences or population differences that account for the decrease in usage.

This does not imply that results from different contexts are not relevant, but the relevance has to be challenged by evaluating the context of the state of the Web, the Web browsing environment and the user characteristics of the population studied. There are aspects of Web browsing behavior that may be relatively stable. For example, a decrease in revisitation rates of Web pages has been found over the years; however, the changes may not so much be due to a difference in behavior as to differences in how the data is recorded and compared, particularly with the increase in dynamic URLs (Herder, 2005). What is important is that sufficient contextual information is reported so that these determinations may be made.

Methods of Observing Web Browsing Behavior

A variety of methods have been used for learning about Web browsing behavior. One of the most common approaches is the use of Web logging, which can be client-side, server-side, or through a proxy. Other approaches include direct researcher observations, diary studies, interviews and questionnaires. Each technique has its own set of advantages and disadvantages and its use is often dictated by the goal and setting of the research (McGrath, 1995). Whichever method is selected, there are implications for the interpretation of results.

Several research domains have used client-side logging to examine Web browsing behavior. These include information seeking behavior on the Web (Choo, Detlor, & Turnbull, 2000), usability evaluation (Hilbert & Redmiles, 2000), and the evaluation of implicit indicators of interest (Claypool, Le, Waseda, & Brown, 2001). Approaches for client-side logging include commercial "spyware" tools (Kelly & Belkin, 2004; Kim & Allen, 2002), custom logging tools (Hawkey & Inkpen, 2005; Obendorf, Weinreich, & Hass, 2004; Reeder, Pirolli, & Card, 2001; Turnbull, 1998), and custom browsers (Claypool, Le, Waseda, & Brown, 2001; Kellar, Watters, & Shepherd, 2006). Client-side logging offers the richest exploration of user behavior. However, many client-side logging tools are designed to work with a specific browser and may be consuming and costly to update as new versions of the browser are introduced. There may also be performance issues due to the lack of robustness of research tools (Kellar, Hawkey, Inkpen, & Watters, 2008).

Server-side logs do not capture the same level of detail as is possible with client-side logging; however, benefits include a reduction in cost and time of implementation. Server-side logging has proved useful in the study of search engine use (Anick, 2003; Spink, Wolfram, Jansen, & Saracevic, 2001), information seeking (Zhang, Zambrowicz, Zhou, & Roderer, 2004), and general Web behavior (Huberman, Pirolli, Pitkow, & Lukose, 1998; Pitkow, 1997). This method is ideal for research with large populations, remote users, or for field studies. The data recorded by server logs includes the IP address of users and the time and address of Web page requests. The use of dynamic IP addresses makes it difficult to distinguish between distinct users; however, cookies can alleviate this problem (Anick, 2003). Caching can also be an issue as pages that are loaded from the Web browser cache do not reach the server and are therefore not logged (Fenstermacher & Ginsburg, 2003).

Proxy-logging is a compromise between client-side logging and server-side logging and provides some of the advantages of each. By allowing participants to log into the system instead of downloading and installing software, proxy solutions such as WebQuilt (Hong, Heer, Waterson, & Landay, 2001) allow participants to work within their normal browsing environment. However, traditional proxy servers do not capture the full spectrum of user interactions with the browser and may not capture access to pages that have been cached at the browser level (Barford, Bestavros, Bradley, & Crovella, 1999). Proxy-side logging may also be problematic when trying to collect fine-grained measurements. Kelly and Belkin (2004) found a large discrepancy between a client-side logging tool and a proxy-based logging tool while collecting Web page dwell times. The data generated by the proxy-based logger was found to be neither reliable nor accurate. One emerging method of data logging is to embed Javascript into delivered web pages through the proxy. This method can be used to capture the user's navigation as well as such user interactions as mouse movement, scroll bar use, and key presses (Atterer, Wnuk, & Schmidt, 2006).

Several other approaches are used to capture Web browsing behavior. Direct researcher observations have been used in laboratory settings (Card et al., 2001; Holscher & Strube, 2000) as well as in the field where researchers can observe participants in their natural setting (Teevan, Alvarado, Ackerman, & Karger, 2004; Thury, 1998). The use of video cameras (Byrne, John, Wehrle, & Crow, 1999) or video capture software (Hargittai, 2002; Jenkins, Corritore, & Wiedenbeck, 2003) provides a record of a user's behavior and its context, but can be extremely time consuming to code. Furthermore, the user's motivation and thoughts may still be unclear. Direct researcher observation is only feasible for small groups of participants and for studies that are qualitative in nature. Diary Studies (Rieh, 2003), surveys (Heinström, 2003; Schiano, Stone, & Bectarte, 2001) and interviews (Jones, Dumais, & Bruce, 2002) are other methods of self-reporting used to obtain a qualitative view of user behavior on the Web.

Qualitative data can be an important component in understanding Web browsing behavior. One drawback to server-side logging is that researchers typically have very little information about the participants being studied; researchers can report on artifactual behaviors, but have little context for those behaviors (Spink, Wolfram, Jansen, & Saracevic, 2001). Additional studies in the form of interviews or surveys can help researchers gain a better understanding of users' cognitive perspectives and the overall environment in which the Web tasks are taking place (Zhang, Zambrowicz, Zhou, & Roderer, 2004). For example, Choo et al. (2000) conducted interviews after analyzing their Web usage logs. The logs were used to guide the discussions with participants about the tasks they were performing. Sellen et al. (2002) interviewed participants about their previous two days' Web activities, while participants were seated in front of their browser history. Participant annotation of Web log data can also provide an understanding of task or user concerns (Kellar, Hawkey, Inkpen, & Watters, 2008; Kelly & Belkin, 2004).

IMPORTANCE OF REPORTING CONTEXTUAL INFORMATION

As presented in the timeline, the World Wide Web is relatively young and is continually evolving. Technological innovations have changed the Web browsing environment: as the state of hardware (Unix boxes, desktop PCs, laptop computers, handheld, cellular phones), Web software (browsers), and Web systems (search engines) progresses, the experience of the end user changes. Internet access is no longer restricted to those with a high income and level of education. As a result, Internet usage patterns are continually changing and their study must also be ongoing.

As discussed in the background, gathering data about a user's Web browsing behavior is a difficult task and there are tradeoffs inherent with the methods selected (McGrath, 1995). Depending on the data collection method, there may be different metrics captured that must then be interpreted to gather an understanding of the user's actual behavior. The task and goals of a user may affect their behavior while Web browsing. There are also individual differences that may have an impact.

It is therefore imperative when reporting the results of a study, that the study design and methodology be sufficiently described so that the reader can see the impact on the results of decisions made. The inclusion of these important details also allows researchers to compare and replicate previous work. Replication and extension studies have the potential to provide insight into how the rapidly changing and dynamic environment of the Web is affecting its users.

Current reporting practices can make it difficult to compare new results with previous results in this area due to inadequate reporting of context, both temporal and methodological. For example, results from a recent field-study (Hawkey & Inkpen, 2005) updated per-session and per-browser window usage (e.g., the number of pages visited, the speed of browsing) from those figures previously reported. However, the researchers experienced difficulty finding previous studies with enough contextual details to allow meaningful comparisons of results. Those publications that did contain sufficient details allowed them to know when comparisons were inappropriate and to reflect upon changes in the context of browsing that may account for the differences noted. This ability to place results in the context of previous work is crucial and the responsibility lies with the research community to make sure that sufficient details are presented.

RECOMMENDATIONS FOR REPORTING CONTEXTUAL INFORMATION

Contextual information consists of the set of information that provides context about a particular piece of research relating to Web browsing behavior. This section presents eight categories of contextual information crucial to the reporting of results: user characteristics, temporal context, Web browsing environment, nature of the Web browsing task, data collection measures, descriptive reporting, statistical analysis, and placing results in context. Without these details, researchers may be unable to replicate previous work, make comparisons between their current work and previous work, and build upon previous work to advance the field.

Although many of the recommendations for reporting contextual information presented in this chapter may appear to be common sense, they are routinely omitted from publications. This was demonstrated by Hawkey & Kellar (2004) in a survey of 44 publications, published in either 2003 or early 2004, dealing with individual user behavior on the Web. Of these 44 papers, 17 were solely applied uses of Web usage (e.g. validating a model). The 27 remaining papers in the survey presented 31 distinct studies. The studies surveyed dealt with evaluation of tools, techniques and interfaces of Web browsers (42%), information seeking behavior on the Web (39%), Web navigation behavior (13%), and general Web use (10%). Each of the surveyed studies were characterized according to the experimental strategy, using McGrath's (1995) definitions. The most common experimental strategy was laboratory experiment (45%), followed by field experiment (23%), experimental simulation (15%), field study (13%), and survey sample (3%).

Hawkey and Kellar (2004) surveyed the studies for the level of contextual information provided according to the eight categories of contextual information established in this section. A summary of the results for each category is given in Table 1. As a general basis for comparison, the authors computed scores for the results, assigning binary (0-not reported, 1-reported) or tertiary (0-not reported, 1-partial details, 2-full details) scores as appropriate for each category. The total score was normalized by computing the ratio of points earned to potential maximum score, taking into consideration those points that were not applicable for the study. There was a wide range in the overall level of contextual data reported in the studies surveyed, with a mean normalized total score of 0.65 (range of 0.38 to 0.93). It is important to acknowledge that the space constraints of a given publication may not allow for this recommended level of detail. While space limitations were found to account for some of the lack of detail (i.e., journal publications tended to report more details than short conference papers), there was still a great deal of variability within each publication venue. In cases where space limitations are an issue, it is recommended that authors create technical reports from experimental design documents to divulge methodological details including task descriptions, study instruments, and well-defined metrics. This detail will ensure that the reported results can be used as a basis for, and compared with, future works.

Recommendations for reporting each category of contextual information are now presented, along with a discussion of how this information (or lack thereof) can impact interpretation of reported results. The recommendations in this chapter are supported throughout with results from Hawkey and Kellar's (2004) survey of the level of contextual reporting provided in publications of Web browsing studies (as summarized in Table 1). These results demonstrate the variability in reporting of methodology, analysis, and results in this domain. The authors expect that the set of reporting recommendations presented in this chapter can serve as a useful tool for both new and veteran researchers in the field as they endeavor to share their research findings effectively.

Recommendation 1: Report User Characteristics

When conducting research examining the behavior of individual Web users, details about the sample population provide important information about the significance of the results. These measures help to determine the external validity of a study and give insight into how well the results can generalize to other populations. User characteristics of interest may include: size and sex of the sample population, age, background, occupation, and Web experience.

The impact of individual differences on Web browsing behavior is a growing research area. For example, Herder and Juvina (2004) collected extensive data on cognitive abilities (spatial, episodic memory, working memory), internet expertise, and affective disposition of participants and correlated this data with self-reports of satisfaction and perception of lost-ness during Web-assisted personal finance tasks. They identified two navigation styles (flimsy and laborious) that predict the perceived disorientation of Web users. Kellar et al. (2006) found individual differences in the use of Web browser navigation tools.

However, individual differences have not received a great deal of attention in previous research. Even in cases where individual user behavior is distinguishable from one another, it has typically been aggregated in order to develop a general user model for general purposes (Grace-Martin & Gay, 2001). Issues arise when individuals' Web behavior exhibits large variability, as in (Cockburn & McKenzie, 2001). In this study participants were recruited from within the academic community, but one person was employed as a webmaster and had a much higher level of Web usage. Web experience, age, occupation, and background play a role in a user's behavior and can contribute to large differences between users. In order to facilitate interpretation of results in light of advances in understanding on the role of individual differences of Web brows-

Table 1. Summary of the results from a survey of the level of contextual reporting in studies of Web browsing behavior (Hawkey and Kellar, 2004)

Contextual Information	Percent Reported	Details
User Characteristics		
Sample size	93.5%	Mean 40.4 (4 to 305)
Sex	41.9%	55% male
Age	35.5%	Various metrics reported: mean age, range, categories
Background	90.3%	75% used academic participants
Web experience	54.8%	Not directly comparable (metrics not standardized)
Temporal Information		
Study dates	25.8%	Dates typically 1-3 years prior to publication
Duration	74.2%	Single session (52%), 1-7 days (9%), 1-4 weeks (9%), 1-12 months (22%), 18 months (9%)
Web Browsing Environment		
Location (explicit or inferable)	87.1%	Only 32% explicitly reported. Lab setting (64%), natural environment (23%)
Browsing software used	93.3%	77% web browsers (21% with augmented functionality), custom software (13%)
Nature of the Web Browsing Task		
Purpose of browsing (explicit or inferable)	100.0%	Researcher-mandated (42%), personal (23%), school (23%), work (19%), navigation (19%)
Data Collection		
Data collection method	96.8%	Observations and/or self-reports (77%), trace measures (10%), archival records (6%)
Data collection software	85.0%	(If using) Specific software (50%), partial details (35%)
Impact of collection on metrics	75.0%	Full details (40%), partial discussion (35%)
Descriptive Reporting of Web Browsing Data		
Types of data reported)	100.0%	Often multiple types of data. Aggregate data (84%), raw data (48%), measures of variability (48%), quotes (29%), anecdotes (19%)
Statistical Analysis of Results		
Statistical analysis addressed	93.5%	Fully explained (26%), statistics given (36%), only significance stated (6%), not appropriate (32%)
Results in Context of Prior Work		
Discussed results in context	61.3%	In-depth discussion (45%), brief discussion (16%), no discussion (39%)

ing behavior, it is important that as much detail as possible is reported.

Details about the user characteristics may not be available to the researchers depending on the type of data collected. For instance, Web usage studies that use server data typically cannot report much information about participants. If this is the case, it is important to explain why this information is not available so the reader understands why the information was omitted.

Sample Size and Sex

Sample size is important due to the high degree of variability between individual Web users. It is one of the most commonly reported pieces of contextual information (Table 1). Large sample sizes can help lessen the effect of individual differences and provide enough data points to aid in the identification of outliers in the population.

Although it is not always possible or appropriate to balance a sample population by sex, it is still important to report the ratio of males to females to help place the results in context. A primarily male population was appropriate with older studies conducted when most Web users were male; however, now that the population of Web users more closely matches the general population, a sample balanced by sex is preferable. The exception is research within a specific domain that may have an inherently uneven balance of males and females (e.g., nursing). The sex of participants is often omitted when study populations are described (Table 1).

Age

As the Web has evolved, so have the key characteristics of users of the Web. As demonstrated in the timeline, the 'typical' user of the Web has shifted from young computer professionals to a varied assortment of users, ranging from young children to grandparents. The method of reporting population age includes mean or median ages, a range of ages, and age categories.

Although it may be convenient to conduct research on 18-22 year old university students, this demographic is only a subset of the average Web users. Sample populations must begin to reflect the actual age range of the general Web user population to maintain external validity. It can be difficult for readers to judge the validity of results as the age of participants is often not reported (Table 1).

Participant Background/Occupation

Although the academic community was at one time representative of the average Web user, this is no longer the case. However, the tendency is to use convenience samples drawn from academic populations. Previous research has found that domain expertise does have an effect on a users' Web behavior (Holscher & Strube, 2000; Ihadjadene, Chaudiron, & Martins, 2003). Therefore, awareness of the background and occupation of the sample population is important. If this information is unknown, it can be difficult to interpret unexpected or surprising results. Fortunately, this is one area that is generally well reported (Table 1).

It is important that researchers attempt to target populations other than the academic community. Small focused studies are also necessary to examine behavioral differences with respect to Web browsing between populations of different backgrounds. Identification of explicit differences could assist other researchers in understanding the limitations resulting from selecting a homogenous sample. It may be the case that the background of users or other individual differences do not impact Web behavior for a class of tasks, but without empirical validation this cannot be assumed.

Web Experience

In addition to domain experience, Web experience also affects a user's behavior on the Web. For example, Cothey (2002) conducted a ten month longitudinal study of browser history logs and found that as students became more experienced they began to visit a more distinct set of Web pages, accessed the Web less frequently, and exhibited a lower rate of search queries (relying more on browsing strategies). Aula, Jhaveri, and Kaki (2005) found that expert searchers often use multiple windows or tabs while searching to support revisitation and to maintain a search history. They also report that expert searchers tend to save links and documents relevant to their search for later revisitation.

Assessing Web experience is difficult as it is constantly evolving. In 1995, a year of Web use may have indicated an individual with a high level of Web experience. Today, this is not the case. Furthermore, length of Web usage does not always imply 'expert' Web usage. Users may develop expertise in a subset of Web related applications and activities.

Web experience is not an easily quantifiable measure but reporting detailed information about Web experience allows other researchers to make judgments. In addition to Web experience, which often is general, researchers can define experience in terms of the task or device. For instance, if investigating Web behavior on a mobile device, it may be important to collect and report information regarding the participants' experience with a mobile device and with Web browsing on a mobile device.

Details about the Web experience of participants is often omitted (Table 1). Furthermore, researchers describe Web experience quite differently, making it difficult to compare the experience of participants from different studies. In a study for which Web experience is particularly important, more concrete measures of Web experience may be necessary. For instance, GVU's WWW User Surveys (1997) included questions that measure Web experience.

Recommendation 2: Report Temporal Information about the Study

Studies examining Web browsing behavior must be interpreted in the temporal context of the state of the Web at the time of the study. Providing the date that a study was conducted is essential to allow future researchers to place the results of studies in context. Furthermore, the duration of the study should also be recorded. There are temporal patterns in Web activity associated with work days, weekends, holidays, and leisure time. Knowing the duration that the Web activity was logged aids in identifying what types of Web usage and patterns may have been captured.

The date of the study was rarely included in the studies of Web browsing behavior surveyed (Table 1); only 26% of the studies provided information regarding the date(s) during which the study was conducted. Although study dates can be inferred from publication dates, research is often published a year or two after the study is carried out. For example, for those papers published in 2003 that provided the dates of the studies, the range of study executions was from early 2000 to mid 2002. Some indication of duration was reported in 74% of the surveyed studies.

Recommendation 3: Report Details of the Study Web Browsing Environment

Details regarding a study's Web browsing environment allow others to replicate previous work and properly interpret study results. This includes information such as the study's setting and the tools used.

Setting of the Study

The setting of a study (lab/home/work/school) may influence a user's Web browsing behavior and provides information regarding the potential completeness of the user's data. For instance, a lab setting is a controlled environment in which a participant may not be acting as they normally would (McGrath, 1995). In a field situation, if a user is studied while only at work, then much of their personal Web usage/behavior may not be captured. Indeed, a user's Web browsing activities and browser settings have been found to vary according to the location of use (i.e., home, work, school) (Hawkey, 2007). Rieh (2003) conducted one of the first studies examining Web searching behavior in the home and found that users searched differently than in previous research conducted in the workplace. The participants searched the Web more frequently, but for shorter periods of time, and the types of searches conducted were much broader. These details about a study's environment are often omitted but give great insight into the realism of the study and the type of browsing tasks in which users might be engaged. While details about the setting of a study can often be gleaned from other details reported, relatively few studies provided concrete details regarding the setting of the study (Table 1).

Browsing Software Used By Participants

One of the biggest challenges in studying Web browsing behavior is employing software that records the appropriate information, while not impeding the user's natural behavior. Often, Web browsers used for research purposes are augmented with new tools or the ability to track a user's behavior. In some instances, this can be accomplished without changing the user's browsing environment (e.g., a Browser Helper Object that works with Microsoft's Internet Explorer) (Hawkey & Inkpen, 2006). However, if the browser used in a study differs from a participant's usual browser, or does not contain their normal tools and data, this may influence the user experience (Kellar, Hawkey, Inkpen, & Watters, 2008). This information is often provided, with differing levels of detail (Table 1).

Recommendation 4: Report Details about the Nature of the Web Browsing Task

Details regarding the nature of the Web browsing task(s) that participants complete for the study are also important to allow others to replicate previous work and properly interpret study results. This includes the task motivation and a rich description of the tasks.

Task Motivation

It is important to include whether the study tasks were personally motivated or motivated by the experiment as Web browsing behavior can be affected by motivation. Laboratory studies allow researchers to observe participants in a controlled fashion. However, it may be challenging to provide a realistic environment, particularly when web activities are not personally motivated. Participants may not make the same effort and take the same actions in a lab study as they would if the Web activities and associated personal data was their own (Whalen & Inkpen, 2005). Loeber and Cristea (2003) describe the effect of motivation on the extensiveness of information searches and include motivation as a factor in their model of navigation on the Internet. This information is often possible to infer based on information implied through descriptions of the study methodology or through participants' quotes and anecdotes (Table 1); making the information explicit would improve understanding of the findings and their generalizability.

Task Details

It is also crucial for researchers to provide a rich description of the tasks performed by participants. This helps give an understanding about the types of behaviors that might have occurred during the experiment and evaluate the realism of the task. Furthermore, the type of Web browsing task (i.e., fact finding, information gathering, browsing, communications, transactions, maintenance) has been found to impact which Web browser navigation tools are used (Kellar, 2007).

If specific Web sites are used during the task, details such as the navigation system available within the site can lend insight into the performance of participants. Ahuja and Webster (2001) found a correlation between participants' perceived disorientation in a Web search task and whether the website had a simple or global navigation scheme. Danielson (2002) found that, in addition to the confidence level of users correlating with the availability of a site overview, their patterns of behavior also changed. Participants abandoned fewer information-seeking tasks, went deeper into the site structure, made large navigation leaps in the site hierarchy, and made less use of the Web browser's back button.

Recommendation 5: Report Details of the Measures Used to Collect Data

Data Collection Methods

The methods of capturing user data about Web browsing behavior provide context for the interpretation of results. The measure types defined by McGrath (1995) are used to frame this discussion. With *self-reports*, participants knowingly report on their own behavior. Examples include questionnaires and semi-structured interviews. *Observations* consist of records of behavior collected by a researcher (or software). Observations can be either overt or covert. Examples include client-side logging software and researcher field notes. *Trace measures* are records of behavior inadvertently left by participants. Examples include data collected from Web server logs. *Archival records* are records of user behavior collected not for the intended purpose of research. The records may be either public or private knowledge. Examples include blogs or Web browser bookmarks.

There are inherent biases and limitations possible with each type of measure (McGrath, 1995) so it is important to provide information about the type of measures chosen. Also important is to explicitly discuss the biases and limitations when describing measures and interpreting results. While these are overall categories of measures, a description of the study instruments selected or designed, and discussions of their validity should be included. Most studies report the general data collection methods used, but fewer details are given about the specific data collection software (Table 1).

Study Metrics

It is also important to report and define the specific metrics collected with the study instruments. Depending on the type of data collection, there may be subtle changes in the interpretation of the metric. For example, when counting the number of pages viewed, a different count may be recorded depending on whether the data was collected at the client, proxy, or server due to caching issues. Frames within a Web page are often handled differently by logging software and change the nature of what is counted when calculating page visits.

The W3C has developed recommendations for Web characterization terminology (W3C, 1999) but they are somewhat abstract. Metrics defined at a finer-grained level would remove any ambiguity. An explicit definition of each metric can greatly contribute to the ability to compare results between studies; however, as seen in Table 1, only 40% of the studies fully reported on how the data collection impacted the metrics they reported, while 35% gave a partial discussion.

Recommendation 6: Provide Descriptive Reporting of the Data

There are several methods of describing the data included in the presentation of results about Web browsing behavior. Many papers report multiple data types (Table 1). Raw data allows other researchers to get a good sense of the data, view outliers and variability, ranges of "normal behavior", and generally gain a better understanding of what was measured. In most studies of user behavior on the Web, there may be raw data that was captured but not pertinent to the study at hand. However, this data may help to characterize general browsing behavior (pages visited, page views, time, actions); and, if made available, could be valuable to other researchers. Additionally, this would also allow the community as a whole to monitor how behavior is changing over time. Care must be taken when sharing participant data as evidenced by the recent controversy over the public release of search data by AOL (McCullagh, 2006). While the data had been anonymized, it was found that the queries often contained information (such as names, addresses, social insurance numbers) that could potentially identify searchers.

Aggregate data provides an overall picture of a sample population's behavior. However, a danger exists in reporting aggregate data because there may be individual participants who skew the data. For example, Hawkey and Kellar (2004) observed instances of aggregate data reporting in which a single participant accounted for a large percentage of Web activity (25% to 40%).For this reason, variability measures, such as standard deviations and quartiles are highly informative. For measurements of frequency, it may be appropriate to normalize the data at the participant level before determining mean frequencies to minimize the impact of outliers.

Participant quotes, obtained through talk aloud protocols, interviews, and general dialog provide valuable insight. Anecdotal stories can also provide this same insight. Hawkey and Kellar (2004) found several instances where studies that included quotes of user dialog and anecdotal passages enabled them to gain more information about the methodology and characteristics of the sample population.

Recommendation 7: Provide Details of Statistical Analysis

Presenting quantitative results about Web browsing behavior without appropriate statistical analysis reduces the validity of the reported results. Without descriptions of the statistics used and the results found, it is impossible for other researchers to judge the suitability of the analysis. In the case of data analysis that is not straight-forward due to characteristics of the data, providing additional details about the selection of the statistical tests and the assumptions behind the tests will aid other researchers in understanding the analysis. In general, most studies provide an adequate description of the statistical analyses performed and the results obtained (Table 1).

Recommendation 8: Report the Results in Context of Prior Studies

Finally, it is important to place the results found in the context of previous research into Web browsing behavior. Where possible, results should be compared and contrasted with previous studies. This may be difficult if previous researchers have not provided full details of the studies. Reflecting on current results in the context of previous research is necessary in order to advance the field, especially within research domains that are still evolving. It also helps other researchers understand the contribution of the work to the field. Despite reviewer guidelines for many publication venues including this facet of reporting, authors often fail to provide an in-depth discussion of their Web browsing behavior results in the context of prior work (Table 1).

DISCUSSION

The results of the survey by Hawkey and Kellar (2004) highlighted the areas of reporting Web browsing behavior done well and those that need some improvement. Some details about user characteristics such as sample size, and background information were generally well reported; but the ratio of male to female participants and their age was reported infrequently. The reporting of Web experience is an area that needs improvement in both including the information and providing detail as to the classification of users. In many other research domains, the date of the study may not bear much importance. However, in the domain of user behavior on the Web, dates and duration of studies are crucial to give temporal context to the study, but these details were lacking in the majority of studies surveyed.

When there are large individual differences in behavior, as exemplified by highly variable data, it is important to get a sense of the underlying data. Only half of the studies surveyed gave a sense of the raw data and reported the amount of variance in the data (Table 1). Technical reports or public Web sites can be a means of disclosing raw data collected in the study. However, the nature of Web usage data, especially when collected in a field situation, often means it may contain personal or identifying information. It may be possible to blind the data sufficiently so that privacy is protected. If the data cannot be blinded and must remain private, providing measures of variance can be helpful.

Much of the detail found lacking in published studies of Web browsing behavior should not require a great deal of space to report. The date of the study, for instance, is crucial for research in this area, yet was omitted in almost 75% of the studies surveyed (Table 1). Clarifications about the population being studied, the environment of the study and the nature of the Web browsing task are all aspects that can be addressed briefly and make a great deal of difference in the ability of the audience to understand the research and compare and contrast it with other results.

More complete descriptions of the logging software employed and its impact on the metrics reported would assist other researchers in their determination of what type of logging software is appropriate for studies under design. Only half of the studies surveyed that used logging software gave full identifying details about the software (Table 1). Commercial products often do not log all the aspects of Web browsing that need to be captured, so custom software is often required. However, it can be challenging to build custom logging software, as it must work with existing Web browsers and tools or provide equivalent functionality. This is particularly challenging when the software must be robust enough to be employed client-side on multiple user computers in a field study. With current reporting practices, it can sometimes be difficult to determine the approach taken, let alone the specific methods of capturing the data.

In the majority of Web browsing behavior studies surveyed, participants tended to be convenience samples recruited through the academic community (Table 1). These users no longer represent typical Web users and care must be taken when generalizing results to the general community. Researchers may still need to conduct tightly constrained studies that, although they may not be reflective of the population, offer valuable insight, especially for exploratory studies. However, there is a need for follow-up research that explores the generalizability of the results. This can be either through a large study of a heterogeneous population or a series of smaller, more focused studies comparing the Web browsing behavior of different types of participants.

There is also a need for complementary experimental strategies. Broad field studies are necessary to discover natural browsing behaviors, but more closely controlled experiments are also needed to isolate specific aspects of browsing and effects of task and environment. If metrics from each study are fully defined, complementary strategies employed within the research community can be more easily assimilated to advance the overall state of research.

CONCLUSION

Currently there is a lack of contextual information, including temporal information being reported in studies of Web browsing behavior, as supported by a survey of published papers (Hawkey & Kellar, 2004). This survey highlighted the need for a set of recommendations to provide structure in reporting. This chapter provided recommendations for including eight categories of contextual information when reporting the results of studies of Web usage. A summary of these recommendations appears in Table 2. We believe this contextual information is crucial to include in the reporting of any studies of Web browsing behavior so that the readers can gain a fuller understanding of the research being presented. For each of the recommendations, we have discussed the impact on the interpretation of results if the contextual details are not reported.

Although the community as a whole may argue that these recommendations are obvious and elementary, the fact of the matter is that they are often not followed. As a result it can be difficult to learn the current knowledge about Web browsing behaviors and assess if and how these behaviors are changing over time. In order to advance research in the field, it is important that researchers are able to find areas for investigation and that is difficult when previous research is not well defined. It is also difficult for researchers and practitioners to use the results to guide the development of algorithms, tools, or applications in this area. The authors hope that the discussions about the impact of not providing this contextual information will motivate others to more fully provide this information. It is our hope that these recommendations will serve as a check list for future researchers conducting and reporting on studies of web browsing behavior.

REFERENCES

Ahuja, J. S., & Webster, J. (2001). Perceived disorientation: an examination of a new measure to assess web design effectiveness. *Interacting with Computers, 14*(1), 15-29.

Anick, P. (2003). Using Terminological Feedback for Web Search Refinement - A Log-based Study. In *26th annual international ACM SIGIR conference on research and development in information retrieval* (pp. 88-95). Toronto, Canada: ACM.

Atterer, R., Wnuk, M., & Schmidt, A. (2006). Knowing the user's every move: user activity tracking for website usability evaluation and implicit interaction. In *15th International Conference on World Wide Web* (pp. 203-212). Edinburgh, Scotland: ACM.

Aula, A., Jhaveri, N., & Kaki, M. (2005). Information Search and Re-access Strategies of Experienced Web Users. In *14th international conference on World Wide Web* (pp. 583-592). Chiba, Japan: ACM.

Table 2. Summary of recommendation appearing in this chapter

	Recommendation Summary
1.	Report sample size and participant characteristics, such as sex, age, background/occupation, and web experience.
2.	Provide the date that the study was conducted, as well as the duration.
3.	Provide details about the study environment and the browsing software used by participants.
4.	Provide rich descriptions of the tasks performed by participants, including whether the tasks were personally motivated or motivated by the experiment.
5.	Provide information about the type of measures chosen, a description of the study instruments, and discuss the study biases and limitations. Also report and define the specific metrics collected with the study instruments.
6.	Provide descriptive reporting of results through raw data, aggregate data, and participant quotes and anecdotes (where appropriate).
7.	Provide additional details about the selection of the statistical tests and the assumptions behind the tests.
8.	Place results in the context of previous work.

Barford, P., Bestavros, A., Bradley, A., & Crovella, M. (1999). Changes in Web Client Access Patterns: Characteristics and Caching Implications. *World Wide Web, 2*(1-2), 15-28.

Byrne, M., John, B., Wehrle, N., & Crow, D. (1999). The Tangled Web We Wove: A Taskonomy of WWW Use. In *SIGCHI conference on human factors in computing systems* (pp. 544-551). Pittsburgh, PA: ACM.

Card, S., Pirolli, P., Van Der Wege, M., Morrison, J., Reeder, R., Schraedley, P., et al. (2001). Information Scent as a Driver of Web Behavior Graphs: Results of a Protocol Analysis Method for Web Usability. In *SIGCHI conference on human factors in computing systems* (pp. 498-505). Seattle, WA: ACM.

Catledge, L., & Pitkow, J. (1995). Characterizing Browsing Strategies in the World-Wide Web. In *3rd international World-Wide Web conference on technology, tools, and applications* (pp. 1065 - 1073). Darmstadt, Germany: Elsevier North-Holland, Inc.

Choo, C. W., Detlor, B., & Turnbull, D. (2000). Information Seeking on the Web: An Integrated Model of Browsing and Searching. *First Monday, 5*(2), Retrieved August 3, 2004, from http://firstmonday.org/issues/issue2005_2002/choo/index.html.

Claypool, M., Le, P., Waseda, M., & Brown, D. (2001). Implicit Interest Indicators. In *6th international conference on intelligent user interfaces* (pp. 33-40). Santa Fe, NM: ACM.

ClickZStatsStaff. (2002). *Internet Usage Stats.* Online at: www.clickz.com/stats/big_picture/traffic_patterns/article.php/960101. Retrieved January 1, 2008.

Cockburn, A., & McKenzie, B. (2001). What do web users do? An empirical analysis of web use. *International Journal of Human-Computer Studies, 54*(6), 903-922.

Cothey, V. (2002). A Longitudinal Study of World Wide Web Users' Information-Searching Behavior. *Journal of the American Society for Information Science and Technology, 53*(2), 67-78.

Danielson, D. R. (2002). Web navigation and the behavioral effects of constantly visible site maps. *Interacting with Computers, 14*(5), 601-618.

Fenstermacher, K., & Ginsburg, M. (2003). Client-Side Monitoring for Web Mining. *Journal of the American Society for Information Science and Technology, 54*(7), 625-637.

Google. (2007). *Google Corporate Information: Google Milestones.* Online at: http://www.google.ca/corporate/history.html. Retrieved January 1, 2008.

Grace-Martin, M., & Gay, G. (2001). Web Browsing, Mobile Computing and Academic Performance. *Educational Technology & Society, 4(3),* Retrieved February 19, 2006, from http://ifets.ieee.org/periodical/vol_2003_2001/grace_martin.html.

GVUOnlineSurvey. (1997). *GVU's 8th WWW User Survey.* Online at: http://www.cc.gatech.edu/gvu/user_surveys/survey-1997-10. Retrieved August 3, 2004.

Hargittai, E. (2002). Beyond Logs and Surveys: In-Depth Measures of People's Web Use Skills. *Journal of the American Society for Information Science and Technology, 53*(14), 1239-1244.

Hawkey, K. (2007). *Managing the visual privacy of incidental information in web browsers.* Unpublished PhD Dissertation, Dalhousie University, Halifax, Nova Scotia.

Hawkey, K., & Inkpen, K. (2005). Web Browsing Today: The impact of changing contexts on user activity. In *CHI '05 extended abstracts on Human Factors in Computing Systems* (pp. 1443-1446). Portland, Oregon: ACM.

Hawkey, K., & Inkpen, K. M. (2006). Examining the Content and Privacy of Web Browsing Incidental Information. In *15th International Conference on World Wide Web* (pp. 123-132). Edinburgh, Scotland: ACM.

Hawkey, K., & Kellar, M. (2004). *Recommendations for reporting context in studies of web browsing behaviour* (No. CS-2004-16). Halifax, NS: Dalhousie University.

Heinström, J. (2003). Fast Surfers, Broad Scanners and Deep Divers as Users of Information Technology - Relating Information Preferences to Personality Traits. In *Annual Meeting of the American Society for Information Science and Technology* (pp. 247-253). Long Beach, CA.

Herder, E. (2005). Characterizations of User Web Revisit Behavior. In *the Workshop on Adaptivity and User Modeling in Interactive Systems (ABIS 2005).* Saarbrücken, Germany.

Herder, E., & Juvina, I. (2004). Discovery of Individual User Navigation Styles. In *the Workshop on Individual Differences in Adaptive Hypermedia (Adaptive Hypermedia 2004).* Eindhoven, The Netherlands.

Hilbert, D. M., & Redmiles, D. F. (2000). Extracting Usability Information from User Interface Events. *ACM Computing Surveys, 32*(4), 384-421.

Holscher, C., & Strube, G. (2000). Web Search Behavior of Internet Experts and Newbies. In *9th International World Wide Web conference on Computer Networks* (pp. 337-346). Amsterdam, The Netherlands: North-Holland Publishing Co.

Hong, J. I., Heer, J., Waterson, S., & Landay, J. A. (2001). WebQuilt: A Proxy-based Approach to Remote Web Usability Testing. *ACM Transactions on Information Systems, 19*(3), 263-285.

Huberman, B., Pirolli, P., Pitkow, J., & Lukose, R. (1998). Strong Regularities in World Wide Web Surfing. *Science, 280*, 95-97.

Ihadjadene, M., Chaudiron, S., & Martins, D. (2003). The Effect of Individual Differences on Searching the Web. In *Annual Meeting of the American Society for Information Science and Technology* (pp. 240-246). Long Beach, CA.

Infoplease. (2001). *Internet use from Any Location by Individuals Age Three and Older.* Online at: http://www.infoplease.com/ipa/A0901651.html. Retrieved November 4, 2004.

Infoplease. (2004a). *Daily Internet Activities.* Online at: http://www.infoplease.com/ipa/A0921860.html. Retrieved November 4, 2004.

Infoplease. (2004b). *Internet Timeline.* Online at: http://www.infoplease.com/ipa/A0193167.html. Retrieved November 4, 2004.

Jansen, B. J., & Pooch, U. (2000). A review of Web searching studies and a framework for future research. *Journal of the American Society for Information Science and Technology, 52*(3), 235-246.

Jenkins, C., Corritore, C., & Wiedenbeck, S. (2003). Patterns of Information Seeking on the Web: A Qualitative Study of Domain Expertise and Web Expertise. *IT & Society, 1*(3), 64-89.

Jones, W., Dumais, S., & Bruce, H. (2002). Once Found, What Then?: A Study of "Keeping" Behaviors in the Personal Use of Web Information. In *Annual Meeting of the American Society for Information Science and Technology* (pp. 391-402). Philadelphia, PA.

Kehoe, C. M., Pitkow, J., Sutton, K., Aggarwal, G., & Rogers, J. D. (1999). *Results of GVU's Tenth World Wide Web User Survey.* Online at: http://www.cc.gtech.edu/gvu/user_surveys/survey-1998-10/tenthreport.html. Retrieved August 4, 2004.

Kellar, M. (2007). *An Examination of User Behaviour during Web Information Tasks.* Unpublished PhD Dissertation, Dalhousie University, Halifax, Nova Scotia.

Kellar, M., Hawkey, K., Inkpen, K. M., & Watters, C. (2008). Challenges of Capturing Natural Web-based User Behaviours. *International Journal of Human Computer Interaction, 24*(4), 385-409.

Kellar, M., Watters, C., & Shepherd, M. (2006). The Impact of Task on the Usage of Web Browser Navigation Tools. In *Graphics Interface* (pp. 235-242). Quebec City, Canada: Canadian Information Processing Society.

Kellar, M., Watters, C., & Shepherd, M. (2007). A Field Study Characterizing Web-based Information Seeking Tasks. *Journal of the American Society for Information Science and Technology, 58*(7), 999-1018.

Kelly, D., & Belkin, N. (2004). Display Time as Implicit Feedback: Understanding Task Effects. In *27th Annual International ACM SIGIR Conference on Research and Development in Information Retrieval* (pp. 377-384). Sheffield, UK: ACM.

Kerner, S. M. (2004). *More Broadband Usage Means More Online Spending*. Online at: www.clickz.com/stats/markets/broadband/article.php/3419281. Retrieved August 4, 2004.

Kim, K.-S., & Allen, B. (2002). Cognitive and Task Influences on Web Searching Behavior. *Journal of the American Society for Information Science and Technology, 53*(2), 109-119.

Laskowski, S., Morse, E., & Gray, W. (2001). *CIFter Project Main Page*. Online at: http://zing.ncsl.nist.gov/cifter/. Retrieved April 18, 2005.

Lenhart, A., & Fox, S. (2006). *Bloggers: A portrait of the internet's new storytellers*. Pew Internet & American Life Project, http://www.pewinternet.org. Retrieved July 19, 2006.

Loeber, S. C., & Cristea, A. (2003). A WWW Information Seeking Process Model. *Educational Technology & Society, 6*(3), 43-52.

Lycos. (1999). *The Lycos 50 Daily Report*. Online at: http://50.lycos.com/083099.html. Retrieved August 4, 2004.

Madden, M., & Fox, S. (2006). *Riding the Waves of "Web 2.0"*. Pew Internet & American Life Project, http://www.pewinternet.org. Retrieved October 5, 2006.

Marsh, D. (2003). *History of the Internet*. Online at: http://www.internetvalley.com/archives/mirrors/davemarsh-timeline-1.htm. Retrieved August 4, 2004.

McCullagh, D. (2006). *AOL's disturbing glimpse into user's lives*: CNET News.com, Online at: http://news.com.com/2100-1030_3-6103098.html. Retrieved October 5, 2006.

McGrath, J. E. (1995). Methodology matters: doing research in the behavioral and social sciences. In J. G. R. Baeker, W. Buxton, and S. Greenberg (Ed.), *Human-Computer Interaction: Toward the Year 2000* (pp. 152-169).

Milic-Frayling, N., Jones, R., Rodden, K., Smyth, G., Blackwell, A., & Sommerer, R. (2004). SmartBack: Supporting Users in Back Navigation. In *13th International World Wide Web Conference* (pp. 63-71). New York, NY: ACM.

Nielsen//NetRatings. (2004a). *United States: Average Web Usage, Month of September 2004, Home Panel*. Online at: www.nielsen-netratings.com. Retrieved October 5, 2006.

Nielsen//NetRatings. (2004b). *United States: Average Web Usage, Month of September 2004, Work Panel*. Online at: www.nielsen-netratings.com. Retrieved October 5, 2006.

Obendorf, H., Weinreich, H., & Hass, T. (2004). Automatic Support for Web User Studies with SCONE and TEA. In *CHI '04 extended abstracts on Human Factors in Computing Systems* (pp. 1135-1138). Vienna, Austria: ACM.

Pastore, M. (1998a). *Microsoft Leads Browser Race*. Online at: www.clickz.com/stats/big_picture/hardware/article.php/151351. Retrieved October 5, 2006.

Pastore, M. (1998b). *Online Users Need Speed.* Online at: www.clickz.com/stats/markets/broadband/article.php/151701. Retrieved October 5, 2006.

Pastore, M. (2000a). *E-Commerce, Mobile Access Drawing Interest from Net Users.* Online at: www.clickz.com/stats/big_picture/geographics/article.php/5911_494701. Retrieved October 5, 2006.

Pastore, M. (2000b). *Internet Usage Stats.* Online at: www.clickz.com/stats/big_picture/traffic_patterns/article.php/291211. Retrieved October 5, 2006.

Pastore, M. (2000c). *Slow Modems Still Dominate Home Internet Scene.* Online at: www.clickz.com/stats/big_picture/hardware/article.php/277191. Retrieved October 5, 2006.

Pastore, M. (2001). *Online Consumers Now the Average Consumer.* Online at: www.clickz.com/stats/big_picture/demographics/article.php/5901_800201. Retrieved October 5, 2006.

Pirolli, P., Pitkow, J., & Rao, R. (1996). Silk from a Sow's Ear: Extracting Usable Structures from the Web. In *SIGCHI Conference on Human Factors in Computing Systems* (pp. 118 - 125). Vancouver, Canada: ACM.

Pitkow, J. (1997). In Search of Reliable Usage Data on the WWW. In *6th International Conference on World Wide Web* (pp. 1343-1355). Santa Clara, CA: Elsevier Science Publishers Ltd.

Pitkow, J., & Recker, M. M. (1994). Using the Web as a Survey Tool: Results from the Second WWW Survey. *Computer Networks and ISDN Systems, 27*(6), 809-822.

Pitkow, J. E., & Kehoe, C. M. (1996). Emerging Trends in the WWW User Population. *Communications of the ACM, 39*(6), 106 - 108.

Rainie, L. (2007). *Forget Dewey and His Decimals, Internet Users are Revolutionizing the Way We Classify Information -- And Make Sense of It.* Pew Internet and American Life Project, http://www.pewinternet.org. Retrieved January 31, 2007.

Reeder, R., Pirolli, P., & Card, S. (2001). WebEyeMapper and WebLogger: tools for analyzing eye tracking data collected in Web-use studies. In *CHI '01 Extended Abstracts on Human Factors in Computing Systems* (pp. 19-20). Seattle, WA: ACM.

Rieh, S. Y. (2003). Investigating Web Searching Behavior in Home Environments. In *Annual Meeting of the American Society for Information Science and Technology* (pp. 255-264). Long Beach, CA.

Schiano, D., Stone, M., & Bectarte, R. (2001). Search and the Subjective Web. In *CHI '01 Extended Abstracts on Human Factors in Computing Systems* (pp. 165-166). Seattle, WA: ACM.

Sellen, A. J., Murphy, R., & Shaw, K. L. (2002). How Knowledge Workers Use the Web. In *SIGCHI Conference on Human Factors in Computing Systems* (pp. 227-234). Minneapolis, MN: ACM.

Spink, A., Wolfram, D., Jansen, M. B. J., & Saracevic, T. (2001). Searching the Web: the Public and their Queries. *Journal of the American Society for Information Science and Technology, 52*(3), 226-234.

Tauscher, L., & Greenberg, S. (1997). How People Revisit Web Pages: Empirical Findings and Implications for the Design of History Systems. *International Journal of Human-Computer Studies, 47*(1), 97-137.

Teevan, J., Alvarado, C., Ackerman, M., & Karger, D. (2004). The Perfect Search Engine is Not Enough: A Study of Orienteering Behavior in Directed Search. In *SIGCHI Conference on Human Factors in Computing Systems* (pp. 415-422). Vienna, Austria: ACM.

Thury, E. M. (1998). Analysis of student Web browsing behavior: implications for designing and evaluating Web sites. In *16th Annual International Conference on Computer Documentation* (pp. 265-270). Quebec City, Canada: ACM.

Turnbull, D. (1998). *WebTracker: A Tool for Understanding Web Use.* Online at: http://www.ischool.utexas.edu/~donturn/research/webtracker/. Retrieved October 5, 2006.

W3C. (1999). *Web Characterization Terminology & Definitions Sheet.* Online at: http://www.w3.org/1999/05/WCA-terms/01. Retrieved June 1, 2005.

Weinreich, H., Obendorf, H., Herder, E., & Mayer, M. (2006). Off the Beaten tracks: Exploring Three Aspects of Web Navigation. In *15th International Conference on World Wide Web* (pp. 133-142). Edinburgh, Scotland: ACM.

Whalen, T., & Inkpen, K. M. (2005). *Gathering evidence: use of visual security cues in web browsers.* In *Graphic Interface* (pp. 137-145). Victoria, British Columbia: Canadian Human-Computer Communications Society.

Wildemuth, B., Barry, C., Luo, L., Crystal, A., & Oh, S. (2004). *Establishing a Research Agenda for Studies of Online Search Behaviors: A Delphi Study.* Online at: http://ils.unc.edu/sig_use_delphi/. Retrieved April 18, 2005.

Zhang, D., Zambrowicz, C., Zhou, H., & Roderer, N. (2004). User Information Seeking Behavior in a Medical Web Portal Environment: A Preliminary Study. *Journal of the American Society for Information Science and Technology, 55*(8), 670-684.

KEY TERMS

Browsing Environment: Description of the context within which Web browsing occurs. For studies of Web usage this includes the Web browser and its associated tools (e.g., history, specialized toolbars), the task, and the motivation for conducting the browsing.

Browsing Task: Details about the browsing task given to the participant, including the participant's goals. The task can be focused (e.g. information searching), more casual browsing, or may be purely navigational. The task can be directed closely by the researcher or be opportunistic and motivated by the needs of the participant.

Descriptive Data Reporting: Providing descriptive details about the raw data gathered to afford readers with a rich understanding of the Web browsing behaviors captured.

Population Characteristics: Attributes of the participant population including such factors as age, sex, background, occupation, Web experience and sample size. Individual differences in Web browsing behaviour may arise as a result of such characteristics.

Study Context: Contextual factors which may impact results of a study. For studies of Web usage, these factors include the temporal context of the study, the study setting, the browsing environment, the task, the data collection methods used, the study instruments and metrics captured, and the characteristics of the population studied.

Study Instruments: The research tools used to collect the study data. For studies of Web usage, these usually include logging software which may be located client-side, server-side or accessed through a proxy server.

Study Setting: Description of the study environment including the location and experimental setup. For studies of web usage, this includes the browsing environment as well as any visible data collection methods.

Temporal Context: Temporal information which may impact interpretation of a study. At different points in time, different browsing environments and activities emerge and become part of users' experiences. Temporal factors which can be reported include the date of the study and duration of the study.

Section III
Behavior Analysis

Chapter XI
From Analysis to Estimation of User Behavior

Seda Ozmutlu
Uludag University, Turkey

Huseyin C. Ozmutlu
Uludag University, Turkey

Amanda Spink
Queensland University of Technology, Australia

ABSTRACT

This chapter summarizes the progress of search engine user behavior analysis from search engine transaction log analysis to estimation of user behavior. Correct estimation of user information searching behavior paves the way to more successful and even personalized search engines. However, estimation of user behavior is not a simple task. It closely relates to natural language processing and human computer interaction, and requires preliminary analysis of user behavior and careful user profiling. This chapter details the studies performed on analysis and estimation of search engine user behavior, and surveys analytical methods that have been and can be used, and the challenges and research opportunities related to search engine user behavior or transaction log query analysis and estimation.

INTRODUCTION

Search engines are the most important tools for reaching information over the Web and the effective use of search engines is a challenge (Liaw and Huang, 2006). Search engine query analysis and user behavior analysis through search engine queries is a very important task, since it is directly related to developing search engines with better performance and also personalized search engines. Analysis of user behavior is important in the sense that each service provider (and search engines are service providers) benefits from knowing its customer base and the way the customers use its services. Enhanced search engine structures and algorithms suitable for the search engine users can be developed after analyzing the behavior of the user base of the search engine.

In addition, a new trend in search engine research is the development of personalized search engines. Including personalization features into search engines has been recognized as a major research area (Liu, et al., 2004). Radlinski and Dumais (2006) state that personalizing search results for individual users is increasingly being recognized as an important future direction for searching. Agichtein, Brill, Dumai and Ragno (2006) state that accurate modeling and interpretation of user behavior have important applications to ranking, click spam detection, search personalization, and other tasks.

However, it is a real challenge to capture user information behavior, since people have different and changing information needs, and they utilize different information seeking strategies to solve their information seeking problems (Gremett, 2006). Many search studies at the human information behavior level explore the factors that influence search within the context of human information seeking (Spink and Jansen, 2004). Excellent reviews on searching exist, which we will point to within the chapter. It should also be mentioned that the chapter is restricted to studies on search engine transaction log analysis and search engine user behavior analysis and does not cover usage mining in general, which is a very wide topic.

However, it is not adequate to only analyze the user interactions with the search engine; it is also necessary to reflect the results of user query analysis to real-time information retrieval algorithms, which have estimation power of the users' upcoming actions and transactions with the search engine. Along this direction, search engine transaction log analysis, and user behavior analysis have progressed from pure analysis of user queries to studies on estimation of content-based behavior of users, and development of personalized information retrieval algorithms.

This chapter provides the summary on the progress of search engine transaction log analysis and user behavior analysis to estimation of search engine user behavior. The chapter begins with a detailed literature review of search engine user behavior studies and continues with a detailed presentation of the methodologies used for analyzing search behavior. Then, the studies on the estimation of search use behavior will be summarized, along with the explanation of the methodologies used for these studies. The chapter is concluded with a discussion of future research opportunities.

SEARCH ENGINE USER BEHAVIOR ANALYSIS

Literature Review of Search Engine User Behavior Studies

In this chapter, we will summarize studies on search behavior. However, the reader should note that there are excellent reviews on search behavior, such as that of Spink and Jansen (2004). Therefore, we will briefly touch on the most important aspects of search behavior and emphasize content-based user behavior.

The early studies on searching behavior were performed during the mid-1990s. Initial studies on search behavior emphasized how the users searched the Web and how to measure search effectiveness. Tillotson, Cherry and Clinton (1995), He and Jacobson (1995), Catledge and Pitkow (1995), Nahl (1998) and Hill and Hannafin (1997) studied the relationships between user demographic characteristics and found that demographic characteristics, such as gender and computer expertise were factors in Internet use.

In subsequent years, a larger scale of studies for search behavior are noted, as well as a more technical nuance on the analysis of search engine logs, such as the integration of stochastic and statistical methods in search engine user behavior analysis. Also, the range of the studies has diversified to include cognitive and behavior studies using transaction log, experimental, single Web site and longitudinal studies. A large number of studies focused on search engine transaction log analysis, and how the searching process worked. These studies strongly emphasized the analysis of statistical characteristics of user queries such as duration of sessions and queries, number of queries per session and number of terms per query. There are many large-scaled studies within this domain, such as those of Silverstein, Henzinger, Marais and Moricz (1999), Cooley, Mobasher and Srivastava (1999), Spink, Bateman and Jansen (1999), Spink, Wolfram, Jansen and Saracevic (2001), Spink, Jansen, Wolfram and Saracevic (2002a), Jansen and Spink (2004), Wolfram, Spink, Jansen and Saracevic (2001) and Jansen, Spink and Saracevic (2000). Jansen and Spink (2004) and Markey (2007a) provide an excellent review of the studies on user behavior and search engine transaction log behavior. After reviewing many studies, Markey (2007a) states that end users enter a few short search statements into online IR systems (two to four terms), relevance feedback is uncommon, the only advanced search features that figure into end-user searches on a regular basis are quotes for bound phrases and the plus and minus operators.

Besides the statistical analysis of search engine queries, one of the most important dimensions of search engine user information seeking behavior is content-based behavior. The number of studies on content-based behavior is relatively few, the reason generally being the effort required to manually process the queries for topic identification (Pu, Chuang and Yang, 2002). Content-based behavior of search engine user queries can be analyzed along a few basic directions. Jansen outlines the level of analysis for transaction logs: At the term level, query level and session level. Similarly, the first level of content-based analysis is the analysis of query terms. Another level is analysis of query topics. Some studies analyzed and summarized the topic of the queries (such as those of Jansen, Spink, Bateman and Saracevic, 1998, Jansen, Spink and Saracevic, 2000, Spink, Wolfram, Jansen and Saracevic, 2001, Silverstein, Henzinger, Marais and Moricz, 1999) and other studies analyzed specific types of search engine queries, such as queries on multimedia, question-format queries and sexual queries. Search engine user queries have also been analyzed in terms of other aspects, such as the effect of time on search engine queries' statistical characteristics, and multitasking behavior of search engine users. Studies on content-based behavior of search engine users range from basic analysis of topics and terms of search engine queries to studies analyzing different types of search engine queries and will be included in the literature review.

Along the first dimension of content-based analysis of search engine transaction logs, some researchers, such as Silverstein, Henzinger, Marais and Moricz (1999), Jansen, Spink, Bateman and Saracevic (1998), Jansen, Spink and Saracevic (2000), have performed content analysis of search engine data logs at the term level, hence analyzed the frequency of terms and term pairs in search engine queries. These researchers have observed that the high-frequency terms reveal interest in current events, but still the highest ranking terms are related to topics of pornography, entertainment and education. Spink, Wolfram, Jansen and Saracevic (2001) analyzed an Excite transaction log collected in 1999 for terms and have discovered that the top category in subject of queries was entertainment and recreation, closely followed by sex and pornography. Interestingly, the distribution of topics of queries, as reported by Spink, Wolfram, Jansen and Saracevic (2001), does not coincide with the distribution of information on the publicly indexable Web, as reported by Lawrence and Giles (1999). They found that about 83 percent of servers contain commercial content, 6 percent scientific/educational content, close to 3 percent health content, 2 percent personal content, slightly more than 1 percent pornographic content. The servers that are about 1 percent of the entire number of servers attract the attention of a large number of users.

Besides term analysis, Jansen, Spink and Saracevic (2000) and Spink, Wolfram, Jansen and Saracevic (2001) have also performed analysis of a sample of queries at the conceptual or topical level and discovered that the top category in subject of queries was entertainment and recreation, closely followed by sex and pornography. Spink, Jansen, Wolfram and Saracevic (2002) analyzed Excite datasets from 1997, 1999 and 2001 for content and found that information problems and search topics have evolved from 1997 to 2001; for example users' interests have shifted from entertainment and pornography to travel and commerce. Ozmutlu, Ozmutlu and Spink (2004b) and Beitzel, Jensen, Chowdhury, Grossman and Frieder (2004) have found that the popularity of topics vary throughout the day.

Other researchers have analyzed the search engine queries on specific topics, such as multimedia queries, sexual queries, question and request-format queries, e-commerce queries. Multitasking queries have also been an important research area.

Multimedia Queries

Regarding multimedia queries, research on image retrieval utilizing indexed image collections (Goodrum and Kim, 1998), various aspects of audio and video retrieval (Brown, Foote, Jones, Sparck Jones and Young, 1996), and the demand for seeking video when designing a multimedia classroom (Smith, Ruocco and Jansen, 1998) have appeared during the late 90s. Jansen, Goodrum, and Spink (2000) conducted a major 1997 user study of multimedia searching using large-scale query data from the Excite search engine. Image queries were the most common multimedia searches with longer sessions than video and audio sessions. Goodrum and Spink (2001) found that Excite image queries in 1997 contained a large number of unique terms. Ozmutlu, Spink and Ozmutlu (2002) analyzed search queries on multimedia from the Excite search engine collected in 2001, and Ozmutlu, Ozmutlu and Spink (2003) report findings from a major study of trends in multimedia searching by Excite users from 1997 to 2001, including changes in queries and session characteristics, and changes or differences in image, video and audio searching. Ozmutlu, Spink and Ozmutlu (2003) found that the percentage of multimedia queries from the Excite data log decreased from 3.7 percent in 1997 and 1999 to 1.79 percent in 2001. Jansen, Spink and Pedersen (2003, 2005) report the results of a research study evaluating the effect of separate multimedia collections on individual searching behavior and investigate the characteristics of multimedia searching on AltaVista. Their results show (similar to Ozmutlu, Ozmutlu and Spink's (2003)) that multimedia searching is complex relative to general searching.

Sexual Queries

Jansen, Spink, and Saracevic (2000) found that sexual queries are only a small proportion of all searches but were the top frequency in the Excite 1999 dataset. About 25 percent of the highest used terms were sexual terms. The diversity of subjects searched is very high within sexual terms, ranging from sexual health to pornography. Spink, Ozmultu, and Lorence (2004) and Spink, Koricich, Jansen and Cole (2004) found that sexually related searches were longer than non-sexual searches and included viewing more pages of sites, especially those related to images.

Question and Request Format Queries

A group of studies investigated the search engine queries in question and request-format. With the emergence of a more Q and A approach to querying, queries in question format are becoming important and significant to the development of more effective Information Retrieval systems. Spink and Ozmutlu (2001) report findings from a study examining the nature of queries submitted to Ask Jeeves-a Q and A search engine. The analysis showed that many queries are not in question or request format. Spink and Ozmutlu (2002) compared Excite and Ask Jeeves question queries from transaction logs recorded in 1999. Most question format queries are about seven terms in length, and non-question/request queries are less than five terms long, and contain few Boolean operators or modifiers. To enhance previous research, Ozmutlu, Ozmutlu and Spink (2003) conducted a comparative study to examine the current use of question and request format queries submitted to Excite and AlltheWeb.com. Their results showed little use of question or request queries by both US and European search engine users in non-Q and A search engines.

E-Commerce Searching

The number of e-commerce queries has increased from 1997 to 2001 (Spink and Guner, 2001; Spink and Jansen, 2004; Spink, Jansen, Wolfram, and Saracevic (2002)). Spink, Jansen, Wolfram, and Saracevic (2002) found that in 2001 the largest category of searches were e-commerce-related. Spink and Guner (2001) discovered that e-commerce or business queries usually include more search terms; lead to fewer pages viewed, are less modified, and include less advanced search features. Company or product name queries were the most common form of business or e-commerce queries.

Multitasking Searching

Another dimension of topic-related information retrieval is multitasking. During a search session, some users can be interested in multiple topics. In terms of information retrieval, multitasking information seeking and searching processes are defined as "the process of searches over time in relation to more than one, possibly evolving, set of information problems" (Spink, Ozmutlu and Ozmutlu, 2002). Spink, Bateman and Jansen (1999) found that 3.8 percent of Excite users responding to a Web-based survey reported multitasking searches. In other studies, it was observed that in a datalog of the Excite search engine collected in 1999, 11.4 percent of users performed multitasking searches and in a datalog of the FAST search engine collected for a day in 2001, 31.8 percent of users performed multitasking searches (Ozmutlu, Ozmutlu and Spink, 2003). Ozmutlu, Ozmutlu and Spink (2003) also reported that (1) multitasking sessions often included more than three topics per session (2) multitasking sessions are longer in duration and number of queries and regular searching sessions and (3)most of the topics in multitasking searches were on general information, computers and entertainment (4) both Excite and AllTheWeb users search for about 3 topics per session and submit 4-5 queries per topic.

In another study, Spink, Park, Jansen and Pedersen (2002) found that 81 percent of two-query Excite and Altavista search sessions were multitasking searches, and there were a broad variety of searching topics. Spink et al. (2006) examined multitasking during Excite and AlltheWeb.com searching. They showed that the mean queries per multitasking search session were 14.9 for Excite and 14.3 for AlltheWeb.com users. The mean queries per session for the entire Excite sample was 10, making Excite multitasking sessions about 50 percent longer than regular search sessions. The same statistics for the AlltheWeb.com dataset show that the mean queries were 10.3 for the entire sample and 14.3 for multitasking sessions. The queries in multitasking sessions were categorized with respect to the topics provided in Spink, Ozmutlu, and Ozmultu (2002). Spink, Park and Jansen (2006) showed that Excite users preferred the categories of hobbies, shopping, and business that form about 47 percent of all queries in multitasking sessions. Spink, Park and Jansen (2006) found that multitasking search sessions included more than three topics per search session.

Detailed Explanation of Methodologies Used for Web Log and User Behavior Analysis

The previous section emphasized the scope and the results of the studies on search behavior and especially content-based behavior. This chapter will focus on the techniques used in the studies listed in the previous section.

Exploratory Data Analysis

Most of the studies available in search behavior analysis and transaction log analysis are based on EDA (Exploratory data analysis) (Jansen, Spink and Saracevic, 2000; Spink, Wolfram, Jansen and Saracevic, 2001). Almost all these studies use EDA measures, such as averages, standard deviation, median, maximum and minimum values, frequency distributions and percentages to investigate the number of queries per session, number of sessions, duration of queries and sessions, number of terms per query and distribution of terms per query. No stochastic, operational research or other advanced statistical techniques were used. We do not include the explanation of these exploratory data analysis techniques in this chapter. Interested readers can see Walpole, Myers and Myers (1998).

Correlation and Test of Independence

The number of studies using more advanced techniques is very few in search behavior analysis. Silverstein, Henzinger, Marais and Moricz (1999) use correlation coefficients and the χ^2 test for independence to evaluate the relationship between term pairs occurring in the same query. Correlation coefficients show the strength of the linear relationship between two or more variables or data strings, and can be given as in Equation (1):

$$\rho = \frac{\sum_{i=1}^{n}(x_i - \bar{x})(y_i - \bar{y})}{\sqrt{\sum_{i=1}^{n}(x_i - \bar{x})\sum_{i=1}^{n}(y_i - \bar{y})}} \qquad (1)$$

where X and Y are the different variables, x_i is the value of the ith data point of the X variable, y_i is the value of the ith data point of the Y variable, $\bar{x}$ and $\bar{y}$ are the averages of the values in the X and Y variables. The correlation coefficient gives a value of -1 and 1, and a value close to 1 or -1 represents a strong linear relationship between the variables X and Y (Walpole, Myers and Myers, 1998).

The χ^2 test for independence is used to test the hypothesis whether two variables of classification are independent, and can be given as in Equation 2:

$$\chi^2 = \frac{\sum_i (o_i - e_i)^2}{ei} \qquad (2)$$

"where the summation extends over r c cells in a r x c contingency table. If $\chi^2 > \chi^2_\alpha$ with v=(r-1)(c-1) degrees of freedom, reject the null hypothesis of independence at the α level of significance; otherwise accept the null hypothesis" (Walpole, Myers and Myers, 1998, pp. 346), and also where o_i is the actual frequency, e_i is the expected frequency.

Markov Models

Ozmutlu, Ozmutlu and Spink (2004b) and Jansen, Spink and Ozmultu (2000) used Markovian analysis to investigate the transitions between unique, modified and next page queries. Markov chains are a stochastic process that considers a finite number of values and states (for example, in Ozmutlu, Ozmutlu and Spink (2004b) and Jansen, Spink and Ozmultu (2000) queries unique, modified and next page queries are states). Also, Kammenhuber, Luxenburger, Feldmann and Weikum (2006) model user behavior during a search session as a Markov model. The Markov model relates the hyperlinks between the documents with the clickstream and the properties of the documents. Each state in their Markov model include index of search query in session, index of result page and position of result click. Manavoglu, Pavlov and Giles (2003) used a mixture and maximum entropy- based approach to model user behavior models for Cite-Seer. They also investigated the use of first order Markov mixture models. They concluded that the Markov model performed better for predicting the behavior of the known users, whereas the maximum entropy model was better at modeling the global behavior model and unknown users.

Markov chains use the transition probability from one state to another. There is always a fixed probability that the processes switched from state i to state j. "We suppose that P $\{X_{n+1}=j \mid X_n=i, X_{n-1}=i_{n-1}, \ldots X_1=i_1, X_0=i_0\} = P_{ij}$ for all states $i_0, i_1, \ldots, i_{n-1}, i, j$ and all $n \geq 0$. Such a stochastic process is known as a Markov chain". The conditional distribution of any future state X_{n+1}" given the past states $X_0, X_1, \ldots X_{n-1}$ and the present state X_n, is independent of the past states and depends only on the present state" (Ross, 1993, pp. 137).

Poisson Sampling

Poisson sampling provides a basis for sampling from large-scale data logs, while preserving the characteristics of the main dataset (Ozmutlu, Spink, Ozmutlu, 2002). Poisson sampling algorithms, widely applied in stochastic research, select sample points from a certain dataset by skipping a random number of observations that is distributed according to a Poisson process versus systematic sampling algorithms skipping a constant number of observations.

The Poisson sampling process is a useful random sampling process as it includes the following properties: 1) Unbiased Sampling, 2) Proportional Sampling, 3) Comparability of Heterogeneous Poisson sampling Arrivals and 4) Flexibility on the Stochastic Arrival Process from which the Sample is Selected.

Poisson sampling can be applied in two different cases: continuous time sampling and discrete time sampling. For continuous time sampling, random timing of the next sample is generated according to an exponential distribution with parameter λ (interarrival time of the next sample $x \sim \text{Exp}(\lambda)$).The formulation for the random number generator for exponential distribution can be derived from the cumulative density function (cdf) of the exponential distribution, given in Equation 3:

$$F(x) = \int_{-\infty}^{x} f(y)dy = \begin{cases} 1-e^{-\lambda x}, & x \geq 0 \\ 0, & x<0 \end{cases} \quad (3)$$

If x is generated according to an exponential distribution, then the outcome of cdf, $F(x)$ for $x \geq 0$, has a Uniform (0,1) distribution. Since random variables $u \sim$ Uniform (0,1) are fairly easy to obtain, it is logical to use a formula where the interarrival time $x \sim \text{Exp}(\lambda)$ can be obtained by a variable $u \sim$ Uniform (0,1). By calculating the analytical inverse of the exponential cdf in Equation 1, the desired formula, which is stated in Equation 2, is developed. After each sample point, a new uniform number u has to be generated to calculate the next exponentially distributed interarrival time using Equation 4:

$$F^{-1}(u) = \begin{cases} -(1/\lambda)*\ln(1-u), & 0 \leq u \leq 1 \\ 0, & u<0 \text{ or } u>1 \end{cases} \quad (4)$$

The other case of the Poisson sampling, discrete time sampling is used where the stochastic process under observations has discrete arrivals. For discrete stochastic arrival processes, sampling is done by randomly generating a number $u \sim$ Uniform (0,1) and then find the corresponding n, the number of arrivals to skip before the next sample, using Poisson Process with parameter $\lambda > 0$, $\{N(t), t \geq 0\}$. The probability mass function of the Poisson process is given in Equation 5:

$$F(x) = \frac{\lambda^k \exp(-\lambda)}{k!}, \quad \lambda > 0, k = 0,1,\ldots, \tag{5}$$

However, the analytical inverse of the Equation 3 is not available. Therefore the following algorithm is used to generate the Poisson variate n (Mann, Schafer and Singpurwalla, 1974):

Step 1: Set $j = 0$ and $y_j = u_0$, where $u_j \sim$ Uniform $(0,1), j = 0,1,\ldots$,
Step 2: If $y_j \leq \exp(-\lambda)$, return $n=j$ and terminate.
Step 3: $j = j+1$, and $y_j = u_j y_j$-1
Goto Step 2

As in the continuous sampling case, another random n is generated using the algorithm stated above.

The query sessions arrive according to a discrete stochastic process. Although, there is no available data study on the type of stochastic process that query sessions follow, the sampling strategy is not affected due to the fourth property of Poisson sampling. The search transaction logs has time stamps for each query entry, however it is not sensitive enough to determine the stochastic arrival process. For example, the smallest time unit of the time stamps in the Excite 1999 dataset was seconds, and on average, there were 31.8 arrivals in each second. One can argue that if the sampling time units are set in seconds, the arrival process can be considered as continuous time. Consequently, continuous time sampling becomes applicable. However, this discussion is not addressed in this study. To be on the safe side, it is appropriate to apply discrete time Poisson sampling for the analysis of transaction logs.

ESTIMATION

Literature Review of Studies Estimating Search Engine User Behavior

There are many studies analyzing user behavior of search engines and many others that analyze the user behavior of OPACs (online public access catalogues), digital libraries and Web site search engines, that are not included in this study. However, there are few studies that estimate the user behavior based on the history of use. Analyzing user behavior is important, however unless the information retrieved from analysis of user behavior is utilized for estimation of the user behavior, it is redundant and ineffective.

There are relatively few studies on estimating user behavior. One of the main elements of content-based behavior is new topic identification or session identification. New topic identification is discovering when the user has switched from one topic to another during a single search session to group sequential log entries that are related to a common topic (He, Goker and Harper, 2002). In order to find useful patterns in user sessions, it is necessary to group the queries on the transaction logs into clusters. After the query clusters have been identified, the common usage patterns can be discovered by statistical tools (Huang, Peng, An and Schuurmans, 2004). Other implications of new topic identification in terms of personalized services, caching systems and site design, are well-documented by Huang, Peng, An and Schuurmans (2004).

There are several studies on new topic identification presented in more detail in the next section. The studies generally analyzed the queries semantically. Defining topic boundaries by relying on semantics of query terms are "dangerously circular" and conceal persistence of users' long-term information needs (Murray, Lin, Chowdhury, 2006). Another possible approach for automatic new topic identification is non-semantic methodologies, where the statistical characteristics of queries, such as query duration or search pattern are used to estimate an upcoming topic change.

Automatic New Topic Identification

New topic identification is the process of discovering when the user has switched from one topic to another during a single search session. If the search engine is aware that the user's new query is on the same topic as the previous query, the search engine could provide the results from the document cluster relevant to the previous query. Alternatively, if the user is on a new topic, the search engine could resort to searching other document clusters. Consequently, search engines can decrease the time and effort required to process the query and increase the quality of the results.

A user may perform searches on one or many topics during a single search session (Spink, Ozmutlu and Ozmutlu, 2002). It should also be noted that although there is a controversy about the definition of session in literature, we define session as a group or entire sequence of queries submitted by a single user (Jansen and Spink, 2004, Ozmutlu, Ozmutlu and Spink 2004b). We define topic as a subject area of interest in a session (Spink, Ozmutlu and Ozmutlu, 2002). Another group of researchers define a topic in a session as a session, such as He, Goker and Harper (2002).

Most query clustering and session identification methods are focused on the interpretation of keywords, which complicates the process of query clustering. An alternative approach is to use statistical characteristics of queries, such as the time intervals between subsequent queries or the reformulation of queries, to cluster queries into different groups. The initial indications of the relationship between statistical characteristics of queries and topic change were shown in Spink, Ozmutlu and Ozmutlu (2002) and He and Goker (2000). Ozmutlu (2006) showed that the statistical characteristics of the queries were effective on topic shifts and continuations using analysis of variance and formulated the relationship between topic shifts/continuations and the statistical characteristics of queries using a multiple linear regression equation.

He, Goker and Harper (2002) proposed a new topic identification algorithm (or session identification algorithm) that uses Dempster-Shafer Theory (Shafer, 1976). Their algorithm automatically identifies topic changes using statistical data from search logs. He, Goker and Harper's (2002) approach was replicated on Excite search engine data (Ozmutlu and Cavdur, 2005a) and Fast search engine data (Ozmutlu, Cavdur and Ozmutlu, 2006). The queries in the sample were marked as topic continuation and shift by a human expert, after which the queries were classified according to their statistical characteristics, ie. search pattern and time interval of the queries. Then, the sample dataset is divided into two parts; the first for training and the second for testing the new topic identification algorithms. The topic identification algorithm is tested with respect to the performance measures of precision, recall, and a fitness function.

Ozmutlu and Cavdur (2005) and Ozmutlu, Cavdur and Ozmutlu (2006) used Dempster-Shafer Theory that enables the combination of two separate probabilistic events related to a single property (such as the topic change). The finding of Ozmutlu and Cavdur (2005) and Ozmutlu, Cavdur and Ozmutlu (2006) was that the application of Dempster-Shafter theory and genetic algorithms were valuable, but there were some problems with application.

Ozmutlu, Cavdur, Spink and Ozmutlu (2004a) and Ozmutlu and Cavdur (2005b) also applied neural networks to automatically identify topic changes. The neural network is trained using the first half of the datasets and tested on the second half of the datasets. In these studies, Ozmutlu, Cavdur, Ozmutlu and Spink (2004a) and Ozmutlu and Cavdur (2005a) showed that neural networks also identified topic shifts successfully, estimating 98 percent of topic shifts and 87 percent of topic continuations correctly. However, the number of topic shifts was overestimated.

Ozmutlu, Ozmutlu and Buyuk (2007) applied conditional probabilities for automatic new topic identification. Ozmutlu, Ozmutlu and Buyuk (forthcoming) also used Monte-Carlo simulation based on conditional probabilities for automatic new topic identification. Another methodology used for automatic new topic identification is Markov chains (Ozmutlu, Ozmutlu and Spink, forthcoming). A still further methodology used for automatic new topic identification is SVM (Ozmutlu, Ozmutlu, Spink (2007), where the statistical characteristics of the search queries are used to maximize the distance between two clusters, where the queries are clustered as topic shift and continuation.

Topic Estimation

Another group of studies is on estimating the topic of a query. Topic identification and estimation is a much more complex problem than new topic identification or session identification. There are several studies in this area.

Pu, Chuang and Yang (2002) developed an automatic classification methodology to classify search queries into broad subject categories. They formed a subject taxonomy and fit each search query into one of the categories in the taxonomy. Ozmutlu, Spink and Ozmutlu (2006) classified search queries into 17 categories: news, government/politics, business, medical, arts and humanities, hobbies, entertainment, employment, education, shopping, computers, individual/family, sexual, science, travel, general information and inexplicit, then calculated the topic-to-topic transition probabilities from the topic-to-topic query frequencies, and used the topic-to-topic transition probabilities and Monte-Carlo simulation to estimate the topic of a consequent query given the topic of the current query.

Shen, Dumais and Horvitz (2005) used Marginal models and Markovian models to analyze and predict topic-to-topic transitions in the MSN transaction logs. Maximum likelihood techniques and Jelinek-Mercer smoothing are used to estimate the probability distributions of the user queries. The authors do not specify the probability distributions used for the topics. Shen, Dumais and Horvitz (2005) also employed individual models, groups models and population models to analyze the data, and found that groups models and Markov models provided favorable results in terms of prediction accuracy of topics (around 40 percent).

Detailed Explanation of Methodologies Used for User Behavior Estimation

There are many probabilistic, statistical learning and artificial intelligence techniques used for query clustering, session identification, new topic identification and topic estimation of search engine queries. These methodologies can be listed as below:

Probabilistic and Statistical Methods

Dempster-Shafer Theory

He, Goker and Harper (2002), Ozmutlu and Cavdur (2005), and Ozmutlu, Cavdur, Ozmutlu (2006) use Dempster-Shafer Theory for automatic new topic identification. Dempster-Shafer Theory enables the combination of two separate probabilistic events related to a single property (such as the topic change). The Dempster Shafer theory would be explained with the new topic identification application in this chapter. Application of Dempster-Shafer Theory requires two sets of information:

- The probabilities of each event (for the new topic identification problem, the events are shift and continuation for a given time interval or a search pattern of a query)

- The weights of separate probabilistic events and a threshold value used to identify a topic shift

Probabilities are easily obtained through the analysis of the data logs, and are used to obtain the parameters of w_{ti}, w_{sp} and t_{shift}, so as to maximize the fitness function F_{β}. P(Search Pattern) and P(Time Interval) show the distribution of search patterns and time intervals, respectively. P(shift|SP) and P(contin|SP) present the conditional probabilities of having a session shift and continuation, respectively, for each pattern category. P(shift|TI) and P(contin|TI) show the conditional probabilities of having a session shift or a session continuation, respectively, for each time interval category. The probabilities are combined by the Dempster-Shafer Theory as follows (He, Goker and Harper, 2002):

$$m_{TI\&SP} = \frac{m_{TI}(P_s)m_{SP}(P_s) + m_{TI}(P_s)m_{SP}(\Theta) + m_{TI}(\Theta)m_{SP}(Ps)}{1 - (m_{TI}(Ps)m_{SP}(P_c) + m_{TI}(P_c)m_{SP}(P_s))} \quad (6)$$

where, i is TI (time interval) or SP(search pattern), P_s denotes a topic shift, P_c denotes a topic continuation, and where:

$mi(P_s)$ =P(shift|i)* wi ;
$mi(P_c)$= P(contin|i)* wi ;
$m_{TI}(\Theta)= 1- m_{TI}(P_s)- m_{TI}(P_c)$;
$m_{sp}(\Theta)= 1- m_{SP}(P_s)- m_{SP}(P_c)$;
$m_{TIandSP}$ =combined score for shift or continuation

The next step is to compare $m_{TIandSP}$ to the threshold value t_{shift} to convert the score to a binary decision, whether there is a topic shift or continuation between queries.

Multiple Linear Regression and Analysis of Variance

Ozmutlu (2006) used multiple linear regressions to characterize the relationships between the statistical characteristics of queries and showed topic shifts and continuations are dependent on the statistical characteristics of the queries.

Multiple linear regression characterizes the relationship between independent and dependent factors of a system. In case there exists more than one independent factor, multiple linear regression is applied. The problem is to fit a model of the following form to the available data, which characterizes a hyper plane in a k-dimensional space (Montgomery, 1991):

$$Y = \beta_0 + \beta_1 x_1 + \beta_2 x_2 + \ldots\ldots + \beta_k x_k + \varepsilon \quad (7)$$

where there are k independent factors, β_i, i=1,..... k is the coefficient of the ith independent factor and β_0 is a constant value.

The coefficients of the regression equation are determined using the least squares method. The objective is to minimize the squared error that occurs between the fitted equation and the actual data. In this chapter, the detailed explanation of how the equations for the regression coefficients are derived using the least squares method are skipped; the interested reader can refer to Montgomery (1991). The coefficients of the regression equation are calculated using the following equations and matrices (Montgomery, 1991). Consider the matrices shown in Box 1, where **y** is a vector of the response (or values of dependent factors obtained as a result of experiments), **X** is a matrix of the values of the independent factors, x_{ij} is the value of the ith independent factor, i=1,...k, at the jth experiment or data point, j=1,...n, β is the vector of the regression coefficients and $\boldsymbol{\varepsilon}$ is the error vector. In this case, the least squares estimator for the regression coefficients is (Montgomery, 1991):

Box 1.

$$\mathbf{y}=\begin{bmatrix} y_1 \\ y_2 \\ \cdots \\ y_n \end{bmatrix}, \mathbf{X}=\begin{bmatrix} 1 & (x_{11}-\bar{x}_1) & (x_{21}-\bar{x}_2) & \cdots\cdots & (x_{k1}-\bar{x}_k) \\ 1 & (x_{12}-\bar{x}_1) & (x_{22}-\bar{x}_2) & \cdots\cdots & (x_{k2}-\bar{x}_k) \\ .. & \cdots\cdots & \cdots\cdots & \cdots\cdots & \cdots\cdots \\ .. & \cdots\cdots & \cdots\cdots & \cdots\cdots & \cdots\cdots \\ 1 & (x_{1n}-\bar{x}_1) & (x_{2n}-\bar{x}_2) & \cdots\cdots & (x_{kn}-\bar{x}_k) \end{bmatrix}, \boldsymbol{\beta}=\begin{bmatrix} \beta_0 \\ \beta_1 \\ \cdots \\ \beta_n \end{bmatrix}, \boldsymbol{\varepsilon}=\begin{bmatrix} \varepsilon_0 \\ \varepsilon_1 \\ \cdots \\ \varepsilon_n \end{bmatrix}$$

$$\beta = \mathbf{(X'X)^{-1}X'y} \quad (8)$$

where **X'** is the transpose of matrix **X**.

The analysis of variance indicates whether the developed regression equation effectively explains the dependent factor, as well as which independent factor has a statistically significant effect on the dependent factor. First, the effectiveness of the regression equation in explaining the dependent factor is considered. To test this situation, the following hypothesis test is used (Montgomery, 1991):

H_0: $\beta_1 = \beta_2 = \ldots\ldots = \beta_k = 0$ (9)
H_1: $\beta_i \neq 0$, for at least one *i*, *i*=1,....*k*, where *k* is the number of independent factors.

Analysis of variance (ANOVA) is conducted to accomplish this hypothesis test. If H_0 is rejected, this means that at least one of the regression coefficients is not equal to zero, and the independent factors have some power of estimation on the dependent factor. ANOVA is a procedure, where the total variation in the dependent factor is partitioned into meaningful components (Walpole, Myers and Myers, 1998). The ANOVA components are usually summarized by the ANOVA table, which are as in Table 1 (Montgomery, 1991). The computed F-value is compared to a critical F value, namely $F_{0.05,k-1,n-k-1}$, which is the significance level of hypothesis testing. If the computed F-value is greater than the critical $F_{0.05,k-1,n-k-1}$, then H_0 is rejected, otherwise H_0 cannot be rejected.

The second application area of ANOVA is to test whether a certain independent factor is effective on the dependent factor. In this study, the regression approach to ANOVA is discussed. The hypothesis test that tests the significance of any individual coefficient is as follows (Montgomery, 1991):

H_0: $= \beta_i = 0$ (10)
H_1: $= \beta_i \neq 0$, i=1,....k, where k is the number of independent factors.

The regression approach to ANOVA is testing the significance of a term in the model, where other terms are already in the model, hence testing the impact of adding the new term to the model.

Table 1. ANOVA table

Source of Variation	Sum of Squares	Degrees of Freedom	Mean Square	F-value
Regression	SSR	K	SSR/k	(SSR/k)/ (SSE/ n-k-1)
Error	SSE	n-k-1	SSE/ n-k-1	
Total	SST	n-1		

Suppose, in matrix notation, the regression model is $\mathbf{y} = \mathbf{X}\beta + \varepsilon$, and β is partitioned as:

$$\beta = \begin{bmatrix} \beta_1 \\ \beta_2 \end{bmatrix} \quad (11)$$

In this case, the full model can be re-written as

$$\mathbf{y} = \mathbf{X_1\beta_1} + \mathbf{X_2\beta_2} + ... + \varepsilon \quad (12)$$

where $\mathbf{X_i}$ represents the columns of matrix $\mathbf{X}$ associated with $\boldsymbol{\alpha}_i$, i=1 and 2.

For the model, which includes β_1 and β_2:

$$\text{SSR}(\beta) = \beta\, \mathbf{X'y} \quad (13)$$

where β is as in Eq. (8), **X** is a matrix of the values of the independent factors and **y** is a vector of the response. SSR (β) is the regression sum of squares relevant to β. Then a reduced model is introduced (Montgomery, 1991). The reduced model is:

$$\mathbf{y} = \mathbf{X_2\beta_2} + ... + \varepsilon \quad (14)$$

The sum of squares for the reduced model is:

$$\text{SSR}(\boldsymbol{\beta}_2) = \boldsymbol{\beta}_2\, \mathbf{X_2'y} \quad (15)$$

The full model is as in Eq. (12), and the SSR for the full model is as in Eq. (13). The difference between the reduced and full sum of squares (sum of squares contributed by the terms in $\boldsymbol{\beta}_1$ given that the terms in $\boldsymbol{\beta}_2$ are already in the model) is:

$$\text{SSR}(\boldsymbol{\beta}_1|\boldsymbol{\beta}_2) = \text{SSR}(\boldsymbol{\beta}) - \text{SSR}(\boldsymbol{\beta}_2) \quad (16)$$

After calculating the sum of squares for each independent factor, the ANOVA components are usually summarized by the ANOVA table, which is given in Table 2 (Walpole, Myers and Myers, 1998). If the computed F-value is greater than the critical $F_{0.05,\ 1,\ n-k-1}$, then H_0 is rejected, otherwise H_0 cannot be rejected.

Conditional Probability

Ozmutlu and Buyuk (2007) use conditional probabilities to estimate topic shifts and continuations given the statistical characteristics of the transaction log queries.

"The probability of an event B occurring when it is known that some event A has occurred is called a conditional probability and is denoted by P(B|A)" (Walpole, Myers and Myers, 1998, pp. 35). The application of conditional probabilities for automatic new topics identification is as follows: Each query in the transaction logs is categorized with respect to its time interval and search pattern combination. Since all the queries have previously been tagged by the human expert as shifts and continuations, it is possible to determine the breakdown of shifts and continuations with respect to the query categories. Using the breakdown of the shifts and continuations with respect to query

Table 2. ANOVA table for the regression approach to ANOVA

Source of Variation	Sum of Squares	Degrees of Freedom	Mean Square	F-value
X_1	SSR (β_1)	1	SSR(β_1) /1	(SSR(β_1)/1)/ (SSE/ n-k-1)
....	....	....	....	....
X_k	SSR (β_k)	1	SSR (β_k) /1	(SSR(β_k)/1)/ (SSE/ n-k-1)
Error	SSE	n-k-1	SSE/ n-k-1	
Total	SST	n-1		

categories, the conditional probability of a topic shift and continuation given the query category is computed by dividing the number of shifts in a certain category to the total number of queries in that category.

Monte-Carlo Simulation

Monte-Carlo simulation is a static simulation scheme that employs random numbers, and is used for solving stochastic or deterministic problems, where time plays no substantial role (Law and Kelton, 1991). Monte-Carlo simulation is used to solve many problems that are analytically complex. In the Monte-Carlo technique, artificial data is generated via the use of a random number generator and the cumulative distribution of interest (Pegden, et al. 1995). A reasonable and acceptable random number generator is important, since the random numbers generated are not actually random, but pseudorandom, meaning that random number sequence is actually reproducible (Pegden, et al., 1995). For Monte-Carlo simulation, random numbers are usually generated from Uniform (0,1) distribution.

Support Vector Machines

Ozmutlu, Ozmutlu and Spink (forthcoming in ASIST 2007) used SVM to classify queries into topic shift and continuation clusters. Support vector machines, introduced by Vladimir Vapnik (1995), is a methodology based on statistical learning theory, and is known to be the most accurate classifier methods for text (Chakrabarti, 2003). Support vector machines are based on generating functions from a set of labeled training data. The function can be a classification function; where the response is in binary form. The function can also be a general regression function.

For classification purposes, SVMs function by finding a hyper surface in the space of possible inputs, which attempts to separate the different classes of data from each other. The training data is initially mapped nonlinearly into a higher-dimensional feature space, and then a separating hyper surface is constructed such that the negative and positive examples of the training data are separated with maximum margin (Osuna, Freund and Girosi, 1996). This results in a nonlinear decision boundary in input space. By using kernel functions, the separating hyper surface can be computed without carrying out the map into the feature space (Hearst, Schölkopf, Dumais, Osuna and Platt, J., 1998). Even though, the problem is complex, such as text classification and pattern recognition, the computations are rather basic (Hearst, Schölkopf, Dumais, Osuna and Platt, J., 1998). For text classification problems, linear SVMs are generally considered adequate (Chakrabarti, 2003). To get more information on the theoretical background, different types and different formulations of SVM, the interested reader can refer to Vapnik (1995), Osuna, Freund and Girosi (1996), Burges (1998), Chakrabarti (2003) and Chang and Lin (2001).

Markov Models

The information on Markov chains was provided in the analysis section.

Artificial Intelligence Methods

Artificial Neural Networks

A neural network is an algorithm, which imitates the human brain, in terms of learning a specific concept and functioning with respect to what it has learnt. Haykin (1994) defines a neural network as "a massively parallel distributed processor that has a natural propensity for storing experiential knowledge and making it available for use." The learning or training process of an artificial neural network is established through a learning algorithm. During the learning/training process, the input and the output of the problem to be solved are provided to the neural network. Knowing the input and the output, the neural network establishes a relationship between them. This relationship is represented with synaptic weights. Then, only the inputs are provided to the neural network and the network provides the answers or output using the pre-determined relationship.

Each neural network has neurons or computing cells, which process the information given to the neural network. The way that the neurons are organized form the structure of the neural network, such as single-layer feedforward networks, multilayer-feedforward networks, recurrent networks and lattice structures (Haykin, 1994).

Neural networks are usually used to solve complex problems of parallel processing nature that involve processing elements interconnected in network architecture. They can overcome various complications that make it difficult to solve some problems, such as non-linear relationships. Since automatic new topic identification is related to user behavior, it is a complex problem like other behavioral problems, and therefore is suitable to apply neural networks. Ozmutlu and Cavdur (2005), Ozmutlu, Cavdur, Spink and Ozmutlu (2004a) applied neural networks for automatic new topic identification.

DISCUSSION: CHALLENGES AND FUTURE DIRECTIONS

Analysis of search engine user behavior has been performed on many datasets successfully. However, estimating search engine user behavior is a challenge. Collecting objective and intervention-free information on search engine users and their information-seeking behavior, with a wide variety of test subjects requires more studies to be performed.

Search engine user studies are either intrusive, where the researcher instructs the users, or totally intervention-free where the transaction logs are analyzed. Intrusive studies might restrict the users to perform some searching tasks, and even if they do not, the user might feel under pressure and might not act naturally. Moreover, such studies are performed over a small number of test subjects, usually college students and graduate students or academicians. Besides, the number of test subjects, the range of characteristics of the test subjects is important. It is hard to say that a group of students from the same university is a representative sample set.

On the other hand, transaction logs only offer a limited amount of information on the users and it is impossible to relate them to the characteristics of the users. There are problems in session definition and identification, and therefore it is challenging to figure out the boundaries of queries submitted by a single user especially if the users are submitting queries from public access computers residing in libraries.

There are many research opportunities that lie ahead relevant to transaction log analysis and user behavior estimation, as detailed in Markey (2007). Other research areas can be listed as:

- Few methodologies are used in analysis of search engine transaction logs, i.e. exploratory data analysis, correlation and Markov models. There are many other techniques that can be used to analyze search engine transaction logs. Multivariate techniques can be especially useful in clustering user queries with respect to several characteristics.
- It should be further investigated whether search engine user behavior and query patterns conform to any statistical distributions or stochastic models in terms of statistical characteristics of queries.
- The time-based behavior of queries should be analyzed. There is only one study (Ozmutlu, et al., 2004b) investigating the characteristics of queries with respect to hours of the day, however no studies exist that analyze the queries with respect to seasons, years, holiday-non-holiday time, and other time patterns.
- The estimation of content-based behavior is very challenging, and is directly related to natural language processing. More studies on estimation of content-based behavior,

employing artificial intelligence and statistical learning methods, can be performed.

- Although, there are a myriad of studies on information retrieval and search engine algorithms, there are no studies that take into account the user behavior when developing these algorithms. The researchers that analyze search engine user behavior state that the results of such analysis would be helpful in developing retrieval algorithms. There is a great research opportunity in building the bridge between user behavior studies and information retrieval algorithms.
- User behavior estimation algorithms and user-centric information retrieval algorithms need not only be successful, but also computationally efficient, and should be performed in real-time.

CONCLUSION

It is critical to analyze and estimate the behavior of search engine users to develop more successful search engines and personalized search engines. Understanding the behavior of search engine users is a challenge, and developing user-centric information retrieval algorithms based on the user characteristics is a major research opportunity. This chapter provides a literature review on transaction log analysis and search engine user behavior estimation, with an emphasis on statistical, probabilistic and artificial intelligence methodologies used. Challenges and research opportunities regarding transaction log analysis and search engine user behavior estimation are also outlined.

ACKNOWLEDGMENT

Part of the research mentioned in this chapter has been funded by TUBITAK, Turkey and is a National Young Researchers Career Development Project 2005: Fund Number: 105M320: "Application of Web Mining and Industrial Engineering Techniques in the Design of New Generation Intelligent Information Retrieval Systems".

REFERENCES

Agichtein, E., Brill, E., Dumais, S., and Ragno, R. (2006). Learning user interaction models for predicting web search result preferences. *Proceedings of the Twenty-Ninth Annual International ACM SIGIR Conference on Research and Development in Information Retrieval,* Seattle, WA, 3-10.

Beitzel, S.M., Jensen, E.C., Chowdhury, A., Grossman, D., and Frieder, O. (2004). Efficiency and Scaling: Hourly Analysis of a Very Large Topically Categorized Web Query Log. *Proceedings of the 27th Annual International Conference on Research and Development in Information Retrieval*, Sheffield, UK, 321-328.

Bilinkis, I., and Mikelsons A. (1992). *Randomized signal processing.* New York, NY: Prentice Hall.

Brown, M., Foote, J., Jones, G., Sparck Jones, K., and Young, S. (1996). Open-vocabulary speech indexing for voice and video mail retrieval. *Proceedings of the fourth ACM international multimedia conference, ACM multimedia '96,* 307–316.

Burges, C. J. C. (1998). A tutorial on support vector machines for pattern recognition. *Data Mining and Knowledge Discovery. 2,* 121–167.

Catledge, L., and Pitkow, J. (1995). Characterizing Browsing Strategies in the World Wide Web, *Proceedings of the 3rd International World Wide Web Conference*, Darmstadt, Germany.

Chakrabarti, S. (2003). *Mining the Web.* Morgan Kaufmann Publishers, San Francisco, CA.

Chang, C.-C., and Lin, C.-J. (2001). *LIBSVM: A library for support vector machines.* Available from http://www.csie.ntu.edu.tw/~cjlin/libsvm.

Cooley, R., Mobasher, B., and Srivastava, J. (1999). Data preparation for mining world wide web browsing patterns. *Knowledge and Information Systems. 1*, 5–32.

Goodrum, A. and Kim, C. (1998). *Visualizing the history of chemistry: queries to the CHF pictorial collection.* Report to the Chemical Heritage Foundation Pictorial Collection.

Goodrum, A., and Spink, A. (2001). Image searching on the Excite Web search engine. *Information Processing and Management. 37(2)*, 295-312.

Gremett, P. (2006). Utilizing a User's Context to Improve Search Results. *Journal of the American Society for Information Science and Technology, 57(6)*, 808–812.

Haykin, S. (1994). *Neural networks.* Englewood Cliffs, NJ: Macmillan College Publishing Company.

He, D., and Goker, A. (2000). Detecting session boundaries from Web user logs. *Proceedings of the BCS-IRSG 22nd Annual Colloquium on Information Retrieval Research, Cambridge, UK*, 57-66.

He. D., Goker, A. and Harper, D.J. (2002). Combining evidence for automatic Web session identification. *Information Processing and Management*, 38, 727-742

He, P.W., and Jacobson, T.E. (1996). What are they doing with the Internet? A Study of User Information Seeking Behaviors. *Internet Reference Services Quarterly, 1*, 31-51

Hearst, M.A, Schölkopf, B., Dumais, S., Osuna, E. and Platt, J. (1998) Trends and Controversies - Support vector machines. *IEEE Intelligent Systems, 13(4)*, 18-28.

Hill, J.R., and Hannafin, M.J. (1997). Cognitive Strategies and Learning from the World Wide Web. *Educational Technology Research and Development, 45*, 37-64

Huang, X., Peng, F., An, A., and Schuurmans, D. (2004). Dynamic web log session identification with statistical language models. *Journal of the American Society for Information Science and Technology, 55(14)*, 1290 - 1303

Jansen, B. J., Goodrum, A., and Spink, A. (2000). Searching for multimedia: analysis of audio, video and image Web queries. *World Wide Web, 3*, 249–254.

Jansen, B.J., Spink, A., Bateman, J., and Saracevic, T. (1998). Real life information retrieval: A study of user queries on the Web. *SIGIR Forum, 33(1)*, 5–17.

Jansen, B. J., Spink, A. and Ozmultu, C. (2000). Use of query reformulation and relevance feedback by Web users. *Internet Research: Electronic Networking Applications and Policy, 10(4)*, 317 - 328.

Jansen, B.J., Spink, A., and Pedersen, J. (2003). An Analysis of Multimedia Searching on Alta Vista. *Proceedings of the 5th ACM SIG Multimedia International Workshop on Multimedia Information Retrieval.* Berkeley, CA, 186 – 192.

Jansen, B. J., Spink, A, and Pedersen, J. (2005). The Effect of Specialized Multimedia Collections on Web Searching. *Journal of Web Engineering. 3(3/4)*, 182-199.

Jansen, B. J., Spink, A., and Saracevic, T. (2000). Real life, real users, and real needs: A study and analysis of user queries on the web. *Information Processing and Management. 36(2)*, 207-227.

Kammenhuber, N., Luxenburger, J., Feldmann, A., and Weikum, G. (2006). Web Search Clickstreams. *IMC'06,* October 25-27, 2006, Rio de Janeiro, Brazil.

Law, A.M., and Kelton, W.D. (1991). *Simulation Modeling and Analysis.* New York: McGraw-Hill

Lawrence, S. and Giles, C.L. (1999). Accessibility of information on the web. *Nature*, 400, 107–109.

Liaw S-S and Huang, H-M. (2006). Information retrieval from the World Wide Web: a user-focused approach based on individual experience with search engines. *Computers in Human Behavior, 22(3)*, 501-517.

Manavoglu, E., Pavlov, D. and Giles, C.L., (2003). Probabilistic user behavior models. *Proceedings of the ICDM 2003: Third IEEE International Conference on Data Mining 2003*, 203- 210.

Mann, N.R., Schafer, R.E., and Singpurwalla N.D. (1974). *Methods for statistical analysis of reliability and life data.* New York: John Wiley and Sons.

Markey, K. (2007a). Twenty-Five Years of End-User Searching, Part 1: Research Findings. *Journal of the American Society for Information Science and Technology. 58(8)*, 1071–1081.

Markey, K. (2007b). Twenty-Five Years of End-User Searching, Part 2: Future Research Directions, *Journal of the American Society for Information Science and Technology. 58(8)*, 1123–1130.

Montgomery, D.C. (1991). *Design and Analysis of Experiments.* New York: John Wiley and Sons

Murray, G. C., Lin, J., and Chowdhury, A. (2006). Identification of user sessions with hierarchical agglomerative clustering. *Proceedings of ASIST 2006: Annual Meeting of the American Society for Information Sciences and Technology.*

Nahl, D. (1998). Ethnography of Novices First use of Web search engines: Affective Control in Cognitive Processes. *Internet Reference Services Quarterly,* 51-72

Osuna, E. E., Freund, R., and Girosi, F. (1996). *Support vector machines: Training and applications.* Massachusetts Institute of Technology, Artificial Intelligence Laboratory Technical Report No. 1602, Center for Biological and Computational Learning, Technical Report No. 144.

Ozmutlu, S. (2006). Automatic new topic identification using multiple linear regression. *Information Processing and Management, 42(4)*, 934-950.

Ozmutlu, H. C., and Cavdur, F. (2005a). Application of automatic topic identification on Excite web search engine data logs. *Information Processing and Management*, 41, 1243-1262.

Ozmutlu, S., and Cavdur, F. (2005b). Neural network applications for automatic new topic identification. *Online Information Review, 29*, 35-53

Ozmutlu, H.C., Cavdur, F., and Ozmutlu, S. (2006). Automatic new topic identification in search engine datalogs. *Internet Research, 16*, 323-338

Ozmutlu, H.C., Cavdur, F., Ozmutlu, S., and Spink, A., (2004a). Neural network applications for automatic new topic identification on Excite Web search engine datalogs. *ASIST'04: Proceedings of the Annual Meeting of the American Society for Information Science and Technology,* (pp. 310-316). Providence, RI.

Ozmutlu, S., Ozmutlu, H.C. and Spink, A. (2007). Using conditional probabilities for automatic new topic identification. *Online Information Review*, 31(4), 491-515.

Ozmutlu, S., Ozmutlu, H. C., and Spink, A., (2003). Are people asking questions of general web search engines. *Online Information Review*, 27, 396-406.

Ozmutlu, S., Ozmutlu, H. C., and Spink, A. (2002). Multimedia Web Searching/ *Proceedings of ASIST 2002: 65th American Society of Information*

Science and Technology Annual Meeting, Long Beach October 2003, 403-408.

Ozmutlu, S., Ozmutlu, H. C., and Spink, A. (2003). Multitasking Web Searching and Implications for Design, *Proceedings of ASIST 2003: 66th American Society of Information Science and Technology Annual Meeting*, Long Beach October 2003.

Ozmutlu, S., Ozmutlu, H. C., and Spink, (2004b). A day in the life of Web searching: an exploratory study. *Information Processing and Management. 40*, 319-345.

Ozmutlu, S., Ozmutlu, H.C. and Spink, A. (forthcoming). *Using Markovian Analysis for Automatic New topic identification.*

Ozmutlu, S., Ozmutlu, H.C. and Spink, A. (2007). Using Support vector machines for Automatic New topic identification, *Proceedings of ASIST 2007: American Society of Information Science and Technology Annual Meeting*, 403-408.

Ozmutlu, S., Ozmutlu, H.C. and Spink, A.(2006). Topic Estimation of Web Search Transaction Log Queries Using Monte-Carlo simulation. *Proceedings of AUSWEB 2006: Australasian World Wide Web Conference.*

Ozmutlu, S., Spink, A., and Ozmutlu, H. C. (2003). Trends in multimedia web searching: 1997-2001, *Information Processing and Management*, 39, 611-621.

Ozmutlu, S., Spink A., and Ozmutlu, C. (2002). Trends in multimedia Web searching: Excite Queries, *IEEE ITCC 2002: Proceedings of the International Conference on Information Technology: Coding and Computing.* Las Vegas, NV, 40-45.

Ozmutlu, S., Spink, A. And Ozmutlu, H.C. (2002). Analysis of large data logs: an application of Poisson sampling on excite web queries. *Information Processing and Management*, 38, 473-490.

Pegden, C.D., Shannon, R.E., and Sadowski, R.P. (1995). *Introduction to Simulation using Siman*, McGraw-Hill, New York

Pu, H.T., Chuang, S-L., and Yang, C. (2002). Subject categorization of query terms for exploring web users' search interests. *Journal of the American Society for Information Science and Technology. 53*, 617–630.

Radlinski, F., and Dumais, S. (2006). Improving personalized Web search using result diversification. *Proceedings of the Twenty-Ninth Annual International ACM SIGIR Conference on Research and Development in Information Retrieval*, Seattle, WA, 691-692.

Ross, S.M. (1993). *Introduction to Probability Models*, 5th Edition, Academic Press, London 1993.

Shen, X, Dumais, S. and Horvitz, E. (2005). Analysis of topic dynamics in web search, *Proceedings of the 14th international conference on World Wide Web*, 1102 - 1103.

Silverstein, C., Henzinger, M., Marais, H., and Moricz, M. (1999). Analysis of a very large Web search engine query log. *ACM SIGIR Forum. 33*, 6-12.

Smith, T., Ruocco, A., and Jansen, B. J. (1998). Digital video in education. *Proceedings of the thirteenth SIGCSE technical symposium on computer science education.* (pp. 122–126).

Spink, A., Bateman, J., and Jansen, B. J. (1999). Searching the Web: Survey of EXCITE users. *Internet Research: Electronic Networking Applications and Policy. 9(2)*, 117-128.

Spink, A., and Guner, O. (2001). E-commerce Web queries: Excite and Ask Jeeves study. *First Monday. 6(7).*

Spink, A., and Jansen, B. J. (2004). *Web Search: Public Searching of the Web.* Kluwer Academic Publishing.

Spink, A., Park, M. Jansen, B.J. and Pedersen, J. (2002). Multitasking on AltaVista. *Proceedings of the IEEE ITCC 2004: International Conference on Coding and Computing*, Las Vegas, NV, 309.

Spink, A., Jansen, B. J., Wolfram, D., and Saracevic, T. (2002). From e-sex to e-commerce: Web search changes. *IEEE Computer, 35*, 133-135.

Spink, A., Koricich, A., Jansen, B. J., and Cole, C. (2004). Sexual searching on Web search engines. *Cyberpsychology and Behavior, 7(1)*, 65-72.

Spink, A., and Ozmutlu, H. C. (2001). What do people ask on the Web and how do they ask it: Ask Jeeves Study. *Proceedings of ASIST 2001: Annual Meeting of the American Society for Information Science and Technology*, Washington, DC.

Spink, A., and Ozmultu, H.C. (2002). Characteristics of question format Web queries: an exploratory study. *Information Processing and Management. 38(4)*, 453-471.

Spink, A., Ozmutlu, H. C., and Lorence, D. P. (2004). Web searching for sexual information: An exploratory study. *Information Processing and Management. 40(1)*, 113-124.

Spink, A., Ozmutlu, H. C., and Ozmutlu, S. (2002). Multitasking information seeking and searching processes. *Journal of the American Society for Information Science and Technology. 53(8)*, 639-652.

Spink, A., Park, M., and Jansen, B. J. (2006). Multitasking during Web search sessions. *Information Processing and Management. 42(1)*, 264-275.

Spink, A., Wolfram, D., Jansen, B. J., and Saracevic, T. (2001). Searching the Web: The public and their queries. *Journal of the American Society for Information Science and Technology. 53*, 226–234.

Tillotson, J., Cherry, J., and Clinton, M. (1995). Internet use through the University of Toronto Library: Demographics, Destinations and Users' Reactions. *Information Technology and Libraries. 14*, 190-198

Vapnik, V. (1995), *The nature of statistical learning theory.* New York: Springer-Verlag.

Walpole, R. E., Myers, R. H., and Myers, S. L. (1998). *Probability and Statistics for Engineers and Scientists.* Upper Saddle River, NJ: Prentice Hall.

Wolff, R.W. (1982). Poisson arrivals see time averages. *Operations Research, 30 (2)*, 223-231.

Wolfram, D., Spink, A., Jansen, B. J., and Saracevic. T. (2001). Vox Populi: The Public Searching of the Web. *Journal of the American Society for Information Science and Technology. 52(12)*, 1073 – 1074

KEY TERMS

Analysis of Variance: Analysis of variance is a procedure, where the total variation in the dependent factor is partitioned into meaningful components (Walpole, Myers and Myers, 1998).

Markov Models: Markov models or chains are a stochastic process that considers a finite number of values and states.

Monte-Carlo Simulation: Monte-Carlo simulation is a static simulation scheme that employs random numbers, and is used for solving stochastic or deterministic problems, where time plays no substantial role (Law and Kelton, 1991).

Neural Networks: A neural network is "a massively parallel distributed processor that has a natural propensity for storing experiential knowledge and making it available for use." (Haykin, 1994).

New Topic Identification: New topic identification is discovering when the user has switched from one topic to another during a single search session to group sequential log entries that are related to a common topic (He, Goker and Harper, 2002), session identification.

Poisson Sampling: The Poisson sampling process is a useful random sampling process as it includes the properties of (1) Unbiased Sampling (2) Proportional Sampling (3) Comparability of Heterogeneous Poisson sampling Arrivals, and (4) Flexibility on the Stochastic Arrival Process From Which the Sample is Selected.

Regression: Regression is an approach that generates a model characterizing the relationship between independent and dependent factors of a system from sample data representing a certain observable fact.

Session Identification: Session identification is discovering the group of sequential log entries that are related to a common user or topic; new topic identification.

Support Vector Machines: Support vector machines is a methodology of statistical learning theory, which is based on generating functions from a set of labeled training data.

Chapter XII
An Integrated Approach to Interaction Design and Log Analysis

Gheorghe Muresan
Microsoft Corporation, USA

ABSTRACT

In this chapter, we describe and discuss a methodological framework that integrates analysis of interaction logs with the conceptual design of the user interaction. It is based on (i) formalizing the functionality that is supported by an interactive system and the valid interactions that can take place; (ii) deriving schemas for capturing the interactions in activity logs; (iii) deriving log parsers that reveal the system states and the state transitions that took place during the interaction; and (iv) analyzing the user activities and the system's state transitions in order to describe the user interaction or to test some research hypotheses. This approach is particularly useful for studying user behavior when using highly interactive systems. We present the details of the methodology, and exemplify its use in a mediated retrieval experiment, in which the focus of the study is on studying the information-seeking process and on finding interaction patterns.

LOGGING THE USER INTERACTION: AN INTRODUCTION

A good understanding of people – what they are like, why they use a certain piece of software, and how they might interact with it – is essential for successful design of interactive systems, which help people achieve their goals. While each user is unique, and may have a particular background, context, interest and motivation to use a system, it is necessary to learn what is generally true about the users of a system and what behavioral patterns are common. Specifically, the designer should learn (1) the users' goals in using a system; (2) the specific tasks undertaken in order to achieve some goals; (3) the language or terminology used by users to describe what they are doing; and (4) the users' experience and skills at using a certain kind of system (Tidwell, 2006). Some common methods and techniques used before and during system design in order to understand the users' needs and to establish system requirements, as well as during the implementation and testing in order to evaluate the usability and effectiveness of a system, are direct observation, interviews, surveys, personas, focus groups.

While these methods are excellent tools for evaluating the quality of the interaction between human and system, the quality of the system in supporting the users to achieve their goals and the user satisfaction, they have a number of drawbacks. First, people are often incapable of accurately assessing their own behaviors, especially when removed from the context of their activities (Pinker, 1999) and therefore interviews and surveys may not provide true answers. Second, direct observation may be obtrusive – the users may be distracted, or they may not behave naturally. Third, they are expensive to run, and therefore provide information from a rather limited sample of users, so the results are often informative, but may lack statistical significance, may miss unusual cases, and may not capture behavioral patterns or trends.

Logging the user interaction with the system provides a complementary tool for analyzing the interaction and evaluating a system. It provides the means to acquiring large quantities of data about patterns of interface usage, speed of user performance, rate of errors, or frequency of requests for online assistance (Shneiderman & Plaisant, 2005). An important ethical issue, which indirectly affects user behavior and therefore the validity of the results, is whether users are told and know that their activity is logged. However, when logging is done in order to evaluate a system rather than user preferences or private activities, and when no personal information is captured, this problem is minimal.

An interesting set of constraints on what data can practically be logged, and on designing a logging system, is dictated by the software architecture of the system being investigated. The simpler situation is that of a standalone system, when the entire user activity runs on the same machine, and where all the data resides. In such situations, if the logging module is designed and built as part of the system, then all user actions, all user events and all data being generated or manipulated can potentially be logged. Logging the interaction with third-party software is more challenging: while operating system-level actions such as keystroke or mouse events, or opening/closing a file, or starting/stopping a certain application can be captured and logged, semantic events specific to a certain application are usually impossible to capture. For example, while it is possible to capture the text typed by a user, it is not easy or even possible to determine if the text was typed as a query for a search engine, or for filling in a form. This problem can be addressed by video-recording the interaction or by using screen-capturing software (e.g., Morae: http://www.techsmith.com/morae.asp; TaskTracer: http://eecs.oregonstate.edu/TaskTracer; uLog: http://www.noldus.com, so that the researchers can subsequently examine the interaction, interpret what is happening, insert annotations or mark significant events. While these tools can be helpful in analyzing the captured data, they rely on the manual-intellectual annotation done by the researcher, and are therefore very labor intensive and error-prone. Moreover, the format used for the logs is usually proprietary, which forces the researchers to buy proprietary analysis software that is not customizable. So, in order to fully benefit from the power of user activity logging, it is preferable that the designer of the logging module has access to the source code of the system being evaluated.

A more complex situation arises in the case of client-server architectures, common for using Web services. The client tier, usually a Graphical User Interface (GUI) application such as a Web browser or an email tool, runs on the user's machine and supports the interaction between the user and the system. Therefore, a logging module running on the client could capture all the user actions and system events (keystrokes, mouse moves, etc). This could even be synchronized with an eye tracking device to disambiguate some of the user's actions. On the other hand, the server tier runs on a server and provides services such as Web search or access to an email repository. Therefore, a logging module running on the server could capture such service requests, and possibly the results of these requests.

The data captured by server-side and client-side logging are complementary (with some overlap) and are typically used to answer different research questions. Moreover, data from the two types of logs is owned by different entities: server logs are owned by the operator of the server services, e.g. search engines, while the client logs may belong to the institution or research group that installed the client software and logging module on a number of workstations. Ideally, the two entities should collaborate and share data, so that answers to research questions can be corroborated. What is easier to corroborate is results obtained based on data from client-side logging, which support quantitative analysis of a user interface, with complementary results obtained from the qualitative methods and techniques discussed at the beginning of this section.

When talking about logging in a client-server architecture, one needs to clarify whether logging is done at the client side, or at the server side, or both. In the **Information Retrieval** (IR) context that interests us, search engine operators do server-side logging in order to capture, for example, trends in topical user interest or in the sophistication of the query formulation, e.g. the use of query Boolean operators. The users' selection of search results can also be used as feedback for adjusting the estimated quality of search results and thus the order of the search hits, or the algorithm for generating Webpage summaries. While capturing a large amount of data about service requests coming from a high number of clients, server-side logging misses the details of the user-system interaction. On the other hand, a client-side logging module is able to capture the intricacies of the interaction, but only for the user running the user interface. Such data can be used for evaluating the usability and effectiveness of a user interface, typically with the purpose of improving it.

Log Analysis in IR and the Motivation for Our Work

While much of the research work in Information Retrieval has focused on the systemic approach of developing and evaluating models and algorithms for identifying documents relevant to a well-defined information need, there is increasing consensus that such work should be placed in an Information Seeking framework in which a searcher's context, task, personal characteristics and preferences should be taken into account (Ingwersen & Jarvelin, 2005).

Since Robertson and Hancock-Beaulieu (1992) described the cognitive, relevance and interactive "revolutions" expected to take place in IR evaluation, the focus in interactive IR experimentation has shifted to exploring the dynamic information need that evolves during the search process, the situational context that influences the relevance judgments and the strategies and tactics adopted by information seekers in satisfying their information need. This paradigm shift to a cognitive approach to exploring search interactions and to studying Human Information Behavior has generated a large number of theories that attempt to model the search interaction and to predict the user's behavior in different contexts and at different stages of the interaction (Fisher, Erdelez, & McKechnie, 2005).

Of particular interest to this author are models of the search interaction process and empirical work to validate such models by observing consistent patterns of user behavior (Ellis, 1989; Kuhlthau, 1991; Belkin et al., 1995; Saracevic, 1996; Xie, 2000; Vakkari, 1999, 2001; Olah, 2005). The interest is not simply in validating theoretical models, but also in (1) developing methodologies to explore behavioral models; and (2) designing systems that implement appropriate interaction design patterns (Cooper, Reinmann, & Cronin, 2007), that better respond to user needs, that can adapt to support various search strategies, and that offer different functionality in different stages of the information seeking process.

Therefore, we are interested in methodologies for running interactive IR experiments, and especially in client-side logging of the interactions and analyzing the log data in such a way that the meaningful details of the interaction are captured and used for quantitative analysis. Let us clarify that we are not dismissing the techniques used for capturing qualitative data about the user interaction, such as direct observation and note-taking, questionnaires and interviews; such data is particularly useful for understanding the users' goals and motivation and for disambiguating user actions. However, we believe that the quantitative analysis of interaction logs is more suitable for observing patterns of behavior, for building a model of the interaction and possibly for predicting user behavior in certain contexts, or simply for testing the usability of a user interface. For example, we can capture the users' predilection for a certain kind of retrieval strategy (e.g. query-based searching vs. browsing), the users' use of advanced query operators or advanced terminology, or the common mistakes made by users, and correlate these with the users' search experience, familiarity with a domain, training, motivation, etc. in order to predict factors that could improve retrieval effectiveness and user satisfaction.

It is often recommended that the retrieval session be evaluated from multiple viewpoints, so that quantitative and qualitative measures are corroborated, and so that objective measures of performance are compared to users' subjective perception of success and satisfaction (Belkin & Muresan, 2004; Sauro, 2004). However, there is no consensus on methodologies and measures for estimating retrieval effectiveness or success, especially for interactive retrieval on the Web. Therefore, there is no consensus on what data an interaction log should capture.

IR experiments are often run in order to answer some research hypotheses or questions, so capturing just the data predicted to answer these questions sounds reasonable. However, limiting the logging to such data may be too restrictive in the long run: new, more detailed questions may arise from the initial analysis, and richer data may be needed to answer them. On the other hand, one may be tempted to capture "all" that happens, in order to be able to conduct any post-hoc analysis. However, this approach may produce too much useless data and may be counter-productive. For example, if the state of the system is captured in tenth of a second increments, most of the data would probably be useless. On the one hand, capturing only changes in the system state, when they occur, would produce data that is relevant and easier to analyze. Also, capturing all mouse moves and clicks may be useless without context: while knowing that the user clicked on the "Search" button to submit a query is essential, knowing that the user clicked on the screen at position *(x, y)* is hard or impossible to interpret.

What we propose is that what should be logged is all semantic events and actions, i.e. events and actions that make sense and are interpretable for a certain system or user interface. For example, mouse moves or clicks are only semantic events if they represent interface actions such as button clicks, selection from a list or menu, copying or pasting, or scrolling of a list of search results. The essential question "*Which are the semantic events for a certain user interface ?*" is addressed by our **integrated approach to interaction design and logging**. During the conceptual design of the interaction and of the user interface, the design team builds the interaction model of the system, i.e. the functionality supported by the user interface and the valid sequences of actions and events that implement the model.

In particular, in the common case that the **Model View Controller (MVC)** design pattern (Gamma et al., 2005) is used for reifying the conceptual model of the system, the design of the controller drives the design of the logging module: the events that affect the model (which maintains the application data) and the views (for displaying data on the screen) are the semantic events that need to captured in the logs. The consequence is a tight coupling between the design of the controller and that of the logger: all the events to which the controller reacts, and which affect the model or views, must be logged. Optionally, in order to increase the efficiency of the log analysis and to support testing of the log accuracy, intermediary data resulting from these effects can also be logged. Logging such data becomes necessary, rather than optional, when the data depends on the context and the time when the event occurs (e.g. the list of results returned by a Web search engine). The consequence is that the complete interaction flow and the changes of the system's state can be "re-played", analyzed and interpreted based on the log data.

A FRAMEWORK FOR MODELING THE INTERACTION AND THE LOGGING

What we propose is a formal procedure that integrates the modeling of the interaction, the logging process and the log analysis, so that (i) a conceptual model of the interaction is developed to capture the functionality of the system, its states, the valid user actions in each state, and the possible flow of the interaction as the system is used; (ii) the user interface accurately implements the conceptual model of the interaction intended to be supported; (iii) the valid, semantic events are captured in the logs, together with the state transitions, so that the sequence of state can be re-created when analyzing the logs (optionally, the states of the system can also be captured explicitly); and (iv) the logs can be analyzed in a systematic and at the same time flexible way. When applied to a particular kind of interaction (such as interactive information retrieval), the proposed procedure can be used to investigate user behavior or to test the usability of a user interface.

Naturally, the proposed approach is most suitable for standalone architectures, or for client logging in a client-server architecture, when the source code of the logger and of the actual application can be integrated easily, so that all the details of the human-computer interaction can be captured. In other configurations, a more restricted version of the approach could, in principle, be applied, based on the observable semantic events. For example, if user interaction with a third party system is studied (e.g. accessing a commercial search engine via a Web browser), then some effort is needed to recognize significant, semantic events and actions among the keyboard and mouse events that take place during the interaction.

Figure 1 captures the proposed experimental setting. What distinguishes this model from the typical experimental setting is the requirement for a conceptual model of the system and of the interaction, from which the design of the logger and of the log parser and analyzer are deterministically derived. It is common in experimental IR, especially for small teams and small budgets, to skip the formal modeling of the interaction, and to insert logging instructions in the application code in an ad-hoc, un-systematic fashion, rather than to formally design the logging module. Therefore, when analyzing the logs, it is difficult to relate the captured events to the states of the system or to the stages of the interaction.

While our approach means more work at the onset, and may seem un-necessary when the experimental schedule is tight, it pays off in the

Figure 1. Integrated approach to design, logging and analysis

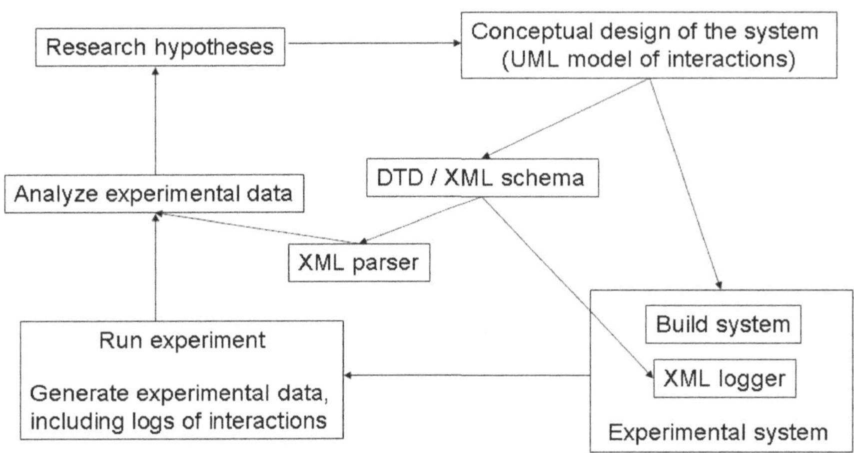

long run. Moreover, the entire research team can participate in the conceptual design, with the advantages that some mistakes and omissions may be avoided, the team members have a better understanding of the underlying interaction model, and the work can be more easily shared. This contrasts with the common situation when the designated programmers build the system and other members of the research team do the log analysis, with insufficient collaboration.

In practice, our approach is based on statecharts (Harel, 1988) or, in the more modern Unified Modeling Language (UML)[1] terminology, on state diagrams. These are extensions of finite state machines (Wagner, 2006), in which the use of memory and conditional transitions make it practical to describe system behavior in reasonably compact diagrams. Such a model of a system describes: (i) a finite number of existence conditions, called **states**; (ii) the **events** accepted by the system in each state; (iii) the **transitions** from one state to another, triggered by an event; (iv) the **actions** associated with an event and/or state transition (Douglass, 1999; Fowler, 2004). Such diagrams have the advantage that they describe in detail the behavior of the system and, being relatively easy to learn and use, allow the participation of the entire research team in developing the conceptual model of the IR system to be employed in an experiment. It also makes it easier for the designated programmers to implement and test the system, as the logic is captured in the model.

While UML is well suited to design the interaction supported by a user interface, XML is an excellent choice of format for logging user actions and state transitions. The Extensible Markup Language (XML)[2] is a World Wide Web Consortium (W3C)[3] standard for document markup that offers the possibility of cross-platform, long-term data storage and interchange. XML is more than a mark-up language: it is a meta-markup language, in the sense that it can define the tags and elements that are valid for a particular document or set of documents. For our purposes, it has the advantage that it is non-proprietary and can be examined with any text editor or open-source XML editor. Also, there are plenty of XML parsers available, written in various programming languages, so processing the logs and extracting relevant information is easy. Moreover, it allows a variety of access modes: (i) sequential access to each event in the log (via SAX[4]); (ii) random access to certain kinds of events, relevant for a certain research hypothesis (via XPath)[5]; and (iii) complex visiting patterns (via DOM)[6].

Closely related to XML are two other standards, Document Type Definitions (DTD) and the W3C XML Schema Language, which are used to describe the vocabulary and language of an XML document. A DTD or an XML Schema, (or simply "schema", to refer to either) can be used by a human to understand or to impose the format of an XML document, or by a machine to validate the correctness of an XML document. Moreover, it can be used by an increasing number of tools (such as the open-source IDE NetBeans) to generate parsers for such XML documents.

While in principle both DTD and XML Schema can be used, there are some differences between the two. DTD's are advantageous in that they are easier to write and interpret by a human, and since they have been around for longer, there are more tools to process them for XML validation and code generation (most commonly for Java or C++). The newer XML schemas allow more specificity in defining types of elements and attributes, but that comes at the cost of reduced readability and more human effort. It is envisaged that the two will co-exist in the future, and that a pragmatic choice can always be made according to the context as to which is more appropriate to use.

UML is ideally suited to support the design of systems, and XML for recording the activity logs. The problem is bridging the gap between the two. One approach fully supported by existing technology is to use the Java Architecture for Data Binding (JAXB)[7] specification to derive Java classes (or rather skeletons of Java classes, specifying name, attributes and method prototypes) from UML diagrams, and then XML DTDs or XML schemas from the Java classes. This approach has the advantage that the skeletons of the Java classes can be expanded with code either for implementing the user interface, or for processing the logs.

An alternative solution is to use the Object Management Group's (OMG) XML Metadata Interchange (XMI)[8] specification. Initially created as an open source specification that allowed modeling tools from different vendors (such as Rational Rose, TogetherJ) to export/import design models, XMI has grown to wider applicability by supporting the production of XML vocabularies and languages that enable the integration of many e-business applications (Carlson, 2001, 2006). XMI specifies a set of mapping rules between UML and XML in terms of elements, attributes and relationships. It must be noted that mapping UML to XMI is not an exact science, and different levels of strictness can be applied, and tradeoffs between a number of mapping decisions can be specified. For example, attributes specified in a UML class diagram can be converted to either XML elements or XML attributes. Carlson (2001) discusses at length such tradeoffs, as well as the use of XPath, XPointer[9] and XLink[10] in implementing more complex relationships from UML diagrams, such as inheritance, association or composition.

Figure 2 captures this approach. UML class diagrams provide the blueprints for UML object diagrams, and XML schemas provide the template for XML documents. XMI specifies the translation of UML class models into XML schemas and of UML object models into XML documents. The obvious and direct application of this approach to logging the interaction appears to be the following: (i) derive UML class diagrams from state diagrams (this is trivial, as the states at different levels of granularity correspond to classes); (ii) use XMI to derive XML schemas from the UML class diagrams; and (iii) capture in XML logs the successive states of the user interfaces, after each event or user action. The approach that we actually propose is a variation of this and will be described later in this section, after we discuss various design decisions.

Finally, in order to avoid the learning curve imposed by the JAXB or XMI automatic alternatives, a "manual-intellectual" approach is feasible for relatively small projects. We followed such

Figure 2. Mapping UML models to XML schemas and documents

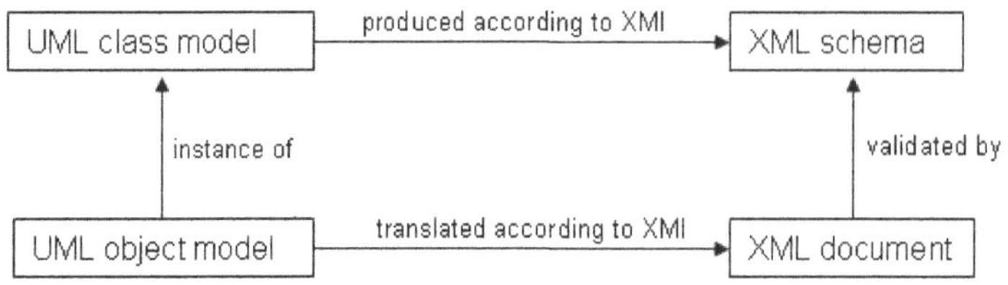

a procedure on the case study described in the next section, deriving the design of the logger and of the log parser from the state diagram of the interaction.

In summary, the expected gains of our vision are:

- Generating user interfaces that accurately implement a certain interaction model.
- Client-side logs that accurately capture user interactions, such as a search session.
- Support for building user models that capture usability problems as well as user preferences. This in turn can contribute to building better interfaces, and to building personalized systems that adapt to the user's needs and preferences.

An apparent disadvantage of this approach is the limitation of what events are logged. One may argue that, once a first log analysis is conducted, the set of research hypotheses/questions may be extended, so data initially viewed as irrelevant may become important. First of all, let us clarify that it is not the research hypotheses that determine if an event is semantic or not, but the interaction model: all the events to which the interaction is designed to respond are logged, whether they are considered relevant to the research questions or not. Secondly, the designers of the experiment have the option of logging additional, non-semantic events for the sake of completeness, and such data can prove useful: e.g. the amount of mouse moving may indicate the frustration of the user; the number of invalid actions attempted by the user may reveal problems with the usability of the user interface, etc. It is up to the designers to reach a balance between logging "everything" and potentially wasting time and resources, and logging only events and actions that have an effect.

Explicit vs. Implicit Logging of States

An essential design decision is whether the logs should capture the states explicitly, or whether logging just the events or actions that trigger state transitions is sufficient, or perhaps even preferred. Figure 3 depicts the conceptual difference between the two cases; of course, the details about a certain trigger will be described in proper XML.

At first sight, explicitly logging the system states appears natural, so that someone examining the logs can clearly see what happened while the system was in a certain state, and when a state transition occurred. However, logs are usually so large and contain so many details, that the researcher is unlikely to gain much knowledge from examining them visually. Rather, the logs should be processed automatically and the information pertinent to a certain research question should be summarized, and possibly visualized, so that it can be interpreted by the researcher. Therefore, *explicitly* capturing the states in the logs is not necessary, as long as they can be re-created at analysis time, based on the events and actions captured in the logs, and on the model captured by the state diagrams. As a result, capturing just

Figure 3. Explicit vs. Implicit capturing of states in interaction logs

```
<StateX>
   <trigger> ... details for trigger to StateX ... </trigger>
</StateX>
<StateY>
   <trigger> ... details for trigger to StateY ... </trigger>
</StateY>
```

```
<trigger> ... details for trigger to StateX ... </trigger>
<trigger> ... details for trigger to StateY ... </trigger>
```

the triggers to states may be sufficient, as long as the state diagrams capture the determinism of the transitions.

One can argue that the data captured in the logs, such as the buttons clicked, the text typed or the menu items selected by the user, are all attributes of user events rather than attributes of the states. Therefore, logging the events, with their attributes, makes it possible to log all the data relevant to the interaction. Let us now consider some more complex situations and design decisions.

In the case of hierarchic states, if we explicitly log states, then a further decision is needed, as depicted in Figure 4. If StateX1 and StateX2 are substates of StateX, then a decision is needed as to whether to explicitly capture the state hierarchy; in practice, one needs to decide whether to log all the levels of the state hierarchy, or only the leaf nodes. For a visual inspection, the explicit choice appears better: the log makes it obvious that, when in StateX1, the system is also in StateX. Again, for the automatic processing of the logs, that is not an advantage; on the contrary, a more complex DTD, and therefore parser, is a disadvantage. Note that, if only the triggers are logged, then the parsing of the log is even simpler, and the knowledge about the state hierarchy is only relevant in the data analysis stage.

Another special situation is the transition to the same state; for example, while the user types the words of a query, the system stays in the same state until the query is submitted.

Figure 5 describes this situation. If the system stays in the same state, it does not make sense to capture multiple instances of the same StateX in the logs; the states can be "collapsed". The problem that appears is that, in this case, a state will appear to have multiple triggers, which makes the DTD more complicated. Again, logging just the triggers removes this problem.

One more situation that we are considering is that of complex systems with orthogonal states, e.g. the state diagram captures, in parallel "swim-lanes", the actions of the user scrolling a document, and the actions of a graphical module rendering a visual display of the search results. The problem is that state transitions in different swim-lanes are independent, so a situation like that depicted in Figure 6 can occur (where StateX and StateY are in one swim lane, and StateA and StateB are in another). It is apparent that the resulting log is not well-formed XML, so parsing it is not possible with regular XML parsers. On the other hand, if only the triggers are captured, this problem is removed.

Overall, there seems to be overwhelming evidence in support of logging just the events and actions that trigger state transitions, rather than explicitly capturing the system states in the logs, and to re-create the states when the logs are parsed and analyzed.

Figure 4. Explicit vs. Implicit capturing of state hierarchy

```
<StateX>
  <StateX1>
    <trigger> ... details for trigger to StateX1 ... </trigger>
  </StateX1>
  <StateX2>
    <trigger> ... details for trigger to StateX2 ... </trigger>
  </StateX2>
</StateX>
<StateY>
  <trigger> ... details for trigger to StateY ... </trigger>
</StateY>
```

```
<StateX1>
  <trigger> ... details for trigger to StateX1 ... </trigger>
</StateX1>
<StateX2>
  <trigger> ... details for trigger to StateX2 ... </trigger>
</StateX2>
<StateY>
  <trigger> ... details for trigger to StateY ... </trigger>
</StateY>
```

```
<trigger> ... details for trigger to StateX1 ... </trigger>
<trigger> ... details for trigger to StateX2 ... </trigger>
<trigger> ... details for trigger to StateY ... </trigger>
```

Figure 5. Collapsing identical states

```
<StateX>
  <trigger> ... details for trigger to StateX ... </trigger>
</StateX>
<StateX>
  <trigger> ... details for trigger to StateX ... </trigger>
</StateX>
```

```
<StateX>
  <trigger> ... details for trigger to StateX ... </trigger>
  <trigger> ... details for trigger to StateX ... </trigger>
</StateX>
```

```
<trigger> ... details for trigger to StateX ... </trigger>
<trigger> ... details for trigger to StateX ... </trigger>
```

Design Patterns for System Design and Log Analysis

The **State** design pattern (Gamma et al., 1995) is a natural choice for a system whose behavior depends on its state, and may change its behavior during execution, based on a state change. It localizes state-specific behavior in different classes, one for each state, avoiding the need for complex *if* or *switch* statements in the code implementing behavior. If the statechart model of the system is available, coding it is relatively simple, as the states, the events and the state transitions are already identified.

One essential decision is whether to use just one set of classes, corresponding to the states of the system, both for implementing the functionality of the system and for analyzing the logs, or to use two sets of classes with the same names, in different packages, one for the system functionality and one for log analysis. Using a unique set of classes can have the advantage that some of the analysis, and the computation of summaries describing the interaction can be done during the interaction, rather than as a separate, offline procedure. However, we prefer the advantage of simplicity and clarity offered by two sets of classes with distinct purposes.

Another essential decision is how the state objects are created and stored when analyzing the logs. One solution is to apply the **Singleton** design pattern (Gamma et al., 1995), so that a unique (singleton) object is created for each state. This is typically the preferred solution when an application has a small number of states and a large number of state transitions: state objects

Figure 6. Capturing transitions between orthogonal states

```
<StateX>
    <trigger> ... details for trigger to StateX ... </trigger>
<StateA>
    <trigger> ... details for trigger to StateA ... </trigger>
</StateX>
<StateY>
    <trigger> ... details for trigger to StateY ... </trigger>
</StateA>
<StateB>
    <trigger> ... details for trigger to StateB ... </trigger>
</StateB>
```

```
<trigger> ... details for trigger to StateX ... </trigger>
<trigger> ... details for trigger to StateA ... </trigger>
<trigger> ... details for trigger to StateY ... </trigger>
<trigger> ... details for trigger to StateB ... </trigger>
```

can be reused rather than new objects created, which makes the application more efficient. Also, a state object can accumulate information over multiple occurrences of the same conceptual state. While in most situations using the singletons is the better solution, for our specific application that solution is not appropriate, due to the level of detail that we want to capture. For example, for an IR application, the researchers may want to analyze not only how many queries were edited and submitted overall, but also how much time was spent formulating each of them, if words were typed or pasted into the query box, the number of corrections that were made on the query, etc. For capturing specific information for each instance of a state, the better solution is to create a new state object every time a state transition occurs.

Finally, it is common for XML parsers generated automatically based on DTD (such as the one produced by NetBeans[11]) to implement the **Visitor** software design pattern. This allows flexibility in specifying which elements of the log tree should be visited and in what order, in order to collect, process and summarize information.

The Procedure

The previous sub-sections have covered the vision of our approach, as well as a discussion of alternatives, with a number of preferences stated. In this sub-section we revisit the conceptual model of our approach, shown in Figure 1, and comment on the implementation of the specific steps.

Building the conceptual model of the interaction is the crucial step of this approach, as everything else depends upon it. The statechart captures the state, the events and the state transitions. Note that the states and the events allow the specification of attributes (e.g. a QuerySubmission event, for example, could specify the text of the query, the targeted search engine, the number of desired hits, etc). While the diagram may become overcrowded if too many details are displayed explicitly, these attributes need to be specified in order to support the next steps.

The list of possible events, together with their attributes, are extracted from the state diagram and used for two purposes: (i) for *specifying a logging module*, which has a function associated to each event so that, when one of these functions is called, it logs the appropriate event and its details; (ii) for *specifying the DTD or XML schema* of the interaction. These two sub-steps should be done in sync, as the DTD specifies the format of the log files written by the logging module. They can be performed either manually, for small systems, or automatically, based on XMI or JAXB technology. An *XML parser specific for the modeled interaction*, and therefore for the log file, can be derived immediately from the DTD model; in fact, there are a number of open-source tools that perform the code generation automatically (such as NetBeans).

The names of the states, extracted from the state diagram, constitute the names of the classes for *building the log analysis module*. It uses the log parser to identify events and to derive state transitions, and it creates instances of the subsequent states, virtually re-creating the interaction. These state objects, which contain useful data read from logs as attributes of events (and possibly of states) can be stored in a list (or another data structure) which can be subsequently filtered according to the research questions investigated, and the information stored by them can be summarized and analyzed.

CASE STUDY: MEDIATED INFORMATION RETRIEVAL

In order to help the reader more easily understand the proposed methodology, we are going to describe its application on our **MIR** (Mediated Information Retrieval) project. The focus of this chapter is the experimental methodology that we designed and employed, rather than the actual research questions and the experimental results of that project. Therefore, the description of the project will be limited to the minimum necessary. A more complete description of the project and an analysis of the results appear elsewhere (Lee, 2006).

The Mediated Retrieval Model

We proposed the concept of **mediated information retrieval** (or access) in previous work (Muresan & Harper, 2001, 2004; Muresan, 2002) as a way to address the problem of exploratory searches, when the searcher may be unfamiliar with a problem domain, uncertain of what information may be useful for solving a particular task, or unsure as to what query terms would be helpful in retrieving relevant information. The idea is to emulate the function of the librarian or intermediary searcher, who interacts with the information seeker, elicits more information and helps the searcher refine, clarify and formulate her information need.

Our reification of the mediation interaction model is based on so-called source collections, specialized collections of abstracts or documents that cover the searcher's problem domain. These collections, which emulate the librarian's knowledge of a certain domain, are either manually

Figure 7. The interaction model in mediated information retrieval

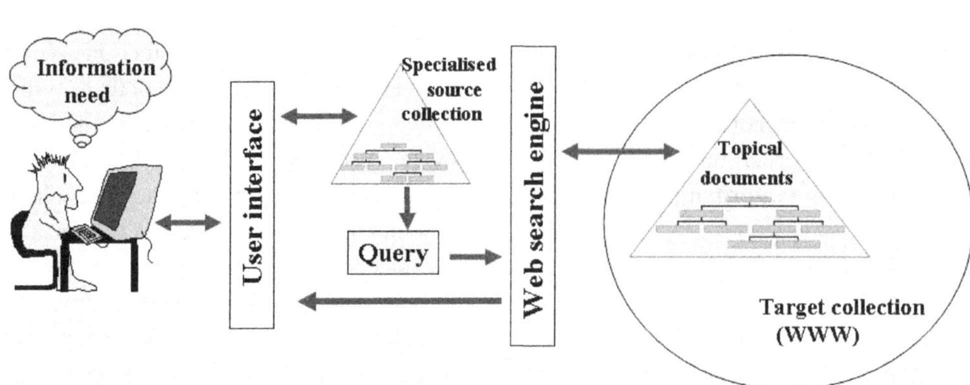

structured (based on some ontology that describes that domain) or are automatically clustered in order to reveal the concepts and structure of the domain, in order to inform and educate the searcher.

The interaction model is captured in Figure 7. In the first stage the searcher interacts with the *source collection* so that (i) she becomes more familiar with the terminology, concepts and structure of the problem domain, and better able to convey her information need; and (ii) the system monitors the user's interaction and her selection of documents, and learns the type of documents that she is interested in. Following the mediation stage, the search target moves to the Web or any other *target collection* where the user hopes to find new information to satisfy her need and complete some task. At this point the system is able to support the searcher by suggesting query terms; also, the user is expected to be more familiar with the problem domain, and able to formulate better queries than before the mediation.

The MIR Project

In previous work we demonstrated the *potential* effectiveness of mediation through pilot studies and user simulations. In the MIR project, we run formal user studies to verify if mediation can indeed improve retrieval effectiveness. Moreover, we are interested in observing patterns of interaction, which could help us design better interfaces.

In the first stage of the project, which we have completed, the human searcher did not get any support from the system in formulating their queries to be submitted to the Web search engine. The mediation consisted in the user exploring the source collection in order to better understand the topic investigated and to enrich her vocabulary. In a future stage of our investigation, the system will suggest a "mediated query" and the searcher will be able to edit it before submitting it to the search engine.

From among the candidate source collections that we were able to obtain, we selected the New Jersey Environmental Digital Library (NJEDL) collection because: (i) with approximately 1,300 documents, it is relatively small so, once clustered, it can be searched and browsed relatively easily in a reasonable amount of time; (ii) it provides a good coverage of environmental issues; (iii) we were able to generate a number of training and test topics for the experiment. A good test topic is one for which there are relevant documents in the target collection (the Web), but finding them requires good queries.

Our experimental design was inspired by work in Interactive TREC[12] (Dumais & Belkin, 2005). We compared a baseline system, with no mediation, against the experimental system, based on mediation. Each of the 16 subjects was randomly assigned a condition that specified the systems to be used and the topics to be investigated, two with the first system and another two with the second system. The systems and the queries were rotated in a latin square design, in order to avoid any order effect. Figures 8 and 9 depict the user interfaces for the baseline and experimental systems.

An effort was made to make the systems identical, with the exception of the mediation functionality, so that any differences in results can be attributed to mediation. Each interface has a *Task control* panel where the task is displayed, and where the subject can formulate their information needs and submit them as queries. Search results from the target collection are shown in the "WEB" tab of the *Search results* panel. When a document is selected, it is displayed in the Web browser. The subject can use the right mouse button to save a document from the hit list; the document snippet will be shown in the *Saved documents* panel. When a document is saved, the searcher is asked to specify the aspects of the topic that the document deals with. Retrieval effectiveness is measured both by recall (the number of relevant Web documents saved by the searcher, relative to the total number of relevant documents known

Figure 8. The baseline MIR interface (no mediation)

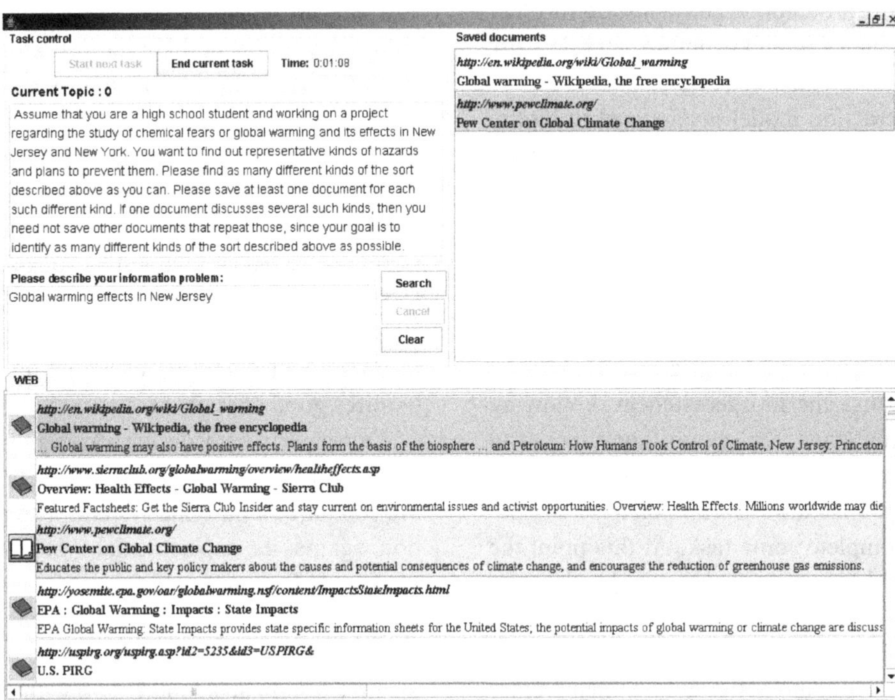

Figure 9. The experimental system (with mediation)

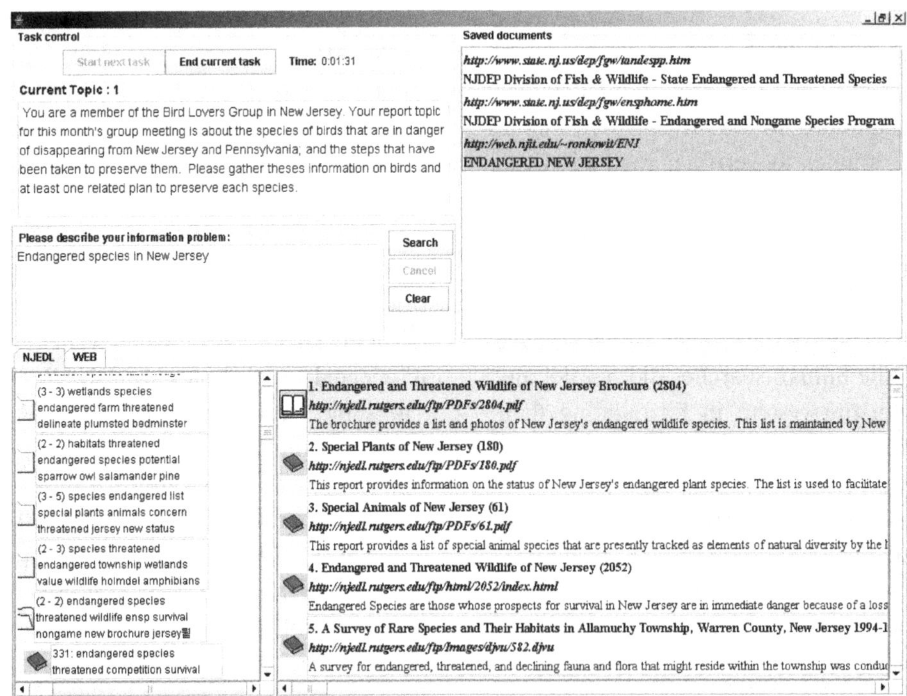

by the researchers to be relevant) and aspectual recall (the number of distinct topical aspects identified by the searcher, relative to the total number of aspects found by the researchers). In order to identify relevant documents and aspects, we employed a pooling procedure similar to what has become a standard procedure in such IR experiments (Voorhees & Harman, 2005): we judged the relevance of the documents saved by all the subjects, and of the candidate documents identified by ourselves when exploring candidate test topics.

The experimental system has an additional tab, "NJEDL", which supports the exploration of the full source collection. The source collection is clustered, and the subjects can use a combination of searching and browsing for its exploration. On the one hand, searching can provide starting points for browsing: when a document snippet in the result list is selected, not only is the full document shown in the Web browser, but the cluster hierarchy is expanded and scrolled automatically, so that the user can investigate the neighborhood of the selected document. On the other hand, browsing the clusters and documents of the source collection is expected to reveal serendipitous relevant information and to suggest new query terms.

At the beginning of the experiment subjects are given a tutorial, and the experimental system is demonstrated to subjects through the prescribed mediation interaction: after seeing the current topic, the searcher explores the source collection available in the NJEDL tab, in order to understand the topic and its context better, and to grasp its terminology. Then, the interaction moves to the WWW tab, where a query can be submitted to the Web search engine, like in the baseline system. In the experiment the user is not forced to adopt this interaction model: if the topic is familiar and formulating a good query is perceived as easy, she may choose to go straight to the WWW tab and search the Web. However, the source collection is always available, and the searcher can always explore it; this may happen if the Web search is perceived as unsuccessful, and more ideas for query terms are sought.

While the focus here is on methodology rather than on the experimental results, let us briefly describe some types of research questions and hypotheses investigated in the MIR project, with the purpose of highlighting the type of data needed to be captured in the logs and analyzed:

- **RH:** "During the mediation stage (exploration of the source collection) users are able to find documents relevant to their problem."

In order to answer this research hypothesis, the logs need to capture the identifiers of the documents opened by the user, so that their relevance can be judged by the researchers. Additionally, capturing time-stamps in the logs allows the investigation of supplementary research questions: "Do users spend more time reading relevant documents than non-relevant documents ?" Moreover, as the browsing of the hierarchically clustered source collection is captured, we can look at common behavior (e.g. depth-first vs. breadth-first exploration) and can compare searching with browsing in terms of efficiency (e.g. effort measured as amount of time spent, number of documents opened, etc.) and effectiveness (successful navigation to relevant documents).

- **RH:** "The mediation stage helps the user formulate better queries and thus achieve better retrieval effectiveness."

While the research design is responsible for separating searchers that use mediation from searchers that do not use mediation, the logs have to capture the actual queries submitted to the search engine, the hits returned, the snippets clicked by the searchers and the saved documents (the relevance of the saved documents is then evaluated by the researchers for a more complete evaluation of search effectiveness). This data can support additional research investigation, for example looking for correlations between query length, more extended vocabulary, query clarity and search effectiveness. Moreover, such data can also be correlated with data from user questionnaires, for example to investigate the effect of search experience or familiarity with a certain topic on time to complete a search, on the number and quality of query submitted, and on task success.

It is apparent that, even if a research experiment is initiated with a small number of research hypotheses, the logging of all semantic events can support the exploration of many additional research hypotheses and questions.

State-Based Design of Interaction and Logging in MIR

To exemplify our procedure on the case study, Figure 10 shows the state diagram that depicts the system states during the MIR interaction. We believe that such a diagram is fairly easy to understand or design even for a researcher not trained in software engineering. In the Idle state between search sessions, the user may perform related activities such as filling in questionnaires required by the experiment. When the session starts, triggered by an evStartTask event, the system displays the current search task and enters the Thinking state, in which the subject reads the task description and thinks of appropriate queries

Figure 10. State diagram for the MIR project

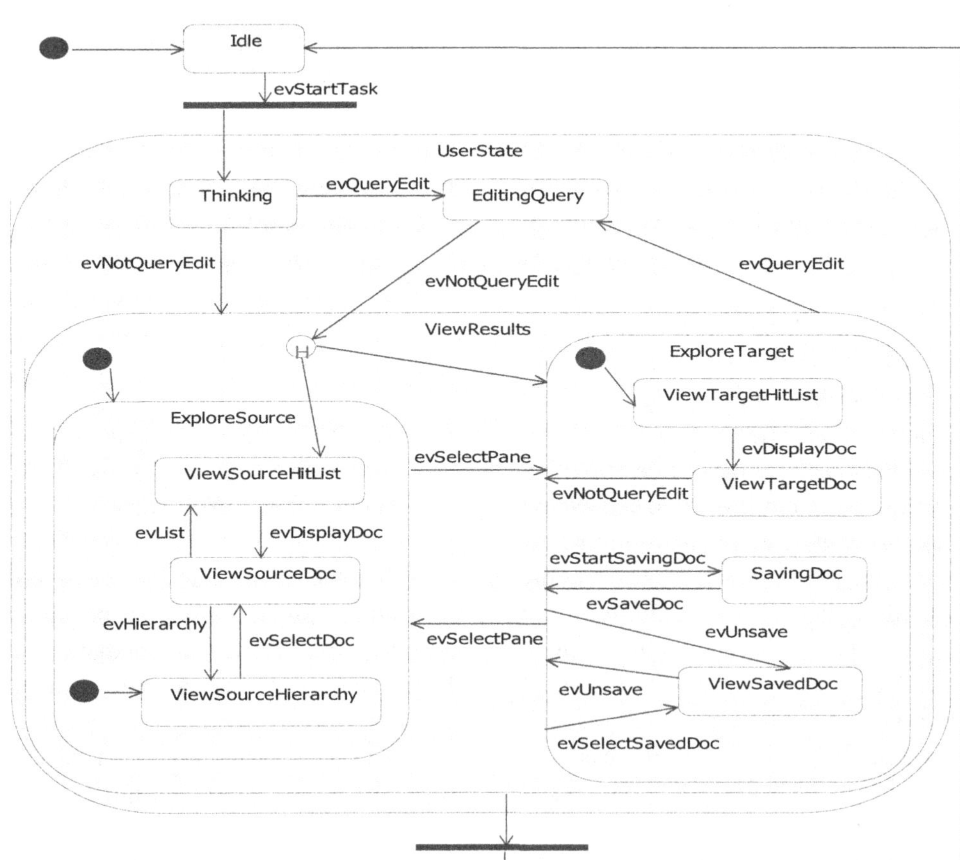

(or alternative actions) to be used. If the user starts typing a query (marked by an evQueryEdit event), there is a transition into the EditingQuery state. On the other hand, in the case of using the mediation system, the user has the choice of starting to browse the source collection first (marked by expanding the cluster hierarchy or selecting a cluster, i.e. an event different from query editing). While the user is editing the query (i.e. typing or using copy-and-paste), the system stays in the EditingQuery state. When the "Search" button is pressed, the history (H) pseudo-state will indicate which of the collections was being explored prior to editing the query; thus the query is submitted to the appropriate collection, the search results are displayed in the *Search results* panel of the appropriate tab, and the system enters the ViewResult state. This is a "superstate", which has a number of "substates": the ExploreSource state corresponds to the exploration of the source collection (NJEDL), while the ExploreTarget state corresponds to the exploration of the target collection (the Web). The searcher may choose between the two collections (and therefore between the two sub-states) by selecting one of the tabs, or the sub-state may be set automatically by the history mechanism.

Not depicted in this diagram are the orthogonal (or parallel) states, corresponding to different components of the system such as the *Task control* panel and the *Search results* panel. These states can also be modeled at different levels of granularity in order to support the design and implementation of the system. For example, the Query panel can be in a Valid state, when a query can be submitted, or an Invalid state, when there is no query, or a query has just been submitted and the search results are expected from the search engine. These system states, parallel to the user states (and hence the two synchronizations bars in the diagram), are essential in designing the functionality of the system. However, they are omitted here for space reasons.

A couple of clarifications are in order:

- Although think-aloud protocols can help, it is not possible to have a perfect image of the searcher's cognitive process. Therefore, what is represented in the diagrams is not the user's cognitive states, but system states. However, the user's actions and the sequence of system states do reflect the decisions taken by the user, and can therefore be used in modeling user behavior.
- The labels assigned to system states reflect the researchers' understanding of the interaction, and specify their understanding of what is going on. Similar to variable names in programming, these labels should convey the semantics of the interaction; however, a perfectly accurate depiction of the user's cognitive process is not necessary. In the example, the label "Thinking" was assigned to the state in which the searcher was instructed to read the assigned task and to think of a search query to submit. There is no guarantee that the user follows the instructions and is indeed thinking; conversely, it does not mean that this is the only state in which the user has to think. The label simply attempts to depict the researcher's best description of what is going on.

From the state diagram, we extract the names and attributes of the events, in order to specify the log format in a DTD and implement the functions of the logging module. Note that, especially for the manual version of the procedure, some adjustments of the names are acceptable, e.g. "evSelectPane" becomes "SelectPane" as XML element in the log file, and as class in the code.

Figure 11 presents a sample of the DTD that describes the MIR interaction, and Figure 12 depicts a sample extracted from a MIR log. It is apparent that the attributes of the events, such as the editing or submission of a query, are captured in the logs and can be used to address the

Figure 11. DTD sample for MIR Log

```
<?xml version="1.0" encoding="UTF-8"?>

<!ELEMENT log (record)*>

<!ELEMENT record (date, millis, message)>

<!ELEMENT date (#PCDATA)>

<!ELEMENT millis (#PCDATA)>

<!ELEMENT message (StartSession|EndSession|
EditQuery|SubmitQuery|SearchResults|SelectPane|
DisplayDoc|StartSaveDoc|SaveDoc|UnsaveDoc|
TouchCluster|ShowMessage)>

<!ELEMENT StartSession EMPTY>
<!ATTLIST StartSession
    task CDATA #IMPLIED
  >

<!ELEMENT EndSession EMPTY>

<!ELEMENT EditQuery EMPTY>
<!ATTLIST EditQuery
    query CDATA #IMPLIED
    querySize CDATA #IMPLIED
    text CDATA #IMPLIED
    offset CDATA #IMPLIED
    count CDATA #IMPLIED
    action CDATA #IMPLIED
  >
```

research hypotheses. Moreover, based on the state diagram, the states can be re-created while the logs are parsed and the events interpreted. This supports research in analyzing state transitions and modeling user behavior.

Apart from being the source of the DTD / XML schema, the interaction state diagram also provides the state names and attributes that support the automatic or manual generation of the class skeletons (e.g. in Java) for the module running the application and for the log analyzer. The two sets of classes have the same names but are in different packages and have different purposes: (i) an application module, tightly coupled with the logging module which writes the XML log files; and (ii) the log analysis module, tightly coupled with an XML parser that recognizes the log elements specified by the DTD file.

Note that the code generated is just a skeleton, and the research team needs to fill in the class methods with actual code that writes or reads data into or from a file. However, such code is trivial after the design of classes and methods has been generated. For writing, if Java is the implementation language, then the standard logging package[13] makes it extremely simple to output logs in XML: a Logger object uses XML by default to write logs into a file, adds a time-stamp automatically, and displays as content of a "**message**" element the text passed to it for logging (see Figure 12).

Even if not used directly in generating the XML schema of the interaction and subsequently the code for log recording and log parsing, the original state diagram describing the states of the system (Figure 10) can be used for automatically generating code for modeling state transitions and, for example, building a Markov model of user behavior (Jurafsky, 2000). Note that the classes depicted in Figure 13, corresponding to the states of the interaction, are actual classes (in an object-oriented programming language such as Java) of the log analyzer, and of the software for state modeling. State objects can capture events that took place for the duration of that state, and additional data structures can capture the sequence of states in chronological order.

Discussion and Evaluation

The effectiveness of a methodological framework is best demonstrated by its flexibility as well as its ability to solve the problem it was designed for. In this section we highlight its power based on evidence from our experiments, as exemplified by the kind of data analysis and research hypotheses investigation that it supports. A more comprehensive analysis of the MIR logs and of the research hypotheses investigated is available elsewhere.[14]

Figure 12. Sample from a MIR Log

```
<?xml version="1.0" encoding="windows-1252" standalone="no"?>
<!DOCTYPE log SYSTEM "logger.dtd">
<log>
<record>
  <date>2005-05-31T16:08:19</date>
  <millis>1117570099901</millis>
  <message><StartSession task='2'/></message>
</record>
<record>
  <date>2005-05-31T16:08:21</date>
  <millis>1117570101833</millis>
  <message><SelectPane title='NJEDL'/></message>
</record>
<record>
  <date>2005-05-31T16:08:30</date>
  <millis>1117570110185</millis>
  <message><TouchCluster op='select'><Cluster id='1413' level='2' parentId='1415'/></TouchCluster></message>
</record>
<record>
  <date>2005-05-31T16:08:31</date>
  <millis>1117570111026</millis>
  <message><TouchCluster op='collapse'><Cluster id='1413' level='2' parentId='1415'/></TouchCluster></message>
</record>
<record>
  <date>2005-05-31T16:08:42</date>
  <millis>1117570122001</millis>
  <message><EditQuery action='add' count='1' offset='0' text='n' querySize='1' query ='n'/></message>
</record>
```

First of all, let us distinguish between two fundamentally different approaches to analyzing the logs. The "atemporal" approach can be applied when the interest is in processing information about a certain kind of event, with no regard to state transitions, or to the order of the states in the logs. Examples of such situations are: getting the list of all the documents viewed or saved by the user, getting the list of all queries submitted to the search engine, etc. In such situations, probably the most efficient solution is to implement an XPath-LogAnalyzer, which uses XPath to visit only the XML nodes in the log tree that are of interest (for example, the SaveDoc events can be visited by specifying "/log/record/message/SaveDoc" as the path to the nodes of interest).

If the time factor is essential in answering a certain research hypothesis or in getting a certain kind of information, then a DOMLogAnalyzer[15] can be employed instead, which will traverse and process the nodes of the log tree (in XML format) in the desired (usually chronological) order. For more flexibility, the task of actually traversing the log tree can be delegated to a separate class (LogScanner in Figure 13), so that the function of traversing the log is decoupled from the function of taking action for each node. An even more flexible solution is to apply the **Strategy** design pattern (Gamma et al., 1995), by making LogScanner an abstract class and having different visiting strategies implemented by its concrete subclasses.

Let us now have a look at a sample of results obtained by applying this methodology in MIR. Box 1 shows a sample report obtained by listing the class names for each state object inferred from a log file, together with the duration of that state (in seconds). Subsequent processing could consist, for example, in building a transition matrix by compiling the states from all the log files in order to (i) observe patterns of behavior and be

Figure 13. State classes used in the MIR log analyzer

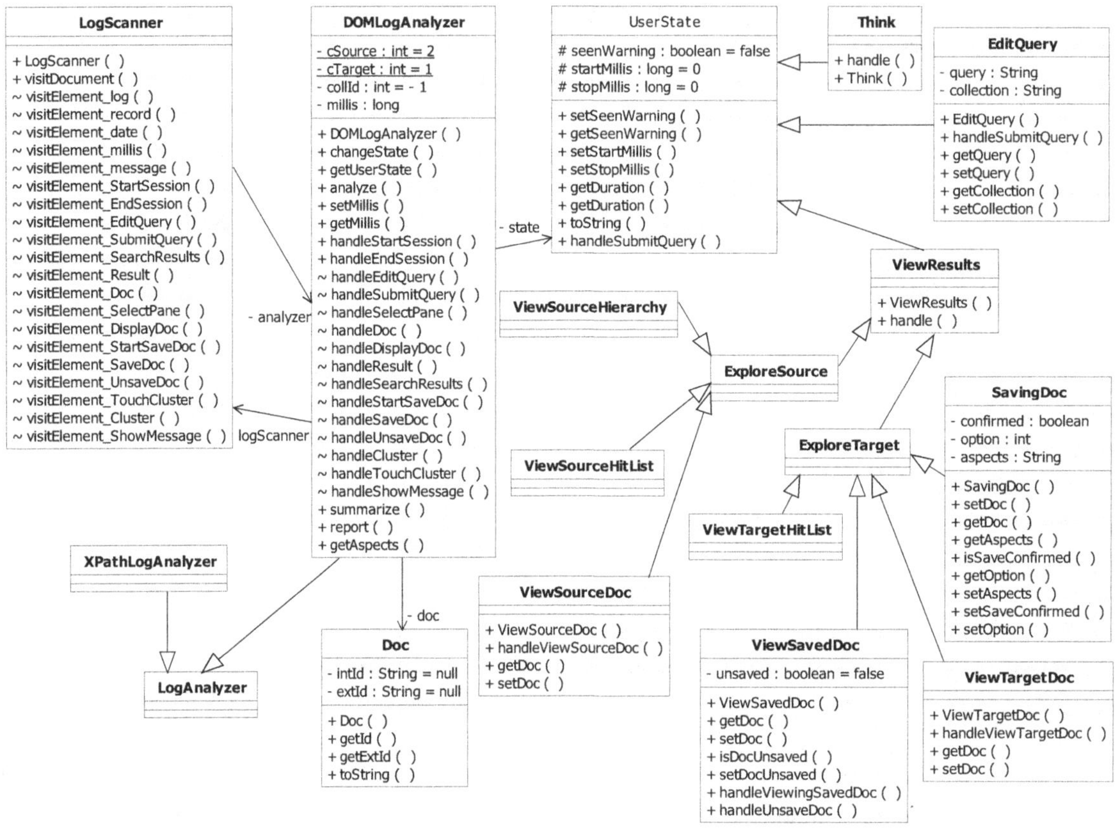

able to predict the next state at a given point; or to (ii) find the most common states and the most common transitions, and optimize the use of the interface for those situations; or to (iii) detect and correct usability problems (e.g. detect transitions that never happen, because some functions are not sufficiently visible in the user interface).

Note that the modeling and analysis of the state transitions can be done at various levels of granularity. For example, the sequence (EditQuery 9, ViewTargetHitList 15, ViewTargetDoc 78, SavingDoc 16, ViewTargetHitList 6, EditQuery 5) could be viewed as (EditQuery 9, ExploreTarget 115, EditQuery 5) if the details of exploring the target are considered irrelevant.

An essential piece of analysis for the MIR project regards the effectiveness of retrieval; we are interested to see whether mediation improves effectiveness. The computation of recall and aspectual recall requires relevance judgments. Even without those, a simple extraction and comparison of data from the logs can give us an idea of how well our expectations were met. Note that in previous experiments, run as part of Interactive TREC, a high correlation was observed between recall and the raw number of documents saved by the subjects (Belkin et al, 2001). Moreover, in the current experiment, the subjects were asked to support their decision to save each document by stating the aspects addressed by the document; therefore, one can expect most saved documents to be relevant, and a higher than usual correlation between recall and number of documents saved. Obtaining from the logs the number of saved

Box 1.

Think	4
EditQuery	9
ViewTargetHitList	15
ViewTargetDoc	78
SavingDoc	16
ViewTargetHitList	6
ViewTargetDoc	31
ViewTargetDoc	9
ViewTargetDoc	35
SavingDoc	11
ViewTargetHitList	3
ViewTargetDoc	173
SavingDoc	16
ViewTargetHitList	14
EditQuery	7
ViewTargetHitList	4
ViewTargetDoc	17
ViewTargetDoc	59
ViewTargetDoc	51
ViewTargetDoc	39
EditQuery	13
ViewTargetHitList	25
ViewTargetDoc	38
SavingDoc	15
...	

documents and the number of queries submitted is trivial.

For the sake of exemplifying some of the statistical analysis supported by our approach, let us report that a set of ANOVA tests shows that most differences between the non-mediated and the mediated conditions are not statistically significant. Surprisingly, slightly more documents were saved on average in the non-mediated condition (m = 3.94, sd = 1.76) than in the mediated condition (m = 3.13, sd = 1.62) despite visibly more effort in the mediation condition. While spending roughly the same total amount of time in the overall search session (m = 1166.16, sd = 185.98 compared to m = 1190.91, sd = 168.91)[16], the mediation subjects submitted significantly more queries (m = 8.69, sd = 4.90 compared to m = 5.69, sd = 3.22; F = 8.377, p = 0.005). In the mediation condition, subjects submitted an average of 2.22 queries to the source collection, and an average of 6.47 queries to the target collection.

Unfortunately, this is a bad result for the mediation hypothesis. Possible explanations are that (i) the subject could not find relevant documents in the source collection; or (ii) the subjects did not have time to read the identified source documents in order to improve their understanding of the topic or to enhance their terminological vocabulary in order to submit better queries. In order to answer these questions, our next steps are to examine the source documents viewed by the users (captured in the interaction logs) and to judge their relevance to the test topics. This will allow us to check if the statistical language models of the queries submitted following mediation show any significant difference. The power and flexibility of our methodology is obvious – the accurate logging of all semantic events, even those not related to the research hypotheses, affords the extension of the original hypotheses, and extra analysis not planned at the outset.

CONTRIBUTIONS AND FUTURE WORK

The proposed methodology is a novel and significant contribution to experimental research in interactive systems, with applications in areas such as Human Computer Interaction or Information Seeking and Retrieval. It is particularly suitable for studying exploratory searching, where the research questions are usually related to understanding patterns of behavior in different stages of the interaction. This approach has been successfully applied in Interactive TREC work and in our Mediated Information Retrieval project.

One interesting issue to consider is the generality of our approach. What kind of systems can it be applied to? Is it not rather limiting to restrict logging to semantic events? Is it possible to log everything that happens during the interaction? We will start addressing these issues by re-iterating the purpose of our work.

Our goal is to integrate the design of the user-system interaction (and implicitly of the user interface) with the design of the logger and of the log analyzer. This means the following:

- The user should be limited to performing actions judged by the system designer to be valid in a certain context; e.g. the user cannot submit an empty query, or save a document repeatedly, etc; this improves the usability of the system and, from a software perspective, it reduces the potential for bugs. It means that only valid actions need to be recorded in the logs. During testing, assertions in the log parsing software can help make sure that the XML documents perfectly match the interaction specification (the XML schema), and that all the recorded events and state transitions are valid.
- It is debatable whether user attempts to perform invalid actions (e.g. the attempt to re-submit a query while the search is active), or events ignored by the system (erratic moves of the mouse) should be logged. On the one hand, only lack of imagination as to what should be logged can limit the system designer, so the danger of recording too much irrelevant data is real (e.g. if a dedicated thread records the state of the system second by second). On the other hand, recording data that is judged irrelevant at the onset may be valuable if the relevance judgment is reconsidered, for example if new research hypotheses are proposed following the initial analysis of an experiment's logs. While recommending a balance between the extremes, we have addressed this issue by including a special action called *ShowMessage* (see the DTD in Figure 11), which records "other" events, i.e. events not included among the valid semantic events in the interaction design. In our own research experiment, we used this capability to record when the task panel's timer alerts the subject that just two minutes are left for completing the task; this is an event that does not affect the state of the system and can be ignored by the user. However, recording that event allows us to determine if the reminder affected the user's subsequent search behavior.
- On a related note, the designers need to decide the granularity of the events to be logged. For example, should the system log each keystroke used to edit a query, or just the final query ? Our recommendation is to let the research hypotheses under investigation inform the decision. For example, we were interested in the effect of topic familiarity on the searcher's query formulation behavior (copying and pasting vs. typing, number of corrections made, etc), so we logged all keystrokes. On the other hand, we only logged the mouse events that had semantic interpretation (selection, cluster expansion, etc).
- Similarly, the system designer needs to decide whether orthogonal events (e.g. the search thread becoming active, or the Internet connection being lost, etc) are worth logging, at the expense of more design and implementation time. Our approach is applicable in two ways: (i) the state diagrams are built separately, and the logging is done in separate files; synchronization of logs, based on time-stamps may be required at analysis time; (ii) more complex state diagrams are used, with parallel swim-lanes, and all the events are logged into the same file; the disadvantage is the increased complexity of the software.

Our proposed approach is appropriate for client-side logging, especially when the research team design and implement both the user interface software (which includes the conceptual interaction design) and the log analyzer. In this situation, the same class hierarchy, representing system states, can be used for implementing both the interaction with the user (keystrokes and mouse actions are interpreted in terms of semantic actions according to the state of the system) and the log analyzer (logged events are interpreted in order to re-create the system states). The proposed approach can be adapted in the following situations, with gradually increasing levels of difficulty:

- For adding logging and analysis functionality to existing code. The state diagram of the interaction needs to be reverse-engineered based on the code and on observing the functionality of the system. Although the benefits of an integrated design are lost, the logging of the events and analysis of the logs can work well.
- For analyzing existing logs produced by a different system. The success of our state-based approach depends on the quality of the user interface that generated the logs (whether or not it allows invalid events to take place and to be logged) and the amount of events logged (whether the sequence of events can unambiguously predict the sequence of system states).
- For server-side logging, our approach is only feasible if the logged information is sufficient to determine the client that generated each event, and if the states of the client can be predicted based on the logged events.

Related Work

A clear distinction needs to be made between different stages of creating interactive systems when discussing and comparing approaches, methodologies or techniques, as these are different for (i) specifying the requirements of the system; (ii) designing the user interface; and (iii) designing and implementing the software. The actual stage of designing the user interface (Tidwell, 2006), although essential for building usable and ultimately successful interfaces, is not one of the concerns of our work. We are interested in linking the system specification to the software design; therefore, we are only going to discuss work relevant to this activity.

Most often, the specification of an interactive system is in the designer's natural language, such as English, accompanied by a set of the sketches of the interface at different stages of the interaction. Unfortunately, natural-language specifications tend to be lengthy, vague and ambiguous, and therefore are often difficult to prove complete, consistent and correct (Shneiderman and Plaisant, 2004). Use cases use a graphical notation to describe user goals, but the emphasis is more on the user-system interaction than in the task itself (Sharp et al, 2007). Task analysis provides a more concise and systematic way to describe and analyze the underlying rationale and purpose of what people are doing: what they are trying to achieve, why they are trying to achieve it and how they are going about it. Task analysis produces models of the world and of the work or activities to be performed in it: it describes the entities in the world, at different levels of abstraction, and the relationship between them, either conceptual or communicative (Diaper & Stanton, 2004). Actually, "task analysis" is a rather generic term, an umbrella for a set of related methodologies such as Hierarchical Task Analysis (HTA), Goals, Operators, Methods and Selection rules (GOMS), Groupware Task Analysis (GTA), etc. Limbourg and Vanderdonckt (2004) provide a description of these, as well as a syntactic and semantic comparison.

The specifications above are generally at a high level of abstraction and task granularity. While useful in guiding the design of the system, they do not provide sufficient support for automatic processing in order to prove completeness or correctness of a system, or for code generation. A possible exception is Paterno's (2001, 2004) work on graphical representation of task specification. He proposes the use of ConcurTaskTrees (CTT) and discusses a variety of ways to integrate task models which describe the activities that should be performed in order to reach users' goals; he employs UML diagrams, created for supporting object-oriented software design, but focused on the internal parts of the software system. Possible approaches discussed are: (i) to represent CCT models with standard UML notation, e.g. with class diagrams; (ii) to develop automatic converters between UML and task models; (iii) to extend UML by building a new type of diagram. Paterno favors the latter approach, proposing a notation for tasks similar to the existing UML activity diagrams, but that also captures hierarchic relationships between tasks. These could be used together with other UML diagrams such as use cases, which define pieces of coherent user behavior without revealing the details of the interactions with the system, and sequence diagrams, which reveal details of the interactions for a certain task or sub-task.

Paterno's work is related to ours in the sense that he also tries to bridge the gap between different levels of abstraction, moving from user tasks towards software implementation. Apart from the application of our methodology being rather different, a distinction is that we are looking at a more detailed level of the interaction, which connects keystrokes and mouse events to semantic actions, in the context of solving a certain task.

Shneiderman and Plaisant (2004) also discuss more specific and formal approaches such as grammars, transition diagrams or statecharts, which provide a more fine-grained view of the human-system interaction and provide support for automatic processing and a connection to software design. Winckler and Palangue (2003) propose a formal description technique based on statecharts, dedicated to modeling navigation in Web application. That work is indeed related to ours, but they focus and limit their attention to modeling the interaction, with no interest to log it and further analyze it.

More closely related to our goal and approach is Trætteberg's (2003) work on DiaMODL, a dialog modeling hybrid language that combines a dataflow-oriented notation with statecharts that focus on behavior. This work is complementary to ours: rather than proposing a new notation or language, our intent is to use and integrate existing notations and languages in order to combine the advantages that they offer. In that direction, we were inspired by Carlson's (2001, 2006) work on linking UML and XML, which we already mentioned in the previous sub-section. However, his view is data-centric, with application in transferring data between applications, while we are mainly interested in modeling, representing, logging and analyzing user-system interactions. Similarly, Crawle and Hole (2003) propose an Interface Specification Meta-Language (ISML) which appears to be related but more generic than our Interaction Modeling Language, plus they also restrict their focus to modeling, rather than logging, the interaction.

In terms of logging and log analysis, our work also falls outside the mainstream research effort. Jansen's (2006) recent review of search log analysis research indicates that most work concentrates on the collection, preparation and analysis of logs, while we focus our attention on designing and/or generating log formats appropriate for certain interaction models, as well as matching parsers for validating the logs and for extracting relevant data from such logs in an efficient, effective and flexible manner.

Jansen concludes, based on an analysis of the literature, that transaction log analysis (TLA) refers, in general, to the use of data collected in transaction logs in order to investigate particular research questions concerning interactions among Web users, the Web search engine, or the Web content during searching episodes. Moreover, transaction logs are most often a server-side data collection method, capturing requests for services from a large number of clients, but missing details of the user-interface interaction. In contrast, we are interested in capturing and analyzing the details of the interaction with client-side logging.

In order to address the drawbacks of server-side logging, a number of researchers have combined them with online questionnaires designed to clarify the users' motivations and intentions, and to disambiguate their behaviors (Hancock-Beaulieu, 2000). Others have used client-side logging. However, most of them did not attempt to capture semantic details of the interaction. For example, Choo, Detlor, & Turnbull (2000) used their WebTracker to log Web browser actions such as "Open URL or File," "Reload," "Back," "Forward," "Add to Bookmarks," "Go to Bookmark," "Print," and "Stop", while Jansen et al. (2006) used their Wrapper to capture operating system level events such as keystrokes, browser requests for URLs, and the start/end of desktop applications. Such tools do not capture the semantic interaction between user and system.

Efforts by Gonçalves et al. (2003) and Klas et al. (2006) toward standardization of log formats in certain types of applications, such as user interfaces for digital libraries, appear closest to ours (with the caveat that their publications focus on their research objectives, and not on the implementation details that could make a comparison possible). Moreover, we suggest that our approach of deriving logging formats from user interface design should help those efforts: the functionality provided by such user interfaces should be first standardized in UML format, and then standardization of the log formats can be achieved as an immediate consequence.

Future Research Directions

One issue that we are currently investigating is an extension of this methodology to studying patterns of behavior by building Hidden Markov Models (HMM) based on the analysis of state transitions recorded in the logs (Jurafsky, 2000). One decision in building such models regards the computation of the transition probabilities. The two potential approaches are based on: (i) macro statistics – the transitions are counted and the probabilities are computed for each individual user, then the probabilities are averaged over the users; and (ii) micro statistics – the transitions are counted and the probabilities computed over all the user logs. The former approach is expected to highlight the differences between individual subjects, and the latter to show common behavior. Both approaches should probably be used so that together they paint a better picture of what is happening. Moreover, where the difference between individual and common behavior is significant, correlations with individual factors (such as familiarity with the topic) should be sought.

Considering the hierarchical structure of states, it is obvious that another issue to consider is state granularity. Taking into account just the top levels may give too coarse a view of the interaction and may not provide sufficient details to answer research questions. On the other hand, the leaf states may provide too much detail and may hide patterns in higher levels. Moreover, due to the limited amount of data generated in a lab user experiment, some of the leaf states may appear infrequently, so drawing conclusions from such sparse data may be dangerous. It is probably better to repeat the analysis for different levels of granularity or to smooth detailed interaction models with models built for transitions between coarse granularity states.

Actually, the analysis described above may prove that, for complex interactions such as information seeking, pure Markov Models are inappropriate, and that more complex extensions should be considered. It may be the case that state transitions are not determined just by the current state and certain events, but also by some parameters of the state, such as the amount of time spent, or the number of documents examined.

A very different research direction is to investigate ways to automatically generate graphical diagrams that show the frequency of each state transition and thus give a visual display of user behavior. So far we have extracted transition frequencies with the log analyzer, but have built such visualizations manually.

Finally, we intend to investigate a number of IR user interfaces and to compare their state diagrams, trying to identify common patterns. This would allow us to provide support, in the form of reusable toolkits of frameworks, for researchers designing and evaluating user interfaces for Information Retrieval.

ACKNOWLEDGMENT

The methodology proposed and discussed here was successfully used in designing the user interfaces and analyzing the logs for the Mediated Information Retrieval (MIR) project, conducted in the School of Communication, Information and Library Studies, Rutgers University, the author's previous affiliation. This author thanks Hyuk-Jin Lee, who conducted the user experiment, Nicholas J. Belkin and Dan O'Connor, supervisors, and David J. Harper[17] from the School of Computing, The Robert Gordon University, UK, external advisor.

REFERENCES

Belkin, N. J., Cool, C., Kelly, D., Lin, S.-J., Park, S., Perez-Carballo, J., & Sikora, C. (2001). Iterative exploration, design and evaluation of support for query reformulation in interactive information retrieval, *Information Processing & Management, 37*(3): 403-434.

Belkin, N.J., Cool, C., Stein, A., & Thiel, U. (1995). Cases, scripts, and information-seeking strategies: on the design of interactive information retrieval systems. *Expert Systems with Applications, 9*(3), 379-395.

Belkin, N.J., & Muresan, G. (2004). Measuring Web search effectiveness: Rutgers at Interactive TREC. In *Measuring Web Search Effectiveness: The User Perspective*, workshop at WWW 2004, May 2004, New York.

Carlson, D. (2001). *Modeling XML applications with UML: Practical e-Business applications.* Addison-Wesley.

Carlson D. (2006). Semantic models for XML schema with UML tooling. *Proceedings of the 2nd International Workshop on Semantic Web Enabled Software Engineering (SWESE)*, Nov 2006, Athens, GA..

Choo, C. W., Detlor, B., & Turnbull, D. (2000). Information seeking on the Web: An integrated model of browsing and searching, *First Monday, 5*(2).

Cooper, A., Reinmann, R., & Cronin, D. (2007). *About Face 3: The essentials of interaction design.* Wiley.

Crowle, S., & Hole, L. (2003). ISML: An interface specification meta-language, *10th International Workshop on Design, Specification and Verification of Interactive Systems*, Madeira.

Diaper, D., & Stanton, N. (2004). *The handbook of task analysis of Human-Computer Interaction.* Lawrence Erlbaum Associates.

Douglass, B. P. (1999). *Doing hard time: Developing real-time systems with UML, objects, frameworks, and patterns.* Addison-Wesley.

Dumais, S. T., & Belkin, N. J. (2005). The TREC interactive tracks: Putting the user into search. In Voorhees, E. M., & Harman, D. K. (Eds.), *TREC – Experiment and evaluation in Information Retrieval*, MIT Press.

Ellis, D. (1989). A behavioral approach to information retrieval system design. *The Journal of Documentation, 45*(3), 171-212.

Fisher, K. E., Erdelez S., & McKechnie, L. (2005). *Theories of Information Behavior.* Information Today.

Fowler, Martin (2004). *UML distilled: A brief guide to the standard object modeling language* (3rd ed.). Addison-Wesley/Pearson Education.

Gamma, E., Helm, R., Johnson, R., & Vlissides, J. (1995). *Design Patterns – Elements of Reusable Object-Oriented Software.* Addison-Wesley.

Gonçalves, M. A., Panchanathan, G., Ravindranathan, U., Krowne, A., Fox, E. A., Jagodzinski, F., & Cassel, L. (2003). The XML log standard for digital libraries: Analysis, evolution, and deployment. *The Third Joint Conference in Digital Libraries (JCDL)*, Houston, TX.

Hancock-Beaulieu, M. (2000). Interaction in Information Searching and Retrieval, *Journal of Documentation, 56*, 431-439.

Harel, D. (1988). On visual formalisms, *Communications of the ACM, 31*(5), 514-530.

Horrocks, I. (1999). *Constructing the user interface with statecharts.* Addison-Wesley.

Ingwersen, P., & Jarvelin, K. (2005). *The Turn – Integration of information seeking and retrieval in context.* Springer.

Jansen, B. J. (2006). Search log analysis: What it is, what's been done, how to do it, *Library & Information Science Research, 28*, 407-432.

Jansen, B. J., Ramadoss, R. Zhang, M., & Zang, N. (2006). Wrapper: An Application for Evaluating Exploratory Searching Outside of the Lab, *SIGIR 2006 Workshop on Evaluating Exploratory Search Systems*, Seattle, WA.

Jurafsky, D., & Martin, J. H. (2000). *Speech and language processing.* Prentice-Hall.

Klas, C.-P., Albrechtsen, H., Fuhr, N., Hansen, P., Kapidakis, S., Kovacs, L., et al. (2006). A logging scheme for comparative digital library evaluation, In *Proceedings of the 10th European conference on research and advanced technology for digital libraries (ECDL 2006)*, Alicante.

Kuhlthau, C. (1991). Inside the search process: information seeking from the user's perspective. *Journal of the American Society for Information Science, 42*(5), 361-371.

Lee, H.-J. (2006). Mediated Information Retrieval for the Web Environment, Ph.D. dissertation, School of Communication, Information and Library Studies, Rutgers University, New Brunswick, NJ, May 2006.

Limbourg, Q., & Vanderdonckt, J. (2004). Comparing task models for user interface design. In Diaper, D., & Stanton, N. (Eds.) *The Handbook of Task Analysis of Human-Computer Interaction.* Lawrence Erlbaum.

Muresan, G. (2002). Using document clustering and language modelling in mediated information retrieval, Ph.D. dissertation, School of Computing, The Robert Gordon University, Aberdeen, Scotland, January 2002.

Muresan, G., & Harper, D. J. (2001). Document clustering and language models for system-mediated information access. In *Proceedings of the 5th European Conference on Digital Libraries (ECDL)*, Darmstadt.

Muresan, G., & Harper, D. J. (2004). Topic modelling for mediated access to very large document collections, *Journal of the American Society for Information Science and Technology, 55*(10), 892-910.

Olah, J. (2005). Shifts Between Search Stages During Task-Performance in Mediated Information-Seeking Interaction. In *Proceedings of the 68th Annual Meeting of the American Society for Information Science (ASIST)*, Charlotte, NC.

Paterno, F. (2001). Towards a UML for Interactive systems. In *Proceedings of the 8th IFIP*

International Conference on Engineering for Human-Computer Interaction, Toronto.

Paterno, F. (2004). ConcurTaskTrees: an engineered notation for task models. In Diaper, D., & Stanton, N. (Eds.) *The Handbook of Task Analysis of Human-Computer Interaction*, Lawrence Erlbaum Associates.

Pinker, S. (1999). *How the mind works.* W.W. Norton &Co.

Robertson, S.E., & Hancock-Beaulieu, M. M. (1992). On the evaluation of IR systems. *Information Processing and Management, 28*(4), 457-466.

Saracevic, T. (1996). Interactive models in information retrieval (IR). A review and proposal. In *Proceedings of the 59th Annual Meeting of the American Society for Information Science (ASIST), 33*, 3-9.

Sauro, J. (2004). Premium usability: Getting the discount without paying the price, *Interactions, 11*(4).

Sharp, H., Rogers, Y., & Preece, J. (2007). *Interaction design.* Wiley.

Shneiderman, B., & Plaisant, C. (2005). *Designing the User Interface.* Addison-Wesley / Pearson Education.

Tidwell, J. (2006). *Designing interfaces.* O'Reilly.

Trætteberg, H. (2003). Dialog modelling with interactors and UML Statecharts - A hybrid approach. In *10th International Workshop on Design, Specification and Verification of Interactive Systems*, Madeira.

Vakkari, P. (1999). Task complexity, problem structure and information actions, integrated studies on information seeking and retrieval. *Information Processing and Management, 35*, 819-837.

Vakkari, P. (2001). Changes in search tactics and relevance judgments when preparing a research proposal: a summary and generalization of a longitudinal study. *Journal of Documentation, 57*(1), 44-60.

Voorhees, E. M., & Harman (2005). *TREC – Experiment and Evaluation in Information Retrieval.* MIT Press.

Wagner, F. (2006). *Modeling software with finite state machines: A practical approach.* Auerbach Publications.

Winckler, M., & Palanque, P. (2003). StateWebCharts: a formal description technique dedicated to navigation modelling of Web applications. In *10th International Workshop on Design, Specification and Verification of Interactive Systems*, Madeira.

Xie, H. (2000). Shifts of interactive intentions and information-seeking strategies in interactive information retrieval. *Journal of the American Society for Information Science, 51*(9), 841-857.

KEY TERMS

Interaction Design: Designing interactive systems that support certain functionality and a range a user behaviors.

Interaction Schema/Model: A formalized description of interaction rules and actions allowed in specific contexts.

Log Analysis: The analysis of user behavior based on the actions recorded during interaction.

Logging Module/System: Component of an interactive system that logs/records relevant interaction between the user and the system (events, user actions, system responses).

Mediated Information Retrieval: A model of IR interaction in which the systems supports the user's exploration of the information space and the formulation of queries.

State Diagram (Statecharts): Model of an interactive system that describes (i) a finite number of existence conditions, called states; (ii) the events accepted by the system in each state; (iii) the transitions from one state to another, triggered by an event; (iv) the actions associated with an event and/or state transition.

User Behavior: The set of actions taken by a user interacting with the system in order to reach a goal or complete a task.

ENDNOTES

1 http://www.uml.org/
2 http://www.w3.org/XML/
3 http://www.w3.org
4 http://www.saxproject.org/
5 http://www.w3.org/TR/xpath
6 http://www.w3.org/DOM/
7 http://java.sun.com/webservices/jaxb/
8 http://www.omg.org/technology/documents/formal/xmi.htm
9 http://www.w3.org/TR/WD-xptr
10 http://www.w3.org/TR/xlink/
11 http://www.netbeans.org/
12 The Text Retrieval Conference (TREC) is an open evaluation event organized annually by the National Institute for Standards and Technology (NIST) which provides an evaluation framework for research groups worldwide. The experimental model and the evaluation metrics developed in TREC have been widely adopted as standards for IR evaluation. See http://trec.nist.gov/.
13 http://java.sun.com/javase/6/docs/technotes/guides/logging/index.html
14 Detailed results and conclusions from the MIR project are reported in Lee's Ph.D. dissertation (2006), supervised by this author.
15 Names such as XPathLogAnalyzer or DOMLogAnalyzer are by no means standard names. They were chosen in the MIR project to indicate that the scanning of the logs was based on XPath, respectively on traversing the DOM tree.
16 The subjects were told that they had 20 minutes (or 1200 seconds) for investigating each topic.
17 Currently affiliated with Google.

Chapter XIII
Tips for Tracking Web Information Seeking Behavior

Brian Detlor
McMaster University, Canada

Maureen Hupfer
McMaster University, Canada

Umar Ruhi
University of Ottawa, Canada

ABSTRACT

This chapter provides various tips for practitioners and researchers who wish to track end-user Web information seeking behavior. These tips are derived in large part from the authors' own experience of collecting and analyzing individual differences, task, and Web tracking data to investigate people's online information seeking behaviors at a specific municipal community portal site (myhamilton.ca). The tips discussed in this chapter include: (1) the need to account for both task and individual differences in any Web information seeking behavior analysis; (2) how to collect Web metrics through deployment of a unique ID that links individual differences, task, and Web tracking data together; (3) the types of Web log metrics to collect; (4) how to go about collecting and making sense of such metrics; and (5) the importance of addressing privacy concerns at the start of any collection of Web tracking information.

INTRODUCTION

Upon first consideration, employing Web tracking to better understand end-user experiences with the Web seems to be a simple process of installing the tracking software, collecting the data over a certain period of time, and conducting the analysis. However, our own experience in setting up, collecting, and analyzing Web tracking data has shown us that the process is surprisingly more difficult than originally expected.

To share what we have learned to help others set up and better utilize Web tracking tools, we have reflected upon what we believe are key tips concerning the use of Web tracking in any Web information seeking analysis. Thus, the overall purpose of this chapter is to discuss the practicalities and usefulness of collecting Web tracking data to help measure and assess the performance and usage of a Website or application, particularly with respect to Web information seeking.

Note that the ideas presented in this chapter are grounded in a research project conducted by the authors over the last three years that investigates people's online behaviors at a municipal community portal site called myhamilton.ca (www.myhamilton.ca). The ultimate goal of the project is to understand the relationships among individual user characteristics such as demographics and personality traits, user attitudes toward and perceptions about accomplishing certain tasks (Web services) online, and actual usage behavior. We believe that an understanding of these relationships will provide insight into how characteristics of the individual, the task, and utilization behaviors affect task performance in an online community environment. We also believe that the capture and analysis of Web tracking data is imperative to reaching such an understanding.

The difficulty in utilizing Web tracking data successfully is in knowing how to position its collection and use within the larger confines of Web information seeking analysis. Web tracking is just one tool that needs to be coordinated with other data collection methods to yield a more comprehensive understanding than Web tracking alone could ultimately provide.

The objective of this chapter is to raise awareness of this point and to suggest techniques and approaches for the collection and analysis of Web tracking information that will aid practitioners in their performance measurement initiatives and understanding of how end-users seek information on the Web. Various tips are presented:

- The need to account for both task and individual differences in any Web information seeking analysis assessment
- The benefits of using a unique ID to link individual differences, task, and Web tracking data
- The types of Web metrics to collect
- How to gather and make sense of the Web metric information that is collected in Web logfiles
- The importance of addressing privacy concerns right up-front in the collection of Web tracking information

We begin by providing background on the need to take both task and individual differences into consideration when investigating end-user Web information seeking behavior. To do this, we provide a general model that describes how task and individual differences affect information seeking behavior. Next, methods to conduct a Web information seeking analysis that allows for the collection of both task and individual differences data are presented. Importantly, these methods include the collection of Web tracking data via the use of Web logs. Using a selective subset of variables from the general model presented earlier, our own myhamilton.ca project serves as a point of illustration. We also provide details with respect to the types of Web metrics to collect and what needs to be done to make sense of these data. Finally, the importance of addressing privacy in any Web information seeking analysis is highlighted.

To help clarify things, find below the following definitions of terms:

- *Information seeking behavior* refers to how people seek information in different contexts (Fisher, Erdelez & McKechnie, 2005).
- *Web information seeking behavior* refers to information seeking behaviors that occur over the Web. Choo, Detlor & Turnbull (2000) identify four main modes of infor-

mation seeking on the Web ranging from wayward browsing to goal-directed search (undirected viewing, conditioned viewing, informal search, and formal search) where each mode is characterized by predominant information seeking moves or activities (undirected viewing: starting and chaining; conditioned viewing: browsing and differentiating; informal search: differentiating, monitoring, and extracting; and formal search: monitoring and extracting).

- *Individual differences* are the demographic and psychological characteristics of people that distinguish one person from another.
- *Task* in this chapter refers to the information seeking task an individual user experiences that instills a need for information and motivates the user to satisfy this information need through some sort of information seeking behavior. Task is the context surrounding a person's information need.
- *Web tracking* refers to the automated collection of Web information seeking behavioral data.
- *Web metrics* pertains to the measures by which to assess a person's Web information seeking behavior or to assess and monitor activity on a Website. Examples of commonly used Web metrics include page views, page transitions, and session times.

INDIVIDUAL DIFFERENCES, TASKS, AND INFORMATION SEEKING BEHAVIOR

Research concerning online information seeking in both information science and marketing has shown that information seeking strategy depends on the type of information seeking task or its context (e.g., Bhatnagar & Ghose, 2004; Moe 2003; Toms & Trifts, 2006; Wildemuth & Hughes, 2005). Scholars in both fields, as well as those in psychology, also have begun to examine the role of individual differences in online behavior (e.g., Bhatnagar & Ghose, 2004; Das, Echambadi, McCardle, & Luckett, 2003; Dillon & Watson, 1996; Ford, Miller & Moss 2001, 2005a, 2005b; Gugerty, Treadaway & Rubinstein, 2006; Heinström, 2005; Ho, 2005; Martin, Sherrard & Wentzel, 2005; Tuten & Bosnjak 2001). Unfortunately, the study of individual differences in information seeking has tended to take a haphazard approach that has failed to link findings with broader theoretical frameworks concerning information seeking behavior and has neglected to study the effects of individual differences in conjunction with specific seeking contexts (Saracevic, 1991). The work of Ford et al. (2001, 2005a, 2005b) is a notable exception both for its use of Wilson's model of information behavior (Wilson & Walsh, 1996) as a basis for investigation and for its examination of how information seeking complexity and individual differences in cognitive style interact to result in differing information seeking strategies (Ford et al., 2005b).

To situate individual differences within the Web information seeking context, we propose our own model of information seeking behavior that utilizes Wilson's (1999) model as a theoretical foundation (see Figure 1). According to this model, task (analogous to Wilson's "context of the information need" construct) leads to information seeking behavior that is mediated by individual differences variables. The purpose of the model is to illustrate how task and individual differences fit into and influence the end-user information seeking process, and to stress the importance of the need to take both task and individual differences into account when planning any type of Web information seeking analysis assessment.

As Figure 1 shows, with respect to **task**, there are a variety of characteristics about a task that can influence an end-user's information seeking behavior. For instance, prior research has found substantial differences in information seeking patterns across tasks and between product categories or information domains (e.g., Bhatnagar

Figure 1. How task and individual differences affect information seeking behavior

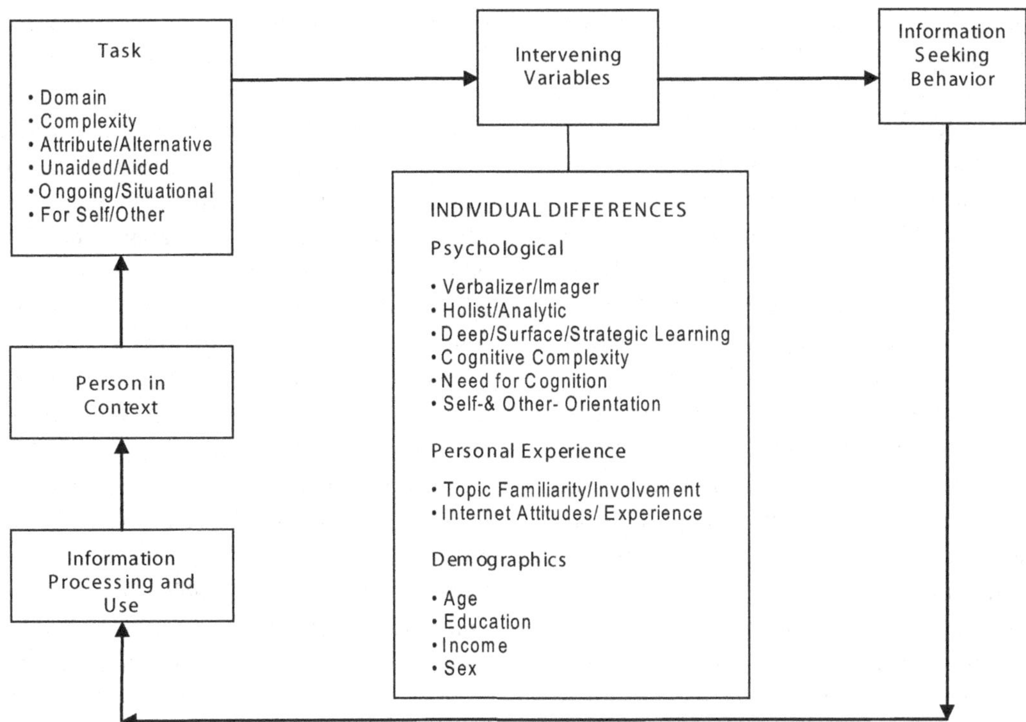

& Ghose, 2004; Trifts & Toms, 2006; Wildemuth & Hughes, 2005). These differences, in part, can be explained by the complexity of the information seeking task, the extent to which the task is clearly structured, whether one is seeking information for oneself or for someone else (Hupfer & Detlor, 2006), and semantic differences between search domains (Byström & Järvelin, 1995; Vakkari, 1999, pp. 825). Ford et al. (2003) suggest that complex tasks require a conceptual broadening of useable terminology to reflect broader search concepts. Conversely, simple tasks would be ones in which all essential concepts necessary to complete the information seeking task are fully specified in the task instructions. In a consumer decision making context, this conceptual broadening may be closely related to how well a consumer is able to mentally formulate the parameters of an information search. For example, consumers who are well aware of their current product needs may be easily able to articulate this need in the form of a search query (e.g., buying a particular DVD), but a decision made with less specificity (e.g., planning a vacation with no particular destination in mind) may require broadening of the search parameters to learn more about the various alternatives available.

Even within a specified information domain, task complexity is influenced by such factors as the number of alternatives available, the number of dimensions of information on which the alternatives vary, and time pressure (Payne, Bettman & Johnson, 1993). Greater complexity in an information seeking task often leads to more heuristic-based processing of information. Decision strategies that require processing information by attribute as opposed to alternative are thought to be easier to undertake.

In the context of online information seeking, tasks that require people to search by attribute as opposed to alternative may be cognitively less complex and require less time at the general search tool level. Therefore, even within a specified domain, differences in information seeking effort allocation may occur, depending upon a person's information seeking orientation (Huneke, Cole & Levin, 2004). That is, whether an individual is engaging in attribute-based or alternative-based processing of information affects the allocation of information seeking effort between general search engines versus specific Websites (Toms & Trifts 2006). Those who are engaged in alternative-based processing are more focused on finding an appropriate source of information and thus allocate a greater amount of their information seeking effort at a general search engine as opposed to in-site search.

Other characteristics of the task shown in Figure 1 that can affect information seeking behavior are whether the information seeking task is aided/unaided or ongoing/situational. The former refers to the extent to which Web information seeking is assisted by interactive decision aids. For example, in the domain of online shopping, Haubl and Trifts (2000) found that interactive tools that assisted consumers in their initial screening of alternatives substantially reduced the amount of information seeking undertaken and improved decision making. Despite the initial learning that is required, in the long run the use of interactive decision aids should reduce task complexity such that users will be able to devote less effort to obtain the required information than they would expend if unassisted. The latter refers to whether information is needed on an ongoing basis, such as when an individual has an interest in a product category or topic but does not intend to make a decision immediately, or whether information is needed for present use, such as a pre-purchase situation in which a decision is imminent.

As Figure 1 shows, **individual differences** play an important role in terms of mediating the effect of task on information seeking behavior in terms of the information seeking strategy or process chosen, as well as its effectiveness. These differences may include an individual's familiarity or level of involvement with the information topic (Moorthy, Ratchford & Talukdar,1997), experience with the Internet (Bhatnar & Ghose, 2004), perceptions of Web-based information seeking (Ford & Miller, 1996), and enduring psychological traits (e.g., Ford et al., 2001; 2005a; 2005b).

For example, Bhatnar and Ghose (2004) found that users with greater experience with the Internet and more education utilized the Internet more frequently. Other demographic characteristics, including age and sex, also have been associated with differences in Web information seeking patterns. Ford et al. (2001) established that information retrieval effectiveness was associated with males while retrieval failure was associated with females. Women felt that they were not in control of their information seeking; they were unable to avoid irrelevant material and stay on target. Men, however, were confident that they were in control and could bypass extraneous content. Educational research conducted with children also has found sex differences in information seeking such that boys searched differently from girls and were able to acquire more target-specific and target-related information. Boys filtered information at an early stage but girls were linear and more thorough navigators (Roy & Chi, 2003).

As Figure 1 illustrates, there are several psychological differences that may influence information seeking behavior in terms of an individual's propensity to engage in elaborate, effortful processing versus effort minimization and reliance on heuristics. Explained below, these include: verbalizer /imager and holistic/analytic cognitive styles; deep, surface and strategic learning approaches; cognitive complexity; Need for Cognition; and Self- and Other-Orientation.

Cognitive Style

Individuals differ in the strategies that they use to seek and process information, and they tend to favor certain strategies, or cognitive styles, on a consistent basis. Among these styles, verbalizer/imager and holist/analytic are the two dominant dimensions (Riding & Cheema, 1991). The verbalizer/imager dimension refers to a preference for and facility with tasks and information that are presented in a verbal versus visual format; verbal and spatial ability are closely related measures (Ekstrom, French & Harman, 1976). Analytic individuals perceive components of complex stimuli as discrete elements and are better able to analyze and impose structure than those who are holist, with their tendency to perceive stimuli in a holistic or global manner. Where Internet searching is concerned, Wang, Hawk and Tenopir (2000) found that holist searchers experienced more difficulty and confusion than analytic users. Ford et al. (2001) found that poor retrieval was linked to a verbalizer cognitive style, as well as perceptions that the Internet's graphic elements were of little value. Similarly, Gugerty et al. (2006) demonstrated that superior spatial, rather than verbal, ability was associated with more favorable computer and Internet attitudes, and also had an indirect effect on information seeking performance. Ford et al. (2001) found no relationships between holist or analytic cognitive styles and retrieval effectiveness, but did find relationships among holists, imagers and Boolean searching and among analytics, verbalizers and Best-match searching (2005a; 2005b). It also appears that cognitive style effects are more important for novice than for experienced Internet searchers (Palmquist & Kim, 2000). Such evidence suggests that individual differences in cognitive style affect not only the information seeking process but also its effectiveness.

Learning Style

Those with a surface approach describe learning as knowledge reproduction achieved through rote learning and memorization. They are passive uncritical learners who devote relatively little effort to information seeking (Ford, 1986; Entwistle & Tait, 1995). Deep learners, on the other hand, view learning as a process that creates knowledge through the synthesis and assimilation of new information. They seek a broad range of information sources using a variety of information seeking strategies. Strategic learners are able to choose either deep or surface learning approaches as appropriate to the task at hand. Analysis of self-reported information seeking behavior has found that a surface approach to learning was associated with a fast surfing information seeking strategy in which users experienced problems with critical analysis and had difficulty judging the relevance of retrieved documents (Heinström, 2005). They also demonstrated confirmatory bias and preferred to access information using only a few documents. In contrast, a deep diving approach characterized those with either deep or strategic learning styles; these individuals were effortful information seekers who sought high quality documents. In addition, Ford et al. (2005a) have found that individual items in the surface learning style (fear of failure and poor time management) were linked to poor retrieval. As with cognitive style, it appears that learning style affects both the information seeking process and its outcomes.

Cognitive Complexity

Those who are cognitively simple tend to see the world in binary terms such as black and white or right and wrong, while those who are cognitively complex are able to see shades of grey and recognize that the validity of a given viewpoint may vary with circumstances. Higher levels of cognitive complexity appear to be associated with poor retrieval (Ford et al., 2001).

Need for Cognition

Individuals with a high Need for Cognition (NFC) enjoy thinking and have a greater tendency to elaborate upon, structure and evaluate information (Cacioppo, Petty & Kao, 1984). They engage in more effortful decision making than those who are low NFC and arrive at better information seeking outcomes (Bailey, 1997). High NFC users also have more favorable attitudes toward Websites with complex verbal and simple visual elements (Martin et al., 2005). NFC is positively correlated with Web information usage (Tuten & Bosnjak 2001) and has a direct impact on self-reported information seeking behavior (Das et al., 2003). Finally, investigation of information seeking at online grocery stores has found that high NFC shoppers, compared with low NFC consumers, investigated more URLs and spent more time reading (Ho, 2005).

Self- and Other-Orientation

These characteristics describe differences in an individual's propensity to be concerned with oneself versus others by tapping gender-related traits that pertain to an independent (Self-Orientation) versus interdependent (Other-Orientation) self-concept orientation (Hupfer, 2001). Self- and Other-Orientation predict Internet use frequency and preferences that male-female indicators often fail to explain. The two scales interact to predict how often individuals seek information online (Hupfer & Detlor, 2006) both for themselves (self-relevant information) and for those close to them (other-relevant information). Other-Orientation also is positively related to usage rates for Internet applications with relationship implications, such as greeting cards (Hupfer & Detlor, 2007a). Furthermore, the two scales interact to predict the importance to an individual of Website characteristics that imply an information-rich environment versus navigational aids that ease processing and maximize efficiency (Hupfer & Detlor, 2007b).

METHODS FOR COLLECTING INDIVIDUAL DIFFERENCES, TASK, AND WEB TRACKING DATA

Recognizing the importance of both task and individual differences in Web information seeking behavior, attention now turns to the methods that allow for the collection of task, individual differences, and information seeking behavior data in a Web information seeking analysis. These methods invariably involve the collection of Web tracking activity via the use of Web logs, but tracking alone is insufficient for a thorough information seeking analysis. Web tracking captures information seeking behavior with Web logfiles, but other data collection instruments, such as questionnaires and interviews, are required to collect individual differences and other task-related data.

In closed environments, like laboratories, researchers can control research participants' information seeking tasks by giving them explicit descriptions or instructions for their tasks and can ask them to complete surveys to collect individual differences data. Closed environments also allow researchers to require that participants use specific software in the lab where their Web activity will be tracked. Other advantages of the closed environment include the opportunity to modify the information seeking tools that are used (e.g., browsers, interfaces), control the available functionality and even provide interactive decision aids. However, closed environments are not without their drawbacks. Processing large numbers of participants through laboratory sessions requires considerable time and resources. In addition, requiring subjects to conduct contrived searches in an artificial setting or scenario may compromise the validity and generalizability of any research results.

Richer Web information seeking analyses are more likely to be found in open environments where end-users can conduct real-life information seeking tasks that are of relevance and importance to them and that take place within natural environments and settings (e.g., the workplace, the home). In open environments, researchers are able to observe natural behavior patterns and collect data that affords greater validity and generalizability. However, conducting Web information seeking investigations in open environments presents its own challenges for the proper collection and analysis of task and individual differences data. For example, dynamic IP addressing prevents the linking of a person's Web tracking data with any individual differences data that is collected through user profiles or questionnaires. Knowing what task prompted a user to turn to the Web to seek information also is problematic in terms of understanding the type of task and its attributes.

There are various ways to go about capturing task, individual differences, and Web behavior data, but a critical component is the ability to link all three types of data together for a specific individual. It probably is easiest to create this linkage in a closed environment. However, if researchers and practitioners want to take advantage of the benefits afforded by Web information seeking analyses conducted in open environments, they must devise a means of connecting these various data sources. We did this, quite successfully, in our own research project at a municipal/community portal site called myhamilton.ca. The project involved the use of two surveys (one pertaining to task; the other pertaining to individual differences) and the collection of Web tracking data to yield a robust understanding of Web user information seeking behavior. Note that a selective subset of task and individual differences variables from the general model presented above were used in our myhamilton.ca research project. Importantly, a unique identification feature linked participants' actual portal activity to demographic, personality and attitude data. To do this, we had to work closely with the portal development group to ensure that the study's data collection instruments (i.e., Web tracking and online surveys) were incorporated directly within the portal's design.

We believe that the use of a unique ID to link data collected in the user surveys to the Web tracking metrics collected in the Web logs is a key strength of our research project. By linking these data sources and triangulating results, we are able to arrive at a rich understanding of end-user online behavior. For example, regressions or path analyses are being used to determine how well individual differences predict task self-reports and actual usage behavior. Further, cluster or discriminant analysis techniques are being used to establish the characteristics of low, medium and high usage groups.

As mentioned above, two types of Web surveys were administered to people who consented to participate in the project. The first of these was an individual differences (user characteristics) survey that collected basic demographic information, personality traits, and technology background on each participant. Items were based on those found in a recent investigation by the authors (Hupfer & Detlor, 2006), the Georgia Institute of Technology's annual GVU WWW User Surveys (cc.gatech.edu/gvu/user_surveys), and Ford and Miller's (1996) scales that measure perceptions of Web-based information seeking (see Appendix A for a list of the individual differences questions used in this project).

The second type of survey was a brief user task evaluation. Eliciting attitudes towards conducting a specific online activity and perceptions of the task's importance, these surveys were administered after participants had completed a given activity on the portal interface (see Appendix B for the actual questions used to measure participants' attitudes toward and perceptions of tasks). These data were collected during short time windows pertaining to a few specific portal activities, such as paying a fine or purchasing a dog license.

In terms of Web tracking, like the two surveys, metrics were collected only from portal users who had agreed to participate in the study. The portal was designed to facilitate metric collection through third party applications hosted on the portal's back-end Web servers. Specific detail concerning the type of Web metrics that were collected and analyzed are discussed in the following section.

WEB METRICS TO COLLECT AND TECHNIQUES FOR ANALYZING THEM

In general, the various sources of Web logs can be classified as either server-level or client-level data sources (Srivastava et al., 2000). The primary metrics in our study were based on server-level data generated through a custom programmed server-side plug-in, and first-party cookies stored on the client-side. These metrics included the following: page attributes such as page views, page transitions, and HTTP referrer information; temporal attributes such as history time stamps, and session times; and visitor attributes such as user identification tags, and remote host information. Consequently, a composite of these primary Web log metrics provided us with the desired analytics output related to information seeking behaviors of end users. Table 1 shows the interrelationships among the various Web log metrics that we used and their sources, as well as the associations among the Web log metrics and their resulting composite analytics.

Table 1. Summary of Web log sources, metrics, and composite analytics

Web Log Metrics	Sources of Web Log Metrics			Composite Analytics		
	Server Object	Session Cookies	Persistent Cookies	Visitor Footprints	Navigation Tracks	Information Seeking
Page Views	•	•		•	•	•
Page Transitions	•				•	•
HTTP Referrer Information	•				•	•
History Time Stamps	•	•	•		•	•
Session Time	•	•			•	•
User Identification Tags	•		•	•		•
Remote Host Information	•			•		•

The advantage of using a customized server-side plug-in rather than other available logging methods such as Web server logs, client-side tracking utilities, and page tagging scripts is that the overall process affords more control for updates and modifications, and also entails less time and effort to clean the data and prepare it for further analysis (e-consultancy, 2003). Compared to Web server logs, custom logfiles suffer from fewer inaccuracies and redundancies (e-consultancy, 2003; Murata & Saito, 2006). With respect to control, a server-side plug-in allows greater autonomy than a client-side remote tracking utility where there is increased dependency on client platform capabilities and end user intentions (Winett, 1998). Similarly, vis-à-vis page tagging scripts where the deployed solution is typically outsourced to an application service provider (Beasley, 2002; e-consultancy, 2003), a server-side plug-in offers more control over the development and maintenance of an application interface.

In our study, the server-side plug-in was designed to poll several collections and properties of the server-side objects including request, response, and session objects in order to retrieve values pertaining to attributes of visited site pages, times spent on each page and in each user session, and unique visitor identification values stored in client-side cookies.

In addition to using a customized server-side plug-in for the collection of Web metrics data, our study utilized first-party cookies to track visitors. This method is regarded as more reliable than using third-party cookies used by hosted analytics vendors as recent Internet statistics show that 12%-17% of Internet users block third-party cookies while only 2%-5% block first-party cookies (WebTrends, 2005). By storing automatically generated unique identifiers on users' workstations, persistent cookies allow the identification of unique site visitors which can prove to be extremely valuable in determining the reach and audience penetration of a Website.

To generate the composite metrics described in Table 1, we created and utilized our own *Web analytics toolkit*. Overall, the collection of singular Web log metrics through server objects and cookies, as shown in Table 1, facilitates the formation of a Web data warehouse, which is regarded as the first step in devising a Web analytics toolkit (Sen et al., 2006). The formation of a Web data warehouse enables simple decision support services through channel traffic reports.

The second step in developing a Web analytics toolkit is to aid sophisticated visitor behavior tracking (Sen et al., 2006) which can only be enabled through additional structured statistical procedures and logic querying methods. In our research study, we did this by following the three phases suggested for Web usage mining studies, namely: 1) *pre-processing*, 2) *pattern discovery*, and 3) *pattern analysis* (Srivastava et al., 2000). The pre-processing phase cleanses, sorts and formats the raw data into organized segments of information (e.g., establishing sequence of activities through sorting first by cookie-based user identifiers and then by server session identifiers). This information feeds into the pattern discovery phase which converts raw logs into data abstractions that are pivotal to the analysis of usage patterns (e.g., deriving session length information from time stamps and page views). The pattern analysis phase calculates descriptive statistics and usage metrics that can help to identify different user clusters based on their patterns of information seeking. Overall, these three phases enable the transformation of dimensions of Web activities that are measurable into those that are meaningful within the context of the analysis of users' information seeking behaviors.

Unlike other Web analytics studies that undertake the development of a self-contained prototypical Web usage mining system as part of the overall research project (Srivastava et al., 2000; Wu et al., 1998; Zaiane et al., 1998), the Web analytics engine used in our study was based on a selection of self-programmed application macros, third party tools, and customized scripts.

Figure 2 shows a high level schematic of the Web analytics engine depicting the various functional modules that were used to operationalize the three phases of Web usage mining. While the data cleanser module enabled the pre-processing phase, the URL filter and crawler, as well as the metrics calculator, enabled the pattern discovery and pattern analysis phases.

In terms of custom applications, server side scripts using SQL (structured query language) were deployed to extract data from tables in the data warehouse and to export into a format suitable for spreadsheets and statistical analysis applications. In the data cleanser module, Excel macros were utilized to cleanse the data and organize it into meaningful segments that were to be used in metrics calculations. The URL filter allowed us to form clusters of Webpages based on their frequency and mode of access. For instance, Website landing pages were identified by noting external referrer Websites, and search tools were recognized by query information such as keywords contained in URLs. Ultimately, a dictionary of landing pages was compiled to facilitate page lookups during the analysis of online user activities.

The information derived from the URL filter was further refined by mapping the URLs to the title of the Webpages. These titles were obtained by running the list of URLs through an Internet-based Web crawler utility which parses Webpages for various types of metadata. In this case, the only metadata that was of interest was the title tag pertaining to the Webpages referenced by the URLs. Finally, the metrics calculator module comprised spreadsheet functions and macros in Excel and analysis widgets in the SPSS statistical application. The metrics calculator was used primarily to report descriptive statistics and produce cluster analysis results that could be viewed in text, table or graphical formats through the metrics viewer module.

The Web analytics engine allowed us to perform a composite analysis of Web log metrics from server-side and client-side sources. Specifically, as shown in Table 1, the Web analytics engine allowed us to define a hierarchical view of user activities based on visitor footprints, navigation tracks, and information seeking trails.

At the lowest level of user information seeking pattern identification, a *visitor footprint* represents "a single clickstream record created by the interaction of the visitor with a page on a Website" (Sen et al., 2006). In establishing visitor footprints, various clickstream metrics such as unique cookie based user identification, server based session identification, time stamp information, referrer page URLs and destination page URLs can be

Figure 2. Components of the Web analytics engine

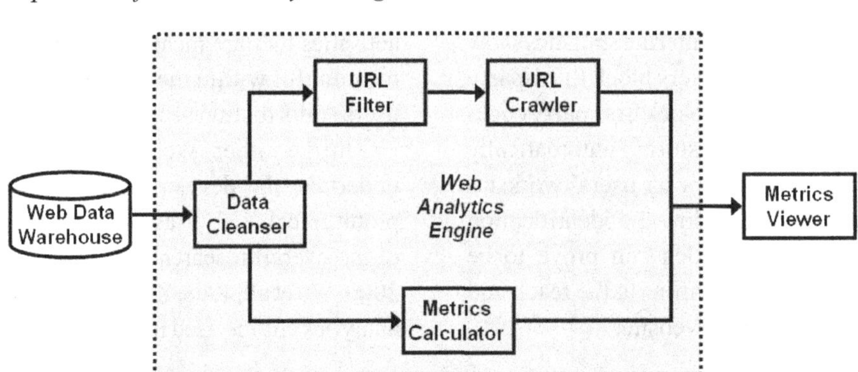

compiled into simple records of online user activities. In our study, the data cleanser and URL crawler modules in the analytics engine were utilized to establish these visitor footprints. Figure 3 shows an extract of nine footprints pertaining to a sample user, User-34.

An aggregation of visitor footprints enables the formation of *navigation tracks* which provide a chronological history of a user's activities on a Website (Sen et al., 2006). In our study, the configuration of each visitor navigation track comprised the entry point to the Website, the path of Webpages that were traversed in each user session, along with the average time spent per page, content page requests per session, search queries per session, and the exit point from the Website. Custom programmed spreadsheet macros in the metrics calculator module of the analytics engine processed the visitor footprint information to reveal these navigation tracks. Figure 4 shows the extract of navigation tracks pertaining to the visitor footprints shown in Figure 3.

Based on information from visitor footprints and navigation tracks, *information seeking trails* characterize the deepest level of pattern discovery employed in our study. Information seeking trails can be discerned by using clustering algorithms which can group similar user beliefs, attitudes and behaviors (Sen et al., 2006). In our study, the information seeking trails were analyzed through composite analytics that acted as surrogate measures to identify scanning, searching and browsing moves on Websites. These information seeking moves were further assembled and classified into modes of information seeking such as undirected viewing, conditioned viewing, informal search, and formal search (Aguilar, 1988; Choo et al., 2000). Episodes of information seeking were analyzed using recursive procedures in spreadsheet macros that hinged on multiple passes through

Figure 3. Extract of visitor footprints

User Cookie ID	Server Session ID	Webpage Alias	Time Stamp
30570681-8208-40e7-8742-a4b5203e2c56	ugxqppfw51j3t4b0b51w2cqo	Portal Homepage	10/02/2006 8:08
30570681-8208-40e7-8742-a4b5203e2c56	ugxqppfw51j3t4b0b51w2cqo	City & Government Subpage 1	10/02/2006 8:11
30570681-8208-40e7-8742-a4b5203e2c56	ugxqppfw51j3t4b0b51w2cqo	City & Government Subpage 2	10/02/2006 8:15
30570681-8208-40e7-8742-a4b5203e2c56	fztodda1r1c2wq55wx2v2h55	Personalized Portal Homepage	28/09/2006 14:50
30570681-8208-40e7-8742-a4b5203e2c56	fztodda1r1c2wq55wx2v2h55	Education & Careers Subpage 1	28/09/2006 14:50
30570681-8208-40e7-8742-a4b5203e2c56	fztodda1r1c2wq55wx2v2h55	Search	28/09/2006 14:54
30570681-8208-40e7-8742-a4b5203e2c56	fztodda1r1c2wq55wx2v2h55	Search Results	29/09/2006 14:54
30570681-8208-40e7-8742-a4b5203e2c56	fztodda1r1c2wq55wx2v2h55	Education & Careers Subpage 2	28/09/2006 14:56
30570681-8208-40e7-8742-a4b5203e2c56	fztodda1r1c2wq55wx2v2h55	Portal Homepage	28/09/2006 15:01

User ID	Session ID	Webpage ID	Time on Page
User-34	Session-3-A	PH	180
User-34	Session-3-A	CG1	246
User-34	Session-3-A	CG2	
User-34	Session-4-A	PPH	62
User-34	Session-4-A	EC1	242
User-34	Session-4-A	SP	61
User-34	Session-4-A	SR	123
User-34	Session-4-A	EC2	301
User-34	Session-4-A	PH	

Figure 4. Extract of visitor navigation tracks

User ID	Track ID	Page Path	Entry Point	Exit Point	Session Length	Avg Time / Page	Page Requests	Search Queries
User-34	1	PH,CG1,CG2	PH	CG2	426	142	3	0
User-34	2	PPH,EC1,SP,SR,EC2,PH	PPH	PH	789	131.5	4	1

visitor footprints and navigation tracks. Figure 5 shows an extract of the additional surrogate metrics that were used to formulate the archetypical information seeking episodes.

Undirected viewing episodes can be identified by observing the most common entry points in visitor navigation tracks and calculating the average number of page requests and the average time spent on Webpages. Since users engaged in undirected viewing modes demonstrate broad scanning web moves (Choo et al., 2000), these modes typically consist of navigation tracks that start at main landing pages such as the Website homepages and sitemaps, and exhibit high average number of page requests and low average time spent per Webpage.

Conditioned viewing episodes can be tallied by identifying similarities in entry and exit points between visitor navigation tracks for the same user. This can be accomplished by calculating the dot product of page paths in visitor navigation paths. Since users engaged in conditioned viewing episodes are interested in selected topics and specific types of information (Choo et al., 2000), these episodes also will typically exhibit a lower ratio of search queries to page requests.

Informal search episodes show signs of unstructured search efforts (Choo et al., 2000) and can be identified by using surrogate measures such as observing navigation tracks that consist of references to external search engines, high average number of sessions with multiple search queries, and low average time spent per Webpage.

Formal search episodes are emblematic of users who make a purposeful and planned effort to acquire specific information (Choo et al., 2000). Using information available in visitor navigation tracks and other surrogate measures of information seeking modes, these episodes can be expected to exhibit a high average number of sessions that started with a search page, a low average number of page requests, and high average time spent per page.

The next step in our research study will involve further examination of the four archetypical episodes of information seeking outlined above. Specifically, we plan on linking the Web analytics information we collected in terms of visitor footprints, navigation tracks and information seeking trails to the data we collected through the individual differences questionnaire and task attitudes survey. Doing so will allow us to

Figure 5. Extract of surrogate metrics and frequencies of archetypical information seeking modes

User ID	Avg. Session Length	Avg. Page Requests Per Session	Avg. Search Queries Per Session	Ratio of Search Queries to Page Requests	Frequency of Sessions Starting with Search	Frequency of Sessions with Multiple Searches
User-33	445.5	6.5	0	0	0	0
User-34	606.4	4.5	1.8	0.4	0	1
User-35	612.6	8.8	3.2	0.36	1	2

User ID	Frequency of Undirected Viewing Episodes	Frequency of Conditioned Viewing Episodes	Frequency of Informal Search Episodes	Frequency of Formal Search Episodes
User-33	3			
User-34	2	1	1	1
User-35	2			2

better understand the associations between Web behavior and the specific characteristics of users or groups of users.

ADDRESSING PRIVACY IN WEB INFORMATION SEEKING ANALYSIS

A final tip for any person wishing to conduct Web information seeking analysis in real-world settings (i.e., non-laboratory environments) is the need to address privacy concerns during the project's initial stages and to design Web data collection and analysis methods with privacy in mind. Ethics boards at academic institutions have always cautioned researchers about the need for anonymity and/or confidentiality. Academics, industry analysts and privacy advocates also have raised concerns about the vast amount of data that is collected using passive devices, such as adware, cookies, spyware and Web viruses, to record online behavior (Marshall & Swartwout, 2006). Such calls for privacy protection are warranted.

For example, the need to preserve privacy with Web log analysis became a highly public debate in the summer of 2006 after America-On-Line (AOL) posted query log data (approximately 20 million search inquiries obtained from over 650,000 users over a three month period) to a publicly accessible Website. These data, which were intended for academic use, assigned each user a unique ID and included the date and time of each query as well as addresses of Websites that were visited after searching was concluded. The AOL team that released the data intended to provide researchers with the opportunity to analyze search patterns and strategies over time without having to disclose any personally identifiable information.

Unfortunately, it rapidly became apparent that the specification of search parameters could in some cases permit the identification of individuals (Barbaro & Zeller, 2006; Hansell 2006a). These data were quickly removed from the site, but not before the data had been downloaded and circulated (Barbaro & Zeller, 2006). The ensuing media furor informed readers about how much data is stored by major search engines (Zeller, Jr. 2006a), how advertisers used search history for segmentation and targeting purposes (Hansell, 2006b) and also advised them as to how they could protect their identity online by using proxy servers and by deleting browser cookies (Biersdorfer, 2006). In late August 2006, AOL dismissed a researcher and project manager, and their chief technology officer resigned (Zeller, 2006b). AOL also announced plans for the implementation of new technologies that would protect privacy and restrict access. Academic opinion concerning the data's use has been divided; the very real privacy concerns have been acknowledged, but at the same time, the availability of a very large and current data set has immeasurable value for those who investigate personalization and information retrieval (Hafner, 2006).

With our own myhamilton.ca research project, we were very aware of the need to address privacy issues at the outset. In our initial discussions with the portal project team, we agreed that each user would be assigned a unique ID that would allow us to link tracking logs with survey data. Participant identities would not be released to us and the portal staff would handle the distribution of incentives to those who participated in our research. While these measures ensured anonymity, we later were confronted with the ramifications of municipal privacy legislation requirements. These concerns were further exacerbated by a portal privacy breach that resulted in the inadvertent broadcasting of people's personal dog licensing information and the attendant negative press in the local media. The ensuing privacy impact assessment conducted on our research project required documentation of the flow and storage of both the survey and tracking data. This documentation included the names of all tables where data was stored, a description of the programs that accessed and updated the data, and the process by which the data would be sent to our research team. The city also planned to delete all data once our research team confirmed its safe receipt at the conclusion of the data collection period.

The city's privacy assessment identified one particularly important outstanding issue in that the city had no means to control or prevent the possible misuse of the survey's demographic information and Web tracking information, both of which resided in the city's databases. This situation arose because participants' unique IDs were stored within the city's databases and thereby created the potential for unauthorized linking of this information. Addressing this concern required extensive and costly program code and database changes. Consequently, rather than storing participants' unique IDs within the user profile table in the city's database, unique IDs were embedded in session cookies that were transmitted between a user's computer and the City of Hamilton's servers. Using session cookies that contained unique IDs allowed us to track user behavior individually but eliminated the need to store a unique ID in a database resident on one of the city's servers that possibly could have been used as a foreign key to access and link together a person's private information.

Elimination of unique IDs within the user profile table also caused us to rethink the way we handled the distribution of participant incentives. Some mechanism was required to identify which participants had participated in the study so that we could contact them and distribute gift certificates. To facilitate this, a field was created in the user profile table to simply act as a flag that would indicate whether or not a particular user had agreed to participate in our research project. This flag allowed us to identify those people who participated in the study but it did not allow us to associate a person's research data with their personally identifying (contact) information.

These changes to our data collection methods required an additional review of our protocol by the McMaster research ethics board and the amendment of our call for participation and consent form in order to clarify privacy implications. Specifically, potential participants were informed that privacy had been built into the methods by which data would be collected and stored. In terms of databases, the unique ID would be stored only in three raw data tables that contained the Web tracking and survey data. No link would exist between these tables and any other contained in the myhamilton.ca database, and no personally identifiable information would be sent to the McMaster research team. All of these revisions, the additional ethics review, and further testing of our data collection instruments delayed the project's launch for over six months. A better understanding of privacy legislation and its impact for our research would have allowed us to avoid both the delay and the expense.

CONCLUSION

To provide insight into methods for conducting a Web information seeking analysis, we presented several tips. First, we raised awareness of the importance of individual differences and tasks in understanding information seeking behavior. We encourage practitioners and researchers to include the collection and analysis of task, individual differences, and behavioral data in any Web information seeking analysis design. The second tip spoke to devising methods that collect task, individual differences, and Web tracking data and provide a means to link these data sets together. We provided our own research project at myhamilton.ca as an example for others to follow in this regard. The two surveys (see Appendices A and B) may help others structure similar research instruments to collect data on tasks and individual differences. The third and fourth tips provided guidelines on which Web metrics to collect and how to go about analyzing them. Though many alternative Web metrics and methods of analysis exist, we anticipate that our description of the Web metrics we collected and our illustration of their analysis will assist others in their own investigations. Finally, we discussed the need to address privacy concerns right up-front in the collection of Web tracking information so as to avoid lengthy and costly delays in conducting a Web information seeking analysis. By paying attention to these five tips, both academic researchers and practitioners can ensure that their Website performance measurement initiatives run smoothly.

REFERENCES

Aguilar, F. J. (1988). *General managers in action*. New York: Oxford University Press.

Bailey, J.R. (1997). Need for cognition and response mode in the active construction of an information domain. *Journal of Economic Psychology, 18*(1), 69-85.

Barbaro, M. & Zeller Jr., T. (2006). A face is exposed for AOL searcher No. 4417749. *The New York Times*, August 9, 1.

Beasley, C. (2002). *It's a hit! Gauging success through traffic analysis*, Retrieved May 7, 2007 from http://www.sitepoint.com/article/success-traffic-analysis

Bhatnagar A., & Ghose, S. (2004). Online information search termination patterns across product categories and consumer demographics. *Journal of Retailing, 80*(3), 221-228.

Biersdorffer, J.D. (2006). How to digitally hide (somewhat) in plain sight. *The New York Times*, August 12, 9.

Byström, K. & Järvelin, K. (1995). Task complexity affects information seeking and use. *Information Processing and Management, 31*(2), 191-213.

Cacioppo, J.T., Petty, R.E. & Kao, C.F. (1984). The efficient assessment of need for cognition. *Journal of Personality Assessment, 48*, 306-307.

Choo, C. W., Detlor, B., & Turnbull, D. (2000). *Web work: Information seeking and knowledge work on the world wide web*. Netherlands: Kluwer Academic Publishers.

Das, S., Echambadi, R., McCardle, M. & Luckett, M. (2003). The effect of interpersonal trust, need for cognition, and social loneliness on shopping, information seeking and surfing on the Web. *Marketing Letters, 14*(3), 185-202.

Dillon, A. & Watson, C. (1996). User analysis HCI. The historical lessons from individual differences research. *International Journal of Human-Computer Studies, 45*(6), 619-638.

e-consultancy. (2003). *Web measurement and analytics*. London, UK: e-consultancy.

Ekstrom, R.B, French, J.W., & Harman, H.H. (1976). *Manual for kit of factor-referenced cognitive tests*, 109-113, 173-177.

Entwistle, H. & Tait, N.J. (1995). *The revised approaches to studying inventory*. Edinburgh: Centre for Research on Learning and Instruction, University of Edinburgh.

Fisher, K. E., Erdelez, S., & McKechnie, L. E. F. (Eds.). (2005). *Theories of information behavior*. Medford, NJ: Information Today.

Ford, N. (1986). Psychological determinants of information needs: A small-scale study of higher education students. *Journal of Librarianship, 18*(1), 47-61.

Ford, N., & Miller, D. (1996). Gender differences in internet perception and use. In *Papers from the 3rd Electronic Library and Visual Information Research (ELVIRA) conference, April 30* (pp. 87-202). London: ASLIB.

Ford, N., Miller, D., & Moss, N. (2001). The role of individual differences in internet searching:

An empirical study. *Journal of the American Society for Information Science and Technology, 52*(12), 1049-1066.

Ford, N., Miller, D., & Moss, N. (2003). Web search strategies and approaches to studying. *Journal of the American Society for Information Science and Technology, 54*(6), 473-489.

Ford, N., Miller, D., & Moss, N. (2005a). Web search strategies and human individual differences: Cognitive and demographic factors, internet attitudes, and approaches. *Journal of the American Society for Information Science and Technology, 56*(7), 741-756.

Ford, N., Miller, D., & Moss, N. (2005b). Web search strategies and human individual differences: A combined analysis. *Journal of the American Society for Information Science and Technology, 56*(7), 757-764.

Gugerty, L., Treadaway C., & Rubinstein, J.S. (2006). Individual differences in internet search outcomes and processes. *CHI 2006*, April, 815-820.

Hafner, K. (2006). Researchers yearn to use AOL logs, but they hesitate. *The New York Times*, August 23, 1.

Hansell, S. (2006a). AOL removes search data on vast group of web users. *The New York Times*, August 8, 4.

Hansell, S. (2006b). Advertisers trace paths users leave on internet. *The New York Times*, August 15, 1.

Häubl, G. & Trifts, V. (2000). Consumer decision making in online shopping environments: The effect of interactive decision aids. *Marketing Science, 19*(1), 4-21.

Heinström, J. (2005). Fast surfing, broad scanning and deep diving: The influence of personality and study approach on students' information-seeking behavior. *Journal of Documentation, 61*(2), 228-247.

Ho, S.Y. (2005). An exploratory study of using a user remote tracker to examine web users' personality traits. *ICEC '05*, August 15-17.

Huneke, M.E., Cole, C. & Levin, I.P. (2004). How varying levels of knowledge and motivation affect search and confidence during consideration and choice. *Marketing Letters, 15*(2&3), 67-79.

Hupfer, M.E. (2001). *Self-Concept orientation and response to agentic and communal advertising messages.* Unpublished Doctoral Thesis, University of Alberta, Edmonton.

Hupfer, M.E., & Detlor, B. (2006). Gender and web information seeking: A self-concept orientation model. *Journal of the American Society for Information Science & Technology, 57*(8), 1105-1115.

Hupfer, M.E., & Detlor, B. (2007a). Beyond gender differences: Self-concept orientation and relationship-building applications on the Internet. *Journal of Business Research, 60*(6), 613-619.

Hupfer, M.E., & Detlor, B. (2007b). Sex, gender and self-concept: Predicting web shopping site design preferences. In Detlor, B., Hassanein, K., & Head M. (Eds.), *Proceedings of the 8th World Congress on the Management of E-Business (WCMeB),* July 11-13, Toronto, Canada. Los Alamitos, California: IEEE Computer Society.

Marshall, K.P. & Swartwout N. (2006). Marketing and internet professionals' fiduciary responsibility: A perspective on spyware. *Journal of Internet Commerce, 5*(3), 109-128.

Martin, B.A.S., Sherrard, M.J., & Wentzel, D. (2005). The role of sensation seeking and need for cognition on web-site evaluations: A resource-matching perspective. *Psychology and Marketing, 22*(2), 109-126.

Moe, W.W. (2003). Buying, searching or browsing: differentiating between online shoppers using in-store navigational clickstream. *Journal of Consumer Psychology, 13*(1&2), 29-40.

Moorthy, S., Ratchford, B.T., & Talukdar, D. (1997). Consumer information search revisited: Theory and empirical analysis. *Journal of Consumer Research, 23*(4), 263-277.

Murata, T., & Saito, K. (2006). Extracting users' interests from web log data. *Proceedings of the IEEE/WIC/ACM International Conference on Web Intelligence (WI'06).*

Palmquist, R.A. & Kim, K.S. (2000). Cognitive style and on-line database search experience as predictors of web search performance. *Journal of the American Society for Information Science, 51*(6), 558-566.

Payne, J.W., Bettman, J.R., and Johnson, E.J. (1993), *The adaptive decision maker.* Cambridge UK: Cambridge University Press.

Riding, R.J., & Cheema I. (1991). Cognitive styles – an overview and integration. *Educational Psychology, 11,* 193-215.

Roy, M., & Chi, M. T. H. (2003). Gender differences in patterns of searching the web. *Journal of Educational Computing Research, 29*(3), 335-348.

Saracevic, T. (1991). Individual differences in organizing, searching and retrieving information. *Proceedings of the American Society for Information Science, 28,* 82-86.

Sen, A., Dacin, P. A., & Pattichis, C. (2006). Current Trends in Web Data Analysis. *Communications of the ACM, 49*(11), 85-91.

Srivastava, J., Cooley, R., Deshpande, M., & Tan, P.N. (2000). Web usage mining: Discovery and applications of usage patterns from web data. *ACM SIGKDD Explorations, 1*(2), 12-23.

Toms, E. & Trifts, V. (2006). When limited cognitive resources meet unlimited information sources: Factors influencing consumers' allocation of web-based search effort. *Proceedings of the 7th World Congress on the Management of eBusiness*, July, Halifax, Canada.

Tuten, T.L. & Bosnjak. M. (2001). Understanding differences in web usage: The role of need for cognition and the five-factor model of personality. *Social Behavior and Personality, 29*(4), 391-398.

Vakkari, P. (1999). Task complexity, problem structure and information actions: Integrating studies on information seeking and retrieval. *Information Processing and Management, 35*(6), 819-837.

Wang, P., Hawk, W.B. & Tenopir, C. (2000). Users' interaction with world wide web resources: An exploratory study using a holistic approach. *Information Processing and Management, 36,* 229-251.

WebTrends. (2005). *Best practices for accurate web analytics: Avoiding third-party cookie rejection and deletion.* Portland, OR: WebTrends

Wildemuth, B. & Hughes, A. (2005). Perspectives on the tasks in which information behaviors are embedded. In Fisher, K.E., Erdelez, S. & McKechnie, L. (Eds.), *Theories of information behavior.* Medford, NJ: Information Today, for the American Society for Information Science & Technology, 275-279.

Wilson, T. D. (1999). Models in information behaviour research. *Journal of Documentation, 55*(3), 249-270.

Wilson, T.D., & Walsh, C. (1996), *Information behavior: An interdisciplinary perspective.* Sheffield: University of Sheffield Department of Information Studies.

Winett, B. (1998). *Tracking your visitors.* Retrieved May 10, 2007, from WebMonkey Tracking Tutorial, http://www.webmonkey.com/e-business/tracking/tutorials/tutorial2.html.

Wu, K.-l., Yu, P. S., & Ballman, A. (1998). Speedtracer: A web usage mining and analysis tool. *IBM Systems Journal, 37*(1), 89-105.

Zaiane, O. R., Xin, M., & Han, J. (1998). Discovering web access patterns and trends by applying olap and data mining technology on web logs. *Proceedings of the IEEE Forum on Reasearch and Technology Advances in Digital Libraries*, Santa Barbara, CA.

Zeller Jr., T. (2006a). Privacy vs. viewing the internet user as a commodity. *The New York Times*, August 12, 1.

Zeller Jr., T. (2006b). AOL acts on release of data. *The New York Times*, August 22, 1.

KEY TERMS

Individual Differences: The demographic and psychological characteristics of people that distinguish one person from another.

Information Seeking Behavior: Refers to how people seek information in different contexts (Fisher, Erdelez & McKechnie, 2005).

Task: In this chapter, refers to the information seeking task an individual user experiences that instills a need for information and motivates the user to satisfy this information need through some sort of information seeking behavior. Task is the context surrounding a person's information need.

Web Information Seeking Behavior: Refers to information seeking behaviors that occur over the Web. Choo, Detlor & Turnbull (2000) identify four main modes of information seeking on the Web ranging from wayward browsing to goal-directed search (undirected viewing, conditioned viewing, informal search, and formal search) where each mode is characterized by predominant information seeking moves or activities (undirected viewing: starting and chaining; conditioned viewing: browsing and differentiating; informal search: differentiating, monitoring, and extracting; and formal search: monitoring and extracting).

Web Metrics: Pertains to the measures by which to assess a person's Web information seeking behavior or to assess and monitor activity on a Website. Examples of commonly used Web metrics include page views, page transitions, and session times.

Web Tracking: Refers to the automated collection of Web information seeking behavioral data.

APPENDIX A: INDIVIDUAL DIFFERENCES QUESTIONNAIRE

Note that some of these questions and their responses pertain to the City of Hamilton and a Canadian context. Modifications would be necessary if administered to a different sample population.

Age
How old are you?
- Under 18
- 18-24
- 25-29
- 30-34
- 35-39
- 40-44
- 44-49
- 50-54
- 55-59
- 60-64
- 65+
- Prefer not to say

Sex
Are you?
- Male
- Female
- Prefer not to say

Race
How would you classify yourself?
- Aboriginal
- Asian
- Black
- East Indian
- Hispanic/Latino
- Middle Eastern
- Multi-Racial
- West Indian
- White
- Other
- Prefer not to say

Kind of area you live in
Which of the following best describes the area you live in?
- Urban
- Suburban

Rural
Prefer not to say

Location in Hamilton

Which geographical area of Hamilton best categorizes the area you live in?

Hamilton East
Hamilton Central
Hamilton West
Dundas
Ancaster
Flamborough
Stoney Creek
Mountain West
Mountain East
Mountain Central
Other
Prefer not to say

Language

At a general conversational level, which of the following languages do you speak? Indicate all that apply.

English
French
Arabic
Bengali
Cantonese
German
Hindi/Urdu
Indonesian
Italian
Japanese
Mandarin
Polish
Portuguese
Russian
Spanish
Other
Prefer not to say

Marital Status

What is your current marital status?

Single (never married)
Co-habiting
Married

Separated/Divorced
Widow/Widower
Prefer not to say

Education

What is your highest education level obtained?

Primary School
Secondary (High) School
Vocational/Technical/Community College
University Undergraduate (bachelors degree)
University Graduate (masters/professional/doctoral degree)
Prefer not to say

Occupation

Your current primary employment status is

Employed
Unemployed
Student
Retired
Other
Prefer not to say

Occupation (cont'd)

Which of the following categories best describes the **industry** you primarily work in (regardless of your actual position)?

Agriculture
Arts, Entertainment, and Recreation
Broadcasting
Construction
Fishing & Hunting
Education
    College, University, and Adult Education
    Primary/Secondary (K-12) Education
    Other Education Industry
Finance and Insurance
Forestry,
Government and Public Administration
Health Care and Social Assistance
Homemaker
Hotel and Food Service
Information Industry
    Information Services and Data Processing
    Other Information Industry
Legal Services

Manufacturing
Computer and Electronics Manufacturing
Other Manufacturing
Military
Mining
Publishing
Software
Telecommunications
Transportation and Warehousing
Real Estate, Rental and Leasing
Religious
Retail
Scientific or Technical Services
Utilities
Wholesale
Other Industry
Prefer not to say

Which of the following best describes your role in industry?

Administrative Staff
Consultant
Junior Management
Middle Management
Researcher
Self-employed/Partner
Skilled Laborer
Student
Support Staff
Temporary Employee
Trained Professional
Upper Management
Other
Prefer not to say

The organization you work for is in which of the following:

Public sector (e.g., government)
Not-for-profit sector
Other
Private sector (e.g. most businesses and individuals)
Don't know
Prefer not to say

Household Composition

What is the number of adults 18 and over living in your household?

0 1 2 3+ Prefer not not say

What is the number of children age 4 and under living in your household?:

0 1 2 3+ Prefer not not say

What is the number of children ages 5 to 9 living in your household?:

0 1 2 3+ Prefer not not say

What is the number of children ages 10 to 13 living in your household?:

0 1 2 3+ Prefer not not say

What is the number of children ages 14 to 17 living in your household?:

0 1 2 3+ Prefer not not say

Household Income

What is your household income before taxes?

Less than $20,000
$20,000-$39,999
$40,000-$59,000
$60,000-$79,999
$80,000-$99,999
$100,000-$119,999
$120,000-$139,999
$140,000-$159,999
$160,000-$179,999
$180,000-$199,999
More than $200,000
Prefer not to say

Years on the Internet

How long have you been using the Internet (including using email, gopher, ftp, etc.)?

Less than 6 months
6 to 12 months
1 to 3 years
4 to 6 years
7 years or more
Prefer not to say

Community Building

Complete the following sentence in the way that comes closest to your own views: 'Since getting on the Internet, I have...'

Become MORE connected with people like me
Become LESS connected with people like me
Become EQUALLY connected with people like me
Don't know
Prefer not to say

Self- versus Other-Orientation *(taken from Hupfer, 2001)*
Rate each item below according to how well you think these statements describe you.
(Utilize a 9-point scale: "never true of me" 1 2 3 4 5 6 7 8 9 "always true of me"; 0 = "Prefer not to say"):
I am a nurturing person
I am a self-sufficient person
I am understanding
I make my own choices
I am a compassionate person
I am my own person
I am self-reliant
I am sympathetic
I am sensitive to the needs of others
I am an independent person

Computer Proficiency
Indicate the extent to which you agree with the following statements (Utilize a 7-point scale of "strongly disagree 1 2 3 4 5 6 7 strongly agree; 0 = "Prefer not to say"):

I am highly competent at...
... creating and editing documents in a word processor
... creating and maintaining electronic spreadsheets of data
... creating and maintaining data tables & records in a database progra
... sending and receiving email messages
... searching for information utilizing a Web search engine (like 'Google')

Web Skill Test
Which of the following have you done? (Check all that apply)

- Ordered a product / service from a business, government or educational entity by filling out a form on the web
- Made a purchase online for more than $100
- Created a Webpage
- Customized a Webpage for yourself (e.g. MyYahoo, CNN Custom News)
- Changed your browser's "startup" or "home" page
- Changed your "cookie" preferences
- Participated in an online chat or discussion (not including email)
- Listened to a radio broadcast online
- Made a telephone call online
- Used a nationwide online directory to find an address or telephone number
- Taken a seminar or class about the Web or Internet
- Bought a book to learn more about the Web or Internet
- Did Internet banking
- Prefer not to say

Technology Comfort

How comfortable do you feel using computers, in general?

- Very comfortable
- Somewhat comfortable
- Neither comfortable nor uncomfortable
- Somewhat uncomfortable
- Very uncomfortable
- Prefer not to say

How comfortable do you feel using the Internet?

- Very comfortable
- Somewhat comfortable
- Neither comfortable nor uncomfortable
- Somewhat uncomfortable
- Very uncomfortable
- Prefer not to say

How satisfied are you with your current skills for using the Internet?

- Very satisfied - I can do everything that I want to do
- Somewhat satisfied - I can do most things I want to do
- Neither satisfied nor unsatisfied
- Unsatisfied - I can't do many things I would like to do
- Very unsatisfied - I can't do most things I would like to do
- Prefer not to say

Frequency of Accessing the Web from Different Locations

From home (including a home office)

- Daily
- Weekly
- Monthly
- Less than once a month
- Never
- Prefer not to say

From work:

- Daily
- Weekly
- Monthly
- Less than once a month
- Never
- Prefer not to say

From school:

- Daily
- Weekly
- Monthly

Less than once a month
Never
Prefer not to say

From public terminals (e.g., a library terminal, public kiosk):
Daily
Weekly
Monthly
Less than once a month
Never
Prefer not to say

From other places:
Daily
Weekly
Monthly
Less than once a month
Never
Prefer not to say

Connection to the Internet

Which of the following connection speeds do you primarily use to connect to the Internet? (Round to the closest value if necessary.) If you access the Internet at home via a commercial provider, choose the speed from you to your Internet provider:

Regular dial-up (through your phone company)
DSL low-speed (through your phone company)
DSL high-speed (through your phone company)
Cable (through your cable provider)
Do not know
Prefer not to say

Number of personal computers

How many personal computers are in your household (including laptops, but not including electronic organizers)?:

0 1 2 3 or more Prefer not not say

Perceptions of Web-based Information Seeking *(taken from Ford & Miller, 1996)*

Rate each item below according to how well you think these statements describe you. (Utilize a 5-point scale: "strongly agree" 1 2 3 4 5 "strongly disagree"; 0 = "Prefer not to say")

- I usually only look at things on the Internet that have been suggested to me.
- Despite its complexity, I generally manage to find my way around the Internet fairly effectively.
- I rarely find anything useful on the Internet.
- I usually manage to keep 'on target' and avoid too much irrelevant material when using the Internet.
- I'm prepared to plough through quite a lot of irrelevant information in case there's something useful I might otherwise miss on the Internet.

- If I had to choose only one, I'd prefer keyword searching to browsing (hypertext) on the Internet.
- The Internet is too unstructured for my liking.
- I personally think that the graphical elements of the World Wide Web (i.e., pictures, icons, graphics, etc. as opposed to just text) make me much more likely to use the Internet than if it were just text-based.
- When I use the Internet, I feel as though I'm not as 'in control' as I would like.
- My advice to someone like me would be: The best way to learn to use the Internet is to explore everything broadly to get a comparative 'feel' of the various aspects/tools before getting down to mastering one in any depth.
- I tend to get lost when using the Internet.
- It's best to use the Internet only when you have a well-defined plan (rather than just browsing around).

APPENDIX B: THE TASK SURVEY

Perception of task importance

For you personally,

1. How important is it to do this task online?
   "not important at all" 1 2 3 4 5 6 7 8 9 "very important"
2. How useful is it to do this task online?
   "not useful at all" 1 2 3 4 5 6 7 8 9 "very useful"
3. How critical is it do this task online?
   "not critical at all" 1 2 3 4 5 6 7 8 9 "very critical"

Attitude towards a particular task

4. I have positive feelings towards doing this task online.
   "strongly disagree" 1 2 3 4 5 6 7 8 9 "strongly agree"
5. The thought of doing this task online is appealing to me.
   "strongly disagree" 1 2 3 4 5 6 7 8 9 "strongly agree"
6. It is a good idea to be able to do that task online.
   "strongly disagree" 1 2 3 4 5 6 7 8 9 "strongly agree"

Chapter XIV
Identifying Users Stereotypes for Dynamic Web Pages Customization

Sandro José Rigo
Universidade Federal do Rio Grande do Sul (UFRGS), Brazil

José Palazzo M. de Oliveira
Universidade Federal do Rio Grande do Sul (UFRGS), Brazil

Leandro Krug Wives
Universidade Federal do Rio Grande do Sul (UFRGS), Brazil

ABSTRACT

Adaptive Hypermedia is an effective approach to automatic personalization that overcomes the difficulties and deficiencies of traditional Web systems in delivering the appropriate content to users. One important issue regarding Adaptive Hypermedia systems is the construction and maintenance of the user profile. Another important concern is the use of Semantic Web resources to describe Web applications and to implement adaptation mechanisms. Web Usage Mining, in this context, allows the generation of Websites access patterns. This chapter describes the possibilities of integration of these usage patterns with semantic knowledge obtained from domain ontologies. Thus, it is possible to identify users' stereotypes for dynamic Web pages customization. This integration of semantic knowledge can provide personalization systems with better adaptation strategies.

INTRODUCTION

With the enormous quantity of documents that are now available on the Web, accessing and collecting the desired and relevant data has become a difficult task that produces low quality results. The Websites adaptation allows the minimization of this problem as an adaptive application generates

Website content or the structure in accordance with a class of users. In fact, the personalization aspects are a critical factor for the successful user experience. As a personalization example, it is common now to find several customization options in an increasing number of Websites. The reasons for this are due to the diversity of users and its experience, intents, needs, preferences and even available equipment and software. The design of a Website with thousands of daily visitors will face hard time to fulfill these very different expectations. The personalization resources available can help users to have a more personal interaction, by observing their needs and preferences.

There are many different definitions for "Web personalization" in the literature. In a more general sense, it is considered as a set of actions that fine-tune the results of some user interaction, regarding this user or a set of similar users (Mobasher, 2005). The practical personalization depends on the context. For an e-Commerce Website it may be related to the set of products that are shown to the user each time he logs on, but for other applications it may refer to the interface organization, the navigational structure and content options. All approaches have their specific problems and some of them are hybrid, combining their better techniques (Middleton, 2004; Kleinberg 2004). It is important to notice that a superior result for the personalization requires not only an efficient approach to the analysis of the contents or users behaviors, but it is also dependent on the Website life cycle. The personalization application should be integrated with tasks such as content management, users profile management, adaptation strategies and interface generation. These tasks are well known in Adaptive Hypermedia initiatives.

Adaptive Hypermedia (Brusilovsky, 2004, 2001; De Bra, 1999) has as its objective the establishment of better user experiences by adapting hyper-documents and hypermedia to the users' needs, preferences and goals. Usability improvement is achieved with the construction of models that represent the users' objectives, preferences, previous knowledge, and skills. The use of these models, together with some complementary information as context, usage records or adaptation rules, allows the identification of possible topics of interest, restrictions and personalization options. In addition, domain information is very important in this process and drives the adaptation choices. This can be with respect to different aspects of a Website, such as its content or structure. Briefly put, this adaptation is based on the relationship between information concerning the application domain and information regarding the user profile.

One important topic in Adaptive Hypermedia systems research is the generation and maintenance of the users' profiles. Some approaches create the user profile from data obtained at the registration process, others incorporate the results of interviews and some perform automatic acquisition of information tracking the resources usage. In general, the profile based on the user identification tends to generate information valid over long periods. In some circumstances, short-term information can also be very useful and this kind of profile relies almost exclusively on the user interaction.

Web Usage Mining originates in prior Data Mining research with the purpose of automatic or semi-automatic discovery of Websites users' access patterns to generate information to be used by recommendation systems or by personalization systems (Mobasher, 2005). Analyzing the approaches to the generation of users' profiles by Web Usage Mining, a general pattern is identified and involves several stages (Markelou, 2005; Woon, 2005) that are briefly cited. The first is the acquisition of usage data. The second stage is dedicated to the pre-processing of data and the identification of access sessions amongst other necessary adjustments due to the Web environment (proxy servers, cookies or access errors, for example). At the end of the second stage, data is organized in appropriate formats for patterns mining where association rules and clusters can be generated or frequent pathways indicated. The third and last stage deals with the analysis and handling of these patterns in specific applications or contexts.

From the analysis of the obtained patterns, clusters identified or validated association rules, it is possible to generate complementary information to support the adaptation stage of Adaptive Hypermedia systems. Nevertheless, it should be clarified that the patterns are obtained mainly with the access information present in the data for each user session. As mentioned, Web Usage Mining makes possible the capture and analysis of the behavior characteristics of Website users allowing the use of mechanisms directed toward personalization and adaptation (Aldenderfer, 1984; Brusilovsky, 2004). Despite being appropriate, this approach can be extended and improved by the use of semantic information associated with content access and navigation information.

An Adaptive Hypermedia application can discover better personalization choices by relating the semantic knowledge of a domain application, such as structural relations, with the usage information, such as navigation patterns. Some complex objects and some specific relation will not be treated with content-based or user-based techniques, as they have no representation in these systems. The representation of such complex objects and relations is possible with a domain ontology, which provides constructs for concepts and its relations definition. In a Website case, ontology provides the content concepts description, the hierarchies between them and the representation of some other existing relations. Domain ontology can be constructed by experts, manually. It can also be accomplished by using Machine Learning, Web Mining and Natural Language Processing techniques. The nature of the application can suggest the more suitable technique or combination.

The use of semantic knowledge, along with usage information, can lead to better knowledge discovery, by treating relations not applied in the other techniques. In general, this improvement takes two forms, which are the use of the semantic information in the pre-processing stage, enriching the pattern generation, or the use of the semantic information in the last stage, in combination with the adaptation itself (De Bra, 2004).

This chapter describes some possibilities for the acquisition of user profiles based on Web Usage Mining and domain ontologies. The main objective is to present the integration of semantic information obtained through the Website domain ontology with usage information obtained from the data gathered from user sessions. In addition, there is the intention to bring information to discuss if it is possible to identify more precisely the interests and needs of a typical user with these resources. The following sections provide some important background information on the Web personalization and Web Mining, ontology construction and semantic integration possibilities. The requirements for the semantic knowledge and usage information integration are discussed and finally some aspects of an Adaptive Hypermedia application based on the concepts of semantic application modeling are presented.

BACKGROUND

This section describes some concepts related to the main topic of this chapter. It provides the necessary background to the analysis of related works presented in the next section and to understand the integration approach described.

Web Personalization

The definition of Web personalization is found in the literature with some variations. In a general form, it is considered as a set of actions that adjust the results of user interaction, regarding this user or a set of users (Mobasher, 2000). In some cases, like an online bookstore, it corresponds to products indications. The scope for this kind of personalization can be very broad, ranging from items such as books or music to stocks, computers or cars. Another personalization example is the flexible organization of the user interface or the selection of contents. For example, the layout elements can be presented with more textual information, with differences in graphic elements, the options displayed in menus or the hyperlinks may be organized in more adequate manner for some user and the content may be more concise or have more details.

The approaches for the personalization can be grouped in content-based, collaborative-filtering or in some hybrid forms with both characteristics. Its differences rely on the strategies and information used to the personalization options generation.

In the content-based approach, the users' personal profiles represent mainly their interests. The Websites content is classified with respect to some subjects. Some metrics to evaluate the subject proximity to the users' interests are then applied for the generation of personalization. This approach can be found in several works, with small variations, but the principal aspect is the adaptation of a Website based on the preferences of the user (Lieberman, 1995; Mladenic, 1999; Mikroyannidis, 2004). Some advantages are found in this approach in situations as Web Information Retrieval, allowing the filtering of a large amount of pages based on the user profile. For example, a Website about movies can personalize the user navigation based on the previous shown interests and the options in the movies database. While this advantage can be relevant, it may also characterize some ineffective situations, when the user has a new interest, in an area not yet described in the profile. Another problem is that some useful semantic relations cannot be applied, as in cases of a more specific or more general approach for the same topic or in cases of different objects used in the same process and thus related.

The collaborative filtering techniques do not perform analysis in the content, but instead they focus on the preferences or activities associated with a specific user. These are then compared with all the other users and can lead to the identification of a set of users with common interests and preferences. There are several options to identify these relations, as the access to similar Web pages, the purchase of related items, the choice of similar options, the selection of similar feedback in ratings options and so on. Once the set of users with similar interests is defined, the personalization can be carried out by observing items not purchased or pages not accessed by a specific user, for instance. As the set of users is found to have the same preferences, it is assumed that one individual in this set can be interested in the same operations performed by the others. This technique, also known as user-based, can present problems in some situations, as in the publication of a new page or the release of a new product. Since the users do not have the necessary time to access, the item cannot be associated with some personalization action (Konstan, 1997; Balabanovic, 1997; Sugiyama 2004).

Some approaches using both techniques are known (Middleton, 2001; Kleinberg, 2004) and can be found as a way of reducing the limitations of each one. With both content and user preferences information the personalization system can be adapted to perform its tasks in a more efficient way.

Web Mining

Web Mining is defined as the discovery and analysis of useful information on the Web, with the objective of identifying behavior, characteristics, trends and navigation patterns (Cook, 2000; Kosala, 2000). There are three main areas of interest in Web Mining, described as Web Content Mining, Web Structure Mining and Web Usage Mining (Zaiane, 2000; Mobasher, 2005). Each of these is associated with some specific data collection originated in the records of Web Server activity, in the Website structure or in its content.

Web Content Mining is the process of extracting useful information from the content of Web documents. The Web content can be unstructured (plain text documents), structured (when dynamic pages exhibits content from databases) or semi-structured (HTML documents). The results can help information retrieval operations and personalization systems (Popov, 2003; LeGrand, 2002; Alani, 2003; Loh, 2000). The main advantage of this approach is the possibility to discover and classify documents and Web pages with respect to their content.

The Web Structure mining is the process of knowledge discovery driven by the Websites links structure. The topology of a site, its organization and the link structure are used to identify patterns. Some useful information extracted from these patterns can be, for instance, the identification of pages that represents collection of specific information, or collections of general information, with a large number of references, like in the concept of hubs and authorities. There are some examples of algorithms such as HITS (Kleinberg, 1999) and PageRank (Brin, 1998), that are based on this kind of data.

The objective of Web Usage Mining is to identify browsing patterns. This is achieved by analyzing the navigational behavior of a group of users. The information necessary to do this is available mainly in Web server log files. Web Usage Mining is carried out in well-defined stages, already mentioned in the text. These are the acquisition of usage data, pre-processing, analysis and usage. In the following sections, these stages are briefly described and discussed.

The first phase involved in the process of Web Usage Mining is concerned with the usage data processing. The processed data is extracted from the Web Server access log files or is generated from a script code included in the Web pages. One of the advantages of both forms of data collection is that they allow a Data Mining approach to the generation of user models for a specific Website, given the ability to obtain the data that is automatically generated when the pages of a Web site are accessed.

These access log files, created by Web Server software, were originally meant to aid debugging and to perform some simple statistics operations (Kohavi, 2001). The Common Log Format (Nielsen, 1995) is widely used, despite the existence of some improvements in other similar formats, like in the Extended Common Log Format and in other proprietary options. The Common Log Format is structured in text documents where each line represents a request or part of one. The main fields are the remote host identification, the remote user identification and login name, the date and time of the request, the exact request line received from the client, a code which indicates whether or not the file was successfully retrieved and the number of bytes actually transferred. The Extended Common Log Format adds two fields, the referrer and the user agent. The first indicates the URL accessed by the client browser before the request. The second indicates the browser software used in the request. In these formats, when some information is not available, it is replaced in the log with a minus sign ('-'). A few lines of a typical log file are shown in Figure 1.

Figure 1. Extended Common Log Format example

```
66.249.64.47 - - [13/Feb/2005:04:15:13 -0200] "GET /cursos/intercambios/apresentacao/corpo.htm HTTP/1.0" 304 - "-"
"Googlebot/2.1 (+http://www.google.com/bot.html)"
10.21.213.93 - - [13/Feb/2005:04:15:20 -0200] "GET /_imagens/capa/banners/ban_extravest.jpg HTTP/1.1" 200 2968
"https://www1.unisinos.br/" "Mozilla/4.0 (compatible; MSIE 6.0; Windows NT 5.2; .NET CLR 1.1.4322)"
```

Some problems can be observed. The verbose structure of these log files tend to be very expensive to process, because each single transaction made by the Web Server is stored in the file. Some of these are not relevant for the mining activity, for example, the retrieval of an individual image file, CSS (Cascading Style Sheet) or a script file. There is also a difficulty in the user identification, which requires some extra processing. Since the user identification and its sessions are important information, the mining systems need to use some heuristics. The date and time, along with the remote host identification are applied to separate the session log information.

To overcome some limitations observed in the log files processing, there is another approach that uses some specific script code, embedded in the pages displayed to the users. This process allows the recording of the real actions performed, without cache or proxy problems, and in real time, while the log file approach involves an offline processing step (Peterson, 2005). The preprocessing phase is simplified with these systems, because the transaction data is already stored in an appropriate form. However, this is achieved with some additional costs in each page view. These costs are due to the scripts embedded in the pages. Some are executed when the page is generated, while others are executed at the page restitution by the Web browser, by client-side script languages such as JavaScript (Netscape, 1998).

The tasks involved in this first preprocessing phase starts with data cleaning, when the log file is examined and some irrelevant entries are removed. Examples are the entries related to software robots doing crawling activities, or related to the structure of the pages as in the case of frames utilization. The next task is the user and session identification. Since the log files can be employed without user identification, there exists the necessity of processing the records to identify users, in general with information such as IP (Internet Protocol) numbers, date and time of the access. When some user, an individual accessing the site not a specific person, is identified, there is also the necessity of session identification, because it can be of importance for some mining process to identify different sessions of a user. There are also peculiar situations to deal with, as in the case of the use of cache mechanisms in the client software (the Web navigator), in the occurrence of errors or in the case of missing stored information in cookies.

After the processing and adjustments in the original data available, different techniques are applied in the knowledge discovery, such as sequential pattern mining, association rule mining, clustering and classification. The most frequent are the association rule and the sequential pattern mining. The first relates items and are used to identify groups of pages visited in similar ways by users. The second allows the most employed sequences of pages to be found. The other techniques are applied to group users into similar interest sets and to identify users in predefined interests groups.

Each technique mentioned can present results that are adequate to different tasks in the final phase, the adaptation or personalization. More details are described in the following sections.

Semantic Web

The Semantic Web initiative has the objective of solving some deficiencies observed in the traditional Web and implementing some improvements to the present possibilities of automated Web content processing. The first task in this direction is the description of documents in a more structured manner, allowing software agents to automatically manipulate such documents. In less structured languages, such as HTML, it is not possible to automatically perform tasks that depend on the documents content. As stated by Berners-Lee et al. (2001), these structured documents along with domain ontologies and inferences mechanisms can overcome the actual weakness of the Web. Documents in the Web are easily accessed by humans, but are not available to some automatic use.

One of the main requirements is the use of URI (Universal Resource Identifier). Another is the use of Unicode (Unicode Consortium, 2006) for codification, in order to ensure platform interoperability. The proper separation between structure and content in the documents is achieved with the use of XML language (Freitas, 2003). If some metadata pattern, such as RDF (Resource Description Framework) (Herman, 2007), is utilized, it is also possible to describe information about the document. This can be very useful and helps to annotate the semantics of documents with information that can be automatically processed enabling a large number of new applications. When this metadata are described in accordance with some user's community standard, they provide the means for a consistent terminology to be at the disposal of several applications. As an example, the "Dublin Core Metadata Initiative" (Dublin Core, 2007) can be cited. It was originated from an open organization engaged in the development of metadata standards that created the "Dublin Core Metadata Element Set" which is widely known and used in resources descriptions. In this metadata set, elements as "creator", "contributor", "coverage", "date", "subject" and others are described with a precise meaning. Its adoption by communities allows precise information exchange, by documents with metadata annotation.

For some operations, the minimal metadata annotation can be insufficient. Descriptions that are more effective can be done with ontologies, in which a set of concepts and relations belonging to a particular domain may be shared. In this case it is possible to achieve more effective treatment of the documents information, with diverse objectives, as Information Retrieval, Electronic Commerce, Distance Learning or Data Integration, to name a few possibilities (Hendler, 2002; Nilsson, 2003). There exist some specific languages for the ontology description, as the OWL (Ontology Web Language) (Herman, 2006) which have the objective of precise concepts and relations description. According to Heflin (2004), this language supports the ontology description and integration, along with inference and query operations. The ontology creation can be done manually, by an expert in the specific domain, or automatically, using some Machine Learning techniques (Fensel, 2001; Fensel, 2002). Some principles, already indicated by Grubber (1993), must be adopted, including coherence, clear description of terms or facilities for ontology extension. The ontology editor usually verifies some other principles, as its correction.

The possibilities for ontology application depend on the knowledge acquisition operation, which can be a difficult task. Some Websites have a large number of pages and the manual creation of an ontology that describes the Website can be unfeasible. For this situation, it is useful to apply automatic creation mechanisms.

Adaptive Hypermedia

Several Adaptive Hypermedia systems were developed by different research groups and address different application areas. The best known are those for education, information retrieval and tourism, library and museum support. Some systems have identification options that connect the users with the profile information. Others are driven by non-invasive techniques and try to get the information for the profile generation in an automatic way (Dolog, 2004). The large volume, the diversity in formats and the great rate of information generation and update makes it hard to treat manually in an adequate form to the different users. In addition, the great number of users and diversity in interests and preferences makes it difficult to generate an efficient and usable interface in a system without adaptive options (De Bra, 2004).

The research in the Adaptive Hypermedia field has the objective of improving the users' satisfaction while using these systems. This usability improvement is achieved by the construction of models that can represent the knowledge, skills, objectives and preferences of the users. Besides the user modeling, some specific techniques are observed in the interface construction and in the usage recording. Some complementary information, as the application context, usage data, adaptation rules, allows for the identification of possible topics of interest and useful adaptations (Brusilovsky, 1996; De Bra, 1999).

To make possible the adaptation, the documents should be related to the domain model and its concepts. These can be more general (broad concepts), can represent groups with topics about a general subject or can describe specific information about some topic. The possible relations will be at the system disposal and the contents can be related to the domain model (Wu, 2002).

The system's generic operation can use these descriptions, in different tasks. The first one is the recording of the users' behavior. In Internet systems, this behavior can be associated with sequences of page accesses, for instance. A second task is to apply some processing method over the user model to classify the content information, regarding its profile. The third one is to combine this information to generate the interface, according to the identified possibilities.

The user profile can be composed of information that is valid over long or short time periods. Normally data with a long period of validity requires the identification of the user to be correctly acquired. In the context of educational systems, it is desirable and even necessary that the system user be identified to allow the update of the profile of the accessed information. In other circumstances, however, this identification could be undesirable for the users, and even be unnecessary given that it is also possible to obtain good results when the adaptation of a Web site is based on a class of users, represented by stereotypes, rather than on specific users. The user profile can be generated based on knowledge or behavior. The knowledge-based approach, that tends to make use of static models, can apply tools as interviews, tests and questionnaires. The behavior-based approach employs data from the users' interaction. These data can be from different periods and are applied in order to extract useful patterns (Middleton, 2004; Kobsa, 1993).

The adaptation in Adaptive Hypermedia systems refers to the contents and its presentation form - information is presented with different details. In addition, the information can be shown in an interface with more text or more images, some specific color configuration or with auxiliary media, as sound, video or animations (Christopher, 2002). Also the new devices' capabilities requires that some specific information initially applied to only one context will be sent now to a diversity of devices, with varied capabilities in memory, display and processing power (Petrelli, 2005). The possibilities of integrating sensors as input to these systems also can be very useful because of the effective interest delimitation that it allows the generation and short cycle of recording, and the inference and adapting process (Zimmerman, 2005).

RELATED WORKS

The Web Mining process can be related to the discovery of knowledge in sources such as the content, the usage records or the structure of Websites. This knowledge can be analyzed and, if considered useful, applied in adaptation or personalization tasks. Some details about the information obtained with these sources can be helpful to identify limitations observed in traditional systems using Web Mining. These limitations are described and related to possible solutions, with the use of some complementary semantic knowledge.

When the content of the pages is treated like a bag of words, it is difficult to the mining process to identify a relation between different pages dealing with the same concept but described with synonyms or hyponyms. As an example, one page can present the term "exercises" and another page can use the term "learning activities" referring to the same concept. Another example is the case of pages with the terms "car" and "gear-box", which, in this approach, will have no relation (in fact, they are composite objects). These situations are treated in several different ways; in some research works, such as Loh et al (2000), concepts are used to describe the contents of documents (which may be Web pages). Concepts are higher-level abstractions that represent ideas, objects and events. They are described by a set of words or even by semantic networks containing synonyms, quasi-synonyms, lexical variations, plural, verb derivations, semantic related words, proper nouns, named entities and abbreviations, multi-words, lexical compounds or noun phrases. Each concept has only one set as a descriptor, but one term may be present in more than one descriptor set. Thus, associated to each term in a concept there must be a weight, describing the relative importance of the term in this concept.

Another limitation found in the traditional process is related with the usage data acquisition and treatment. In this case, the access patterns computed with data from the Web server logs or some other acquisition form can also have some important information for the mining process that is not correctly treated. Since the traditional systems work with the page view concepts, the common results are a cluster of pages or a frequent access pattern. However, the information is restricted to access only. None of the possible relations between the page views is taken into account. As stated before, some interesting conclusions can be obtained from the page views relations analysis. For example, a cluster of visited pages can be used to discover the relations between its pages.

The integration of semantic knowledge, as a way to overcome these limitations, can be found in works that are referred to "Semantic Web Mining", as described by Stumme (2002). The main objective is the integration of domain knowledge with the mining process. Web Usage Mining makes possible the capture and analysis of the behavior characteristics of Website users, for mechanisms directed toward personalization and adaptation (Koutri, 2004; Mobasher and Dai, 2005). This approach is improved with semantic information associated with the Web usage information. The semantic information can be used in the pre-processing stage, enriching the pattern generation, or in the adaptation process (Stume, 2002; Eirinaki, 2006).

The construction of models that are able to represent the knowledge, abilities, goals and preferences of users can be seen in Adaptive Hypermedia systems (Christopher, 2002; Petrelli, 2005; Wu, 2002). Many of these systems maintain identification interfaces and profile characterization of each user, while others use non-invasive techniques and aim to automatically obtain data for the generation and maintenance of the user model (Dolog, 2004). Morales (2006) describes an interesting approach aimed to acquire user models by a specific subsystem that applied semantic Web technologies. The system developed to model learners' behavior is closely coupled with a Web-based educational system and all the user actions are treated as events and related to content elements. This treatment has the objective to create beliefs about the learner that can be validated and stored in the model. In Cantador (2006) there is the description of a strategy to automatically cluster users' profiles based on an ontology that describes domain concepts. As these concepts are used, the system can generate several layers of clusters, each representing some group of users with particular interests.

Some interesting results may be achieved by the collaboration between systems. Since different systems can have partial information about the users, it is interesting to have some form of mediation or collaboration. The systems can benefit from enriching the stored User Model information. Some works are known in this field, as in Berkovsky (2006) and Musa (2005), which suggests the use of resources as Web-services and mediation approaches. Dolog (2004), Nejdl (2003) and Arroyo (2006) present a more detailed discussion about the possibilities of interoperability in personalization systems. The user model is implemented in diverse forms, using the semantic Web resources, as RDF for metadata description. In addition, this metadata annotation can be related to standards for learning modeling, such as PAPI (IEEE LTSC, 2001) and IMS LIP (IMS, 2001). The application of semantic Web resources in the description of elements for the user models is proposed in Ounnas (2006), where some known standards as PAPI, IMS LIP and FOAF (FOAF, 2000) are studied and an extension to FOAF is proposed. From this extension, it is possible to relate information in these models.

In addition to user modeling there are known techniques for the construction of interfaces in a flexible manner and following the usage of these interfaces. These models and complementary information such as the application context, usage data covering user or user group interactions, and adaptation rules, amongst others, permit the identification of possible topics of interest, access restrictions and adaptations of content and format (DeBra, 2004; Brusilovsky, 2004). One example in this direction is the GLAM system (Jacquiot, 2006), that uses a layered model, in order to facilitate the adaptation. The main objective is to implement navigation adaptation, provided by means of actions selection.

The integration of usage information in combination with semantic information produces better results, as reported in the work of Mobasher (2002), where semantic information contained in the ontology of a Website, together with the usage data, is applied in the analysis and generation of clusters and association rules. Thus, the clusters and association rules generated allow correlating the relevant details of each section of the Website. The case study used is a film Website, and with this treatment, the user's choice of a page containing a film description can be associated to several possible actors of user interest, which would not be possible without the semantic description of the pages.

The usage information is also related with some structural data or annotation information. An example can be seen in the work described by Bateman (2006), where the annotation problem is addressed. This work suggests the collaborative annotation approach (CommonFolks) together with document annotation, in an e-learning context. The RDF and LOM patterns are applied. Another example is described in Bechofer (2006), related to conceptual browsing. Ontologies in OWL Language automatically relate hyperlinks from different Websites. This allows the use of the hyperlink structure of Websites in order to discover interesting relations. The metadata and reasoning components can dynamically relate resources.

The problem of content adaptation to users' preferences can also be treated with semantic knowledge, as demonstrated by Aroyo (2006). In this work, ontologies about a domain application allow inferring some specific relations associated with time or lexical relations. This facilitates the recommendations to the user, as it allows the conceptual navigation. Another example is the "Poncelet Project" (Habel, 2006) that applies an ontology describing the concepts in the educational material at the student's disposal. The ontology classifies the resources and relates it to concepts. Then it can provide multiple paths to different students. In addition, it may help in the administration of the resources.

Other works deal with the processing of specific characteristics involved in this process, such as the use of Description Logic techniques as an aid to the processing of semantic information (Esposito, 2004). There are also approaches to the more specific usage of semantic information (for example, similarity) in mining, as in the case of the *Semantically Similar Data Mining*

(SSDM) algorithm (Vieira, 2005), for the mining of association rules taking into account synonym information. Mechanisms for the treatment of sets of data accessed by the user to construct a conceptual map with the objective of revealing their interests can also be observed (Zhong, 2006). There are methods for the identification of users based on the Web usage with the integration of this information with semantic information (Zhou, 2006; Jin, 2005).

In some works the employment of usage information integrated with semantic information is associated with the use of clustering techniques that take into account the set of concepts identified in a group of pages that has been previously reported as a commonly followed path with associative rules or as a cluster (Eirinaki, 2003; Esposito, 2004; Mobasher, 2005). In other cases, the ontology capabilities are used to provide semantic bridges between data resources, as RSS feeds. This can be seen in Conlan (2006), as domain ontologies are applied to personalize the exhibition of news items.

AN INTEGRATION APPROACH

The main purpose of this chapter consists in the description of the integration of Web usage information with semantic information. This integration makes it possible to obtain user classes that are associated with well-defined behavior, observed in the usage of Websites and, finally, to employ this information to generate adaptations without the need to identify specific users. An experiment that illustrates this approach is described. An open source Web Content Management system is used to implement the Web usage data acquisition and to generate the structure adaptations. The pre-processing and the Web Usage Mining steps were implemented independently, and a domain ontology provides the semantic description of the application. Details of the integration process are described below.

Web Usage Mining and Semantic Information Integration

The approach described here intends to be more complete, including not only the usage information adaptations. To accomplish this objective, the process also involves some semantic information regarding the Website structure and some complementary relations, such as content type, precedence and requisites. This information is maintained in a domain ontology, which is described below.

The usage information considered in this approach consists on the frequent sequential paths of the Website users. Considering a set $P = \{p_1, p_2, p_3, ..., p_n\}$ as the set of *n* pages in a Website, then the user access in a session allows the generation of a non empty set $L = \{l_1, l_2, l_3, ..., l_m\}$, where each l_i belong to P. A frequent sequential pattern is the set of repetitive accesses, observed some defined limits of occurrences. The identification of frequent sequential patterns in this work is implemented as an additional stage, using the algorithm known as Spade with the improvements described in the literature (Zaki, 2001; Leleu, 2003).

In the application used for the experiment, the published pages have a specific code that allows the recording of access information. This data is processed in a way that describes the path taken by each user in their visit to the Website (Oliveira, 2006). Figure 2 shows an example of the format and data applied in the access recording process. This format allows the recording of date, time and browser, the page URL, IP number and access parameter. The access origin is recorded in the "userid" element, generated by a cookie created at the first user access. The element "adapt" distinguishes the access between normal or suggested pages.

When the adaptation is based only in the usage information, these frequent sequential patterns are typically consulted at each user interaction in order to verify if the user path have some similarity with the considered patterns. In the case of a

Figure 2. Usage data example


```
<acess>
<ip>201.37.126.43</ip>
<page>/cms01/index.php</page>
<parameter>34</parameter>
<agent>Mozilla/5.0 (...) Gecko/20050717 Firefox/1.0.6</agent>
<date>12/11/2006</date><time>13:04:23</time>
<userid>f4b3173f4a4efb248f6f200c5ce678e3</userid>
<adapt>0</adapt>
</acess>
```


Figure 3. Some access patterns and its interpretation

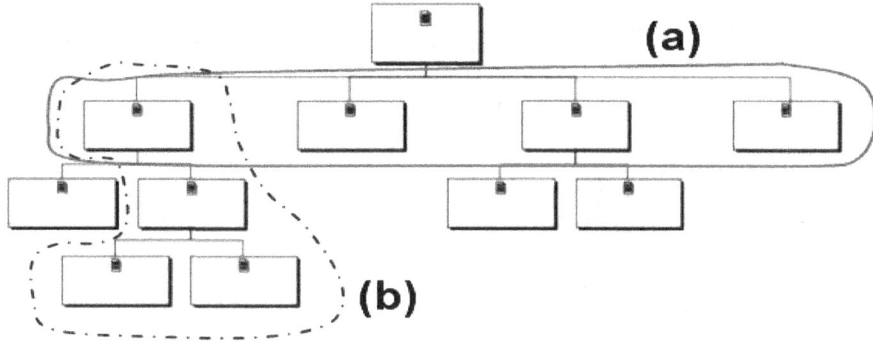

correct match, the system assumes that this user can have some interest for the subsequent pages in the pattern and they are suggested as structure adaptations. Figure 3 shows two different access patterns in a simplified Website structure: the first (a) is composed by the pages indicated by the set with continuous line. The second (b) is identified by the dashed-line set. When using the access information only, it is not possible to identify that the first represents a browsing over general topics and the second represents the navigation inside a specific topic. This information is very important since it allows us to improve the adaptation process.

The ontology allows the definition of concepts, relations and restrictions regarding some application domain, which can be more general or specific. In this work, a more specific approach was chosen. In this case, the ontology is also known as a "domain ontology" and one of its advantages is the possibility of having a more precise mapping of the important concepts and its relations, given the target domain. This choice demands the ontology to be reviewed and rewritten to each (new) application domain.

An experiment to allow the validation of this approach was developed in the educational field. The domain ontology created had as objective to describe relevant concepts to the educational field. The same approach can be applied to different areas, with specific ontologies. The ontology was manually constructed by application domain experts using the Protégé ontology editor (Protégé, 2007), with the OWL language. This representation form facilitates posterior manipulation. In this case, part of the information described in the ontology can be seen in Figure 4 and represents the content available on a Website with educational

Figure 4. Part of the domain ontology used in the experiment

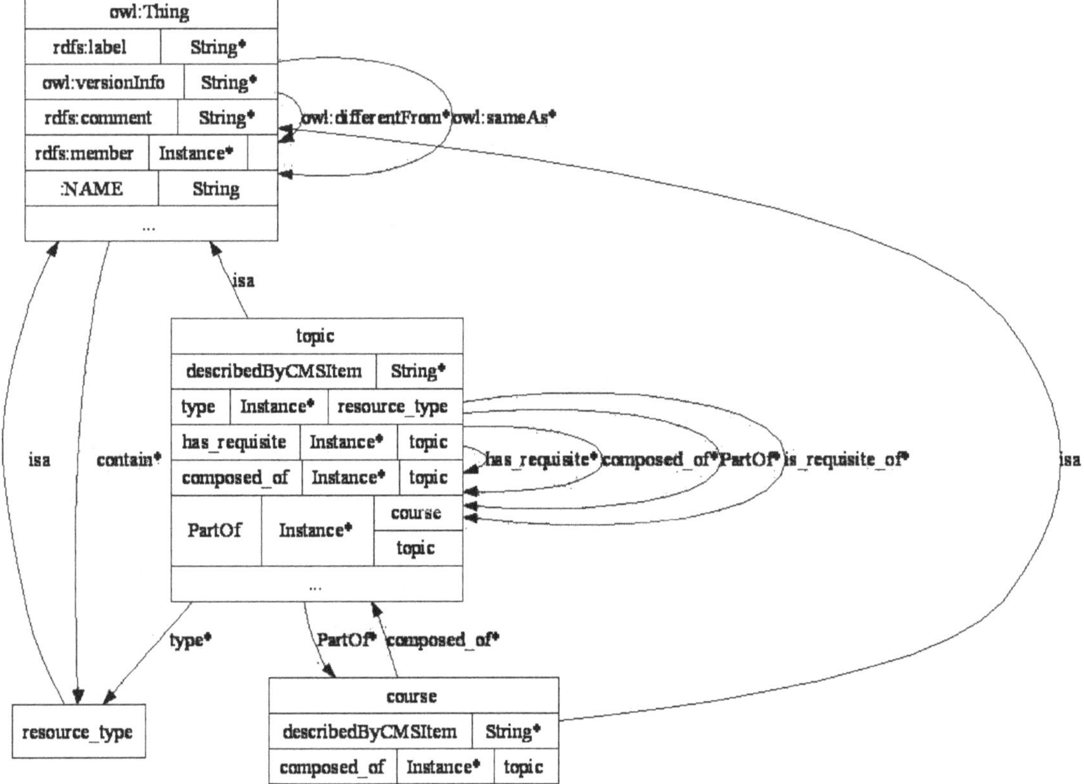

material. There it is possible to observe the relations between "topic" and "course". The relations "part_of" and "composed_of" indicates the type of the composition. The relations "has_requisite" or "is_requisite_of" indicate dependency between the topics of one course. The relation "contain" allows qualification of each component in the Website. The relation between the Website and the ontology is established by the semantic annotation of the Website elements. Each page of the Website is described as an ontology instance, along with the necessary relations. These instances are used in the integration process along with the usage information, as described below.

The instances in the ontology can be manipulated by inference mechanisms or by query languages, such as SPARQL language (Seaborne, 2007), which was the case in this work. The SPARQL language verifies the occurrence of interesting relations in the ontology instances. As an example, it is possible to identify, given a specific instance, all the relations associated to it. Also it is possible to recover, given a specific property, all the instances related to it. Finally, it is possible to discover all the relations that exist between two known instances.

To illustrate how the SPARQL language and the semantic annotation were used in this work, we will use Figure 5 that illustrates the description of one element of the application domain ontology.

Figure 5 shows part of the OWL representation of the instances in the ontology. The items "*T05_ACTIVITIES*" and "*T05_01_MENU*" are

Figure 5. Part of the domain ontology instances

```
<topic rdf:ID="ID_24">
  <part_of rdf:resource="#DATABASE"/>
  <composed_of>
   <topic rdf:ID="ID_25">
     <part_of rdf:resource="#ID_24"/>
     <describedbyCMSItem>24</ describedbyCMSItem >
     <rdfs:comment >T05_01_MENU</rdfs:comment>
   </topic>
  </composed_of>
  < describedbyCMSItem >24</ describedbyCMSItem >
  <rdfs:comment >T05_ACTIVITIES</rdfs:comment>
</topic>
```

Figure 6. Part of the SPARQL queries

```
a) PREFIX v:<http://www..../.../...owl>
     SELECT ?x, ?y WHERE  (v:ID_24, ?x, ?y),
          (v:ID_25, ?x, ?y)

b) PREFIX v:<http://www..../.../...owl>
     SELECT ?x WHERE (v:ID_24, ?x, v:ID_25)
```

identified respectively as "*ID_24*" and "*ID_25*", based on the RDF ID element. This identification relates the elements to the corresponding pages in the Website. The "*composed_of*" relation defines the hierarchy between the items. The property "*describedbyCMSItem*" allows the semantic annotation of the contents, as they are stored in the Web Content Management System applied in the experiment. The relation "*part_of*" identifies the topic described as "ID_24" as part of the course titled "Database". This information can be accessed using the following SPARQL statements.

Figure 6 illustrates some possibilities for the identification of relations using the SPARQL language. The topic identifiers in the ontology match the browsing parameters used in the Website navigation. This allows the integration between the access information and the ontology information, in queries performed with the previously identified frequent sequential patterns. The first example (a) identifies all relations and instances associated with the two topics indicated ("ID_24" and "ID_25"). The second example (b) recovers all the relations between these two topics. The outcome of these queries allows the identification of the context that is not accessible from the usage patterns alone. This context is applied to identify users' stereotypes, which are then associated to specific adaptation rules.

The result is the identification of more interesting patterns, related both with the usage and with the Website structure. By associating these patterns with specific rules, adaptations that are more expressive can be reached. Some examples of these results are the identification of users looking for specific topics, general view of the Website or complementary contents.

Figure 7. Integration of semantic information with Web Usage Mining

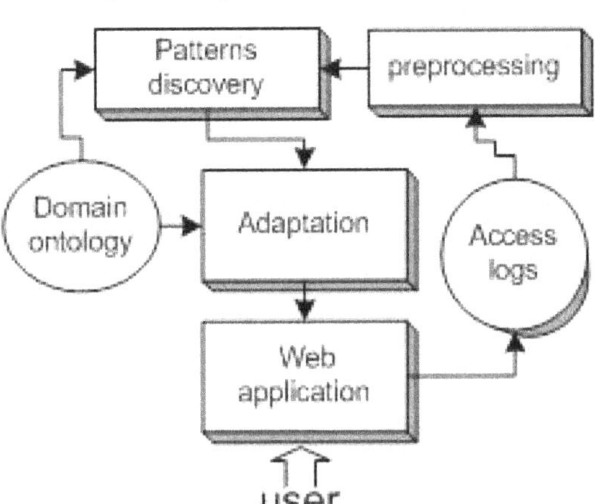

Figure 7 illustrates this process in a general form. The adaptation stage receives information from the domain ontology as well, in addition to the frequent sequential patterns already obtained from the processing of the access log data. With these two sources of information, it is possible not only to identify the page access sequences, but also to identify the concepts present in each page and their relationship. From the interaction with the user, the Web application collects the usage data, storing them in the 'access logs' component.

The pre-processing integrates the usage information, making it available to the next stage, the patterns discovery. After their validation, these patterns are available for the adaptation component, which interacts with the Web application generating adaptations of the structure of the Web pages. This action takes into account the existence of a domain ontology for the application in question.

Structure and Content Adaptation

The information originated in the observed frequent sequential patterns is added to the original structure of the Website. Following the information already collected and processed, the system has a description of frequent sequential paths and specific relationships derived from the domain ontology. Based on the behavior observed from a user session the information is employed as complement to the original structure of the site and is published in specific areas of the interface. Thus, the pages accessed by the user are correlated by frequent sequential patterns. The identification that a certain number of pages accessed during a user session belong to a pattern can be assumed to indicate that the user in question is part of a group of users of the Website that share a specific content interest, and found this set of pages.

The identification of frequent sequential paths is applied in this work to minimize the need for specific rules for the generation of adaptation. In some systems, and particularly in those directed toward education, it is necessary to identify users and even to record the actions they make on the system. As consequence, in these cases it can be easy to specify the adaptation mechanism using rules (Paramythis, 2005). In the experiment that we have carried out, the identification of the users and their details is avoided, as was the use of this information to generate rules. An argument to justify this approach can be found in the behavior of users of Websites with domains different to those directed toward education, where in general there exists no desire to provide identification information.

The pre-processing of usage data and the generation of patterns is carried out periodically. During the user sessions, the system detects, from a recent access history that includes only accesses made in the current session, any coincidence of the observed behavior with the behavior patterns previously established and, if there exists such coincidence, carries out the associated adaptation. In these cases, as covered in the experiment, the adaptation was composed of alterations applied to the structure of the resulting page with the addition of new navigation possibilities derived from the patterns that have been established.

Content adaptation could be carried out by the addition of material related to the content being accessed on the basis of some relationship given in the ontological description. The semantic annotation of the content permits the identification of specific situations, from the identification of the type of complementary resources.

Experimental Results

Adaptive Hypermedia systems can pose several problems when the question is the performance and quality evaluation. The adaptations implemented can be associated with quality attributes and with efficiency parameters. In this case, since the main objective of this work is the identification of the useful Website adaptations, based on users' stereotypes related to a set of users, some tests were conducted in order to evaluate the quantity of generated adaptations and the quantity of accesses to these suggested adaptations.

The experiment in discussion was carried out over a period of six months during which the material was available for access, with the necessary information for the adaptation being generated.

The results obtained indicate that some frequent patterns were related to specific behavior. One of these cases is associated to the overall navigation, where the user accesses the main topics available in the Website structure. This information is obtained from browsing frequent patterns that returns, when integrated with the semantic information described in the domain ontology, a relationship with an upper concept, usually the Website initial content. The kind of relation verified in the ontology in this case is mostly the "part_of". Another frequent case is the situation in which the items in the frequent pattern are related mostly with the "part of" relation, but in a way that an antecedent and subsequent item are associated. In this situation, the behavior detected is described as a navigation in which the user accesses the related and internal items of one specific topic.

Some of these situations are identified below and can be used as examples of the improvements obtained with the approach. The analysis of different frequent sequential patterns, with the same number of elements, allows the identification of different contexts. These contexts can only be distinguished when the domain ontology relations are used together with usage information. Some examples are summarized in Figure 8. In this figure, it is possible to identify elements that correspond to frequent patterns, with a number indicating their access order. The arcs between the elements indicate the ontology relations found for the items. Comparing the items "a" and "b", it can be seen that the first item ("a") is the representation of a browsing in the same level of the Website, the equivalent of a general view of the contents in this level. However, the second item ("b") indicates the access to more detailed information in one specific Website topic.

Based on this identified context, different adaptations procedures can be chosen. Another example of different contexts discovery can also be observed (items "c" and "d"). In the first case ("c"), the browsing started in a more general level and was directed to a more detailed level. In the second case ("d") there is more activity browsing in a general level, followed by the choice of a more detailed level.

The suggested adaptations are monitored and the access to these items can be compared with the normal Website items. In this case, the results indicate a useful set of adaptations generated. The proposed method can generate valuable information by relating the Web usage data and the semantic information. It is also possible to insert of new relations in the domain ontology, in a way that can be appropriated and effective to different application domains.

Figure 8. Semantic contexts obtained

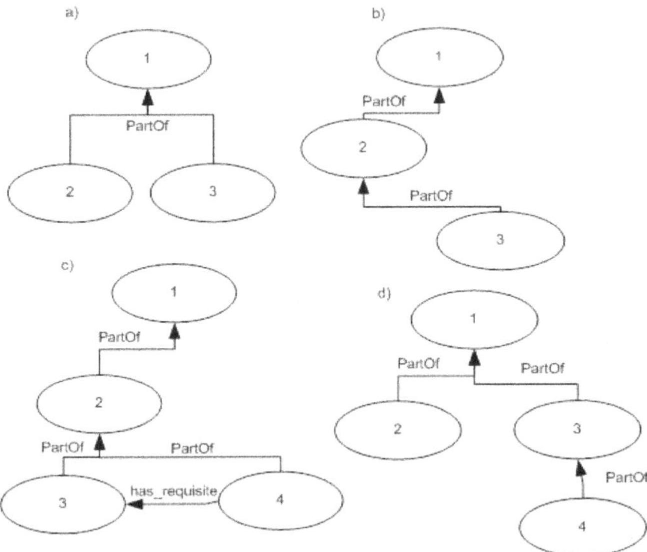

CONCLUSION

This chapter presented an approach for the acquisition of user stereotypes based on Web Usage Mining and domain ontologies. In this case, the domain ontology describes important relations for the application. The relations in the ontology are combined with the usage patterns obtained by Web Mining techniques. The integration of semantic information with usage information was described and some related works were presented, in order to illustrate the possibilities of better identification of the interests and needs of a typical user with these resources.

The cognitive overload observed in the process of Internet users searching for information can be related to the difficulties of automatic acquisition of needed information. As the Internet standards were developed to human usage, there is the necessity of more adequate resources to the structured and more formal description of the documents and contents. In addition, there is the necessity for formal mechanisms to documents annotations. This allows the use of metadata and gives support to a great number of possible applications that would benefit from this information. The operations that become possible with a structured and properly identified (annotated) document are far more interesting than those possible with non-structured or un-annotated documents. Some difficulties in this case are observed in the annotation process, which can be manual and dependent on users' effort, or can be automatic and rely on Text Mining techniques. Resources such as ontologies and inference mechanisms can improve this scenario, with even better possibilities, as they can describe domain applications concepts and its relations. In this case, the knowledge described in ontologies can be associated with the existing documents for better manipulation.

These semantic resources are also used in a great number of experimental applications, but there are also diverse industrial initiatives. The Adaptive Hypermedia applications are among those that benefit from these resources. This can be observed in several aspects, as in the application descriptions, interface generation, user and context models construction or adaptation mechanism.

Some of the tasks of Adaptive Hypermedia applications are carried out with information generated from fields as Web Usage Mining. Specifically the user stereotype can be enriched by observing significant access patterns, related to the pages of a Website, obtained from the user navigation pattern. In this sense, these patterns can be treated as evidences of specific needs or goals, and then used to identify classes of users. It has also been shown that the use of a domain ontology, in which the pages can be associated to specific concepts or stages of repetitive processes on the Website, is more general than just the use of access information, without the related semantic information. That can justify the integration of Web Mining, ontology description and semantic integration possibilities. The requirements for the semantic knowledge and usage information integration are discussed and related with Adaptive Hypermedia application. There are even better possibilities for improvements when the application has a more formal description, such as an ontology, and associated to specific models that help, for example, in the identification of concepts associated to the application domain or to stages of routine tasks.

The handling of a user model and the direct identification of a specific user makes adequate results possible, because information concerning their interests, knowledge and goals are taken into account. Despite that, it is considered important to also evaluate the possibilities that arise from the data collection being uncoupled from a specific user. With this procedure, repetitive behavior is identified, which can also serve to identify goals and interests, with no specific user identification. In many application areas, it is not feasible or desired to obtain the user identification.

REFERENCES

Alani, H., Kim, S., Millard, D., Weal, M. Hall, W. Lewis, P. & Shadbolt. (2003). *Automatic Extraction of Knowledge from Web Documents*. Workshop on Human Language Technology for the Semantic Web and Web Services, 2 Int. Semantic Web Conf. Sanibel Island, Florida, USA.

Aldenderfer, M. S., & Blashfield, R. K. (1984). *Cluster Analysis*. Beverly Hills, CA: Sage, 1984. 88 p.

Aroyo, L., Bellekens, P., Björkman, M., Broekstra, J. & Houben, G. J. (2006). *Ontology based personalization in User-adaptive systems*. In 2nd International Workshop on Web Personalization, Recommender Systems and Intelligent User Interfaces (WPRSIUI'06), Dublin, Ireland.

Aroyo, L., Dolog, P., Houben, G-J., Kravcik, M., Naeve, A., Nilsson, M. & Wild, F. (2006). *Interoperability*. In Personalized Adaptive Learning. Educational Technology & Society, 9 (2), 4-18.

Balabanovic, M. & Shoham, Y. (1997). *Content-based collaborative recommendation*. Communications. Of the ACM. 40(3): 66-72. March 1997.

Bateman, S., Brooks, C. & Mccalla, G. (2006). *Collaborative Tagging Approaches for Ontological Metadata in Adaptive E-Learning Systems*. Proceedings of the Fourth International Workshop on Applications of Semantic Web Technologies for E-Learning (SW-EL 2006). pages 3-12.

Bechhofer, S., Yesilada, Y., Horan, B. & Goble, C. A. (2006). *Knowledge-Driven Hyperlinks: Linking in the Wild*. Sean Bechhofer. AH 2006, 1-10. 'http://dx.doi.org/10.1007/11768012_1', pages 1-10,2006.

Berkovsky, S., Kuflik, T. & Ricci, T. (2006). *Cross-Technique Mediation of User Models*, in proceedings of the AH Conference, 2006.

Berners-Lee, T., Hendler, J. & Lassila, O. (2001), The Semantic Web, *Scientific American*, May 2001, pp. 28-37.

Brin, S. & Page, L. (1998). *The anatomy of a large-scale hypertextual Web search engine*, Computer Networks, 30(1-7): 107-117, Proceedings of the 7th International World Wide Web Conference (WWW7).

Brusilovsky, P. (2001). *Adaptive Hypermedia.* User Modeling and User-Adapted Interaction, 11:87-110, 2001.

Brusilovsky, P. (1996) *Methods and techniques of adaptive hypermedia.* User Modeling and User-adapted interaction, 6(2/3), 87-129.

Brusilovsky, P., Karagiannidis, C. & Sampson, D. (2004). *Layered evaluation of adaptive learning systems.* International Journal of Continuing Engineering Education and Lifelong Learning 14 (4/5), 402 - 421. 2004.

Cantador, I. & Castells, P. (2006). *Multilayered Semantic Social Network Modeling by Ontology-Based User Profiles Clustering: Application to Collaborative Filtering.* 15th International Conference on Knowledge Engineering and Knowledge Management - Managing Knowledge in a World of Networks (EKAW 2006). Podebrady, Czech Republic, October 2006.

Christopher, D. (2002). *Staff: The hypercontext framework for adaptive Hypertext.* Conference on Hypertext and Hypermedia. Proceedings of the thirteenth ACM conference on Hypertext and hypermedia. Maryland, USA. Pages: 11 – 20.

Conlan, O., O'Keeffe, I. & Tallon, S. (2006), *Combining Adaptive Hypermedia Techniques and Ontology Reasoning to produce Dynamic Personalized News Services*, Proceedings of the Fourth International Conference on Adaptive Hypermedia and Adaptive Web-Based Systems (AH2006), Dublin, Ireland (2006).

Cook, D. J., & Holder, L. B. (2000). *Graph-based data mining.* IEEE Intelligent Systems, Los Alamitos, v.15, n.2, p. 32-41.

De Bra, P. et al. (2003). *AHA! The adaptive hypermedia architecture.* Conference on Hypertext and Hypermedia. Proceedings of the fourteenth ACM conference on Hypertext and hypermedia.. Nottingham, UK, Pages: 81 – 84. 2003. ISBN:1-58113-704-4.

De Bra, P., Arroyo, L. & Chepegin, V. (2004). *The next big thing: adaptive Web-based systems.* Journal of Digital Information, V(5)N(1).

De Bra, P., et al. (1999). *Adaptive hypermedia: From systems to framework.* ACM Computing Surveys, 31(4). 1999.

Dolog, P. (2004). *Identifying relevant fragments of learner profile on the semantic Web.* In Proceedings of SWEL'2004 — Intl. Workshop on Semantic Web for eLearning, Intl. Semantic Web Conference 2004, Hiroshima.

Dolog, P., Henze, N. & Nejdl, W. (2004). *Personalization in distributed e-learning environments.* In Proceedings of WWW2004 --- The Thirteen International World Wide Web Conference, New York, May 2004. P.85-94. ACM Press.

Dublin Core. (2007). *The Dublin Core Metadata Initiative.* Retrieved september, 20, 2007, from http://dublincore.org/.

Eirinaki, M. (2003). *SEWeP: Using Site Semantics and a Taxonomy to Enhance the Web Personalization Process* (2003). In Proc. of the 9th SIGKDD Conf., 2003.

Eirinaki, M., Mavroedis, D., Tsatsaronis, G. & Vazirginannis, M. (2006). *Introducing Semantics in Web Personalization: the role of ontologies.* M Ackermann et al. (Eds.): EWMF/KDO 2005, LNAI, pp.147-162,2006. Springer Verlag, Berlin Heidelberg 2006.

Esposito, F. & Lisi, A. (2004). *An ILP Approach to semantic Web mining.* In P.Buitelaar, et al (Eds.), Notes of the ECML/PKDD, 2004 Workshop on Knowledge Discovery and Ontologies, 139-144, Pisa, Italy.

Fensel, D. (2001). Ontologies: Silver Bullet for Knowledge Management and Electronic Commerce. Springer-Verlag.

Fensel, D. (2002). Ontology-Based Knowledge Management. IEEE Computer, 35(11), pages 56-59.

FOAF. (2000). *The Friend of A Friend Project.* Retrieved september, 20, 2007, from http://www.foaf-project.org/index.html.

Freitas, F. L. G. (2003). *Ontologias e a Web Semântica.* XXIII Congresso da Sociedade Brasileira de Computação. JAI. Campinas, São Paulo, Junho de 2003.

Gruber, T. (1993). *What is an Ontology?* Retrieved May, 01 2007, from http://www.ksl.stanford.edu/kst/what-is-an-ontology.html.

Habel, G. Reyes, M. L., Magnan, F. & Reyes, G. (2006). *General Poncelet meets the Semantic Web: A concrete example of the usage of ontologies to support creation and dissemination of eLearning contents.* Workshop on Applications of Semantic Web Technologies for e-Learning (SW-EL@AH'06), June 21-23 2006, Dublin, Ireland.

Heflin, J. (2004). *OWL Web Ontology Language Use Cases and Requirements.* Retrieved May, 01, 2007 from em http://www.w3.org/TR/Webont-req/, 2004.

Hendler, J., Berners-Lee, T. & Miller, E. (2002). *Integrating Applications on the semantic Web.* Journal of the institute of electrical Engenieers of japan, Vol 122(10), October, 2002, p. 676-680.

Herman, I. (2006). *Web Ontology Language.* Retrieved september, 20, 2007, from http://www.w3.org/2004/OWL/.

Herman, I. (2007). *Resource Description Framework.* Retrieved september, 20, 2007, from http://www.w3.org/RDF/.

IEEE LTSC. (2001). *Learning Technology—Public and Private Information.* Retrieved september, 20, 2007, from http://edutool.com/papi/drafts/08/IEEE_1484_02_02_D08_PAPI_rationale.doc.

IMS Consortium. (2001). *Learner Information Package Specification.* Retrieved september, 20, 2007, from http://www.imsglobal.org/profiles/index.html.

Jacquiot, C. Bourda, Y., Popineau, F., Delteil, A. & Reynaud, C. (2006). *GLAM: A Generic Layered Adaptation Model for Adaptive Hypermedia Systems.* AH 2006: 131-140.

Jin, X., Zhou, Y., & Mobasher, B. (2005). *Task-Oriented Web User Modeling for Recommendation.* Proceedings of the 10th International Conference on User Modeling (UM'05) Edinburgh, Scotland, July 2005.

Kleinberg, J. M. & Sandler, M. (2004). *Using Mixture Models for Collaborative Filtering.* Proc. 36th ACM Symposium on Theory of Computing, 2004. STOC'04, June 13.15, 2004, Chicago, Illinois, USA. Copyright 2004 ACM 1581138520/04/0006.

Kleinberg, J. M. (1999). *Authoritative sources in a hyperlinked environment.* Journal of the ACM,volume 46, number 5, pages 604—632.

Kobsa, A . (1993). *User Modeling: Recent Work, Prospects and Hazards.* M. Schneider-Hufschmidt, T. Kühme and U. Malinowski, eds. (1993): Adaptive User Interfaces: Principles and Practice. North-Holland, Amsterdam, 1993. Copyright © North-Holland.

Kohavi, R. (2001). *Mining e-commerce data: the good, the bad and the ugly.* Proceeding of the 7th ACM SIGKDD Inernational COnference on Knowledge Discovery and Data Mining, San Francisco, California, 8-13.

Konstan, J., Miller, B., Maltz, D., Herlocker, J., Gordon, L. & Riedl, J. (1997). *Grouplens: Applying collaborative filtering to usenet news.* Communications of the ACM, 40(3).

Kosala, R. & Blockeel, H. (2000). *Web Mining Research: a survey.* Sigkdd explorations. ACM SIGKDD, Vol 2, Issue 1, July, 2000.

Koutri, M., Avouris, N. & Daskalaki, S. (2004). *A survey on Web usage mining techniques for Web-based adaptive hypermedia systems.* Adaptable and Adaptative Hypermedia Systems. Idea Inc. Hershey, 2004.

LeGrand, B. & Soto, M. (2002). *XML Topic Maps and Semantic Web Mining.* Semantic Web Mining Workshop, Conference ECML/PKDD 2001. Freiburg, Germany. January, 2002.

Leleu, M. (2003). *GO-SPADE: Mining sequential patterns over datasets with consecutive repetitions*, LNAI 2743, pp. 293-306, 2003. Springer Verlag Berlin Heildeberg.

Lieberman, H. (1995). *Letizia: An Agent That Assists Web Browsing* (1995) Proceedings of the Fourteenth International Joint Conference on Artificial Intelligence (IJCAI-95).

Loh, S., Wives, L. & Oliveira, J. P. M. (2000). *Concept –based knowledge Discovery in texts extracted from the Web.* SigKDD Explorations, 2(1), p.29-30. 2000.

Markellou, P., Rigou, M. & Sirmakessis, S. (2005). *Mining for Web personalization.* In Web Mining: Applications and Techniques. Anthony Scime (ed.), Idea Group Publishing, p.27-49.

Middleton, S. DeRoure, D. & Shadbolt, N. (2001). *Capturing knowledge of user preferences: Ontologies in recommender systems.* In Proceedings of the ACM K-CAP'01, Victoria, Canada, 2001. ACM Press.

Middleton, S. E., Shadbolt, N. R. & De Roure, D.C. (2004). *Ontological user profiling in recommender systems.* ACM Transactions on Information Systems,22 (1), 54–88.

Mikroyannidis, A. & Theodoulidis, B. (2004). *A Theoretical Framework and an Implementation Architecture for Self Adaptive Web Sites.* In Proc. Of IEEE/WIC/ACM International Conference on Web Intelligence (WI'04). 2004. Beijing, China, p.558-561.

Mladenic, D. (1999). *Machine learning used by Personal WebWatcher. Proceedings of ACAI-99 Workshop on Machine Learning and Intelligent Agents*, Chania, Crete, July 5-16, 1999.

Mobascher B. & Daí, H. (2005). *Integrating Semantic Knowledge with Web Usage Mining for Personalization.* In Web Mining: Applications and Techniques. Anthony Scime (ed.), Idea Group Publishing.

Mobascher, B. (2005). *Web Usage Mining and personalization.* Practical Handbook of Internet Computing Munindar P. Singh (ed.), CRC Press.

Mobasher, B., Cooley, R., & Srivastava, J.(2000). *Automatic Personalization Based on Web Usage Mining. Communication of ACM.* Volume 43, Issue 8, August, 2000.

Mobasher, P., Dai, H. (2002). *Using Ontologies to Discover Domain-Level Web Usage Profiles.* Proceedings of the 2nd Workshop on Semantic Web Mining. Held at PKDD'02, Helsinki, Finland, August 2002.

Morales, R., Van Labeke, N. & Brna, P. (2006). *Towards a Learner Modelling Engine for the Semantic Web* , International Workshop on Applications of Semantic Web Technologies for E-Learning (SW-EL). AH2006.

Musa, D. L. & Oliveira, J.P.M. (2005). *Sharing Learner Information through a Web Services-based Learning Architecture.* Journal Of Web Engineering, Princeton, New Jersey, v. 4, n. 3, p. 263-278, 2005.

Nejdl, W. Dolog, P. (2003). *Challenges and Benefits of the Semantic Web for User Modelling* In Proc. of AH2003 workshop, WWW 2003.

Netscape Communications Corporation. (1998). *JavaScript Guide*. Retrieved september, 20, 2007, from http://wp.netscape.com/eng/mozilla/3.0/handbook/javascript/.

Nielsen, H. F. (1995). *Logging in W3C httpd*. Retrieved september, 20, 2007, from http://www.w3.org/Daemon/User/Config/Logging.html#common-logfile-format.

Nilsson, M., Palmer, M. & Brase, J. (2003). *The LOMRDf binding-principles and implementation*. Technical report, Information system institute, University of hannover, germany, 2003. 3rd Annual Ariadne Conference, 20-21 November 2003, Leuven, Belgium.

Oliveira, J. P. M. & Rigo, S. J. (2006). *Mineração de uso em sites Web para a descoberta de classes de usuários*. In: CLEI 2006.Santiago, Chile, 19-25 October 2006.

Ounnas, A. (2006) Towards a Semantic Modeling of Learners for Social Networks. In *Proceedings of International Workshop on Applications of Semantic Web Technologies for E-Learning (SW-EL) at the AH2006 Conference*, pp. 102-108, Dublin, Ireland.

Paramythis, A. Stephanidis, C. (2005). *A generic adaptation framework for Web-based hypermedia systems*. In Adaptable and adaptive Hypermedia Systems. Anthony Scime (ed.), Idea Group Publishing, p.80-103. 2005.

Peterson, E. T. (2005). *Web Site Measurement Hacks*. O'Reilly (2005), ISBN 0-596-00988-7.

Petrelli, D. (2005). *User-Centred Design of Flexible Hypermedia for a Mobile Guide: Reflections on the HyperAudio Experience*. User Modeling and User-Adapted Interaction (2005) 15:303–338. Springer.

Popov, B. et al. (2003). *Towards Semantic Web Information Extraction*. Second International Semantic Web Conference (ISWC-03). Sanibel Island, Florida, October 20, 2003.

Protégé. (2007). *The Protege Plataform*. Retrieved september, 20, 2007, from http://protege.stanford.edu.

Seaborne, A. & Prud'hommeaux, E. (2006). *SPARQL Query Language for RDF*. Retrieved september, 20, 2007, from http://www.w3.org/TR/rdf-sparql-query/.

Stumme, G., Berendt, B., & Hotho, A. (2002). *Usage Mining for and on the Semantic Web. Next Generation Data Mining*. Proc. NSF Workshop, Baltimore, Nov. 2002, 77-86.

Sugiyama, K. & Yoshikawa, K. H. (2004). *Adaptive Web Search Based on User Profile Constructed without Any Effort from Users* WWW2004, May 17–22, 2004, New York, New York, USA. ACM 1-58113-844-X/04/0005.

Unicode Consortium. (2006). *The Unicode Standard*. Retrieved september, 20, 2007, from http://www.unicode.org.

Vieira, T., P. (2005). *SSDM : a semantically similar data mining algorithm*. XX Simpósio Brasileiro de Banco de Dados - 2005 - Uberlândia, MG, Brasil.

Woon Y., et al. (2005). *Web Usage mining: algorithms and results*. 2005 In Web Mining: Applications and Techniques. Anthony Scime (ed.), Idea Group Publishing, p.373-394.

Wu, H. (2002). *A reference architecture for adaptive hypermedia applications*. Eindhoven: Technische Universiteit Eindhoven, 2002. ISBN 90-386-0572-2.

Zaiane, O. R. (2000). *Web Mining: Concepts, Practices and Research*. In:SIMPÓSIO BRASILEIRO DE BANCO DE DADOS, SBBD, 15., 2000,João

Pessoa. Tutorial... João Pessoa: CEFET-PB; Porto Alegre: PUCRS,2000. p. 410-474.

Zaki, M. (2001). *SPADE:An eficient algorithm for mining frequent sequences.* Machine Learning, 42, 31-60, 2001, Kluver Academic Publishers. 2001.

Zhong, N. & Li, Y. (2006). *Mining Ontology for Automatically Acquiring Web User Information Needs.* IEEE Trans. Knowl. Data Eng. 18(4): 554-568.

Zhou, Y. & Mobasher, B. (2006). *Web User Segmentation Based on a Mixture of Factor Analyzers.* Proceedings ECWeb'06. Krakow, Poland, September 2006.

Zimmermann, A. et al. (2005). *Personalization and Context Management.* User Modeling and User-Adapted Interaction (2005) 15:275–302 Springer.

KEY TERMS

Adaptive Hypermedia: Approach to automatic personalization.

Domain Ontologies: Description of concepts and relations regarding some knowledge field.

Personalization: Process that adjust the results obtained by users when accessing Web systems.

Semantic Web: Set of resources intended to improve the actual possibilities of Web applications.

User Profile: Set of information regarding user preferences, necessities and knowledge.

Web Systems: Any application designed to be used on the Web.

Web Usage Mining: Set of techniques to generate patterns and discover knowledge from the web usage data.

Chapter XV
Finding Meaning in Online, Very-Large Scale Conversations

Brian K. Smith
Pennsylvania State University, USA

Priya Sharma
Pennsylvania State University, USA

Kyu Yon Lim
Pennsylvania State University, USA

Goknur Kaplan Akilli
Pennsylvania State University, USA

KyoungNa Kim
Pennsylvania State University, USA

Toru Fujimoto
Pennsylvania State University, USA

Paula Hooper
TERC, USA

ABSTRACT

Computers and networking technologies have led to increases in the development and sustenance of online communities, and much research has focused on examining the formation of and interactions within these virtual communities. The methods for collecting data and analyzing virtual online communities, especially very large-scale online discussion forums can be varied and complex. In this chapter, we describe two analytical methods—qualitative data analysis and Social Network Analysis (SNA)–that we used to examine conversations within ESPN's Fast Break community, which focuses on fantasy basketball sports games. Two different levels of analyses—the individual and community level—allowed us to examine individual reflection on game strategy and decision-making as well as characteristics of the community and patterns of interactions between participants within community. The description of our use of these two analytical methods can help researchers and designers who may be attempting to analyze and characterize other large-scale virtual communities.

INTRODUCTION

The use of computer media to support collaboration and communication has increased in recent years. Electronic mail, instant messaging (IM), chat rooms, discussion forums, and social networking platforms (e.g., Facebook, MySpace, Twitter) all support people in conversing with others regardless of geographic and/or temporal proximity. Understanding how people come together to form online or virtual communities and how knowledge flows between participants over time has been a concern for researchers since the early days of computer-mediated collaboration (Curtis, 1992; Hiltz, 1985; Rheingold, 1995). Studies of online communities span many research questions from why people engage in them (Ridings, 2004) to content analyses of specific interests forums such as breast cancer (e.g., Rodgers & Chen, 2005; Sharf, 1997) and teacher professional development (e.g., Barab, MaKinster, & Scheckler, 2004; Renninger & Shumar, 2002; Schlager, Fusco, & Schank, 2002).

This chapter describes methods to collect and analyze conversations associated with such online, virtual communities, especially those that can be described as very large-scale conversations (VLSCs). Sack (2002) describes three characteristics of these online spaces:

1. **Size.** VLSCs involve interchanges betweens hundreds and thousands of people. Newsgroups, chat forums, and Weblogs are examples of spaces where the volume of messages posted can range in the tens and hundreds of thousands.
2. **Networked communities.** VLSCs support network-based communities that have few, if any, geographic and/or temporal boundaries. Individuals within these communities come together over similar interests rather than spatial concerns one might find in neighborhoods and cities. It is also clear that when actors, their activities, and the places where these occur are closely examined, they provide evidence that these communities are complex and multifaceted structures (Schweir, 2001; Wellman & Gulia, 1999; Wenger, 1998).
3. **Public.** Conversations can occur between many individuals behind closed walls, e.g., a company's employees working on a major project. But many VLSCs are open and accessible to anyone. These are particularly interesting because individuals choosing to contribute to them are likely to be engaged in the conversation topic, enough that they are willing to expend long periods of time and effort in exchanges with others.

These three properties make VLSCs interesting artifacts for research. First, because these networked conversations typically revolve around specific topics and interests, their content can be analyzed to understand how people use, express, and learn knowledge over time. Their public nature makes them accessible to researchers. And their size provides opportunities for large conversational studies that could be difficult to collect and analyze in other media (e.g., face-to-face conversations).

The techniques described in this chapter focus on two levels of analysis. The first focuses on the content of conversations with the goal of understanding what people are sharing during collaborative discourse. The second level of social network analysis provides ways to understand how knowledge is disseminated in conversation spaces. Together, these analytical lenses allow researchers to study both the content of and the participants in VLSCs.

We will illustrate the use of these methods with a specific case, a discussion forum that is associated with an online, fantasy basketball game (*Fast Break*). The discussion forum meets each of Sack's VLSC criteria: 1300+ people contribute 50,000 - 80,000 messages to it each year, those contributors are distributed throughout the world, and the forum is accessible to anyone with a computer, a Web browser, and an interest in the subject material. We will use this case to show how conversations can be collected from VLSCs and analyzed to understand discussion content and participant practices. Specifically, we examine 1) related messages, threads, to understand the activities expressed in conversations; and 2) the relationships between actors as they engage in discussion. Both approaches help us select samples of the larger dataset for analysis. Moreover, they provide two ways to study VLSCs, merge the results, and develop a more holistic sense of the conversation space.

RESEARCH FRAMEWORK

Ethnography is a methodological technique for examining and understanding community life (Marcus, 1998). Our analyses are based on ethnographic methodologies that examine discourse practices to understand how discussion forum participants construct knowledge over time (e.g., Gee & Green, 1998; Herring, 2004; Hutchins, 1996). This process involved examining online discussions through participant observation to provide grounded and thick descriptions of community (Geertz, 1983; Marcus, 1998).

Participant observation occurs in social situations and can be decomposed into three elements: a place, its actors, and their activities (Spradley, 1980). All VLSCs, whether they are collections of email messages, discussions in chat rooms, or Weblog postings and comments, are situated in a place, albeit one that exists online. These online places exist because of a collection of actors who initiate and respond to conversations. The conversations that flow between actors in the place can be characterized as activities since they are deliberate communication acts. These conversations can also be classified into patterns

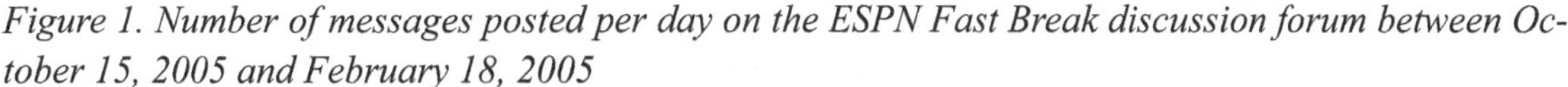

Figure 1. Number of messages posted per day on the ESPN Fast Break discussion forum between October 15, 2005 and February 18, 2005

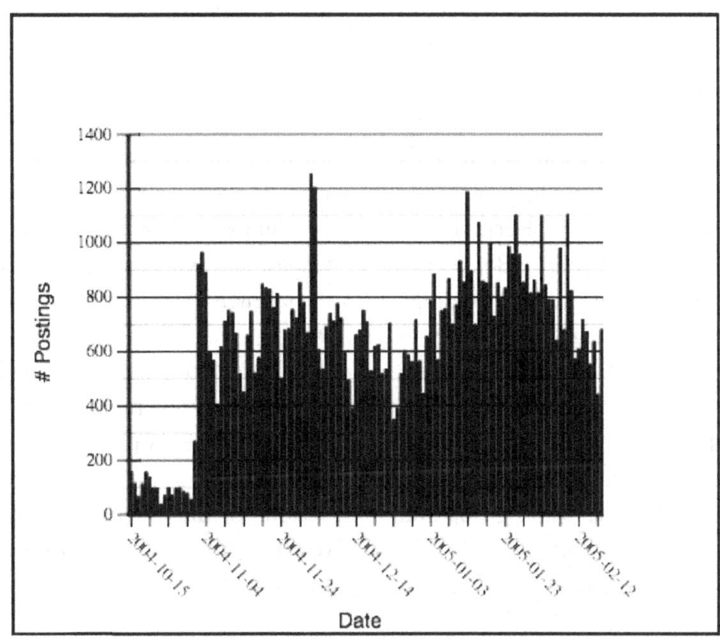

of activity, such as requesting more information, making and justifying claims, reflecting on past conversations, and so on. Participant observation allows us to describe online spaces as communities and to understand the nature of "life" within them. That is, what activities do people engage in? What kinds of conversations do people engage in? What type of language do they use? Who are the people who are part of this community? How can we characterize their interactions with each other and within the larger community? These and other related questions may be of interest to those seeking to understand the purpose of online conversations and what motivates people to contribute to them.

Researcher as Participant Observer

Building an ethnography involves extended engagement with the community being researched, collecting field notes, locating and interviewing informants, examining artifacts, and interviewing community members, frequently as a participant observer (Emerson, Fretz, & Shaw, 1993). Because our discussion forum was associated with an online game, we were able to engage with and become immersed in the community by playing the actual game, which contributed to our understanding in three ways.

First, we became acquainted with the language used by members of the discussion forum. This language can appear cryptic to outsiders due to its sports related terminology (Bernhard & Eade, 2005; Hiltner & Walker, 1996). Basketball knowledge is required to interpret the postings since players use nicknames (e.g., "KG" = Kevin Garnett) and abbreviations ("D" = defense) when describing their rosters. Becoming a participant in (or observer of) this and other networked conversation often requires understanding the linguistic and cultural norms of the discussion group and expressing ideas in similar language.

Second, playing the game helped us understand its rules, mechanics, and the sorts of decisions players must make. There were numerous instances of players discussing their strategies in the discussion forum. This was somewhat surprising given the competitive nature of fantasy sports. However, peer collaboration is often mentioned as motivation for playing the games (Shipman, 2001). Players may find sharing their winning teams engaging: It is a way to display a competitive edge, but it also exposes potentially good strategies to others in the forum. For instance, the following example shows several players responding to Ian's request about Kobe Bryant:

Ian: Thoughts please. Do you think he <Kobe Bryant> will play well?

Duncan: no man the D is going to be up him and he gets personal Defense from Bowen and under the ring is Duncan waiting for him, and if Bowen gets tired we have Ginobili

Booger: he will still get at least 20 fastbreaks, but there could be better tomorrow.

Rico: I think Kobe has almost gained KG status by losing Shaq (It's always asking for disaster to not pick him), but I think that the Spurs can stop him from being too productive. I have decided to not pick him.

Jason: he will still get at least 20 fastbreaks wtf!? Most TEAM doesn't even get 20 fastbreak point a game (Lakers have 19 and 13 in their last two), and you think Kobe's gonna have AT LEAST 20 fastbreaks agianst the Spurs, one of the better defensive team in the league?

These conversations provide insights into activities that players engage in during game play. Our experiences playing the fantasy basketball game made it easier to identify and interpret actions in the discussion texts. In many cases, researchers may need to spend time to become immersed in the subject matter and culture of discussion forums in order to analyze their content.

Finally, our immersion in the game helped us to identify relevant data from the community that corresponds to the following seven characteristics of a community extracted from the literature (Haythornthwaite, Kazmer, Robins & Shoemaker, 2000; Jones, 1995a, 1995b; Reid, 1991, 1994, 1999; Riel & Polin, 2004; Herring, 2004):

1. Active and self-sustaining participation
2. A core of regular participants
3. Shared history, purpose, culture, norms and values
4. Solidarity, support, reciprocity among participants
5. Criticisms, conflict and means of conflict resolution
6. Self-awareness of group as an entity distinct from other groups
7. Emergence of roles, hierarchy, governance, rituals

All of these characteristics are interesting to study, but the methods we describe in this chapter are primarily concerned with sharing and critiquing decision-making (3, 4, 5) and the ways that players initiate and/or contribute to knowledge sharing (7).

DATA COLLECTION

The *Fast Break* discussion forum will be our main example throughout the chapter. We focus on conversations during the period of October 15, 2004 (the start of the 2004-2005 NBA season) and February 18, 2005 (the beginning of the NBA All-Star break). There were 1344 participants in the chat room, contributing 82,104 messages (Figure 2, μ=55.33, σ=316.06). At the low end, 536 players contributed a single message, while the top contributor posted 7253 messages.

The first challenge associated with analyzing VLSCs is collecting and cleaning the data. There are a number of ways to collect online discussion messages for further analysis. The simplest method would be to cut and paste the text from each entry into a text document. This may be viable if the number of messages being analyzed is

Figure 2. List of conversation topics (threads) in the Fast Break discussion forum

Topics	Posted by	Replies	Last Post
Mr Hawaii super tips......		7	Nov 30 2006, 10:58 pm
I really shudda taken Kobe!		0	Nov 30 2006, 10:56 pm
Greatest single FBP performance?		3	Nov 30 2006, 10:53 pm
SHOULD'VE WENT...		2	Nov 30 2006, 10:50 pm
Dorell Wright		8	Nov 30 2006, 10:50 pm
MY GARBAGE DUMP!!!!!!!!!!!1		1	Nov 30 2006, 10:26 pm
lineup input appreciated		0	Nov 30 2006, 10:24 pm
new lineup for tomorrow...		0	Nov 30 2006, 10:17 pm
why noone ever takes Billups		6	Nov 30 2006, 10:00 pm
Anybody took Kwame Brown?		2	Nov 30 2006, 9:58 pm

relatively small. This becomes impractical when studying places like the *Fast Break* discussion forum where 80,000+ messages were posted over five months. Specialized computer programs may be required to collect and process very large-scale conversational data for storage and analysis.

We wrote a simple Web robot in the Perl scripting language to collect our discussion data. Web robots, also called spiders, crawlers, or wanderers, recursively follow hyperlinked pages, extracting and processing information (Cheong, 1996; Hemenway & Calishain, 2003). The robot started from the first thread contained in the discussion forum, read the HTML to find URLs that linked to player messages, and extracted the message content from the HTML source code. The recursive nature of the robot led to a small program that traversed the message hierarchy to completion. The general algorithm is shown in Box 1.

The *Fast Break* discussion board consists of multiple pages listing topics of conversation (Figure 2). One of these page URLs was provided as input to the robot for it to begin looking for the actual message content. The hyperlinks on the page were extracted and loaded to reveal the thread's messages (Figure 3). The robot then parsed the thread's HTML source to find individual messages and extract their relevant features (e.g., message URL, subject, author, date and time when the message was posted, and the message content). Once a message's features were found, they were written to a text file in XML format:

```
<message>
    <author>____</author>
    <date>Nov 30 2006</date>
    <time>9.25 pm</time>
    <content>i wish you would have wrote that yesterday.
thanks for future reference though.</content>
</message>
```

The robot's next task was to parse the XML-encoded messages and format them for analysis. Because we were dealing with tens of thousands of messages, we decided to store the content in a relational database, specifically the open source MySQL database. MySQL is free, has strong customer and developer support, and can run on all major computer operating systems. Moving the XML messages into the MySQL database was straightforward: The robot used an XML reader to find each message, extract its tags, and insert these into a database table. The result was a database that could be accessed and searched in multiple ways.

INDIVIDUAL LEVEL ANALYSIS: ANALYZING PLAYER DISCUSSIONS AND ACTIONS

It would have been a formidable task to apply discourse analysis to all of the postings in the *Fast Break* forum since it and other VLSCs have large numbers of participants and messages that make

Box 1. Generic algorithm for retrieving discussion messages with Web robots

```
for all pages listing discussion threads do
    for all threads on the page do
        open thread URL
        for all messages in the thread do
                extract message features from the message HTML code
        next
    next
next
```

Figure 3. List of messages contained within a Fast Break thread

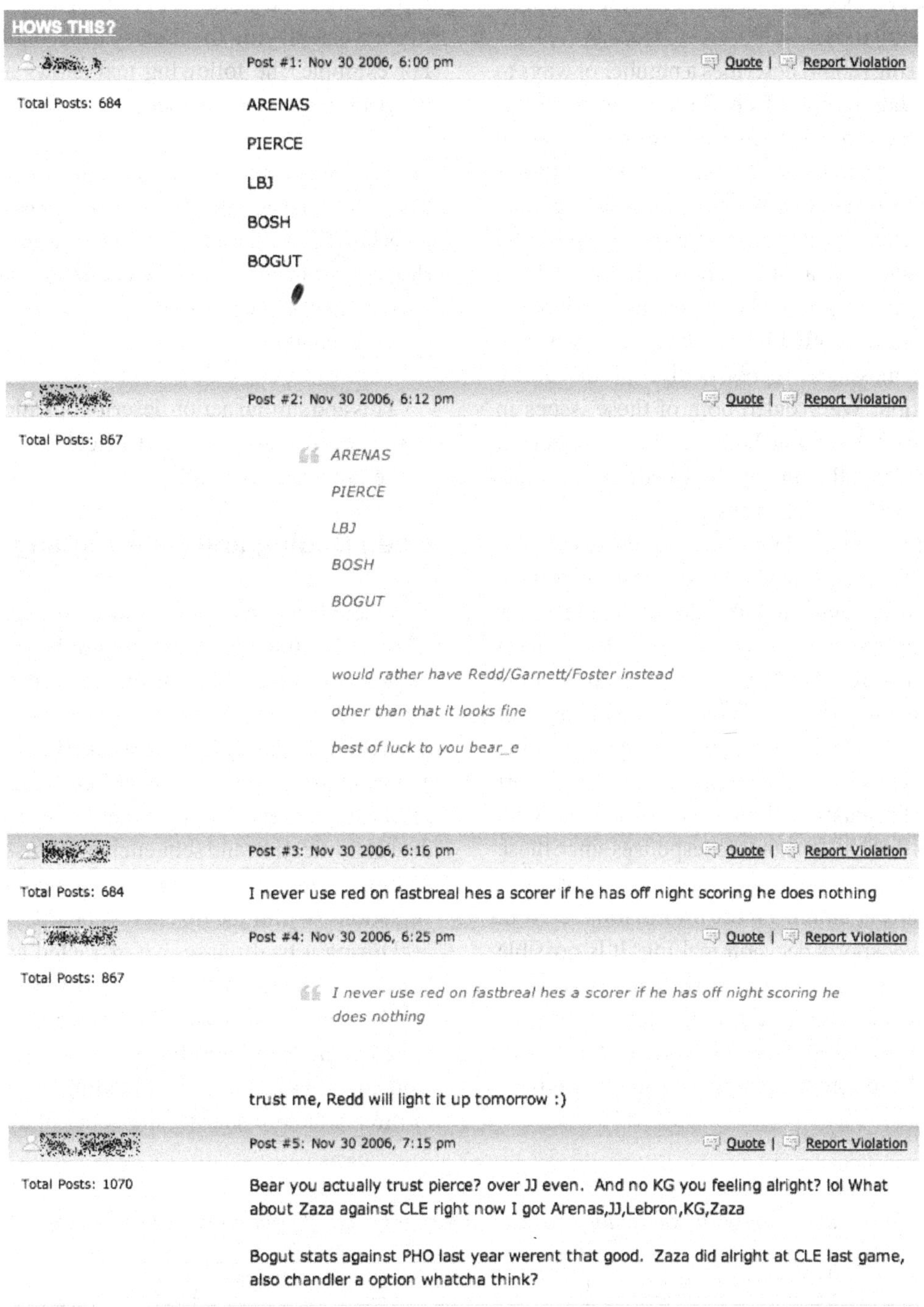

comprehensive analyses difficult. Therefore, it was necessary to select a sample from the complete set of textual data.

Herring (2004) describes a number of ways to collect data samples from online conversations. Random sampling, often used in empirical social science research, is difficult in VLSC studies since the context in which a message appears is important for its interpretation. Sampling by convenience is another approach that allows researchers to study what is readily available to them, but it is often unsystematic and may not include messages representative of the entire population. We avoided both of these issues in our work by writing Web robots to collect all discussions, allowing us the freedom to sample messages in multiple ways.

Our first method for analyzing the discussion forum examined threads, that is, consecutive messages posted about a particular topic. Messages receiving the most discussion (i.e., the longest threads) were a small percentage of all discussion threads (7.7%, see Table 1). The majority of the threads consisted of singleton messages that went unanswered by other participants or of short bursts of discussion. We started our analysis with threads that had ten or more responses since those longer threads indicate sustained discussions, potentially containing more information relevant to fantasy sports decision making. It is possible for consecutive messages in a thread to have little or no relationship to the initial topic (Herring, 1999; Hewitt, 2005), but we found few instances of unrelated follow-up messages in our studies.

Messages contained in these threads of related topics often describe the actions that players make when playing the fantasy basketball game. For example, the following text shows a player describing his roster choices:

ok. hey i was debating weather to take wade (who has been sleeping lately) or sam or arenas. i will probably stick with wade (he is due for a good game) shaq against bumby should be interesting. hope mia doesn't blow out denver so shaq and wade will both get good minutes!

This and similar action descriptions allowed us to see how players make and articulate decisions in the fantasy basketball game.

Open Coding and Data Tagging

Initial analyses consisted of open coding, which involves reading and comparing individual data units so as to label similar units into categories (Strauss & Corbin, 1990). Open coding can be applied to any meaningful unit of data (Flick, 2002), and we chose individual discussion threads as the smallest coherent data unit that could facilitate data classification and sequencing. We used open coding to examine the content and focus of conversations within the discussion board.

During a trial phase, we extracted and analyzed 15 discussion threads from the previous year's discussion archive. The data were manually edited using Word and Excel. Eight researchers worked individually on open-coding the same set of threads before sharing the codes at a weekly

Table 1. Discussion threads in the fantasy basketball forum by length, quantity, and percentage of total

Thread Length	Number of Threads	% of Total Threads
< 4	16595	74.3
5-9	4013	18.0
10-15	1149	5.1
> 15	587	2.6

review session. The group review was useful in clarifying ambiguous sections of the data and aligning interpretation criteria. In this trial phase, we attempted to differentiate and categorize threads based on their intent within the fantasy game environment, a standard procedure within qualitative analysis. For example, a thread with the title "Please join my group," was easily classified as related to recruitment, while threads with titles such as "Roster for tomorrow" or "Why not Dwayne Wade today?" were categorized as discussions about teams and athletes.

During a second round of open coding, longer threads were extracted and filtered to focus on citations of statistics or numbers and evidence of strategic conversations (i.e., comparisons of teams or athletes, descriptions of strengths or weaknesses of specific lineups or athletes, etc.). Interactions within the thread were also considered to understand how players posed questions and responded to each other about game and team strategies. By compiling and comparing various instances of strategic discourse forms, we were able to refine and code the categories illustrated by the conversations.

A set of ten initial action codes were identified as being recurrent, including: predict, claim, support/agree, reflect, question, correction (of others' information), suggest, clarify, raising assurance, and disagree. In addition, most of these actions were accompanied by a description or explanation of reasoning for the action.

This led to a coding structure that consisted of an action plus a descriptor (e.g., Box 2). This structure allowed us to tag messages more efficiently, and to parse and refine the action codes.

Having determined a coding structure during the trial phase, we began to code the actual set of discussion data for the 2005-2006 year. Here too, the discussion threads were distributed and individually coded by one of the eight researchers. We met every week to discuss the codes and our understanding of their meaning. Through these weekly meetings and over a period of six months, we eventually refined the initial group of 10 codes and reduced them to six action codes that were exclusive and clearly focused on a single action. Boyatzis (1998) suggests that for high inter-rater reliability, a good code should have a label, a definition of what characteristics constitute or define the code, as well as examples and non-examples to clarify meaning and eliminate confusion while coding. Table 2 identifies our attempt to formalize these code definitions and provide examples to guide our final coding.

Categorizing Data

After all codes were tagged appropriately, our next step was to compile and compare messages within each category to identify relationships between sub-categories. This process is generally referred to as axial coding or categorization of tagged data (Baptiste, 2001). We began by compiling all messages tagged with the reflect code. We compiled the codes in a document, and began to re-examine each message with special attention to the definitions provided in Table 1. Our initial document consisted of 81 pages of messages coded with the reflect tag: Through a process of clarification and elimination, our final set of message data was contained in a document of 24 pages. Thus, almost 70% of the initially coded data were rejected as being too ambiguous or inappropriate to code as a reflection.

After eliminating irrelevant messages, we examined each message in more detail to identify the types of reflection that were being exhibited. For example, note the expanded code in Box 3.

The more detailed analysis led us to sort reflect codes into three main sub-categories based on similar intents: reflections on one's own strategies for athlete selection, reflections on one's own strategy as compared to strategies of other players, and reflections on one's own performance in the context of the fantasy game. Although we are still

Box 2. Example of coding a message into an action plus descriptor

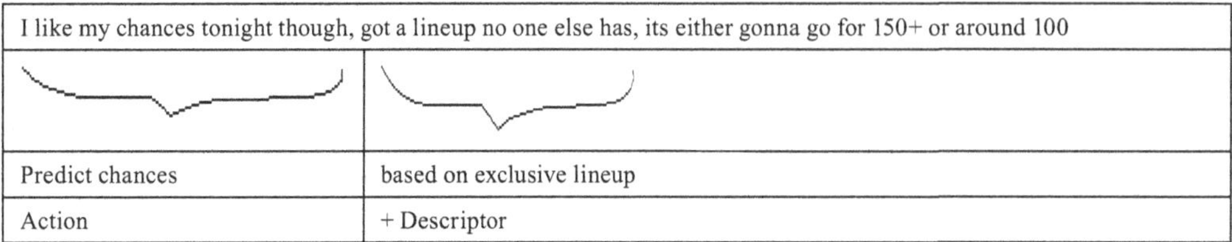

I like my chances tonight though, got a lineup no one else has, its either gonna go for 150+ or around 100	
Predict chances	based on exclusive lineup
Action	+ Descriptor

Table 2. Actions used to categorize conversations in the fantasy basketball discussion forum

Action	Definition	Example
Predict	1. Explicitly, try to predict players or team performance 2. Must be phrased in the future 3. Can be with or without justification (descriptors)	"Tomorrow's game Kobe will.."
Claim	1. To express one's own opinion 2. Not to predict, select, or eliminate players 3. With or without justification	"I think…"
Reflect	1. When going over their own previous actions or selections 2. References to previous strategies and possible change	"Looking back at yesterdays scores. I would have"
Select and Eliminate	1. Direct references to selecting and eliminating players for lineup 2. Names of players are mentioned 3. With or without justification	"This is my lineup vs. Kobe is good here is my line up"
Clarify	1. Clarifying something they previously said on the board or asking for clarification on something someone else said 2. Cues would be a reference to previous posts (you said, did you mean, etc.,)	"Are you sure.." "When you said…"
Suggest	1. Suggest a player or team to someone else with the intent of convincing them 2. Provides directives by saying "If I were you.." or "You should or shouldn't" etc., 3. With or without justification	"You should.." "If I were you.."

in the process of describing these categorizations and deriving more overarching relationships, Table 3 shows part of the structure that emerged from this second level of axial coding within the reflect category.

At this stage, open and axial coding provide a process for us to determine and describe evidence for reflection within the discussion board. Our next step will be to formalize and integrate these categories into themes that describe how and when reflection takes place in online fantasy games discussion boards.

COMMUNITY LEVEL ANALYSIS: ANALYZING ACTOR RELATIONSHIPS AND PATTERNS OF INTERACTION

The first phase of our analysis focused on exploring the content of discussions and the ways that individuals expressed meaning. We were also interested in studying the patterns of communication between individuals in the discussion forum. Online conversations will likely include participants that initiate a majority of the discourse, others that primarily respond to inquiries, and many that lurk in the background. Identifying the various participant roles in conversation spaces can assist in understanding how online communities develop and flourish (or wither away) over time.

Social Network Analysis

Social network analysis (SNA) is a technique used to study the interactions between individuals in a community. Unlike other approaches such as content analysis for in-depth exploration of dialogue, or quantification of messages for frequency estimation (Hara *et al.*, 2000; Henri, 1992; Hewitt & Teplovs, 1999; Levin *et al.*, 1990; Marra *et al.*, 2004), social network analysis focuses on the patterns of collective interaction and relationships among actors in the network (Scott, 2000; Scott *et al.*, 2005; Wasserman & Faust, 1994). For

Box 3. Example of coding a message into a coding sub-category

Individual message thread	A Very Droll 113... The Ban on Miller is On!! If I had Known,for Sure,that Bogut was gonna be the Starter,I would got Him & AI!!
Expanded description for reflect code	How information about player position would have changed strategy/ selection (reflect)

Table 3. Reflection categories after axial coding

REFLECT
1. On player selection strategies
1.1. How information about player position would have changed strategy/selection
1.1.1. Selecting a lower coach to afford a better athlete for a position
1.1.2. Selecting a lower center to afford a better athlete for a position
1.1.3. Selecting a lower athlete for a position to afford a coach
1.2. Whom to dump, whom to switch
1.2.1. Observation on TV (watching the real basketball games)
1.3. Advice from other gamers
1.3.1. Regretting advice that decreases one's score
1.3.2. Advice that increases one's score
1.4. w.r.t. one's own estimation about other gamers' pick
2. On differences in own vs. other's strategies
2.1. Reflection on other player's choice vs. own reasoning-conflict with scores? values?
3. On one's performance with reference to other fantasy games

example, SNA has been used to investigate patterns of friendships between individuals (Moreno, 1953; Rapoport & Horvath, 1961), co-authorship between scholars (Price, 1965; Otte & Rousseau, 2002), and socio-communicational structure between politicians (Park *et al.*, 2004).

The content of discussion forum messages becomes less important in social network analysis than the relational data representing the contacts, ties, and connections that relate one actor to others in the network, and which cannot be reduced to the properties of the individual agent themselves (Scott, 2000). Rather than focusing on the subject matter of messages, SNA is concerned with identifying recurring communications between actors and the primary contributors in the social network. Ties between actors that suggest the organization of an online community are generally implicit, but they can be discovered and made explicit for analysis.

Social network analyses derive social structure based on observed relationships between actors rather than on a priori classifications (Haythornthwaite, 1996). VLSCs may lack pre-defined groups, hierarchies, and rules, but these may be implicit in the interactions between participants. SNA allows researchers to determine the emerging organizational structures and to visualize the formation of communities over time. In a social network, each actor has different levels of accessibility to other actors depending on his or her location in the network as well as the pattern of ties. In other words, key communicators in a network hold the potential to influence other actors. This otherwise hidden information becomes explicit through social network analyses.

Overview of Relationships and Patterns in Data

SNA can be used to analyze conversational data in (at least) two ways. We used SNA to guide our analyses of the data in two ways. The first perspective examined the network for group cohesion, including interconnection between all actors in the network. The second perspective identified central and peripheral actors in the network. These approaches enable us to understand information flow between actors and to examine the relationships between actors in the network.

Creating and Visualizing Social Networks

Making social relationships explicit begins with the construction of adjacency matrices. In an adjacency matrix, the scores in the cells of the matrix indicate the ties between each pair of actors (Wasserman & Faust, 1994), representing who is adjacent to whom in the social space. The label for each column and row is an actor in the network. A matrix constructed in this way has two cells representing the intersection of any two actors, one above and one below the diagonal (Scott, 2000; Scott et al., 2005). If a tie exists between two actors, then a 1 is entered in the matrix cell representing the intersection of these two players. If no tie exists, a 0 is entered. Multiple ties between individuals can be represented by adding the number of ties and placing that value in the relevant cells. An example adjacency matrix can be seen in Table 4.

A directional (or asymmetric) and weighted (or valued) adjacency matrix is generally used for VLSCs due to the nature of online discussion. In a directional matrix, it is not necessary that the two cells for each pair of nodes have the same value (Scott et al., 2005). For example, in Table 4, A sent a message to B, but B did not send a message to A. Note that in a directional matrix, the sender of a tie is the row and the target of the tie is the column (Scott, 2000). The matrix is directional since participants in discussion forums can both send and receive replies.

A common practice in social network analysis is to render adjaceny matrices into *sociograms* that visually convey relationships between actors. These sociograms make network structure explicit as collections of nodes with links that portray directionality and connection strength (Harary, 1969). The visual representations provide researchers with new insights about network structures and have helped them to communicate those insights to others (Freeman, 2000). The visualized analysis of the network is especially useful when an intuitive representation of the quantity and direction of participation in online venues is required. Figure 4 shows the sociogram for the matrix appearing in Table 4. Each actor is represented by a node, and interactions between nodes are represented by directed links.

Due to the size of the dataset, we wrote a computer program to automate the process of creating an adjacency matrix for the *Fast Break* discussions. That program stepped through the database of conversations to record the number of responses to each actor's postings and the number of times that actors posted responses to others. We focused only on the reply postings rather than the initiating postings, because replies include an explicit direction (to the sender) whereas initial messages are open to anyone in the network. Consequently, the 1 in Row A, Column B indicates that A replied once to the thread initiated by B. Positive numbers represent the strength of the tie, the number of postings, and these are entered in each cell. When one posted a message under his or her own thread, then 1 or any weighted number was entered in the diagonal.

At this point, one could use social network analysis software to visualize the adjacency matrix. Unfortunately, most VLSCs have considerably more actors than the matrix shown in Table 4, leading to sociograms that are densely

Figure 4. Sociogram representation of the adjacency matrix in Table 4

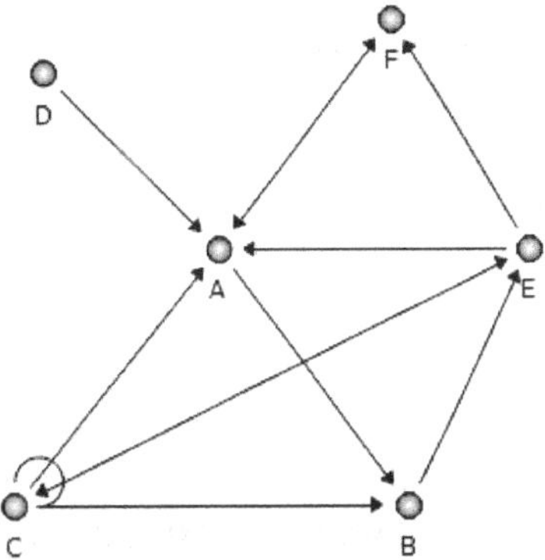

Table 4. Directed and weighted adjacency matrix

	A	B	C	D	E	F
A	0	1	0	0	0	1
B	0	0	0	0	2	0
C	3	1	1	0	3	0
D	2	0	0	0	0	0
E	1	0	3	0	0	1
F	1	0	0	0	0	0

populated by intersecting links that are difficult to follow. Although visually appealing, sociograms are most effective for smaller networks. For large networks common to VLSCs, we need to use statistical techniques to discover social relationships. A subset of those techniques are described below.

Analyzing Group Cohesiveness

Group-level cohesion can be used to identify who was communicating with whom in a discussion forum. Cohesiveness describes the whole network in terms of the presence of strong, direct, intense, or frequent relationships among network members (Haythornthwaite, 1996; Wasserman & Faust, 1994). We used density and cliques to measure cohesiveness.

- **Density.** Density describes the general level of linkage among the actors in the entire network. The density of a network is defined as the number of ties in a network divided by the maximum number of all possible ties (Scott, 2000). By definition, the density of a complete network where every node is directly connected to every other node is 1. Density is an important measure since it reveals the overall information flow in a network (Haythornthwaite, 1996). For example, in our Fast Break discussion board, the network density is 9.1%, suggesting that information tends to flow through a relatively small number of people.
- **Cliques.** In any network, there are subgroups with highly interconnected players, which are known as clusters. When these clusters are fully connected, clusters become cliques. A clique is defined as a maximal complete subgroup of three or more actors (Wasserman & Faust, 1994). Analyzing cohesive subgroups informed us about what was happening in the unstructured VLSC, especially in terms of the number of subgroups that emerged, the members of the subgroups, and the strength of the connection. The cohesion index describes the degree to which there are strong links within the clique rather than outside of it. If the index is greater than 1, the intra-clique connectivity is stronger than the inter-clique connectivity (Bock & Husain, 1950). To analyze cliques and cohesion index, we converted the adjacency matrix from directional to non-directional, and weighted to non-weighted. In this way, we can focus on the connectedness between players rather than the direction and weight of who is sending out messages to whom in a clique.

Four major cliques were identified in the *Fast Break* network, each consisting of 22 participants (Table 5). Note that members of one clique often appear in others. This is expected given the low density of the *Fast Break* network where a few players are contributing the majority of the discussion messages. This phenomenon is explicitly explained by the cohesion index. The index of 60.058 from the first clique indicates that there were very strong ties, which reflect the number

Table 5. The four largest cliques in the Fast Break network

Cliques	Members	Size	Cohesion Index
K1	7,4,22,23,14,11,2,9,36,12,52,61 ,78,3,32,8,60,62,69,5,33,75	22	60.058
K2	7,4,22,23,14,11,2,9,36,12,52,61 ,78,3,10,33,62,8,5,60,69,75	22	58.125
K3	7,4,22,23,14,11,2,9,36,12,52,61 ,41,8,32,60,3,62,75,5,69,33	22	60.99
K4	7,4,22,23,14,11,2,9,36,12,182,3 ,8,62,60,78,10,75,33,69,61,5	22	59.631

of replies within the clique rather than outside of it. The *Fast Break* network consists of a few strongly cohesive sub-groups and isolates which makes the network density low. Identifying these cliques allows us to focus our discourse analyses on highly active contributors in VLSCs.

Analyzing Individual Prominence

Prominence informs us who has influence or power in a network (Haythornthwaite, 1996; Wasserman & Faust, 1994). In other words, prominent actors are located in strategic locations in a network, playing a central role in the information sharing process. An actor's prominence or importance can be measured by assessing an individual's centrality. Centrality is measured by counting the number of relationships maintained by each actor in a network (Freeman, 1979; Wasserman & Faust, 1994). Although there are several different definitions on centrality, we measured degree centrality and betweenness centrality of each player to identify the major players in the *Fast Break* community.

Degree centrality is defined as the number of immediate ties that an actor has. In a directed network, in-degree centrality is the number of nominations an actor receives, while out-degree centrality is the number of nominations an actor gives (Freeman, 1979). In the case of VLSCs, a person who received many replies from others is said to have high in-degree centrality, whereas a person who replied frequently to others' postings is said to have high out-degree centrality.

Figure 5 shows a diagram of in-degree centrality for the *Fast Break* network. Nodes in the center of the circle represent participants receiving the most replies to their discussion messages. These are the conversation starters or the main initiators of discussion in the forum. Nodes further from the center represent players that participate less in leading new topics of conversation.

Figure 5. Concentric display of in-degree. Nodes in the center of the figure represent participants in the discussion forum receiving the largest number of replies to their postings

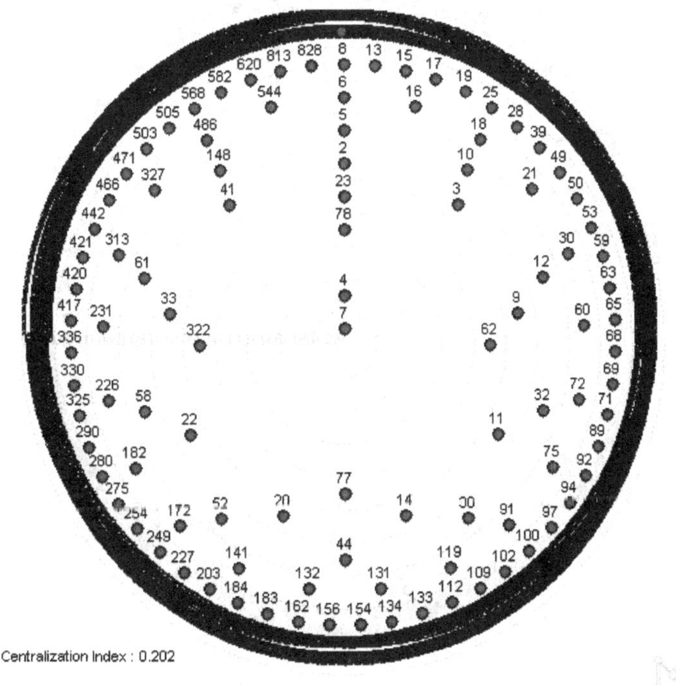

Figure 6 shows out-degree centrality for the network. Central nodes in this diagram correspond to participants who respond the most to messages in the discussion forum. These people are most likely responding to queries about team selections. Focusing on them in a VLSC analysis is important since they may have greater amounts of expertise than other group members.

The central players in the in- and out-degree visualizations are also members of the major cliques that we discussed earlier.

Betweenness Centrality

Interactions between nonadjacent actors might depend on other actors in the network, especially those who lie on the paths between the two actors (Wasserman & Faust, 1994). Actors who sit between others become important since they are gatekeepers for the information flow (Scott, 2000). Freeman (1979) defined betweenness as the frequency that an actor is found in the shortest path between two other actors. Betweenness centrality represents the strategic importance of location in a network, rather than the quantity of connections. In the *Fast Break* forum, a player with high betweenness is more likely to be located between two important (or prominent) players and is more likely to eventually facilitate information sharing by connecting them.

Figure 7 shows betweenness for the network. Nodes in the center of the circle represent participants in the discussion forum that facilitate a large number of conversations between others. While in- and out-degree centrality measures show an actor's involvement in initiating or re-

Figure 6. Concentric display of out-degree. Nodes in the center of the figure represent participants in the discussion forum responding the largest number of messages

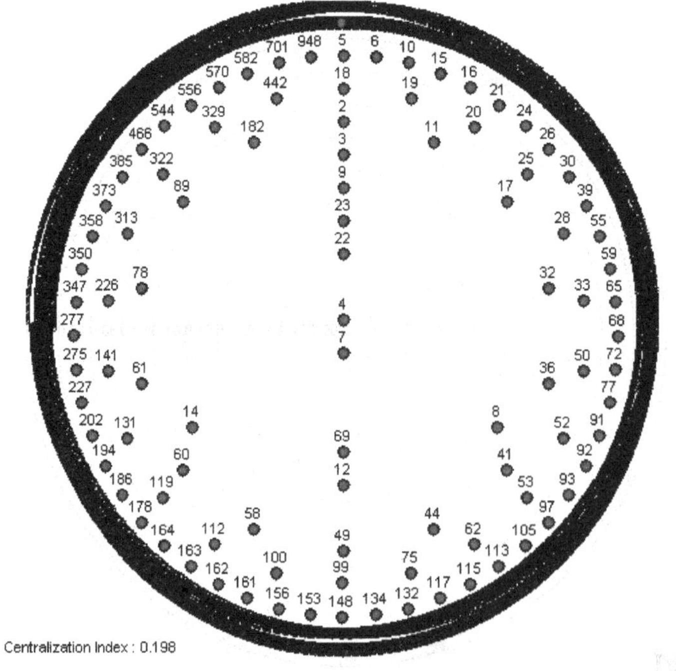

sponding to messages, the betweenness measure combines these to find the most important actors in the network's information flow. In other words, researchers can use this measure to discover those individuals that are responsible for relaying messages within the social network.

DISCUSSION

The *Fast Break* discussion forum described in this chapter is just one instance of a very large-scale conversation that occurs on the Internet. We described two approaches to finding meaning in VLSCs. Threads, collections of messages related by topic, offer insights into the major conversational themes. Individual messages related to these themes can be analyzed and categorized to discover the major discussion topics. We also focused on relationships between actors in the discussion forum using social network analysis. SNA can identify major contributors in the discussion forum and understand how knowledge is spread throughout an online community.

A key aspect for analyzing VLSC data is identifying a coherent set of methods/perspectives that allow parsing of data to answer specific questions. While our focus was consistently ethnographic, we pursued our analyses by first using a micro-lens (individual threads, messages, content) and then gradually widened it into a macro-lens (who, where, how types of questions about connections in the community). One set of challenges faced during analysis was conceptual—that is, how could we select a method that allowed us to answer the questions we had posed? A second set of challenges related to the technical feasibility of dealing with such a large volume of messages.

Figure 7. Concentric display of betweenness. Nodes in the center represent participants that convey the most information between players in the discussion forum

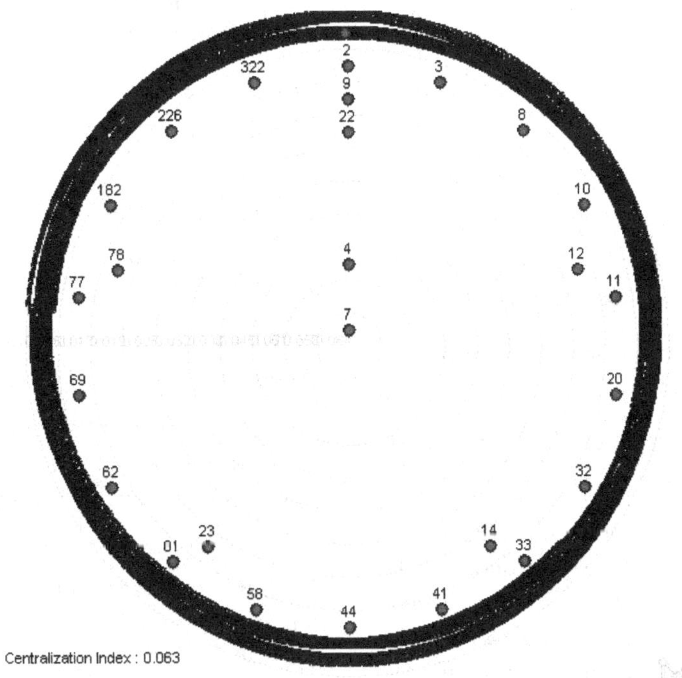

While some of the data collection and cleaning was managed through the creation of Web programs, we still lacked an efficient tool that allowed multiple researchers to collectively code and tag such a large volume of data, especially when our focus was on the individual threads and messages. While software for conducting SNA is more easily available, researchers attempting to code large-scale data must account for technical considerations in open-coding minute data chunks, especially within a group.

In this chapter, we explicated some of the strategies and foci that allowed us to manage and elucidate large volumes of data. That is, we described how we adapted the use of extant methodologies such as ethnography and SNA to answer specific questions about the online community of interest. Using ethnography, we elucidated a description of the place and the types of conversations and reasoning visible online, while SNA allowed us to describe the structure of the online community and identify prominent actors and networks. Although both these methodologies proved useful in answering our questions, we envision the need for development of additional methods and strategies to make the data collection and analyses processes more efficient and effective.

REFERENCES

A.T. Kearney Inc. (2003). *The New Sports Consumer.* Chicago, IL: A.T. Kearney, Inc.

Ballard, C. (2004, June 21). Fantasy world. *Sports Illustrated, 100,* 80-89.

Babbie, E. (2002). *The practice of social research.* Stamford, CT: Wadsworth.

Baptiste, Ian (September, 2001). Qualitative data analysis: common phases, strategic differences [42 paragraphs]. *Forum: Qualitative Sozialforschung / Forum: Qualitative Social Research* [On-line Journal], 2(3). Available at: http://www.qualitative-research.net/fqs/fqs-eng.htm

Barab, S. A., MaKinster, J. G., & Scheckler, R. (2004). Designing system dualities: Characterizing an online professional development community. In S. A. Barab, R. Kling & J. H. Gray (Eds.), *Designing for Virtual Communities in the Service of Learning* (pp. 53-90). Cambridge, UK: Cambridge University Press.

Bock, R. D., & Husain, S. Z. (1950). An adaptation of holzinger's b-coefficients for the analysis of sociometric data. *Sociometry, 13*, 146-153.

Cheong, F.-C. (1996). *Internet Agents: Spiders, Wanderers, Brokers, and Bots.* Indianapolis, IN: New Riders Publishing.

Cross, R., Parker, A., & Borgatti, S. (2002). *A bird's-eye view: Using social network analysis to improve knowledge creation and sharing.* IBM Institute for Business Value.

Curtis, P. (1992). Mudding: Social phenomena in text-based virtual realities. In *Proceedings of Directions and Implications of Advanced Computing (DIAC 92) Symposium.* Berkeley, CA.

Cyram Company Ltd. (2005). NetMiner (Version 2.6). Seoul, Korea: Cyram Company Ltd.

Flick, U. (2002). *An Introduction to Qualitative Research.* Thousand Oaks, CA: Sage Publications.

Freeman, L.C. (1979). Centrality in social networks: I. Conceptual clarification. *Social Networks, 1*, 215-239.

Freeman, L.C. (2000). Visualizing social networks. *Journal of Social Structure, 1*(1).

Garton, L., Haythornthwaite, C., & Wellman, B. (1997). Studying online social networks. *Journal of Computer-Mediated Communication, 3*(1).

Gee, J. P., & Green, J. L. (1998). Discourse analysis, learning, and social practice: A methodological study. *Review of Research in Education, 23*, 119-169.

Granovetter, M. S. (1983). The strength of weak ties: A network theory revisited. *Sociological Theory, 1*, 201-233.

Hara, N., Bonk, C. J., & Angeli, C. (2000). Content analysis of online discussion in an applied educational psychology course. *Instructional Science, 28*(2), 115-152.

Harary, F. (1969). *Graph Theory.* Reading, MA: Addison-Wesley.

Haythornthwaite, C. (1996). Social network analysis: An approach and technique for the study of information exchange. *Library and Information Science Research, 18*, 323-342.

Hemenway, K., & Calishain, T. (2003). *Spidering Hacks: 100 Industrial-Strength Tips and Tools.* Sebastopol, CA: O'Reilly & Associates, Inc.

Henri, F. (1992). Computer conferencing and content analysis. In A. R. Kaye (Ed.), *Collaborative Learning through Computer Conferencing: The Najaden Papers* (pp. 115-136). New York: Springer.

Herring, S. C. (2004). Computer-mediated discourse analysis: An approach to researching online behavior. In S. A. Barab, R. Kling & J. H. Gray (Eds.), *Designing for Virtual Communities in the Service of Learning* (pp. 338-376). Cambridge, UK: Cambridge University Press.

Herring, S. (1999). Interactional coherence in CMC. *Journal of Computer-Mediated Communication, 4*(4).

Hewitt, J. (2005). Toward an understanding of how threads die in asynchronous computer conferences. *The Journal of the Learning Sciences, 14*(4), 567-589.

Hewitt, J., & Teplovs, C. (1999). An analysis of growth patterns in computer conferencing threads. In C. M. Hoadley & J. Roschelle (Eds.), *Proceeedings of Computer Support for Collaborative Learning 1999* (pp. 232-241). Mahwah, NJ: Lawrence Erlbaum Associates.

Hiltz, S. R. (1985). *Online Communities A Case Study of the Office of the Future.* Norwood, NJ: Ablex Publishing Corp.

Hutchins, E. (1996). *Cognition in the Wild.* Cambridge, MA: The MIT Press.

Levin, J. A., Kim, H., & Riel, M. M. (1990). Analyzing instructional interactions on electronic message networks. In L. M. Harasim (Ed.), *Online Education: Perspectives on a New Environment* (pp. 185–214). New York: Praeger.

Marcus, G. E. (1998). *Ethnography Through Thick and Thin.* Princeton, NJ: Princeton University Press.

Marra, R. M., Moore, J. L., & Klimczak, A. K. (2004). Content analysis of online discussion forums: A comparative analysis of protocols. *Educational Technology Research and Development, 52*(2), 23-40.

Moreno, J. L. (1953). *Who Shall Survive? Foundations of Sociometry.* Boston, MA: Beacon House.

Otte, E., & Rousseau, R. (2002). Social network analysis: A powerful strategy, also for the information sciences. *Journal of Information Science, 28*(6), 441-453.

Park, H. W., Kim, C. S., & Barnett, G. A. (2004). Socio-communicational structure among political actors on the web in south korea: The dynamics of digital presence in cyberspace. *New Media & Society, 6*(3), 403-423.

Price, D.J. de Solla (1965). Networks of scientific papers. *Science, 149*, 510-515.

Rapoport, A., & Horvath, W. J. (1961). A study of a large sociogram. *Behavioral Science, 6*, 279 -291.

Renninger, K. A., & Shumar, W. (2002). Community building with and for teachers at The Math Forum. In K. A. Renninger & W. Shumar (Eds.), *Building Virtual Communities: Learning and Change in Cyberspace* (pp. 60-95). Cambridge, UK: Cambridge University Press.

Rheingold, H. (1993). *The Virtual Community: Homesteading on the Electronic Frontier.* Cambridge, MA: The MIT Press.

Ridings, C. M., & Gefen, D. (2004). Virtual community attraction: Why people hang out online. *Journal of Computer-Mediated Communication, 10*(1), Article 4.

Rodgers, S., & Chen, Q. (2005). Internet community group participation: Psychosocial benefits for women with breast cancer. *Journal of Computer-Mediated Communication, 10*(4), Article 5.

Schlager, M. S., Fusco, J., & Schank, P. (2002). Evolution of an online education community of practice. In K. A. Renninger & W. Shumar (Eds.), *Building Virtual Communities: Learning and Change in Cyberspace* (pp. 129-158). Cambridge, UK: Cambridge University Press.

Scott, J. G. (2000). *Social Network Analysis: A Handbook* (2nd ed.). Thousand Oaks, CA: Sage Publications.

Scott, J. G. (1998). Trend report: Social network analysis. *Sociology, 22*(1), 109-127.

Scott, J. G., Tallia, A. F., Crosson, J. C., & et al. (2005). Social network analysis as an analytic tool for interaction patterns in primary care practices. *Annals of Family Medicine, 3*(5), 443-448.

Sharf, B. F. (1997). Communicating breast cancer on-line: Support and empowerment on the Internet. *Women & Health, 26*(1), 65-84.

Strauss, A. L., & Corbin, J. (1990). *Basics of Qualitative Research: Grounded Theory Procedures and Techniques.* Newbury Park, CA: Sage Publications.

Spradley, J. P. (1980). *Participant Observation.* London, UK: Wadsworth Publishing.

Valente, T. (1995). *Network Models of the Diffusion of Innovation.* Cresskill, NJ: Hampton Press.

Wasserman, S., & Faust, K. (1994). *Social Network Analysis: Methods and Applications.* Cambridge, UK: Cambridge University Press.

Wellman, B. (2001). Computer networks as social networks. *Science, 293*(14), 2031-2034.

AUTHOR NOTE

This material is supported in part by a grant from the National Science Foundation (ESI-0515494) to the first and second authors. Any opinions, findings, and conclusions or recommendations expressed in this material are those of the author(s) and do not necessarily reflect the views of the National Science Foundation.

KEY TERMS

Density describes the general level of linkage among the actors in a social network.

Ethnography is a methodological technique for examining and understanding community life.

Group-Level Cohesion can be used to identify who was communicating with whom in a discussion forum.

Networked Communities are those support network-based communities that have few, if any, geographic and/or temporal boundaries, which VLSCs support.

Online or Virtual Communities are sets of people that interact primarily using information communication technology (e.g., listserv, email, social networking applications) instead of face to face.

Open Coding involves reading and comparing individual data units so as to label similar units into categories.

Public Conversations are those that are open and accessible to anyone. Conversations can occur between many individuals behind closed walls, e.g., a major company's employees working on a major project.

Social Network Analysis (SNA) is a technique used to study the interactions between individuals in a community.

Sociograms visually convey relationships between actors. These sociograms make network structure explicit as collections of nodes with links that portray directionality and connection strength.

Very Large-Scale Conversations (VLSCs) are those that involve interchanges betweens hundreds and thousands of people. Newsgroups, chat forums, and Weblogs are examples of spaces where the volume of messages posted can range in the tens and hundreds of thousands.

Section IV
Query Log Analysis

Chapter XVI
Machine Learning Approach to Search Query Classification

Isak Taksa
Baruch College, City University of New York, USA

Sarah Zelikovitz
The College of Staten Island, City University of New York, USA

Amanda Spink
Queensland University of Technology, Australia

ABSTRACT

Search query classification is a necessary step for a number of information retrieval tasks. This chapter presents an approach to non-hierarchical classification of search queries that focuses on two specific areas of machine learning: short text classification and limited manual labeling. Typically, search queries are short, display little class specific information per single query and are therefore a weak source for traditional machine learning. To improve the effectiveness of the classification process the chapter introduces background knowledge discovery by using information retrieval techniques. The proposed approach is applied to a task of age classification of a corpus of queries from a commercial search engine. In the process, various classification scenarios are generated and executed, providing insight into choice, significance and range of tuning parameters.

INTRODUCTION

Machine learning for text classification is an active area of research, encompassing a variety of learning algorithms (Sebastiani, 2002), classification systems (Barry et al., 2004) and data representations (Spink and Jansen, 2004). Classification of search queries is one example of text classification that is particularly complex and challenging. Typically, search queries are short, reveal very few features per single query and are therefore a weak source for traditional machine learning. This chapter focuses on two specific areas of machine learning: short text classification problems and using a small set of labeled documents. We examine the issues of non-hierarchical (Cesa-Bianchi et al., 2006) classification and introduce a method that combines limited manual labeling, computational linguistics and information retrieval to classify a large collection of search queries. We discuss classification proficiency of the proposed method on a large search engine query log, and the implication of this approach on the advancement of short-text classification.

For this discussion we view query logs as sets of textual data on which we perform classification (Jansen, 2006). Observed in this way, each query in a log can be seen as a document that is to be classified according to some pre-defined set of labels, or *classes*. The approach described in this chapter classifies a corpus of search queries from the Excite search engine, by retrieving from the Web a set of background knowledge to learn additional features that are indicative of the classes. Viewing the initial log with the search queries as a document corpus $\boldsymbol{D} = \{d_1, d_2, \ldots d_i \ldots d_n\}$, we create a set of classes that indicate a personal demographic characteristic of the searcher, $\boldsymbol{C} = \{c_1, c_2, \ldots c_j \ldots c_m\}$. We present an approach that allows classification or the assignment of a class from the set *C* to many of the documents in the set *D*. This approach consists of the following five steps:

I. Select (from the print and the online media) a short set of manually chosen terms $\boldsymbol{T}_{init} = \{t_1, t_2, \ldots, t_j, \ldots, t_m\}$ consisting of terms t_j that are known a priori to be descriptive of a particular class c_j
II. Use this initial set *T* to classify a small subset of (search queries) set D thereby creating an initial set of classified queries $\boldsymbol{Q}_{init} = \{q_1, q_2, \ldots q_j \ldots q_l\}$
III. Submit these queries q_j to a commercial search engine and use the returned search results to build a temporary corpus of background knowledge $\boldsymbol{B}_{temp} = \{b_1, b_2, \ldots b_j \ldots b_{l*10}\}$
IV. Use an algorithm to select from *B* more class related terms *T*
V. Use this newly created set *T* to classify more documents (search queries) in corpus D thereby adding more classified queries to set *Q*.

While steps I and II are executed only once, steps III through V are repeated continuously until the classification process is terminated (Figure 1).

We focus on validating our approach to the classification of a set of short documents, namely search queries. This approach uses a combination of techniques: we first look at developing a method to obtain relevant background knowledge for a set of web queries; then we build the background knowledge to acquire ranked terms for improved information retrieval; we then investigate the impact of the new terms' selection algorithms on the effectiveness of the classification process.

BACKGROUND

Text classification (or alternatively, text categorization) can be defined as follows: Given a set of

Figure 1. Steps in a classification process

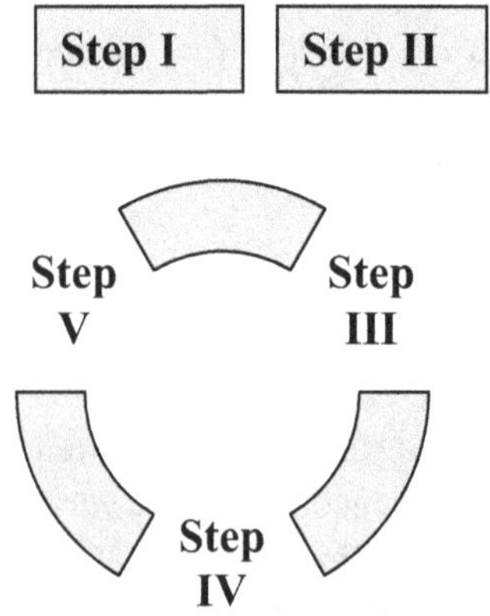

documents *D* and a set of *m* classes (or labels) *C*, define a function *F* that will assign a value from the set of *C* to each document in *D*. For example, *D* might consist of the set of all Mathematics paper titles, and *C* could therefore be the set of sub-areas of Mathematics in which these papers lie. Problems in text classification vary widely in many aspects. Some documents to be classified are very short text strings such as titles of Web pages, titles of papers or articles, or even simply names of companies. Others may consist of entire Web pages, email contents, or news articles, sometimes spanning many pages. There are document classification problems with many possible classes that overlap. Other problems may have only two or three classes with clear and unique definitions for the classes.

Instead of hand-crafting rules, the machine learning community approaches text classification problems as *supervised* learning problems. In this case the human expert simply has to label a set of examples with appropriate classes. This set of labeled examples is called the *training set*, which we will refer to as the set *T*. Once a training corpus of correctly labeled documents is available, there are a variety of techniques that can be used to create a set of rules or a model of the data that will allow future documents to be classified correctly. The techniques can be optimized and studied independently of the domains and specific problems that they will be used to address. A plethora of different learning algorithms have been applied to many different representations of textual documents, successfully allowing for the classification of documents in varied domains (Slattery & Mitchell, 2000; Sebastiani, 2002; Joachims 2002; Barry et al., 2004).

A common problem when using machine learning for text classification is dealing with an insufficient number of training examples to correctly classify instances with unknown classes. If there are too few examples, machine learning algorithms often cannot represent the classes properly, and therefore have a high error rate when attempting to classify new examples. In essence, few examples do not allow for the creation of a model of the data that generalizes well for new examples in the domain. There are a number of approaches that may be taken to aid in the creation of more accurate classifiers. Researchers have noted that although it is often the case that there are very few labeled examples, there are often many unlabeled examples readily available (Joachims, 1999; Nigam et al., 2000). An approach that has been taken by a number of researchers has been to choose, in some way, a *small* number of additional training examples that should be hand-labeled in order to add particular examples to the *labeled* training set that will improve learning. Uncertainty sampling has been used in this way (Lewis and Catlett, 1994) where specific examples are chosen out of a large pool of unlabeled examples to be given to humans to be classified. These hand labeled examples then become part of the training corpus. In this way fewer examples must be given to an expert to be labeled than if the examples were simply randomly sampled.

Even if we do not wish to give these unlabeled examples to experts to label, they can be used in a *semi-supervised* learning paradigm, in various ways and in conjunction with a variety of classifiers (Lanquillon, 2000) to improve classification. Work using naïve Bayes text classifiers use the labeled training examples to assign probabilistic classes to many unlabeled examples. These newly classified examples are then used in the classifier creation process (Nigam et al., 2000; Schneider, 2005; Nigam et al., 2006). Unlabeled examples have also been used to create new features for the set of labeled examples. In that, the set of labeled examples is enhanced by the information provided in the set of unlabeled examples (Szummer and Jaakkola, 2000).

If a small set of training examples can be re-expressed using different views (Ghani, 2002; Nigam and Ghani, 2000), or if two distinct learning algorithms can be used on the same small set of training data (Goldman and Zhou, 2000), the combination of the labeled and unlabeled sets can be used to achieve a highly accurate classifier. Semi-supervised Support Vector Machines (SVM) have been studied extensively as well (Joachims, 1999; Bennett and Demirez, 1998; Liu et al., 2004; Sindhwani and Keerthi, 2006). Unlabeled examples have also been used in conjunction with sets of known positive examples in two-class problems to improve classification (Li and Liu, 2003).

There are some problems for which unlabeled examples might not be particularly useful. Specifically, for short-text classification problems, unlabeled examples may be too short to learn new features, and too short to obtain proper word statistics. Machine learning algorithms depend on the co-occurrences of terms to provide understanding as to the probability of which terms fall into which classes. Text classification problems with short text entries in the training set do not allow for these types of generalizations. Furthermore, unlabeled examples or new examples to be classified might not share any terms with the training set.

Other approaches have been taken in these hard-to-classify domains. There have been studies of the incorporation of domain knowledge by selection and creation (Li and Liu 2003), cross-referencing query and domain documents (Wen et al., 2002), or reweighing of features using related information such as ontologies (Gabrilovich and Markovich, 2005) or user feedback (Raghavan et al., 2005; 2006). Domain knowledge has also been incorporated into text classifiers by modification of the classifiers to include prior results (Schapire et al., 2002; Wu and Srihari, 2005; Dayanik et al., 2006). There has also been work done using query-expansion type techniques to incorporate additional knowledge into text classifiers (Sahami and Heilman, 2006) and query formulation techniques using terms found in previously retrieved documents (Zhu et al., 2003). For additional review of relevant work in query classification we refer the reader to another chapter in this book ("Analytical approaches for topic analysis and identification of web search engine transaction logs" by Ozmutu, S., Ozmutu, H. & Spink, A).

Our research uses what we term as *background knowledge* to aid a short-text classifier. We define background knowledge for a text-classification task to be a set of text documents that is related to the task, but that does not consist simply of unlabeled examples. Background knowledge has been previously used (Zelikovitz et al., 2007; Zelikovitz and Kogan, 2006) to improve classification of unknown instances. These sets of background text are not of the same length and form as the training and unlabeled examples, but can be used to find common co-occurrences of terms, as well as terms that are indicative of specific classes.

The work that we present here is specifically related to text classification of *short* textual documents. Short text classification is a challenging type of classification because very little information (i.e. words) is known for each example that is to be classified. Because short text examples tend to share few terms, it is particularly difficult to classify new instances and common comparisons between texts often yield no useful results. Two pieces of text that could actually be of the same class in *C* can share no terms, since each of them contains only a few terms that do not overlap. Simply comparing a training set to unknown examples using traditional methods such as cosine similarities can therefore be useless. An example of short text classification that is receiving interest lately is the query classification (Sahami and Heilman, 2006; Sarawagi, 2005). Different approaches have been taken in these short text classification tasks to provide longer related knowledge to each one, by using web searches, synonyms, and statistical methods (Sarawagi, 2005).

METHODOLOGY

Our approach in this chapter is different from the traditional machine learning approaches described above. Instead of actually incorporating the background knowledge set into the learning algorithm, we use background knowledge for the purpose of finding previously unknown class related terms. As described earlier, we begin with only a small set of manually selected class related terms (or phrases). These terms are used to label a small set of documents – search queries extracted from a large Excite query log collected in the morning and afternoon hours of December 20, 1999 and contains close to 2.5 million queries (Excite, 1999). This small set of labeled documents is then used as search queries to retrieve a much larger set of longer, related documents. We analyze the larger set of related documents to learn additional class related terms for the classification task.

Bootstrapping from Known Class-Related Terms

To create the set of classes we used Levinson's *Life Structure Theory*. After studying a group of men and women Levinson introduced his theory (Levinson, 1986) as consisting of equilibrium/disequilibrium periods during which a man builds/questions his life structure. At the center of his theory is the *life structure*, the underlying pattern of an individual's life at any particular time. For our classes we use Levinson's seasonal cycles as shown in Table 1 below.

Using the abbreviations we get a set of classes as follows: *C= {EA, AW, SD, MA, CL, LA}*. We search for terms that are indicative of each of these classes. In particular, we obtained the terms (words or phrases) from well-known printed publications (Seventeen, Parenting, Family Circle, American Association of Retired Persons Magazine, etc.) and popular blogs (MySpace, The Chronicle, BloggingMommies, etc.). For each of the classes in set *C*, we manually selected a list of 10 words and phrases that are indicative of each of these classes. A partial example of these terms can be seen in Table 2.

Using the list of terms for each class, we culled a set of queries from the Excite log that contained these age-indicative terms. We began with a very small set of returned labeled queries; 60 in all, 10 per each of the six classes. This set of queries is our set of classified training documents that we use to start the classification of many other queries that do not contain the original list of class related terms. An example of a query selected

Table 1. Age categories

Levinson's Life Structure Theory		
AGE	*STAGE*	*SEASONAL CYCLE*
17-22	Early adult transition	Early adulthood (EA)
22-28	Enter adult world	Adult world (AW)
28-33	Age 30 transition	
33-40	Settle down	Settle down (SD)
40-45	Midlife transition	
45-50	Enter middle adulthood	Middle adulthood (MA)
50-55	Age 50 transition	
55-60	Culmination of middle adulthood	Culmination (CL)
60-65	Late adult transition	
65+	Late adulthood	Late adulthood (LA)

Table 2. Age indicative query terms

CLASS	*AGE INDICATIVE TERMS/PHRASES*
EA (17-22)	Cliff notes, Prom, College admission, Spring break, Internship, Summer job
AW (22-33)	Job, Wedding, Pregnancy, Child care, Housing, Mortgage, Graduate school
SD (33-45)	Investments, Family vacation, Summer home, 401(K), Prep schools, Schools
MA (45-55)	Retirement, Travel, Personal health, Elder care, Cosmetic surgery, Politics
CL (55-65)	Inheritance tax, Estate planning, Wills, Grand parenting, Cruises, Heart attack
LA (65+)	Philosophy, Persistent pain, Hip replacement, Medicare, Leisure

Table 3. Excite log queries

CLASS	*QUERY*
EW (17-22)	cliff notes Wuthering heights
AW (22-33)	Hotel catered wedding
SD (33-45)	Investment policy statement
MA (45-55)	retirement community Florida
CL (55-65)	IRS inheritance tax
LA (65+)	Arthritis pain

from the log for each of the classes in the set *C* is shown in Table 3.

Automatic Retrieval of Background Sets

We submitted the classified queries to the Google search engine to automatically create a background set of knowledge. For each of the classified queries we created a pool of documents, each of which was the text of a search result obtained by submitting the classified query to Google. We restricted search results to documents written in the English language. Google returned the top results of the search on the classified query that were downloaded and stored. We saved the textual sections of the pages that were downloaded, and each one became a document, classified according to the class of the query that generated it. We limited our returned results to the top 10 pages returned for each query since users frequently examine just the first page (top 10 results) (Spink and Jansen, 2004; Taksa, 2005). After downloading search results we had a set of ten text documents for each one of our queries. These were then used as a corpus for analysis. This method allows for the retrieval of documents that are class related, but are much longer than the original queries. The queries from the search log are an average length of ~3 words, whereas the new documents that were downloaded had an average length of several thousand words, and hence more could be learned from them.

An example of a query that was classified as an *EA (17-22)* query is:

Cliff Notes Wuthering Heights

The top page returned by Google was: http://www.cliffsnotes.com/WileyCDA/LitNote/id-164.html - the official Cliff Notes site. The first paragraph of this page is:

Call it a Cliff Note, Cliffs Note, or CliffsNotes, if you're looking for the original literature study guide series then you've come to the right place. Use the links below to find free summaries, character analyses, essay suggestions, important quotes, and more to help you get the very most from your study time.

As can be seen from this example, there are other terms here that high school students might search on, namely *essay*, or *study guide*, or even alternate spellings of *Cliff Notes*.

Finding New Class Related Terms

Each page that was returned by Google was labeled with the class category of the query that produced it. This set of pages can be looked at as a new and different document *training* corpus with known labels. The training set T consists of the returned search pages, and the classes C are the classes that were used to label the original small set of hand-labeled queries. However, the properties of this training corpus are markedly different than the original query training set. Essentially, this newly created training corpus does not consist of short-text examples. As opposed to our original data set, where examples were queries only a few words long, this larger returned corpus contains entries that are web-page length. Hence there is much more generalization that we can do from the words in this larger returned document corpus.

What is especially interesting is the new, larger, document corpus vocabulary. A serious disadvantage of short-text corpora is that they do not contain a rich enough vocabulary to facilitate learning, however, with a longer document corpus we can learn much about the domain from the set of words that are in it. In essence, our method of page retrieval allows us to swap a short-text corpus for one with longer entries from which we can learn.

Our approach studies the set of terms that composes the returned document corpus to find those particular terms that are related to our classification problem. We began by using the information gain (IG) criterion to rank *all* terms in the corpus; no stemming was used to facilitate query creation later. For a supervised text classification task, each term that is present in the training corpus can be seen as a feature that can be used individually for classification. For example, suppose that the term *investment* occurs in the training corpus. We can partition the training corpus into two disjoint subsets, one of which contains the word *investment*, and one of which does not. Given the training set of classified examples, T, we can partition it by the presence or absence of each term, t that exists in these examples. We can then determine how closely related this term is to the classification task.

To do this, we borrow a concept from Information Theory, called *information gain*, which has been used by machine learning researchers for the purposes of classification (Quinlan, 1986). Given a probability distribution $P = (p_1, p_2, ..., p_n)$ then the information conveyed by this distribution, also called the *entropy* of P, is:

$$entropy(P) = -(p_1 \times \log(p_1) + p_2 \times \log(p_2) + \ldots p_n \times \log(p_n))$$

Essentially, this measure is a measure of the randomness of the distribution. High entropy signifies that the distribution is random, whereas low entropy signifies that there is some pattern in the data. In the field of information theory, the entropy is a measure of how many bits it takes to transmit a message with the probability distribution P. If we wish to discover the entropy of a training set T, then the probability distribution P is simply the set of probabilities that a training example fits into any of the classes of set C. From these training set probabilities we can compute *entropy (T)*.

Each term *t* gives a partition of the training set *T*, $\{T_0, T_1\}$, where T_0 consists of those training examples that contain the term *t*, and T_1 consists of those training examples that do not contain the term *t*. For each of these subsets, we can compute individual entropies, and the summation of those entropies, weighted by the probability distribution gives us the information needed to identify the class of a training example after the partition is done.

The information gain (*IG*) for a term *t* tells us how much information is gained by partitioning the training set *T* on the term *t*. It is defined as the subtraction:

$$IG(t) = entropy(T) - (entropy(T_0) \times \frac{|T_0|}{|T|} + entropy(T_1) \times \frac{|T_1|}{|T|})$$

Terms with high information gain create partitions of the original training set that overall have lower entropy, and therefore are reflective of the particular classification scheme.

The computation of the *IG* value for each of these terms allows us to learn important features in this background corpus. However, our challenge was to determine which of these features best reflected each class. To discover which terms give us information about particular classes, we sorted all terms in the corpus in descending order based upon the *IG* value. We labeled each of the terms with the class whose training examples most reflected this term, i.e. whose training examples actually most often contained that term. See Table 4 for a partial list of the terms with the highest information gain (IG) for the class *AW (22-33)*.

We then chose the top terms for each of the classes. At this point we selected a list of fifty terms (per class) to classify queries that were not classified before. An example of some of the derived terms for all of the classes can be seen in Table 5.

It is important to note that some of the text documents did not contain the terms that were associated with their class. We are not concerned with this fact, however, because we are simply looking for good indicative terms that are related to particular classes.

DISCUSSION

To assess the effectiveness of the proposed approach we designed and implemented several evaluation scenarios (Table 6). By successively modifying parameters (one at a time) that describe each scenario, we identified parameters that affect the classification process.

Creating Evaluation Scenarios

Five parameters describe every scenario. The first parameter, not shown in the table and constant for all scenarios, is the number of manually selected class terms used to bootstrap the process. As specified above the number is 10. Other parameters are

Table 4. Terms with highest IG for class AW (22-33)

TERM	*IG*
Bride	0.61277
Planner	0.55563
Menu	0.55034

Table 5. Derived classification terms

CLASS	*NEW TERMS/PHRASES*
EW (17-22)	Essay, guide, college, character
AW (22-33)	Bride, planner, menu, romantic, flowers
SD (33-45)	Dividends, long term, interest, monthly
MA (45-55)	Golf, builder, luxury, villa, condominium
CL (55-65)	Bequest, valuation, income, gift, publication
LA (65+)	Chronic pain, joints, painkillers

modifiable, and their values are listed in Table 6. We started with Scenario-A (base scenario) and modified only one of the parameters at a time to generate three groups of additional scenarios. The first, ***Group α***, varies the quantity of queries (*Column I*) and query selection process (*Column II*). The second, ***Group β***, uses two contrasting numbers (*Column III*) of newly acquired terms for the classification process. The third, ***Group γ***, modifies the order (*Column IV*) of top 100 classifications terms used for the classification process.

The first parameter *Number of queries to retrieve background knowledge* (column I) represents the number of queries that are selected from the queries classified in the prior iteration of our algorithm. These queries are submitted to Google to retrieve "background knowledge". In all the scenarios this number is 10 except for Scenario-B where the number is 20. We want to examine whether increasing the size of the retrieved background knowledge would generate better quality classification terms.

The next parameter *Query selection process* (column II) specifies the process of selecting new search queries from amongst the newly classified queries. In most scenarios the process is random, which means that from a pool of queries classified we select (via a random number generator) a small set of queries to add to our labeled training set. The process is changed for Scenario-C. The majority of the queries in the log are 2 to 3 words long. We sort the queries that match our list of class-related terms in descending order of their length (number of terms in the query, excluding stop words). We use the top 10 longest queries for the retrieval of the background knowledge. For example, in Table 7, we list four sample queries that have terms related to wedding planning. Query #2 is the longest query – it has four meaningful terms.

On the other hand, for Scenario-D we are looking for "lighter" queries. We take the four queries in Table 7 and submit each term to Google

Table 7. Sample queries

QUERY #1	Catered hotel wedding
QUERY #2	Wedding reception menu ideas
QUERY #3	Wedding planner in Dallas
QUERY #4	Party planner in Dallas

Table 6 Classification scenarios

TYPE	***SCENARIO***	***Number of queries to retrieve background knowledge***	***Query selection process***	***Number of top classification terms***	***Terms selection process***
		I	***II***	***III***	***IV***
Base	**Scenario-A**	10	Random	50	Top
Group α	**Scenario-B**	20	Random	50	Top
	Scenario-C	10	"Longer"	50	Top
	Scenario-D	10	"Lighter"	50	Top
Group β	**Scenario-E**	10	Random	30	Top
	Scenario-F	10	Random	100	Top
Group γ	**Scenario-G**	10	Random	50	"Lightest" of the top 100
	Scenario-H	10	Random	50	"Heaviest" of the top 100

to find document frequency for every term. See results in Table 8. We use this frequency as the query weight. For example, the "lightest" query in this table is Query#1 (its "lightest" term has the smallest frequency). The heaviest is Query#4 (same reasoning). To break the tie between Query#3 and Query#4 we have to go down to the third term.

The next parameter *Number of top classification terms* (column III) represents the number of new terms that will be used in the next classification iteration. After calculating the Information Gain (IG) for every term in background knowledge, we sort the list in descending order of IG. The list is long and we use the top 50 terms only. For Scenario-E we use only the top 30 terms and for Scenario-F we use the top 100 terms.

The final parameter *Terms selection process* (column IV) specifies the selection of new classification terms from the sorted list produced by IG calculations. For all scenarios we use Top-50, but for the last two scenarios we take the Top-100 and go to Google to find their frequencies. For Scenario-G we sort the Top-100 list in ascending order of the frequencies and pick the 50 "lightest" queries and for Scenario-H the other half of the list or the 50 "heaviest" queries.

Appraising Classification Results

To start (bootstrap) Scenario-A (and all other scenarios), we used a manually selected set consisting of 60 terms (10 per each class). Even though this set is negligible in size, it allowed for classification of over 8% of the query log. The number of queries that can be classified for the bootstrap step and for the subsequent six unsupervised iterations are shown in Table 9.

The second row of numbers in all cells shows the number of classified queries (per iteration) as a percent of the class total after all classification iterations. The chart (Figure 2) for the second set of numbers demonstrates a) highly fluctuating individual class/iteration classification results and b) steady decline of iteration classification results for all classes combined.

Table 10 exhibits classification results of all eight scenarios. Overall, only one scenario demonstrated slightly better results than the base Scenario-A. All other scenarios, while demonstrating measurable improvements for individual classes, failed to produce any improvement for the complete scenario.

In the first of three groups, ***Group a***, we tried two different approaches: the increased number of newly classified queries used to retrieve the background knowledge (Scenario-B) and different methodologies of selecting these queries (Scenario-C and Scenario-D). Scenario-B showed a slight overall improvement over the base Scenario-A (1%), while demonstrating an individual improvement in two out of the six classification classes. On the other hand, Scenario-C (longer queries) showed improvement in only one class

Table 8. Determining query's size and weight

QUERY#1		*QUERY#2*		*QUERY#3*		*QUERY#4*	
TERM	FREQ.*	TERM	FREQ.*	TERM	FREQ.*	TERM	FREQ.*
catered	8.2	reception	101	planner	59	planner	59
wedding	176	wedding	176	Dallas	117	Dallas	117
hotel	453	ideas	344	wedding	176	party	553
		menu	664				

**frequency in millions*

Table 9. Scenario A - classification results

	NUMBER OF CLASSIFIED QUERIES							
CLASS	**Bootstrap Step**	**Unsupervised Iterations**						
		1	**2**	**3**	**4**	**5**	**6** **29,374** **11,472** **9,656**	**Class Total**
EA (17-22)	84,541 **(32%)**	52,540 **(20%)**	22,427 **(8%)**	38,464 **(15%)**	26,275 **(10%)**	15,264 **(6%)**	23,374 **(9%)**	262,885 **(100%)**
AW (22-33)	37,344 **(25%)**	23,421 **(16%)**	14,438 **(10%)**	21,783 **(15%)**	13,642 **(9%)**	21,643 **(15%)**	14,472 **(10%)**	146,743 **(100%)**
SD (33-45)	49,473 **(31%)**	34,212 **(21%)**	22,427 **(14%)**	18,953 **(12%)**	11,378 **(7%)**	14,562 **(9%)**	9,656 **(6%)**	160,661 **(100%)**
MA (45-55)	28,136 **(17%)**	32,652 **(20%)**	26,538 **(16%)**	21,642 **(13%)**	22,455 **(13%)**	18,713 **(11%)**	17,210 **(10%)**	167,346 **(100%)**
CL (55-65)	11,350 **(27%)**	6,427 **(15%)**	8,259 **(19%)**	6,230 **(15%)**	3,174 **(8%)**	4,215 **(10%)**	2,721 **(6%)**	42,376 **(100%)**
LA (65+)	6,713 **(33%)**	3,247 **(16%)**	1,521 **(8%)**	2,874 **(14%)**	3,943 **(19%)**	1,379 **(7%)**	562 **(3%)**	20,239 **(100%)**
Iteration Total	217,557 **(27%)**	152,499 **(19%)**	95,610 **(12%)**	109,946 **(14%)**	80,867 **(10%)**	75,776 **(9%)**	67,995 **(9%)**	800,250 **(100%)**
% of all queries	***8.70***	***6.09***	***3.82***	***4.40***	***3.23***	***3.03***	***2.72***	***32.01***

Figure 2. Individual class/iteration classification results

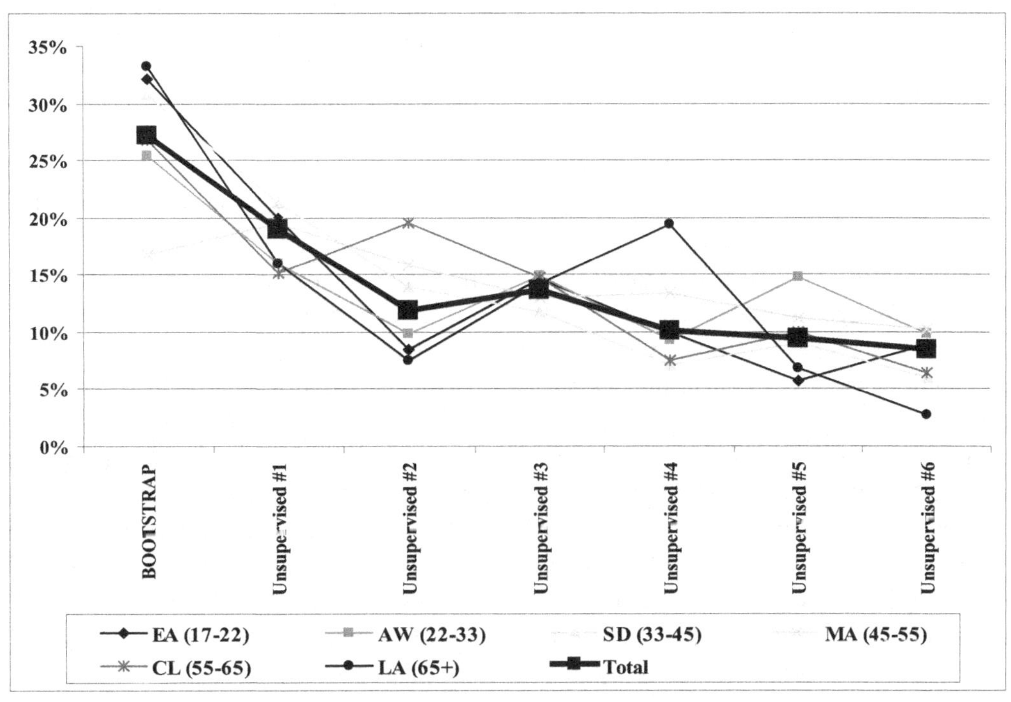

Table 10. Comparison of all classification results (class/scenario). Items in bold font show increase vs. the base Scenario-A.

	SCENARIO							
CLASS	*A*	*B*	*C*	*D*	*E*	*F*	*G*	*H*
EA (17-22)	262,885	**291,575**	**270,536**	254,210	255,471	**274,213**	259,574	247,533
AW (22-33)	146,743	129,073	133,278	139,541	129,843	126,913	144,526	137,728
SD (33-45)	160,661	**165,240**	153,544	159,257	158,474	157,618	146,711	156,390
MA (45-55)	167,346	162,548	132,549	148,232	143,269	161,431	129,550	152,479
CL (55-65)	42,376	45,216	37,050	38,672	25,846	35,341	29,535	39,542
LA (65+)	20,239	14,753	16,492	13,561	15,847	19,540	15,236	17,220
CLASS TOTAL	*800,250*	*808,405*	*743,449*	*753,473*	*728,750*	*775,056*	*725,132*	*750,892*
% CHANGE	*0%*	1%	-7%	-6%	-9%	-3%	-9%	-6%

and Scenario-D ("lighter" queries) showed no improvements in individual classes. Both scenarios fell by 7% and 6% respectively in overall performance vs. the base Scenario-A. There are several interesting observations that came from these experiments. The largest class *EA (17-22)* was the biggest beneficiary of either Scenario-B (more queries) or Scenario-C (longer queries) used to generate background knowledge. While these approaches were beneficial for one class, they produced inferior results for others. Similarly, looking for less frequent queries (Scenario-D), either produced negative improvement or no improvement at all. This is intuitively the case because many of the less frequent queries are variations of more common popular queries, and our background sets were unable to produce new, previously unknown terms, with high information gain. For example, no matter what literary work follows the term *CliffNotes*, the "Top 10" results are either identical or very similar. Although a query containing *Cliff Notes* and some obscure work might be uncommon in the query log, the set of 10 background texts that it returned are not new.

In the second group, ***Group β***, we examined the influence, or actually lack of any, by varying the number of new classification terms produced by the retrieved background knowledge. Instead of the usual 50 terms, used throughout all other scenarios, we first reduced this number to 30 (Scenario-E) and overall scenario results dropped by 9% vs. the base scenario. And after increasing this number to 100 (Scenario-F), the drop in performance was only 3%. While the overall scenario's performance went down, only one class showed improved performance when this number was increased to 100.

In the third group, ***Group γ***, we used two distinct ordering schemas of the terms produced by the retrieved background knowledge. As usual, we selected the 100 terms with the highest information gain (IG). But instead of using the top 50 (as we did in other scenarios) we reordered the top 100 terms according to the document frequencies returned by Google for each term. We used the frequency as the "weight" of the term and sorted the top 100 list in ascending order of the term's "weight" for Scenario-G and descending order for Scenario-H. In both scenarios we used the top 50 terms. Again, both scenarios produced results inferior to the base Scenario-A. While investigating the effectiveness of these two scenarios, we observed that the most common terms in our Excite corpus are often scattered throughout the *IG* sorted list of words. Many of the most common terms in the Excite corpus do not have high information gain in any iteration. This is intuitive, because many common search terms are generic in the sense that queries of all classes of *C* may contain them. These terms are not really useful when classifying documents and our *IG* method that ranks terms will discover that these terms are not class related.

Furthermore, as we reflect on the nature of the data that we are using for our approach, there are several objective factors that make this classification task and our approach to it, a difficult one. First, according to a topical study of the same log, a large number of queries are intra-class in nature (e.g. 20.3% People and places, 7.5% Sex and pornography, 6.8% Non-English or unknown) (Spink et al., 2002), and therefore are not easily classifiable according to our original set of classes, *C*. In particular, many of the queries in the Excite log may contain no terms that can be deemed class related, or may contain terms that fit two or more classes. It would be impossible to classify these types of queries. The other important factor that affects the match of queries in the log and terms in the background set, is the fact that we are using today's Web collection and search engine to produce the background set, but the query log was collected in 1999. The Web collection grew tenfold in the last seven years; search engines are fine-tuned to return results that reflect contemporary culture and language (Spink et al., 2004).

Finally it is essential to keep in mind the season (Chaw at al., 2005). Five days before Christmas the users are searching for very specific things, such as *candles* for a party, *recipes* for holiday meals, tree *decorations and ornaments* or holiday *gifts* or *presents* for friends.

CONCLUSION AND FUTURE RESEARCH

We develop and demonstrate an approach to semi-supervised classification of unlabeled short documents (search queries). We start with a small manually selected training set and expand it by developing background knowledge that provides a new set of classification terms. By iteratively applying this approach and improving performance of the ranking algorithm we are able to classify many queries in a large query log.

There are several promising directions for future research. Temporal study of the proposed approach is the first that comes to mind. It will show the impact of the current Web collection and search technology on classification of older logs. While the size of the training set doesn't seem to be an issue, a better selection of terms and the inclusion of appropriately classified inter-class terms require further study.

Evaluation of our classification results in terms of the comparison of classified queries to well known, age-related sites is also a direction that we are currently exploring.

REFERENCES

Barry, A. M., Holmes J., & Llor`a, X. (2004). Data mining using learning classifier systems. In L. Bull (Ed.), *Applications of Learning Classifier Systems, Lecture Notes in Computer Science: Studies in Fuzziness and Soft Computing*, 15–67. Berlin, Germany: Springer.

Bennett, K. & Demiriz, A. (1998). Semi-Supervised Support Vector Machines. In *Advances in Neural Information Processing Systems 11*. MIT Press.

Cesa-Bianchi, N., Gentile, C. & Zaniboni, L. (2006). Hierarchical Classification: Combining Bayes with SVM. In *Proceedings of the 23rd International Conference on Machine Learning,* 177–184. Pittsburgh, PA.

Chau, M., Fang, X., & Sheng, O. R. L., (2005). Analysis of the Query Logs of a Web Site Search Engine. *Journal of the American Society for Information Science and Technology*, 56(13), 1363–1376

Dayanik, A., Lewis, D. D., Madigan, D., Menkov, V. & Genkin, A. (2006). Constructing informative prior distributions from domain knowledge in text classification. In *Proceedings of the 29th Annual international ACM SIGIR Conference on Research and Development in Information Retrieval,* 493–500. ACM Press, New York

Excite (1999). Excite and other more recent data sets can be downloaded from http://ist.psu.edu/faculty_pages/jjansen/academic/transaction_logs.html

Gabrilovich, E., & Markovitch, S. (2005). Feature generation for text categorization using world knowledge. In *Proceedings of the Nineteenth International Joint Conference of Artificial Intelligence*, 1048–1053.

Ghani, R. (2002). Combining Labeled and Unlabeled Data for MultiClass Text Categorization. In *Proceedings of the Nineteenth International Conference on Machine Learning*, 187–194. Morgan Kaufmann.

Goldman S., & Zhou, Y. (2000). Enhancing Supervised Learning with Unlabeled Data. In *Proceedings of the Seventeenth International Conference on Machine Learning*, 327–334. Morgan Kaufmann.

Jansen, B. J. 2006. Search log analysis: What is it; what's been done; how to do it. *Library and Information Science Research*, 28(3), 407–432.

Joachims T. (2002). The Maximum-Margin Approach to Learning Text Classifiers. In *Ausgezeichnete Informatikdissertationen*, D. Wagner et al. (Hrsg.), *GI-Edition - Lecture Notes in Informatics (LNI)*, Köllen Verlag, Bonn, 2002.

Lanquillon, C. (2000). Learning from Labelled and Unlabeled Documents: A Comparative Study on Semi-Supervised Text Classification. In *Proceedings of PKDD-00, 4th European Conference on Principles of Data Mining and Knowledge Discovery*, 490–497. Springer Verlag, Heidelberg, DE.

Levinson, D.J.(1986). *The Seasons of a Man's Life*. New York: Ballantine Books.

Lewis, D. D., & Catlett, J. (1994). Heterogeneous Uncertainty Sampling for Supervised Learning. In *Proceedings of the Eleventh International Conference on Machine Learning,* 148–156. Morgan Kaufmann.

Li, X., & Liu, B. (2003). Learning to Classify Text Using Positive and Unlabeled Data. In *Proceedings of the Eighteenth International Joint Conference on Artificial Intelligence,* 587–594). Morgan Kaufmann.

Liu, X., Croft, W. B., Oh, P. & Hart, D. (2004). Automatic recognition of reading levels from user queries. *Proceedings of the 27th ACM International Conference on Research and Development in Information Retrieval*, 548–549, Sheffield, United Kingdom.

Nigam, K., & Ghani, R. (2000). Analyzing the Effectiveness and Applicability of Co-training. In *Proceedings of the Ninth International Conference on Information and Knowledge Management*, 86–93. ACM.

Nigam, K., McCallum, A. K., Thrun, S., & Mitchell, T. (2000). Text Classification from Labeled and Unlabeled Documents using EM. *Machine Learning, 39*(2/3), 103–134.

Nigam K., McCallum A., & Mitchell T. (2006) Semi-Supervised Text Classification Using EM. In *Semi-Supervised Learning*, Olivier Chapelle, Bernhard Schölkopf, & Alexander Zien (Eds.), 31-51, MIT Press.

Quinlan, J. R. (1986). Induction of Decision Trees. *Machine Learning*, 1, 81–106.

Raghavan, H., Madani, O., & Jones, R. (2006). Active Learning with Feedback on Both Features and Instances. *Journal of Machine Learning Research*, Volume 7, 1655–1686.

Raghavan, H., Madani, O., & Jones, R. (2005). Interactive Feature Selection. In *Proceedings of the Nineteenth International Joint Conference of Artificial Intelligence*, 841–846.

Sahami M., & Heilman, T. D. (2006). A Web-based Kernel Function for Measuring the Similarity of Short-text Snippets. In *Proceedings of the Fifteenth International World Wide Web Conference*, 377–386. ACM.

Sarawagi, S. (Ed.). (2005). *SIGKDD Explorations, Newsletter of the ACM Special Interest Group on Knowledge Discovery and Data Mining.* Addison Wesley.

Schapire, R. E., Rochery, M., Rahim, M., & Gupta, N. (2002) Incorporating Prior Knowledge into Boosting. In *Proceedings of the International Conference on Machine Learning*, 538–545. Morgan Kaufmann.

Schneider, K.-M. (2005). Techniques for Improving the Performance of Naïve Bayes for Text Classification. *Sixth International Conference on Intelligent Text Processing and Computational Linguistics.* LNCS 3406, 682–693.

Sebastiani, F. (2002). Machine learning in automated text categorization. *ACM Computer Surveys, 34*(1), 1–47.

Sindhwani, S., & Keerthi, S. (2006) Large scale semi-supervised linear SVMs. In *Proceedings of the 29th annual international ACM SIGIR conference on Research and Development in Information Retrieval*, 477–484. ACM Press.

Slattery, S., & Mitchell, T. (2000). Discovering Test Set Regularities in Relational Domains. In *Proceedings of the Seventeenth International Conference on Machine Learning*, 895–902. Morgan Kaufmann.

Spink, A., & Jansen, B. J. (2004). *Web search, public searching of the web.* New York: Kluwer.

Spink, A., Wolfram, D., Jansen, B. J., & Saracevic, T. (2001). The public and their queries. *Journal of the American Society for Information Science and Technology*, 52(3), 226–234.

Spink, A., Jansen, B. J., Wolfram, D., & Saracevic, T. (2002). From E-Sex to E-Commerce: Web Search Changes. *IEEE Computer*, 35(3), 107–109.

Szummer, M., & Jaakkola T. (2000). Kernel expansions With Unlabeled Examples. In *Advances in Neural Information Processing Systems* 13, 626–632. MIT Press.

Taksa, I. (2005). Predicting the Cumulative Effect of Multiple Query Formulations, In *Proceedings of the IEEE International Conference on Information Technology: Coding and Computing,* Volume II, April 2005, 491–496.

Wen, J-R., Nie, J-Y. & Zhang, H-J. (2002). Query clustering using user logs. *ACM, Transactions on Information Systems*, 20(1), 59–81.

Wu, X., & Srihari, R. K. (2004). Incorporating prior knowledge with weighted margin support vector machines. In *Proceedings of KDD*, 326–333. ACM Press.

Zelikovitz, S., Cohen, W. W., & Hirsh H. (2007). Extending WHIRL with Background Knowledge for Improved Text Classification. *Information Retrieval, 10*(1), 35–67.

Zelikovitz, S. & Kogan, M. (2006). Using Web Searches on Important Words to Create Background Sets for LSI Classification. In *Proceedings of the Nineteenth International FLAIRS Conference*, 598–603. AAAI Press.

Zhu, T., Greiner, R. & Haeubl, G. (2003). Learning a model of a web user's interests. *Proceedings of the 9th International Conference on User Modeling, Lecture Notes in Computer Science,* 2702, 65–75, Springer.

KEY TERMS

Background Knowledge: Body of text, images, databases, or other data that is related to a particular machine learning classification task. The background knowledge may contain information about the classes; it may contain further examples; it may contain data about both examples and classes.

Entropy: Measurement that can be used in machine learning on a set of data that is to be classified. In this setting it can be defined as the amount of uncertainty or randomness (or noise) in the data. If all data is classified with the same class, the entropy of that set would be 0. The entropy of a set *T* that has a probability distribution of classes $\{p_1, p_2, \ldots p_n\}$ can be defined as $-(p_1 \times \log(p_1) + p_2 \times \log(p_2) + \ldots p_n \times \log(p_n))$.

Information Gain: The amount of information in a given set of data can be defined as (1 – *entropy)*. If any observation about the given data is made, new information can then be recomputed. The difference between the two information values is the "information gain". In other words, the change of entropy is the information that is gained by the observation. If we partition a set T into T_1 and T_0, based upon some characteristic of the data then the information gain of that partition can be defined as:

$$IG(t) = entropy\,(T) - (entropy\,(T_0) \times \frac{|T_0|}{|T|} + entropy\,(T_1) \times \frac{|T_1|}{|T|})$$

Labeled Set: Set of item-label pairs. The item consists of an actual example that can be classified, and the label is the classification. In a supervised learning paradigm this set is sometimes referred to as the "training set".

Machine Learning: The area of artificial intelligence that studies the algorithms and processes that allow machines to learn. These algorithms use a combination of techniques to learn from examples, from prior knowledge, or from experience.

Text Classification: Process of assigning classes (or labels) to textual data. Textual data can range from short phrases to much longer documents. Sometimes referred to as "text categorization", a text classification task can be defined as follows: Given a set of documents $D = \{d_1, d_2, \ldots, d_n\}$ and a set of classes $C = \{c_1, c_2, \ldots, c_m\}$ assign a label from the set *C* to each element of set *D*.

Unlabeled Set: Set of examples whose labels or classes are unknown. If the class of an unlabeled example is learned, it can then be added to a "labeled set".

Chapter XVII
Topic Analysis and Identification of Queries

Seda Ozmutlu
Uludag University, Turkey

Huseyin C. Ozmutlu
Uludag University, Turkey

Amanda Spink
Queensland University of Technology, Australia

ABSTRACT

This chapter emphasizes topic analysis and identification of search engine user queries. Topic analysis and identification of queries is an important task related to the discipline of information retrieval which is a key element for the development of successful personalized search engines. Topic identification of text is also no simple task, and a problem yet unsolved. The problem is even harder for search engine user queries due to real-time requirements and the limited number of terms in the user queries. The chapter includes a detailed literature review on topic analysis and identification, with an emphasis on search engine user queries, a survey of the analytical methods that have been and can be used, and the challenges and research opportunities related to topic analysis and identification.

INTRODUCTION

There are billions of pages over the Internet, and it would virtually be impossible to retrieve information from the Web efficiently unless search engines were available. This chapter emphasizes one of the most intriguing facets of search engine user query or transaction log analysis, topic analysis and identification of user queries. Topic analysis of queries is a very important dimension of transaction log analysis, since it is directly related to effective use of search engines, considering that the advances in search engine design are geared towards the development of personalized and topic-specific search engine algorithms.

The obvious potential improvements in search engine design are the personalization and specialization of search engines. Specialized search engines ideally provide only and all the Web pages relevant to a specified topic. Personalized search engines are designed considering individual user needs, and it is a real challenge to capture user information behavior, since people have different and changing information needs, and they utilize different information seeking strategies to solve their information seeking problems (Gremett, 2006). In order to develop successful personalized search engines, it is important to capture the content-based behavior of users, and thus analyze the topics of transaction log queries.

One of the most important dimensions of search engine user information seeking behavior is content-based behavior. The ideal point in analyzing the content-based behavior of search engine users is to successfully perform topic identification of user queries. Had topic identification of user queries been successfully performed in real-time, it would be possible to develop search engine algorithms that can cluster and rank results in real-time based on user topics and needs, hence personalize the search results. Such algorithms would be an effective step in building the link between user information-seeking needs and personalized search engines by personalizing search results. Radlinski and Dumais (2006) and Agichtein, Brill, Dumais and Ragno (2006) state that personalizing search results for individual users is increasingly being recognized as an important future direction for Web search, and that accurate modeling and interpretation of user behavior has important applications to ranking, search personalization, and other tasks. Along these lines, several studies have flourished that bridge the gap between user behavior information and personalized search engine algorithms, such as those of Agichtein, Brill and Dumais (2006). Also, Google launched its personalized search engine in October 2006.

The chapter begins with a detailed literature review of the methods related to topic identification of user queries in transaction logs, continues with a detailed explanation of the models used for topic identification, and ends with a discussion and conclusion.

LITERATURE REVIEW FOR TOPIC ANALYSIS AND IDENTIFICATION OF USER QUERIES

In this chapter, we include a literature review of the state-of-the-art on topic analysis and identification. Topic analysis and identification studies ranging from basic analysis of topics and terms of search engine queries, to query clustering, session identification, automatic new topic identification and query topic identification models, and then to the more general context of text classification, categorization and mining, will be included in the literature review.

Topic Analysis of Search Engine Queries

Several researchers have analyzed search engine transaction logs at the term level and at the conceptual level. A detailed review of these studies and their content-based analysis is given in the other chapter by Ozmutlu, Ozmutlu and Spink in this handbook (i.e. "From Analysis To Estimation of User Behavior"). Silverstein, Henzinger, Marais and Moricz (1999), Jansen, Spink, Bateman and Saracevic (1998), Jansen, Spink and Saracevic (2000) have performed content analysis of search engine data logs at the term level, and have observed that some of the high-frequency terms reflect interest in current events, but still the highest ranking terms are related to topics of pornography, entertainment and education. Spink, Wolfram, Jansen and Saracevic (2001) analyzed

Excite transaction logs collected in 1999 for terms and have discovered that the top category subject of queries was entertainment and recreation, closely followed by sex, pornography and preferences. Besides term analysis, Jansen, Spink and Saracevic (2000) and Spink, Wolfram, Jansen and Saracevic (2001) have also performed analysis of a sample of queries at the conceptual or topical level and discovered that the top category in subject of queries was entertainment and recreation, closely followed by sex, pornography and preferences. Spink, Jansen, Wolfram and Saracevic (2002) analyzed Excite datasets from 1997, 1999 and 2001 and found that users' interests have shifted from entertainment and pornography to travel and commerce.

Other researchers have analyzed the search engine queries in specific topics, which can be listed as follows:

- Multimedia queries (Jansen, Goodrum, and Spink, 2000; Goodrum and Spink, 2001; Ozmutlu, Spink and Ozmutlu, 2003; Ozmutlu, Ozmutlu and Spink, 2002; Jansen, Spink and Pedersen, 2003, 2005)
- Sexual queries (Spink, Ozmultu, and Lorence, 2004; Spink, Koricich, Jansen and Cole, 2004)
- Question and request-format queries (Spink and Ozmutlu, 2001; Spink and Ozmutlu, 2002; Ozmutlu, Ozmutlu and Spink, 2003)
- E-commerce queries (Spink and Guner, 2001; Spink and Jansen, 2004)
- Medical queries (Spink, Yang, Nykanen, Lorence, Jansen, Ozmutlu, and Ozmutlu, 2004)

Multitasking queries have also been an important research area in transaction log analysis. Search engine users might be interested in multiple topics over time, and in terms of information retrieval, multitasking information seeking and searching processes are defined as "the process of searches over time in relation to more than one, possibly evolving, set of information problems including changes or shifts in beliefs, cognitive, affective, and/or situational states" (Spink, Ozmutlu and Ozmutlu, 2002). A detailed review on multitasking is available in the other chapter by Ozmutlu, Ozmutlu and Spink in this handbook (i.e. "From Analysis To Estimation of User Behavior").

There are relatively few studies on topic identification. These studies can be summarized under session identification, query clustering and automatic new topic identification. Although mentioned with different terms, these studies cater to the same objective, grouping the queries such as to divide a session into different clusters, where each cluster depicts a new topic. One of the main elements of content-based behavior is new topic identification or session identification (these terminologies have been used widely in literature to define the same concept). New topic identification or session identification is discovering when the user has switched from one topic to another during a single search session to group sequential log entries that are related to a common topic (He, Goker and Harper, 2002). In order to find useful patterns in user sessions, it is necessary to group the queries on the transaction logs into clusters. Other implications of session and new topic identification in terms of personalized services, caching systems and Web site design, are well-documented by Huang, Peng, An and Schuurmans (2004).

Session Identification

Session identification is one of the main research areas related to content-based behavior. It is difficult to identify user sessions due to the stateless nature of the client-server relationship. It should also be noted that although there is a controversy about the definition of session in literature, we define session as a group or entire sequence of queries submitted by a single user (Jansen and Spink, 2004, Ozmutlu, Ozmutlu and Spink 2004). We define topic as a subject area of interest in a session (Spink, Ozmutlu and Ozmutlu, 2002). Another group of researchers define a topic in a session as a session, such as He, Goker and Harper (2002).

A single IP address might not mean a single user, due to dynamic IP applications and use of search engines at common-access computers such as libraries, computer labs, etc (Jansen, Spink, Blakely and Koshman, 2007). The most commonly used session identification method is timeout, in which a user session is defined as a sequence of requests from the same user such that two consecutive requests separated by an interval more than a predefined threshold define a new session. The time-out method suffers from the problem that it is difficult to set the time threshold (Cooley, Mobasher and Srivastava, 1999, Huang, Peng, An and Schuurmans, 2004). Search engine researchers have also used cookies, along with IP addresses, for user identification.

The use of cookies reduces the session identification problem, but with common-access computers the problem remains. Also, due to the multitasking nature of the users explained in the previous paragraphs, a user might be interested in several topics. Therefore, some search engines also use a temporal boundary along with cookies to help address the session identification problem, with the idea that temporal boundaries help minimize the common user terminal issue, and delineate repeat searchers to a search engine who have returned with a new information need. However, this approach does not address the user with multiple information needs during a single searching episode. The method of IP address; IP and cookie; and IP, cookie, and temporal boundary all employ a mechanical definition of a session rather than a conceptual definition that defines a searching session within an information seeking task (Jansen, Spink, Blakely and Koshman, 2007). Jansen, Spink, Blakely and Koshman (2007) compare the methods of IP address; IP and cookie; and IP, cookie, and temporal boundary in their paper. Another session identification method is based on statistical language models (Huang, et al., 2004). The method uses an information theoretic approach to identifying session boundaries dynamically by measuring the change of information in the sequence of requests.

Query Clustering and Classification

Another research area of information retrieval is developing query clustering models based on content information. Beeferman and Berge (2000) and Wen, Nie and Zhang (2002) applied query clustering that uses search engine query logs including click-through data, which provides the documents that the user have selected as a result of the search query. Query similarities are proposed based on the common documents that users have selected. The difference of Beeferman and Berge's (2000) study is that it is non-semantic. Pu, Chuang and Yang (2002) developed an automatic classification methodology to classify search queries into broad subject categories. They formed a subject taxonomy and fit each search query into one of the categories in the taxonomy.

Wen, Nie and Zhang (2002) claimed that query clustering based on cross-referencing of queries and documents is more successful than basic keyword-based clustering. Zhu, Greiner and Haubl (2003) proposed a link based system that generates queries from terms contained in the previously accessed documents. Their algorithm assumed that the last accessed document is the only relevant document and was based on predicting whether a term is likely to occur in the last accessed relevant document. Muresan and Harper (2004) proposed a topic modeling system for developing mediated queries. They performed a statistical analysis of terms in documents available in a source collection and a statistical representation of the lexicographic model of the query. This step is followed by context analysis, which relates topics and terms considering weights, and then developing mediated queries based on the similarity of the terms to specific topics.

Recently, Liu, Croft, Oh and Hart (2004) used Support Vector Machines (SVMs) to classify queries in different groups. Some syntactic features of the queries, such as sentence length, average number of characters per word, average number of syllables per word, percentage of various part-of-speech tags, and various readability indices, as well as semantic features, such as frequency of numerous 1-, 2-, and 3-word sequences, were used to classify the queries. Results showed that SVM achieved recognition accuracy around 80 percent for queries. Metzler and Croft (2005) also performed classification of question queries using SVM and prior knowledge on the correlation values between question words and types.

Li, Zheng and Dai (2005) define the rules, framework and results for the KDDCUP 2005 competition to classify 800,000 queries into 67 categories. Shen, Pan, Sun, Pan, Wu, Yin and Yang (2005, 2006) proposed a query classification scheme, Q^2C@UST, which won the KDDCUP 2005 award. They used a two-phase framework to classify the queries considering their semantics. Two types of classifiers, synonym-based and statistics-based, are developed in the first phase of their framework to act as the training stage. In the second phase of their framework, a query's related Web pages and its category information are fetched through search engines. Then, the queries are classified through the base classifiers. Kardkovacs, Tikk, Bansaghi (2005) had runner-up awards at the KDDCUP competition with their Ferrety algorithm. The Ferrety algorithm uses the Internet and a set of clue words and modified tf-idf calculations to categorize queries, and combined a web search based categorizer and a taxonomy mapper. Shen, Sun, Yang and Chen (2006) proposed a bridging classifier on an intermediate taxonomy in an offline mode, which is then used in online mode to cluster user queries. It is adequate to train the bridging classifier only once. They claimed that their classification algorithm outperformed the Q^2C@UST classification scheme. Vogel, Bickel, Haider, Schimpfky, Siemen, Bridges and Scheffer (2005) proposed an architecture to cluster queries to an arbitrary subject taxonomy. Manual effort is required to instantiate a given taxonomy. The classification system of queries uses a web directory to identify the subject context.

Automatic New Topic Identification and Topic Estimation

Automatic new topic identification studies aim to divide user sessions into topics clusters, hence apply query clustering at the semantic level. There are several studies, which perform automatic new topic identification and also topic estimation based on the statistical characteristics of search engine queries. These studies are given in detail in the other chapter by Ozmutlu, Ozmutlu and Spink in this handbook (i.e. "From Analysis To Estimation of User Behavior").

Text Classification and Categorization Models

Topic identification of search engine queries might be considered within the broader context of text categorization and classification. Filtering the documents as relevant and not relevant to a certain topic is seen as a binary classification problem. For the binary classification problem, SVM has been extensively used (Chai, Ng and Cheiu, 2002; Joachims, 1998; Sebastini, 2002; Tax and Duin, 2001; Yang and Liu, 1999) and has been successful for text categorization (Yu, Zhai and Ha, 2003). Recently, Yu, Zhai and Ha (2003) classify unlabeled text into categories using SVMC (support vector mapping convergence), an efficient extension of SVM. They found that when the number of positive documents in the document space is insufficient, SVMC outperforms other methods, whereas it provides poorer results when the number of positive documents increases in the sample space. Swan and Jensen (2000) proposed a system called Time-Mines that use the date tags on the documents and the statistical characteristics of term usage to successfully group documents in separate clusters. Lawrie, Croft and Rosenberg (2001) compared different hierarchy models to categorize documents, and found that the dominating set technique performed better compared to other techniques in terms of finding topic words for hierarchical categorization of documents.

Jin, Si and Zhai (2003) perform user-centric information retrieval by making use of relevance feedback information. Hu, Bandhkavi and Zhai (2003) studied the precision and average rank of hard TREC-topics. Sayyadian, Shakery, Doan and Zhai (2004) attempt to solve the problem of entity retrieval, which is retrieving extra information about an entity such as a person, or place from text and structured data; given some level of information about that certain entity.

Zhai, Velivelli and Yu (2004) study the comparative text mining problem that is searching for common themes in various collections of text. They proposed a generative probabilistic mixture model for comparative text mining. Kelly, Diaz, Belkin and Allan (2004) investigated the techniques used for topic clustering of documents and discovered that most methods performed poorly when evaluated according to the user-defined topic classes. Mei and Zhai (2005) used statistical language models to perform a special temporal text mining task, which is studying the patterns of themes in text. They showed that the statistical methods used in the study, the Kullback-Leibler divergence and a hidden Markov chain model can successfully provide temporal theme structures.

Wang, Mohanty and McCallum (2005) showed that the Group-Topic model can be successfully used to search for clusters of topics of events within collections of documents. Li and McCallum (2005) successfully used a semi-supervised learning method to generate syntactic and semantic word clusters. Shen, Tan and Zhai (2005) studied how to utilize feedback information to improve retrieval performance. They used four language models for context-sensitive retrieval, and showed that feedback information can improve retrieval performance. Metzler and Croft (2005) used a Markov random field model to analyze term dependencies in text. They showed that modeling the term dependencies significantly increased the performance of information retrieval.

Another application of text mining is Topic Detection and Tracking (TDT), which is to process news streams and gather information in different news topics. TDT consists of five tasks, topic tracking, link detection, topic detection, first story detection and story segmentation (Feng and Allan, 2005). Topic modeling has been performed significantly in the context of Topic Detection and Tracking (Kelly, et al., 2004). The significant works on TDT can be listed as those of Feng and Allan (2005), Larkey, Feng, Connell and Lavrenko (2004), and Kumaran and Allan (2004, 2005).

Most query and document clustering methods, as described above, are focused on interpretation of keywords or understanding the topic or the contents of the query. This significantly complicates the process of query clustering and increases the potential noise of the results.

EXPLANATION OF METHODOLOGIES USED FOR TOPIC IDENTIFICATION OF SEARCH ENGINE QUERIES

To perform the query clustering, automatic new topic identification and topic estimation tasks detailed in the literature review section, statistical learning methods, such as regression and SVMs, artificial intelligence methods, such as neural networks, statistical and stochastic methods, such as Markov chains, Dempster-Shafer theory and methods based on conditional probabilities, have been used. These methods have also been used for document categorization. A detailed review of these methods has been provided in the other chapter by Ozmutlu, Ozmutlu and Spink in this handbook, (i.e. "From Analysis To Estimation of User Behavior").

Within the more general context of text classification, information extraction and topic detection, methods of supervised learning, unsupervised learning and semi-supervised learning have recently been actively used. Unsupervised learning methods do not rely on labeled data and are based on calculating the document vector similarity based on several document similarity indexes, such as the cosine coefficient. Semi-supervised learning uses large amounts of unlabeled data, together with the labeled data, to build classifiers. Supervised learning methods require large amounts of labeled data, which might be hard to provide or develop (Zhu, 2006). Due to its advantage of not requiring labeled data, semi-supervised learning has recently been popular in classification tasks, as well as text classification.

Popular methods of semi-supervised training used for text categorization are self-training and co-training. In self-training, a classifier is initially trained with the small amount of labeled data, and is then used to classify unlabeled data. Afterwards, the most confident unlabeled points, together with their predicted labels, are added to the training set, the classifier is re-trained and the procedure is repeated (Zhu, 2006). Co-training (Blum and Mitchell, 1998, Mitchell, 1999) requires two conditionally independent sets sufficient to train a good classifier. Separate classifiers are trained on the two labeled sets of data. Then, each classifier classifies unlabeled data, and provides the other classifier with t several additional unlabeled examples and their predicted labels, and each classifier is re-trained (Zhu, 2006).

Supervised learning consists of machine learning or statistical learning algorithms, where the algorithm is initially trained over a large dataset and then inference is performed over other datasets. Supervised learning algorithms that have been applied for text categorization and information extraction are support vector machines, neural networks, Bayesian network classifier, the naïve Bayes classifier, maximum entropy modeling, hidden Markov models and conditional random fields. Naïve Bayes classifiers are a class of classifiers based on probability theory, used especially when there are a large number of inputs. Prior probabilities are calculated with respect to the initial state of the system. Then, the likelihood of a new object is calculated given its surroundings. The final classification is performed by combining the likelihood values and the prior probabilities to obtain the posterior probabilities. Bayesian network classifiers are based on finding the best network that represents a training set of labeled data according to some objective function. Generally, this problem could be infeasible, however algorithms are available to solve the problem for certain types of networks (Friedman, Geiger and Goldszmidt, 1997).

One of the most popular models for text categorization and document clustering is support vector machines and its variants. Explanation of support vector machines and Markov models have been provided in the other chapter by Ozmutlu, Ozmutlu and Spink in this handbook (i.e. "From Analysis To Estimation of User Behavior"). We will present a brief explanation of Maximum entropy modeling, Hidden Markov models and conditional random fields in this chapter. More detailed explanation can be found in various natural language processing and text processing books such as that of Moens (2002).

Maximum Entropy Modeling

Maximum entropy modeling is motivated by the principle of generating probability distributions from a training dataset, and is based on calculating the conditional probability $P(y|x)$, which is the probability that event y occurs given that event x has occurred. Using the concept of conditional probability, maximum entropy modeling aims to model random and stochastic events. Initially a training dataset is used to define the conditional probabilities $P(y|x)$ for all x and y's of interest, i.e. to train the data. After the conditional probabilities are formed, they are expressed as constraints to define the possible and potential phenomenon in the data. The aim is to choose the most uniform solution conforming to these constraints. This solution principle resembles that of constrained optimization. The solution is sought within a feasible region defined by the constraints, and the objective is to maximize uniformity of the solution. The uniformity of the solution is represented by the conditional entropy equation of the conditional probabilities, as:

$$H(p) \equiv -\sum_{x,y} \tilde{p}(x)p(y|x)\log\ p(y|x)$$

where $\tilde{p}(x)$ is the empirical distribution of x in the training data set (Berger, Pietra and Pietra, 1996). The application to natural language processing and topic identification is based on assigning specific words to x and y, and investigating the conditional probability of one word occurring given that another word has occurred.

Hidden Markov Models

A Hidden Markov model is a stochastic model, where the system can be modeled by a discrete-time, discrete-space Markov process with unknown parameters. There is a list of observable outputs or parameters for each state. The Hidden Markov model is a stochastic process, where the underlying process or parameters are not observable, but can only be monitored through another stochastic process with observable parameters (Rabiner, 1989). Consequently, the Hidden Markov model requires the hidden parameters to be determined from the observable parameters, and the result is a model for the underlying process.

A Hidden Markov model is characterized by the number of states in the model, the number of distinct observation parameters per state, the state transition probabilities, the observation parameter distribution in a state and the initial state probability distribution (Rabiner, 1989).

Hidden Markov models are widely applied in pattern recognition for speech, handwriting and image recognition tasks. Given the current observable patterns for speech, handwriting or images, Hidden Markov models are used to determine the underlying model. For example, in natural language processing, words can be the observable parameters and the syntactic states for words could be the hidden parameters.

Conditional Random Fields

Conditional random fields (Lafferty, McCallum and Pereira, 2001) are a probabilistic framework for labeling and segmenting sequential data, based on conditional probabilities (Wallach, 2004). A conditional random field includes a single exponential model for the joint probability of the sequence of labels given the observation sequence (Lafferty, McCallum and Pereira, 2001). The structure of the underlying hidden process is known, and the hidden process is emitting observable parameters, as seen in Hidden Markov models. Within this scenario, learning and inference can be performed. Learning is determining the best potential probability functions to maximize some objective function, given a sample set of the observable parameters along with the values of the hidden labels/parameters. Inference is finding the most likely set of hidden parameters for any given observable parameters and the probability function derived as a result of learning. The conditional random fields have advantages over hidden Markov models, since they relax the independence assumptions required by Hidden Markov models (Wallach, 2004).

DISCUSSION: CHALLENGES AND FUTURE DIRECTIONS

Although, there are many successful methodologies on text categorization and information extraction, several challenges and research opportunities also lie ahead. The main research opportunity lies in applying text categorization algorithms on search engine user queries. None of the fairly successful algorithms of text categorization and information extraction, such as those listed in the previous section, i.e. maximum entropy modeling, hidden Markov models and conditional random fields, have been applied to topic identification of search engine user queries. Such an application comprises two aspects:

- Natural language processing or text categorization algorithms are usually applied on larger segments of text such as paragraphs. Semantic or content analysis of a full piece of text is usually based on analyzing salient portions of texts, such as abstract or first sentence of paragraphs, but search engine user queries usually only consists of a few keywords (Spink, et al., 1999, 2001). Therefore, it might be very difficult to interpret the query and apply text categorization algorithms on few words. It is also difficult to fit the keywords to any subject taxonomy, due to problems such as the number of keywords, as well as word ambiguity and mismatch and other problems. There is also the problem of overlapping topics in topic identification. Therefore, a real research opportunity lies in reducing the dimension of text categorization to search engine queries.
- Another main challenge in query clustering or query topic identification is performing in real-time. This issue also lies at the heart of the personalized search engine concept. Topic identification algorithms need not only be successful, but also computationally efficient. Available and newly developed topic identification and text categorization methods should be tested for their computational efficiency in a real search engine setting.

Finally, combining all the issues and challenges listed above, a very important research direction in information retrieval is developing personalized search engine algorithms that can successfully rank and cluster the results in real-time, and increase user satisfaction of the results.

CONCLUSION

This chapter includes a detailed literature review of the state-of-the-art in topic identification and analysis, with an emphasis on methods and techniques. Topic identification of search engine queries relate to many studies, ranging from term analysis of search engine queries, to topic estimation, automatic new topic identification, session identification and query clustering and then to the broader concept of text categorization and natural language processing. Challenges and research opportunities related to topic identification of search engine queries are also outlined. Topic analysis and identification is a challenging task, since it is directly related to natural language processing, a task not yet fully successfully performed. It is a major research opportunity to reduce text categorization tasks to user query level, and perform topic identification in real-time and in a real search engine setting. If topic identification of search engine user queries can be performed successfully, it can pave the way to more effective personalized search engines, the most recent progress in search engine design.

ACKNOWLEDGMENT

This research has been funded by TUBITAK, Turkey and is a National Young Researchers Career Development Project 2005: Fund Number: 105M320: "Application of Web Mining and Industrial Engineering Techniques in the Design of New Generation Intelligent Information Retrieval Systems".

REFERENCES

Agichtein, E., Brill, E. and Dumais, S. (2006), Improving Web search ranking by incorporating user behavior information. *Proceedings of the Twenty-Ninth Annual International ACM SIGIR Conference on Research and Development in Information Retrieval*, pp.19-26.

Agichtein, E., Brill, E., Dumais, S. and Ragno, R. (2006), Learning user interaction models for predicting Web search result preferences. *Proceedings of the Twenty-Ninth Annual International ACM SIGIR Conference on Research and Development in Information Retrieval*, pp. 3-10.

Beeferman, D. and Berger, A. (2000). Agglomerative clustering of a search engine query log. *Proceedings of the 6th ACM SIGKDD International Conference on Knowledge Discovery and Data Mining,* Boston, MA, 407 – 416.

Berger, A.L., Pietra, S.A.D. and Pietra, V.J.D. (1996). A Maximum Entropy Approach to Natural Language Processing. *Computational Linguistics, 22(1).*

Blum, A., and Mitchell, T. (1998). Combining labeled and unlabeled data with co-training. COLT, *Proceedings of the Workshop on Computational Learning Theory.*

Chai, K. M. A., Ng, H. T. and Cheiu, L. (2002). Bayesian online classifiers for text classification and filtering. *SIGIR'02: Proceedings of 25th ACM International Conference on Research and Development in Information Retrieval,* Tampere, Finland, 97–104.

Cooley, R., Mobasher, B. and Srivastava, J. (1999). Data preparation for mining world wide Web browsing patterns. *Knowledge and Information Systems. 1*, 5–32.

Feng, A. and Allan, J. (2005). *Hierarchical Topic Detection in TDT.* CIIR Technical Report, University of Massachusetts.

Friedman, N., Geiger, D. and Goldszmidt, M. (1997). Bayesian network classifiers. *Machine Learning,* 29, 131—163.

Gremett, P. (2006). "Utilizing a User's Context to Improve Search Results. *Journal of the American Society for Information Science and Technology, 57(6)*, 808–812.

Goodrum, A. and Spink, A. (2001). Image searching on the Excite Web search engine. *Information Processing and Management, 37(2)*, 295-312.

He. D., Goker, A. and Harper, D.J. (2002). Combining evidence for automatic Web session identification. *Information Processing and Management,* 38, 727-742

Huang, X., Peng, F., An, A. and Schuurmans, D. (2004). Dynamic Web log session identification with statistical language models. *Journal of the American Society for Information Science and Technology, 55(14)*, 1290 - 1303

Jansen, B. J., Goodrum, A. and Spink, A. (2000). Searching for multimedia: analysis of audio, video and image Web queries. *World Wide Web, 3*, 249–254.

Jansen, B.J., Spink, A., Bateman, J. and Saracevic, T. (1998). Real life information retrieval: A study of user queries on the Web. *SIGIR Forum, 33(1)*, 5–17.

Jansen, B. J., Spink, A., Blakely, C. and Koshman, S. (2007). Defining a session on Web search engines. *Journal of the American Society for Information Science and Technology. 58(6)*, 862-871.

Jansen, B.J., Spink, A. and Pedersen, J. (2003). An Analysis of Multimedia Searching on Alta Vista. *Proceedings of the 5th ACM SIG Multimedia International Workshop on Multimedia Information Retrieval*, Berkeley, CA, 186 – 192.

Jansen, B. J., Spink, A. and Pedersen, J. (2005). The Effect of Specialized Multimedia Collections on Web Searching. *Journal of Web Engineering. 3*, 182-199.

Jansen, B. J., Spink, A. and Saracevic, T. (2000). Real life, real users, and real needs: A study and analysis of user queries on the web. *Information Processing and Management, 36(2)*, 207-227.

Jin, R., Si, L. and Zhai, C. (2003). Preference-based graphic models for collaborative filtering. *Proceedings of the 19th Conference in Uncertainty in Artificial Intelligence,* Acapulco, Mexico, 329-336.

Joachims, T. (1998). Text categorization with support vector machines. *ECML'98: Proceedings of the 10th European Conference on Machine Learning,* Chemnitz, Germany, 137-142.

Hu, X., Bandhakavi, S. and Zhai, C. (2003). Error analysis of difficult TREC topics. *SIGIR'03: Proceedings of 26th ACM International Conference on Research and Development in Information Retrieval,* Toronto, Canada, 407-408.

Kardkovács, Z.T., Tikk, D. and Bánsághi, Z. (2005). The Ferrety algorithm for the KDD Cup 2005 problem. *ACM SIGKDD Explorations Newsletter*, 7(2), 111-116.

Kelly, D., Diaz, F., Belkin, N. J., and Allan, J. (2004). A user-centered approach to evaluating topic models. *Lecture Notes in Computer Science, 2997*, 27-41.

Kumaran, G. and Allan, J. (2004). Text classification and named entities for new event detection. *SIGIR '04: Proceedings of 27th ACM International Conference on Research and Development in Information Retrieval,* Sheffield, UK, 297-304.

Kumaran, G. and Allan, J. (2005). Using names and topics for new event detection. *Proceedings of Human Language Technology Conference/Conference on Empirical Methods in Natural Language Processing,* Vancouver, B.C., Canada.

Lafferty, J., McCallum, A. and Pereira, F. (2001). Conditional random fields: probabilistic models for segmenting and labeling sequence data. *Proceedings of the International Conference on Machine Learning.*

Larkey, L.S., Feng, F., Connell, M. and Lavrenko, V. (2004), Language-specific models in multilingual topic tracking. *SIGIR'04: Proceedings of 27th ACM International Conference on Research and Development in Information Retrieval,* Sheffield, UK, 402-409.

Lawrie, D., Croft, W. B. and Rosenberg, A., (2001). Finding topic words for hierarchical summarization. *SIGIR'01: Proceedings of 24th ACM International Conference on Research and Development in Information Retrieval*, New Orleans, LA, 349-357.

Li, Y., Zheng, Z. and Dai, H. (2005). KDD CUP-2005 report: facing a great challenge. *ACM SIGKDD Explorations Newsletter*, 7(2), 91-99.

Li, W. and McCallum, A. (2005). Semi-supervised sequence modeling with syntactic topic models. *Proceedings of the 12th Conference on Artificial Intelligence,* 813-818.

Liu, X., Croft, W. B., Oh, P. and Hart, D. (2004). Automatic recognition of reading levels from user queries. *SIGIR'04: Proceedings of the 27th ACM International Conference on Research and Development in Information Retrieval,* 548-549.

Mei, Q. and Zhai, C. (2005). Discovering evolutionary theme patterns from text an exploration of temporal text mining. *Proceedings of the 11th ACM SIGKDD International Conference on Knowledge Discovery and Data Mining, Chicago,* Illinois, USA, 198-207.

Metzler, D. and Croft, W. B. (2005). Analysis of statistical question classification for fact-based questions. *Information Retrieval, 8*, 481-504.

Metzler, D. and Croft, W. B. (2005). A Markov random field model for term dependencies. *SIGIR'05: Proceedings of the 28th Annual International ACM SIGIR conference on Research and Development in Information Retrieval,* Salvador, Brazil, 472-479.

Mitchell, T. (1999). The role of unlabeled data in supervised learning. *Proceedings of the Sixth International Colloquium on Cognitive Science.* San Sebastian, Spain.

Moens, M-F. (2002), *Automatic Indexing and Abstracting of Document Texts.* Kluwer Academic publishers, New York.

Muresan, G. and Harper, D.J. (2004). Topic modeling for mediated access to very large document collections. *Journal of the American Society for Information Science and Technology. 55*, 892–910.

Ozmutlu, S., Ozmutlu, H. C. and Spink, A. (2002). Multimedia Web Searching, *Proceedings of ASIST 2002: 65th American Society of Information Science and Technology Annual Meeting,* Long Beach October 2003, 403-408.

Ozmutlu, S., Ozmutlu, H. C. and Spink, A., (2003). Are people asking questions of general web search engines. *Online Information Review,* 27, 396-406.

Ozmutlu, S., Ozmutlu, H. C. and Spink, (2004). A day in the life of Web searching: an exploratory study. *Information Processing and Management. 40*, 319-345.

Ozmutlu, S., Spink, A. and Ozmutlu, H. C. (2003). Trends in multimedia web searching: 1997-2001, *Information Processing and Management*, 39, 611-621.

Rabiner, L.R. (1989). A tutorial on Hidden Markov models and selected applications in speech recognition. In Rabiner, L.R. (Ed.) *Proceedings of the IEEE*, 77(2), 257 - 286

Radlinski, F. and Dumais, S. (2006). Improving Personalized Web Search using Result Diversification. *Proceedings of SIGIR'06*, August 6–11, 2006, Seattle, Washington, USA.

Sayyadian, M., Shakery, A., Doan, A., and Zhai, C. (2004). Toward entity retrieval over structured and text data. *WIRD'04: 1st Workshop on the Integration of Information Retrieval and Databases,* Sheffield, UK, 47-54.

Sebastiani, F. (2002). Machine learning in automated text categorization. *ACM Computing Surveys, 34*, 1–47.

Shen, X., Tan, B. and Zhai, C. (2005). Context sensitive information retrieval using implicit feedback. *SOGIR'05: Proceedings of the 28th ACM International Conference on Research and Development in Information Retrieval,* Salvador, Brazil, 43-50.

Shen, D., Pan, R., Sun, J-T., Pan, J.J., Wu, K., Yin, J. and Yang, Q. (2006). Query enrichment for web-query classification. *ACM Transactions on Information Systems (TOIS)*, 24(3), 320-352.

Shen, D., Pan, R., Sun, J-T., Pan, J.J., Wu, K., Yin, J. and Yang, Q. (2005). Q2C@UST: our winning solution to query classification in KDDCUP 2005. *ACM SIGKDD Explorations Newsletter,* 7(2), 100-110.

Shen, D., Sun, J-T., Yang, Q. and Chen, Z. (2006). Building bridges for web query classification. *Proceedings of the 29th annual international ACM SIGIR conference on Research and development in information retrieval,* Seattle, Washington, 131 – 138.

Silverstein, C., Henzinger, M., Marais, H., and Moricz, M. (1999). Analysis of a very large Web search engine query log. *ACM SIGIR Forum, 33*, 6-12.

Spink, A. and Guner, O. (2001). E-commerce Web queries: Excite and Ask Jeeves study. *First Monday, 6(7).*

Spink, A. and Jansen, B. J. (2004). *Web Search: Public Searching of the Web.* Kluwer Academic Publishing.

Spink, A., Jansen, B. J., Wolfram, D. and Saracevic, T. (2002). From e-sex to e-commerce: Web search changes. *IEEE Computer, 35,* 133-135.

Spink, A., Koricich, A., Jansen, B. J. and Cole, C. (2004). Sexual searching on Web search engines. *Cyberpsychology and Behavior, 7(1),* 65-72.

Spink, A. and Ozmutlu, H. C. (2001). What do people ask on the Web and how do they ask it: Ask Jeeves Study. *Proceedings of ASIST 2001: Annual Meeting of the American Society for Information Science and Technology,* Washington, DC. Nov. 2001.

Spink, A. and Ozmultu, H.C. (2002). Characteristics of question format Web queries: an exploratory study. *Information Processing and Management. 38(4),* 453-71.

Spink, A., Ozmutlu, H. C. and Lorence, D. P. (2004). Web searching for sexual information: An exploratory study. *Information Processing and Management, 40(1),* 113-124.

Spink, A., Ozmutlu, H. C. and Ozmutlu, S. (2002). Multitasking information seeking and searching processes. *Journal of the American Society for Information Science and Technology, 53(8),* 639-652.

Spink, A., Wolfram, D., Jansen, B. J. and Saracevic, T. (2001). Searching the Web: The public and their queries. *Journal of the American Society for Information Science and Technology, 53,* 226–234.

Spink, A., Yang, Y., Nykanen, P., Lorence, D. P., Jansen, B. J., Ozmutlu, S., and Ozmutlu, H. C. (2004). A study of medical and health queries to a Web search engine. *Health Information and Libraries Journal, 21(1),* 44-51

Swan, R. and Jensen, D. (2000). TimeMines: Constructing timelines with statistical models of word usage. *Proceedings of the 6th ACM SIGKDD International Conference on Knowledge Discovery and Data Mining,* Boston, MA, 73-80.

Tax, D. M. J. and Duin, R. P. W. (2001).Uniform object generation for optimizing one-class classifiers. *Journal of Machine Learning Research, 2,* 155–173.

Vogel, D., Bickel, S., Haider, P., Schimpfky, R., Siemen, P., Bridges, S. and Scheffer, T. (2005). Classifying search engine queries using the web as background knowledge. *ACM SIGKDD Explorations Newsletter,* 7(2), 117-122.

Wallach, H.M. (2004). *Conditional random fields: An Introduction.* Technical Report MS-CIS-04-21. Department of Computer and Information Science, University of Pennsylvania.

Wang, X., Mohanty, N. and McCallum, A. (2005). Group and topic discovery from relations and text. *LinkKDD-05: Proceedings of the 11th ACM SIGKDD International Conference on Knowledge Discovery and Data Mining Workshop on Link Discovery: Issues, Approaches and Applications,* Chicago, IL, 28-35.

Wen, J. R., Nie, J. Y. and Zhang, H. J. (2002). Query clustering using user logs. *ACM Transactions on Information Systems, 20,* 59–81.

Yang, Y. and Liu, X. (1999). A re-examination of text categorization methods. *SIGIR'99: Proceedings of the 22nd ACM International Conference on Research and Development in Information Retrieval,* Berkeley, CA, 42-49.

Yu, H., Zhai, C. and Ha, J., (2003). Text classification from positive and unlabeled documents. *CIKM'03: Proceedings of the 2003 ACM CIKM International Conference on Information and*

Knowledge Management, New Orleans, LA, 232-239.

Zhai, C., Velivelli, A. and Yu, B. (2004). A cross-collection mixture model for comparative text mining. *Proceedings of the 10th ACM SIGKDD International Conference on Knowledge Discovery and Data Mining,* Seattle, WA, 743-748.

Zhu, X. (2006). *Semi-Supervised Learning Literature Survey.* Available at http://pages.cs.wisc.edu/~jerryzhu/pub/ssl_survey.pdf

Zhu, T., Greiner, R. and Haubl, G. (2003). Learning a model of a web user's interests. *Proceedings of the 9th International Conference on User Modeling*, Johnstown, USA.

KEY TERMS

Conditional Random Fields: Conditional random fields are a probabilistic framework for labeling and segmenting sequential data, based on conditional probabilities (Wallach, 2004).

Hidden Markov Models: The Hidden Markov model is a stochastic process, where the underlying process or parameters are not observable, but can only be monitored through another stochastic process with observable parameters (Rabiner, 1989).

Maximum Entropy Modeling: Maximum entropy modeling is a methodology aiming to model random and stochastic events, that is motivated by the principle of generating probability distributions from a training dataset, and calculating the conditional probability that event y occurs given that event x has occurred.

New Topic Identification: New topic identification is discovering when the user has switched from one topic to another during a single search session to group sequential log entries that are related to a common topic (He, Goker and Harper, 2002), session identification.

Query Clustering: Grouping the sequential log entries into different clusters in terms of topics or users.

Session Identification: Session identification is discovering the group of sequential log entries that are related to a common user or topic; new topic identification.

Topic Analysis: Analysis aiming to identify the topic of search engine queries.

Topic Identification: Automatically identifying or estimating the topic of search engine queries without human intervention.

Chapter XVIII
Query Log Analysis in Biomedicine

Elmer V. Bernstam
University of Texas Health Science Center at Houston, USA

Jorge R. Herskovic
University of Texas Health Science Center at Houston, USA

William R. Hersh
Oregon Health & Science University, USA

ABSTRACT

Clinicians, researchers and members of the general public are increasingly using information technology to cope with the explosion in biomedical knowledge. This chapter describes the purpose of query log analysis in the biomedical domain as well as features of the biomedical domain such as controlled vocabularies (ontologies) and existing infrastructure useful for query log analysis. We focus specifically on MEDLINE, which is the most comprehensive bibliographic database of the world's biomedical literature, the PubMed interface to MEDLINE, the Medical Subject Headings vocabulary and the Unified Medical Language System. However, the approaches discussed here can also be applied to other query logs. We conclude with a look toward the future of biomedical query log analysis.

INTRODUCTION

Biology and medicine are becoming information disciplines. One of the key drivers of the transformation is development of high-throughput techniques in molecular biology that generate large volumes of data quickly. For example, using a microarray costing a few hundred dollars, a single person can obtain expression data on thousands of genes within a few days. Briefly, a single gene expression microarray experiment can determine whether a large number of genes are more or less active in a particular state (e.g., cancer or some other disease) compared to normal.

These and other advances in biomedicine have led to an information explosion. No human can possibly manipulate data regarding thousands of genes without the aid of information technology. As a result, computers are now essential tools in biomedicine.

The vast amount of knowledge in many areas of biomedicine, and science in general, far exceeds the cognitive capacity of any human. Therefore, the paradigm must shift from knowing all of the answers *before* being asked the question, to "just in time learning" (i.e., retrieve knowledge *after* being asked the question). The only practical way to access the published literature in biomedicine is to rely on books, journals and electronic resources rather than human memory (Slawson & Shaughnessy, 2005). Fortunately, biomedicine benefits from relatively well-developed information retrieval resources based on controlled terminologies (ontologies). In this chapter, we will briefly review biomedical information retrieval, focusing on retrieval from the MEDLINE database. We discuss biomedical knowledge sources to which query log analysis has been applied. We then turn to problems and solutions in biomedical query log analysis. Finally, we discuss the contributions that query log analysis can make to the development of biomedical information retrieval systems.

BACKGROUND

The US National Library of Medicine (NLM) of the National Institutes of Health (NIH) developed and maintains many critical resources including databases, knowledge sources and software tools intended to allow access to biomedical information. The NLM "collects materials and provides information and research services in all areas of biomedicine and healthcare" ("About the National Library of Medicine," 2007). When working with query logs in the biomedical domain, we make extensive use of NLM resources including MEDLINE, a variety of services via the Unified Medical Language System and PubMed, a search interface onto the biomedical literature indexed in MEDLINE.

MEDLINE

MEDLINE is the largest and most comprehensive database of biomedical literature in the world. MEDLINE is maintained by the NLM and is available via multiple interfaces created by a variety of commercial and non-commercial vendors such as Ovid, MD Consult and the NLM itself.

MEDLINE currently indexes over 16 million articles from over 5,000 journals and is growing by over 500,000 articles per year. Since these statistics change continuously, the interested reader should visit http://www.nlm.nih.gov/pubs/factsheets/medline.html for the latest data. For each article, MEDLINE contains bibliographic information including title, authors, journal, publication date and tags from a controlled vocabulary known as the **Me**dical **S**ubject **H**eadings or MeSH (see below).

MEDLINE contains reference information, abstract (if available) and links to full-text articles when available, but does not contain the full-text articles themselves. It is therefore a *bibliographic database*. In contrast to full-text collections, users identify potentially interesting articles within MEDLINE, but obtain the actual article text elsewhere such as a physical library or journal Website. Biomedical journals increasingly provide online versions of content, therefore medical libraries are shifting from providing primarily print journals and photocopying facilities to providing access to online materials including journals, textbooks, databases and consulting services.

It is hard to overstate the significance of MEDLINE to biomedical researchers, students and clinicians. Indeed, if a biomedical journal is not indexed in MEDLINE, its quality is suspect and authors may think twice before publishing in that journal ("Annals of Family Medicine Selected for Indexing in Index Medicus and MEDLINE,"

2004). Biomedical researchers sometimes "interview" potential colleagues, research groups or even institutions by reviewing their "MEDLINE profiles". Clinical dilemmas often send the practitioner to MEDLINE in search of an answer.

Biomedical Controlled Vocabularies

The biomedical domain is associated with many (relatively) well-developed *controlled terminologies* and *ontologies* that have been applied to log analysis. A *terminology* is a set of terms. *Terms* are linguistic labels for concepts. *Concepts* are cognitive constructs based on entities in the real world such as "nose" [A09.531] or "anatomy" [A]. Labels in square brackets ([ ]) refer to entries in the **Me**dical **S**ubject **H**eadings (MeSH) vocabulary, see below. A *classification or taxonomy* is a terminology where terms are arranged by "is_a" or "is_member_of" relationships into classes (de Keizer, Abu-Hanna, & Zwetsloot-Schonk, 2000). For examples, a "nose" is_a "sense organ". Terminologies are *controlled* in the sense that the list of terms is fixed for some period of time, often with periodic updates designed to maintain usability (i.e., applications designed for version 1.0 of the vocabulary should still work with version 2.1). Designated authorities govern the update and maintenance process. For example, the NLM has responsibility for the MeSH. In other words, users cannot simply rename the term "anatomy" to "body parts."

We will focus our attention on one specific controlled vocabulary important to biomedical information retrieval, the MeSH. Then we turn to the more general **U**nified **M**edical **L**anguage **S**ystem or UMLS that provides a metathesaurus to allow cross-referencing between multiple biomedical controlled vocabularies, a semantic network that facilitates reasoning about biomedical concepts and tools for natural language processing (Specialist Lexicon).

MEDLINE Indexing Using the Medical Subject Headings (MeSH)

In order to facilitate information retrieval by users, every article in MEDLINE is manually indexed using a controlled vocabulary called the **Me**dical **S**ubject **H**eadings (MeSH). MeSH was developed and is being maintained by the National Library of Medicine. Its first edition was in 1954, when it was called "Subject Heading Authority List" (U.S. National Library of Medicine, 2006b). Its 2005 edition, the latest for which data are available, contains almost 23,000 unique descriptors and more than 151,000 supplemental records. It also has thousands of cross-references that point to the actual MeSH term (U.S. National Library of Medicine, 2005). For example, "Acetylsalicylic Acid" is a cross-reference for "Aspirin."

MeSH terms are divided into 16 categories including anatomic terms, organisms, diseases and so forth (Table 1). Each category contains multiple subcategories arranged in a hierarchy, as shown in Figure 1. A term can appear in more than one hierarchy. For example "Blood-Brain Barrier" appears under "Cardiovascular System" [A07.035] and "Brain" [A08.186.211.035].

MeSH is updated annually. Qualifiers and terms may merge, disappear, or be added to the MeSH. Whenever terms are removed or merged, the NLM updates existing MEDLINE records to reflect the updated MeSH. Specifically, deletions of MeSH headings and changes in the preferred term of a MeSH heading may require changes in existing MEDLINE records. There are three general types of maintenance tasks. *Preferred term* changes are simple substitutions. For example, in 2007 the preferred term for the heading "Nutrition" changed to "Nutrition Physiology." To reflect this change, every citation in the database that was previously tagged with "Nutrition" was updated to "Nutrition Physiology." *Automatic tasks* are algorithmic replacements (or deletions) that are performed without manual review of individual records. For example, the descriptor record for

Figure 1. MeSH hierarchy

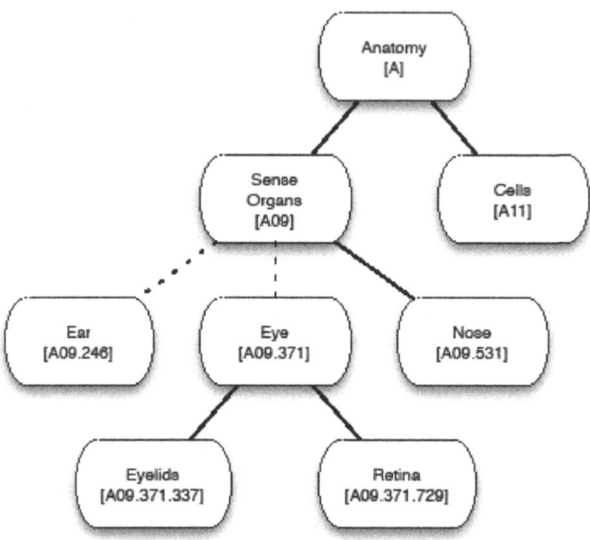

Table 1. MeSH Tree Structures (2007)

Anatomy [A]
Organisms [B]
Diseases [C]
Chemicals and Drugs [D]
Analytical, Diagnostic and Therapeutic Techniques and Equipment [E]
Psychiatry and Psychology [F]
Biological Sciences [G]
Natural Sciences [H]
Anthropology, Education, Sociology and Social Phenomena [I]
Technology, Industry, Agriculture [J]
Humanities [K]
Information Science [L]
Named Groups [M]
Healthcare [N]
Publication Characteristics [V]
Geographicals [Z]

"Tendons, Para-Articular" was deleted in 2007. Tags within existing citations that referenced "Tendons, Para-Articular" were replaced with references to another record "Tendons." *Manual tasks* are performed by a (human) MeSH specialist who determines the proper action on a case-by-case basis. Manual tasks sometimes "fine tune" the results of automatic tasks. Therefore, indexing of MEDLINE records always reflects the latest edition of MeSH (U.S. National Library of Medicine, 2006a).

MEDLINE indexers train for months to index articles efficiently and correctly. Indexing is performed on the basis of the full text article, rather than the bibliographic information contained in MEDLINE. Since human indexing is expensive and labor-intensive, the NLM has developed Natural Language Processing (NLP) tools to help indexers be more efficient. Presently, the NLM's Medical Text Indexer (MTI) suggests terms for the indexer's consideration but its performance is well below human standards and therefore it cannot replace a human indexer. Traditional NLP techniques are unable to detect the most important concepts in an article (Gay, Kayaalp, & Aronson, 2005). Therefore, the system is designed to suggest many MeSH terms and human indexers must choose the most important concepts. However, inter-rater reliability for human indexers averages 30-70% depending on the granularity of the MeSH term (i.e., general terms are applied more reliably than specific terms) (Funk & Reid, 1983). The gold standard is therefore ill defined, as is the case in many areas of natural language processing and information retrieval.

Unified Medical Language System (UMLS)

The UMLS provides tools for biomedical text analysis. Since query logs are text, the UMLS can be very useful in their analysis. The UMLS consists of three components referred to as "knowledge sources" which are available via the Web after (free) licensing from http://umlsks.nlm.nih.gov. Alternatively, users can create local UMLS installations by requesting the UMLS on DVD from the NLM.

Briefly, the *metathesaurus* inter-relates over 100 "source vocabularies." For example, a query to the metathesaurus can identify the MeSH terms and ICD-9 codes (a terminology often used for representing clinical diagnoses for medical billing) most closely describing the concept "bacterial pneumonia." The *semantic network* allows computable inference of categories. Using the semantic network, we can automatically determine that a "neoplastic process" is a "disease or syndrome." Finally, the *Specialist Lexicon* provides lexical information useful for natural language processing tools. For example, the verb "treat" has three inflectional variants (treats, treated and treating).

The UMLS is an ambitious project that attempts to cover the entire biomedical domain without intentional preference for specific topic areas. Since it aggregates multiple source vocabularies that it does not manage, the utility of the UMLS for natural language processing (and query log analysis) is limited by the quality of the source vocabularies as well as potential UMLS errors. More generally, projects that depend on controlled vocabularies are limited by the scope and quality of the controlled vocabulary.

PubMed

PubMed is a freely available NLM interface to MEDLINE located at: http://www.pubmed.gov. Total MEDLINE usage via all vendors is difficult to determine. However, PubMed alone accounted for more than 675 million searches over the first nine months of 2006; a nearly 12% increase from the same time period in 2005 ("Resource statistics," 2007).

The majority of citations in PubMed are from MEDLINE. However, PubMed also includes citations from publishers, citations from PubMed Central (a full text, freely available collection of articles) and other citations dating back to 1865. As of May 2007, PubMed contains over 17 million citations growing by over 700,000 per year (see Figure 2 and Figure 3).

Over the years, PubMed developers added multiple advanced features. Perhaps the most relevant feature for query log analysis is query re-formulation. When a user enters a query via

Figure 2. Number of articles in PubMed

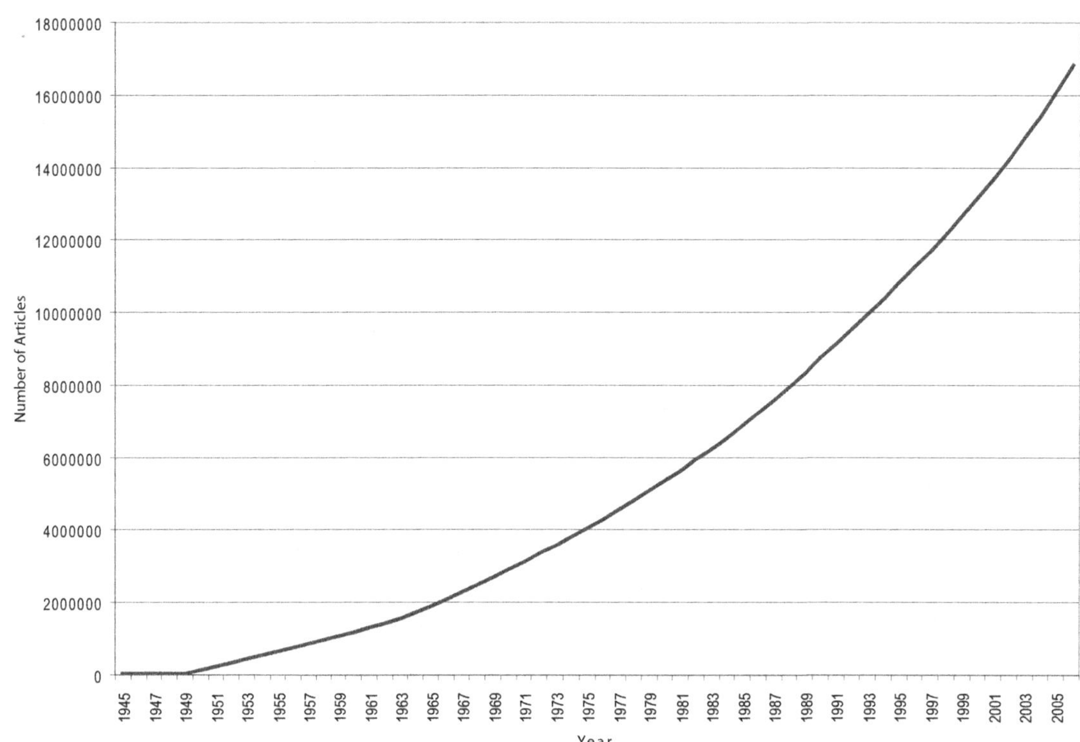

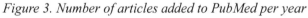

Figure 3. Number of articles added to PubMed per year

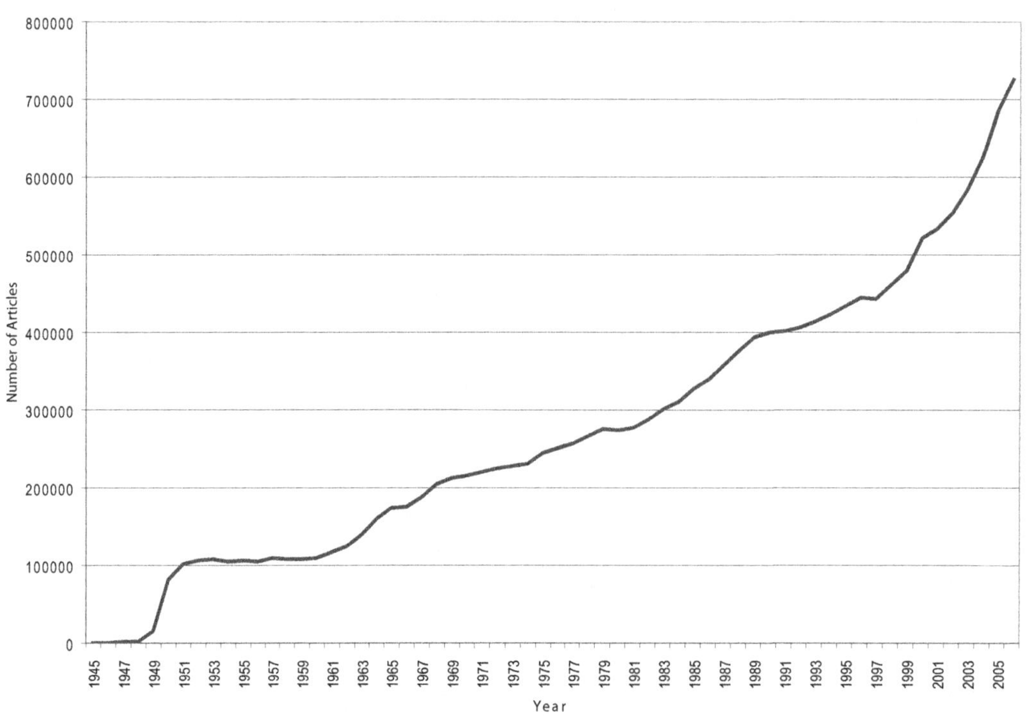

the PubMed search box, the query is modified according to a complex set of rules that are designed to provide users with the best results. For example, if one searches for "query log" (in quotes, designating search for a literal string), PubMed finds no results and, instead, executes "query[All Fields] AND log[All Fields]." In addition, since use of MeSH in MEDLINE queries have been shown to improve performance (W. Hersh & Hickam, 1994), PubMed maps user queries to MeSH whenever possible. Users' queries are re-formulated even if the original query result set is not empty (e.g., query = [query log] without quotes). However, the user can avoid reformulation by explicitly specifying the query using operators, quotes and/or tags (e.g., query = "query log" [tw]). The rules for PubMed query processing are discussed fully on the PubMed Website (http://www.pubmed.gov).

MEDLINE and the PubMed interface are widely used and are therefore worthy of study. Further, healthcare consumers are increasingly searching online for health information (Fox & Rainie, 2002). The NLM estimates that approximately one third of all MEDLINE queries via its PubMed interface are issued by members of the general public rather than clinicians or researchers (Lacroix, 2000). We will discuss the use of resources intended for professionals by healthcare consumers later in this chapter.

MAIN THRUST OF CHAPTER

Query logs in the biomedical domain are derived from three major categories of search engines: 1) MEDLINE interfaces such as PubMed or Ovid (http://www.ovid.com), 2) search interfaces intended for healthcare consumers such as MEDLINEplus (http://MEDLINEplus.gov/) and 3) other. The third category includes search engines within electronic medical records (e.g., searching based on the clinical situation of a specific patient), integrated information providers such as MD Consult that provide access to multiple resources via a single interface, detecting health-related queries in general-purpose Web search engine logs, etc.

In this chapter, we will focus on approaches to query log analysis for data obtained from publicly available MEDLINE interfaces. However, studies have shown that biomedical queries are qualitatively similar to queries issued on Web search engines (Herskovic, Tanaka, Hersh, & Bernstam, 2007; Zeng, Kogan, Ash, Greenes, & Boxwala, 2002). Specifically, they are generally short (1-2 terms), unlikely to contain operators (e.g. Boolean operators) even when these are allowed and cover a wide range of topics. Therefore, techniques developed for MEDLINE log analysis will probably generalize to other search engine types (e.g., Web) and vice versa.

Questions Addressed by Query Log Analysis

As in other fields, biomedical query log analysis attempts to understand information retrieval from the users' perspective. What do users search for? How do they search (formulate queries)? Do they find what they are looking for (are searches successful)? What are the causes and potential remedies for search failures?

The limitations of query log analysis described in other fields apply to the biomedical domain. Query logs tell us the terms that users included in their queries, query length and other query characteristics. However, query logs are only indirect reflections of user information needs (i.e., the reason that the search engine is being used). Indeed, understanding information needs from query logs is a difficult task. Query logs can be complemented by other analyses such as field studies and instrumented user panels. In field studies and instrumented user panels, a subset of users are studied in more detail than can be obtained from query logs (Grimes, Tang, & Russell, 2007). Unlike query log analyses, field/lab studies and instrumented user panels require user participation or at least require users to agree to be monitored. Therefore, users are often compensated for their time and effort.

Field or laboratory studies generally examine relatively small samples (tens) of users either in their natural environment (field) or in a laboratory over a short period of time. Users can be interviewed to understand why they searched and whether their search was successful. Users' behavior beyond the single search engine being studied can also be evaluated. For example, a user may search MEDLINE, retrieve a specific article on aspirin treatment of coronary disease, then consult a textbook for an overview of coronary disease and another resource for the pharmacology of aspirin.

Instrumented user panels employ some means of recording user activity such as keystroke logging software or browser applications (plug-ins) that record activity on the Web. For example, ComScore Networks (http://www.comscore.com) is a for-profit online research company that maintains an instrumented user panel. Aggregated information is used to understand online behavior. Such studies can involve hundreds or thousands of users that are observed for variable periods of time. Depending on the study design, users may be asked to record their information need and whether their search was successful. Instrumented user panels differ from field/laboratory studies in that there is no requirement for direct subject-researcher contact. However, one can imagine hybrid study designs that combine elements of field/lab studies and instrumented user panels.

Different search use cases, such as obtaining the results of the latest clinical trial or learning about a topic in preparation for a test, require different kinds of literature. For example, the results of the latest clinical trial will be published in a journal and indexed in MEDLINE. In contrast, a textbook will present summary information that can help a user get an overview of a topic organized in a manner that facilitates learning. As the rapidly expanding biomedical literature overwhelms our ability to keep up, even with relatively specific topics, we often turn to *synthetic literature*, such as textbooks or systematic reviews that summarize primary literature (journal articles indexed in MEDLINE) (Haynes, 2001). It is important to note that the relative utility of different information resources will not be reflected in the query logs of a search engine that accesses that single resource.

In spite of such limitations, analysis of query logs cannot be fully replaced by other kinds of studies. Query logs contain enormous amounts of data over long periods of time. In contrast to field/laboratory studies or instrumented user panels, query logs reflect real search engine usage without the possibility of behavior change due to observation. Further, queries in search engine logs reflect real information needs and their analysis does not burden users.

Techniques for Analyzing Biomedical Query Logs

Traditional query log analysis focuses on *terms* within *queries* and queries within *sessions*. A query is a string, composed of one or more terms, submitted to a search engine. A query with zero terms is empty and generally excluded from analysis. A user may issue one or more queries during a single session. Previous query log analyses show that single-query sessions are quite common (Herskovic et al., 2007; Jansen, Spink, & Saracevic, 2000). Although one can imagine counter-examples such as browsing, a single session is generally assumed to reflect a user trying to satisfy a single information need (Silverstein, Henzinger, Marais, & Moricz, 1998).

Term-oriented analyses can be performed automatically on very large log files and can be very informative. For example, term frequency analyses can provide insight into user vocabularies. One of the reasons that healthcare consumers have difficulty accessing information intended for professionals is a language mismatch. Consumers' language is known to be different from the language used by healthcare professionals and designers of biomedical information resources (Zeng et al., 2002). For example, a professional's "myocardial infarction" is a layman's "heart attack." They share no terms yet mean essentially the same thing.

Traditional analysis techniques have been extensively documented in scientific reports (e.g., (Jansen et al., 2000; Silverstein et al., 1998)) and in other chapters of this book. Therefore, this chapter will focus on analysis techniques that are particularly applicable to analysis of logs from biomedical search engines.

Semantic Analysis

Mapping to controlled taxonomies allows us to automatically group terms into meaningful, well-defined categories. Therefore, in addition to traditional term frequency and association analysis, we can automatically perform *semantic analysis* to understand the meaning of queries. However, we cannot necessarily assume that the query represents a user's intended information need. For example, a query for "nose" may represent an interest in properties of smell, allergic disorders causing a "runny nose," or trauma to the nose. Semantic analysis is complementary to traditional analysis and provides an additional method for understanding user information needs and for computing session boundaries.

Controlled vocabularies and taxonomies are not unique to biomedicine. For example, the freely-available WordNet database of English words (http://wordnet.princeton.edu) provides capabilities that can be used to perform semantic analysis on non-biomedical query logs. Indeed, since queries executed by biomedical search engines can contain non-biomedical terms, general terminologies such as WordNet can be quite helpful for biomedical query log analysis.

Understanding User Information Needs Using Semantic Analysis

Since MeSH is a classification (i.e., a hierarchical terminology), we can group query terms by abstracting from specific terms found in queries to general categories. For example, we can automatically determine that queries including terms that map to MeSH headings "ear" [A09.246] and "eye" [A09.371] are both requesting information about the more general category of "sense organs" [A09] and not to "cells" [A11] (see Figure 1). We can compare general categories. For example, we can determine the percentage of queries that relate to "anatomy" [A] (as opposed to "diseases" [C]).

The UMLS semantic network can help us understand user information needs by defining relationships between queries. The semantic network allows us to determine the semantic relationships between concepts such as drugs that treat diseases. For example, consider a user searching for "aspirin," "heart attack," "hip pain" and "stroke." One way to interpret the user's information need is "therapeutic applications of aspirin." Of course, as with all query log analyses, interpretation of user information needs remains an extrapolation from available data. It is possible that the user issued these queries without any relationship between them; i.e., they were first interested in the side effects of aspirin, then in prognosis in the setting of a heart attack, etc.

Session Boundary Determination Using Semantic Distance

Query log analyses have generally divided data into *sessions*. Sessions are thought to represent an individual user searching to satisfy a single information need. Session boundaries have traditionally been defined by time cutoffs (Jansen et al., 2000; Silverstein et al., 1998). Queries from a single user that fall within a certain time interval (e.g. five minutes) of each other are considered to belong to the same session. If queries are separated by more than the pre-determined amount of time, they are presumed to belong to separate sessions and therefore reflect separate information needs.

Understanding sessions has implications for search engine design. For example, if users issue a single query per session, then they are either satisfied with the results or stop searching for some other reason, e.g., they are frustrated and give up. On the other hand, finding multiple queries per session implies that users may be pursuing some strategy to satisfy their information need. We can then turn our attention to understanding user strategies such as broadening the query, narrowing the query or substituting terms. For example, if users are often narrowing queries, perhaps a query formulation assistant that can help users issue more specific queries would be helpful. On the other hand, if users' queries often retrieve no results, a query formulation assistant that suggests broader terms may be more useful.

Clearly, we can think of exceptions such as browsing where a user may not have a specific information need, or the information need can change in light of previously retrieved results. Further, the session boundary is difficult to determine objectively. How many minutes of inactivity signals a change in information need? Two minutes? Five minutes? Ten minutes?

Semantic analysis provides an alternative method for identifying session boundaries that is more closely tied to our understanding of what a session means. Specifically, we can determine the *semantic distance* between queries. Semantic distance reflects the difference in meaning between queries and can be calculated in a number of ways (Cooper, 2000). For example, the query "nose" is closer to "ear" (both are sense organs) than it is to "myocardial infarction" (heart attack, a disease of the heart). If the semantic distance between terms found in a pair of queries is large, then we assume that the information need has changed. Therefore, a semantic session boundary algorithm can be expressed as: consecutive queries from the same user belong to the same session if the semantic distance is less than some threshold; otherwise they belong to different sessions.

We can compute semantic distance between queries using the MeSH hierarchy. Specifically, we can map query terms to MeSH and then determine the number of steps (edges between nodes in the graph) on the shortest path between concepts (Herskovic et al., 2007). When there were no MeSH mappings, we can fall back on WordNet, a hierarchy of English words. Note that this is an example of a non-biomedical vocabulary used for biomedical query log analysis.

Steps closer to the top of the tree represent a greater semantic distance compared to steps closer to the bottom of the tree. For example, "nose" and "ear" are two steps apart but are similar (they are both sense organs). Similarly, "anatomy" and "diseases" are two steps apart but are relatively dissimilar. To account for this, we need a depth-sensitive measure of semantic distance. A depth-sensitive measure has precedents in the literature and, in particular, is similar to the Leacock-Chodorow distance (Budanitsky & Hirst, 2001). The pseudo-code for one such algorithm that has been used successfully for MEDLINE query log analysis is shown in Figure 4 (Herskovic et al., 2007). In this algorithm, the MeSH tree is assumed to have a "top" represented by a single node that links to the 16 concepts listed in Table 1.

How well does this MeSH-based semantic session boundary algorithm work? To answer this question, we compared the performance of semantic and time-based thresholds to human judgment of where session boundaries should occur. Two reviewers independently identified session boundaries in a random sample of 2,390 actual PubMed queries issued by 351 individual users. Sessions were defined as sets of queries in which the user appeared to be pursuing the same information need. We compared the results of this exercise to dividing the queries into sessions using a variety of time cutoffs (0 to 120 minutes

Figure 4. Pseudo-code for session boundary computation algorithm based on semantic distance

```
Let Q be the set of queries from a single user
Let S be an empty set of session boundaries

Begin
   Pop the first query from Q into q
   Send q to PubMed and retrieve its translation q'
   While there are queries left in Q
      Let q'' = q'
      Pop the first query from Q into q
      Send q to PubMed and retrieve its translation q'
      Precompute the semantic distance D for each possible combination of MeSH terms from q' and q''
      Pair every MeSH term in q'' with the MeSH term closest to it in q'
      Let SD = the sum of all distances between pairs of MeSH terms
      If SD is greater than a predefined threshold,
         Append a session boundary immediately before q to S

   Return S
End
```

in 1 minute increments) and to our MeSH-based semantic algorithm. We found that the semantic algorithm had better concordance with human judgment than any time cutoff. We also used these results to determine the best semantic distance threshold between sessions (3.8).

Navigational vs. Informational Queries

Three kinds of queries have been characterized according to their underlying intent (Broder, 2002). *Informational queries* are intended to satisfy information needs on a particular topic. For example, a user may search for "myocardial infarction." Although MEDLINE does not contain the full text of articles, users can issue informational queries on the abstract text and MeSH tags to identify articles of interest. Once interesting articles are identified, they can be accessed either via links (present in PubMed), on journal Websites or in printed journals (e.g., at the library). A similar query could be issued for the Web using a Web search engine. In contrast, *navigational queries* are intended to retrieve a specific document or set of documents. For example, the PubMed query "j am med inform assoc [journal] AND 2006 [dp] AND 96 [pg]" (where dp=date of publication, pg=page) intends to retrieve a specific article. On the Web, users might search for the Website of a particular company (e.g., http://www.porsche.com). When users issue *transactional queries*, they want to perform Web-mediated activities such as shopping or banking. Transactional queries do not have a direct MEDLINE/PubMed equivalent.

The distinction between informational and navigational queries reflects the distinction between information retrieval and database access. Information retrieval focuses on access to relatively unstructured data (e.g., free text). In contrast, database management systems provide access to highly structured data (e.g., numerical data in a table). Therefore, identifying which records to return is a critical issue for information retrieval systems. On the other hand, compact storage and efficient retrieval are important database issues. If users issue primarily navigational queries, then researchers should focus on optimizing database access. However, if informational queries are common, then information retrieval issues must be addressed.

Although there are a number of algorithms to operationalize the distinction between navigational and informational queries, for biomedical query logs the presence of MeSH terms is likely to represent informational queries. In other words, if a query includes biomedical concepts then the user is likely to have a general information need, rather than to be looking for a particular reference (e.g., author=Sorensen, journal=Science, year=2007, volume= 316, issue=5828, page=1122). However, if the query does not contain MeSH terms, we cannot conclude that it is navigational. It may simply contain concepts that cannot be mapped to MeSH using current technology. Therefore, we look for bibliographic tags (E.g., page number, journal, volume, etc.) – if we find these, then the query is navigational. This algorithm is depicted as a flowchart in Figure 5 and has also been used successfully in a MEDLINE query log analysis (Herskovic et al., 2007).

Published Query Log Analysis in the Biomedical Domain (Brief Literature Review)

Surprisingly few analyses of biomedical search engine query logs have been published in the peer-reviewed literature. Most studies attempted to understand information needs of clinicians or the language of healthcare consumers.

Figure 5. Algorithm for distinguishing navigational queries (data retrieval) from information queries (information retrieval)

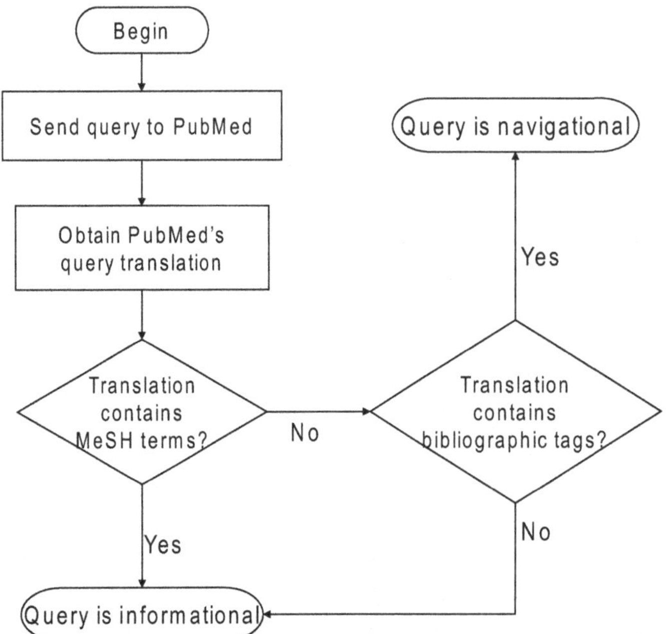

Query Log Analyses Focused on the Information Needs of Clinicians

Strasberg, et al. (Strasberg, Hubbs, Rindfleisch, & Melmon, 1999) reviewed queries from an early Web-based integrated information resource called SHINE (Stanford Health Information Network for Education). SHINE was designed for clinicians at an academic medical center and provided access to information from a textbook, MEDLINE, drug information, clinical practice guidelines and other resources via a single user interface. The authors found that 25% of queries concerned drug information or infectious disease. The remaining 75% of queries concerned a broad range of topics. They concluded that future information retrieval systems should include drug information among a broad range of knowledge sources covering a wide range of topics.

The largest query log analysis in the biomedical domain was an analysis of PubMed queries by Herskovic, et al. (Herskovic et al., 2007). As with many other domains, access to query log data is limited by privacy concerns. Specifically, unusual individual queries or a pattern formed by multiple queries can be used to identify individuals (Nakashima, 2006); a particular concern for the healthcare domain. Similarly, competitive concerns limit the availability of commercial data. Therefore, only very limited query log data are available. However, the NLM has made available a single day's PubMed query log (24 hour period, exact date not made public by the NLM). Although a single day's queries doesn't sound like very much, for PubMed the log file includes approximately 3 million queries. In summary, the authors found that users issued queries on a broad range of topics without dominant search terms or topics. Like Web search engine sessions, most PubMed sessions consisted of a single query. However, the average PubMed query contained more terms than the average general Web search engine query. The majority of PubMed queries were informational (rather than navigational), suggesting that information retrieval remains important.

Query Log Analyses of Search Engines Intended for Healthcare Consumers

MEDLINEplus (http://www.MEDLINEplus.gov) is a consumer-oriented online medical information resource developed and maintained by the NLM. To some extent, MEDLINEplus was a reaction to the large number of healthcare consumers that accessed PubMed when it became freely available via the Web. Consequently, MEDLINEplus might be considered a response to internal NLM analyses of PubMed query logs.

Zeng et al., (Zeng et al., 2002) analyzed a MEDLINEplus query log in conjunction with NLM staff and found that consumers' information retrieval performance was poor; perhaps resulting from mismatches between consumer terminology and the terminologies used to create and index content. Based on their analysis, the authors concluded that mismatches implied that consumers and professionals had different mental models as well as different language. Therefore, to improve consumers' information retrieval performance, consumers require support at all levels (lexical, semantic and mental models).

UMLS coverage of consumer terms has also been studied using a variety of methods with different results. For example, (Brennan & Aronson, 2003) attempted to map text from consumer email messages to UMLS concepts and concluded that "large amounts of the free text messages of lay people do not include concepts from the standardized vocabularies present in the UMLS and that the mapping of these ... terms ... remains imprecise at best." On the other hand, (Smith, Stavri, & Chapman, 2002) found that 96% of concepts from consumer emails could be mapped to UMLS using NLP tools from the NLM.

ISSUES AND CONTROVERSIES

Healthcare consumer information needs seem to focus on medical topics, even in the case of resources that were not designed to meet such information needs. For example, a consumer may search the Website of the National Library of Medicine looking for information about the treatment of a broken wrist (McCray, Loane, Browne, & Bangalore, 1999). In spite of documented problems with information retrieval (Zeng et al., 2002), consumers are satisfied with their online experience and are making choices based on the information that they encounter (Fox & Rainie, 2000; Helft, Hlubocky, Gordon, Ratain, & Daugherty, 2000). In some cases, such as complementary and alternative medicine (CAM), patients may not discuss their use of treatments found online with their physician (Eisenberg et al., 2001). On the other hand, clinicians are increasingly faced with patients who have been informed (or misinformed) by the Web. As a result, clinicians, researchers and healthcare consumers are concerned about the quality and accuracy of online health information (Biermann, Golladay, Greenfield, & Baker, 1999; Fox & Rainie, 2000; Jadad & Gagliardi, 1998; Price & Hersh, 1999).

Multiple approaches to identifying problematic information online have been proposed including lists of quality criteria to be used by consumers for judging Websites (see (Eysenbach, Powell, Kuss, & Sa, 2002) for a review), centralized "clearing-houses" for manual Website review, certification authorities and attempts at automated reliability evaluation. However, to date such efforts have had little success. Indeed, a systematic evaluation of commonly cited health information quality measures found that no quality measures (alone or in combination) could screen out inaccurate online information about CAM (Walji et al., 2004). Fortunately, there is only limited published evidence of harm from online information (Crocco, Villasis-Keever, & Jadad, 2002). It is not yet clear whether this lack of published evidence reflects lack of harm or under-reporting.

SOLUTIONS AND RECOMMENDATIONS

Perhaps the more general issue is that people have an insatiable need for biomedical information. Although there is controversy regarding the percentage of searches that are health related (Eysenbach & Kohler, 2004), there is widespread agreement that the absolute number of searches is enormous. Healthcare consumers turn to search engines, both general-purpose search engines such as Google and biomedical search engines such as PubMed, when they want to understand a disease, learn how to stay well or cope with another's illness.

Analyzing search engine query logs can help to identify important topics that need to be addressed by biomedical information resources including the mass media and (human) clinicians. In other words, understanding the information needs of healthcare consumers can help us identify topics that should be addressed by clinicians in their discussions with patients. Query log analyses can help us understand consumer vocabularies and to design information retrieval systems that mediate between the language of consumers and the professional terminologies that are inherent in biomedical information resources.

FUTURE TRENDS

Information Explosion in Biomedicine as an Information Challenge

The influence of biological knowledge on clinical medicine is increasing every year. Completion of a draft sequence of the human genome project in 2003 resulted in new diagnostic tests based on genetic data entering clinical practice. Therapies based on genetic data are not far behind. For example, molecular tests are already affecting the treatment of breast cancer (Paik et al., 2004). Potentially actionable knowledge is generated and deposited in information resources at an accelerating rate (Figures 2 and 3).

This trend poses an information challenge. For researchers, finding information to inform their work is increasingly difficult as the sheer amount of information grows. Further, scientists must increasingly function in inter-disciplinary teams. Therefore, they must search for information on topics outside of their immediate domain. For example, molecular modeling requires biologists to interact with statisticians, mathematicians, physicists and computer scientists. Concepts such as computability and computational complexity of algorithms that were previously the domain of theoretical computer science are now directly relevant to biologists. Interdisciplinary fields of computational biology and biomedical informatics reflect the changing nature of biomedicine.

For healthcare consumers, biomedical information resources on the Web have made information available that was previously restricted to healthcare professionals. There is ample evidence that consumers are taking advantage of this in increasing numbers (Lacroix & Mehnert, 2002). However, access to information does not necessarily imply access to accurate, actionable knowledge for researchers, clinicians or consumers. Researchers and clinicians have access to the information, but may have difficulty retrieving it from large databases such as MEDLINE. Indeed, MEDLINE queries formulated by sophisticated users are more effective than queries formulated by novice users (W. R. Hersh & Hickam, 1998). Analysis of query logs can be a first step toward understanding information needs, ways to improve search engines and translate between user and resource terminologies. In the future, terminologies used for information retrieval (such as MeSH) can include entry terms (i.e., terms that cause a concept to be retrieved) derived from query log analyses.

For clinicians, as the amount of information grows, it can no longer be learned ahead of time. Clinicians must now turn to information resources to learn answers AFTER they have been asked the question. Multiple systems have been developed that were technically successful but were never used by clinicians. However, clinicians have shown a willingness to adopt useful technologies.

The shift to "just in time" learning for clinicians is a complex problem with social, political and technical aspects. Exploring the implications of this shift is beyond the scope of this chapter. However, it is worth noting that if physicians must access information at the point of care and if patients can access the same information, there may be a shift away from traditional "paternalistic" doctor-patient relationships where the physician makes decisions for patients. Indeed, there have been efforts to increase active patient participation in decision-making, sometimes conflicting with patient wishes (A. Robinson & Thomson, 2001). With consumer empowerment (consumerism), there have also been discussions of increasing consumer financial responsibility for healthcare (J. C. Robinson, 2001). Finally, available information retrieval tools are not well suited for "just in time" decision making. For example, searching PubMed for "breast cancer" yields over 160,000 citations ordered by date – not useful for making a specific patient decision in real time. New tools must be developed that rely on synthetic literature and novel user interfaces.

CONCLUSION

In summary, biomedical query log analysis can help us understand user information needs and perhaps help match user terminology with the terminology of the resources that they hope to access. Researchers, clinicians and healthcare consumers (general public) are faced with an exponential increase in biomedical information. This is reflected in the size of biomedical databases such as MEDLINE and poses new challenges. Instead of relying on human memory as the repository of biomedical knowledge, we must transition to "just in time" learning and rely on search engines to retrieve information in non-emergency settings.

Query log analysis in biomedicine has a relatively short history compared to the Web. However, biomedical controlled terminologies such as MeSH and knowledge sources such as the UMLS allow researchers to ask questions about the meaning of queries as well as the terms that were used. In turn, query log analysis can help enhance terminologies by providing entry terms that match the mental models of users. As biomedical researchers, clinicians and healthcare consumers come to rely on search engines, query log analyses become increasingly important to help satisfy user information needs.

REFERENCES

About the National Library of Medicine. (2007). Retrieved September 9, 2007, from http://www.nlm.nih.gov/about/index.html

Annals of Family Medicine Selected for Indexing in Index Medicus and MEDLINE. (2004). Retrieved September 9, 2007, from http://www.aafp.org/annals/x28117.html

Anonymous. (2004, 08/08/2006). Searching PubMed. *PubMed Help* Retrieved 09/25/2006, 2006, from http://www.ncbi.nlm.nih.gov/books/bv.fcgi?rid=helppubmed.section.pubmedhelp.Searching_PubMed#pubmedhelp.Combining_search_ter

Biermann, J. S., Golladay, G. J., Greenfield, M. L., & Baker, L. H. (1999). Evaluation of cancer information on the Internet. *Cancer, 86*(3), 381-390.

Brennan, P. F., & Aronson, A. R. (2003). Towards linking patients and clinical information: detecting UMLS concepts in e-mail. *J Biomed Inform, 36*(4-5), 334-341.

Broder, A. (2002). A taxonomy of web search. *SIGIR Forum, 36*(2), 3-10.

Budanitsky, A., & Hirst, G. (2001). *Semantic distance inWordNet: An experimental, application-oriented evaluation of five measures.* Paper presented at the North American Chapter of the Association for Computational Linguistics. from http://citeseer.ist.psu.edu/budanitsky01semantic.html

Cooper, M. C. (2000). Semantic distance measures. *Computational Intelligence, 16*(1), 79-94.

Crocco, A. G., Villasis-Keever, M., & Jadad, A. R. (2002). Analysis of cases of harm associated with use of health information on the Internet. *JAMA, 287*, 2869-2871.

de Keizer, N. F., Abu-Hanna, A., & Zwetsloot-Schonk, J. H. (2000). Understanding terminological systems. I: Terminology and typology. *Methods Inf Med, 39*(1), 16-21.

Eisenberg, D. M., Kessler, R. C., Rompay, M. I. V., Kaptchuk, T. J., Wilkey, S. A., Appel, S., et al. (2001). Perceptions about complementary therapies relative to conventional therapies among adults who use both: results from a national survey. *Annals of Internal Medicine, 135*(5), 344-351.

Eysenbach, G., & Kohler, C. (2004). Health-related searches on the Internet. *Jama, 291*(24), 2946.

Eysenbach, G., Powell, J., Kuss, O., & Sa, E. R. (2002). Empirical studies assessing the quality of health information for consumers on the world wide web: a systematic review. *JAMA, 287*(20), 2691-2700.

Fox, S., & Rainie, L. (2000). *The online healthcare revolution: How the Web helps Americans take better care of themselves.* Washington DC: Pew

Internet and American Life Project: Onlineo. Document Number)

Fox, S., & Rainie, L. (2002). *Vital decisions: how internet users decide what information to trust when they or their loved ones are sick*. Washington, DC: Pew Internet & American Life Projecto. Document Number)

Funk, M. E., & Reid, C. A. (1983). Indexing consistency in MEDLINE. *Bull Med Libr Assoc, 71*(2), 176-183.

Gay, C. W., Kayaalp, M., & Aronson, A. R. (2005). *Semi-automatic indexing of full text biomedical articles*. Paper presented at the AMIA Annu Symp Proc.

Grimes, C., Tang, D., & Russell, D. M. (2007, May 8-12, 2007). *Query logs alone are not enough*. Paper presented at the WWW 2007, Banff, Canada.

Haynes, R. B. (2001). Of studies, syntheses, synopses, and systems: the "4S" evolution of services for finding current best evidence. *ACP J Club, 134*(2), A11-13.

Helft, P. R., Hlubocky, F. J., Gordon, E. J., Ratain, M. J., & Daugherty, C. (2000, 2000). *Hope and the media in advanced cancer patients*. Paper presented at the American Society of Clinical Oncology 36th annual meeting, New Orleans, LA.

Hersh, W., & Hickam, D. (1994). Use of a multi-application computer workstation in a clinical setting. *Bull Med Libr Assoc, 82*(4), 382-389.

Hersh, W. R., & Hickam, D. H. (1998). How well do physicians use electronic information retrieval systems? A framework for investigation and systematic review. *Jama, 280*(15), 1347-1352.

Herskovic, J. R., Tanaka, L. Y., Hersh, W., & Bernstam, E. V. (2007). A day in the life of PubMed: analysis of a typical day's query log. *J Am Med Inform Assoc, 14*(2), 212-220.

Jadad, A. R., & Gagliardi, A. (1998). Rating health information on the Internet: navigating to knowledge or to Babel? *JAMA, 279*(8), 611-614.

Jansen, B. J., Spink, A., & Saracevic, T. (2000). Real Life, Real Users, and Real Needs: A Study and Analysis of User Queries on the Web *Information Processing and Management, 36*(2), 207-227.

Lacroix, E.-M. (2000). *Expanding world access to health literature*. Paper presented at the 8th International congress on Medical Librarianship, London.

Lacroix, E.-M., & Mehnert, R. (2002). The US National Library of Medicine in the 21st century: expanding collections, nontraditional formats, new audiences. *Health Information and Libraries Journal, 19*(3), 126-132.

McCray, A. T., Loane, R. F., Browne, A. C., & Bangalore, A. K. (1999). Terminology issues in user access to Web-based medical information. *Proc AMIA Symp*, 107-111.

Nakashima, E. (2006, August 8, 2006). AOL takes down site with users' search data. *Washington Post,* p. D01, from http://www.washingtonpost.com/wp-dyn/content/article/2006/08/07/AR2006080701150.html

Paik, S., Shak, S., Tang, G., Kim, C., Baker, J., Cronin, M., et al. (2004). A multigene assay to predict recurrence of tamoxifen-treated, node-negative breast cancer. *N Engl J Med, 351*(27), 2817-2826.

Price, S. L., & Hersh, W. R. (1999). Filtering Web pages for quality indicators: an empirical approach to finding high quality consumer health information on the World Wide Web. *Proc AMIA Symp*, 911-915.

Resource statistics. (2007). Retrieved May 15, 2007, from http://www.ncbi.nlm.nih.gov/About/tools/restable_stat_pubmeddata.htm

Robinson, A., & Thomson, R. (2001). Variability in patient preferences for participating in medical decision making: implication for the use of decision support tools. *Qual Healthcare, 10 Suppl 1*, i34-38.

Robinson, J. C. (2001). The end of managed care. *JAMA, 285*(20), 2622-2628.

Silverstein, C., Henzinger, M., Marais, H., & Moricz, M. (1998). *Analysis of a Very Large AltaVista Query Log* (Technical Note No. SRC Technical Note 1998-014): Digital Equipment Corporationo. Document Number)

Slawson, D. C., & Shaughnessy, A. F. (2005). Teaching evidence-based medicine: should we be teaching information management instead? *Acad Med, 80*(7), 685-689.

Smith, C. A., Stavri, P. Z., & Chapman, W. W. (2002). In their own words? A terminological analysis of e-mail to a cancer information service. *Proc AMIA Symp*, 697-701.

Strasberg, H. R., Hubbs, P. R., Rindfleisch, T. C., & Melmon, K. L. (1999). Analysis of information needs of users of the Stanford Health Information Network for Education. *Proc AMIA Symp*, 965-969.

U.S. National Library of Medicine. (2005, May 27). *MeSH Fact Sheet.* Retrieved March 30, 2007, from http://www.nlm.nih.gov/mesh/intro_preface2007.html#pref_hist

U.S. National Library of Medicine. (2006a, May 27). *Citation Maintenance Tasks in XML format.* Retrieved April 5, 2007, from http://www.nlm.nih.gov/mesh/gcmdoc2007.html

U.S. National Library of Medicine. (2006b, November 27). *MeSH history.* Retrieved March 30, 2007, from http://www.nlm.nih.gov/mesh/intro_preface2007.html#pref_hist

Walji, M., Sagaram, S., Sagaram, D., Meric-Bernstam, F., Johnson, C., Mirza, N. Q., et al. (2004). Efficacy of quality criteria to identify potentially harmful information: a cross-sectional survey of complementary and alternative medicine web sites. *J Med Internet Res, 6*(2), e21.

Zeng, Q., Kogan, S., Ash, N., Greenes, R. A., & Boxwala, A. A. (2002). Characteristics of consumer terminology for health information retrieval. *Methods Inf Med, 41*(4), 289-298.

KEY TERMS

Biomedicine: The broad domain of biology and healthcare including research and practice related to living organisms often focused on, but not limited to, human health and disease.

Classification or Taxonomy: A terminology where terms are arranged by "is_a" or "is_member_of" relationships into classes (de Keizer, Abu-Hanna, & Zwetsloot-Schonk, 2000).

Concept: A cognitive construct based on entities in the real world such as "nose" or "anatomy" (de Keizer, Abu-Hanna, & Zwetsloot-Schonk, 2000).

Consumer (of healthcare): A member of the lay public, as opposed to a researcher or clinician. Therefore, a consumer is not an expert in biomedical science or terminology.

Informational Query: Query intended to satisfy a general information need, as opposed to an attempt to locate a specific article or group of articles (navigational query) (Broder, 2002).

MEDLINE: A database of biomedical literature created and maintained by the US National Library of Medicine (NLM, a unit of the National Institutes of Health). MEDLINE is a bibliographic database, meaning that it contains the reference information needed to find articles, but not the actual full-text articles.

MeSH: Medical Subject Headings.

Navigational Query: Query intended to locate a particular article or group of articles, as opposed to satisfying a general information need (informational query) (Broder, 2002).

PubMed: A freely-available interface onto MEDLINE created and maintained by the NLM.

Semantic: Of or relating to meaning in language (http://www.merriam-webster.com/dictionary/semantic accessed September 18, 2007).

Term: Linguistic label for concepts (de Keizer, Abu-Hanna, & Zwetsloot-Schonk, 2000).

Terminology: A set of terms (de Keizer, Abu-Hanna, & Zwetsloot-Schonk, 2000).

UMLS: Unified Medical Language System.

Chapter XIX
Processing and Analysis of Search Query Logs in Chinese

Michael Chau
The University of Hong Kong, Hong Kong

Yan Lu
The University of Hong Kong, Hong Kong

Xiao Fang
The University of Toledo, USA

Christopher C. Yang
Drexel University, USA

ABSTRACT

More non-English contents are now available on the World Wide Web and the number of non-English users on the Web is increasing. While it is important to understand the Web searching behavior of these non-English users, many previous studies on Web query logs have focused on analyzing English search logs and their results may not be directly applied to other languages. In this Chapter we discuss some methods and techniques that can be used to analyze search queries in Chinese. We also show an example of applying our methods on a Chinese Web search engine. Some interesting findings are reported.

INTRODUCTION

Search engines have been widely used for finding useful information on the World Wide Web. Many users start their Web activities using popular search engines such as Google (http://www.google.com). Many search engines were originally designed for English Web pages. While English content is popular on the Web, the number of Web users speaking other languages is increasing rapidly (Global Reach, 2004). To satisfy the information needs of non-English speaking users, most large commercial search engines support multilingual searching. However, the underlying technologies used in these search engines may not be the best technique for searching non-English documents.

For instance, in mainland China, Google's share of the search engine market is smaller than that of the market leader Baidu (http://www.baidu.com), a search engine tailor-made for Chinese Web pages (CNNIC, 2006). Because of such reasons, there are many language-specific search engines designed for particular languages. For example, the search engine Fireball (http://www.fireball.de) was designed for German Web pages, Goo (http://www.goo.ne.jp) for Japanese, and Ayna (http://www.ayna.com) for Arabic. The information needs and search behavior of non-English users are different from those of native English users because of different languages and different cultures (Chau et al., 2007). More importantly, some languages, such as Asian languages, have different characters, grammars, and structures that are significantly different from those of English. Consequently, the methods and techniques for processing search logs in these languages can be quite different from those for processing English search logs. In this chapter, we discuss methods and issues involved in processing search logs in Chinese. As one of the most widely used non-English languages, Chinese has its unique characteristics. On the other hand, it shares similar characteristics with some other Asian languages such as Japanese and Korean. We believe that we can extend methods in this chapter across these languages.

The chapter is structured as follows. In the next section, we give some background knowledge about the characteristics of the Chinese language. Then we discuss the methods and techniques used to analyze Chinese search queries. The section that follows presents the application of our methods on a Chinese Web search engine called Timway. The last section provides a summary of this chapter.

BACKGROUND

The analysis of search engine logs can be classified into the area of Web usage mining. Study on search engine logs usually has focused on how users use the search engines on the Web to find the information they need. On the other hand, it also has a strong root in information retrieval research. Before the Web became popular, many studies had reported analysis of user information behavior, search queries, and search sessions with various information retrieval and digital library systems (e.g., Fenichel, 1981; Bates et al., 1993). In recent years, we have seen many studies devoted to search engines and information systems on the Web. The first category of Web search engine log research focused on analyzing the search logs submitted to general-purpose search engines. In 1998, Jansen, Spink, and several others started a series of research projects on the search logs that were made available by Excite. Their first study analyzed a set of 51,473 queries submitted to the Excite search engine in 1997 (Jansen et al., 1998; Jansen et al., 2000). Subsequently, they expanded their research and analyzed three sets of data collected in 1997, 1999 and 2001, each containing at least one million queries submitted to the Excite search engine (Spink et al., 2001; 2002; Wolfram et al., 2001). Many interesting findings have been identified from these search logs, such as the trends in Web searching (Spink et al., 2002), sexual information searching on the Web (Spink et al., 2004), and Web queries in question format (Spink & Ozmultu, 2002). Another large-scale Web query analysis was performed by Silverstein et al. (1999) on a set of 993 million requests submitted to the AltaVista search engine over a period of 43 days in 1998. Most of these studies used a set of similar metrics or statistics in their studies, including number of sessions, number of queries, number of queries in a session, number of terms in a query, percentage of queries using Boolean queries, number of result pages viewed by each user, etc. These metrics allow researchers to compare their findings across different types of search engines at different times.

The second category of Web search analysis focused on the search logs of a specific Web site or system. One example is the study of Croft et al. (1995), which investigated the search queries submitted to the THOMAS system, an online searchable database consisting of U.S. legislative information. They analyzed 94,911 queries recorded in their system and identified the top 25 queries. They also found that 88% of all queries contained three or fewer words, a number much lower than that of traditional information retrieval systems. Jones et al. (1998) analyzed the transaction logs of the New Zealand Digital Library that contained a collection of computer science technical reports. They obtained similar results regarding the number of words in queries: almost 82% of queries were composed of three or fewer words. Their study also found that most users use the default settings of search engines without any modifications. Chau et al. (2005) studied the search queries submitted to the search engine on a government Web site, and Wang et al. (2003) analyzed the search queries submitted to the search engine of a university. In both studies, it was demonstrated that seasonal patterns exist in Website searching. They also found that the search queries submitted to a general-purpose search engine were quite different from those submitted to a Website search engine, in terms of search topics, search term distribution, the mean number of queries per session, and the mean length of queries.

Most search log studies have focused on search queries in English or in other Western languages. For example, previous studies on the Excite search logs and the Altavista search logs were conducted on English queries (Jansen et al., 2000; Spink et al., 2001; Silverstein et al., 1999). The Fireball study analyzed Web search queries in German (Hoelscher, 1998). Because of language differences, the results of these search query analysis studies may not be applicable to Chinese Web searching. For example, the mean number of query length, measured as the number of words in an English query, would become difficult to interpret in Chinese, which uses characters. The usage of operators could also be different. It is more natural to form a query "information AND systems" in English than a query "資訊 AND 系統" in Chinese because of the language difference. Cultural differences may also result in different information seeking behaviors, especially for search topics. It is thus important to conduct studies on non-English search query logs in order to understand the needs of these non-English users. (For a comprehensive review of the history of and existing work in search log analyses, please refer to Section I of this book.)

There were only a few studies that focused on Asian languages. One example is the study performed by the Academia Sinica in Taiwan on Chinese search engines. Rather than studying users' information needs and searching behaviors, they analyzed the query logs to provide term suggestion to users. Huang et al. (2003) analyzed the query logs submitted to several general-purpose Web search engines in Taiwan, including Yahoo-Taiwan (http://tw.yahoo.com), Sina-Taiwan (http://www.sina.com.tw), PChome (http://www.pchome.com.tw) and Yam (http://www.yam.com). A total of 2,369,282 queries and 218,362 unique terms were collected in a period of 126 days. They found that 74% of their search sessions contained only one query, which was similar to the number in the AltaVista study (Silverstein et al., 1999). Pu et al. (2002) also performed analysis on the query logs from three Chinese search engines in Taiwan, namely Dreamer, GAIS, and Openfind (http://www.openfind.com.tw). They found that the average length of the Chinese queries in their logs was 3.18 characters. They also reported that advanced search functions were seldom used, and that less than five percent of queries covered almost three-quarters of the total frequencies (Pu et al., 2002).

The processing methods for English search queries might not perform well in analyzing Chinese search queries. Many previous studies on non-English text processing have shown that existing techniques need to be revised or completely redesigned for Chinese documents. We noted that character-based processing methods were often used for the analysis of Chinese text. The reason is that the language structure between Chinese and English is very different. One of the most notable features is that Chinese is an ideographical, character-based language, while English is an alphabetical, word-based language. For character-based languages, most of the meaningful words are built up by combining single characters, and an individual character may deliver different meanings in different words. Moreover, in Chinese the syntax of words is quite different from that in English. There is no space between terms in Chinese, making it difficult to correctly perform segmentation, whereas in English every word is basically delimited by space. This specific characteristic of Chinese would result in many different searching behaviors, such as the average number of terms or characters used in a query.

ANALYSIS METHODS

In this section, we discuss the analysis methods that can be applied in some Asian languages. There are a large number of Asian languages, such as Chinese, Japanese, Korean, Thai, Vietnamese, Hindi, and Malay. Among them, Chinese is the most popular and is discussed here. We believe the method can be applied to some other Asian languages that share similar characteristics with Chinese.

Data Collecting and Pre-Processing

One of the characteristics of a Chinese search log is that the Chinese queries are often received in different character encodings. GB-2312, GBK, and BIG 5 are the three most popular Chinese language encoding schemes. They are used in different Chinese speaking regions with different popularity. For example, Traditional Chinese, usually encoded in BIG 5, is widely used in Hong Kong and Taiwan, while Simplified Chinese, usually encoded in GB-2312, is more commonly used in mainland China and Singapore. While some search engines may convert all encodings into one (e.g., Unicode) in their search logs, it is common for log files from one search engine to contain queries with different encoding schemes. To facilitate the analysis of Chinese queries, all queries should be converted into one encoding scheme.

In encoding conversion, the most important step is to detect what encoding a raw query is in. Because the encodings have different character sets, encoding methods, choice of characters, vocabulary, and semantics, detection is a complex process rather than a straightforward mapping, and cannot be performed with 100% accuracy (Halpern & Kerman, 1999). Detection is often done by analyzing the likelihood of the terms based on the frequencies of each character as well as the frequencies of each word by look-up in standard corpuses. One example of encoding conversion tools is the one available online from Mandarin Tools (http://www.mandarintools.com/) (Peterson, 2004).

General Analysis

The metrics used in analyzing Chinese search logs are similar to those used in the studies on English search logs (Spink et al., 2001; Silverstein et al., 1999; Jansen et al., 2000). They can be classified into three levels - session, query, and term level. The statistics at the session and query levels, such as the mean number of queries per session and the mean number of terms per query, reveal user's searching behaviors and should be applied to Chinese search query logs directly. The use of similar metrics allows researchers to compare their findings across different types of search engines at different times. It also facilitates the comparison between Chinese search queries and English search queries. For example, it has been found that average length of Chinese Web search queries is often larger than that of English queries (Pu et al., 2002; Chau et al., 2007).

Zipf Distribution Analysis

Many studies have applied the Zipf distribution to analyze the distribution of search terms. Zipf distribution, traditionally often applied to extensive textual passages, has been investigated for database contents in bibliographic and full text databases (Zipf, 1949). Let f be the frequency of a word in a corpus and γ be the rank of the word. According to the Zipf distribution:

$$f = k / \gamma \qquad (1)$$

where k is a constant for a corpus. Zipf curves follow a straight line when plotted on a double-logarithmic diagram, which means when $log(f)$ is drawn against $log(r)$ in a graph, a straight line is obtained with a slope of -1. A number of theoretical developments of Zipf's law were later derived (Fedorowicz, 1982). A more general form of the Zipf distribution is as follows (Mandelbrot, 1953):

$$f = k / (\gamma + \alpha)^{\beta} \qquad (2)$$

where α and β are constants for a corpus being analyzed. Generally, the constants α and β were found to have only small statistical deviations from the original law by Zipf (Smith & Devine, 1985).

Earlier Web search analysis studies have suggested that the distribution of terms used in Web search engines largely followed the Zipf distribution. Spink et al. (2001) used a double log rank-frequency plot to determine the accordance of the Excite search log data with a Zipf distribution. The study found that the resulting distribution is slightly unbalanced for the high and low ranking terms. The findings concur with those of other previous studies (Nelson, 1989; Wolfram, 1992). Jansen et al. (2000) also found that the resulting distribution seemed to be unbalanced at the ends of the graph of rank-frequency distribution. The curve fell off very gently at the beginning and showed discontinuities and an unusually long tail toward the end. Wang et al. (2003) used Zipf's curve to analyze the usage of English search terms. Different from other studies, they plotted a second line by ranking words based on unique frequencies and compared this with the original line. The drastic drop of this second line indicated that the number of words with low frequency increased as the frequency decreased. It is interesting to apply Zipf's distribution analysis to Chinese search queries. However, the unit of analysis would be different; instead of using word rank and frequencies, it is more reasonable to use characters in conducting Zipf's analysis in Chinese, as discussed in the next subsection.

Term Analysis

Term-level analysis of queries in Chinese languages can be quite different from that of English queries. As discussed above, Chinese languages are character-based languages. The concept of "term" in these languages is quite different from that in English. In English query analysis, a search term is often used to refer to an English word. However, in Chinese, words are not separated by spaces. Therefore, term-related analysis often cannot be directly applied in the analysis of Chinese queries. Instead, character-based processing has been widely used (e.g., Chau et al., 2005). Character-based processing methods are often based on a statistical model (e.g., Chien, 1997). Among these methods, character-based bigrams or n-grams analysis are often conducted for Chinese text.

The idea of bigram analysis is to extract all sequences of two adjacent words in each query. For n-gram analysis, all sequences of n adjacent words will be extracted. For example, let us consider a query "數碼相機" (digital camera). If we perform bigram analysis, the tokens are "數碼", "碼相", and "相機". Two of these tokens "數碼" (digital) and "相機" (camera) are valid terms while "碼相" is invalid. Similarly, for trigrams analysis, "數碼相" and "碼相機" (both are invalid tokens) will be extracted. For unigram (character-level) analysis, the characters "數", "碼", "相" and "機" are indexed. The analysis of n-grams for other values of n can be performed in a similar fashion. The frequencies of these tokens (grams) are then recorded for the whole corpus. Because tokens with low frequencies are often filtered out, it is expected that some of the invalid terms will be filtered. The tokens (including bigrams, trigrams, and possibly n-grams) with high frequencies correspond to English words with high frequencies. Analyses on search topics, search term distribution, and character distribution can be performed on these tokens.

More advanced analysis, such as natural language processing, Hidden Markov Model, or Mutual Information (Chien, 1997), also can be applied to Chinese text analysis. These models allow better word segmentation in such languages as Chinese. However, one problem is that Web query logs mostly consist of short queries and the corpus is somewhat limited. The effectiveness of these techniques on Chinese queries has yet to be evaluated.

TIMWAY: AN EXAMPLE

In this Section, we present an example of how we analyzed the search logs of a search engine in Hong Kong called Timway (http://www.timway.com/). Timway is a search engine established in 1997 and is primarily designed for searching Web sites in Hong Kong. Timway indexes Web pages in both English and Chinese and accepts search queries in both languages. Chinese queries can be submitted in Big 5 as well as GB encodings. About 1.2 million search queries were collected from December 1, 2003 to March 2, 2004. Detailed analysis on this data set was presented in Chau et al. (2007).

The data were first pre-processed for data cleansing and session identification. We followed the method proposed by Silverstein (1999) in segmenting sessions. After dividing the queries into sessions, we were able to perform descriptive analyses such as number of sessions, mean and median numbers of queries per session, number of empty queries, and so on. The methods of finding these numbers are the same as those in English search query logs.

The encoding conversion tools available from Mandarin Tools (Peterson, 2004) as discussed above were then used to detect the language (English or Chinese) of the queries and the encoding (Big5, GB2312, GBK, Unicode) of the Chinese queries. By converting all Chinese queries to the same encoding, further analysis such as bigram analysis could be performed more easily. In order to test the accuracy of the detection program on the data set, a set of 137 randomly selected Chinese queries were extracted from our data. The detection program was used to detect the encoding of each of the queries in this set. A Chinese native speaker was then asked to judge whether the encoding detected by the program was correct by looking at each query in both the original encoding scheme and the detected encoding scheme and deciding which one was more likely to be a search query. In our test, the program correctly detected 136 out of the 137 queries, demonstrating an accuracy of 99.27%. Using this software, the queries were all converted to Big 5 for further analysis.

After the encoding conversion, we could then perform such analyses as finding the number of unique queries, the mean and median number of unique queries per session, the mean and median numbers of characters per query, and other analyses at the character level. A simple Java program was developed to perform character-based analysis and n-gram analysis on the data for n up to 10. Zipf's distribution analysis, search topic analysis, and other query-level and term-level analysis were then performed on the data.

The top queries are shown in Table 1. Many of these queries are related to pornography, which corroborates with earlier findings in English search logs. In addition, we can also identify the most popular Chinese words/phrases in the search queries. The top bigrams, trigrams, and quadragrams are shown in Table 2. No significant queries were revealed for terms with n greater than 6 as these queries had low frequencies.

As can be seen in Table 2, some trigrams (like 有限公 and 限公司) are incomplete Chinese words. Together they form the meaningful quadragram 有限公司 (Limited Company). Such incomplete terms can affect the results of our analyses. One way to deal with these incomplete terms was to perform statistical analyses such as mutual information on the search queries. By using such techniques, infrequent terms will be filtered. However, the problem is that we will run the risk of missing some complete terms with low frequencies. More testing will be needed in this aspect.

Double-log rank-frequency plots were used to determine whether the Timway data would fit with a Zipf distribution. To plot the curve, the terms of interest are first ranked by their frequencies. The natural logarithm of a term's rank is then plotted against the natural logarithm of the term's frequency.

Since Chinese words consist of sequences of characters, it is interesting to analyze the characteristics of unigrams and n-grams in search queries in order to determine the accordance with the Zipf distribution and to understand users' usage of terms and characters. Because there is no clear word boundary in Chinese like the "space" counterpart in English, it is not trivial to automate the accurate extraction of compound words (semantically complete words) in a Chi-

Table 1. Top 5 Chinese queries in the Timway search logs

Top 5 Chinese Queries	Frequency (%)
一樓一 (prostitution)	6,841 (0.54%)
成人 (adult)	4,621 (0.37%)
色情 (pornography)	3,995 (0.32%)
走光 (wardrobe malfunction)	2,869 (0.23%)
內衣 (underwear)	2,558 (0.20%)

Table 2. Top 5 bigrams, trigrams, and quadragrams in the Timway search logs

Top 5 Bigrams	Freq.	Top 5 Trigrams	Freq.	Top 5 Quadragrams	Freq.
香港 (Hong Kong)	17,134	六合彩 (Mark Six Lottery)	3,177	有限公司 (Limited Company)	1,812
成人 (adult)	13,768	有限公 (*incomplete)	1,816	手提電話 (cellular phone)	864
色情 (pornography)	9,922	限公司(*incomplete)	1,815	數碼相機(digital camera)	746
公司 (company)	5,045	學生妹 (female student)	1,814	情色文學(porn literature)	736
下載 (download)	4,858	旅行社 (travel agency)	1,631	成人漫畫(adult comics)	726

nese query. Without using techniques such as mutual information for automatic Chinese word segmentation, we directly tokenized the search queries into characters and all occurrences of any consecutive characters (up to 12) were extracted and the frequencies were recorded.

We calculated the frequencies of all n-grams (with n = 1 to 6) in the Timway query logs and put them in rank order. We found that the n-gram Zipf curves approximately follow straight lines and can be represented by a single Mandelbrot form (Ha et al., 2002). We found that the values of β for unigrams and bigrams are higher than the standard magnitude of the negative slope of Zipf distribution ($\beta = 1$), showing that the relative frequencies of unigrams and bigrams are slightly higher than those of a standard Zipf distribution for high-ranking terms. The relatively low β-values of n-grams (n = 3, 4, 5, 6) indicate that the relative frequencies of words in n-grams are much lower than those of a standard Zipf distribution for high-ranking terms.

Another issue that we could study was about queries that consisted of both languages, e.g., "卡拉 ok" (Karaoke) and "明星 wallpaper" (celebrities wallpaper). These are often known as bilingual queries or mixed queries and need to be treated separately. By detecting these queries, we were able to perform further analysis and understand the nature of these queries (Lu et al., 2006). It is interesting to investigate: Why do users submit such bilingual queries? What are the characteristics of these queries? How can we improve Web search engines to work with these queries?

Mixed queries can be roughly categorized into six types. The first type of mixed queries consists of names of magazines, placements, and firms such as "東 touch" (East touch), "UA 時代廣場" (UA time square), and "ACM 又一城" (ACM festival walk) etc. For the second type of mixed queries, the English part of the queries does not have a popular Chinese translation and thus can not be replaced by simple Chinese translation. Examples are "mp3", "bt", "dvd", "midi", and "ICQ". Most of them are related to computer systems. For the third type, the English part has been translated into Chinese but the term phrase contains English due to the special culture in Hong Kong, which is often said to be the place where "East meets West". People in Hong Kong are used to utilizing English words in ways of both speaking and writing. They often combine Chinese and English together to form phrases and sentences, and thus search queries reflect this practice. Some examples are "成人 game" (adult game) and "明星 wallpaper" (celebrities wallpaper). In the fourth type of mixed queries, the English parts are the abbreviations of certain English phrases and are popularly used by people. For example, "3G" in "3G 手機" (3G mobile phone) is the shortened form of "third generation", "IQ" in "IQ 題"(IQ test) refers to "intelligence quotient", and "AV" in "日本 AV" (Japan AV) stands for "adult video". In the fifth type, the queries are mixed with Chinese words and their corresponding English terms, and their English part and Chinese part have the same meaning, such as "Yuen Long 元朗", "Bowie Lam 林保怡". They might intend to get a high recall rate. The last type of mixed queries consists of the English form of the brand and the Chinese form of the product, such as "Canon 鏡頭" (Canon lens), "Sharp 手機" (Sharp cell phone), and "Panasonic 數碼攝錄機" (Panasonic Digital Video). The top 5 mixed queries are shown in Table 3.

Overall, the results of this analysis revealed interesting findings about Chinese Web queries

Table 3. Top 5 Mixed queries in the Timway search logs

Top 5 Mixed Queries	Frequency (%)
頭文字D (name of a comics)	98
BT下載 (BT download)	96
mp3機 (mp3 player)	91
bt下載 (bt download)	86
卡拉ok (Karaoke)	84

(Chau et al., 2007). The findings suggested that some characteristics identified in the search log, such as search topics and the mean number of queries per session, are similar to those in English Web search engines. However, some other characteristics, such as the use of operators in query formulation, are significantly different. One possible reason is that it is less natural to apply Boolean operators such as AND/OR and +/- in such Asian languages as Chinese. The analysis also shows that only a very small number of unique Chinese characters are used in search queries because Chinese characters are a closed set – the number of characters is more or less restricted. As the findings are not a major focus of this Chapter, interested readers are referred to Chau et al. (2007) and Lu et al. (2006) for more details of the findings.

CONCLUSION AND FUTURE RESEARCH

In this chapter we have presented some issues to be noted when analyzing search queries in Chinese. In particular, a study of Chinese Web search queries in Hong Kong is used as an example. The results of the analyses showed that the proposed methods can reveal some interesting characteristics of Chinese Web searching that can be compared and contrasted with previous findings in English Web searching. While the techniques presented cannot be applied to all Asian languages directly, we believe that it can be applied to some languages that are similar to Chinese, such as Japanese. As there was only limited previous research on Asian search log analysis, it will be interesting to perform more studies in this area, especially for languages other than Chinese. These studies will enable the comparison between English and non-English search queries and their characteristics, and lead to better understanding of the searching behavior of users using these languages. These findings can help us design better search interfaces and search engines for the Web.

REFERENCES

Chau, M., Qin, J., Zhou, Y., Tseng, C., and Chen, H. (2005). SpidersRUs: Automated Development of Vertical Search Engines in Different Domains and Languages, in *Proceedings of the ACM/IEEE-CS Joint Conference on Digital Libraries*, Denver, Colorado, USA, June 7-11, 2005.

Chau, M., Fang, X., and Yang, C. C. (2007). Web Searching in Chinese: A Study of a Search Engine in Hong Kong, *Journal of the American Society for Information Science and Technology* (JASIST), accepted for publication, 58(7), 1044-1054, 2007.

Chien, L.-F. (1997). PAT-Tree-Based Keyword Extraction for Chinese Information Retrieval, in *Proceedings of the 1997 ACM SIGIR*, Philadelphia, PA, USA, pp. 50-58.

CNNIC – China Internet Network Information Center, *Chinese Search Engine Market Survey Report 2006.*

Fedorowicz, J. (1982). A Zipfian Model of an Automatic Bibliographic System: an Application to MEDLINE. *Journal of American Society of Information Science*, (33), pp 223-232.

Global Reach (2004). "Global Internet Statistics," available at: http://www.glreach.com/globstats/

Ha, L. Q., Sicilia-Garcia, E. I., Ming, J. and Smith, F. J. (2002) Extension of Zipf's law to words and phrases. *Proceedings of the 19th International Conference on Computational Linguistics*, 2002, pp. 315–320.

Halpern, J. and Kerman, J. (1999) "The Pitfalls and Complexities of Chinese to Chinese Conversion," in *Proceedings of the 14th International*

Unicode Conference, Cambridge, Massachusetts, USA, March 1999.

Hölscher, C., How Internet Experts Search for Information on the Web, in Proceedings of the World Conference of the World Wide Web, Internet, and Intranet, Orlando, Florida, USA, 1998.

Huang, C. K., Chien, L. F., Oyang, Y. J. (2003). Relevant Term Suggestion in Interactive Web Search Based on Contextual Information in Query Session Logs, *Journal of the American Society of Information Science and Technology*, 54(7), 638-649.

Jansen, B. J., Spink, A., and Saracevic, T. (2000). Real Life, Real Users, and Real Needs: A Study and Analysis of User Queries on the Web. *Information Processing and Management*, 36, 207-227.

Jansen, B. J., Spink, A., Bateman, J., and Saracevic, T. Real Life Information Retrieval: A Study of User Queries on the Web. *ACM SIGIR Forum*, (32:1), 1998, pp. 5-17.

Lu, Y. and Chau, M., Fang, X., and Yang, C. C. Analysis of the Bilingual Queries in a Chinese Web Search Engine, in *Proceedings of the Fifth Workshop on E-Business (WEB 2006)*, Milwaukee, Wisconsin, USA, December 9, 2006.

Mandelbrot, B. An Information Theory of the Statistical Structure of Language, in *Communication Theory*, edited by Willis Jackson, New York: Academic Press, 1953, pp. 486-502.

Peterson, E. (2004). Chinese Encoding Converter, [Online], retrieved from http://www.mandarintools.com/ on October 7, 2004.

Pu, H. T., Chuang, S.-L., and Yang, C. (2002). Subject Categorization of Query Terms for Exploring Web Users' Search Interests. *Journal of the American Society for Information Science and Technology*, 53(8), 617-630.

Salton, G. (1989). *Automatic Text Processing*. Reading, Addison-Wesley, Boston, MA, USA.

Silverstein, C., Henzinger, M., Marais, H. and Moricz, M. (1999) Analysis of a Very Large Web Search Engine Query Log. *ACM SIGIR Forum*, 33(1), 6-12.

Smith, F. J. & Devine, K. Storing and Retrieving Word Phrases. *Information Processing & Management*, (21:3), 1985, pp. 215-224.

Spink, A., Jansen, B. J., Wolfram, D., and Saracevic, T. (2002). From E-Sex to E-Commerce: Web Search Changes, *IEEE Computer*, 35(3), 107-109.

Spink, A. and Ozmultu, H. C. (2002). Characteristics of Question Format Web Queries: An Exploratory Study. *Information Processing and Management*, 38, 453-471.

Spink, A., Ozmutlu, H. C., and Lorence, D. P. (2004). Web Searching for Sexual Information: An Exploratory Study. *Information Processing and Management*, 40, 113-123.

Spink, A., Wolfram, D., Jansen, B. J., and Saracevic, T. (2001). Searching the Web: The Public and Their Queries. *Journal of the American Society for Information Science and Technology*, 52(3), 226-234.

Wang, P., Berry, M. W., and Yang, Y. Mining Longitudinal Web Queries: Trends and Patterns. *Journal of the American Society for Information Science and Technology*, (54:8), 2003, pp.743-758.

Wolfram, D., Spink, A., Jansen, B. J., and Saracevic, T., (2001). Vox Populi: The Public Searching of the Web. *Journal of the American Society for Information Science and Technology*, 52(12), 1073-1074.

Zipf, G. K. *Human behavior and the principle of least effort*. Cambridge: Addison-Wesley, 1949.

KEY TERMS

Bigram Analysis: The analysis of all sequences of two adjacent words in each query.

Chinese Search Logs: Contain the Chinese queries that are often received in different character encodings. GB-2312, GBK, and BIG 5 are the three most popular Chinese language encoding schemes. They are used in different Chinese speaking regions with different popularity. For example, Traditional Chinese, usually encoded in BIG 5, is widely used in Hong Kong and Taiwan, while Simplified Chinese, usually encoded in GB-2312, is more commonly used in mainland China and Singapore.

N-Gram Analysis: The analysis of all sequences of n adjacent words in each query.

Zipf Distribution: A distribution in which the frequency of any object is inversely proportional to its frequency rank. It has been observed in text corpora, database contents, and other natural phenomena.

Chapter XX
Query Log Analysis for Adaptive Dialogue-Driven Search

Udo Kruschwitz
University of Essex, UK

Nick Webb
SUNY Albany, USA

Richard Sutcliffe
University of Limerick, Ireland

ABSTRACT

The theme of this chapter is the improvement of Information Retrieval and Question Answering systems by the analysis of query logs. Two case studies are discussed. The first describes an intranet search engine working on a university campus which can present sophisticated query modifications to the user. It does this via a hierarchical domain model built using multi-word term co-occurrence data. The usage log was analysed using mutual information scores between a query and its refinement, between a query and its replacement, and between two queries occurring in the same session. The results can be used to validate refinements in the domain model, and to suggest replacements such as domain-dependent spelling corrections. The second case study describes a dialogue-based question answering system working over a closed document collection largely derived from the Web. Logs here are based around explicit sessions in which an analyst interacts with the system. Analysis of the logs has shown that certain types of interaction lead to increased precision of the results. Future versions of the system will encourage these forms of interaction. The conclusions of this chapter are firstly that there is a growing literature on query log analysis, much of it reviewed here, secondly that logs provide many forms of useful information for improving a system, and thirdly that mutual information measures taken with automatic term recognition algorithms and hierarchy construction techniques comprise one approach for enhancing system performance.

INTRODUCTION

The Web is growing at an incredible speed and has become an active research area in its own right (Spink & Jansen, 2004). Search engines such as Google (Brin & Page, 1998) enable users to process, access and navigate vast amounts of information. Such engines are built upon the well-established principles of Information Retrieval (IR) (Baeza-Yates & Ribeiro-Neto, 1999). While an IR system takes as input a user query and returns a ranked list of documents considered relevant to it, a Question Answering (QA) system goes one stage further and returns an exact answer extracted from one of the documents. Since its adoption at the Text REtrieval Conference (TREC) (Voorhees, 1999), the Cross Language Evaluation Forum (CLEF) (Magnini, Romagnoli, Vallin, Herrera, Peñas, Peinado, Verdejo & de Rijke, 2003) and the National Test Collection for Information Retrieval (NTCIR) (Sasaki, Chen, Chen & Lin, 2005), in concert with targeted funding under the Advanced Research Development Agency (ARDA) Advanced QUestion Answering for INTelligence (AQUAINT) program, QA has developed rapidly to the stage at which commercial systems such as Qristal are beginning to appear (Laurent, Séguéla & Nègre, 2006).

A considerable amount of the work in IR and QA has been devoted to the retrieval of results for individual queries. Increasingly, however, users need Interactive Information Systems (IIS) capable of converging on a person's information need by stages, using methods such as Interactive QA (Webb, 2006; Webb & Webber, 2008; Small, Strzalkowski, Liu, Ryan, Salkin, Shimizu, Kantor, Kelly, Rittman & Wacholder, 2004) and dialogue driven search (Kruschwitz, 2003; Kruschwitz, 2005; Kruschwitz & Al-Bakour, 2005). Traditional artificial dialogue systems already allow users to interact with simple, structured data such as train or flight timetables (Zue, Glass, Goodine, Leung, Phillips, Polifroni & Seneff, 1990; Goddeau, Brill, Glass, Pao, Phillips, Polifroni, Seneff & Zue, 1994; Allen, Schubert, Ferguson, Heeman, Hwang, Kato, Light, Martin, Miller, Poesio & Traum, 1995; Aust, Oerder, Seide & Steinbiss, 1995). Such models make extensive use of corpora containing both Human-Computer (H-C) and increasingly Human-Human (H-H) interactions (Hardy, Biermann, Inouye, Mckenzie, Strzalkowski, Ursu, Webb & Wu, 2004). Such corpora can be used to study and capture the phenomena, vocabulary and style of such interactions and hence to develop appropriate machine models.

By contrast, IR and QA systems often operate in much wider domains for which appropriate corpora are not available. As a result, query logs are potentially an extremely valuable resource for increasing our understanding of the complex interactions involved and hence in developing more sophisticated systems. Logs contain a huge amount of information but effective methods for extracting it are only now being developed.

In this chapter we will focus on interactive systems which retrieve information via a dialogue with the user. We will first discuss previous work on log analysis, on interactive information systems and on the use of such analysis to improve interaction. We will then present two case studies which show how an analysis of query logs can be used to improve the underlying domain model and the model of interaction, and hence the *quality* of interaction in a system. The first study deals with UKSearch (Udo Kruschwitz Search) which performs IR working on a University intranet and is aimed at faculty, staff and students. The second focuses on HITIQA (High Quality Interactive Question Answering) which performs QA over Web documents and is aimed at benefiting the Intelligence community, and those with an analytical approach to information. Finally we will draw the findings of both studies together to identify how log analysis can be used to improve interactive systems in future and to establish what challenges must be overcome in the process.

RELATED WORK

General Log Analysis

So far, Web log analysis has centred typically around finding interesting usage patterns or query patterns such as query length, word distribution or even trends. Early studies performed on log files of the *Excite* and *AltaVista* search engines have given us interesting insights into the users' search behaviour such as the average query length of about 2.35 words (Jansen, Bateman & Saracevic, 1998; Silverstein, Henzinger & Marais, 1998). Interestingly, more recent studies have confirmed a lot of the early findings (Beitzel, Jensen, Chowdhury, Grossman & Frieder, 2004; Beitzel, Jensen, Chowdhury, Frieder & Grossman, 2007). Other log analysis studies also investigate trends (Spink & Jansen, 2004). However, all these investigations aim largely at describing the users' search behaviour, understanding what the users have in mind and (possibly) how these trends change over time. This type of Web log analysis has also been conducted on local Web sites (Wang, Berry & Yang, 2003; Chau, Fang & Sheng, 2005), and it is by no means restricted to public Web search. Intranet search log analysis is a related area which nevertheless has attracted much less attention (Stenmark & Jadaan, 2006).

There is a separate area of Web log analysis which investigates the log files of slightly more pro-active search engines which make suggestions as to how to modify the original query. Anick, for example, analysed such log files and found that even if the search engine presents the user with query modification suggestions (in this case via *AltaVista's Prisma* tool), then the vast majority of reformulations are still done manually (Anick, 2003). Results from other studies also cast some doubt on the uptake of interactive user suggestions made by the system (Koshman, Spink & Jansen, 2006). Different studies have found that users do indeed make use of the system's reformulation assistance (Jansen, Spink & Koshman, 2007).

All this existing work indicates that Web log analysis has grown into a very active research area. Nevertheless, most of this work has so far remained on a descriptive level. To our knowledge, there has been very little work on utilising the log files for feeding back into the search process. Dialogue-driven search systems are an emerging area which can benefit directly from knowledge automatically derived from log files. The aim is to improve the system suggestions by exploiting the log files that record previous user interactions with the search system.

Log Analysis for Improving IIS

For the emerging field of Interactive Information Systems, it would be extremely beneficial to utilise corpora that reflect the actions of real users engaged in complex information seeking and browsing tasks. Such actions go beyond human-machine communication, to include retrieval and browsing tasks, which when taken together can be used to determine strategies and evaluation techniques for the information seeking process. We need to be able to analyze and extract prototypical information seeking behaviours, generalised beyond specific domain applications, to find those sequences of events or actions which users make use of to reliably discover and use key concepts in a large data collection.

To apply these techniques to large, unstructured information such as the open Web seems at present unfeasible, however there is a large number of electronic document collections and private intranets, within companies, universities and other institutions, and search in this type of collections has attracted much less attention. Locating relevant information within such collections can be as difficult as the open Web. Nevertheless, these collections contain a huge amount of valuable knowledge that is encoded implicitly and can not therefore be applied directly in the search and discovery process.

There are two direct challenges within this data. One is to identify and extract such knowledge automatically, and the other is to make it usable by incorporating it in an interactive search system. A search engine that offers the user suggestions, to widen or narrow the search, has the potential to be a more useful tool (Kruschwitz & Al-Bakour, 2005; Small, Strzalkowski, Liu, Ryan, Salkin, Shimizu, Kantor, Kelly, Rittman & Wacholder, 2004). A student who searches a university Web site for "exam results" may be presented with a list of module names or numbers to choose from. To be a feasible, general approach, these query modification options must be constructed automatically, based on encoded knowledge derived from the underlying documents. Automatically constructed knowledge can never be as good as manually created structures, therefore an equally important challenge is to improve and maintain this knowledge. Web log analysis gives us the ability to mine log files in order to automatically improve suggestions made by the system, in other words to *adapt* to the users' search behaviour.

Equally importantly, an analysis of real users' Web logs can provide direction toward a new evaluation strategy for interactive systems of this kind. Traditional Information Retrieval metrics such as precision and recall have only tangential meaning with respect to system suggested items that are known a-priori to be only somewhat related to the original query. It would be interesting if we were able to capture the value of these information items to the individual user, which requires that the data search process be coupled with a notion of how the search data is to be used, using the information gained from interaction with the system (Wacholder, Small, Bai, Kelly, Rittman, Ryan, Salkin, Song, Sun, Ting, Kantor & Strzalkowski, 2004; Wacholder, Kelly, Rittman, Sun, Kantor, Small & Strzalkowski, 2007).

There are three main aspects we wish to address in this chapter: Building adaptive domain models, modelling human interaction with data, and evaluating Interactive Information Systems.

Log Analysis for Building Adaptive Domain Models

More and more search engines offer users ways to refine queries, such as *Yahoo!*, the clustering search engine *Vivisimo*, the meta-search engine *Dogpile* and the scientific search engine *Scirus*. Even *Google* now offers query modification suggestions for certain queries. Generally speaking, we can expect to see much more such *faceted* search applications in the future, i.e. applications that guide the user in the search process by proposing query modifications (Dale, 2006). Our interactive information retrieval work, however, focuses on fairly constrained domains such as intranets and local Web sites. Despite the similarity of problems that search engines for intranets and general Web search engines have to address, there are significant differences too and it has been acknowledged that there is a need for more in-depth studies of intranet searching (Stenmark, 2005). Once we move from the Web to smaller collections we expect very different queries and interactions; and results obtained for one collection will not necessarily be applicable to another one. General purpose knowledge structures appear to be even less useful in an intranet setting where the documents are typically drawn from a smaller set of topics.

Different techniques exist to extract domain knowledge for such document collections (Sanderson & Croft, 1999; Anick & Tipirneni, 1999; Kruschwitz, 2005). These domain models can be incorporated into a standard search engine, to suggest query modification terms to the user in an interactive search process, but there has been very little work on updating such a domain model based on either explicit or implicit user feedback. As an automatically extracted domain model will inherently be incomplete and contain a lot of "noise", adjusting it is essential if the recommendations provided by the system are to be improved. Modifications are required in particular in situations where the pool of documents is not static, but dynamic. Continuously recreating the domain model seems inappropriate, however, as there exists the question of how often this should be done. Instead we require a more flexible method that will enable us to filter this noise from useful information. Analysis of logged user information appears to be the most promising option. The users' search behaviour can be used as input into this process of adjusting the domain model so that it becomes more accurate.

Log Analysis for Modelling Human Interaction with Data

When we talk about user modelling, or more accurately in this sense, interaction modelling, there are two distinct issues. The first is modelling the interactions of a single user, to adapt system performance to better assist that user. More generally however, there is the notion of strategies of interaction which enable groups of users to achieve their goals using interaction methods which are more closely aligned to those deployed in human-human interaction. A simple example of this can be seen in recommender systems (Montaner, Lopez & Rosa, 2003), such as those deployed on *Amazon* , which point users towards products and services which are judged to be most interesting to them based on prior behaviour. By Interactive Information Systems, we mean those that are able to enter into a negotiation with the user to determine the size, shape and possible trajectory of their information need. We do not mean to limit the role of the user to disambiguation, but rather assume that the user has an under-specified description of their information requirement, which cannot be fully expressed a-priori, and indeed may evolve over time, where the system needs to co-operate with the user to explore the information space. Clearly, it is impossible to set all modes of this co-operation in advance – so as one source of knowledge we use logs of user interactions – indicators of future information paths and negotiation steps based on prior behaviour and success, to learn models of interaction which will in some sense be unavoidably domain dependent but will also, we hope, contain clues to general models of interaction for information seeking tasks.

Log Analysis for Evaluating IIS

Interactive Information Systems are inherently difficult to evaluate. Any process that includes interaction with live users has to make a distinction between objective evaluation of system performance, and the subjective analysis of how the system performs in assisting the user with their goals. This problem has been initially tackled with spoken language dialogue systems (Dybkjær, Bernsen, Carlson, Chase, Dahlbäck, Failenschmid, Heid, Heisterkamp, Jönsson, Kamp, Karlsson, v. Kuppevelt, Lamel, Paroubek & Williams, 1998; den Os & Bloothooft, 1998; Antoine, Zeiliger & Caelen, 1998; Walker, Kamm & Litman, 2000), but there are gaps in these approaches, which need to be addressed. These include the introduction of performance bottlenecks, such as speed of response, which can have a disproportionate effect on user satisfaction.

Having considered previous work on log analysis we now turn to the core of the chapter: two case studies in which query logs are used to determine how the quality of interaction in an IIS can be improved. The first study is concerned with IR (UKSearch) and the second with QA (HITIQA). In each case we provide background information on the system itself before describing the query log and the way in which it was used.

CASE STUDY: UKSEARCH

Overview

UKSearch is an Interactive Information System that guides users through a document collection (such as an academic intranet) by retrieving matching documents and presenting them alongside query modification suggestions which, for example, allow the user to widen or narrow down the original query. A detailed log of each interaction is kept which includes the original query, the various suggestions made by UKSearch, and a record of those accepted by the user. We will outline later how this information can be used to improve the system.

Whilst we contend that some of the search behaviours we identify inside constrained domain intranets are specific to those small collections, we hope that some part of these will be generalisable to wider, open-domain problems. Therefore, we need user data for different collections, to discover which strategies are transferable and which are domain specific. We have made a start by running a prototype of our own search system that combines a standard search engine with automatically extracted domain knowledge. The main observations that influenced the design of our system are:

- Sophisticated search engines without any dialogue component are sufficient for a large number of queries.
- Queries submitted to a Web search engine are usually very short (typically between one and three words).
- The majority of queries result in a large set of matching documents even in small domains.

The last two of these points strongly support the use of a dialogue component. The first suggests the use of a standard search engine. As a consequence, our approach does not aim to abandon established search technology but instead to deal with the remaining percentage of queries that cannot be answered with a one-shot query. The main principle underlying the system design is that we construct a domain model for the entire collection in an offline process prior to making the system available to the user, but we also acquire knowledge on-the-fly for those queries the user actually submits. A dialogue manager selects suitable query modifications based on the relations encoded in the domain model and presents them as a flat list of terms alongside those extracted from the best matching documents. This means that most user requests can be satisfied by a single search engine call. However, if the expected documents are not among the most highly ranked ones, the user can pick a query refinement term to modify the query.

Modelling of Domain Structure

In order to guide a user through the document space in the information seeking process we need explicit knowledge about the document collection encoded in some electronic form. However, typically such knowledge is not available for specific collections such as intranets or the Web site of a small company. There are at least two solutions to address this problem; we either construct such knowledge manually or we employ some automatic knowledge acquisition process. Both manual and automatic construction of domain knowledge come with their own problems. Manually constructed knowledge sources such as ontologies are very difficult to maintain (Maedche, Motik, Stojanovic, Studer & Volz, 2003). The quality of automatically constructed knowledge on the other hand relies very much on the data it is derived from. Nevertheless, a fully automated process is very appealing.

We acquire a domain model automatically exploiting the markup structure of the document collection. This process is described in more detail elsewhere (Kruschwitz, 2005), but we want to give a brief summary here. There are two stages both of which can be performed offline prior to employing the domain model. We first identify a set of "concepts" in the document collection which are then arranged in tree structures (one tree per concept). We detect these concepts by defining a concept as words or phrases that are found in at least two different markup contexts in the same document (a markup context could be the title of a document, a heading, some anchor text, etc.). Exploiting the fact that our concepts are likely to turn up as real user queries (Kruschwitz, 2003), the model-construction process is a sequence of user request simulations starting with an initial query and subsequently adding terms to the query. For example, Figure 1 can be interpreted as follows: there are documents in the collection in which the term *"fees"* was identified as a concept. Furthermore, there are documents that contain concepts *"fees"* and *"payment"*; other documents contain concepts *"fees"* and *"student"* and *"information"* etc. It should become clear that such a model does *not* capture the actual *semantic* relations that exist between concepts but only the fact *that* there is some relation, one that can be used to guide a user in the search process. We can now derive query modification suggestions directly from the domain model if a user query matches one of the root nodes. Assume the user started by searching for *"fees"* (which is in fact one of the most frequently submitted queries in the sample domain discussed below). This query would trigger the search system to offer query refinement terms such as *"student"*, *"payment"*, *"phd"* and *"postgraduate"*.

Note that other similarly structured domain models could be considered instead (Sanderson & Croft, 1999; Anick & Tipirneni, 1999; Lawrie & Croft, 2003).

Interaction with UKSearch

The overall system architecture (reflected in Figure 2) has already been used for our task-based evaluation trials of *UKSearch* (Kruschwitz & Al-Bakour, 2005). The figure is a simplified overview of what happens inside the search system:

- The user query is submitted simultaneously to the search engine and to the domain model that has been constructed using the documents' markup structure.
- The search engine results are displayed alongside the query modification options which are derived from both the domain model and the additional terms extracted from the best matching documents (i.e. pseudo-relevance feedback).

We will briefly describe how our system constructs query modifications (i.e. relaxations and refinements). Every time the user interacts with the system these steps are performed:

- Calculate query refinements.
- Calculate query relaxations.

Figure 1. Part of the domain model

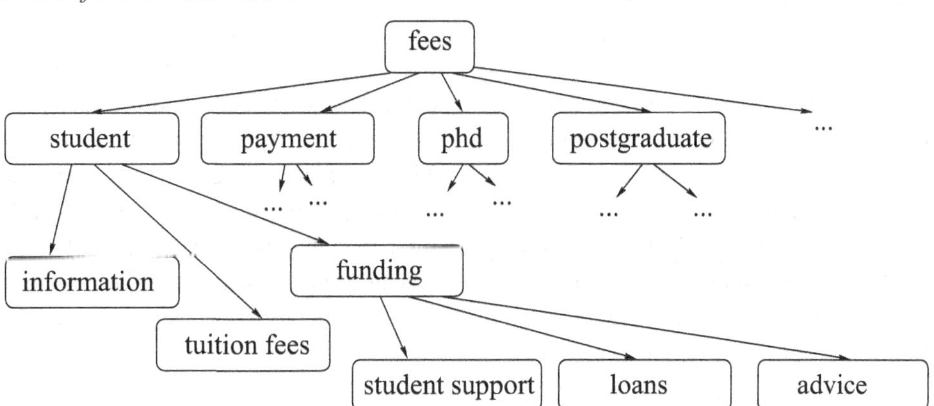

Figure 2. Sketch of information flow in UKSearch

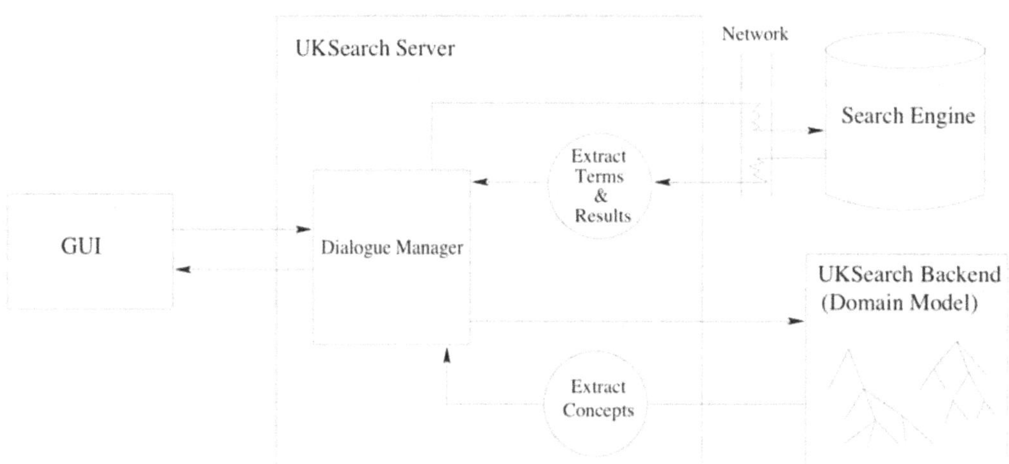

- Rank all query modifications.
- Select the highest ranked query modifications and construct potential choices.

We apply the domain model to explore a fairly restricted space of query modifications. This is because the domain model is custom-built for exactly this process, i.e. finding refinement or relaxation terms for a given query. The ranking function ignores all query relaxations if there are potential query refinements. This is based on the observation that queries are much more likely to be too general than too specific (Kruschwitz, 2003). Furthermore, we only employ pseudo-relevance feedback (i.e. extract any terms on-the-fly) for query refinement. Otherwise we simply present query relaxations, i.e. suggestions for partial queries.

For the extraction of terms from matching documents we use the titles and snippets returned by the search engine. We assign parts of speech and select nouns and certain noun phrases (the idea is to use patterns that can identify collocations in documents). We consider nouns and noun phrases to be the most useful phrases for retrieval tasks. For the detection of noun phrases we look for particular patterns, i.e. sequences of part-of-speech tags based on the algorithm for the detection of terminological terms described in (Justeson & Katz, 1995). Finally we select the most frequent nouns and noun phrases we identified and add them to the refinement terms suggested by the domain model. We display up to 10 terms derived from the domain model followed by the (up to) 20 most frequent ones calculated on-the-fly. Note that the user can also choose to replace the current query by any one of the suggested refinement terms. More details on how the dialogue manager selects query modification terms are discussed elsewhere (Kruschwitz, 2003).

Our system has been running on a university intranet for more than a year. Our examples are drawn from more than 20,000 queries collected over a six-month period. The log files are an extremely valuable resource because they are a reflection of real user interests (in contrast to TREC-like scenarios which are always somewhat artificial). Nevertheless, it can be more difficult to interpret what the user was actually after. Figure 3 is a sample screenshot of the system following the user query *"fees"*.

Figure 3. System response to user query "fees"

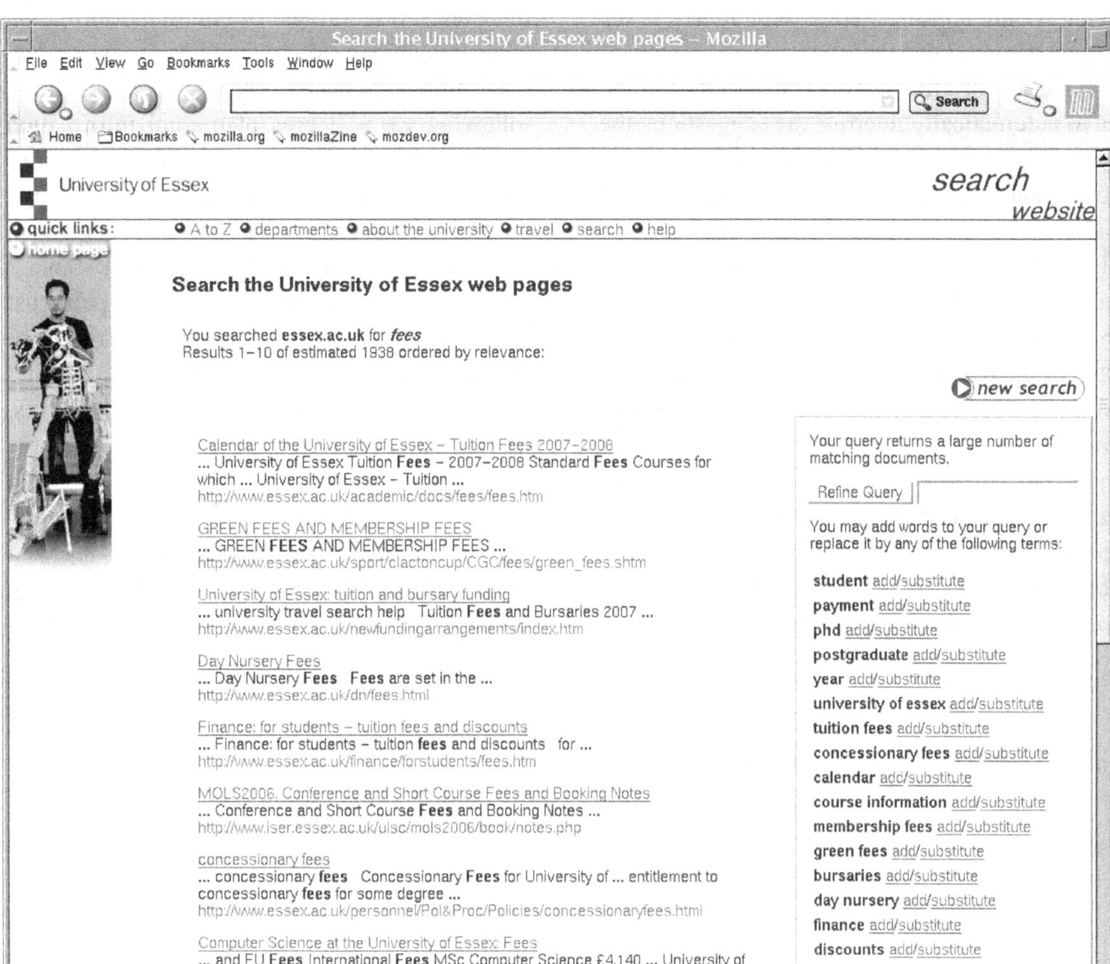

Adaptive Modelling of Interactions using Query Logs

The data collected so far are a justification for a system that guides a user in the search process: more than 10% of user queries are query modification steps, i.e. the user either replaces the initial query or adds terms to the query to make it more specific. The majority of these modifications are terms suggested by the system (the others are additional query terms provided by the user). The log files which record the user interaction with the system allow us to figure out which suggestions are typically picked by users and which ones are not. That way we identify those usage patterns which can help the next user with the same request. These log files tell us that the commonly submitted query modification patterns are very domain-specific (making log files acquired from general Web search appear much less applicable for adaptive dialogue-driven intranet search). Moreover, there is a long tail of modifications submitted only once.

Counting frequencies of events is one thing. What we are aiming at however is to assess the degree of association between a query modification and the original query. This will then allow us to automatically improve the suggestions the system makes, by adapting the originally constructed domain structures. As an example, Table 1 lists the three most frequent query refinements alongside some less frequent ones (i.e. *additions* to a query) as they were submitted by the users.

This is very sparse data. Nevertheless, to assess the degree of association between these pairs we can calculate how probable it is that a query *contains* any of the query terms or corresponding modifications listed in Table 1 (instead of doing this for exact matches only). This data is less sparse. Maximum likelihood estimates (over the corpus of all queries) can be used to measure *Pointwise Mutual Information (I)* of pairs of terms. A high value reflects closely related terms. Of course, there are shortcomings with mutual information measures, in particular when run on sparse data (Manning & Schütze, 1999). Therefore, in the following we will present mutual information values alongside the corresponding *p values* of significance tests using chi-square (χ^2) (although one needs to be careful with these values as well when dealing with rather sparse data). Table 2 presents the results for the refinement pairs just discussed. We list the number of occurrences of each term as well as the number of times we find both in a query (we preserve the order of terms, i.e. there are exactly 90 queries which contain the string "printing credit").

Our interpretation of these results is that the users (reflected by information such as selected or ignored modification terms recorded in the log files) leave largely implicit relevance feedback on

Table 1. Selection of query refinement steps

Query	Refinement	Frequency
parking	car parking	9
printing	credit	4
printer	accounting	4
...	...	...
time table	timetable	3
subscription list	smallads	2
dog day care	pet care	2

Table 2. Pointwise mutual information and χ^2 results for selected query refinements

Query q1 (Frequency)	Query q2 (Freq.)	Freq. q1q2	I(q1,q2)	p (χ^2)
parking (205)	car parking (116)	19	2.80	≤ 0.001
printing (267)	credit (201)	90	3.54	≤ 0.001
printer (170)	accounting (59)	34	4.25	≤ 0.001
...				
time table(50)	timetable (455)	3	1.00	not sign.
subscription list (14)	smallads (45)	3	4.58	≤ 0.001
dog day care (4)	pet care (2)	2	8.55	≤ 0.001

system suggestions which should be exploited to guide the next user with a similar request. Query refinement terms are an indication of closely associated terms. This statement on its own may sound trivial. However, such information as collected from the user interaction can be utilised to automatically improve query refinement suggestions offered by the system. The aim is not to replace the query suggestions derived from pseudo-relevance feedback but to improve them since user log information and terms extracted on-the-fly can complement each other, in particular in informational queries and for rare user queries (White, Clarke & Cucerzan, 2007).

So far we were only concerned with query refinements, i.e. terms that are added to some user query (suggested by the system or manually added by the user). In line with other studies, we observe a large number of spelling errors in the log files. If there are no matching documents for a user query, then the system will try to break the query into individual parts and also present an input field for query modification. Such input can be used to automatically derive spelling corrections from user provided input, e.g. see the examples included in Table 3. Note that a general purpose spell checker would not necessarily give us the right suggestions for domain-specific terms (e.g. *alresford court*, one of the student residences). Note also that the type of application discussed here results in very sparse data unlike log files and language models that can be derived from general Web search logs (Cucerzan & Brill, 2004). Apart from spelling corrections, query replacements can also be utilised to derive closely related domain-specific concepts (e.g. in Table 3: a user replaced *uploading coursework* by *ocs* which is the local *online coursework submission system*).

We can derive domain knowledge not just from individual dialogues but also from session logs. But again we are faced with data that is more sparse than the search logs collected on Web search engines which have been employed to derive query substitutions using session information (Jones, Rey, Madani & Greiner, 2006). Table 4 presents pairwise mutual information values for the most frequent (non-identical) pairs of queries submitted in the same session, irrespective of whether the second query (*Query q2*) is a completely new query, a refinement for *Query q1*, or a replacement. The table also lists examples of misspelled queries which were then corrected by the user as a *new* query (not necessarily as a query modification) within the same session, i.e. the user went back to the input screen and started a new query. Unlike previously (e.g. Table 2), this time we selected exactly matching queries only, in other words only where the query *"parking"* was followed by *"car parking"* was it considered in Table 4 and not if these were part of some longer queries.

One way of selecting promising relations out of all user-system interactions is by choosing term pairs whose distribution has shown significance using the χ^2 test (or has a correspondingly high pointwise mutual information value). The goal

Table 3. Pointwise mutual information and χ^2 results for selected query replacements

Query q (Frequency)	Replacement r (Freq.)	Freq. qr	I(q, r)	p (χ^2)
un iversity weeks (1)	university weeks (47)	1	6.08	≤ 0.001
parking permitt (1)	parking (205)	1	4.61	≤ 0.001
arlesford court (1)	alresford court (2)	1	9.24	≤ 0.001
uploading coursework (1)	ocs (80)	1	5.55	≤ 0.001
small adds (16)	small ads (58)	3	4.20	≤ 0.001

Table 4. Pointwise mutual information and χ^2 results for pairs of queries in the same session

Query q1 (Frequency)	**Query q2 (Freq.)**	**Freq. q1q2**	**I(q1, q2)**	**p (χ^2)**
parking (38)	car parking (63)	11	4.55	≤ 0.001
time table (28)	timetable (305)	9	3.08	≤ 0.001
smallads (31)	subscription list (10)	7	6.14	≤ 0.001
map (83)	campus map (61)	7	3.35	≤ 0.001
timetable (305)	timetables (122)	4	0.79	not sign.
...				
plagarism (13)	academic offence (5)	3	6.86	≤ 0.001
plagarism (13)	plagiarism (48)	2	4.19	≤ 0.001
plagerism (4)	plagiarism (48)	2	5.37	≤ 0.001
about jisc plgiarism (1)	about jisc plagiarism (1)	1	9.93	≤ 0.001

is to derive useful query modification options by observing the users' search behaviour. For example, whenever a user searches for *"parking"*, the system will suggest *"car parking"* as a potential query modification (see Table 4). Based on the same table we would not however present the term *"timetables"* if the query was *"timetable"* since that query pair has not been found to be significant.

The same method will permit us to select query modification options for frequently misspelled user queries.

Findings of UKSearch Study

The log files of our dialogue-driven retrieval system are an invaluable source of information because they record real user-computer interactions. This data informs us about how to improve the domain model and hence the suggestions made by the system. In other words, the log files provide us with *implicit feedback* from the users, sufficient to adjust the domain knowledge automatically without having to rely on other forms of explicit or implicit user feedback (Ruthven & Lalmas, 2003). However, the use of implicit relevance feedback described here is different from previous approaches in that it is not utilised in a particular search task but instead the feedback of the entire pool of users of the system is collected in order to adjust the domain model of a particular document collection. In essence, the behaviour of the user population – as recorded in the log files – is observed and thus the domain model improved in a collaborative way. We also want to stress that the aim is *not* to build up individual user profiles which is a whole research field on its own (Teevan, Dumais & Horvitz, 2005).

The strength of the approach lies in the fact that the acquired knowledge is domain-specific while the actual methods are domain-independent and can be applied unobtrusively in any similar search context.

These directions of research will move us more towards adaptive information retrieval systems, something recognised as an exciting development in information retrieval (Markey, 2007).

CASE STUDY: HITIQA

Overview

HITIQA (High Quality Interactive Question Answering) is a system to assist analysts in finding answers to complex intelligence problems, both efficiently and thoroughly. It is an advanced Question Answering (QA) system that helps analysts to produce high quality reports for complex intelligence problems in less time and with lower cognitive load (Small, Strzalkowski, Liu, Shimizu & Yamrom, 2004). HITIQA uses event-based, data-driven semantic processing and natural language dialogue, coupled with an advanced information visualisation interface, to deliver accurate answers to an analyst's questions, along with related contextual information. The goal of using a system such as HITIQA is to write a structured report at the end of the allotted investigation and research phase, detailing the answer to the specific scenario or question. The primary function then of HITIQA is to supply composite answers to complex, exploratory questions such as "What is the state of development of long range missiles in North Korea?". This makes HITIQA different from standard factoid QA systems, which try to return the single best answer to a limited set of questions - often "who", "what", "where" or "which". Complex questions are those that often require more than a single answer, providing instead a snapshot of the information landscape. An analyst often requires justification, in terms of supporting documents or hypothesis, to back up any answer or conclusion.

Although not discussed in detail here, the architecture of HITIQA is similar to the majority of question answering systems, in that it consists of a retrieval phase to target potential answer bearing passages, with subsequent steps using a range of Information Extraction (IE) techniques to highlight and capture elements of potential interest to the analyst. During operation, HITIQA automatically logs a wide range of information, including questions asked, passages retrieved, passages opened, relevance changes initiated by the analyst, time spent and data items copied to the private space. As will be seen later, we use this information both to conduct internal evaluation of performance, and to model improved interaction behaviour based on prior analytical actions.

Modelling of Domain Structure

Unlike the closed domain scenario of UKSearch, it is impractical for HITIQA to build a model of the domain a-priori (indeed, HITIQA can operate over the open web). However, some method of retrieving and evaluating nuggets of data is necessary. HITIQA is an example of a system that builds a just-in-time representation of the underlying data, in response to an information retrieval step based on keywords in the query. Retrieved documents are split into paragraphs, from which candidate passages are selected and duplicate or irrelevant passages removed. The top 200 passages become our final set of candidate answer passages.

HITIQA employs a method called framing for imposing partial structure on textual data. Framing allows HITIQA to systematically compare different passages, both against each other and against the user question. HITIQA clusters the candidate answer passages using a combination of hierarchical clustering and n-bin classification (Hardy, Shimizu, Strzalkowski, Liu, Wise & Zhang, 2002), where each cluster represents a topic theme within the retrieved set. Two types of frames are used in this process: un-typed GENERAL-frames and typed EVENT-frames instantiated by triggers typically based on specific verb types. The result of using a typed frame is the assignment of roles to some of the attributes. Examples of typed frames include: the TRANSFER frame with roles including SOURCE, DESTINATION and OBJECT; the DEVELOP frame with AGENT and OBJECT roles; and the ATTACK frame, with roles including AGENT, TARGET, INSTRUMENT (Hardy, Kanchakouskaya & Strzalkowski, 2006). Should a GENERAL-frame be used, and an example can be seen in Figure 4, no attribute information is lost, but the roles of these attributes are unassigned. Attributes are extracted from text passages using BBN's IdentiFinder (Miller, Schwartz, Weischedel & Stone, 1999), which tags 24 types of named entity classes.

The framing process is also applied to the analyst's question, resulting in one or more GOAL-frames, representations of the user need which are then compared to the DATA-frames obtained from retrieved text passages, as seen in Figure 5.

A GOAL-frame can be a GENERAL-frame or any of the EVENT-frames. HITIQA automatically judges a particular DATA-frame as relevant, and subsequently the corresponding segment of text as relevant, by comparison with one or more GOAL-frames. DATA-frames are scored based on the number of conflicts found with the GOAL-frames. The conflicts are mismatches on values of corresponding attributes, including direct incompatibilities (e.g., different locations), role mismatch (e.g. from Korea vs. to Korea) and missing or under-specified attribute values.

Frame conflict scores are increased by 1 for each mismatched GENERAL-frame attribute, hence frames with a perfect match are called 0-conflict frames (or just 0-frames), those with a single attribute mismatch are called 1-frames, and so on. Frames that are judged to have no match to the question, either by the system, or by the user through interaction, are scored as 99-frames. When comparing attributes we are utilizing basic string matching techniques, expansions to synonyms using WordNet, and gazetteers for typical location attributes. The framing process is the mechanism through which HITIQA uncovers topics or aspects within the answer space that the user has not explicitly asked for. If these topics or aspects align closely with the user's question (i.e. they match many of the salient attributes), HITIQA will attempt to make the user aware of them and

Figure 4. A sample text passage and the corresponding GENERAL frame in HITIQA

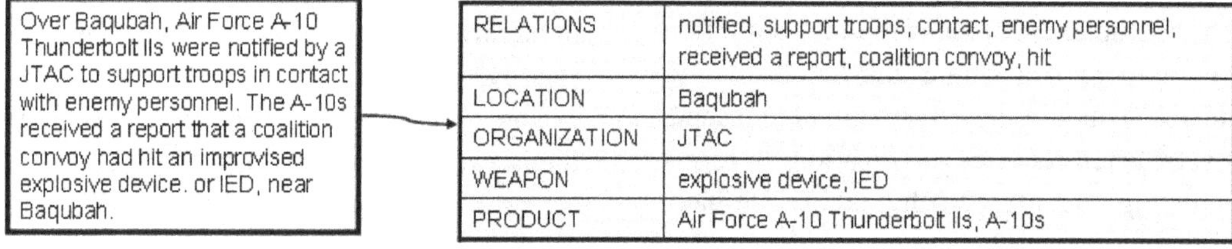

Over Baqubah, Air Force A-10 Thunderbolt IIs were notified by a JTAC to support troops in contact with enemy personnel. The A-10s received a report that a coalition convoy had hit an improvised explosive device. or IED, near Baqubah.

RELATIONS	notified, support troops, contact, enemy personnel, received a report, coalition convoy, hit
LOCATION	Baqubah
ORGANIZATION	JTAC
WEAPON	explosive device, IED
PRODUCT	Air Force A-10 Thunderbolt IIs, A-10s

Figure 5. An example of matching between the GOAL frame extracted from an input query and a DATA frame extracted from a text passage in HITIQA

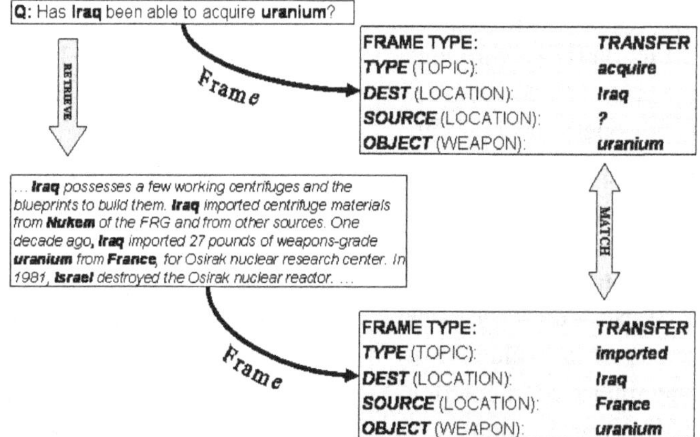

let them decide if they should be included in the final answer space.

This framing process is domain independent, in the sense that any information not captured by specific EVENT-frames falls into a GENERAL-frame. A current version of HITIQA works over the open Web, without topic restriction. Further details of the framing process can be seen in Small and Strzalkowski (2008).

Interaction with HITIQA

Whilst our data-driven framing approach enables us to derive ad-hoc structure on the underlying text documents, we still need to determine the analyst's individual information need. We do this by entering into an interaction with them to negotiate the resulting answer space as defined by the framing process. This interaction takes place both through verbal interactive dialogue and through a visualisation panel, as can be seen in Figure 6.

HITIQA uses frames to initiate a clarification dialogue with the analyst, which in turn enables the system to properly classify information. An example of HITIQA interaction can be seen in Figure 7. Once all potential DATA-frames have been scored against the GOAL-frame, the system has a structured set of scored data that it can use to initiate dialogue with the analyst. Frames that are seen as possibly containing highly related information to the analyst's question, but are not an exact match, that is the 1- or 2-conflict frames, may be used to generate dialogue with the analyst.

Figure 6. Interaction through a visualisation panel in HITIQA

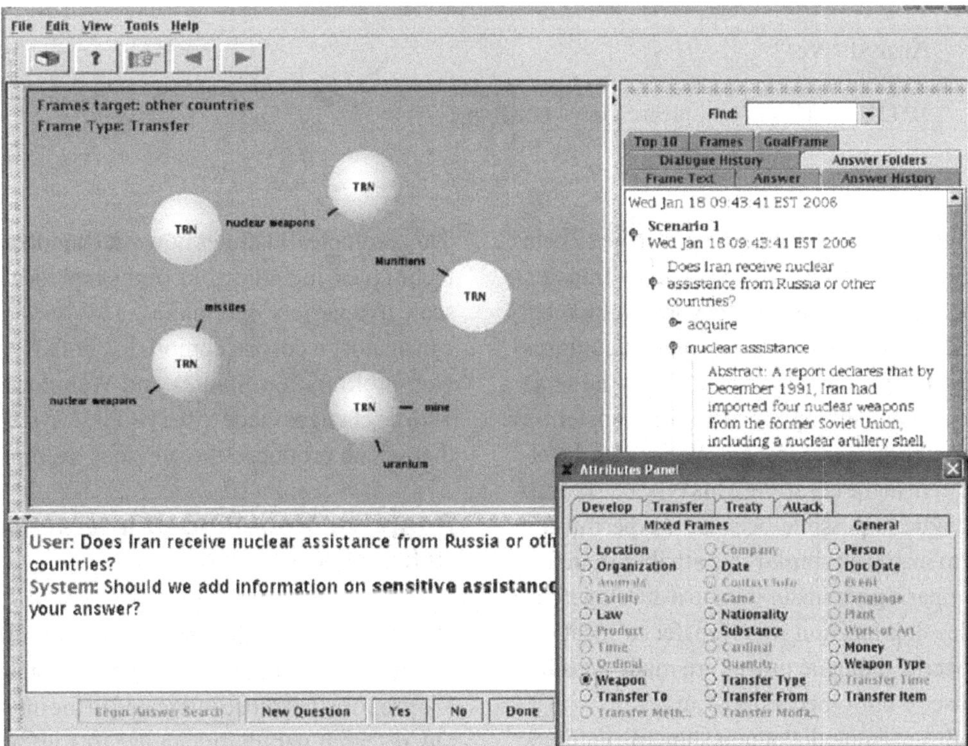

Figure 7. Actual excerpt taken from the HITIQA logs during an interaction with a United States Navy Reserve analyst. Note: atropine is an antidote for sarin exposure

> Analyst: "Who is at greatest risk for a sarin gas attack?"
>
> [*exact match answer displayed*]
>
> HITIQA: "Would you be interested in atropine?"
>
> Analyst: "Yes"
>
> HITIQA: "Do you want to see information on gas mask?"
>
> Analyst: "Yes"
>
> HITIQA: "Thank you, please view your answer"

Figure 8. Excerpt taken from the HITIQA logs

> Analyst: "How are South Africa's weapons of mass destruction (WMD) programs developing?"
>
> [*exact match answer displayed*]
>
> HITIQA: "Can we also add material on the transfer of WMD and intelligence between South Africa and other countries to your answer?"
>
> Analyst: "Yes"
>
> HITIQA: "Thank you, please view your answer"

In Figure 8, we show an example of the system expanding to a new event type, namely transfer, from the analyst's initial question on development of WMD in South Africa. The system recognises that there is a location of interest that is the same in both events: develop location and transfer to. Additionally, the transfer event overlaps the development item in the question. This type of expanding dialogue is possible because we permit the system to match on similar role attributes, in this case comparing a transfer item to a develop item, and a develop location to a transfer to location. Such specific dialogue moves are made possible by the use of our typed EVENT-frames.

Another example dialogue is shown in Figure 9. This example illustrates how well our data driven techniques, including our frame representations, scale to a variety of domains. This question was run against a corpus comprising both Centre for Non-proliferation Studies and Web documents, with no changes made to the HITIQA system from that which produced the previous examples.

Adaptive Modelling of Interactions using Query Logs

HITIQA captures the entire interaction process – from exploratory drills through to report writing. We propose that those interested in the interactive QA research paradigm can use this information to, for example, correlate between steps in the

Figure 9. Question interaction with the HITIQA system as demonstrated live to the ARDA AQUAINT community, Washington D.C.

Analyst: "What is the status of the Social Security System?"

[*exact match answer displayed*]

HITIQA: "Would you be interested in information on retirement relative to your question?"

Analyst: "Yes"

HITIQA: "Do you want to see information on private accounts?"

Analyst: "Yes"

HITIQA: "Thank you, please view your answer"

interaction and quality of report. We want to show that through exploratory interaction, users discover nuggets of information that would otherwise have been missed, or examine how users adapt their own queries (and the studies presented for UKSearch will help us in this regard), to see how best HITIQA should present and handle query modification. By collecting a wealth of information from users, about the actual search and discovery strategies using an interactive QA system, across a range of scenarios, we want to be able to abstract, from our corpus annotation, stereotypical information seeking actions, and highlight those interaction steps, mechanism and styles which consistently lead to positive information outcomes.

Once analysts have completed their reports, they cross evaluate all reports on the topic, with respect to a number of parameters:

- **Completeness:** Covers all relevant content
- **Precision:** Avoids irrelevant material
- **Coherence:** Is well organized
- **Usefulness:** Includes crucial information

HITIQA also captures quantitative metrics through internal system logs, such as:

- Time spent
- Questions asked
- Material presented, seen, saved and rejected

The nature of the data generated using HITIQA is general enough that we expect it to be highly useful to answer a range of generic open problems relating to interaction and the QA process – that is, this data is applicable to a range of developing systems and underlying interaction models, beyond the functionality represented in the HITIQA system.

In order to make better suggestions to the user, we need to understand the current actions and deliberations of the analyst, and to do so we are examining our logs of user interactions. By collecting interaction events, in combination with knowledge of the material gathered by each individual analyst (as captured automatically in the HITIQA logs) we aim to capture regular interaction moves made by experienced information seeking users, as they sift and search through massive data streams. We do so in order that we might capture and generalise those actions, and replicate them (or facilitate human users' use of them) in automatic information seeking systems.

Such a collection of interactions can provide the basis for a variety of machine learning applications that can acquire models of information seeking behaviour. Further, we want to assess the presentation of information to the user, to discover which information is best conveyed through language or through visualisation, and to determine the ranking that can be assigned to the presentation of information. By collecting all interactions, including indirect actions such as the information they browsed, and making the assumption that any action on a user's part communicates something, we want to be able to determine some correlation between the quality of answers returned and the interaction process.

To extract such patterns of interaction, we need to have an understanding of the range of user actions that are performed over data. We are using a set of annotations to capture analyst interactions, based around *dialogue acts* – a well-understood notation for representing aspects of discourse structure. We are using an extension of an existing set of dialogue acts (DAMSL) (Core & Allen, 1997), to include the set of actions analysts can perform on data items, which we intend to interpret as implicit communication about the data. Automatic annotation of dialogue acts can be performed at a relatively high level using straightforward statistical classification techniques (Samuel, Carberry & Vijay-Shanker, 1998; Stolcke, Ries, Coccaro, Shriberg, Bates, Jurafsky, Taylor, Martin, Ess-Dykema & Meteer, 2000; Webb, Hepple & Wilks, 2005). Figure 10 gives an indication of what such a sequence of interactions looks like from an analytical perspective.

From this example, we can see that the analyst browsed the first document (3), but did not copy any information. If the analyst had asked a new question at this stage, we could surmise

Figure 10. Sequence of analyst actions over data

(1) Analyst ▶ "What are the names of the senior al-Qaida leaders?"
<wh_question>
(2) HITIQA ▶ Displays a series of short summary answers and related documents.
<offer>
(3) Analyst ▶ Opens offered document 1
<browse>
(4) Analyst ▶ Closes document 1
<close>
(5) HITIQA ▶ "Would you be interested in information on new operational cells relative to your question?"
<yes-no question>
(6) Analyst ▶ "Yes"
<accept>
(7) HITIQA ▶ Adds new document to folder
<update>
(8) Analyst ▶ Opens document 2
<open>
(9) Analyst ▶ Copies material from document 2
<copy>
(10) Analyst ▶ Closes document 2
<close>
(11) HITIQA ▶ "Should we add information on law enforcement official to your answer?"
<yes-no question>
(12) Analyst ▶ "No"
<rejection>

it as a clarification or reformulation. Instead, the analyst chose to allow the system to guide them (6), presumably because the question the system previously posed (5) is relevant in the current context. Indeed, the question provided material that was subsequently copied by the analyst (9). However, a further follow up question was then rejected (12).

We are interested in seeking common, repeated actions of analysts, so as to be able to interpret their actions more effectively, and decide automatically under what circumstances we can deduce that the search space needs to be expanded. We also wish to spot when the current line of enquiry is stale, or complete. What is not included in this example is the interaction the user can have through visualisation or other available modalities, although this can be annotated in the same way. We want to be able to understand at what points in the interaction the analyst feels the visualisation is a better modality of interaction than the alternatives. This may be analyst independent but we may be able to determine *classes* of users, based on analytical behaviour – those analysts who prefer more verbose, exploratory interaction, as against those who prefer to drill down into data using an interactive visualisation. It is worth reinforcing that we intend to refer to the contents of the evaluated reports in our logs so that we are aware of where each nugget came from, be it through direct interaction, clarification dialogue or through the visualisation.

Findings of the HITIQA Study

HITIQA has progressed through a range of evaluations. We use the logs of analyst actions to compute intrinsic measures of system performance – such as the number of questions asked, and time spent using the system. This data is vital for evaluation of a system where there is a substantial subjective measure in any grading of performance. New models and paradigms of evaluation are required to combine these metrics together. To establish usage models for existing log information, HITIQA participated in the ARDA Metrics Challenge workshop, run by NIST in 2004. It focused on two aspects of interaction for the evaluation: the analyst's process and the analyst's products. The objective measures of efficiency and effectiveness are measures of the process, whereas the more subjective rating of the analyst's reports assess if better quality information is being located and used in the final product. The data set for this evaluation was created by NIST, and was approximately 4 GB in size, the majority of files being mined from the web, in addition to a set received from the Center for Non-proliferation Studies (CNS). Four systems participated in the study, which included the NIST chosen baseline system, GNIST – analysts using the Google Information Retrieval system over the same data. Eight United States Naval Reserve (USNR) analysts were recruited to be the subjects in the study and Air Force Rome Labs (AFRL) created eight scenarios, each of which was reviewed by a panel of experts. Each analyst had two days in total to work with each system, following a training session. Analysts used each system for two and a half hours in order to produce an analytical report for a given scenario, and after each session there were evaluations. Two scenarios were completed by each analyst for each system. While still preliminary, the evaluations suggest two important advantages of HITIQA over keyword based document retrieval systems such as Google (see Figure 11):

1. The HITIQA interactive approach is significantly more efficient because it requires the analyst to ask fewer questions (nearly 60% fewer than using Google) and consequently spend less time to obtain a report of equal or better content; and
2. HITIQA is more effective because it produces more usable information per user question, evidenced by analysts saving more material for their reports and doing so more

Figure 11. Comparison of HITIQA with the baseline GNIST system

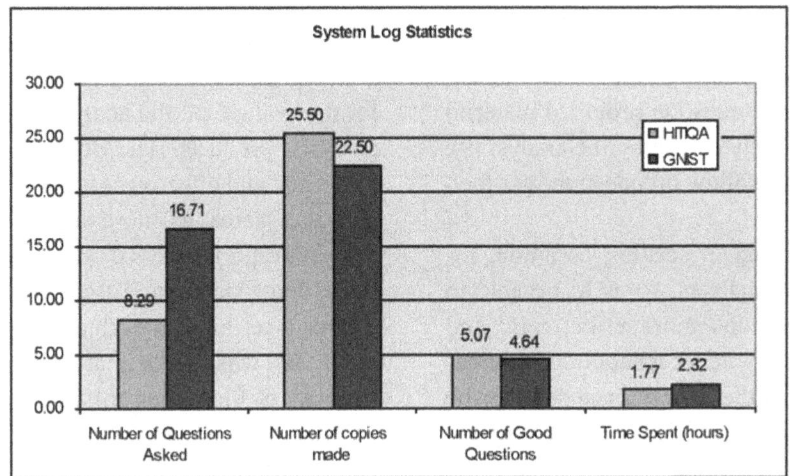

often. It makes the collection process twice as effective as searching with Google.

With respect to this chapter, we wanted to use the logs of analytical behaviour to determine if our method of interaction was both successful and useful to the analyst. We needed to test our hypothesis that a system that could uncover both highly related topics and relevant pieces of information, and offer them to the analyst in an efficient and reliable way, would be useful for analytical question answering.

We wanted to evaluate the component of our system that selects candidate frames, and offers them to the analyst. As this was a preliminary, intrinsic evaluation, we chose to run this experiment without analysts. Instead, the system automatically replied "Yes" to each of its own clarification questions. While this experiment is quite informative, it is important to keep in mind that in real operation the analyst guides the dialogue process, in that each answer determines the next question that the system generates. Therefore the evaluation in this section can only be seen as an indicative baseline evaluation. Using a corpus annotated for this task (Small & Strzalkowski, 2008) we were able to compare the precision of the frames pre-"dialogue" versus post-"dialogue", Figure 12, with the hypothesis being that precision should increase after a dialogue if valid and interesting passages (with respect to the question and the scenario) are being automatically offered to the analyst.

We were pleased to see a substantial increase in the precision of our 0-conflict frames. This confirmed our assumption that the system was finding and offering relevant frames to the analyst. We achieved a 26.2% increase in the precision of passages that are relevant to just the question and a 10.1% increase in the precision of passages that are relevant only to other topics of the scenario. This confirms that our base level of interaction is successful – and provides a good basis for exploring expanded interaction using the modelling approaches outlined in the previous section.

CONCLUSION

This chapter has been concerned with Interactive Information Systems and how they can be improved by the analysis of query logs. We have looked at two such systems, UKSearch and HI-

Figure 12. Precision before and after dialogue

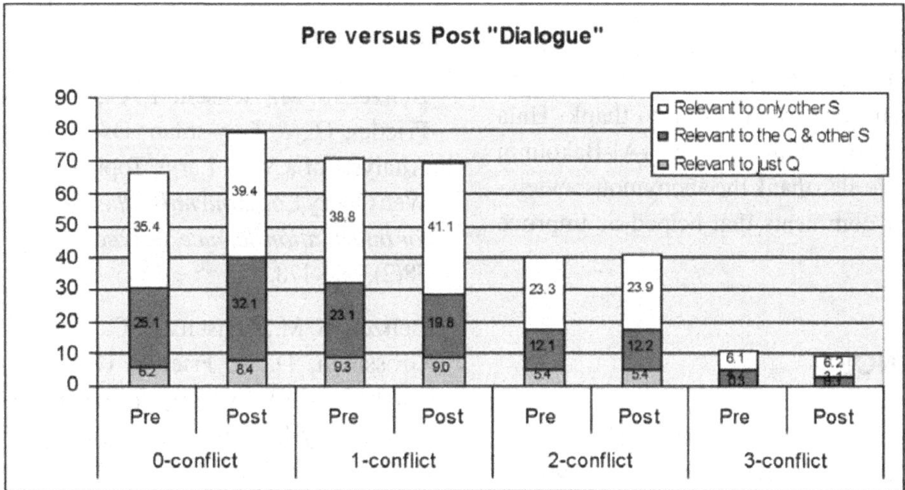

TIQA, and discussed how logs from these systems have been used for performance analysis and enhancement. The main conclusions which can be drawn from this work are as follows:

Firstly, there is a growing literature on query log analysis which we have reviewed in our early sections. However, most of the work described does not aim to use the results to improve the system. Instead the objective is usually to determine general trends of usage.

Concerning UKSearch, there are several important findings:

- Commonly submitted query modification patterns for UKSearch are domain specific.
- It was possible to analyse the log using mutual information scores between a query and its refinement, between a query and its replacement, and between two queries occurring in the same session.
- The results of the analysis were used to validate refinements in the domain model, and to suggest replacements such as domain-dependent spelling corrections.

Concerning HITIQA, the following can be concluded:

- Based on the logs, we can see that certain types of interaction lead to retrieval results of increased precision.
- Future versions of the system can thus be built to encourage these forms of interaction.
- We can use the log file information to try to build generic models of analytic interaction over data.
- Log files can be used to evaluate both overall system performance, and component based evaluation.

Overall, we can say that the use of log files is an area of research which will continue to grow. Log files will expand in both size and complexity, through increased use and the capture of a wider range of interaction information, to better characterize users and tasks. Outstanding challenges include the need to find an evaluation strategy that can take logged user information and determine some correlate between the information retrieved, the interaction performance, and the level of user satisfaction with the underlying system.

ACKNOWLEDGMENT

We would like to thank all colleagues who have participated in the development and evaluation of the search systems. We want to thank Hala Al-Bakour, Patrick Mills, and Dyaa Al-Bakour in particular. We also thank the anonymous reviewers for their comments that helped us improve the chapter.

REFERENCES

Allen, J., Schubert, L., Ferguson, G., Heeman, P., Hwang, C., Kato, T., Light, M., Martin, N., Miller, B., Poesio, M., & Traum, D. (1995). The TRAINS project: A Case Study in Building a Conversational Planning Agent. *Journal of Experimental and Theoretical Artificial Intelligence*, 7, 7-48.

Anick, P. (2003). Using Terminological Feedback for Web Search Refinement - A Log-based Study. In *Proceedings of the 26 Annual International ACM SIGIR Conference on Research and Development in Information Retrieval, Toronto, Canada* (pp. 88-95).

Anick, P. G., & Tipirneni, S. (1999). The Paraphrase Search Assistant: Terminological Feedback for Iterative Information Seeking. In *Proceedings of the 22 Annual International ACM SIGIR Conference on Research and Development in Information Retrieval, Berkeley, CA* (pp. 153-159).

Antoine, J. Y., Zeiliger, J., & Caelen, J. (1998). DQR Test Suites for a Qualitative Evaluation of Spoken Dialogue Systems: from Speech Understanding to Dialogue Strategy. In *Proceedings of the 1 International Conference on Language Resources and Evaluation, Granada, Spain* (pp. 59-66).

Aust, H., Oerder, M., Seide, F., & Steinbiss, V. (1995). The Philips Automatic Train Timetable Information System. *Speech Communication*, 17, 249-262.

Baeza-Yates, R., & Ribeiro-Neto, B. (1999). *Modern Information Retrieval*. Boston, MA: Addison Wesley.

Beitzel, S. M., Jensen, E. C., Chowdhury, A., Frieder, O., & Grossman, D. (2007). Temporal Analysis of a Very Large Topically Categorized Web Query Log. *Journal of the American Society for Information Science and Technology (JASIST)*, 58(2), 166-178.

Beitzel, S. M., Jensen, E. C., Chowdhury, A., Grossman, D., & Frieder, O. (2004). Hourly Analysis of a Very Large Topically Categorized Web Query Log. In *Proceedings of the 27 Annual International ACM SIGIR Conference on Research and Development in Information Retrieval, Sheffield, UK* (pp. 321-328).

Brin, S., & Page, L. (1998). The Anatomy of a Large-Scale Hypertextual Web Search Engine. In *Proceedings of the Seventh International World Wide Web Conference (WWW7)*, Brisbane, Australia (pp. 107-117).

Chau, M., Fang, X., & Sheng, O. (2005). Analysis of the Query Logs of a Web Site Search Engine. *Journal of the American Society for Information Science and Technology (JASIST)*, 56(13), 1363-1376.

Core, M. G., & Allen, J. (1997). Coding Dialogs with the DAMSL Annotation Scheme. In *AAAI Fall Symposium on Communicative Action in Humans and Machines*, MIT, Cambridge, MA.

Cucerzan, S., & Brill, E. (2004). Spelling Correction as an Iterative Process that Exploits the Collective Knowledge of Web Users. In *Proceedings of EMNLP'04* (pp. 293-300).

Dale, R. (2006). Industry Watch. *Natural Language Engineering*, 12(4), 391-395.

den Os, E., & Bloothooft, G. (1998). Evaluating Various Spoken Dialogue Systems with a Single Questionnaire: Analysis of the ELSNET Olympics. In *Proceedings of the 1 International*

Conference on Language Resources and Evaluation, Granada, Spain (pp. 51-54).

Dybkjær, L., Bernsen, N. O., Carlson, R., Chase, L., Dahlbäck, N., Failenschmid, K., Heid, U., Heisterkamp, P., Jönsson, A., Kamp, H., Karlsson, I., v. Kuppevelt, J., Lamel, L., Paroubek, P., & Williams, D. (1998). The DISC Approach to Spoken Language Systems Development and Evaluation. In *Proceedings of the 1 International Conference on Language Resources and Evaluation*, Granada, Spain (pp. 185-189).

Goddeau, D., Brill, E., Glass, J., Pao, C., Phillips, M., Polifroni, J., Seneff, S., & Zue, V. (1994). GALAXY: A Human-Language Interface to On-line Travel Information. In *Proceedings International Conference on Spoken Language Processing*, Yokohama, Japan.

Hardy, H., Shimizu, N., Strzalkowski, T., Liu, T., Wise, B., & Zhang, X. (2002). Cross-Document Summarization by Concept Classification. In *Proceedings of ACM SIGIR '02 Conference*, Tampere, Finland (pp. 121-128).

Hardy, H., Biermann, A., Inouye, R. B., Mckenzie, A., Strzalkowski, T., Ursu, C., Webb, N., & Wu, M. (2004). Data Driven Strategies for an Automated Dialogue System. In *Proceedings of the 42nd Annual Meeting of the Association for Computational Linguistics*, Barcelona, Spain *(ACL 2004)*.

Hardy, H., Kanchakouskaya, V., & Strzalkowski, T. (2006). Automatic Event Classification using Surface Text Features. In *Proceedings of the AAAI Workshop on Event Extraction and Synthesis.*

Jansen, B. J., Bateman, J., & Saracevic, T. (1998). Real Life Information Retrieval: A Study of User Queries on the Web. *SIGIR Forum*, 32(1), 5-17.

Jansen, B. J., Spink, A., & Koshman, S. (2007). Web Server Interaction with the Dogpile.com Metasearch Engine. *Journal of the American Society for Information Science and Technology (JASIST)*, 58(5), 744-755.

Jones, R., Rey, B., Madani, O., & Greiner, W. (2006). Generating Query Substitutions. In *Proceedings of the 15th International Conference on World Wide Web (WWW'06)* (pp. 387-396).

Justeson, J. S., & Katz, S. M. (1995). Technical Terminology: some Linguistic Properties and an Algorithm for Identification in Text. *Natural Language Engineering*, 1(1), 9-27.

Koshman, S., Spink, A., & Jansen, B. J. (2006). Web Searching on the Vivisimo Search Engine. *Journal of the American Society for Information Science and Technology (JASIST)*, 57(14), 1875-1887.

Kruschwitz, U. (2003). An Adaptable Search System for Collections of Partially Structured Documents. *IEEE Intelligent Systems*, 18(4), 44-52.

Kruschwitz, U. (2005). *Intelligent Document Retrieval: Exploiting Markup Structure*, volume 17 of The Information Retrieval Series. New York, NY: Springer-Verlag.

Kruschwitz, U., & Al-Bakour, H. (2005). Users Want More Sophisticated Search Assistants – Results of a Task-Based Evaluation. *Journal of the American Society for Information Science and Technology (JASIST)*, 56(13), 1377-1393.

Laurent, D., Séguéla, P., & Nègre, S. (2006). QA better than IR? In A. Peñas and R. F. E. Sutcliffe (Eds.), *Proceedings of the Workshop on Multilingual Question Answering, MLQA'06, 11th Conference of the European Chapter of the Association for Computational Linguistics*, Trento, Spain (pp. 1-8).

Lawrie, D. J., & Croft, W. B. (2003). Generating Hierarchical Summaries for Web Searches. In *Proceedings of the 26 Annual International ACM SIGIR Conference on Research and Development in Information Retrieval*, Toronto, Canada (pp. 457-458).

Maedche, A., Motik, B., Stojanovic, L., Studer, R., & Volz, R. (2003). An Infrastructure for Searching, Reusing and Evolving Distributed Ontologies. In *Proceedings of the Twelfth International World Wide Web Conference (WWW2003)*, Budapest, Hungary (pp. 439-448).

Magnini, B., Romagnoli, S., Vallin, A., Herrera, J., Peñas, A., Peinado, V., Verdejo, F., & de Rijke, M. (2003). The Multiple Language Question Answering Track at CLEF 2003. In *Working Notes for the CLEF 2003 Workshop*, Trondheim, Norway.

Manning, C. D., & Schütze, H. (1999). *Foundations of Statistical Natural Language Processing.* Cambridge, MA: MIT Press.

Markey, K. (2007). Twenty-Five Years of End-User Searching, Part 2: Future Research Directions. *Journal of the American Society for Information Science and Technology (JASIST)*, 58(8), 1123-1130.

Miller, D., Schwartz, R., Weischedel, R., & Stone, R. (1999). Named Entity Extraction from Broadcast News. In *Proceedings of DARPA Broadcast News Workshop.*

Montaner, M., Lopez, B., & Rosa, J. L. D. L. (2003). A Taxonomy of Recommender Agents on the Internet. *Artificial Intelligence Review*, 19, 285-330.

Ruthven, I., & Lalmas, M. (2003). A Survey on the Use of Relevance Feedback for Information Access Systems. *Knowledge Engineering Review*, 18(2), 95-145.

Samuel, K., Carberry, S., & Vijay-Shanker, K. (1998). Dialogue Act Tagging with Transformation-Based Learning. In *Proceedings of the 36th Annual Meeting of the Association for Computational Linguistics and 17th International Conference on Computational Linguistics*, Montreal.

Sanderson, M., & Croft, B. (1999). Deriving Concept Hierarchies from Text. In *Proceedings of the 22 Annual International ACM SIGIR Conference on Research and Development in Information Retrieval*, Berkeley, CA (pp. 206-213).

Sasaki, Y., Chen, H.-H., h. Chen, K., & Lin, C.-J. (2005). Overview of the NTCIR-5 Cross-Lingual Question Answering Task (CLQA1). In *Proceedings of the Fifth NTCIR Workshop Meeting on Evaluation of Information Access Technologies,* Tokyo, Japan.

Silverstein, C., Henzinger, M., & Marais, H. (1998). *Analysis of a Very Large AltaVista Query Log* (Digital SRC Technical Note 1998-014). Palo Alto, CA: Digital Systems Research Center.

Small, S., Strzalkowski, T., Liu, T., Ryan, S., Salkin, R., Shimizu, N., Kantor, P., Kelly, D., Rittman, R., & Wacholder, N. (2004a). HITIQA: Towards Analytical Question Answering. In *Proceedings of The 20th International Conference on Computational Linguistics (Coling 2004),* Geneva, Switzerland.

Small, S., Strzalkowski, T., Liu, T., Shimizu, N., & Yamrom, B. (2004). A Data Driven Approach to Interactive QA. In M. Maybury (Ed.), *New Directions in Question Answering* (pp. 129-140). Cambridge, MA: MIT Press.

Small, S., & Strzalkowski, T. (2008). HITIQA: High-Quality Intelligence through Interactive Question Answering. *Journal of Natural Language Engineering: Special Issue on Interactive Question Answering* (forthcoming, 2008).

Spink, A., & Jansen, B. (2004). *Web Search: Public Searching of the Web, volume 6 of The Information Science and Knowledge Management Series.* Dordrecht, The Netherlands: Kluwer Academic Publishers.

Stenmark, D. (2005). One Week with a Corporate Search Engine: A Time-Based Analysis of Intranet Information Seeking. In *Proceedings of the Eleventh Americas Conference on Information Systems*, Omaha, Nebraska.

Stenmark, D., & Jadaan, T. (2006). Intranet Users' Information-Seeking Behaviour: A Longitudinal Study of Search Engine Logs. In *Proceedings of the Annual Meeting of the American Society for Information Science and Technology*, Austin, TX.

Stolcke, A., Ries, K., Coccaro, N., Shriberg, E., Bates, R., Jurafsky, D., Taylor, P., Martin, R., Ess-Dykema, C. V., & Meteer, M. (2000). Dialogue Act Modeling for Automatic Tagging and Recognition of Conversational Speech. In *Computational Linguistics* 26(3), 339-373.

Teevan, J., Dumais, S. T., & Horvitz, E. (2005). Personalizing Search via Automated Analysis of Interests and Activities. In *Proceedings of the 28 Annual International ACM SIGIR Conference on Research and Development in Information Retrieval*, Salvador, Brazil (pp. 449 456).

Traum, D. R., Robinson, S., & Stephan, J. (2004). Evaluation of Multi-Party Virtual Reality Dialogue Interaction. In *Proceedings of Fourth International Conference on Language Resources and Evaluation (LREC)* (pp. 1699-1702).

Voorhees, E. (1999). The TREC-8 Question Answering Track Report. In *Proceedings of the Eighth Text Retrieval Conference (TREC-8)*, pages 77-82, NIST Special Publication 500-246.

Wacholder, N., Kelly, D., Rittman, R., Sun, Y., Kantor, P., Small, S., & Strzalkowski, T. (Forthcoming, 2007). A Model for Realistic Evaluation of an End-to-End Question Answering System. *Journal of the American Society for Information Science and Technology.*

Wacholder, N., Small, S., Bai, B., Kelly, D., Rittman, R., Ryan, S., Salkin, R., Song, P., Sun, Y., Ting, L., Kantor, P., & Strzalkowski, T. (2004). Designing a Realistic Evaluation of an End-to-End Interactive Question Answering System. In *Proceedings of the Fourth International Conference on Language Resources and Evaluation (LREC '04).*

Walker, M., Kamm, C., & Litman, D. (2000). Towards Developing General Models of Usability with PARADISE. *Natural Language Engineering*, 6(3), 363-377.

Wang, P., Berry, M., & Yang, Y. (2003). Mining Longitudinal Web Queries: Trends and Patterns. *Journal of the American Society for Information Science and Technology (JASIST)*, 54(8), 743-758.

Webb, N. (Ed.) (2006). *HLT-NAACL Workshop on Interactive Question Answering.* East Stroudsburg, PA: Association for Computational Linguistics.

Webb, N., Hepple, M., & Wilks, Y. (2005). Dialogue Act Classification Based on Intra- Utterance Features. In *Proceedings of the AAAI Workshop on Spoken Language Understanding.*

Webb, N., & Webber, B., editors (Forthcoming, 2008). *Special Issue of the Journal of Natural Language Engineering on Interactive Question Answering.*

White, R. W., Clarke, C. L. A., & Cucerzan, S. (2007). Comparing Query Logs and Pseudo-Relevance Feedback for Web-Search Query Refinement. In *Proceedings of the 30th Annual International ACM SIGIR Conference on Research and Development in Information Retrieval (SIGIR'07)* (pp. 831-832).

Zue, V., Glass, J., Goodine, D., Leung, H., Phillips, M., Polifroni, J., & Seneff, S. (1990). The VOYAGER Speech Understanding System: Preliminary Development and Evaluation. In *Proceedings of IEEE International Conference on Acoustics, Speech and Signal Processing* (pp. 73-76).

KEY TERMS

Domain Knowledge is the knowledge possessed or required of a person or system within a specific topical area.

Interactive Information Systems (IIS) are capable of converging on a person's information need by stages.

Query Modification is the modification by a search of a previous query.

Question Answering (QA) Systems go one step fruther than an information retrieval system that takes as input a user query and returns a ranked list of documents considered relevant to it. QA) systems return an exact answer extracted from one of the documents.

Section V
Contextual and Specialized Analysis

Chapter XXI
Using Action-Object Pairs as a Conceptual Framework for Transaction Log Analysis

Mimi Zhang
Pennsylvania State University, USA

Bernard J. Jansen
Pennsylvania State University, USA

ABSTRACT

In this chapter, we present the action-object pair approach as a conceptual framework for conducting transaction log analysis. We argue that there are two basic components in the interaction between the user and the system recorded in a transaction log, which are action and object. An action is a specific expression of the user. An object is a self-contained information object, the recipient of the action. These two components form one interaction set or an action-object pair. A series of action-object pairs represents the interaction session. The action-object pair approach provides a conceptual framework for the collection, analysis, and understanding of data from transaction logs. We believe that this approach can benefit system design by providing the organizing principle for implicit feedback and other interactions concerning the user and delivering, for example, personalized service to the user based on this feedback. Action-object pairs also provide a worthwhile approach to advance our theoretical and conceptual understanding of transaction log analysis as a research method.

MOTIVATION

The ultimate purpose of search engine designers is to devise Web search engines that provide the most relevant information to each individual user. Since the user decides whether information is relevant or if the system is suitable, it is critical to understand the user's system evaluation. Sun Tzu (n.d./1971), an ancient Chinese military strategist, said "know the enemy, know yourself;

your victory will never be endangered" (p.129). This advice can be applied on the battlefield, but it can also apply to building information technology systems.

In a broad sense, one can understand Sun's maxim as if you can know your own capability, and the characteristics and capabilities of people you deal with, it will be easier to devise processes appropriate to the situation. Therefore, in order to fulfill users' information needs and serve them better, we should know the users, understand their goals, and recognize their information search tactics. If we can recognize users' needs and their ways of approaching information, we can provide users with more suitable searching systems.

There are multiple ways to identify the individual user and provide tailored information systems. Search engines can learn about the users both explicitly and implicitly (Keenoy & Levene, 2005). In an explicit fashion, the users provide the necessary information to the system. The basis of this approach is that users would like to answer the questions, fill in a series of forms, or set up the profiles themselves. However, according to Keenoy and Levene (2005, p. 205), explicit feedback has low implementation rates due to the high cost of time and energy, unpredictable and unobvious benefits, and privacy concerns. This is in accordance with Zipf's Law – an individual will only perform actions that cost "the least effort" (Case, 2002, p. 140). Zipf's Law is a grounded and fundamental theoretical construct for information seeking studies. Zipf's Law is used to guide user studies and understanding of human behaviors, as well as the development of information systems.

Rather than relying on explicit feedback by users, implicit feedback based on the analysis of interactions between the user and the system may be a better approach (Keenoy & Levene, 2005; Khopkar, Spink, Giles, Shah, & Debnath, 2003). Although it certainly depends on the design goals, the implicit approach is in many ways superior since the user does not need to perform more actions such as answering questions or setting up profiles. It is an unobtrusive method; therefore, the approach has less chance of altering users' behavior.

The implicit approach is also highly dynamic. Since it analyzes and models current user interactions, it adapts well even if the users' information needs change over time. White, Ruthven, and Jose (2001) compared the effectiveness of explicit and implicit feedback techniques and claimed no statistical difference between the two approaches. In addition, according to Zipf's Law (1949), to users, the implicit feedback approach seems to be superior to the explicit feedback approach considering it costs them nothing but has the same effectiveness as the explicit feedback.

A search engine transaction log is "an electronic record of interactions that have occurred during a searching episode between a Web search engine and users searching for information on that Web search engine" (Jansen, 2006, p. 408). One can use the record of these interactions as a source of the implicit feedback. Dumais (2002) believes this is the only method for obtaining considerable amounts of data about users in a complex environment like the Web. Therefore, transaction log analysis seems a practical and convenient way to know the interactions of users with information systems. One can develop the user model by analyzing the data in transaction logs. Using this data, the system can make backward inferences to model the user and then make forward inferences to assist them with their information need.

However, there is a lack of theoretical frameworks for collecting, analyzing, and understanding data from transaction logs. Do we really need to analyze users' every communication with the computer? If not, what kinds of user-system interactions do the transaction logs need to contain? Log files are usually huge and messy. How can we effectively and efficiently organize and analyze them? How can we get the data to make sense and understand users via the log file? A modeling framework is needed to address these problems. In this chapter, we propose the action-object pair approach as a conceptual method to collect, analyze and understand transaction log data.

In the following section, we present the relevant concepts and the theoretical foundations of the action-object pair approach. We will provide a detailed description of the approach in the method section and its potential applications in the application section. We then describe a series of studies on applying the action-object pair approach to show its practical and theoretical values in the case study section. In the conclusion section, we sum up the issues, the underpinnings, and the advantages of the action-object pair approach.

SCIENTIFIC FOUNDATIONS

The foundational concepts of the action-object pair approach include user modeling in information searching, interaction, implicit feedback, and adaptive hypermedia system. User modeling in information searching allows us to conceptualize the interaction between the user and the system. However, there are various forms of interactions. For the system design purposes, we are interested in modeling interactions as actions performing upon information objects presented via the system. Implicit feedback explores the way to comprehend users in an unobtrusive fashion. Actions and objects together can inform us about the user and provide ways to capitalize on the implicit feedback. The implicit feedback can be used in system design, especially for personalization. Adaptive hypermedia system design is a promising way to utilize the implicit feedback and fits well with the action-object pairs approach. All of these concepts lead to the idea of using the action-object pair approach to conceptualize the analysis of transaction log data.

Modeling in Information Searching

Information scientists have contributed to theorizing the interaction process and modeling searchers in information retrieval and seeking. Wilson (1999) defines a model in the following way: "A model may be described as a framework for thinking about a problem and may evolve into a statement of the relationships among theoretical propositions. Most models in the general field of information behavior are of the former variety: they are statements, often in the form of diagrams, that attempt to describe an information-seeking activity, the causes and consequences of that activity, or the relationships among stages in information-seeking behaviour." (p. 250)

The action-object pair approach is similar to Wilson's (1999, p. 250) concept of a model. It provides a framework for thinking about transaction log analysis, which can uncover the interactive relationship between the user and the system. It attempts to describe an information-seeking activity and depicts the relationships between different sessions of information seeking. The action-object approach is theoretically based on Saracevic's stratified model (Saracevic & Kantor, 1997a, 1997b; Saracevic, Kantor, Chamis, & Trivison, 1988; Saracevic, Mokros, Su, & Spink, 1991; Spink & Saracevic, 1997).

Saracevic and his colleagues (Saracevic & Kantor, 1997a, 1997b; Saracevic et al., 1988; Saracevic et al., 1991; Spink & Saracevic, 1997) developed the stratified model of information retrieval interaction from a series of studies (refer to Figure 1). It describes the interactions between the user and the computer or system during retrieval at a surface level. Saracevic (1997) defined the interaction as "a dialogue between the participants - user and computer - through an interface, with the main purpose to affect the cognitive state of the user for effective use of information in connection with an application at hand" (p.316). It shows that information retrieval (IR) interaction is not a batch process but a deliberate exchange procedure. The exchange occurs on the surface level (i.e. interface). It includes two participants: the user and the computer.

Saracevic (1996, 1997) argued that the user and the computer have different levels or strata. The user side has at least three levels including cognitive, affective, and situational. The cognitive level refers to users' cognitive structures. Users interact with computers and process information cognitively including query development, query modification, relevance judgment, and such. The affective level refers to users' intentions and intentionality including beliefs, motivations, feelings, desires, urgency and so on. It mediates the interaction process. The situational level refers to the context the user is situated in. The context produces the users' information need and influences the way they approach information.

To Saracevic (1996, 1997), the computer side includes at least three strata, which are engineering, processing, and content. The engineering level includes the hardware and its attributes. The analysis will focus on the influence of the attributes on the interaction process. The processing level includes the software and algorithm. The analysis focuses on their effectiveness and evaluation. The content level refers to the information resources and meta-information. The potential analysis could include the adequacy or nature of information, its representation, and so on. The interaction takes place while different levels interact with each other. The adaptations happen to both participants and meet on the interface. The manner that information is used is determined by levels ranging from content toward situation.

Figure 1. Elements in the stratified model of Information Retrieval Interaction (Saracevic, 1997, p. 316)

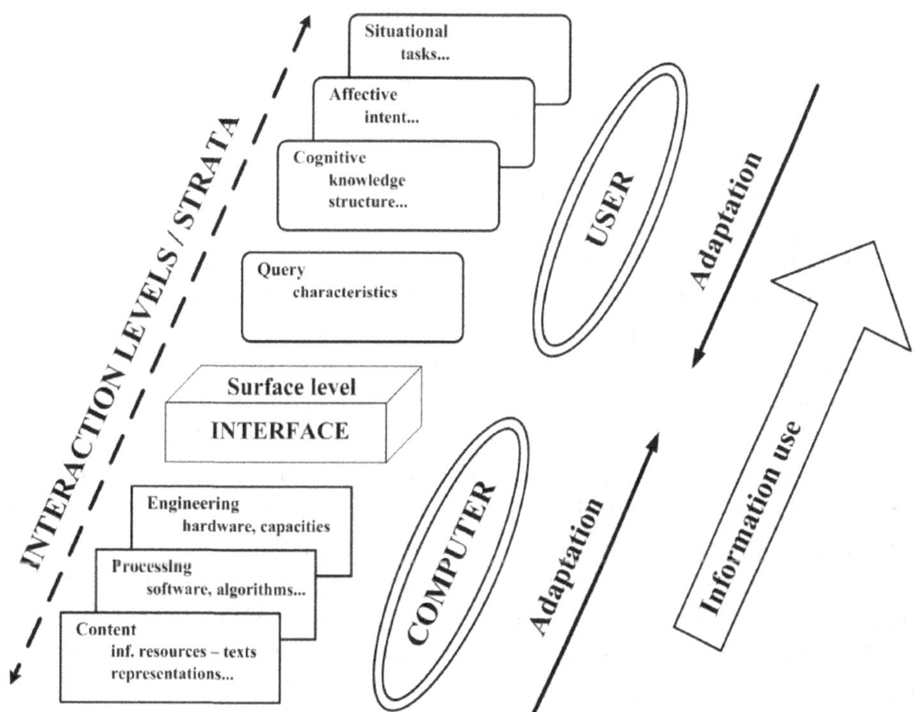

The strength of the stratified model is its high relevance with the information searching systems. It has a detailed description of the interaction processes and decompositions of both participants into strata, which makes it more relevant to system design compared to most IR models. It focuses exclusively on the query. Saracevic (1997, p. 317) believes "query is the most important aspect of user modeling". One can easily acquire the query via transaction logs. However, the stratified model fails to address the interactive and dynamic nature of the information seeking process beyond labeling it as a communication process. Therefore, we incorporate the action-object pairs into the stratified model and develop the action-object pair approach. We argue that the information seeking process is an interactive and dynamic process as described above. However, what do we mean by "interactive" and "dynamic"? Why is this important for a model?

Interaction

In the area of information searching (i.e., people using online information systems to locate data or information), researchers many times focus on the interactions between people and information searching systems. They picture interactions from different perspectives. Efthimiadis and Robertson (1989) categorized interactions at various stages in the information retrieval process. Bates (1990) presented four levels of interaction (move, tactic, stratagem, and strategy). Belkin and fellow researchers (1995) extensively explored user interaction within an information session. Lalmas and Ruthven (1999) presented interaction as that which occurs across sessions and that which occurs within a session. Jansen and Spink (2006) considered an interaction as any specific exchange between the searcher and the system. The searcher may be multitasking (Spink, 2004) within a searching episode, or the episode may be an instance of the searcher engaged in successive searching (Lin, 2002; Spink, Wilson, Ellis, & Ford, 1998).

While these definitions of interaction are descriptive at a high level, a more practical definition of interaction from the transaction log analysis perspective can benefit both the theoretical understanding and the system design. We propose defining interaction by using an action-object pair. It describes interactions between people and information searching systems as a set of action-object pairs. The interaction process is composed of a series of searchers' actions enabled by the information search systems over some information objects. Action and object set is the basic component of interaction. Our definition can be viewed as a combination of multidisciplinary views of interaction. Action is relevant to research in human-computer interaction and computer science. Object is related to studies in information science. Together they provide a conceptual view of interactions from the user's perspective.

From the discussions above, we have a conceptual understanding of the action-object pair approach. It also has some practical value for system design and development. It can provide implicit feedback to the system in an organized way.

Implicit Feedback

Transaction logs are a method of recording interactions between users and system, and for deriving implicit feedbacks. Implicit feedback is an unobtrusive way to get inputs from users. Researchers have explored various aspects of interactions as measurements of implicit feedback. Goecks and Shavlik (2000) used hyperlinks clicked, scrolling performed and processor cycles consumed. Seo and Zhang (2000) studied reading time, scrolling, link selection and bookmarking as potential implicit feedbacks, and found that bookmarking had the strongest relationship with interesting documents but scrolling had no relationship. Claypool and colleagues (2001) measured mouse clicks, mouse movement, scrolling and elapsed time as the implicit feedback metrics. Kelly and Belkin (2001) studied reading time, scrolling, and interaction. Kelly and Belkin (2004) also examined the display time as the implicit feedback and found no direct relationship between the display time and the usefulness of documents. Shen, Tan, and Zhai (2005) employed previous queries and click through information as the implicit feedback measures.

Oard and Kim (2001) considered all users' behaviors as a form of implicit feedback and proposed a framework for observed behaviors to improve system performance (refer to Table 1). The framework has two axes: behavior category and minimal scope. Behavior category includes four types of observable behavior: examine, retain, reference, and annotate. Examine refers to searchers' behaviors of checking the information content. It can be view, listen, and select. Retain is about the behaviors of preserving the information content for future usage. It can be print, bookmark, save, delete, purchase, and subscribe. Reference is to create linkage between information contents. It can be copy-paste, quote, forward, reply, link, and cite. Annotate refers to intended behaviors to add personal values to the information content. It can be mark up, rate, publish, and organize. Most follow-on implicit feedback classifications have adhered to this conceptual presentation.

Minimal scope is "the smallest unit normally associated with the behavior" (Oard & Kim, 2001, p. 484). It has three levels, which are segment, object, and class. A segment is a portion of an information object. An object is a self-contained information entity. A class is a set of objects. For example, a Webpage can be an object. A sentence or a paragraph on the Webpage is a segment. A Website including several Webpages is a class. (Oard & Kim, 2001)

Kelly and Teevan (2003) further developed this framework (refer to Table 2) by adding a fifth behavior category: create, which refers to the generation of the information content. It can be type, edit, and author. They also added scroll, find, and query as actions of examining the information segment; browse as action of examining the information class; and email as action of retaining the information object.

Table 1. Potentially observable behaviors (Oard & Kim, 2001, p. 484)

		MINIMAL SCOPE		
		Segment	Object	Class
BEHAVIOR CATEGORY	Examine	View	Select	
		Listen		
	Retain	Print	Bookmark	Subscribe
			Save	
			Delete	
			Purchase	
	Reference	Copy-paste	Forward	
		Quote	Reply	
			Link	
			Cite	
	Annotate	Mark up	Rate	Organize
			Publish	

Jansen and McNeese (2005) further refined this framework and applied it specifically in the Web searching domain (refer to Table 3). They extended the minimal scope axis by adding interface as the minimal scope of the system. The original components are mainly about the Internet content in the information searching area.

In addition, they dropped annotate and create on the behavior category axis because they are more related to the manipulation of information content and less related to information searching. They added two other behavior categories: execute and navigate. These are common behaviors during Web search. Jansen and McNeese's (2005)framework is exclusively tailored for information searching. The actions in each cell also have been altered accordingly. This modified version of the framework is a version of the action-object approach per se. The minimal scope axis is the object. The behavior category axis is the action in a broad term. In each cell, there are actions on the ground level. Using the action-object approach, one could acquire the implicit feedback from searchers.

With the implicit feedback available, what can this information do for the system design? How can we effectively utilize the implicit feedback acquired by using the action-object approach? Adaptive hypermedia system design techniques address these questions, which we can leverage for transaction log analysis and the design of Web searching systems.

Adaptive Hypermedia System

With the implicit feedback, we could personalize a system by utilizing the adaptive hypermedia system design techniques. The adaptive hyper-

Table 2. Modified potentially observable behaviors by Kelly and Teevan (2003, p. 19)

		MINIMAL SCOPE		
		Segment	Object	Class
BEHAVIOR CATEGORY	Examine	View	Select	*Browse*
		Listen		
		Scroll		
		Find		
		Query		
	Retain	Print	Bookmark	Subscribe
			Save	
			Delete	
			Purchase	
			Email	
	Reference	Copy-paste	Forward	
		Quote	Reply	
			Link	
			Cite	
	Annotate	Mark up	Rate	Organize
			Publish	
	Create	*Type*	*Author*	
		Edit		

Table 3. Classification of implicit feedback on system and content during information searching process (Jansen & McNeese, 2005, p. 1482)

		MINIMAL SCOPE			
		SYSTEM	CONTENT		
		Interface	Segment	Object	Class
BEHAVIOR CATEGORY	Execute	Query	Click	Select	
		Open	Scroll		
		Close			
		Resize			
	Examine		View	Open	Browse
			Find		
	Navigate	Back		GoTo	
		Forward		Previous	
				Next	
	Retain	Create	Print	Bookmark	
		Name		Save	
				Purchase	
				E-mail	
	Reference		Copy-Paste		

media systems are defined as "all hypertext and hypermedia systems which reflect some features of the user in the user model and apply this model to adapt various visible aspects of the system to the user" (Brusilovsky, 1996, p. 88). They combine system design with user modeling to fulfill the heterogeneous information needs of each individual user (Bailey, Hall, Millard, & Weal, 2007; Brusilovsky, 1996; Cannataro, Cuzzocrea, & Pugliese, 2001). The hypermedia system is designed to adapt to users' goals, knowledge, background, hyperspace experience and preferences (Brusilovsky, 1996, p. 93-96).

Brusilovsky (1996, pp. 96-100) states that system adaptation can be on two levels: content-level (adaptive presentation) and link-level (adaptive navigation). The adaptive presentation can include technologies such as adaptive multimedia presentation and adaptive text presentation. The adaptive navigation support can contain technologies such as direct guidance, adaptive sorting of links, adaptive hiding of links, adaptive annotation of links, and map adaptation.

Cannataro, Cuzzocrea, and Pugliese (2001) proposed that the adaptive hypermedia system has three basic components: "the Application Domain Model, the User Model, and the techniques to adapt presentations with respect to the user's behavior and to the content provider's goals" (p. 411). The Application Domain Model refers to the descriptions of the hypermedia contents and their organization architecture. Datacentric is the most promising modeling approach. The user modeling is used to uncover "the user's characteristics and preferences and his/her expectations in the browsing of hypermedia" (Cannataro et al., 2001, p. 411).

Cannataro, Cuzzocrea, and Pugliese (2001, p. 411) claimed that this approach to profile users was different from the overlay model and stereotype model. The former approach typically utilizes a series of attribute-value pairs to present the user's characteristics. The latter approach usually classifies users into different groups. The adaptive presentation tailors the presentation of the Application Domain according to the User Model. It is "a manipulation of information fragments, adaptive navigation support" (Cannataro et al., 2001, p. 411) and "a manipulation of the links presented to the user" (Cannataro et al., 2001, p. 411). Ceri and his peers (Ceri, Daniel, Matera, & Facca, 2007) described that the adaptive actions can be adaptive page contents, adaptive navigation, adaptive site view, and adaptive presentation style.

De Bra and Calvi (1998) proposed the concept-value pair method to model users. The adaptive system learns users based on their actions or the answers to the system's questions and employs these actions to predict their needs and desires. Concept-value pairs are used to build up models of the user. In a (*c*, *v*) pair, *c* is a *concept* and *v* is a *value*. The pair represents the amount of knowledge that the user has about a certain concept. The term concept is used in a broad way here, which can also refer to the user's preference. Values can be described in different fashions including numbers, descriptions, and Booleans. For example, the concept is "something", and the value can be a percentage (for instance, 99%), "no knowledge, somewhat knows about, familiar", or "true or false". De Bra and Calvi (1998) believed the representation system with many values cannot be simulated in a practical sense. It would be impossible to simulate "something" with an infinite number of percentages as values. Therefore, the concept should be defined in a fine-grained way for the purpose of simulation. This is a simple but practical user modeling approach. It simulates users in a programmable way. We also draw the action-object pair approach from it.

ACTION–OBJECT PAIR APPROACH DESCRIPTION

Successful log analysis is determined by "conducting the analysis with an organized approach" (Jansen, 2006, p. 420). The question is how to define "organized". Most of the previous search logs are organized and analyzed to address some research questions. The typical research questions are at the aggregate level, including the length of query, number of queries per search session, query reformulation pattern, and such (Park, Bae, & Lee, 2005; Silverstein, Henzinger, Marais, & Moricz, 1999; Wang, Berry, & Yang, 2003). These analyses are research question oriented and organize user data according to the research questions addressed. It is an organized approach but has little direct value to the design of personalized systems. Another "organized" approach is individual user oriented. The log analysis is conducted according to each user. This approach is more suitable for the personalized system design. Therefore, we propose the action-object pair approach.

The action-object pair approach is a conceptual framework for transaction log analysis. It is developed based on extending Saracevic's stratified model and modifying the concept-value approach (refer to Figure 2 and 3). The stratified model allows us to describe the interaction process between the user and the system. Its user modeling part does not fit our purpose of developing a conceptual framework for transaction log analysis. Therefore, we replace the user modeling portion with the action-object pairs, which are developed from the concept-value approach.

The conceptual component in the action-object pair approach is (a, o) pair. In a (*a*, *o*) pair, *a* stands for action and *o* stands for object. An action is a specific expression of the user. An object is a self-contained information object, the receipt of the action. One (*a*, *o*) pair represents one interaction between the user and the system. Action can be *submit*, *copy*, *paste*, *print*, *save*, *submit*, *scroll*, *modify*, *click*, *resize*, and such. An action

Figure 2. Extension of stratified model by using action-object pair

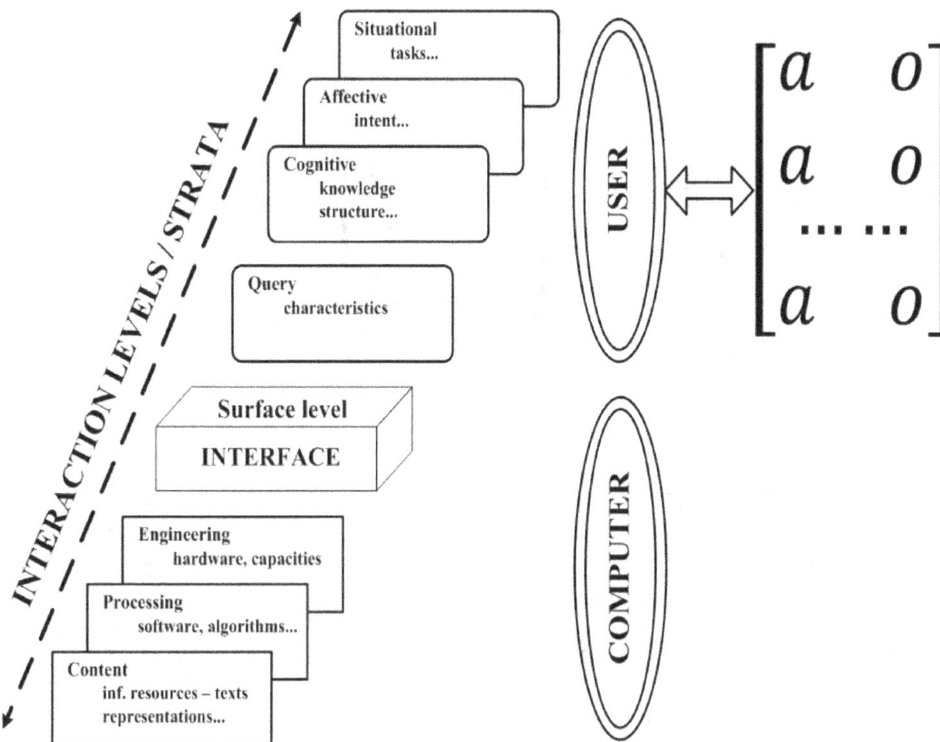

can be derived from analyzing different strata of users and computers. A detailed list of potential actions is in Table 3.

An object can be *query*, *URL*, *result*, *Webpage*, *scrollbar*, *window*, and such. Objects can be acquired by studying different strata of computers, especially the content level. For example, a user is interested in purchasing a Canon G9, a digital camera and looking for some reviews before placing the order. The user submits the query "canon g9 review". We can organize this interaction by using action-object pair. Action is *submit* and object is *a query*. The (*a*, *o*) pair is (*submit*, *canon g9 review*).

One (*a*, *o*) pair is one interaction between the user and the system. A series of (*a*, *o*) pairs or an *a-o* matrix can represent the interaction session, which is defined as a series of interactions between the user and the system to fulfill the user's certain information need. According to the stratified model, the interaction session is the product of situational, affective, and cognitive strata interacting with a search engine via queries on the surface level (Saracevic, 1996, 1997). Therefore, an *a-o* matrix can also be viewed as such a product. We can use backward inference from the product to acquire insight about the user's three strata. Thus, Saracevic's stratified model can be modified by using *a-o* matrix to inform on the strata of the user (refer to Figure 2 and 3). The *a-o* matrix development rules of thumb are: the more (*a*, *o*) pairs, the more complicated the model will be (Jansen & Pooch, 2001, p. 22); the more (*a*, *o*) pairs, the more accurate the model will be.

This approach provides a novel and efficient way to link interactions between the user and the system together. It can be applied to collecting, analyzing and understanding transaction logs. It

Figure 3. Modified version of stratified model

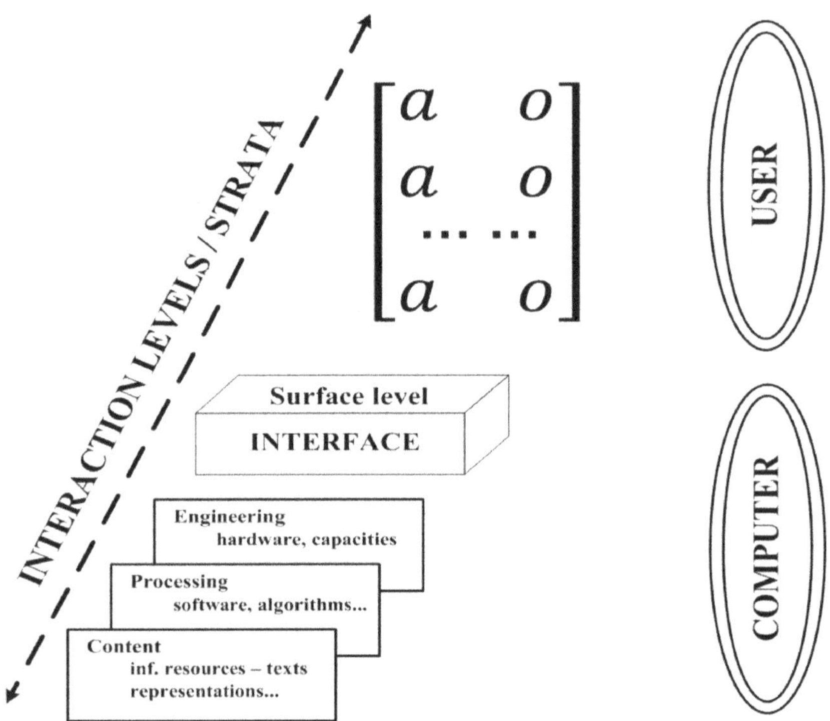

provides guidance to understand the records of interactions. We can analyze the log by creating an *a-o* matrix. We can analyze the frequency of action-object pairs. Once the frequent co-occurrences of action-object pairs are identified, they can be recommended if they do not appear together. The frequent co-occurrences of action-object pair orders can be recommended when the *a-o* pairs are not presented in those orders. Some low-performance actions can be improved by triggering the recommendation mechanisms. The analysis result can be understood by using a modified version of the stratified model.

The action-object pair approach can be used in designing adaptive search engines. It is an approach developed for the information searching domain from the concept-value pair method, which originally was used to model users and design adaptive hypermedia systems (De Bra & Calvi, 1998; Jansen & Pooch, 2001). Thus, we can use the action-object pair approach to develop adaptive search engines. Adaptive search engine help fulfill the information searching needs of the individual user. They can provide adaptive presentation and adaptive navigation. For example, the search engine can provide different link summaries on the search engine result page to different users. These are potential ways to improve users' information relevance judgment.

We believe the action-object pair approach is an extremely workable method since the user does not need to perform more actions such as answering questions or setting up profiles. It is an unobtrusive method. This approach is also highly dynamic. It can model the user in a timely manner, considering that the users' information needs change all the time. Their actions and the objects they act on are the products of the cognition, affection and situation altogether. It can benefit system design since users' actions are recorded in a way convertible into code to modify the system. In the next section, we will present the potential applications of the action-object pair approach to show its practical value.

APPLICATION

There are three major applications for the action-object pair approach. It can be applied to transaction log collection, transaction log analysis, and understanding users. The action-object pair approach addresses the question on what types of interactions need to be recorded in the transaction log. It accounts for how the transaction log should be analyzed. It uncovers a new way to understand users via data collected in the transaction log.

Transaction Log Collection

The action-object pair approach can be used to guide the transaction log creation. Early in the history of system design, the transaction log was created primarily for system maintenance purposes. It was not utilized for other purposes concerning the user. Jansen, Spink, and Saracevic (2000) published one of the first journal papers using a Web log to understand various aspects of user interactions during Web searching. There are two types of search logs: server-side logs and client-side logs. Server-side logs are generated by Web server applications and record the interactions between the user and search engines via browsers on the computer. Typical server-side logs usually include user identification, date, time, and query. Client-side logs are generated by applications on a user's computer and include the full range of interactions between user-system compared with the server-side logs. W3C (Hallam-Baker & Behlendorf, n.d.) defines the standard format of transaction logs. However, there is a lack of framework to guide the user-system interactions, which the serve-side logs and the client-side logs should capture, especially for system design and user understanding purposes.

The action-object pair approach can address this data collection issue. Transaction logs do not include every user-system interaction. Detailed records of the user-system interactions indeed can bring us a comprehensive and more accurate interaction model. However, it is costly in terms of systems resources. In addition, different people have different standards about degree of comprehensiveness and accuracy. One will agree that the most suitable record is the one that is comprehensive and accurate, while the least costly. Therefore, the right amount of data really depends on the purposes of the transaction log. If you want to use the data to study the collaborative information behavior of a distributed group, you may want to record the communicative actions among group members. These communications have great influence over how the group conducts search. If you are only interested in the individual search behavior, you can ignore these communicative actions. Thus, the action-object pair you are interested in will decide the interactions that the log files should capture. Potential recordable interaction actions are shown in Table 3.

Transaction Log Analysis

Transaction logs are typically messy and large files. How to organize the data in order to conduct an efficient analysis is the starting point of log analysis. It is fundamental and critical in the log analysis process. We propose the using action-object pair approach to organize the transaction log. Every interaction can be transformed to be an action-object pair. A set of action-object pairs can be placed in the modified version of the stratified model (refer to Figure 3). Action-object pairs help frame the analysis and benefits system design. Based on the action-object pairs model, one can consider what kinds of design should be made to support the action-object pairs on the engineering, processing, and content strata.

The action-object pairs can be created in a codable fashion. This characteristic will benefit system design. Action-object pairs can be generated automatically by the software packages. Therefore, the system can conduct transaction log analysis in real time. Based on the analysis results, the system can provide some potential live suggestions or some adaptive personalization to the user. For example, certain action-object pairs can trigger certain system actions. A (*submit, query*) can initiate the spelling check function. The spelling suggestions can remind the user to check on some possible mistakes. This feedback and engagement will make sure the user employs the right word to describe his/her information needs and frame the query.

User Modeling

The action-object pair approach can be applied to knowing users and understanding users. In the stratified model, Saracevic (1996, 1997) argued the user's actions were the products of the situation, affection, and cognition combination from the user side. Profilers picture people based on their actions. One can then compose the user file based on the action-object pair approach via the transaction log (refer to Figure 2).

As we have pointed out above, each item in the transaction log can be converted to an action-object pair. Each pair informs us of the user. Based on categorizing the information objects, you can know the domains in which he/she will have an interest. Based on the user's actions and previous studies on the implicit feedback, you can infer if the user finds the relevant information. Based on the user's frequent actions on processing relevant information, one can predict what the user will do the next time in such a situation.

In order to further explain the practical value of the action-object pair, we will present applicable research in the following case study section.

CASE STUDY

The action-object approach has been extensively applied in a series of studies by Jansen (Jansen, 2003, 2005, 2007; Jansen & McNeese, 2005; Jansen & Pooch, 2004). The researchers (Jansen, 2003, 2005; Jansen & Pooch, 2004) employed the action-object approach to design a software agent as plug-in to monitor and support users' interactions. The agent monitored five actions: *bookmark, copy, print, save, and submit*; and identified three objects: *documents, passages from documents*, and *queries*. The agent monitors the log file. When a certain action-object pair appears, the assistance will be triggered. For example, the action is *submit* and the object is *query*. The action-object pair is (*submit, query*). The assistance triggered can be spell-checking and providing the spelling modification suggestions.

The agent provided assistance on five major issues: structuring queries, spelling, query refinement, managing results, and relevance feedback (Jansen, 2003, pp. 746-747, 2005, p. 914; Jansen & Pooch, 2004, pp. 22-24).

Structuring Queries

Users find it hard to properly structure queries, especially applying the rules of a particular system. In particular, they do not know how to and when to use Boolean operators (e.g., AND, OR, NOT) (Proctor, 2002) and term modifier symbols (e.g. '+', '!') (Spink, Jansen, Wolfram, & Saracevic, 2002) in an appropriate way on certain systems.

Agent Assistance

If the user submits a query, the agent recognizes this as a (*submit, query*) pair. It checks the query's structure based on the system's syntactic rules and corrects any mistake to make sure the query is properly structured before submitting it to the search engine.

Spelling

Users often make spelling mistakes in queries (Jansen et al., 2000; Yee, 1991), which can potentially reduce the number of results returned. However, it is usually difficult to detect these spelling errors because people can make the same mistakes while creating the documents, and especially in large document collections like the Internet, the probability of making the same spelling mistakes is extremely high. Therefore, these misspelled queries frequently retrieve results. The user may even not notice the query includes a spelling mistake.

Agent Assistance

A (*submit, query*) pair alerts the agent to check for spelling. The agent parses the query into terms, examining each term using an online dictionary. If the agent fails to locate the term in the dictionary, it will provide spelling suggestions or remind the users to check the spelling themselves. The agent's current online dictionary is *ispell* (Gorin, 1971). It can employ any online dictionary by using the proper application program interface (API).

Query Refinement

Searchers do not modify their query, although there may be other terms that relate directly to or better describe their information needs (Bruza, McArthur, & Dennis, 2000). Studies by Jansen and his colleagues (1998) disclose that searchers rarely refine their queries, or do so incrementally. They usually modify their queries only one or two times.

Agent Assistance

By identifying a (*submit, query*) pair, the agent analyzes each query term and looks into a thesaurus to suggest synonyms and the contextual definitions of the query terms. The agent uses WordNet (Miller, 1998) but can utilize any online thesaurus with proper modifications.

Managing Results

Users have difficulty managing the number of results (Gauch & Smith, 1993). They have difficulty in increasing the number of results when there are not enough results and decreasing the number of results when there are too many results (Yee, 1991). Roughly speaking, user queries are very broad. Broad queries usually result in an unmanageable number of results. However, Silverstein and his colleagues (1999) claimed that few searchers view more than the first ten or twenty documents from the result list.

Agent Assistance

Recognizing the (*submit, query*) pair and the number of results, the agent provides suggestions to refine the query. When the number of results is larger than twenty, the agent provides guidance to refine the query to reduce the length of the result list. When the number of results is less than twenty, the agent provides suggestions to expand the query to increase the results returned by the system.

Relevance Feedback

Harman (1992) pointed out that relevance feedback provided effective search assistance. However, searchers seldom use it even if it is offered. Koenemann and Belkin (1996) proposed to automate this process. Mitra and his peers (1998) suggested automating this process by using term relevance feedback.

Agent Assistance

Upon recognizing a (*bookmark, document*), (*print, document*), (*save, document*) or (*copy, passage*) pair, the agent executes a version of relevance feedback by using terms from the document or passage object. For example, when the user goes over a document from the results list and conducts bookmarking, printing, or saving, the agent recommends terms from the document that the user can have potential interest in adding to the query.

According to Jansen and his peers (2003, 2004, 2005), the agent can be enabled or disabled by users. The empirical test shows this agent could significantly improve the system's performance in terms of precision. All the participants employed the agent feedback at least once. Users were willing to accept automated assistance especially after locating the relevant information. Query refinement was the most frequently used assistance and relevance feedback was least frequently used. The average workload was measured by using the SWAT method (Boff & Lincoln, 1988) and the result was 5.37 out of 9. The potential source of workload was the inappropriate feedback supply manner.

Jansen and McNeese (2005) further developed this agent. They refined the term used to describe action and object. They replaced *copy* as *copy-paste*, *submit* as *execute*, *passages from documents* as segment. It records more actions including *send to*, *view*, *scroll*, *next*, *goto*, and *previous*, although the agent does not utilize them to make any inference. The reason was due to a lack of consensus on the implicit feedback from these actions. They add a module called tracking module to formulate the action-object pair and then send it to a certain module of the agent. They dropped the query structuring module and added a new module called similar queries. Search engines such as AltaVista (Anick, 2003) recommends similar queries from previous users for current users to reformulate the queries. The agent recognizes the (*submit*, *query*) pair and searches for queries containing all or some of this query submitted by previous users. It displays the top three unique queries as recommended modifications.

According to Jansen and McNeese (2005), the modules in the agent have been improved. Spelling assistance is taken care of by the query term module. The agent triggered by the (*submit*, *query*) pair not only parses query into terms but also removes query operators (such as MUST APPEAR, MUST NOT APPEAR, and PHASE). The dictionary has been switched from *ispell* (Gorin, 1971) to Microsoft Office Dictionary. The query refinement module has also been changed. If there are more than 30 results returned by the system, the agent initiated by the (*submit*, *query*) pair will try to locate AND, MUST APPEAR, and PHRASE operators. If there is no such operator, the agent will reformulate queries with existing terms and appropriate usage of AND, MUST APPEAR, and PHRASE operators. If the query has AND or MUST APPEAR operators, the agent will reformulate the query with PHRASE operator. If the query has PHRASE operator, there is no action from the agent. If the number of results returned by the search engine is less than 20, a similar process as above will happen by replacing AND with OR. The managing results module was renamed as a query reformulation module. Instead of using 20 results returned by the search engine as a boundary of too many or too few results, they used 10 and 30 (i.e. if the number of the results is less than 10, then there are too few results; if the number of results is larger than 30, then there are too many results). The agent will make certain recommendations accordingly. In addition, the agent now preprocesses each term in the query with the assistance of the Microsoft Office thesaurus before sending it to the thesaurus API.

Jansen and McNeese (2005) empirically evaluated the second version of the agent. They found that the system performance had increased about 20% measured by the number of user-selected relevant documents. The users interacted with the system in a predictable way. The most common three-state pattern is Execute Query - View Results: With Scrolling - View Assistance. The implementation rate of the agent was 71%. However, there was no obvious correlation between the use of assistance and previous searching performance. Jansen (2007) conducted another user study by using the second version of the agent to test the effectiveness of automated searching assistance based on the implicit feedback. The conclusion was that the searching performance indeed improved and increased about 30% but the result depended on the evaluation metric used.

In the case study above, the action-object pair approach has shown its values in terms of providing a theoretical framework for collecting, analyzing, and understanding the search log file. It also facilitated the system design and improved the system performance. The participants did not reject of using the agent. All of these indicate the action-object pair approach is a promising conceptual framework for data collection, transaction log analysis, and user modeling.

CONCLUSION

Understanding users is critical for effective system design. Implicit feedback functions better than explicit feedback in many situations since it is an unobtrusive and burden-free method for users. A transaction log is a direct and convenient way to record implicit feedback from users. Researchers and designers can exploit this resource. The question is "how". How can one get the most value from large and messy log files? How can one know if the data in the log is recorded in an appropriate fashion to provide the implicit feedback? How can one know what is an efficient and effective way to make sense of the log? How can one know if the transaction log is processed in the right way to get the implicit feedback? There is a lack of frameworks for providing guidance for collecting, analyzing, and understanding data from transaction logs. Therefore, we propose the action-object pair approach as a conceptual framework for transaction log analysis.

The action-object pair approach is an extension of Saracevic's stratified model and developed by modifying the concept-value approach. We use the stratified model as a starting point for this modeling approach. The user component of the stratified model is adjusted to fit the purpose of transaction log analysis. We modify the concept-value approach, converting it to the action-object pair approach. This approach is utilized to replace the user component in the stratified model. From this, one gets a modified version of the stratified model (refer to Figure 3). In the action-object approach, an action is defined as a specific expression of the user. An object is a self-contained information object, the receipt of the action. One (a, o) pair is one interaction between the user and the system. A set of (a, o) pairs or *a-o* matrix can represent the interaction session, in which a particular information need gets satisfied.

The action-object pair approach provides a novel way to guide the transaction log collection, organize the transaction log, and deliver the implicit feedback to the system. The log file must have enough data to build the action-object pairs. The more (a, o) pairs, the more accurately one can model the user. Therefore, the log can be organized as (a, o) pairs. The system can use the (a, o) pairs as the implicit feedback. Based on it, the system can provide adaptive services to the users. The system can model users in a timely fashion, which means the system can potentially provide timely adaptation to the user. This is very important. In a series of queries, a user can refer to 'Amazon' as an online store for one query and as a river in the next query. In addition, the action-object pair approach advances our conceptual understanding of collecting, analyzing, and comprehending transaction logs. It sheds some theoretical light on questions such as what to collect and how to organize, analyze, and understand the log file.

REFERENCES

Anick, P. (2003, July-August). *Using terminological feedback for Web search refinement - A log-based study.* Paper presented at the Twenty-Sixth Annual International ACM SIGIR Conference on Research and Development in Information Retrieval, Toronto, Canada.

Bailey, C., Hall, W., Millard, D. E., & Weal, M. J. (2007). Adaptive hypermedia through contextualized open hypermedia structures [Electronic Version]. *ACM Transactions on Information Systems, 25*(4), Article 16. Retrieved October 20, 2007, from http://doi.acm.org/10.1145/1281485.1281487

Bates, M. J. (1990). Where should the person stop and the information search interface start? *Information Processing and Management, 26*(5), 575-591.

Belkin, N., Cool, C., Stein, A., & Thiel, S. (1995). Cases, scripts, and information-seeking strategies: On the design of interactive information retrieval systems. *Expert Systems with Applications, 9*(3), 379-395.

Boff, K. R., & Lincoln, J. E. (1988). *Engineering Data Compendium: Human Perception and Performance.* Wright-Patterson A.F.B. Dayton, Ohio: Harry G. Armstrong Aerospace Medical Research Laboratory.

Brusilovsky, P. (1996). Methods and techniques of adaptive hypermedia. *User Modeling and User-Adapted Interaction, 6*(2-3), 87-129.

Bruza, P., McArthur, R., & Dennis, S. (2000, July). *Interactive Internet search: Keyword, directory and query reformulation mechanisms compared.* Paper presented at the Twenty-third Annual International ACM SIGIR Conference on Research and Development in Information Retrieval, Athens, Greece.

Cannataro, M., Cuzzocrea, A., & Pugliese, A. (2001). A probabilistic adaptive hypermedia system. *Proceedings of the International Conference on Information Technology: Coding and Computing (ITCC '01)*, USA, 411-415.

Case, D. (2002). *Looking for information: a survey of research on information seeking, needs, and behavior.* San Diego, CA: Academic Press.

Ceri, S., Daniel, F., Matera, M., & Facca, F. M. (2007). Model-driven development of context-aware Web applications [Electronic Version]. *ACM Transactions on Internet Technology,* 7(1), Article 2. Retrieved October 20, 2007, from http://doi.acm.org/10.1145/1189740.1189742

Claypool, M., Le, P., Wased, M., & Brown, D. (2001, January). *Implicit interest indicators.* Paper presented at the Sixth International Conference on Intelligent User Interfaces, Sanata Fe, NM.

De Bra, P., & Calvi, L. (1998, June). *AHA: A generic adaptive hypermedia system.* Paper presented at the Second Workshop on Adaptive Hypertext and Hypermedia, HYPERTEXT'98, Pittsburgh, PA.

Dumais, S. T. (2002). *Web experiments and test collections.* Retrieved April 20, 2003, from http://www2002.org/presentations/dumais.pdf

Efthimiadis, E. N., & Robertson, S. E. (1989). Feedback and interaction in information retrieval. In C. Oppenheim (Ed.), *Perspectives in information management* (pp. 257-272). London: Butterworths.

Gauch, S., & Smith, J. (1993). An expert system for automatic query reformulation. *Journal of the American Society for Information Science, 44*(3), 124-136.

Goecks, J., & Shavlik, J. (2000, January). *Learning users' interests by unobtrusively observing their normal behavior.* Paper presented at the Fifth International Conference on Intelligent User Interfaces, New Orleans, LA.

Gorin, R. E. (1971). *Developer of ispell.* Retrieved 12 February, 2000, from http://fmg-www.cs.ucla.edu/geoff/ispell.html

Harman, D. (1992, June). *Relevance Feedback Revisited.* Paper presented at the Fifteenth Annual International ACM SIGIR Conference on Research and Development in Information Retrieval, Copenhagen, Denmark.

Jansen, B. J. (2003, October). *Designing automated help using searcher system dialogues.* Paper presented at the 2003 IEEE International Conference on Systems, Man and Cybernetics, Washington, DC.

Jansen, B. J. (2005). Seeking and implementing automated assistance during the search process. *Information Processing and Management, 41*(4), 909-928.

Jansen, B. J. (2006). Search log analysis: What is it; what's been done; how to do it. *Library and Information Science Research, 28*(3), 407-432.

Jansen, B. J. (2007). *Evaluating the effectiveness of automated searching assistance.* Manuscript submitted for publication.

Jansen, B. J., & McNeese, M. D. (2005). Evaluating the effectiveness of and patterns of interactions with automated searching assistance. *Journal of the American Society for Information Science and Technology, 56*(14), 1480-1503.

Jansen, B. J., & Pooch, U. (2001). Web user studies: A review and framework for future work. *Journal of the American Society for Information Science and Technology, 52*(3), 235-246.

Jansen, B. J., & Pooch, U. (2004). Assisting the Searcher: Utilizing Software Agents for Web Search Systems. *Internet Research - Electronic Networking Applications and Policy, 14*(1), 19-33.

Jansen, B. J., & Spink, A. (2006). How are we searching the World Wide Web? A comparison of nine search engine transaction logs. *Information Processing and Management, 42*(1), 248-263.

Jansen, B. J., Spink, A., & Saracevic, T. (2000). Real life, real users, and real needs: A study and analysis of user queries on the Web. *Information Processing and Management, 36*(2), 207-227.

Keenoy, K., & Levene, M. (2005). Personalisation of Web search. In B. Mobasher and S. S. Anand (Eds.), *Intelligent Techniques for Web Personalization* (pp. 201-228). Berlin, German: Springer-Verlag.

Kelly, D., & Belkin, N. J. (2001, Sepetmber). *In reading time, scrolling and interaction: Exploring implicit sources of user preferences for relevance feedback.* Paper presented at the Twenty-fourth Annual International ACM SIGIR Conference on Research and Development in Information Retrieval, New Orleans, LA.

Kelly, D., & Belkin, N. J. (2004, July). *In display time as implicit feedback: Understanding task effects.* Paper presented at the Twenty-seventh Annual International Conference on Research and Development in Information Retrieval, Sheffield, England.

Kelly, D., & Teevan, J. (2003). Implicit feedback for inferring user preference: A bibliography. *SIGIR Forum, 37*(2), 18-28.

Khopkar, Y., Spink, A., Giles, C. L., Shah, P., & Debnath, S. (2003). Search engine personalization: An exploratory study [Electronic Version]. *First Monday,* 8. Retrieved October 20, 2007, from http://firstmonday.org/issues/issue8_7/khopkar/index.html

Koenemann, J., & Belkin, N. (1996, April). *A case for interaction: A study of interactive information retrieval behavior and effectiveness.* Paper presented at the ACM SIGCHI '96 Conference on Human Factors in Computing Systems, Vancouver, Canada.

Lalmas, M., & Ruthven, I. (1999, May). *A framework for investigating the interaction in information retrieval.* Paper presented at the Ninth European-Japanese Conferences on Information Modeling and Knowledge Bases, Japan.

Lin, S. J. (2002, August). *Design space of personalized indexing: Enhancing successive web searching for transmuting information problem,* Paper presented at the American Conference on Information Systems, Dallas, TX.

Miller, G. (1998). *WordNet: An electronic lexical database.* Cambridge, MA: MIT Press.

Mitra, M., Singhal, A., & Buckley, C. (1998, August). *Improving automatic query expansion.* Paper presented at the Twenty-first Annual International ACM SIGIR Conference on Research and Development in Information Retrieval, Melbourne, Australia.

Oard, D., & Kim, J. (2001). Modeling information content using observable behavior. *Proceedings of the Sixty-fourth American Society for Information Science Annual Meeting, 38*, 481-488.

Park, S., Bae, H., & Lee, J. (2005). End user searching: A Web log analysis of NAVER, a Korean Web search engine. *Library and Information Science Research, 27*(2), 203-221.

Proctor, E. (2002). Boolean operators and the naive end-user: Moving to AND. *Online, 26*(4), 34-37.

Saracevic, T. (1996, October). *Modeling interaction in information retrieval (IR): A review and proposal.* Paper presented at the Fifty-ninth American Society for Information Science, Baltimore, MD.

Saracevic, T. (1997). The stratified model of information retrieval interaction: Extension and applications. *Proceedings of the Sixtieth American Society for Information Science Annual Meeting, 34*, 313-327.

Saracevic, T., & Kantor, P. (1997a). Studying the value of library and information services: I. Establishing a theoretical framework. *Journal of the American Society for Information Science, 48*(6), 527-542.

Saracevic, T., & Kantor, P. (1997b). Studying the value of library and information services: II. Methodology and taxonomy. *Journal of the American Society for Information Science, 48*(7), 543-563.

Saracevic, T., Kantor, P., Chamis, A. Y., & Trivison, D. (1988). Study of information seeking and retrieving: I. Background and methodology. *Journal of the American Society for Information Science, 39*(3), 161-176.

Saracevic, T., Mokros, H., Su, L., & Spink, A. (1991). Interaction between users and intermediaries during online searching. *Proceedings of the Twelfth Annual National Online Meeting, 12*, 329-341.

Seo, Y. W., & Zhang, B. T. (2000, June). *Learning users' preferences by analyzing Web-browsing behavior.* Paper presented at the Fourth International Conference on Autonomous Agents, Barcelona, Spain.

Shen, X., Tan, B., & Zhai, C. (2005, August). *Context-sensitive information retrieval using implicit feedback.* Paper presented at the Twenty-eighth Annual International ACM SIGIR Conference on Research and Development in Information Retrieval, Brazil.

Silverstein, C., Henzinger, M., Marais, H., & Moricz, M. (1999). Analysis of a very large Web search engine query log. *SIGIR Forum, 33*(1), 6-12.

Spink, A. (2004). Multitasking information behavior and information task switching: An exploratory study. *Journal of Documentation, 60*(3), 336-345.

Spink, A., Jansen, B. J., Wolfram, D., & Saracevic, T. (2002). From E-sex to E-commerce: Web search changes. *IEEE Computer, 35*(3), 107-111.

Spink, A., & Saracevic, T. (1997). Interaction in information retrieval: Selection and effectiveness of search terms. *Journal of the American Society for Information Science, 48*(8), 741-761.

Spink, A., Wilson, T., Ellis, D., & Ford, F. (1998). Modeling Users' Successive Searches in Digital Environments study [Electronic Version]. *D-Lib Magazine.* Retrieved October 20, 2007, from http://www.dlib.org/dlib/april98/04spink.html

Sun, T. (1971). *The Art of War* (S. B. Griffith Trans.). New York: Oxford University Press. (Original work published n.d.)

Hallam-Baker, M. P. & Behlendorf, B. (n.d.). *Extended logfile format.* Retrieved October 15, 2007, from http://www.w3.org/TR/WD-logfile.html

Wang, P., Berry, M., & Yang, Y. (2003). Mining longitudinal Web queries: Trends and patterns. *Journal of the American Society for Information Science and Technology, 54*(8), 743-758.

White, R. W., Ruthven, I., & Jose, M. J. (2001, November). *Comparing implicit and explicit feedback techniques for Web retrieval: TREC-10 interactive track report.* Paper presented at the Tenth Text Retrieval Conference (TREC-10), Gaithersburg, MD.

Wilson, T. D. (1999). Models in information behaviour research. *Journal of Documentation, 55*(3), 249-270.

Yee, M. (1991). System design and cataloging meet the user: User interfaces to online public access catalogs. *Journal of the American Society for Information Science, 42*(2), 78-98.

Zipf, G. K. (1949). *Human behavior and the principle of least effort.* Cambridge, MA: Addison-Wesley Press.

KEY TERMS

Action: An action is a specific utterance of the user.

Action Object (*a*, *o*) Pair: In (*a*, *o*) pair, *a* stands for action and *o* stands for object.

Action-Object Pair Approach: One (*a*, *o*) pair is one interaction between the user and the system. A series of (*a*, *o*) pairs or *a*-*o* matrix can represent the interaction session, which is defined as a series of interactions between the user and the system to fulfill the user's certain information need.

Object: An object is a self-contained information object, the receipt of the action.

Chapter XXII
Analysis and Evaluation of the Connector Website

Paul DiPerna
The Blau Exchange Project, USA

ABSTRACT

This chapter proposes a new theoretical construct for evaluating Websites that facilitate online social networks. The suggested model considers previous academic work related to social networks and online communities. This study's main purpose is to define a new kind of social institution, called a "connector Website", and provide a means for objectively analyzing Web-based organizations that empower users to form online social networks. Several statistical approaches are used to gauge Website-level growth, trend lines, and volatility. This project sets out to determine whether or not particular connector Websites can be mechanisms for social change, and to quantify the nature of the observed social change. The author hopes this chapter introduces new applications for Web log analysis by evaluating connector Websites and their organizations.

PREMISE

In February 2000, Malcolm Gladwell published his best-selling book *The Tipping Point* to much controversy as well as popular acclaim. Gladwell's thesis, building on the work of epidemiologists and social scientists before him, stated that a social "tipping point" is characterized by: (1) the contagiousness and subsequent "stickiness" of an idea, product, or message; (2) small causes leading to big effects and social change; and (3) a resulting social change that occurs quickly and exponentially (Gladwell, 2000).

How does tipping theory work? A disease epidemic is the metaphor. According to Gladwell, social tipping happens as a viral process by which ideas, products, and messages spread and infect a population. Gladwell's "Connector" is a key human agent in social epidemics. Connectors are important because they know a lot of people, and the people they know come from diverse social networks and subcultures. Simply put, Connectors bring many people together who otherwise would have little chance to make an acquaintance. If these people casually interact by exchanging ideas, products, or messages (relying on the first factor of contagiousness and stickiness), interactions should exponentially increase across a defined population and lead to a social tipping point.

A classic social networking model put forth more than thirty years ago by Mark Granovetter explains one of the general processes driving tipping point theory. In an article published in the *American Journal of Sociology*, Granovetter explored how limited small-scale social interactions (he termed "weak ties") can lead to large-scale phenomena such as diffusion of influence and information, social mobility, community and political organization, and social cohesion (Granovetter, 1973). Weak ties tend to be low maintenance in terms of time, commitment, and energy. These relationships often provide a broad range of sources that are quick references for new information and opportunities. Gladwell's Connectors enable the weak ties between people.

INTRODUCTION

Today many millions of Americans are utilizing "connector Websites" to serve as a proxy for Gladwell's Connector. The connector Website is a proposed theoretical construct and is defined in this report. This type of Website is a new kind of social institution, and its public availability coincided with the emergence of the Internet in the mid-1990s. A connector Website has the capacity and function to provide contacts and facilitate social exchanges between people, and effectively build communities of users. It boosts timely and relevant interactions between individuals while enlarging the scale of social exchange processes, by way of online social search and social networking.

Social exchange applications (and technologies) collectively fortify the infrastructural backbone for connector Websites. To some degree, each Website allows for "social search" *and* "social networking". It is an empirical question beyond the scope of this report to parse out to what extent a Website is used specifically for one purpose or the other. In general, connectors allow users to create self-identifying profiles, while also empowering them to search for others based on needs, interests, mutual "friends", contacts, or other points of focus.

In the mid-to-late 1990s, the first connector Websites were those emphasizing social search, and more specifically, online dating (e.g. Match.com), online trading and classifieds (e.g. Craigslist), and online auctions (e.g. eBay). A second generation of connectors gained national media attention around 2002, offering more explicit social networking options for professional/career networking (e.g. LinkedIn, Ryze), and for making new friends through mutual friends or interests (e.g. Friendster, MySpace, Facebook). In 2004 industry-leading companies like Google, Yahoo!, MSN, and AOL started testing their own connector Websites to enhance their existing online communities.

The research on connector Websites is largely qualitative and restricted to social networks and online communities *within* Websites. Most researchers have focused their energies modeling the design of online communities, observing online identity formation and social interactions within one Website or a small number of Websites, and using social network analysis to measure the kinds of relationships in a community's social networks (Adamic et al., 2003; Barnes, 2006; Boyd, 2004; Boyd & Heer, 2006; Donath & Boyd, 2004; Dwyer, 2007; Garton et al., 1997; Kollock & Smith, 1999; Preece & Maloney-Krichmar, 2003; Rheingold, 1993; Rosen et al., 2003; Wellman & Gulia, 1999; Wellman & Hampton, 1999; Stutzman, 2006a; Stutzman, 2006c). In recent years, the Pew Internet & American Life Project has conducted large scale surveys offering valuable information about human behavior in online communities (Boase et al., 2006; Horrigan, 2001; Lenhart & Madden, 2007). However there is little social science research on Websites, functioning as social organizations and producing social networks and online communities.

When arguing the importance for studying institutions in economics, legendary economist Ronald Coase stated: "... it is the institutions that govern the performance of an economy, and it is this that gives the [study of institutions] its importance for economists" (Coase, 1998). Likewise, this study assumes the general importance of studying social institutions to the performance of a social system. In this chapter connector Websites are treated as institutions whose social context – development, operations, culture, and governance – have real world implications for the performance of their respective social networks and online communities, as well as the larger social system that is the Internet.

The current social science research does not take the broad view, examining tangible implications of connector Websites. This chapter's core objectives are definition, discovery, exploration, and description. The chapter examines four questions:

1. What is the connector Website model?
2. Which Websites have pioneered the connector Website model?
3. Do connector Website trends demonstrate exponential social change?
4. Do lessons of existing connector Websites have future implications?

By building on useful social theories, case studies, survey research, and the snapshot reporting of journalists, bloggers, and market analysts, the author hopes to better understand Websites whose broad implications are unknown. This study should contribute to Web log analysis methodology, assessing the impact of a connector Website in terms of its aggregate effects.

THE CONNECTOR WEBSITE MODEL

In early October 2005, at the annual Online Community Summit, enthusiasm abounded for the potential of online collaboration, social networks, and community-building. Many in attendance viewed the Internet's quickly evolving social applications as a boon for Website development. Many attendees left the conference with an optimism believing that online social networks and communities can do social good, whether through private, nonprofit, or public sector organizations. A new kind of Website had emerged allowing people to communicate, organize, and coordinate with each other in new ways.

The connector Website model is based on James Coleman's reasoning that a person making even a limited social connection will affect the status quo (Coleman, 1988). There are several essential aspects when describing a connector Website.

The following is an operational definition:

- The connector Website provides a relatively simple means of interaction for users who seek to offer or obtain goods, services, or information.
- It is an intermediary offering peer-to-peer Web applications that collectively make up an infrastructure for social exchange, networking, and diffusion processes.
- Over time, user-to-user interactions gradually generate a majority portion of the Website content, the regulation of which is governed jointly between the host organization and the online community of users.
- Depending on the surrounding social and economic conditions, as well as site design and development, the connector Website is capable of facilitating the discovery and coordination of context-based communications and transactions.

The Journal of Computer-Mediated Communication (JCMC) recently published a special thematic issue on social network Websites, and so it is important to make a distinction between the terms "connector Website" and "social network site". JCMC guest editors Danah Boyd and Nicole Ellison define a "social network site" in their insightful introduction:

We define social network sites as Web-based services that allow individuals to (1) construct a public or semi-public profile within a bounded system, (2) articulate a list of other users with whom they share a connection, and (3) view and traverse their list of connections and those made by others within the system. The nature and nomenclature of these connections may vary from site to site. (Boyd & Ellison, 2007)

Social network sites are viewed here as a subset of the connector Website universe – they are the focus for data analysis later in this chapter. Generally speaking, the definition for a social network site is structural. Implementation of a particular kind of social networking platform is necessary for a Website to be categorized as a social network site. It should "enable users to articulate and make visible their social networks" (Boyd & Ellison, 2007). The six degrees computing concept, which Friendster made popular by 2004, is the origin for publicly visible social networks on Websites.

For better or worse, the connector Website's definition is broader, containing both structural and operational elements. Connectors will have searchable profiles, including but not confined to "six degrees" social search. Other conditions require some combination of structural features such as social networking platforms, blogs, forums, RSS feeds, tags, wikis, and widgets with observable social processes such as visits, search, networking, exchange, diffusion, and governance.

A little more elaboration about connector Websites might be useful. First, interpersonal communications and transactions are relatively simple. Specifically, connectors allow users to look for others by targeting online profiles either through mutual contacts or customized search parameters. A user can also perform a search on one or more preference criteria, or keywords, specifying which qualities he or she most desires in another user. Depending on the level of detail, a person can search for others based on one category (e.g. zip code) or multiple categories (e.g. gender, career interest, favorite sports, favorite movies, likes to cook, etc.). Interactive classifieds and discussion boards are other applications that facilitate interactions. These early Website applications were rooted in social search. Several years later, a more explicit social networking application added another dimension to the connector Website.

Second, a connector Website serves as a key intermediary for its users. It serves this function by actively bridging users who act as "consumers" with those users who are "producers". In an idealized model, consumer-users create the demand for information and other goods, and the producer-users supply the timely and relevant information or goods. For example, eBay or Craigslist can easily connect a user wanting a U2 poster or a GE microwave with other users who can supply these goods. Facebook, MySpace, and Classmates.com are intermediaries for making human contacts. Connectors tend to tap into a previously underserved supply and demand market, mediating frequent and new exchanges within its online community.

Third, most connector Website content is generated by the online community. A useful metaphor is a professional conference. The connector is the host of an online "conference" that never adjourns, running twenty-four hours a day, seven days a week. The connector Website enables the introductions and establishes the structure, goals, usability, and social norms and values for the conference. However the attendees (users) significantly contribute and add value to the

Table 1. Use and time commitment for connector websites

Short Term	Medium Term	Long Term
- advice - affirmation - commerce - corroboration - elaboration - peer support - reference - research - resources - self-expression - trading	- collaboration - focus groups - interviews - mobilization - peer support - research - self-expression - working relationships	- collaboration - organization - peer support - research - self-expression - working relationships

proceedings (Website content) as time moves on. This could mean establishing new working relationships or cultivating existing ones, presenting products and personal/professional information, advancing reputation, and offering any number of other informal services.

The connector Website's content responsibilities alternate between its host organization and its group of users. Initially, right after Website launch, it is important for the Website to supply content and the "rules of the game" for the community. Online tutorials help users to learn to navigate and use the Website. The connector ideally supplies online material to spark discussions or ideas for other interactions. Managing user expectations is also critical. As connectors mature over time, a significant amount of content begins to be directly generated by the online community – examples are user profile pages, blogs, tags, wikis, forums, "real simple syndication" (RSS) feeds, ratings, reviews, classifieds, and replicable widgets. There are also connector-community interactions such as group blogs, group wikis, chat sessions, surveys, and polls. The connector may offer timely and relevant classifieds, Website links, blogs, and interviews. User interactions drive the Website's dynamics, and in the process, further build the online community.

Finally, online communities gradually become jointly self-regulating with the host organization once social norms are clear and well-established. This means the users collectively take on more responsibility for enforcing Website and community values with respect to the user-posted content. Accountability systems fueled by feedback and reputation-building technologies (providing cues like ratings and reviews) signal important information about a user and his or her content. By implementing some kind of accountability system a connector subtly structures online incentives in such a way as to guide user behavior. There is a cautionary note, however. Evidence exists of connectors applying heavy-handed top-down regulation, and as result, Websites have lost users. To some degree, connectors with some self-regulation have user leaders or mavens who volunteer to enforce the connector's norms and values. These members function like online neighborhood watchdogs.

The connector Website adds substantial value to online communities when executing two processes: discovery and coordination. Connectors make *discovery* more powerful and accurate through social search and trust-building applications. Joe Cothrel, an online community expert at Lithium Technologies, has suggested that "with these tools, a user not only finds that someone has something they need – [he or she] also finds out something about the quality of that product and the likelihood this party will deliver it" (J.

Figure 1. Connector website dimensions

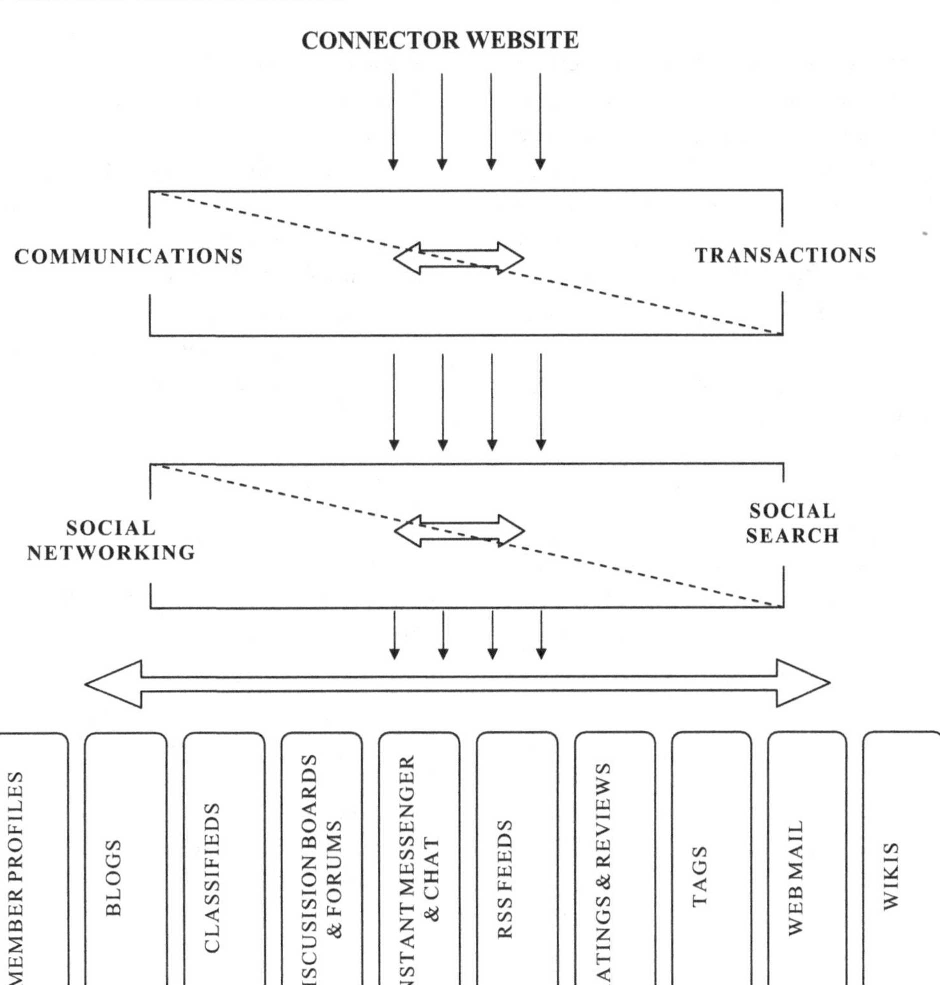

Cothrel, personal communication, 2005). In terms of *coordination*, connectors are more efficient than other online community Websites because they have the capacity to network specialized communications and transactions for users in specific situations (DiPerna, 2006; Stutzman, 2006b). Often social search and social networking applications are mixed together on connector Websites and previously have been regarded by and large as a single application.

Why is a connector Website appealing? The connector saves time and energy for people, offering effective ways to link up with others based on common needs, interests, and priorities. The model seizes on the low transaction costs of using the Internet. It also has the potential to forge weak (but important) contacts and to develop lasting relationships. The connector empowers the individual. The frequency, diversity, and informality of online social exchanges expose people to new perspectives and experiences. A diffusion process could lead to larger scale, possibly exponential social change. This study attempts to be a starting point for new research on Websites as social organizations and online social networks and communities as social systems.

Research on Connector Websites

The existing research literature on Websites – meeting this chapter's definition of a connector Website – is sparse. Generally, projects have been grounded in theoretical and formal modeling, social network analysis, or case study. University of California-Berkeley, Michigan State, and Massachusetts Institute of Technology researchers have described Website applications within connectors, namely Friendster (Boyd, 2004; Boyd, 2006; Boyd & Heer, 2006; Donath & Boyd, 2004; Boyd & Ellison, 2007). They have given an early overview of social Websites; conducted ethnographic fieldwork to describe the simultaneous evolutionary patterns of a connector's online community and its Web-based social applications; and studied the roles of online profiles and identity for communications and social networking.

The interest in examining connector Websites, particularly social network sites, has exploded in the last couple of years. Fred Stutzman (2006a; 2006c) has uncovered interesting trends with respect to Facebook registration and self-identification behavior. Nicole Ellison, Charles Steinfield, and Cliff Lampe (2007) have explored the formation and maintenance of social capital on Facebook. Larry Rosen (2006), a psychologist based at California State University-Dominguez Hills, recently studied the behavior of Los Angeles area MySpace users. In August 2006, Cornell University researchers presented a conference paper discussing the challenges of collecting and analyzing longitudinal data on online social groups and communities, specifically investigating the connector Website LiveJournal and a smaller online conference community (Backstrom et al., 2006). They used social networking analysis and formal modeling techniques to consider the ways in which communities in online social networks grow over time. In the previously mentioned special issue of JCMC, Internet researchers investigated the cultures and online behaviors exhibited on MySpace, BlackPlanet.com, Cyworld, and YouTube (Byrne, 2007; Kim & Yun, 2007; Liu, 2007; Lange, 2007). To date most studies on connectors have focused on one or two Websites at a time.

However, Eszter Hargittai (2007) offered a compelling comparative analysis when looking for systematic differences between people who use social network sites and those who do not use them. While analyzing survey data, Hargittai was able to break out distinct user characteristics for people on Facebook, MySpace, Friendster, and Xanga. This chapter later provides a comparative traffic analysis for connector Websites.

PIONEERING CONNECTOR WEBSITES

Connector Websites target both general and particular communities whose members are interested in individual expression, trading and auctioning of goods, matchmaking and dating, building social/friend networks, professional/career networking, civic organization, event planning, and other social activities. For nearly all of these Websites, word-of-mouth referrals have been an effective marketing tool. Connectors' registration numbers and business activities are sizable – they have social exchange applications that appeal to tens of millions of people, as well as investors.

First Generation Connectors

About ten years ago, connectors established an Internet presence on several fronts in social search – online auctions, classifieds, and online dating. In the first case, transactions-based connectors surfaced on the Internet in 1995. eBay (www.ebay.com), built by Pierre Omidyar and Jeff Skoll, is the alpha Website of this group. A decade old and now boasting more than a hundred million active members, the service is known to most Americans. eBay's mission is "...to provide a global trading platform where practically anyone can trade practically anything." So far it has worked to unparalleled success on the Internet. Millions of items are listed in an online auction format. A seller can upload photos and other descriptive materials for whatever he or she would like to sell. That person sets an initial bidding price and period of time for the auction. Many sellers also can set a fixed price to forego the auction process. On the other side of the transaction process, buyers either casually browse or selectively search through items for their desired consumption. Today eBay serves as an auction house and shopping mall. If ever the cliché might be appropriate, Omidyar and Skoll were able to deliver an idea whose time had come – a hyper efficient trading community guided by online social search applications and accountability mechanisms.

One of the many innovations at eBay is the way it provides information to sellers and buyers about each other. The Website relies heavily on a feedback system that builds user (buyer or seller) reputation, and as a result, installs a useful accountability system. After a transaction, the buyer and the seller are allowed to rate the person or some other entity on the other end of the transaction on a one-to-five star scale. Accumulating these ratings, good or bad, contribute to additional signals about a user's trustworthiness. This important information establishes a known value, which is important when making any transaction. People are more likely to make rational choices than irrational ones, and so they want as much information as possible about whom and what they are dealing with in order to base an economic decision to serve their interests.

Maybe one of eBay's largest social contributions is how it has helped the general Internet population to recognize new norms in social exchange. eBay is not the only Website responsible for this phenomenon, but it likely can share the credit. The Website service constructed an online system of "trust cues" about its members, and in the process, they possibly have helped establish ratings and feedback banks as Web currency. Not only did eBay install a system to valuate transaction items, but it also systemized the valuation of its community members.

Craigslist (www.craigslist.org) is a conceptual cousin of eBay, though without the nested accountability system. Craigslist uses an interactive online classifieds format rather than eBay's online auctions format – a simple online bulletin board display, which is highly functional, and is easy to use. The searchable classifieds are within a chosen city of interest (in contrast to employing a profile or keyword matching and sorting method like other social search applications). Craigslist offers an organized directory of topics, and a familiar classifieds display to enable a swift user learning curve. Users post announcements or submit responses with ease, and so the social exchanges are quick and direct. Unlike eBay, Craigslist does not use feedback or ratings mechanisms to build trust. Most transactions tend to be conducted face-to-face whether someone wants concert tickets, an apartment, jobs, or other items and services.

At about the same time eBay and Craigslist started out their paths on the Internet, online dating Websites started to gain social acceptance. Match.com (www.match.com) has been a premier online dating Website since 1995. Today the Website boasts that millions use its social search applications for dating and relationships. Match.com has been successful because it attracts highly motivated and engaged people – those who could be lonely, looking to find dates, or hoping to start a romantic relationship.

Classmates.com (www.classmates.com), also launched in 1995, served implicit social networking goals, but it technically relied on a social search application. This early connector's stated mission was (and still is) "...connecting millions of members throughout the U.S. and Canada with friends and acquaintances from school, work, and the military." Classmates.com could be considered a precursor to a later generation of connector Websites because it helped familiarize U.S. Internet users with the notion of social networking by way of the Web. Now more than 14 million different people visit Classmates.com each month (*MarketWatch*, 2006). Social search made inroads for online trading, dating, and reunion, but a few more years would go by before discrete social networking tools emerged on Websites, offering a new way for social exchange.

Second Generation Connectors: Emergence of Social Network Sites

In 2003-2004, Friendster (www.friendster.com) ushered in a new wave of connector Websites and garnered a lot of publicity. Friendster offered a novel social networking application that was partly based on dating Websites' use of searchable online profiles, as well as the six degrees email networking technology introduced in 1997 by Sixdegrees.com. Friendster allowed users to make their online friends publicly visible, as well as view and even contact friends of friends in the order of first, second, and third degrees. Friendster's rapid user growth inspired many copycat Websites. Big Internet companies, like Yahoo!, Google, and Microsoft – entered the online social network site space by 2004.

There were fascinating upsides and downsides in Friendster's early story. To its credit, Friendster had been used for purposes ranging from online dating to meeting people based on personal background, location, interests, or pre-existing friendships. On the other hand, Friendster did not have much in the way of original content, nor did it seem to have a core understanding of one or more distinguishable groups of its users. As a result, when faced with competition, the connector had to scramble to brand itself.

Friendster includes many of the features of online dating connectors, but its main appeal has been functionality. The Website offers searches for people or groups across an unlimited number of social networks or topic categories. On Friendster, contacting the friends of friends is based in part on Stanley Milgram's famous "six degrees of separation" experiment (Dodds, Muhamad, & Watts, 2003; Milgram, 1967). The process is simple and repetitive to find an "nth degree" friend. When a user starts at his or her own profile home page, this person can readily see his or her first degree friends. It is then possible to go to a first degree friend's profile and see all of that person's first degree friends, the originating user's second degree friends. The process can begin again with a second degree friend's profile in order to find third degree friends, and so on.

Friendster makes social search very easy, connecting people by particular demographics and keywords. For example, if a person wants to find others who have liked reading the *Da Vinci Code* or someone who happens to follow the Pittsburgh Steelers, Friendster is a sure bet for matching with other like-minded people based on those parameters. The Website enables a high likelihood of finding other people with a mutual interest in a short amount of time. Because of this creative mixture of social search and social networking applications, after three years of service, Friendster publicized on its Website that it had more than 20 million registered users. In an effort to broaden its appeal, Friendster began to offer blogging, classifieds, bookmark sharing, and other interactive capabilities.

Competition and internal strife switched fortunes for Friendster. After an initial splash of success, the connector Website began having a number of nagging problems. The Website earned the unwanted reputation for technical miscalculations and poor customer service. Friendster's online infrastructure was not ready for its early surging user growth rates. People complained about major lag times between making profile edits and those edits being officially posted on the Website. Another problem was Friendster's lack of brand or theme. It became a lot like a mall food court, a purely functional place that tries to offer many different things to many different people. Demographics emerged as the most defining character of the Website – urban twenty-somethings, who by and large looked for dates or competed with each other to create the largest friend network. At best, this was passive branding – Friendster did not actively target these groups of users.

Over time, Friendster's functionality did not seem enough to earn user loyalty. Many users defected to newer connector Websites like MySpace and Facebook. Competitors could provide the same social exchange applications, and to growing online communities, while also doing more to engage on themes or targeted demographics. Friendster accomplished two necessary ingredients for success – early entry into a new industry and offering a disruptive technology and innovation – but the Website to this day continues to search for competitive advantage and long term sustainability.

Over the past few years, MySpace (www.myspace.com) and some other competitors capitalized on Friendster's problems. On the surface, MySpace started out similar to Friendster – it was a connector Website primarily based on social search and social networking applications for the purpose of context-based communications. At one time the demographic of the two sites were alike, targeting teens and twenty-somethings. However MySpace went a step further than Friendster by seeking out a niche community of users by specifically focusing on music and popular entertainment interests. The Website enabled people to discover music online in the same way they find out about music in person – through friends. At an early stage, MySpace offered file downloads, direct connections to bands, testimonials and ratings, and career networking capabilities for musicians. At first a seeming benign derivative of Friendster, MySpace catapulted way ahead of its predecessor in terms of membership growth, user log time on the Website, and user satisfaction. On July 11, 2006, it was reported that MySpace dethroned Yahoo! as the most heavily visited Website on the Web.

Like MySpace, Facebook (www.facebook.com) also utilized Friendster's social networking model, but focused on a more targeted audience – college students. Mark Zuckerberg, Dustin Moskovitz, and Chris Hughes, all students at Harvard University, launched the Website in early 2004. Danah Boyd has described Facebook as a "closed" network – memberships restricted only to those people with academic email addresses and searching only locally within schools and not across schools (D. Boyd, personal communication, 2005). In just over two years, Facebook was able to claim at least 80% participation on nearly every major college campus in America.

LinkedIn (www.linkedin.com) also features social networking capabilities and uses an even more restricted network model for nurturing its online community. LinkedIn facilitates business and professional networking. The company describes its connecting protocol as "...users can be approached [only] if one of their trusted contacts forwards a contact request to them because they believe it is an opportunity their contact will appreciate." In essence LinkedIn constrains access to its members. This is quite more restrictive than MySpace, Friendster, and other more social or friends-based Websites. Reid Hoffman, founder of LinkedIn, converted a common offline social process into an online process. Both LinkedIn and Facebook have taken steps to structure their online communities keeping in mind certain needs, interests, and priorities, while establishing large and somewhat closed social networks.

To sum up this section, first and second generation connector Websites clearly set out to enable weak ties between users, first by social search, and then by phasing in social networking. Following the successes of pioneering connectors, many of the 2005 and 2006 startup connectors embedded social networking applications into their platforms. Given the premise stated earlier that a connector generally enables social processes that can lead to exponential change, we should expect these Websites to produce evidence of exponential trends. Longitudinal Website traffic data and user growth rates should be adequate measures. Little research has been conducted to systematically evaluate Website traffic to determine whether or not a Website demonstrates exponential change over time.

Can user traffic data for a connector Website offer evidence of emergent online social structures and behaviors leading to online communities? This question is explored for the remainder of this study.

DATA & METHODS

Monthly Website traffic data for thirteen connector Websites are analyzed for the following analysis. Most of these connectors are part of the highly-publicized "Web 2.0" phenomenon, a term popularized by Tim O'Reilly and the Internet trade media for peer-to-peer-oriented Websites, which emphasize interaction, collaboration, and user-generated content. A panel of comScore Media Metrix Website traffic data (U.S. only) is used for longitudinal analysis. Observations are restricted by the availability of data for comScore-selected connectors that have, to some degree, installed social networking and social search applications. Connectors also had to meet the following conditions: (1) the Website's online community generates a substantial amount of content, mostly by profiles; and (2) the Websites launched before July 2005. The observed time period spanned twenty

Table 2. Selected connector Websites

NAME	Online since*	Social Search/Networking for**
CLASSMATES.COM	Jan-1995	Maintaining School, Work, Military Connections
LIVEJOURNAL	Mar-1999	Blogging – Ratings
XANGA	Nov-1999	Blogging; Exploring/Sharing Photos
FRIENDSTER	Apr-2002	General / Pop Culture Interests
LINKEDIN	May-2003	Business Networking (in more than 130 industries)
MYSPACE	Sep-2003	General / Pop Culture Interests
HI5	Dec-2003	General / Latin America, Europe, North America, Australia
ORKUT	Jan-2004	Converting Offline Networks Into Online Networks (Google affiliate)
FACEBOOK	Feb-2004	College and High School Students
FLICKR	Mar-2004	Folksonomy/Tagging – Organizing/Sharing/Suggesting Photos and Images
TAGGED	Oct-2004	Tagging – Exploring/Sharing Photos, Videos, Bookmarks
WINDOWS LIVE SPACES	Dec-2004	Blogging, Sharing Photos
BEBO	Jan-2005	United Kingdom – Teens – Schools, Colleges, and Music Interests

** Information obtained by following this sequence of sourcing: direct email with Website's media relations; on the website itself; doing a Google search using "[website name] launched" and then verifying across multiple sources.*

*** Information inferred from the website's main webpage, "About Us" webpage, and (if applicable) Wikipedia entry.*

nine months, May 2005 through September 2007. The unit of analysis is the connector Website, and the key dependent variable is "Monthly Unique Visitors" – estimated counts of individual users who view a Website in a particular month.

This study is an exercise in Web log analysis. Admittedly, monthly unique visitors could be one of the most basic pieces of data for doing such work. However it is possible to glean insightful findings from even the most basic type of measurement, especially when a given body of research for these new Websites is so young. The data also allow for interesting derivative measures for extending analysis and understanding.

Do connector Websites offer evidence of exponential social change over time? This is the key empirical question for this chapter. This study considers month-to-month traffic changes as a snapshot of social change for a given Website's online community. The comScore Website traffic data lead to traffic trend estimations for each of the thirteen connector Websites. At the end of this section, a judgment is made on whether or not a given connector demonstrated exponential change in the time period May 2005 through September 2007. The determination is based on the following observations:

1. Percentage change over the time period, May 2005 to September 2007
2. Traffic trend estimation with respect to an exponential function;
3. Website volatility
4. Website age and maturity

A couple of cautions and limitations should be mentioned at this point. The following Web log analysis is exploratory and descriptive - causality cannot be asserted using the methods employed here. The study is unable to distinguish between the characteristics attributed to the host organization from those of the online community of users. The Website organization and the online community are a single symbiotic entity and viewed as a type of social institution. This analysis is strongly suggestive, but not conclusive, since there is a relatively small number of connector Websites contained in the dataset. In any case it should be possible to learn more about longitudinal trends on thirteen popular connector Websites and see if traffic trends have implications for social change.

COMSCORE MEDIA METRIX ANALYSIS

Table 3 lists the connector Websites in rank order of monthly unique visitors (hereafter, traffic)

Table 3. Monthly unique visitors on connector Websites. SEPTEMBER 2007*

CONNECTOR WEBSITE	No. Unique Visitors (000)
MYSPACE	68,449
FACEBOOK	30,601
FLICKR	13,150
CLASSMATES.COM	13,084
WINDOWS LIVE SPACES	9,763
BEBO	4,389
LIVEJOURNAL	4,185
XANGA	3,123
HI5	2,833
LINKEDIN	2,386
TAGGED	1,741
FRIENDSTER	1,645
ORKUT	503
U.S Internet Usage	181,858

** Data provided by comScore Media Metrix: http://www.comscore.com*

in September 2007. MySpace clearly separates itself from the pack, having more than twice the number of users when compared to Facebook, its nearest competing connector in this sample. More than 1 out of 3 American Internet users visited MySpace in the last observed month. Facebook claims roughly 17% of U.S. Internet users. Flickr and Classmates.com attract about 7%. Moving down the table, the connectors from Windows Live Spaces to LinkedIn attract between 5% and 1% of the U.S. Internet usage market. Tagged, Friendster, and Orkut are beneath the 1% threshold.

In Table 4 some connector Websites illustrate large total growth and impressive average monthly growth rates. Eight Websites at least doubled their monthly traffic over the course of twenty nine months. Flickr and LinkedIn are standout examples. Flickr increased its traffic more than thirteen times its baseline. LinkedIn shot up more than eleven times. Interestingly, affinity social network site rivals MySpace and Facebook demonstrated identical growth rates (339.4%) over the observed time period. Four connectors lost users during the time period, three of them (Classmates.com, Xanga, and LiveJournal) are the oldest in the sample. Both of these connectors also maintained an average monthly traffic growth rate above 10%.

At this point, the study models each of the connector Website trends with respect to an exponential function, using the equation: $y = ae^{bx}$. In the equation x is the value of the independent

Table 4. Which are the fastest growing connector websites? MAY 2005 to SEPTEMBER 2007*

WEBSITE	Total Period % Traffic Change	Average Monthly % Traffic Change
FLICKR	1,324.0 %	11.2 %
LINKEDIN	1,116.9 %	12.9 %
ORKUT	343.3 %	8.7 %
FACEBOOK	339.4 %	6.0 %
MYSPACE	339.4 %	5.6 %
TAGGED	282.2 %	7.4 %
WINDOWS LIVE SPACES	211.0 %	4.6 %
BEBO	118.0 %	4.8 %
FRIENDSTER	29.6 %	2.2 %
HI5	-4.3 %	2.0 %
CLASSMATES.COM	-22.9 %	-0.1 %
LIVEJOURNAL	-43.4 %	-1.4 %
XANGA	-62.8 %	-2.3 %
U.S. Internet Usage	9.9 %	0.3 %

** Raw data provided by comScore Media Metrix: http://www.comscore.com*

variable (month), and *y* is the value of the dependent variable (monthly unique visitors). The value *e* (approximately 2.7182) is the base of natural logarithms. A statistical program calculates the values of *a* and *b* that best fit the connector's data. If the observed data points closely correlate to the newly generated exponential curve, then this pattern (illustrated by a high R^2 value) indicates that exponential growth does a good job of explaining a connector Website's trend during the time period.

Table 5 summarizes the trends and the exponential function tests. Appendix B lays out the trend graphs for the connector Websites in the sample. To err on the side of caution, $R^2 \geq .8$ to be a "strong" fit; $.5 \leq R^2 < .8$ to be "moderate" fit; and $0 \geq R^2 < .5$ to be a "weak" fit. Six of the trends correlate nicely with its exponential model, indicating strong fit. Two of them – Flickr and LinkedIn – displayed staggering growth over twenty nine months. Orkut, Facebook, and MySpace all more than tripled, but also importantly, showed modest downturns like the other two higher growth Websites. Xanga is the only Website indicating what seems to be very serious decline. Tagged, Windows Live Spaces, and Bebo also demonstrated solid growth spurts in this period, but the fluctuating rhythms of their trends likely hurt the correlation to their respective exponential models. As a result, these three

Table 5. Does the connector Website demonstrate exponential change?

	Based on trend estimation, did the connector website demonstrate exponential change over the observed time period? (Y/N)		
WEBSITE	**MAY-05 to SEPT-07 % Traffic Change**	**Goodness of Fit Exponential Function (R^2)**	**Final Estimation**
FLICKR	1,324.0 %	0.9208 = STRONG	Y
LINKEDIN	1,116.9 %	0.9219 = STRONG	Y
ORKUT	343.3 %	0.8818 = STRONG	Y
FACEBOOK	339.4 %	0.9468 = STRONG	Y
MYSPACE	339.4 %	0.8794 = STRONG	Y
TAGGED	282.2 %	0.6013 = MODERATE	N
WINDOWS LIVE SPACES	211.0 %	0.5596 = MODERATE	N
BEBO	118.0 %	0.7635 = MODERATE	N
FRIENDSTER	29.6 %	0.1384 = WEAK	N
HI5	-4.3 %	0.1792 = WEAK	N
CLASSMATES.COM	-22.9 %	0.3845 = WEAK	N
LIVEJOURNAL	-43.4 %	0.3493 = WEAK	N
XANGA	-62.8 %	0.8289 = STRONG	Y

connectors fall within the "moderate" category. The other Websites did not show a dramatic percentage growth nor did they fit particularly well with their exponential models. Seven connector Websites do not pass this empirical test.

Traffic Volatility

Trend volatility might explain in part why Tagged misses the cut, and why MySpace, Facebook, and Orkut (showing only slightly greater relative growth) fit their exponential models. Table 6 lists the connector Websites in ascending order, from least to most volatile. Volatility is defined here simply as the variance of a Website's "monthly percentage change" over the twenty nine month time period. We see LinkedIn and Orkut are at the bottom of the list, having the steepest upturns and downturns on their respective month-to-month rates of change. It is not clear how volatility affects connector Websites. Orkut and LinkedIn, still relatively small in total users and achieving among the highest growth rates, exhibit the most trend volatility. On the other hand MySpace and Facebook, the two most populated connectors, have relatively moderate growth rates and are low volatility. It's interesting that LiveJournal, the poorest performing connector, also sits at the top of the table with a low volatility score. It may be that volatility is the wild ride host organizations need to experience before reaching some stabilizing threshold of monthly traffic.

In terms of growth and numbers, volatility might be a necessary condition to become a successful connector Website. High to moderate volatility could be a characteristic at start-up and while a Website escalates operations and activities. Though volatility is probably viewed as a liability after some kind of scale has presumably been reached, either in terms of community-building or organizational capacity. Following this line of thought, low to moderate volatility is probably a characteristic of the most highly visited Websites where they should have earned some level of core online community and user loyalty. Admittedly, this is mostly speculation. There is a solid pathway for future research beyond the range of this study.

Website Age and Maturity

The age of the connector Website appears associated with traffic growth differences. There is a moderate negative association (r=-.38) between a Website's age (in months) and its percentage growth over the time period – meaning that older age may bring slower growth. This is not a big surprise. It is quite possible the older Websites boomed at an earlier time before the observed time period. A maturation period may be a characteristic for these Websites as they approach long term sustainability. It is also interesting to note that there is a moderate negative association (r=-.32) between a Website's age and its volatility across the time period – meaning that older sites may experience less severe shifts in monthly rates of change. It is intuitive to think that a connector's host organization would eventually get past some of the early bumps and bruises that come as a start-up entity, leading to less severe traffic swings.

DISCUSSION & IMPLICATIONS

One basic finding stands out. Connector Websites experience exponential changes in Website traffic over time. At least five out of the thirteen connectors showed rapid growth, and one other displayed substantial shrinkage. So six connectors have produced rather unexpected social epidemics in terms of huge gains (or loss) in user traffic.

As a side note, it would seem impossible to sustain the kind of Flickr or LinkedIn traffic growth in the long-term. Take Flickr as an example. The site is approximately 43 months old. Hypothetically, if the Website kept escalating at the current pace of about 500% per year, it would approach

Table 6. How volatile are the connector websites in the sample? MAY 2005 to SEPTEMBER 2007

LESS VOLATILE → MORE VOLATILE

WEBSITE	Volatility*
MYSPACE	.0039
WINDOWS LIVE SPACES	.0115
LIVEJOURNAL	.0116
FACEBOOK	.0124
CLASSMATES.COM	.0177
FRIENDSTER	.0247
XANGA	.0267
FLICKR	.0308
BEBO	.0440
HI5	.0531
TAGGED	.0641
ORKUT	.0657
LINKEDIN	.0872
U.S. Internet Usage	.0001

**Volatility defined here as the variance of "monthly percentage change" for a website over the twenty nine month time period.*

1.6 billion unique monthly users in September 2010 – that would be nearly 1 out of 5 people on the planet! Eventually growth has to decelerate. Therefore it seems to be important for any connector Website's host organization to forecast its market (or online community scale) at the early stages of the connector's operations. Over time, sustaining a level relative to the forecasted scale might be more prudent than seeking constant rapid growth. This is not to understate the difficulty of making such projections and calculations. Quite the contrary, for a general service like Flickr (i.e. photo sharing), forecasting for scale will likely be difficult.

Why does it look like some connector Websites illustrate exponential change, and others do not? The average age of the connectors that exhibit positive exponential growth is approximately 47 months. Based on their large online constituencies and relative "maturity", it is a reasonable guess that Classsmates.com, LiveJournal, and Xanga (all three launched before 2000) may have shown sizable growth long before the time period in this analysis. There is anecdotal evidence that Friendster hit hyper growth in 2003-2004. It would be interesting to test whether or not there is a clear maturation process for these Websites and their host organizations. The moderate correlations presented in the preceding analysis give suggestive evidence on the importance of time and age with respect to exponential trends.

What do the Lessons of Existing Connector Websites Imply for Future Startups?

Connector Websites have to contend with a number of issues. First, personal security and fraud are serious issues. A host organization's need to maintain reliability and trust with its online community, and any direct or perceived breach can be death to the community. Connectors are virtual open markets for social exchanges of information or other goods and services, and they largely rely on self-policing and reporting of Website abuses. Not long ago Friendster was notorious for its users creating fictional profiles and even defamatory profiles, also known as "fakesters". Fortunately new Web services are becoming available to enable connectors to conduct verifications for online profiles as a means to prevent fakesters, harassers, and underage users.

A lot of connectors ask for photos to go with online profiles, and sometimes these photos are quite explicit. Match.com has a fairly strict screening process that mandates a waiting period before photos are posted. Employees scrutinize submitted photos as a means of quality control. So the problem is resolvable, albeit likely requiring more labor and cost. For some connectors, photos may not be necessary for facilitating interactions among users. The creation of an avatar is a good example of side-stepping the pitfalls of providing profile photos. Users create an animated image to build a virtual self-portrait. A connector called Stardoll uses avatars for its online community of seven-to-seventeen year-olds, where the members can dress and change the outfits of their personal online doll. Inappropriate and misrepresenting images are largely eliminated. In the case of consumer fraud, eBay is trying to prevent fake listings of expensive consumer goods like plasma televisions and mountain bikes. Sustainable connectors actively address privacy and security dangers, and they are committed to quality control.

A mostly self-regulating online community is the desired means for enforcing Website rules and norms. However, online vigilantism is an unintended consequence for such bottom-up enforcement of the community's norms and values. eBay has been struggling with this issue over the past few years. eBay users have taken accountability measures into their own hands mainly by alerting buyers that a listing is fake. eBay encourages reporting fake listings to the company, but they do not approve of user-to-user alerts or self-styled sting operations. These actions may undermine eBay's accountability system, which is the primary signal for a given user's reputation and trustworthiness. The lesson here is that extreme regulation, bottom-up or top-down, is unhealthy for a connector's long term development. Online security violations and fraud take many forms, but there is no doubt that quality control of user-generated content will be a major concern for connectors. As time passes, it is conceivable that host organizations adapt by encouraging online community rules, norms, and self-regulation, contributing to the maturation period suggested in the study's analysis.

Second, a key challenge for connector Websites is to attract a great quantity of users that provide an expansive range of perspectives and experiences. Otherwise the utility of the connector diminishes. For example, if someone is an elementary school principal looking for information in order to adopt a new reading program, it would be most valuable if there are many reading specialists, many textbook salespeople, and many principals who at the least can serve as points of reference. In order to assure the registration of new members, it would seem beneficial to commit to strategic marketing during the initial stages of Web development – especially if the connector specializes its networking purpose and organizing themes.

There can be a downside to ambitiously seeking out as many new users as quickly as possible, and the allure of exponential network growth rates is tempered by some recent experiences. Friendster shows how good fortunes can quickly reverse. With its "six degrees of separation" networking technology, Friendster became more popular literally by the week, but technical problems multiplied as the Website could not keep up with its growing community of users. Writing in *The New York Times*, Gary Rivlin quoted a former Friendster employee saying:

The service was growing faster than we could keep up with, so we spent all this time making sure the service was stable... A lot of people were frustrated because we weren't rolling out a lot of features but instead working on infrastructure. (Rivlin, 2005)

Another risk for connectors is overestimating and over-reliance of the viral / word-of-mouth marketing approach. Certainly there are plenty of examples of viral messaging by way of connectors, but they are exceptions to what is believed to be the rule for existing connectors. Pursuing a viral strategy is a fascinating social experiment, but it is likely a long-term liability for the host organization. Sites can cede too much of the online community's development and management to the discretion and rationale of its users. Orkut is an interesting case in point, having a significant proportion of its user base located in South America. Orkut launched in early 2004 as a challenger to Friendster and MySpace, and it is doubtful that this Google service initially aimed to have the bulk of its online community building take place in South America. The viral marketing approach may be effective for exponential growth over a time period, but it can lead to greater long term concerns for Website control, development, management, and direction.

Third, newly launched connectors should seriously consider their scale and benchmarks for sustainable growth. Otherwise, as shown by Friendster, a lack of preparedness may cause a customer service meltdown and threaten the Website's survival. At the outset of Website development, it is useful to understand the planned online community's needs, interests, and priorities as best as possible. Within these parameters, stable connectors prepare and develop the Website according to a community scale, hoping to serve the projected maximum number of users for that online community. Connectors ought to plan for exponential growth rates, but also plan for deceleration of traffic growth and effectively manage user (and investor) expectations.

Fourth, a connector needs to establish a recognizable brand, or else it will likely face fickle users. Three types of branding come to mind for these Websites, either in terms of the online community's social context (i.e. needs, interests, priorities), in terms of community demographics (i.e. age, gender, race, ethnicity, location), or timing of the Websites launch and entry into targeted market(s). Connectors like Classmates.com (alumni connections), Match.com (online dating), and LinkedIn (professional networking) explicitly focus on the social context of users. A social network site like Facebook (teens/college) brands itself based on demographics. Sites like eBay and Craigslist have probably benefited a great deal by the timing of their launches, as well as how long they have remained relatively unchallenged by significant competitors.

Connectors that do not plan for branding can be criticized for taking the "if you build it, they will come" approach. Friendster seems to be one such example that has not clearly defined a brand. The novel applications of social networking, blogging, or tagging, may not be good enough in the long term to draw new users and to be sticky for bringing back users for repeat visits. These Websites risk being perceived as overly superficial and faddish, lacking substantive understanding of its community of users.

This may be so, but what about some of the general connectors identified in this report's data analysis that showed rapid growth? For example, it is possible that Flickr will establish itself as *the* photo sharing and networking service on the Internet. Like eBay and Craigslist, Flickr entered early in the photo-sharing genre, has had few competitors, and built a sizable online community very quickly. The barriers to market entry are probably considerable for competitors. However, the same could have been said for Friendster. It will be interesting to see whether or not Flickr fortified market barriers that are higher than what Friendster had built at its peak before the emergence of MySpace and Facebook. Other connectors like Orkut, Tagged, and Windows Live Spaces do not appear to neatly fit into any of the three branding categories. Though all three have had tremendous growth since 2005, their sustainability in the long term may be shakier than connectors with recognizable brands.

Fifth, reputation-building mechanisms and accountability systems likely contribute to traffic growth. A connector's legitimacy and value depend on how well its feedback systems satisfy user expectations. Feedback takes many forms, ranging from discrete to subtle signals. Ratings and rankings on connectors like eBay, Facebook, and MySpace give explicit cues about other community members. In effect, these social metric systems quantify reputation, and more specifically social capital. James Coleman, a very influential sociologist in the late twentieth century, suggested social capital as "... relations among persons that facilitate action... it exists in the relations among persons." Ratings and rankings, in particular, quantify social capital. They give clear cues, representing a given set of relations between two users. They are observable on a connector Website, and as a consequence, influence the actions of other users.

For example, a user with a 4.8 rating on a 5.0 scale will be viewed as trustworthy and reliable, but someone scoring at 2.2 much less so. Within the social structure consisting of the Website and its community, users have a higher incentive to seek out User 4.8 rather than User 2.2 for online communications or transactions. User 4.8's social capital is actually visible and comes across as more attractive to others.

There are qualitative means for gauging trust and reputation on connector Websites. Reviews (also called testimonials, bulletins, and recommendations) exist on connectors such as Facebook, Friendster, MySpace, and Tribe.net. This user-generated text is an explicit cue. More subtle signals are found on a given user's profile page, such as the appearance of the profile page; disclosed frequency of a user's online activity; quantity and quality of listed friends/contacts; response quality in the profile's categories; and user postings or comments to message boards. Such information can signal personal characteristics in much the same way we get impressions from email. Patricia Wallace has discussed the impressionistic tendencies that people exhibit online (Wallace, 1999). She explains that given a fixed amount of online information (what could be on a connector profile page), people have the tendency to try to maximize their "impression formation shortcuts" – exerting the least possible amount of energy and work, people will try to learn as much information as possible about others who are online.

It seems reasonable that a connector Website's online community would like both explicit and implicit user cues to be as valid and reliable as possible. If this occurs, trust should develop between users, and between the community and the Website. If there is little validity and reliability in these cues, user flight to a competing connector should likely occur over time. Well-constructed accountability mechanisms probably temper trend volatility and add to a Website's stickiness.

Although connectors have had a measurable impact in a variety of social areas (commerce and trading; dating; teenage and collegiate socializing; professional networking), in the future the model will likely be used for more specific interests and topics in which people are regularly engaged or for people in life transition phases. Themes could organize around occupations, education, healthcare, parenting, religious or spiritual living, volunteering, politics, hobbies, and residence. In fact, connectors that launched in late 2005 and 2006 appeared to follow this path toward differentiation.

Table 7 displays some emerging norms among current connector Websites, summarizing the main ideas in this section. Thoughtful business practice underscores most of these strategies. Connectors add value when identifying communities that either have been underserved in some way or unrecognized by conventional (i.e. offline) commercial, government, or nonprofit institutions.

CONCLUSION

A new application for Web log analysis is presented in this chapter, and it clearly shows that connector Websites matter a great deal to Americans. This is evident when observing connectors' monthly traffic trends and correlating their actual trends with an exponential model. They demonstrate dramatic traffic change over time. Millions of people actively use these Websites as intermediaries to find people, information, services, or other goods.

The numbers of people using connectors continue to swell. Each of at least five (almost six) connectors more than tripled user traffic growth from May 2005 to September 2007. Standout examples are Flickr (1,324 %) and LinkedIn (1,117 %). Five connectors – Flickr, LinkedIn, Orkut, Facebook, and MySpace – showed exponential growth over the time period. Xanga and LiveJournal were the only connectors to substantially lose users. Volatility clearly exists as a characteristic of connectors, but counter-intuitively, it may be a good thing for exponential growth. More research is needed to understand this characteristic, and what it means for connector Websites. It is somewhat speculative here, but connector Websites and their online communities may need time to mature for attaining sustainability in terms of traffic trends. Young connector Websites may want to learn from the coming-of-age experiences of first and second generation connectors.

The evidence here is not conclusive, but the Web log analysis does suggest it would be a mistake to overlook the social implications of connector Websites. Recent developing stories point to future areas for possible research and further examination:

Table 7.

Emerging Norms for Connector Websites
• Understand community in terms of needs, interests, and priorities.
• Plan early for community scale.
• Clearly set rules of the game to cultivate website norms and values.
• Manage user expectations.
• Institute accountability systems and trust-building mechanisms.
• Structure online incentives to support the website's norms and values.
• Encourage community self-regulation.
• Develop infrastructure and capacity as quickly as possible.
• Make the website sticky.
• Create simple and functional webpages. Optimize user-interface.
• Mix content: Content is created by the host, individual users, and host-user collaborations. Features may include user profiles, blogs, wikis, discussion boards, ratings, reviews, rankings, tags, bookmarks, classifieds, chat, interviews, surveys, polls, and web widgets.
• Keep pace with fast changing website technologies.
• Commit to marketing by word-of-mouth referrals, partnerships, and advertisements.
• Synchronize online activities with offline activities.
• Establish a brand as quickly as possible.

1. **Social Values and Tradeoffs:** Connector Websites offer convenience of choice, reliability of personal judgment, efficiency of communications and transactions, and the potential for tapping into others' experiences and resources. What is the downside to these expanded freedoms? Issues of personal privacy and security have hit the headlines in 2006. Stories grow about pedophiles stalking on teen connector Websites like MySpace ready to prey on vulnerable or overly trusting young girls and boys. A public reaction was inevitable. The U.S. House Committee on Energy and Commerce Subcommittee on Oversight and Investigation held several hearings from June 21-28, 2006, which included testimony from the Federal Trade Commissioner, federal and state law enforcement officials, and executives from Facebook, MySpace, Xanga, Google, Yahoo!, Microsoft, and market research organizations. Major concerns aired about the confidentiality of members' personal data and how Websites monitor and enforce safety, rules, online community best practices, and adherence to the Children's Online Privacy Protection Act (COPPA). The Federal Trade Commission now has a "Facts for Consumers" bulletin for parents posted on the agency Website. It is unclear which direction public policy will turn at this point, but it is possible state and federal government officials may seek to directly regulate connector Websites.
2. **Differentiation and Specialization:** As connector Websites evolve, they appear to be differentiating with respect to their organizational missions and focusing branding efforts on users' needs, interests, and priorities. This started to happen in 2006. A sampling of new connector themes and organizing topics are related to: political campaigns and elections; religious expression and sharing; car and truck enthusiasts; female professionals; family-based networks; pet ownership; the World Cup; mental health issues; youth social initiatives; wedding preparations and references; and world travel. Many of these connectors will never approach the size of an eBay, MySpace or Match.com. However they are likely establishing a core competency and competitive advantage based on substance, and not relying solely on the novelty of their social networking application, or the timing of their Website launch. Increased specialization should continue in the future, and the community scale of connector Websites on average will probably shrink as the overall sector matures.

Connector Websites continue to adapt to the prevailing social and economic circumstances of the day. They have been at the forefront of the so-called Web 2.0 online expansion era. In terms of participation numbers, Website traffic trends, and unorthodox business practices and strategies, connector Websites are a timely topic.

The overarching goal here has been to bridge the somewhat disconnected information pools and audiences coming out of academia, the mainstream news media, bloggers, and the Internet industry's insiders and analysts. Other objectives included: (1) Propose and define the connector Website as a new type of social institution and intermediary; (2) Describe how the connector Website model is playing out in the real world; (3) Apply an institutional approach to analyze the behavior of connector Websites and their online communities; (4) Determine whether or not connector Websites have demonstrated exponential change over time; and (5) Suggest the implications of existing connector Websites, pointing to future trends and possible areas for research. The use of Web log analysis in this study should enable us to better evaluate connector Websites as they evolve in the future.

ACKNOWLEDGMENT

I would like to thank the following people for helpful discussions, reviews, and suggestions over the past two years: Joe Carney, Jim Cashel, Joe Cothrel, Sunil Dasgupta, Jim DiPerna, Matt Dull, Katie Field-Mateer, Patrick Gavin, Joe Geraghty, Daniel Harrison, Jim Harvey, Eszter Hargittai, Jim Jansen, Ben Klemens, Katharine Kravetz, Andrew Lee, Amanda Lenhart, Kate Mazukelli, Sarah-Kay McDonald, Anjetta McQueen, Elana Mintz, Alan Murphy, Erin Murphy, Jason Palmer, Jonathan Rauch, Stephen Rose, Judy Smith-Davis, Fred Stutzman, Russell Wheeler, Dave Witzel, Danny Yagan, and participants at the 2005 Online Community Summit in Sonoma, CA. Their unique perspectives and experiences have been invaluable resources for writing this report.

A big thank you to Andrew Lipsman and comScore Media Metrix for providing me with the website traffic data used in my analysis. comScore Media Metrix is a leading website tracking organization that is based in Reston, Virginia.

Finally, words cannot express how grateful I am to my wife Christy for her support, honesty, and comments throughout this entire research project.

REFERENCES

Adamic, L. A., Buyukkokten, O., & Adar, E. (2003). A social network caught in the Web. *First Monday*, *8*(6).

Backstrom, L., Huttenlocher, D., Kleinberg, J., & Lan, X. (2006). Group formation in large social networks: Membership, growth, and evolution. *Proceedings from the Annual International Conference on Knowledge Discovery and Data Mining (Association for Computing Machinery KDD).* Philadelphia, Pennsylvania.

Barnes, S. (2006). A privacy paradox: Social networking in the United States. *First Monday,* 11(9).

Boase, J., Horrigan, J., Wellman, B., & Rainie, L. (2006). *The strength of Internet ties.* Washington, DC: Pew Internet & American Life Project.

Boyd, D. (2004). Friendster and publicly articulated social networks. *Proceedings of ACM Conference on Human Factors in Computing Systems*, New York: ACM Press, 1279-1282.

Boyd, D. (2006). Friends, Friendsters, and MySpace Top 8: Writing community into being on social network sites. *First Monday,* 11(12).

Boyd, D., & Heer, J. (2006). Profiles as conversation: Networked identity performance on Friendster. *Proceedings of Thirty-Ninth Hawai'i International Conference on System Sciences.* Los Alamitos, CA: IEEE Press.

Boyd, D., & Ellison, N. (2007). Social network sites: Definition, history, and scholarship. *Journal of Computer-Mediated Communication*, 13(1), article 11.

Byrne, D. N. (2007). Public discourse, community concerns, and civic engagement: Exploring black social networking traditions on BlackPlanet.com. *Journal of Computer-Mediated Communication*, 13(1), article 16.

Coase, R. (1998). The new institutional economics. *The American Economic Review*, 88(2), 72-74.

Coleman, J. S. (1988). Social capital in the creation of human capital. *American Journal of Sociology: Supplement: Organizations and Institutions: Sociological and Economic Approaches to the Analysis of Social Structure,* 94, S100-S101.

Coleman, J. S. (1990). *Foundations of social theory.* Cambridge: Harvard University Press, 300-316.

DiPerna, P. (2006). K-12 encounters the Internet. *First Monday*, 11(5).

Dodds, P., Muhamad, R., & Watts, D. (2003). An experimental study of search in global social networks. *Science*, 301, 827-829.

Donath, J., & Boyd, D. (2004). Public displays of connection. *BT Technology Journal, 22*(4), 71-82.

Dwyer, C. (2007). Digital relationships in the 'MySpace' generation: Results from a qualitative study. *40th Hawaii International Conference on System Sciences (HICSS).* Waikoloa, HI.

Ellison, N., Steinfield, C., & Lampe, C. (2007). The benefits of Facebook "friends": Exploring the relationship between college students' use of online social networks and social capital. *Journal of Computer-Mediated Communication,* 12(3), article 1.

Garton, L., Haythornwaite, C., & Wellman, B. (1997). Studying online social networks. *Journal of Computer Mediated Communications, 3*(1).

Gladwell, M. (2000). *The tipping point.* New York: Little, Brown, & Company.

Granovetter, M. (1973). The strength of weak ties. *American Journal of Sociology*, 78(6), 1360-1380.

Hargittai, E. (2007). Whose space? Differences among users and non-users of social network sites. *Journal of Computer-Mediated Communication*, 13(1), article 14.

Horrigan, J. (2001). *Online communities: Networks that nurture long distance relationships and local ties.* Washington, DC: Pew Internet & American Life Project.

Kim, K.-H., & Yun, H. (2007). Cying for me, Cying for us: Relational dialectics in a Korean social network site. *Journal of Computer-Mediated Communication*, 15(1), article 11.

Kollock, P., & Smith, M. A. (1999). Communities in cyberspace. In P. Kollock & M. A. Smith (Eds.), *Communities in cyberspace* (3-28). New York: Routledge.

Lange, P. G. (2007). Publicly private and privately public: Social networking on YouTube. *Journal of Computer-Mediated Communication*, 13(1), article 18.

Lenhart, A., & Madden, M. (2007). *Teens, privacy & online social networks.* Washington, DC: Pew Internet & American Life Project.

Liu, H. (2007). Social network profiles as taste performances. *Journal of Computer-Mediated Communication*, 13(1), article 13.

MarketWatch. (2006, June 15). Social networking sites continue to attract record numbers as MySpace.com surpasses 50 million U.S. visitors in May. *MarketWatch.*

Milgram, S. (1967). The small world problem. *Psychology Today*, 1, 60-67.

Pew Internet & American Life Project. (2005). *Internet: The mainstreaming of online life: Trends 2005.* Washington, DC: Pew Internet & American Life Project.

Preece, J., & Maloney-Krichmar, D. (2003). Online communities. In J. Jacko & A. Sears (Eds.), *Handbook of Human-Computer Interaction* (596-620). Mahwah, NJ: Lawrence Erlbaum Associates Inc. Publishers.

Preece, J., & Maloney-Krichmar, D. (2005). Online communities: Design, theory, and practice. *Journal of Computer-Mediated Communication,* 10(4), article 1.

Rheingold, H. (1993). *The virtual community: Homesteading on the electronic frontier.* Reading, MA: Addison-Wesley.

Rivlin, G. (2005, January 24). Users lose the thrill of 'social networking'. *The New York Times*, p. C1.

Rosen, D., Woelfel, J., Krikorian, D., & Barnett, G. A. (2003). Procedures for analyses of online communities. *Journal of Computer-Mediated Communication*, 8(4).

Stutzman, F. (2006a). An evaluation of identity-sharing behavior in social network communities. *iDMAa Journal*, 3(1).

Stutzman, F. (2006b). Situational relevance in social networking Websites. Retrieved January 12, 2006, from http://chimprawk.blogspot.com/2006/01/situational-relevance-in-social.html

Stutzman, F. (2006c). Student life on Facebook. (Ph.D. working paper, University of North Carolina, 2006).

Wallace, P. (1999). *The psychology of the Internet*. Cambridge: Cambridge University Press, 14-37.

Wellman, B., & Gulia, M. (1999). Net surfers don't ride alone: Virtual communities as communities. In P. Kollock & M. A. Smith (Eds.), *Communities in cyberspace* (167-194). New York: Routledge.

Wellman, B., & Hampton, K. (1999). Living networked on and offline. *Contemporary Sociology, 28*(6), 648-654.

KEY TERMS[1]

Blog: Shorthand for Weblog. A frequent and chronological publication of comments and thoughts on the Internet. It is a journal that may be instantly published to a host Web site.

Chat: Also known as instant messaging. Allows people to communicate online by broadcasting messages to people in real time, often as one-on-one channel, but also in a group forum sometimes called a chat room.

Connector Website: A Website providing a relatively simple means of interaction for users who seek to offer or obtain goods, services, or information. It is an intermediary offering peer-to-peer Web applications that collectively make up an infrastructure for social exchange, networking, and diffusion processes. Over time, user-to-user interactions gradually generate a majority portion of the Website content and the regulation of which is governed jointly between the host organization and the online community of users. Depending on the surrounding social and economic conditions, as well as site design and development, the connector Website should excel in facilitating the discovery and coordination of context-based communications and transactions.

Discussion Board: Also known as forum, message board, and bulletin board. For the purpose of exchanging information only. A Website location where users may post text communication for one another. Not sensitive to time constraints or structures.

Feedback: Website "currency" that builds or detracts reputation for users or specific content. Within a Website's feedback system, for example, a user may give positive or negative point(s) to another user or that user's posted content based on some interaction.

Folksonomy: A word combining "folk" and "taxonomy," meaning the "people's classification management". Refers to the collaborative but unsophisticated way in which information is being categorized on the Web. Instead of using a centralized form of classification, users are encouraged to assign freely chosen keywords (called tags) to pieces of information or data, a process known as tagging.

Instant Messenger: An online service that alerts users when friends or colleagues are online and allows them to communicate with each other in real time on a private online chat window.

Online Community: Also known as virtual community. A group of people communicating or interacting with each other by means of information technologies, typically the Internet, rather than face to face. Online communities can be used loosely for a variety of social groups interacting via the Internet. The concept does not necessarily mean that there is a strong bond among the members. The term *virtual community* is attributed to the book of the same title by Howard Rheingold in 1993.

Rating: Net feedback; an indicator of reputation on a particular Website.

Review: Also known as testimonial, bulletin, and wall. A structured discussion board that allows users to submit critical text about an idea, user, product, or message. Often supplements ratings. See Amazon.com.

RSS Feed: Shorthand for Real Simple Syndication. A family of XML file formats for Web syndication used by news Websites and blogs.

Social Networking: A term describing an online process. It is a Website technology that allows users to search, identify, and communicate with other people as contacts, fitting closest to their specified preferences and criteria.

Social Network Site: Web-based services that allow individuals to (1) construct a public or semi-public profile within a bounded system, (2) articulate a list of other users with whom they share a connection, and (3) view and traverse their list of connections and those made by others within the system. The nature and nomenclature of these connections may vary from site to site (Boyd & Ellison, 2007).

Stickiness: A popular term for marketing a message. Short-term stickiness describes a Website's ability to keep a user on the Website for as long as possible. Long-term stickiness refers to a Website's ability to motivate a user to return to that particular Website.

Tag: In the practice of collaborative categorization using freely chosen keywords, these are descriptors that individuals assign to objects. Tags can be used to specify properties of an object that are not obvious from the object itself. They can then be used to find objects with some desired set of properties, or to organize objects.

User: One who uses a computer system, software application, or Website. Users may need to identify themselves for the purposes of accounting, security, logging and resource management. In order to identify oneself, a user has a *user account* and a *user name*, and in most cases also a *password*. Users employ the user interface for access to a system or Website, and the process of identification is often referred to as *log in*.

Webmail: Email received and sent only locally on a particular Website. The user's other email accounts remain unaffected.

Widget: A Web widget is a portable chunk of code that can be installed and executed within any separate HTML-based Web page by an end user without requiring additional compilation. They are derived from the idea of reusable code that has existed for years. Nowadays other terms used to describe Web widgets including: gadget, badge, module, capsule, snippet, mini and flake. Web widgets often but not always use DHTML, Adobe Flash or JavaScript programming languages.

Wiki: A series of Web pages that allows users to generate content, but also allows others (often unrestricted) to edit the content. A tool for online collaboration and without constraints of time.

ENDNOTE

1 Adapted or verbatim from Wikipedia, unless otherwise noted.

APPENDIX A

comScore Media Metrix Methodology

(cited directly from comScore Media Metrix. See the following comScore Media Metrix URL: http://www.comscore.com/method/method.asp)

With more than 2 million participants under continuous measurement, the comScore Global Network is the largest consumer panel of its kind, and delivers the most comprehensive view available of consumer activity – both online and offline.

comScore has developed a statistical methodology to ensure the accuracy and reliability of projections to the total population based on its network. Ultimately this provides comScore clients with confidence in the quality of information that drives important business decisions every day.

At the heart of the comScore Global Network is a sample of consumers enlisted via Random Digit Dial (RDD) recruitment - the methodology long endorsed by many market and media researchers. comScore also employs a variety of online recruitment programs, which have been time-tested through the years in which the comScore Global Network has been in operation. The reliance upon comScore services by hundreds of clients stands as testament to the strength and reliability of this combined approach.

Participants in the comScore Global Network receive a package of benefits that have proven to be broadly appealing to all demographic segments:

- Server-based virus protection
- Attractive sweepstakes prizes
- Opportunity to impact and improve the Internet

Participants are protected by industry-leading privacy policies that ensure anonymity of personal information. Membership is provided through an efficient sign-up process.

All demographic segments of the online population are represented in the comScore Global Network, with large samples of participants in each segment. For example, our network includes hundreds of thousands of high-income Internet users - one of the most desirable and influential groups to measure, yet also one of the most difficult to recruit.
comScore determines the size and characteristics of the total online population via a continuous survey spanning tens of thousands of persons over the course of a year. The sample of participants in this enumeration survey is selected via RDD methodology. Respondents are asked a variety of questions about their Internet use, as well as descriptive information about themselves and their households. The result is an accurate and up-to-date picture of the universe to which the comScore sample is projected.
The resulting combination of large samples across all segments, and a reliable view of the total universe, allows comScore to eliminate the effects of over- or under-representation of any group in the network.

comScore services are based either on the complete Global Network database or from components relevant to client needs. For example, comScore's industry-leading, RDD-based Media Metrix 2.0 audience measurement system is founded upon 120,000 U.S. panelists. Media Metrix Global Services are produced using the behavior of 500,000 panelists outside of the U.S. And Media Metrix XPC (eXPanded Coverage) adds visibility of smaller Web sites and local market activity through data captured from the balance of the comScore panel.

APPENDIX B

Exponential Function Tests for Connector Website Trends

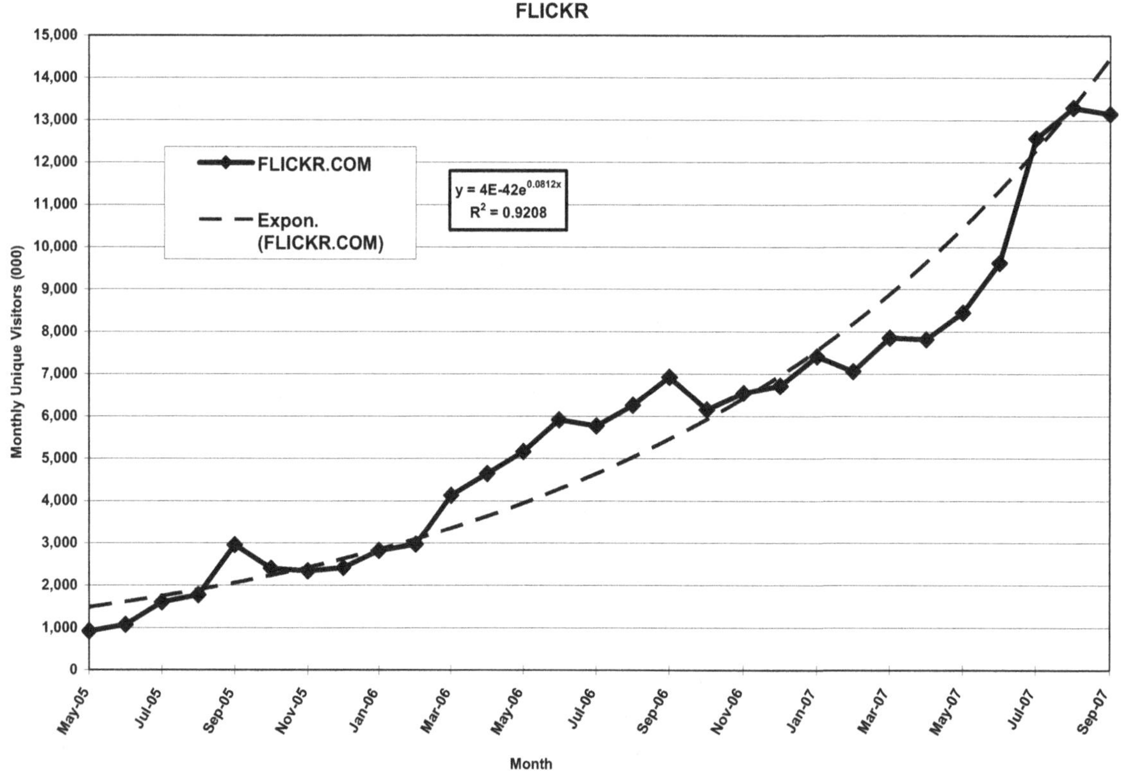

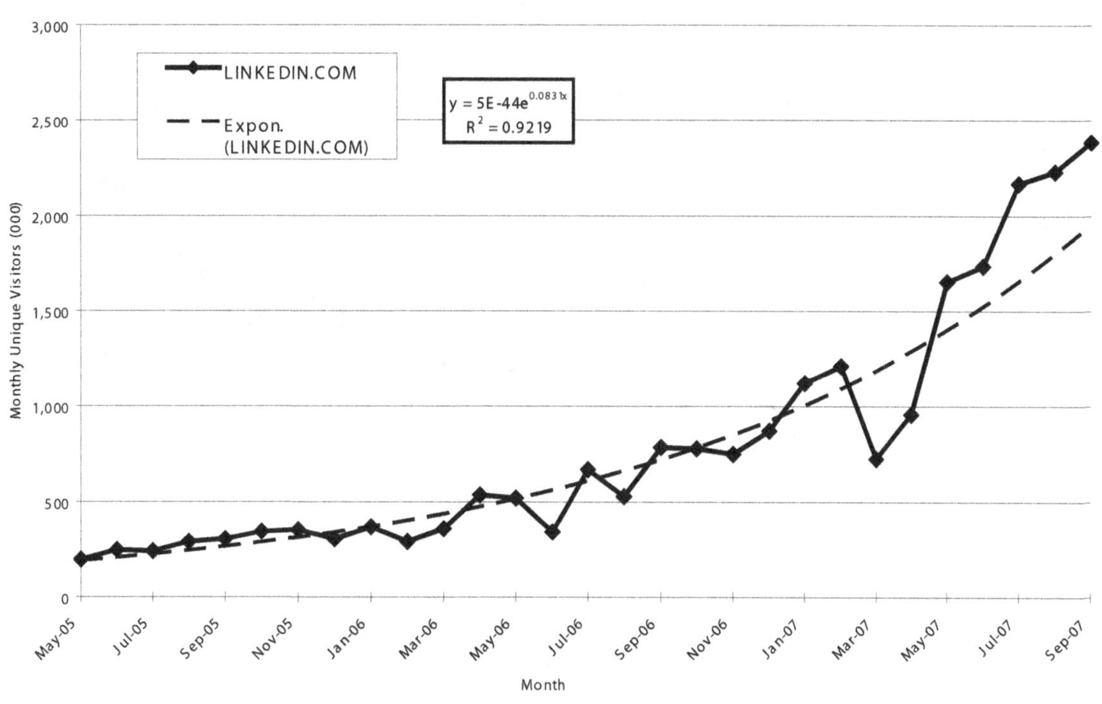
LINKEDIN
LINKEDIN.COM
Expon. (LINKEDIN.COM)
y = 5E-44e^0.0831x
R^2 = 0.9219
Monthly Unique Visitors (000)
3,000
2,500
2,000
1,500
1,000
500
0
May-05
Jul-05
Sep-05
Nov-05
Jan-06
Mar-06
May-06
Jul-06
Sep-06
Nov-06
Jan-07
Mar-07
May-07
Jul-07
Sep-07
Month

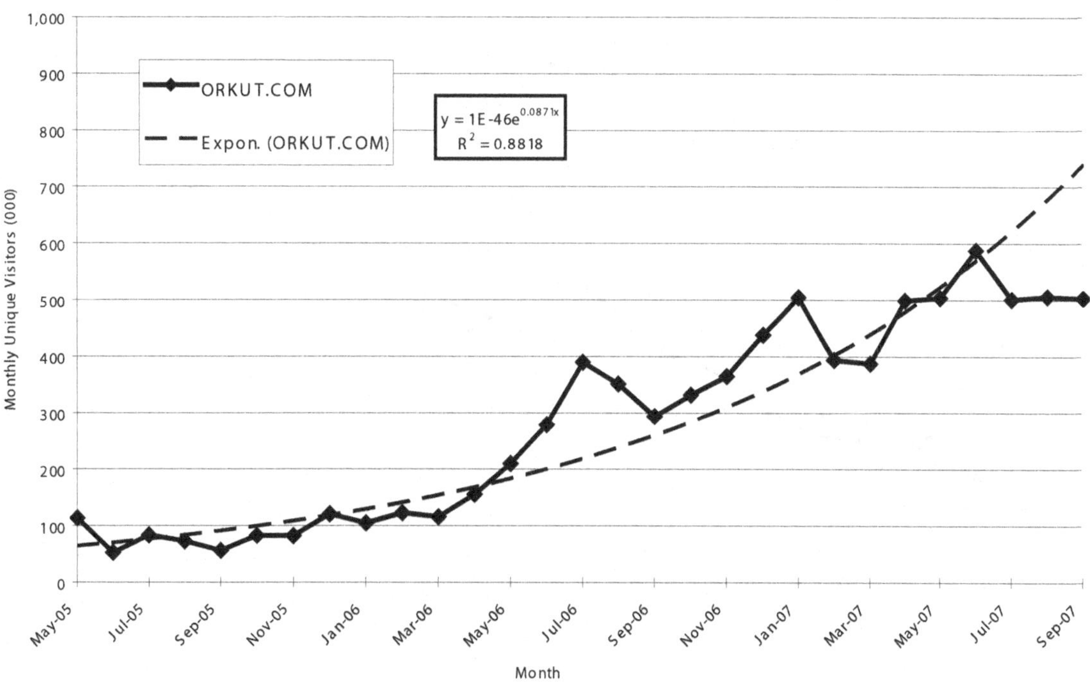
ORKUT
ORKUT.COM
Expon. (ORKUT.COM)
y = 1E-46e^0.0871x
R^2 = 0.8818
Monthly Unique Visitors (000)
1,000
900
800
700
600
500
400
300
200
100
0
May-05
Jul-05
Sep-05
Nov-05
Jan-06
Mar-06
May-06
Jul-06
Sep-06
Nov-06
Jan-07
Mar-07
May-07
Jul-07
Sep-07
Month

FACEBOOK

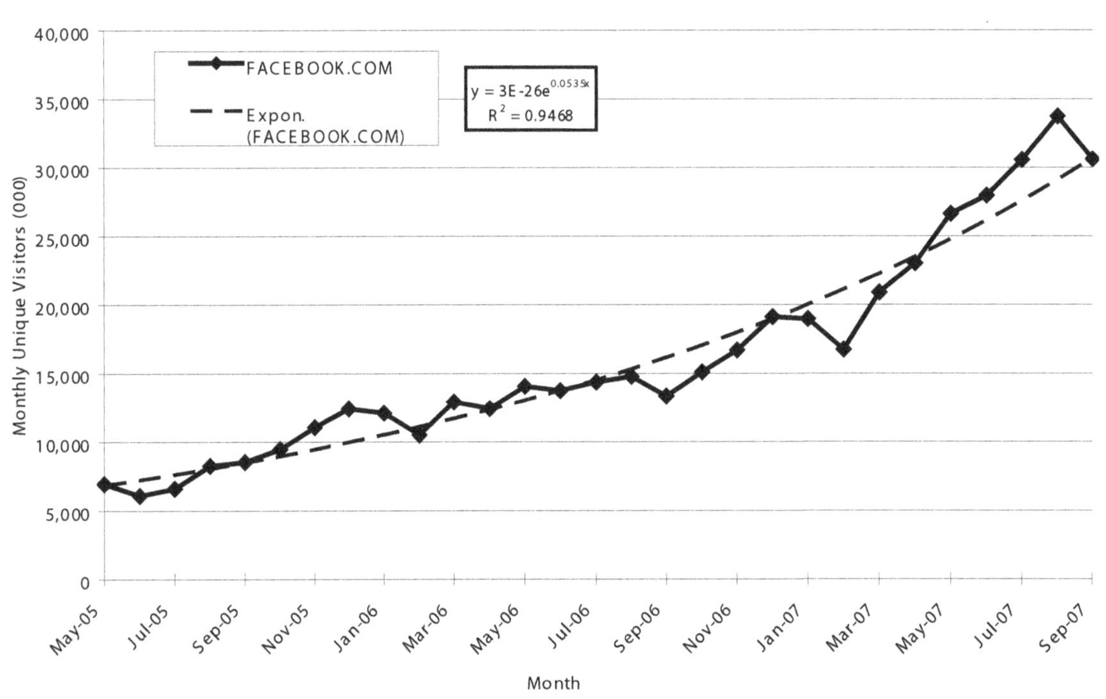
FACEBOOK.COM
Expon. (FACEBOOK.COM)
y = 3E-26e^0.0535x
R^2 = 0.9468
Monthly Unique Visitors (000)
40,000
35,000
30,000
25,000
20,000
15,000
10,000
5,000
0
May-05
Jul-05
Sep-05
Nov-05
Jan-06
Mar-06
May-06
Jul-06
Sep-06
Nov-06
Jan-07
Mar-07
May-07
Jul-07
Sep-07
Month

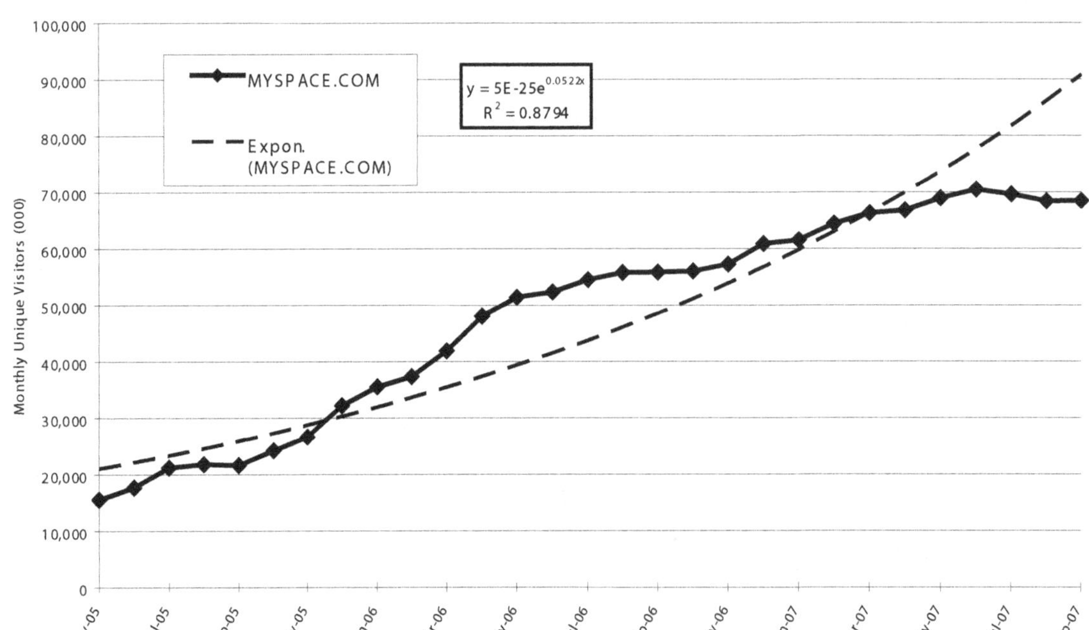
MYSPACE
MYSPACE.COM
Expon. (MYSPACE.COM)
y = 5E-25e^0.0522x
R^2 = 0.8794
Monthly Unique Visitors (000)
100,000
90,000
80,000
70,000
60,000
50,000
40,000
30,000
20,000
10,000
0
May-05
Jul-05
Sep-05
Nov-05
Jan-06
Mar-06
May-06
Jul-06
Sep-06
Nov-06
Jan-07
Mar-07
May-07
Jul-07
Sep-07
Month

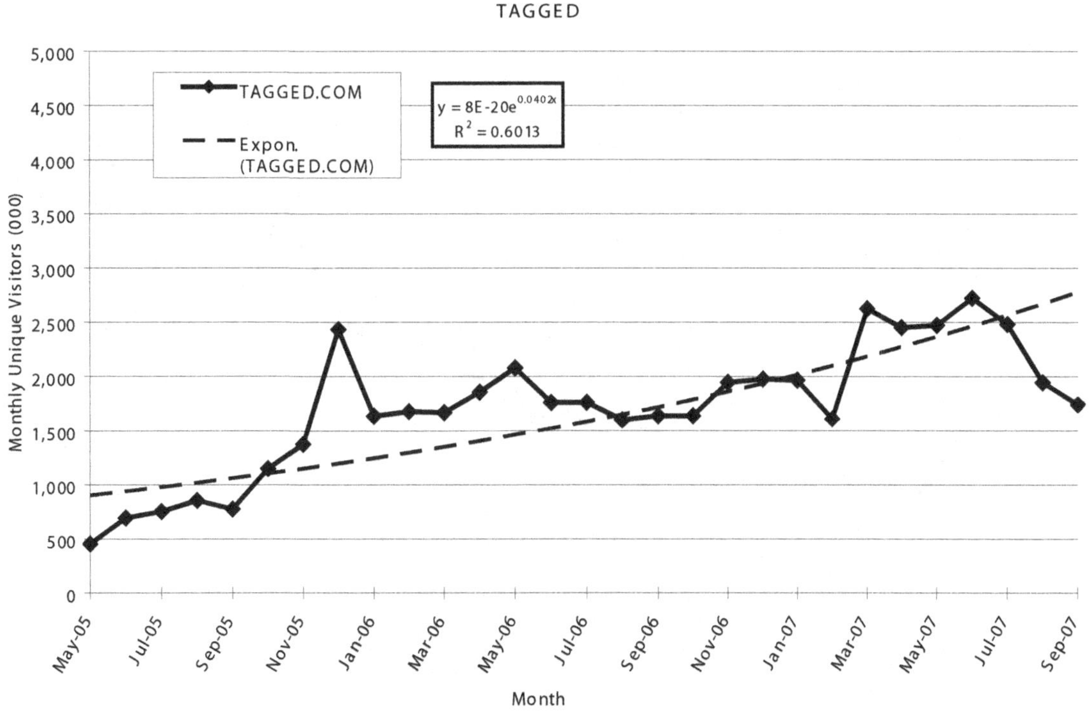
TAGGED
TAGGED.COM
Expon. (TAGGED.COM)
y = 8E-20e^0.0402x
R² = 0.6013
Monthly Unique Visitors (000)
5,000
4,500
4,000
3,500
3,000
2,500
2,000
1,500
1,000
500
0
May-05
Jul-05
Sep-05
Nov-05
Jan-06
Mar-06
May-06
Jul-06
Sep-06
Nov-06
Jan-07
Mar-07
May-07
Jul-07
Sep-07
Month

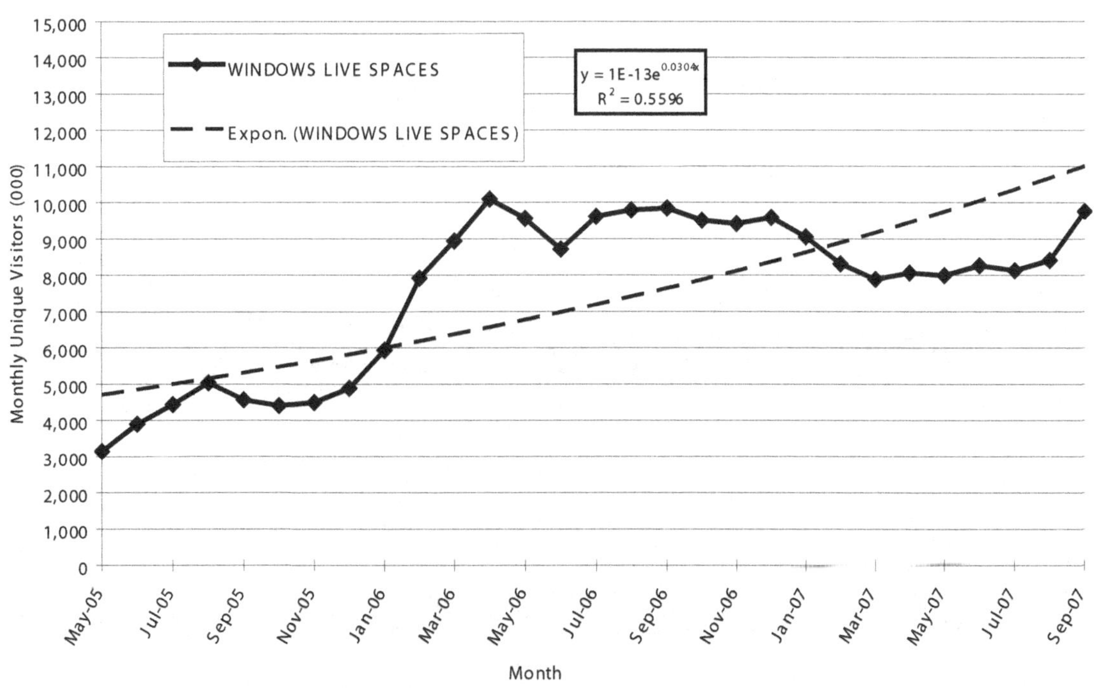
WINDOWS LIVE SPACES
WINDOWS LIVE SPACES
Expon. (WINDOWS LIVE SPACES)
y = 1E-13e^0.0304x
R² = 0.5596
Monthly Unique Visitors (000)
15,000
14,000
13,000
12,000
11,000
10,000
9,000
8,000
7,000
6,000
5,000
4,000
3,000
2,000
1,000
0
May-05
Jul-05
Sep-05
Nov-05
Jan-06
Mar-06
May-06
Jul-06
Sep-06
Nov-06
Jan-07
Mar-07
May-07
Jul-07
Sep-07
Month

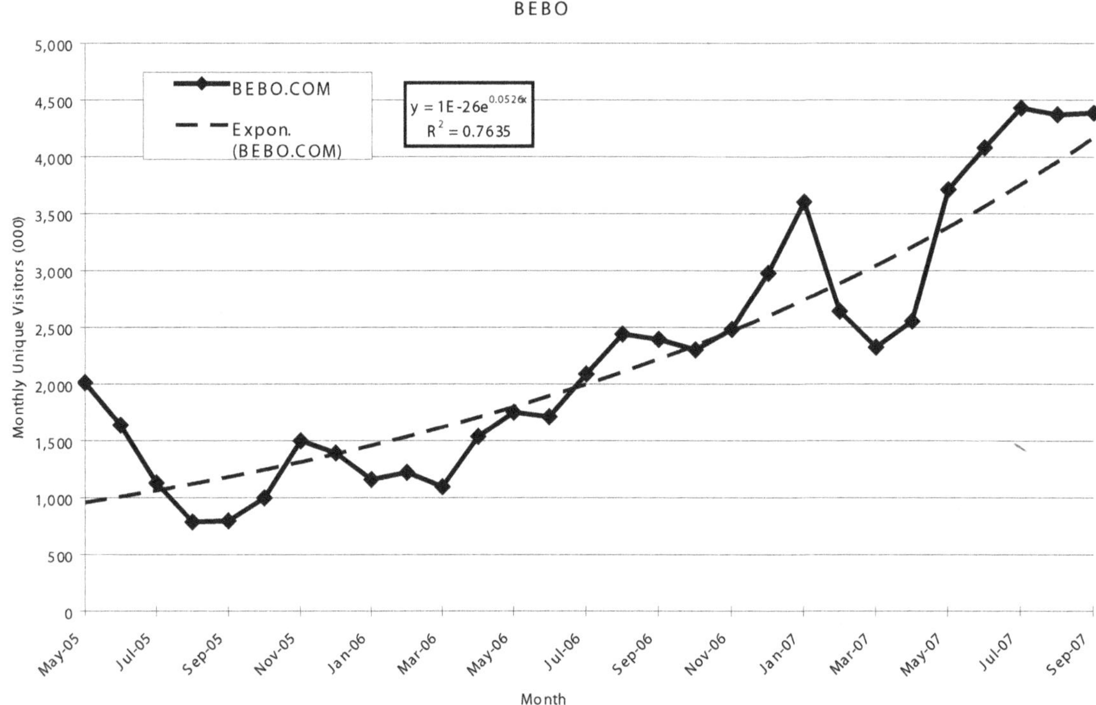
BEBO
BEBO.COM
Expon. (BEBO.COM)
y = 1E-26e^0.0526x
R^2 = 0.7635
Monthly Unique Visitors (000)
5,000
4,500
4,000
3,500
3,000
2,500
2,000
1,500
1,000
500
0
May-05
Jul-05
Sep-05
Nov-05
Jan-06
Mar-06
May-06
Jul-06
Sep-06
Nov-06
Jan-07
Mar-07
May-07
Jul-07
Sep-07
Month

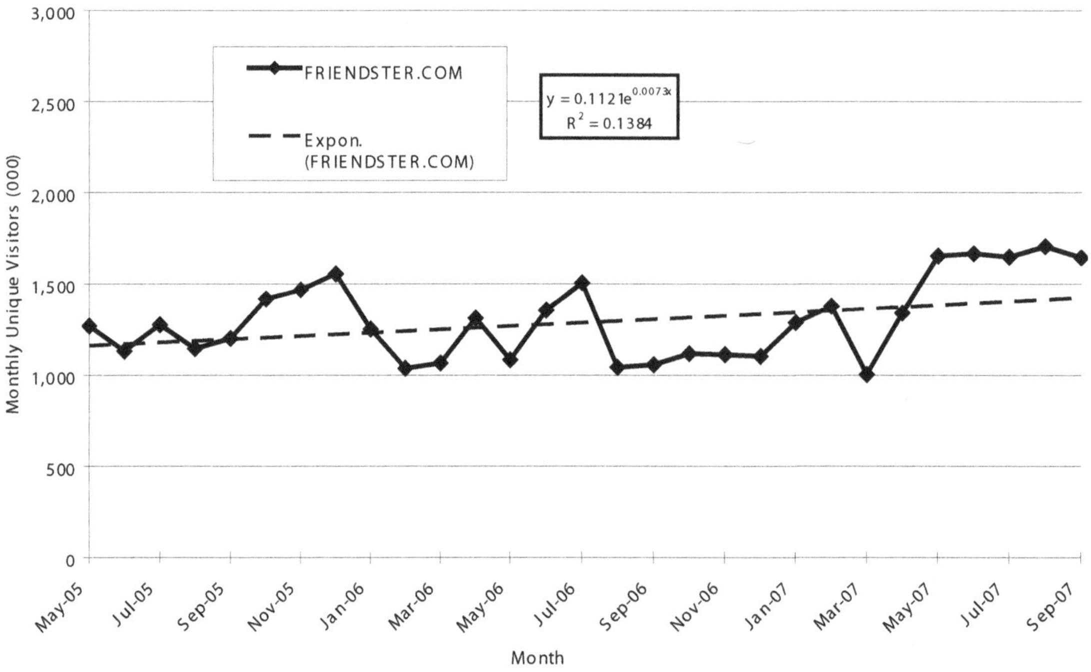
FRIENDSTER
FRIENDSTER.COM
Expon. (FRIENDSTER.COM)
y = 0.1121e^0.0073x
R^2 = 0.1384
Monthly Unique Visitors (000)
3,000
2,500
2,000
1,500
1,000
500
0
May-05
Jul-05
Sep-05
Nov-05
Jan-06
Mar-06
May-06
Jul-06
Sep-06
Nov-06
Jan-07
Mar-07
May-07
Jul-07
Sep-07
Month

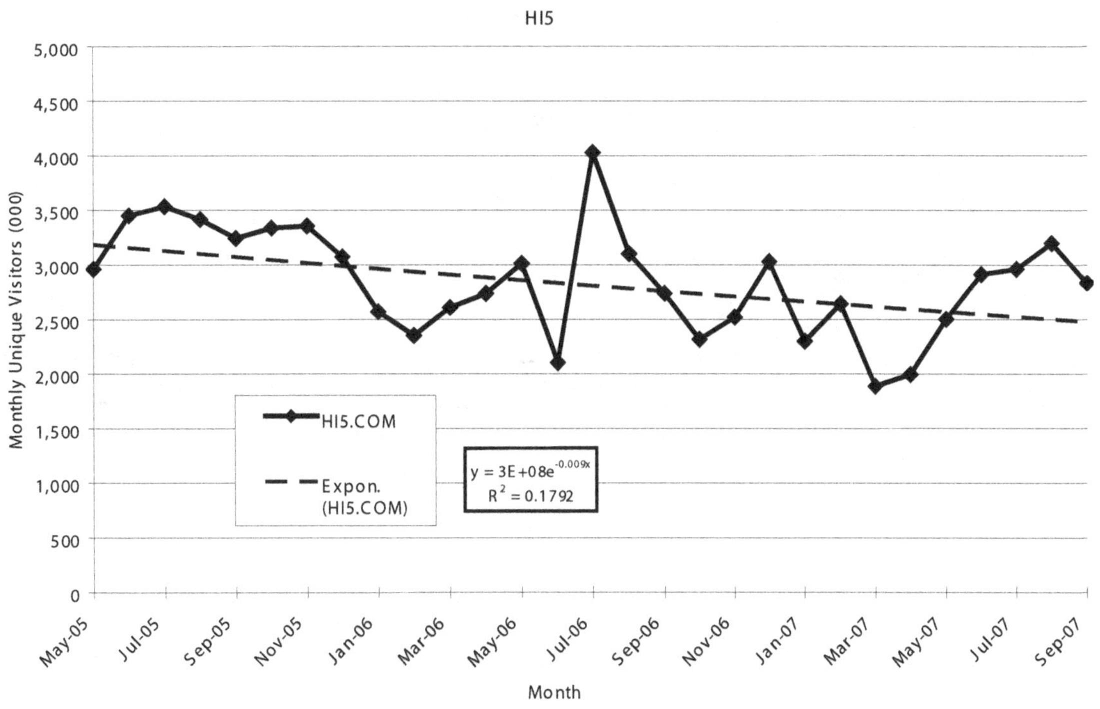
HI5
5,000
4,500
4,000
3,500
3,000
2,500
2,000
1,500
1,000
500
0
Monthly Unique Visitors (000)
HI5.COM
Expon. (HI5.COM)
y = 3E+08e^-0.009x
R² = 0.1792
May-05
Jul-05
Sep-05
Nov-05
Jan-06
Mar-06
May-06
Jul-06
Sep-06
Nov-06
Jan-07
Mar-07
May-07
Jul-07
Sep-07
Month

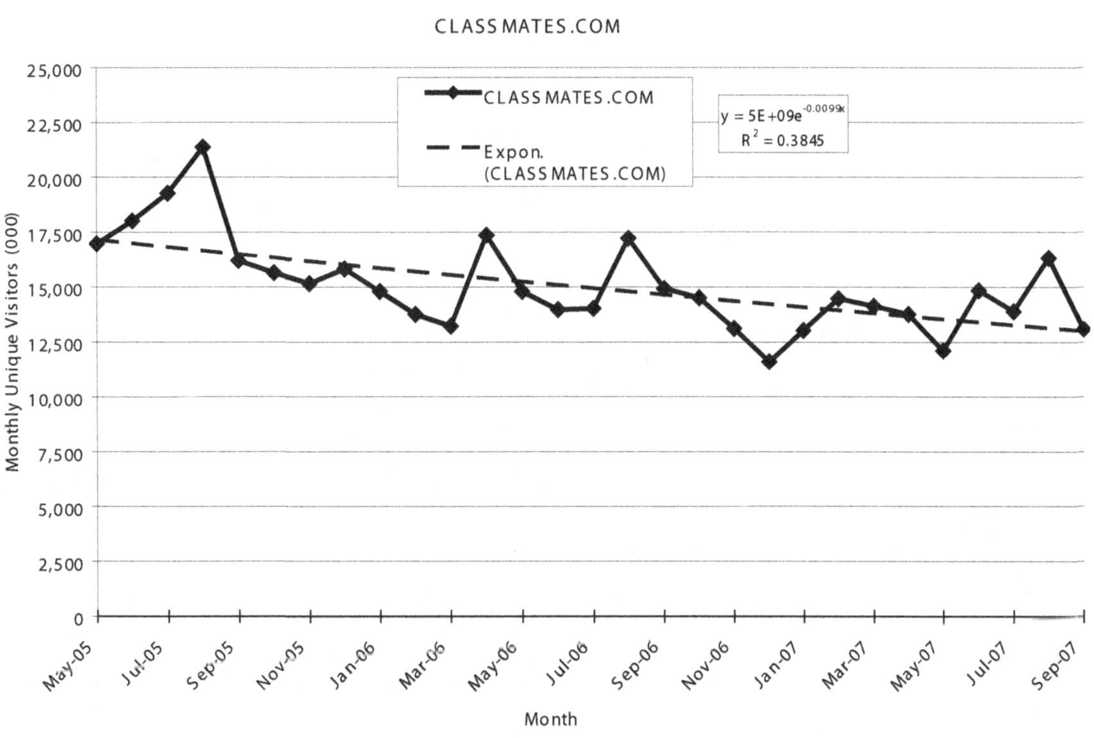
CLASSMATES.COM
25,000
22,500
20,000
17,500
15,000
12,500
10,000
7,500
5,000
2,500
0
Monthly Unique Visitors (000)
CLASSMATES.COM
Expon. (CLASSMATES.COM)
y = 5E+09e^-0.0099x
R² = 0.3845
May-05
Jul-05
Sep-05
Nov-05
Jan-06
Mar-06
May-06
Jul-06
Sep-06
Nov-06
Jan-07
Mar-07
May-07
Jul-07
Sep-07
Month

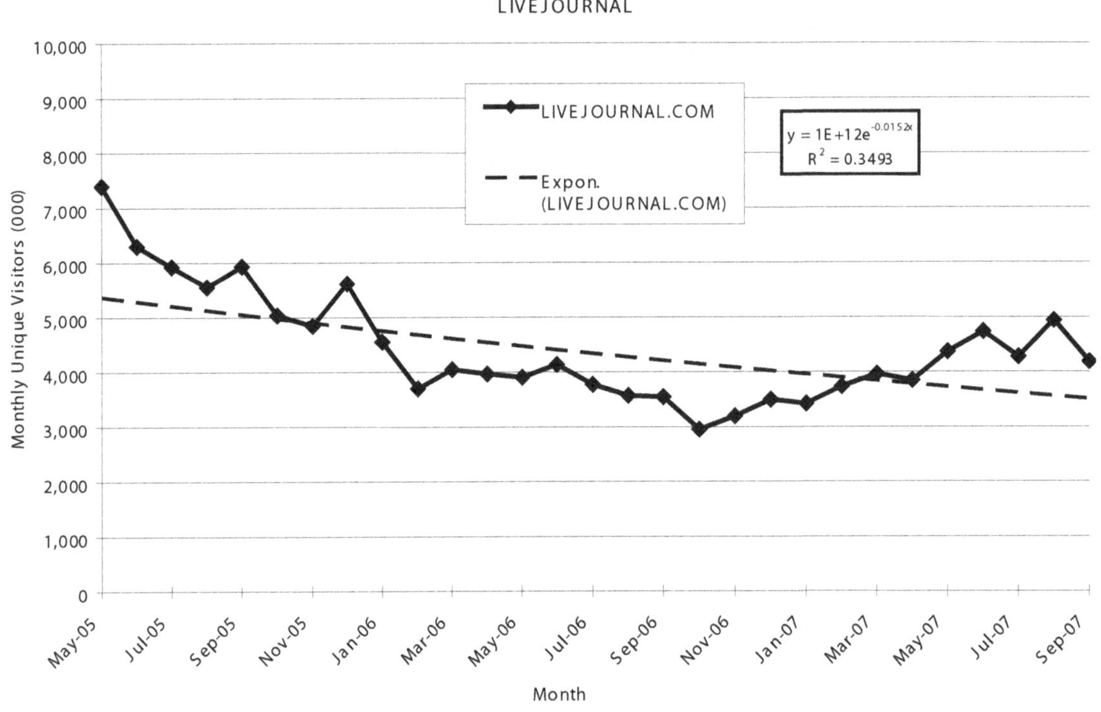
LIVEJOURNAL
LIVEJOURNAL.COM
Expon. (LIVEJOURNAL.COM)
y = 1E+12e^-0.0152x
R² = 0.3493
Monthly Unique Visitors (000)
10,000
9,000
8,000
7,000
6,000
5,000
4,000
3,000
2,000
1,000
0
May-05
Jul-05
Sep-05
Nov-05
Jan-06
Mar-06
May-06
Jul-06
Sep-06
Nov-06
Jan-07
Mar-07
May-07
Jul-07
Sep-07
Month

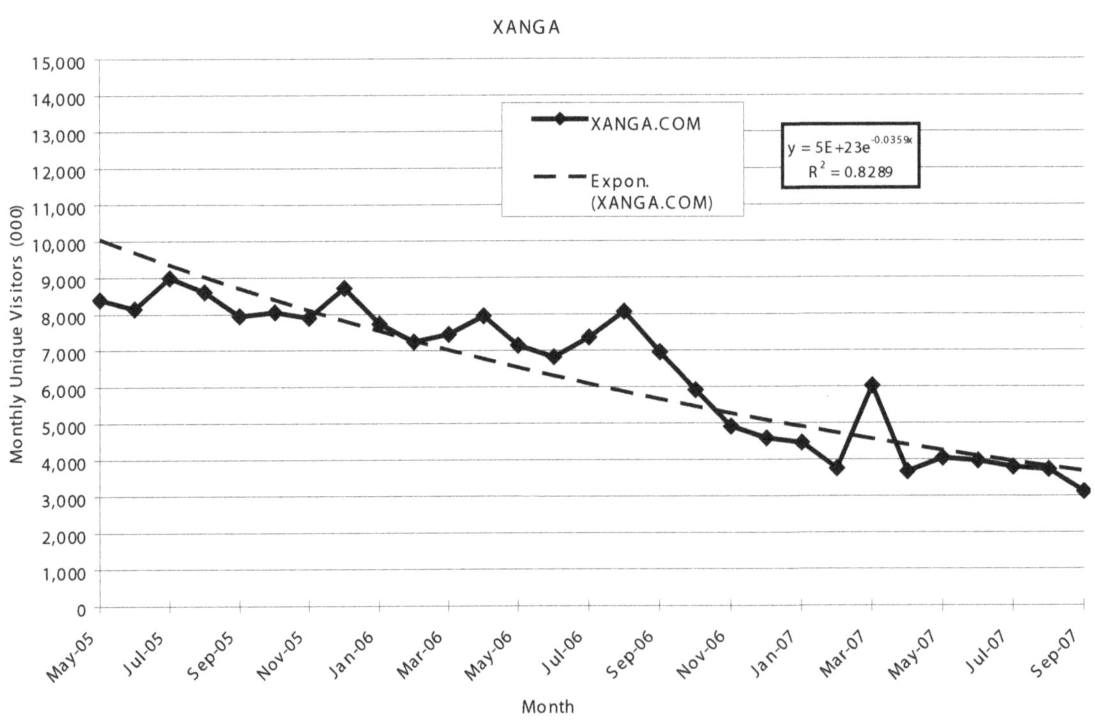
XANGA
XANGA.COM
Expon. (XANGA.COM)
y = 5E+23e^-0.0359x
R² = 0.8289
Monthly Unique Visitors (000)
15,000
14,000
13,000
12,000
11,000
10,000
9,000
8,000
7,000
6,000
5,000
4,000
3,000
2,000
1,000
0
May-05
Jul-05
Sep-05
Nov-05
Jan-06
Mar-06
May-06
Jul-06
Sep-06
Nov-06
Jan-07
Mar-07
May-07
Jul-07
Sep-07
Month

Chapter XXIII
Information Extraction from Blogs

Marie-Francine Moens
Katholieke Universiteit Leuven, Belgium

ABSTRACT

This chapter introduces information extraction from blog texts. It argues that the classical techniques for information extraction that are commonly used for mining well-formed texts lose some of their validity in the context of blogs. This finding is demonstrated by considering each step in the information extraction process and by illustrating this problem in different applications. In order to tackle the problem of mining content from blogs, algorithms are developed that combine different sources of evidence in the most flexible way. The chapter concludes with ideas for future research.

INTRODUCTION

A *blog* (short for Web log) is a Web based publication consisting primarily of periodic content. The content is usually displayed in a reverse chronological order. Blogs are typically social media and provide commentary on a large variety of topics on a particular subject, such as products (e.g., cars, food), people (e.g., politicians, celebrities), politics, news or health. The communication medium is primarily text, although we see an increasing focus on photographs (photoblog), sketchblogs, videos (vlog) or audio (podcasting), or on combinations of these media. A descriptive textual component is usually present, because text is an important component in human communication. Many blogs are built in an interactive dialogue setting, but a blog can also have the form of a personal diary. Other people engage themselves to complement, freely tag or comment the content, and authors of blogs prefer to link to other content. The people who write the blogs are usually not professionals.

Blogs are very *creative forms of human expression* and have in our society an influence on our convictions, political opinions and societal relationships that is often underestimated. Blogs are a mirror of a society, and many different parties have an interest in monitoring their content. Businesses, lawyers, sociologists and politicians want to know the topics that are of most concern to citizens. Police and intelligence services might find valuable links or cues to crime tracking. Citizens are interested in finding soul mates with common interests. We humans have no trouble aggregating the different media and inferring messages and interpretations from them. If we design machines that help people to search blogs, to monitor blogs, mine or summarize them, we expect from these machines a certain degree of understanding of the blog contents. Assigning a semantic meaning to blogs brings us to the domain of artificial intelligence. This chapter will treat the topic of information extraction from blogs. In previous work we have defined information extraction as:

Information extraction is the identification, and consequent or concurrent classification and structuring into semantic classes, of specific information found in unstructured data sources providing additional aids to access and interpret the unstructured data by information systems. (Moens, 2006, p. 225)

Information extraction is used to get some information out of *unstructured data.* Written and spoken text, pictures, video and audio are all forms of unstructured data. *Unstructured* does not imply that the data is structurally incoherent (in that case it would simply be nonsense), but rather that its information is encoded in such a way that makes it difficult for computers to immediately interpret it. Information extraction is the process that adds meaning to unstructured, raw data, whether that is text, images, video or audio. Consequently, the data becomes structured or semi-structured and can be more easily processed by the computer.

In other words, information extraction presupposes that although the semantic information in a text and its linguistic organization is not *immediately* computationally transparent, it can nevertheless be retrieved by taking into account surface regularities that reflect its computationally opaque internal organization. An information extraction system will use a set of extraction patterns, which are either manually constructed or automatically learned, to take information out of a source and put it in a more structured format. When structuring this information, it is not the purpose to replace the unstructured data by the extracted information, which would be equal to imposing a certain view on the data. The goal is to complement the unstructured low level data with semantic labels so that their automated retrieval, linking, mining and visualization become more effective (Moens, 2006).

The unstructured data sources we are mainly concerned with in this chapter are *written texts,* possibly enriched with *free tags, comments* and hypermedia *links*. Information extraction aims here at identifying certain information for use in subsequent information systems. State-of-the-art information extraction techniques are applied to well-formed texts, i.e., consistent with the standards of an official language. However, blog data is notorious for being incoherent and full of grammatical and spelling errors. Sometimes a community or jargon language is used. The focus of this chapter is on the problems encountered by using a state of the art information extraction system when dealing with blogs.

This chapter is organized as follows. We continue with some background (next section) on information extraction in general and information extraction from blogs in particular. We outline the history of information extraction. In a subsequent section we consider the different steps in an information extraction task and focus on particular issues when dealing with blog data. We discuss tokenization and lexical analysis, natural language processing and finally information extraction. In the latter part of the chapter we go deeper into a few specific applications: topic and thread detection, opinion mining, and argumentation detection. Wherever possible, we illustrate our findings with our own research experiences. We conclude with a number of prospects for further research.

BACKGROUND

Let us first give a few examples of information extraction from blogs.

A new consensus statement from the American Diabetes Association (ADA) has now suggested consideration of metformin, 850 mg twice daily, as a treatment option for people with prediabetes. (Yahoo! Health blog)

Suppose people question the blogs in a search for a treatment of prediabetes: identifying that metformin is a drug and linking the drug to the treatment of prediabetes are information extraction tasks.

I've owned several SUVs. They all felt tippy--seeing some flip over in news programs certainly didn't help. It's physics, right? The Q7 decouples sitting high and feeling like you're going to tip over. And it's also got permanent all-wheel drive ("Quattro"). If I were in charge of Audi's marketing, I would focus on the concept that Audi is the German car manufacturer with all-wheel drive. Very reassuring. (Guy Kawazaki)

Audi marketing services might mine blogs in order to know what people write about the sitting position in an Audi Q7. This requires extracting the information regarding sitting and coupling it to the Audi Q7.

HRC introduces bill to make possession of a concealed weapon mandatory when voting or getting driver's license. Have banner (and Ted Nugent) ready for announcement: "Hillary '08: She'll Blow You Away." Question: is it legal for HRC to wear a holster and revolver on the floor of the Senate? If so, which plays better: waist, shoulder, or strapped to calf? (The Huffington Post)

From this blog text it is interesting to extract the names of senators who introduced bills with regard to weapon possession in order to write a summary on this legal issue.

... It turned out that there was not nearly as much overlap between the infrared absorption spectra of water vapour and CO2 as thought. In 1956, calculations by Gilbert Plass proved that Ångström had got it wrong: adding more and more CO2 to the atmosphere would trap more and more heat. ... So by the 1950s, it was starting to become clear that human activity was causing CO2 levels to rise and that this rise would reduce the loss of heat into space. The implication seemed clear: provided all the other factors affecting the climate did not change, the Earth would warm. (Newscientist blogs)

For fast reading, it could be interesting to visualize in a catching way the argumentation structure of this discourse: The conclusion "the Earth would warm" and the used arguments (e.g., "adding more and more CO2 to the atmosphere would trap more and more heat."), and constraints (e.g., "provided all factors affecting the climate did not change").

Information extraction from text has quite a long history. The work of Roger Schank (Schank, 1975) and Marvin Minsky (1975) in the 1970s is very important in this respect. They taught us that content in texts is composed of small elements, which the author(s) of the texts has combined in order to communicate a certain message. The *Message Understanding Conferences* (MUC), held in the 1980s and 1990s were the first large-scale effort to boost research into automatic information extraction and has defined the research field for decades. The MUC legacy still resounds very strongly in Riloff and Lorenzen's definition of information extraction:

IE systems extract domain-specific information from natural language text. The domain and types of information to be extracted must be defined in advance. IE systems often focus on object identification, such as references to people, places, companies, and physical objects. [...] Domain-specific extraction patterns (or something similar) are used to identify relevant information. (Riloff & Lorenzen, 1999, p. 169)

This definition represents a traditional view on what information extraction is and it more or less captures what this discipline is about: The extraction of information that is semantically defined from a text, using a set of extraction rules that are tailored to a very closed domain. However, the scope of Riloff and Lorenzen's definition has become much too limited. Information extraction is not necessarily domain specific. In practice, the domain of the information to be extracted is often determined in advance, but this has more to do with technological limitations than with the long-term goals of the research discipline. An ideal information extraction system should be *domain independent* or at least portable to any domain with a minimum of engineering effort. As a result, Cowie and Lehnert see information extraction as a process that involves the extraction of fragments of information from natural language texts and the linking of these fragments into a coherent framework. In their view, information extraction:

[...] isolates relevant text fragments, extracts relevant information from the fragments, and then pieces together the targeted information in a coherent framework. [...] The goal of information extraction research is to build systems that find and link relevant information while ignoring extraneous and irrelevant information. (Cowie & Lehnert, 1996, p. 81)

Cowie and Lehnert's interpretation of information extraction is close to what we need, when processing blog data. But, text is not the only source of unstructured information in blog documents: fragments can be pieced together from tags, comments or linked content, and other media (e.g., image, video). Information extraction, for instance, also regards the automatic recognition of faces and objects in images and their labeling, or the cross-media recognition of content (Berg et al., 2007; Deschacht & Moens, 2007).

Extraction of factual information from text is a mature technology. MUC is currently succeeded by the *Automatic Content Extraction* (ACE) competition. A solid stimulus for developing extraction technology currently originates from the *biomedical field* where content becomes manageable only with the help of this technology. In this field, for instance, names of genes and their interactions are automatically detected in texts.

From its early beginnings information extraction has relied on *symbolic knowledge* that is *handcrafted* by a knowledge engineer. The knowledge patterns regard characteristics of the content to extract and the typical context in which the information is found. Lexical (e.g., words), syntactic (part-of-speech tags which signal the syntactical word category, dependencies found in the syntactic parse of a sentence), orthographic and layout patterns are commonly combined to form the patterns to be extracted. Such an approach is especially valuable for extracting information from texts in a limited domain, which is characterized by a limited set of extraction patterns. Typically the knowledge engineer manually inspects a corpus of domain relevant texts and handcrafts knowledge rules or frames possibly assisted by a domain expert. Frames are a popular knowledge format. A frame stores the properties or characteristics of an entity, action or event. It typically consists of a number of slots to refer to the properties named by a frame, each of which contains a value (or is left blank). The number and type of slots will be chosen according to the particular knowledge to be represented. A slot may contain a reference to another frame.

Other features of frames have advantages: They include the provision of a default value for a particular slot in all frames of a certain type, the use of more complex methods for inheriting values and properties between frames, and the use of procedural attachments to the frame slots. When frames have mutual relationships, a semantic net of frames can represent them.

Many different information extraction systems have been implemented based on a symbolic approach, most of them developed within the MUC initiatives. Perhaps the most famous system in this category is the FASTUS system developed by Hobbs et al. (1996).

Notwithstanding the success of the information extraction systems in the 1980s and 1990s, there was a growing concern in making the information extraction systems easily portable to domains other than the one a system was built for, and eventually to use information extraction in open domains. The high cost of the manual pattern drafting in the knowledge acquisition stage made researchers investigate the possibilities of *machine learning* approaches. Among early approaches of machine learning in information extraction is the work of Riloff and Lehnert (1993) on the famous AutoSlog system.

Most of these systems use *supervised* techniques to learn *extraction patterns*. The pattern recognizers or classifiers train from a set of previously classified examples. The general idea is that a human expert annotates fragments that should be extracted in a small corpus of training documents with semantic labels, and then the learning system generalizes from these examples to produce a function or rule that can be applied on previously unseen instances. The underlying idea is that it is easier to annotate documents than to write extraction rules, since the latter requires some degree of programming expertise, and usually relies on the skills of the knowledge engineer to anticipate extra patterns. Although for some applications symbolic, handcrafted knowledge that is sharable across applications, is more convenient, we see a gradually increasing interest in machine learning techniques from the second half of the 1990s onwards. The most current and the most successful algorithms are *Support Vector Machines* (Christianini & Shawe-Taylor, 2000), *maximum entropy modeling* (Berger, Della Pietra & Della Pietra, 1996), and *conditional random fields* (Lafferty, McCallum & Pereira, 2001).

Parallel with the development of supervised approaches, there is interest in using *unsupervised* or *semi-supervised learning* for information extraction that respectively requires no or few annotated examples. The cost of annotation is still a major handicap in developing large-scale information extraction systems or in porting an existing system to another domain. The most common unsupervised techniques attempt clustering, where instances with similar characteristics are grouped. Many semi-supervised technologies build classification models that bootstrap from a few annotated instances. In the cases of self-training and co-training new classification patterns are discovered in the unlabeled examples when they occur frequently in correlation with already known patterns (as for instance in Collins and Singer (1999)). In the case of active learning, the machine selects examples to annotate based on the uncertainty of classification of the example by the current classifier, representativeness of the example for a set of unlabeled examples, or divergence of the example from the current learned model of the classifier (e.g., Boiy, Hens, Deschacht & Moens, 2007).

Current information extraction systems classify entities (e.g., as persons, organizations, locations, cf. above the examples in the biomedical domain), detect relationships between entities among which are coreferring relations (e.g., "Hillary Clinton is a senator") and recognize circumstantial attributes such as temporal expressions. These systems commonly focus on well-formed texts in standard languages. While information extraction in open domains is already limited, extraction from noisy and ever changing media symbols is even scarcer. Often, we are confronted with *informal texts* from which we want to extract information. Examples are transcribed speech, spam texts, instant messages that were generated through mobile services, and blogs. These types of texts are characterized by spelling errors, novel words, use of abbreviations, inconsistent use of capitalization patterns, and malformed and ungrammatical sentences and phrases. In many cases information extraction patterns change continuously (e.g., different authors have different informal styles) or deliberately (e.g., in spam mail), making their processing especially difficult. Also, natural language processing techniques on which information extraction often relies, will not perform as well as they should. In messages and blogs content is often left implicit because readers and writers might share common knowledge or context, or content is found in contextual sources (threads of a conversation or comment and tags). Studies on information extraction from informal texts are very limited. Jansche and Abney (2002) studied extraction of caller names and phone numbers from voice mail transcripts. Rennie and Jaakkola (2005) extracted named entities from e-mails. Minkov et al. (2004) inferred background knowledge in e-mails. As we will see below, the properties of informal texts such as blogs restrict the use of many of the common techniques for information extraction. Finally, textual information is increasingly interweaved with other media such as images, audio fragments or other symbolic communication languages.

INFORMATION EXTRACTION TECHNIQUES

Overview

Let us first summarize the extraction process. Figure 1 shows two phases in this process. In the *training phase*, the knowledge engineer or the system acquires the necessary extraction patterns; the latter situation referring to the use of machine learning. In the *testing phase*, the learned model is applied to unseen examples. In the first step, a text corpus is selected that is representative of the intended task. Before the text can be used for extrapolating extraction patterns, it often requires preprocessing. Preprocessing usually consists of tokenization, lexical analysis and possible normalization. Another step belonging to the preprocessing phase is the enrichment of the textual data with linguistic metadata such as part-of-speech tags and dependency information of sentence constituents by means of natural language processing tools. The preprocessing step gives us the features by which we describe extraction patterns of training and test examples.

In the manual approach, an information specialist will use the preprocessed training corpus during the learning phase as a basis for writing an *extraction grammar.* In a machine learning approach, the training corpus is first manually annotated to indicate which elements in the texts are relevant for the extraction task, and the machine learning module will use these annotations in the learning phase to automatically induce the extraction grammar from the corpus. The extraction grammar can be in the form of a mathematical function that will predict the class of an example in the testing phase. It is also possible that the training corpus is not manually labeled or only partially annotated referring to respectively unsupervised and weakly supervised techniques.

In the following sections we focus on the current methods for information extraction.

Tokenization and Lexical Analysis

Tokenization breaks a text into tokens or words. It distinguishes words, components of multipart words and multiword expressions. In space-delimited languages (such as most European languages) a word or token can be defined as a string of characters separated by white space. During this process, lemmatization (i.e., bring-

Figure 1. Schematic representation of an information extraction task

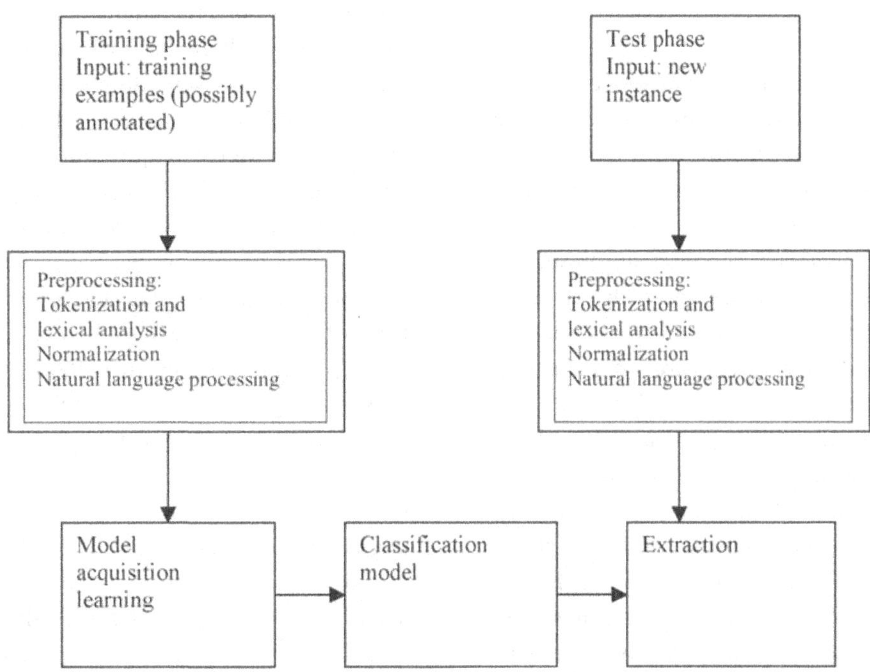

ing a word to its dictionary form) or stemming (i.e., conflating a word to its stem) based on affix and suffix removal can be performed. In certain languages such as German and Dutch, multipart words might be split in their components by means of a word splitter (e.g., "tuinfeest" (garden party) in Dutch is split in tuin (garden) and feest (party)). Multiword expressions (e.g., "carbon dioxide emission") can be based on cooccurrence statistics (e.g., use of the mutual information statistic, chi-square statistic, etc.) in a large corpus. During this analysis a form of normalization of acronyms, abbreviations and capitalizations is performed. Tokenization and lexical analysis are often combined with *sentence splitting*.

Overall, tokenization and lexical analysis are considered to be necessary processing steps in any application that involves textual data. In the case of blogs or other community texts this is not a trivial task as is shown in the following examples.

Example in French:

Voici tt ce ki me pasione ds ma petite vi!!!é tt mé pote é pll dotre truk!!!Avou de Dcouvrir. (Skyrock blog)

Possible translation in standard French and English:

Voici tout ce qui me passionne dans ma petite vie. Tout m'a ... et plusieurs autres trucs. A vous de découvrir.

Here everything which fascinates me in my small life. Everything has me ... and multiple other tricks. For you to explore.

Example in English:

WB really seems to be spilling the beans on a lot of stuff we didnt think we hand if this is their warm up, what is going to get us frothing in December? (The movie blog)

We illustrate the difficulties of processing these texts with our own research, where we automatically created a folksonomy from blogs written in a dialect from the Belgian city of Hasselt (De Smet & Moens, 2007).

Because of the lack of consensus on spelling, dialect words are not present in standard lexicons. A first category of dialect words have the same origin as standard words, but are pronounced differently and their written equivalent mimics the dialect pronunciation. In other cases, completely new words appear in dialects that do not necessarily have a one-to-one translation to standard words. In our own experiments in the A4MC3 project we *constructed a dictionary* of dialect words based on blog data. We defined a dialect edit distance by which the words of a text are processed. Upon sufficient similarity of an unknown word with a known standard Dutch word, it is accepted as a spelling variant of that word. On the other hand, if this difference is larger than a threshold value and the occurrence of the word in the corpus is important, the word is added as a new word to the lexicon. In the former case, the dialect and standard word have the same roots, the dialect word, however, has evolved to a different spelling by following a set of rules that determine the pronunciation. These rules comprise, for example, contractions or alterations of vowels, and are often (but not always) dependent on the context of characters they appear in. The alterations are however not exclusive: The same phonetic entity can be expressed by several combinations of characters. We have therefore adapted the edit-distance algorithm, as developed by Levenshtein; this distance efficiently calculates the minimal cost when transforming one character string into another by deleting, inserting and substituting characters. To improve the accuracy of the matching, we learn the cost of each operation by making use of a hand-built representative seed set of dialect words and their standard equivalents. We take into account both the change in characters and the contextual characters. We defined a function for estimating the operation cost that decreases monotonically with increasing frequency of the contextual pattern in question. This approach also detects completely new words that have a root that is different from known words.

In our experiments we had access to some bootstrapping knowledge about spelling variations of words in a certain dialect. Often we do not have this knowledge available. If we have access to a large corpus, we can rely on techniques used in automatic thesaurus construction where synonyms are detected when they frequently occur in the same lexical and grammatical context (e.g., Crouch & Yang, 1992).

For dialect or community jargon there are no standard resources, which are available for standard languages. Standard language can rely on lexical resources in machine readable form that offer knowledge of, for instance, synonymy, hypernymy (broader term), hyponymy (more specific term) and meronymy (part-of-relation).

Natural Language Processing

Another step is the enrichment of the textual data with linguistic metadata that will be used as features in the extraction process. For this purpose, a number of natural language processing tools can be used. For most applications, they include part-of-speech (POS) tagging (i.e., detecting the syntactic word class such as noun, verb, etc.) and phrase chunking (i.e., detecting base noun and verb phrases). Syntactic structure is often indicative of the information distribution in a sentence. For many applications, a rudimentary syntactic analysis is sufficient, which is often referred to as shallow parsing. Shallow parsing aims to recover fragments of syntactic structures as efficiently and as correctly as possible. It can be implemented in different ways. For example, phrasal analysis can be accomplished by bracketing the output of a part-of-speech tagger. In some cases additional parsing (i.e., breaking up a sentence into its constituents and building the dependency tree of a sentence), or even full parsing might be desirable. Full parsing aims at providing a maximally detailed analysis of a sentence's structure. This might include the translation into a canonical structure (e.g., syntactical argument structure) in which processes (e.g., as expressed by verbs) of sentences and their arguments are delimited. In addition, sentence constituents can be classified (e.g., subject, object, semantic roles). These resources often use tree banks to train from. A treebank can be defined as a syntactically processed corpus that contains annotations of natural language data at various linguistic levels (word, phrase, clause and sentence levels). A treebank provides mainly the morphosyntactic and syntactic structure of the utterances within the corpus and consists of a bank of linguistic trees, thereby its name.

There are linguistic resources that combine lexical and semantic information. For instance, the Berkeley *FrameNet* project is creating an online lexical resource for English (Fillmore and Baker, 2001). The aim is to document the range of semantic and syntactic combinatory possibilities (valences) of each word in each of its senses. The FrameNet database can be seen both as a dictionary and as a thesaurus. The former signals, for instance, the definition of a lexical item and gives access to annotated examples illustrating each syntactic pattern found in the corpus and the kinds of semantic information instanced with such patterns. The database acts also as a thesaurus, in that, by being linked to frames, each word is directly connected with other words in its frame(s), and further extensions are provided by working out the ways in which a word's basic frames are connected with other frames through relations of inheritance (possibly multiple inheritance) and phrase composition.

All the above resources are difficult to use if the blog language diverges from standard language. Very often the sentences in blogs are syntactically (and lexically) not well-formed, and words might be used metaphorically making them more difficult to disambiguate. Part-of-speech taggers, sentence chunkers or parsers that are trained for standard language fail to attain sufficient accuracy levels, and sometimes they are not robust enough to process the "dirty" language. We could retrain these tools on annotated blog data, but this requires a substantial annotation effort given the variety of blog "language" patterns.

Information Extraction

Information extraction regards a further semantic processing of the texts. It identifies and classifies information, links equivalent content, or detects other relationships between content.

The training examples and any new test example that will be classified with a learned model are usually represented as a vector of features capturing the characteristics of the examples obtained from the above preprocessing techniques. Nearest neighbor classifiers such as Support Vector Machines can use more complex, structured objects instead of feature vectors (e.g., trees that represent dependency information of sentences or of html pages) and use kernel functions in their computations.

Currently, we see a preference for using machine learning techniques when extracting information. First of all, a number of state of the art algorithms have interesting properties and advantages for natural language processing. There is a *lesser building effort* compared to extraction systems that rely on handcrafted extraction patterns. Annotation is usually considered to be easier than knowledge engineering. Moreover, many learning techniques allow a *probabilistic assignment of semantic labels*. If we want to reduce the computational complexity, we may use simple algorithms such as naïve Bayes classification. Because sufficient training data or knowledge rules are usually not available in order to cover all linguistic phenomena, or the system is confronted with unsolved ambiguities of the language due to content left implicit or purposely left ambiguous by the author, there is an advantage of using learning techniques that adhere to the *maximum entropy principle.* This principle states that, when we make inferences based on incomplete information, we should draw them from that probability distribution that has the maximum entropy permitted by the information that we do have. Examples of such classifiers are the *maximum entropy model* (Berger et al., 1996) and *conditional random fields* (Lafferty et al., 2001). Learning techniques that can deal with a large set of features that on occasion might be noisy, such as a *Support Vector Machine* (Christianini & Shawe Taylor, 2000), are also very valuable. Machine learning techniques can also incorporate context dependency. Context-dependent classifiers (e.g., conditional random fields) recognize patterns when the assignment of one class not only depends on a certain configuration of features, but also on other semantic classes assigned, i.e., on other feature vectors of objects in the context.

Machine learning naturally allows considering many more contextual features than is usually the case with handcrafted rules. All these advantages become especially relevant when we process blog texts. We are dealing here with a highly dynamic medium, changing and implicit contents, various styles, language use, etc., demanding very adaptive methods of processing. This does not mean that we cannot use handcrafted symbolic patterns, when the effort of their construction is worthy and they can be shared across different applications.

There are a number of typical information extraction tasks that lately have been extensively researched with regard to open domain information extraction and that are starting to be included in commercial applications. They include named entity recognition, noun phrase coreference resolution, entity relation recognition and timeline recognition.

Named entity recognition classifies named expressions in text (such as person, company, location or protein names). In the example "Mary Smith works for Concentra," "Mary" is recognized as a person and "Concentra" as a company. Named entity recognition – and more specifically recognition of persons, organizations and locations – in news texts is fairly well developed, yielding performance in terms of F-measure[1] above 95% (e.g., Bikel, Schwartz & Weischedel, 1997). The performance of named entity taggers on written documents such as Wall Street Journal articles is thus comparable to human performance, the latter being estimated in the 94-96% F-measure range. In the biomedical domain named entity recognition is a very common task because of the absolute necessity to recognize names of genes, proteins, gene products, organisms, drugs, chemical compounds, diseases, symptoms, etc. Depending on the semantic class, F-measures range up to 80% (e.g., Zhang et al., 2004).

Another important task is *noun phrase coreferent resolution.* Two or more noun phrases are coreferent, when they refer to the same situation described in the text. Many references in a text are encoded as phoric references, i.e., linguistic elements that rather than directly encode the meaning of an entity, refer to a direct description of the entity earlier (anaphoric) or later (cataphoric) in the text. In the example, "Bill Clinton went to New York, where he was invited for a keynote speech. The former president ..."., "Bill Clinton", "he" and "the former president" refer in this text to the same entity. "He" refers to an anaphoric reference. This is a quite difficult task with F-measures somewhat exceeding the 70% (e.g., Ng & Cardie, 1999).

Relationships between entities can be discovered. In the example, "John Smith works for IBM", the relation "employee" between John Smith and IBM is detected. This task is closely related to semantic role recognition (Gildea &

Jurafsky, 2002) where sentence constituents are labeled with semantic functions (i.e., processes, their actors and circumstances). Entity relation recognition receives a large attention in the biomedical domain. The named entity recognition is a first step for more advanced extraction tasks such as the detection of protein-protein interaction, gene regulation events, subcellular location of proteins and pathway discovery. Performance of relationship detection depends on the type of relation that is extracted. Performance decreases with insufficient annotated training examples (e.g., Culotta & Sorensen, 2004).

There is also some current work on the *recognition of temporal expressions* or timexes which is useful for resolving the time line of narrative stories (Mani, Pustejovsky & Gaizauskas, 2005). Detecting temporal expressions in text is not too complicated and compares to the above information extraction tasks in terms of performance numbers. Resolving the timexes into an absolute or relative time line is much more difficult.

The above extraction tasks (with the exception of domain-specific entity and relation recognition) have the advantage of being rather domain independent, so the learned models can be applied to a variety of texts, including blog texts.

Currently, simple levels of meaning are extracted, but these techniques are already sufficient to extract factual information from texts. Limited work is done in using information extraction techniques for semantically classifying information in blogs (Sood, Owsley, Hammond & Birnbaum, 2007). Below we see how information extraction is used in valuable applications of blog mining that are the result of our own research. However, first we turn our attention to a number of interesting particularities of blog documents.

Additional Particularities of Blogs

Due to available social software and "Web 2.0" social services, the addition of comments, tags and links to blog entries became very popular. Their popularity is partly due to the freedom of adding whatever content one wants to add. *Tagging* is a common way of associating keywords (tags) to organize blog content. The collection of tags within a specific system or application defines a folksonomy and the tags help users search and navigate. Tags can also be obtained from a controlled vocabulary, but most of the time people use free-tagging, and tag or *comment* in their own words and phrases. An interesting study of Berendt and Hanser (2007) found that tags select or highlight aspects of meaning and might add more content to documents (at least for some of the readers) for instance, in case they are added by other users. In addition, people link content for a variety of reasons (e.g., illustrations, definitions, motivations).

The success of these additions is greatly due to the *freedom* that people experience. Whatever content they find useful, they can add. Because all these utterances are free and naturally generated, they form a kind of "natural blog language". When humans create content, the result is often far away from a logical and structured representation that would be easy to process by the machine. We create content in an intuitive and natural way. Our creations are often full of *ambiguities* (i.e., the same expressions have different meanings) and of *paraphrases* (i.e., similar content is expressed in a variety of ways). We see these characteristics also in blogs, their texts and added data (Golder & Huberman, 2006). The power of human understanding of these data lies in recognizing the patterns of communication and interpreting them according to our linguistic, cultural and other background knowledge, and in making inferences, even when different tags, comments and links (combined with the malformedness discussed above) are present. Our human brain manages to understand and to interpret the content, because it makes the right contextual disambiguation, associations and inferences. Having the machine make sense out of such data is a real challenge.

We lack research that *integrates the different sources* of content in blogs when extracting information from blogs. How could tags, comments and links be integrated in more refined and more difficult classification tasks such as information extraction? First of all, these data sources can contain additional content that complements the original blog text and which is left implicit in this source. Moreover, the additional data could contain paraphrases of source content. Both cases can improve matching with a learned information extraction model. Finally, the data can fulfill a disambiguating function by making certain information more explicit or adding content, which forms additional context for disambiguating the text. The use of these sources of evidence opens many avenues for future research. In this respect, studies on joint citation and text mining (Glenisson, Glänzel, Janssens & De Moor, 2005), cross-media content recognition (Deschacht & Moens, 2007) and on cross-lingual content recognition in comparable corpora might be inspiring (Munteanu & Marcu, 2006).

APPLICATIONS

We illustrate this chapter with a number of applications of information extraction in blogs.

Topic and Thread Detection

A first task involves identifying the topic or subject that people write about. So we can, for instance, monitor "buzz" about a certain product or person. This seems like a trivial task: We just use a search engine to find instances of a certain name in the blogs and compute some statistics of the occurrences that are possibly monitored over time. In most cases this approach works fine, but there are some points of attention.

First of all, names can be *ambiguous* (e.g., Michael Jordan) or written with *spelling variants* (e.g., Hillary Rodham Clinton and Hillary Clinton). We respectively use the context of the names when disambiguating (e.g., by grouping or clustering names when the contextual words in a window match) and use variations on the edit distance to find spelling variants. Li, Morie and Roth (2004) train a probabilistic inference model for these tasks. In addition, there are many coreferring expressions in a text that refer to the same object or person (e.g., Hillary Clinton can be referred to as "she" or the "senator" or "former first lady" in the text). Solving these co-referring expressions within and across documents is the subject of ongoing research (e.g., Angheluta & Moens, 2007). Tracking persons across blogs is helpful in building profiles of these people (e.g., to find their functions or expertise).

Secondly, blog texts are not in the form of continuous discourse. Their genre has some characteristics of a *dialogue* as persons reply to or comment on certain statements. The blog messages are usually short, incomplete and characterized by partially threaded and interwoven topics making thread detection combined with topic detection a non-trivial task. The most common approach is using clustering algorithms. The features used in the clustering consist of content words, but also of linguistics-oriented features such as the leading type of sentence in the short message (e.g., declarative, interrogative, imperative or conditional, the category and person of a pronoun, proper names, noun phrase heads, etc.) (Feng & Hovy, 2006).

Finally, blogs exhibit *special* models as content is created and updated by different authors in a collaborative way. These *discourse* models have seldom been studied from a linguistic point of view. Such studies could give additional insights on how to extract information.

Opinion Mining

One of the most interesting information extraction tasks when processing blogs is *opinion mining.* People share their experiences on-line, ventilate their opinions (and frustrations), or simply talk about anything. The large amount of available data creates opportunities for automatic mining and analysis. Especially, politicians and companies are interested in what people think about certain topics or issues. And when politicians and companies start ventilating their opinions, it is the man in the street who wants to extract the ideas on a certain subject.

Opinion mining or attitude recognition currently attracts a great deal of research and commercial interest (an overview of this work can be found in (Shanahan & Wiebe, 2006). Current systems rely on *handcrafted symbolic patterns* (such as words and their sentiment polarity) or on *machine learning* techniques. They mainly detect positive, negative and neutral feelings in a text, passage or sentence. A sentiment is not unambiguously expressed in a text; it is often represented in subtle and complex ways. In addition, we are interested in detecting the attitude towards a certain topic or attribute of that topic (e.g., "the fuel consumption of a Toyota Prius"), but the text might express different contradictory emotions (e.g., "for city traffic it is low, but on freeways I expected it to be less."), or the emotions cited in one sentence might be directed towards several *topics* (e.g., "an Audi Q7 consumes a lot of fuel in comparison with my Prius") and their *attributes*.

There has been little research in identifying the direction of a certain emotion and in linking it to a certain topic and its attributes. This requires the detection of structural links between the emotion and a topic or its attributes. In natural language such structural links are often expressed by dependencies in the parse tree of a sentence. Boiy et al. (2007) (research of the TIME project) demonstrate that such parse information is valuable in improving the accuracy of sentences in which contradictory emotions are present. In this project we determined positive, negative and neutral sentiments towards a given topic with an accuracy of more than 80 percent on blog data using a cascade of classifiers, where about 30% of the classified sentences were not well-formed. In these experiments, traditional sentence parsers failed to process certain sentences.

Argumentation Mining

A very new information extraction task is *argumentation mining*. Argumentative texts are found in our daily discourse. We use arguments each time that we want to persuade a party in the communication process. Arguments are also found in blogs. It is interesting to automatically detect what people, politicians or other parties argue about and what argument they use to sustain a certain opinion or to counter another argument. Moens, Boiy, Mochales Palau and Reed (2007) give first results on the classification of sentences as being argumentative as part of the ACILA project. For this task, simple features such as couples of two words, verbs and text statistics on sentence length, average word length and number of punctuation marks were used to classify the sentences with an accuracy of more than 76% with a multinomial naïve Bayes classifier, when processing news texts. When we look at the errors, we obtain interesting insights. The linguistic markers that we detect (e.g., the adverb "but") are sometimes ambiguous. Many sentences do not give any clue to whether it contains an argument or not. Some reasoning steps are left implicit, and the precise logical connection between individual reasoning steps is not spelled out. The most difficult case to solve is when there are no linguistic markers in the text and the argument detection depends on world and common sense knowledge, which is not present in the text. These difficulties also play a role when we want to recognize different types of arguments and their relations in a discourse, demanding accurate techniques for detecting the rhetorical discourse structure of a text, and perhaps having a better understanding of its semantics in order to infer that, for instance, one statement is countering another one.

In blogs the *argumentation structure* (i.e., argumentative content and its relations) might be distributed across different texts, as the argumentation might follow a kind of dialogue with several participants. Later comments might constitute additional pro or contra arguments. Argumentation detection in such an interactive setting seems a challenging task, which has not been studied yet.

FUTURE RESEARCH

More problems than solutions have been cited with regard to information extraction from blogs, thus leaving much room for future research. First of all, it would be interesting to *combine the different sources* of evidence found in blog texts, their tags, comments and links. Because much of the content we detect is uncertain, Bayesian inference models (e.g., Pearl, 1988, Blei, Bagnell & McCallum, 2002, Manning, 2006) seem well suited. As seen above, blog data are often complementary, but in order to make inferences with these data, it is important to know which textual content of a blog entry precisely relates to the tags, comment, of linked content, and with which types of relationships these data connect. This refers to automatically typing tags, comments or tags with their rhetorical role (e.g., explanation, summarization, contrast), so that data can be optimally aggregated. This is a very novel and challenging task taking into account that the data and thus their semantic meaning can change over time.

The most difficult cases for information extraction are those that are written in some *community language* that is barely understandable by the machine. The processing of these texts comes close to a machine translation task. However, compared to machine translation, we do not have parallel corpora for training translation dictionaries of words and phrases.

With regard to the applications, interesting *monitoring tasks* can be designed, such as detecting propaganda speech, hate discourse and other unlawful content.

Many new challenges can be thought of. For instance, when in the future, content of blogs is monitored and perhaps filtered, a lot of effort will be spent to make the blogs even more obscure for machine processing by *adding irrelevant content*. Additional content can be added in order to mislead filters and this content might really be hidden from the readers of the blogs (cf. De Beer & Moens, 2007).

In addition, blogs are increasingly built of *multimedia objects*. Here also we need techniques to align and integrate these content sources in order to make sense of the whole.

One approach to follow would be to normalize content as well as possible (i.e., lexical and syntactic reconstruction), hereby perhaps considering several confident normalization hypotheses as is done for speech transcription in Mamou, Carmel and Hoory (2006). Compared to figure 1, the normalization component becomes more important during the preprocessing. In addition, we will have to foresee a component that aligns and integrates text, tags, comments, and possible content identified in linked media. Because of a foreseen large uncertainty, when processing the blogs, the classification or extraction model that we build might rely on probabilistic inferences. The above ideas can be tested and expanded in future research.

CONCLUSION

We have defined information extraction as structuring and classifying unstructured data. Blogs are a typical example of such unstructured data. We have focused in this chapter especially on blogs that are spontaneously and instantaneously created and that can change over time through the addition of tags, comments and links.

Humans like to create content and the digital age has given us wonderful tools to generate masses of it. We like to explore this creativity when expressing how we perceive the world around us. Our natural language is a first, important example. Although our utterances are structured to a certain degree, there are a myriad of ways of how we can express ideas by combining a very large set of words and syntactic constructs, possibly illustrated with images, video and audio. We are continuously very creative in finding new words and novel linguistic constructions, apart from innovative forms of communications. Blogs are often written in the form of natural language statements, but the language is subject to many variations that are bound to persons or communities. In addition, the traditional document format or even traditional hypertext medium is exchanged for innovative forms of communication. Threads of conversations are not uncommon, people comment on each other's writings or add tags in a very leisured and flexible way. The result is a labyrinth of content, hardly understandable by the machine.

Information extraction brings some structure to the data, so that they can be more effectively searched, linked, mined and visualized by the machine. In other words, we want to identify specific information and semantically label it on top of the low level (word) data.

Whereas information extraction – especially fact extraction - from texts written in standard natural language is becoming a realistic task, information extraction from blogs is far from solved. Natural utterances are characterized by ambiguity and synonymy. The former refers to the situation where an element is ambiguous, and we need context to disambiguate it. The latter refers to the situation where many different content elements or phrases have the same meaning. On one hand information from blogs seems more difficult because we use many more different expressions than in standard language and they are augmented with links, comments, tags and other media. On the other hand the task should be easier because of the wealth of evidence sources that help to assign meaning, to disambiguate and to link content. However, we have not yet researched information extraction that is based on an alignment and integration of these different data sources.

Citizens, professionals, governments and companies have an increasing interest to search, mine and synthesize blog data. Given their enormous amounts, we need machines to process them. Extracting information from the data is a valuable step.

ACKNOWLEDGMENT

We are very grateful to the organizations that sponsored the research mentioned in this chapter: A4MC3 (Architectures for Mobile Community Content Creation), sponsored by IBBT, in collaboration with Concentra Media; ACILA (Automatic Detection and Classification of Arguments in a Legal Case) sponsored by K.U.Leuven Onderzoeksfonds (OT/06/03); AntiPhish (Anticipatory Learning for Reliable Phishing Prevention) sponsored by EU-FP6; and TIME (Advanced Time-Based Text Analytics) sponsored by IWOIB, in collaboration with Attentio, Belgium. We thank the reviewers for their valuable comments.

REFERENCES

Angheluta, R. and Moens, M.-F., 2007, Cross-document entity tracking, In G. Amati, C. Carpineto & G. Romano (Eds.), *Advances in Information Retrieval - 29th European Conference on IR Research ECIR - Lecture Notes in Computer Science 4425* (pp. 670-674), Berlin: Springer.

Berendt, B. and Hanser, C., 2007, Tags are not metadata, but "just more content" – to some people, In *Proceedings of the International Conference on Weblogs and Social Media ICWSM* (pp. 19-26), Omnipress.

Berg, T. et al., 2007, *Names and faces*, University of California Berkeley. Technical report.

Berger, A.D., Della Pietra, S.A. and Della Pietra, V.J., 1996, A maximum entropy approach to natural language processing, *Computational Linguistics,* 22(1), 39-71.

Bikel, D. M., Schwartz, R. and Weischedel, R.M., 1999, An algorithm that learns what's in a name, *Machine Learning,* 34, 211-231.

Blei, D., Bagnell, J. and McCallum, A., 2002, Learning with scope, with application to information extraction and classification, In *Uncertainty in Artificial Intelligence: Proceedings of the Eighteenth Conference* (UAI-2002) (pp. 53–60), San Francisco, CA: Morgan Kaufmann.

Boiy, E., Hens, P., Deschacht, K. and Moens, M.-F., 2007, Automatic sentiment analysis of on-line text, In *Proceedings of the 11th International Conference on Electronic Publishing, Openness in Digital Publishing: Awareness, Discovery & Access 2007, Vienna Austria.*

Cardie, C. and Wagstaff, K., 1999, Noun phrase coreference as clustering, In *Proceedings of the Joint Conference on Empirical Methods in Natural Language Processing and Very Large Corpora* (pp. 82-89), ACL.

Christianini, N. and Shawe-Taylor, J., 2000, *An Introduction to Support Vector Machines and Other Kernel Based Learning Methods*, Cambridge, UK: Cambridge University Press.

Collins, M. and Singer, Y., 1999, Unsupervised models for named entity classification, In *Proceedings of Empirical Methods in Natural Language Processing (EMNLP)*, College Park, MD.

Cowie, J. and Lehnert, W., 1996, Information extraction, *Communications of the ACM,* 39 (1), 80-91.

Crouch, C.J. and Yang, B., 1992, Experiments in automatic statistical thesaurus construction. In *Proceedings of the 15th Annual International ACM SIGIR Conference on Research and Development of Information Retrieval* (pp. 77-88), New York: ACM.

Cullota, A. and Sorensen, J., 2004, Dependency tree kernels for relation extraction, In *Proceedings of the 42nd Annual Meeting of the Association for Computational Linguistics* (pp. 424-430), East Stroudsburg, PA: ACL.

De Beer, J. and Moens, M.-F., 2007, A general solution of (hidden) text salting. Technical Report K.U.Leuven.

De Smet, W. and Moens, M.-F., 2007, Generating a topic hierarchy from dialect texts. In *Proceedings of the 4th International Workshop on Text-based Information Retrieval* (*TIR-07*), IEEE Computer Society.

Deschacht, K. and Moens, M.-F., 2007, Text analysis for automatic image annotation, In *Proceedings of the 45th Annual Meeting of the Association for Computational Linguistics*, East Stroudsburg: ACL.

Feng, D. and Hovy, E.D., 2006, Learning to detect conversation focus of threaded discussions, in *Proceedings of the Human Language Technology / North American Association of Computational Linguistics conference* (HLT-NAACL 2006), New York, NY.

Fillmore, C.J. and Baker, C.F., 2001, Frame semantics for text understanding, In *Proceedings of WordNet and Other Lexical Resources Workshop.*

Gildea, D. and Jurafsky, D., 2002, Automatic labeling of semantic roles. *Computational Linguistics*, 28(3), 245-288.

Glenisson, P., Glänzel, W., Janssens, F. and De Moor, B., 2005, Combining full text and bibliometric information in mapping scientific disciplines, *Information Processing & Management*, 41 (6), 1548-1572.

Golder, S. and Huberman, B.A., 2007, The structure of collaborative tagging systems, *Journal of Information Science,* 32 (2): 198-208.

Hobbs, J. H. et al., 1996, FASTUS: A cascaded finite-state transducer for extracting information from natural-language text, In *Finite State Devices for Natural Language Processing*, Cambridge MA: The MIT Press.

Jansche, M. and Abney, S.P., 2002, Information extraction from voicemail transcripts, In *Proceedings of Empirical Methods in Natural Language Processing.* East Stroudsburg, PA: ACL.

Lafferty, J., McCallum, A. and Pereira, F.C.N., 2001, Conditional random fields: Probabilistic models for segmenting and labelling sequence data. In *Proceedings of the 18th International Conference on Machine Learning* (pp. 282-289), San Francisco, CA: Morgan Kaufmann.

Li, X., Morie, P. and Roth, D., 2006, Identification and tracing of ambiguous names. In *Proceedings of the Human Language Technology – North American Chapter of the Association for Computational Linguistics* (pp. 17-24).

Mamou, J., Carmel, D. and Hoory R., 2006, Spoken document retrieval from call-center conversations, In *Proceedings of Twenty-Ninth Annual International ACM SIGIR Conference on Research and Development of Information Retrieval* (pp. 51-58), New York: ACM.

Mani, I., Pustejovsky, J. and Gaizauskas, R. (Eds.), 2005, *The Language of Time: A Reader.* Oxford University Press.

Minkov, E., Wang, R.C. and Cohen, W.W., 2004, Extracting personal names from emails, In *Proceedings of the Human Language Technology Conference and Conference on Empirical Methods in Natural Language Processing (HLT/EMNLP)* (pp. 443–450), East Stroudsburg, PA: ACL.

Minsky, M. , 1975, A framework for representing knowledge, In P.H. Winston (Ed.), *The Psychology of Computer Vision* (pp. 211-277), New York: McGraw-Hill.

Moens, M.-F., 2006, *Information Extraction: Algorithms and Prospects in a Retrieval Context (The Information Retrieval Series* 21). New York: Springer.

Moens, M.-F., Boiy, E., Mochales Palau, R. and Reed, C. , 2007, Automatic detection of arguments in legal texts. In *Proceedings of the Eleventh International Conference on Artificial Intelligence and Law,* New York: ACM.

Munteanu, D.S. and Marcu, D., 2006, Extracting parallel sub-sentential fragments from comparable corpora, In *Proceedings of ACL-2006, Sydney, Australia* (pp. 81-88).

Pearl, J. ,1988, *Probabilistic Reasoning in Intelligent Systems*, Morgan-Kaufmann.

Rennie, J.D.M. and Jaakkola, T., 2005, Using term informativeness for named entity detection. In *Proceedings of the Twenty-Eight Annual International ACM SIGIR Conference on Research and Development in Information Retrieval* (pp. 353-360), New York: ACM.

Riloff, E. and Lorenzen, J., 1999, Extraction-based text categorization: Generating domain-specific role relationships automatically, In T. Strzalkowski (Ed.), *Natural Language Information Retrieval* (pp. 167-196), Dordrecht, The Netherlands: Kluwer Academic Publishers.

Schank, R. C., 1975, *Conceptual Information Processing*, Amsterdam: North Holland.

Shanahan, G., Qu, Y. and Wiebe, J. , 2006, *Computing Attitude and Affect in Text: Theory and Applications* (*The Information Retrieval Series* 20), Berlin: Springer.

Sood, S.C., Owsley, S., Hammond, K.J. and Birnbaum, L. , 2007, TagAssist: Automatic tag suggestion for blog posts. In *Proceedings of the International Conference on Weblogs and Social Media ICWSM 2007* (pp. 177-183), Omnipress.

Zhang, J., Shen, D., Zu, G., Jian, S., and Tan, C.L., 2004, Enhancing HMM-based biomedical named entity recognition by studying special phenomena, *Journal of Biomedical Informatics*, 37, 411-422.

KEY TERMS

Argumentative Mining: The detection of an argumentative structure in a discourse and the recognition of its composing elements such as the premises and conclusions of an argument; possibly the integration of the found arguments into a knowledge structure used for reasoning.

Blog (Short for Web Log): A Web based publication consisting primarily of periodic content.

Conditional Random Field (CRF): Learning system for classification often used for labeling sequential data (such as natural language data); as a type of Markov random field, it is an undirected graphical model in which each vertex represents a random variable, whose distribution is to be inferred, and each edge represents a dependency between two variables.

Information Extraction: The identification, and consequent or concurrent classification and structuring into semantic classes, of specific information found in unstructured data sources providing additional aids to access and interpret the unstructured data by information systems.

Maximum Entropy Model: Learning system used for classification that computes the probability distributions corresponding to an object and its class based on training examples, and that selects the one with maximum entropy, where the computed probability distributions satisfy the constraints set by the training examples.

Named Entity Recognition: Classifies named expressions in text (such as person, company, location or protein names).

Noun Phrase Coreferent: Two or more noun phrases are coreferent when they refer to the same situation described in the text.

Opinion Mining: The detection of the opinion or subjective assessment in a certain medium (mostly text) where the opinion is usually expressed towards a certain entity or an entity's attribute; possibly the aggregation of the found opinions into a score that reflects the opinion of a community.

Parser: Software program which analyses the grammatical structure of a sentence according to the grammar of the language; a parser is often automatically trained from annotated examples; it captures the implied hierarchy of the input sentence and transforms it into a form suitable for further processing (e.g., a dependency tree).

Part-of-Speech: Word class or category (also called lexical class) which is generally defined by the syntactic or morphological behaviour of the word in question; common classes are noun, verb and adjective among others.

Support Vector Machine (SVM): Learning system used for classification and regression that uses a hypothesis space of linear functions in a high dimensional feature space, trained with a learning algorithm from optimisation theory; special property of an SVM is that it simultaneously minimizes the empirical classification error and maximizes the geometric margin that separates two classes; hence SVMs are known as maximum margin classifiers.

Tokenization: Breaks a text into tokens or words. It distinguishes words, components of multipart words and multiword expressions.

Treebank: A syntactically processed corpus that contains annotations of natural language data at various linguistic levels (word, phrase, clause and sentence levels). A treebank provides mainly the morphosyntactic and syntactic structure of the utterances within the corpus and consists of a bank of linguistic trees, thereby its name.

ENDNOTE

1 F-measure refers here to the harmonic mean, a measure that combines recall and precision where recall and precision are equally weighted (also referred to as F_1-measure).

Chapter XXIV Nethnography: A Naturalistic Approach Towards Online Interaction

Adriana Andrade Braga
Pontifícia Universidade Católica do Rio de Janeiro, Brazil

ABSTRACT

This chapter explores the possibilities and limitations of nethnography, an ethnographic approach applied to the study of online interactions, particularly computer-mediated communication. In this chapter, a brief history of ethnography, including its relation to anthropological theories and its key methodological assumptions is addressed. Next, one of the most frequent methodologies applied to Internet settings, that is to treat logfiles as the only or main source of data, is explored, and its consequences are analyzed. In addition, some strategies related to a naturalistic perspective for data analysis are examined. Finally, an example of an ethnographic study, which involves participants of a Weblog, is presented to illustrate the potential for nethnography to enhance the study of CMC.

INTRODUCTION

The introduction of computing technology in recent times produced deep changes on communication processes and practices. The first generations of analysts presented a range of positions regarding the study of these new media environments, evidencing very often the limitations of deterministic evaluations of these social facts (e.g. Lévy, 1993; Rheingold, 1993; Turkle, 1995). The concrete uses of these new technological resources created other negotiations regarding meanings and identities. The introduction of the personal computer connected to the worldwide Web brought new ways of dealing with old matters. The interaction protocols and the identity production devices presented by these phenomena demand proper techniques of interpretation. Far from the speculation about the impact of computing technology on human communication, this chapter wishes to present some ways to investigate the social uses of digital environments.

In ordinary interaction, face to face or by telephone, people know how to behave in order to sustain or to cause a certain impression among their acquaintances. Even if there are no formally codified rules, there are tacit methods (Garfinkel, 1967) that allow ordinary members of society to expect some specific responses during social situations. Computer-mediated communication (CMC), as a novel medium, demands from its participants a certain degree of improvisation when facing unexpected or new situations. In these cases, patterns of conduct taken from other contexts are adapted, in order to create new tacit rules for behavior within these settings. As these new social environments demand improvisation and adaptation from the participants to deal with unexpected situations, it is argued that it also demands from the analyst a combination or adaptation of methods originally designed to investigate different contexts, in order to fully grasp the specificity of CMC.

The study of social behavior on Internet environments presents a great methodological challenge. A first remark on method refers to the historical period in which the research takes place. These forms of interaction are recent phenomena, and they depart from individual and group strategies not inherited, but acquired through the use and adaptation of already-existing rules, taken from other relational contexts. Such strategies are applied on a case-by-case basis, according to situational demands, prior to an explicit formal or even tacit codification. These rules-in-the-making will consolidate later, as online cultural activities go on.

Thus, the aim of this chapter is to present a methodological perspective through which social interaction in online environments can be studied naturalistically, that is, focusing mainly on the observation of naturally occurring phenomena.

In order to explore the possibilities and limitations of an ethnographic approach applied to the study of online interaction, a brief history of ethnography will first be addressed, including its relation with anthropological theories, and its key methodological assumptions. Next, one of the most frequent methodologies applied to Internet settings is discussed, that is to treat logfiles as the only or main source of data, and some of its consequences are analyzed. In addition, some strategies related to a naturalistic perspective for data analysis are examined. Finally, an example of an ethnographic study is presented which involves participants of a Weblog to illustrate the potential for nethnography to enhance the study of CMC.

This chapter presents aspects of the methodology developed in a research project concluded in 2006 that investigated communicational interaction within an Internet environment, the 'guestbook' of a Brazilian Weblog dedicated to contemporary motherhood, called "Mothern" (mother + modern), available at www.mothern.blogspot.com. This Weblog was chosen because of its unique combination of both traditional and modern concepts of femininity, coping with all the contradictions derived from this perspective. Besides that, the Weblog Mothern had an astonishing career on the Internet, generating two best-selling books, an editorial section on a feminine magazine, and a TV show – now in its second season. The multi-method perspective detailed in this chapter was designed to grasp the concrete uses and consumption of this communication technology by the participants. Its key assumptions, once taken with proper care, can be applied to the study of online interaction in other Internet settings, such as social networking sites.

THE ETHNOGRAPHIC TRADITION

Ethnography was conceived and historically applied to the study of groups in face-to-face contact with the ethnographer, in which his/her experience is taken as a data source. The unique interpersonal exchange occurring on the Internet is a sort of novelty, that brings methodological challenges to the application of this traditional research method, making it necessary to adjust some premises of ethnography to these new objects.

In the late nineteenth century, ethnography referred to a clear division of scientific labor, in which the "ethnologist" stays in his/her office sending questionnaires to missionaries, merchants or travelers on the way to distant and exotic places such as New Guinea, Africa or Australia. These informers were asked also to acquire objects for "ethnographic collections" in museums in Europe. Many pieces from this period can be found in places like "The British Museum," in England or "Le Musée de l'Homme," in France.

Although the collection of first-hand data among exotic groups and its written description can be taken as an ancient procedure – as the famous and sometimes fantastic "travelers stories," like those of Marco Polo and Hans Staden – the creation and full development of ethnography as a research technique has happened only in the late XIX and early XX Centuries. Even though some of the theoretical basis of cultural evolutionists (like Sir James George Frazer (2000, 1890), Sir Edward Burnett Tylor (1924, 1870) and Lewis Henry Morgan (1985, 1877), to name a few) were in fact convergent with ethnographic fieldwork, mainly regarding the prescription of an empirical foundation, their works were most of the time mere speculation about the "origins" of Humanity, written after second or third-hand information about "primitive" peoples that they never actually saw personally. It was just after the severe methodological criticism posed by Franz Boas (1901) to this theoretical scheme that the premises of ethnographic fieldwork had a first sketch. Boas emphasized the importance of the personal presence of the researcher in the field, considering the acquired skill in the natives' language and long-term permanence among them as fundamental capacities for a successful investigation. The strong empiricist position of Boas had established a tradition in Cultural Anthropology: a generation of great anthropologists had graduated under the direct supervision of Boas in Columbia University, like Ruth Benedict, Margaret Mead and Edward Sapir.

The first major theoretical formulation of the ethnographic method was published in 1922, in the classic "The Argonauts of the Western Pacific," by Bronislaw Malinowski (1953, 1922). In this book, written after a four-year period among the natives of the Trobriand Islands, a few miles East of New Guinea, Malinowski laid the foundations of the ethnographic method, structuring it with the application of two techniques: participant observation and ethnographic fieldwork.

Malinowski's classic study was described by Yves Winkin (1998) as the first of three revolutions in Social Anthropology, intending to catch the native's point of view from within. This attitude marks this revolution, in which the ethnographer stays for long periods in the field, and in which the people observed are not taken as an exotic specimen, but as respectable human beings, whose social activities deserve to be reported. The second revolution is set in the early 1930s, when Lloyd Warner, an American anthropologist, after studying Australian Aborigine tribes under the supervision of Radcliffe-Brown, started to use ethnography to analyze small towns in Massachusetts and Illinois, on the so-called "community studies." This application was revolutionary because, for the first time, ethnographic technique was applied to a 'civilized' society.

Traditionally, ethnography was designed to analyze 'primitive' cultures, whose lack of written documents led to direct observation of behavior as a data source. Community studies like this broadened the theoretical range of Social Anthropology, bringing it closer to the Department of Sociology of the University of Chicago, the renowned "Chicago School." In the1950s, there is the third revolution when some Chicago sociologists, such as Ward Goodenough, Howard Becker and Erving Goffman, apply a notion of culture that broadens even more the scope of ethnography, overcoming the study of isolated communities, like ethnic ghettos or small mid-west towns.

Defining culture as what is needed for someone to be a member (Goodenough, 1957), the object of ethnography was the system of social regulation, the implicit and explicit rules, the latent and manifest knowledge that should be acquired in order of 'being a member', in such a way that an individual can act in a predictable way towards his/her group. Ethnographic fieldwork relies on the idea that the universal is in the heart of the particular, and that analytic precision allows generalization. Since this "third revolution," ethnography can be potentially applied wherever systems of rules (tacit or not) can be identified, defining inclusion and exclusion, members and not-members, insiders and outsiders.

NETHNOGRAPHY: POSSIBILITIES AND LIMITS OF A NON-PARTICIPANT OBSERVATION

In order to employ ethnography for the study of CMC, researchers should have an in-depth understanding of the theoretical assumptions which support this methodology and engage in an interdisciplinary exchange with researchers employing the same research design in conventional settings. The potential of ethnography for CMC resides in the centrality of the researcher as the main source of data through her/his experience within the site and presupposes an extensive and deep exposure to the setting. Therefore, in this section, the status of the researcher as a participant in Internet sites is discussed, as well as the potential uses and limitations that such strategy entails.

The notion of sociability, originally defined by Georg Simmel (1983, 1911) as 'the play-form of sociation,' is widely used by Internet researchers when dealing with digital environments, sometimes raising arguments and contradictions, for instance, on the notion of "virtual communities." Very often the notion of community draws upon a nostalgic concept of an ideal, natural and homogeneous type of social gathering. The utopia of an ideal community, intelligent and cosmopolitan presents some contradictions, however. How can the conception of a shelter for the individual among his/her peers be taken along with one of a space for tolerance with diversity? Such a nostalgic view upon pre-industrial communities had been criticized under the argument of the destructive power of homogeneous groups, which tend to expel 'strangers' trying to replace the original order.

In this sense, at the same time that a limitless freedom of expression for the Internet is claimed, there is the need for rules that allow the collective co-existence, albeit these rules are still being structured. In being so, the patterns of verbal expression held on these settings are in some way submitted to the social control of participants. The freedom created by anonymity, the absence of physical presence that would expose body, gender or class predicates – typical features of online behavior – can serve either as an incentive to friendship and intimacy or to aggression and disrespect towards others. In many discussion lists, assertively open to new members, newcomers are often ignored for not presenting the desired profile for a member, a condition for welcoming and belonging. On occasions, it is possible to perceive situations in which the lack of affinity of a newcomer with the regular participants' norms leads to reactions that can vary from ostracism to open aggression.

Currently, researchers who investigate social interactions on the Internet do not pay much attention to the discussion on the methodological procedures they employ in their analysis. However, to think about the cultural dynamics of the Internet requires a previous reflection on its empirical specificities. The ethnographic method can be pertinent and operational in this sense, in spite of its demanding of complementary methodologies.

In a classic text of Social Anthropology, "The Interpretation of Cultures," Clifford Geertz (1973) makes a standpoint between those who worry about the limitation and the specificity of the notion of culture, trying to keep it within a frame that warrants its pertinence. In trying to define the ethnographic procedures – in order to fit it into the conception of Anthropology as a form of knowledge – Geertz states clearly that, beyond mere technique, such as selection of informers, mapping of the field, transcription of texts, keeping a diary, etc, the defining feature of ethnography is what Gilbert Ryle called "thick description." The notion of "thick description" was originally used by the British philosopher Gilbert Ryle (1968), in a lecture about the description of thought as action. To Ryle, there are different levels of thickness in a description. To a thin description, that perceives only a single level of meaning for a given action – one that could be captured by a camera, for instance – he opposes the possibility of a thick description, in which the multiple layers of meaning of a given phenomenon can be interpreted.

Between what Ryle called thin and thick description lies the object of ethnography, a hierarchical stratification of meaningful structures. The analyst must choose between the different structures of meaning, and, from then on, define its relevance. The ethnographer, then, faces multiple complex conceptual structures, overlaid and interconnected, that need to be understood and presented.

Considering culture in such terms, the personal experience of ethnography would be to stand within a given cultural environment, in order to accomplish the scientific undertaking: the formulation of a basis that could contribute to the enlargement of the universe of human discourse. It is important to remark that culture as a natural fact is different from culture as a theoretical entity. Being so, the ethnographer interprets the given facts of culture, materializing social discourse into words, a document that can be retrieved at any time, keeping the moment for study and research.

Ethnographic technique, for its emphasis on the experience of the researcher as a data source, has become a promising theoretical approach towards research objects related to CMC. Such a choice demands theoretical deepening, impregnation on fieldwork data and, possibly, interdisciplinary dialogue with researchers that use this method in a more traditional way.

The application of ethnographic-based techniques wishes to build up a report about a micro-level communicational situation focusing on the circumstances. To do so, the researcher should do direct observation as a source of data collection in a fieldwork diary, selection of informers for open interviews and participation in the activities of the group. Generalization, in this case, is made possible by the subtlety of distinctions, not by the dimension of abstractions: conclusions are taken from small facts. Through the examination of the social facts and the system of symbols related to them, the ethnographer seeks to understand the informal logic that compound the cultural forms. In such an interlocution environment, an interpretive analysis of the discourses would explore the Web of meanings through an attitude of selective distance, resulting in a rigorous report, however inherently incomplete and questionable.

The neologism "nethnography" (net + ethnography) was originally coined by a group of American researchers, Bishop, Star, Neumann, Ignacio, Sandusky and Schatz in 1995, to describe a methodological challenge: to preserve the rich details of ethnographic fieldwork observations while using the electronic media to "follow the actors." Their study tested new equipment for a digital library at the University of Illinois.

Recently, other researchers had adopted some of the different terms designed to cover the application of ethnography to study digital environments. Most of them focus on data collected on logfiles (Kozinets, 2002, 2005; Langer and Beckman, 2005, Dicks et al., 2005), although a more naturalistic position, closer to traditional ethnography can also be found (Hine, 2005, Rutter and Smith, 2005, Greiffenhagen and Watson, 2005).

The usage of ethnographic technique towards Internet interaction, however, raises some methodological issues that must be dealt with. In methodological terms, ethnography is grounded in the notion of participant observation, taking for granted that it is impossible, in face-to-face situations, to have observation without participation. Now, digital environments of CMC are characterized by the physical absence of its participants, being perfectly possible to be there "invisible."(such a practice is denominated as "lurking"). In being so, is it possible to fully understand the culture of a group without participating in it, just watching? Is a non-participant observation possible?

I depart from the perspective that it is impossible to observe without participating, that is, observation itself could be a form of participation. However, what matters here is that, definitely, it is a very peculiar sort of participation, since it is possible for the observer to be "invisible," observe without being observed, not interfering, in principle, in the dynamics of the situation, although one must take into account that the possibility of lurkers are considered by participants. It is this participation in the group (even if invisible) that will allow the understanding of aspects of that culture, in the way of elaborating a thick description of the situation, a procedure that demands a detailed comprehension of the members' shared meanings.

The condition that makes ethnography possible is the immersion and the experience of effective participation in the fieldwork situation. It includes participation, observation, and description: categories that form the unity of ethnography. So, is lurking considered "participation?" Yes, it is, but of a very special kind. I understand online participant observation as a "special participation" because, in terms of presence/absence, the information about the observer on the setting is not immediately accessible to other participants, although the presence of lurkers can be inferred through the discrepancy between the number of accesses and the number of registered comments, as well as through the possibility of identification of the internet providers or IP numbers of visitors.

Rutter and Smith (2002a) give an interesting example in this sense. Discussing the particularities of interaction on a text-based environment, the newsgroup they called "RunCom.local," they present some advantages of ethnography in online settings:

...online ethnography is surely a researcher's dream. It does not involve leaving the comforts of your office desk; there are no complex access privileges to negotiate; field data can be easily recorded and saved for later analysis; large amounts of information can be collected quickly and inexpensively. (Rutter & Smith, 2002a, p. 3)

Rutter and Smith do not recognize their work as a participant observation, at least not as it is conventionally understood. They acknowledge having practiced much more observation than participation, and this took them to question the very notion of the research setting (Rutter and Smith, 2002a: 4). They warn about the importance of the researcher being conscious about where we are studying as electronic ethnographers, since, as in a phone call, relationships on the Internet are defined by acts of communication, considering that there is no "place" on the Internet beyond metaphor.

Another pertinent topic regarding this perspective deals with the ethics implications they bring along. In a physical setting, the very presence of the ethnographer is an aspect to be negotiated in the fieldwork, while the "net presence" (Agre, 1994) seems to be something quite indistinct (Barnes, 2004). Regarding traditional ethnography, Winkin (1998) sustains that the ethnographer should be absolutely clear about his/her identity in field situations, and a reasonably open about his/her research agenda. The fact is that the relation between presence/absence has specific implications for Internet research.

THE LOGFILE TEMPTATION

One of the most frequent analytical approaches to Internet settings is to treat logfiles as the only or main source of data (for instance, Dicks and Mason, 1998, Dicks et al. 2005, Kozinets, 2002, 2005) In this section, I will explore some of the consequences of such an approach. In addition, I will examine some strategies related to a naturalistic perspective for data analysis. Logfiles present a general view of the situation in which data is usually interpreted from the researcher's perspective rather than from CMC's participants. In addition, seldom interaction processes that take place over time are captured by such analysis. Computers are involved in many everyday life activities and the communication established through this means may have distinct meanings, beyond communication *per se*. For this reason, the exclusive use of logfiles represents a risk of de-contextualising, and thus misrepresenting, CMC.

Standing in opposition to those that present the introduction of computer technology as producing a radical transformation in society, Greiffenhagen and Watson (2005) consider online activities as transformations, complements or supplements of non-online activities, and are rarely substitutions or something completely without precedents. In the study of social actions, the sense of these actions – for the members – is seen as being locally situated and practical, that is, involve a range of practical considerations for being used, in what Schutz (1962) calls "the everyday life attitude." Such activities are characterized more for their practical than theoretical nature. Thus, proceeding through an adequate empirical analysis on an instance-by-instance basis is recommended.

From an ethnomethodological perspective, it is important to study "locally-situated" instances of CMC uses, a phenomenon that cannot be interpreted through a global and abstract theoretical description:

> *the term 'CMC' suggests that we are dealing with a single phenomenon. In contrast, we suggest that CMC is not a single, unitary, or self-contained phenomenon. Instead, we are dealing with diverse instances where CMC features in some particular activity or complex of activities. These instances may well show some similarities, overlaps, etc. – but will not be exactly identical. This is why ethnomethodology considers it important to examine single, locally-situated instances of, in this case, CMC use. For us, then, CMC is not a unitary phenomenon which can be rendered through an abstract, overall theoretical depiction.* (Greiffenhagen & Watson 2005, p. 91)

In terms of method, ethnomethodology implies the notion of 'unique adequacy requirement,' a competence demanded from the analyst on the concerning activity. Such competence can avoid the researcher describing the activities of members as a mere stipulation or focus on the difficulties of the beginner. That is, what may appear as familiar or obvious to regular participants of a specific situation may seem 'strange' or 'extraordinary' to an observer not competent in that field.

Logfiles, an outcome of CMC technology, are very often taken as "the" data, solving many problems of collecting information. However, Greiffenhagen and Watson point out some risks of such a methodological choice. Logfiles present a "bird's eye" perspective on the situation, that is, a point of view typical from the analyst, not from the participants of the CMC, besides the fact that it misses the possibility of grasping how participants establish their contacts over time. Computers are implied in wider activities of everyday life, communication established through this medium may have other purposes than communication itself. Thus, depending only on logfiles leads to a de-contextualization that may not allow the phenomenon to be properly understood. The choice of some analysts of taking logfiles as independent information, and granting priority exclusively to their contents erases the specificities of CMC.

In this sense, researchers that take logfiles as the only data source, according to Greiffenhagen and Watson, could be characterized as what Roy Turner (1974) once called 'archaeologists by choice,' analysts that choose to consider only fragments and traces of a society in their studies, while the society itself is still available for examination.

Many studies are designed as a 'comparison' between natural-occurrence speech (e. g., everyday conversations) and online chatting, highlighting its similarities and differences. Such choice can be criticized under the argument that, although oral-listening conversation is one of the evident models for CMC activities, it certainly is not the only one. The application of models conceived specifically for natural oral-listening conversation by researchers of digital environments has caused many mistakes in CMC studies. It is evident that aspects of natural conversations can be identified in online communication; however, aspects of other instances such as letter-writing, telephone calls, walkie-talkie or written notes can either be identified in such communications. Being so, these models must be used carefully, on an instance-by-instance basis. They are a possible resource among others locally-situated. Under the risk of taking deviations to the original model on trivial communicational flow between participants being taken as 'confuse,' 'interruptive' and so on, they are being posed against a standard that does not consider the specificities of CMC activities.

ETHNOGRAPHY APPLIED TO ONLINE COMMUNICATION: A METHODOLOGICAL PERSPECTIVE

In this section, I will present the research design of an ethnographic study which involved participants of a Weblog. This methodology can be adapted to analyze other social networking sites, once care is taken to account for local differences in contexts, topics of interest or activities carried on by participants. The researcher has employed a series of online data collection methods taking into account the communication tools employed by the participants (Weblogs, photologs, Orkut, e-mail, instant messenger, etc), in addition to other strategies, such as cell phone, digital camera, regular mail, and face-to-face meetings. Such diversity has required from both the participants and the researcher some degree of improvisation, given the novelty entailed by the combination of these communication devices. Furthermore, the researcher has created an analytical process to account for the relationship between content and means of communication.

The limits and possibilities pointed out above make evident the need for developing a composition of techniques for every research, a specific methodological device, that Howard Becker (1993) calls "multimethod." I would like to point out a specific feature of the wide universe of feminine culture, as an illustration of the application of ethnography to online interactions: feminine computer-mediated communication. To do so, I chose as a point for observation the environment around a successful Weblog, called 'Mothern.' The title connects the words 'mother' and 'modern,' relating the semantic field of motherhood to that of modernity. The focus group seems to be emblematic in Brazilian context, since these women represent the first generation in contact with computer technology in everyday work life.

Participants of CMC accomplish their activities using resources taken from many former communicational practices that can be analyzed by different methods, complementary to ethnography. In this case, the use and consumption of the Internet by participants led to the specific methodological composition employed, that is a combination of ethnography with discourse analysis.

On the Weblog Mothern, as in many others on the Internet, it is possible to verify the recurrence of a communication circuit that includes gathering and dispersion of participants throughout the digital environments, with intense exchange of links and files of text, sound and image, the use of complementary media that surpasses the digital frontiers, like telephone, mobile phones, standard mail, cameras, etc, and face-to-face meetings. The configuration of this course, that I called "blog-circuit" points to the pertinence of the methodological arrangement proposed in this chapter as a promising model for the analysis of social interaction on Internet environments.

In the configuration of this methodological proposal, there are two key-concepts that are operational, the notions of "social interaction" (Goffman, 1967) and "enunciation" (Benveniste, 1989). These concepts were produced in quite distinct contexts. The notion of social interaction was formulated in the so-called "Chicago School of Sociology," trying to understand the processes of symbolic exchange between participants in the same social situation; the concept of enunciation refers to a descriptive dimension of the ways through which discourses are produced.

Social situations on the Internet present some specificity that need to be described. Erving Goffman (1959: 22), using the so called "dramaturgic metaphor," separates the places in which social behavior takes place into two wide categories that he calls "backstage" and "front," respectively, the region where social action is prepared for presentation to others, and the region where action is represented. According to his theory, when people are in the front, presenting themselves to others, they are generally polite, while in the backstage they may criticize, mock up or complain about them. Communication on the Weblog Mothern many times deal with personal, even intimate, topics, expressed through a backstage language, closer to speech than to writing, although their communication activity relies more in written text than in any other medium (Barnes, 2004). Being so, online activities, particularly those occurring on Weblogs are described by some analysts as if they would happen in an indistinct frontier between "public" and "private." However, an ethnographic perspective of the object reveals that participants are completely aware of this distinction, separating "public" topics and positions for the guestbook, while "private" ones are sent by e-mail or telephone.

Data such as telephone numbers are never published in the guestbook, although there are references to the exchange of numbers by e-mail, making mobile phones the most important medium when it comes to face to face meetings. The same information control over telephone numbers is exerted towards residential addresses of participants. Even the e-mail addresses shown in the guestbook are very often created just for that purpose, preserving the "main" e-mail address just for trusty people, that is, those who were personally introduced by an acquaintance. It is worth noting that such private information could only be retrieved for research purposes by the participation in personal meetings and interviews, as logfiles are too "public" for such a confession.

Communication activity in the Mothern environment motivated many participants to create their own Weblogs, presenting the personal experience of each new blogger with motherhood. So, during these years of activity, there were dozens of new Weblogs, shaping a circuit of online interaction among these women. However, it is interesting to remark that this intense online activity does not exclude face to face contact. Participants very often promote meetings in different Brazilian cities, in which conversation concerns mainly their online activity. Complimentarily, these meetings are described and discussed on the Weblogs and guestbooks, and pictures taken are posted on photologs.

Communication in an online environment does not substitute communication in other Internet places or face to face meetings, but participation as technical resources motivated by socialization. It must be remarked, however, that this circulation outside the guestbook is promoted by subgroups within the community, while many other participants, although active, do not surpass the digital environment. The creation of a parallel discussion list only available to the pioneers of the community shows some limits of the alleged openness of this public environment.

The Internet offers many different environments, each with its specificities, in which different forms of social interaction take place. The guestbook's intense activity evidences the preference of participants for the comment-organization system, for its simplicity and quickness in sending and reading messages. Internet providers and email addresses of participants are often changed, evidencing the stage of development and testing of these technologies for them. The basic form of contact participants establish with computing technology is of "tryout." Very often, participants ask for feedback of their experiences in the guestbook.

An important feature of online behavior is a reciprocity system, in which a visit to a Weblog – registered with a comment in its guestbook – must have retribution by the blogger, with a visit to the visitor's own Weblog and the posting of a comment. Of course this reply is related to the degree of symbolic importance of the visited towards the visitor. A visitor considered annoying or indifferent will probably not receive a reply to his/her visit even if a written invitation was posted. Similar dynamics occur with the list of recommended Websites through available links on Weblogs homepages.

A word must be said about instant messenger. This technology complements the online activity of participants. The intensive use of instant messenger by participants can be observed since the beginning of this Internet tool. When the guestbook activities started to register increasing numbers of comments, instant messenger was used in the creation of sub-groups, people that shared affinities and looked for privacy.

The categorization of instant messenger by participants as a "live" medium is noteworthy. Being a text-based communication tool, instant messenger evidently operate with a gap between a statement and its reply. What's "live" on instant messenger is that two – or more – participants know they are simultaneously online and interconnected on the screen. So, it is a very peculiar kind of "live" medium whose features eventually make it preferable to telephonic conversation, as the gap between statements allows a lapse of time for thinking about or reviewing what has been "said" while in an almost simultaneous response. This medium can be combined with other gadgets, such as microphones, speakers or Webcams and software, such as Skype or the same instant messenger, in newer versions. Such continuous development of possibilities for computer-mediated communication makes the contact with technological novelties and the exchange of information about them a constant topic among the participants.

Participants of the Mothern blog-circuit can be considered lay users of computer technology. They have found a way of expression through the facilities of novel Internet tools and interfaces. In private environments of cyberspace, such as the parallel discussion list, they meet for chatting on intimate issues, disguising the existence of the list on the Internet provider, so that they can not be found by regular search engines.

A myriad of groups of interest use the social spaces available on the Internet. However, these places seem to be structurally incomplete. In the comments left on the guestbook, as well as in interviews with regular participants, the recognition is that if it war not for the Internet, all those people would never notice the existence of the others. However, when the situation demands the expression of true affection, they use a traditional medium, such as the telephone, or, preferably, physical presence, in the form of a visit or a gift sent by regular mail, evidencing the lack of legitimacy or trust attributed to online communication.

Even if the topics on the Weblog seem to be quite far from what would be of journalistic interest, and much closer to intimacy, the use participants make of this environment states clearly the limits between what is intimate and personal and what can be published. On the Weblog, there are plenty of links for definitely private communication: personal e-mails of each of the "bloggers" and of every participant that wishes to publicize this information. Within the dynamics of this Weblog, it can be perceived that really intimate topics are not dealt with in the guestbook, taken by participants as an undoubtedly public place. To them, the guestbook is a meeting point, among others, but they definitely do not see it as an intimate forum.

On "The Presentation of Self in Everyday Life," Goffman considers that "information about the individual helps to define the situation, enabling others to know in advance what he will expect of them and what they may expect of him." (Goffman, 1959: 1) In the presentation of self by newcomers it is possible to identify some patterns that distinguish the entrance on that setting that may vary from praise to open criticism. It is worth noting that, although the Weblog Mothern is dedicated to motherhood, this topic is not always evident on the presentation of self by newcomers. Even if the topic is present in most of the messages left, praising the Weblog and its contents seems to be the most frequent pattern.

The specific research object analyzed in this chapter demanded a specific methodological device. I did not work with the Weblog as a whole, but rather chose some structures, taken as dynamic spots of the communication being held there, along with complementary data: i) the content of the guestbook linked to the Weblog, a starting point that lead to the other data sources; ii) transcriptions of interviews with informers selected by the contact established on the guestbook; iii) fieldwork notes taken during participation in face-to-face meetings promoted by the participants; iv) video recordings of natural situations of computer use during communicative practices on the Weblog. Interviewing privileges "fresh talk" as much as possible, avoiding survey-like questionnaires. Thus, a face to face meeting or even a phone call are preferable as interviewing situations than email or live messenger, since the dilemmas and contradictions of the situation may arise in the form of laughter, uneasiness, nodding, silence and so on. By e-mail or instant messenger, the possibility of editing the text before sending favors the expression of more reflexive answers, missing an important part of the phenomenon. Beyond the more evident elements of the Weblog – posts, links, layout and guestbook – it is possible to perceive a set of principles, values and interpretations of events, dynamic negotiations of meaning and definitions of the situation carried on by participants.

Thus, fractions of definitions of reality appear as topics for debate in the guestbook, followed by other related positions, structuring "threads," defined by Rutter and Smith (2002a) as a sequence of comments motivated by a given topic in online interactions. A thread, in this sense, is the result of a double contingency: the discursive order (in its political dimension of negotiation of meanings) and the interaction order (in its dynamics of presentation of self of participants).

I took as a starting point the content of the guestbook, as it concentrates the main dynamic points of the Mothern blog-circuit. In the guestbook, the analysis centered on: i) the first comments, the entrance of newcomers; ii) comments that introduce a new topic which generated reactions or a new thread. To analyze this data, mainly composed by written messages, I used techniques of discourse analysis.

The strong interactional dimension of the phenomenon analyzed pointed out the need to relate discourse analysis to ethnographic fieldwork, in such a way that the complex interactional

Figure 1. Data sources of nethnography

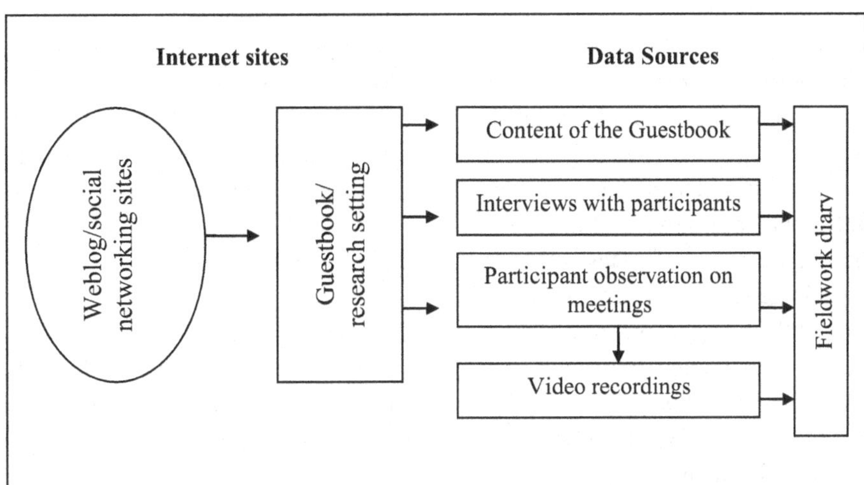

dynamics could be understood. So, there were analyzed transcriptions of interviews – face-to-face, by telephone or e-mail – with the bloggers and regular participants, fieldnotes taken on 'Mothern meetings,' periodically promoted by participants, written interactions found on other Weblogs related to Mothern and the content of an ethnographic fieldwork diary, started on the first session of fieldwork and that followed throughout the research process.

In summary, to properly study the digital environment of Mothern, I focused on the relation between guestbook/regular posts; Mothern/other Weblogs and subsidiary communities; personal meetings among participants/photologs; and fieldwork diary/transcription of interviews with selected informers. All these connections allowed a characterization of the social interaction circuit established by the group.

AN ANALYTIC APPLICATION

Motherhood as a topic of conversation nowadays can easily be taken as something outdated, connected to a traditional perspective of femininity, and related to the triad husband-household-children. As an example, we could think of Miranda, of the late 'Sex and the City' television show, who apologized to her friends for allowing matters of motherhood to enter into their interaction, while accounting for baby pictures on her walls. Once motherhood as a topic of conversation seems to find no place in modern times, it is interesting to think that the Internet can provide a meeting point for discussions on this subject, without the prejudice and articulated with the positively-valued meanings of technological updating and participation in the public sphere.

There are many different forms of using the digital environment allowed by Weblogs. In this case, rescuing a traditional feminine practice that, under a masculine perspective, could easily be taken as futile and unnecessary. In workplaces, from where most of the participants access the Internet, feminine sociability – epiphenomenon of online work – finds a way of expression.

The distinction of two "orders" in the organization of this Weblog can be applied to other Weblogs and digital environments: the Interaction Order, formal modalities that structure the social interaction, such as conflicts, entrance of newcomers and visitors behavior; and the Discourse Order, the field of meanings, socio-symbolic dimension in which relations of power between participants are managed. I would now like to describe some interactional modalities that take place within this Weblog.

Online communication has peculiar interaction rituals, different from those held in face to face interaction. The arrival of a newcomer in the guestbook is in general motivated by: i) the exposure of one of the bloggers on conventional media, ii) by recommendation of friends that already interact on the guestbook or – in the beginning of the Weblog, iii) by friends and relatives congratulating them for the novelty.

In the beginning of the Weblog Mothern, the average number of comments in the guestbook per month was around 250. After a successful work of publicity, with acquaintances and other Weblog owners, the number of visitors rose to a peak of 2000 comments, returning after that to a stable flow of about 500 comments per month. After the first appearances of the Weblog owners in the media – newspapers and magazines – there was a rapid increase of this rate, raising the average to about 4000 comments per month.

In these comments left by newcomers there are some identifiable interactional patterns, both on the entrance and on the reaction to this entrance. Between usual participants, the interaction taking place on this guestbook seems to avoid conflicts, framing the general situation as what Georg Simmel called 'sociability' (Simmel, 1983). For Goffman (1959), most of social interaction is possible by the voluntary engagement of participants in what he calls "working consensus" (1959, p. 10), a sort of superficial agreement in which each participant gives up part of his/her personal positions to hold a shared definition of the situation common to all. However, sometimes disruption can emerge due to the entrance of a hostile newcomer or to the proposal of a polemic subject.

These polemic topics are usually related to the 'feminine universe,' such as abortion, drinking during pregnancy, homosexuality, children education, and so on. In summary, by mixing uncompromising leisure and proposing topics for discussion, definitions for each situation debated are proposed and defended or attacked within this environment, defined by the participants as a place for freedom of expression.

The Entrance

The Weblog has been online for the past four years, and compiling a guestbook for the same time, in which participants enter as newcomers, writing an initial comment, that can receive comments from other participants. Most of these first time comments use praise as a 'password' to the interactional environment. Motherhood as a topic is rather frequent, but the pure praise (as in many other Weblogs) is the major resource for acceptance between other participants. The reaction to praise is usually a kind reply by the bloggers, which evidences the sequence praise-welcoming. Sometimes, the entrance is held without praise, the newcomer asks directly for advice, information or poses a suggestion, a form that I call 'no-praise,' which is also usually welcome.

However, in some cases the entrance is rather turbulent, with harsh critiques to the topics discussed in the guestbook. In these cases – not many – the reaction of the regular participants is quick and full-strength. They face any critique to their contents claiming the guestbook as a place for absolute freedom of expression, framing the critiques as outrageous assaults to their freedom. It is worth noting that when a disagreement like this happens, the replies tend to define the public space of the guestbook as a private one. This defensive pattern can be seen in many other conflicts in the guestbook, defined by its usual participants as private property, in which they make the rules, and let discontents go away. Hence, as it could be observed in many different Weblogs, the entrance of newcomers usually follows one of these modalities: praise, no-praise or criticism, producing reactions accordingly.

Conflicts

Eventually, the usual kindness rules of this interactional environment are challenged by conflicts between participants. These conflicts often rise due to opposite positions regarding polemic topics. In such cases, there are long series of comments in which positions are radically taken, hesitating members are challenged, accusations are exchanged, and participants decide to go away or are banished, in a dynamic ruled by conflict. Although this kind of situation does not define the regular atmosphere within the guestbook, several conflicts have been observed in its four years of activity.

One example occurred when a young participant asked for advice, complaining she was pregnant, but still lived with her parents, just like her boyfriend, who was unemployed, and she asked the other participants whether she should abort or not. In two days, hundreds of comments were posted. The specific topic lost its relevance and was changed by a metaphysical matter, with divided opinions between "pro-life" versus "pro-choice." The episode ended with the voluntary departure of two participants who radically condemned the pro-choice position.

During conflicts, as in other Weblogs, the behavior of participants tends to align towards a consensual position, in which minor differences are set aside in order to act in unity against the opponents. As Simmel (1983) points out, conflict is at the same time a force of destruction and cohesion. The actions in such a situation may vary from open aggression to ostracism, according to the relative status of the opponent involved.

Informal Theorization of Femininity

Of the three categories presented, this is the most specific of the discourse order regarding the Weblog Mothern. Every Weblog has its own specificity, which makes it assemble specific readers and participants. Hierarchies of relevance are, thus, locally situated and must be studied on a case by case basis. Considering the dynamic process of updating feminine culture, it is interesting to remark the 'encyclopedic' dimension of the topics discussed within the guestbook. They talk about several issues concerning motherhood: alcohol-drinking in the presence of children, smoking, illegal drug using, homosexual experiences, alternative medicine, dieting, children nurturing, breastfeeding, toys, gender roles, media products for children, and many more. In doing so, these young mothers seem to re-think motherhood, creating a sort of informal theorization that aims to negotiate contemporary definitions about femininity, available in the context of this mediated public sphere.

Examining these informal theoretical statements, can be seen as a general intention to re-think habits, practices and morals in society, but usually these proposals are thought of as programs for individual action, and not as a project of political transformation.

FINAL REMARKS

Emergent social practices such as computer-mediated communications demand new methodological devices to analyze them. This chapter proposed a methodological position grounded on naturalistic observation, an ethnographic perspective applied to online interactions.

It seems necessary to enhance naturalistic studies of Internet settings in which the rich experiences of the ethnographic tradition are taken into consideration. Much research self-presented as (n)ethnographic disregards essential dimensions of ethnographic fieldwork, such as patience and long term observation thereby misunderstanding the phenomenon. As online activities do not happen exclusively online, it is difficult to grab their full significance for its participants without leaving the researcher's office.

Ethnography represents a promising design for the empirical study of CMC, if properly adapted. After all, these emergent social practices present particular features that demand a considerable mediation regarding the rules of the traditional ethnographic method. The mere transposition of participant observation to CMC can be very problematic, given the potential non-participant role of the researcher in online exchanges. Another risk consists of assuming that online communication occurs exclusively online and that all that is said or exchanged is available through Webfiles, easily accessed and stored. One of the key contributions of nethnography is to move the researcher beyond the temptation of a one-stop data collection strategy; rather it proposes the researcher should actively search for the meanings produced and shared by the group of participants in their forms of CMC and beyond. The techniques to be employed for data collection and analysis may vary depending on the phenomenon under research; however the nethnographic design is a powerful guideline to enhance the study of CMC.

If, on one hand, the logfiles made available by Internet technology seems to offer "everything" that happen on CMC activities, which seems to minimize or even solve the problems of data collection, on the other hand the use of this resource as the only source of data can make the analyst miss the inter-subjective meanings shared by the group under investigation. The analysis of CMC activities demands a combination of research techniques for every different case at hand.

One point to be remarked is that the social environments offered by the Internet are used as alternatives, among others, for inter-personal relationships. However, from the perspective of participants, online interactions present a lack of legitimacy, trust and credibility that can never substitute for face to face interaction. Once it is assumed that on the other side of computer screens there are people interacting, and that through these interactions there are power relations, social hierarchies, conflicts, socialization and feelings involved, nethnography can be a powerful methodological device for understanding the social order expressed in computer-mediated communication.

REFERENCES

Agre, Phil. (1994) *Net Presence, Computer-Mediated Communication Magazine*, 1-4. Available at: http://www.december.com/cmc/mag/1994/aug/presence.html

Barnes, Susan. (2004) *Goffman and the Internet: Applying Goffman's Concepts to Online Communication.* Paper presented at IAMCR Conference. Porto Alegre, PUCRS.

Boas, Franz. (1901) The Mind of Primitive Man. *The Journal of American Folklore*, 14, 1-11.

Becker, Howard S. (1993) *Métodos de Pesquisa em Ciências Sociais.* São Paulo, Hucitec.

Benveniste, Émile. (1989) *Problemas de Lingüística Geral II.* Campinas, Pontes.

Bishop, Ann P., Star, Susan L., Neumann, Laura, Ignacio, Emily, Sandusky, Robert J., & Schatz, Bruce. (1995). Building a university digital library: Understanding implications for academic institutions and their constituencies. In: *Higher Education and the NII: From vision to reality. Proceedings of the Monterey Conference*, Sept. 26-29. Washington, DC, Coalition for Networked Information.

Dicks, Bella and Mason, Bruce. (1998). Hypermedia and ethnography: reflections on the construction of a research approach. *Sociological Research Online.* 3/3, available at: http://www.socresonline.org.uk

Dicks, Bella; Bruce Mason & Amanda Coffey et al. (2005) *Qualitative Research and Hypermedia:*

Ethnography for the Digital Age. London, Sage Publications.

Frazer, James G. (2000) [orig. 1870] *The Golden Bough: a study on magic and religion.* New York: Bartleby.com.

Garkinkel, Harold. (1967) *Studies in Ethnomethodology.* New Jersey: Prentice Hall.

Geertz, Clifford. (1973) *The Interpretation of Cultures.* New York: Basic Books.

Goffman, Erving. (1959) *The Presentation of Self in Everyday Life.* New York: Doubleday Anchor Books.

Goffman, Erving. (1967) *Interaction Ritual: Essays in Face-to-Face Behavior.* Garden City, Doubleday.

Goodenough, Ward. (1957) Cultural Anthropology and Linguistics. *Report of the Seventh Annual Round Table Meeting on Linguistics and Language Studies.* Paul Gavin (org.) (Reprinted in HYMES, Dell (ed.). (1964) *Language in culture and society: a reader in linguistics and anthropology.* New York, Harper and Row).

Greiffenhagen, Christian. & Watson, Rod. (2005) 'Teoria' e 'Método' na CMC: identidade, género, e tomada-de-turno – uma abordagem etnometodológica e analítico-conversacional. In: Braga, Adriana (Ed.) *CMC, Identidades e Género: teoria e método.* Colecção Estudos em Comunicação. Covilhã, Universidade da Beira Interior, Portugal.

Hine, Christine M. (2000) *Virtual Ethnography,* London, Sage Publications.

Hine, Christine. (2005) Virtual Methods and the Sociology of Cyber-Social-Scientific Knowledge. In: HINE, Christinc (Org.). *Virtual Methods. Issues in Social Research on the Internet.* Oxford: Berg.

Kozinets, Robert V. (2002). The field behind the screen: Using netnography for marketing research in online communications. *Journal of Marketing Research,* 39, 61–72.

Kozinets, Robert V. (2005) 'Communal Big Bangs and the Ever-Expanding Netnographic Universe,' *Thexis,* 3, 38-41.

Langer, Roy and Beckman, Suzanne. (2005) Sensitive Research Topics: netnography revisited. In: *Qualitative Marker Research: An International Journal.* 8,2, 189-203.

Levy, Pierre. (1993) *As Tecnologias da Inteligência.* Rio de Janeiro: Editora 34.

Malinowsky, Bronislaw. (1953) [orig. 1922] *Argonauts of the Western Pacific.* New York: E. F. Dutton.

Morgan, Lewis H. (1985) [orig. 1877] *Ancient Society.* Tucson: University of Arizona Press.

Miller, Hugh. (1995) *The Presentation of Self in Electronic Life: Goffman on the Internet.* Paper presented at Embodied Knowledge and Virtual Space Conference. University of London.

Rheingold, Howard. (1993) *The Virtual Community: Homesteading of the Electronic Frontier.* Reading, MA: Addison-Wesley.

Rutter, Jason & Smith, Greg. (2002a) *Ethnografic Presence in Nebulous Settings: A Case Study.* Paper presented at ESRC Virtual Methods Seminar Series. Brunel University.

Rutter, Jason and Smith, Greg. (2002b) *Spinning Threads: Rituals of Sociability in CMC.* Available at: http://les.man.ac.uk/cric/Jason_Rutter/papers

Ryle, Gilbert. (1968) "*The thinking of thoughts – What is 'Le Penseur' doing?*" in: University Lectures Series, 18, University of Saskatchewan.

Schutz, Alfred. (1962) *Collected Papers.* The Hague, Martinus Nijhoff.

Simmel, Georg. (1983) [orig. 1911] *Sociologia.* São Paulo, Ática.

Smith, Greg. (2004) "Instantâneos 'sub specie aeternitatis:' Simmel, Goffman e a sociologia formal." In: Gastaldo, É. (Ed.) *Erving Goffman, desbravador do cotidiano.* Porto Alegre: Tomo Editorial.

Turkle, Sherry. (1995) *Life on the Screen: Identity in the Age of the Internet.* New York: Simon & Schuster.

Turner, Roy. (1974) *Ethnomethodology.* Canada: Penguin Books.

Tylor, Edward B. (1924) [orig. 1871] *Primitive Culture.* New York: Brentano's.

Winkin, Yves. (1998) *A Nova Comunicação – da teoria ao trabalho de campo.* Campinas, Papirus.

KEY TERMS

Blog-Circuit: Communicational circuit established among participants of different social networking sites, accomplished through links exchange and reciprocal visits.

Blogger: Person who creates and maintains a Weblog.

Computer-Mediated Communication (CMC): Communications that occur via computer-mediated formats (i.e., Weblogs, instant messages, e-mails, chat rooms) between two or more individuals.

Digital Environment: Social setting produced through computer technology.

Ethnography: Research technique used traditionally in Anthropology, in which long term permanence of the researcher in the field and systematic description of social situations provides data for analyzing the culture of a given group or society.

Ethnomethodology: Term coined by Harold Garfinkel in the 1960s, that refers to a branch of Sociology that examines the ways in which people make sense of their world, share their understandings and produce collectively the social order in which they live.

Fieldwork: Ethnographic activity held in a given period and place in which the researcher collects data through direct contact with the group being studied.

Fieldwork Diary: Research technique in which the ethnographer take systematic notes describing fieldwork situations.

Interactional: (in the field of Social Sciences) related to or proper of the social interaction.

Logfile: log kept by a Web server regarding registers left on a Website.

Naturalistic Perspective: Empiricist approach of the Social Sciences based on the premise of collecting data essentially from "natural" situations, those that happen despite the presence or participation of the researcher.

Nethnography: Ethnographic research concerning digital environments.

Online Interaction: Social interaction held by co-participants of a digital environment.

Participant Observation: Research strategies based on a close and intimate familiarity with a group and its practices in their natural environment, usually over an extended period of time.

Research Setting: Social situations in which an ethnographer develops his/her fieldwork.

Social Interaction: Mutual action and/or influence among co-participants of the same social situation.

Weblog: Also known as blog, is a Web page in which the author(s) publish constantly updated contents. Entries are written in chronological order and commonly displayed in reverse chronological order, in the form of posts, usually describing personal experiences. A typical Weblog combines text, images, links to other Weblogs, Web pages and other media, and provides means of interaction with readers, using e-mail, guestbook or comments linked to single posts.

Chapter XXV
Web Log Analysis:
Diversity of Research Methodologies

Isak Taksa
Baruch College, City University of New York, USA

Amanda Spink
Queensland University of Technology, Australia

Bernard J. Jansen
Pennsylvania State University, USA

ABSTRACT

Web log analysis is an innovative and unique field constantly formed and changed by the convergence of various emerging Web technologies. Due to its interdisciplinary character, the diversity of issues it addresses, and the variety and number of Web applications, it is the subject of many distinctive and diverse research methodologies. This chapter examines research methodologies used by contributing authors in preparing the individual chapters for this handbook, summarizes research results, and proposes new directions for future research in this area.

INTRODUCTION

The Web has become the environment where people of all ages, languages and cultures conduct their daily digital lives. Working or entertaining, learning or socializing, home or on the road, individually or as a group, Web users are ubiquitously surrounded by an infrastructure of devices, networks and applications. This infrastructure combined with the perpetually growing amount of every imaginable type of information supports the user's intellectual or physical activity. Whether searching, using or creating and disseminating the information, users leave behind a great deal of data revealing their information needs, attitudes, personal and environmental facts. Web designers collect these artifacts in a variety of Web logs for subsequent analysis.

The Handbook of Web Log Analysis reflects on the multifaceted themes of Web use and demonstrates an equally diverse range of research methodologies. The next section briefly reviews research methodologies applied by contributing authors. Subsequent sections report research results obtained using these methodologies and propose directions for future research in the field of Web log analysis.

RESEARCH METHODOLOGIES

What are the research methodologies frequently applied in Web-based research? Some researchers focus on collection and preparation of information for data analysis (Jansen, 2006), while others concentrate on elicitation; reduction and visualization for user-profiling (Romano et al., 2003). Researchers also benefit from a new, aggressively growing source of personal communication – blogs (Jing, 2006; Rossler, 2002).

In a different direction, there are a number of studies that focus on analysis of research methodologies. Powel (1999) uses a comprehensive classification developed by Kim (1996) to review, define and discuss quantitatively and qualitatively-driven methodologies. Another publication (Palvia et al., 2007) provides a slightly different but equally comprehensive classification of research methodologies. Using these three sources, we identified the following methodologies used by this handbook's authors:

- **Conceptual Framework / Inquiry:** Concepts are introduced and defined, and subsequently used to construct conceptual frameworks that provide study directions.
- **Phenomenology / Ethnomethodology:** An interpretive methodology that examines users' behavior. Ethnomethodology, an extension of phenomenology, examines individual and group interactions within a social structure.
- **Content Analysis:** A methodical and replicable methodology used to determine, quantify, and analyze the presence of research objects within a large data set.
- **Ethnography:** A qualitative study in which the researcher observes members of a chosen group in a natural environment over a long period of time.
- **Historical Method:** Collects and examines facts about events, people and the environment of the past.
- **Discourse Analysis:** A scientific argument evaluation method.
- **Case Study:** A comprehensive study of a single subject, influenced by a proper selection of unit of analysis.

CONCEPTUAL FRAMEWORK / INQUIRY

Many research studies clearly specify and explain the methodologies used to describe or explain the subject under study. These studies usually introduce a set of concepts related to an existing (or future systems), or to a set of objects, or to behavior aspects of participants. Concepts are then used to construct conceptual frameworks, which provide the plan, purpose and direction for the study. Depending on the goals, data and technology, the conceptual frameworks offer a choice of methodologies: surveys, data analysis, literature review or many others. The conceptual frameworks methodology is widely used in many Web studies including information retrieval (Jansen 2006; Jansen et al, 2000), Web log analysis in e-commerce (Meersman et al., 2003), education and library studies (Nicholson 2004; Vrana, 2002).

Transaction Log Analysis

Transaction log analysis is a broad category of methods used for macro and micro analysis of transaction logs - electronic records of interactions that have occurred between a system and users of that system. Among others, these methods include Web log analysis, (i.e., analysis of Web system logs), blog analysis (i.e., analysis of Web blogs) and search log analysis (i.e., analysis of search engine logs).

Chapter I "Research and Methodological Foundations of Transaction Log Analysis" introduces, outlines and discusses the theoretical and methodological foundations for transaction log analysis. The chapter addresses the fundamentals of transaction log analysis from a research viewpoint and the concept of transaction logs as a data collection technique from the perspective of behaviorism. The chapter continues with the methodological aspects of transaction log analysis and examines the strengths and limitations of transaction logs as trace data. It reviews the conceptualization of transaction log analysis as an unobtrusive approach to research, and presents both the power and deficiency of the unobtrusive methodological concept, including benefits and risks of transaction log analysis specifically from the perspective of an unobtrusive method. The chapter concludes with some essential ethical and legal questions: use of the logs for research, ownership, and user consent and access control.

Complementing the Web Log Analysis Methodology

Whether to validate or to substantiate existing research results, or to gain a new perspective on an existing issue, researchers often need complementary sources and methodologies to collect subject data.

Chapter III "Surveys as a Complementary Method to Web Log Analysis" examines surveys as a viable complementary method for transaction log analysis. The chapter presents a brief overview of survey research literature, with a focus on the use of surveys for Web-related research. It continues with a comprehensive overview of a 10 - step process to plan and conduct a survey and a comprehensive guide to designing a survey instrument. To illustrate the benefits of a survey in conjunction with transaction logs, a case study (including data analysis) of a large electronic survey is presented. The chapter concludes by stressing complementary capabilities of a survey specifically in the areas of understanding the underlying motivations, affective characteristics, cognitive factors, and contextual aspects that influence user behavior.

Search Logs Analysis

The data stored in search logs of Web search engines, Intranets, and Websites provides important insights into understanding the information searching tactics of online searchers. This understanding can assist information system designers and interface developers.

Chapter VI "The Methodology of Search Log Analysis" presents a review of, and foundation for, conducting Web search transaction log analysis. A search log analysis methodology is outlined consisting of three stages: collection (the process of collecting the interaction data for a given period in a transaction log including *User Identification, Date, Time, and Search query terms*), preparation (the process of preparing the transaction log data for analysis including *cleaning, parsing and normalizing*), and analysis (the process of analyzing the prepared data including *Term, Query, and Session level analysis*). The chapter continues with possible venues for analysis and concludes with suggestions for further research consisting of unobtrusive data collection to preserve the unaltered behavior of searchers, use of cookies to identify individual sessions, and use of survey data to get reasonable estimations of needed demographic data.

Website Analytics

Operational Website management necessitates a way to track and measure visitors' traffic, visitors' behavior and even more importantly how this behavior compares to the expected behavior.

Chapter VII "Uses, Limitations, and Trends in Web Analytics" focuses on measuring the performance of a Website. The measuring includes tracking the traffic (number of visitors), and visitors' activity and behavior while visiting the site. The chapter discusses current methodologies to log data and evaluate Website performance, stressing the limitations of log file analysis (e.g. lack of personal information, missing duration of the visit); clarifying new techniques (e.g. site overlay, Geo-mapping) in Web analytics that supplement traditional log file analysis; and analyzing trends in Web analytics as related to Web 2.0 technologies (social networking, tagging, blogging). As part of the Web 2.0 discussion the authors touch on the issue of "long tail". The chapter is concluded with suggestions to improve the accuracy of existing metrics (by using cookies and page tagging) and identifying the need for a new set of metrics and analytics for the Web 2.0.

Website Key Performance Indicators

Web analytics studies visitor behavior on a Website. By collecting various Web analytics metrics one can develop key performance indicators (KPIs) – a versatile analytic model that measures visitor trends.

Chapter VIII "A Review of Methodologies for Analyzing Websites" provides an overview of the process of Web analytics. The chapter outlines how visitor information such as number of visits, number of visitors and visit duration can be collected through the use of log files and page tagging. This information is then combined to create important key performance indicators that are tailored not only to the business goals of the company running the Website, but also to the goals and content of the Website. First, the authors discuss the metrics that can be collected from the Website visitor, its types and potential uses. Then, they analyze the two primary methods for gathering visitor information - log files and page tagging, detailing advantages and disadvantages of each method, and enumerating types of support information, and examples of data format. Once the data is collected, the selection and construction of KPIs is discussed and followed up by a description of the entire process with advice for Web analytics integration. The chapter is concluded with suggestions on what to look for when choosing analytics tools, as well as a comparison of several specific tools.

Action-Object Pairs

There are two basic components in the interaction between the user and the system that are recorded in a transaction log, they are action and object. An action is a specific expression of the user. An object is a self-contained information object. These two components form one interaction set or an action-object pair. A series of action-object pairs represents the interaction session.

Chapter XXI "Using Action-Object Pairs as a Conceptual Framework for Transaction Log Analysis" presents the action-object pair approach as a conceptual framework for three major steps of log analysis: the i) collection, ii) analysis, and iii) understanding of data from transaction logs. The authors present the scientific foundation and provide a detailed description of the proposed concept, and use the above three steps to illustrate the concept's applicability. The chapter is concluded with several case studies using the action-object pair approach. The studies illustrate the benefits of the approach and also how it facilitated the system performance. The authors suggest ways of using this approach to answer many questions still facing researchers involved in transaction log analysis.

PHENOMENOLOGY / ETHNOMETHODOLOGY

The design and acceptance of information systems is usually determined by a dichotomy between technology and behavior. While some approaches stress technological advance, others focus on users' behavior (Verbeek & Slob, 2006). Phenomenology is an interpretive methodology that examines users' behavior. It examines events and actions by which individual users give meaning to, and make sense of, interactions with technology (Budd, 2005). Phenomenology uses an interdisciplinary approach to investigate the reason, purpose and analysis of users' actions while searching for and deciding on the relevance of search results (Nicolas et al., 2007); it relies on technological mediation to explain amplification and reduction – "an increased capacity to engage with the world in a particular way, accompanied by a reduced capacity to engage with it in other ways" (Arnold, 2003; p. 240). It aims at supporting and improving the quality of interaction in an action-centric environment (Fernaeus, 2008). Ethnomethodology, an extension of phenomenology, examines individual and group interactions in transitory social structures created by on-demand connectivity (Westbrook, 2004).

Estimating User Behavior

Correct estimation of user information searching behavior paves the way to more successful and even personalized search engines. However, estimation of user behavior is not a simple task. It closely relates to natural language processing and human computer interaction, and requires preliminary analysis of user behavior and careful user profiling.

Chapter XI "From Analysis to Estimation of User Behavior" details the studies performed on analysis and estimation of search engine user behavior, and surveys analytical methods that have been used to accomplish this task. The first part of the chapter is devoted to a review of existing search engine user behavior studies including multimedia, multitasking and e-commerce searches followed by detailed explanation of methodologies used for Web log and user behavior analysis including correlation and test of independence, Markov models, and Poisson sampling.

The second part follows the same process. First, the authors provide a detailed overview of studies estimating search engine user behavior including topic and session identification, and topic estimation, followed by detailed explanation of methodologies used for user behavior estimation including probabilistic and statistical methods, Monte-Carlo simulation and artificial intelligence methods. The chapter is concluded with specific ideas for further research such as the use of multivariate techniques to cluster user queries, the analysis of time-based behavior of users (seasons, holidays. etc.), and use of artificial intelligence and statistical learning methods for studying the content-based behavior.

Interaction Design for Studying User Behavior

A good understanding of people – what they are like, why they use a certain piece of software, and how they might interact with it – is essential for successful design of interactive systems, which help people achieve their goals.

Chapter XII "An Integrated Approach to Interaction Design and Log Analysis" describes a methodological framework that integrates analysis of interaction logs with the conceptual design of the user interaction. This approach is particularly useful for studying user behavior when using highly interactive systems. The author proposes a formal procedure that integrates the modeling of the interaction, the logging and the analysis of logged data. The procedure allows for capture of the functionality, states, and user action in each state. When applied to a particular kind of interaction (such as interactive information retrieval), the proposed procedure can be used to investigate user behavior or to test the usability of a user interface. To demonstrate the capability of this procedure the author uses a case study of a MIR (Mediated Information Retrieval) project.

The chapter is concluded with a comprehensive plan for future research, including studying patterns of behavior by building Hidden Markov Models (HMM) based on the analysis of state transitions recorded in the logs, granularity of hierarchical structure of states and visualization of user behavior.

Tips for Tracking Web User Behavior

Developing and employing Web tracking to better understand end-user experiences with the Web portal seems to be a simple process. However, setting up, collecting, and analyzing Web tracking data is surprisingly more difficult than originally expected.

Chapter XIII "Tips for Tracking Web Information Seeking Behavior" provides various tips for practitioners and researchers who wish to track end-user Web information seeking behavior. These tips are derived from the authors' own experience in collecting and analyzing individual differences, tasks, and Web tracking data to investigate people's online information seeking behaviors at a specific municipal community portal site (myhamilton.ca). The tips proposed and discussed in this chapter include: i) the need to account for both task and individual (learning and cognitive) differences in any Web information seeking behavior analysis; ii) how to collect Web metrics through deployment of a unique ID (a key strength of this research project) that links individual differences, task, and Web tracking data together; iii) the types of Web log metrics to collect (including raw metrics and composite analytics); iv) how to go about collecting and making sense of such metrics (visitor footprints, navigation tracks and information seeking trails); and v) the importance of addressing privacy concerns (including location, privacy legislation requirements, and privacy impact assessment) at the start of any collection of Web tracking information. The chapter is complemented with an extensive questionnaire to assist portal developers in tracking users' behavior.

User Profiling for Dynamic Page Customization

Adaptive Hypermedia is an effective approach to establishing better user experience and delivering user relevant content.

Chapter XIV "Identifying Users Stereotypes for Dynamic Web Pages Customization" explores adaptive hypermedia as an effective approach to automatic personalization that overcomes the complexities and deficiencies of traditional Web systems in delivering user-relevant content.

The chapter focuses on three major tasks regarding adaptive hypermedia systems:

i. The construction and maintenance of the user profile, which is achieved through integration of semantic information obtained from the Website domain ontology with usage information obtained from the data gathered from user sessions.
ii. The use of Semantic Web resources to describe Web applications (Universal Resource Identifier, Resource Description Framework, Ontology Web Language).
iii. Implementation of adaptation mechanisms (e.g. education, information retrieval and tourism). Web Usage Mining, in this context, allows the discovery of Website access patterns.

The chapter describes the possibilities of integration of these usage patterns with semantic knowledge obtained from domain ontology. Thus, it is possible to identify users' stereotypes for dynamic Web pages customization. This integration of semantic knowledge can provide personalization systems with better adaptation strategies. To illustrate their approach the authors use an open source Web Content Management system to implement the Web usage data acquisition and to generate the structure adaptations.

Social Networks

The latest developments in Web design introduced a connector Website – a Website that facilitates social (or business) interactions among participants.

Chapter XXII "Analysis and Evaluation of the Connector Website" proposes a new theoretical model for evaluating Websites that facilitate online social networks. The chapter reviews previous academic work related to social networks and online communities, defines a new kind of social institution called a connector Website, and provides a brief history of several generations of the connector Websites. To conduct the analysis the author collected monthly Website traffic data from thirteen connector Websites and applied several statistical approaches to gauge Website-level growth, trend lines, and volatility. One interesting finding that the author is trying to explain is worth mentioning here "six connectors have produced rather unexpected social epidemics in terms of huge gains (or loss) in user traffic". The chapter is concluded with some lessons learned and their implications for future connector Websites. Important directions for further research are indicated, specifically, social values and tradeoffs, and differentiation and specialization of existing connector Websites.

CONTENT ANALYSIS

Content analysis is defined as a methodical and replicable methodology (Stemmer, 2001) used to i) determine presence of research objects within a large data set; ii) quantify and categorize the presence of the objects; iii) analyze the validity (Rourke & Anderson, 2004), reliability (Lombard et al.,2002), and significance of the obtained results for meaning and relationships of objects; and conjecture the demographics (age, gender), time and location of an activity that creates the object, and behavior patterns (needs, intent, attitude) of owners or creators of these objects (Krippendorf, 2004). Objects are usually defined as prearranged or derived terms, phrases or topics (in any language), and images. There are two basic types of content analysis: conceptual (looking to quantify and categorize objects) and semantic (looking to find and predict meaning) in the set of objects (Murphy & Ciszewska-Carr, 2005).

Query Classification

Usually search queries are very short (2 - 3 search terms), display little class specific information per single query, and are therefore a weak source for machine learning an established tool for classification tasks.

Chapter XVI "Machine Learning Approach to Search Query Classification" presents a novel method of non-hierarchical classification of search queries that focuses on two specific areas of machine learning: short text classification and limited manual labeling. To improve the effectiveness of the proposed method the chapter introduces background knowledge discovery by using information retrieval techniques. The uniqueness of this method is that instead of actually incorporating the newly retrieved background knowledge into the learning algorithm, it is used for the purpose of finding previously unknown class related terms. By iteratively applying this process, a large number of classification terms was developed and successfully applied to a task of age classification of a corpus of queries from a commercial search engine.

Since query classifications are done on earlier recorded logs it is interesting to see how calendar dates (e.g. "back to school" season, New Year, etc.) and current events (e.g. Elections) impinge on the effectiveness of the process. Another issue that possibly affects the classification process is the use of current Web collections (significantly larger collections, language of new Websites reflecting social and cultural shifts) to classify older logs. Another promising direction is the creation and expansion of a definitive set of age related terms and phrases.

Topic Analysis

Topic analysis and identification of queries is an important task related to the discipline of information retrieval that is a key element for the development of successful personalized search engines. The problem is more difficult for search engine user queries due to real-time requirements and the limited number of terms in the user queries. Topic identification of search engine queries relates to many studies, ranging from term analysis of search engine queries, to topic estimation, automatic new topic identification, session identification and query clustering, and then to the broader concept of text categorization and natural language processing.

Chapter XVII "Topic Analysis and Identification of Queries" includes (a) a detailed literature review on topic analysis and identification, with an emphasis on search engine user queries, (b) a survey of the analytical methods that have been and can be used, and (c) outlines the challenges and research opportunities related to topic analysis and identification. A comprehensive review covers domain specific search queries (medical, e-commerce, sexual), generic session/topic identification and query clustering approaches and concludes with text classification and categorization models.

The second part of the chapter is devoted to the overview of methodologies used for topic identification including statistical learning methods (regression and Support Vector Machines), artificial intelligence methods (neural networks), statistical and stochastic methods (Markov chains, Dempster-Shafer theory) and methods based on conditional probabilities. The chapter is concluded with suggestions for future research, which include reducing the dimension of text categorization to search engine queries and improving the computational complexity of the topic identification algorithms.

Domain Specific Log Analysis

Clinicians, researchers and members of the general public are increasingly using information technology to cope with the explosion in biomedical knowledge. The vast amount of this knowledge in many areas of biomedicine, and science in general, far exceeds the cognitive capacity of any human. Fortunately for the search engine user, the biomedical domain is associated with many (relatively) well-developed controlled terminologies and vocabularies (ontologies) that make the search process easier and more structured.

Chapter XVIII "Query Log Analysis in Biomedicine" discusses these features of the biomedical domain. The chapter focuses specifically on MEDLINE, which is the most comprehensive bibliographic database of the world's biomedical literature, the PubMed interface to MEDLINE, the Medical Subject Headings vocabulary and the Unified Medical Language System. While biomedical query log analysis is similar to other domains in its limitations it also exhibits a major advantage – query logs can be complemented by other analyses such as field studies and instrumented user panels. Additionally, mapping the layman's query to controlled taxonomies allows for semantic analysis to understand the meaning of queries.

While assessing the success of the human genome project, the authors predict the explosion of biomedical information and foresee an information challenge facing health care providers and health care consumers. Both groups have sometimes conflicting views, "paternalistic" vs. participative, and may need different interfaces while searching for identical/similar information. The chapter is concluded with ideas for new tools and user interfaces for biomedical information retrieval.

Language Specific Log Analysis

More and more non-English content is now available on the World Wide Web and the number of non-English users on the Web is increasing. Many previous studies on Web query logs have focused on analyzing English search logs and their results may not be directly applied to other languages.

Chapter XIX "Processing and Analysis of Search Query Logs in Chinese" discusses various methods and techniques that can be used to analyze search queries in Chinese. Stressing the one most notable feature of the Chinese language (an ideographical, character-based language) vs. the English language (an alphabetical, word-based language), the authors explain the difficulty of using traditional log analysis methods for Chinese query logs. For character-based languages, most of the meaningful words are built up by combining single characters, and an individual character may deliver different meanings in different words.

Moreover, in Chinese the syntax of words is quite different from that in English. There is no space between terms in Chinese, making it difficult to correctly perform segmentation, whereas in English every word is basically delimited by space. This specific characteristic of Chinese would result in many apparently different searching behaviors. The discussion is complemented by an example of log analysis based on the Timway search engine which indexes and searches the collection in both languages: Chinese and English. The chapter is concluded with an observation that not all Asian languages follow the analysis pattern and therefore need a different infrastructure for data collection and log analysis.

Goal Specific Query Analysis

Information retrieval and question answering systems often operate in much wider domains for which appropriate corpora are not available. As a result, query logs are an extremely valuable resource for increasing our understanding of the complex interactions involved and hence in developing more sophisticated systems. Logs contain a huge amount of information but effective methods for extracting it are only now being developed.

Chapter XX "Query Log Analysis for Adaptive Dialogue-Driven Search" analyses two case studies, both aimed at improving Information Retrieval and Question Answering systems. The first describes an intranet search engine (UKSearch) that offers sophisticated query modifications to the user. It does this via a hierarchical domain model that was built using multi-word term co-occurrence data. The usage log is analyzed using mutual information scores between a query and its refinement, between a query and its replacement, and between two queries occurring in the same session. The second case study (HITIQA - High Quality Interactive Question Answering) describes a dialogue-based Question Answering system working over a closed document collection largely derived from the Web.

Logs are based around explicit sessions in which an analyst interacts with the system. Analysis of the logs has shown that certain types of interaction lead to increased precision of the results and therefore can be used to improve the underlying domain model and the model of interaction, and hence the quality of interaction in a system. Authors conclude with critique of the large body of log analysis literature (extensively reviewed in the chapter) that usually concentrates on determining general trends of usage instead of trying to improve the system under study. Several improvements of domain-dependent spelling correction are suggested as well as a need for generic models of analytic interaction over data.

ETHNOGRAPHY

Ethnography is a qualitative study in which the researcher observes members of a chosen group in a natural environment over a long period of time. It relies on the researcher gaining and maintaining entry into an active group, a challenging (Gorman & Clayton, 2005) and time consuming (Labaree, 2002) process. Whether as an active face-to-face member or as an unobtrusive observer, the researcher plays a variety of roles in order to monitor and register group members' actions and behavior. Nethnography, a portmanteau of net and ethnography, is a recent phenomenon born with the advent of computer-mediated communication (CMC). Analyzing the content of asynchronous or synchronous CMC allows for the discovery and understanding of conventions and types of human interaction, finding meaning and comprehension of the context, discerning topics and distinguishing multiple discussion threads (Hewitt, 2003). The following three chapters demonstrate several methods and frameworks for analysis of three distinct types of Web logs.

Nethnography

While its predecessor – ethnography – relies on active, face-to-face participation of the observer in the study process, nethnography relies on Web logs as the sole source of data.

Chapter XXIV "Nethnography: a Naturalistic Approach towards Online Interaction" explores the potential and limitations of nethnography, an ethnographic approach applied to the study of online interactions, particularly computer-mediated communication (CMC). The chapter presents a brief history of ethnography, including its relation to anthropological theories and its key methodological assumptions. The presentation focuses on common methodologies that treat log files as the only or main source of data and discusses results of such an approach. In addition, it examines some strategies related to a naturalistic perspective of data analysis. To illustrate the potential of nethnography to enhance the study of CMC, the author presents an example of an ethnographic study. The chapter is concluded with suggestions on how the nethnography methodology can be adapted to analyze other social networking sites, once care is taken to account for local differences in contexts, topics of interest or activities carried on by participants.

The Blogs

A blog (short for Web log) is part of the network of social media designed and popularized by participants to exchange information, express opinions or discuss just about any topic under the sun. According to blog search engine Technorati there are over 100 million blogs.

Chapter XXIII "Information Extraction from Blogs" introduces information extraction from textual blogs. The author argues that the classic techniques for information extraction that are commonly used for mining well-formed texts lose some of their validity in the context of blogs. With the addition of Web 2.0 applications (e.g. tagging) the blog "language" became less structured, more ambiguous and difficult to understand. These findings are demonstrated by considering each step in the information extraction process and by illustrating these problems in different blog applications such as topic and thread detection, opinion mining, and argumentation mining. In order to tackle the problem of mining content from blogs, the author suggests ideas for future research including combining different sources of evidence found in blog texts, their tags, comments and links. The author also suggests some novel applications such as a translator for blogs using community languages and an anti-spammer with the ability to detect and ignore irrelevant content added to mislead filtering and monitoring software.

Finding Meaning in Online Discussions

Proliferation of networking technologies, applications and Web based services allowed for the increase in the number of virtual communities where members join to share common ideas, interests or just desire to express themselves. Much research has been focused on examining the formation of and interactions within these virtual communities. However, the methods for collecting and analyzing data in very large-scale online discussion forums can be varied and complex.

Chapter XV "Methods to Find Meaning in Online Discussion" provides an understanding of how participants come together to form large scale virtual communities and how knowledge flows between participants over time. In this chapter, two analytical methods are described: qualitative data analysis and Social Network Analysis (SNA). Both are used to examine conversations within ESPN's *Fast Break* community, which focuses on fantasy basketball sports games. The first method of analysis, qualitative data analysis, examines threads and collections of messages related by topic and offers insights into the major conversational themes. Individual messages related to these themes are categorized and analyzed to discover the major discussion topics. This method also reflects the individual's game strategy and decision-making.

On the other hand, social network analysis is not focused on the subject matter of the discussion; rather it is concerned with recurring communications between occasional and frequent participants, identifying the primary contributors in the social network and explaining the spread of knowledge in the discussion forum. The chapter is concluded with interesting directions for future research including the need for algorithms and technology to deal with the large number of messages, design of collaborative tools for data collection and analysis, and use of ethnography and SNA to answer specific questions about the online community of interest.

HISTORICAL METHOD

The historical method (historiography) collects and examines facts about events, people and the environment of the past. It attempts to narrate, understand, and interpret the historical data (Godfrey, 2006). It analyzes historical facts and recreates participants' behavior and environment in time and space (Barab & Squire, 2004).

Historic Perspective

What started as transaction log analysis evolved in name and in practice into analysis of Web logs in general and informational retrieval logs in particular.

Chapter II "Historic Perspective of Log Analysis" provides an historical review of the birth and progress of transaction log analysis applied to information retrieval systems. It offers a detailed discussion of the early work (mid-1960's to the late 1970's) evaluating systems performance; explains how this work has migrated (late 1970's through the mid-1980's) to Online Public Access Catalogues evaluation with emphasis on both system use and user behavior; followed by a decade (mid-1980's through the mid-1990's) of data base evaluation; and finally into the evaluation of World Wide Web usage (mid-1990's and on) in countless research directions limited only by imaginations and technology constraints. A discussion of privacy issues with a framework for addressing the same is presented. The chapter is concluded with ideas for research directions (including merging transaction logs with demographic data), new domains (marketing and e-commerce), and suggestions for hybrid research designs that combine the highly quantitative approach of stochastic modeling with the more qualitative approaches available.

DISCOURSE ANALYSIS

Discourse analysis (DA) challenges the conventional thinking along interdisciplinary lines (Weiss & Weiss, 2003) and it shapes the construction and approval of information systems (Vasconcelos, 2007). DA is also used as a scientific argument evaluation method (Acuff, 2007) sometimes understating the underlying scientific or technological concepts. Introducing ontology and epistemology (Hirschheim et al., 1995) into discourse analysis enhances the thoroughness and authenticity of this research method.

Web-Traffic Measurement

Web-traffic measurement is the analysis of data between client and server computers. It provides insight into how people use computers and is commonly used in research.

Chapter V "Watching the Web: An Ontological and Epistemological Critique of Web-Traffic Measurement" provides a brief history of the topic, presents and compares two dominant forms of Web-traffic measurement - log file analysis and ASP-based tools, and critically evaluates the implicit and largely unexamined ontological and epistemological claims of both methods. This evaluation suggests that like all research methods, Web-traffic measurement has implicit ontological and epistemological assumptions embedded within it, albeit to a limited degree. To remedy "ontological and epistemological difficulties" the author suggests several improvements: the Web-traffic measurement must include a systematic method of reflexivity and Web traffic researchers ought explicitly to adopt a more interpretivist stance, based on qualitative approaches. On the applied side, the author also suggests periodically scheduled "reliability tests" whereby Web-traffic researchers can review shifts in traffic patterns.

CASE STUDY

A case study is a comprehensive study of a single subject. Selecting the appropriate unit of analysis to investigate a single subject or a single hypothesis significantly impacts the compilation and explanation of experimental data (Henning et al., 2004). Frequently, the selection and identification of unit of analysis is a complex process that requires additional and sometimes intensive studies (Dubé & Paré, 2003). These additional studies often shift the choice of unit of analysis from larger units to much smaller units, affecting the validity of final results. Lack of consensus among researchers conducting investigation in the same field, as to what the unit of analysis should be, leads to disparate results in longitudinal studies (Yin, 2000).

Unit of Analysis and Validity of Web Log Data

It is a common belief, and a reasonable assumption, that the Web log traces left by the individual Website visitor and collected by the server provide a tremendous amount of quality data. Two issues which concern researchers are what data to measure and how accurate (valid) is the data.

Chapter IX "The Unit of Analysis and the Validity of Web Log Data" examines these issues and explains limitations of the data collection and interpretation processes, as well as sources of such data. The authors define the measurement units to trace (interaction time, frequency of logins, active/passive involvement, page requests), then they discuss two types of log files (client and server) and explain methodological challenges such as caching, user recognition, and session's length calculation that result in questioning the validity of collected data. The authors suggest guidelines for selecting units of analysis and insuring the validity of log data such as: examine the content structure, consider site specifications, realize and compensate for time inaccuracy at the server level.

DIVERSE RESEARCH METHODOLOGIES, COMMON ISSUES

There are two key issues that influence the design and administration of a research study: privacy of the user and reporting study results. There is growing awareness and concern in the scientific community that careful consideration should be given to the protection of privacy and confidentiality of on-line users (Akram, 2006). Unfamiliar with or uncertain about Web site privacy and security policy, users/visitors tend to reveal personal demographic and environmental data (Gates & Whalen, 2006; Ward et al., 2005). Storing, sharing, and protecting users' information is a frequent topic in scientific research (Patil et al., 2006; Karat et al., 2005; Ngai & Wat, 2002). While self-regulation is an accepted policy for privacy protection in the United States, the European Community favors a legislative approach and tight government supervision (O'Connor, 2006). Another point of agreement among the majority of researchers is the need for improved structure and composition of scientific reporting. Researchers in the medical field responded to this need with several "checklist" standards such as CONSORT (Moher et al., 2001) and CHERRIES (Gunther, 2004). On the other hand, general science researchers use less comprehensive "checklists" such as IMRAD (Sollaci & Pereira, 2004) for reporting research results in addition to a set of writing guidelines popular among researchers (Holliday, 2001). Further needs were also identified for reporting longitudinal research (Tooth et al., 2005).

Privacy and Web Logging

Privacy is a significant concern when planning research that examines human behavior. There are two aspects of privacy that play an important role in conducting such research: strict compliance with existing regulations and alleviation of users' uneasiness with being observed during the experiments.

Chapter IV "Privacy Issues Associated with Web Logging Data" examines these two aspects of privacy. The chapter briefly examines the first aspect as it applies to the Canadian Personal Information Protection and Electronic Documents Act (PIPEDA) and organizational regulations, such as a university's local research ethics board (REB), and then devotes the major part of the chapter to the second aspect – privacy enhancing mechanisms and assurances to encourage natural Web browsing behavior. The author offers an expansive literature overview of general privacy theory while addressing privacy concerns and challenges associated with Web browsing data. The chapter is concluded with numerous recommendations for increasing understanding and trust during observational data collection and suggestions for future analysis of privacy issues impacting collaborative and context browsing.

Recommendations for Reporting Web Usage Studies

Since the advent of Internet, the Web, and search engines, studies of users' use of systems are a hot topic of research and generate a wide variety of studies and reports.

Chapter X "Recommendations for Reporting Web Usage Studies" presents recommendations for reporting context in studies of Web usage including Web browsing behavior. These recommendations consist of eight categories of contextual information crucial to the reporting of results: user characteristics, temporal information, Web browsing environment, nature of the Web browsing task, data collection methods, descriptive data reporting, statistical analysis, and results in the context of prior work. This chapter argues that the Web and its user population are constantly growing and evolving. This changing temporal context can make it difficult for researchers to evaluate previous work in the proper context, particularly when detailed information about the user population, experimental methodology, and results is not presented. The adoption of these recommendations will allow researchers in the area of Web browsing behavior to more easily replicate previous work, make comparisons between their current work and previous work, and build upon previous work to advance the field.

CONCLUSION

Web logs are increasingly being used, by academic and industry researchers, to study, understand and improve the interaction between the user and Web services. The Handbook of Research on Web Log Analysis focuses on complex issues and answers many hard questions. The handbook tackles issues of privacy, social interaction, and community building. It focuses on analysis of the user's behavior during Web activities, and also investigates current methodologies and metrics for Web log analysis.

This chapter reviewed various quantitative and qualitative research methodologies used by contributing authors. It summarized results reported in individual chapters and presented new research directions and novel applications of existing knowledge.

REFERENCES

Acuff, J. M. (2007). *Ontological and Epistemological Pluralism in the Evaluation of Scientific Arguments.* Presented at 103rd Annual Meeting of the American Political Science Association, Chicago, IL, August 30-September 2. http://www.allacademic.com/meta/p211986_index.html

Akram, A. A., (2006). Electronic Privacy: Patient Concerns, *Communications of the IIMA,* Vol. 6 (1), 67-82.

Arnold, M. (2003). On the phenomenology of technology: the "Janus-faces" of mobile phones, *Information and Organization*, Vol. 13 (4), 231–256.

Barab, S., & Squire, K. (2004). Design-Based Research: Putting a Stake in the Ground, *The Journal of the learning sciences*, Vol. 13 (1), 1-14

Budd, J. M. (2005). Phenomenology and information studies, *Journal of Documentation,* Vol. 61 (1), 44-59.

Dick, P. (2004), Discourse analysis, in Cassell, C., Symon, G. (Eds), *Essential Guide to Qualitative Methods in Organizational Research*, Sage, London, 203-213.

Dubé, L., & Paré, G. (2003). Rigor in Information Systems Positivist Case Research: Current Practices, Trends, and Recommendations, *MIS Quarterly,* Vol. 27 (4), 597-636.

Fernaeus, Y, Tholander, J., & Jonsson, M. (2008). Towards a New set of Ideals: Consequences of the Practice Turn in Tangible Interaction, *Proceedings of the Second International Conference on Tangible and Embedded Interaction (TEI'08),* 223-230.

Gates, C. & Whalen, T. (2006) Personal Information on the Web: Methodological Challenges and Approaches. *CHI 2006 Workshop on Privacy and HCI: Methodologies for Studying Privacy Issues.*

Godfrey, D. G. (2006). *Methods of Historical Analysis in Electronic Media.* Mahwah, NJ: Erlbaum, 2006

Gorman, G. E., & Clayton, P. (2005). *Qualitative research for the information professional.* London: Facet.

Guther, E. (2004). Improving the quality of Web surveys: The Checklist for Reporting Results of Internet E-Surveys (CHERRIES). *Journal of Medical Internet Research*, Vol. 6 (3) e34. Retrieved March 23, 2008, from http://www.jmir.org/2004/3/e34/.

Henning, E. ,Van Rensburg, W., & Smit, B. (2004). *Finding your way in qualitative inquiry*. Pretoria: Van Schaik.

Hewitt, J. (2003). How Habitual Online Practices Affect the Development of Asynchronous Discussion Threads, *Journal of Educational Computing Research*, Vol. 28 (1), 31-45.

Hirschheim, R. A., H.-K. Klein, H. K. & Lyytinen K. (1995) *Information Systems Development and Data Modeling: Conceptual and Philosophical Foundations*. Cambridge; New York: Cambridge University Press.

Holliday, A. (2001). *Doing and Writing Qualitative Research,* London: Sage.

Jansen, B. J. (2006). Search log analysis: What it is, what's been done, how to do it, *Library & Information Science Research*, Vol. 28 (3), 407–432.

Jansen, B. J. & Spink, A. (2006).How are we searching the world wide Web?: a comparison of nine search engine transaction logs, *Information Processing and Management,* Vol. 42 (1), 248-263.

Jansen, B. J., Spink, A. & Saracevic, T. (2000). Real Life, Real Users, and Real Needs: A Study and Analysis of User Queries on the Web. *Information Processing and Management*, Vol. 36 (2), 207-227.

Jing, T. Y. (2006). Supporting Research with Weblogs: A Study on Web-Based Research Support Systems, *Proceedings of Web Intelligence and Intelligent Agent Technology Workshops, IEEE/WIC/ACM International Conference*, 161-164.

Karat, C-M., Karat, J., & Brodie, C. (2005). Why HCI research in privacy and security is critical now, *International Journal of Man-Machine Studies*, Vol. 63 (1-2), 1-4

Kim, M. (1996). Research Record, *Journal of Education for Library and Information Science*, Vol. 37, 378-380

Krippendorf, K. (2004). *Content analysis: An introduction to its methodology* (2nd), Thousand Oaks, CA: Sage.

Labaree, R. V. (2002). The risk of "going observationalist": Negotiating the hidden dilemmas of being an insider participant observer. *Qualitative Research,* Vol. 2 (1), 97-122.

Lombard, M., Snyder-Duch, J., & Bracken, C. C. (2002). Content analysis in mass communication: Assessment and reporting of intercoder reliability. *Human Communication Research*, Vol. 28 (4), 587-604.

Meersman, R., Aberer, K., & Dillon, T. (2003). Semantic Issues in e-Commerce Systems. Series: *IFIP International Federation for Information Processing*, Vol. 111.

Moher, D., Schulz, K. F., & Altman, D. G. (2001). The CONSORT statement: Revised recommendations for improving the quality of reports of parallel-group randomised trials. *The Lancet*, 357, 1191-1194.

Murphy, E., & Ciszewska-Carr, J. (2005). Contrasting syntactic and semantic units in the analysis of online discussions. *Australasian Journal of Educational Technology,* Vol. 21 (4), 546-566.

Naidu, S. & Järvelä, S. (2006). Analyzing CMC content for what? *Computers & Education,* Vol. 46 (1), 96-103.

Ngai , E. W. T. & Wat, F. K. T. (2002). A literature review and classification of electronic commerce research, *Information & Management*, Vol. 39 (5), 415–429.

Nicholas, D., Huntington, P., & Jamali, H. R. (2007). Diversity in the Information Seeking Behaviour of the Virtual Scholar: Institutional Comparisons, *Journal of Academic Librarianship*, Vol. 33 (6), 629-638.

Nicholson, S. (2004). A conceptual framework for the holistic measurement and cumulative evaluation of library services, *Journal of Documentation*, Vol. 60 (2), 164-182.

O'Connor, P. (2006). An International Comparison of Approaches to Online Privacy Protection: Implications for the Hotel Sector, *Journal of Services Research*, Vol. 6, 7-26.

Palvia, P., Pinjani, P., & Sibley, E. H. (2007). A profile of information systems research. *Information & Management, Information & Management*, Vol. 44 (1), 1-11.

Patil, S., Romero, N. A. & Karat, J. (2006). Privacy and HCI: methodologies for studying privacy issues, *CHI Extended Abstracts*, 1719-1722.

Powell R.R., (1999). Recent Trends in Research: A Methodological Essay. *Library and Information Science Research,* Vol. 21 (1) 91-119.

Romano, N. C., Donovan, C., Chen, H. C., & Nunamaker, J. F. (2003). A methodology for analyzing Web-based qualitative data. *Journal of Management Information Systems*, Vol. 19 (4), 213-246.

Rossler, P. (2002). Content analysis in online communication: A challenge for traditional methodology. In Batinic, B., Reips, U. D., & Bosnjak, M. (Eds.), *Online social sciences,* Seattle, WA: Hogrefe & Huber.

Rourke, L., & Anderson, T. (2004). Validity in quantitative content analysis. *Educational Technology Research and Development, 52* (1), 5-18.

Sollaci, L. B. & Pereira, M. G. (2004). The introduction, methods, results, and discussion (IMRAD) structure: a fifty-year survey, *Journal of the Medical Library Association*, Vol. 92 (3), 364-371

Stemler, S. (2001). An overview of content analysis. *Practical Assessment, Research & Evaluation*, 7(17), Retrieved March 15, 2008 from http://pareonline.net/getvn.asp?v=7&n=17

Spink, A., & Jansen, J. (2004). *Web Search: Public Searching of the Web.* Springer.

Strijbos, J-W., Martens, R. L. Prins, F.J. & Jochems, W. M. G. (2006), Content analysis: What are they talking about? *Computers & Education*, Vol. 46 (1), 29-48.

Tooth, L., Ware, R., Bain, C., Purdie, D. M. & Dobson, A. (2005). Quality of reporting of observational longitudinal research. *American Journal of Epidemiology*, Vol. 161 *(3), 280-288.*

Vasconcelos, A. C. (2007). The role of professional discourses in the organizational adaptation of information systems, *International Journal of Information Management*, Vol. 27 (4), 279-293.

Verbeek, P. P. & Slob, A. (2006), *User Behavior and Technology Development – Shaping Sustainable Relations between Consumers and Technologies*, Dordrecht: Springer.

Vrana, R. (2002). *Digital Libraries - Creating Information Space Excellence: Is It Already Time for Benchmarking?* Paper presented at the 2002 CARNet Users Conference.

Ward, S., Bridges, K., & Chitty, B. (2005). Do incentives matter? An examination of On-line privacy concerns and willingness to provide personal and financial information, *Journal of Marketing Communications*, Vol. 11 (1), 21-40.

Weiss, G. & Weiss. R. (2003). Critical Discourse Analysis. Theory and Interdisciplinarity, New York: Palgrave.

Westbrook, J.I., Braithwaite, J., Iedema, R.A., & Coiera, E.W. (2004). Evaluating the impact of information communication technologies on complex organizational systems: a multi-disciplinary, multi-method framework, *Proceedings of the 11th World Congress on Medical Informatics*, Fieschi M, Coiera E & Yu-Chan J, (Eds.), IOS, Washington, USA, 1323 -1327.

Yin, R. K. (2000). Rival explanations as an alternative to reforms as "experiments". In Bickman, L., ed. *Validity and Social Experimentation. Donald Campbell's Legacy*, vol. 1. Thousand Oaks, CA/ London/New Delhi: Sage, 239-266.

KEY TERMS

Conceptual Framework/Inquiry: Methodology to build and use conceptual framework as a plan and direction for research.

Content Analysis: Methodical and replicable methodology to determine, quantify and analyze presence of research objects within large data sets.

Discourse Analysis: Scientific argument evaluation method.

Ethnography: A qualitative study in which the researcher observes members of a chosen group in a natural environment over a long period of time.

Historical Method: Collects and examines, and interprets facts about events, people and environment of the past.

Phenomenology: An interpretive methodology that examines users' behavior.

Research Methods: Specific approaches employed in research that are typically derived from the research questions or aims.

Glossary

Abandonment Rate is a KPI that measures the percentage of visitors who got to that point on the site but decided not to perform the target action.

Action is an action is a specific utterance of the user.

Action Object (*a*, *o*) Pair stands for action and *o* stands for object.

Action-Object Pair Approach is where one (*a*, *o*) pair is an interaction between the user and the system. A series of (*a*, *o*) pairs or *a-o* matrix can represent the interaction session, which is defined as a series of interactions between the user and the system to fulfill the user's certain information need.

Adaptive Hypermedia is an approach to automatic personalization.

Adaptive Prompting is a context sensitive method of issuing diagnostics based on patterns of actions as well as individual actions by the user

Alignment-Centric Performance Management is a method of defining a site's business goals by choosing only a few key performance indicators.

Analysis – First Order is an analysis of transaction patterns in which state pairs are evaluated and the immediately previous state is used to predict the current state

Analysis – Higher Order is an analysis of transaction patterns in which a sequence of states greater than two are evaluated and the current state is predicted on the basis of previous states (for example, a second-order process analysis would look at two previous states to predict the current state, a third order would look at three previous states, and so forth)

Analysis of Variance is a procedure, where the total variation in the dependent factor is partitioned into meaningful components.

Analysis –Zero Order is an analysis of transactions in which only the current state is evaluated. This is usually characterized by studies in which frequency counts of particular states are reported irrespective of their context.

Anonymized Data has been collected with identifying information, but has had subsequent removal of any links between the data and identifying information so that the researcher can no longer discern the specific owner of the data. Also, Anonymous data is the data that is collected without any associated identifying information.

Argumentative Mining is the detection of an argumentative structure in a discourse and the recognition of its composing components such as the premises and conclusions of the argument; possibly the integration of the found arguments into a knowledge structure used for reasoning.

Average Order Value is a KPI that measures the total revenue to the total number of orders.

Average Time on Site (ATOS): See visit length.

Background Knowledge is the body of text, images, databases, or other data that is related to a particular machine learning classification task. The background knowledge may contain information about the classes; it may contain further examples; it may contain data about both examples and classes.

Behavioral Targeting is a technique used by online publishers and advertisers to increase the effectiveness of their campaigns. The idea is to observe a user's online behavior anonymously and then serve the most relevant advertisement based on their behavior. Theoretically, this helps advertisers deliver their online advertisement to the users who are most likely to be influenced by them.

Behaviorism is a research approach that emphasizes the outward behavioral aspects of thought. For transaction log analysis, we take a more open view of behaviorism. In this more encompassing view, behaviorism emphasizes the observed behaviors without discounting the inner aspects that may accompany these outward behaviors.

Bigram Analysis is the analysis of all sequences of two adjacent words in each query.

Bigram is a group of two words or characters.

Bilingual query is a search query that contains words in more than one language.

Biomedicine is the broad domain of biology and health care including research and practice related to living organisms often focused on, but not limited to, human health and disease.

Blog (short for Web Log) is a Web based publication consisting primarily of periodic content. Also, Blog is shorthand for Weblog. A frequent and chronological publication of comments and thoughts on the Internet. It is a journal that may be instantly published to a host web site.

Blog-Circuit is the communicational circuit established among participants of different social networking sites, accomplished through links exchange and reciprocal visits.

Blogger is a person who creates and maintains a Weblog.

Cache Busting is a techniques used to prevent browsers or proxy servers from serving content from their cache, in order to force the browser or proxy server to fetch a fresh copy for each user request. Cache busting is used to provide a more accurate count of the number of requests from users.

Cached Files are some files that are saved and retrieved by browsers or proxy servers to save network resources

Chat is also known as instant messaging. Allows people to communicate online by broadcasting messages to people in real time, often as one-on-one channel, but also in a group forum sometimes called a chat room.

Checkout Conversion Rate is a KPI that measures the percent of total visitors who begin the checkout process.

Chinese Search Logs contain the Chinese queries are often received in different character encodings. GB-2312, GBK, and BIG 5 are the three most popular Chinese language encoding schemes. They are used in different Chinese speaking regions with different popularity. For example, Traditional Chinese, usually encoded in BIG 5, is widely used in Hong Kong and Taiwan, while Simplified Chinese, usually encoded in GB-2312, is more commonly used in mainland China and Singapore.

Classification or Taxonomy is a terminology where terms are arranged by "is_a" or "is_member_of" relationships into classes

Clickstream Data/Clicktrail is the recording of Web pages that a computer user clicks on while Web browsing or using a personal computer.

Clickstream Tracking is the passive collection of data that computer users generated when they click the mouse on a Web site. A computer user's "clickstream" is the list of events they have initiated by clicking their mouse.

Client-Side Log are all users' computer activities saved in a client's computer as a computer file.

Client-Side Logging is the software that records Web browsing behavior at the user's computer. This is generally achieved either through a custom web browser or through browser plug-ins such as tool bars or browser helper objects.

Commerce Website is a type of Website where the goal is to get visitors to purchase goods or services directly from the site.

Committed Visitor Index is a KPI that measures the percentage of visitors that view more than one page or spend more than 1 minute on a site (these measurements should be adjusted according to site type).

Computer-Mediated Communication (CMC) is communications that occur via computer-mediated formats (i.e., Weblogs, instant messages, e-mails, chat rooms) between two or more individuals.

Concepts are cognitive constructs based on entities in the real world such as "nose" or "anatomy"

Conceptual Framework/Inquiry is a methodology to build and use conceptual framework as a plan and direction for research.

Conditional Random Field (CRF) is a learning system for classification often used for labeling sequential data (such as natural language data); as a type of Markov random field, it is an undirected graphical model in which each vertex represents a random variable, whose distribution is to be inferred, and each edge represents a dependency between two variables.

Conditional Random Fields are a probabilistic framework for labeling and segmenting sequential data, based on conditional probabilities (Wallach, 2004)

Connector Website is a Website providing a relatively simple means of interaction for users who seek to offer or obtain goods, services, or information. It is an intermediary offering peer-to-peer web applications that collectively make up an infrastructure for social exchange, networking, and diffusion processes. Over time, user-to-user interactions gradually generate a majority portion of the website content and the regulation of which is governed jointly between the host organization and the online community of users. Depending on the surrounding social and economic conditions, as well as site design and development, the connector website should excel in facilitating the discovery and coordination of context-based communications and transactions.

Consumer (of Healthcare) is assumed to be a member of the lay public, as opposed to a researcher or clinician. Therefore, a consumer is not an expert in biomedical science or terminology.

Content Analysis is a methodical and replicable methodology to determine, quantify and analyze presence of research objects within large data sets.

Content/Media Website is a type of Website focused on advertising.

Contextual Privacy concerns: privacy concerns vary in any given instance according to the inherent privacy concerns of the user and the situational factors at play. These include the viewer of the information, level of control retained over the information, and the type of information. Furthermore, these factors can vary according to the device in use and the location.

Conversion Rate is a KPI that measures the percentage of total visitors to a Website that perform a specific action.

Cookies (HTTP cookies or Web cookies) are parcels of text left by a Website on the computer user's hard disk drive; these data are then accessed by the Website's computer server each time the user re-visits the Website. Cookies are used to authenticate, track, and maintain specific information about users, such as site preferences and the contents of their electronic shopping carts.

Cost Per Lead (CPL) is a KPI that measures the ratio of marketing expenses to total leads and shows how much it costs a company to generate a lead.

Customer Loyalty is a KPI that measures the ratio of new to existing customers.

Customer Satisfaction Metrics are KPI items that measures how the users rate their experience on a site.

Demographics and System Statistics is a metric that measures the physical location and information of the system used to access the Website.

Density describes the general level of linkage among the actors in a social network.

Depth of Visit is a KPI that measures the ratio between page views and visitors.

Digital Environment is the social setting produced through computer technology.

Discourse Analysis is a scientific argument evaluation method.

Discussion Board is also known as forum, message board, and bulletin board, for the purpose of exchanging information only. A Website location where users may post text communication for one another. Not sensitive to time constraints or structures.

Domain Knowledge is the knowledge possessed or required of a person or system within a specific topical area.

Domain Ontologies are the description of concepts and relations regarding some knowledge field.

Electronic Commerce Research is all forms of investigation of online selling of goods or services.

Electronic Survey is one in which a computer plays a major role in both the delivery of a survey to potential respondents and the collection of survey data from actual respondents.

Entropy is the measurement that can be used in machine learning on a set of data that is to be classified. In this setting it can be defined as the amount of uncertainty or randomness (or noise) in the data. If all data is classified with the same class, the entropy of that set would be 0. The entropy of a set T that has a probability distribution of classes $\{p_1, p_2, \ldots p_n\}$ can be defined as:

$$-(p_1 \times \log(p_1) + p_2 \times \log(p_2) + \ldots p_n \times \log(p_n))$$

Episode of Use is a time frame used to measure a specific occasion of use.

Ethnography is a methodological technique for examining and understanding community life. Also, Ethnography is a research technique used traditionally in Anthropology, in which long term permanence of the researcher in the field and systematic description of social situations provides data for analyzing the culture of a given group or society.

Ethnomethodology is a term coined by Harold Garfinkel in the 1960s, that refers to a branch of sociology that examines the ways in which people make sense of their world, share their understandings and produce collectively the social order in which they live.

Ethogram is an index of the behavioral patterns of a unit. An ethogram details the different forms of behavior that an actor displays. In most cases, it is desirable to create an ethogram in which the categories of behavior are objective, discrete, not overlapping with each other. The definitions of each behavior should be clear, detailed and distinguishable from each other. Ethograms can be as specific or general as the study or field warrants.

Feedback is Website "currency" that builds or detracts reputation for users or specific content. Within a website's feedback system, for example, a user may give positive or negative point(s) to another user or that user's posted content based on some interaction.

Fieldwork Diary is the research technique in which the ethnographer take systematic notes describing fieldwork situations.

Fieldwork is the ethnographic activity held in a given period and place in which the researcher collects data through direct contact with the group being studied.

Flash Cookies are similar to "cookies" (above), but coded with Macromedia Flash software; Flash cookies are more difficult to remove than traditional cookies, and as a result, they tend to be more reliable.

Folksonomy is a word combining "folk" and "taxonomy," meaning the "people's classification management". Refers to the collaborative but unsophisticated way in which information is being categorized on the web. Instead of using a centralized form of classification, users are encouraged to assign freely chosen keywords (called tags) to pieces of information or data, a process known as tagging.

Geo-Mapping is a visual representation of the geographical location of Website visitors layered on top of map or satellite imagery.

Group-Level Cohesion can be used to identify who was communicating with whom in a discussion forum.

Hidden Markov Model is a stochastic process, where the underlying process or parameters are not observable, but can only be monitored through another stochastic process with observable parameters.

Historical Method collects and examines, and interprets facts about events, people and environment of the past.

Identical Query is a query within a session that is a copy of a previous query within that session.

Individual Differences are the demographic and psychological characteristics of people that distinguish one person from another.

Information Extraction is the identification, and consequent or concurrent classification and structuring into semantic classes, of specific information found in unstructured data sources providing additional aids to access and interpret the unstructured data by information systems.

Information Gain is the amount of information in a given set of data can be defined as (1 – entropy). If any observation about the given data is made, new information can then be recomputed. The difference between the two information values is the "information gain". In other words, the change of entropy is the information that is gained by the observation.

Information Seeking Behavior refers to how people seek information in different contexts.

Informational Query is a query intended to satisfy a general information need, as opposed to an attempt to locate a specific article or group of articles (navigational query).

Inherent Privacy Concerns: An individual's general privacy concerns; their disposition to privacy. Factors which may impact a person's disposition to privacy include their age and computer experience.

Initial Query is the first query submitted in a session by a given user.

Instant Messenger is an online service that alerts users when friends or colleagues are online and allows them to communicate with each other in real time on a private online chat window.

Interaction Design is designing interactive systems that support certain functionality and a range a user behaviors.

Interaction Schema/model is a formalized description of interaction rules and actions allowed in specific contexts.

Interactional (in the field of Social Sciences) related to or property of the social interaction.

Interactions are the physical expressions of communication exchanges between the searcher and the system.

Interactive Information Systems (IIS) are capable of converging on a person's information need by stages.

Internal Search is a metric that measures information on keywords and results pages viewed using a search engine embedded in the Website.

Interpretivism is a tradition in social and humanities research that assumes findings are to be interpreted by the researcher. This contrasts with positivism, which assumes the researcher "finds" or simply "observes" findings.

IS Research Methodologies refers to the common research methods used by information scientists.

Key Performance Indicator (KPI) is a combination of metrics tied to a business strategy.

Labeled Set is a set of item-label pairs. The item consists of an actual example that can be classified, and the label is the classification. In a supervised learning paradigm this set is sometimes referred to as the "training set".

Lead Generation Website is a type of Website that is used to obtain user contact information in order to inform them of a company's new products and developments, and to gather data for market research.

Lifestyle Time Frame is the general media use during the lifetime.

Log Analysis is the analysis of user behavior based on the actions recorded during interaction. In addition, log file analysis is a method of gathering metrics that uses information gathered from a log file to gather Website statistics. Also, Log File Analysis is the analyze of log files (Web server logs) to review the aggregate results.

Log File is a log kept by a Web server of information about requests made to the Website including (but not limited to) visitor IP address, date and time of the request, request page, referrer, and information on the visitor's Web browser and operating system. Also, Logfile is a log kept by a Web server regarding registers left on a Website. Also, Log Files or Web Server Logs are files automatically created and maintained by a computer server on which a Website is hosted of the activity on that Website (traffic, hits, etc.). A typical example is a Web server log which maintains a history of page requests.

Logging Module/System is the component of an interactive system that logs/records relevant interaction between the user and the system (events, user actions, system responses).

Machine Learning is the area of artificial intelligence that studies the algorithms and processes that allow machines to learn. These algorithms use a combination of techniques to learn from examples, from prior knowledge, or from experience.

Markov Models or Chains are a stochastic process that considers a finite number of values and states.

Markov Process is a stochastic process in which the transition probabilities can be estimated on the basis of first order data. Such a process is also stationary in that probability estimates do not change across the sample (generally across time).

Maximum Entropy Model is a learning system used for classification that computes the probability distributions corresponding to an object and its class based on training examples, and that selects the one with maximum entropy, where the computed probability distributions satisfy the constraints set by the training examples.

Maximum Entropy Modeling is a methodology aiming to model random and stochastic events, that is motivated by the principle of generating probability distributions from a training dataset, and calculating the conditional probability that event y occurs given that event x has occurred.

Mediated Information Retrieval is a model of IR interaction in which the systems supports the user's exploration of the information space and the formulation of queries.

MEDLINE is a database of biomedical literature created and maintained by the US National Library of Medicine (NLM, a unit of the National Institutes of Health). MEDLINE is a bibliographic database, meaning that it contains the reference information needed to find articles, but not the actual full-text articles.

MeSH stands for Medical Subject Headings.

Metrics is a statistical data collected from a Website such as number of unique visitors, most popular pages, etc.

Monte-Carlo Simulation is a static simulation scheme that employs random numbers, and is used for solving stochastic or deterministic problems, where time plays no substantial role.

Multi-Episode Segment of Time is the media use during the particular segments of the lifetime such as hours, weeks, or months.

Named Entity Recognition classifies named expressions in text (such as person, company, location or protein names).

Naturalistic Perspective is an empiricist approach of the Social Sciences based on the premise of collecting data essentially from "natural" situations, those that happen despite the presence or participation of the researcher.

Navigational Query is a query intended to locate a particular article or group of articles, as opposed to a general information need (informational query)

Nethnography refers to ethnographic research concerning digital environments.

Networked Communities are those support network-based communities that have few, if any, geographic and/or temporal boundaries, which VLSCs support.

Neural Networks are massively parallel distributed processor that has a natural propensity for storing experiential knowledge and making it available for use.

New Topic Identification is discovering when the user has switched from one topic to another during a single search session to group sequential log entries that are related to a common topic or session identification.

New Visitor is a user who is accessing a Website for the first time.

New Visitor Percentage is a KPI that measures the ratio of new visitors to unique visitors.

N-Gram Analysis is the analysis of all sequences of n adjacent words in each query.

N-Gram is a group of n words or characters.

Noun Phrase Coreferent is when two or more noun phrases are coreferent, when they refer to the same situation described in the text.

Object is an object is a self-contained information object, the receipt of the action.

Online Business Performance Management (OBPM) is a method of defining a site's business goals that emphasizes the integration of business tools and Web analytics to make better decisions quickly in an ever-changing online environment.

Online Community (also known as virtual community) is a group of people communicating or interacting with each other by means of information technologies, typically the Internet, rather than face to face. Online communities can be used loosely for a variety of social groups interacting via the Internet. The concept does not necessarily mean that there is a strong bond among the members. The term virtual community is attributed to the book of the same title by Howard Rheingold in 1993. Also, Online or virtual communities are sets of people that interact primarily using information communication technology (e.g., listserv, email, social networking applications) instead of face to face.

Online Interaction is social interaction held by co-participants of a digital environment.

Open Coding involves reading and comparing individual data units so as to label similar units into categories.

Opinion Mining is the detection of the opinion or subjective assessment in a certain medium (mostly text) where the opinion is usually expressed towards a certain entity or an entity's attribute; possibly the aggregation of the found opinions into a score that reflects the opinion of a community.

Order Conversion Rate is a KPI that measures the percent of total visitors who place an order on a Website.

Page Access is users' one screen access to the Web server content.

Page Depth is a KPI that measures the ratio of page views for a specific page and the number of unique visitors to that page.

Page Requests are users' requests to the Web server to send files to the users' browser.

Page Tagging (Web Bug/Beacon) is an object that is embedded in a Web page or e-mail and is usually invisible to the user but allows checking that a user has viewed the page or e-mail. Also, Page tagging is a method of gathering metrics that uses an invisible image to detect when a page has been successfully loaded and then uses JavaScript to send information about the page and the visitor back to a remote server.

Parser is a software program which analyses the grammatical structure of a sentence according to the grammar of the language; a parser is often automatically trained from annotated examples; it captures the implied hierarchy of the input sentence and transforms it into a form suitable for further processing (e.g., a dependency tree).

Participant Observations are the research strategies based on a close and intimate familiarity with a group and its practices in their natural environment, usually over an extended period of time.

Part-of-Speech is a word class or category (also called lexical class) which is generally defined by the syntactic or morphological behaviour of the word in question; common classes are noun, verb and adjective among others.

Personalization is the process that adjust the results obtained by users when accessing Web systems.

Phenomenology is an interpretive methodology that examines users' behavior.

Poisson Sampling is a useful random sampling process as it includes the properties of (1) Unbiased Sampling (2) Proportional Sampling (3) Comparability of Heterogeneous Poisson sampling Arrivals, and (4) Flexibility on the Stochastic Arrival Process from Which the Sample is Selected.

Positivist Epistemology (also referred to as positivism) refers to the school of research thought that sees observable evidence as the only form of defensible scientific findings. Positivist epistemology, therefore, assumes that only "facts" derived from the scientific method can make legitimate knowledge claims. It also assumes the researcher is separate from and not affecting the outcomes of research.

Privacy is the claim of an individual to determine what information about himself or herself should be known to others.

Prospect Rate is a KPI that measures the percentage of visitors who get to the point in a site where they can perform the target action (even if they do not actually complete it).

Protocol Analysis is the systematic evaluation of protocols using automated or manual content analysis tools.

Protocol is in this domain, a protocol is the "verbatim" record of user/system interaction for the entire user session (or selected portions) generally with time stamps on each action and perhaps some indication of system resources in use at the time.

Proxy Logging is the software that serves as an intermediary between the user's web browser and the web site servers. Users generally have to log-in to the proxy and the proxy server can be used to augment retrieved web pages.

Public Conversations are those that are open and accessible to anyone. Conversations can occur between many individuals behind closed walls, e.g., a major company's employees working on a major project.

PubMed is a freely-available interface onto MEDLINE created and maintained by the NLM.

Query Clustering is grouping the sequential log entries into different clusters in terms of topics or users.

Query is a string of terms submitted by a searcher in a given instance.

Query Length is the number of terms in the query. May or may not include stop words.

Query Modification is the modification by a search of a previous query.

Question Answering (QA) Systems go one step further than a typical information retrieval system that takes as input a user query and returns a ranked list of documents considered relevant to it. QA) systems return an exact answer extracted from one of the documents.

Rating or Net Feedback is an indicator of reputation on a particular Website.

Referrers and Keyword Analysis is a metric that measures which sites have directed traffic to the Website and which keywords visitors are using to find the Website.

Regression is an approach that generates a model characterizing the relationship between independent and dependent factors of a system from sample data representing a certain observable fact.

Repeat Query is a query submitted more than once during the data collection period, irrespective of the user.

Repeat Visitor is a user who has been to a Website before and is now returning.

Research Methodology is the general knowledge approaches to conducting and designing research.

Research Methods are specific approaches employed in research that are typically derived from the research questions or aims.

Research Setting is the social situations in which an ethnographer develops his/her fieldwork.

Returning Visitors is a KPI that measures the ratio of unique visitors to total visits.

Review, also known as Testimonial, Bulletin, and Wall is a structured discussion board that allows users to submit critical text about an idea, user, product, or message. Often supplements ratings. See Amazon.com.

RSS Feed is shorthand for Real Simple Syndication. A family of XML file formats for Web syndication used by news websites and blogs.

Search Engine is a software program that searches one or more databases and gathers the results related to the search query

Search Engine Referrals are KPI metrics that measures the ratio of referrals to a site from specific search engines compared to the industry average.

Search log Analysis (SLA) is the use of data collected in a search log to investigate particular research questions concerning interactions among Web users, the Web search engine, or the Web content during searching episodes. Also, SLA is defined as the use of data collected in a search log to investigate particular research questions concerning interactions among Web users, the Web search engine, or the Web content during searching episodes.

Search Log Analysis (SLA) Process is a three stage process of collection, preparation and analysis.

Search Log is an electronic record of interactions that have occurred during a searching episode between a Web search engine and users searching for information on that Web search engine. Also, a search log is an electronic record of interactions that have occurred during a searching episode between a Web search engine and users searching for information on that Web search engine.

Searching Episode is a set of interactions between a user and a search engine. An searching episode is composed on one or more sessions.

Semantic is of or relating to meaning in language.

Semantic Web is the set of resources intended to improve the actual possibilities of Web applications.

Server Logs: See log files.

Server-Side Logging is the software that records Web browsing behavior at the server. Data collection is generally limited to navigation information.

Server-Side Logs are all users' Web access activities on a Web server saved in a Web server as a computer file.

Session Duration is the period from the time of the first interaction to the time of the last interaction for a searcher interacting with a search engine.

Session Identification is discovering the group of sequential log entries that are related to a common user or topic or new topic identification.

Session is a set of sequentially or semantically related clicks. Also, Session is the series of queries submitted by a user during one interaction with the Web search engine.

Session Length is the number of queries submitted by a searcher during a defined period of interaction with the search engine.

Single Access Ratio is a KPI that measures the ratio of total single access pages (or pages where the visitor enters the site and exits immediately from the same page) to total entry pages.

Site Overlay is any type of content that is superimposed over a Web page; for the purpose of Web analytics, the site overlay typically shows click and conversion data superimposed over the links on a Web page.

Social Interaction is the mutual action and/or influence among co-participants of the same social situation.

Social Network Analysis (SNA) is a technique used to study the interactions between individuals in a community.

Social Network Site is a Web-based services that allow individuals to (1) construct a public or semi-public profile within a bounded system, (2) articulate a list of other users with whom they share a connection, and (3) view and traverse their list of connections and those made by others within the system. The nature and nomenclature of these connections may vary from site to site.

Social Networking is a term describing an online process. It is a website technology that allows users to search, identify, and communicate with other people as contacts, fitting closest to their specified preferences and criteria.

Sociograms visually convey relationships between actors. These sociograms make network structure explicit as collections of nodes with links that portray directionality and connection strength.

Sociology of Computing is a stream in sociology that researches the interactions between humans and computers as well as the social effects of using computers.

State Diagram (state charts) is the model of an interactive system that describes (i) a finite number of existence conditions, called states; (ii) the events accepted by the system in each state; (iii) the transitions from one state to another, triggered by an event; (iv) the actions associated with an event and/or state transition.

Stickiness is a KPI that measures how many people arrive at a homepage and proceed to traverse the rest of the site. Also, stickiness is a popular term for marketing a message. Short-term stickiness describes a website's ability to keep a user on the website for as long as possible. Long-term stickiness refers to a website's ability to motivate a user to return to that particular website.

Stochastic Process is a process that is probabilistic rather than deterministic in behavior. In the current context, a user state can be estimated but not determined with certainty when a sequence of previous states is available (e.g. a partial transaction log).

Support Vector Machine (SVM) is a learning system used for classification and regression that uses a hypothesis space of linear functions in a high dimensional feature space, trained with a learning algorithm from optimisation theory; special property of an SVM is that it simultaneously minimizes the empirical classification error and maximizes the geometric margin that separates two classes; hence SVMs are known as maximum margin classifiers. Also, SVM is a methodology of statistical learning theory, which is based on generating functions from a set of labeled training data.

Support/Self Service Website is a type of Website that focuses on helping users find specialized answers for their particular problems.

Survey Instruments are a data collection procedure that one can use in a variety of research designs.

Survey Research is a method for gathering information by directly asking respondents about some aspect of themselves, others, objects, or their environment.

Tag: In the practice of collaborative categorization using freely chosen keywords, these are descriptors that individuals assign to objects. Tags can be used to specify properties of an object that are not obvious from the object itself. They can then be used to find objects with some desired set of properties, or to organize objects.

Task refers to the information seeking task an individual user experiences that instills a need for information and motivates the user to satisfy this information need through some sort of information seeking behavior. Task is the context surrounding a person's information need.

Term is a linguistic label for concepts. Also: a series of characters separated by white space or other separator.

Term Pair is two terms that occur within the same query.

Terminology is a set of terms.

Text classification is the process of assigning classes (or labels) to textual data. Textual data can range from short phrases to much longer documents. Sometimes referred to as "text categorization", a text classification task can be defined as follows: Given a set of documents $D = \{d_1, d_2, \ldots, d_n\}$ and a set of classes $C = \{c_1, c_2, \ldots, c_m\}$ assign a label from the set C to each element of set D.

TLA is the study of electronically recorded interactions between on-line information retrieval systems and the persons who search for information found in those systems.

Tokenization breaks a text into tokens or words. It distinguishes words, components of multipart words and multiword expressions.

Top Pages is a metric that measures the pages in a Website that receive the most traffic.

Topic Analysis is analysis aiming to identify the topic of search engine queries.

Topic Identification is automatically identifying or estimating the topic of search engine queries without human intervention.

Total Bounce Rate is a KPI that measures the percentage of visitors who scan the site and then leave.

Trace Data or measures offer a sharp contrast to directly collected data. The greatest strength of trace data is that it is unobtrusive. The collection of the data does not interfere with the natural flow of behavior and events in the given context. Since the data is not directly collected, there is no observer present in the situation where the behaviors occur to affect the participants' actions. Trace data is unique; as unobtrusive and nonreactive data it can make a very valuable research course of action. In the past, trace data was often time consuming to gather and process, making such data costly. With the advent of transaction logging software, trace data for the studying of behaviors of users and systems has really taken off.

Traffic Concentration is a KPI that measures the ratio of number of visitors to a certain area in a Website to total visitors.

Transaction is a two-item set consisting of a query and a response, in which the IR system contributes either the query or the response and in which the response may be null. This definition allows human-to-machine, machine-to-human, and machine-to-machine transactions. It also allows for unanswered queries.

Transaction Log Analysis is a broad categorization of methods that covers several subcategorizations, including Web log analysis (i.e., analysis of Web system logs), blog analysis and search log analysis (analysis of search engine logs). In addition, transaction log analysis is the study of electronically recorded interactions between online information retrieval systems and the persons who search for information found in those systems.

Transaction Log is an autonomous file (or log) containing records of the individual transactions processed by a computerized IR system. Also, transaction logs are an electronic record of interactions that have occurred between a system and users of that system. These log files can come from a variety of computers and systems (Websites, OPAC, user computers, blogs, listserv, online newspapers, etc.), basically any application that can record the user – system – information interactions.

Treebank is a syntactically processed corpus that contains annotations of natural language data at various linguistic levels (word, phrase, clause and sentence levels). A treebank provides mainly the morphosyntactic and syntactic structure of the utterances within the corpus and consists of a bank of linguistic trees, thereby its name.

UMLS stands for Unified Medical Language System.

Unique Term is a term submitted one or more times in the data set.

Unique Visit is a single visit to a Website (regardless of if the user has previously visited the site); an alternative to unique visitors.

Unique Visitor is a specific user who accesses a Website.

Unlabeled Set is a set of examples whose labels or classes are unknown. If the class of an unlabeled example is learned, it can then be added to a "labeled set".

Unobtrusive Methods are research practices that do not require the researcher to intrude in the context of the actors. Unobtrusive methods do not involve direct elicitation of data from the research participants or actors. This approach is in contrast to obtrusive methods such as laboratory experiments and surveys requiring that the researchers physically interject themselves into the environment being studied.

User Behavior is the set of actions taken by a user interacting with the system in order to reach a goal or complete a task.

User Experience refers to the immersive character of technology use and is typically evoked by designers of technology. The "user experience" is assumed to be architected by interaction designers.

User is a person who uses a computer system, software application, or website. Users may need to identify themselves for the purposes of accounting, security, logging and resource management. In order to identify oneself, a user has a user account and a user name, and in most cases also a password. Users employ the user interface for access to a system or website, and the process of identification is often referred to as log in.

User profiles are the set of information regarding user preferences, necessities and knowledge.

Very Large-Scale Conversations (VLSCs) are those that involve interchanges betweens hundreds and thousands of people. Newsgroups, chat forums, and Weblogs are examples of spaces where the volume of messages posted can range in the tens and hundreds of thousands.

Visit Length is a metric that measures total amount of time a visitor spends on the Website.

Visit Value is a KPI that measures the total number of visits to total revenue.

Visitor Path is a metric that measures the route a visitor uses to navigate through the Website.

Visitor Type is a metric that measures users who access a Website. Each user who visits the Website is a unique user. If it is a user's first time to the Website, that visitor is a new visitor, and if it is not the user's first time, that visitor is a repeat visitor.

Web 2.0 is a second generation of Web-based communities and hosted services, such as social-networking sites, wikis and blogs, which facilitate collaboration and sharing between users.

Web Analyst is a job title used by private-sector practitioners, which typically involves analyzing Web-traffic data.

Web Analytics is the measurement of visitor behavior on a Website. Also, Web Analytics is the study of the behavior of Website visitors; the use of data collected from a Website to determine which aspects of the Website work towards the business objectives (for example, which landing pages encourage people to make a purchase).

Web Browsing Behaviors are user behaviors on the Web including their browsing activities and Web browser interactions. Privacy concerns have been found to impact Web browsing behaviors.

Web Browsing Environment is the context within which Web browsing occurs. For studies of Web usage this includes the Web browser and its associated tools (e.g., history, specialized toolbars), the task, and the motivation for conducting the browsing.

Web Information Seeking behavior refers to information seeking behaviors that occur over the Web. There are four main modes of information seeking on the Web ranging from wayward browsing to goal-directed search (undirected viewing, conditioned viewing, informal search, and formal search) where each mode is characterized by predominant information seeking moves or activities (undirected viewing: starting and chaining; conditioned viewing: browsing and differentiating; informal search: differentiating, monitoring, and extracting; and formal search: monitoring and extracting).

Web Metrics are a generic term for the many types of measurements that can be made about a Website and its visitors. Also, Web metrics pertains to the measures by which to assess a person's Web information seeking behavior or to assess and monitor activity on a Website. Examples of commonly used Web metrics include page views, page transitions, and session times.

Web Systems are any application designed to be used on the Web.

Web Tracking refers to the automated collection of Web information seeking behavioral data.

Web Usage Mining is the set of techniques to generate patterns and discover knowledge from the web usage data.

Weblog is also known as blog and is a Web page in which the author(s) publish constantly updated contents. Entries are written in chronological order and commonly displayed in reverse chronological order, in the form of posts, usually describing personal experiences. A typical Weblog combines text, images, links to other Weblogs, Web pages and other media, and provides means of interaction with readers, using e-mail, guestbook or comments linked to single posts.

Webmail is email received and sent only locally on a particular website. The user's other email accounts remain unaffected.

Widget is a Web widget is a portable chunk of code that can be installed and executed within any separate HTML-based web page by an end user without requiring additional compilation. They are derived from the idea of reusable code that has existed for years. Nowadays other terms used to describe web widgets including: gadget, badge, module, capsule, snippet, mini and flake. Web widgets often but not always use DHTML, Adobe Flash or JavaScript programming languages.

Wiki is a series of Web pages that allows users to generate content, but also allows others (often unrestricted) to edit the content. A tool for online collaboration and without constraints of time.

Zipf Distribution is a distribution in which the frequency of any object is inversely proportional to its frequency rank. It has been observed in text corpora, database contents, and other natural phenomena.

Compilation of References

A.T. Kearney Inc. (2003). *The New Sports Consumer.* Chicago, IL: A.T. Kearney, Inc.

Abdinnour-Helm, S. F., Chaparro, B. S., & Farmer, S. M. (2005). Using the end-user computing satisfaction (eucs) instrument to measure satisfaction with a Web site. *Decision Sciences, 36*(2), 341-364.

Abdulla, G., Liu, B., & Fox, E. (1998). Searching the World-Wide Web: implications from studying different user behavior. *Paper presented at the World Conference of the World Wide Web, Internet, and Intranet, Orlando, FL.*

About the National Library of Medicine. (2007). Retrieved September 9, 2007, from http://www.nlm.nih.gov/about/index.html

Abramson, A. D. (1998). Monitoring and evaluating use of the World Wide Web in an academic library: an exploratory study. In *Proceedings of the Annual Meeting of the American Society for Information Science* (pp. 315-326). Medford, N.J.: Information Today, Inc.

Ackerman, M., Cranor, L., & Reagle, J. (1999). Privacy in E-Commerce: Examining User Scenarios and Privacy Preferences. In *1st ACM conference on Electronic commerce* (pp. 1-8). Denver, CO: ACM.

Acuff, J. M. (2007). *Ontological and Epistemological Pluralism in the Evaluation of Scientific Arguments.* Presented at 103rd Annual Meeting of the American Political Science Association, Chicago, IL, August 30-September 2. http://www.allacademic.com/meta/p211986_index.html

Adamic, L. A., Buyukkokten, O., & Adar, E. (2003). A social network caught in the Web. *First Monday, 8*(6).

Agichtein, E., Brill, E. and Dumais, S. (2006), Improving Web search ranking by incorporating user behavior information. *Proceedings of the Twenty-Ninth Annual International ACM SIGIR Conference on Research and Development in Information Retrieval*, pp.19-26.

Agichtein, E., Brill, E., Dumais, S. and Ragno, R. (2006), Learning user interaction models for predicting Web search result preferences. *Proceedings of the Twenty-Ninth Annual International ACM SIGIR Conference on Research and Development in Information Retrieval*, pp. 3-10.

Agichtein, E., Brill, E., Dumais, S., and Ragno, R. (2006). Learning user interaction models for predicting web search result preferences. *Proceedings of the Twenty-Ninth Annual International ACM SIGIR Conference on Research and Development in Information Retrieval*, Seattle, WA, 3-10.

Agre, Phil. (1994) *Net Presence, Computer-Mediated Communication Magazine*, 1-4. Available at: http://www.december.com/cmc/mag/1994/aug/presence.html

Aguilar, F. J. (1988). *General managers in action.* New York: Oxford University Press.

Ahuja, J. S., & Webster, J. (2001). Perceived disorientation: an examination of a new measure to assess web design effectiveness. *Interacting with Computers, 14*(1), 15-29.

Akram, A. A., (2006). Electronic Privacy: Patient Concerns, *Communications of the IIMA,* Vol. 6 (1), 67-82.

Alani, H., Kim, S., Millard, D., Weal, M. Hall, W. Lewis, P. & Shadbolt. (2003). *Automatic Extraction of Knowledge from Web Documents*. Workshop on Human Language Technology for the Semantic Web and Web Services, 2 Int. Semantic Web Conf. Sanibel Island, Florida, USA.

Alasuutari, P. (1995). *Researching Culture: Qualitative Methods and Cultural Studies*. Thousand Oaks: Sage.

Aldenderfer, M. S., & Blashfield, R. K. (1984). *Cluster Analysis*. Beverly Hills, CA: Sage, 1984. 88 p.

Aldrich, S. E. (2006, May 2). *The Other Search: Making the Most of Site Search to Optimize the Total Customer Experience*. Patricia Seybold Group. Retrieved March 7, 2007, from WebSideStory database.

Allen, J., Schubert, L., Ferguson, G., Heeman, P., Hwang, C., Kato, T., Light, M., Martin, N., Miller, B., Poesio, M., & Traum, D. (1995). The TRAINS project: A Case Study in Building a Conversational Planning Agent. *Journal of Experimental and Theoretical Artificial Intelligence*, 7, 7-48.

Anderson, C. (2006). *The long tail: Why the future of business is selling less of more*. New York, NY: Hyperion.

Angheluta, R. and Moens, M.-F., 2007, Cross-document entity tracking, In G. Amati, C. Carpineto & G. Romano (Eds.), *Advances in Information Retrieval - 29th European Conference on IR Research ECIR - Lecture Notes in Computer Science 4425* (pp. 670-674), Berlin: Springer.

Anick, P. (2003). Using Terminological Feedback for Web Search Refinement - A Log-based Study. In *Proceedings of the 26 Annual International ACM SIGIR Conference on Research and Development in Information Retrieval, Toronto, Canada* (pp. 88-95).

Anick, P. G., & Tipirneni, S. (1999). The Paraphrase Search Assistant: Terminological Feedback for Iterative Information Seeking. In *Proceedings of the 22 Annual International ACM SIGIR Conference on Research and Development in Information Retrieval, Berkeley, CA* (pp. 153-159).

Annals of Family Medicine Selected for Indexing in Index Medicus and MEDLINE. (2004). Retrieved September 9, 2007, from http://www.aafp.org/annals/x28117.html

Anonymous. (2004, 08/08/2006). Searching PubMed. *PubMed Help* Retrieved 09/25/2006, 2006, from http://www.ncbi.nlm.nih.gov/books/bv.fcgi?rid=helppubmed.section.pubmedhelp.Searching_PubMed#pubmedhelp.Combining_search_ter

Ansari, S., Kohavi, R., Mason, L., & Zheng, Z. (2001). Integrating E-Commerce and Data Mining: Architecture and Challenges. *IEEE International Conference on Data Mining*.

Antoine, J. Y., Zeiliger, J., & Caelen, J. (1998). DQR Test Suites for a Qualitative Evaluation of Spoken Dialogue Systems: from Speech Understanding to Dialogue Strategy. In *Proceedings of the 1 International Conference on Language Resources and Evaluation, Granada, Spain* (pp. 59-66).

Archive.org. (1997). Features, Technology and Strategy Overview: Why WebTrends v3.0 is the best solution for your business. http://web.archive.org/web/19970415212525/http://webtrends.com/: [April 7, 2007].

Arnold, M. (2003). On the phenomenology of technology: the "Janus-faces" of mobile phones, *Information and Organization*, Vol. 13 (4), 231–256.

Aroyo, L., Bellekens, P., Björkman, M., Broekstra, J. & Houben, G. J. (2006). *Ontology based personalization in User-adaptive systems*. In 2nd International Workshop on Web Personalization, Recommender Systems and Intelligent User Interfaces (WPRSIUI'06), Dublin, Ireland.

Aroyo, L., Dolog, P., Houben, G-J., Kravcik, M., Naeve, A., Nilsson, M. & Wild, F. (2006). *Interoperability*. In Personalized Adaptive Learning. Educational Technology & Society, 9 (2), 4-18.

Atterer, R., Wnuk, M., & Schmidt, A. (2006). Knowing the user's every move: user activity tracking for website usability evaluation and implicit interaction. In *15th International Conference on World Wide Web* (pp. 203-212). Edinburgh, Scotland: ACM.

Aula, A., Jhaveri, N., & Kaki, M. (2005). Information Search and Re-access Strategies of Experienced Web Users. In *14th international conference on World Wide Web* (pp. 583-592). Chiba, Japan: ACM.

Aust, H., Oerder, M., Seide, F., & Steinbiss, V. (1995). The Philips Automatic Train Timetable Information System. *Speech Communication*, 17, 249-262.

Avinash, A. (2007, June 26). *Bounce Rate: Sexiest Web Metric Ever?* Retrieved December 2, 2007, from http://www.mpdailyfix.com/2007/06/bounce_rate_sexiest_web_metric.html.

Babbie, E. (2002). *The practice of social research.* Stamford, CT: Wadsworth.

Babbie, E. (2004). *The Practice of Social Research.* Belmont, CA: Wadsworth Publishing.

Back, H. B. (1976). *The design and evaluation of an interactive reference retrieval system for the management sciences.* Unpublished doctoral dissertation, Carnegie Mellon University.

Backstrom, L., Huttenlocher, D., Kleinberg, J., & Lan, X. (2006). Group formation in large social networks: Membership, growth, and evolution. *Proceedings from the Annual International Conference on Knowledge Discovery and Data Mining (Association for Computing Machinery KDD).* Philadelphia, Pennsylvania.

Baeza-Yates, R., & Castillo, C. (2001, 1-5 May). *In Relating Web structure and user search behavior* (pp. 1-2). Paper presented at the 10th World Wide Web Conference, Hong Kong, China. ACM.

Baeza-Yates, R., & Ribeiro-Neto, B. (1999). *Modern Information Retrieval.* Boston, MA: Addison Wesley.

Baeza-Yates, R., Calderón-Benavides, L., & Gonźalez, C. (2006, 11-13 October). The intention behind web queries. *Paper presented at the String Processing and Information Retrieval (SPIRE 2006), Glasgow, Scotland.*

Bailey, C., Hall, W., Millard, D. E., & Weal, M. J. (2007). Adaptive hypermedia through contextualized open hypermedia structures [Electronic Version]. *ACM Transactions on Information Systems, 25*(4), Article 16. Retrieved October 20, 2007, from http://doi.acm.org/10.1145/1281485.1281487

Bailey, J.R. (1997). Need for cognition and response mode in the active construction of an information domain. *Journal of Economic Psychology, 18*(1), 69-85.

Bains, S. (1997). End-user searching behavior: Considering methodologies. *The Katharine Sharp Review,* 1(4), http://www.lis.uiuc.edu/review/winter1997/bains.html.

Balabanovic, M. & Shoham, Y. (1997). *Content-based collaborative recommendation.* Communications. Of the ACM. 40(3): 66-72. March 1997.

Ballard, C. (2004, June 21). Fantasy world. *Sports Illustrated, 100,* 80-89.

Baptiste, Ian (September, 2001). Qualitative data analysis: common phases, strategic differences [42 paragraphs]. *Forum: Qualitative Sozialforschung / Forum: Qualitative Social Research* [On-line Journal], 2(3). Available at: http://www.qualitative-research.net/fqs/fqs-eng.htm

Barab, S. A., MaKinster, J. G., & Scheckler, R. (2004). Designing system dualities: Characterizing an online professional development community. In S. A. Barab, R. Kling & J. H. Gray (Eds.), *Designing for Virtual Communities in the Service of Learning* (pp. 53-90). Cambridge, UK: Cambridge University Press.

Barab, S., & Squire, K. (2004). Design-Based Research: Putting a Stake in the Ground, *The Journal of the learning sciences*, Vol. 13 (1), 1-14

Barbaro, M. & Zeller Jr., T. (2006). A face is exposed for AOL searcher No. 4417749. *The New York Times,* August 9, 1.

Barber, A. S., & Riccalton, C. (1988). The use of the LS/2000 online public access catalogue at Newcastle University Library (Grant No. SI/G/816): *British Library Research and Development Department Report.*

Barford, P., Bestavros, A., Bradley, A., & Crovella, M. (1999). Changes in Web Client Access Patterns: Characteristics and Caching Implications. *World Wide Web, 2*(1-2), 15-28.

Barnes, S. (2006). A privacy paradox: Social networking in the United States. *First Monday,* 11(9).

Barnes, Susan. (2004) *Goffman and the Internet: Applying Goffman's Concepts to Online Communication.* Paper presented at IAMCR Conference. Porto Alegre, PUCRS.

Barry, A. M., Holmes J., & Llor'a, X. (2004). Data mining using learning classifier systems. In L. Bull (Ed.), *Applications of Learning Classifier Systems, Lecture Notes in Computer Science: Studies in Fuzziness and Soft Computing,* 15–67. Berlin, Germany: Springer.

Bateman, S., Brooks, C. & Mccalla, G. (2006). *Collaborative Tagging Approaches for Ontological Metadata in Adaptive E-Learning Systems.* Proceedings of the Fourth International Workshop on Applications of Semantic Web Technologies for E-Learning (SW-EL 2006). pages 3-12.

Bates, M. J. (1990). Where should the person stop and the information search interface start? *Information Processing and Management, 26*(5), 575-591.

Batista, P., & Silva, M. J. (2001). Web access mining from an on-line newspaper logs. *Paper presented at the 12th International Meeting of the Euro Working Group on Decision Support Systems (EWG-DSS 2001),* Cascais, Portugal.

Beasley, C. (2002). *It's a hit! Gauging success through traffic analysis,* Retrieved May 7, 2007 from http://www.sitepoint.com/article/success-traffic-analysis

Becher, J. D. (2005, March). Why Metrics-Centric Performance Management Solutions Fall Short. *DMReview Magazine.* Retrieved March 7, 2007, from http://www.dmreview.com/article_sub.cfm?articleId=1021509.

Bechhofer, S., Yesilada, Y., Horan, B. & Goble, C. A. (2006). *Knowledge-Driven Hyperlinks: Linking in the Wild.* Sean Bechhofer. AH 2006, 1-10. 'http://dx.doi.org/10.1007/11768012_1', pages 1-10,2006.

Becker, Howard S. (1993) *Métodos de Pesquisa em Ciências Sociais.* São Paulo, Hucitec.

Beeferman, D. and Berger, A. (2000). Agglomerative clustering of a search engine query log. *Proceedings of the 6th ACM SIGKDD International Conference on Knowledge Discovery and Data Mining,* Boston, MA, 407 – 416.

Beitzel, S. M., Jensen, E. C., Chowdhury, A., Grossman, D., & Frieder, O. (2004, 25-29 July). Hourly analysis of a very large topically categorized web query log. *Paper presented at the 27th Annual International Conference on Research and Development in Information Retrieval, Sheffield, U.K.*

Beitzel, S. M., Jensen, E. C., Lewis, D. D., Chowdhury, A., & Frieder, O. (2007). Automatic classification of Web queries using very large unlabeled query logs. *ACM Transactions on Information Systems, 25*(2), Article No. 9.

Beitzel, S. M., Jensen, E. C., Chowdhury, A., Frieder, O., & Grossman, D. (2007). Temporal Analysis of a Very Large Topically Categorized Web Query Log. *Journal of the American Society for Information Science and Technology (JASIST),* 58(2), 166-178.

Beitzel, S. M., Jensen, E. C., Chowdhury, A., Grossman, D., & Frieder, O. (2004). Hourly Analysis of a Very Large Topically Categorized Web Query Log. In *Proceedings of the 27 Annual International ACM SIGIR Conference on Research and Development in Information Retrieval, Sheffield, UK* (pp. 321-328).

Beitzel, S.M., Jensen, E.C., Chowdhury, A., Grossman, D., and Frieder, O. (2004). Efficiency and Scaling: Hourly Analysis of a Very Large Topically Categorized Web Query Log. *Proceedings of the 27th Annual International Conference on Research and Development in Information Retrieval,* Sheffield, UK, 321-328.

Belkin, M. (2006, April 8). *15 Reasons why all Unique Visitors are not created equal.* Retrieved March 7, 2007, from http://www.omniture.com/blog/node/16.

Belkin, N. J., Cool, C., Kelly, D., Lin, S.-J., Park, S., Perez-Carballo, J., & Sikora, C. (2001). Iterative exploration, design and evaluation of support for query reformulation in interactive information retrieval, *Information Processing & Management, 37*(3): 403-434.

Belkin, N., Cool, C., Stein, A., & Theil, S. (1995). Cases, scripts, and information-seeking strategies: On the design of interactive information retrieval systems. *Expert Systems With Applications,* 9(3), 379-395.

Belkin, N.J., & Muresan, G. (2004). Measuring Web search effectiveness: Rutgers at Interactive TREC. In *Measuring Web Search Effectiveness: The User Perspective*, workshop at WWW 2004, May 2004, New York.

Bennett, K. & Demiriz, A. (1998). Semi-Supervised Support Vector Machines. In *Advances in Neural Information Processing Systems 11.* MIT Press.

Benveniste, Émile. (1989) *Problemas de Lingüística Geral II.* Campinas, Pontes.

Berendt, B. and Hanser, C., 2007, Tags are not metadata, but "just more content" – to some people, In *Proceedings of the International Conference on Weblogs and Social Media ICWSM* (pp. 19-26), Omnipress.

Berg, T. et al. , 2007, *Names and faces*, University of California Berkeley. Technical report.

Berger, A.D., Della Pietra, S.A. and Della Pietra, V.J., 1996, A maximum entropy approach to natural language processing, *Computational Linguistics,* 22(1), 39-71.

Berger, A.L., Pietra, S.A.D. and Pietra, V.J.D. (1996). A Maximum Entropy Approach to Natural Language Processing. *Computational Linguistics, 22(1).*

Berkovsky, S., Kuflik, T. & Ricci, T. (2006). *Cross-Technique Mediation of User Models*, in proceedings of the AH Conference, 2006.

Berners-Lee, T., Hendler, J. & Lassila, O. (2001), The Semantic Web, *Scientific American*, May 2001, pp. 28-37.

Berry, M. W. and Browne, M. (2005). *Understanding search engines mathematical modeling and text retrieval, Second edition.* Philadelphia: Society For Industrial and Applied Mathematics.

Bertot, J. C., & McClure, C. R. (1997). Web usage statistics: measurement issues and analytical techniques. *Government Information Quarterly*, 14(4), 373-396.

Bhatnagar A., & Ghose, S. (2004). Online information search termination patterns across product categories and consumer demographics. *Journal of Retailing, 80*(3), 221-228.

Biermann, J. S., Golladay, G. J., Greenfield, M. L., & Baker, L. H. (1999). Evaluation of cancer information on the Internet. *Cancer, 86*(3), 381-390.

Biersdorffer, J.D. (2006). How to digitally hide (somewhat) in plain sight. *The New York Times*, August 12, 9.

Bikel, D. M., Schwartz, R. and Weischedel, R.M., 1999, An algorithm that learns what's in a name, *Machine Learning*, 34, 211-231.

Bilinkis, I., and Mikelsons A. (1992). *Randomized signal processing.* New York, NY: Prentice Hall.

Bishop, Ann P., Star, Susan L., Neumann, Laura, Ignacio, Emily, Sandusky, Robert J., & Schatz, Bruce. (1995). Building a university digital library: Understanding implications for academic institutions and their constituencies. In: *Higher Education and the NII: From vision to reality. Proceedings of the Monterey Conference*, Sept. 26-29. Washington, DC, Coalition for Networked Information.

Blecic, D., Bangalore, N.S., Dorsch, J.L., Henderson, C.L., Koenig, M.H., & Weller, A.C. (1998). Using transaction log analysis to improve opac retrieval results. *College & Research Libraries,* 59(1), 39 - 50.

Blei, D., Bagnell, J. and McCallum, A., 2002, Learning with scope, with application to information extraction and classification, In *Uncertainty in Artificial Intelligence: Proceedings of the Eighteenth Conference* (UAI-2002) (pp. 53–60), San Francisco, CA: Morgan Kaufmann.

Blum, A., and Mitchell, T. (1998). Combining labeled and unlabeled data with co-training. COLT, *Proceedings of the Workshop on Computational Learning Theory.*

Boas, Franz. (1901) The Mind of Primitive Man. *The Journal of American Folklore*, 14, 1-11.

Boase, J., Horrigan, J., Wellman, B., & Rainie, L. (2006). *The strength of Internet ties.* Washington, DC: Pew Internet & American Life Project.

Bock, R. D., & Husain, S. Z. (1950). An adaptation of holzinger's b-coefficients for the analysis of sociometric data. *Sociometry, 13*, 146-153.

Boff, K. R., & Lincoln, J. E. (1988). *Engineering Data Compendium: Human Perception and Performance.* Wright-Patterson A.F.B. Dayton, Ohio: Harry G. Armstrong Aerospace Medical Research Laboratory.

Boiy, E., Hens, P., Deschacht, K. and Moens, M.-F., 2007, Automatic sentiment analysis of on-line text, In *Proceedings of the 11th International Conference on Electronic Publishing, Openness in Digital Publishing: Awareness, Discovery & Access 2007, Vienna Austria.*

Booske, B. C., & Sainfort, F. (1998). Relation between quantitative and qualitative measures of information use. *International Journal of Human-Computer Interaction*, 10(1), 1-21.

Borgman, C. L. (1982). Online monitoring of users of the Ohio State University online catalog: methodological issues and results. In A. E. Petrarca, C.E. Taylor, and R. S. Kohn (Eds.), Information Interaction: Proceedings of the 45th ASIS annual meeting: Vol. 19 (pp. 35-36). White Plains, NY: Knowledge Industry Publications.

Borgman, C. L. (1983). *End user behavior on The Ohio State University libraries' online catalog* (Research report prepared for OCLC). Dublin, OH: Office of Research, OCLC.

Borgman, C. L. (1984). *The user's mental model of an information retrieval system: effects on performance.* Unpublished doctoral dissertation, Stanford University.

Borgman, C. L. (1986). Why are online catalogs hard to use? Lessons learned from information retrieval studies. *Journal of the American Society for Information Science, 37(6)*, 387-400.

Borgman, C. L. (1996). Why are online catalogs *still* hard to use? *Journal of the American Society for Information Science, 47(7)*, 493-503.

Borgman, C. L., Case, D. O., & Meadow, C. T. (1989). The design and evaluation of a front-end interface for energy researchers. *Journal of the American Society for Information Science, 40(2)*, 99-109.

Borgman, C. L., Hirsh, S. G., & Hiller, J. (1996). Rethinking online monitoring methods for information retrieval systems: From search product to search process. *Journal of the American Society for Information Science, 47(7)*, 568-583.

Boyd, D. (2004). Friendster and publicly articulated social networks. *Proceedings of ACM Conference on Human Factors in Computing Systems*, New York: ACM Press, 1279-1282.

Boyd, D. (2006). Friends, Friendsters, and MySpace Top 8: Writing community into being on social network sites. *First Monday*, 11(12).

Boyd, D., & Ellison, N. (2007). Social network sites: Definition, history, and scholarship. *Journal of Computer-Mediated Communication*, 13(1), article 11.

Boyd, D., & Heer, J. (2006). Profiles as conversation: Networked identity performance on Friendster. *Proceedings of Thirty-Ninth Hawai'i International Conference on System Sciences.* Los Alamitos, CA: IEEE Press.

Brennan, P. F., & Aronson, A. R. (2003). Towards linking patients and clinical information: detecting UMLS concepts in e-mail. *J Biomed Inform, 36*(4-5), 334-341.

Brin, S. & Page, L. (1998). *The anatomy of a large-scale hypertextual Web search engine*, Computer Networks, 30(1-7): 107-117, Proceedings of the 7th International World Wide Web Conference (WWW7).

Brin, S., & Page, L. (1998). The Anatomy of a Large-Scale Hypertextual Web Search Engine. In *Proceedings of the Seventh International World Wide Web Conference (WWW7)*, Brisbane, Australia (pp. 107-117).

Broder, A. (2002). A taxonomy of web search. *SIGIR Forum, 36*(2), 3-10.

Brooks, N. (2004, July). *The Atlas Rank Report I: How Search Engine Rank Impacts Traffic.* Retrieved 1 August, 2004, from http://www.atlasdmt.com/media/pdfs/insights/RankReport.pdf

Brooks, N. (2004, October). *The Atlas Rank Report II: How Search Engine Rank Impacts Conversions.* Retrieved 15 January, 2005, from http://www.atlasonepoint.com/pdf/AtlasRankReportPart2.pdf

Brophy, P. (2004) Narrative-based librarianship. In *The area of information and social communication: Festschrift for Professor Wanda Pindlova (Studies in Library and Information Sciences Vol.10)* (pp. 188-195). Krakow: Jagiellonian University Press.

Brown, M., Foote, J., Jones, G., Sparck Jones, K., and Young, S. (1996). Open-vocabulary speech indexing for voice and video mail retrieval. *Proceedings of the fourth ACM international multimedia conference, ACM multimedia '96,* 307–316.

Bruno, Fernanda. (2005) Quem está olhando? Variações do público e do privado em Weblogs, fotologs e reality shows. In *Revista Contemporânea* (3/2), Salvador, EDUFBA.

Brusilovsky, P. (2001). *Adaptive Hypermedia.* User Modeling and User-Adapted Interaction, 11:87-110, 2001.

Brusilovsky, P. (1996). Methods and techniques of adaptive hypermedia. *User Modeling and User-Adapted Interaction*, *6*(2-3), 87-129.

Brusilovsky, P., Karagiannidis, C. & Sampson, D. (2004). *Layered evaluation of adaptive learning systems.* International Journal of Continuing Engineering Education and Lifelong Learning 14 (4/5), 402 - 421. 2004.

Bruza, P., McArthur, R., & Dennis, S. (2000, July). *Interactive Internet search: Keyword, directory and query reformulation mechanisms compared.* Paper presented at the Twenty-third Annual International ACM SIGIR Conference on Research and Development in Information Retrieval, Athens, Greece.

Bryman, A. (2004). *Social Research Methods* (2nd ed.). Oxford: Oxford University Press.

Budanitsky, A., & Hirst, G. (2001). *Semantic distance inWordNet: An experimental, application-oriented evaluation of five measures.* Paper presented at the North American Chapter of the Association for Computational Linguistics. from http://citeseer.ist.psu.edu/budanitsky-01semantic.html

Budd, J. M. (2005). Phenomenology and information studies, *Journal of Documentation,* Vol. 61 (1), 44-59.

Burby, J. & Brown, A. (2007). *Web Analytics Definitions.* Retrieved October 30, 2007, from http://www.webanalyticsassociation.org/attachments/committees/5/WAA-Standards-Analytics-Definitions-Volume-I-20070816.pdf.

Burby, J. (2004, July 20). *Build a Solid Foundation With Key Performance Indicators, Part 1: Lead-Generation Sites.* Retrieved March 7, 2007, from http://www.clickz.com/showPage.html?page=3382981.

Burges, C. J. C. (1998). A tutorial on support vector machines for pattern recognition. *Data Mining and Knowledge Discovery. 2,* 121–167.

Burton, M. C., & Walther, J. B. (2001). The value of Web log data in use-based design and testing. *Journal of Computer-Mediated Communication*, 6(3).

Byrne, D. N. (2007). Public discourse, community concerns, and civic engagement: Exploring black social networking traditions on BlackPlanet.com. *Journal of Computer-Mediated Communication*, 13(1), article 16.

Byrne, M., John, B., Wehrle, N., & Crow, D. (1999). The Tangled Web We Wove: A Taskonomy of WWW Use. In *SIGCHI conference on human factors in computing systems* (pp. 544-551). Pittsburgh, PA: ACM.

Byström, K. & Järvelin, K. (1995). Task complexity affects information seeking and use. *Information Processing and Management, 31*(2), 191-213.

Cacheda, F., & Viña, Á. (2001, July). *In Experiences retrieving information in the World Wide Web* (pp. 72-79). Paper presented at the 6th IEEE Symposium on Computers and Communications, Hammamet, Tunisia. IEEE.

Cacioppo, J.T., Petty, R.E. & Kao, C.F. (1984). The efficient assessment of need for cognition. *Journal of Personality Assessment*, *48*, 306-307.

Cannataro, M., Cuzzocrea, A., & Pugliese, A. (2001). A probabilistic adaptive hypermedia system. *Proceedings of the International Conference on Information Technology: Coding and Computing (ITCC '01)*, USA, 411-415.

Cantador, I. & Castells, P. (2006). *Multilayered Semantic Social Network Modeling by Ontology-Based User Profiles Clustering: Application to Collaborative Filtering.* 15th International Conference on Knowledge Engineering and Knowledge Management - Managing Knowledge in a World of Networks (EKAW 2006). Podebrady, Czech Republic, October 2006.

Card, S., Pirolli, P., Van Der Wege, M., Morrison, J., Reeder, R., Schraedley, P., et al. (2001). Information Scent as a Driver of Web Behavior Graphs: Results of a Protocol Analysis Method for Web Usability. In *SIGCHI conference on human factors in computing systems* (pp. 498-505). Seattle, WA: ACM.

Cardie, C. and Wagstaff, K., 1999, Noun phrase coreference as clustering, In *Proceedings of the Joint Conference on Empirical Methods in Natural Language Processing and Very Large Corpora* (pp. 82-89), ACL.

Carlisle, J. H. (1974). *Man computer interactive problem solving – relationships between user characteristics and interface complexity.* Unpublished doctoral dissertation, Yale University.

Carlson D. (2006). Semantic models for XML schema with UML tooling. *Proceedings of the 2nd International Workshop on Semantic Web Enabled Software Engineering (SWESE)*, Nov 2006, Athens, GA..

Carlson, D. (2001). *Modeling XML applications with UML: Practical e-Business applications.* Addison-Wesley.

Case, D. (2002). *Looking for information: a survey of research on information seeking, needs, and behavior.* San Diego, CA: Academic Press.

Catledge, L., & Pitkow, J. (1995). Characterizing Browsing Strategies in the World-Wide Web. In *3rd international World-Wide Web conference on technology, tools, and applications* (pp. 1065 - 1073). Darmstadt, Germany: Elsevier North-Holland, Inc.

CCMedia. (2007, August 30). *How to Obtain a Cost-effective Operational Model for Support/ Self-service Websites?* Retrieved December 5, 2007, from www.webnibbler.com/en/WhitePaper/Online%20Support%20Website.pdf.

Ceri, S., Daniel, F., Matera, M., & Facca, F. M. (2007). Model-driven development of context-aware Web applications [Electronic Version]. *ACM Transactions on Internet Technology,* 7(1), Article 2. Retrieved October 20, 2007, from http://doi.acm.org/10.1145/1189740.1189742

Cesa-Bianchi, N., Gentile, C. & Zaniboni, L. (2006). Hierarchical Classification: Combining Bayes with SVM. In *Proceedings of the 23rd International Conference on Machine Learning,* 177–184. Pittsburgh, PA.

Chai, K. M. A., Ng, H. T. and Cheiu, L. (2002). Bayesian online classifiers for text classification and filtering. *SIGIR'02: Proceedings of 25thACM International Conference on Research and Development in Information Retrieval,* Tampere, Finland, 97–104.

Chakrabarti, S. (2003). *Mining the Web.* Morgan Kaufmann Publishers, San Francisco, CA.

Chamberlain, K. (1995, 6 November). *What is grounded theory?* Retrieved 17 September, 2005, from http://kerlins.net/bobbi/research/qualresearch/bibliography/gt.html

Chang, C.-C., and Lin, C.-J. (2001). *LIBSVM: A library for support vector machines.* Available from http://www.csie.ntu.edu.tw/~cjlin/libsvm.

Chapman, J. L. (1981). A state transition analysis of online information-seeking behavior. *Journal of the American Society for Information Science, 32(5),* 325-333.

Chatham, B. (2004). *A Primer on A/B Testing.* Cambridge: Forrester Research.

Chatham, B. (2005). *What's On Web Analytics Users' Minds?* : Forrester Research.

Chatterjee, P., Hoffman, D. L., & Novak, T. P. (2003). Modeling the Clickstream: Implications for Web-Based

Advertising Efforts. *Marketing Science, 22*(4), 520-541.

Chau, M., Fang, X., & Sheng, O. R. L., (2005). Analysis of the Query Logs of a Web Site Search Engine. *Journal of the American Society for Information Science and Technology*, 56(13), 1363–1376

Chau, M., Fang, X., and Yang, C. C. (2007). Web Searching in Chinese: A Study of a Search Engine in Hong Kong, *Journal of the American Society for Information Science and Technology* (JASIST), accepted for publication, 58(7), 1044-1054, 2007.

Chau, M., Qin, J., Zhou, Y., Tseng, C., and Chen, H. (2005). SpidersRUs: Automated Development of Vertical Search Engines in Different Domains and Languages, in *Proceedings of the ACM/IEEE-CS Joint Conference on Digital Libraries*, Denver, Colorado, USA, June 7-11, 2005.

Chen, H. M. & Cooper, M. D. (2001). Using clustering techniques to detect usage patterns in a Web-based information system. *Journal of the American Society for Information Science, 52(11),* 888-904.

Cheong, F.-C. (1996). *Internet Agents: Spiders, Wanderers, Brokers, and Bots.* Indianapolis, IN: New Riders Publishing.

Chien, L.-F. (1997). PAT-Tree-Based Keyword Extraction for Chinese Information Retrieval, in *Proceedings of the 1997 ACM SIGIR*, Philadelphia, PA, USA, pp. 50-58.

Choo, C. W., Detlor, B., & Turnbull, D. (2000). Information Seeking on the Web: An Integrated Model of Browsing and Searching. *First Monday, 5*(2), Retrieved August 3, 2004, from http://firstmonday.org/issues/issue2005_2002/choo/index.html.

Choo, C. W., Detlor, B., & Turnbull, D. (2000). *Web work: Information seeking and knowledge work on the world wide web.* Netherlands: Kluwer Academic Publishers.

Choo, C., Detlor, B., & Turnbull, D. (1998). A behavioral model of information seeking on the web: Preliminary results of a study of how managers and IT specialists use the web. *Paper presented at the 61st Annual Meeting of the American Society for Information Science, Pittsburgh, PA.*

Chowdhury, A., & Soboroff, I. (2002). Automatic evaluation of world wide web search services. *Paper presented at the 25th Annual International ACM SIGIR Conference on Research and Development in Information Retrieval, Tampere, Finland.*

Christianini, N. and Shawe-Taylor, J., 2000, *An Introduction to Support Vector Machines and Other Kernel Based Learning Methods*, Cambridge, UK: Cambridge University Press.

Christopher, D. (2002). *Staff: The hypercontext framework for adaptive Hypertext.* Conference on Hypertext and Hypermedia. Proceedings of the thirteenth ACM conference on Hypertext and hypermedia. Maryland, USA. Pages: 11 – 20.

Claypool, M., Le, P., Wased, M., & Brown, D. (2001, January). *Implicit interest indicators.* Paper presented at the Sixth International Conference on Intelligent User Interfaces, Sanata Fe, NM.

ClickZStatsStaff. (2002). *Internet Usage Stats.* Online at: www.clickz.com/stats/big_picture/traffic_patterns/article.php/960101. Retrieved January 1, 2008.

CNNIC – China Internet Network Information Center, *Chinese Search Engine Market Survey Report 2006.*

Coase, R. (1998). The new institutional economics. *The American Economic Review*, 88(2), 72-74.

Cockburn, A., & McKenzie, B. (2001). What do web users do? An empirical analysis of web use. *International Journal of Human-Computer Studies, 54*(6), 903-922.

Cohen, L. B. (2003). A Two-tiered model for analyzing library Web site usage statistics, part 1: Web server logs. *Libraries and The Academy, 3*(2), 315.

Cohen, L. B. (2003). A Two-tiered model for analyzing library Web site usage statistics, part 2: log file analysis. *Libraries and The Academy, 3*(3), 517.

Coleman, J. S. (1988). Social capital in the creation of human capital. *American Journal of Sociology: Supple-*

ment: Organizations and Institutions: Sociological and Economic Approaches to the Analysis of Social Structure, 94, S100-S101.

Coleman, J. S. (1990). *Foundations of social theory.* Cambridge: Harvard University Press, 300-316.

Collins, M. and Singer, Y., 1999, Unsupervised models for named entity classification, In *Proceedings of Empirical Methods in Natural Language Processing (EMNLP)*, College Park, MD.

Conlan, O., O'Keeffe, I. & Tallon, S. (2006), *Combining Adaptive Hypermedia Techniques and Ontology Reasoning to produce Dynamic Personalized News Services,* Proceedings of the Fourth International Conference on Adaptive Hypermedia and Adaptive Web-Based Systems (AH2006), Dublin, Ireland (2006).

ConnectUsDirect.com. (2006). Online newsletter on Web analytics. (April).

Cook, D. J., & Holder, L. B. (2000). *Graph-based data mining.* IEEE Intelligent Systems, Los Alamitos, v.15, n.2, p. 32-41.

Cooley, R., Mobasher, B. and Srivastava, J. (1999). Data preparation for mining World Wide Web browsing patterns. *Knowledge and Information Systems. 1,* 5–32.

Cooper, A., Reinmann, R., & Cronin, D. (2007). *About Face 3: The essentials of interaction design.* Wiley.

Cooper, M. C. (2000). Semantic distance measures. *Computational Intelligence, 16*(1), 79-94.

Cooper, M.D. (1998). Design considerations in instrumenting and monitoring Web-based information retrieval systems. *Journal of the American Society for Information Science,* 49(10), 903–919.

Core, M. G., & Allen, J. (1997). Coding Dialogs with the DAMSL Annotation Scheme. In *AAAI Fall Symposium on Communicative Action in Humans and Machines,* MIT, Cambridge, MA.

Cothey, V. (2002). A longitudinal study of World Wide Web users' information searching behavior. *Journal of the American Society for Information Science and Technology, 53*(2), 67-78.

Couper, M. (2000). Web surveys: A review of issues and approaches. *Public Opinion Quarterly, 64*(4), 464-494.

Couper, M., Traugott, M., & Lamias, M. (2001). Web Survey Design and Administration. *Public Opinion Quarterly, 65*(2), 230-253.

Cowie, J. and Lehnert, W., 1996, Information extraction, *Communications of the ACM,* 39 (1), 80-91.

Cranor, L. F. (1999). Internet Privacy. *Communications of the ACM, 42*(2), 28-31.

Creswell, J. W. (1994). *Research Design: Qualitative and Quantitative Approaches.* Thousand Oaks: Sage.

Crocco, A. G., Villasis-Keever, M., & Jadad, A. R. (2002). Analysis of cases of harm associated with use of health information on the Internet. *JAMA, 287,* 2869-2871.

Croft, W. B., Cook, R., & Wilder, D. (1995, 11- 13 June). Providing government information on the internet: Experiences with THOMAS. *Paper presented at the Digital Libraries Conference, Austin, TX.*

Cross, R., Parker, A., & Borgatti, S. (2002). *A bird's-eye view: Using social network analysis to improve knowledge creation and sharing.* IBM Institute for Business Value.

Crouch, C.J. and Yang, B., 1992, Experiments in automatic statistical thesaurus construction. In *Proceedings of the 15th Annual International ACM SIGIR Conference on Research and Development of Information Retrieval* (pp. 77-88), New York: ACM.

Crowle, S., & Hole, L. (2003). ISML: An interface specification meta-language, *10th International Workshop on Design, Specification and Verification of Interactive Systems*, Madeira.

Cucerzan, S., & Brill, E. (2004). Spelling Correction as an Iterative Process that Exploits the Collective Knowledge of Web Users. In *Proceedings of EMNLP'04* (pp. 293-300).

Cullota, A. and Sorensen, J., 2004, Dependency tree kernels for relation extraction, In *Proceedings of the 42nd Annual Meeting of the Association for Computational Linguistics* (pp. 424-430), East Stroudsburg, PA: ACL.

Curtis, P. (1992). Mudding: Social phenomena in text-based virtual realities. In *Proceedings of Directions and Implications of Advanced Computing (DIAC 92) Symposium*. Berkeley, CA.

Cyram Company Ltd. (2005). NetMiner (Version 2.6). Seoul, Korea: Cyram Company Ltd.

Dale, R. (2006). Industry Watch. *Natural Language Engineering*, 12(4), 391-395.

Dalhousie Research Services. (2006). *Directives to Researchers regarding Compliance with the University Policy for the Protection of Personal Information from Access Outside Canada*. Retrieved July 29, 2007 from http://researchservices.dal.ca/files/Personal_Information_Protection_Guide.pdf.

Danaher, P. J. (1995). What happens to television ratings during commercial breaks?, *Journal of Advertising Research*, 35(1), 37-47.

Danielson, D. R. (2002). Web navigation and the behavioral effects of constantly visible site maps. *Interacting with Computers, 14*(5), 601-618.

Das, S., Echambadi, R., McCardle, M. & Luckett, M. (2003). The effect of interpersonal trust, need for cognition, and social loneliness on shopping, information seeking and surfing on the Web. *Marketing Letters, 14*(3), 185-202.

Davis, M. P. (2004). Information-seeking behavior of chemists: A Transaction Log Analysis of referral URLs, *Journal of the American Society for Information Science and Technology*, 55(3), 326-332.

Dayanik, A., Lewis, D. D., Madigan, D., Menkov, V. & Genkin, A. (2006). Constructing informative prior distributions from domain knowledge in text classification. In *Proceedings of the 29th Annual international ACM SIGIR Conference on Research and Development in Information Retrieval,* 493–500. ACM Press, New York

De Beer, J. and Moens, M.-F., 2007, A general solution of (hidden) text salting. Technical Report K.U.Leuven.

De Bra, P. et al. (2003). *AHA! The adaptive hypermedia architecture.* Conference on Hypertext and Hypermedia. Proceedings of the fourteenth ACM conference on Hypertext and hypermedia.. Nottingham, UK, Pages: 81 – 84. 2003. ISBN:1-58113-704-4.

De Bra, P., & Calvi, L. (1998, June). *AHA: A generic adaptive hypermedia system.* Paper presented at the Second Workshop on Adaptive Hypertext and Hypermedia, HYPERTEXT'98, Pittsburgh, PA.

De Bra, P., Arroyo, L. & Chepegin, V. (2004). *The next big thing: adaptive Web-based systems.* Journal of Digital Information, V(5)N(1).

De Bra, P., et al. (1999). *Adaptive hypermedia: From systems to framework.* ACM Computing Surveys, 31(4). 1999.

de Keizer, N. F., Abu-Hanna, A., & Zwetsloot-Schonk, J. H. (2000). Understanding terminological systems. I: Terminology and typology. *Methods Inf Med, 39*(1), 16-21.

De Silva, S. M. (1997). A review of expert systems in library and information science. *Malaysian Journal of Library & Information Science, 2(2),* 57-92.

De Smet, W. and Moens, M.-F., 2007, Generating a topic hierarchy from dialect texts. In *Proceedings of the 4th International Workshop on Text-based Information Retrieval* (*TIR-07*), IEEE Computer Society.

De, S. K., & Krishna, P. R. (2004). Clustering web transactions using rough approximation. *Fuzzy Sets and Systems, 148,* 131-138.

den Os, E., & Bloothooft, G. (1998). Evaluating Various Spoken Dialogue Systems with a Single Questionnaire: Analysis of the ELSNET Olympics. In *Proceedings of the 1 International Conference on Language Resources and Evaluation*, Granada, Spain (pp. 51-54).

Denzin, N., & Lincoln, Y. (2000). Introduction: The Discipline and Practice of Qualitative Research. In N.

Denzin & Y. Lincoln (Eds.), *Handbook of Qualitative Research* (2nd ed., pp. 1-30). Thousand Oaks: Sage.

Deschacht, K. and Moens, M.-F., 2007, Text analysis for automatic image annotation, In *Proceedings of the 45th Annual Meeting of the Association for Computational Linguistics*, East Stroudsburg: ACL.

Dhyani, D., Ng, W. G. & Bhowmick, S. (2002). A survey of web metrics. *ACM Computing Survey, 34*(December), 469-503.

Diaper, D., & Stanton, N. (2004). *The handbook of task analysis of Human-Computer Interaction.* Lawrence Erlbaum Associates.

Dick, P. (2004), Discourse analysis, in Cassell, C., Symon, G. (Eds), *Essential Guide to Qualitative Methods in Organizational Research*, Sage, London, 203-213.

Dicks, Bella and Mason, Bruce. (1998). Hypermedia and ethnography: reflections on the construction of a research approach. *Sociological Research Online.* 3/3, available at: http://www.socresonline.org.uk

Dicks, Bella; Bruce Mason & Amanda Coffey et al. (2005) *Qualitative Research and Hypermedia: Ethnography for the Digital Age.* London, Sage Publications.

Dillman, D. A. (1978). *Mail and telephone surveys.* New York: John Wiley & Sons.

Dillon, A. & Watson, C. (1996). User analysis HCI. The historical lessons from individual differences research. *International Journal of Human-Computer Studies, 45*(6), 619-638.

DiPerna, P. (2006). K-12 encounters the Internet. *First Monday*, 11(5).

Dodds, P., Muhamad, R., & Watts, D. (2003). An experimental study of search in global social networks. *Science*, 301, 827-829.

Dodoo, M. (2006, March 3). *Privacy & Google Analytics.* Retrieved March 7, 2007, from http://www.marteydodoo.com/2006/05/03/privacy-google-analytics/.

Dolog, P. (2004). *Identifying relevant fragments of learner profile on the semantic Web.* In Proceedings of SWEL'2004 — Intl. Workshop on Semantic Web for eLearning, Intl. Semantic Web Conference 2004, Hiroshima.

Dolog, P., Henze, N. & Nejdl, W. (2004). *Personalization in distributed e-learning environments.* In Proceedings of WWW2004 --- The Thirteen International World Wide Web Conference, New York, May 2004. P.85-94. ACM Press.

Dominick, W. D. (1987). A performance measurement and evaluation environment for information systems. *Information Processing and Management, 23(10,* 7-15.

Dominick, W. D. (1974). *The man/machine interface, system monitoring and performance evaluation methodology for on-line interactive systems.* Unpublished masters thesis, Northwestern University.

Dominick, W. D. (1990). The NASA RECON educational-program in interactive information-retrieval systems. *Computers & Education, 14(2),* 103-112.

Donath, J., & Boyd, D. (2004). Public displays of connection. *BT Technology Journal, 22*(4), 71-82.

Douglass, B. P. (1999). *Doing hard time: Developing real-time systems with UML, objects, frameworks, and patterns.* Addison-Wesley.

Drott, M.C. (1998). *In Using Web server logs to improve site design* (pp. 43 - 50). Paper presented at the the 16th Annual International Conference on Computer Documentation, Quebec, Canada. ACM.

Drummond, M. E. (1973). *Evaluation and Measurement Techniques for Digital Library Systems.* Englewood Cliffs, NJ: Prentice-Hall, Inc.

Dubé, L., & Paré, G. (2003). Rigor in Information Systems Positivist Case Research: Current Practices, Trends, and Recommendations, *MIS Quarterly,* Vol. 27 (4), 597-636.

Dublin Core. (2007). *The Dublin Core Metadata Initiative.* Retrieved September, 20, 2007, from http://dublincore.org/

Dumais, S. T. (2002). *Web experiments and test collections.* Retrieved April 20, 2003, from http://www2002.org/presentations/dumais.pdf

Dumais, S. T., & Belkin, N. J. (2005). The TREC interactive tracks: Putting the user into search. In Voorhees, E. M., & Harman, D. K. (Eds.), *TREC – Experiment and evaluation in Information Retrieval,* MIT Press.

Dumais, S.T. (2002, 7-11 May). *Web experiments and test collections.* Retrieved 20 April, 2003, from http://www2002.org/presentations/dumais.pdf

Dwyer, C. (2007). Digital relationships in the 'MySpace' generation: Results from a qualitative study. *40th Hawaii International Conference on System Sciences (HICSS).* Waikoloa, HI.

Dybkjær, L., Bernsen, N. O., Carlson, R., Chase, L., Dahlbäck, N., Failenschmid, K., Heid, U., Heisterkamp, P., Jönsson, A., Kamp, H., Karlsson, I., v. Kuppevelt, J., Lamel, L., Paroubek, P., & Williams, D. (1998). The DISC Approach to Spoken Language Systems Development and Evaluation. In *Proceedings of the 1 International Conference on Language Resources and Evaluation,* Granada, Spain (pp. 185-189).

e-consultancy. (2003). *Web measurement and analytics.* London, UK: e-consultancy.

Efthimiadis, E. N., & Robertson, S. E. (1989). Feedback and interaction in information retrieval. In C. Oppenheim (Ed.), *Perspectives in information management* (pp. 257-272). London: Butterworths.

Eirinaki, M. (2003). *SEWeP: Using Site Semantics and a Taxonomy to Enhance the Web Personalization Process* (2003). In Proc. of the 9th SIGKDD Conf., 2003.

Eirinaki, M., Mavroedis, D., Tsatsaronis, G. & Vazirginannis, M. (2006). *Introducing Semantics in Web Personalization: the role of ontologies.* M Ackermann et al. (Eds.): EWMF/KDO 2005, LNAI, pp.147-162, 2006. Springer Verlag, Berlin Heidelberg 2006.

Eisenberg, B. (2005). How To Improve A/B Testing. www.clickz.com/experts/crm/traffic/article.php/3500811: [November 10, 2006].

Eisenberg, B. (2005, April 1). *Web Analytics: Exciting Times Ahead.* Retrieved March 7, 2007, from http://www.clickz.com/showPage.html?page=3493976

Eisenberg, D. M., Kessler, R. C., Rompay, M. I. V., Kaptchuk, T. J., Wilkey, S. A., Appel, S., et al. (2001). Perceptions about complementary therapies relative to conventional therapies among adults who use both: results from a national survey. *Annals of Internal Medicine, 135*(5), 344-351.

Ekstrom, R.B, French, J.W., & Harman, H.H. (1976). *Manual for kit of factor-referenced cognitive tests,* 109-113, 173-177.

Ellis, D. (1989). A behavioral approach to information retrieval system design. *The Journal of Documentation, 45*(3), 171-212.

Ellison, N., Steinfield, C., & Lampe, C. (2007). The benefits of Facebook "friends": Exploring the relationship between college students' use of online social networks and social capital. *Journal of Computer-Mediated Communication,* 12(3), article 1.

Enright, A. (2006). Real-time analytics boost ROI, accountability. *Marketing News,* (October 1), 20-24.

Entwistle, H. & Tait, N.J. (1995). *The revised approaches to studying inventory.* Edinburgh: Centre for Research on Learning and Instruction, University of Edinburgh.

Esposito, F. & Lisi, A. (2004). *An ILP Approach to semantic Web mining.* In P.Buitelaar, et al (Eds.), Notes of the ECML/PKDD, 2004 Workshop on Knowledge Discovery and Ontologies, 139-144, Pisa, Italy.

Etgen, M., & Cantor, J. (1998). *What does getting WET (Web Event-logging Tool) mean for Web usability?,* [Online]. Available: http://www.itl.nist.gov/iaui/vvrg/hf-web/proceedings/etgen-cantor/index.html [22 October, 2002].

Eveland, W. P., Jr., & Dunwoody, S. (1998). Surfing the Web for science: Early data on the users and uses of The Why Files. *NISE Brief,* 2(2), 1-10.

Eveland, W. P., Jr., & Dunwoody, S. (1998). Users and navigation patterns of a science World Wide Web site for the public. *Public Understanding of Science*, 7, 285-311.

eVision. (2007, September 27). *Websites that convert visitors into customers: Improving the ability of your Website to convert visitors into inquiries, leads, and new business.* Retrieved March 7, 2007, from http://www.evisionsem.com/marketing/webanalytics.htm

Excite (1999). Excite and other more recent data sets can be downloaded from http://ist.psu.edu/faculty_pages/jjansen/academic/transaction_logs.html

Eysenbach, G., & Kohler, C. (2004). Health-related searches on the Internet. *Jama, 291*(24), 2946.

Eysenbach, G., Powell, J., Kuss, O., & Sa, E. R. (2002). Empirical studies assessing the quality of health information for consumers on the world wide web: a systematic review. *JAMA, 287*(20), 2691-2700.

Fedorowicz, J. (1982). A Zipfian Model of an Automatic Bibliographic System: an Application to MEDLINE. *Journal of American Society of Information Science*, (33), pp 223-232.

Feng, A. and Allan, J. (2005). *Hierarchical Topic Detection in TDT.* CIIR Technical Report, University of Massachusetts.

Feng, D. and Hovy, E.D., 2006, Learning to detect conversation focus of threaded discussions, in *Proceedings of the Human Language Technology / North American Association of Computational Linguistics conference* (HLT-NAACL 2006), New York, NY.

Fenichel, C. H. (1979). *Online information retrieval: Identification of measures that discriminate among users with different levels and types of experience.* Unpublished doctoral dissertation, Drexel University.

Fenichel, C. H. (1981). On-line searching measures that discriminate among users with different types of experiences. *Journal of the American Society for Information Science, 32(1),* 23-32.

Fensel, D. (2001). Ontologies: Silver Bullet for Knowledge Management and Electronic Commerce. Springer-Verlag.

Fensel, D. (2002). Ontology-Based Knowledge Management. IEEE Computer, 35(11), pages 56-59.

Fenstermacher, K., & Ginsburg, M. (2003). Client-Side Monitoring for Web Mining. *Journal of the American Society for Information Science and Technology, 54*(7), 625-637.

Fernaeus, Y, Tholander, J., & Jonsson, M. (2008). Towards a New set of Ideals: Consequences of the Practice Turn in Tangible Interaction, *Proceedings of the Second International Conference on Tangible and Embedded Interaction (TEI'08),* 223-230.

Fillmore, C.J. and Baker, C.F., 2001, Frame semantics for text understanding, In *Proceedings of WordNet and Other Lexical Resources Workshop.*

Fink, A. (1995). *The survey handbook (vol. 1).* Thousands Oaks, CA: Sage Publications.

Fisher, K. E., Erdelez, S., & McKechnie, L. E. F. (Eds.). (2005). *Theories of information behavior.* Medford, NJ: Information Today.

Fisher, R. J. (1993). Social Desirability Bias and the Validity of Indirect Questioning. *Journal of Consumer Research, 20*(2), 303-315.

Flick, U. (2002). *An Introduction to Qualitative Research.* Thousand Oaks, CA: Sage Publications.

FOAF. (2000). *The Friend of A Friend Project.* Retrieved september, 20, 2007, from http://www.foaf-project.org/index.html.

Ford, N. (1986). Psychological determinants of information needs: A small-scale study of higher education students. *Journal of Librarianship, 18*(1), 47-61.

Ford, N., & Miller, D. (1996). Gender differences in internet perception and use. In *Papers from the 3rd Electronic Library and Visual Information Research (ELVIRA) conference, April 30* (pp. 87-202). London: ASLIB.

Ford, N., Miller, D., & Moss, N. (2001). The role of individual differences in internet searching: An empirical study. *Journal of the American Society for Information Science and Technology, 52*(12), 1049-1066.

Ford, N., Miller, D., & Moss, N. (2003). Web search strategies and approaches to studying. *Journal of the American Society for Information Science and Technology, 54*(6), 473-489.

Ford, N., Miller, D., & Moss, N. (2005). Web search strategies and human individual differences: Cognitive and demographic factors, internet attitudes, and approaches. *Journal of the American Society for Information Science and Technology, 56*(7), 741-756.

Ford, N., Miller, D., & Moss, N. (2005). Web search strategies and human individual differences: A combined analysis. *Journal of the American Society for Information Science and Technology, 56*(7), 757-764.

FoundPages. (2007, October 25). *Increasing Conversion Rates.* Retrieved October 31, 2007, from http://www.foundpages.com/calgary-internet-marketing/search-conversion.html

Fourie, I. (2002, 24 -25 October). *A review of Web information-seeking/searching studies (2000 - 2002): Implications for research in the south african context* (pp. 49-75). Paper presented at the Progress in Library and Information Science in Southern Africa: 2d Biannial DISSAnet Conference, Pretoria, South Africa. SAOUG.

Fourie, I., & van den Berg, H. (2003, June). *A story told by nexus transaction logs: What to make of it* (pp. 1 - 19). Paper presented at the 7th Southern African Online Meeting, Muldersdrift, South Africa. SAOUG.

Fowler, F. J. (1995). *Improving survey questions: Design and evaluation (vol. 38).* Thousand Oaks, CA.: Sage Publications.

Fowler, Martin (2004). *UML distilled: A brief guide to the standard object modeling language* (3rd ed.). Addison-Wesley/Pearson Education.

Fox, S., & Rainie, L. (2000). *The online healthcare revolution: How the Web helps Americans take better care of themselves.* Washington DC: Pew Internet and American Life Project: Onlineo. Document Number)

Fox, S., & Rainie, L. (2002). *Vital decisions: how internet users decide what information to trust when they or their loved ones are sick.* Washington, DC: Pew Internet & American Life Projecto. Document Number)

Frazer, James G. (2000) [orig. 1870] *The Golden Bough: a study on magic and religion.* New York: Bartleby.com.

Freeman, L.C. (1979). Centrality in social networks: I. Conceptual clarification. *Social Networks, 1*, 215-239.

Freeman, L.C. (2000). Visualizing social networks. *Journal of Social Structure, 1*(1).

Freitas, F. L. G. (2003). *Ontologias e a Web Semântica.* XXIII Congresso da Sociedade Brasileira de Computação. JAI. Campinas, São Paulo, Junho de 2003.

Friedman, N., Geiger, D. and Goldszmidt, M. (1997). Bayesian network classifiers. *Machine Learning,* 29, 131—163.

Funk, M. E., & Reid, C. A. (1983). Indexing consistency in MEDLINE. *Bull Med Libr Assoc, 71*(2), 176-183.

Gabrilovich, E., & Markovitch, S. (2005). Feature generation for text categorization using world knowledge. In *Proceedings of the Nineteenth International Joint Conference of Artificial Intelligence*, 1048–1053.

Gamma, E., Helm, R., Johnson, R., & Vlissides, J. (1995). *Design Patterns – Elements of Reusable Object-Oriented Software.* Addison-Wesley.

Garfinkel, S., & Spafford, G. (2001). *Web Security, Privacy & Commerce, 2nd Edition*: O'Reilly.

Garkinkel, Harold. (1967) *Studies in Ethnomethodology.* New Jersey: Prentice Hall.

Garton, L., Haythornthwaite, C., & Wellman, B. (1997). Studying online social networks. *Journal of Computer-Mediated Communication, 3*(1).

Gassman, B. (2005). *How to Choose An Advanced Solution for Web Analytics.* Stamford: Gartner Research.

Gates, C. & Whalen, T. (2006) Personal Information on the Web: Methodological Challenges and Approaches. *CHI 2006 Workshop on Privacy and HCI: Methodologies for Studying Privacy Issues.*

Gauch, S., & Smith, J. (1993). An expert system for automatic query reformulation. *Journal of the American Society for Information Science, 44*(3), 124-136.

Gay, C. W., Kayaalp, M., & Aronson, A. R. (2005). *Semi-automatic indexing of full text biomedical articles.* Paper presented at the AMIA Annu Symp Proc.

Gee, J. P., & Green, J. L. (1998). Discourse analysis, learning, and social practice: A methodological study. *Review of Research in Education, 23*, 119-169.

Geertz, Clifford. (1973) *The Interpretation of Cultures.* New York: Basic Books.

Ghani, R. (2002). Combining Labeled and Unlabeled Data for MultiClass Text Categorization. In *Proceedings of the Nineteenth International Conference on Machine Learning*, 187–194. Morgan Kaufmann.

Gildea, D. and Jurafsky, D., 2002, Automatic labeling of semantic roles. *Computational Linguistics*, 28(3), 245-288.

Gladwell, M. (2000). *The tipping point.* New York: Little, Brown, & Company.

Glaser, B., & Strauss, A. (1967). *The discovery of grounded theory: Strategies for qualitative research.* Chicago, IL: Aldine Publishing Co.

Glenisson, P., Glänzel, W., Janssens, F. and De Moor, B., 2005, Combining full text and bibliometric information in mapping scientific disciplines, *Information Processing & Management*, 41 (6), 1548-1572.

Global Reach (2004). "Global Internet Statistics," available at: http://www.glreach.com/globstats/

Goddeau, D., Brill, E., Glass, J., Pao, C., Phillips, M., Polifroni, J., Seneff, S., & Zue, V. (1994). GALAXY: A Human-Language Interface to On-line Travel Information. In *Proceedings International Conference on Spoken Language Processing*, Yokohama, Japan.

Godfrey, D. G. (2006). *Methods of Historical Analysis in Electronic Media.* Mahwah, NJ: Erlbaum, 2006

Goecks, J., & Shavlik, J. (2000, January). *Learning users' interests by unobtrusively observing their normal behavior.* Paper presented at the Fifth International Conference on Intelligent User Interfaces, New Orleans, LA.

Goffman, E. (1959). *The Presentation of Self in Everyday Life.* Garden City, New York: Doubleday Anchor Books.

Goffman, Erving. (1967) *Interaction Ritual: Essays in Face-to-Face Behavior.* Garden City, Doubleday.

Goldberg, J. (2001, 5/18). *Why Web usage statistics are (worse than) meaningless*, [Online]. Available: http://www.goldmark.org/netrants/webstats/ [15 October 2002].

Golder, S. and Huberman, B.A., 2007, The structure of collaborative tagging systems, *Journal of Information Science,* 32 (2): 198-208.

Goldman S., & Zhou, Y. (2000). Enhancing Supervised Learning with Unlabeled Data. In *Proceedings of the Seventeenth International Conference on Machine Learning*, 327–334. Morgan Kaufmann.

Gonçalves, M. A., Panchanathan, G., Ravindranathan, U., Krowne, A., Fox, E. A., Jagodzinski, F., & Cassel, L. (2003). The XML log standard for digital libraries: Analysis, evolution, and deployment. *The Third Joint Conference in Digital Libraries (JCDL)*, Houston, TX.

Goodenough, Ward. (1957) Cultural Anthropology and Linguistics. *Report of the Seventh Annual Round Table Meeting on Linguistics and Language Studies.* Paul Gavin (org.) (Reprinted in HYMES, Dell (ed.). (1964) *Language in culture and society: a reader in linguistics and anthropology.* New York, Harper and Row).

Goodrum, A. and Kim, C. (1998). *Visualizing the history of chemistry: queries to the CHF pictorial collection.* Report to the Chemical Heritage Foundation Pictorial Collection.

Goodrum, A. and Spink, A. (2001). Image searching on the Excite Web search engine. *Information Processing and Management, 37(2)*, 295-312.

Goodwin, H. B. (1959). Some thoughts on improved technical information service. *Special Libraries, 50(9),* 443-446.

Google. (2007). *Google Corporate Information: Google Milestones.* Online at: http://www.google.ca/corporate/history.html. Retrieved January 1, 2008.

Gorge, M. (2007). Making sense of log management for security purposes – an approach to best practice log collection, analysis and management. *Computer Fraud & Security, 2007(5),* 5-10.

Gorin, R. E. (1971). *Developer of ispell.* Retrieved 12 February, 2000, from http://fmg-www.cs.ucla.edu/geoff/ispell.html

Gorman, G. E., & Clayton, P. (2005). *Qualitative research for the information professional.* London: Facet.

Gove, N. B. (1973). Some good and bad features of present and future systems. In M. B. Henderson(Ed.) *Interactive Bibliographic Systems* (pp. 26-31). U.S. Atomic Energy Commission: Office of Information Services.

Grace-Martin, M., & Gay, G. (2001). Web Browsing, Mobile Computing and Academic Performance. *Educational Technology & Society, 4(3),* Retrieved February 19, 2006, from http://ifets.ieee.org/periodical/vol_2003_2001/grace_martin.html.

Granovetter, M. (1973). The strength of weak ties. *American Journal of Sociology,* 78(6), 1360-1380.

Granovetter, M. S. (1983). The strength of weak ties: A network theory revisited. *Sociological Theory, 1,* 201-233.

Graziano, A. M., & Raulin, M. L. (2004). *Research methods: A process of inquiry* (5th ed.). Boston: Pearsono.

Greenfield, M. (2006, January 1). *Use Web Analytics to Improve Profits for New Year: Focus on four key statistics.* Retrieved March 7, 2007, from http://www.practicalecommerce.com/articles/132/Use-Web-Analytics-to-Improve-Profits-for-New-Year/

Greiffenhagen, Christian. & Watson, Rod. (2005) 'Teoria' e 'Método' na CMC: identidade, género, e tomada-de-turno – uma abordagem etnometodológica e analítico-conversacional. In: Braga, Adriana (Ed.) *CMC, Identidades e Género: teoria e método.* Colecção Estudos em Comunicação. Covilhã, Universidade da Beira Interior, Portugal.

Gremett, P. (2006). "Utilizing a User's Context to Improve Search Results. *Journal of the American Society for Information Science and Technology, 57(6),* 808–812.

Gremett, P. (2006). Utilizing a User's Context to Improve Search Results. *Journal of the American Society for Information Science and Technology, 57(6),* 808–812.

Griffiths, J. R., Hartley, R. J., & Willson, J. P. (2002). An improved method of studying user-system interaction by combining transaction log analysis and protocol analysis. *Information Research, 7(4).* Available at: http://InformationR/ir/7-4/paper139.html

Grignetti, M. C., Hausmann, C., & Gould, L. (1975). An intelligent online assistant and tutor – NLS Scholar. In *AFIPS Conference Proceedings NCC* (pp. 775-781)

Grimes, C., Tang, D., & Russell, D. M. (2007, May 8-12, 2007). *Query logs alone are not enough.* Paper presented at the WWW 2007, Banff, Canada.

Gruber, T. (1993). *What is an Ontology?* Retrieved May, 01 2007, from http://www.ksl.stanford.edu/kst/what-is-an-ontology.html.

Gugerty, L., Treadaway C., & Rubinstein, J.S. (2006). Individual differences in internet search outcomes and processes. *CHI 2006,* April, 815-820.

Guther, E. (2004). Improving the quality of Web surveys: The Checklist for Reporting Results of Internet E-Surveys (CHERRIES). *Journal of Medical Internet Research,* Vol. 6 (3) e34. Retrieved March 23, 2008, from http://www.jmir.org/2004/3/e34/.

GVUOnlineSurvey. (1997). *GVU's 8th WWW User Survey.* Online at: http://www.cc.gatech.edu/gvu/user_surveys/survey-1997-10. Retrieved August 3, 2004.

Ha, L. Q., Sicilia-Garcia, E. I., Ming, J. and Smith, F. J. (2002) Extension of Zipf's law to words and phrases.

Proceedings of the 19th International Conference on Computational Linguistics, 2002, pp. 315–320.

Habel, G. Reyes, M. L., Magnan, F. & Reyes, G. (2006). *General Poncelet meets the Semantic Web: A concrete example of the usage of ontologies to support creation and dissemination of eLearning contents.* Workshop on Applications of Semantic Web Technologies for e-Learning (SW-EL@AH'06), June 21-23 2006, Dublin, Ireland.

Hafner, K. (2006). Researchers yearn to use AOL logs, but they hesitate. *The New York Times*, August 23, 1.

Hallam-Baker, P. M. & Behlendorf, B. (1999,February 4). *Extended Log File Format.* Retrieved March 7, 2007, from http://www.w3.org/TR/WD-logfile.html

Halpern, J. and Kerman, J. (1999) "The Pitfalls and Complexities of Chinese to Chinese Conversion," in *Proceedings of the 14th International Unicode Conference*, Cambridge, Massachusetts, USA, March 1999.

Hancock-Beaulieu, M. (2000). Interaction in information searching and retrieval. *Journal of Documentation*, 56(4), 431-439.

Hancock-Beaulieu, M., Robertson, S., & Nielsen, C. (1990). *Evaluation of online catalogues: An assessment of methods* (bl research paper 78). London: The British Library Research and Development Department.

Handschuh, S. & Staab, S. (2002). Authoring and annotation of Web pages in CREAM. *Proceedings of the 11th International Conference on World Wide Web*, Honolulu, Hawaii.

Hansell, S. (2006). AOL removes search data on vast group of web users. *The New York Times*, August 8, 4.

Hansell, S. (2006). Advertisers trace paths users leave on internet. *The New York Times*, August 15, 1.

Hara, N., Bonk, C. J., & Angeli, C. (2000). Content analysis of online discussion in an applied educational psychology course. *Instructional Science, 28*(2), 115-152.

Harary, F. (1969). *Graph Theory.* Reading, MA: Addison-Wesley.

Hardy, H., Biermann, A., Inouye, R. B., Mckenzie, A., Strzalkowski, T., Ursu, C., Webb, N., & Wu, M. (2004). Data Driven Strategies for an Automated Dialogue System. In *Proceedings of the 42nd Annual Meeting of the Association for Computational Linguistics*, Barcelona, Spain *(ACL 2004).*

Hardy, H., Kanchakouskaya, V., & Strzalkowski, T. (2006). Automatic Event Classification using Surface Text Features. In *Proceedings of the AAAI Workshop on Event Extraction and Synthesis.*

Hardy, H., Shimizu, N., Strzalkowski, T., Liu, T., Wise, B., & Zhang, X. (2002). Cross-Document Summarization by Concept Classification. In *Proceedings of ACM SIGIR '02 Conference,* Tampere, Finland (pp. 121-128).

Harel, D. (1988). On visual formalisms, *Communications of the ACM, 31*(5), 514-530.

Hargittai, E. (2002). Beyond logs and surveys: In-depth measures of people's web use skills. *Journal of the American Society for Information Science and Technology,* 53(14), 1239-1244.

Hargittai, E. (2004). Classifying and coding online actions. *Social Science Computer Review, 22*(2), 210-227.

Hargittai, E. (2007). Whose space? Differences among users and non-users of social network sites. *Journal of Computer-Mediated Communication,* 13(1), article 14.

Harman, D. (1992, June). *Relevance Feedback Revisited.* Paper presented at the Fifteenth Annual International ACM SIGIR Conference on Research and Development in Information Retrieval, Copenhagen, Denmark.

Häubl, G. & Trifts, V. (2000). Consumer decision making in online shopping environments: The effect of interactive decision aids. *Marketing Science, 19*(1), 4-21.

Hawkey, K. (2007). *Managing the visual privacy of incidental information in web browsers.* Unpublished PhD Dissertation, Dalhousie University, Halifax, Nova Scotia.

Hawkey, K., & Inkpen, K. (2005). Privacy Gradients: Exploring ways to manage incidental information during co-located collaboration. In *CHI '05 Extended Abstracts of Human Factors in Computing Systems* (pp. 1431-1434). Portland, Oregon: ACM.

Hawkey, K., & Inkpen, K. (2005). Web Browsing Today: The impact of changing contexts on user activity. In *CHI '05 extended abstracts on Human Factors in Computing Systems* (pp. 1443-1446). Portland, Oregon: ACM.

Hawkey, K., & Inkpen, K. M. (2006). Examining the Content and Privacy of Web Browsing Incidental Information. In *15th International Conference on World Wide Web* (pp. 123-132). Edinburgh, Scotland: ACM.

Hawkey, K., & Inkpen, K. M. (2006). Keeping Up Appearances: Understanding the Dimensions of Incidental Information Privacy. In *SIGCHI Conference on Human Factors in Computer Systems* (pp. 821-830). Montreal, Quebec: ACM.

Hawkey, K., & Kellar, M. (2004). *Recommendations for reporting context in studies of web browsing behaviour* (No. CS-2004-16). Halifax, NS: Dalhousie University.

Hawkins, R. P., & Pingree, S. (1997). Measuring time frames of communication behaviors in computer use. *Paper presented at the International Communication Association*, Montreal, Canada.

Haykin, S. (1994). *Neural networks.* Englewood Cliffs, NJ: Macmillan College Publishing Company.

Haynes, R. B. (2001). Of studies, syntheses, synopses, and systems: the "4S" evolution of services for finding current best evidence. *ACP J Club, 134*(2), A11-13.

Haythornthwaite, C. (1996). Social network analysis: An approach and technique for the study of information exchange. *Library and Information Science Research, 18*, 323-342.

He, D., and Goker, A. (2000). Detecting session boundaries from Web user logs. *Proceedings of the BCS-IRSG 22nd Annual Colloquium on Information Retrieval Research, Cambridge, UK*, 57-66.

He, D., Göker, A., & Harper, D.J. (2002). Combining evidence for automatic Web session identification. *Information Processing & Management, 38*(5), 727-742.

He, P.W., and Jacobson, T.E. (1996). What are they doing with the Internet? A Study of User Information Seeking Behaviors. *Internet Reference Services Quarterly, 1*, 31-51

He. D., Goker, A. and Harper, D.J. (2002). Combining evidence for automatic Web session identification. *Information Processing and Management*, 38, 727-742

Hearst, M.A, Schölkopf, B., Dumais, S., Osuna, E. and Platt, J. (1998) Trends and Controversies - Support vector machines. *IEEE Intelligent Systems, 13(4)*, 18-28.

Heck, M. (2005, February 18). *Chart Your Website's Success.* Retrieved March 7, 2007, from http://www.infoworld.com/Omniture_SiteCatalyst_11/product_56297.html?view=1&curNodeId=0&index=0

Heflin, J. (2004). *OWL Web Ontology Language Use Cases and Requirements.* Retrieved May, 01, 2007 from em http://www.w3.org/TR/Webont-req/, 2004.

Heinström, J. (2003). Fast Surfers, Broad Scanners and Deep Divers as Users of Information Technology - Relating Information Preferences to Personality Traits. In *Annual Meeting of the American Society for Information Science and Technology* (pp. 247-253). Long Beach, CA.

Heinström, J. (2005). Fast surfing, broad scanning and deep diving: The influence of personality and study approach on students' information-seeking behavior. *Journal of Documentation, 61*(2), 228-247.

Helft, P. R., Hlubocky, F. J., Gordon, E. J., Ratain, M. J., & Daugherty, C. (2000, 2000). *Hope and the media in advanced cancer patients.* Paper presented at the American Society of Clinical Oncology 36th annual meeting, New Orleans, LA.

Hemenway, K., & Calishain, T. (2003). *Spidering Hacks: 100 Industrial-Strength Tips and Tools.* Sebastopol, CA: O'Reilly & Associates, Inc.

Hendler, J., Berners-Lee, T. & Miller, E. (2002). *Integrating Applications on the semantic Web.* Journal of the institute of electrical Engenieers of japan, Vol 122(10), October, 2002, p. 676-680.

Henning, E. ,Van Rensburg, W., & Smit, B. (2004). *Finding your way in qualitative inquiry.* Pretoria: Van Schaik.

Henri, F. (1992). Computer conferencing and content analysis. In A. R. Kaye (Ed.), *Collaborative Learning through Computer Conferencing: The Najaden Papers* (pp. 115-136). New York: Springer.

Herder, E. (2005). Characterizations of User Web Revisit Behavior. In *the Workshop on Adaptivity and User Modeling in Interactive Systems (ABIS 2005).* Saarbrücken, Germany.

Herder, E., & Juvina, I. (2004). Discovery of Individual User Navigation Styles. In *the Workshop on Individual Differences in Adaptive Hypermedia (Adaptive Hypermedia 2004).* Eindhoven, The Netherlands.

Herman, I. (2006). *Web Ontology Language.* Retrieved september, 20, 2007, from http://www.w3.org/2004/OWL/.

Herman, I. (2007). *Resource Description Framework.* Retrieved september, 20, 2007, from http://www.w3.org/RDF/.

Herring, S. (1999). Interactional coherence in CMC. *Journal of Computer-Mediated Communication, 4*(4).

Herring, S. C. (2004). Computer-mediated discourse analysis: An approach to researching online behavior. In S. A. Barab, R. Kling & J. H. Gray (Eds.), *Designing for Virtual Communities in the Service of Learning* (pp. 338-376). Cambridge, UK: Cambridge University Press.

Hersh, W. R., & Hickam, D. H. (1998). How well do physicians use electronic information retrieval systems? A framework for investigation and systematic review. *Jama, 280*(15), 1347-1352.

Hersh, W., & Hickam, D. (1994). Use of a multi-application computer workstation in a clinical setting. *Bull Med Libr Assoc, 82*(4), 382-389.

Herskovic, J. R., Tanaka, L. Y., Hersh, W., & Bernstam, E. V. (2007). A day in the life of PubMed: analysis of a typical day's query log. *J Am Med Inform Assoc, 14*(2), 212-220.

Hewitt, J. (2003). How Habitual Online Practices Affect the Development of Asynchronous Discussion Threads, *Journal of Educational Computing Research*, Vol. 28 (1), 31-45.

Hewitt, J. (2005). Toward an understanding of how threads die in asynchronous computer conferences. *The Journal of the Learning Sciences, 14*(4), 567-589.

Hewitt, J., & Teplovs, C. (1999). An analysis of growth patterns in computer conferencing threads. In C. M. Hoadley & J. Roschelle (Eds.), *Proceeedings of Computer Support for Collaborative Learning 1999* (pp. 232-241). Mahwah, NJ: Lawrence Erlbaum Associates.

Hilbert, D. M., & Redmiles, D. F. (2000). Extracting usability information from user interface events. *ACM Computing Surveys 32*(4), 384-421.

Hilbert, D., & Redmiles, D. (1998, 10-13 May). *Agents for collecting application usage data over the Internet* (pp. 149-156). Paper presented at the Second International Conference on Autonomous Agents (Agents '98), Minneapolis/St. Paul, MN.

Hilbert, D., & Redmiles, D. (2001, 9-13 July). *Large-scale collection of usage data to inform design* (pp. 569-576). Paper presented at the Eight IFIP TC 13 Conference on Human-Computer Interaction (INTERACT 2001), Tokyo, Japan.

Hildreth, C. R. (1991). Advances toward the E3OPAC: The imperative and the path. In *Proceedings of the Think Tank on the Present and Future of the Online Catalog* (pp. 17-38) Chicago: Reference and Adult Services Division, American Library Association.

Hill, J.R., and Hannafin, M.J. (1997). Cognitive Strategies and Learning from the World Wide Web. *Educational Technology Research and Development, 45*, 37-64

Hiltz, S. R. (1985). *Online Communities A Case Study of the Office of the Future.* Norwood, NJ: Ablex Publishing Corp.

Hine, Christine M. (2000) *Virtual Ethnography*, London, Sage Publications.

Hine, Christine. (2005) Virtual Methods and the Sociology of Cyber-Social-Scientific Knowledge. In: HINE, Christine (Org.).*Virtual Methods. Issues in Social Research on the Internet.* Oxford: Berg.

Hirschheim, R. A., H.-K. Klein, H. K. & Lyytinen K. (1995) *Information Systems Development and Data Modeling: Conceptual and Philosophical Foundations.* Cambridge; New York: Cambridge University Press.

Ho, S.Y. (2005). An exploratory study of using a user remote tracker to examine web users' personality traits. *ICEC '05*, August 15-17.

Hobbs, J. (2007). *Communal computing and shared spaces of usage: a study of Internet Cafes in developing contexts.* Paper presented at the American Society for Information Science and Technology. Las Vegas Nevada. Retrieved.

Hobbs, J. H. et al., 1996, FASTUS: A cascaded finite-state transducer for extracting information from natural-language text, In *Finite State Devices for Natural Language Processing*, Cambridge MA: The MIT Press.

Holliday, A. (2001). *Doing and Writing Qualitative Research,* London: Sage.

Hölscher, C., & Strube, G. (2000). Web search behavior of internet experts and newbies. *International Journal of Computer and Telecommunications Networking, 33*(1-6), 337-346.

Holst, O. R. (1969). *Content Analysis for the Social Sciences and Humanities.* Reading, Massachusetts: Perseus Publishing.

Hong, J. I., Heer, J., Waterson, S., & Landay, J. A. (2001). WebQuilt: A Proxy-based Approach to Remote Web Usability Testing. *ACM Transactions on Information Systems, 19*(3), 263-285.

Horrigan, J. (2001). *Online communities: Networks that nurture long distance relationships and local ties.* Washington, DC: Pew Internet & American Life Project.

Horrocks, I. (1999). *Constructing the user interface with statecharts.* Addison-Wesley.

Hu, X., Bandhakavi, S. and Zhai, C. (2003). Error analysis of difficult TREC topics. *SIGIR'03: Proceedings of 26th ACM International Conference on Research and Development in Information Retrieval,* Toronto, Canada, 407-408.

Huang, C. K., Chien, L. F., Oyang, Y. J. (2003). Relevant Term Suggestion in Interactive Web Search Based on Contextual Information in Query Session Logs, *Journal of the American Society of Information Science and Technology*, 54(7), 638-649.

Huang, M.-H. (2003). Designing website attributes to induce experiential encounters. *Computers in Human Behavior, 19*(4), 425-442.

Huang, X., Peng, F., An, A. and Schuurmans, D. (2004). Dynamic Web log session identification with statistical language models. *Journal of the American Society for Information Science and Technology, 55(14)*, 1290 - 1303

Huberman, B., Pirolli, P., Pitkow, J., & Lukose, R. (1998). Strong Regularities in World Wide Web Surfing. *Science, 280*, 95-97.

Huizingh, E. K. R. E. (2002). The antecedents of Web site performance. *European Journal of Marketing, 36*(11/12), 1225-1247.

Huneke, M.E., Cole, C. & Levin, I.P. (2004). How varying levels of knowledge and motivation affect search and confidence during consideration and choice. *Marketing Letters, 15*(2&3), 67-79.

Hunter, R. N. (1991). Successes and failures of patrons searching the online catalog at a large academic library: a transaction log analysis. *RQ 30(Spring),* 395-402.

Hupfer, M.E. (2001). *Self-Concept orientation and response to agentic and communal advertising messages.* Unpublished Doctoral Thesis, University of Alberta, Edmonton.

Hupfer, M.E., & Detlor, B. (2006). Gender and web information seeking: A self-concept orientation model. *Journal of the American Society for Information Science & Technology, 57*(8), 1105-1115.

Hupfer, M.E., & Detlor, B. (2007). Beyond gender differences: Self-concept orientation and relationship-building applications on the Internet. *Journal of Business Research, 60*(6), 613-619.

Hupfer, M.E., & Detlor, B. (2007). Sex, gender and self-concept: Predicting web shopping site design preferences. In Detlor, B., Hassanein, K., & Head M. (Eds.), *Proceedings of the 8th World Congress on the Management of E-Business (WCMeB),* July 11-13, Toronto, Canada. Los Alamitos, California: IEEE Computer Society.

Huseby, S. H. (2004). *Innocent Code: A Security Wake-Up Call for Web Programmers.* UK: John Wiley & Sons Ltd.

Hutchins, E. (1996). *Cognition in the Wild.* Cambridge, MA: The MIT Press.

IBM. (2004, May 19). *Log File Formats.* Retrieved October 29, 2007, from http://publib.boulder.ibm.com/tividd/td/ITWSA/ITWSA_info45/en_US/HTML/guide/c-logs.html

IEEE LTSC. (2001). *Learning Technology—Public and Private Information.* Retrieved september, 20, 2007, from http://edutool.com/papi/drafts/08/ IEEE_1484_02_02_D08_PAPI_rationale.doc.

Ihadjadene, M., Chaudiron, S., & Martins, D. (2003). The Effect of Individual Differences on Searching the Web. In *Annual Meeting of the American Society for Information Science and Technology* (pp. 240-246). Long Beach, CA.

Immon, B. (2001). Why clickstream data counts. *e-Business Advisor,* (April)

IMS Consortium. (2001). *Learner Information Package Specification.* Retrieved september, 20, 2007, from http://www.imsglobal.org/profiles/index.html.

Infoplease. (2001). *Internet use from Any Location by Individuals Age Three and Older.* Online at: http://www.infoplease.com/ipa/A0901651.html. Retrieved November 4, 2004.

Infoplease. (2004). *Daily Internet Activities.* Online at: http://www.infoplease.com/ipa/A0921860.html. Retrieved November 4, 2004.

Infoplease. (2004). *Internet Timeline.* Online at: http://www.infoplease.com/ipa/A0193167.html. Retrieved November 4, 2004.

Ingwersen, P., & Jarvelin, K. (2005). *The Turn – Integration of information seeking and retrieval in context.* Springer.

Jacka, R. *Getting Results From Your Website.* Retrieved October 30, 2007, from http://www.panalysis.com/downloads/gettingresults.pdf

Jackson, M. (2007, January 22). *Analytics: Deciphering the Data.* Retrieved March 7, 2007, from http://www.ecommerce-guide.com/resources/article.php/3655251

Jacquiot, C. Bourda, Y., Popineau, F., Delteil, A. & Reynaud, C. (2006). *GLAM: A Generic Layered Adaptation Model for Adaptive Hypermedia Systems.* AH 2006: 131-140.

Jadad, A. R., & Gagliardi, A. (1998). Rating health information on the Internet: navigating to knowledge or to Babel? *JAMA, 279*(8), 611-614.

Jaillet, H. F. (2006). Web metrics: measuring patterns in online shopping. *Journal of Consumer Behavior, 2(4),* 369-381.

Jansche, M. and Abney, S.P., 2002, Information extraction from voicemail transcripts, In *Proceedings of Empirical Methods in Natural Language Processing.* East Stroudsburg, PA: ACL.

Jansen, B. J. & Pooch, U. (2001). A review of Web searching studies and a framework for future research. *Journal of the American Society for Information Science, 52(3),* 235-246.

Jansen, B. J. & Spink, A. (2000). Methodological approach in discovering user search patterns through Web log analysis. *Bulletin of the American Society for Information Science, 27(1),* 15-17.

Jansen, B. J. & Spink, A. (2006). How are we searching the world wide Web?: a comparison of nine search engine transaction logs, *Information Processing and Management,* Vol. 42 (1), 248-263.

Jansen, B. J. (2003, October). *Designing automated help using searcher system dialogues.* Paper presented at the 2003 IEEE International Conference on Systems, Man and Cybernetics, Washington, DC.

Jansen, B. J. (2005). Seeking and implementing automated assistance during the search process. *Information Processing and Management, 41*(4), 909-928.

Jansen, B. J. (2006). Search log analysis: What is it; what's been done; how to do it. *Library and Information Science Research, 28*(3), 407-432.

Jansen, B. J. (2006). Using temporal patterns of interactions to design effective automated searching assistance. *Communications of the ACM, 49(4),* 72-74.

Jansen, B. J. (2007). *Evaluating the effectiveness of automated searching assistance.* Manuscript submitted for publication.

Jansen, B. J., & McNeese, M. D. (2005). Evaluating the effectiveness of and patterns of interactions with automated searching assistance. *Journal of the American Society for Information Science and Technology, 56*(14), 1480-1503.

Jansen, B. J., & Pooch, U. (2000). A review of Web searching studies and a framework for future research. *Journal of the American Society for Information Science and Technology, 52*(3), 235-246.

Jansen, B. J., & Pooch, U. (2001). Web user studies: A review and framework for future work. *Journal of the American Society for Information Science and Technology, 52*(3), 235-246.

Jansen, B. J., & Pooch, U. (2001). Web user studies: A review and framework for future work. *Journal of the American Society of Information Science and Technology,* 52(3), 235-246.

Jansen, B. J., & Pooch, U. (2004). Assisting the Searcher: Utilizing Software Agents for Web Search Systems. *Internet Research - Electronic Networking Applications and Policy, 14*(1), 19-33.

Jansen, B. J., & Resnick, M. (2005). Examining searcher perception of and interactions with sponsored results. *Paper presented at the ACM Conference on Electronic Commerce*, Vancouver, Canada.

Jansen, B. J., & Spink, A. (2003, 23 - 26 June). *An analysis of Web information seeking and use: Documents retrieved versus documents viewed* (pp. 65-69). Paper presented at the 4th International Conference on Internet Computing, Las Vegas, Nevada.

Jansen, B. J., & Spink, A. (2005). An analysis of Web searching by European AlltheWeb.com users. *Information Processing and Management*, 41, 361-381.

Jansen, B. J., & Spink, A. (2005). How are we searching the World Wide Web? A comparison of nine search engine transaction logs. *Information Processing & Management,* 42(1), 248-263.

Jansen, B. J., & Spink, A. (2006). How are we searching the World Wide Web? A comparison of nine search engine transaction logs. *Information Processing and Management, 42*(1), 248-263.

Jansen, B. J., Goodrum, A. and Spink, A. (2000). Searching for multimedia: analysis of audio, video and image Web queries. *World Wide Web, 3*, 249–254.

Jansen, B. J., Jansen, K., & Spink, A. (2005). Using the Web to look for work: Implications for online job seeking and recruiting. *Internet Research*, 15(1), 49-66.

Jansen, B. J., Ramadoss, R. Zhang, M., & Zang, N. (2006). Wrapper: An Application for Evaluating Exploratory Searching Outside of the Lab, *SIGIR 2006 Workshop on Evaluating Exploratory Search Systems*, Seattle, WA.

Jansen, B. J., Ramadoss, R., Zhang, M., & Zang, N. (2006). Wrapper: An application for evaluating exploratory searching outside of the lab, SIGIR 2006 Workshop on Evaluating Exploratory Search Systems. *The 29th Annual International ACM SIGIR Conference on Research & Development on Information Retrieval (SIGIR2006).* Seattle, Washington, USA.

Jansen, B. J., Spink, A, and Pedersen, J. (2005). The Effect of Specialized Multimedia Collections on Web Searching. *Journal of Web Engineering. 3(3/4),* 182-199.

Jansen, B. J., Spink, A. and Ozmultu, C. (2000). Use of query reformulation and relevance feedback by Web users. *Internet Research: Electronic Networking Applications and Policy, 10(4)*, 317 - 328.

Jansen, B. J., Spink, A. and Pedersen, J. (2003). An Analysis of Multimedia Searching on Alta Vista. *Proceedings of the 5th ACM SIG Multimedia International Workshop on Multimedia Information Retrieval*, Berkeley, CA, 186 – 192.

Jansen, B. J., Spink, A. and Pedersen, J. (2005). The Effect of Specialized Multimedia Collections on Web Searching. *Journal of Web Engineering. 3*, 182-199.

Jansen, B. J., Spink, A., & Pedersen, J. (2005). A temporal comparison of AltaVista Web searching. *Journal of the American Society for Information Science and Technology*, 56(6), 559-570.

Jansen, B. J., Spink, A., & Pedersen, J. (2005). Trend analysis of AltaVista Web searching. *Journal of the American Society for Information Science and Technology*, 56(6), 559-570.

Jansen, B. J., Spink, A., & Saracevic, T. (2000). Real life, real users, and real needs: A study and analysis of user queries on the Web. *Information Processing and Management, 36*(2), 207-227.

Jansen, B. J., Spink, A., & Saracevic, T. (2000). Real life, real users, and real needs: A study and analysis of user queries on the Web. *Information Processing & Management,* 36(2), 207-227.

Jansen, B. J., Spink, A., and Pedersen, J. (2003). An Analysis of Multimedia Searching on Alta Vista. *Proceedings of the 5th ACM SIG Multimedia International Workshop on Multimedia Information Retrieval*. Berkeley, CA, 186 – 192.

Jansen, B. J., Spink, A., Blakely, C. and Koshman, S. (2007). Defining a session on Web search engines. *Journal of the American Society for Information Science and Technology. 58(6)*, 862-871.

Jansen, B. J., Bateman, J., & Saracevic, T. (1998). Real Life Information Retrieval: A Study of User Queries on the Web. *SIGIR Forum*, 32(1), 5-17.

Jansen, B. J., Spink, A., & Koshman, S. (2007). Web Server Interaction with the Dogpile.com Metasearch Engine. *Journal of the American Society for Information Science and Technology (JASIST)*, 58(5), 744-755.

Jansen, K. J., Corley , K. G., & Jansen, B. J. (2006). E-survey methodology: A review, issues, and implications. In J. D. Baker & R. Woods (Eds.), *Encyclopedia of electronic surveys and measurements (eesm)* (pp. 1-8). Hershey, PA.: Idea Group Publishing.

Jenkins, C., Corritore, C., & Wiedenbeck, S. (2003). Patterns of Information Seeking on the Web: A Qualitative Study of Domain Expertise and Web Expertise. *IT & Society, 1*(3), 64-89.

Jeong, M., Oh, H., & Gregoire, M. (2003). Conceptualizing Web site quality and its consequences in the lodging industry. *Hospitality Management 22*(2), 161-175.

Jin, R., Si, L. and Zhai, C. (2003). Preference-based graphic models for collaborative filtering. *Proceedings of the 19th Conference in Uncertainty in Artificial Intelligence,* Acapulco, Mexico, 329-336.

Jin, X., Zhou, Y., & Mobasher, B. (2005). *Task-Oriented Web User Modeling for Recommendation.* Proceedings of the 10th International Conference on User Modeling (UM'05) Edinburgh, Scotland, July 2005.

Jing, T. Y. (2006). Supporting Research with Weblogs: A Study on Web-Based Research Support Systems, *Proceedings of Web Intelligence and Intelligent Agent Technology Workshops, IEEE/WIC/ACM International Conference*, 161-164.

Joachims T. (2002). The Maximum-Margin Approach to Learning Text Classifiers. In *Ausgezeichnete Informatikdissertationen*, D. Wagner et al. (Hrsg.), *GI-Edition - Lecture Notes in Informatics (LNI)*, Köllen Verlag, Bonn, 2002.

Joachims, T. (1998). Text categorization with support vector machines. *ECML'98: Proceedings of the 10th European Conference on Machine Learning,* Chemnitz, Germany, 137-142.

Joachims, T., Granka, L., Pan, B., Hembrooke, H., & Gay, G. (2005, 15-19 August). Accurately interpreting clickthrough data as implicit feedback. *Paper presented at the 28th Annual International ACM SIGIR conference on Research and Development in Information Retrieval, Salvador, Brazil.*

Joinson, A. N., Paine, C., Reips, U.-D., & Buchanan, T. (2006). Privacy and Trust: The role of situational and dispositional variables in online disclosure. In *Privacy, Trust, and Identity Issues for Ambient Intelligence Workshop, Pervasive 2006* (pp. 1-6). Dublin, Ireland.

Jones, R., Rey, B., Madani, O., & Greiner, W. (2006). Generating Query Substitutions. In *Proceedings of the 15th International Conference on World Wide Web (WWW'06)* (pp. 387-396).

Jones, S., Cunningham, S. J., & McNab, R. (1998). Usage analysis of a digital library. *Paper presented at the Digital Libraries 98, Third ACM Conference on Digital Libraries*, Pittsburgh, PA.

Jones, S., Cunningham, S. J., McNab, R., & Boddie, S. (2000). A transation log analysis of a digital library. *International Journal of Digital Libraries*, 3, 152-169.

Jones, S., Cunningham, S., & McNab, R. (1998, June 1998). *In Usage analysis of a digital library* (pp. 293-294). Paper presented at the the Third ACM Conference on Digital Libraries, Pittsburgh, PA. ACM.

Jones, W., Dumais, S., & Bruce, H. (2002). Once Found, What Then?: A Study of "Keeping" Behaviors in the Personal Use of Web Information. In *Annual Meeting of the American Society for Information Science and Technology* (pp. 391-402). Philadelphia, PA.

Jurafsky, D., & Martin, J. H. (2000). *Speech and language processing.* Prentice-Hall.

Justeson, J. S., & Katz, S. M. (1995). Technical Terminology: some Linguistic Properties and an Algorithm for Identification in Text. *Natural Language Engineering*, 1(1), 9-27.

Kammenhuber, N., Luxenburger, J., Feldmann, A., and Weikum, G. (2006). Web Search Clickstreams. *IMC'06,* October 25-27, 2006, Rio de Janeiro, Brazil.

Kanerva, A., Keeker, K., Risden, K., Schuh, E., & Czerwinski, M. (2004). *Web usability research at Microsoft Corporation.* Microsoft Corporation [Online]. Available: http://research.microsoft.com/users/marycz/webchapter.html [12 January 2004].

Karat, C-M., Karat, J., & Brodie, C. (2005). Why HCI research in privacy and security is critical now, *International Journal of Man-Machine Studies*, Vol. 63 (1-2), 1-4

Kardkovács, Z.T., Tikk, D. and Bánsághi, Z. (2005). The Ferrety algorithm for the KDD Cup 2005 problem. *ACM SIGKDD Explorations Newsletter*, 7(2), 111-116.

Kaushik, A (2006, November 13). *Excellent Analytics Tip #8: Measure the Real Conversion Rate & 'Opportunity Pie.'* Retrieved November 3, 2007, from http://www.kaushik.net/avinash/2006/11/excellent-analytics-tip-8-measure-the-real-conversion-rate-opportunity-pie.html

Kaushik, A. (2007, January 23). *Web Analytics Tool Selection: 10 Questions to ask Vendors.* Retrieved March 7, 2007, from http://www.kaushik.net/avinash/2007/01/web-analytics-tool-selection-10-questions-to-ask-vendors.html

Kay, J., & Thomas, R. C. (1995). Studying long-term system use. *Communications of the ACM, 38*(7), 61-69.

Keenoy, K., & Levene, M. (2005). Personalisation of Web search. In B. Mobasher and S. S. Anand (Eds.), *Intelligent Techniques for Web Personalization* (pp. 201-228). Berlin, German: Springer-Verlag.

Kehoe, C. M., & Pitkow, J. (1996). Surveying the territory: Gvu's five WWW user surveys. *The World Wide Web Journal, 1*(3), 77-84.

Kehoe, C. M., Pitkow, J., Sutton, K., Aggarwal, G., & Rogers, J. D. (1999). *Results of GVU's Tenth World Wide Web User Survey.* Online at: http://www.cc.gtech.edu/gvu/user_surveys/survey-1998-10/tenthreport.html. Retrieved August 4, 2004.

Kellar, M. (2007). *An Examination of User Behaviour during Web Information Tasks.* Unpublished PhD Dissertation, Dalhousie University, Halifax, Nova Scotia.

Kellar, M., Hawkey, K., Inkpen, K. M., & Watters, C. (2008). Challenges of Capturing Natural Web-based User Behaviours. *International Journal of Human Computer Interaction, 24*(4), 385-409.

Kellar, M., Watters, C., & Shepherd, M. (2006). The Impact of Task on the Usage of Web Browser Navigation Tools. In *Graphics Interface* (pp. 235-242). Quebec City, Canada: Canadian Information Processing Society.

Kellar, M., Watters, C., & Shepherd, M. (2007). A field study characterizing Web-based information seeking tasks. *Journal of the American Society for Information Science and Technology, 58*(7), 999-1018.

Kelly, D. (2004). *Understanding implicit feedback and document preference: A naturalistic user study.* New Brunswick: Rutgers, The State University of New Jersey.

Kelly, D., & Belkin, N. (2004). Display Time as Implicit Feedback: Understanding Task Effects. In *27th Annual International ACM SIGIR Conference on Research and Development in Information Retrieval* (pp. 377-384). Sheffield, UK: ACM.

Kelly, D., & Belkin, N. J. (2001, Sepetmber). *In reading time, scrolling and interaction: Exploring implicit sources of user preferences for relevance feedback.* Paper presented at the Twenty-fourth Annual International ACM SIGIR Conference on Research and Development in Information Retrieval, New Orleans, LA.

Kelly, D., & Belkin, N. J. (2004, July). *In display time as implicit feedback: Understanding task effects.* Paper presented at the Twenty-seventh Annual International Conference on Research and Development in Information Retrieval, Sheffield, England.

Kelly, D., & Teevan, J. (2003). Implicit feedback for inferring user preference: A bibliography. *SIGIR Forum, 37*(2), 18-28.

Kelly, D., Diaz, F., Belkin, N. J., and Allan, J. (2004). A user-centered approach to evaluating topic models. *Lecture Notes in Computer Science, 2997*, 27-41.

Kerner, S. M. (2004). *More Broadband Usage Means More Online Spending.* Online at: www.clickz.com/stats/markets/broadband/article.php/3419281. Retrieved August 4, 2004.

Khopkar, Y., Spink, A., Giles, C. L., Shah, P., & Debnath, S. (2003). Search engine personalization: An exploratory study [Electronic Version]. *First Monday*, 8. Retrieved October 20, 2007, from http://firstmonday.org/issues/issue8_7/khopkar/index.html

Kiesler, S., & Sproull, L. S. (1986). Response effects in the electronic survey. *Public Opinion Quarterly, 50*, 402-413.

Kim, K.-H., & Yun, H. (2007). Cying for me, Cying for us: Relational dialectics in a Korean social network site. *Journal of Computer-Mediated Communication*, 15(1), article 11.

Kim, K.-S., & Allen, B. (2002). Cognitive and Task Influences on Web Searching Behavior. *Journal of the American Society for Information Science and Technology, 53*(2), 109-119.

Kim, M. (1996). Research Record, *Journal of Education for Library and Information Science*, Vol. 37, 378-380

Kim, S., & Stoel, L. (2004). Apparel retailers: Website quality dimensions and satisfaction. *Journal of Retailing and Consumer Services 11*(2), 109-117.

Kinsella, J., & Bryant, P. (1987). Online public access catalogue research in the united kingdom: An overview. *Library Trends,* 35(4), 619 - 629.

Klas, C.-P., Albrechtsen, H., Fuhr, N., Hansen, P., Kapidakis, S., Kovacs, L., et al. (2006). A logging scheme for comparative digital library evaluation, In *Proceedings of the 10th European conference on research and advanced technology for digital libraries (ECDL 2006)*, Alicante.

Kleinberg, J. M. & Sandler, M. (2004). *Using Mixture Models for Collaborative Filtering.* Proc. 36th ACM Symposium on Theory of Computing, 2004. STOC'04, June 13.15, 2004, Chicago, Illinois, USA. Copyright 2004 ACM 1581138520/04/0006.

Kleinberg, J. M. (1999). *Authoritative sources in a hyperlinked environment.* Journal of the ACM,volume 46, number 5, pages 604—632.

Kobsa, A. (1993). *User Modeling: Recent Work, Prospects and Hazards.* M. Schneider-Hufschmidt, T. Kühme and U. Malinowski, eds. (1993): Adaptive User Interfaces: Principles and Practice. North-Holland, Amsterdam, 1993. Copyright © North-Holland.

Koenemann, J., & Belkin, N. (1996, April). *A case for interaction: A study of interactive information retrieval behavior and effectiveness.* Paper presented at the ACM SIGCHI '96 Conference on Human Factors in Computing Systems, Vancouver, Canada.

Kohane, I. S., Mandl, K. D., Taylor, P. S., Holm, I. A., Nigrin, D. J., Kunkel, L. M. (2007). Reestablishing the Researcher-Patient Compact. *Science, 316(5826),* 836-837.

Kohavi, R. (2001). *Mining e-commerce data: the good, the bad and the ugly.* Proceeding of the 7th ACM SIGKDD Inernational COnference on Knowledge Discovery and Data Mining, San Francisco, California, 8-13.

Kollock, P., & Smith, M. A. (1999). Communities in cyberspace. In P. Kollock & M. A. Smith (Eds.), *Communities in cyberspace* (3-28). New York: Routledge.

Konstan, J., Miller, B., Maltz, D., Herlocker, J., Gordon, L. & Riedl, J. (1997). *Grouplens: Applying collaborative filtering to usenet news.* Communications of the ACM, 40(3).

Korfhage, R. (1997). *Information storage and retrieval.* New York: Wiley.

Kosala, R. & Blockeel, H. (2000). *Web Mining Research: a survey.* Sigkdd explorations. ACM SIGKDD, Vol 2, Issue 1, July, 2000.

Koshman, S., Spink, A., & Jansen, B. J. (2006). Web Searching on the Vivisimo Search Engine. *Journal of the American Society for Information Science and Technology (JASIST),* 57(14), 1875-1887.

Koufaris, M. (2002). Applying the technology acceptance model and flow theory to online consumer behavior. *Information Systems Research 13*(2), 205-223.

Koutri, M., Avouris, N. & Daskalaki, S. (2004). *A survey on Web usage mining techniques for Web-based adaptive hypermedia systems.* Adaptable and Adaptative Hypermedia Systems. Idea Inc. Hershey, 2004.

Kozinets, Robert V. (2002). The field behind the screen: Using netnography for marketing research in online communications. *Journal of Marketing Research,* 39, 61–72.

Kozinets, Robert V. (2005) 'Communal Big Bangs and the Ever-Expanding Netnographic Universe,' *Thexis,* 3, 38-41.

Krippendorf, K. (2004). *Content analysis: An introduction to its methodology* (2nd), Thousand Oaks, CA: Sage.

Krosnick, J. A. (1999). Survey research. In *Annual review of psychology* (Vol. 50, pp. 537-367): Annual Review.

Kruschwitz, U. (2003). An Adaptable Search System for Collections of Partially Structured Documents. *IEEE Intelligent Systems,* 18(4), 44-52.

Kruschwitz, U. (2005). *Intelligent Document Retrieval: Exploiting Markup Structure,* volume 17 of The Information Retrieval Series. New York, NY: Springer-Verlag.

Kruschwitz, U., & Al-Bakour, H. (2005). Users Want More Sophisticated Search Assistants – Results of a Task-Based Evaluation. *Journal of the American Society for Information Science and Technology (JASIST),* 56(13), 1377-1393.

Kuhlthau, C. (1991). Inside the search process: information seeking from the user's perspective. *Journal of the American Society for Information Science, 42*(5), 361-371.

Kumaran, G. and Allan, J. (2004). Text classification and named entities for new event detection. *SIGIR '04: Proceedings of 27th ACM International Conference on Research and Development in Information Retrieval,* Sheffield, UK, 297-304.

Kumaran, G. and Allan, J. (2005). Using names and topics for new event detection. *Proceedings of Human Language Technology Conference/Conference on Empirical Methods in Natural Language Processing,* Vancouver, B.C., Canada.

Kuniavsky, M. (2003). *Observing the User Experience: A Practioner's Guide to User Research.* San Francisco: Morgan Kaufman.

Kurth, M. (1993). The limits and limitations of transaction log analysis. *Library Hi Tech, 11*(2), 98-104.

Labaree, R. V. (2002). The risk of "going observationalist": Negotiating the hidden dilemmas of being an insider participant observer. *Qualitative Research,* Vol. 2 (1), 97-122.

Lacroix, E.-M. (2000). *Expanding world access to health literature.* Paper presented at the 8th International congress on Medical Librarianship, London.

Lacroix, E.-M., & Mehnert, R. (2002). The US National Library of Medicine in the 21st century: expanding collections, nontraditional formats, new audiences. *Health Information and Libraries Journal, 19*(3), 126-132.

Lafferty, J., McCallum, A. and Pereira, F. (2001). Conditional random fields: probabilistic models for segmenting and labeling sequence data. *Proceedings of the International Conference on Machine Learning.*

Lalmas, M., & Ruthven, I. (1999, May). *A framework for investigating the interaction in information retrieval.* Paper presented at the Ninth European-Japanese Conferences on Information Modeling and Knowledge Bases, Japan.

Lange, P. G. (2007). Publicly private and privately public: Social networking on YouTube. *Journal of Computer-Mediated Communication,* 13(1), article 18.

Langer, Roy and Beckman, Suzanne. (2005) Sensitive Research Topics: netnography revisited. In: *Qualitative Marker Research: An International Journal.* 8,2, 189-203.

Lanquillon, C. (2000). Learning from Labelled and Unlabeled Documents: A Comparative Study on Semi-Supervised Text Classification. In *Proceedings of PKDD-00, 4th European Conference on Principles of Data Mining and Knowledge Discovery,* 490–497. Springer Verlag, Heidelberg, DE.

Larkey, L.S., Feng, F., Connell, M. and Lavrenko, V. (2004), Language-specific models in multilingual topic tracking. *SIGIR'04: Proceedings of 27th ACM International Conference on Research and Development in Information Retrieval,* Sheffield, UK, 402-409.

Larson, R. R. (1991). Between Scylla and Charybdis: Subject searching in the online catalog. *Advances in Librarianship,* 15, 175-236.

Laskowski, S., Morse, E., & Gray, W. (2001). *CIFter Project Main Page.* Online at: http://zing.ncsl.nist.gov/cifter/. Retrieved April 18, 2005.

Lau, E. P. & Goh, D. H-L, (2006). In search of query patterns: A case study of a university OPAC. *Information Processing and Management, 42(5),* 1316-1329.

Laurent, D., Séguéla, P., & Nègre, S. (2006). QA better than IR? In A. Peñas and R. F. E. Sutcliffe (Eds.), *Proceedings of the Workshop on Multilingual Question Answering, MLQA'06, 11th Conference of the European Chapter of the Association for Computational Linguistics,* Trento, Spain (pp. 1-8).

Law, A.M., and Kelton, W.D. (1991). *Simulation Modeling and Analysis.* New York: McGraw-Hill

Lawrence, S. and Giles, C.L. (1999). Accessibility of information on the web. *Nature,* 400, 107–109.

Lawrie, D. J., & Croft, W. B. (2003). Generating Hierarchical Summaries for Web Searches. In *Proceedings of the 26 Annual International ACM SIGIR Conference on Research and Development in Information Retrieval,* Toronto, Canada (pp. 457-458).

Lawrie, D., Croft, W. B. and Rosenberg, A., (2001). Finding topic words for hierarchical summarization. *SIGIR'01: Proceedings of 24th ACM International Conference on Research and Development in Information Retrieval,* New Orleans, LA, 349-357.

Lecompte, M., & Shenshul, J. (1999). *Designing and Conducting Ethnographic Research.* Walnut Creek: Altamira Press.

Lederer, S., Hong, J. I., Dey, A. K., & Landay, J. A. (2004). Personal privacy through understanding and action: five pitfalls for designers. *Personal and Ubiquitous Computing, 8*(6), 440-454.

Lederer, S., Mankoff, J., & Dey, A. K. (2003). Towards a Deconstruction of the Privacy Space. *Workshop on Ubicomp Communities: Privacy as Boundary Negotiation, UBICOMP 2003*: Retrieved August 12, 2005 from http://guir.berkeley.edu/pubs/ubicomp2003/privacy-workshop/papers/lederer-privacyspace.pdf

Lee, H.-J. (2006). Mediated Information Retrieval for the Web Environment, Ph.D. dissertation, School of Communication, Information and Library Studies, Rutgers University, New Brunswick, NJ, May 2006.

LeGrand, B. & Soto, M. (2002). *XML Topic Maps and Semantic Web Mining.* Semantic Web Mining Workshop, Conference ECML/PKDD 2001. Freiburg, Germany. January, 2002.

Leleu, M. (2003). *GO-SPADE: Mining sequential patterns over datasets with consecutive repetitions,* LNAI 2743, pp. 293-306, 2003. Springer Verlag Berlin Heildeberg.

Lemos, André. (1998) *Ciber-socialidade: tecnologia e vida social na cultura contemporânea.* São Paulo, VII Compós.

Lenhart, A., & Fox, S. (2006). *Bloggers: A portrait of the internet's new storytellers.* Pew Internet & American Life Project, http://www.pewinternet.org. Retrieved July 19, 2006.

Lenhart, A., & Madden, M. (2007). *Teens, privacy & online social networks.* Washington, DC: Pew Internet & American Life Project.

Levin, J. A., Kim, H., & Riel, M. M. (1990). Analyzing instructional interactions on electronic message networks. In L. M. Harasim (Ed.), *Online Education: Perspectives on a New Environment* (pp. 185–214). New York: Praeger.

Levinson, D.J.(1986). *The Seasons of a Man's Life.* New York: Ballantine Books.

Levy, Pierre. (1993) *As Tecnologias da Inteligência.* Rio de Janeiro: Editora 34.

Lewis, D. D., & Catlett, J. (1994). Heterogeneous Uncertainty Sampling for Supervised Learning. In *Proceedings of the Eleventh International Conference on Machine Learning,* 148–156. Morgan Kaufmann.

Li, W. and McCallum, A. (2005). Semi-supervised sequence modeling with syntactic topic models. *Proceedings of the 12th Conference on Artificial Intelligence,* 813-818.

Li, X., & Liu, B. (2003). Learning to Classify Text Using Positive and Unlabeled Data. In *Proceedings of the Eighteenth International Joint Conference on Artificial Intelligence,* 587–594). Morgan Kaufmann.

Li, X., Morie, P. and Roth, D., 2006, Identification and tracing of ambiguous names. In *Proceedings of the Human Language Technology – North American Chapter of the Association for Computational Linguistics* (pp. 17-24).

Li, Y., Zheng, Z. and Dai, H. (2005). KDD CUP-2005 report: facing a great challenge. *ACM SIGKDD Explorations Newsletter,* 7(2), 91-99.

Liaw S-S and Huang, H-M. (2006). Information retrieval from the World Wide Web: a user-focused approach based on individual experience with search engines. *Computers in Human Behavior, 22(3),* 501-517.

Lieberman, H. (1995). *Letizia: An Agent That Assists Web Browsing* (1995) Proceedings of the Fourteenth International Joint Conference on Artificial Intelligence (IJCAI-95).

Limbourg, Q., & Vanderdonckt, J. (2004). Comparing task models for user interface design. In Diaper, D., & Stanton, N. (Eds.) *The Handbook of Task Analysis of Human-Computer Interaction.* Lawrence Erlbaum.

Lin, S. J. (2002, August). *Design space of personalized indexing: Enhancing successive web searching for transmuting information problem,* Paper presented at the American Conference on Information Systems, Dallas, TX.

Lin, S.-J. (2002, 9-11 August). *In Design space of personalized indexing: Enhancing successive Web searching for transmuting information problems* (pp. 1092 - 1100). Paper presented at the Eighth Americas Conference on Information Systems, Dallas, Texas. AIS.

Lin, X., Liebscher, P., & Marchionini, G., (1991). Graphical representations of electronic search patterns. *Journal of the American Society for Information Science, 42(7),* 469-478.

Liu, C., Marchewka, J. T., Lu, J., & Yu, C.-S. (2004). Beyond concern: a privacy-trust-behavioral intention model of electronic commerce. *Information & Management, 42*(1), 127-142.

Liu, H. (2007). Social network profiles as taste performances. *Journal of Computer-Mediated Communication,* 13(1), article 13.

Liu, X., Croft, W. B., Oh, P. & Hart, D. (2004). Automatic recognition of reading levels from user queries. *Proceedings of the 27th ACM International Conference on Research and Development in Information Retrieval,* 548–549, Sheffield, United Kingdom.

Liu, X., Croft, W. B., Oh, P. and Hart, D. (2004). Automatic recognition of reading levels from user queries. *SIGIR'04: Proceedings of the 27th ACM International Conference on Research and Development in Information Retrieval,* 548-549.

Loeber, S. C., & Cristea, A. (2003). A WWW Information Seeking Process Model. *Educational Technology & Society, 6*(3), 43-52.

Loh, S., Wives, L. & Oliveira, J. P. M. (2000). *Concept –based knowledge Discovery in texts extracted from the Web.* SigKDD Explorations, 2(1), p.29-30. 2000.

Lombard, M., Snyder-Duch, J., & Bracken, C. C. (2002). Content analysis in mass communication: Assessment and reporting of intercoder reliability. *Human Communication Research,* Vol. 28 (4), 587-604.

Lu, Y. and Chau, M., Fang, X., and Yang, C. C. Analysis of the Bilingual Queries in a Chinese Web Search Engine, in *Proceedings of the Fifth Workshop on E-Business (WEB 2006),* Milwaukee, Wisconsin, USA, December 9, 2006.

Lycos. (1999). *The Lycos 50 Daily Report.* Online at: http://50.lycos.com/083099.html. Retrieved August 4, 2004.

Mackenzie, I. S., Kauppinen, T., & Silfverberg, M. (2001). Accuracy measures for evaluating computer printing devices. *CHI2001,* 9-16.

Madden, M., & Fox, S. (2006). *Riding the Waves of "Web 2.0".* Pew Internet & American Life Project, http://www.pewinternet.org. Retrieved October 5, 2006.

Maedche, A., Motik, B., Stojanovic, L., Studer, R., & Volz, R. (2003). An Infrastructure for Searching, Reusing and Evolving Distributed Ontologies. In *Proceedings of the Twelfth International World Wide Web Conference (WWW2003),* Budapest, Hungary (pp. 439-448).

Magnini, B., Romagnoli, S., Vallin, A., Herrera, J., Peñas, A., Peinado, V., Verdejo, F., & de Rijke, M. (2003). The Multiple Language Question Answering Track at CLEF 2003. In *Working Notes for the CLEF 2003 Workshop,* Trondheim, Norway.

Malhotra, N. K., Kim, S. S., & Agarwal, J. (2004). Internet Users' Information Privacy Concerns (IUIPC): The Construct, the Scale, and a Causal Model. *Information Systems Research, 15*(4), 336-355.

Malinowsky, Bronislaw. (1953) [orig. 1922] *Argonauts of the Western Pacific.* New York: E. F. Dutton.

Mamou, J., Carmel, D. and Hoory R., 2006, Spoken document retrieval from call-center conversations, In *Proceedings of Twenty-Ninth Annual International ACM SIGIR Conference on Research and Development of Information Retrieval* (pp. 51-58), New York: ACM.

Manavoglu, E., Pavlov, D. and Giles, C.L., (2003). Probabilistic user behavior models. *Proceedings of the*

ICDM 2003: Third IEEE International Conference on Data Mining 2003, 203- 210.

Mandelbrot, B. An Information Theory of the Statistical Structure of Language, in *Communication Theory*, edited by Willis Jackson, New York: Academic Press, 1953, pp. 486-502.

Mani, I., Pustejovsky, J. and Gaizauskas, R. (Eds.), 2005, *The Language of Time: A Reader*. Oxford University Press.

Mann, N.R., Schafer, R.E., and Singpurwalla N.D. (1974). *Methods for statistical analysis of reliability and life data*. New York: John Wiley and Sons.

Manning, C. D., & Schütze, H. (1999). *Foundations of Statistical Natural Language Processing*. Cambridge, MA: MIT Press.

Manning, H. (2004). *Persona Best Practices*. Cambridge: Forrester Research.

Marcus, G. E. (1998). *Ethnography Through Thick and Thin*. Princeton, NJ: Princeton University Press.

Marcus, R. S. (1982). *Investigation of computer-aided document search strategies* (Report LIDS-R-1233). Boston:Laboratory for Information and Decision Systems, Massachusetts Institute of Technology.

Markellou, P., Rigou, M. & Sirmakessis, S. (2005). *Mining for Web personalization*. In Web Mining: Applications and Techniques. Anthony Scime (ed.), Idea Group Publishing, p.27-49.

MarketingSherpa. (2007, October 20). *Security Logo in Email Lifts Average Order Value 28.3%*. Retrieved December 4, 2007, from https://www.marketingsherpa.com/barrier.html?ident=30183

MarketWatch. (2006, June 15). Social networking sites continue to attract record numbers as MySpace.com surpasses 50 million U.S. visitors in May. *MarketWatch*.

Markey, K. (1984). *Subject searching in library catalogs: before and after the introduction of online catalogs*. Dublin, OH: OCLC.

Markey, K. (2007). Twenty-Five Years of End-User Searching, Part 1: Research Findings. *Journal of the American Society for Information Science and Technology. 58(8)*, 1071–1081.

Markey, K. (2007). Twenty-Five Years of End-User Searching, Part 2: Future Research Directions. *Journal of the American Society for Information Science and Technology (JASIST)*, 58(8), 1123-1130.

Marra, R. M., Moore, J. L., & Klimczak, A. K. (2004). Content analysis of online discussion forums: A comparative analysis of protocols. *Educational Technology Research and Development, 52*(2), 23-40.

Marsh, C. (1984). Problems with surveys: method or epistemology? In M. Blumer (Ed.), *Sociological Research Methods: An Introduction* (2nd ed., pp. 82-102). London: MacMillan.

Marsh, D. (2003). *History of the Internet*. Online at: http://www.internetvalley.com/archives/mirrors/davemarsh-timeline-1.htm. Retrieved August 4, 2004.

Marshall, J. *Seven Deadly Web Analytics Sins*. Retrieved March 7, 2007, from http://www.clicktracks.com/insidetrack/articles/7_deadly_webanalytics_sins01.php

Marshall, K.P. & Swartwout N. (2006). Marketing and internet professionals' fiduciary responsibility: A perspective on spyware. *Journal of Internet Commerce, 5*(3), 109-128.

Martin, B.A.S., Sherrard, M.J., & Wentzel, D. (2005). The role of sensation seeking and need for cognition on web-site evaluations: A resource-matching perspective. *Psychology and Marketing, 22*(2), 109-126.

Martin, T. H. (1977). Monitoring and Individual Rights. In *Information management in the 1980's: Proceedings of the American Society for Information Science annual meeting* (p. 64) White Plains, NY: Knowledge Industry Publications.

Marx, G. T. (2003). A Tack in the Shoe: Neutralizing and Resisting the New Surveillance. *Journal Of Social Issues, 59*(2), 369-390.

Mason, N. (2007, February 6). *Customer Loyalty Improves Retention.* Retrieved March 7, 2007, from http://www.clickz.com/showPage.html?page=3624868

McCorkel, J., & Myers, K. (2003). What difference does difference make? Position and privilege in the field. *Qualitative Sociology, 26*(2), 199-231.

McCray, A. T., Loane, R. F., Browne, A. C., & Bangalore, A. K. (1999). Terminology issues in user access to Web-based medical information. *Proc AMIA Symp*, 107-111.

McCullagh, D. (2006). *AOL's disturbing glimpse into user's lives.* CNET News.com, Online at: http://news.com.com/2100-1030_3-6103098.html. Retrieved October 5, 2006.

McFadden, C. (2005, July 6). *Optimizing the Online Business Channel with Web Analytics.* Retrieved March 7, 2007, from http://www.Webanalyticsassociation.org/en/art/?9

McGrath, J. E. (1994). Methodology matters: Doing research in the behavioral and social sciences. In R. Baecker & W. A. S. Buxton (Eds.), *Readings in Human-Computer Interaction: An Interdisciplinary Approach* (2nd ed., pp. 152-169). San Mateo, CA: Morgan Kaufman Publishers.

McGrath, J. E. (1995). Methodology matters: doing research in the behavioral and social sciences. In J. G. R. Baeker, W. Buxton, and S. Greenberg (Ed.), *Human-Computer Interaction: Toward the Year 2000* (pp. 152-169).

McKinney, V., Yoon, K., & Zahedi, F. (2002). The measurement of Web-customer satisfaction: An expectation and disconfirmation approach. *Information Systems Research, 13*(3), 296-315.

McTavish, F., Pingree, S., Hawkins, R., & Gustafson, D. (2003). Cultural differences in use of an electronic discussion group. *Journal of Health Psychology*, 8(1), 105-117.

Meadow, C. T. (1990). The making of an information retrieval interface. In *Information Technology 1990. Next decade in information technology, Proceedings of the 5th Jerusalem conference on information technology* (pp. 787-795). Los Alamitos, CA.: IEEE Computer Society.

Meadow, C. T. et al. (1977) *Individualized Instruction for Data Access (IIDA)* Final Design Report. Philadelphia, PA: Drexel University, Graduate School of Library Science, Franklin Institute Research Laboratories.

Meadow, C. T., Hewett, T. T. & Aversa, E. S. (1982). A computer intermediary for interactive database searching. Part I: Design. *Journal of the American Society for Information Science, 33(5),* 325-332.

Meadow, C. T., Hewett, T. T. & Aversa, E. S. (1982). A computer intermediary for interactive database searching. Part II: Evaluation. *Journal of the American Society for Information Science, 33(6),* 357-364.

Meersman, R., Aberer, K., & Dillon, T. (2003). Semantic Issues in e-Commerce Systems. Series: *IFIP International Federation for Information Processing*, Vol. 111.

Mehta, R., & Sivadas, E. (1995). Comparing response rates and response content in mail vs. Electronic mail surveys. *Journal of the Market Research Society, 37*(4), 429-439.

Mei, Q. and Zhai, C. (2005). Discovering evolutionary theme patterns from text an exploration of temporal text mining. *Proceedings of the 11th ACM SIGKDD International Conference on Knowledge Discovery and Data Mining, Chicago,* Illinois, USA, 198-207.

Meier, J. D., Mackman, A., Dunner, M., Vasireddy, S., Escamilla, R., & Murakan, A. (2003). *Improving Web Application Security: Threats and Countermeasures*: Microsoft Press.

Meister, D., & Sullivan, D. J. (1967) *Evaluation of user reactions to a prototype on-line information retrieval system* (Report No. NASA CR-918). Report to NASA by Bunker-Ramo Corporation under Contract No. NASA-1369, ERIC ED 019 094.

Metzler, D. and Croft, W. B. (2005). A Markov random field model for term dependencies. *SIGIR'05: Proceedings of the 28th Annual International ACM SIGIR conference on Research and Development in Information Retrieval,* Salvador, Brazil, 472-479.

Metzler, D. and Croft, W. B. (2005). Analysis of statistical question classification for fact-based questions. *Information Retrieval, 8*, 481-504.

Michaelidou, N., & Dibb, S. (2006). Using email queeztionnaires for research: good practice in tackling non-response. *Journal of Targeting, Measurement, and Analysis for Marketing, 14*(4), 289.

Microsoft. (2005, August 22). *W3C Extended Log File Examples.* Retrieved March 7, 2007, from http://technet2.microsoft.com/WindowsServer/en/library/b5b8a519-8f9b-456b-9040-018358f2c0c01033.mspx?mfr=true

Middleton, S. DeRoure, D. & Shadbolt, N. (2001). *Capturing knowledge of user preferences: Ontologies in recommender systems.* In Proceedings of the ACM K-CAP'01, Victoria, Canada, 2001. ACM Press.

Middleton, S. E., Shadbolt, N. R. & De Roure, D.C. (2004). *Ontological user profiling in recommender systems.* ACM Transactions on Information Systems,22 (1), 54–88.

Mikroyannidis, A. & Theodoulidis, B. (2004). *A Theoretical Framework and an Implementation Architecture for Self Adaptive Web Sites.* In Proc. Of IEEE/WIC/ACM International Conference on Web Intelligence (WI'04). 2004. Beijing, China, p.558-561.

Milgram, S. (1967). The small world problem. *Psychology Today*, 1, 60-67.

Milic-Frayling, N., Jones, R., Rodden, K., Smyth, G., Blackwell, A., & Sommerer, R. (2004). SmartBack: Supporting Users in Back Navigation. In *13th International World Wide Web Conference* (pp. 63-71). New York, NY: ACM.

Miller, D., Schwartz, R., Weischedel, R., & Stone, R. (1999). Named Entity Extraction from Broadcast News. In *Proceedings of DARPA Broadcast News Workshop.*

Miller, G. (1998). *WordNet: An electronic lexical database.* Cambridge, MA: MIT Press.

Miller, Hugh. (1995) *The Presentation of Self in Electronic Life: Goffman on the Internet.* Paper presented at Embodied Knowledge and Virtual Space Conference. University of London.

Millsap, L., & Ferl, T. (1993). Search patterns of remote users: An analysis of opac transaction logs. *Information Technology and Libraries,* 11(3), 321-343.

Minkov, E., Wang, R.C. and Cohen, W.W., 2004, Extracting personal names from emails, In *Proceedings of the Human Language Technology Conference and Conference on Empirical Methods in Natural Language Processing* (*HLT/EMNLP*) (pp. 443–450), East Stroudsburg, PA: ACL.

Minsky, M. , 1975, A framework for representing knowledge, In P.H. Winston (Ed.), *The Psychology of Computer Vision* (pp. 211-277), New York: McGraw-Hill.

Mitchell, T. (1999). The role of unlabeled data in supervised learning. *Proceedings of the Sixth International Colloquium on Cognitive Science.* San Sebastian, Spain.

Mitra, M., Singhal, A., & Buckley, C. (1998, August). *Improving automatic query expansion.* Paper presented at the Twenty-first Annual International ACM SIGIR Conference on Research and Development in Information Retrieval, Melbourne, Australia.

Mittman, B., & Dominick, W. D. (1973) Developing monitoring techniques for an on-line information retrieval system. *Information Processing and Management, 9(6),* 297-307.

Miwa, M. (2001, 2-4 February). *In User situations and multiple levels of users goals in information problem solving processes of askeric users* (Vol. 38, pp. 355-371). Paper presented at the the 2001 Annual Meeting of the American Society for Information Sciences and Technology, San Francisco, CA, USA. ASIS.

Mladenic, D. (1999*). Machine learning used by Personal WebWatcher. Proceedings of ACAI-99 Workshop on Machine Learning and Intelligent Agents*, Chania, Crete, July 5-16, 1999.

Mobascher B. & Daí, H. (2005). *Integrating Semantic Knowledge with Web Usage Mining for Personalization.* In Web Mining: Applications and Techniques. Anthony Scime (ed.), Idea Group Publishing.

Mobascher, B. (2005). *Web Usage Mining and personalization.* Practical Handbook of Internet Computing Munindar P. Singh (ed.), CRC Press.

Mobasher, B., Cooley, R., & Srivastava, J.(2000). *Automatic Personalization Based on Web Usage Mining. Communication of ACM.* Volume 43, Issue 8, August, 2000.

Mobasher, P., Dai, H. (2002). *Using Ontologies to Discover Domain-Level Web Usage Profiles.* Proceedings of the 2nd Workshop on Semantic Web Mining. Held at PKDD'02, Helsinki, Finland, August 2002.

Moe, W. W., & Fader, P. S. (2004). Capturing evolving visit behavior in clickstream data. *Journal of Interactive Marketing, 18(1),* 5-19.

Moe, W.W. (2003). Buying, searching or browsing: differentiating between online shoppers using in-store navigational clickstream. *Journal of Consumer Psychology, 13*(1&2), 29-40.

Moens, M.-F., 2006, *Information Extraction: Algorithms and Prospects in a Retrieval Context* (*The Information Retrieval Series* 21). New York: Springer.

Moens, M.-F., Boiy, E., Mochales Palau, R. and Reed, C. , 2007, Automatic detection of arguments in legal texts. In *Proceedings of the Eleventh International Conference on Artificial Intelligence and Law,* New York: ACM.

Moens, M-F. (2002), *Automatic Indexing and Abstracting of Document Texts.* Kluwer Academic publishers, New York.

Moher, D., Schulz, K. F., & Altman, D. G. (2001). The CONSORT statement: Revised recommendations for improving the quality of reports of parallel-group randomised trials. *The Lancet,* 357, 1191-1194.

Mohr, J, Sengupta, S. and Slater, S. (2005). *Marketing of high-technology products and innovations,* Upper Saddle River, NJ: Prentice Hall.

Montaner, M., Lopez, B., & Rosa, J. L. D. L. (2003). A Taxonomy of Recommender Agents on the Internet. *Artificial Intelligence Review,* 19, 285-330.

Montgomery, A., & Faloutsos, C. (2001). Identifying web browsing trends and patterns. *IEEE Computer,* 34(7), 94-95.

Montgomery, D.C. (1991). *Design and Analysis of Experiments.* New York: John Wiley and Sons

Moorthy, S., Ratchford, B.T., & Talukdar, D. (1997). Consumer information search revisited: Theory and empirical analysis. *Journal of Consumer Research, 23*(4), 263-277.

Morales, R., Van Labeke, N. & Brna, P. (2006). *Towards a Learner Modelling Engine for the Semantic Web* , International Workshop on Applications of Semantic Web Technologies for E-Learning (SW-EL). AH2006.

Moreno, J. L. (1953). *Who Shall Survive? Foundations of Sociometry.* Boston, MA: Beacon House.

Morgan, Lewis H. (1985) [orig. 1877] *Ancient Society.* Tucson: University of Arizona Press.

Moukdad, H., & Large, A. (2001). Users' perceptions of the web as revealed by transaction log analysis. *Online Information Review,* 25(6), 349-358.

Munteanu, D.S. and Marcu, D., 2006, Extracting parallel sub-sentential fragments from comparable corpora, In *Proceedings of ACL-2006, Sydney, Australia* (pp. 81-88).

Murata, T., & Saito, K. (2006). Extracting users' interests from web log data. *Proceedings of the IEEE/WIC/ACM International Conference on Web Intelligence (WI'06).*

Muresan, G. (2002). Using document clustering and language modelling in mediated information retrieval, Ph.D. dissertation, School of Computing, The Robert Gordon University, Aberdeen, Scotland, January 2002.

Muresan, G. and Harper, D.J. (2004). Topic modeling for mediated access to very large document collections. *Journal of the American Society for Information Science and Technology. 55,* 892–910.

Muresan, G., & Harper, D. J. (2001). Document clustering and language models for system-mediated information access. In *Proceedings of the 5th European Conference on Digital Libraries (ECDL)*, Darmstadt.

Murphy, E., & Ciszewska-Carr, J. (2005). Contrasting syntactic and semantic units in the analysis of online discussions. *Australasian Journal of Educational Technology,* Vol. 21 (4), 546-566.

Murray, G. C., Lin, J., and Chowdhury, A. (2006). Identification of user sessions with hierarchical agglomerative clustering. *Proceedings of ASIST 2006: Annual Meeting of the American Society for Information Sciences and Technology.*

Musa, D. L. & Oliveira, J.P.M. (2005). *Sharing Learner Information through a Web Services-based Learning Architecture.* Journal Of Web Engineering, Princeton, New Jersey, v. 4, n. 3, p. 263-278, 2005.

Nahl, D. (1998). Ethnography of Novices First use of Web search engines: Affective Control in Cognitive Processes. *Internet Reference Services Quarterly,* 51-72

Naidu, S. & Järvelä, S. (2006). Analyzing CMC content for what? *Computers & Education,* Vol. 46 (1), 96-103.

Nakashima, E. (2006, August 8, 2006). AOL takes down site with users' search data. *Washington Post,* p. D01, from http://www.washingtonpost.com/wp-dyn/content/article/2006/08/07/AR2006080701150.html

Napier, H. A., Judd, P., Rivers, O., & Adams, A. (2001). *Creating a winning E-business* (pp. 364-369). Boston, MA: Thomas Course Technology.

Napier, H. A., Judd, P., Rivers, O., & Adams, A. (2003). *E-business technologies.* (pp. 372-380). Boston, MA: Thomas Course Technology.

Nejdl, W. Dolog, P. (2003). *Challenges and Benefits of the Semantic Web for User Modelling* In Proc. of AH2003 workshop, WWW 2003.

Netscape Communications Corporation. (1998). *JavaScript Guide.* Retrieved september, 20, 2007, from http://wp.netscape.com/eng/mozilla/3.0/handbook/javascript/.

Ngai, E. W. T. & Wat, F. K. T. (2002). A literature review and classification of electronic commerce research, *Information & Management,* Vol. 39 (5), 415–429.

Nicholas, D., Huntington, P., & Jamali, H. R. (2007). Diversity in the Information Seeking Behaviour of the Virtual Scholar: Institutional Comparisons, *Journal of Academic Librarianship,* Vol. 33 (6), 629-638.

Nicholas, D., Huntington, P., Jamali, H. R., & Dobrowolski, T. (2007). Characterizing and evaluating information seeking behavior in a digital environment: Spotlight on the 'bouncer'. *Information Processing and Management, 43,* 1085-1102

Nicholas, D., Huntington, P., Lievesley, N., & Withey, R. (1999). Cracking the code: Web log analysis. *Online and CD ROM Review,* 23(5), 263-269.

Nicholson, S. (2004). A conceptual framework for the holistic measurement and cumulative evaluation of library services, *Journal of Documentation,* Vol. 60 (2), 164-182.

Nielsen, B. (1986). What they say they do and what they do: Assessing online catalog use instruction through transaction monitoring. *Information Technology and Libraries,* 5, 28-34.

Nielsen, H. F. (1995). *Logging in W3C httpd.* Retrieved september, 20, 2007, from http://www.w3.org/Daemon/User/Config/Logging.html# common-logfile-format.

Nielsen//NetRatings. (2004). *United States: Average Web Usage, Month of September 2004, Home Panel.* Online at: www.nielsen-netratings.com. Retrieved October 5, 2006.

Nigam K., McCallum A., & Mitchell T. (2006) Semi-Supervised Text Classification Using EM. In *Semi-Supervised Learning,* Olivier Chapelle, Bernhard Schölkopf, & Alexander Zien (Eds.), 31-51, MIT Press.

Nigam, K., & Ghani, R. (2000). Analyzing the Effectiveness and Applicability of Co-training. In *Proceedings of the Ninth International Conference on Information and Knowledge Management,* 86–93. ACM.

Nigam, K., McCallum, A. K., Thrun, S., & Mitchell, T. (2000). Text Classification from Labeled and Unlabeled Documents using EM. *Machine Learning, 39*(2/3), 103–134.

Nilsson, M., Palmer, M. & Brase, J. (2003). *The LOM RDf binding-principles and implementation.* Technical report, Information system institute, University of hannover, germany, 2003. 3rd Annual Ariadne Conference, 20-21 November 2003, Leuven, Belgium.

O'Connor, P. (2006). An International Comparison of Approaches to Online Privacy Protection: Implications for the Hotel Sector, *Journal of Services Research*, Vol. 6, 7-26.

Oard, D., & Kim, J. (2001). Modeling information content using observable behavior. *Proceedings of the Sixty-fourth American Society for Information Science Annual Meeting, 38*, 481-488.

Obendorf, H., Weinreich, H., & Hass, T. (2004). Automatic Support for Web User Studies with SCONE and TEA. In *CHI '04 extended abstracts on Human Factors in Computing Systems* (pp. 1135-1138). Vienna, Austria: ACM.

Olah, J. (2005). Shifts Between Search Stages During Task-Performance in Mediated Information-Seeking Interaction. In *Proceedings of the 68th Annual Meeting of the American Society for Information Science (ASIST)*, Charlotte, NC.

Oliveira, J. P. M. & Rigo, S. J. (2006). *Mineração de uso em sites Web para a descoberta de classes de usuários.* In: CLEI 2006.Santiago, Chile, 19-25 October 2006.

Ollman, B. (2001). Critical Realism in the Light of Marx's Process of Abstraction. In J. Lopez & G. Potter (Eds.), *After Postmodernism: An Introduction to Critical Realism* (pp. 285-298). London: Athlone Press.

Olson, J. S., Grudin, J., & Horvitz, E. (2005). A Study of Preferences for Sharing and Privacy, *in CHI '05 Extended Abstracts of Human Factors in Computing Systems* (pp. 1985-1988). Portland, Oregon: ACM.

Olson-Buchanan, J. B., & Boswell, W. R. (2006). Blurring boundaries: Correlates of integration and segmentation between work and nonwork. *Journal of Vocational Behavior, 68*(3), 432-445.

Omniture. (2007). Omniture Site Catalyst. http://www.omniture.com/products/web_analytics/sitecatalyst: [April 18, 2007].

Osuna, E. E., Freund, R., and Girosi, F. (1996). *Support vector machines: Training and applications.* Massachusetts Institute of Technology, Artificial Intelligence Laboratory Technical Report No. 1602, Center for Biological and Computational Learning, Technical Report No. 144.

Otte, E., & Rousseau, R. (2002). Social network analysis: A powerful strategy, also for the information sciences. *Journal of Information Science, 28*(6), 441-453.

Ounnas, A. (2006) Towards a Semantic Modeling of Learners for Social Networks. In *Proceedings of International Workshop on Applications of Semantic Web Technologies for E-Learning (SW-EL) at the AH2006 Conference*, pp. 102-108, Dublin, Ireland.

Ozmutlu, H. C., and Cavdur, F. (2005a). Application of automatic topic identification on Excite web search engine data logs. *Information Processing and Management*, 41, 1243-1262.

Ozmutlu, H.C., Cavdur, F., and Ozmutlu, S. (2006). Automatic new topic identification in search engine datalogs. *Internet Research, 16*, 323-338

Ozmutlu, H.C., Cavdur, F., Ozmutlu, S., and Spink, A., (2004). Neural network applications for automatic new topic identification on Excite Web search engine datalogs. *ASIST '04: Proceedings of the Annual Meeting of the American Society for Information Science and Technology,* (pp. 310-316). Providence, RI.

Ozmutlu, S. (2006). Automatic new topic identification using multiple linear regression. *Information Processing and Management, 42(4)*, 934-950.

Ozmutlu, S., and Cavdur, F. (2005). Neural network applications for automatic new topic identification. *Online Information Review, 29*, 35-53

Ozmutlu, S., Ozmutlu, H. C. and Spink, (2004). A day in the life of Web searching: an exploratory study. *Information Processing and Management. 40*, 319-345.

Ozmutlu, S., Ozmutlu, H. C. and Spink, A. (2002). Multimedia Web Searching, *Proceedings of ASIST 2002: 65th American Society of Information Science and Technology Annual Meeting*, Long Beach October 2003, 403-408.

Ozmutlu, S., Ozmutlu, H. C. and Spink, A., (2003). Are people asking questions of general web search engines. *Online Information Review*, 27, 396-406.

Ozmutlu, S., Ozmutlu, H. C., and Spink, A. (2002). Multimedia Web Searching/ *Proceedings of ASIST 2002: 65th American Society of Information Science and Technology Annual Meeting*, Long Beach October 2003, 403-408.

Ozmutlu, S., Ozmutlu, H. C., and Spink, A. (2003). Multitasking Web Searching and Implications for Design, *Proceedings of ASIST 2003: 66th American Society of Information Science and Technology Annual Meeting*, Long Beach October 2003.

Ozmutlu, S., Ozmutlu, H. C., and Spink, A., (2003). Are people asking questions of general web search engines. *Online Information Review*, 27, 396-406.

Ozmutlu, S., Ozmutlu, H.C. and Spink, A. (2007). Using conditional probabilities for automatic new topic identification. *Online Information Review*, 31(4), 491-515.

Ozmutlu, S., Ozmutlu, H.C. and Spink, A. (2007). Using Support vector machines for Automatic New topic identification, *Proceedings of ASIST 2007: American Society of Information Science and Technology Annual Meeting*, 403-408.

Ozmutlu, S., Ozmutlu, H.C. and Spink, A. (forthcoming). *Using Markovian Analysis for Automatic New topic identification.*

Ozmutlu, S., Ozmutlu, H.C. and Spink, A.(2006). Topic Estimation of Web Search Transaction Log Queries Using Monte-Carlo simulation. *Proceedings of AUSWEB 2006: Australasian World Wide Web Conference.*

Özmutlu, S., Özmutlu, H.C., & Spink, A. (2003, 23 - 26 June). *In A study of multitasking Web searching* (pp. 145-150). Paper presented at the the IEEE ITCC'03: international Conference on information Technology: Coding and Computing, Las Vegas, Nevada. IEEE.

Ozmutlu, S., Spink A., and Ozmutlu, C. (2002). Trends in multimedia Web searching: Excite Queries, *IEEE ITCC 2002: Proceedings of the International Conference on Information Technology: Coding and Computing.* Las Vegas, NV, 40-45.

Ozmutlu, S., Spink, A. and Ozmutlu, H. C. (2003). Trends in multimedia web searching: 1997-2001, *Information Processing and Management*, 39, 611-621.

Ozmutlu, S., Spink, A. And Ozmutlu, H.C. (2002). Analysis of large data logs: an application of Poisson sampling on excite web queries. *Information Processing and Management*, 38, 473-490.

Ozmutlu, S., Spink, A., and Ozmutlu, H. C. (2003). Trends in multimedia web searching: 1997-2001, *Information Processing and Management*, 39, 611-621.

P&AB. (2003). Consumer Privacy Attitudes: A Major Shift Since 2000 and Why. *Privacy & American Business Newsletter, 10*(6), 1,3-5.

Page, S. (2000). Community research: The lost art of unobtrusive methods. *Journal of Applied Social Psychology, 30*(10), 2126- 2136.

Paik, S., Shak, S., Tang, G., Kim, C., Baker, J., Cronin, M., et al. (2004). A multigene assay to predict recurrence of tamoxifen-treated, node-negative breast cancer. *N Engl J Med, 351*(27), 2817-2826.

Palen, L., & Dourish, P. (2003). Unpacking "Privacy" for a Networked World. In *SIGCHI Conference on Human Factors in Computing Systems* (pp. 129-136). Ft. Lauderdale, FL: ACM.

Palmquist, R.A. & Kim, K.S. (2000). Cognitive style and on-line database search experience as predictors of web search performance. *Journal of the American Society for Information Science, 51*(6), 558-566.

Palvia, P., Pinjani, P., & Sibley, E. H. (2007). A profile of information systems research. *Information & Management, Information & Management*, Vol. 44 (1), 1-11.

Paramythis, A. Stephanidis, C. (2005). *A generic adaptation framework for Web-based hypermedia systems.* In Adaptable and adaptive Hypermedia Systems. Anthony Scime (ed.), Idea Group Publishing, p.80-103. 2005.

Park, H. W., Kim, C. S., & Barnett, G. A. (2004). Socio-communicational structure among political actors on the web in south korea: The dynamics of digital presence in cyberspace. *New Media & Society, 6*(3), 403-423.

Park, S., Bae, H., & Lee, J. (2005). End user searching: A Web log analysis of NAVER, a Korean Web search engine. *Library & Information Science Research,* 27(2), 203-221.

Parker, E. B., & Paisley, W. J. (1966). Research for Psychologists at the Interface of the Scientist and His Information System. *American Psychologist, 21(11),* 1061-1071.

Pastore, M. (1998). *Microsoft Leads Browser Race.* Online at: www.clickz.com/stats/big_picture/hardware/article.php/151351. Retrieved October 5, 2006.

Pastore, M. (1998). *Online Users Need Speed.* Online at: www.clickz.com/stats/markets/broadband/article.php/151701. Retrieved October 5, 2006.

Pastore, M. (2000). *E-Commerce, Mobile Access Drawing Interest from Net Users.* Online at: www.clickz.com/stats/big_picture/geographics/article.php/5911_494701. Retrieved October 5, 2006.

Pastore, M. (2000). *Internet Usage Stats.* Online at: www.clickz.com/stats/big_picture/traffic_patterns/article.php/291211. Retrieved October 5, 2006.

Pastore, M. (2000). *Slow Modems Still Dominate Home Internet Scene.* Online at: www.clickz.com/stats/big_picture/hardware/article.php/277191. Retrieved October 5, 2006.

Pastore, M. (2001). *Online Consumers Now the Average Consumer.* Online at: www.clickz.com/stats/big_picture/demographics/article.php/5901_800201. Retrieved October 5, 2006.

Paterno, F. (2001). Towards a UML for Interactive systems. In *Proceedings of the 8th IFIP International Conference on Engineering for Human-Computer Interaction*, Toronto.

Paterno, F. (2004). ConcurTaskTrees: an engineered notation for task models. In Diaper, D., & Stanton, N. (Eds.) *The Handbook of Task Analysis of Human-Computer Interaction*, Lawrence Erlbaum Associates.

Patil, S., Romero, N. A. & Karat, J. (2006). Privacy and HCI: methodologies for studying privacy issues, *CHI Extended Abstracts*, 1719-1722.

Payne, J.W., Bettman, J.R., and Johnson, E.J. (1993), *The adaptive decision maker.* Cambridge UK: Cambridge University Press.

Pearl, J. ,1988, *Probabilistic Reasoning in Intelligent Systems*, Morgan-Kaufmann.

Pegden, C.D., Shannon, R.E., and Sadowski, R.P. (1995). *Introduction to Simulation using Siman*, McGraw-Hill, New York

Penniman, W. D. & Perry J. C. (1976). *Tempo of on-line user interaction.* Paper presented at the 5th Mid-year meeting of the American Society for Information Science, Nashville, TN.

Penniman, W. D. (1971, January). *BASIS-70 Design, Implementation, and Operation.* Paper presented at the joint meeting of the Central Ohio Chapters of the American Society for Information Science and the Association for Computing Machinery, Columbus, OH.

Penniman, W. D. (1974, October). *Rhythms of dialogue in BASIS – a preliminary report on doctoral research in human-computer conversational interaction.* Paper presented at the 37th annual meeting of the American Society for Information Science.

Penniman, W. D. (1975). *Rhythms of dialog in human-computer conversation.* Unpublished doctoral dissertation, The Ohio State University.

Penniman, W. D. (1975). A stochastic process analysis of on-line user behavior. In *Proceedings of the American Society for Information Science Vol. 12* (pp. 147-148). Washington, D.C.: ASIS.

Penniman, W. D. (1976). *A conceptual framework for adaptive prompting in interactive computer systems.* Unpublished paper included in correspondence to Dr. Sarah Rhodes, National Science Foundation, May 19, 1976.

Penniman, W. D. (1982). Modeling and evaluation of on-line user behavior. In *Proceedings American Society for Information Science, Vol. 19* (pp. 231-235).

Penniman, W. D. (1984). A methodology for evaluating interactive system usage. *SIGCHI Bulletin, 15(4),* 6-11.

Penniman, W. D. (1991). System interfaces revisited. In M. A. Siegel (Ed.), *Design and evaluation of computer/human interfaces: Issues for librarians and information scientists* (pp. 69-78). Urbana, IL: Graduate School of Library and Information Science, University of Illinois.

Penniman, W. D. and Dominick, W. D. (1980). Monitoring and evaluation of on-line information system usage. *Information Processing and Management, 16(1),* 17-35.

Permadi, F. (2005, June 19). *Introduction to Flash Local Shared-Object.* Retrieved March 7, 2007, from http://www.permadi.com/tutorial/flashSharedObject/index.html

Peters, T. (1993). The history and development of transaction log analysis. *Library Hi Tech, 42*(11), 41-66.

Peters, T. A. (1989). When smart people fail: an analysis of the transaction log of an online public access catalog. *The Journal of Academic Librarianship, 15(November),* 267-273.

Peters, T. A. (1998). Remotely familiar: Using computerized monitoring to study remote use. *Library Trends, 47(1),* 7-20.

Peters, T. A., Kaske, N. K., & Kurth, M. (1993) Transaction log analysis. *Library Hi Tech Bibliography, 8(9),* 151-183.

Peters, T. A., Kurth, M., Flaherty, P., Sandore, B., & Kaske, N. K. (1993) An introduction to the special section on transaction log analysis. *Library Hi Tech Issue 42, 11(2),* 38-40.

Petersen, E. (2004). *Web Analytics Demystified*: Celilo Group Media/Cafe Press.

Petersen, E. (2005). *US Web Analytics forecast 2004-2009*: Jupiter Research.

Petersen, E. (2005). *Web Site Measurement Hacks.* San Franscisco: O'Reilly Media.

Petersen, E., Bayriamova, Z., Evans, P. F., Levy, M., & Matiesanu, C. (2004). *Key Performance Indicators: Using Analytics to Drive Action.* New York: Jupiter Research.

Peterson, E. (2004). Chinese Encoding Converter, [Online], retrieved from http://www.mandarintools.com/ on October 7, 2004.

Peterson, E. T. (2004). *Web Analytics Demystified.* Celilo Group Media.

Peterson, E. T. (2005). *Web Site Measurement Hacks.* O'Reilly (2005), ISBN 0-596-00988-7.

Peterson, E. T. (2005, July 31). *Average Order Value.* Retrieved November 3, 2007, from Web Analytics Demystified Blog Website: http://blog.webanalyticsdemystified.com/weblog/2005/07/average-order-value.html

Petrelli, D. (2005). *User-Centred Design of Flexible Hypermedia for a Mobile Guide: Reflections on the HyperAudio Experience.* User Modeling and User-Adapted Interaction (2005) 15:303–338. Springer.

Pew Internet & American Life Project. (2005). *Internet: The mainstreaming of online life: Trends 2005.* Washington, DC: Pew Internet & American Life Project.

Phillips, D. J. (2002). Context, identity, and privacy in ubiquitous computing environments. In *Workshop on socially-informed design of privacy-enhancing solutions, Ubicomp 2002.* Goteborg, Sweden.

Phippen, A. (2004). An evaluation methodology for virtual communities using Web analytics. *Paper pre-*

sented at the Proceedings of the International Networks Conference, Plymouth, UK.

Phippen, A., Sheppard, L., & Furnell, S. (2004). A practical evaluation of Web analysis. *Internet Research*, 14(4), 284-293.

Picard, E. (2006). *Ajax Counting Nightmares*. Retrieved 9/14/2007, http://www.clickz.com/showPage.html?page=3610786

Pinker, S. (1999). *How the mind works*. W.W. Norton &Co.

Pirolli, P., Pitkow, J., & Rao, R. (1996). Silk from a Sow's Ear: Extracting Usable Structures from the Web. In *SIGCHI Conference on Human Factors in Computing Systems* (pp. 118 - 125). Vancouver, Canada: ACM.

Pitkow, J. (1997). In Search of Reliable Usage Data on the WWW. In *6th International Conference on World Wide Web* (pp. 1343-1355). Santa Clara, CA: Elsevier Science Publishers Ltd.

Pitkow, J. E., & Kehoe, C. M. (1996). Emerging Trends in the WWW User Population. *Communications of the ACM, 39*(6), 106 - 108.

Pitkow, J., & Recker, M. M. (1994). Using the Web as a Survey Tool: Results from the Second WWW Survey. *Computer Networks and ISDN Systems, 27*(6), 809-822.

Pitkow, J.E. (1997, 7-11 April). *In search of reliable usage data on the www* (pp. 1343-1355). Paper presented at the Santa Clara, CA, the Sixth International World Wide Web Conference. Elsevier.

Popov, B. et al. (2003). *Towards Semantic Web Information Extraction*. Second International Semantic Web Conference (ISWC-03). Sanibel Island, Florida, October 20, 2003.

Potter, G., & Lopez, J. (2001). General Introduction: After Postmodernism: the Millennium. In J. Lopez & G. Potter (Eds.), *After Postmodernism: An Introduction to Critical Realism*. London: Athlone Press.

Powell R.R., (1999). Recent Trends in Research: A Methodological Essay. *Library and Information Science Research,* Vol. 21 (1) 91-119.

Preece, J., & Maloney-Krichmar, D. (2003). Online communities. In J. Jacko & A. Sears (Eds.), *Handbook of Human-Computer Interaction* (596-620). Mahwah, NJ: Lawrence Erlbaum Associates Inc. Publishers.

Preece, J., & Maloney-Krichmar, D. (2005). Online communities: Design, theory, and practice. *Journal of Computer-Mediated Communication,* 10(4), article 1.

Price, D.J. de Solla (1965). Networks of scientific papers. *Science, 149*, 510-515.

Price, S. L., & Hersh, W. R. (1999). Filtering Web pages for quality indicators: an empirical approach to finding high quality consumer health information on the World Wide Web. *Proc AMIA Symp*, 911-915.

Proctor, E. (2002). Boolean operators and the naive end-user: Moving to AND. *Online, 26*(4), 34-37.

Protégé. (2007). *The Protege Plataform*. Retrieved september, 20, 2007, from http://protege.stanford.edu.

Pu, H.T., Chuang, S-L., and Yang, C. (2002). Subject categorization of query terms for exploring web users' search interests. *Journal of the American Society for Information Science and Technology. 53*, 617–630.

Qiu, L. (1993). Markov models of search state patterns in a hypertext information retrieval system. *Journal of the American Society for Information Science, 44(7),* 413-427.

QuestionPro. *Measuring Customer Loyalty and Customer Satisfaction*. Retrieved November 21, 2007, from http://www.questionpro.com/akira/showArticle.do?articleID=customerloyalty.

Quinlan, J. R. (1986). Induction of Decision Trees. *Machine Learning*, 1, 81–106.

Rabiner, L.R. (1989). A tutorial on Hidden Markov models and selected applications in speech recognition. In Rabiner, L.R. (Ed.) *Proceedings of the IEEE*, 77(2), 257 - 286

Radlinski, F., and Dumais, S. (2006). Improving personalized Web search using result diversification. *Proceedings of the Twenty-Ninth Annual International ACM SIGIR Conference on Research and Development in Information Retrieval,* Seattle, WA, 691-692.

Raghavan, H., Madani, O., & Jones, R. (2005). Interactive Feature Selection. In *Proceedings of the Nineteenth International Joint Conference of Artificial Intelligence*, 841–846.

Raghavan, H., Madani, O., & Jones, R. (2006). Active Learning with Feedback on Both Features and Instances. *Journal of Machine Learning Research*, Volume 7, 1655–1686.

Rainie, L. (2007). *Forget Dewey and His Decimals, Internet Users are Revolutionizing the Way We Classify Information -- And Make Sense of It.* Pew Internet and American Life Project, http://www.pewinternet.org. Retrieved January 31, 2007.

Rapoport, A., & Horvath, W. J. (1961). A study of a large sociogram. *Behavioral Science, 6*, 279 -291.

Reeder, R., Pirolli, P., & Card, S. (2001). WebEyeMapper and WebLogger: tools for analyzing eye tracking data collected in Web-use studies. In *CHI '01 Extended Abstracts on Human Factors in Computing Systems* (pp. 19-20). Seattle, WA: ACM.

Reips, U.-D. (2000). The Web experiment method: advantages, disadvantages, and solutions. (*In* M. H. Birnbaum (eds.), *Psychological Experiments on the Internet,* San Diego, CA: Academic Press. p. 89-117.)

Rennie, J.D.M. and Jaakkola, T., 2005, Using term informativeness for named entity detection. In *Proceedings of the Twenty-Eight Annual International ACM SIGIR Conference on Research and Development in Information Retrieval* (pp. 353-360), New York: ACM.

Renninger, K. A., & Shumar, W. (2002). Community building with and for teachers at The Math Forum. In K. A. Renninger & W. Shumar (Eds.), *Building Virtual Communities: Learning and Change in Cyberspace* (pp. 60-95). Cambridge, UK: Cambridge University Press.

Resource statistics. (2007). Retrieved May 15, 2007, from http://www.ncbi.nlm.nih.gov/About/tools/restable_stat_pubmeddata.htm

Rheingold, H. (1993). *The virtual community: Homesteading on the electronic frontier.* Reading, MA: Addison-Wesley.

Rice, R. E., & Borgman, C. L. (1983). The use of computer-monitored data in information science and communication research. *Journal of the American Society for Information Science, 34(4),* 247-256.

Riding, R.J., & Cheema I. (1991). Cognitive styles – an overview and integration. *Educational Psychology, 11,* 193-215.

Ridings, C. M., & Gefen, D. (2004). Virtual community attraction: Why people hang out online. *Journal of Computer-Mediated Communication, 10*(1), Article 4.

Rieh, S. Y. (2003). Investigating Web Searching Behavior in Home Environments. In *Annual Meeting of the American Society for Information Science and Technology* (pp. 255-264). Long Beach, CA.

Riloff, E. and Lorenzen, J., 1999, Extraction-based text categorization: Generating domain-specific role relationships automatically, In T. Strzalkowski (Ed.), *Natural Language Information Retrieval* (pp. 167-196), Dordrecht, The Netherlands: Kluwer Academic Publishers.

Rivlin, G. (2005, January 24). Users lose the thrill of 'social networking'. *The New York Times*, p. C1.

Robertson, S.E., & Hancock-Beaulieu, M. M. (1992). On the evaluation of IR systems. *Information Processing and Management, 28*(4), 457-466.

Robinson, A., & Thomson, R. (2001). Variability in patient preferences for participating in medical decision making: implication for the use of decision support tools. *Qual Healthcare, 10 Suppl 1,* i34-38.

Robinson, J. C. (2001). The end of managed care. *JAMA, 285*(20), 2622-2628.

Rodgers, S., & Chen, Q. (2005). Internet community group participation: Psychosocial benefits for women with breast cancer. *Journal of Computer-Mediated Communication, 10*(4), Article 5.

Romano, N. C., Donovan, C., Chen, H. C., & Nunamaker, J. F. (2003). A methodology for analyzing Web-based qualitative data. *Journal of Management Information Systems*, Vol. 19 (4), 213-246.

Rose, D. E., & Levinson, D. (2004, 17–22 May). Understanding user goals in web search. *Paper presented at the World Wide Web Conference (WWW 2004), New York, NY, USA.*

Rose, G. M., Meuter, M. L., & Curran, J. L. (2005). On-line waiting: The role of download time and other important predictors on attitude toward e-retailers. *Psychology & Marketing Research, 22*(2), 127-151.

Rosen, D., Woelfel, J., Krikorian, D., & Barnett, G. A. (2003). Procedures for analyses of online communities. *Journal of Computer-Mediated Communication*, 8(4).

Rosenfeld, L., & Wiggins, R. (2007). *Using Search Analytics To Diagnose What's Ailing Your IA.* Paper presented at the American Society for Information Science and Technology. Las Vegas Nevada. Retrieved.

Rosenkrans, L. G. (2006). Online banner ads and metrics challenges. *International Journal of Internet Marketing and Advertising, 3*(3), 193-218.

Ross, N., & Wolfram, D. (2000). End user searching on the internet: An analysis of term pair topics submitted to the excite search engine. *Journal of the American Society for Information Science,* 51(10), 949-958.

Ross, S.M. (1993). *Introduction to Probability Models*, 5th Edition, Academic Press, London 1993.

Rossler, P. (2002). Content analysis in online communication: A challenge for traditional methodology. In Batinic, B., Reips, U. D., & Bosnjak, M. (Eds.), *Online social sciences,* Seattle, WA: Hogrefe & Huber.

Roster, C., Rogers, R., Hozler, G. C., Baker, K., & Albaum, G. (2007). Management of marketing research projects: does delivery method matter anymore in survey research? *Journal of Marketing Theory and Practice, 15*(2), 127.

Rourke, L., & Anderson, T. (2004). Validity in quantitative content analysis. *Educational Technology Research and Development, 52* (1), 5-18.

Roy, M., & Chi, M. T. H. (2003). Gender differences in patterns of searching the web. *Journal of Educational Computing Research, 29*(3), 335-348.

Ruthven, I., & Lalmas, M. (2003). A Survey on the Use of Relevance Feedback for Information Access Systems. *Knowledge Engineering Review*, 18(2), 95-145.

Rutter, Jason & Smith, Greg. (2002) *Ethnografic Presence in Nebulous Settings: A Case Study.* Paper presented at ESRC Virtual Methods Seminar Series. Brunel University.

Rutter, Jason and Smith, Greg. (2002) *Spinning Threads: Rituals of Sociability in CMC.* Available at: http://les.man.ac.uk/cric/Jason_Rutter/papers

Ryle, Gilbert. (1968) "*The thinking of thoughts – What is 'Le Penseur' doing?*" in: University Lectures Series, 18, University of Saskatchewan.

Sackmann, S., Struker, J., & Accorsi, R. (2006). Personalization in Privacy-Aware Highly Dynamic Systems. *Communications of the ACM, 49*(9), 32-38.

Sahami M., & Heilman, T. D. (2006). A Web-based Kernel Function for Measuring the Similarity of Short-text Snippets. In *Proceedings of the Fifteenth International World Wide Web Conference*, 377–386. ACM.

Salton, G. (1989). *Automatic Text Processing.* Reading, Addison-Wesley, Boston, MA, USA.

Samuel, K., Carberry, S., & Vijay-Shanker, K. (1998). Dialogue Act Tagging with Transformation-Based Learning. In *Proceedings of the 36th Annual Meeting of the Association for Computational Linguistics and 17th International Conference on Computational Linguistics*, Montreal.

Sanderson, M., & Croft, B. (1999). Deriving Concept Hierarchies from Text. In *Proceedings of the 22 Annual International ACM SIGIR Conference on Research and Development in Information Retrieval*, Berkeley, CA (pp. 206-213).

Sandore, B. (1993). Applying the results of Transaction Log Analysis. *Library Hi Tech*, 42, 87-97.

Sandore, B., Flaherty, P., & Kaske, N.K. (1993). A manifesto regarding the future of transaction log analysis. *Library Hi Tech,* 11(2), 105-111.

Sandore, B., Flaherty, P., Kaske, N. K., Kurth, M., & Peters, T. (1993). A manifesto regarding the future of transaction log analysis. *Library Hi Tech, Issue 42 11(2),* 105-106.

Sapir, D. (2004, August). Online Analytics and Business Performance Management. *BI Report.* Retrieved March 7, 2007, from http://www.dmreview.com/editorial/dmreview/print_action.cfm?articleId=1008820

Saracevic, T. (1991). Individual differences in organizing, searching and retrieving information. *Proceedings of the American Society for Information Science*, *28*, 82-86.

Saracevic, T. (1996). Interactive models in information retrieval (IR). A review and proposal. In *Proceedings of the 59th Annual Meeting of the American Society for Information Science (ASIST), 33*, 3-9.

Saracevic, T. (1996, October). *Modeling interaction in information retrieval (IR): A review and proposal.* Paper presented at the Fifty-ninth American Society for Information Science, Baltimore, MD.

Saracevic, T. (1997). The stratified model of information retrieval interaction: Extension and applications. *Proceedings of the Sixtieth American Society for Information Science Annual Meeting, 34*, 313-327.

Saracevic, T. (1997, 1-6 November). *In Extension and application of the stratified model of information retrieval interaction* (Vol. 34, pp. 313-327). Paper presented at the The Annual Meeting of the American Society for Information Science, Washington, DC.

Saracevic, T., & Kantor, P. (1997). Studying the value of library and information services: I. Establishing a theoretical framework. *Journal of the American Society for Information Science*, *48*(6), 527-542.

Saracevic, T., & Kantor, P. (1997). Studying the value of library and information services: II. Methodology and taxonomy. *Journal of the American Society for Information Science*, *48*(7), 543-563.

Saracevic, T., Kantor, P., Chamis, A. Y., & Trivison, D. (1988). Study of information seeking and retrieving: I. Background and methodology. *Journal of the American Society for Information Science*, *39*(3), 161-176.

Saracevic, T., Mokros, H., Su, L., & Spink, A. (1991). Interaction between users and intermediaries during online searching. *Proceedings of the Twelfth Annual National Online Meeting*, *12*, 329-341.

Sarawagi, S. (Ed.). (2005). *SIGKDD Explorations, Newsletter of the ACM Special Interest Group on Knowledge Discovery and Data Mining.* Addison Wesley.

Sasaki, Y., Chen, H.-H., h. Chen, K., & Lin, C.-J. (2005). Overview of the NTCIR-5 Cross-Lingual Question Answering Task (CLQA1). In *Proceedings of the Fifth NTCIR Workshop Meeting on Evaluation of Information Access Technologies,* Tokyo, Japan.

Sauro, J. (2004). Premium usability: Getting the discount without paying the price, *Interactions, 11*(4).

Sayyadian, M., Shakery, A., Doan, A., and Zhai, C. (2004). Toward entity retrieval over structured and text data. *WIRD'04: 1st Workshop on the Integration of Information Retrieval and Databases,* Sheffield, UK, 47-54.

Schank, R. C., 1975, *Conceptual Information Processing*, Amsterdam: North Holland.

Schapire, R. E., Rochery, M., Rahim, M., & Gupta, N. (2002) Incorporating Prior Knowledge into Boosting. In *Proceedings of the International Conference on Machine Learning*, 538–545. Morgan Kaufmann.

Schiano, D., Stone, M., & Bectarte, R. (2001). Search and the Subjective Web. In *CHI '01 Extended Abstracts on Human Factors in Computing Systems* (pp. 165-166). Seattle, WA: ACM.

Schlager, M. S., Fusco, J., & Schank, P. (2002). Evolution of an online education community of practice. In K. A. Renninger & W. Shumar (Eds.), *Building Virtual Communities: Learning and Change in Cyberspace* (pp. 129-158). Cambridge, UK: Cambridge University Press.

Schneider, G. (2007). *Electronic commerce.* (7th ed., pp. 380). Boston, MA: Thomson Course Technology.

Schneider, K.-M. (2005). Techniques for Improving the Performance of Naïve Bayes for Text Classification. *Sixth International Conference on Intelligent Text Processing and Computational Linguistics.* LNCS 3406, 682–693.

Schutz, Alfred. (1962) *Collected Papers.* The Hague, Martinus Nijhoff.

Schwandt, T. A. (2000). Three Epistemological Stances for Qualitative Inquiry: Interpretivism, Hermeneutics, and Social Constructionism. In N. Denzin & Y. Lincoln (Eds.), *Handbook of Qualitative Research* (pp. 189-215). Thousand Oaks: Sage.

Scott, J. G. (1998). Trend report: Social network analysis. *Sociology, 22*(1), 109-127.

Scott, J. G. (2000). *Social Network Analysis: A Handbook* (2nd ed.). Thousand Oaks, CA: Sage Publications.

Scott, J. G., Tallia, A. F., Crosson, J. C., & et al. (2005). Social network analysis as an analytic tool for interaction patterns in primary care practices. *Annals of Family Medicine, 3*(5), 443-448.

Seaborne, A. & Prud'hommeaux, E. (2006). *SPARQL Query Language for RDF.* Retrieved september, 20, 2007, from http://www.w3.org/TR/rdf-sparql-query/.

SearchCRM. (2007, May 9). *Measuring Customer Loyalty.* Retrieved November 4, 2007, from http://searchcrm.techtarget.com/general/0,295582,sid11_gci1253794,00.html

Sebastiani, F. (2002). Machine learning in automated text categorization. *ACM Computer Surveys, 34*(1), 1–47.

Sellars, W. (1963). Philosophy and the scientific image of man. In *Science, Perception, and Reality* (pp. 1 - 40). New York: Ridgeview Publishing Company.

Sellen, A. J., Murphy, R., & Shaw, K. L. (2002). How Knowledge Workers Use the Web. In *SIGCHI Conference on Human Factors in Computing Systems* (pp. 227-234). Minneapolis, MN: ACM.

Sen, A., Dacin, P. A., & Pattichis, C. (2006). Current Trends in Web Data Analysis. *Communications of the ACM, 49*(11), 85-91.

Seo, Y. W., & Zhang, B. T. (2000, June). *Learning users' preferences by analyzing Web-browsing behavior.* Paper presented at the Fourth International Conference on Autonomous Agents, Barcelona, Spain.

Sex and the Internet – devices and desires. (2007). *Economist, 383(8525),* 74.

Shanahan, G., Qu, Y. and Wiebe, J. , 2006, *Computing Attitude and Affect in Text: Theory and Applications* (*The Information Retrieval Series* 20), Berlin: Springer.

Shankar, V., & Malthouse, E. C. (2007). The growth of interactions and dialogs in interactive marketing. *Journal of Interactive Marketing, 21(2),* 2-4.

Sharf, B. F. (1997). Communicating breast cancer on-line: Support and empowerment on the Internet. *Women & Health, 26*(1), 65-84.

Sharp, H., Rogers, Y., & Preece, J. (2007). *Interaction design.* Wiley.

Shen, D., Pan, R., Sun, J-T., Pan, J.J., Wu, K., Yin, J. and Yang, Q. (2006). Query enrichment for web-query classification. *ACM Transactions on Information Systems (TOIS)*, 24(3), 320-352.

Shen, D., Pan, R., Sun, J-T., Pan, J.J., Wu, K., Yin, J. and Yang, Q. (2005). Q2C@UST: our winning solution to query classification in KDDCUP 2005. *ACM SIGKDD Explorations Newsletter*, 7(2), 100-110.

Shen, D., Sun, J-T., Yang, Q. and Chen, Z. (2006). Building bridges for web query classification. *Proceedings of the 29th annual international ACM SIGIR conference on Research and development in information retrieval,* Seattle, Washington, 131 – 138.

Shen, X, Dumais, S. and Horvitz, E. (2005). Analysis of topic dynamics in web search, *Proceedings of the 14th international conference on World Wide Web,* 1102 - 1103.

Shen, X., Tan, B. and Zhai, C. (2005). Context sensitive information retrieval using implicit feedback. *SOGIR'05: Proceedings of the 28th ACM International Conference on Research and Development in Information Retrieval,* Salvador, Brazil, 43-50.

Shen, X., Tan, B., & Zhai, C. X. (2007). Privacy protection in personalized search. *SIGIR forum, 41(1),* 4-17.

Shneiderman, B., & Plaisant, C. (2005). *Designing the User Interface.* Addison-Wesley / Pearson Education.

Silverstein, C., Henzinger, M., & Marais, H. (1998). *Analysis of a Very Large AltaVista Query Log* (Digital SRC Technical Note 1998-014). Palo Alto, CA: Digital Systems Research Center.

Silverstein, C., Henzinger, M., Marais, H. and Moricz, M. (1999) Analysis of a Very Large Web Search Engine Query Log. *ACM SIGIR Forum,* 33(1), 6-12.

Silverstein, C., Henzinger, M., Marais, H., & Moricz, M. (1998). *Analysis of a Very Large AltaVista Query Log* (Technical Note No. SRC Technical Note 1998-014): Digital Equipment Corporationo. Document Number)

Silverstein, C., Henzinger, M., Marais, H., & Moricz, M. (1999). Analysis of a very large Web search engine query log. *SIGIR Forum, 33*(1), 6-12.

Simmel, Georg. (1983) [orig. 1911] *Sociologia.* São Paulo, Ática.

Sindhwani, S., & Keerthi, S. (2006) Large scale semi-supervised linear SVMs. In *Proceedings of the 29th annual international ACM SIGIR conference on Research and Development in Information Retrieval,* 477–484. ACM Press.

Skinner, B. F. (1953). *Science and Human Behavior.* New York: Free Press.

Slack, F. (1996). End-user searches and search path maps: a discussion. *Library Review 45(2).* 41-51.

Slack, F. E. (1991) *OPACs: Using enhanced transaction logs to achieve more effective online help for subject searching.* Unpublished doctoral dissertation, Council for National Academy Awards, United Kingdom.

Slattery, S., & Mitchell, T. (2000). Discovering Test Set Regularities in Relational Domains. In *Proceedings of the Seventeenth International Conference on Machine Learning,* 895–902. Morgan Kaufmann.

Slawson, D. C., & Shaughnessy, A. F. (2005). Teaching evidence-based medicine: should we be teaching information management instead? *Acad Med, 80*(7), 685-689.

Sloan, P. (2007). The quest for perfect online ad. *Business 2.0,* (February)

Smaglik, P., Hawkins, R. P., Pingree, S., Gustafson, D. H., Boberg, E., & Bricker, E. (1998). The quality of interactive computer use among HIV-infected individuals. *Journal of Health Communication,* 3, 53-68.

Small, S., & Strzalkowski, T. (2008). HITIQA: High-Quality Intelligence through Interactive Question Answering. *Journal of Natural Language Engineering: Special Issue on Interactive Question Answering* (forthcoming, 2008).

Small, S., Strzalkowski, T., Liu, T., Ryan, S., Salkin, R., Shimizu, N., Kantor, P., Kelly, D., Rittman, R., & Wacholder, N. (2004a). HITIQA: Towards Analytical Question Answering. In *Proceedings of The 20th International Conference on Computational Linguistics (Coling 2004),* Geneva, Switzerland.

Small, S., Strzalkowski, T., Liu, T., Shimizu, N., & Yamrom, B. (2004). A Data Driven Approach to Interactive QA. In M. Maybury (Ed.), *New Directions in Question Answering* (pp. 129-140). Cambridge, MA: MIT Press.

Smith, C. A., Stavri, P. Z., & Chapman, W. W. (2002). In their own words? A terminological analysis of e-mail to a cancer information service. *Proc AMIA Symp,* 697-701.

Smith, D. E. (2005). *Institutional ethnography: a sociology for people.* Walnut Creek, CA: AltaMira Press.

Smith, F. J. & Devine, K. Storing and Retrieving Word Phrases. *Information Processing & Management,* (21:3), 1985, pp. 215-224.

Smith, Greg. (2004) "Instantâneos 'sub specie aeternitatis:' Simmel, Goffman e a sociologia formal." In:

Gastaldo, É. (Ed.) *Erving Goffman, desbravador do cotidiano*. Porto Alegre: Tomo Editorial.

Smith, T., Ruocco, A., and Jansen, B. J. (1998). Digital video in education. *Proceedings of the thirteenth SIGCSE technical symposium on computer science education*. (pp. 122–126).

Sollaci, L. B. & Pereira, M. G. (2004). The introduction, methods, results, and discussion (IMRAD) structure: a fifty-year survey, *Journal of the Medical Library Association*, Vol. 92 (3), 364-371

Sood, S.C., Owsley, S., Hammond, K.J. and Birnbaum, L. , 2007, TagAssist: Automatic tag suggestion for blog posts. In *Proceedings of the International Conference on Weblogs and Social Media ICWSM 2007* (pp. 177-183), Omnipress.

Spink, A. (2004). Multitasking information behavior and information task switching: An exploratory study. *Journal of Documentation*, *60*(3), 336-345.

Spink, A. and Guner, O. (2001). E-commerce Web queries: Excite and Ask Jeeves study. *First Monday, 6(7).*

Spink, A. and Jansen, B. J. (2004). *Web Search: Public Searching of the Web*. Kluwer Academic Publishing.

Spink, A. and Ozmultu, H. C. (2002). Characteristics of Question Format Web Queries: An Exploratory Study. *Information Processing and Management*, 38, 453-471.

Spink, A. and Ozmultu, H.C. (2002). Characteristics of question format Web queries: an exploratory study. *Information Processing and Management. 38(4)*, 453-71.

Spink, A. and Ozmutlu, H. C. (2001). What do people ask on the Web and how do they ask it: Ask Jeeves Study. *Proceedings of ASIST 2001: Annual Meeting of the American Society for Information Science and Technology*, Washington, DC. Nov. 2001.

Spink, A., & Jansen, B. (2004). *Web Search: Public Searching of the Web, volume 6 of The Information Science and Knowledge Management Series*. Dordrecht, The Netherlands: Kluwer Academic Publishers.

Spink, A., & Jansen, B. J. (2004). *Web search, public searching of the web*. New York: Kluwer.

Spink, A., & Saracevic, T. (1997). Interaction in information retrieval: Selection and effectiveness of search terms. *Journal of the American Society for Information Science*, *48*(8), 741-761.

Spink, A., and Guner, O. (2001). E-commerce Web queries: Excite and Ask Jeeves study. *First Monday. 6(7).*

Spink, A., and Jansen, B. J. (2004). *Web Search: Public Searching of the Web*. Kluwer Academic Publishing.

Spink, A., and Ozmultu, H.C. (2002). Characteristics of question format Web queries: an exploratory study. *Information Processing and Management. 38(4)*, 453-471.

Spink, A., and Ozmutlu, H. C. (2001). What do people ask on the Web and how do they ask it: Ask Jeeves Study. *Proceedings of ASIST 2001: Annual Meeting of the American Society for Information Science and Technology*, Washington, DC.

Spink, A., Bateman, J., & Jansen, B. J. (1999). Searching the Web: A survey of excite users. *Journal of Internet Research: Electronic Networking Applications and Policy, 9*(2), 117-128.

Spink, A., Jansen, B. J., Wolfram, D. and Saracevic, T. (2002). From e-sex to e-commerce: Web search changes. *IEEE Computer, 35*, 133-135.

Spink, A., Jansen, B. J., Wolfram, D., & Saracevic, T. (2002). From E-sex to E-commerce: Web search changes. *IEEE Computer*, *35*(3), 107-111.

Spink, A., Koricich, A., Jansen, B. J. and Cole, C. (2004). Sexual searching on Web search engines. *Cyberpsychology and Behavior, 7(1)*, 65-72.

Spink, A., Ozmutlu, H. C. and Lorence, D. P. (2004). Web searching for sexual information: An exploratory study. *Information Processing and Management, 40(1)*, 113-124.

Spink, A., Ozmutlu, H. C. and Ozmutlu, S. (2002). Multitasking information seeking and searching processes. *Journal of the American Society for Information Science and Technology, 53(8)*, 639-652.

Spink, A., Ozmutlu, H. C., and Lorence, D. P. (2004). Web searching for sexual information: An exploratory study. *Information Processing and Management. 40(1)*, 113-124.

Spink, A., Park, M. Jansen, B.J. and Pedersen, J. (2002). Multitasking on AltaVista. *Proceedings of the IEEE ITCC 2004: International Conference on Coding and Computing*, Las Vegas, NV, 309.

Spink, A., Park, M., and Jansen, B. J. (2006). Multitasking during Web search sessions. *Information Processing and Management. 42(1)*, 264-275.

Spink, A., Wilson, T., Ellis, D., & Ford, F. (1998). Modeling Users' Successive Searches in Digital Environments study [Electronic Version]. *D-Lib Magazine.* Retrieved October 20, 2007, from http://www.dlib.org/dlib/april98/04spink.html

Spink, A., Wilson, T., Ellis, D., & Ford, F. (1998, April 1998). Modeling users' successive searches in digital environments. *D-Lib Magazine.*

Spink, A., Wolfram, D., Jansen, B. J., & Saracevic, T. (2001). The public and their queries. *Journal of the American Society for Information Science and Technology*, 52(3), 226–234.

Spink, A., Wolfram, D., Jansen, M. B. J., & Saracevic, T. (2001). Searching the Web: the Public and their Queries. *Journal of the American Society for Information Science and Technology, 52*(3), 226-234.

Spink, A., Yang, Y., Nykanen, P., Lorence, D. P., Jansen, B. J., Ozmutlu, S., and Ozmutlu, H. C. (2004). A study of medical and health queries to a Web search engine. *Health Information and Libraries Journal, 21(1)*, 44-51

Sponder, M. (2006). *ComScore working on web 2.0 metrics.* Retrieved 4/20/2007, from http://www.web-metricsguru.com/2006/12/comscore_working_on_web_20_met.html

Spors, K. (2007, May 13). For the web, choose your words carefully. [Electronic version]. *Wall Street Journal,*

Spradley, J. P. (1980). *Participant Observation.* London, UK: Wadsworth Publishing.

Sproull, L. S. (1986). Using electronic mail for data collection in organizational research. *Academy of Management Journal, 29*(1), 159-169.

Srivastava, J., Cooley, R., Deshpande, M., & Tan, P.N. (2000). Web usage mining: Discovery and applications of usage patterns from web data. *ACM SIGKDD Explorations, 1*(2), 12-23.

Stabell, C. B. (1974). *Individual differences in managerial decision making processes: A study of conversational computer system usage.* Unpublished doctoral dissertation, Massachusetts Institute of Technology.

Stemler, S. (2001). An overview of content analysis. *Practical Assessment, Research & Evaluation*, 7(17), Retrieved March 15, 2008 from http://pareonline.net/getvn.asp?v=7&n=17

Stenmark, D. (2005). One Week with a Corporate Search Engine: A Time-Based Analysis of Intranet Information Seeking. In *Proceedings of the Eleventh Americas Conference on Information Systems*, Omaha, Nebraska.

Stenmark, D., & Jadaan, T. (2006). Intranet Users' Information-Seeking Behaviour: A Longitudinal Study of Search Engine Logs. In *Proceedings of the Annual Meeting of the American Society for Information Science and Technology*, Austin, TX.

Sterne, J. *10 Steps to Measuring Website Success.* Retrieved March 7, 2007, from http://www.marketingprofs.com/login/join.asp?adref=rdblk&source=/4/sterne13.asp

Stolcke, A., Ries, K., Coccaro, N., Shriberg, E., Bates, R., Jurafsky, D., Taylor, P., Martin, R., Ess-Dykema, C. V., & Meteer, M. (2000). Dialogue Act Modeling for Automatic Tagging and Recognition of Conversational Speech. In *Computational Linguistics* 26(3), 339-373.

Strasberg, H. R., Hubbs, P. R., Rindfleisch, T. C., & Melmon, K. L. (1999). Analysis of information needs of users of the Stanford Health Information Network for Education. *Proc AMIA Symp*, 965-969.

Strauss, A. L., & Corbin, J. (1990). *Basics of Qualitative Research: Grounded Theory Procedures and Techniques.* Newbury Park, CA: Sage Publications.

Strijbos, J-W., Martens, R. L. Prins, F.J. & Jochems, W. M. G. (2006), Content analysis: What are they talking about? *Computers & Education*, Vol. 46 (1), 29-48.

Stumme, G., Berendt, B., & Hotho, A. (2002). *Usage Mining for and on the Semantic Web. Next Generation Data Mining.* Proc. NSF Workshop, Baltimore, Nov. 2002, 77-86.

Stutzman, F. (2006). An evaluation of identity-sharing behavior in social network communities. *iDMAa Journal*, 3(1).

Stutzman, F. (2006). Situational relevance in social networking Websites. Retrieved January 12, 2006, from http://chimprawk.blogspot.com/2006/01/situational-relevance-in-social.html

Stutzman, F. (2006). Student life on Facebook. (Ph.D. working paper, University of North Carolina, 2006).

Sudman, S., Bradburn, N. M., & Schwarz, N. (1996). *Thinking about answers: The application of cognitive processes to survey methodology.* San Francisco: Jossey-Bass Publishers.

Sugiyama, K. & Yoshikawa, K. H. (2004). *Adaptive Web Search Based on User Profile Constructed without Any Effort from Users* WWW2004, May 17–22, 2004, New York, New York, USA. ACM 1-58113-844-X/04/0005.

Sullivan, D. (2001, November 6). *Spiderspotting: When a search engine, robot or crawler visits.* Retrieved 5 August, 2003, from http://www.searchenginewatch.com/webmasters/article.php/2168001

Sun, T. (1971). *The Art of War* (S. B. Griffith Trans.). New York: Oxford University Press. (Original work published n.d.)

Swan, R. and Jensen, D. (2000). TimeMines: Constructing timelines with statistical models of word usage. *Proceedings of the 6th ACM SIGKDD International Conference on Knowledge Discovery and Data Mining*, Boston, MA, 73-80.

Sweiger, M. (2002). *Clickstream data warehousing.* New York: Wiley.

Szummer, M., & Jaakkola T. (2000). Kernel expansions With Unlabeled Examples. In *Advances in Neural Information Processing Systems* 13, 626–632. MIT Press.

Taha, A. (2004). Wired Research: Transaction Log Analysis of E-journal databases to assess the research activities and trends in UAE university. *Paper presented at the Nordic Conference on Information and Documentation*, Aalborg, Denmark.

Taksa, I. (2005). Predicting the Cumulative Effect of Multiple Query Formulations, In *Proceedings of the IEEE International Conference on Information Technology: Coding and Computing,* Volume II, April 2005, 491–496.

Tang, J. C., Liu, S. B., Muller, M., Lin, J., & Drews, C. (2006). Unobtrusive but invasive: using screen recording to collect field data on computer-mediated interaction. In *20th anniversary conference on Computer supported cooperative work* (pp. 479-482). Banff, Alberta: ACM.

Tauscher, L., & Greenberg, S. (1997). How People Revisit Web Pages: Empirical Findings and Implications for the Design of History Systems. *International Journal of Human-Computer Studies, 47*(1), 97-137.

Tax, D. M. J. and Duin, R. P. W. (2001).Uniform object generation for optimizing one-class classifiers. *Journal of Machine Learning Research, 2*, 155–173.

Teevan, J., Alvarado, C., Ackerman, M., & Karger, D. (2004). The Perfect Search Engine is Not Enough: A Study of Orienteering Behavior in Directed Search. In *SIGCHI Conference on Human Factors in Computing Systems* (pp. 415-422). Vienna, Austria: ACM.

Teevan, J., Dumais, S. T., & Horvitz, E. (2005). Personalizing Search via Automated Analysis of Interests and Activities. In *Proceedings of the 28 Annual International ACM SIGIR Conference on Research and Development in Information Retrieval*, Salvador, Brazil (pp. 449 456).

Teltzrow, M., & Kobsa, A. (2004). Impacts of user preferences on personalized systems: a comparative study. In *Designing personalized user experiences in eCommerce* (pp. 315-332). Norwell, MA, USA: Kluwer Academic Publishers.

Thomas, I. (2007, January 9). *The rumors are true: Microsoft 'Gatineau' exists*. Retrieved March 7, 2007, from http://www.liesdamnedlies.com/2007/01/the_rumors_are_.html

Thury, E. M. (1998). Analysis of student Web browsing behavior: implications for designing and evaluating Web sites. In *16th Annual International Conference on Computer Documentation* (pp. 265-270). Quebec City, Canada: ACM.

Tidwell, J. (2006). *Designing interfaces*. O'Reilly.

Tillotson, J., Cherry, J., and Clinton, M. (1995). Internet use through the University of Toronto Library: Demographics, Destinations and Users' Reactions. *Information Technology and Libraries*. *14*, 190-198

Tolle, J. E. (1983). *Current utilization of online catalogs: transaction analysis* (Final report to the Council on Library Resources, Vol. 1). Dublin, OH.: OCLC

Tolle, J. E. (1983). Transaction log analysis online catalogs. In *Proceedings of the 6th annual international ACM SIGIR conference on research and development in information retrieval* (pp. 147-160). New York: ACM Press.

Tolle, J. E. (1984). Monitoring and evaluation of information systems via transaction log analysis. In *Proceedings of the 7th annual international ACM SIGIR conference on research and development in information retrieval* (pp. 247-258). Swinton, U.K.: British Computer Society.

Tolle, J. E. (1985a). Performance measurement and evaluation of online information systems. In *proceedings of the 1985 ACM thirteenth annual conference on computer science* (pp. 196-203). New York: ACM Press.

Tolle, J. E. (1985b). Online search patterns: NLM CATLINE database. *Journal of the American Society for Information Science, 36(2)*, 82-93.

Toms, E. & Trifts, V. (2006). When limited cognitive resources meet unlimited information sources: Factors influencing consumers' allocation of web-based search effort. *Proceedings of the 7th World Congress on the Management of eBusiness*, July, Halifax, Canada.

Toms, E.G., Freund, L., & Li, C. (2004). Wiire: The Web interactive information retrieval experimentation system prototype. *Information Processing & Management*, 40(4), 655-675.

Tooth, L., Ware, R., Bain, C., Purdie, D. M. & Dobson, A. (2005). Quality of reporting of observational longitudinal research. *American Journal of Epidemiology*, Vol. 161 *(3), 280-288.*

Trætteberg, H. (2003). Dialog modelling with interactors and UML Statecharts - A hybrid approach. In *10th International Workshop on Design, Specification and Verification of Interactive Systems*, Madeira.

Traum, D. R., Robinson, S., & Stephan, J. (2004). Evaluation of Multi-Party Virtual Reality Dialogue Interaction. In *Proceedings of Fourth International Conference on Language Resources and Evaluation (LREC)* (pp. 1699-1702).

Treiblmaier, H. (2007). Web site analysis: A review and assessment of previous research. *Communications of the Association for Information Systems, 19*, 806-843.

Treu, S. (1971). A conceptual framework for the searcher-system interface. In Walker, D. E. (Ed.), *Interactive bibliographic search: the user/computer interface* (pp. 53-66). Montvale, N.J.:AFIPS Press.

Treu, S. (1973) Techniques and tools for improving the interactive system interface. In *Interactive bibliographic systems: Proceedings of a forum held at Gaithersburg, Md. October 4-5, 1971* (pp.32-38). Oak ridge, TN: United States Atomic Energy Commission, Office of Information Services.

Tsai-Youn, H. (2006). *Search strategies for image retrieval in the field of journalism*. Unpublished doctoral dissertation, Rutgers The State University of New Jersey.

Tse, A. C. B., Tse, K. C., Yin, C. H., Ting, C. B., Yi, K. W., Yee, K. P., et al. (1995). Comparing two methods of sending out questionnaires: E-mail vs. Mail. . *Journal of the Market Research Society, 37*(4), 441-446.

Turkle, Sherry. (1995) *Life on the Screen: Identity in the Age of the Internet.* New York: Simon & Schuster.

Turnbull, D. (1998). *WebTracker: A Tool for Understanding Web Use.* Online at: http://www.ischool.utexas.edu/~donturn/research/webtracker/. Retrieved October 5, 2006.

Turner, Roy. (1974) *Ethnomethodology.* Canada: Penguin Books.

Tuten, T.L. & Bosnjak. M. (2001). Understanding differences in web usage: The role of need for cognition and the five-factor model of personality. *Social Behavior and Personality, 29*(4), 391-398.

Tylor, Edward B. (1924) [orig. 1871] *Primitive Culture.* New York: Brentano's.

U.S. National Library of Medicine. (2005, May 27). *MeSH Fact Sheet.* Retrieved March 30, 2007, from http://www.nlm.nih.gov/mesh/intro_preface2007.html#pref_hist

U.S. National Library of Medicine. (2006, May 27). *Citation Maintenance Tasks in XML format.* Retrieved April 5, 2007, from http://www.nlm.nih.gov/mesh/gcmdoc2007.html

U.S. National Library of Medicine. (2006, November 27). *MeSH history.* Retrieved March 30, 2007, from http://www.nlm.nih.gov/mesh/intro_preface2007.html#pref_hist

Unicode Consortium. (2006). *The Unicode Standard.* Retrieved september, 20, 2007, from http://www.unicode.org.

Vakkari, P. (1999). Task complexity, problem structure and information actions: Integrating studies on information seeking and retrieval. *Information Processing and Management, 35*(6), 819-837.

Vakkari, P. (2001). Changes in search tactics and relevance judgments when preparing a research proposal: a summary and generalization of a longitudinal study. *Journal of Documentation, 57*(1), 44-60.

Valente, T. (1995). *Network Models of the Diffusion of Innovation.* Cresskill, NJ: Hampton Press.

Vapnik, V. (1995), *The nature of statistical learning theory.* New York: Springer-Verlag.

Vasconcelos, A. C. (2007). The role of professional discourses in the organizational adaptation of information systems, *International Journal of Information Management,* Vol. 27 (4), 279-293.

Verbeek, P. P. & Slob, A. (2006), *User Behavior and Technology Development – Shaping Sustainable Relations between Consumers and Technologies,* Dordrecht: Springer.

Vieira, T., P. (2005). *SSDM : a semantically similar data mining algorithm.* XX Simpósio Brasileiro de Banco de Dados - 2005 - Uberlândia, MG, Brasil.

Vogel, D., Bickel, S., Haider, P., Schimpfky, R., Siemen, P., Bridges, S. and Scheffer, T. (2005). Classifying search engine queries using the web as background knowledge. *ACM SIGKDD Explorations Newsletter,* 7(2), 117-122.

Voorhees, E. (1999). The TREC-8 Question Answering Track Report. In *Proceedings of the Eighth Text Retrieval Conference (TREC-8),* pages 77-82, NIST Special Publication 500-246.

Voorhees, E. M., & Harman (2005). *TREC – Experiment and Evaluation in Information Retrieval.* MIT Press.

Vrana, R. (2002). *Digital Libraries - Creating Information Space Excellence: Is It Already Time for Benchmarking?* Paper presented at the 2002 CARNet Users Conference.

W3C. (1999). *Web Characterization Terminology & Definitions Sheet.* Online at: http://www.w3.org/1999/05/WCA-terms/01. Retrieved June 1, 2005.

Wacholder, N., Kelly, D., Rittman, R., Sun, Y., Kantor, P., Small, S., & Strzalkowski, T. (Forthcoming, 2007). A Model for Realistic Evaluation of an End-to-End Question Answering System. *Journal of the American Society for Information Science and Technology.*

Wacholder, N., Small, S., Bai, B., Kelly, D., Rittman, R., Ryan, S., Salkin, R., Song, P., Sun, Y., Ting, L., Kantor, P., & Strzalkowski, T. (2004). Designing a Realistic Evaluation of an End-to-End Interactive Question Answering System. In *Proceedings of the Fourth International Conference on Language Resources and Evaluation (LREC '04).*

Wagner, F. (2006). *Modeling software with finite state machines: A practical approach.* Auerbach Publications.

Waite, K., & Harrison, T. (2002). Consumer expectations of online information provided by bank websites. *Journal of Financial Services Marketing* 6(4), 309-322.

Walji, M., Sagaram, S., Sagaram, D., Meric-Bernstam, F., Johnson, C., Mirza, N. Q., et al. (2004). Efficacy of quality criteria to identify potentially harmful information: a cross-sectional survey of complementary and alternative medicine web sites. *J Med Internet Res, 6*(2), e21.

Walker, D. E. (Ed.). (1971). *Interactive bibliographic search: the user/computer interface.* Montvale, N.J.: AFIPS Press.

Walker, M., Kamm, C., & Litman, D. (2000). Towards Developing General Models of Usability with PARADISE. *Natural Language Engineering*, 6(3), 363-377.

Wallace, P. (1999). *The psychology of the Internet.* Cambridge: Cambridge University Press, 14-37.

Wallace, P. M. (1993). How do patrons search the online catalog when no one's looking? Transaction log analysis and implications for BI and system design. *RQ 30(Winter),* 239-252.

Wallach, H.M. (2004). *Conditional random fields: An Introduction.* Technical Report MS-CIS-04-21. Department of Computer and Information Science, University of Pennsylvania.

Walpole, R. E., Myers, R. H., and Myers, S. L. (1998). *Probability and Statistics for Engineers and Scientists.* Upper Saddle River, NJ: Prentice Hall.

Wang, P. L., Hawk, W. B. & Tenopir, C. (2000). Users' interaction with the World Wide Web resources: an exploratory study using a holistic approach. *Information Processing and Management, 36(2),* 229-251.

Wang, P. L., Tenopir, C., Layman, E., Penniman, W. D., & Collins, S. (1998). An exploratory study of user searching of the World Wide Web: A holistic approach. In *Proceedings of the Annual Meeting of the American Society for Information Science* (pp. 389-399). Medford, N.J.: Information Today, Inc.

Wang, P., Berry, M. W., and Yang, Y. Mining Longitudinal Web Queries: Trends and Patterns. *Journal of the American Society for Information Science and Technology*, (54:8), 2003, pp.743-758.

Wang, P., Berry, M., & Yang, Y. (2003). Mining longitudinal Web queries: Trends and patterns. *Journal of the American Society for Information Science and Technology, 54*(8), 743-758.

Wang, P., Hawk, W.B. & Tenopir, C. (2000). Users' interaction with world wide web resources: An exploratory study using a holistic approach. *Information Processing and Management, 36*, 229-251.

Wang, X., Mohanty, N. and McCallum, A. (2005). Group and topic discovery from relations and text. *LinkKDD-05: Proceedings of the 11th ACM SIGKDD International Conference on Knowledge Discovery and Data Mining Workshop on Link Discovery: Issues, Approaches and Applications,* Chicago, IL, 28-35.

Ward, S., Bridges, K., & Chitty, B. (2005). Do incentives matter? An examination of On-line privacy concerns and willingness to provide personal and financial information, *Journal of Marketing Communications*, Vol. 11 (1), 21-40.

Wasserman, S., & Faust, K. (1994). *Social Network Analysis: Methods and Applications.* Cambridge, UK: Cambridge University Press.

Watson, J. B. (1913). Psychology as the behaviorist views it. *Psychological Review, 20*, 158-177.

Web Analytics Association. (2006). Retrieved 09/14/2007, http://www.webanalyticsassociation.org/attachments/committees/5/WAA-Standards-Analytics-Definitions-Big-3-20061206.pdf.

Web Analytics Association. *Onsite Behavior - Path Analysis.* Retrieved March 7, 2007, from http://www.Webanalyticsassociation.org/attachments/contentmanagers/336/1%20Path%20AnAnalys.doc

Webb, E. J., Campbell, D. T., Schwartz, R. D. D., Sechrest, L., & Grove, J. B. (1981). *Nonreactive Measures in the Social Sciences* (2nd ed.). Boston, MA: Houghton Mifflin.

Webb, E. J., Campbell, D. T., Schwarz, R. D., & Sechrest, L. (2000). *Unobtrusive Measures (Revised Edition).* Thousand Oaks, California: Sage.

Webb, N. (Ed.) (2006). *HLT-NAACL Workshop on Interactive Question Answering.* East Stroudsburg, PA: Association for Computational Linguistics.

Webb, N., & Webber, B., editors (Forthcoming, 2008). *Special Issue of the Journal of Natural Language Engineering on Interactive Question Answering.*

Webb, N., Hepple, M., & Wilks, Y. (2005). Dialogue Act Classification Based on Intra- Utterance Features. In *Proceedings of the AAAI Workshop on Spoken Language Understanding.*

WebSideStory. (2004). *Use of Key Performance Indicators in Web Analytics.* Retrieved December 2, 2007, from www.4everywhere.com/documents/KPI.pdf

WebSideStory. (2007). Web Site Analytics: On Demand Web Analytics for Optimizing Online Business Performance. http://www.websidestory.com/products/web-analytics/hbx-analytics/overview.html: [April 18, 2007].

WebTrends. (2001). WebTrends eBusiness Intelligence Solution Named "Best of 2000" By PC Magazine. [April 4, 2007].

WebTrends. (2005). *Best practices for accurate web analytics: Avoiding third-party cookie rejection and deletion.* Portland, OR: WebTrends

Weinreich, H., Obendorf, H., Herder, E., & Mayer, M. (2006). Off the Beaten tracks: Exploring Three Aspects of Web Navigation. In *15th International Conference on World Wide Web* (pp. 133-142). Edinburgh, Scotland: ACM.

Weir, C., Anderson, J., & Jack, M. (2006). On The Role Of Metaphor And Language In Design of Third Party Payments in eBanking: Usability and Quality. *International Journal of Human-Computer Studies, 64*, 770-787.

Weischedel., B., Matear, S., & Deans, K. (2005). The use of e-metrics in strategic marketing decisions: A preliminary investigation. *International Journal of Internet Marketing and Advertising, 2*(1/2), 109-125.

Weiss, G. & Weiss. R. (2003). Critical Discourse Analysis. Theory and Interdisciplinarity, New York: Palgrave.

Wellman, B. (2001). Computer networks as social networks. *Science, 293*(14), 2031-2034.

Wellman, B., & Gulia, M. (1999). Net surfers don't ride alone: Virtual communities as communities. In P. Kollock & M. A. Smith (Eds.), *Communities in cyberspace* (167-194). New York: Routledge.

Wellman, B., & Hampton, K. (1999). Living networked on and offline. *Contemporary Sociology, 28*(6), 648-654.

Wen, J-R., Nie, J-Y. & Zhang, H-J. (2002). Query clustering using user logs. *ACM, Transactions on Information Systems*, 20(1), 59–81.

Westbrook, J.I., Braithwaite, J., Iedema, R.A., & Coiera, E.W. (2004). Evaluating the impact of information communication technologies on complex organizational systems: a multi-disciplinary, multi-method framework, *Proceedings of the 11th World Congress on Medical Informatics*, Fieschi M, Coiera E & Yu-Chan J, (Eds.), IOS, Washington, USA, 1323 -1327.

Westin, A. F. (2003). Social and Political Dimensions of Privacy. *Journal of Social Issues, 59*(2), 431-453.

Whalen, T., & Inkpen, K. M. (2005). *Gathering evidence: use of visual security cues in web browsers.* In *Graphic Interface* (pp. 137-145). Victoria, British Columbia: Canadian Human-Computer Communications Society.

White, K. (2006, May 10). *Unique vs. Returning Visitors Analyzed.* Retrieved March 7, 2007, from http://newsletter.blizzardinternet.com/unique-vs-returning-visitors-analyzed/2006/05/10/#more-532

White, R. W., Clarke, C. L. A., & Cucerzan, S. (2007). Comparing Query Logs and Pseudo-Relevance Feedback for Web-Search Query Refinement. In *Proceedings of the 30th Annual International ACM SIGIR Conference on Research and Development in Information Retrieval (SIGIR'07)* (pp. 831-832).

White, R. W., Ruthven, I., & Jose, M. J. (2001, November). *Comparing implicit and explicit feedback techniques for Web retrieval: TREC-10 interactive track report.* Paper presented at the Tenth Text Retrieval Conference (TREC-10), Gaithersburg, MD.

Wiggins, A. (2007). *Data Driven Design: Using Web Analytics To Improve Information Architecture.* Paper presented at the American Society for Information Science and Technology. Las Vegas Nevada. Retrieved.

Wildemuth, B. & Hughes, A. (2005). Perspectives on the tasks in which information behaviors are embedded. In Fisher, K.E., Erdelez, S. & McKechnie, L. (Eds.), *Theories of information behavior.* Medford, NJ: Information Today, for the American Society for Information Science & Technology, 275-279.

Wildemuth, B., Barry, C., Luo, L., Crystal, A., & Oh, S. (2004). *Establishing a Research Agenda for Studies of Online Search Behaviors: A Delphi Study.* Online at: http://ils.unc.edu/sig_use_delphi/. Retrieved April 18, 2005.

Williams, E. (2006). Retrieved 06/12/2007, from www.evhead.com/2006/08/pageviews-are-obsolete.asp

Wilson, T. D. (1999). Models in information behaviour research. *Journal of Documentation, 55*(3), 249-270.

Wilson, T.D., & Walsh, C. (1996), *Information behavior: An interdisciplinary perspective.* Sheffield: University of Sheffield Department of Information Studies.

Winckler, M., & Palanque, P. (2003). StateWebCharts: a formal description technique dedicated to navigation modelling of Web applications. In *10th International Workshop on Design, Specification and Verification of Interactive Systems*, Madeira.

Winett, B. (1998). *Tracking your visitors.* Retrieved May 10, 2007, from WebMonkey Tracking Tutorial, http://www.webmonkey.com/e-business/tracking/tutorials/tutorial2.html.

Winkin, Yves. (1998) *A Nova Comunicação – da teoria ao trabalho de campo.* Campinas, Papirus.

Wobus, J. (1998). *DHCP FAQ.* [Online] Available: http://www.dhcp-handbook.com/dhcp_faq.html [15 February 2004].

Wolff, R.W. (1982). Poisson arrivals see time averages. *Operations Research, 30 (2)*, 223-231.

Wolfram, D. (1999). Term co-occurrence in internet search engine queries: An analysis of the Excite data set. *Canadian Journal of Information and Library Science, 24*(2/3), 12-33.

Wolfram, D., Spink, A., Jansen, B. J., and Saracevic. T. (2001). Vox Populi: The Public Searching of the Web. *Journal of the American Society for Information Science and Technology. 52(12),* 1073 – 1074

Woon Y., et al. (2005). *Web Usage mining: algorithms and results.* 2005 In Web Mining: Applications and Techniques. Anthony Scime (ed.), Idea Group Publishing, p.373-394.

World Wide Web Consortium. (2007). A Little History of the World Wide Web. http://www.w3.org/History.html: [February 19, 2007].

Wu, H. (2002). *A reference architecture for adaptive hypermedia applications.* Eindhoven: Technische Universiteit Eindhoven, 2002. ISBN 90-386-0572-2.

Wu, K.-l., Yu, P. S., & Ballman, A. (1998). Speedtracer: A web usage mining and analysis tool. *IBM Systems Journal, 37*(1), 89-105.

Wu, X., & Srihari, R. K. (2004). Incorporating prior knowledge with weighted margin support vector machines. In *Proceedings of KDD*, 326–333. ACM Press.

Wyly, B. J. (1996). From access point to materials: a transaction log analysis of access point value for online catalog users. *Library Resources & Technical Services, 40(July),* 211-236.

Xie, H. (2000). Shifts of interactive intentions and information-seeking strategies in interactive information retrieval. *Journal of the American Society for Information Science, 51*(9), 841-857.

Yang, Y. and Liu, X. (1999). A re-examination of text categorization methods. *SIGIR'99: Proceedings of the 22nd ACM International Conference on Research and Development in Information Retrieval,* Berkeley, CA, 42-49.

Yee, M. (1991). System design and cataloging meet the user: User interfaces to online public access catalogs. *Journal of the American Society for Information Science, 42*(2), 78-98.

Yin, R. K. (2000). Rival explanations as an alternative to reforms as "experiments". In Bickman, L., ed. *Validity and Social Experimentation. Donald Campbell's Legacy*, vol. 1. Thousand Oaks, CA/London/New Delhi: Sage, 239-266.

Young, D. (2007, August 15). Site Search: Increases Conversion Rates, Average Order Value And Loyalty. *Practical Ecommerce*, Retrieved November 15, 2007, from http://www.practicalecommerce.com/articles/541/Site-Search-Increases-Conversion-Rates-Average-Order-Value-And-Loyalty/

Yu, H., Zhai, C. and Ha, J., (2003). Text classification from positive and unlabeled documents. *CIKM'03: Proceedings of the 2003 ACM CIKM International Conference on Information and Knowledge Management,* New Orleans, LA, 232-239.

Yu, H.-F., Chen, Y.-M., & Tseng, L.-M. (2004). Archive knowledge discovery by proxy cache. *Internet Research*, 14(1), 34-47.

Yuan, W., & Meadow, C.T. (1999). A study of the use of variables in information retrieval user studies. *Journal of the American Society for Information Science,* 50(2), 140-150.

Yun, G. W. (2007). Interactivity concepts examined: Response time, hypertext, role taking, and multimodality. *Media Psychology, 9*(5), 527-548

Yun, G. W., Ford, J., Hawkins, R. P., Pingree, S., & McTavish, F. (2006). On the validity of client-side vs server-side web log data analysis. *Internet Research, 16*(5), 537-552.

Yun, G. W., Ford, J., Hawkins, R. P., Pingree, S., McTavish, F., Gustafson, D., & Berhe, H. (2006). On the validity of client-side vs. server-side Web log data analysis. *Internet Research*, 16(5), 537-552.

Zaiane, O. R. (2000). *Web Mining: Concepts, Practices and Research.* In: SIMPÓSIO BRASILEIRO DE BANCO DE DADOS, SBBD, 15., 2000, João Pessoa. Tutorial... João Pessoa: CEFET-PB; Porto Alegre: PUCRS, 2000. p. 410-474.

Zaiane, O. R., Xin, M., & Han, J. (1998). Discovering web access patterns and trends by applying olap and data mining technology on web logs. *Proceedings of the IEEE Forum on Reasearch and Technology Advances in Digital Libraries*, Santa Barbara, CA.

Zaki, M. (2001). *SPADE: An eficient algorithm for mining frequent sequences.* Machine Learning, 42, 31-60, 2001, Kluver Academic Publishers. 2001.

Zawodny, J. (2006). *Hit counter 2.0, or web 2.0 metrics.* Retrieved 02/16/2007, from http://jeremy.zawodny.com/blog/archives/007665.html.

Zelikovitz, S. & Kogan, M. (2006). Using Web Searches on Important Words to Create Background Sets for LSI Classification. In *Proceedings of the Nineteenth International FLAIRS Conference*, 598–603. AAAI Press.

Zelikovitz, S., Cohen, W. W., & Hirsh H. (2007). Extending WHIRL with Background Knowledge for Improved Text Classification. *Information Retrieval, 10*(1), 35–67.

Zeller Jr., T. (2006). Privacy vs. viewing the internet user as a commodity. *The New York Times*, August 12, 1.

Zeller Jr., T. (2006). AOL acts on release of data. *The New York Times*, August 22, 1.

Zeng, Q., Kogan, S., Ash, N., Greenes, R. A., & Boxwala, A. A. (2002). Characteristics of consumer terminology for health information retrieval. *Methods Inf Med, 41*(4), 289-298.

Zhai, C., Velivelli, A. and Yu, B. (2004). A cross-collection mixture model for comparative text mining. *Proceedings of the 10th ACM SIGKDD International Conference on Knowledge Discovery and Data Mining*, Seattle, WA, 743-748.

Zhang, D., Zambrowicz, C., Zhou, H., & Roderer, N. (2004). User Information Seeking Behavior in a Medical Web Portal Environment: A Preliminary Study. *Journal of the American Society for Information Science and Technology, 55*(8), 670-684.

Zhang, J., Shen, D., Zu, G., Jian, S., and Tan, C.L., 2004, Enhancing HMM-based biomedical named entity recognition by studying special phenomena, *Journal of Biomedical Informatics*, 37, 411-422.

Zhong, N. & Li, Y. (2006). *Mining Ontology for Automatically Acquiring Web User Information Needs*. IEEE Trans. Knowl. Data Eng. 18(4): 554-568.

Zhou, Y. & Mobasher, B. (2006). *Web User Segmentation Based on a Mixture of Factor Analyzers.* Proceedings ECWeb'06. Krakow, Poland, September 2006.

Zhu, T., Greiner, R. & Haeubl, G. (2003). Learning a model of a web user's interests. *Proceedings of the 9th International Conference on User Modeling, Lecture Notes in Computer Science,* 2702, 65–75, Springer.

Zhu, X. (2006). *Semi-Supervised Learning Literature Survey.* Available at http://pages.cs.wisc.edu/~jerryzhu/pub/ssl_survey.pdf

Zimmermann, A. et al. (2005). *Personalization and Context Management.* User Modeling and User-Adapted Interaction (2005) 15:275–302 Springer.

Zipf, G. K. (1949). *Human behavior and the principle of least effort.* Cambridge, MA: Addison-Wesley Press.

Zue, V., Glass, J., Goodine, D., Leung, H., Phillips, M., Polifroni, J., & Seneff, S. (1990). The VOYAGER Speech Understanding System: Preliminary Development and Evaluation. In *Proceedings of IEEE International Conference on Acoustics, Speech and Signal Processing* (pp. 73-76).

About the Contributors

Bernard J. Jansen is an assistant professor in the College of Information Sciences and Technology at The Pennsylvania State University. Jim has more than 150 publications in information technology and systems across a multi-disciplinary range of journals and conferences. His areas of expertise are Web searching, sponsored search, and personalization for information searching. He is co-author of the book, Web Search: Public Searching of the Web. Jim is a member of the editorial boards of six international journals. He has received awards and honors, including an ACM Research Award and six application development awards, along with other writing, publishing, research, and leadership honors. Several agencies and corporations have supported his research. He teaches both undergraduate and graduate courses, as well as mentoring students in various research and educational efforts. He also has successfully conducted numerous consulting projects.

Isak Taksa is an associate professor in the Department of Computer Information Systems at Baruch College of the City University of New York (CUNY). His primary research interests include information retrieval, knowledge discovery and text and data mining. He has published extensively on theoretical and applied aspects of information retrieval and search engine technology in journals including Information Retrieval, Journal of the American Society for Information Science.

Amanda Spink is professor in the Faculty of Information Technology at the Queensland University of Technology and co-leader of the Information Science Cluster. Her primary research includes: basic, applied, industry and interdisciplinary studies in information science, information behavior, cognitive information retrieval; Web retrieval, including relevance, feedback and multitasking models. Professor Amanda Spink has published over 300 journal articles, refereed conference papers and book chapters, and 5 books. She is a member of numerous journal editorial boards including: Information Processing and Management, Journal of Documentation, Journal of Information Systems Education and Webology.

* * *

Goknur Kaplan Akilli is a PhD student in the professor in the Instructional Systems Program at the Pennsylvania State University.

Elmer Bernstam is an associate professor of health informatics and internal medicine at the University of Texas Health Science Center at Houston. Dr. Bernstam heads the clinical informatics focus at the School of Health Information Sciences. His research currently focuses on information retrieval, consumer informatics and informatics in translational research. In addition to his MD, Dr. Bernstam holds Master's degrees in computer engineering and biomedical informatics. He completed a National Library of Medicine post-doctoral fellowship in informatics at Stanford Medical Informatics. Dr. Bernstam is board-certified in internal medicine and maintains an active clinical practice. He is a fellow of the American College of Physicians.

Danielle Booth is a graduate of The Pennsylvania State University with a BS in information sciences and technology with a minor in Japanese, and she is now an analyst at comScore. Danielle's research deals mainly with analyzing human online searching behavior, and she is currently the coauthor of four publications in various journal and conferences.

Adriana A. Braga, PhD, is a Brazilian researcher with a Bachelor's degree in Psychology and Master's and Doctorate studies in Communication Sciences. She is Assistant Professor at the Pontifícia Universidade Católica/Rio de Janeiro (PUC-RJ). Her PhD Thesis *Computer-Mediated Femininity: social interaction in a blog-circuit* was the recipient of the 2007 Media Ecology Association's Harold A. Innis Award and CAPES Award for best dissertation on Social Sciences 2007. Dr. Braga is the editor of the book *CMC, Identidades e Género: teoria e método* (Portugal, Editora UBI, 2005) and author of *Personas Materno-Eletrônicas: uma análise do blog Mothern* (Editora Sulina [forthcoming] 2008).

Michael Chau is an assistant professor in the School of Business at the University of Hong Kong. He received his PhD degree in management information systems from the University of Arizona and a bachelor degree in computer science and information systems from the University of Hong Kong. His current research interests include information retrieval, Web mining, data mining, knowledge management, electronic commerce, security informatics, and intelligence agents. He has published more than 60 research articles in leading journals and conferences, including *IEEE Computer, ACM Transactions on Information Systems, Journal of the America Society for Information Science and Technology, Annual Review of Information Science and Technology, Decision Support Systems, Journal of the Association for Information Systems, International Journal of Human-Computer Studies, and Communications of the ACM.* More information can be found at http://www.business.hku.hk/~mchau/

Brian Detlor is an Associate Professor of Information Systems in the DeGroote School of Business at McMaster University in Hamilton, Ontario, Canada. His research interests center on Web information seeking, portal adoption and use, information literacy, electronic government, and knowledge management. Brian teaches a large introductory course on information systems to undergraduate students and currently serves as the Director of the Ph.D. program at the DeGroote School of Business. He recently co-authored the first Canadian edition of an MIS textbook entitled "Business-Driven Information Systems" published by McGraw-Hill Ryerson in 2008.

Paul DiPerna is a host and moderator for the Blau Exchange Project. For more than six years DiPerna worked as a researcher and administrator at The Brookings Institution. He was a research analyst for the first five issues of the Brown Center Report on American Education (2000-2004) and served as the administrator for the National Working Commission on Choice in K-12 Education. DiPerna currently serves as a director at the Friedman Foundation for Educational Choice in Indianapolis. His publications have appeared in First Monday, Journal of Information Technology Impact, Education Next, and The Washington Examiner.

Anthony (Tony) Ferrini is currently an MBA student at the University of Montana. He has extensive experience in the world of search engine positioning and Web-based marketing, having run a successful company, AcquireMarketing.com, for the past 6 years. (Acquire Marketing delivers competitive placements for keyword results in the top search engines and directories.) In addition, he was the information technology manager for the University of Montana's Continuing Education Department, overseeing all use of on-line course delivery modules through that program. He currently serves as the on-line course support liaison for all distance learning in the University of Montana's MBA program.

Xiao Fang is an assistant professor of information systems at the College of Business Administration, University of Toledo. He received his PhD degree in management information systems from the University of Arizona in 2003. His current research interests are in the areas of business intelligence and knowledge management. He has published in such journals as *Journal of Management Information Systems, ACM Transactions on Information Systems, ACM Transactions on Internet Technology, Communications of the ACM, INFORMS Journal on Computing, and Journal of the American Society for Information Science and Technology.*

Toru Fujimoto is a PhD student in the professor in the Instructional Systems Program at the Pennsylvania State University.

Kirstie Hawkey is a postdoctoral research fellow in the Departments of Computer Science and Electrical & Computer Engineering at the University of British Columbia. She received her PhD in computer science from Dalhousie University in 2007. Her research interests include personal information management and usable privacy and security, particularly within the context of group work. As part of her dissertation research, Kirstie conducted two field studies investigating privacy concerns for web browsing activity for which she developed client-side logging software and an electronic diary for participant annotation of log data.

William Hersh is professor and chair of the Department of Medical Informatics & Clinical Epidemiology at Oregon Health & Science University (OHSU) in Portland, Oregon, USA. Dr. Hersh's main research focus has been in the area of information retrieval, where he has authored over 100 scientific papers as well as the book, Information Retrieval: A Health & Biomedical Perspective, now in its second edition. He is well known for his work looking at how clinicians and researchers search for and use information to improve their work. Most recently, he has focused his efforts in biomedical image retrieval, assessing the best methods for indexing and retrieval of images.

Jorge Herskovic is a Doctoral candidate at the University of Texas School of Health Information Sciences at Houston. In addition to his research, which focuses on biomedical information retrieval, Dr. Herskovic is an instructor for the Foundations of Health Informatics Course at the same school. He holds an MD and an MS in health informatics. Dr. Herskovic completed a two-year Keck Doctoral Fellowship and is currently preparing his dissertation. He is fully dedicated to the research and practice of informatics.

Paula Hooper received her PhD from MIT's Media Laboratory in 1998 and is currently a senior research fellow at TERC. Her research investigates the role of cultural resources and computational media in children's scientific and mathematical sense-making. Dr. Hooper has also worked on school reform efforts as a teacher, principal, and researcher.

Maureen Hupfer is an associate professor of marketing in the DeGroote School of Business at McMaster University. In addition to social marketing and the consumption of visual imagery, her research with Brian Detlor addresses the effects of gender and self-concept in online environments. Specifically, they have examined how gender-related self-concept traits predict a) how often individuals search for information that is important to themselves versus someone close to them, b) how frequently individuals use online applications with relationship implications, and c) individuals' importance ratings for shopping site features that promote efficiency and effort minimization versus those that allow more elaborate processing.

Melanie Kellar is a user experience researcher with Google. She received her PhD in computer science from Dalhousie University in 2007. Her research interests include information seeking, web browser tools, and methodologies for studying user behavior on the Web. Melanie's dissertation investigated how people use their web browsers to satisfy their information needs, providing new understanding of the high level tasks in which users engage on the Web as well as how people interact with their web browsers in the context of task. As part of her PhD research, Melanie developed a custom browser that logged user interactions on the Web.

KyoungNa Kim is a PhD student in the Instructional Systems Program at the Pennsylvania State University.

Udo Kruschwitz received a diploma in computer science from Humboldt University Berlin and a PhD in computer science from University of Essex. He is now a lecturer in the Department of Computing and Electronic Systems at the University of Essex. His main research is in natural language processing (NLP), information retrieval (IR) and the implementation of such techniques in real applications. He gained prior research experience in the Verbmobil and Yellow Pages Assistant projects, the latter funded by BT, for whom he also worked as a consultant. Dr. Kruschwitz is the author of the monograph "Intelligent Document Retrieval: Exploiting Markup Structure", published in Springer's Information Retrieval series.

Sam Ladner is currently a doctoral candidate in the Department of Sociology at York University. She researches the intersections between technology, work and organizations and is particularly interested in new, online social research methods. She has ten years' experience working on the Web, with a specialty in qualitative and quantitative user research, including web analytics, ethnographic observation, and usability testing. She has consulted major media and financial services companies on their online strategies and design, as well as taught hundreds of undergraduate students on social theory and social research methods.

Kyu Yon Lim is a PhD student in the Instructional Systems Program at the Pennsylvania State University.

Yan Lu is a graduate student and a research assistant in the School of Business at the University of Hong Kong. She received her BSc in management information systems from Xi'an Jiaotong University, China. Her research interests include information retrieval, Web mining, and electronic commerce. She has published research articles in the 10th Pacific Asia Conference on Information Systems (PACIS 2006) and the 5th Workshop on e-Business (WeB 2006).

Marie-Francine Moens is an associate professor at the Department of Computer Science of the Katholieke Universiteit Leuven, Belgium. She holds a MSc and a PhD degree in computer science from this university. She currently leads a research team of 10 researchers and PhD students who study topics of text based information retrieval. Her main interests are in the domain of automated content retrieval from texts using a combination of statistical, machine learning and symbolic techniques, and exploiting insights from linguistic and cognitive theories.

Jakki J. Mohr is the Jeff and Martha Hamilton Distinguished Faculty Fellow and professor of marketing at the University of Montana-Missoula. Before beginning her academic career, she worked in Silicon Valley in the advertising area for both Hewlett Packard's Personal Computer Group and TeleVideo Systems. An innovator in the field of marketing high-technology products and services, Mohr's book, "*Marketing of High-Technology Products and Innovations*," has achieved international acclaim. In addition to her numerous teaching and research awards, she provides consulting to a variety of companies (ranging in size from Fortune 500 companies to small high-tech start-ups) in the area of technology and marketing.

Gheorghe Muresan is a senior software development engineer in Microsoft's Live Search. At the time of submission he was an assistant professor in the School of Communication, Information and Library Studies at the Rutgers University. His research interest are in Web IR, user modeling for personalizing information retrieval, studying the user interaction in the information-seeking context, and in methodologies for evaluating search success.

José Palazzo Moreira de Oliveira is full professor of computer science at Federal University of Rio Grande do Sul - UFRGS. He as a doctor degree in computer science from Institut National Politechnique - IMAG (1984), Grenoble, France, a MSc degree in computer science from PPGC-UFRGS (1976) and has graduated in electronic engineering (1968). His research interests include information systems, e-learning, database systems and applications, conceptual modeling and ontologies, applications of database technology and distributed systems. He has published about 160 papers, has been an advisor of 11 PhD and 49 MSc students.

Seda Ozmutlu is an associate professor in the Industrial Engineering Department of Uludag University. She has a BS degree in management engineering from Istanbul Technical University, and MS and PhD dual degrees in industrial engineering and operations research, both from Penn State University. Her research interests include application of artificial intelligence and statistical techniques on information science problems and information retrieval. She is a researcher and principal investigator in several projects sponsored by TUBITAK (Turkish Science and Technology Foundation), and has published over 30 papers in her research areas of interest.

H. Cenk Ozmutlu is an associate professor in the Industrial Engineering Department of Uludag University. He has a BS degree in management engineering from Istanbul Technical University, an MS degree in operations research from George Washington University, and a PhD degree in industrial engineering from The Pennsylvania State University. His research interests include application of operations research and artificial intelligence techniques on information science problems, information retrieval and telecommunication. He is a researcher and principal investigator in several projects sponsored by TUBITAK (Turkish Science and Technology Foundation), and has published over 30 papers in his research areas of interest.

W. David Penniman is executive director of Nylink, a statewide library cooperative for the State of New York promoting collaboration and innovation via technology in libraries, museums, and other cultural heritage institutions. He has conducted information systems research, design, and development for industry, government, academic institutions, and other not-for-profits. He resides in Albany, N.Y. where he restores antique cars as a hobby.

Lee Rainie is the director of the Pew Internet & American Life Project. Since December 1999, the Washington D.C. research center has examined how people's internet use affects their families, communities, health care, education, civic and political life, and work places. The Project has issued more than 120 reports based on its surveys that monitor people's online activities and the internet's role in their lives. Prior to launching the Pew Internet Project, Lee was managing editor of U.S. News & World Report. He is a graduate of Harvard College and has a Master's degree in political science from Long Island University.

Sandro José Rigo is adjunct professor of computer science at UNISINOS - Universidade do Vale do Rio dos Sinos. He is a Doctoral student at Federal University of Rio Grande do Sul – UFRGS; has a MSc degree in computer science from PGCC-UFRGS (1994) and graduated in computer science in 1991 at the Catholic University of Rio Grande do SUL - PUCRS. His research interests include Semantic Web mining, adaptive hypermedia, Web development and human-computer interaction.

Umar Ruhi is a lecturer in the Telfer School of Management at the University of Ottawa. He teaches various undergraduate and graduate level courses in management information systems and e-business. Additionally, he teaches in the University's interdisciplinary graduate program in e-business technologies. His primary research interests include community informatics, computer-mediated-communication and e-business strategies. For the past three years, Umar has been involved in consulting, advisory, and analytical roles in conducting research in the areas of e-government, community portals and knowledge management. He has been involved in the authorship of several academic and practitioner journal articles and book chapters related to his research projects, and has presented at various international conferences. More information about Umar is available at http://www.umar.biz

Priya Sharma is an assistant professor in the Instructional Systems Program at the Pennsylvania State University. Before moving to academia, she worked in the corporate sector in India and the U.S. for over 5 years designing, developing, and evaluating multimedia training and instruction. Her current research focuses on the enabling role of technologies in fostering reflection and self-organized learning.

Brain Smith is a professor in the College of Information Sciences and Technology, the Pennsylvania State University. Dr. Smith's research studies the use of computation to support and augment human performance and learning. He is particularly interested in ways ubiquitous computing technologies can be created to assist people in reflecting on prior beliefs and ways of doing. Examples of his work include video annotation systems for biology education, GPS-enabled cameras and image databases for history education, and interventions around photography and computer visualizations to promote awareness of personal health practices. Current projects are underway to explore information design for informal, everyday decision-making.

Richard Sutcliffe received a BSc in computational science from St. Andrews University and a PhD in computer science from University of Essex. He is now a senior lecturer at the University of Limerick. His research lies within the areas of natural language processing and information retrieval. Since 2002 he has been working on question answering (QA) and has participated in TREC and NTCIR as well as being a co-organiser of the Multiple Language QA Track at CLEF. He has co-chaired workshops at COLING, EACL and elsewhere, and has co-authored many articles. Recent projects have included creating a query collection for parallel evaluation across languages, using decision trees to search document collections, extracting definitions from texts in different genres, investigating the characteristics of IR within QA, and applying QA techniques to the analysis of query logs.

Nick Webb received a BSc in artificial intelligence and a MSc in computer science (natural language understanding), both from the University of Essex, and is completing his PhD in computer science at the University of Sheffield. He is now lead research scientist in the Institute for Informatics, Logics and Security Studies, at the University at Albany, part of the State University of New York. Prior to this, Nick was a research fellow in the NLP Group at the University of Sheffield, and a senior research officer at the University of Essex. Within NLP, his research focus is on dialogue and conversational systems, most recently combining dialogue with information systems to further develop the paradigm of interactive question answering (IQA). Nick is co-editing an upcoming special issue of the Journal of Natural Language Engineering on IQA with Bonnie Webber, to appear in spring 2008.

Leandro Krug Wives is associate professor of computer science at Federal University of Rio Grande do Sul – UFRGS. He has a doctor degree in computer science from PPGC-UFRGS (2004); a MSc degree in computer science from PPGC-UFRGS (1999) and graduated in computer science as well in 1996 at the Catholic University of Pelotas – UCPEL. His research interests include text mining, clustering, recommender systems, information retrieval, information extraction, and digital libraries.

Christopher C. Yang is an associate professor in the Department of Systems Engineering and Engineering Management and the director of the Digital Library Laboratory at the Chinese University of Hong Kong. He received his BS, MS, and PhD in electrical and computer engineering from the University of Arizona. He has also been an assistant professor in the Department of Computer Science and Information Systems at the University of Hong Kong and a research scientist in the Department of Management Information Systems at the University of Arizona. His recent research interests include cross-lingual information retrieval and knowledge management, Web search and mining, security informatics, text summarization, multimedia retrieval, information visualization, digital library, and electronic commerce. He has published over 130 referred journal and conference papers in *Journal of* *the American Society for Information Science and Technology (JASIST), Decision Support Systems (DSS), IEEE Transactions on Image Processing, IEEE Transactions on Robotics and Automation, IEEE Computer, Information Processing and Management, Journal of Information Science, Graphical Models and Image Processing, Optical Engineering, Pattern Recognition, International Journal of Electronic Commerce, Applied Artificial Intelligence, IWWWC, SIGIR, ICIS, CIKM,* and more. He has edited several special issues on multilingual information systems, knowledge management, and Web mining in *JASIST* and *DSS.* He chaired and served in many international conferences and workshops. He has also frequently served as an invited panelist in the NSF Review Panels in US. He was the chairman of the Association for Computing Machinery Hong Kong Chapter.

Gi Woong Yun is an assistant professor at the School of Communication Studies, Bowling Green State University. His research interests are Internet as media. He works on social psychological theories of communication, online interactive forums, Internet research methodology and more. He enjoys thinking about tools and theories developed by communication researchers. Also, he manages to spend his time working on Web applications and he is currently running several Web sites. He likes to incorporate computers in his social psychological approaches in communication field and he likes to have fun with students working on class projects.

Sarah Zelikovitz received her BS with honors and MA degrees in computer information science from Brooklyn College of CUNY, and in 2002, received her PhD in computer science from Rutgers University. She joined the faculty of the Computer Science Department at the College of Staten Island of the City University of New York in 2002 as an assistant professor. Dr. Zelikovitz's research interests lie in the use of unlabeled or background knowledge in the aid of text classification. Over the last few years she has published conference and journal articles in this area.

Mimi Zhang is currently a PhD candidate in the College of Information Sciences and Technology, the Pennsylvania State University. She is interested in information seeking behavior and especially in applying relevant theories from multiple disciplines to gain a better understanding of users and advance the theoretical framework. She has been involved in different types of user studies, ranging from qualitative studies to quantitative studies, surveys to interviews, lab studies to transaction log analysis. She has a number of publications in conferences and journals.

Index

M

N

O

P

Q

R

S

T

U

V

W

Z